THE DEVIL IN THE WHITE CITY

ALSO BY ERIK LARSON

Isaac's Storm

THE
DEVIL IN THE
WHITE CITY

MURDER, MAGIC AND MADNESS
AT THE FAIR THAT CHANGED AMERICA

ERIK LARSON

Doubleday

LONDON · NEW YORK · TORONTO · SYDNEY · AUCKLAND

TRANSWORLD PUBLISHERS
61–63 Uxbridge Road, London W5 5SA
a division of The Random House Group Ltd

RANDOM HOUSE AUSTRALIA (PTY) LTD
20 Alfred Street, Milsons Point, Sydney,
New South Wales 2061, Australia

RANDOM HOUSE NEW ZEALAND LTD
18 Poland Road, Glenfield, Auckland 10, New Zealand

RANDOM HOUSE SOUTH AFRICA (PTY) LTD
Endulini, 5a Jubilee Road, Parktown 2193, South Africa

Published 2003 by Doubleday
a division of Transworld Publishers

A catalogue record for this book is available from the British Library.
ISBN (cased) 0385 602057
(tpb) 0385 602731

Printed in Great Britain by
Mackays of Chatham plc, Chatham, Kent

1 3 5 7 9 10 8 6 4 2

To Chris, Kristen, Lauren, and Erin,
for making it all worthwhile

—and to Molly, whose lust for socks
kept us all on our toes

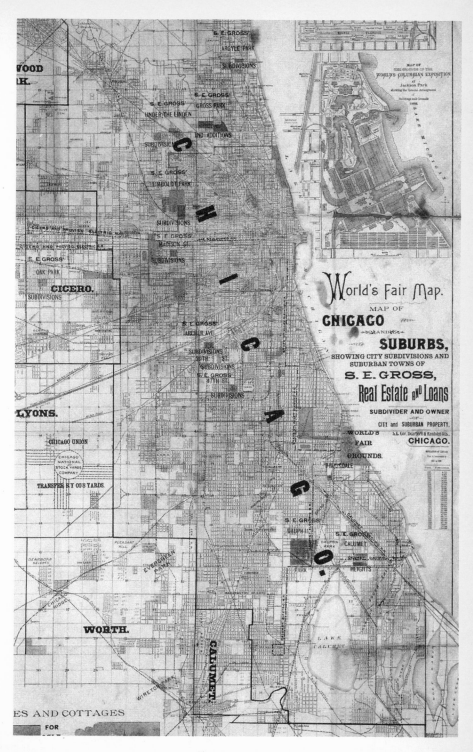

Chicago, 1891.

CONTENTS

EVILS IMMINENT

(A NOTE)

IN CHICAGO AT THE END of the nineteenth century amid the smoke of industry and the clatter of trains there lived two men, both handsome, both blue-eyed, and both unusually adept at their chosen skills. Each embodied an element of the great dynamic that characterized the rush of America toward the twentieth century. One was an architect, the builder of many of America's most important structures, among them the Flat-iron Building in New York and Union Station in Washington, D.C.; the other was a murderer, one of the most prolific in history and harbinger of an American archetype, the urban serial killer. Although the two never met, at least not formally, their fates were linked by a single, magical event, one largely fallen from modern recollection but that in its time was considered to possess a transformative power nearly equal to that of the Civil War.

In the following pages I tell the story of these men and this event, but I must insert here a notice: However strange or macabre some of the following incidents may seem, this is *not* a work of fiction. Anything between quotation marks comes from a letter, memoir, or other written document. The action takes place mostly in Chicago, but I beg readers to forgive me for the occasional lurch across state lines, as when the staunch, grief-struck Detective Geyer enters that last awful cellar. I beg forbearance, too, for the occasional side journey demanded by the story, including excursions into the medical acquisition of corpses and the correct use of Black Prince geraniums in an Olmstedian landscape.

Beneath the gore and smoke and loam, this book is about the evanescence of life, and why some men choose to fill their brief allotment of time engaging the impossible, others in the manufacture of sorrow. In the end it is a story of the ineluctable conflict between good and evil, daylight and darkness, the White City and the Black.

ERIK LARSON
SEATTLE

Make no little plans; they have no magic to stir men's blood.
DANIEL H. BURNHAM
DIRECTOR OF WORKS
WORLD'S COLUMBIAN EXPOSITION, 1893

I was born with the devil in me. I could not help the fact that I was a murderer, no more than the poet can help the inspiration to sing.
DR. H. H. HOLMES
CONFESSION
1896

PROLOGUE

Aboard the Olympic

1912

The architects *(left to right)*: Daniel Burnham, George Post, M. B. Pickett, Henry Van Brunt, Francis Millet, Maitland Armstrong, Col. Edmund Rice, Augustus St. Gaudens, Henry Sargent Codman, George W. Maynard, Charles McKim, Ernest Graham, Dion Geraldine.

Aboard the *Olympic*

THE DATE WAS APRIL 14, 1912, a sinister day in maritime history, but of course the man in suite 63–65, shelter deck C, did not yet know it. What he did know was that his foot hurt badly, more than he had expected. He was sixty-five years old and had become a large man. His hair had turned gray, his mustache nearly white, but his eyes were as blue as ever, bluer at this instant by proximity to the sea. His foot had forced him to delay the voyage, and now it kept him anchored in his suite while the other first-class passengers, his wife among them, did what he would have loved to do, which was to explore the ship's more exotic precincts. The man loved the opulence of the ship, just as he loved Pullman Palace cars and giant fireplaces, but his foot problem tempered his enjoyment. He recognized that the systemic malaise that caused it was a consequence in part of his own refusal over the years to limit his courtship of the finest wines, foods, and cigars. The pain reminded him daily that his time on the planet was nearing its end. Just before the voyage he told a friend, "This prolonging of a man's life doesn't interest me when he's done his work and has done it pretty well."

The man was Daniel Hudson Burnham, and by now his name was familiar throughout the world. He was an architect and had done his work pretty well in Chicago, New York, Washington, San Francisco, Manila, and many other cities. He and his wife, Margaret, were sailing to Europe in the company of their daughter and her husband for a grand tour that was to continue through the summer. Burnham had chosen this ship, the R.M.S. *Olympic* of the White Star Line, because it was new and glamorous and big. At the time he booked passage the *Olympic* was the largest vessel in regular service, but just three days before his departure a sister ship—a slightly longer twin—had stolen that rank when it set off on its maiden voyage. The twin, Burnham knew, was at that moment carrying one of his closest friends, the painter Francis Millet, over the same ocean but in the opposite direction.

As the last sunlight of the day entered Burnham's suite, he and Margaret set off for the first-class dining room on the deck below. They took the elevator to spare his foot the torment of the grand stairway, but he did so with reluctance, for he admired the artistry in the iron scrollwork of its balustrades and the immense dome of iron and glass that flushed the ship's core with natural light. His sore foot had placed increasing limitations on his mobility. Only a week earlier he had found himself in the humiliating position of having to ride in a wheelchair through Union Station in Washington, D.C., the station he had designed.

The Burnhams dined by themselves in the *Olympic*'s first-class salon, then retired to their suite and there, for no particular reason, Burnham's thoughts returned to Frank Millet. On impulse, he resolved to send Millet a midsea greeting via the *Olympic*'s powerful Marconi wireless.

Burnham signaled for a steward. A middle-aged man in knife-edge whites took his message up three decks to the Marconi room adjacent to the officer's promenade. He returned a few moments later, the message still in his hand, and told Burnham the operator had refused to accept it.

Footsore and irritable, Burnham demanded that the steward return to the wireless room for an explanation.

Millet was never far from Burnham's mind, nor was the event that had brought the two of them together: the great Chicago world's fair of 1893. Millet had been one of Burnham's closest allies in the long, bittersweet struggle to build the fair. Its official name was the World's Columbian Exposition, its official purpose to commemorate the four hundredth anniversary of Columbus's discovery of America, but under Burnham, its chief builder, it had become something enchanting, known throughout the world as the White City.

It had lasted just six months, yet during that time its gatekeepers recorded 27.5 million visits, this when the country's total population was 65 million. On its best day the fair drew more than 700,000 visitors. That the fair had occurred at all, however, was something of a miracle. To build it Burnham had confronted a legion of obstacles, any one of which could have—*should* have—killed it long before Opening Day. Together he and his architects had conjured a dream city whose grandeur and beauty exceeded anything each singly could have imagined. Visitors wore their best clothes and most somber expressions, as if entering a great cathedral. Some wept at its beauty. They tasted a new snack called Cracker Jack and a new breakfast food called Shredded Wheat. Whole villages had been imported from Egypt, Algeria, Dahomey, and other far-flung locales, along with their inhabitants. The Street in Cairo exhibit alone employed nearly two hundred Egyptians and contained twenty-five distinct build-ings, including a fifteen-hundred-seat theater that introduced America to a new and scandalous form of entertainment. Everything about the fair was exotic and, above all, immense. The fair occupied over one square mile and filled more than two hundred buildings. A single exhibit hall had enough interior volume to have housed the U.S. Capitol, the Great Pyra-mid, Winchester Cathedral, Madison Square Garden, and St. Paul's Cathedral, all at the same time. One structure, rejected at first as a "mon-strosity," became the fair's emblem, a machine so huge and terrifying that it instantly eclipsed the tower of Alexandre Eiffel that had so wounded America's pride. Never before had so many of history's brightest lights, including Buffalo Bill, Theodore Dreiser, Susan B. Anthony, Jane Addams, Clarence Darrow, George Westinghouse, Thomas Edison, Henry Adams, Archduke Francis Ferdinand, Nikola Tesla, Ignace Paderewski, Philip Armour, and Marshall Field, gathered in one place at one time. Richard Harding Davis called the exposition "the greatest event in the history of the country since the Civil War."

That something magical had occurred in that summer of the world's fair was beyond doubt, but darkness too had touched the fair. Scores of workers had been hurt or killed in building the dream, their families con-signed to poverty. Fire had killed fifteen more, and an assassin had trans-formed the closing ceremony from what was to have been the century's greatest celebration into a vast funeral. Worse had occurred too, although these revelations emerged only slowly. A murderer had moved among the beautiful things Burnham had created. Young women drawn to Chicago by the fair and by the prospect of living on their own had disappeared, last seen at the killer's block-long mansion, a parody of everything architects held dear. Only after the exposition had Burnham and his colleagues learned of the anguished letters describing daughters who had come to the city and then fallen silent. The press speculated that scores of fairgoers must have disappeared within the building. Even the street-hardened members of the city's Whitechapel Club, named for the London stalking grounds of Jack the Ripper, were startled by what detectives eventually found inside and by the fact that such grisly events could have gone undiscovered for so long. The rational explanation laid blame on the forces of change that during this time had convulsed Chicago. Amid so much turmoil it was understandable that the work of a young and handsome doctor would go unnoticed. As time passed, however, even sober men and women began to think of him in less-than-rational terms. He described himself as the Devil and contended that his physical shape had begun to alter. Enough strange things began happening to the men who brought him to justice to make his claim seem almost plausible.

For the supernaturally inclined, the death of the jury foreman alone offered sufficient proof.

Burnham's foot ached. The deck thrummed. No matter where you were on the ship, you felt the power of the *Olympic*'s twenty-nine boilers transmitted upward through the strakes of the hull. It was the one constant that told you—even in the staterooms and dining chambers and smoking lounge, despite the lavish efforts to make these rooms look as if they had been plucked from the Palace of Versailles or a Jacobean mansion—that you were aboard a ship being propelled far into the bluest reaches of the ocean.

Burnham and Millet were among the few builders of the fair still alive. So many others had gone. Olmsted and Codman. McKim. Hunt.

Atwood—mysteriously. And that initial loss, which Burnham still found difficult to comprehend. Soon no one would remain, and the fair would cease to exist as a living memory in anyone's brain.

Of the key men, who besides Millet was left? Only Louis Sullivan: embittered, perfumed with alcohol, resenting who knew what, but not above coming by Burnham's office for a loan or to sell some painting or sketch.

At least Frank Millet still seemed strong and healthy and full of the earthy good humor that had so enlivened the long nights during the fair's construction.

The steward came back. The expression in his eyes had changed. He apologized. He still could not send the message, he said, but at least now he had an explanation. An accident had occurred involving Millet's ship. In fact, he said, the *Olympic* was at that moment speeding north at maximum velocity to come to her aid, with instructions to receive and care for injured passengers. He knew nothing more.

Burnham shifted his leg, winced, and waited for more news. He hoped that when the *Olympic* at last reached the site of the accident, he would find Millet and hear him tell some outrageous story about the voyage. In the peace of his stateroom, Burnham opened his diary.

That night the fair came back to him with extra clarity.

PART I

Frozen Music

Chicago, 1890–91

Chicago, circa 1889.

The Black City

How easy it was to disappear:

A thousand trains a day entered or left Chicago. Many of these trains brought single young women who had never even seen a city but now hoped to make one of the biggest and toughest their home. Jane Addams, the urban reformer who founded Chicago's Hull House, wrote, "Never before in civilization have such numbers of young girls been suddenly released from the protection of the home and permitted to walk unattended upon the city streets and to work under alien roofs." The women sought work as typewriters, stenographers, seamstresses, and weavers. The men who hired them were for the most part moral citizens intent on efficiency and profit. But not always. On March 30, 1890, an officer of the First National Bank placed a warning in the help-wanted section of the *Chicago Tribune,* to inform female stenographers of "our growing conviction that no thoroughly honorable business-man who is this side of dotage ever advertises for a lady stenographer who is a blonde, is good-looking, is quite alone in the city, or will transmit her photograph. All such advertisements upon their face bear the marks of vulgarity, nor do we regard it safe for any lady to answer such unseemly utterances."

The women walked to work on streets that angled past bars, gambling houses, and bordellos. Vice thrived, with official indulgence. "The parlors and bedrooms in which honest folk lived were (as now) rather dull places," wrote Ben Hecht, late in his life, trying to explain this persistent trait of old Chicago. "It was pleasant, in a way, to know that outside their windows, the devil was still capering in a flare of brimstone." In an analogy that would prove all too apt, Max Weber likened the city to "a human being with his skin removed."

Anonymous death came early and often. Each of the thousand trains that entered and left the city did so at grade level. You could step from a curb and be killed by the Chicago Limited. Every day on average two people were destroyed at the city's rail crossings. Their injuries were grotesque. Pedestrians retrieved severed heads. There were other hazards. Streetcars fell from drawbridges. Horses bolted and dragged carriages into crowds. Fires took a dozen lives a day. In describing the fire dead, the term the newspapers most liked to use was "roasted." There was diphtheria, typhus, cholera, influenza. And there was murder. In the time of the fair the rate at which men and women killed one another rose sharply throughout the nation but especially in Chicago, where police found themselves without the manpower or expertise to manage the volume. In the first six months of 1892 the city experienced nearly eight hundred violent deaths. Four a day. Most were prosaic, arising from robbery, argument, or sexual jealousy. Men shot women, women shot men, and children shot one another by accident. But all this could be understood. Nothing like the Whitechapel killings had occurred. Jack the Ripper's five-murder spree in 1888 had defied explanation and captivated readers throughout America, who believed such a thing could not happen in their own hometowns.

But things were changing. Everywhere one looked the boundary between the moral and the wicked seemed to be degrading. Elizabeth Cady Stanton argued in favor of divorce. Clarence Darrow advocated free love. A young woman named Borden killed her parents.

And in Chicago a young handsome doctor stepped from a train, his surgical valise in hand. He entered a world of clamor, smoke, and steam, refulgent with the scents of murdered cattle and pigs. He found it to his liking.

The letters came later, from the Cigrands, Williamses, Smythes, and untold others, addressed to that strange gloomy castle at Sixty-third and Wallace, pleading for the whereabouts of daughters and daughters' children.

It was so easy to disappear, so easy to deny knowledge, so very easy in the smoke and din to mask that something dark had taken root.

This was Chicago, on the eve of the greatest fair in history.

"The Trouble Is Just Begun"

ON THE AFTERNOON OF MONDAY, February 24, 1890, two thousand people gathered on the sidewalk and street outside the offices of the *Chicago Tribune,* as similar crowds collected at each of the city's twenty-eight other daily newspapers, and in hotel lobbies, in bars, and at the offices of Western Union and the Postal Telegraph Company. The gathering outside the *Tribune* included businessmen, clerks, traveling salesmen, stenographers, police officers, and at least one barber. Messenger boys stood ready to bolt as soon as there was news worth reporting. The air was cold. Smoke filled the caverns between buildings and reduced lateral visibility to a few blocks. Now and then police officers cleared a path for one of the city's bright yellow streetcars, called grip-cars for the way their operators attached them to an ever-running cable under the street. Drays full of wholesale goods rumbled over the pavers, led by immense horses gusting steam into the murk above.

The wait was electric, for Chicago was a prideful place. In every corner of the city people looked into the faces of shopkeepers, cab drivers, waiters and bellboys to see whether the news already had come and whether it was good or bad. So far the year had been a fine one. Chicago's population had topped one million for the first time, making the city the second most populous in the nation after New York, although disgruntled residents of Philadelphia, previously in second place, were quick to point out that Chicago had cheated by annexing large expanses of land just in time for the 1890 decadal census. Chicago shrugged the sniping off. Big was big. Success today would dispel at last the eastern perception that Chicago was nothing more than a greedy, hog-slaughtering backwater; failure would bring humiliation from which the city would not soon recover, given how heartily its leading men had boasted that Chicago would prevail. It was this big talk, not the persistent southwesterly breeze, that had prompted New York editor Charles Anderson Dana to nickname Chicago "the Windy City."

In their offices in the top floor of the Rookery, Daniel Burnham, forty-three, and his partner, John Root, newly forty, felt the electricity more keenly than most. They had participated in secret conversations, received certain assurances, and gone so far as to make reconnaissance forays to outlying parts of the city. They were Chicago's leading architects: They had pioneered the erection of tall structures and designed the first building in the country ever to be called a skyscraper; every year, it seemed, some new building of theirs became the tallest in the world. When they moved into the Rookery at La Salle and Adams, a gorgeous light-filled structure of Root's design, they saw views of the lake and city that no one but construction workers had seen before. They knew, however, that today's event had the potential to make their success so far seem meager.

The news would come by telegraph from Washington. The *Tribune* would get it from one of its own reporters. Its editors, rewrite men, and typesetters would compose "extra" editions as firemen shoveled coal into the boilers of the paper's steam-driven presses. A clerk would paste each incoming bulletin to a window, face out, for pedestrians to read.

Shortly after four o'clock, Chicago standard railroad time, the *Tribune* received its first cable.

Even Burnham could not say for sure who had been first to propose the idea. It had seemed to rise in many minds at once, the initial intent simply to celebrate the four hundredth anniversary of Columbus's discovery of the New World by hosting a world's fair. At first the idea gained little momentum. Consumed by the great drive toward wealth and power that had begun after the end of the Civil War, America seemed to have scant interest in celebrating its distant past. In 1889, however, the French did something that startled everyone.

In Paris on the Champ de Mars, France opened the Exposition

Universelle, a world's fair so big and glamorous and so exotic that visitors came away believing no exposition could surpass it. At the heart of the exposition stood a tower of iron that rose one thousand feet into the sky, higher by far than any man-made structure on earth. The tower not only assured the eternal fame of its designer, Alexandre Gustave Eiffel, but also offered graphic proof that France had edged out the United States for dominance in the realm of iron and steel, despite the Brooklyn Bridge, the Horseshoe Curve, and other undeniable accomplishments of American engineers.

The United States had only itself to blame for this perception. In Paris America had made a half-hearted effort to show off its artistic, industrial, and scientific talent. "We shall be ranked among those nations who have shown themselves careless of appearances," wrote the *Chicago Tribune*'s Paris correspondent on May 13, 1889. Other nations, he wrote, had mounted exhibits of dignity and style, while American exhibitors erected a mélange of pavilions and kiosks with no artistic guidance and no uniform plan. "The result is a sad jumble of shops, booths, and bazaars often unpleasing in themselves and incongruous when taken together." In contrast, France had done everything it could to ensure that its glory overwhelmed everyone. "Other nations are not rivals," the correspondent wrote, "they are foils to France, and the poverty of their displays sets off, as it was meant to do, the fullness of France, its richness and its splendor."

Even Eiffel's tower, forecast by wishful Americans to be a monstrosity that would disfigure forever the comely landscape of Paris, turned out to possess unexpected élan, with a sweeping base and tapered shaft that evoked the trail of a skyrocket. This humiliation could not be allowed to stand. America's pride in its growing power and international stature had fanned patriotism to a new intensity. The nation needed an opportunity to top the French, in particular to "out-Eiffel Eiffel." Suddenly the idea of hosting a great exposition to commemorate Columbus's discovery of the New World became irresistible.

At first, most Americans believed that if an exposition honoring the deepest roots of the nation were to be held anywhere, the site should be Washington, the capital. Initially even Chicago's editors agreed. As the notion of an exposition gained shape, however, other cities began to see it as a prize to be coveted, mainly for the stature it would confer, stature being a powerful lure in this age when pride of place ranked second only to pride of blood. Suddenly New York and St. Louis wanted the fair. Washington laid claim to the honor on grounds it was the center of government, New York because it was the center of everything. No one cared what St. Louis thought, although the city got a wink for pluck.

Nowhere was civic pride a more powerful force than in Chicago, where men spoke of the "Chicago spirit" as if it were a tangible force and prided themselves on the speed with which they had rebuilt the city after the Great Fire of 1871. They had not merely restored it; they had turned it into the nation's leader in commerce, manufacturing, and architecture. All the city's wealth, however, had failed to shake the widespread perception that Chicago was a secondary city that preferred butchered hogs to Beethoven. New York was the nation's capital of cultural and social refinement, and its leading citizens and newspapers never let Chicago forget it. The exposition, if built right—if it topped Paris—might dispel that sentiment once and for all. The editors of Chicago's daily newspapers, upon seeing New York enter the contest, began to ask, why *not* Chicago? The *Tribune* warned that "the hawks, buzzards, vultures, and other unclean beasts, creeping, crawling, and flying, of New York are reaching out to get control of the fair."

On June 29, 1889, Chicago's mayor, DeWitt C. Cregier, announced the appointment of a citizens committee consisting of 250 of the city's most prominent men. The committee met and passed a resolution whose closing passage read: "The men who have helped build Chicago want the fair, and, having a just and well-sustained claim, they intend to have it."

Congress had the final say, however, and now the time for the big vote had come.

A *Tribune* clerk stepped to the window and pasted the first bulletin. The initial ballot put Chicago ahead by a big margin, with 115 votes to New York's 72. St. Louis came next, followed by Washington. One congressman opposed having a fair at all and out of sheer cussedness voted for Cumberland Gap. When the crowd outside the *Tribune* saw that Chicago led New York by 43 votes, it exploded with cheers, whistles, and applause. Everyone knew, however, that Chicago was still 38 votes shy of the simple majority needed to win the fair.

Other ballots followed. Daylight faded to thin broth. The sidewalks filled with men and women leaving work. Typewriters—the women who operated the latest business machines—streamed from the Rookery, the Montauk, and other skyscrapers wearing under their coats the customary white blouse and long black skirt that so evoked the keys of their Remingtons. Cab drivers cursed and gentled their horses. A lamplighter scuttled along the edges of the crowd igniting the gas jets atop cast-iron poles. Abruptly there was color everywhere: the yellow streetcars and the sudden blues of telegraph boys jolting past with satchels full of joy and gloom; cab drivers lighting the red night-lamps at the backs of their hansoms; a large gilded lion crouching before the hat store across the street. In the high buildings above, gas and electric lights bloomed in the dusk like moonflowers.

The *Tribune* clerk again appeared in the newspaper's window, this time with the results of the fifth ballot. "The gloom that fell upon the crowd was heavy and chill," a reporter observed. New York had gained fifteen votes, Chicago only six. The gap between them had narrowed. The barber in the crowd pointed out to everyone in his vicinity that New York's additional votes must have come from congressmen who previously had favored St. Louis. This revelation caused an army lieutenant, Alexander Ross, to proclaim, "Gentlemen. I am prepared to state that any person from St. Louis would rob a church." Another man shouted, "Or poison his wife's dog." This last drew wide agreement.

In Washington the New York contingent, including Chauncey Depew, president of the New York Central and one of the most celebrated orators of the day, sensed a tide change and asked for a recess until the next day. On learning of this request the crowd outside the *Tribune* booed and hissed, correctly interpreting the move as an attempt to gain time to lobby for more votes.

The motion was overruled, but the House voted for a brief adjournment. The crowd remained in place.

After the seventh ballot Chicago was only one vote short of a majority. New York had actually lost ground. A stillness settled on the street. Cabs halted. Police ignored the ever-longer chains of grip-cars that stretched left and right in a great cadmium gash. Passengers disembarked and watched the *Tribune* window, waiting for the next announcement. The cables thrumming beneath the pavement struck a minor chord of suspense, and held it.

Soon a different man appeared in the *Tribune* window. He was tall, thin, and young and wore a black beard. He looked at the crowd without expression. In one hand he held a paste pot, in the other a brush and a bulletin sheet. He took his time. He set the bulletin on a table, out of sight, but everyone in the crowd could tell what he was doing by the motion of his shoulders. He took his time unscrewing the paste pot. There was something somber in his face, as if he were looking down upon a casket. Methodically he painted paste onto the bulletin. It took him a good long while to raise it to the window.

His expression did not change. He fastened the bulletin to the glass.

Burnham waited. His office faced south, as did Root's, to satisfy their craving for natural light, a universal hunger throughout Chicago, where gas jets, still the primary source of artificial illumination, did little to pierce the city's perpetual coal-smoke dusk. Electric bulbs, often in fixtures that combined gas and electricity, were just beginning to light the newest buildings, but these in a sense added to the problem, for they required basement dynamos driven by coal-fired boilers. As the light faded, gaslights on the streets and in the buildings below caused the smoke to glow a dull yellow. Burnham heard only the hiss of gas from the lamps in his office.

That he should be there now, a man of such exalted professional stature in an office so high above the city, would have come as a great and satisfying surprise to his late father.

Daniel Hudson Burnham was born in Henderson, New York, on September 4, 1846, into a family devoted to Swedenborgian principles of obedience, self-subordination, and public service. In 1855, when he was nine, the family moved to Chicago, where his father established a successful wholesale drug business. Burnham was a lackluster student: "the records of the Old Central show his average scholarship to be frequently as low as 55 percent," a reporter discovered, "and 81 percent seems the highest he ever reached." He excelled, however, at drawing and sketched constantly. He was eighteen when his father sent him east to study with private tutors to prepare him for the entrance exams for Harvard and Yale. The boy proved to have a severe case of test anxiety. "I went to Harvard for examination with two men not as well prepared as I," he said. "Both passed easily, and I flunked, having sat through two or three examinations without being able to write a word." The same happened at Yale. Both schools turned him down. He never forgot it.

In the fall of 1867, at twenty-one, Burnham returned to Chicago. He sought work in a field where he might be successful and took a job as a draftsman with the architectural firm of Loring & Jenney. He had found his calling, he wrote in 1868, and told his parents he wanted to become the "greatest architect in the city or country." The next year, however, he bolted for Nevada with friends to try his hand at mining gold. He failed. He ran for the Nevada legislature and failed again. He returned to Chicago broke, in a cattle car, and joined the firm of an architect named L. G. Laurean. Then came October 1871: a cow, a lantern, confusion, and wind. The Great Chicago Fire took nearly eighteen thousand buildings and left more than a hundred thousand people homeless. The destruction promised endless work for the city's architects. But Burnham quit. He sold plate glass, failed. He became a druggist, quit. "There is," he wrote, "a family tendency to get tired of doing the same thing very long."

Exasperated and worried, Burnham's father in 1872 introduced his son to an architect named Peter Wight, who admired the young man's skill at drawing and hired him as a draftsman. Burnham was twenty-five. He liked Wight and liked the work; he liked especially one of Wight's other draftsmen, a southerner named John Wellborn Root, who was four years younger. Born in Lumpkin, Georgia, on January 10, 1850, Root was a musical prodigy who could sing before he could talk. During the Civil War, as Atlanta smoldered, Root's father had smuggled him to Liverpool, England, aboard a Confederate blockade-runner. Root won acceptance into Oxford, but before he could matriculate, the war ended and his father summoned him back to America, to his new home in New York City, where Root studied civil engineering at New York University and became a draftsman for the architect who later designed St. Patrick's Cathedral.

Burnham took to Root immediately. He admired Root's white skin and muscular arms, his stance at the drafting table. They became friends, then partners. They recorded their first income three months before the Panic of 1873 snuffed the nation's economy. But this time Burnham stuck with it. Something about the partnership with Root bolstered him. It filled an absence and played to both men's strengths. They struggled for their own commissions and in the meantime hired themselves out to other more established firms.

One day in 1874 a man walked into their office and in a single galvanic moment changed their lives. He wore black and looked ordinary, but in his past there was blood, death, and profit in staggering quantity. He came looking for Root, but Root was out of town. He introduced himself instead to Burnham and gave his name as John B. Sherman.

There was no need to amplify the introduction. As superintendent of the Union Stock Yards, Sherman ruled an empire of blood that employed 25,000 men, women, and children and each year slaughtered fourteen million animals. Directly and indirectly nearly one-fifth of Chicago's population depended on the yards for its economic survival.

Sherman liked Burnham. He liked his strength, his steady blue gaze, and the confidence with which he conducted the conversation. Sherman commissioned the firm to build him a mansion on Prairie Avenue at Twenty-first Street among homes owned by other Chicago barons and where now and then Marshall Field, George Pullman, and Philip Armour could be seen walking to work together, a titanic threesome in black. Root drew a house of three stories with gables and a peaked roof, in red brick, buff sandstone, blue granite, and black slate; Burnham refined the drawings and guided construction. Burnham happened to be standing in the entrance to the house, considering the work, when a young man with a mildly haughty air and an odd strut—not ego, here, but a congenital fault—walked up to him and introduced himself as Louis Sullivan. The name meant nothing to Burnham. Not yet. Sullivan and Burnham talked. Sullivan was eighteen, Burnham twenty-eight. He told Sullivan, in confidence, that he did not expect to remain satisfied doing just houses. "My idea," he said, "is to work up a big business, to handle big things, deal with big business men, and to build up a big organization, for you can't handle big things unless you have an organization."

John Sherman's daughter, Margaret, also visited the construction site. She was young, pretty, and blond and visited often, using as her excuse the fact that her friend Della Otis lived across the street. Margaret did think the house very fine, but what she admired most was the architect who seemed so at ease among the cairns of sandstone and timber. It took a while, but Burnham got the point. He asked her to marry him. She said yes; the courtship went smoothly. Then scandal broke. Burnham's older brother had forged checks and wounded their father's wholesale drug business. Burnham immediately went to Margaret's father to break the engagement, on grounds the courtship could not continue in the shadow of scandal. Sherman told him he respected Burnham's sense of honor but rejected his withdrawal. He said quietly, "There is a black sheep in every family."

Later Sherman, a married man, would run off to Europe with the daughter of a friend.

Burnham and Margaret married on January 20, 1876. Sherman bought them a house at Forty-third Street and Michigan Avenue, near the lake but more importantly near the stockyards. He wanted proximity. He liked Burnham and approved of the marriage, but he did not entirely trust the young architect. He thought Burnham drank too much.

Sherman's doubts about Burnham's character did not color his respect for his skill as an architect. He commissioned other structures. In his greatest vote of confidence, he asked Burnham & Root to build an entry portal for the Union Stock Yards that would reflect the yards' growing importance. The result was the Stone Gate, three arches of Lemont limestone roofed in copper and displaying over the central arch the carved bust—Root's touch, no doubt—of John Sherman's favorite bull, Sherman. The gate became a landmark that endured into the twenty-first century, long after the last hog crossed to eternity over the great wooden ramp called the Bridge of Sighs.

Root also married a daughter of the stockyards, but his experience was darker. He designed a house for John Walker, president of the yards, and met Walker's daughter, Mary. During their courtship she became ill with tuberculosis. The disease rapidly gained ground, but Root remained committed to the engagement, even though it was clear to everyone he was marrying a dead woman. The ceremony was held in the house Root had designed. A friend, the poet Harriet Monroe, waited with the other guests for the bride to appear on the stairway. Monroe's sister, Dora, was the sole bridesmaid. "A long wait frightened us," Harriet Monroe said, "but at last the bride, on her father's arm, appeared like a white ghost at the halfway landing, and slowly oh, so hesitatingly dragging her heavy satin train, stepped down the wide stairway and across the floor to the bay window which was gay with flowers and vines. The effect was weirdly sad." Root's bride was thin and pale and could only whisper her vows. "Her gayety," Harriet Monroe wrote, "seemed like jewels on a skull."

Within six weeks Mary Walker Root was dead. Two years later Root married the bridesmaid, Dora Monroe, and very likely broke her poet-sister's heart. That Harriet Monroe also loved Root seems beyond dispute. She lived nearby and often visited the couple in their Astor Place home. In 1896 she published a biography of Root that would have made an angel blush. Later, in her memoir, *A Poet's Life,* she described Root's marriage to her sister as being "so completely happy that my own dreams of happiness, confirmed by that example, demanded as fortunate a fulfillment, and could accept nothing less." But Harriet never found its equal and devoted her life instead to poetry, eventually founding *Poetry* magazine, where she helped launch Ezra Pound toward national prominence.

Root and Burnham prospered. A cascade of work flowed to their firm, partly because Root managed to solve a puzzle that had bedeviled Chicago builders ever since the city's founding. By solving it, he helped the city become the birthplace of skyscrapers despite terrain that could not have been less suited to the role.

In the 1880s Chicago was experiencing explosive growth that propelled land values to levels no one could have imagined, especially within the downtown "Loop," named for the turn-around loops of streetcar lines. As land values rose, landowners sought ways of improving the return on their investments. The sky beckoned.

The most fundamental obstacle to height was man's capacity to walk stairs, especially after the kinds of meals men ate in the nineteenth century, but this obstacle had been removed by the advent of the elevator and, equally important, by Elisha Graves Otis's invention of a safety mechanism for halting an elevator in free-fall. Other barriers remained, however, the most elemental of which was the bedeviling character of Chicago's soil, which prompted one engineer to describe the challenge of laying foundations in Chicago as "probably not equaled for perverseness anywhere in the world." Bedrock lay 125 feet below grade, too deep for workers to reach with any degree of economy or safety using the construction methods available in the 1880s. Between this level and the surface was a mixture of sand and clay so saturated with water that engineers called it gumbo. It compressed under the weight of even modest structures and drove architects, as a matter of routine, to design their buildings with sidewalks that intersected the first story four inches above grade, in the hope that when the building settled and dragged the sidewalks down with it, the walks would be level.

There were only two known ways to resolve the soil problem: Build short and avoid the issue, or drive caissons down to bedrock. The latter technique required that workers excavate deep shafts, shore the walls, and pump each so full of air that the resulting high pressure held water at bay, a process that was notorious for causing deadly cases of the bends and used mainly by bridge builders who had no other choice. John Augustus Roebling had used caissons, famously, in building the Brooklyn Bridge, but their first use in the United States had occurred earlier, from 1869 through 1874, when James B. Eads built a bridge over the Mississippi at St. Louis. Eads discovered that workers began experiencing the bends at sixty feet below ground, roughly half the depth to which a Chicago caisson would have to descend. Of the 352 men who worked on the bridge's notorious east caisson, pressure-related illness killed twelve, left two crippled for life, and injured sixty-six others, a casualty rate of over 20 percent.

But Chicago's landowners wanted profit, and at the city's center, profit meant height. In 1881 a Massachusetts investor, Peter Chardon Brooks III, commissioned Burnham & Root to build the tallest office building yet constructed in Chicago, which he planned to call the Montauk. Previously he had brought them their first big downtown commission, the seven-story Grannis Block. In that structure, Burnham said, "our originality began to show. . . . It was a wonder. Everybody went to see it, and the town was proud of it." They moved their offices into its top floor (a potentially fatal move, as it happens, but no one knew it at the time). Brooks wanted the new building to be 50 percent taller "if," he said, "the earth can support it."

The partners quickly grew frustrated with Brooks. He was picky and frugal and seemed not to care how the building looked as long as it was functional. He issued instructions that anticipated by many years Louis Sullivan's famous admonition that form must follow function. "The building throughout is to be for use and not for ornament," Brooks wrote. "Its beauty will be in its all-adaptation to its use." Nothing was to project from its face, no gargoyles, no pedimenta, for projections collected dirt. He wanted all pipes left in the open. "This covering up of pipes is all a mistake, they should be exposed everywhere, if necessary painted well and handsomely." His frugal glare extended to the building's bathrooms. Root's design called for cabinets under sinks. Brooks objected: A cabinet made "a good receptacle for dirt, mice too."

The trickiest part of the Montauk was its foundation. Initially Root planned to employ a technique that Chicago architects had used since 1873 to support buildings of ordinary stature. Workers would erect pyramids of stone on the basement slab. The broad bottom of each pyramid spread the load and reduced settlement; the narrow top supported load-bearing columns. To hold up ten stories of stone and brick, however, the pyramids would have to be immense, the basement transformed into a Giza of stone. Brooks objected. He wanted the basement free for the boilers and dynamo.

The solution, when Root first struck it, must have seemed too simple to be real. He envisioned digging down to the first reasonably firm layer of clay, known as hard-pan, and there spreading a pad of concrete nearly two feet thick. On top of this workers would set down a layer of steel rails stretching from one end of the pad to the other, and over this a second layer at right angles. Succeeding layers would be arranged the same way. Once complete, this *grillage* of steel would be filled and covered with Portland cement to produce a broad, rigid raft that Root called a floating foundation. What he was proposing, in effect, was a stratum of artificial bedrock that would also serve as the floor of the basement. Brooks liked it.

Once built, the Montauk was so novel, so tall, it defied description by conventional means. No one knows who coined the term, but it fit, and the Montauk became the first building to be called a skyscraper. "What Chartres was to the Gothic cathedral," wrote Thomas Talmadge, a Chicago architect and critic, "the Montauk Block was to the high commercial building."

This was the heyday of architectural invention. Elevators got faster and safer. Glassmakers became adept at turning out ever larger sheets of plate glass. William Jenney, of the firm Loring & Jenney, where Burnham started his architectural career, designed the first building to have a load-bearing metal frame, in which the burden of supporting the structure was shifted from the exterior walls to a skeleton of iron and steel. Burnham and Root realized that Jenney's innovation freed builders from the last physical constraints on altitude. They employed it to build taller and taller buildings, cities in the sky inhabited by a new race of businessmen, whom some called "cliff-dwellers." These were men, wrote Lincoln Steffens, "who will not have an office unless it is up where the air is cool and fresh, the outlook broad and beautiful, and where there is silence in the heart of business."

Burnham and Root became rich men. Not Pullman rich, not rich enough to be counted among the first rank of society alongside Potter Palmer and Philip Armour, or to have their wives' gowns described in the city's newspapers, but rich beyond anything either man had expected, enough so that each year Burnham bought a barrel of fine Madeira and aged it by shipping it twice around the world on slow freighters.

As their firm prospered, the character of each partner began to emerge and clarify. Burnham was a talented artist and architect in his own right, but his greatest strength lay in his ability to win clients and execute Root's elegant designs. Burnham was handsome, tall, and strong, with vivid blue eyes, all of which drew clients and friends to him the way a lens gathers light. "Daniel Hudson Burnham was one of the handsomest men I ever saw," said Paul Starrett, later to lead construction of the Empire State Building; he joined Burnham & Root in 1888 as an all-purpose helper. "It was easy to see how he got commissions. His very bearing and looks were half the battle. He had only to assert the most commonplace thing and it sounded important and convincing." Starrett recalled being moved by Burnham's frequent admonition: "Make no little plans; they have no magic to stir men's blood."

Burnham understood that Root was the firm's artistic engine. He believed Root possessed a genius for envisioning a structure quickly, in its entirety. "I've never seen anyone like him in this respect," Burnham said. "He would grow abstracted and silent, and a faraway look would come into his eyes, and the building was there before him—every stone." At the same time he knew Root had little interest in the business side of architecture and in sowing the relationships at the Chicago Club and Union League that eventually led to commissions.

Root played the organ every Sunday morning at the First Presbyterian Church. He wrote opera critiques for the *Chicago Tribune*. He read broadly in philosophy, science, art, and religion and was known throughout Chicago's upper echelon for his ability to converse on almost any subject and to do so with great wit. "His conversational powers were extraordinary," a friend said. "There seemed to be no subject which he had not investigated and in which he was not profoundly learned." He had a sly sense of humor. One Sunday morning he played the organ with particular gravity. It was a while before anyone noticed he was playing "Shoo, Fly." When Burnham and Root were together, one woman said, "I used always to think of some big strong tree with lightning playing around it."

Each man recognized and respected the other's skills. The resultant harmony was reflected in the operation of their office, which, according to one historian, functioned with the mechanical precision of a "slaughterhouse," an apt allusion, given Burnham's close professional and personal association with the stockyards. But Burnham also created an office culture that anticipated that of businesses that would not appear for another century. He installed a gym. During lunch hour employees played handball. Burnham gave fencing lessons. Root played impromptu recitals on a rented piano. "The office was full of a rush of work," Starrett said, "but the spirit of the place was delightfully free and easy and human in comparison with other offices I had worked in."

Burnham knew that together he and Root had reached a level of success that neither could have achieved on his own. The synchrony with which they worked allowed them to take on ever more challenging and daring projects, at a time when so much that an architect did was new and when dramatic increases in the height and weight of buildings amplified the risk of catastrophic failure. Harriet Monroe wrote, "The work of each man became constantly more necessary to the other."

As the firm grew, so did the city. It got bigger, taller, and richer; but it also grew dirtier, darker, and more dangerous. A miasma of cinder-flecked smoke blackened its streets and at times reduced visibility to the distance of a single block, especially in winter, when coal furnaces were in full roar. The ceaseless passage of trains, grip-cars, trolleys, carriages—surreys, landaus, victorias, broughams, phaetons, and hearses, all with iron-clad wheels that struck the pavement like rolling hammers—produced a constant thunder that did not recede until after midnight and made the open-window nights of summer unbearable. In poor neighborhoods garbage mounded in alleys and overflowed giant trash boxes that became banquet halls for rats and bluebottle flies. Billions of flies. The corpses of dogs, cats, and horses often remained where they fell. In January they froze into disheartening poses; in August they ballooned and ruptured. Many ended up in the Chicago River, the city's main commercial artery. During heavy rains, river water flowed in a greasy plume far out into Lake Michigan, to the towers that marked the intake pipes for the city's drinking water. In rain any street not paved with macadam oozed a fragrant muck of horse manure, mud, and garbage that swelled between granite blocks like pus from a wound. Chicago awed visitors and terrified them. French editor Octave Uzanne called it "that Gordian city, so excessive, so satanic." Paul Lindau, an author and publisher, described it as "a gigantic peepshow of utter horror, but extraordinarily to the point."

Burnham loved Chicago for the opportunity it afforded, but he grew wary of the city itself. By 1886 he and Margaret were the parents of five children: two daughters and three sons, the last, a boy named Daniel, born in February. That year Burnham bought an old farmhouse on the lake in the quiet village of Evanston, called by some "the Athens of suburbs." The house had sixteen rooms on two floors, was surrounded by "superb old trees," and occupied a long rectangle of land that stretched to the lake. He bought it despite initial opposition from his wife and her father, and did not tell his own mother of his planned move until the purchase was complete. Later he wrote her an apology. "I did it," he explained, "because I can no longer bear to have my children in the streets of Chicago. . . ."

Success came easily to Burnham and Root, but the partners did have their trials. In 1885 a fire destroyed the Grannis Block, their flagship structure. At least one of them was in the office at the time and made his escape down a burning stairway. They moved next to the top floor of the Rookery. Three years later a hotel they had designed in Kansas City collapsed during construction, injuring several men and killing one. Burnham was heartbroken. The city convened a coroner's inquest, which focused its attention on the building's design. For the first time in his career Burnham found himself facing public attack. He wrote to his wife, "You must not worry over the affair, no matter what the papers say. There will no doubt be censure, and much trouble before we get through, all of which we will shoulder in a simple, straightforward, manly way; so much as in us lies."

The experience cut him deeply, in particular the fact his competence lay exposed to the review of a bureaucrat over whom he had no influence. "The coroner," he wrote Margaret three days after the collapse, "is a disagreeable little doctor, a political hack, without brains, who distresses me." Burnham was sad and lonesome and wanted to go home. "I do so long to be there, and be at peace again, with you."

A third blow came in this period, but of a different character. Although Chicago was rapidly achieving recognition as an industrial and mercantile dynamo, its leading men felt keenly the slander from New York that their city had few cultural assets. To help address this lack, one prominent Chicagoan, Ferdinand W. Peck, proposed to build an auditorium so big, so acoustically perfect, as to silence all the carping from the East and to make a profit to boot. Peck envisioned enclosing this gigantic theater within a still larger shell that would contain a hotel, banquet room, and offices. The many architects who dined at Kinsley's Restaurant, which had a stature in Chicago equal to that of Delmonico's in New York, agreed this would be the single most important architectural assignment in the city's history and that most likely it would go to Burnham & Root. Burnham believed likewise.

Peck chose Chicago architect Dankmar Adler. If acoustically flawed, Peck knew, the building would be a failure no matter how imposing the finished structure proved to be. Only Adler had previously demonstrated a clear grasp of the principles of acoustical design. "Burnham was not pleased," wrote Louis Sullivan, by now Adler's partner, "nor was John Root precisely entranced." When Root saw early drawings of the Auditorium, he said it appeared as if Sullivan were about to "smear another façade with ornament."

From the start there was tension between the two firms, although no one could have known it would erupt years later in a caustic attack by Sullivan on Burnham's greatest achievements, this after Sullivan's own career had dissolved in a mist of alcohol and regret. For now, the tension was subtle, a vibration, like the inaudible cry of overstressed steel. It arose from discordant beliefs about the nature and purpose of architecture. Sullivan saw himself as an artist first, an idealist. In his autobiography, in which he always referred to himself in the third person, he described himself as "an innocent with his heart wrapped up in the arts, in the philosophies, in the religions, in the beatitudes of nature's loveliness, in his search for the reality of man, in his profound faith in the beneficence of power." He called Burnham a "colossal merchandiser" fixated on building the biggest, tallest, costliest structures. "He was elephantine, tactless, and blurting."

Workers began building the Auditorium on June 1, 1887. The result was an opulent structure that, for the moment, was the biggest private building in America. Its theater contained more than four thousand seats, twelve hundred more than New York's Metropolitan Opera House. And it was air-conditioned, through a system that blew air over ice. The surrounding building had commercial offices, an immense banquet hall, and a hotel with four hundred luxurious rooms. A traveler from Germany recalled that simply by turning an electric dial on the wall by his bed, he could request towels, stationery, ice water, newspapers, whiskey, or a shoe shine. It became the most celebrated building in Chicago. The president of the United States, Benjamin Harrison, attended its grand opening.

Ultimately these setbacks proved to be minor ones for Burnham and Root. Far worse was to occur, and soon, but as of February 14, 1890, the day of the great fair vote, the partners seemed destined for a lifetime of success.

Outside the *Tribune* building there was silence. The crowd needed a few moments to process the news. A man in a long beard was one of the first to react. He had sworn not to shave until Chicago got the fair. Now he climbed the steps of the adjacent Union Trust Company Bank. On the top step he let out a shriek that one witness likened to the scream of a skyrocket. Others in the crowd echoed his cry, and soon two thousand men and women and a few children—mostly telegraph boys and hired messengers—cut loose with a cheer that tore through the canyon of brick, stone, and glass like a flash flood. The messenger boys raced off with the news, while throughout the city telegraph boys sprinted from the offices of the Postal Telegraph Company and Western Union or leaped aboard their Pope "safety" bikes, one bound for the Grand Pacific Hotel, another the Palmer House, others to the Richelieu, Auditorium, Wellington, the gorgeous homes on Michigan and Prairie, the clubs— Chicago, Century, Union League—and the expensive brothels, in partic- ular Carrie Watson's place with its lovely young women and cascades of champagne.

One telegraph boy made his way through the dark to an unlit alley that smelled of rotted fruit and was silent save for the receding hiss of gaslights on the street he had left behind. He found a door, knocked, and entered a room full of men, some young, some old, all seeming to speak at once, a few quite drunk. A coffin at the center of the room served as a bar. The light was dim and came from gas jets hidden behind skulls mounted on the walls. Other skulls lay scattered about the room. A hang- man's noose dangled from the wall, as did assorted weapons and a blan- ket caked with blood.

These artifacts marked the room as headquarters of the Whitechapel Club, named for the London slum in which two years earlier Jack the Ripper had done his killing. The club's president held the official title of the Ripper; its members were mainly journalists, who brought to the club's meetings stories of murder harvested from the city's streets. The weapons on the wall had been used in actual homicides and were provided by Chicago policemen; the skulls by an alienist at a nearby lunatic asylum; the blanket by a member who had acquired it while covering a battle between the army and the Sioux.

Upon learning that Chicago had won the fair, the men of the Whitechapel Club composed a telegram to Chauncey Depew, who more than any other man symbolized New York and its campaign to win the fair. Previously Depew had promised the members of the Whitechapel Club that if Chicago prevailed he would present himself at the club's next meeting, to be hacked apart by the Ripper himself—metaphorically, he presumed, although at the Whitechapel Club could one ever be certain? The club's coffin, for example, had once been used to transport the body of a member who had committed suicide. After claiming his body, the club had hauled it to the Indiana Dunes on Lake Michigan, where members erected an immense pyre. They placed the body on top, then set it alight. Carrying torches and wearing black hooded robes, they circled the fire singing hymns to the dead between sips of whiskey. The club also had a custom of sending robed members to kidnap visiting celebrities and steal them away in a black coach with covered windows, all without saying a word.

The club's telegram reached Depew in Washington twenty minutes after the final ballot, just as Chicago's congressional delegation began celebrating at the Willard Hotel near the White House. The telegram asked, "When may we see you at our dissecting table?"

Depew sent an immediate response: "I am at your service when ordered and quite ready after today's events to contribute my body to Chicago science."

Although he was gracious in acknowledging defeat, Depew doubted that Chicago really understood the challenge that lay ahead. "The most marvelous exhibit of modern times or ancient times has now just closed successfully at Paris," he told the *Tribune*. "Whatever you do is to be compared with that. If you equal it you have made a success. If you surpass it you have made a triumph. If you fall below it you will be held responsible by the whole American people for having assumed what you are not equal to.

"Beware," he warned. "Take care!"

Chicago promptly established a formal corporation, the World's Columbian Exposition Company, to finance and build the fair. Quietly officials made it clear that Burnham and Root would be the lead designers. The burden of restoring the nation's pride and prominence in the wake of the Paris exposition had fallen upon Chicago, and Chicago in turn had lodged it firmly, if for now discreetly, on the top floor of the Rookery.

Failure was unthinkable. If the fair failed, Burnham knew, the nation's honor would be tarnished, Chicago humiliated, and his own firm dealt a crushing blow. Everywhere Burnham turned there was someone—a friend, an editor, a fellow club member—telling him that the nation expected something tremendous out of this fair. And expected it in record time. The Auditorium alone had taken nearly three years to build and driven Louis Sullivan to the brink of physical collapse. Now Burnham and Root were being called upon to build what amounted to an entire city in about the same amount of time—not just any city, but one that would surpass the brilliance of the Paris exposition. The fair also would have to make a profit. Among Chicago's leading men, profitability was a matter of personal and civic honor.

By traditional architectural standards the challenge seemed an impossible one. Alone neither architect could have done it, but together, Burnham believed, he and Root had the will and the interlocking powers of organization and design to succeed. Together they had defeated gravity and conquered the soft gumbo of Chicago soil, to change forever the character of urban life; now, together, they would build the fair and change history. It could be done, because it had to be done, but the challenge was monstrous. Depew's oratory on the fair quickly grew tiresome, but the man had a way of capturing with wit and brevity the true character of a situation. "Chicago is like the man who marries a woman with a ready-made family of twelve," he said. "The trouble is just begun."

Even Depew, however, did not foresee the true magnitude of the forces that were converging on Burnham and Root. At this moment he and they saw the challenge in its two most fundamental dimensions, time and money, and these were stark enough.

Only Poe could have dreamed the rest.

The Necessary Supply

ONE MORNING IN AUGUST 1886, as heat rose from the streets with the intensity of a child's fever, a man calling himself H. H. Holmes walked into one of Chicago's train stations. The air was stale and still, suffused with the scent of rotten peaches, horse excrement, and partially combusted Illinois anthracite. Half a dozen locomotives stood in the trainyard exhaling steam into the already-yellow sky.

Holmes acquired a ticket to a village called Englewood in the town of Lake, a municipality of 200,000 people that abutted Chicago's southernmost boundary. The township encompassed the Union Stock Yards and two large parks: Washington Park, with lawns, gardens, and a popular racetrack, and Jackson Park, a desolate, undeveloped waste on the lakeshore.

Despite the heat Holmes looked fresh and crisp. As he moved through the station, the glances of young women fell around him like wind-blown petals.

He walked with confidence and dressed well, conjuring an impression of wealth and achievement. He was twenty-six years old. His height was five feet, eight inches; he weighed only 155 pounds. He had dark hair and striking blue eyes, once likened to the eyes of a Mesmerist. "The eyes are very big and wide open," a physician named John L. Capen later observed. "They are blue. Great murderers, like great men in other walks of activity, have blue eyes." Capen also noted thin lips, tented by a full dark mustache. What he found most striking, however, were Holmes's ears. "It is a marvelously small ear, and at the top it is shaped and carved after the fashion in which old sculptors indicated deviltry and vice in their statues of satyrs." Overall, Capen noted, "he is made on a very delicate mold."

To women as yet unaware of his private obsessions, it was an appealing delicacy. He broke prevailing rules of casual intimacy: He stood too close, stared too hard, touched too much and long. And women adored him for it.

He stepped from the train into the heart of Englewood and took a moment to survey his surroundings. He stood at the intersection of Sixty-third and Wallace. A telegraph pole at the corner held Fire Alarm Box No. 2475. In the distance rose the frames of several three-story homes under construction. He heard the concussion of hammers. Newly planted trees stood in soldierly ranks, but in the heat and haze they looked like desert troops gone too long without water. The air was still, moist, and suffused with the burned-licorice scent of freshly rolled macadam. On the corner stood a shop with a sign identifying it as E. S. Holton Drugs.

He walked. He came to Wentworth Street, which ran north and south and clearly served as Englewood's main commercial street, its pavement clotted with horses, drays, and phaetons. Near the corner of Sixty-third and Wentworth, he passed a fire station that housed Engine Company no. 51. Next door was a police station. Years later a villager with a blind spot for the macabre would write, "While at times there was considerable need of a police force in the Stock Yards district, Englewood pursued the even tenor of its way with very little necessity for their appearance other than to ornament the landscape and see that the cows were not disturbed in their peaceful pastures."

Holmes returned to Wallace Street, where he had seen the sign for Holton Drugs. Tracks crossed the intersection. A guard sat squinting against the sun watching for trains and every few minutes lowered a crossing gate as yet another locomotive huffed past. The drugstore was on the northwest corner of Wallace and Sixty-third. Across Wallace was a large vacant lot.

Holmes entered the store and there found an elderly woman named Mrs. Holton. He sensed vulnerability, sensed it the way another man might capture the trace of a woman's perfume. He identified himself as a doctor and licensed pharmacist and asked the woman if she needed assistance in her store. He spoke softly, smiled often, and held her in his frank blue gaze.

He was good with conversation, and soon she revealed to him her deepest sorrow. Her husband, upstairs in their apartment, was dying of cancer. She confessed that managing the store while caring for him had become a great burden.

Holmes listened with moist eyes. He touched her arm. He could ease her burden, he said. Not only that, he could turn the drugstore into a thriving establishment and conquer the competition up the block.

His gaze was so clear and blue. She told him she would have to talk to her husband.

———

She walked upstairs. The day was hot. Flies rested on the window sill. Outside yet another train rumbled through the intersection. Cinder and smoke drifted like soiled gauze past the window. She would talk to her husband, yes, but he was dying, and she was the one who now managed the store and bore its responsibilities, and she had come to a decision.

Just thinking about the young doctor gave her a feeling of contentment she had not experienced in a long while.

———

Holmes had been to Chicago before, but only for brief visits. The city impressed him, he said later, which was surprising because as a rule nothing impressed him, nothing moved him. Events and people captured his attention the way moving objects caught the notice of an amphibian: first a machinelike registration of proximity, next a calculation of worth, and last a decision to act or remain motionless. When he resolved at last to move to Chicago, he was still using his given name, Herman Webster Mudgett.

As for most people, his initial sensory contact with Chicago had been the fantastic stink that lingered always in the vicinity of the Union Stock Yards, a Chinook of putrefaction and incinerated hair, "an elemental odor," wrote Upton Sinclair, "raw and crude; it was rich, almost rancid, sensual and strong." Most people found it repulsive. The few who found it invigorating tended to be men who had waded in its "river of death," Sinclair's phrase, and panned from it great fortunes. It is tempting to imagine that all that death and blood made Mudgett feel welcome but more realistic to suppose it conveyed a sense that here at last was a city that allowed a broader range of behavior than was tolerated in Gilmanton Academy, New Hampshire, the town in which he was born and where he drifted through childhood as a small, odd, and exceptionally bright boy—and where, as a consequence, in the cruel imaginations of his peers, he became prey.

The memory of one episode stayed with him throughout his life. He was five, wearing his first boy's suit, when his parents sent him off to begin his education at the village schoolhouse. "I had daily to pass the office of one village doctor, the door of which was seldom if ever barred," he wrote in a later memoir. "Partly from its being associated in my mind as the source of all the nauseous mixtures that had been my childish terror (for this was before the day of children's medicines), and partly because of vague rumors I had heard regarding its contents, this place was one of peculiar abhorrence to me."

In those days a doctor's office could indeed be a fearsome place. All doctors were in a sense amateurs. The best of them bought cadavers for study. They paid cash, no questions asked, and preserved particularly interesting bits of diseased viscera in large clear bottles. Skeletons hung in offices for easy anatomical reference; some transcended function to become works of art so detailed, so precisely articulated—every bleached bone hitched to its neighbor with brass, under a skull grinning with slap-shoulder bonhomie—that they appeared ready to race chattering down the street to catch the next grip-car.

Two older children discovered Mudgett's fear and one day captured him and dragged him "struggling and shrieking" into the doctor's office. "Nor did they desist," Mudgett wrote, "until I had been brought face to face with one of its grinning skeletons, which, with arms outstretched, seemed ready in its turn to seize me.

"It was a wicked and dangerous thing to do to a child of tender years and health," he wrote, "but it proved an heroic method of treatment, destined ultimately to cure me of my fears, and to inculcate in me, first, a strong feeling of curiosity, and, later, a desire to learn, which resulted years afterwards in my adopting medicine as a profession."

The incident probably did occur, but with a different choreography. More likely the two older boys discovered that their five-year-old victim did not mind the excursion; that far from struggling and shrieking, he merely gazed at the skeleton with cool appreciation.

When his eyes settled back upon his captors, it was they who fled.

Gilmanton was a small farming village in New Hampshire's lake country, sufficiently remote that its residents did not have access to a daily newspaper and rarely heard the shriek of train whistles. Mudgett had two siblings, a brother and sister. His father, Levi, was a farmer, as was Levi's own father. Mudgett's parents were devout Methodists whose response to even routine misbehavior relied heavily on the rod and prayer, followed by banishment to the attic and a day with neither speech nor food. His mother often insisted he pray with her in her room, then filled the air around him with trembly passion.

By his own assessment, he was a "mother's boy." He spent a good deal of time alone in his room reading Jules Verne and Edgar Allan Poe and inventing things. He built a wind-powered mechanism that generated noise to scare birds from the family fields and set out to create a perpetual motion machine. He hid his most favored treasures in small boxes, among them his first extracted tooth and a photograph of his "twelve-year-old sweetheart," although later observers speculated these boxes also contained treasures of a more macabre sort, such as the skulls of small animals that he disabled and then dissected, alive, in the woods around Gilmanton. They based this speculation on the hard lessons learned during the twentieth century about the behavior of children of similar character. Mudgett's only close friend was an older child named Tom, who was killed in a fall while the boys were playing in an abandoned house.

Mudgett gouged his initials into an old elm tree at his grandfather's farm, where the family marked his growth with notches in a doorjamb. The first was less than three feet high. One of his favorite pastimes was to hike to a high boulder and shout to generate an echo. He ran errands for an "itinerant photographer" who stopped for a time in Gilmanton. The man had a pronounced limp and was glad for the help. One morning the photographer gave Mudgett a broken block of wood and asked him to take it to the town wagon maker for a replacement. When Mudgett returned with the new block, he found the photographer sitting beside his door, partly clothed. Without preamble, the photographer removed one of his legs.

Mudgett was stunned. He had never seen an artificial limb before and watched keenly as the photographer inserted the new block into a portion of the leg. "Had he next proceeded to remove his head in the same mysterious way I should not have been further surprised," Mudgett wrote.

Something about Mudgett's expression caught the photographer's eye. Still on one leg, he moved to his camera and prepared to take Mudgett's picture. Just before he opened the shutter, he held up his false leg and waved it at the boy. Several days later he gave Mudgett the finished photograph.

"I kept it for many years," Mudgett wrote, "and the thin terror-stricken face of that bare-footed, home-spun clad boy I can yet see."

At the time Mudgett described this encounter in his memoir, he was sitting in a prison cell hoping to engineer a swell of public sympathy. While it is charming to imagine the scene, the fact is the cameras that existed during Mudgett's boyhood made candid moments almost impossible to capture, especially when the subject was a child. If the photographer saw anything in Mudgett's eyes, it was a pale blue emptiness that he knew, to his sorrow, no existing film could ever record.

At sixteen Mudgett graduated school and, despite his age, took a job as a teacher, first in Gilmanton and then in Alton, New Hampshire, where he met a young woman named Clara A. Lovering. She had never encountered anyone quite like Mudgett. He was young but poised and had a knack for making her feel good even when she was inclined to feel otherwise. He spoke so well and with such warmth, always touching her in small affectionate ways, even in public. His great flaw was his persistent demand that she allow him to make love to her, not as a lover in formal courtship but in that way that was supposed to come only after marriage. She held him off but could not deny that Mudgett aroused within her an intensity of desire that colored her dreams. Mudgett was eighteen when he asked her to elope. She agreed. They married on July 4, 1878, before a justice of the peace.

At first there was passion far beyond what the dour gossip of older women had led Clara to expect, but their relationship chilled rapidly. Mudgett left the house for long periods. Soon he was gone for days at a time. Finally he was just gone. In the wedding registry of Alton, New Hampshire, they remained married, their contract a legal if desiccated thing.

At nineteen Mudgett went to college. Initially he set his sights on Dartmouth but changed his mind and instead went directly into medical school. He enrolled first in the medicine program at the University of Vermont in Burlington but found the school too small and after only one year moved to the University of Michigan in Ann Arbor, one of the West's leading scientific medical schools, noted for its emphasis on the controversial art of dissection. He enrolled on September 21, 1882. During the summer of his junior year he committed what he called, in his memoir, "the first really dishonest act of my life." He took a job as a traveler for a book publisher, assigned to sell a single book throughout northwestern Illinois. Instead of turning in the proceeds, he kept them. At the end of the summer he returned to Michigan. "I could hardly count my Western trip a failure," he wrote, "for I had seen Chicago."

He graduated in June 1884 with a lackluster record and set out to find "some favorable location" in which to launch a practice. To do so he took another job as a traveler, this time with a nursery company based in Portland, Maine. His route took him through towns he might otherwise never have encountered. Eventually he came to Mooers Forks, New York, where, according to the *Chicago Tribune,* the trustees of the grade school, "impressed with Mudgett's gentlemanly manners," hired him as the school principal, a post he held until he at last opened a medical practice. "Here I stayed for one year doing good and conscientious work, for which I received plenty of gratitude but little or no money."

Wherever he went, troubling things seemed to occur. His professors in Michigan had little to say about his academic talents but recalled that he had distinguished himself in a different way. "Some of the professors here recollected him as being a scamp," the university said. "He had a breach of promise with a hairdresser, a widow, who came to Ann Arbor from St. Louis, Mich."

In Mooers Forks there were rumors that a boy seen in his company had disappeared. Mudgett claimed the boy had returned to his own home in Massachusetts. No investigation took place. No one could imagine the charming Dr. Mudgett causing harm to anyone, let alone a child.

At midnight, many nights, Mudgett would pace the street outside his lodging.

Mudgett needed money. Teaching had paid a poverty wage; his medical practice yielded an income only slightly larger. "In the fall of 1885," he wrote, "starvation was staring me in the face."

While in medical school he and a fellow student, a Canadian, had talked about how easy it would be for one of them to buy life insurance, make the other the beneficiary, then use a cadaver to fake the death of the one insured. In Mooers Forks the idea came back to Mudgett. He paid a visit to his former classmate and found that his financial condition was no better. Together they devised an elaborate life insurance fraud, which Mudgett described in his memoir. It was an impossibly complex and gruesome plan, likely beyond the powers of anyone to execute, but his description is noteworthy for what it revealed, without his intention, about his astigmatic soul.

Broadly stated, the plan called for Mudgett and his friend to recruit a couple of other accomplices, who together would fake the deaths of a family of three and substitute cadavers for each person. The bodies would turn up later in an advanced state of decomposition, and the conspirators would divide the $40,000 death benefit (equivalent to more than one million dollars in twenty-first-century valuation).

"The scheme called for a considerable amount of material," Mudgett wrote, "no less than three bodies in fact," meaning he and his friend somehow had to acquire three cadavers roughly resembling the husband, wife, and child.

Mudgett foresaw no difficulty in acquiring the cadavers, although in fact a national shortage of corpses for medical education had by then driven doctors to raid graveyards for the freshly dead. Recognizing that even a doctor could not secure three bodies at once without raising suspicion, Mudgett and his accomplice agreed that each should contribute toward "the necessary supply."

Mudgett claimed to have gone to Chicago in November 1885 and there to have acquired his "portion" of the bodies. Unable to find a job, he placed his portion in storage and left for Minneapolis, where he found work in a drugstore. He remained in Minneapolis until May 1886, when he left for New York City, planning to take "a part of the material there," and to leave the rest in Chicago. "This," he said, "necessitated repacking the same."

He claimed to have deposited one package of dismembered cadaver in the Fidelity Storage Warehouse in Chicago. The other accompanied him to New York, where he lodged it "in a safe place." During his train journey to New York, however, he read two newspaper articles about insurance crime, "and for the first time I realized how well organized and well prepared the leading insurance companies were to detect and punish this kind of fraud." These articles, he claimed, caused him to abandon the plan and to jettison all hope of ever succeeding at such a scheme in the future.

He was lying. In fact, Mudgett was convinced that the fundamentals of the approach had merit—that by faking the deaths of others, he could indeed fleece life insurance companies. As a physician, he knew no means existed for establishing the identities of burned, dismembered, or otherwise disfigured corpses. And he did not mind handling bodies. They were "material," no different from firewood, although somewhat more difficult to dispose of.

He was lying too about needing money. The owner of the house in Mooers Forks where he boarded, D. S. Hays, noticed Mudgett often displayed large sums of cash. Hays grew suspicious and watched Mudgett closely—albeit not closely enough.

Mudgett left Mooers Fork at midnight, without paying his lodging bill to Hays. He made his way to Philadelphia, where he hoped to situate himself in a drugstore and eventually to become a partner or owner. He found nothing suitable, however, and instead took a job as a "keeper" at the Norristown Asylum. "This," he wrote, "was my first experience with insane persons, and so terrible was it that for years afterwards, even now sometimes, I see their faces in my sleep." Within days he quit.

Eventually he did find a position at one of Philadelphia's drugstores. Soon afterward a child died after taking medicine acquired at the store. Mudgett immediately left the city.

He caught a train for Chicago but quickly found that he could not work as a druggist in Illinois until he passed a licensing examination in the state capital in Springfield. There, in July 1886, the year Sir Arthur Conan Doyle introduced his detective to the world, Mudgett registered his name as Holmes.

Holmes understood that powerful new forces were acting upon Chicago, causing a nearly miraculous expansion. The city was growing in all available directions, and where it abutted the lake, it grew skyward, sharply increasing the value of land within the Loop. Everywhere he looked he saw evidence of the city's prosperity. Even the smoke was proof. The city's newspapers loved to crow about the startling increase in the number of workers employed by Chicago's industries, especially meat-packing. Holmes knew—everyone knew—that as skyscrapers soared and the stockyards expanded their butchery, the demand for workers would remain high, and that workers and their supervisors would seek to live in the city's suburbs, with their promise of smooth macadam, clean water, decent schools, and above all air untainted by the stench of rotting offal from the Union Yards.

As the city's population swelled, demand for apartments turned into "flat fever." When people could not find or afford apartments, they sought rooms in private homes and boardinghouses, where typically the rent included meals. Speculators thrived and created eerie landscapes. In Calumet a thousand ornate streetlamps stood in a swamp, where they did nothing but ignite the fog and summon auras of mosquitoes. Theodore Dreiser reached Chicago about when Holmes did and was struck by this landscape of anticipation. "The city had laid miles and miles of streets and sewers through regions where perhaps one solitary house stood out alone," he wrote in *Sister Carrie*. "There were regions, open to the sweeping winds and rain, which were yet lighted throughout the night with long, blinking lines of gas lamps fluttering in the wind."

One of the fastest-growing suburbs was Englewood. Even a newcomer like Holmes could tell that Englewood was booming. Real estate advertisements were full of testimonials to its location and appreciating values. Englewood in fact had been growing quickly ever since the Great Fire of 1871. One resident recalled how immediately after the fire "there was such a rush for homes in Englewood and the population increased so rapidly that it was impossible to keep up with it." Old railroad men still called it Chicago Junction or Junction Grove or simply the Junction, for the eight railroad lines that converged within its borders, but after the Civil War residents grew weary of the industrial resonance of the name. In 1868 a Mrs. H. B. Lewis suggested a new one, Englewood, the name of a New Jersey town in which she previously had lived and which had taken its name from a forest in Carlisle, England, legendary for having sheltered two outlaws of Robin Hood stripe. It was here, in what Chicagoans called a "streetcar" suburb, that stockyard supervisors chose to settle, as did officials of companies headquartered in the skyscrapers of the Loop. They acquired big houses on streets named Harvard and Yale that were lined with elm, ash, sycamore, and linden and posted with signs barring all but essential wagon traffic. They sent their children to school and went to church and attended meetings of the Masons and of forty-five other secret societies having lodges, kingdoms, and hives in the village. On Sundays they wandered among the velvet lawns of Washington Park and, if in the mood for solitude, the wind-blasted ridges of Jackson Park at the easternmost end of Sixty-third Street, on the lakeshore.

They took trains and streetcars to work and congratulated themselves on living upwind of the stockyards. The developer of a large Englewood parcel touted this asset in a catalog promoting the auction of two hundred residential lots called the Bates Subdivision: "To the business men of the Union Stock Yards it is particularly convenient and accessible, and free from the odors that are wafted by the prevailing winds to the most fashionable localities of the City."

⸻

Dr. Holton did die. Holmes made his widow an offer: He would buy the store, and she could continue to reside in the second-floor apartment. He couched his offer in prose that made it seem as if he were proposing the purchase not to benefit himself but solely to free the grieving Mrs. Holton from the burden of work. He touched her arm as he spoke. After she signed the deed over to him, he stood and thanked her with tears in his eyes.

He financed the purchase mainly with money he raised by mortgaging the store's fixtures and stock, agreeing to repay the loan at a rate of one hundred dollars a month (about three thousand dollars in twenty-first-century value). "My trade was good," he said, "and for the first time in my life I was established in a business that was satisfactory to me."

He put up a new sign: H. H. HOLMES PHARMACY. As word spread that a young, handsome, and apparently unmarried young doctor now stood behind the counter, an increasing number of single women in their twenties began to patronize the store. They dressed nicely and bought things they did not need. Longtime customers also liked the new proprietor, although they missed the comforting presence of Mrs. Holton. The Holtons had been there when their children were sick; had comforted them when these illnesses proved mortal. They knew Mrs. Holton had sold the place. But why had they not seen her around town?

Holmes smiled and explained that she had decided to visit relatives in California, something she had long wanted to do but could never find the time or money to accomplish and certainly could not have done with her husband on his deathbed.

As time wore on and the inquiries dwindled, Holmes modified the story a bit. Mrs. Holton, he explained, liked California so much she had decided to settle there permanently.

"Becomingness"

NOTHING. THERE HAD BEEN SO much energy, so much bravado, but now—nothing. It was July 1890, nearly six months since Congress had voted to give the World's Columbian Exposition to Chicago, but the forty-five men on the exposition's board of directors still had not decided where within the city the fair should be built. At the time of the vote, with the city's pride at stake, all Chicago had sung with one voice. Its emissaries had boasted to Congress that the city could deliver a grander and more appropriate setting than anything New York, Washington, or any other city could propose. Now, however, each quarter of Chicago was insisting on a location within its own boundaries, and the squabbling had stymied the board.

The fair's Committee on Grounds and Buildings had asked Burnham, quietly, to evaluate a number of locations in the city. With equal discretion, the committee assured Burnham and Root that ultimately they would direct the design and construction of the fair. For Burnham, each lost moment was a theft from the already scanty fund of time allotted to build the exposition. The final fair bill signed in April by President Benjamin Harrison established a Dedication Day for October 12, 1892, to honor the moment four hundred years earlier when Columbus had first sighted the New World. The formal opening, however, would not occur until May 1, 1893, to give Chicago more time to prepare. Even so, Burnham knew, much of the fair would have to be ready for the dedication. That left just twenty-six months.

A friend of Burnham's, James Ellsworth, was one of the board's directors; he too was frustrated by the stalemate, so much so that on his own initiative, during a business trip to Maine in mid-July, he visited the Brookline, Massachusetts, office of Frederick Law Olmsted to try and persuade him to come to Chicago and evaluate the sites under consideration and perhaps take on the task of designing the fair's landscape. Ellsworth hoped that Olmsted's opinion, backed by his reputation as the wizard of Central Park, would help force a decision.

That Ellsworth, of all people, should be driven to this step was significant. Initially he had been ambivalent about whether Chicago should even seek the world's fair. He agreed to serve as a director only out of fear that the exposition was indeed at risk of fulfilling the meager expectations of the East and becoming "simply a fair as the term generally implies." He believed it imperative that the city protect its civic honor by producing the greatest such event in the world's history, a goal that seemed to be slipping from Chicago's grasp with each sweep of the clock's hands.

He offered Olmsted a consulting fee of one thousand dollars (equivalent to about thirty thousand today). That the money was his own, and that he lacked official authority to hire Olmsted, were two points Ellsworth failed to disclose.

Olmsted declined. He did not design fairs, he told Ellsworth. He doubted, moreover, that enough time remained for anyone to do the fair justice. To produce the kind of landscape effects Olmsted strived to create required not months but years, even decades. "I have all my life been considering distant effects and always sacrificing immediate success and applause to that of the future," he wrote. "In laying out Central Park we determined to think of no result to be realized in less than forty years."

Ellsworth insisted that what Chicago had in mind was something far grander than even the Paris exposition. He described for Olmsted a vision of a dream city designed by America's greatest architects and covering an expanse at least one-third larger than the Paris fair. Ellsworth assured Olmsted that by agreeing to help, he would be joining his name to one of the greatest artistic undertakings of the century.

Relenting slightly, Olmsted said he would think about it and agreed to meet with Ellsworth two days later, on Ellsworth's return from Maine.

Olmsted did think about it and began to see the exposition as an opportunity to achieve something for which he had fought long and hard but almost always with disappointing results. Throughout his career he had struggled, with little success, to dispel the perception that landscape architecture was simply an ambitious sort of gardening and to have his field recognized instead as a distinct branch of the fine arts, full sister to painting, sculpture, and brick-and-mortar architecture. Olmsted valued plants, trees, and flowers not for their individual attributes but rather as colors and shapes on a palette. Formal beds offended him. Roses were not roses but "flecks of white or red modifying masses of green." It irked him that few people seemed to understand the effects he worked so long and hard to create. "I design with a view to a passage of quietly composed, soft, subdued pensive character, shape the ground, screen out discordant elements and get suitable vegetation growing." Too often, however, he would "come back in a year and find destruction: why? 'My wife is so fond of roses;' 'I had a present of some large Norway spruces;' 'I have a weakness for white birch trees—there was one in my father's yard when I was a boy.' "

The same thing happened with large civic clients. He and Calvert Vaux had built and refined Central Park from 1858 through 1876, but forever afterward Olmsted found himself defending the park against attempts to tinker with its grounds in ways he considered tantamount to vandalism. It wasn't just Central Park, however. Every park seemed subject to such abuse.

"Suppose," he wrote to architect Henry Van Brunt, "that you had been commissioned to build a really grand opera house; that after the construction work had been nearly completed and your scheme of decoration fully designed you should be instructed that the building was to be used on Sundays as a Baptist Tabernacle, and that suitable place must be made for a huge organ, a pulpit and a dipping pool. Then at intervals afterwards, you should be advised that it must be so refitted and furnished that parts of it could be used for a court room, a jail, a concert hall, hotel, skating rink, for surgical cliniques, for a circus, dog show, drill room, ball room, railway station and shot tower?" That, he wrote, "is what is nearly always going on with public parks. Pardon me if I overwhelm you; it is a matter of chronic anger with me."

What landscape architecture needed, Olmsted believed, was greater visibility, which in turn would bring greater credibility. The exposition could help, he realized, providing it did rise to the heights envisioned by Ellsworth. He had to weigh this benefit, however, against the near-term costs of signing on. His firm already had a full roster of work, so much, he wrote, that "we are always personally under an agitating pressure and cloud of anxiety." And Olmsted himself had grown increasingly susceptible to illness. He was sixty-eight years old and partly lame from a decades-old carriage accident that had left one leg an inch shorter than the other. He was prone to lengthy bouts of depression. His teeth hurt. He had chronic insomnia and facial neuralgia. A mysterious roaring in his ears at times made it difficult for him to attend to conversation. He was still full of creative steam, still constantly on the move, but overnight train journeys invariably laid him low. Even in his own bed his nights often became sleepless horrors laced with toothache.

But Ellsworth's vision was compelling. Olmsted talked it over with his sons and with the newest member of the firm, Henry Sargent Codman— "Harry"—an intensely talented young landscape architect who had quickly become a trusted adviser and confidant.

When Ellsworth returned, Olmsted told him he had changed his mind. He would join the venture.

⌐══⌐

Once back in Chicago, Ellsworth secured formal authority to hire Olmsted and arranged to have him report directly to Burnham.

In a letter to Olmsted, Ellsworth wrote: "My position is this: The reputation of America is at stake in this matter, and the reputation of Chicago is also at stake. As an American citizen, you have an equal interest in furthering the success of this great and grand undertaking, and I know from talking with you, that on an occasion like this you grasp the whole situation and will be confined to no narrow limits."

Certainly that seemed to be the case when, during later contract negotiations, Olmsted at Codman's urging requested a fee of $22,500 (about $675,000 today) and got it.

On Wednesday, August 6, 1890, three weeks after Ellsworth's Brookline visit, the exposition company telegraphed Olmsted: "When can you be here?"

Olmsted and Codman arrived three days later, on Saturday morning, and found the city ringing from the news that the final census count had confirmed the earlier, preliminary ranking of Chicago as America's second largest city, even though this final tally also showed that Chicago's lead over Philadelphia was a skimpy one, only 52,324 souls. The good news was a salve for a difficult summer. Earlier, a heat wave had brutalized the city, killing seventeen people (including a man named Christ) and neatly eviscerating Chicago's boasts to Congress that the city possessed the charming summer climate—"cool and delicious," the *Tribune* had said—of a vacation resort. And just before the heat wave, a rising young British writer had published a scalding essay on Chicago. "Having seen it," Rudyard Kipling wrote, "I desire never to see it again. It is inhabited by savages."

To Burnham, Codman seemed amazingly young, late twenties at the most. To be so young and have the trust of America's greatest landscape architect, Codman must have been very bright indeed. He had obsidian eyes that looked as if they could punch holes in steel. As for Olmsted, Burnham was struck by the slightness of his frame, which seemed structurally insufficient to support so massive a skull. That head: Bald for most of its surface, trimmed at bottom with a tangled white beard, it resembled an ivory Christmas ball resting on a bed of excelsior. Olmsted looked worn from his travels, but his eyes were large, warm, and bright.

He wanted to start work immediately. Here at last, Burnham saw, was a man who understood the true cost of each lost minute.

Burnham of course knew of Olmsted's achievements: Central Park in Manhattan, Prospect Park in Brooklyn, the grounds of Cornell and Yale, and scores of other projects. He knew also that before launching the field of landscape architecture, Olmsted had been a writer and editor who had journeyed throughout the antebellum South exploring the culture and practice of slavery. Olmsted had a reputation for brilliance and tireless devotion to his work—but also for an acerbic candor that emerged most predictably in the presence of men who failed to understand that what he sought to create were not flower beds and ornamental gardens but expanses of scenery full of mystery, shadow, and sun-stippled ground.

Olmsted, for his part, knew that Burnham had been a leading force in driving buildings into the clouds. Burnham was said to be the business genius of his firm, Root the artist. It was with Burnham that Olmsted felt the greatest kinship. Burnham was decisive, blunt, and cordial; he spoke under a level blue gaze that Olmsted found reassuring. In private communication Olmsted and Codman agreed that Burnham was a man they could work with.

The tour began at once, but it was hardly an objective one. Burnham and Root clearly favored one location in particular: Jackson Park, on Chicago's South Side, due east of Englewood on the lakeshore. As it happened, Olmsted knew this ground. Twenty years earlier, at the request of Chicago's South Park commissioners, Olmsted had studied both Jackson Park and, to its west, Washington Park, and the broad boulevard that connected them, called Midway. In the plans he had produced for the commissioners, he envisioned transforming Jackson Park from a desert of sand and stagnant pools into a park unlike any other in the nation, focused on water and boating, with canals, lagoons, and shady coves. Olmsted finished those plans shortly before the Great Fire of 1871. In the rush to rebuild, Chicago never got around to realizing his vision. The park became part of Chicago during the 1889 annexations, but otherwise, Olmsted saw, little had changed. He knew its flaws, its *many* flaws, but believed that with a lot of deft dredging and sculpting, the park could be transformed into a landscape unlike any that had ever seated an exposition.

For he recognized that Jackson Park had something no other city in the world could equal: the spreading blue plain of Lake Michigan, as comely a backdrop for a fair as anyone could hope for.

On Tuesday, August 12, just four days after he and Codman arrived in Chicago, Olmsted filed a report with the exposition directors, who then to his chagrin made the report public. Olmsted had intended the report for a professional audience, one that would take for granted Jackson Park's fundamental acceptability and value the report as an unflinching guide to the challenges ahead. He was surprised to find the report put to use by opposing cliques as evidence that the fair could not possibly be placed in Jackson Park.

The directors asked for a second report. Olmsted delivered it on Monday, August 18, six days after the first. Burnham saw to his delight that Olmsted had given the directors somewhat more than they perhaps had wished to receive.

Olmsted was no literary stylist. Sentences wandered through the report like morning glory through the pickets of a fence. But his prose revealed the depth and subtlety of his thinking about how landscape could be modified to produce an effect in the mind.

First he had set down a few principles and done a little chiding.

Rather than squabbling over sites, he lectured, the different factions needed to recognize that for the exposition to succeed, everyone had to work together, no matter which location the directors selected. "It is to be desired, let us say, that it should be better understood than it yet seems to be by some of your fellow citizens, that the Fair is not to be a Chicago Fair. It is a World's Fair, and Chicago is to stand before the world as the chosen standard bearer for the occasion of the United States of America.

All Chicago can afford to take nothing less than the very best site that can be found for the fair, regardless of the special local interests of one quarter of the city or another."

Every landscape element of the fair, he argued, had to have one "supreme object, viz., the becomingness: the *becomingness* of everything that may be seen as a modestly contributive part of a grand whole; the major elements of which whole will be in the towering series of the main exhibition structures. In other words, the ground, with all it carries, before, between, and behind the buildings, however dressed with turf, or bedecked with flowers, shrubs or trees, fountains, statues, bric-a-brac, and objects of art, should be one *in unity of design* with the buildings; should set off the buildings and should be set off, in matters of light and shadow and tone, by the buildings."

Clearly certain sites were endowed more richly than others. More would be gained by associating the exposition with some feature of striking natural beauty "than by the most elaborate and costly artificial decorations in the form of gardening features, terraces, fountains and statues, than it is possible for the mind of man to devise or the hand of man to carry out." What the many factions in the battle for the fair seemed to ignore was that Chicago had "but one natural object at all distinctively local, which can be regarded as an object of much grandeur, beauty or interest. This is the Lake."

The lake was beautiful and always changing in hue and texture, but it was also, Olmsted argued, a novelty capable of amplifying the drawing power of the exposition. Many visitors from the heart of the country "will, until they arrive here, never have seen a broad body of water extending to the horizon; will never have seen a vessel under sail, nor a steamboat of half the tonnage of those to be seen hourly passing in and out of Chicago harbor; and will never have seen such effects of reflected light or of clouds piling up from the horizon, as are to be enjoyed almost every summer's day on the lake margin of the city."

Olmsted next considered four specific candidates: a site on the lakeshore above the Loop; two inland sites, one of which was Garfield Park on the western perimeter of the city; and of course Jackson Park.

Although Olmsted himself preferred the northernmost site, he insisted Jackson Park could work and "produce results of a pleasingly becoming character, such as have not hitherto been aimed at in World's Fairs."

Olmsted dismissed the inland sites out of hand as being flat and monotonous and too far from the lake. In critiquing Garfield Park, he again took a moment to express his annoyance at Chicago's inability to select a site, a failure he found all the more exasperating given the elaborate boasts issued by the city's leading men back when they were lobbying Congress for the fair:

"But considering what has been so strenuously urged upon the attention of the country in regard to the number and excellence of sites which Chicago has to offer; considering what advantages the Centennial Fair in Philadelphia possessed in the neighboring scenery; considering what advantages of the same order would have been possessed by the Fair if it had been given a site in the beautiful Rock Creek Valley at Washington, of which the Nation is just taking possession for a Park; considering what superb views were presented of the Palisades and up the valley of the Hudson on the one hand, and the waters and varied shores of Long Island Sound on the other, from the site offered for the Fair by New York; considering all this, we cannot but fear that the choice of a site in the rear of the city, utterly without natural landscape attraction, would be found a disappointment to the country, and that it would give occasion for not a little ironical reference to the claims of an endless extent of *perfect* sites made last winter before Congress."

The emphasis was Olmsted's.

Burnham hoped this second report would at last compel a decision. The delay was maddening, absurd, the hourglass long ago upended. The board seemed unaware that Chicago now risked becoming a national, even global, embarrassment.

⌐━━━⌐

Weeks passed.

At the end of October 1890 the site question remained unresolved. Burnham and Root tended to their fast-growing practice. Contractors had begun erecting two of the firm's newest, tallest Chicago skyscrapers, the Women's Christian Temperance Union Temple and the Masonic Fraternity Temple, at twenty-one stories the tallest building in the world. The foundations of both were nearly finished and awaited the installation of cornerstones. With architecture and construction such a fascination in Chicago, cornerstone ceremonies became extravagant affairs.

The Temperance celebration took place at the corner of La Salle and Monroe, beside a ten-ton boulder of dark New Hampshire granite seven feet square by three feet thick. Here Burnham and Root joined other dignitaries, including Mrs. Frances E. Willard, president of the Union, and Carter Henry Harrison, a former mayor who, with four terms already under his belt, was again running for the office. When Harrison appeared, wearing his usual black slouch hat, his pocket quilled with cigars, the crowd roared a welcome, especially the Irish and union men who saw Harrison as a friend of the city's lower classes. The presence of Burnham, Root, and Harrison beside the Temperance stone was more than a bit ironic. As mayor, Harrison had kept a couple of cases of fine bourbon in his office at city hall. The city's stern Protestant upper class saw him as a civic satyr whose tolerance of prostitution, gambling and alcohol had allowed the city's vice districts, most notably the Levee— home of the infamous bartender and robber Mickey Finn—to swell to new heights of depravity. Root was a notorious bon vivant, whom Louis Sullivan once described as "a man of the world, of the flesh, and considerably of the devil." And Burnham, in addition to monitoring the global passage of his Madeira, each year bottled four hundred quarts of lesser stuff sent to him by a friend and personally selected the wines for the cellar of the Union League Club.

With great ceremony Burnham handed a silver-plated trowel to Mrs. T. B. Carse, president of the Temple Building Association, whose smile suggested she knew nothing of these monstrous habits or at least was willing for the moment to ignore them. She scooped up a mound of mortar previously laid for purposes of the ceremony, then reapplied it and tapped it back into place, prompting a witness to observe, "she patted the mortar as a man sometimes pats the head of a curly-haired boy." She passed the trowel to the fearsome Mrs. Willard, "who stopped the mortar more heartily, and got some of it on her gown."

Root, according to a witness, leaned toward friends and suggested sotto voce that they all cut away for cocktails.

⌐────────⌐

Nearby, at the distribution warehouse of the *Chicago Inter Ocean,* a widely read and respected newspaper, a young Irish immigrant—and staunch supporter of Carter Harrison—completed his workday. His name was Patrick Eugene Joseph Prendergast. He ran a squad of obstreperous newsboys, whom he loathed, and who loathed him in return, as was clear by their taunts and practical jokes. That Prendergast might one day shape the destiny of the World's Columbian Exposition would have seemed ridiculous to these boys, for Prendergast to them was about as hapless and sorry a human being as they could imagine.

He was twenty-two years old, born in Ireland in 1868; his family emigrated to the United States in 1871 and in August that year moved to Chicago, just in time to experience the Great Fire. He was always, as his mother said, "a shy and retiring kind of a boy." He got his grade-school education at Chicago's De La Salle Institute. Brother Adjutor, one of his teachers, said, "While in school he was a remarkable boy in this way, that he was very quiet and took no part in the play of the other students at noon time. He would generally stand around. From the appearance of the boy I would be led to think that he was not well; that he was sick." Prendergast's father got him a job delivering telegrams for Western Union, which the boy held for a year and a half. When Prendergast was thirteen, his father died, and he lost his only friend. For a time his withdrawal from the world seemed complete. He awakened slowly. He began reading books about law and politics and attending meetings of the Single-Tax Club, which embraced Henry George's belief that private landowners should pay a tax, essentially rent, to reflect the underlying truth that land belonged to everyone. At these meetings Prendergast insisted on taking part in every conversation and once had to be carried from the room. To his mother, he seemed to be a different man: well read, animated, involved. She said: "He got smart all of a sudden."

In fact, his madness had become more profound. When he was not working, he wrote postcards, scores of them, perhaps hundreds, to the most powerful men in the city, in a voice that presumed he was their equal in social stature. He wrote to his beloved Harrison and to assorted other politicians, including the governor of Illinois. It's possible even that Burnham received a card, given his new prominence.

That Prendergast was a troubled young man was clear; that he might be dangerous seemed impossible. To anyone who met him, he appeared to be just another poor soul crushed by the din and filth of Chicago. But Prendergast had grand hopes for the future, all of which rested on one man: Carter Henry Harrison.

He threw himself eagerly into Harrison's mayoral campaign, albeit without Harrison's knowledge, sending postcards by the dozens and telling anyone who would listen that Harrison, staunch friend of the Irish and the working man, was the best candidate for the job.

He believed that when Harrison at last won his fifth two-year term— ideally in the upcoming April 1891 election, but perhaps not until the next, in 1893—he would reward Prendergast with a job. That was how Chicago politics worked. He had no doubt that Harrison would come through and rescue him from the frozen mornings and venomous news-boys that for the moment defined his life.

Among the most progressive alienists, this kind of unfounded belief was known as a delusion, associated with a newly identified disorder called paranoia. Happily, most delusions were harmless.

⸻

On October 25, 1890, the site for the fair still unchosen, worrisome news arrived from Europe, the first hint of forces gathering that could do infinitely more damage to the fair than the directors' stalemate. The *Chicago Tribune* reported that increasing turbulence in global markets had raised concerns in London that a recession, even a full-blown "panic," could be in the offing. Immediately these concerns began buffeting Wall Street. Railroad stocks tumbled. The value of Western Union's shares fell by five percent.

The next Saturday news of a truly stunning failure stuttered through the submarine cable that linked Britain and America.

In Chicago, before the news arrived, brokers spent a good deal of time discussing the morning's strange weather. An unusually "murky pall" hung over the city. Brokers joked how the gloom might be the signal that a "day of judgment" was at hand.

The chuckling faded with the first telegrams from London: Baring Brothers & Co., the powerful London investment house, was on the verge of closure. "The news," a *Tribune* writer observed, "was almost incredible." The Bank of England and a syndicate of financiers were racing to raise a fund to guarantee Baring's financial obligations. "The wild rush that followed to sell stocks was something terrible. It was a veritable panic for an hour."

For Burnham and the exposition directors, this wave of financial damage was troubling. If it indeed marked the start of a true and deep financial panic, the timing was abysmal. In order for Chicago to live up to its boasts about surpassing the Paris exposition in both size and attendance, the city would have to spend far more heavily than the French and capture a lot more visitors—yet the Paris show had drawn more people than any other peaceful event in history. In the best of times winning an audience of that scale would be a challenge; in the worst, impossible, especially since Chicago's interior location guaranteed that most visitors would have to buy an overnight train ticket. The railroads had made it known early and forcefully that they had no plans to discount their Chicago fares for the exposition.

Other corporate failures occurred both in Europe and in the United States, but their true meaning remained for the moment unclear—in retrospect, a good thing.

In the midst of this intensifying financial turbulence, on October 30 the exposition board appointed Burnham chief of construction, with a salary equivalent to $360,000; Burnham in turn made Root the fair's supervising architect and Olmsted its supervising landscape architect.

Burnham now possessed formal authority to begin building a fair, but he still had no place to put it.

"Don't Be Afraid"

As ENGLEWOOD GAINED POPULATION, Holmes's sales of tonics and lotions increased. By the end of 1886 the pharmacy was running smoothly and profitably. His thoughts turned now to a woman he had met earlier in the year during his brief stay in Minneapolis, Myrta Z. Belknap. She was young and blond, with blue eyes and a lush figure, but what elevated her above mere beauty was the aura of vulnerability and need that surrounded her. She became an immediate obsession, her image and need locked in his brain. He traveled to Minneapolis, ostensibly on business. He had no doubt he would succeed. It amused him that women as a class were so wonderfully vulnerable, as if they believed that the codes of conduct that applied in their safe little hometowns, like Alva, Clinton, and Percy, might actually still apply once they had left behind their dusty, kerosene-scented parlors and set out on their own.

The city toughened them quickly, however. Best to catch them at the start of their ascent toward freedom, in transit from small places, when they were anonymous, lost, their presence recorded nowhere. Every day he saw them stepping from trains and grip-cars and hansom cabs, inevitably frowning at some piece of paper that was supposed to tell them where they belonged. The city's madams understood this and were known to meet inbound trains with promises of warmth and friendship, saving the important news for later. Holmes adored Chicago, adored in particular how the smoke and din could envelop a woman and leave no hint that she ever had existed, save perhaps a blade-thin track of perfume amid the stench of dung, anthracite, and putrefaction.

To Myrta, Holmes seemed to have stepped from a world far more exciting than her own. She lived with her parents and clerked in a music store. Minneapolis was small, somnolent, and full of Swedish and Norwegian farmers as charming as cornstalks. Holmes was handsome, warm, and obviously wealthy, and he lived in Chicago, the most feared and magnetic of cities. Even during their first meeting he touched her; his eyes deposited a bright blue hope. When he left the store that first day, as motes of dust filled the space he left behind, her own life seemed drab beyond endurance. A clock ticked. Something had to change.

When his first letter arrived, asking sweetly if he might court her, she felt as if a coarse blanket had been lifted from her life. Every few weeks he returned to Minneapolis. He told her about Chicago. He described its skyscrapers and explained how each year the buildings grew taller and taller. He told her pleasantly shocking stories of the stockyards, how the hogs climbed the Bridge of Sighs to an elevated platform where chains were attached to their hind legs and they were swept away, shrieking, along an overhead track down into the bloody core of the slaughter-house. And romantic stories: how Potter Palmer had been so in love with his wife, Bertha, that he had given her a luxurious hotel, the Palmer House, as a wedding present.

There were rules about courtship. Although no one set them down on paper, every young woman knew them and knew instantly when they were being broken. Holmes broke them all—and with such forthright lack of shame that it became clear to Myrta that the rules must be different in Chicago. At first it frightened her, but she found quickly that she liked the heat and risk. When Holmes asked her to be his wife, she accepted immediately. They married on January 28, 1887.

Holmes neglected to tell Myrta that he already had a wife, Clara Lovering, the original Mrs. Herman Webster Mudgett. Two weeks after marrying Myrta, he filed a petition in the Supreme Court of Cook County, Illinois, to divorce Lovering. This was no fine-spirited gesture to clear the record: He charged Lovering with infidelity, a ruinous accusation. He allowed the petition to lapse, however, and eventually the court dismissed it for "failure to prosecute."

In Chicago Myrta saw at once that the stories Holmes had told of the city had only barely captured its glamour and dangerous energy. It was like a cauldron of steaming iron, trains everywhere—jarring, but also a reminder that life had opened to her at last. In Minneapolis there had been only silence and the inevitable clumsy petitions of potato-fingered men looking for someone, anyone, to share the agony of their days. That Holmes lived in Englewood, not the heart of Chicago, was at first a disappointment, but here too there was a vibrancy far beyond what she had experienced at home. She and Holmes settled into the second-floor apartment previously occupied by Mrs. Holton. By the spring of 1888 Myrta was pregnant.

At first she helped run the drugstore. She liked working with her husband and often watched him when he was engaged with a customer. She savored his looks and blue calm and craved the moments when, in the course of routine tasks, their bodies would touch. She admired, too, the charm with which he managed each transaction and how he won the business even of elderly customers loyal to the absent Mrs. Holton. And she smiled, at least initially, as a seemingly endless train of young women entered the store, each insisting that only direct consultation with Dr. Holmes himself would suffice.

Myrta came to see that underneath her husband's warm and charming exterior there flowed a deep current of ambition. He seemed a druggist in name only; he more closely fit the prevailing ideal of the self-made man who through hard work and invention pulled himself rung by rung into the upper strata of society. "Ambition has been the curse of my husband's life," Myrta said later. "He wanted to attain a position where he would be honored and respected. He wanted wealth."

She insisted, however, that his ambition never impaired his character and never distracted him from his role as husband and eventually father. Holmes, she swore, had a gentle heart. He adored children and animals. "He was a lover of pets and always had a dog or cat and usually a horse, and he would play with them by the hour, teaching them little tricks or romping with them." He neither drank nor smoked and did not gamble. He was affectionate and impossible to ruffle. "In his home life I do not think there was ever a better man than my husband," Myrta said. "He never spoke an unkind word to me or our little girl, or my mother. He was never vexed or irritable but was always happy and free from care."

Yet from the start tension suffused their marriage. Holmes expressed no hostility; the heat came from Myrta, who quickly tired of all those young female customers and the way Holmes would smile at them and touch them and channel his blue gaze into their eyes. At first she had found it appealing; then it made her uneasy; finally it made her jealous and watchful.

Her increasing possessiveness did not anger Holmes. Rather he came to see her as an obstacle, just as a sea captain might view an iceberg—something to monitor and avoid. Business was so good, he told Myrta, that he needed her help managing the store's books. She found herself spending more and more time in an office upstairs, writing correspondence and preparing invoices for the drugstore. She wrote to her parents of her sorrow. In the summer of 1888 her parents moved to Wilmette, Illinois, where they occupied a pretty two-story house on John Street, opposite a church. Lonely, sad, and pregnant, Myrta joined them at the house and there bore a daughter, Lucy.

Suddenly Holmes began acting like a dutiful husband. Myrta's parents were cool at first, but he courted their approval with moist-eyed declarations of regret and displays of adoration for his wife and child. He succeeded. "His presence," Myrta said, "was like oil on troubled waters, as mother often said to him. He was so kind, so gentle and thoughtful that we forgot our cares and worries."

He begged their forbearance for his lengthy absences from the Wilmette house. There was so much to do in Chicago. From the way he dressed and the money he gave Myrta, he certainly seemed like a man on the rise, and this perception went a long way to ease the concerns of Myrta's parents. They and Myrta settled into a life marked by increasingly sparse visits from Dr. Holmes, but when he did appear, he brought warmth and gifts and entombed little Lucy in his arms.

"It is said that babies are better judges of people than grown-up persons," Myrta said, "and I never saw a baby that would not go to Mr.

Holmes and stay with him contentedly. They would go to him when they wouldn't come to me. He was remarkably fond of children. Often when we were traveling and there happened to be a baby in the car he would say, 'Go and see if they won't lend you that baby a little while,' and when I brought it to him he would play with it, forgetting everything else, until its mother called for it or I could see that she wanted it. He has often taken babies that were crying from their mothers, and it would hardly be any time until he had them sound asleep or playing as happily as little ones can."

With Englewood booming, Holmes saw an opportunity. Ever since acquiring Holton's drugstore, he had been interested in the undeveloped land across the street. After a few inquiries he learned that it was owned by a woman in New York. In the summer of 1888 he bought the land and, thinking ahead, registered the deed under a false name, H. S. Campbell. Soon afterward he began jotting notes and sketching features for a building he planned to erect on the lot. He did not consult an architect, although a fine one, a Scotsman named A. A. Frazier, had an office in the building that housed Holton's store. To hire an architect would have meant revealing the true character of the structure that suddenly had lodged itself in his imagination.

The building's broad design and its function had come to him all at once, like a blueprint pulled from a drawer. He wanted retail shops on the first floor, to generate income and allow him to employ as many women as possible; apartments would fill the second and third. His personal flat and a large office would occupy the second-floor corner overlooking the intersection of Sixty-third and Wallace. These were the basics. It was the details of the building that gave him the most pleasure. He sketched a wooden chute that would descend from a secret location on the second floor all the way to the basement. He planned to coat the chute with axle grease. He envisioned a room next to his office fitted with a large walk-in vault, with airtight seams and asbestos-coated iron walls. A gas jet embedded in one wall would be controlled from his closet, as would other gas jets installed in apartments throughout the building. There would be a large basement with hidden chambers and a sub-basement for the permanent storage of sensitive material.

As Holmes dreamed and sketched, the features of his building became more elaborate and satisfying. But this was only the dream phase. He could hardly imagine the pleasure that would fill his days when the building was finished and flesh-and-blood women moved among its features. As always, the thought aroused him.

Constructing the building, he knew, would be no small challenge. He devised a strategy that he believed would not only allay suspicions but also reduce the costs of construction.

He placed newspaper advertisements for carpenters and laborers, and soon workers with teams of horses began excavating the land. The resulting hole evoked a giant grave and exuded the same musty chill, but this was not unwelcome for it provided workers with relief from the intensifying summer heat. The men had difficulty with the soil. The top few feet were easy to manage, but lower down the earth became sandy and wet. The sides of the pit had to be shored with timber. The walls bled water. A later report by a Chicago building inspector noted, "There is an uneven settlement of foundations, in some places as much as four inches in a span of 20 feet." Bricklayers set the foundation and laid the exterior walls, while carpenters erected the interior frame. The street resonated with the wheeze of handsaws.

Holmes cast himself as a demanding contractor. As workers came to him for their wages, he berated them for doing shoddy work and refused to pay them, even if the work was perfect. They quit, or he fired them. He recruited others to replace them and treated these workers the same way. Construction proceeded slowly, but at a fraction of the proper cost. The high rate of turnover had the corollary benefit of keeping to a minimum the number of individuals who understood the building's secrets. A worker might be ordered to perform a certain task—for example, to install the gas nozzle inside the big walk-in vault—but in the narrow context within which the worker functioned, the assignment could seem reasonable or at worst merely eccentric.

Even so, a bricklayer named George Bowman found the experience of working for Holmes somewhat chilling. "I don't know what to make of Holmes," Bowman said. "I hadn't been working for him but two days before he came around and asked me if I didn't think it pretty hard work, this bricklaying. He asked me if I wouldn't like to make money easier than that, and of course I told him yes. A few days after, he came over to me and, pointing down to the basement, said, 'You see that man down there? Well, that's my brother-in-law, and he has got no love for me, neither have I for him. Now, it would be the easiest matter for you to drop a stone on that fellow's head while you're at work and I'll give you fifty dollars if you do.'"

What made the incident particularly frightening was Holmes's manner as he made the offer—"about the same manner one would expect from a friend who was asking you the most trivial question," Bowman said.

Whether Holmes truly meant for Bowman to kill the man cannot be known. It would have been wholly within character for Holmes to have first persuaded the "brother-in-law" to take out a life insurance policy with Holmes as beneficiary. It was possible, too, that Holmes was merely testing Bowman to determine how useful he might be in the future. If so, it was a test that Bowman failed. "I was so badly scared I didn't know what to say or do," Bowman said, "but I didn't drop the stone and got out of the place soon after."

Three men did meet Holmes's standard of trustworthiness. Each worked for him throughout the period of construction and continued to associate with him after the building was completed. One was Charles Chappell, a machinist who lived near Cook County Hospital. He first worked for Holmes as a common laborer but soon proved to possess a talent that Holmes found particularly valuable. Another was Patrick Quinlan, who lived at Forty-seventh and Morgan in Englewood until he moved into Holmes's building as its caretaker. He was a small, twitchy man in his late thirties, with light curly hair and a sandy mustache.

The third and most important was Benjamin Pitezel, a carpenter, who joined Holmes in November 1889. He replaced a worker named Robert Latimer, who had quit to take over as gatekeeper at the rail intersection in front of Holmes's drugstore. At first, Latimer said, Pitezel took care of the horses involved in the construction of Holmes's building, but later he became his all-round assistant. Holmes and Pitezel seemed to have a close relationship, close enough at least for Holmes to do Pitezel a costly favor. Pitezel was arrested in Indiana for attempting to pass forged checks. Holmes posted bail and forfeited the amount when Pitezel, as planned, failed to return for trial.

Pitezel had smooth features and a sharp well-defined chin. He might have been handsome if not for a certain hungry gauntness and the way the lids of his eyes cloaked the top of each iris. "In a general way," Holmes said, "I should describe him a man nearly six feet high (at least five feet ten inches), always thin in flesh and weighing from one hundred and forty-five to one hundred and fifty-five lbs., having very black and somewhat coarse hair, very thick, with no tendency to baldness; his mustache was a much lighter color and I think of a red tinge, though I have seen him have it colored black at times, which gave him quite a different appearance."

Pitezel was plagued with various maladies: sore knees from the installation of one too many floors, a wart on his neck that kept him from wearing a stiff collar, and teeth so painful that at one point he had to suspend his work for Holmes. Despite being a chronic alcoholic, he was, in the appraisal of one doctor, a man of "fine physique."

Pitezel was married to Carrie Canning of Galva, Illinois, and the father of a fast-increasing number of children. Photographs of the children show a sweet if sober bunch who seem ready at a moment's notice to swing into action with brooms and dishcloths. The couple's first daughter, Dessie, had been born out of wedlock, an event entirely within the realm of what Pitezel's parents had come to expect of their son. In a last plea for Pitezel to take a more righteous path, his father wrote: "Come with me and I will do the good is the Savior's command. Will you go? I will take that wicked nature out of you, and I will wash from you all stains, and I will be a father to you and you shall be a son and an heir." The pain in his father's words was palpable. "I love you," he wrote, "although you have gone far astray."

Alice, the second child, was born soon after the marriage. Another daughter and three sons followed, although one boy died of diphtheria shortly after birth. Three of the children—Alice, Nellie, and Howard—would become so well known throughout America that headline writers would refer to them by their first names alone, confident that even the most remote reader understood exactly who they were.

Pitezel too would achieve a certain fame because of Holmes. "Pitezel was his tool," a district attorney said, "his creature."

Construction of Holmes's building occurred in ragged stages and more or less halted each winter at the close of what workers called the "building season," although Holmes had read how architects in the Loop were using techniques that allowed construction year-round. Eventually, much would be made of the fact that Holmes had erected his building during the same period in which Jack the Ripper, thousands of miles away, began his killings.

The first of Jack's murders occurred on August 31, 1888, the last on the night of November 9, 1888 when he met a prostitute named Mary Kelly and accompanied her back to her rooms. He slashed her throat in a Van Gogh stroke that nearly removed her head from her spine. Over the next few hours, secure within walls, he carved off her breasts and placed these on a table along with her nose. He slashed her from throat to pubis, skinned her thighs, removed her internal organs, and arranged them in a pile between her feet. He cut off a hand, which he then thrust into her bisected abdomen. Kelly had been three months' pregnant at the time.

Abruptly the murders stopped, as if that tryst with Mary Kelly had sated the killer's need at last. Five confirmed victims, only five, and Jack the Ripper became the embodiment, forever, of pure evil.

Every Chicago resident who could read devoured these reports from abroad, but none with quite so much intensity as Dr. H. H. Holmes.

On June 29, 1889, when Holmes's building was half completed, Chicago annexed Englewood and soon afterward established a new police precinct, the Tenth, Second Division, at Sixty-third and Wentworth, seven blocks from Holmes's pharmacy. Soon patrolmen under the command of Captain Horace Elliott began making regular walks past the store, where in accord with custom they stopped to chat with the young and personable owner. Periodically the officers ambled across the street to watch construction of the new building. Englewood already had a number of substantial structures, including the YMCA, the Cook County Normal School, which trained teachers, and the lavish Timmerman Opera House, now nearing completion at Sixty-third and Stewart, but the village still had a lot of open terrain, and any building destined to occupy an entire block was a topic of conversation.

Construction took another year, with the usual hiatus for winter. By May 1890 the building was largely finished. The second floor had six corridors, thirty-five rooms, and fifty-one doors, the third another three dozen rooms. The building's first floor had space for five retail stores, the best of which was a large and inviting corner shop on the intersection of Sixty-third and Wallace.

One month after moving into his building, Holmes sold the former Holton drugstore and assured the buyer that he would face little competition.

To the buyer's chagrin, Holmes promptly opened a new drugstore just across the street, in his own corner shop.

Holmes installed a variety of other businesses in his remaining first-floor stores, including a barbershop and restaurant. City directories also listed at Holmes's address the office of a doctor named Henry D. Mann, possibly a Holmes alias, and the headquarters of the Warner Glass Bending Company, which Holmes formed ostensibly to enter the booming new business of making and shaping the large sheets of plate glass suddenly in so much demand.

Holmes equipped his shops with furniture and fixtures that he bought on credit. He had no intention of paying his debts and was confident he could evade prosecution through guile and charm. When creditors came by demanding to see the owner of the building, Holmes referred them happily to the fictive H. S. Campbell.

"He was the smoothest man I ever saw," said C. E. Davis, whom Holmes had hired to manage the drugstore's jewelry counter. Creditors, Davis said, would "come here raging and calling him all the names imaginable, and he would smile and talk to them and set up the cigars and drinks and send them away seemingly his friends for life. I never saw him angry. You couldn't have trouble with him if you tried."

Davis gestured toward the store. "If all the writs of mechanic's lien that have been levied on this structure were pasted on these three walls, the block would look like a mammoth circus billboard. But I never heard of a lien being collected. Holmes used to tell me he had a lawyer paid to keep him out of trouble, but it always seemed to me that it was the courteous, audacious rascality of the fellow that pulled him through. One day he bought some furniture for his restaurant and moved it in, and that very evening the dealer came around to collect his bill or remove his goods. Holmes set up the drinks, took him to supper, bought him a cigar and sent the man off laughing at a joke, with a promise to call the next week for his money. In thirty minutes after he took his car Holmes had wagons in front loading up that furniture and the dealer never got a cent. Holmes didn't go to jail, either. He was the only man in the United States that could do what he did."

Holmes had the money to pay his debts. Davis estimated that Holmes made $200,000 through his drugstore and other business ventures, most of which were fraudulent. Holmes attempted, for example, to sell investors a machine that turned water into natural gas. He secretly connected his prototype to city gas lines.

He was always charming and cordial, but there were times when even these traits failed to put his business associates at ease. A druggist named Erickson recalled how Holmes used to come into his store to buy chloroform, a potent but unpredictable anesthetic in use since the Civil War. "I sometimes sold him the drug nine or ten times a week and each time it was in large quantities. I asked him what he used it for on several occasions, but he gave me very unsatisfactory answers. At last I refused to let him have any more unless he told me, as I pretended that I was afraid that he was not using it for any proper purpose."

Holmes told Erickson he was using the chloroform for scientific experiments. Later, when Holmes returned for more chloroform, Erickson asked him how his experiments were coming.

Holmes gave him a blank look and said he was not conducting any experiments.

"I could never make him out," Erickson said.

A woman named Strowers occasionally did Holmes's laundry. One day he offered to pay her $6,000 if she would acquire a $10,000 life insurance policy and name him beneficiary. When she asked why he would do such a thing, he explained that upon her death he'd make a profit of $4,000, but in the meantime she'd be able to spend her $6,000 in whatever manner she chose.

To Mrs. Strowers, this was a fortune, and all she had to do was sign a few documents. Holmes assured her it was all perfectly legal.

She was healthy and expected to live a good long while. She was on the verge of accepting the offer when Holmes said to her, softly, "Don't be afraid of me."

Which terrified her.

In November 1890 Holmes learned along with the rest of Chicago that the directors of the World's Columbian Exposition had at last reached a decision as to where to build the fair. To his delight, he read that the main site was to be Jackson Park, due east of his building at the lake end of Sixty-third, with exhibits also in downtown Chicago and Washington Park and along the full length of Midway Boulevard.

Holmes knew the parks from his bicycle journeys. Like most Americans, he had become caught up in the bicycle craze that was ignited by the advent of the "safety" bicycle, with its same-sized wheels and chain-and-sprocket drive. Unlike most Americans, however, Holmes sought also to capitalize on the craze by buying bicycles on credit, then reselling them without ever paying off the initial purchase. He himself rode a Pope.

The Exposition Company's decision raised a groundswell of greed throughout Chicago's South Side. An advertisement in the *Tribune* offered a six-room house for sale at Forty-first and Ellis, a mile or so north of Jackson Park, and boasted that during the fair the new owner could expect to let four of the six rooms for nearly a thousand dollars a month (about $30,000 in twenty-first-century currency). Holmes's building and land were valuable to begin with, given Englewood's continued growth, but now his property seemed the equivalent of a seam of gold ore.

An idea came to him for a way to mine that ore and also satisfy his other needs. He placed a new advertisement seeking more construction workers and once again called for the help of his loyal associates, Chappell, Quinlan, and Pitezel.

Pilgrimage

On Monday evening, December 15, 1890, a day noteworthy in Chicago for its extraordinary warmth and elsewhere for the gunshot death of Sitting Bull, Daniel Burnham stepped aboard a train bound for New York and what he knew would be the most crucial encounter of the exposition odyssey.

He entered a bright green coach, one of George Pullman's Palace cars, where the air hung with the stillness of a heavy tapestry. A bell clanged and continued clanging in a swinging rhythm as the train surged at grade level into the heart of the city at twenty miles an hour, despite the presence at arm's reach of grip-cars, carriages, and pedestrians. Everyone on the street paused to watch as the train leaped past crossing gates waving a raccoon's tail of white and black smoke. The train clicked by the Union Stock Yards, doubly pungent in the day's strange warmth, and skirted sierras of black coal capped with grimy melting snow. Burnham treasured beauty but saw none for miles and miles and miles, just coal, rust, and smoke in endless repetition until the train entered the prairie and everything seemed to go quiet. Darkness fell, leaving a false twilight of old snow.

The exposition directors' decision on where to locate the fair had caused a rapid acceleration of events that was encouraging but also unsettling, because suddenly the whole thing had become more real, its true magnitude more daunting. Immediately the directors had ordered a rough plan of the fair, to be delivered to them within twenty-four hours. John Root, guided by Burnham and Olmsted, had produced a drawing on a sheet of brown paper measuring forty square feet, which the men delivered to the committee with a barbed aside to the effect that the designers of the Paris exposition had been able to spend a whole year thinking, planning, and sketching before reaching the same point. The drawing envisioned a mile-square plain on the lakeshore sculpted by dredges into a wonderland of lagoons and canals. Ultimately, the designers knew, the exposition would have hundreds of buildings, including one for each state of the union and for many countries and industries, but on the drawing they sketched only the most important, among them five immense palaces sited around a central Grand Court. They also made room for a tower to be built at one end of the court, although no one knew exactly who would build this tower or what it would look like, only that it would have to surpass Eiffel's tower in every way. The directors and their federal overseers, the National Commission, approved the plan with uncharacteristic speed.

For outsiders, it was the sheer size of the exposition that made it seem such an impossible challenge. That the fair's grounds would be vast and its buildings colossal was something every Chicago resident took for granted; what mystified them was how anyone could expect to build the biggest thing ever constructed on American soil, far bigger than Roebling's Brooklyn Bridge, in so little time. Burnham knew, however, that the fair's size was just one element of the challenge. The gross features of the fair envisioned in the plan concealed a billion smaller obstacles that the public and most of the exposition's own directors had no idea existed. Burnham would have to build a railroad within the fairgrounds to transport steel, stone, and lumber to each construction site. He would have to manage the delivery of supplies, goods, mail, and all exhibit articles sent to the grounds by transcontinental shipping companies, foremost among them the Adams Express Company. He would need a police force and a fire department, a hospital and an ambulance service. And there would be horses, thousands of them—something would have to be done about the tons of manure generated each day.

Immediately after the brown-paper plan received approval, Burnham requested authority to build "at once cheap wooden quarters in Jackson Park for myself and force," quarters in which he would live almost continuously for the next three years. This lodging quickly became known as "the shanty," though it had a large fireplace and an excellent wine cellar stocked by Burnham himself. With a power of perception that far outpaced his era, Burnham recognized that the tiniest details would shape the way people judged the exposition. His vigilance extended even to the design of the fair's official seal. "It may not occur to you how very important a matter this Seal is," he wrote in a December 8, 1890, letter to George R. Davis, the fair's director-general, its chief political officer. "It will be very largely distributed throughout foreign countries, and is one of those trivial things by which these people will judge the artistic standard of the Fair."

All these, however, were mere distractions compared to the single most important task on Burnham's roster: the selection of architects to design the fair's major buildings.

He and John Root had considered designing the whole exposition themselves, and indeed their peers jealously expected they would do so. Harriet Monroe, Root's sister-in-law, recalled how one evening Root came home "cut to the quick" because an architect whom he had considered a friend "had apparently refused to recognize Mr. Burnham when they met at a club." Root grumbled, "I suppose he thinks we are going to hog it all!" He resolved that to preserve his credibility as supervising architect, a role in which he would be compelled to oversee the work of other exposition architects, he would not himself design any of the buildings.

Burnham knew exactly whom he wanted to hire but was less aware of how incendiary his selections would prove. He wanted the best architects America had to offer, not just for their talent but also for how their affiliation instantly would shatter the persistent eastern belief that Chicago would produce only a country fair.

In December, though he lacked an official mandate to do so, Burnham secretly mailed inquiries to five men, "feeling confident that I would carry my point." And indeed soon afterward the fair's Grounds and Buildings Committee authorized him to invite the men to join the exposition. Unquestionably they were five of the greatest architects America had produced, but of the five, three were from the land of "unclean beasts" itself:

George B. Post, Charles McKim, and Richard M. Hunt, the nation's most venerable architect. The others were Robert Peabody of Boston and Henry Van Brunt, Kansas City.

None was from Chicago, even though the city took great pride in its architectural pioneers, in Sullivan, Adler, Jenney, Beman, Cobb, and the others. Somehow, despite his powers of anticipation, Burnham failed to realize that Chicago might see his choices as betrayal.

⌐⟶

What troubled Burnham at the moment, as he rode in his Pullman compartment, was the fact that only one of his candidates, Van Brunt of Kansas City, had replied with any enthusiasm. The others had expressed only a tepid willingness to meet once Burnham arrived in New York.

Burnham had asked Olmsted to join him for the meeting, aware that in New York the landscape architect's reputation exerted a force like gravity, but Olmsted could not get away. Now Burnham faced the prospect of having to go alone to meet these legendary architects—one of them, Hunt, a man also of legendary irascibility.

Why were they so unenthusiastic? How would they react to his attempts at persuasion? And if they declined and word of their refusal became public, what then?

The landscape outside his windows gave him little solace. As his train roared across Indiana, it overtook a cold front. Temperatures plunged. Strong gusts of wind buffeted the train, and ghostly virga of ice followed it through the night.

⌐⟶

There was something Burnham did not know. Soon after receiving his letter the eastern architects, Hunt, Post, Peabody, and McKim, had held a meeting of their own in the offices of McKim, Mead and White in New York to discuss whether the fair would be anything more than a display of overfed cattle. During the meeting Hunt—the architect Burnham most hoped to recruit—announced that he would not participate. George Post persuaded him at least to hear what Burnham had to say, arguing that if Hunt stood down, the others would feel pressed to do likewise, for such was Hunt's influence.

McKim had opened this meeting with a wandering talk about the fair and its prospects. Hunt cut him off: "McKim, damn your preambles. Get down to facts!"

⸺

In New York the wind blew hard and harsh all week. On the Hudson ice produced the earliest halt to navigation since 1880. Over breakfast at his hotel on Thursday morning, Burnham read with uneasiness about the failure of S. A. Kean & Co., a private bank in Chicago. It was one more sign of a gathering panic.

⸺

Burnham met the eastern architects Monday evening, December 22, at the Players Club, for dinner. Their cheeks were red from the cold. They shook hands: Hunt, McKim, Post, and Peabody—Peabody, down from Boston for the meeting. Here they were, gathered at one table, the nation's foremost practitioners of what Goethe and Schelling called "frozen music." All were wealthy and at the peaks of their careers, but all also bore the scars of nineteenth-century life, their pasts full of wrecked rail cars, fevers, and the premature deaths of loved ones. They wore dark suits and crisp white collars. All had mustaches, some dark, some gray. Post was huge, the largest man in the room. Hunt was fierce, a frown in a suit, with a client list that included most of America's richest families. Every other mansion in Newport, Rhode Island, and along Fifth Avenue in New York seemed to have been designed by him, but he also had built the base for the Statue of Liberty and was a founder of the American Institute of Architects. All the men had one or more elements of shared background. Hunt, McKim, and Peabody had all studied at L'Ecole des Beaux Arts in Paris; Van Brunt and Post had studied under Hunt; Van Brunt had been Peabody's mentor. For Burnham, with his failed attempts at getting into Harvard and Yale and his lack of formal architectural training, sitting down to dinner with these men was like being a stranger at someone else's Thanksgiving.

The men were cordial. Burnham described his vision of a fair larger and grander than the Paris exposition. He played up the fact of Olmsted's participation. Both Olmsted and Hunt were hard at work on George Washington Vanderbilt's manor, Biltmore, near Asheville, North Carolina, and together had built the Vanderbilt family's mausoleum. But Hunt was skeptical and not shy about expressing his doubts. Why should he and the others interrupt their already full schedules to build temporary structures in a far-off city where they would have little control over the final product?

Their skepticism shook Burnham. He was accustomed to the headlong civic energy of Chicago. He wished Olmsted and Root were beside him: Olmsted, to counter Hunt; Root because of his wit, and because the other architects all knew him from his role as secretary of the American Institute of Architects. Ordinarily it was in situations like this that Burnham could be most effective. "To himself, and indeed to most of the world in general, he was always right," wrote Harriet Monroe, "and by knowing this so securely he built up the sheer power of personality which accomplished big things." But this night he felt ill at ease, a choirboy among cardinals.

He argued that Chicago's fair, unlike any other before it, would be primarily a monument to architecture. It would awaken the nation to the power of architecture to conjure beauty from stone and steel. Olmsted's plans alone would make the exposition unique, with lagoons, canals, and great lawns all set against the cobalt-blue steppe of Lake Michigan. In exhibit space, he told them, the fair would be at least one-third larger than what the French had allotted in Paris. This was no mere dream, he said. Chicago had the resolve to make this exposition a reality, the same resolve that had made the city the second largest in America. And, he added, Chicago had the money.

The architects' questions became slightly less challenging, more practical. What kind of structures did he envision, and in what style? The issue of the Eiffel Tower arose: What could Chicago do to equal that? On this score Burnham had no plan other than somehow to surpass Eiffel. Secretly, he was disappointed that the engineers of America had not yet stepped forward with some novel but feasible scheme to eclipse Eiffel's achievement.

The architects worried that anyone who joined the fair would find himself in the grip of innumerable committees. Burnham guaranteed complete artistic independence. They wanted to know in detail how Olmsted felt about the sites selected for the fair, in particular about a central feature called the Wooded Island. Their insistence prompted Burnham to telegraph Olmsted immediately and urge him once again to come. Again Olmsted demurred.

One question came up repeatedly throughout the evening: Was there enough time?

Burnham assured them that ample time remained but that he had no illusions. The work had to start at once.

He believed he had won them. As the evening ended, he asked, would they join?

There was a pause.

Burnham left New York the next morning on the North Shore Limited. Throughout the day his train pushed through a landscape scoured by snow as a blizzard whitened the nation in a swath from the Atlantic to Minnesota. The storm destroyed buildings, broke trees, and killed a man in Baberton, Ohio, but it did not stop the Limited.

While aboard the train, Burnham wrote a letter to Olmsted that contained a less-than-candid description of the meeting with the architects. "They all approved the proposition to have them take hold of the artistic part of the main buildings. . . . The general layout seemed to meet the hearty approval, first of Mr. Hunt then of the others, but they were desirous of knowing your views of the landscape on and about the island. Therefore I telegraphed you urgently to come. They were very much disappointed, as was I, when it was found impossible to get you. The gentlemen are all to be here on the 10th of next month and at that time they urgently request, as do I, that you will be here personally. I find that Mr. Hunt especially lays large stress upon your opinions in the entire matter."

In fact, the evening had ended rather differently. At the Player's Club, sips of cognac and exhalations of smoke had filled that last difficult pause. The dream was an appealing one, the architects agreed, and no one doubted Chicago's sincerity in imagining this fantasy precinct of lagoons and palaces, but the reality was something else entirely. The only real certainty was the disruption that would be caused by long-distance travel and the myriad other difficulties inherent in building a complex structure far from home. Peabody did commit to the fair, but Hunt and the others did not: "they said," as Burnham later revealed, "they would think it over."

They did, however, agree to come to the January 10 meeting in Chicago to confer again and examine the chosen ground.

None of the architects had been to Jackson Park. In its raw state, Burnham knew, it was not a setting likely to win anyone's heart. This time Olmsted had to be present. In the meantime Root too would have to become involved in the courtship. The architects respected him but were leery of his powers as supervising architect. It was critical that he go to New York.

Outside the sky was blank, the light pewter. Despite Pullman's vestibules ice as fine as dust settled between coaches and filled Burnham's train with the tang of deep winter. Wind-felled trees appeared beside the railbed.

⚬⟝⟞⚬

Daniel Burnham arrived in Chicago to find the city's architects and members of the exposition board outraged that he had gone outside the city—to New York, of all godforsaken places—to court architects for the fair; that he had snubbed the likes of Adler, Sullivan, and Jenney. Sullivan saw it as a sign that Burnham did not truly believe Chicago had the talent to carry the fair by itself. "Burnham had believed that he might best serve his country by placing all of the work exclusively with Eastern architects," Sullivan wrote; "solely, he averred, on account of their surpassing culture." The chairman of the Grounds and Buildings Committee was Edward T. Jefferey. "With exquisite delicacy and tact," Sullivan said, "Jefferey, at a meeting of the Committee, persuaded Daniel, come to Judgment, to add the Western men to the list of his nominations."

Hastily, Root and Burnham conferred and chose five Chicago firms to join the effort, among them Adler & Sullivan. Burnham visited each the next day. Four of the five put aside their hurt feelings and accepted immediately. Only Adler & Sullivan resisted. Adler was sulking. "I think he, Adler, had hoped to be in the position I was in," Burnham said. "He was rather disgruntled and did 'not know.' "

Ultimately, Adler did accept Burnham's invitation.

Now it was Root's turn to go to New York. He had to go anyway to attend a meeting of the directors of the American Institute of Architects and planned afterward to take a train to Atlanta to inspect one of the firm's buildings. Root was in his office at the Rookery on the afternoon of New Year's Day 1891, shortly before his departure, when an employee stopped by to see him. "He said he was tired," the man recalled, "and felt inclined to resign the secretaryship of the Institute. This was alarming, as he had never been heard to complain of too much work, and while it only indicated extreme physical exhaustion and before he went home he became cheerful and hopeful again, it has its significance in the light of subsequent events."

In New York, Root assured the architects again and again that he would do nothing to interfere with their designs. Despite his charm—the *Chicago Inter Ocean* once called him "another Chauncey M. Depew in postprandial wit and humor"—he failed to arouse their enthusiasm and left New York for Atlanta feeling the same degree of disappointment Burnham had felt two weeks earlier. His journey south did little to cheer him up. Harriet Monroe saw him upon his return to Chicago. He was depressed, she said, "by the attitude of the Eastern men, whom he found singularly apathetic, utterly incredulous that any association of Western businessmen would give art a free hand in the manner he set forth. The dream was too extravagant ever to be realized, and they were extremely reluctant to undertake its realization against the hampering and tampering, the interferences petty and great, which they felt were certain to ensue."

Root was tired and discouraged. He told Monroe he just could not get the men interested. "He felt that this was the greatest opportunity ever offered to his profession in this country, and he could not make them appreciate it," she said. The architects did plan to come to Chicago for the January meeting, he told her, "but reluctantly; their hearts were not in it."

On January 5, 1891, the Committee on Grounds and Buildings authorized Burnham to offer formal commissions to all ten architects and pay each $10,000 (equivalent today to about $300,000). It was a rich fee, considering that all Burnham wanted them to do was provide working drawings and make a few visits to Chicago. Burnham and Root would see to the construction of the buildings and manage the niggling details that typically haunted an architect's life. There would be no artistic interference.

The eastern men gave their tentative acceptance, but their concerns had not diminished.

And they still had not seen Jackson Park.

A Hotel for the Fair

HOLMES'S NEW IDEA WAS TO turn his building into a hotel for visitors to the World's Columbian Exposition—no Palmer House or Richelieu, certainly, but just comfortable enough and cheap enough to lure a certain kind of clientele and convincing enough to justify a large fire insurance policy. After the fair he intended to burn the building to collect the insurance and, as a happy dividend, destroy whatever surplus "material" might remain in its hidden storage chambers, although ideally, given other disposal measures available to him, the building by then would contain nothing of an incriminating nature. The thing was, one never knew. In the most transcendent moment, it was easy to make a mistake and forget some little thing that a clever detective might eventually use to propel him to the gallows. Whether the Chicago police even possessed that kind of talent was open to question. The Pinkerton National Detective Agency was the more dangerous entity, but its operatives of late seemed to be spending most of their energy battling strikers at coalfields and steel mills around the country.

Again acting as his own architect, Holmes early in 1891 began planning the necessary modifications, and soon carpenters were at work on the second and third floors. Once again Holmes's method of segregating tasks and firing workers was proving successful. Clearly none of the workers had gone to the police. Patrolmen from the new Chicago police precinct house on Wentworth walked past Holmes's building each day. Far from being suspicious, the officers had become friendly, even protective. Holmes knew each man by name. A cup of coffee, a free meal in his restaurant, a fine black cigar—policemen valued these gestures of affinity and grace.

Holmes was, however, beginning to feel mounting pressure from cred-itors, in particular from several furniture and bicycle dealers. He could still charm them and commiserate over their inability to locate the elusive deedholder, H. S. Campbell, but Holmes knew they soon would lose patience and in fact was a bit surprised they had not pursued him more forcefully than had been the case thus far. His techniques were too new, his skills too great, the men around him too naïve, as if they had never before experienced a falsehood. For every business that now refused to sell him goods, there were a dozen more that fawned over him and accepted his notes endorsed by H. S. Campbell or secured by the assets of the Warner Glass Bending Company. When pressed, sensing that a particular creditor was on the verge of legal action, even violence, Holmes paid his bills in cash using money harvested from his own ven-tures, such as lease income from his apartments and stores, sales from his pharmacy, and the proceeds from his newest venture, a mail-order med-icine company. In a parody of Aaron Montgomery Ward's fast-growing empire in central Chicago, Holmes had begun selling sham drugs that he guaranteed would cure alcoholism and baldness.

He was always open to new financial opportunities but was especially so now, since he knew that no matter how deftly he kept labor costs down, he still would have to pay for at least some of the transformation of his building. When Myrta's great-uncle, Jonathan Belknap of Big Foot Prairie, Illinois, came to Wilmette for a visit, that challenge suddenly seemed likely to resolve itself. Belknap was not a rich man, but he was well off.

Holmes began appearing more frequently at the Wilmette house. He brought toys for Lucy, jewelry for Myrta and her mother. He filled the house with love.

Belknap had never met Holmes but knew all about his troubled mar-riage to Myrta and was prepared to dislike the young doctor. On first meeting he found Holmes far too smooth and self-assured for a man of so few years. He was struck, however, by how enthralled Myrta seemed to be whenever Holmes was around and by how even Myrta's mother—Belknap's niece by marriage—appeared to glow in Holmes's presence. After several more encounters Belknap began to appreciate why Myrta had fallen so thoroughly for the man. He was handsome and clean and dressed well and spoke in fine sentences. His gaze was blue and forthright. In conversation he listened with an intensity that was almost alarming, as if Belknap were the most fascinating man in the world, not just an elderly uncle visiting from Big Foot Prairie.

Belknap still did not like Holmes, but he found his candor sufficiently disarming that when Holmes asked him to endorse a note for $2,500 to help cover the cost of a new house in Wilmette for himself and Myrta, Belknap agreed. Holmes thanked him warmly. A new house, away from Myrta's parents, might be all the couple needed to end their growing estrangement. Holmes promised to pay the money back as soon as his business affairs allowed.

Holmes returned to Englewood and promptly forged Belknap's signature to a second note for the same amount, intending to use the proceeds for his hotel.

On Holmes's next visit to Wilmette, he invited Belknap to visit Englewood for a tour of his building and of the newly chosen site for the World's Columbian Exposition.

Although Belknap had read much about the world's fair and did want to see its future home, he did not relish the idea of spending a full day with Holmes. Holmes was charming and gracious, but something about him made Belknap uneasy. He could not have defined it. Indeed, for the next several decades alienists and their successors would find themselves hard-pressed to describe with any precision what it was about men like Holmes that could cause them to seem warm and ingratiating but also telegraph the vague sense that some important element of humanness was missing. At first alienists described this condition as "moral insanity" and those who exhibited the disorder as "moral imbeciles." They later adopted the term "psychopath," used in the lay press as early as 1885 in William Stead's *Pall Mall Gazette,* which described it as a "new malady" and stated, "Beside his own person and his own interests, nothing is sacred to the psychopath." Half a century later, in his path-breaking book *The Mask of Sanity,* Dr. Hervey Cleckley described the prototypical psychopath as "a subtly constructed reflex machine which can mimic the human personality perfectly. . . . So perfect is his reproduction of a whole and normal man that no one who examines him in a clinical setting can point out in scientific or objective terms why, or how, he is not real." People exhibiting this purest form of the disorder would become known, in the jargon of psychiatry, as "Cleckley" psychopaths.

When Belknap refused Holmes's offer, Holmes seemed to crumble with hurt and disappointment. A tour was necessary, Holmes pleaded, if only to bolster his own sense of honor and to demonstrate to Belknap that he really was a man of means and that Belknap's note was as secure an investment as any man could make. Myrta too looked crestfallen.

Belknap gave in. During the train journey to Englewood, Holmes pointed out landmarks: the skyscrapers of the city, the Chicago River, the stockyards. Belknap found the stench overpowering, but Holmes seemed not to notice it. The men exited the train at Englewood station.

The town was alive with movement. Trains rumbled past every few minutes. Horse-drawn streetcars moved east and west along Sixty-third, amid a dense traffic of carriages and drays. Everywhere Belknap looked some building was under construction. Soon the level of construction would increase even more, as entrepreneurs prepared to cash in on the expected crush of exposition visitors. Holmes described his own plans. He took Belknap on a tour of his pharmacy, with its marble countertops and glass containers filled with wildly colored solutions, then took him up to the second floor, where he introduced him to the building's caretaker, Patrick Quinlan. Holmes walked Belknap through the building's many corridors and described how the place would look as a hotel. Belknap found it bleak and strange, with passages that struck off in unexpected directions.

Holmes asked Belknap if he would like to see the roof and the construction already under way. Belknap declined, claiming falsely that he was too old a man to climb that many steps.

Holmes promised stirring views of Englewood, perhaps even a glimpse of Jackson Park off to the east, where the buildings of the fair soon would begin to rise. Again Belknap resisted, this time with more force.

Holmes tried a different approach. He invited Belknap to spend the night in his building. At first Belknap declined this offer as well, but feeling perhaps that he had been overly rude in avoiding the roof, he relented.

After nightfall Holmes led Belknap to a room on the second floor. Gas lamps had been installed at haphazard intervals along the corridor, leaving pockets of gloom whose borders shivered as Belknap and Holmes moved past. The room was furnished and comfortable enough and overlooked the street, which was still reassuringly busy. As far as Belknap could tell, he and Holmes were by now the only occupants of the building. "When I went to bed," Belknap said, "I carefully locked the door."

Soon the street sounds receded, leaving only the rumble of trains and the hollow clip-clop of an occasional horse. Belknap had difficulty sleeping. He stared at the ceiling, which was bathed in the shifting light of the streetlamps below his window. Hours passed. "Presently," Belknap said, "I heard my door tried and then a key was slipped into the lock."

Belknap called out, asking who was at the door. The noise stopped. He held his breath and listened and heard the sound of feet moving down the hall. He was certain that initially two men had been outside his door, but now one of them had left. He called again. This time a voice answered. Belknap recognized it as belonging to Patrick Quinlan, the caretaker.

Quinlan wanted to come in.

"I refused to open the door," Belknap said. "He insisted for a time and then went away."

Belknap lay awake the rest of the night.

Soon afterward he discovered Holmes's forgery. Holmes apologized, claiming a dire need for money, and was so persuasive and abject that even Belknap felt mollified, although his distrust of Holmes persisted. Much later Belknap realized why Holmes had wanted so badly to show him the building's roof. "If I'd gone," Belknap said, "the forgery probably wouldn't have been discovered, because I wouldn't have been around to discover it.

"But I didn't go," he said. "I'm afraid of heights."

◦━━━◦

As carpenters and plasterers worked on his building, Holmes turned his attention to the creation of an important accessory. He sketched a number of possible designs, relying perhaps on past observations of similar equipment, then settled on a configuration that seemed likely to work: a large rectangular box of fireproof brick about eight feet deep, three feet high, and three feet wide, encased within a second box of the same material, with the space between them heated by flames from an oil burner. The inner box would serve as an elongated kiln. Although he had never built a kiln before, he believed his design would generate temperatures extreme enough to incinerate anything within. That the kiln would also be able to destroy any odors emanating from the interior box was singularly important.

He planned to install the kiln in the basement and hired a bricklayer named Joseph E. Berkler to do the job. He told him he intended to use the kiln to produce and bend plate glass for his Warner Glass Bending Company. At Holmes's instructions Berkler added a number of components made of iron. He worked quickly, and soon the kiln was ready for its first test.

Holmes ignited the burner. There was a satisfying whoosh. A wave of warmth rolled from the chamber to the far walls of the basement. The scent of partially combusted oil suffused the air.

But the test was disappointing. The box did not generate as much heat as Holmes had hoped. He adjusted the burner and tried again but achieved little improvement.

He used the city directory to locate a furnace company and requested an appointment with an experienced man. He identified himself as the founder of Warner Glass. If for some reason officials of the furnace company felt moved to verify that Warner Glass existed, all they had to do was check the 1890 Englewood directory to find the company's listing, with Holmes named as proprietor.

The manager of the furnace company—his name was never made public—decided to attend to the matter personally and met Holmes at his building. He found a young good-looking man, almost delicate, who conveyed an air of confidence and prosperity. He had striking blue eyes. His building was on the gloomy side, the construction obviously below the standards of structures rising elsewhere on Sixty-third, but it was well located in a community that clearly was booming. For so young a man to own most of a city block was itself an accomplishment.

The manager followed Holmes to his second-floor office and there in the pleasant cross breeze from the corner windows studied Holmes's drawings of his kiln. Holmes explained that he could not obtain "the necessary amount of heat." The manager asked to see the apparatus.

That wasn't necessary, Holmes said. He did not wish to trouble the manager, only to seek his advice, for which he would pay an appropriate fee.

The furnace man insisted he could do nothing without actually examining the kiln.

Holmes smiled. Of course. If the manager did not mind spending the extra time, he would be glad to show it to him.

Holmes led his visitor down the stairs to the first floor and from there down another, darker flight to the basement.

They entered a large rectangular cavern that ran the entire length of the block, interrupted only by beams and posts. In the shadows stood vats and barrels and mounds of dark matter, possibly soil. A long narrow table with a steel top stood under a series of unlit lamps and two worn leather cases rested nearby. The cellar had the look of a mine, the smell of a surgeon's suite.

The furnace man examined the kiln. He saw that it contained an inner chamber of firebrick constructed in a manner that kept flames from reaching the interior, and he noted the clever addition of two openings in the top of the inner box that would allow gases from the box to flow into the surrounding flames, where they would then be consumed. It was an interesting design and seemed likely to work, although he did observe to himself that the shape of the kiln seemed unsuited to the task of bending glass. The inner box was too small to admit the broad panes now appearing in storefronts throughout the city. Otherwise, he noticed nothing unusual and foresaw no difficulty in improving the kiln's operation.

He returned with a work crew. The men installed a more powerful burner that, once ignited, heated the kiln to three thousand degrees Fahrenheit. Holmes seemed pleased.

Only later did the furnace man recognize that the kiln's peculiar shape and extreme heat made it ideal for another, very different application. "In fact," he said, "the general plan of the furnace was not unlike that of a crematory for dead bodies, and with the provision already described there would be absolutely no odor from the furnace."

But again, that was later.

Holmes's absences from Wilmette lengthened once again, although at regular intervals he sent Myrta and his daughter enough money to keep them comfortable. He even insured the girl's life, since children after all were such fragile things and could be taken from the world in a heartbeat.

His businesses were doing well. His mail-order company brought in a surprising amount of cash, and he began trying to find a way to capitalize on the latest medical rage, a cure for alcoholism invented by a physician named Keeley in Dwight, Illinois. The corner drugstore ran smoothly and profitably, although one woman in the neighborhood observed that he seemed to have difficulty retaining the young and typically attractive women he often hired as clerks. These clerks, as far as she could tell, had an unfortunate habit of departing without warning, sometimes even leaving their personal belongings in their rooms on the second floor. She saw such behavior as a troubling sign of the rising shiftlessness of the age.

The work of turning Holmes's building into a hotel proceeded slowly, with the usual bouts of rancor and delay. Holmes left the task of finding replacement workers to his three helpers, Quinlan, Chappell, and Pitezel.

They seemed to have little difficulty finding new men for each new opening. Thousands of workers laid off elsewhere had come to Chicago hoping for jobs building the fair, only to find that too many workers had gotten the same idea, thus leaving a large pool of men available for work—any work, at any price.

Holmes turned his attention to other, more pleasant distractions. Sheer fate had brought two new women into his life, one of them nearly six feet tall and possessed of a rapturous body, the other, her sister-in-law, a lovely young woman with black hair and exquisite dark eyes.

That the tall one came equipped with a husband and daughter made the situation infinitely more appealing.

The Landscape of Regret

THE EASTERN ARCHITECTS LEFT New Jersey at 4:50 P.M., January 8, 1891, in car 5, section 6, of the North Shore Limited, which Hunt had reserved so that they all could travel together. Olmsted had come down from Boston the night before in order to join them.

It was a bewitching moment: a gorgeous train rocketing through the winter landscape carrying five of history's greatest architects, all in the same car, gossiping, joking, drinking, smoking. Olmsted used the opportunity to describe in detail Jackson Park and the trials of dealing with the exposition's many layers of committees that for the moment seemed to have so much power. He respected Burnham for his candor, his directness, and the air of leadership he exuded, and no doubt he told the architects as much. That he spent a good deal of time asserting his own vision of the exposition's landscape is also beyond doubt, especially his belief that the Wooded Island should remain entirely free of conspicuous manmade structures.

Two hours before the train reached Chicago, during a brief stop, McKim received a cable notifying him that his mother, Sarah McKim, had died unexpectedly in her home, at seventy-eight. The two had been very close. He left the group and caught a return train.

The architects arrived in Chicago late Friday night, January 9, and took carriages to the Wellington Hotel, where Burnham had arranged rooms for all. Van Brunt, arriving from Kansas City, joined them there. The next morning they boarded carriages for the journey south to Jackson Park. Root, absent, was to return that day from Atlanta.

The ride to the park took about an hour. "It was one of those cold winter days," Burnham recalled. "The sky was overcast with clouds and the lake covered with foam."

At the park the architects eased from the carriages puffing blasts of steam into the frigid air. The wind picked up motes of sand that stung their cheeks and forced them to shield their eyes. They stumbled over the frozen ground, Hunt wincing from gout, cursing, disbelieving; Olmsted, his teeth inflamed, his night an ordeal of wakefulness, limping from his long-ago carriage accident.

The lake was gray, darkening to a band of black at the horizon. The only color in the vicinity was the frost rouge on the men's cheeks and the blue of Burnham's and Olmsted's eyes.

Olmsted watched for the architects' reactions. Now and then he and Burnham caught each other's glances.

The architects were stunned: "they gazed," Burnham said, "with a feeling almost of despair."

Jackson Park was one square mile of desolation, mostly treeless, save for pockets of various kinds of oak—burr, pin, black, and scarlet—rising from a tangled undergrowth of elder, wild plum, and willow. In the most exposed portions there was only sand tufted with marine and prairie grasses. One writer called the park "remote and repulsive"; another, a "sandy waste of unredeemed and desert land." It was ugly, a landscape of last resort. Olmsted himself had said of Jackson Park: "If a search had been made for the least parklike ground within miles of the city, nothing better meeting the requirement could have been found."

In fact, the site was even worse than it appeared. Many of the oaks were dead. Given the season, the dead were hard to distinguish from the living. The root systems of others were badly damaged. Test borings showed that the earth within the park consisted of a top layer of black soil about one foot thick, followed by two feet of sand, then eleven feet of sand so saturated with water, Burnham wrote, "it became almost like quicksand and was often given this name." The Chicago men understood the challenge that this soil presented; the New York men, accustomed to bedrock, did not.

The park's gravest flaw, at least from Olmsted's perspective, was that its shoreline was subject to dramatic annual changes in the level of the lake, sometimes as much as four feet. Such fluctuations, Olmsted recognized, would greatly increase the difficulty of planting the banks and shores. If the water level fell, visitors to the fair would be treated to an offensive band of bare earth at the waterline. If it rose too high, the water would submerge and kill shore plantings.

The architects climbed back into their carriages. They drove toward the lake over the park's rough roads at the pace of a funeral cortege and with equal gloom. Burnham wrote: "a feeling of discouragement allied to hopelessness came over those who then first realized the extent and magnitude of the proposed undertaking, and appreciated the inexorable conditions of a time-limitation to the work. . . . Twenty-one months later was the day fixed by Act of Congress for the dedication of the buildings, and in the short space of twenty-seven and one-half months, or on May 1, 1893, the entire work of construction must be finished, the landscape perfected, and the exhibits installed."

At the lake they again left their carriages. Peabody of Boston climbed atop a pier. He turned to Burnham. "Do you mean to say that you really propose opening a Fair here by Ninety-three?"

"Yes," Burnham said. "We intend to."

Peabody said, "It can't be done."

Burnham looked at him. "That point is settled," he said.

But even he did not, and could not, grasp what truly lay ahead.

Root returned to Chicago while the architects were in Jackson Park. It was his forty-first birthday. He went directly from the train station to the Rookery. "He went down to the office in a gay humor," Harriet Monroe said, "and that very day received a commission for a large commercial building."

But that afternoon draftsman Paul Starrett encountered Root in one of the Rookery's elevators "looking ill." His good spirits had fled. He complained again of being tired.

The architects returned from their tour discouraged and full of regret. They gathered again in the firm's library, where Root, suddenly revitalized, now joined them. He was gracious, funny, warm. If anyone could sway these men and ignite their passion, Burnham knew, Root was the one. Root invited the outside men to come to his house on Astor Place the next day, Sunday, for high tea, then went home at last to greet his children and his wife, Dora, who according to Harriet Monroe was in bed "ill almost unto death" from a recent miscarriage.

Root told Dora of his weariness and suggested that in the coming summer they should escape somewhere for a long rest. The last months had been full of frustration and long nights of work and travel. He was exhausted. The trip south had done nothing to ease his stress. He looked forward to the end of the week, January 15, when the architects would conclude their conference and go home.

"After the 15th," he told his wife, "I shall not be so busy."

The eastern and Chicago architects reconvened that night at the University Club for a dinner in their honor hosted by the fair's Grounds and Buildings Committee. Root was too tired to attend. Clearly the dinner was a weapon meant to ignite enthusiasm and show the easterners that Chicago fully intended to follow through on its grand boasts about the exposition. It was the first in a sequence of impossibly rich and voluminous banquets whose menus raised the question of whether any of the city's leading men could possibly have a functional artery.

As the men arrived, reporters intercepted them. The architects were gracious but closemouthed.

They were to sit at a large T-shaped table, with Lyman Gage, president of the exposition, at the center of the topmost table, Hunt on his right, Olmsted on his left. Bundles of carnations and pink and red roses transformed the tables into cutting beds. A boutonniere rested beside each plate. Everyone wore tuxedos. There was not a woman in sight.

At precisely eight P.M. Gage took Hunt and Olmsted by the arm and led the way from the Club's reception room to the banquet hall.

———

Oysters.
A glass or two of *Montrachet.*
Consommé of Green Turtle.
Amontillado.
Broiled Shad à la Maréchel.
Cucumbers. Potatoes à la Duchesse.
Filet Mignon à la Rossini.
Chateau Lafite and *Rinnart Brut.*
Fonds d'Artichaut Farcis.
Pommery Sec.
Sorbet au Kirsch.
Cigarettes.
Woodcock on Toast.
Asparagus Sala.
Ices: Canton Ginger.
Cheeses: Pont l'Eveque; Rocquefort. Coffee. Liquers.
Madeira, 1815.
Cigars.

———

Gage spoke first. He offered a rousing oration on the brilliance of the future exposition and the need now for the great men in the banquet hall to think first of the fair, last of themselves, affirming that only through the subordination of self would the exposition succeed. The applause was warm and enthusiastic.

Burnham spoke next. He described his own vision of the fair and Chicago's resolve to make that vision real. He too urged teamwork and self-sacrifice. "Gentlemen," he said, "1893 will be the third great date in our country's history. On the two others, 1776 and 1861, all true Americans served, and so now I ask you to serve again!"

This time the room erupted. "The men left the banquet hall that night united like soldiers in a campaign," Burnham said.

It was the Chicagoans, however, who did all the marching. At Root's house the next day Harriet Monroe met the eastern architects and came away shaken. "In talking with them I was amazed at their listless and hopeless attitude," she said. "Beautiful effects were scarcely to be expected in buildings so enormous and so cheaply constructed; the level of monotony of ground surfaces in Chicago made effective grouping practically impossible; the time for preparation and construction was too short: these and other criticisms indicated a general feeling of disparagement."

At tea's end Root escorted the visitors to their carriages. It was dark and bitterly cold. A sharp wind scythed along Astor Place. Much was made, in retrospect, of the fact that Root, in evening dress, charged into the rock-cold night without first putting on a coat.

Vanishing Point

AFTER YEARS SPENT DRIFTING from town to town and job to job, a young jeweler named Icilius Conner—he preferred the nickname "Ned"—moved to Chicago with his wife Julia and their eight-year-old daughter Pearl and quickly found that Chicago was indeed a city of opportunity. At the start of 1891 Ned found himself managing a jewelry counter that occupied one wall of a thriving drugstore on the city's South Side, at Sixty-third and Wallace. For once in Ned's adult life, the future gleamed.

The owner of the drugstore, though very young, was prosperous and dynamic, truly a man of the age, and seemed destined for even greater success given that the World's Columbian Exposition was to be built just a short streetcar ride east, at the end of Sixty-third. There was talk too that a new elevated rail line, nicknamed the Alley L for the way its trestles roofed city alleys, would be extended eastward along Sixty-third directly to Jackson Park, thus providing visitors with another means of reaching the future fair. Already traffic on the street had increased sharply, as each day hundreds of citizens drove their carriages to the park to see the chosen site. Not that there was much to see. Ned and Julia had found the park an ugly, desolate place of sandy ridges and half-dead oaks, although Pearl had enjoyed trying to catch tadpoles in its pools of stagnant water. That anything wonderful could rise on that ground seemed beyond possibility, although Ned, like most new visitors to Chicago, was willing to concede that the city was a place unlike any he had encountered. If any city could make good on the elaborate boasts circulated thus far, Chicago was the one. Ned's new employer, Dr. H. H.

Holmes, seemed a perfect example of what everyone called the "Chicago spirit." To be so young, yet own a block-long building, would be incredible in any other place of Ned's experience. Here it seemed an ordinary accomplishment.

The Conners lived in a flat on the second floor of the building, near Dr. Holmes's own suite of rooms. It was not the brightest, most cheerful apartment, but it was warm and close to work. Moreover, Holmes offered to employ Julia as a clerk in the drugstore and to train her to keep his books. Later, when Ned's eighteen-year-old sister, Gertrude, moved to Chicago, Holmes asked to hire her as well, to manage his new mail-order medicine company. With three incomes, the family might soon be able to afford a house of their own, perhaps on one of the wide macadam streets of Englewood. Certainly they'd be able to afford bicycles and trips to Timmerman's theater down the street.

One thing did make Ned uneasy, however. Holmes seemed inordinately attentive to Gertie and Julia. On one level this was natural and something to which Ned had become accustomed, for both women were great beauties, Gertie slim and dark, Julia tall and felicitously proportioned. It was clear to Ned, clear in fact from the first moment, that Holmes was a man who liked women and whom women liked in return. Lovely young women seemed drawn to the drugstore. When Ned tried to help them, they were remote and uninterested. Their manner changed markedly if Holmes happened then to enter the store.

Always a plain man, Ned now seemed to become part of the background, a bystander to his own life. Only his daughter Pearl was as attentive to him as always. Ned watched with alarm as Holmes flattered Gertie and Julia with smiles and gifts and treacly praise—especially Gertie—and how the women glowed in response. When Holmes left them, they appeared crestfallen, their demeanor suddenly brittle and snappish.

Even more disconcerting was the change in how customers responded to Ned himself. It was not what they said but what they carried in their eyes, something like sympathy, even pity.

One night during this period Holmes asked Ned a favor. He led him to the big vault and stepped inside, then told Ned to close the door and listen for the sound of his shouting. "I shut the door and put my ear to the crack," Ned recalled, "but could hear only a faint sound." Ned opened the door, and Holmes stepped out. Now Holmes asked Ned if he would go inside and try shouting, so that Holmes could hear for himself how little sound escaped. Ned did so but got back out the instant Holmes reopened the door. "I didn't like that kind of business," he said.

Why anyone would even want a soundproof vault was a question that apparently did not occur to him.

For the police there were warnings of a different sort—letters from parents, visits from detectives hired by parents—but these were lost in the chaos. Vanishment seemed a Chicago pastime. There were too many disappearances, in all parts of the city, to investigate properly, and too many forces impeding the detection of patterns. Patrolmen, many of them, were barely competent, appointed solely at the direction of ward bosses. Detectives were few, their resources and skills minimal. Class obscured their vision. Ordinary vanishings—Polish girls, stockyard boys, Italian laborers, Negro women—merited little effort. Only the disappearance of moneyed souls drew a forceful response, and even then there was little that detectives could do other than send telegrams to other cities and periodically check the morgue for each day's collection of unidentified men, women, and children. At one point half the city's detective force was involved in investigating disappearances, prompting the chief of the city's central detective unit to announce he was considering the formation of a separate bureau, "a mysterious disappearances department."

Women and men vanished in equal proportion. Fannie Moore, a young visitor from Memphis, failed to return to the home where she was boarding and was never seen again. J. W. Highleyman left work one day, caught a suburban train, and vanished, the *Tribune* said, "as completely as though swallowed by the earth." The women were presumed to have been ravished, the men robbed, their corpses plunged into the turgid waters of the Chicago River or the alleys of Halsted and the Levee and that hard stretch of Clark between Polk and Taylor known to veteran officers as Cheyenne. Found bodies went to the morgue; if unclaimed, they traveled next to the dissection amphitheater at Rush Medical College or perhaps Cook County Hospital and from there to the articulation laboratory for the delicate task of picking flesh and connective tissue from the bones and skull, washing all with bleach, and remounting same for the subsequent use of doctors, anatomy museums, and the occasional private collector of scientific novelties. The hair was sold for wigs, the clothing given to settlement houses.

Like the Union Stock Yards, Chicago wasted nothing.

Alone

THE EASTERN AND CHICAGO ARCHITECTS met again on Monday morning, January 12, in Burnham & Root's library on the top floor of the Rookery. Root was absent. William R. Mead had come from New York to stand in for his grieving partner, McKim. As the men waited for everyone to arrive, the visitors from time to time would drift to the library's east-facing windows and stare out at the vastness of Lake Michigan. The light entering the room was preternaturally intense, carrying with it the surplus radiance of the lake and its frozen shore.

Burnham rose to offer the men a formal welcome, but he did not seem at ease. He was aware of the lingering reticence of the eastern men and seemed hell-bent on winning them with flattery that verged on unction— a tactic that Louis Sullivan had known Burnham to deploy with great effect. "Himself not especially susceptible to flattery except in a sentimental way, he soon learned its efficacy when plastered thick on big business men," Sullivan wrote. "Louis saw it done repeatedly, and at first was amazed at Burnham's effrontery, only to be more amazingly amazed at the drooling of the recipient. The method was crude but it worked."

Said Sullivan, "It soon became noticeable that he was progressively and grossly apologizing to the Eastern men for the presence of their benighted brethren of the West."

Hunt noticed it too. "*Hell*," he snapped, "we haven't come here on a missionary expedition. Let's get to work."

Murmurs of agreement rose through the room. Adler was cheered; Sullivan smirked. Olmsted watched, deadpan, as he listened to a roaring in his ears that would not subside. Hunt grimaced; the trip from New York and the excursion to Jackson Park had worsened his gout.

Hunt's interjection startled Burnham. It brought back in a rush the hurt of the great dual snub by the East, his rejection by Harvard and Yale; but the remark and the obvious support it garnered in the room also caused Burnham to shift focus to the work at hand. As Sullivan saw it, "Burnham came out of his somnambulistic vagary and joined in. He was keen enough to understand that 'Uncle Dick' "—meaning Hunt— "had done him a needed favor."

Burnham told the men that henceforth they would serve as the fair's Board of Architects. He invited them to choose a chairman. They elected Hunt. "The natural dominance of the master again asserted itself without pretension," wrote Van Brunt, "and we once more became his willing and happy pupils."

For secretary they elected Sullivan, who most decidedly was *not* a happy pupil of Hunt's. To him, Hunt was the janissary of a dead vernacular. Burnham, too. Both men symbolized all that stood in the way of Sullivan's own emerging ethos that a building's function should express itself in its design—not merely that form should follow function but that "the function *created* or organized its form."

To Sullivan, Hunt was merely a relic, Burnham something far more dangerous. In him Sullivan saw a kindred capacity for obsession. Sullivan had come to see Chicago architecture as dominated by only two firms: Burnham & Root and Adler & Sullivan. "In each firm was a man with a fixed irrevocable purpose in life, for the sake of which he would bend or sacrifice all else," Sullivan wrote. "Daniel Burnham was obsessed by the feudal idea of power. Louis Sullivan was equally obsessed by the beneficent idea of Democratic power." Sullivan admired both Root and Adler but believed they functioned on a lesser plane. "John Root was so self-indulgent that there was a risk he might never draw upon his underlying power; Adler was essentially a technician, an engineer, a conscientious administrator. . . . Unquestionably, Adler lacked sufficient imagination; so in a way did John Root—that is to say, the imagination of the dreamer. In the dream-imagination lay Burnham's strength and Louis's passion."

Shortly before noon Burnham left the room to take a telephone call from Dora Root. She told him her husband had awakened with a bad cold and would not be able to attend the meeting. Several hours later she called again: A doctor had come and diagnosed pneumonia.

Root's spirits were good. He joked and sketched. "I haven't escaped sickness all my life to get off easily now," he told Harriet Monroe. "I knew when my turn came, it would be a Tartar."

The architects continued to meet but without Burnham, who stayed beside his partner's bed except for occasional departures to help resolve issues back in the library or to visit Hunt, whose gout had grown so painful he was confined to his room in the Wellington Hotel. Root joked with his nurses. At its regular Wednesday meeting the Grounds and Buildings Committee passed a resolution wishing Root a speedy recovery. That day Burnham wrote to a Chicago architect named W. W. Boyington: "Mr. Root is quite low, and there is uncertainty about his recovery, but still a chance for him."

On Thursday Root seemed to rally. Burnham again wrote to Boyington: "am able this morning to give you a little better report. He has passed a pretty good night and is easier. While the danger is not over, we are hopeful."

Enthusiasm among the architects rose. With Hunt still confined to his room, Post stood in as chairman. He and Van Brunt shuttled to and from Hunt's hotel. The architects approved the original brown-paper plan fashioned by Burnham, Olmsted, and Root with few changes. They decided how big the main buildings should be and how they should be situated on the site. They chose a uniform style, neoclassical, meaning the buildings would have columns and pediments and evoke the glories of ancient Rome. This choice was anathema to Sullivan, who abhorred derivative architecture, but during the meeting he made no objection. The architects also made what would prove to be one of the most important decisions of the fair: They set a uniform height, sixty feet, for the cornice of each of the palaces of the Grand Court. A cornice was merely a horizontal decorative projection. Walls, roofs, domes, and arches could rise far higher, but by establishing this one point of commonality the architects ensured a fundamental harmony among the fair's most imposing structures.

At about four o'clock Thursday afternoon Codman and Burnham drove to Root's house. Codman waited in the carriage as Burnham went inside.

Burnham found Root struggling for breath. Throughout the day Root had experienced strange dreams, including one that had come to him many times in the past of flying through the air. When Root saw Burnham, he said, "You won't leave me again, will you?"

Burnham said no, but he did leave, to check on Root's wife, who was in a neighboring room. As Burnham talked with her, a relative also entered the room. She told them Root was dead. In his last moments, she said, he had run his fingers over his bedding as if playing the piano. "Do you hear that?" he whispered. "Isn't it wonderful? That's what I call music."

The house settled into an eerie postmortem quiet broken only by the hiss of gas lamps and the weary tick of clocks. Burnham paced the floor below. He did not know it, but he was being watched. Harriet Monroe's Aunt Nettie sat on a step high on the dark upper curve of the stairway that rose from Root's living room to the second floor. The woman listened as Burnham paced. A fire burned in the hearth behind him and cast large shadows on the opposing wall. "I have worked," Burnham said, "I have schemed and dreamed to make us the greatest architects in the world—I have made him see it and kept him at it—and now he dies—*damn!—damn!—damn!*"

Root's death stunned Burnham, stunned Chicago. Burnham and Root had been partners and friends for eighteen years. Each knew the other's thoughts. Each had come to rely on the other for his skills. Now Root was gone. Outsiders wondered if Root's death might mean the death of the exposition. The newspapers were full of interviews in which the city's leading men described Root as the guiding force behind the fair, that without him the city could not hope to realize its dreams. The *Tribune* said Root was "easily" Chicago's "most distinguished architect, if indeed he had his superior in the whole country." Edward Jefferey, chairman of the Grounds and Buildings Committee, said, "There is no man in the profession of architects who has the genius and ability to take up the Exposition work where Mr. Root left off."

Burnham kept silent. He considered quitting the fair. Two forces warred within him: grief, and a desire to cry out that *he,* Burnham, had been the engine driving the design of the fair; that *he* was the partner who had propelled the firm of Burnham & Root to greater and greater achievement.

The eastern architects departed on Saturday, January 17. On Sunday Burnham attended a memorial service for Root at Root's Astor Place house and his burial in Graceland Cemetery, a charming haven for the well-heeled dead a few miles north of the Loop.

On Monday he was back at his desk. He wrote twelve letters. Root's office next to his was silent, draped in bunting. Hothouse flowers perfumed the air.

The challenge ahead looked more daunting than ever.

———

On Tuesday a large bank failed in Kansas City. The following Saturday Lyman Gage announced that he would quit as president of the fair, effective April 1, to tend to his own bank. The fair's director-general, George Davis, at first refused to believe it. "It's all nonsense," he snapped. "Gage has got to stay with us. We can't do without him."

There was labor unrest. Just as Burnham had feared, union leaders began using the future fair as a vehicle for asserting such goals as the adoption of a minimum wage and an eight-hour day. There was the threat of fire and weather and disease: Already foreign editors were asking who would dare attend the exposition given Chicago's notorious problems with sewage. No one had forgotten how in 1885 fouled water had ignited an outbreak of cholera and typhoid that killed ten percent of the city's population.

Darker forces marshaled in the smoke. Somewhere in the heart of the city a young Irish immigrant sank still more deeply into madness, the preamble to an act that would shock the nation and destroy what Burnham dreamed would be the single greatest moment of his life.

Closer at hand a far stranger creature raised his head in equally intent anticipation. "I was born with the devil in me," he wrote. "I could not help the fact that I was a murderer, no more than the poet can help the inspiration to sing."

PART II

An Awful Fight

Chicago, 1891–93

Manufactures and Liberal Arts Building, after the storm of June 13, 1892.

Convocation

On Tuesday, February 24, 1891, Burnham, Olmsted, Hunt, and the other architects gathered in the library on the top floor of the Rookery to present drawings of the fair's main structures to the Grounds and Buildings Committee. The architects met by themselves throughout the morning, with Hunt serving as chairman. His gout forced him to keep one leg on the table. Olmsted looked worn and gray, except for his eyes, which gleamed beneath his bald skull like marbles of lapis. A new man had joined the group, Augustus St. Gaudens, one of America's best-known sculptors, whom Charles McKim had invited to help evaluate the designs. The members of the Grounds and Buildings Committee arrived at two o'clock and filled the library with the scent of cigars and frosted wool.

The light in the room was sallow, the sun already well into its descent. Wind thumped the windows. In the hearth at the north wall a large fire cracked and lisped, flushing the room with a dry sirocco that caused frozen skin to tingle.

At Hunt's brusque prodding the architects got to work.

One by one they walked to the front of the room, unrolled their drawings, and displayed them upon the wall. Something had happened among the architects, and it became evident immediately, as though a new force had entered the room. They spoke, Burnham said, "almost in whispers."

Each building was more lovely, more elaborate than the last, and all were immense—fantastic things on a scale never before attempted.

Hunt hobbled to the front and displayed his Administration Building, intended to be the most important at the fair and the portal through which most visitors would enter. Its center was an octagon topped by a dome that rose 275 feet from floor to peak, higher than the dome of the U.S. Capitol.

The next structure presented was even bigger. If successfully erected, George B. Post's Manufactures and Liberal Arts Building would be the largest building ever constructed and consume enough steel to build two Brooklyn Bridges. All that space, moreover, was to be lit inside and out with electric lamps. Twelve electric elevators would carry visitors to the building's upper reaches. Four would rise through a central tower to an interior bridge 220 feet above the floor, which in turn would lead to an exterior promenade offering foot-tingling views of the distant Michigan shore, "a panorama," as one guidebook later put it, "such as never before has been accorded to mortals."

Post proposed to top his building with a dome 450 feet high, which would have made the building not only the biggest in the world but also the tallest. As Post looked around the room, he saw in the eyes of his peers great admiration but also something else. A murmur passed among them. Such was this new level of cohesion among the architects that Post understood at once. The dome was too much—not too tall to be built, simply too proud for its context. It would diminish Hunt's building and in so doing diminish Hunt and disrupt the harmony of the other structures on the Grand Court. Without prodding, Post said quietly, "I don't think I shall advocate that dome; probably I shall modify the building." There was unspoken but unanimous approval.

Sullivan had already modified his own building, at Burnham's suggestion. Originally Burnham wanted Adler & Sullivan to design the fair's Music Hall, but partly out of a continued sense of having been wronged by Burnham, the partners had turned the project down. Burnham later offered them the Transportation Building, which they accepted. Two weeks before the meeting Burnham wrote to Sullivan and urged him to modify his design to create "one grand entrance toward the east and make this much richer than either of the others you had proposed. . . . Am sure that the effect of your building will be much finer than by the old method of two entrances on this side, neither of which could be so fine and effective as the one central feature." Sullivan took the suggestion but never acknowledged its provenance, even though that one great entrance eventually became the talk of the fair.

All the architects, including Sullivan, seemed to have been captured by the same spell, although Sullivan later would disavow the moment. As each architect unrolled his drawings, "the tension of feeling was almost painful," Burnham said. St. Gaudens, tall and lean and wearing a goatee, sat in a corner very still, like a figure sculpted from wax. On every face Burnham saw a "quiet intentness." It was clear to him that now, finally, the architects understood that Chicago had been serious about its elaborate plans for the fair. "Drawing after drawing was unrolled," Burnham said, "and as the day passed it was apparent that a picture had been forming in the minds of those present—a vision far more grand and beautiful than hitherto presented by the richest imagination."

As the light began to fade, the architects lit the library's gas jets, which hissed like mildly perturbed cats. From the street below, the top floor of the Rookery seemed aflame with the shifting light of the jets and the fire in the great hearth. "The room was still as death," Burnham said, "save for the low voice of the speaker commenting on his design. It seemed as if a great magnet held everyone in its grasp."

The last drawing went up. For a few moments afterward the silence continued.

Lyman Gage, still president of the exposition, was first to move. He was a banker, tall, straight-backed, conservative in demeanor and dress, but he rose suddenly and walked to a window, trembling with emotion. "You are dreaming, gentlemen, dreaming," he whispered. "I only hope that half the vision may be realized."

Now St. Gaudens rose. He had been quiet all day. He rushed to Burnham and took his hands in his own. "I never expected to see such a moment," he said. "Look here, old fellow, do you realize this has been the greatest meeting of artists since the fifteenth century?"

⁐———⁌

Olmsted too sensed that something extraordinary had occurred, but the meeting also troubled him. First, it confirmed his growing concern that the architects were losing sight of the nature of the thing they were proposing to build. The shared vision expressed in their drawings struck him as being too sober and monumental. After all, this was a world's fair, and fairs should be fun. Aware of the architects' increasing emphasis on size, Olmsted shortly before the meeting had written to Burnham suggesting ways to enliven the grounds. He wanted the lagoons and canals strewn with waterfowl of all kinds and colors and traversed continually by small boats. Not just any boats, however: *becoming* boats. The subject became an obsession for him. His broad view of what constituted landscape architecture included anything that grew, flew, floated, or otherwise entered the scenery he created. Roses produced dabs of red; boats added intricacy and life. But it was crucial to choose the right kind of boat. He dreaded what would happen if the decision were left to one of the fair's many committees. He wanted Burnham to know his views from the start.

"We should try to make the boating feature of the exposition a gay and lively one," he wrote. He loathed the clatter and smoke of steam launches; he wanted electric boats designed specifically for the park, with emphasis on graceful lines and silent operation. It was most important that these boats be constantly but quietly in motion, to provide diversion for the eye, peace for the ear. "What we shall want is a regular service of boats like that of an omnibus line in a city street," he wrote. He also envisioned a fleet of large birchbark canoes paddled by Indians in deerskin and feathers and recommended that various foreign watercraft be moored in the fair's harbor. "I mean such as Malay proas, catamarans, Arab dhows, Chinese sanpans, Japanese pilot boats, Turkish caiques, Esquimaux kiacks, Alaskan war canoes, the hooded boats of the Swiss Lakes, and so on."

A far more important outcome of the Rookery meeting, however, was Olmsted's recognition that the architects' noble dreams magnified and complicated the already-daunting challenge that faced him in Jackson Park. When he and Calvert Vaux had designed Central Park in New York, they had planned for visual effects that would not be achieved for decades; here he would have just twenty-six months to reshape the desolation of the park into a prairie Venice and plant its shores, islands, terraces, and walks with whatever it took to produce a landscape rich enough to satisfy his vision. What the architects' drawings had shown him, however, was that in reality he would have far fewer than twenty-six months. The portion of his work that would most shape how visitors appraised his landscape—the planting and grooming of the grounds immediately surrounding each building—could only be done *after* the major structures were completed and the grounds cleared of construction equipment, temporary tracks and roads, and other aesthetic impedimenta. Yet the palaces unveiled in the Rookery were so immense, so detailed, that their construction was likely to consume nearly all the remaining time, leaving little for him.

Soon after the meeting Olmsted composed a strategy for the transformation of Jackson Park. His ten-page memorandum captured the essence of all he had come to believe about the art of landscape architecture and how it should strive to conjure effects greater than the mere sum of petals and leaves.

He concentrated on the fair's central lagoon, which his dredges soon would begin carving from the Jackson Park shore. The dredges would leave an island at the center of the lagoon, to be called, simply, the Wooded Island. The fair's main buildings would rise along the lagoon's outer banks. Olmsted saw this lagoon district as the most challenging portion of the fair. Just as the Grand Court was to be the architectural heart of the fair, so the central lagoon and Wooded Island were to constitute its landscape centerpiece.

Above all he wanted the exposition landscape to produce an aura of "mysterious poetic effect." Flowers were not to be used as an ordinary gardener would use them. Rather, every flower, shrub, and tree was to be deployed with an eye to how each would act upon the imagination. This was to be accomplished, Olmsted wrote, "through the mingling intricately together of many forms of foliage, the alternation and complicated crossing of salient leaves and stalks of varying green tints in high lights with other leaves and stalks, behind and under them, and therefore less defined and more shaded, yet partly illumined by light reflected from the water."

He hoped to provide visitors with a banquet of glimpses—the undersides of leaves sparkling with reflected light; flashes of brilliant color between fronds of tall grass waving in the breeze. Nowhere, he wrote, should there be "a display of flowers demanding attention as such. Rather, the flowers to be used for the purpose should have the effect of flecks and glimmers of bright color imperfectly breaking through the general greenery. Anything approaching a gorgeous, garish or gaudy display of flowers is to be avoided."

Sedges and ferns and graceful bulrush would be planted on the banks of the Wooded Island to conjure density and intricacy and "to slightly screen, without hiding, flowers otherwise likely to be too obtrusive." He envisioned large patches of cattails broken by bulrush, iris, and flag and pocketed with blooming plants, such as flame-red cardinal flower and yellow creeping buttercup—planted, if necessary, on slightly raised mounds so as to be just visible among the swaying green spires in the foreground.

On the far shore, below the formal terraces of the buildings, he planned to position fragrant plants such as honeysuckle and summersweet, so that their perfume would rise into the nostrils of visitors pausing on the terraces to view the island and the lagoon.

The overall effect, he wrote, "is thus to be in some degree of the character of a theatrical scene, to occupy the Exposition stage for a single summer."

It was one thing to visualize all this on paper, another to execute it. Olmsted was nearly seventy, his mouth aflame, his head roaring, each night a desert of wakefulness. Even without the fair he faced an intimidating portfolio of works in progress, chief among them the grounds of Biltmore, the Vanderbilt estate in North Carolina. If everything went perfectly—*if* his health did not degrade any further, *if* the weather held, *if* Burnham completed the other buildings on time, *if* strikes did not destroy the fair, *if* the many committees and directors, which Olmsted called "that army our hundreds of masters," learned to leave Burnham alone—Olmsted *might* be able to complete his task on time.

A writer for *Engineering Magazine* asked the question no one had raised at the Rookery: "How is it possible that this vast amount of construction, greatly exceeding that of the Paris Exhibition of 1889, will be ready in two years?"

For Burnham, too, the meeting in the Rookery had produced a heightened awareness of how little time remained. Everything seemed to take longer than it should, and nothing went smoothly. The first real work in Jackson Park began on February 11, when fifty Italian immigrants employed by McArthur Brothers, a Chicago company, began digging a drainage ditch. It was nothing, routine. But word of the work spread, and five hundred union men stormed the park and drove the workers off. Two days later, Friday the thirteenth, six hundred men gathered at the park to protest McArthur's use of what they alleged were "imported" workers. The next day two thousand men, many armed with sharpened sticks, advanced on McArthur's workers, seized two, and began beating them. Police arrived. The crowd backed off. McArthur asked Mayor Cregier for protection; Cregier assigned the city's corporation counsel, a young lawyer named Clarence Darrow, to look into it. Two nights later the city's unions met with officers of the fair to demand that they limit the workday to eight hours, pay union-scale wages, and hire union workers before all others. After two weeks of deliberation the fair's directors accepted the eight-hour day but said they'd think about the rest.

There was conflict, too, among the fair's overseers. The National Commission, made up of politicians and headed by Director-General George Davis, wanted financial control; the Exposition Company, run by Chicago's leading businessmen and headed by President Lyman Gage, refused: The company had raised the money, and by God the company would spend it, in whatever way it chose.

Committees ruled everything. In his private practice Burnham was accustomed to having complete control over expenditures needed to build his skyscrapers. Now he needed to seek approval from the Exposition Company's executive committee at every step, even to buy drafting boards. It was all immensely frustrating. "We must push this now," Burnham said. "The delays have seemed interminable."

But he did make progress. For example, he directed a contest to choose a female architect to design the Woman's Building for the fair. Sophia Hayden of Boston won. She was twenty-one years old. Her fee was the prize money: a thousand dollars. The male architects each got ten thousand. There had been skepticism that a mere woman would be able to conceive such an important building on her own. "Examination of the facts show[s] that this woman had no help whatever in working up the designs," Burnham wrote. "It was done by herself in her home."

In March, however, all the architects acknowledged that things were proceeding far too slowly—that if they built their structures as originally planned out of stone, steel, and brick, the buildings could not possibly be finished by Opening Day. They voted instead to clad their buildings in "staff," a resilient mixture of plaster and jute that could be molded into columns and statuary and spread over wood frames to provide the illusion of stone. "There will not be a brick on the grounds," Burnham said.

In the midst of all this, as the workload increased, Burnham realized he could put off no longer the hiring of a designer to replace his beloved John Root. He needed someone to manage his firm's ongoing work while he tended to the exposition. A friend recommended Charles B. Atwood of New York. McKim shook his head. There were stories about Atwood, and questions of dependability. Nonetheless, Burnham arranged to meet Atwood in New York, at the Brunswick Hotel.

Atwood stood him up. Burnham waited an hour, then left to catch his train. As he was crossing the street, a handsome man in a black bowler and cape with black gun-muzzle eyes approached him and asked if he was Mr. Burnham.

"I am," Burnham said.

"I'm Charles Atwood. Did you want to see me?"

Burnham glared. "I am going back to Chicago; I'll think it over and let you know." Burnham caught his train. Once back in Chicago he went directly to his office. A few hours later Atwood walked in. He had followed Burnham from New York.

Burnham gave him the job.

Atwood had a secret, as it happens. He was an opium addict. It explained those eyes and his erratic behavior. But Burnham thought him a genius.

⁐

As a reminder to himself and anyone who visited his office in the shanty, Burnham posted a sign over his desk bearing a single word: RUSH.

⁐

Time was so short, the Executive Committee began planning exhibits and appointing world's fair commissioners to secure them. In February the committee voted to dispatch a young army officer, Lieutenant Mason A. Schufeldt, to Zanzibar to begin a journey to locate a tribe of Pygmies only recently revealed to exist by explorer Henry Stanley, and to bring to the fair "a family of twelve or fourteen of the fierce little midgets."

The committee gave Lieutenant Schufeldt two and a half years to complete his mission.

⁐

Beyond the fairgrounds' new fence, turmoil and grief engulfed Chicago. Union leaders threatened to organize unions worldwide to oppose the fair. *The Inland Architect,* a prominent Chicago journal, reported: "That un-American institution, the trades union, has developed its un-American principle of curtailing or abolishing the personal freedom of the individual in a new direction, that of seeking, as far as possible, to cripple the World's Fair." Such behavior, the journal said, "would be called treason in countries less enlightened and more arbitrary than ours." The nation's financial condition worsened. Offices in the newest of Chicago's skyscrapers remained vacant. Just blocks from the Rookery, Burnham & Root's Temperance Building stood huge and black and largely empty. Twenty-five thousand unemployed workers roamed the city. At night they slept in police stations and in the basement of City Hall. The unions grew stronger.

The old world was passing. P. T. Barnum died; grave-robbers attempted to steal his corpse. William Tecumseh Sherman died, too. Atlanta cheered. Reports from abroad asserted, erroneously, that Jack the Ripper had returned. Closer at hand, a gory killing in New York suggested he might have migrated to America.

In Chicago the former warden of the Illinois State Penitentiary at Joliet, Major R. W. McClaughry, began readying the city for the surge in crime that everyone expected the fair to produce, establishing an office in the Auditorium to receive and distribute Bertillon identifications of known criminals. Devised by French criminologist Alphonse Bertillon, the system required police to make a precise survey of the dimensions and physical peculiarities of suspects. Bertillon believed that each man's measurements were unique and thus could be used to penetrate the aliases that criminals deployed in moving from city to city. In theory, a detective in Cincinnati could telegraph a few distinctive numbers to investigators in New York with the expectation that if a match existed, New York would find it.

A reporter asked Major McClaughry whether the fair really would attract the criminal element. He paused a moment, then said, "I think it quite necessary that the authorities here should be prepared to meet and deal with the greatest congregation of criminals that ever yet met in this country."

Cuckoldry

AT THE HOLMES BUILDING at Sixty-third and Wallace, now known widely in the neighborhood as "the castle," the Conner family was in turmoil. Lovely, dark Gertrude—Ned's sister—one day came to Ned in tears and told him she could not stay in the house another moment. She vowed to catch the first train back to Muscatine, Iowa. Ned begged her to tell him what had occurred, but she refused.

Ned knew that she and a young man had begun courting, and he believed her tears must have resulted from something he had said or done. Possibly the two had been "indiscreet," although he did not think Gertrude capable of so drastic a moral lapse. The more he pressed her for an explanation, the more troubled and adamant she became. She wished she had never come to Chicago. It was a blighted, hellish place full of noise and dust and smoke and inhuman towers that blocked the sun, and she hated it—hated especially this gloomy building and the ceaseless clamor of construction.

When Holmes came by, she would not look at him. Her color rose. Ned did not notice.

Ned hired an express company to collect her trunk and saw her to the station. Still she would not explain. Through tears, she said good-bye. The train huffed from the station.

In Iowa—in safe, bland Muscatine—Gertrude fell ill, an accident of nature. The disease proved fatal. Holmes told Ned how sorry he was to hear of her passing, but in his eyes there was only a flat blue calm, like the lake on a still August morning.

With Gertrude gone, the tension between Ned and Julia increased. Their marriage never had been tranquil. Back in Iowa they had come close to separating. Now, again, their relationship was crumbling. Their daughter, Pearl, became commensurately more difficult to manage, her behavior marked by periods of sullen withdrawal and eruptions of anger. Ned understood none of it. He was "of an easy-going innocent nature," a reporter later observed, "he mistrusted nothing." He did not see what even his friends and regular customers saw. "Some of my friends told me there was something between Holmes and my wife," he said later. "At first I did not believe it."

Despite the warnings and his own mounting uneasiness, Ned admired Holmes. While he, Ned, was but a jeweler in someone else's store, Holmes controlled a small empire—and had yet to turn thirty years old. Holmes's energy and success made Ned feel even smaller than he already was inclined to feel, especially now that Julia had begun looking at him as if he had just emerged from a rendering vat at the stockyards.

Thus Ned was particularly susceptible to an offer from Holmes that seemed likely to increase his own stature in Julia's eyes. Holmes proposed to sell Ned the entire pharmacy, under terms that Ned—naïve Ned—found generous beyond all expectation. Holmes would increase his salary from twelve to eighteen dollars a week, so that Ned could pay Holmes six dollars a week to cover the purchase. Ned wouldn't even have to worry about handling the six dollars—Holmes would deduct it from the new eighteen-dollar salary each week, automatically. Holmes promised also to take care of all the legal details and to record the transfer with city officials. Ned would get his twelve dollars a week just as always, but now he would be the owner of a fine store in a prosperous neighborhood destined to become even wealthier once the world's fair began operation.

Ned accepted, giving no thought to why Holmes would wish to shed such a healthy business. The offer eased his concerns about Holmes and Julia. If Holmes and she were involved in an indiscreet liaison, would he offer Ned the jewel of his Englewood empire?

To Ned's sorrow, he soon found that his new status did nothing to ease the tension between himself and Julia. The ferocity of their arguments only increased, as did the length of the cold silences that filled whatever other time they spent together. Holmes was sympathetic. He bought Ned lunch at the first-floor restaurant and told Ned how certain he was that the marriage would be salvaged. Julia was an ambitious woman and clearly a very beautiful one, but she would come to her senses in short order.

Holmes's sympathy was disarming. The idea that Holmes might be the cause of Julia's discontent seemed more and more improbable. Holmes even wanted Ned to buy life insurance, for surely once his marital strife subsided, he would want to protect Julia and Pearl from destitution in the event of his death. He recommended that Ned also consider insuring Pearl's life and offered to pay the initial premiums. He brought an insurance man, C. W. Arnold, to meet with Ned.

Arnold explained that he was building a new agency and wanted to sell as many policies as possible in order to attract the attention of the biggest insurance companies. To secure a policy, all Ned had to pay was a dollar, Arnold said—just one dollar to begin protecting his family forever.

But Ned did not want a policy. Arnold tried to change his mind. Ned refused and refused and finally told Arnold that if he really needed a dollar, Ned would simply give him one.

Arnold and Holmes looked at each other, their eyes empty of all expression.

Soon creditors began appearing at the pharmacy demanding repayment of mortgages secured by the store's furnishings and its stock of salves and ointments and other goods. Ned was unaware of the existence of these debts and believed the creditors were trying to defraud him— until they presented documents signed by the previous owner, H. H. Holmes. Convinced now that these were bona-fide debts, Ned promised to pay them as soon as he was able.

Here too Holmes was sympathetic, but there was nothing he could do. Any thriving venture accumulated debts. He had assumed that Ned understood at least that much about business. At any rate it was some-thing to which Ned would now have to become accustomed. The sale, he reminded Ned, was final.

———

This latest disappointment rekindled Ned's uneasiness about Holmes and Julia. He began to suspect that his friends might indeed be correct in believing that Holmes and Julia were engaged in an illicit affair. It would explain the change in Julia, certainly, and might even explain Holmes's sale of the pharmacy—an unstated trade: the store in exchange for Julia.

Ned did not yet confront Julia with his suspicions. He told her simply that if her behavior toward him did not change, if her coldness and hos-tility continued, he and she would have to separate.

She snapped, "Separation couldn't come too soon to suit me."

But they remained together a short while longer. Their battles became more frequent. Finally Ned shouted that he was done, the marriage was over. He spent the night in the barbershop on the first floor, directly below their apartment. He heard her footsteps as she moved about on the floor above.

The next morning he told Holmes he was leaving and would abandon his interest in the store. When Holmes urged him to reconsider, Ned merely laughed. He moved out and took a new job with a jewelry store in downtown Chicago, H. Purdy & Co. Pearl remained with Julia and Holmes.

Ned made one more attempt to win back his wife. "I told her after I left the building that if she would return to me and stop her quarreling we would live together again, but she refused to come back."

Ned vowed that one day he would return for Pearl. Soon he left Chicago and moved to Gilman, Illinois, where he met a young woman and began a formal courtship, which compelled him to visit Holmes's building one more time, to seek a divorce decree. He got it but failed to gain custody of Pearl.

———

With Ned gone and the divorce final, Holmes's interest in Julia began to dissipate. He had promised her repeatedly that he would marry her once the decree was confirmed, but now he found the prospect repulsive. Pearl's sullen, accusing presence had become especially unappealing.

At night, after the first-floor stores had closed and Julia and Pearl and the building's other tenants were asleep, he sometimes would descend to the basement, careful to lock the door behind him, and there ignite the flames of his kiln and marvel at its extraordinary heat.

Vexed

BURNHAM SAW HIS FAMILY RARELY now. By the spring of 1891 he was living full time in the shanty at Jackson Park; Margaret stayed in Evanston with a few servants who helped her care for their five children. Only a modest train ride separated the Burnhams, but the mounting demands of the fair made that distance as difficult to span as the Isthmus of Panama. Burnham could send telegrams, but they forced a cold and clumsy brevity and afforded little privacy. So Burnham wrote letters, and wrote them often. "You must not think this hurry of my life will last forever," he wrote in one letter. "I shall stop after the World's Fair. I have made up my mind to this." The exposition had become a "hurricane," he said. "To be done with this flurry is my strongest wish."

Every dawn he left his quarters and inspected the grounds. Six steam-powered dredges the size of floating barns gnawed at the lakeshore, as five thousand men with shovels and wheelbarrows and horse-drawn graders slowly scraped the landscape raw, many of the men wearing bowlers and suitcoats as if they just happened to be passing by and on impulse chose to pitch in. Despite the presence of so many workers, there was a maddening lack of noise and bustle. The park was too big, the men too spread out, to deliver any immediate sense of work being done. The only reliable signs were the black plumes of smoke from the dredges and the ever-present scent of burning leaves from slash piles set aflame by workers. The brilliant white stakes that marked the perimeters of buildings imparted to the land the look of a Civil War burial ground. Burnham did find beauty in the rawness—"Among the trees of the Wooded Island the long white tents of the contractor's camp gleamed in the sun, a soft, white note in the dun-colored landscape, and the pure blue line of the lake horizon made a cheerful contrast to the rugged and barren fore-ground"—but he also found deep frustration.

The work advanced slowly, impeded by the worsening relationship between the fair's two ruling bodies, the National Commission and the Exposition Company, and by the architects' failure to get their drawings to Chicago on time. All the drawings were late. Equally aggravating was the fact that there still was no Eiffel challenger. Moreover, the exposition had entered that precarious early phase common to every great construction project when unexpected obstacles suddenly emerge.

Burnham knew how to deal with Chicago's notoriously flimsy soil, but Jackson Park surprised even him.

Initially the bearing capacity of its ground was "practically an unknown quality," as one engineer put it. In March 1891 Burnham ordered tests to gauge how well the soil would support the grand palaces then on the architects' drafting tables. Of special concern was the fact that the buildings would be sited adjacent to newly dug canals and lagoons. As any engineer knew, soil under pressure tended to shift to fill adjacent excavations. The fair's engineers conducted the first test twelve feet from the lagoon on ground intended to support the northeast corner of the Electricity Building. They laid a platform four feet square and loaded it with iron to a pressure of 2,750 pounds per square foot, twenty-two tons in all. They left it in place for fifteen days and found that it settled only one-quarter of an inch. Next they dug a deep trench four feet from the platform. Over the next two days the platform sank another eighth of an inch but no farther. This was good news. It meant that Burnham could use Root's floating *grillage* for foundations without having to worry about catastrophic settlement.

To make sure these properties were constant throughout the park, Burnham had his chief engineer, Abraham Gottlieb, test locations earmarked for other buildings. The tests yielded similar results—until Gottlieb's men came to the site intended for George Post's gigantic Manufactures and Liberal Arts Building. The soil destined to support the northern half of the building showed total settlement of less than one inch, consistent with the rest of the park. At the southern end of the site, however, the men made a disheartening discovery. Even as workers loaded the platform, it sank eight inches. Over the next four days it settled thirty inches more, and would have continued sinking if the engineers had not simply called off the test.

Of course: Nearly all the soil of Jackson Park was competent to support floating foundations *except* the one portion destined to bear the fair's biggest and heaviest building. Here, Burnham realized, contractors would have to drive piles at least down to hard-pan, an expensive complication and a source of additional delay.

The problems with this building, however, had only just begun.

In April 1891 Chicago learned the results of the latest mayoral election. In the city's richest clubs, industrialists gathered to toast the fact that Carter Henry Harrison, whom they viewed as overly sympathetic to organized labor, had lost to Hempstead Washburne, a Republican. Burnham, too, allowed himself a moment of celebration. To him, Harrison represented the old Chicago of filth, smoke, and vice, everything the fair was designed to repudiate.

The celebrations were tempered, however, by the fact that Harrison had lost by the narrowest of margins, fewer than four thousand votes. What's more, he had achieved this near-victory without the support of a major party. Shunned by the Democrats, he had run as an independent.

Elsewhere in the city, Patrick Prendergast grieved. Harrison was his hero, his hope. The margin was so narrow, however, that he believed that if Harrison ran again, he would win. Prendergast resolved to double his own efforts to help Harrison succeed.

In Jackson Park Burnham faced repeated interruptions stemming from his de facto role as ambassador to the outside world, charged with cultivating goodwill and future attendance. Mostly these banquets, talks, and tours were time-squandering annoyances, as in June 1891 when, at the request of Director-General Davis, Burnham hosted a visit to Jackson Park by a battalion of foreign dignitaries that consumed two full days. Others were purely a pleasure. A few weeks earlier Thomas Edison, known widely as "the Wizard of Menlo Park," had paid a visit to Burnham's shanty. Burnham showed him around. Edison suggested the exposition use incandescent bulbs rather than arc lights, because the incandescent variety produced a softer light. Where arc lights could not be avoided, he said, they should be covered with white globes. And of course Edison urged the fair to use direct current, DC, the prevailing standard.

The civility of this encounter belied a caustic battle being waged outside Jackson Park for the rights to illuminate the exposition. On one side was General Electric Company, which had been created when J. P. Morgan took over Edison's company and merged it with several others and which now proposed to install a direct current system to light the fair. On the other side was Westinghouse Electric Company, with a bid to wire Jackson Park for alternating current, using patents that its founder, George Westinghouse, had acquired a few years earlier from Nikola Tesla.

General Electric offered to do the job for $1.8 million, insisting the deal would not earn a penny's profit. A number of exposition directors held General Electric stock and urged William Baker, president of the fair since Lyman Gage's April retirement, to accept the bid. Baker refused, calling it "extortionate." General Electric rather miraculously came back with a bid of $554,000. But Westinghouse, whose AC system was inherently cheaper and more efficient, bid $399,000. The exposition went with Westinghouse, and helped change the history of electricity.

The source of Burnham's greatest dismay was the failure of the architects to finish their drawings on schedule.

If he had once been obsequious to Richard Hunt and the eastern men, he was not now. In a June 2, 1891, letter to Hunt, he wrote, "We are at a dead standstill waiting for your scale drawings. Can't we have them as they are, and finish here?"

Four days later he again prodded Hunt: "The delay you are causing us by not forwarding scale drawings is embarrassing in the extreme."

That same month a serious if unavoidable interruption hobbled the Landscape Department. Olmsted became ill—severely so. He attributed his condition to poisoning from an arsenic-based pigment called Turkey Red in the wallpaper of his Brookline home. It may, however, simply have been another bout of deep blue melancholia, the kind that had assailed him off and on for years.

During his recuperation Olmsted ordered bulbs and plants for cultivation in two large nurseries established on the fairgrounds. He ordered Dusty Miller, Carpet Bugle, President Garfield heliotrope, Speedwell, Pennyroyal, English and Algerian ivies, verbena, vinca, and a rich palette of geraniums, among them Black Prince, Christopher Columbus, Mrs. Turner, Crystal Palace, Happy Thought, and Jeanne d'Arc. He dispatched an army of collectors to the shores of Lake Calumet, where they gathered twenty-seven traincar loads of iris, sedge, bulrush, and other semiaquatic plants and grasses. They collected an additional four thousand crates of pond lily roots, which Olmsted's men quickly planted, only to watch most of the roots succumb to the ever-changing levels of the lake.

In contrast to the lush growth within the nurseries, the grounds of the park had been scraped free of all vegetation. Workers enriched the soil with one thousand carloads of manure shipped from the Union Stock Yards and another two thousand collected from the horses working in Jackson Park. The presence of so much exposed earth and manure became a problem. "It was bad enough during the hot weather, when a south wind could blind the eyes of man and beast," wrote Rudolf Ulrich, Olmsted's landscape superintendent at the park, "but still worse during wet weather, the newly filled ground, which was still undrained, becoming soaked with water."

Horses sank to their bellies.

It was midsummer 1891 by the time the last of the architects' drawings were completed. As each set came in, Burnham advertised for bids. Recognizing that the architects' delays had put everything behind schedule, he inserted into the construction contracts clauses that made him a "czar," as the *Chicago Tribune* put it. Each contract contained a tight deadline for completion, with a financial penalty for every day beyond. Burnham had advertised the first contract on May 14, this for the Mines Building. He wanted it finished by the end of the year. That left at best about seven months for construction (roughly the amount of time a twenty-first-century homeowner would need to build a new garage). "He is the arbiter of all disputes and no provision is made for an appeal from his decision," the *Tribune* reported. "If in the opinion of Mr. Burnham the builder is not employing a sufficient force of men to complete the work on time, Mr. Burnham is authorized to engage men himself and charge the cost to the builder." The Mines Building was the first of the main exposition buildings to begin construction, but the work did not start until July 3, 1891, with less than sixteen months remaining until Dedication Day.

As construction of the buildings at last got under way, anticipation outside the park began to increase. Colonel William Cody—Buffalo Bill—sought a concession for his Wild West show, newly returned from a hugely successful tour of Europe, but the fair's Committee on Ways and Means turned him down on grounds of "incongruity." Undeterred, Cody secured rights to a large parcel of land adjacent to the park. In San Francisco a twenty-one-year-old entrepreneur named Sol Bloom realized that the Chicago fair would let him at last take advantage of an asset he had acquired in Paris two years earlier. Entranced by the Algerian Village at the Paris exposition, he had bought the rights to display the village and its inhabitants at future events. The Ways and Means Committee rejected him, too. He returned to San Francisco intent on trying a different, more oblique means of winning a concession—one that ultimately would get him a lot more than he had bargained for. Meanwhile young Lieutenant Schufeldt had reached Zanzibar. On July 20 he telegraphed Exposition President William Baker that he was confident he could acquire as many

Pygmies from the Congo as he wished, provided the king of Belgium consented. "President Baker wants these pygmies," the *Tribune* said, "and so does everybody else around headquarters."

On the drafting board the fair did look spectacular. The centerpiece was the Grand Court, which everyone had begun calling the Court of Honor. With its immense palaces by Hunt, Post, Peabody, and the rest, the court by itself would be a marvel, but now nearly every state in the nation was planning a building, as were some two hundred companies and foreign governments. The exposition promised to surpass the Paris exposition on every level—every level that is, except one, and that persistent deficit troubled Burnham: The fair still had nothing planned that would equal, let alone eclipse, the Eiffel Tower. At nearly one thousand feet in height, the tower remained the tallest structure in the world and an insufferable reminder of the triumph of the Paris exposition. "To out-Eiffel Eiffel" had become a battle cry among the directors.

A competition held by the *Tribune* brought a wave of implausible proposals. C. F. Ritchel of Bridgeport, Connecticut, suggested a tower with a base one hundred feet high by five hundred feet wide, within which Ritchel proposed to nest a second tower and, in this one, a third. At intervals a complicated system of hydraulic tubes and pumps would cause the towers to telescope slowly upward, a journey of several hours, then allow them to sink slowly back to their original configuration. The top of the tower would house a restaurant, although possibly a bordello would have been more apt.

Another inventor, J. B. McComber, representing the Chicago-Tower Spiral-Spring Ascension and Toboggan Transportation Company, proposed a tower with a height of 8,947 feet, nearly nine times the height of the Eiffel Tower, with a base one thousand feet in diameter sunk two thousand feet into the earth. Elevated rails would lead from the top of the tower all the way to New York, Boston, Baltimore, and other cities. Visitors ready to conclude their visit to the fair and daring enough to ride elevators to the top would then toboggan all the way back home. "As the cost of the tower and its slides is of secondary importance," McComber noted, "I do not mention it here, but will furnish figures upon application."

A third proposal demanded even more courage from visitors. This inventor, who gave his initials as R. T. E., envisioned a tower four thousand feet tall from which he proposed to hang a two-thousand-foot cable of "best rubber." Attached at the bottom end of this cable would be a car seating two hundred people. The car and its passengers would be shoved off a platform and fall without restraint to the end of the cable, where the car would snap back upward and continue bouncing until it came to a stop. The engineer urged that as a precaution the ground "be covered with eight feet of feather bedding."

Everyone was thinking in terms of towers, but Burnham, for one, did not think a tower was the best approach. Eiffel had done it first and best. More than merely tall, his tower was grace frozen in iron, as much an evocation of the spirit of the age as Chartres had been in its time. To build a tower would be to follow Eiffel into territory he already had conquered for France.

In August 1891 Eiffel himself telegraphed the directors to ask if he might submit a proposal for a tower. This was a surprise and at first a welcome one. Exposition President Baker immediately cabled Eiffel that the directors would be delighted to see whatever he proposed. If the fair was to have a tower, Baker said in an interview, "M. Eiffel is the man to build it. It would not be so much of an experiment if he should be in charge of its construction. He might be able to improve on his design for the Eiffel Tower in Paris, and I think it fair to assume that he would not construct one in any way inferior to that famous structure." To the engineers of America, however, this embrace of Eiffel was a slap in the face. Over the next week and a half telegrams shot from city to city, engineer to engineer, until the story became somewhat distorted. Suddenly it seemed as if an Eiffel Tower in Chicago was a certainty—that Eiffel himself was to do the out-Eiffeling. The engineers were outraged. A long letter of protest arrived at Burnham's office, signed by some of the nation's leading engineers.

Acceptance of "the distinguished gentleman's offer," they wrote, would be "equivalent to a statement that the great body of civil engineers in this country, whose noble works attest their skill abroad as well as throughout the length and breadth of the land, lack the ability to cope with such a problem, and such action could have a tendency to rob them of their just claim to professional excellence."

Burnham read this letter with approval. It pleased him to see America's civil engineers at last expressing passion for the fair, although in fact the directors had promised nothing to Eiffel. His formal proposal arrived a week later, envisioning a tower that was essentially a taller version of what he had built in Paris. The directors sent his proposal out for translation, reviewed it, then graciously turned it down. If there was to be a tower at the fair, it would be an American tower.

But the drafting boards of America's engineers remained dishearteningly barren.

⌒⎯⎯⌒

Sol Bloom, back in California, took his quest for a concession for his Algerian Village to an influential San Franciscan, Mike De Young, publisher of the *San Francisco Chronicle* and one of the exposition's national commissioners. Bloom told him about the rights he had acquired in Paris and how the exposition had rebuffed his petition.

De Young knew Bloom. As a teenager Bloom had worked in De Young's Alcazar Theater and worked his way up to become its treasurer at age nineteen. In his spare time Bloom had organized the ushers, checkers, and refreshment sellers into a more efficient, cohesive structure that greatly increased the theater's profits and his own salary. Next he organized these functions at other theaters and received regular commissions from each. At the Alcazar he inserted into scripts the names of popular products, bars, and restaurants, including the Cliff House, and for this received another stream of income. He also organized a cadre of professional applauders, known as a "claque," to provide enthusiastic ovations, demand encores, and cry *"Brava!"* for any performer willing to pay. Most performers did pay, even the most famous diva of the time, Adelina Patti.

One day Bloom saw an item in a theatrical publication about a novel Mexican band that he believed Americans would adore, and he convinced the band's manager to let him bring the musicians north for a tour. Bloom's profit was $40,000. At the time he was only eighteen.

De Young told Bloom he would investigate the situation. One week later he summoned Bloom back to his office.

"How soon could you be ready to go to Chicago?" he asked.

Bloom, startled, said, "In a couple of days, I guess." He assumed De Young had arranged a second opportunity for him to petition the fair's Ways and Means Committee. He was hesitant and told De Young he saw no value in making the journey until the exposition's directors had a better idea of the kinds of attractions they wanted.

"The situation has advanced since our talk," De Young said. "All we need now is somebody to take charge." He gave Bloom a cable from the Exposition Company that empowered De Young to hire someone to select the concessions for the Midway Plaisance and guide their construction and promotion. "You've been elected," he said.

"I can't do it," Bloom said. He did not want to leave San Francisco. "Even if I did, I've got too much at stake here to consider it."

De Young watched him. "I don't want to hear another word from you till tomorrow," he said.

In the meantime De Young wanted Bloom to think about how much money he would have to be paid to overcome his reluctance. "When you come back you can name your salary," he said. "I will either accept or reject it. There will be no argument. Is that agreeable?"

Bloom did agree, but only because De Young's request gave him a graceful way of refusing the job. All he had to do, he figured, was name such an outrageous sum that De Young could not possibly accept it, "and as I walked down the street I decided what it would be."

Burnham tried to anticipate every conceivable threat to the fair. Aware of Chicago's reputation for vice and violence, Burnham insisted on the creation of a large police force, the Columbian Guard, and placed it under the command of Colonel Edmund Rice, a man of great valor who had faced Pickett's Charge at Gettysburg. Unlike conventional police departments, the Guard's mandate explicitly emphasized the novel idea of preventing crime rather than merely arresting wrongdoers after the fact.

Disease, too, posed dangers to the fair, Burnham knew. An outbreak of smallpox or cholera or any of the other lethal infections that roamed the city could irreparably taint the exposition and destroy any hopes the directors had of achieving the record attendance necessary to generate a profit.

By now the new science of bacteriology, pioneered by Robert Koch and Louis Pasteur, had convinced most public health officials that contaminated drinking water caused the spread of cholera and other bacterial diseases. Chicago's water teemed with bacteria, thanks mainly to the Chicago River. In a monumental spasm of civic engineering the city in 1871 reversed the river's direction so that it no longer flowed into Lake Michigan, but ran instead into the Des Plaines River and ultimately into the Mississippi, the theory being that the immense flows of both rivers would dilute the sewage to harmless levels—a concept downriver towns like Joliet did not wholeheartedly embrace. To the engineers' surprise, however, prolonged rains routinely caused the Chicago River to regress and again pour dead cats and fecal matter into the lake, and in such volume that tendrils of black water reached all the way to the intake cribs of the city water system.

Most Chicago residents had no choice but to drink the water. Burnham, however, believed from the start that the fair's workers and visitors needed a better, safer supply. In this too he was ahead of the age. On his orders his sanitary engineer, William S. MacHarg, built a water-sterilization plant on the fairgrounds that pumped lake water through a succession of large tanks in which the water was aerated and boiled. MacHarg's men set big casks of this sterilized water throughout the park and replenished them every day.

Burnham planned to close the purification plant by Opening Day and give visitors a choice between two other supplies of safe water: lake water purified with Pasteur filters and offered free of charge, or naturally pure water for a penny a cup, piped one hundred miles from the coveted springs of Waukesha, Wisconsin. In November 1891 Burnham ordered MacHarg to investigate five of Waukesha's springs to gauge their capacity and purity, but to do so "quietly," suggesting he was aware that running a pipeline through the village's comely landscape might prove a sensitive issue. No one, however, could have imagined that in a few months MacHarg's efforts to secure a supply of Waukesha's best would lead to an armed encounter in the middle of a fine Wisconsin night.

What most worried Burnham was fire. The loss of the Grannis Block, with his and Root's headquarters, remained a vivid, humiliating memory. A catastrophic fire in Jackson Park could destroy the fair. Yet within the park fire was central to the construction process. Plasterers used small furnaces called salamanders to speed drying and curing. Tinners and electricians used fire pots for melting, bending, and fusing. Even the fire department used fire: Steam engines powered the pumps on the department's horse-drawn fire trucks.

Burnham established defenses that by prevailing standards seemed elaborate, even excessive. He formed an exposition fire department and ordered the installation of hundreds of fire hydrants and telegraphic alarm boxes. He commissioned the construction of a fire boat, the *Fire Queen,* built specifically to negotiate the park's shallow canals and to pass under its many low bridges. Design specifications required that every building be surrounded by an underwater main and be plumbed with interior standpipes. He also banned all smoking on the grounds, although here he made at least two exceptions: one for a contractor who pleaded that his crew of European artisans would quit if denied their cigars, the other for the big hearth in his own shanty, around which he and his engineers, draftsmen, and visiting architects gathered each night for wine, talk, and cigars.

With the onset of winter Burnham ordered all hydrants packed in horse manure to prevent freezing.

On the coldest days the manure steamed, as if the hydrants themselves were on fire.

━━

When Sol Bloom returned to the office of Mike De Young, he was confident De Young could not possibly accept his salary request, for he had decided to ask for the same salary as the president of the United States: $50,000. "The more I thought about it," Bloom recalled, "the more I enjoyed the prospect of telling Mike De Young that no less a sum could compensate me for my sacrifice in leaving San Francisco."

De Young offered Bloom a seat. His expression was sober and expectant.

Bloom said: "Much as I appreciate the compliment, I find that my interests lie right here in this city. As I look ahead I can see myself—"

De Young cut him off. Softly he said, "Now, Sol, I thought you were going to tell me how much you wanted us to pay you."

"I didn't want you to think I didn't appreciate—"

"You said that a minute ago," De Young said. "Now tell me how much money you want."

This was not going quite the way Bloom had expected. With some trepidation, Bloom told him the number: "A thousand dollars a week."

De Young smiled. "Well, that's pretty good pay for a fellow of twenty-one, but I have no doubt you'll earn it."

━━

In August, Burnham's chief structural engineer, Abraham Gottlieb, made a startling disclosure: He had failed to calculate wind loads for the fair's main buildings. Burnham ordered his key contractors—including Agnew & Co., erecting the Manufactures and Liberal Arts Building—to stop work immediately. For months Burnham had been combating rumors that he had forced his men to work at too fast a pace and that as a result some buildings were unsafe; in Europe, press reports held that certain structures had been "condemned." Now here was Gottlieb, conceding a potentially catastrophic error.

Gottlieb protested that even without an explicit calculation of wind loads, the buildings were strong enough.

"I could not, however, take this view," Burnham wrote in a letter to James Dredge, editor of the influential British magazine *Engineering*. Burnham ordered all designs strengthened to withstand the highest winds recorded over the previous ten years. "This may be going to extremes," he told Dredge, "but to me it seems wise and prudent, in view of the great interests involved."

Gottlieb resigned. Burnham replaced him with Edward Shankland, an engineer from his own firm who possessed a national reputation as a designer of bridges.

On November 24, 1891, Burnham wrote to James Dredge to report that once again he was under fire over the issue of structural integrity. "The criticism now," he wrote, "is that the structures are unnecessarily strong."

Bloom arrived in Chicago and quickly discovered why so little had been accomplished at the Midway Plaisance, known officially as Department M. Until now it had been under the control of Frederick Putnam, a Harvard professor of ethnology. He was a distinguished anthropologist, but putting him in charge of the Midway, Bloom said years later, "was about as intelligent a decision as it would be today to make Albert Einstein manager of the Ringling Brothers and Barnum & Bailey Circus." Putnam would not have disagreed. He told a Harvard colleague he was "anxious to get this whole Indian circus off my hands."

Bloom took his concerns to Exposition President Baker, who turned him over to Burnham.

"You are a very young man, a very young man indeed, to be in charge of the work entrusted to you," Burnham said.

But Burnham himself had been young when John B. Sherman walked into his office and changed his life.

"I want you to know that you have my full confidence," he said. "You are in complete charge of the Midway. Go ahead with the work. You are responsible only to me. I will write orders to that effect. Good luck."

By December 1891 the two buildings farthest along were the Mines Building and the Woman's Building. Construction of the Mines Building had gone smoothly, thanks to a winter that by Chicago standards had been mercifully benign. Construction of the Woman's Building, however, had become an ordeal, both for Burnham and its young architect, Sophia Hayden, mainly because of modifications demanded by Bertha Honore Palmer, head of the fair's Board of Lady Managers, which governed all things at the fair having to do with women. As the wife of Potter Palmer, she was accustomed by wealth and absolute social dominance to having her own way, as she had made clear earlier in the year when she suppressed a revolt led by the board's executive secretary that had caused open warfare between factions of elegantly coiffed and dressed women. In the thick of it one horrified lady manager had written to Mrs. Palmer, "I *do* hope that Congress will not become disgusted with our sex."

Hayden came to Chicago to produce final drawings, then returned home, leaving their execution to Burnham. Construction began July 9; workers began applying the final coat of staff in October. Hayden returned in December to direct the decoration of the building's exterior, believing this to be her responsibility. She discovered that Bertha Palmer had other ideas.

In September, without Hayden's knowledge, Palmer had invited women everywhere to donate architectural ornaments for the building and in response had received a museum's worth of columns, panels, sculpted figures, window grills, doors, and other objects. Palmer believed the building could accommodate all the contributions, especially those sent by prominent women. Hayden, on the other hand, knew that such a hodgepodge of materials would result in an aesthetic abomination. When an influential Wisconsin woman named Flora Ginty sent an elaborately carved wooden door, Hayden turned it down. Ginty was hurt and angry. "When I think of the days I worked and the miles I traveled to achieve these things for the Woman's building, my ire rises a little yet." Mrs. Palmer was in Europe at the time, but her private secretary, Laura Hayes, a gossip of virtuosic scope, made sure her employer learned all the details. Hayes also relayed to Palmer a few words of advice that she herself had given the architect: " 'I think it would be better to have the building look like a patchwork quilt, than to refuse these things which the Lady Managers have been to such pains in soliciting.' "

A patchwork quilt was not what Hayden had in mind. Despite Mrs. Palmer's blinding social glare, Hayden continued to decline donations. A battle followed, fought in true Gilded Age fashion with oblique snubs and poisonous courtesy. Mrs. Palmer pecked and pestered and catapulted icy smiles into Hayden's deepening gloom. Finally Palmer assigned the decoration of the Woman's Building to someone else, a designer named Candace Wheeler.

Hayden fought the arrangement in her quiet, stubborn way until she could take it no longer. She walked into Burnham's office, began to tell him her story, and promptly, literally, went mad: tears, heaving sobs, cries of anguish, all of it. "A severe breakdown," an acquaintance called it, "with a violent attack of high nervous excitement of the brain."

Burnham, stunned, summoned one of the exposition surgeons. Hayden was discreetly driven from the park in one of the fair's innovative English ambulances with quiet rubber tires and placed in a sanitarium for a period of enforced rest. She lapsed into "melancholia," a sweet name for depression.

⌐───────◦

At Jackson Park aggravation was endemic. Simple matters, Burnham found, often became imbroglios. Even Olmsted had become an irritant. He was brilliant and charming, but once fixed on a thing, he was as unyielding as a slab of Joliet limestone. By the end of 1891 the question of what kind of boats to allow on the fair's waterways had come to obsess him, as if boats alone would determine the success of his quest for "poetic mystery."

In December 1891 Burnham received a proposal from a tugboat manufacturer arguing the case for steam launches at the exposition. Olmsted got wind of it from Harry Codman, who in addition to being his chief operating man in Chicago served as a kind of spy, keeping Olmsted abreast of all threats to Olmsted's vision. Codman sent Olmsted a copy of the letter, adding his own note that the tugboat maker seemed to enjoy Burnham's confidence.

On December 23 Olmsted wrote to Burnham: "I suspect that even Codman is inclined to think that I make too much of a hobby of this boat question and give an amount of worry, if not thought, to it that would be better expended on other and more critical matters, and I fear that you may think me a crank upon it."

He proceeded, however, to vent his obsession yet again. The tug-maker's letter, he complained, framed the boat question solely in terms of moving the greatest number of passengers between different points at the exposition as cheaply and quickly as possible. "You perfectly well know that the main object to be accomplished was nothing of this sort. I need not try to make a statement of what it was. You are as alive to it as I am. You know that it was a poetic object, and you know that if boats are to be introduced on these waters, it would be perfect nonsense to have them of a kind that would antagonize this poetic object."

Mere transportation was never the goal, he fumed. The whole point of having boats was to enhance the landscape. "Put in the waters unbe-coming boats and the effect would be utterly disgusting, destroying the value of what would otherwise be the most valuable original feature of this Exposition. I say destroy deliberately. A thousand times better [to] have no boats."

⌐━━━⌐

Despite increasing committee interference and intensified conflict between Burnham and Director-General Davis, and with the threat of labor strikes ever present, the main buildings rose. Workers laid founda-tions of immense timbers in crisscrossed layers in accord with Root's *gril-lage* principle, then used steam-powered derricks to raise the tall posts of iron and steel that formed each building's frame. They cocooned the frames in scaffolds of wood and faced each frame with hundreds of thou-sands of wooden planks to create walls capable of accepting two thick layers of staff. As workers piled mountains of fresh lumber beside each building, jagged foothills of sawdust and scrap rose nearby. The air smelled of cut wood and Christmas.

In December the exposition experienced its first death: a man named Mueller at the Mines Building, dead of a fractured skull. Three other deaths followed in short order:

Jansen, fractured skull, Electricity Building;

Allard, fractured skull, Electricity Building;

Algeer, stunned to oblivion by a new phenomenon, electric shock, at the Mines Building.

Dozens of lesser accidents occurred as well. Publicly Burnham struck a pose of confidence and optimism. In a December 28, 1891, letter to the editor of the *Chicago Herald,* he wrote, "A few questions of design and plan are still undetermined, but there is nothing which is not well in hand, and I see no reason why we will not be able to complete our work in time for the ceremonies in October, 1892"—Dedication Day—"and for the opening of the Exposition, May 1st, 1893."

In reality, the fair was far behind schedule, with worse delay forestalled only by the winter's mildness. The October dedication was to take place inside the Manufactures and Liberal Arts Building, yet as of January only the foundation of the building had been laid. For the fair to be even barely presentable in time for the ceremony, everything would have to go perfectly. The weather especially would have to cooperate.

Meanwhile, banks and companies were failing across America, strikes threatened everywhere, and cholera had begun a slow white trek across Europe, raising fears that the first plague ships would soon arrive in New York Harbor.

As if anyone needed extra pressure, the *New York Times* warned: "the failure of the fair or anything short of a positive and pronounced success would be a discredit to the whole country, and not to Chicago alone."

Remains of the Day

In November 1891 Julia Conner announced to Holmes she was pregnant; now, she told him, he had no choice but to marry her. Holmes reacted to her news with calm and warmth. He held her, stroked her hair, and with moist eyes assured her that she had nothing to worry about, certainly he would marry her, as he long had promised. There was, however, a condition that he now felt obligated to impose. A child was out of the question. He would marry her only if she agreed to allow him to execute a simple abortion. He was a physician, he had done it before. He would use chloroform, and she would feel nothing and awaken to the prospect of a new life as Mrs. H. H. Holmes. Children would come later. Right now there was far too much to do, especially given all the work that lay ahead to complete the hotel and furnish each of its rooms in time for the world's fair.

Holmes knew he possessed great power over Julia. First there was the power that accrued to him naturally through his ability to bewitch men and women alike with false candor and warmth; second, the power of social approbation that he now focused upon her. Though sexual liaisons were common, society tolerated them only as long as their details remained secret. Packinghouse princes ran off with parlormaids and bank presidents seduced typewriters; when necessary, their attorneys arranged quiet solo voyages to Europe to the surgical suites of discreet but capable doctors. A public pregnancy without marriage meant disgrace and destitution. Holmes possessed Julia now as fully as if she were an antebellum slave, and he reveled in his possession. The operation, he told Julia, would take place on Christmas Eve.

Snow fell. Carolers moved among the mansions on Prairie Avenue, pausing now and then to enter the fine houses for hot mulled cider and cocoa. The air was scented with woodsmoke and roasting duck. In Graceland Cemetery, to the north, young couples raced their sleighs over the snow-heaped undulations, pulling their blankets especially tight as they passed the tall, gloomy guardian at the tomb of Dexter Graves, *Eternal Silence,* a hooded figure that from a distance seems to have only darkness where the face should have been. To look into this emptiness, legend held, was to receive a glimpse into the underworld.

At 701 Sixty-third Street in Englewood Julia Conner put her daughter to bed and did her best to smile and indulge the child's delighted anticipation of Christmas. Yes, Saint Nicholas would come, and he would bring wonderful things. Holmes had promised a bounty of toys and sweets for Pearl, and for Julia something truly grand, beyond anything she could have received from her poor bland Ned.

Outside the snow muffled the concussion of passing horses. Trains bearing fangs of ice tore through the crossing at Wallace.

Julia walked down the hall to an apartment occupied by Mr. and Mrs. John Crowe. Julia and Mrs. Crowe had become friends, and now Julia helped Mrs. Crowe decorate a Christmas tree in the Crowes' apartment, meant for Pearl as a Christmas-morning surprise. Julia talked of all that she and Pearl would do the next day, and told Mrs. Crowe that soon she would be going to Davenport, Iowa, to attend the wedding of an older sister, "an old maid," Mrs. Crowe said, who to everyone's surprise was about to marry a railroad man. Julia was awaiting the rail pass that the groom was supposed to have put in the mail.

Julia left the apartment late that night, in good spirits, Mrs. Crowe later recalled: "there was nothing about her conversation that would lead any of us to think she intended going away that night."

Holmes offered Julia a cheerful "Merry Christmas" and gave her a hug, then took her hand and led her to a room on the second floor that he had readied for the operation. A table lay draped in white linen. His surgical kits stood open and gleaming, his instruments laid out in a sunflower of polished steel. Fearful things: bonesaws, abdomen retractor, trocar and trepan. More instruments, certainly, than he really needed and all positioned so that Julia could not help but see them and be sickened by their hard, eager gleam.

He wore a white apron and had rolled back his cuffs. Possibly he wore his hat, a bowler. He had not washed his hands, nor did he wear a mask. There was no need.

She reached for his hand. There would be no pain, he assured her. She would awaken as healthy as she was now but without the encumbrance she bore within. He pulled the stopper from a dark amber bottle of liquid and immediately felt its silvery exhalation in his own nostrils. He poured the chloroform into a bunched cloth. She gripped his hand more tightly, which he found singularly arousing. He held the cloth over her nose and mouth. Her eyes fluttered and rolled upward. Then came the inevitable, reflexive disturbance of muscles, like a dream of running. She released his hand and cast it away with splayed fingers. Her feet trembled as if tapping to a wildly beating drum. His own excitement rose. She tried to pull his hand away, but he was prepared for this sudden surge of muscle stimulation that always preceded stupor, and with great force clamped the cloth to her face. She beat at his arms. Slowly the energy left her, and her hands began to move in slow arcs, soothing and sensuous, the wild drums silent. Ballet now, a pastoral exit.

He kept one hand on the cloth and with the other dribbled more of the liquid between his fingers into its folds, delighting in the sensation of frost where the chloroform coated his fingers. One of her wrists sagged to the table, followed shortly by the other. Her eyelids stuttered, then closed. Holmes did not think her so clever as to feign coma, but he held tight just the same. After a few moments he reached for her wrist and felt her pulse fade to nothing, like the rumble of a receding train.

He removed the apron and rolled down his sleeves. The chloroform and his own intense arousal made him feel light-headed. The sensation, as always, was pleasant and induced in him a warm languor, like the feeling he got after sitting too long in front of a hot stove. He stoppered the chloroform, found a fresh cloth, and walked down the hall to Pearl's room.

It took only a moment to bunch the fresh cloth and douse it with chloroform. In the hall, afterward, he examined his watch and saw that it was Christmas.

———

The day meant nothing to Holmes. The Christmas mornings of his youth had been suffocated under an excess of piety, prayer, and silence, as if a giant wool blanket had settled over the house.

———

On Christmas morning the Crowes waited for Julia and Pearl in glad anticipation of watching the girl's eyes ignite upon spotting the lovely tree and the presents arrayed under its boughs. The apartment was warm, the air rouged with cinnamon and fir. An hour passed. The Crowes waited as long as they could, but at ten o'clock they set out to catch a train for central Chicago, where they planned to visit friends. They left the apartment unlocked, with a cheerful note of welcome.

The Crowes returned at eleven o'clock that night and found everything as they had left it, with no evidence that Julia and her daughter had come. The next morning they tried Julia's apartment, but no one answered. They asked neighbors inside and outside the building if any had seen Julia or Pearl, but none had.

When Holmes next appeared, Mrs. Crowe asked him where Julia might be. He explained that she and Pearl had gone to Davenport earlier than expected.

Mrs. Crowe heard nothing more from Julia. She and her neighbors thought the whole thing very odd. They all agreed that the last time anyone had seen Julia or Pearl was Christmas Eve.

This was not precisely accurate. Others did see Julia again, although by then no one, not even her own family back in Davenport, Iowa, could have been expected to recognize her.

Just after Christmas Holmes asked one of his associates, Charles Chappell, to come to his building. Holmes had learned that Chappell was an "articulator," meaning he had mastered the art of stripping the flesh from human bodies and reassembling, or articulating, the bones to form complete skeletons for display in doctors' offices and laboratories. He had acquired the necessary techniques while articulating cadavers for medical students at Cook County Hospital.

During his own medical education Holmes had seen firsthand how desperate schools were to acquire corpses, whether freshly dead or skeletonized. The serious, systematic study of medicine was intensifying, and to scientists the human body was like the polar icecap, something to be studied and explored. Skeletons hung in doctors' offices where they served as visual encyclopedias. With demand outpacing supply, doctors established a custom of graciously and discreetly accepting any offered cadaver. They frowned on murder as a means of harvest; on the other hand, they made little effort to explore the provenance of any one body. Grave-robbing became an industry, albeit a small one requiring an exceptional degree of sang-froid. In periods of acute shortage doctors themselves helped mine the newly departed.

It was obvious to Holmes that even now, in the 1890s, demand remained high. Chicago's newspapers reported ghoulish tales of doctors raiding graveyards. After a foiled raid on a graveyard in New Albany, Indiana, on February 24, 1890, Dr. W. H. Wathen, head of the Kentucky Medical College, told a *Tribune* reporter, "The gentlemen were acting not for the Kentucky School of Medicine nor for themselves individually, but for the medical schools of Louisville to which the human subject is as necessary as breath to life." Just three weeks later the physicians of Louisville were at it again. They attempted to rob a grave at the State Asylum for the Insane in Anchorage, Kentucky, this time on behalf of the University of Louisville. "Yes, the party was sent out by us," a senior school official said. "We must have bodies, and if the State won't give them to us we must steal them. The winter classes were large and used up so many subjects that there are none for the spring classes." He saw no need to apologize. "The Asylum Cemetery has been robbed for years," he said, "and I doubt if there is a corpse in it. I tell you we must have bodies. You cannot make doctors without them, and the public must understand it. If we can't get them any other way we will arm the students with Winchester rifles and send them to protect the body-snatchers on their raids."

Holmes had an eye for opportunity, and with demand for corpses so robust, opportunity now beckoned.

He showed Charles Chappell into a second-floor room that contained a table, medical instruments, and bottles of solvents. These did not trouble Chappell, nor did the corpse on the table, for Chappell knew that Holmes was a physician. The body was clearly that of a woman, although of unusual height. He saw nothing to indicate her identity. "The body," he said, "looked like that of a jack rabbit which had been skinned by splitting the skin down the face and rolling it back off the entire body. In some places considerable of the flesh had been taken off with it."

Holmes explained that he had been doing some dissection but now had completed his research. He offered Chappell thirty-six dollars to cleanse the bones and skull and return to him a fully articulated skeleton. Chappell agreed. Holmes and Chappell placed the body in a trunk lined with duckcloth. An express company delivered it to Chappell's house.

Soon afterward Chappell returned with the skeleton. Holmes thanked him, paid him, and promptly sold the skeleton to Hahneman Medical College—the Chicago school, not the Philadelphia school of the same name—for many times the amount he had paid Chappell.

⌒

In the second week of January 1892 new tenants, the Doyle family, moved into Julia's quarters in Holmes's building. They found dishes on the table and Pearl's clothes hung over a chair. The place looked and felt as if the former occupants planned to return within minutes.

The Doyles asked Holmes what had happened.

With his voice striking the perfect sober note, Holmes apologized for the disarray and explained that Julia's sister had fallen gravely ill and Julia and her daughter had left at once for the train station. There was no need to pack up their belongings, as Julia and Pearl were well provided for and would not be coming back.

Later Holmes offered a different story about Julia: "I last saw her about January 1, 1892, when a settlement of her rent was made. At this time she had announced not only to me, but to her neighbors and friends, that she was going away." Although she had told everyone her destination was Iowa, in fact, Holmes said, "she was going elsewhere to avoid the chance of her daughter being taken from her, giving the Iowa destination to mislead her husband." Holmes denied that he and Julia had ever engaged each other physically, or that she had undergone "a criminal operation," a then-current euphemism for abortion. "That she is a woman of quick temper and perhaps not always of a good disposition may be true, but that any of her friends and relatives will believe her to be an amoral woman, or one who would be a party to a criminal act I do not think."

A Gauntlet Dropped

EIGHTEEN NINETY-TWO BROKE COLD, with six inches of snow on the ground and temperatures falling to ten degrees below zero, certainly not the coldest weather Chicago had ever experienced but cold enough to clot the valves of all three of the city water system's intake valves and temporarily halt the flow of Chicago's drinking water. Despite the weather, work at Jackson Park progressed. Workers erected a heated movable shelter that allowed them to apply staff to the exterior of the Mines Building no matter what the temperature. The Woman's Building was nearly finished, all its scaffolding gone; the giant Manufactures and Liberal Arts Building had begun rising above its foundation. In all, the workforce in the park numbered four thousand. The ranks included a carpenter and furniture-maker named Elias Disney, who in coming years would tell many stories about the construction of this magical realm beside the lake. His son Walt would take note.

Beyond the exposition's eight-foot fence and its two tiers of barbed wire, there was tumult. Wage reductions and layoffs stoked unrest among workers nationwide. Unions gained strength; the Pinkerton National Detective Agency gained revenue. A rising union man named Samuel Gompers stopped by Burnham's office to discuss allegations that the exposition discriminated against union workers. Burnham ordered his construction superintendent, Dion Geraldine, to investigate. As labor strife increased and the economy faltered, the general level of violence rose. In taking stock of 1891, the *Chicago Tribune* reported that 5,906 people had been murdered in America, nearly 40 percent more than in 1890. The increase included Mr. and Mrs. Borden of Fall River, Massachusetts.

The constant threat of strike and the onset of deep cold shaded the new year for Burnham, but what most concerned him was the fast-shrinking treasury of the Exposition Company. In advancing the work so quickly and on such a grand scale, Burnham's department had consumed far more money than anyone had anticipated. There was talk now among the directors of seeking a $10 million appropriation from Congress, but the only immediate solution was to reduce expenditures. On January 6 Burnham commanded his department chiefs to take immediate, in some cases draconian, measures to cut costs. He ordered his chief draftsman, in charge of exposition work under way in the attic of the Rookery, to fire at once any man who did "inaccurate or 'slouchy' work" or who failed to do more than his full duty. He wrote to Olmsted's landscape superintendent, Rudolf Ulrich, "it seems to me you can now cut your force down one-half, and at the same time let very many expensive men go." Henceforth, Burnham ordered, all carpentry work was to be done only by men employed by the fair's contractors. To Dion Geraldine, he wrote, "You will please dismiss every carpenter on your force. . . ."

Until this point Burnham had shown a level of compassion for his workers that was extraordinary for the time. He had paid them even when illness or injury kept them out of work and established an exposition hospital that provided free medical care. He built quarters within the park where they received three large meals a day and slept in clean beds and well-heated rooms. A Princeton professor of political economy named Walter Wyckoff disguised himself as an unskilled laborer and spent a year traveling and working among the nation's growing army of unemployed men, including a stint at Jackson Park. "Guarded by sentries and high barriers from unsought contact with all beyond, great gangs of us, healthy, robust men, live and labor in a marvelous artificial world," he wrote. "No sight of misery disturbs us, nor of despairing poverty out in vain search for employment. . . . We work our eight hours a day in peaceful security and in absolute confidence of our pay."

But now even the fair was laying off men, and the timing was awful. With the advent of winter the traditional building season had come to an end. Competition for the few jobs available had intensified as thousands of unemployed men from around the country—unhappily bearing the label "hobo," derived possibly from the railroad cry "ho, boy"— converged on Chicago in hopes of getting exposition work. The dismissed men, Burnham knew, faced homelessness and poverty; their families confronted the real prospect of starvation.

But the fair came first.

⌒⌒⌒⌒

The absence of an Eiffel challenger continued to frustrate Burnham. Proposals got more and more bizarre. One visionary put forth a tower five hundred feet taller than the Eiffel Tower but made entirely of logs, with a cabin at the top for shelter and refreshment. The cabin was to be a log cabin.

If an engineer capable of besting Eiffel did not step forward soon, Burnham knew, there simply would not be enough time left to build anything worthy of the fair. Somehow he needed to rouse the engineers of America. The opportunity came with an invitation to give a talk to the Saturday Afternoon Club, a group of engineers who had begun meeting on Saturdays at a downtown restaurant to discuss the construction challenges of the fair.

There was the usual meal in multiple courses, with wine, cigars, coffee, and cognac. At one table sat a thirty-three-year-old engineer from Pittsburgh who ran a steel-inspection company that had branch offices in New York and Chicago and that already possessed the exposition contract to inspect the steel used in the fair's buildings. He had an angular face, black hair, a black mustache, and dark eyes, the kind of looks soon to be coveted by an industry that Thomas Edison was just then bringing to life. He "was eminently engaging and social and he had a keen sense of humor," his partners wrote. "In all gatherings he at once became the center of attraction, having a ready command of language and a constant fund of amusing anecdotes and experiences."

Like the other members of the Saturday Afternoon Club, he expected to hear Burnham discuss the challenges of building an entire city on such a short schedule, but Burnham surprised him. After asserting that "the architects of America had covered themselves with glory" through their exposition designs, Burnham rebuked the nation's civil engineers for failing to rise to the same level of brilliance. The engineers, Burnham charged, "had contributed little or nothing either in the way of originating novel features or of showing the possibilities of modern engineering practice in America."

A tremor of displeasure rolled through the room.

"Some distinctive feature is needed," Burnham continued, "something to take the relative position in the World's Columbian Exposition that was filled by the Eiffel Tower at the Paris Exposition."

But not a tower, he said. Towers were not original. Eiffel had built a tower already. "Mere bigness" wasn't enough either. "Something novel, original, daring and unique must be designed and built if American engineers are to retain their prestige and standing."

Some of the engineers took offense; others acknowledged that Burnham had a point. The engineer from Pittsburgh felt himself "cut to the quick by the truth of these remarks."

As he sat there among his peers, an idea came to him "like an inspiration." It arrived not as some half-formed impulse, he said, but rich in detail. He could see it and touch it, hear it as it moved through the sky.

There was not much time left, but if he acted quickly to produce drawings and managed to convince the fair's Ways and Means Committee of the idea's feasibility, he believed the exposition could indeed out-Eiffel Eiffel. And if what happened to Eiffel happened to him, his fortune would be assured.

It must have been refreshing for Burnham to stand before the Saturday Afternoon Club and openly chide its members for their failure, because most of his other encounters over exposition business invariably became exercises in self-restraint, especially when he went before the fair's many and still-multiplying committees. This constant Victorian minuet of false grace consumed time. He needed more power—not for his own ego but for the sake of the exposition. Unless the pace of decision-making accelerated, he knew, the fair would fall irreparably behind schedule, yet if anything the barriers to efficiency were increasing in size and number. The Exposition Company's shrinking war chest had driven its relationship with the National Commission to a new low, with Director-General Davis arguing that any new federal money should be controlled by his commission. The commission seemed to form new departments every day, each with a paid chief—Davis named a superintendent of sheep, for a salary that today would total about $60,000 a year—and each claiming some piece of jurisdiction that Burnham thought belonged to him.

Soon the struggle for control distilled to a personal conflict between Burnham and Davis, its primary battlefield a disagreement over who should control the artistic design of exhibits and interiors. Burnham thought it obvious that the territory belonged to him. Davis believed otherwise.

At first Burnham tried the oblique approach. "We are now organizing a special interior decorative and architectural force to handle this part," he wrote to Davis, "and I have the honor to offer the services of my department to yours in such matters. I feel a delicacy in having my men suggest to yours artistic arrangements, forms and decorations of exhibits, without your full approval, which I hereby respectfully ask."

But Davis told a reporter, "I think it is pretty well understood by this time that no one but the Director-General and his agents have anything to do with exhibits."

The conflict simmered. On March 14 Burnham joined Davis for dinner with Japan's delegate to the fair, at the Chicago Club. Afterward Davis and Burnham remained at the club arguing quietly until five o'clock the next morning. "The time was well spent," he wrote to Margaret, who was then out of town, "and we have come to a better feeling so that the path will be much smoother from this time forward."

An uncharacteristic weariness crept into his letter. He told Margaret he planned to end work early that night and go to Evanston, "and sleep in your dear bed, my love, and I shall dream of you. What a rush this life is! Where do the years go to?"

There were moments of grace. Burnham looked forward to evenings on the grounds when his lieutenants and visiting architects would gather for dinner at the shanty and converse into the night in front of Burnham's immense fireplace. Burnham treasured the camaraderie and the stories. Olmsted recounted the endless trials of protecting Central Park from ill-thought modifications. Colonel Edmund Rice, chief of the exposition's Columbian Guard, described what it was like to stand in a shaded wood at Gettysburg as Pickett launched his men across the intervening field.

Late in March 1892 Burnham invited his sons to join him at the shanty for one of their periodic overnight stays. They failed to arrive at the scheduled time. At first everyone attributed their absence to a routine railroad delay, but as the hours passed, Burnham's anxiety grew. He knew as well as anyone that train wrecks in Chicago were nearly a daily occurrence.

Darkness began to fall, but at last the boys arrived. Their train had been held up by a broken bridge on the Milwaukee & St. Paul line. They reached the shanty, Burnham wrote to Margaret, "just in time to hear Col. Rice tell some yarns about the war and life in the plains among the scouts and Indians."

As Burnham wrote this letter, his sons were near at hand. "They are very happy to be here and are now looking at the large photographic album with Mr. Geraldine." The album was a collection of construction photographs taken by Charles Dudley Arnold, a photographer from Buffalo, New York, whom Burnham had hired as the fair's official photographer. Arnold also was present, and soon the children were to join him in a sketching session.

Burnham closed, "We are all well and satisfied with the amount and variety of work our good fortune has given us to do."

Such peaceful intervals never lasted long.

The conflict between Burnham and Davis again flared to life. The directors of the Exposition Company did decide to seek a direct appropriation from Congress, but their request triggered a congressional investigation of the fair's expenditures. Burnham and President Baker expected a general review but instead found themselves grilled about the most mundane expenses. For example, when Baker listed the total spent on carriage rental, the subcommittee demanded the names of the people who rode in the carriages. At one session in Chicago the committee asked Davis to estimate the final cost of the exposition. Without consulting Burnham, Davis gave an estimate ten percent below the amount Burnham had calculated for President Baker, which Baker had then included in his own statement to investigators. Davis's testimony carried with it the unstated accusation that Burnham and Baker had inflated the amount of money needed to complete the fair.

Burnham leaped to his feet. The subcommittee chairman ordered him to sit. Burnham remained standing. He was angry, barely able to keep himself composed. "Mr. Davis has not been to see me or any of my people," he said, "and any figures he has given he has jumped at. He knows nothing about the matter."

His outburst offended the subcommittee chairman. "I object to any such remarks addressed to a witness before this committee," the chairman said, "and I will ask that Mr. Burnham withdraw his remark."

At first Burnham refused. Then, reluctantly, he agreed to withdraw the part about Davis knowing nothing. But only that part. He did not apologize.

The committee left for Washington to study the evidence and report on whether an appropriation was warranted. The congressmen, Burnham wrote, "are dazed with the size and scope of this enterprise. We gave them each a huge pile of data to digest, and I think their report will be funny, because I know that months would not be enough time for me to work out a report, even with my knowledge."

On paper at least, the fair's Midway Plaisance began to take shape. Professor Putnam had believed the Midway ought first and foremost to provide an education about alien cultures. Sol Bloom felt no such duty.

The Midway was to be fun, a great pleasure garden stretching for more than a mile from Jackson Park all the way to the border of Washington Park. It would thrill, titillate, and if all went well perhaps even shock. He considered his great strength to be "spectacular advertising." He placed notices in publications around the world to make it known that the Midway was to be an exotic realm of unusual sights, sounds, and scents. There would be authentic villages from far-off lands inhabited by authentic villagers—even Pygmies, if Lieutenant Schufeldt succeeded. Bloom recognized also that as czar of the Midway he no longer had to worry about seeking a concession for his Algerian Village. He could approve the village himself. He produced a contract and sent it off to Paris.

Bloom's knack for promotion caught the attention of other fair officials, who came to him for help in raising the exposition's overall profile. At one point he was called upon to help make reporters understand how truly immense the Manufactures and Liberal Arts Building would be. So far the exposition's publicity office had given the press a detailed list of monumental but dreary statistics. "I could tell they weren't in the least interested in the number of acres or tons of steel," Bloom wrote, "so I said, 'Look at it this way—it's going to be big enough to hold the entire standing army of Russia.' "

Bloom had no idea whether Russia even had a standing army, let alone how many soldiers it might include and how many square feet they would cover. Nonetheless, the fact became gospel throughout America. Readers of Rand, McNally's exposition guidebooks eventually found themselves thrilling to the vision of millions of fur-hatted men squeezed onto the building's thirty-two-acre floor.

Bloom felt no remorse.

The Angel from Dwight

IN THE SPRING OF 1892 Holmes's assistant Benjamin Pitezel found himself in the city of Dwight, Illinois, about seventy-five miles southwest of Chicago, taking the famous Keeley cure for alcoholism. Patients stayed in the three-story Livingston Hotel, a red-brick building of simple appealing design, with arched windows and a veranda along the full length of its façade, a fine place to rest between injections of Dr. Leslie Enraught Keeley's "gold cure." Gold was the most famous ingredient in a red, white, and blue solution nicknamed the "barber pole" that employees of the Keeley Institute injected into patients' arms three times a day. The needle, one of large nineteenth-century bore—like having a garden hose shoved into a bicep—invariably deposited a yellow aureole on the skin surrounding the injection site, a badge for some, an unsightly blemish for others. The rest of the formula was kept secret, but as best doctors and chemists could tell, the solution included substances that imparted a pleasant state of euphoria and sedation trimmed with amnesia—an effect the Chicago post office found problematic, for each year it wound up holding hundreds of letters sent from Dwight that lacked important elements of their destination addresses. The senders simply forgot that things like names and street numbers were necessary for the successful delivery of mail.

Pitezel had long been a heavy drinker, but his drinking must have become debilitating, for it was Holmes who sent him to Keeley and paid for his treatment. He explained it to Pitezel as a gesture born of kindness, a return for Pitezel's loyalty. As always, he had other motives. He recognized that Pitezel's drinking impaired his usefulness and threatened to disrupt schemes already in play. Holmes later said of Pitezel, "he was too valuable a man, even with his failings taken into consideration, for me to dispense with." It's likely Holmes also wanted Pitezel to gather whatever intelligence he could about the cure and its labeling, so that he could mimic the product and sell it through his own mail-order drug company. Later, indeed, Holmes would establish his own curative spa on the second floor of his Englewood building and call it the Silver Ash Institute. The Keeley cure was amazingly popular. Thousands of people came to Dwight to shed their intemperate ways; many thousands more bought Dr. Keeley's oral version of the cure, which he marketed in bottles so distinctive that he urged purchasers to destroy the empties, to keep unscrupulous companies from filling them with their own concoctions.

Every day Pitezel joined three dozen other men in the daily ritual of "passing through the line" to receive his injections. Women received theirs in their own rooms and were kept separated from the men to protect their reputations. In Chicago hostesses always knew when guests had taken the cure, because upon being offered a drink, those guests invariably answered, "No, thank you. I've been to Dwight."

Pitezel returned to Englewood in April. The psychotropic powers of Keeley's injections may account for the story Pitezel now told Holmes, of how at Keeley he had met a young woman of great beauty—to hear him tell it, preternatural beauty—named Emeline Cigrand. She was blond, twenty-four years old, and since 1891 had worked as a stenographer in Dr. Keeley's office. Pitezel's almost hallucinatory description must have tantalized Holmes, for he wrote to Cigrand and offered her a job as his personal secretary, at twice the salary she was making in Keeley. "A flattering offer," as a member of the Cigrand family later described it.

Emeline accepted without hesitation. The institute had a certain cachet, but the village of Dwight was no Chicago. To be able to earn twice her salary and live in that city of legendary glamour and excitement, with the world's fair set to open in a year, made the offer irresistible. She left Keeley in May, bringing along her $800 in savings. Upon arriving in Englewood, she rented rooms in a boardinghouse near Holmes's building.

Pitezel had exaggerated Emeline's beauty, Holmes saw, but not by much. She was indeed lovely, with luminous blond hair. Immediately Holmes deployed his tools of seduction, his soothing voice and touch and frank blue gaze.

He bought her flowers and took her to the Timmerman Opera House down the block. He gave her a bicycle. They spent evenings riding together on the smooth macadam of Yale and Harvard streets, the picture of a happy young couple blessed with looks and money. ("White pique hats with black watered-ribbon bands and a couple of knife feathers set at the side are the latest novelty for women cyclists," the *Tribune*'s society column observed.) As Emeline became more accustomed to her "wheel," a term everyone still used even though the old and deadly huge-wheeled bicycles of the past had become thoroughly obsolete, she and Holmes took longer and longer rides and often rode along the willowed Midway to Jackson Park to watch the construction of the world's fair, where inevitably they found themselves among thousands of other people, many of them also bicyclists.

On a few Sundays Emeline and Holmes rode into the park itself, where they saw that construction was still in its early phase—a surprise, given the rapid onset of the fair's two most important deadlines, Dedication Day and Opening Day. Much of the park was still barren land, and the biggest building, Manufactures and Liberal Arts, was barely under way. A few buildings had advanced at a far greater pace and appeared to be more or less complete, in particular the Mines Building and the Woman's Building. There were so many distinguished-looking men in the park these days—statesmen, princes, architects, and the city's industrial barons. Society matrons came as well, to attend meetings of the Board of Lady Managers. Mrs. Palmer's great black carriage often came roaring through the fair's gate, as did the carriage of her social opposite, Carrie Watson, the madam, her coach distinctive for its gleaming white enamel body and yellow wheels and its black driver in scarlet silk.

Emeline found that riding her bicycle was best in the days after a good downpour. Otherwise the dust billowed like sand over Khartoum and sifted deep into her scalp, where even a good brushing failed to dislodge it.

One afternoon as Emeline sat before her typewriter in Holmes's office, a man entered looking for Holmes. He was tall, with a clean jaw and modest mustache, and wore a cheap suit; in his thirties; good looking, in a way, but at the same time self-effacing and plain—though at the moment he appeared to be angry. He introduced himself as Ned Conner and said he had once run the jewelry counter in the pharmacy downstairs. He had come to discuss a problem with a mortgage.

She knew the name—had heard it somewhere, or seen it in Holmes's papers. She smiled and told Ned that Holmes was out of the building. She had no idea when he would return. Could she help?

Ned's anger cooled. He and Emeline "got to talking about Holmes," as Ned later recalled.

Ned watched her. She was young and pretty—a "handsome blonde," as he later described her. She wore a white shirtwaist and black skirt that accentuated her trim figure, and she was seated beside a window, her hair candescent with sunlight. She sat before a black Remington, new and doubtless never paid for. From his own hard experience and from the look of adoration that entered Emeline's eyes when she spoke of Holmes, Ned guessed her relationship involved a good deal more than type-writing. Later he recalled, "I told her I thought he was a bad lot and that she had better have little to do with him and get away from him as soon as possible."

For the time being, at least, she ignored his advice.

On May 1, 1892, a doctor named M. B. Lawrence and his wife moved into a five-room apartment in Holmes's building, where they often encountered Emeline, although Emeline herself did not yet live in the building. She still occupied rooms in a nearby boardinghouse.

"She was one of the prettiest and most pleasant young women I ever met," said Dr. Lawrence, "and my wife and I learned to think a great deal of her. We saw her every day and she often came in for a few minutes' chat with Mrs. Lawrence." The Lawrences often saw Emeline in Holmes's company. "It was not long," Dr. Lawrence said, "before I became aware that the relations between Miss Cigrand and Mr. Holmes were not strictly those of an employer and employee, but we felt that she was to be more pitied than blamed."

Emeline was infatuated with Holmes. She loved him for his warmth, his caresses, his imperturbable calm, and his glamour. Never had she met a man quite like him. He was even the son of an English lord, a fact he had confided in strictest secrecy. She was to tell no one, which dampened the fun quite a bit but added to the mystery. She did reveal the secret to friends, of course, but only after first securing their oaths that they absolutely would tell no one else. To Emeline, Holmes's claim of lordly heritage had credibility. The name Holmes clearly was English—to know that, all one had to do was read the immensely popular stories of Sir Arthur Conan Doyle. And an English heritage would explain his extraordinary charm and smooth manner, so unusual in brutish, clangorous Chicago.

Emeline was a warm and outgoing woman. She wrote often to her family in Lafayette, Indiana, and to the friends she had made in Dwight. She acquired friends easily. She still dined at regular intervals with the woman who ran the first boardinghouse in which she had stayed after her arrival in Chicago and considered the woman an intimate friend.

In October two of her second cousins, Dr. and Mrs. B. J. Cigrand, paid her a visit. Dr. Cigrand, a dentist with an office at North and Milwaukee Avenues on Chicago's North Side, had contacted Emeline because he was working on a history of the Cigrand family. They had not previously met. "I was charmed by her pleasing manners and keen wit," Dr. Cigrand said. "She was a splendid woman physically, being tall, well formed, and with a wealth of flaxen hair." Dr. Cigrand and his wife did not encounter Holmes on this visit and in fact never did meet him face to face, but they heard glowing stories from Emeline about his charm, generosity, and business prowess. Emeline took her cousins on a tour of Holmes's building and told them of his effort to transform it into a hotel for exposition guests. She explained, too, how the elevated railroad being erected over Sixty-third Street would carry guests directly to Jackson Park. No one doubted that by the summer of 1893 armies of visitors would be advancing on Englewood. To Emeline, success seemed inevitable.

Emeline's enthusiasm was part of her charm. She was headlong in love with her young physician and thus in love with all that he did. But Dr. Cigrand did not share her glowing assessment of the building and its prospects. To him, the building was gloomy and imposing, out of spirit with its surrounding structures. Every other building of substance in Englewood seemed to be charged with the energy of anticipation, not just of the world's fair but of a grand future expanding far beyond the fair's end. Within just a couple of blocks of Sixty-third rose huge, elaborate houses of many colors and textures, and down the street stood the Timmerman Opera House and the adjacent New Julien Hotel, whose owners had spent heavily on fine materials and expert craftsmen. In contrast, Holmes's building was dead space, like the corner of a room where the gaslight could not reach. Clearly Holmes had not consulted an architect, at least not a competent one. The building's corridors were dark and pocked with too many doors. The lumber was low grade, the carpentry slipshod. Passages veered at odd angles.

Still, Emeline seemed entranced. Dr. Cigrand would have been a cold man indeed to have dashed that sweet, naïve adoration. Later, no doubt, he wished he had been more candid and had listened more closely to the whisper in his head about the wrongness of that building and the discontinuity between its true appearance and Emeline's perception of it. But again, Emeline was in love. It was not his place to wound her. She was young and enraptured, her joy infectious, especially to Dr. Cigrand, the dentist, who saw so little joy from day to day as he reduced grown men of proven courage to tears.

Soon after the Cigrands' visit, Holmes asked Emeline to marry him, and she accepted. He promised her a honeymoon in Europe during which, of course, they would pay a visit to his father, the lord.

Dedication Day

OLMSTED'S TEETH HURT, HIS EARS roared, and he could not sleep, yet throughout the first months of 1892 he kept up a pace that would have been punishing for a man one-third his age. He traveled to Chicago, Asheville, Knoxville, Louisville, and Rochester, each overnight leg compounding his distress. In Chicago, despite the tireless efforts of his young lieutenant Harry Codman, the work was far behind schedule, the task ahead growing more enormous by the day. The first major deadline, the dedication set for October 21, 1892, seemed impossibly near—and would have seemed even more so had not fair officials changed the original date, October 12, to allow New York City to hold its own Columbus celebration. Given the calumny New York previously had shoveled on Chicago, the postponement was an act of surprising grace.

Construction delays elsewhere on the grounds were especially frustrating for Olmsted. When contractors fell behind, his own work fell behind. His completed work also suffered. Workmen trampled his plantings and destroyed his roads. The U.S. Government Building was a case in point. "All over its surroundings," reported Rudolf Ulrich, his landscape superintendent, "material of any kind and all descriptions was piled up and scattered in such profusion that only repeated and persistent pressure brought to bear upon the officials in charge could gain any headway in beginning the work; and, even then, improvements being well under way, no regard was paid to them. What had been accomplished one day would be spoiled the next."

The delays and damage angered Olmsted, but other matters distressed him even more. Unbelievably, despite Olmsted's hectoring, Burnham still seemed to consider steam-powered launches an acceptable choice for the exposition's boat service. And no one seemed to share his conviction that the Wooded Island must remain free of all structures.

The island had come under repeated assault, prompting a resurfacing of Olmsted's old anger about the compulsion of clients to tinker with his landscapes. Everyone wanted space on the island. First it was Theodore Thomas, conductor of Chicago's symphony, who saw the island as the ideal site, the *only* site, for a music hall worthy of the fair. Olmsted would not allow it. Next came Theodore Roosevelt, head of the U.S. Civil Service Commission and a human gunboat. The island, he insisted, was perfect for the hunting camp exhibit of his Boone and Crockett Club. Not surprisingly, given Roosevelt's power in Washington, the politicians of the fair's National Commission strongly endorsed his plan. Burnham, partly to keep the peace, also urged Olmsted to accept it. "Would you object to its being placed on the north end of the Island, snuggled in among the trees, purely as an exhibit, provided it shall be so concealed as to only be noticed casually by those on the Island and not at all from the shore?"

Olmsted did object. He agreed to let Roosevelt place his camp on a lesser island but would not allow any buildings, only "a few tents, some horses, camp-fire, etc." Later he permitted the installation of a small hunter's cabin.

Next came the U.S. government, seeking to place an Indian exhibit on the island, and then Professor Putnam, the fair's chief of ethnology, who saw the island as the ideal site for several exotic villages. The government of Japan also wanted the island. "They propose an outdoor exhibit of their temples and, as has been usual, they desire space on the wooded island," Burnham wrote in February 1892. To Burnham it now seemed inevitable that something would occupy the island. The setting was just too appealing. Burnham urged Olmsted to accept Japan's proposal. "It seems beyond any question to be the thing fitting to the locality and I cannot see that it will in any manner detract essentially from the features which you care for. They propose to do the most exquisitely beautiful things and desire to leave the buildings as a gift to the City of Chicago after the close of the Fair."

Fearing much worse, Olmsted agreed.

It did not help his mood any that as he battled to protect the island, he learned of another attack on his beloved Central Park. At the instigation of a small group of wealthy New Yorkers, the state legislature had quietly passed a law authorizing the construction of a "speedway" on the west side of the park so that the rich could race their carriages. The public responded with outrage. Olmsted weighed in with a letter describing the proposed road as "unreasonable, unjust and immoral." The legislature backed off.

His insomnia and pain, the crushing workload, and his mounting frustration all tore at his spirit until by the end of March he felt himself on the verge of physical and emotional collapse. The intermittent depression that had shadowed him throughout his adult life was about to envelop him once again. "When Olmsted is blue," a friend once wrote, "the logic of his despondency is crushing and terrible."

Olmsted, however, believed that all he needed was a good rest. In keeping with the therapeutic mores of the age, he decided to do his convalescing in Europe, where the scenery also would provide an opportunity for him to enrich his visual vocabulary. He planned forays to public gardens and parks and the grounds of the old Paris exposition.

He put his eldest son, John, in charge of the Brookline office and left Harry Codman in Chicago to guide the work on the world's fair. At the last minute he decided to bring along two of his children, Marion and Rick, and another young man, Phil Codman, who was Harry's younger brother. For Marion and the boys, it promised to be a dream journey; for Olmsted it became something rather more dark.

They sailed on Saturday, April 2, 1892, and arrived in Liverpool under a barrage of hail and snow.

In Chicago Sol Bloom received a cable from France that startled him. He read it a couple of times to make sure it said what he thought it said. His Algerians, scores of them along with all their animals and material possessions, were already at sea, sailing for America and the fair—one year early.

"They had picked the right month," Bloom said, "but the wrong year."

⌐⸺⸺⸗

Olmsted found the English countryside charming, the weather bleak and morbid. After a brief stay at the home of relatives in Chislehurt, he and the boys left for Paris. Daughter Marion stayed behind.

In Paris Olmsted went to the old exposition grounds. The gardens were sparse, suppressed by a long winter, and the buildings had not weathered well, but enough of the fair remained to give him "a tolerable idea" of what the exposition once had been. Clearly the site was still popular. During one Sunday visit Olmsted and the boys found four bands playing, refreshment stands open, and a few thousand people roaming the paths. A long line had formed at the base of the Eiffel Tower.

With the Chicago fair always in mind, Olmsted examined every detail. The lawns were "rather poor," the gravel walks "not pleasant to the eye nor to the foot." He found the Paris fair's extensive use of formal flower beds objectionable. "It seemed to me," he wrote, in a letter to John in Brookline, "that at the least it must have been extremely disquieting, gaudy & childish, if not savage and an injury to the Exposition, through its disturbance of dignity, and injury to breadth, unity & composure." He reiterated his insistence that in Chicago "simplicity and reserve will be practiced and petty effects and frippery avoided."

The visit rekindled his concern that in the quest to surpass the Paris exposition Burnham and his architects had lost sight of what a world's fair ought to be. The Paris buildings, Olmsted wrote, "have much more color and much more ornament in color, but much less in moulding and sculpture than I had supposed. They show I think more fitness for their purposes, seem more designed for the occasion and to be less like grand permanent architectural monuments than ours are to be. I question if ours are not at fault in this respect and if they are not going to look too assuming of architectural stateliness and to be overbonded with sculptural and other efforts for grandeur and grandiloquent pomp."

Olmsted liked traveling with his youthful entourage. In a letter to his wife in Brookline he wrote, "I am having a great deal of enjoyment, and I hope laying in a good stock of better health." Soon after the party returned to Chislehurst, however, Olmsted's health degraded and insomnia again shattered his nights. He wrote to Harry Codman, who was himself ill with a strange abdominal illness, "I can only conclude now that I am older and more used up than I had supposed."

A doctor, Henry Rayner, paid a social visit to Chislehurst to meet Olmsted. He happened to be a specialist in treating nervous disorders and was so appalled by Olmsted's appearance that he offered to take him to his own house in Hampstead Heath, outside London, and care for him personally. Olmsted accepted.

Despite Rayner's close attention, Olmsted's condition did not improve; his stay at Hampstead Heath became wearisome. "You know that I am practically in prison here," he wrote to Harry Codman on June 16, 1892. "Every day I look for decided improvement and thus far everyday, I am disappointed." Dr. Rayner too was perplexed, according to Olmsted. "He says, with confidence, after repeated examinations, of all my anatomy, that I have no organic trouble and that I may reasonably expect under favorable circumstances to keep at work for several years to come. He regards my present trouble as a variation in form of the troubles which led me to come abroad."

Most days Olmsted was driven by carriage through the countryside, "every day more or less on a different road," to view gardens, churchyards, private parks, and the natural landscape. Nearly every ornamental flowerbed offended him. He dismissed them as "childish, vulgar, flaunting, or impertinent, out of place and discordant." The countryside itself, however, charmed him: "there is nothing in America to be compared with the pastoral or with the picturesque beauty that is common property in England. I cannot go out without being delighted. The view before me as I write, veiled by the rain, is just enchanting." The loveliest scenes, he found, were comprised of the simplest, most natural juxtapositions of native plants. "The finest combination is one of gorse, sweet briar, brambles, hawthorn, and ivy. Even when there is no bloom this is charming. And these things can be had by the hundred thousand at very low prices."

At times the scenes he saw challenged his vision of Jackson Park, at other times they affirmed it. "Everywhere the best ornamental grounds that we see are those in which vines and creepers are outwitting the gardener. We can't have little vines and weeds enough." He knew there was too little time to let nature alone produce such effects. "Let us as much as possible, train out creepers, and branches of trees, upon bridges, pulling down and nailing the branches, aiming to obtain shade and reflection of foliage and broken obscuration of water."

Above all, his sorties reinforced his belief that the Wooded Island, despite the Japanese temple, should be made as wild as possible. "I think more than ever of the value of the island," he wrote to Harry Codman, "and of the importance of using all possible, original means of securing impervious screening, dense massive piles of foliage on its borders; with abundant variety of small detail in abject subordination to general effect. . . . There cannot be enough of bulrush, adlumia, Madeira vine, catbriar, virgin's bower, brambles, sweet peas, Jimson weed, milkweed, the smaller western sunflowers and morning glories."

But he also recognized that the wildness he sought would have to be tempered with excellent groundskeeping. He worried that Chicago would not be up to the task. "The standard of an English laborer, hack driver or cad in respect to neatness, smugness and elegance of gardens and grounds and paths and ways is infinitely higher than that of a Chicago merchant prince or virtuoso," he wrote to Codman, "and we shall be disgraced if we fail to work up to a far higher level than our masters will be prepared to think suitable."

Overall Olmsted remained confident that his exposition landscape would succeed. A new worry troubled him, however. "The only cloud I see over the Exposition now is the Cholera," he wrote in a letter to his Brookline office. "The accounts from Russia and from Paris this morning are alarming."

As Sol Bloom's Algerians neared New York Harbor, workers assigned to the Midway erected temporary buildings to house them. Bloom went to New York to meet the ship and reserved two traincars to bring the villagers and their cargo back to Chicago.

As the Algerians left the ship, they began moving in all directions at once. "I could see them getting lost, being run over, and landing in jail," Bloom said. No one seemed to be in charge. Bloom raced up to them, shouting commands in French and English. A giant black-complected man walked up to Bloom and in perfect House of Lords English said, "I suggest you be more civil. Otherwise I may lose my temper and throw you into the water."

The man identified himself as Archie, and as the two settled into a more peaceful conversation, he revealed to Bloom that he had spent a decade in London serving as a rich man's bodyguard. "At present," he said, "I am responsible for conveying my associates to a place called Chicago. I understand it is somewhere in the hinterland."

Bloom handed him a cigar and proposed that he become his bodyguard and assistant.

"Your offer," Archie said, "is quite satisfactory."

Both men lit up and puffed smoke into the fragrant murk above New York Harbor.

———

Burnham fought to boost the rate of construction, especially of the Manufactures and Liberal Arts Building, which had to be completed by Dedication Day. In March, with just half a year remaining until the dedication, he invoked the "czar" clause of his construction contracts. He ordered the builder of the Electricity Building to double his workforce and to put the men to work at night under electric lights. He threatened the Manufactures contractor with the same fate if he did not increase the pace of his work.

Burnham had all but given up hope of surpassing the Eiffel Tower. Most recently he had turned down another outlandish idea, this from an earnest young Pittsburgh engineer who had attended his lecture to the

Saturday Afternoon Club. The man was credible enough—his company held the contract for inspecting all the steel used in the fair's structures—but the thing he proposed to build just did not seem feasible. "Too fragile," Burnham told him. The public, he said, would be afraid.

A hostile spring further hampered the fair's progress. On Tuesday, April 5, 1892, at 6:50 A.M., a sudden windstorm demolished the fair's just-finished pumping station and tore down sixty-five feet of the Illinois State Building. Three weeks later another storm destroyed eight hundred feet of the south wall of the Manufactures and Liberal Arts Building. "The wind," the *Tribune* observed, "seems to have a grudge against the World's Fair grounds."

To find ways to accelerate the work, Burnham called the eastern architects to Chicago. One looming problem was how to color the exteriors of the main buildings, especially the staff-coated palisades of the Manufactures and Liberal Arts Building. During the meeting an idea arose that in the short run promised a dramatic acceleration of the work, but that eventually served to fix the fair in the world's imagination as a thing of otherworldly beauty.

By all rights, the arena of exterior decoration belonged to William Pretyman, the fair's official director of color. Burnham admitted later that he had hired Pretyman for the job "largely on account of his great friendship for John Root." Pretyman was ill suited to the job. Harriet Monroe, who knew him and his wife, wrote, "His genius was betrayed by lofty and indomitable traits of character which could not yield or compromise. And so his life was a tragedy of inconsequence."

The day of the meeting Pretyman was on the East Coast. The architects proceeded without him. "I was urging everyone on, knowing I had an awful fight against time," Burnham said. "We talked about the colors, and finally the thought came, 'let us make it all perfectly white.' I do not remember who made that suggestion. It might have been one of those things that reached all minds at once. At any rate, I decided it."

The Mines Building, designed by Chicago's Solon S. Beman, was nearly finished. It became the test building. Burnham ordered it painted a creamy white. Pretyman returned and "was outraged," Burnham recalled.

Pretyman insisted that any decision on color was his alone.

"I don't see it that way," Burnham told him. "The decision is mine."

"All right," Pretyman said. "I will get out."

Burnham did not miss him. "He was a brooding sort of man and very cranky," Burnham said. "I let him go, then told Charles McKim that I would have to have a man who could actually take charge of it, and that I would not decide from the point of friendship."

McKim recommended the New York painter Francis Millet, who had sat in on the color meeting. Burnham hired him.

Millet quickly proved his worth. After some experimentation he settled on "ordinary white lead and oil" as the best paint for staff, then developed a means of applying the paint not by brush but through a hose with a special nozzle fashioned from a length of gas pipe—the first spray paint. Burnham nicknamed Millet and his paint crews "the Whitewash Gang."

In the first week of May a powerful storm dropped an ocean of rain on Chicago and again caused the Chicago River to reverse flow. Again the sewage threatened the city's water supply. The decaying carcass of a horse was spotted bobbing near one of the intake cribs.

This new surge underscored for Burnham the urgency of completing his plan to pipe Waukesha spring water to the fair by Opening Day. Earlier, in July 1891, the exposition had granted a contract for the work to the Hygeia Mineral Springs Company, headed by an entrepreneur named J. E. McElroy, but the company had accomplished little. In March Burnham ordered Dion Geraldine, his chief construction superintendent, to press the matter "with the utmost vigor and see that no delay occurs."

Hygeia secured rights to lay its pipe from its springhouse in Waukesha through the village itself but failed to anticipate the intensity of opposition from citizens who feared the pipeline would disfigure their landscape and drain their famous springs. Hygeia's McElroy, under mounting pressure from Burnham, turned to desperate measures.

On Saturday evening, May 7, 1892, McElroy loaded a special train with pipes, picks, shovels, and three hundred men and set off for Waukesha to dig his pipeline under cover of darkness.

Word of the expedition beat the train to Waukesha. As it pulled into the station, someone rang the village firebell, and soon a large force of men armed with clubs, pistols, and shotguns converged on the train. Two fire engines arrived hissing steam, their crews ready to blast the pipelayers with water. One village leader told McElroy that if he went ahead with his plan, he would not leave town alive.

Soon another thousand or so townspeople joined the small army at the station. One group of men dragged a cannon from the town hall and trained it on Hygeia's bottling plant.

After a brief standoff, McElroy and the pipelayers went back to Chicago.

Burnham still wanted that water. Workers had already laid pipes in Jackson Park for two hundred springwater booths.

McElroy gave up trying to run pipes directly into the village of Waukesha. Instead he bought a spring in the town of Big Bend, twelve miles south of Waukesha, just inside the Waukesha County line. Fair visitors would be able to drink Waukesha springwater after all.

That the water came from the county and not the famous village was a subtlety upon which Burnham and McElroy did not dwell.

⌒──⌒

In Jackson Park everyone became caught up in the accelerating pace of construction. As the buildings rose, the architects spotted flaws in their designs but found the forward crush of work so overwhelming, it threatened to leave the flaws locked in stone, or at least staff. Frank Millet unofficially kept watch over the buildings of the eastern architects during their lengthy absences from the park, lest some ad hoc decision cause irreparable aesthetic damage. On June 6, 1892, he wrote to Charles McKim, designer of the Agriculture Building, "You had better write a letter embodying all the ideas of changes you have, because before you know it they'll have you by the umbilicus. I staved them off from a cement floor in the Rotunda to-day and insisted that you must have brick. . . . It takes no end of time and worry to get a thing settled right but only a second to have orders given out for a wrong thing to be done. All these remarks are in strict confidence, and I write in this way to urge you to be explicit and flat-footed in your wishes."

At the Manufactures and Liberal Arts Building workers employed by contractor Francis Agnew began the dangerous process of raising the giant iron trusses that would support the building's roof and create the widest span of unobstructed interior space ever attempted.

The workers installed three sets of parallel railroad tracks along the length of the building. Atop these, on railcar wheels or "trucks," they erected a "traveler," a giant derrick consisting of three tall towers spanned at the top by a platform. Workers using the traveler could lift and position two trusses at a time. George Post's design called for twenty-two trusses, each weighing two hundred tons. Just getting the components to the park had required six hundred railcars.

On Wednesday, June 1, exposition photographer Charles Arnold took a photograph of the building to record its progress. Anyone looking at that photograph would have had to conclude that the building could not possibly be finished in the four and a half months that remained until Dedication Day. The trusses were in place but no roof. The walls were just beginning to rise. When Arnold took the photograph, hundreds of men were at work on the building, but its scale was so great that none of the men was immediately visible. The ladders that rose from one level of scaffold to the next had all the substance of matchsticks and imparted to the structure an aura of fragility. In the foreground stood mountains of debris.

Two weeks later Arnold returned for another photograph and captured a very different scene—one of devastation.

On the night of June 13, just after nine o'clock, another abrupt storm had struck the fairgrounds, and this one also seemed to single out the Manufactures and Liberal Arts Building. A large portion of the building's north end collapsed, which in turn caused the failure of an elevated gallery designed to ring the interior of the building. One hundred thousand feet of lumber crashed to the floor. Arnold's photograph of the aftermath showed a Lilliputian man, possibly Burnham, standing before a great mound of shattered wood and tangled steel.

This, of all buildings.

The contractor, Francis Agnew, acknowledged the wall had been inadequately braced but blamed this condition on Burnham for pushing the men to build too quickly.

Now Burnham pushed them even harder. He made good on his threat and doubled the number of men working on the building. They worked at night, in rain, in stifling heat. In August alone the building took three lives. Elsewhere on the grounds four other men died and dozens more suffered all manner of fractures, burns, and lacerations. The fair, according to one later appraisal, was a more dangerous place to work than a coal mine.

Burnham intensified his drive for more power. The constant clash between the Exposition Company and the National Commission had become nearly unbearable. Even the congressional investigators had recognized that the overlapping jurisdiction was a source of discord and needless expense. Their report recommended that Davis's salary be cut in half, a clear sign that the balance of power had shifted. The company and commission worked out a truce. On August 24 the executive committee named Burnham director of works. Chief of everything.

Soon afterward Burnham dispatched letters to all his department heads, including Olmsted. "I have assumed personal control of the active work within the grounds of the World's Columbian Exposition," he wrote. "Henceforward, and until further notice, you will report to and receive orders from me exclusively."

∘———∘

In Pittsburgh the young steel engineer became more convinced than ever that his challenge to the Eiffel Tower could succeed. He asked a partner in his inspection firm, W. F. Gronau, to calculate the novel forces that would play among the components of his structure. In engineering parlance, it embodied little "dead load," the static weight of immobile masses of brick and steel. Nearly all of it was "live load," meaning weight that changes over time, as when a train passes over a bridge. "I had no precedent," Gronau said. After three weeks of intense work, however, he came up with detailed specifications. The numbers were persuasive, even to Burnham. In June the Ways and Means Committee agreed that the thing should be built. They granted a concession.

The next day the committee revoked it—second thoughts, after a night spent dreaming of freak winds and shrieking steel and two thousand lives gone in a wink. One member of the committee now called it a "monstrosity." A chorus of engineers chanted that the thing could not be built, at least not with any margin of safety.

Its young designer still did not concede defeat, however. He spent $25,000 on drawings and additional specifications and used them to recruit a cadre of investors that included two prominent engineers, Robert Hunt, head of a major Chicago firm, and Andrew Onderdonk, famous for helping construct the Canadian Pacific Railway.

Soon he sensed a change. The new man in charge of the Midway, Sol Bloom, had struck like a bolt of lightning and seemed amenable to just about anything—the more novel and startling the better. And Burnham had gained almost limitless power over the construction and operation of the fair.

The engineer readied himself for a third try.

In the first week of September 1892 Olmsted and his young party left England for home, departing Liverpool aboard the *City of New York*. The seas were high, the crossing difficult. Seasickness felled Marion and left Rick perpetually queasy. Olmsted's own health again declined. His insomnia came back. He wrote, "I was more disabled when I returned than when I left." Now, however, he had no time to recuperate. Dedication Day was only a month away, and Harry Codman was again ill, incapacitated by the same stomach problem that had struck him during the summer. Olmsted left for Chicago to take over direct supervision of the work while Codman recovered. "I am still tortured a good deal with neuralgia and toothache," Olmsted wrote, "and I am tired and have a growing dread of worry & anxiety."

In Chicago he found a changed park. The Mines Building was finished, as was the Fisheries Building. Most of the other buildings were well under way, including, incredibly, the giant Manufactures and Liberal Arts Building, where hundreds of workers swarmed its scaffolds and roof. The building's floor alone had consumed five traincar loads of nails.

Amid all this work, however, the landscape had suffered. Temporary tracks latticed the grounds. Wagons had gouged chasms across paths, roads, and would-be lawns. Litter lay everywhere. A first-time visitor might wonder if Olmsted's men had done any work at all.

Olmsted, of course, knew that tremendous progress had been made, but it was the sort that escaped casual notice. Lagoons existed now where once there had been barren land. The elevated sites upon which the buildings stood had not existed until his grading teams created them. The previous spring his men had planted nearly everything raised in the exposition's nurseries, plus an additional 200,000 trees, aquatic plants, and ferns, and 30,000 more willow cuttings, all this under the direction of his aptly named head gardener, E. Dehn.

In the time left before Dedication Day Burnham wanted Olmsted's men to concentrate on cleaning the grounds and dressing them with flowers and temporary lawns of sod, actions that Olmsted understood were necessary but that clashed with his career-long emphasis on designing for scenic effects that might not be achieved for decades. "Of course the main work suffers," he wrote.

One indisputably positive development had occurred during his absence, however. Burnham had awarded the boat concession to a company called the Electric Launch and Navigation Company, which had produced a lovely electric vessel of exactly the character Olmsted wanted.

On Dedication Day even the press was polite enough to overlook the stark appearance of the grounds and the unfinished feel of the Manufactures and Liberal Arts Building. To have done otherwise would have been an act of disloyalty to Chicago and the nation.

⌀────⌀

The dedication had been anticipated nationwide. Francis J. Bellamy, an editor of *Youth's Companion,* thought it would be a fine thing if on that day all the schoolchildren of America, in unison, offered something to their nation. He composed a pledge that the Bureau of Education mailed to virtually every school. As originally worded, it began, "I pledge allegiance to my Flag and to the Republic for which it stands . . ."

⌀────⌀

A great parade brought Burnham and other dignitaries to the Manufactures and Liberal Arts Building, where a standing army of 140,000 Chicagoans filled the thirty-two-acre floor. Shafts of sunlight struck through the rising mist of human breath. Five thousand yellow chairs stood on the red-carpeted speaker's platform, and in these chairs sat businessmen dressed in black, and foreign commissioners and clerics in scarlet, purple, green, and gold. Ex-mayor Carter Harrison, again running for a fifth term, strode about shaking hands, his black slouch hat raising cheers from supporters in the crowd. At the opposite end of the building a five-thousand-voice choir sang Handel's "Hallelujah" chorus to the accompaniment of five hundred musicians. At one point a spectator recalled, "Ninety thousand people suddenly rose and stood upon their feet and simultaneously waved and fluttered ninety thousand snowy pocket-handkerchiefs; the air was cut into dusty spirals, which vibrated to the great iron-ribbed ceiling. . . . One had a sense of dizziness, as if the entire building rocked."

The chamber was so immense that visual signals had to be used to let the chorus know when a speaker had stopped talking and a new song could begin. Microphones did not yet exist, so only a small portion of the audience actually heard any speeches. The rest, with faces contorted from the strain of trying to listen, saw distant men gesturing wildly into the sound-killing miasma of whispers, coughs and creaking shoe leather. Harriet Monroe, the poet who had been John Root's sister-in-law, was there and watched as two of the nation's greatest speakers, Colonel

Henry Watterson of Kentucky and Chauncey M. Depew of New York, took turns at the podium, "both orators waving their windy words toward a vast, whispering, rustling audience which could not hear."

This was a big day for Miss Monroe. She had composed a lengthy poem for the event, her "Columbian Ode," and pestered her many powerful friends into having it placed on the day's program. She watched with pride as an actress read it to the few thousand people close enough to hear it. Unlike the majority of the audience, Monroe believed the poem to be rather a brilliant work, so much so that she had hired a printer to produce five thousand copies for sale to the public. She sold few and attributed the debacle to America's fading love of poetry.

That winter she burned the excess copies for fuel.

Prendergast

On November 28, 1892, Patrick Eugene Joseph Prendergast, the mad Irish immigrant and Harrison supporter, selected one of his postal cards. He was twenty-four years old now and despite his accelerating mental decline was still employed by the *Inter Ocean* as a delivery contractor. The card, like all the others, was four inches wide by five inches long, blank on one face, with postal insignia and a printed one-cent stamp on the other. In this time when writing long letters was everyday practice, men of normal sensibility saw these cards as the most crabbed of media, little better than telegrams, but to Prendergast this square of stiff paper was a vehicle that gave him a voice in the skyscrapers and mansions of the city.

He addressed this particular card to "A. S. Trude, Lawyer." He sketched the letters of the name in large floral script, as if seeking to dispatch the cumbersome duty of addressing the card as quickly as possible, before advancing to the message itself.

That Prendergast had selected Trude to be one of his correspondents was not surprising. Prendergast read widely and possessed a good grasp of the grip-car wrecks, murders, and City Hall machinations covered so fervently by the city's newspapers. He knew that Alfred S. Trude was one of Chicago's best criminal defense attorneys and that from time to time he was hired by the state to serve as prosecutor, a practice customary in particularly important cases.

Prendergast filled the postcard from top margin to bottom, from edge to edge, with little regard for whether the sentences formed level lines or not. He gripped the pen so tightly it impressed channels into the tips of his thumb and forefinger. "My Dear Mr. Trude," he began. "Were you much hurt?" An accident, reported in the press, had caused Trude minor injuries. "Your humble servant hereby begs leave to tender you his sincere sympathy and trusts that while he does not appear before you in person, you nonetheless will not have any doubts as to his real sympathy for you in your misfortunes—you are wished by him a speedy recovery from the results of the accident which you had the misfortune to meet with."

He wrote with a tone of familiarity that presumed Trude would consider him a peer. As the note progressed, his handwriting shrank, until it seemed like something extruded rather than written. "I suppose Mr. Trude that you do understand that the greatest authority on the subject of law is Jesus Christ—and that you also know that the fulfillment of the whole law depends upon the observance of these two commands thou shalt Love God most of all & your neighbor as your self—these are the greatest commands if you please sir."

The note clicked from theme to theme like the wheels of a train crossing a freightyard. "Have you ever saw the picture of the fat man who looked for his dog while his dog was at his feet and still did not have the wit to see what was the matter—have you observed the cat?"

He did not add a closing and did not sign the note. He simply ran out of room, then posted the card.

Trude read the note and at first dismissed it as the work of a crank. The number of troubled men and women seemed to be increasing with each passing year. The jails were full of them, a warden later would testify. Inevitably some became dangerous, like Charles Guiteau, the man who had assassinated President Garfield in Washington.

For no clear reason, Trude kept the card.

"I Want You at Once"

In late November the young Pittsburgh engineer once again put his proposal for out-Eiffeling Eiffel before the Ways and Means Committee. This time in addition to drawings and specifications he included a list of investors, the names of the prominent men on his board, and proof that he had raised enough money to finance the project to completion. On December 16, 1892, the committee granted him a concession to build his structure in the Midway Plaisance. This time the decision held.

He needed an engineer willing to go to Chicago and supervise the construction effort and thought he knew just the man: Luther V. Rice, assistant engineer of the Union Depot & Tunnel Company, St. Louis. His letter to Rice began, "I have on hand a great project for the World's Fair in Chicago. I am going to build a vertically revolving wheel 250' in dia."

Nowhere in this letter, however, did he reveal the true dimension of his vision: that this wheel would carry thirty-six cars, each about the size of a Pullman, each holding sixty people and equipped with its own lunch counter, and how when filled to capacity the wheel would propel 2,160 people at a time three hundred feet into the sky over Jackson Park, a bit higher than the crown of the now six-year-old Statue of Liberty.

He told Rice, "I want you at once if you can come." He signed the letter: George Washington Gale Ferris.

Chappell Redux

ONE DAY IN THE FIRST week of December 1892 Emeline Cigrand set out for Holmes's building in Englewood bearing a small neatly wrapped parcel. Initially her mood was bright, for the parcel contained an early Christmas present she planned to give to her friends the Lawrences, but as she neared the corner of Sixty-third and Wallace, her spirits dimmed. Where once the building had seemed almost a palace—not for its architectural nobility but for what it promised—now it looked drab and worn. She climbed the stairs to the second floor and went directly to the Lawrences' apartment. The warmth and welcome resurrected her good spirits. She handed the parcel to Mrs. Lawrence, who opened it immediately and pulled from the wrapping a tin plate upon which Emeline had painted a lovely forest.

The gift delighted Mrs. Lawrence but also perplexed her. Christmas was only three weeks off, she said kindly: Why hadn't Emeline simply waited and given the plate then, when Mrs. Lawrence could have offered a gift in return?

Her face brightening, Emeline explained that she was going home to Indiana to spend Christmas with her family.

"She seemed delighted with the anticipation of a visit to them," Mrs. Lawrence said. "She spoke in most affectionate terms of them and seemed as happy as a child." But Mrs. Lawrence also sensed a note of finality in Emeline's voice that suggested Emeline's journey might have another purpose. She said, "You are not going away from us?"

"Well," Emeline said. "I don't know. Maybe."

Mrs. Lawrence laughed. "Why, Mr. Holmes could never get along without you."

Emeline's expression changed. "He could if he had to."

The remark confirmed something for the Lawrences. "It had seemed to me for some time that Miss Cigrand was changing in her feelings toward Holmes," said Dr. Lawrence. "In the light of what has happened since, I believe now that she had found out to a certain extent the real character of Holmes and determined to leave him."

She may have begun to believe the stories she heard in the neighborhood of Holmes's penchant for acquiring things on credit and then not paying for them—stories she had heard all along, for they were rife, but that she at first had dismissed as the gossip of envious hearts. Later there was speculation that Emeline herself had trusted Holmes with her $800 savings, only to have it disappear in a fog of promises of lavish future returns. Ned Conner's warning echoed in her mind. Lately she had begun talking of returning one day to Dwight to resume her work for Dr. Keeley.

Emeline never told the Lawrences good-bye. Her visits simply stopped. That she would leave without a parting word struck Mrs. Lawrence as being very much out of character. She wasn't sure whether to feel wounded or worried. She asked Holmes what he knew about Emeline's absence.

Ordinarily Holmes looked at Mrs. Lawrence with a directness that was unsettling, but now he avoided her gaze. "Oh, she's gone away to get married," Holmes said, as if nothing could have interested him less.

The news shocked Mrs. Lawrence. "I don't see why she didn't mention something to me about getting married."

It was a secret, Holmes explained: Emeline and her betrothed had revealed their wedding plans only to him.

But for Mrs. Lawrence this explanation only raised more questions. Why would the couple want such privacy? Why had Emeline said nothing to Mrs. Lawrence, when together they had shared so many other confidences?

Mrs. Lawrence missed Emeline and the way her effervescence and physical brightness—her prettiness and sunflower hair—lit the sullen halls of Holmes's building. She remained perplexed and a few days later again asked Holmes about Emeline.

He pulled a square envelope from his pocket. "This will tell you," he said.

The envelope contained a wedding announcement. Not engraved, as was customary, merely typeset. This too surprised Mrs. Lawrence. Emeline never would have accepted so mundane a means of communicating news of such magnitude.

The announcement read:

Mr. Robert E. Phelps.
Miss Emeline G. Cigrand.
Married
Wednesday, December 7th
1892
CHICAGO

Holmes told Mrs. Lawrence he had received his copy from Emeline herself. "Some days after going away she returned for her mail," he explained in his memoir, "and at this time gave me one of her wedding cards, and also two or three others for tenants in the building who were not then in their rooms; and in response to inquiries lately made I have learned that at least five persons in and about Lafayette, Ind., received such cards, the post mark and her handwriting upon the envelope in which they were enclosed showing that she must have sent them herself after leaving my employ."

Emeline's family and friends did receive copies of the announcement through the mail, and indeed these appeared to have been addressed by Emeline herself. Most likely Holmes forged the envelopes or else duped Emeline into preparing them by persuading her they would be used for a legitimate purpose, perhaps for Christmas cards.

For Mrs. Lawrence the announcement explained nothing. Emeline had never mentioned a Robert Phelps. And if Emeline had come to the building bearing marriage announcements, she surely would have presented one in person.

The next day Mrs. Lawrence stopped Holmes yet again, and this time asked what he knew about Phelps. In the same dismissive manner Holmes said, "Oh, he is a fellow Miss Cigrand met somewhere. I do not know anything about him except that he is a traveling man."

News of Emeline's marriage reached her hometown newspaper, which reported it on December 8, 1892, in a small chatty bulletin. The item called Emeline a "lady of refinement" who "possesses a character that is strong and pure. Her many friends feel that she has exercised good judgment in selecting a husband and will heartily congratulate her." The item offered a few biographical details, among them the fact that Emeline once had been employed as a stenographer in the county recorder's office. "From there," the item continued, "she went to Dwight, and from there to Chicago, where she met her fate."

"Fate" being the writer's coy allusion to marriage.

In the days that followed Mrs. Lawrence asked Holmes additional questions about Emeline, but he responded only in monosyllables. She began to think of Emeline's departure as a disappearance and recalled that soon after Emeline's last visit a curious change in routine had occurred within Holmes's building.

"The day after Miss Cigrand disappeared, or the day we last saw her, the door of Holmes' office was kept locked and nobody went into it except Holmes and Patrick Quinlan," Mrs. Lawrence said. "About 7 o'clock in the evening Holmes came out of his office and asked two men who were living in the building if they would not help him carry a trunk downstairs." The trunk was new and large, about four feet long. Its contents clearly were heavy and made the big trunk difficult to manage. Holmes repeatedly cautioned his helpers to be careful with it. An express wagon arrived and took it away.

Mrs. Lawrence later claimed that at this point she became convinced Holmes had killed Emeline. Yet she and her husband made no effort to move from the building, nor did they go to the police. No one did. Not Mrs. Lawrence, not Mr. and Mrs. Peter Cigrand, not Ned Conner, and not Julia's parents, Mr. and Mrs. Andrew Smythe. It was as if no one expected the police would be interested in yet another disappearance or, if they were, that they would be competent enough to conduct an effective investigation.

Soon afterward Emeline's own trunk, filled with her belongings and all the clothing she had brought with her when she left home in 1891 to work for Keeley, arrived at a freight depot near her hometown. Her parents at first believed—hoped—she had sent the trunk home because now that she was marrying a wealthy man, she no longer needed such old and worn things. The Cigrands received no further mail from Emeline, not even at Christmas. "This," said Dr. B. J. Cigrand, Emeline's second cousin, the North Side dentist, "in spite of the fact that she was in the habit of writing to her parents two or three times a week."

Emeline's parents still did not imagine murder, however. Peter Cigrand said, "I had at last come to the belief she must have died in Europe and her husband either did not know our address or neglected to notify us."

The Cigrands and Lawrences would have found their anxiety intensified manyfold had they known a few other facts:

That the name Phelps was an alias that Holmes's assistant, Benjamin Pitezel, had used when he first met Emeline at the Keeley Institute;

That on January 2, 1893, Holmes again had enlisted the help of Charles Chappell, the articulator, and sent him a trunk containing the corpse of a woman, her upper body stripped nearly bare of flesh;

That a few weeks later the LaSalle Medical College of Chicago had taken delivery of a nicely articulated skeleton;

And that something peculiar had occurred in the room-sized vault in Holmes's building, a phenomenon that when finally discovered by police three years later would defy scientific explanation.

Somehow a footprint had become etched into the smooth enameled finish on the inside of the vault door at a point roughly two feet above the floor. The toes, the ball, and the heel were so clearly outlined as to leave no doubt that a woman had left the print. The degree of detail mystified the police, as did the print's resilience. They tried rubbing it off by hand, then with a cloth and soap and water, but it remained as clear as ever.

No one could explain it with any certainty. The best guess posited that Holmes had lured a woman into the vault; that the woman was shoeless at the time, perhaps nude; and that Holmes then had closed the airtight door to lock her inside. She had left the print in a last hopeless effort to force the door open. To explain the print's permanence, detectives theorized that Holmes, known to have an avid interest in chemistry, had first poured a sheen of acid onto the floor to hasten by chemical reaction the consumption of oxygen in the vault. The theory held that Emeline had stepped in the acid, then placed her feet against the door, thus literally etching the print into the enamel.

But again, this revelation came much later. As of the start of 1893, the year of the fair, no one, including Holmes, had noticed the footprint on the door.

"The Cold-Blooded Fact"

AT THE START OF JANUARY 1893 the weather turned cold and stayed cold, the temperature falling to twenty degrees below zero. In his dawn tours, Burnham faced a hard pale world. Cairns of frozen horse manure punctuated the landscape. Along the banks of the Wooded Island ice two feet thick locked Olmsted's bulrush and sedge in cruel contortions. Burnham saw that Olmsted's work was far behind. And now Olmsted's man in Chicago, Harry Codman, upon whom everyone had come to depend, was in the hospital recovering from surgery. His recurring illness had turned out to be appendicitis. The operation, under ether, had gone well and Codman was recuperating, but his recovery would be slow. Only four months remained until Opening Day.

The extreme cold increased the threat of fire. The necessary fires alone—the salamanders and tinner's pots—had caused dozens of small blazes, easily put out, but the cold increased the likelihood of far worse. It froze water lines and hydrants and drove workers to break Burnham's ban on smoking and open flame. The men of the Columbian Guard stepped up their vigilance. It was they who suffered most from the cold, standing watch around the clock in far-flung reaches of the park where no shelter existed. "The winter of 1892–3 will always be remembered by those who served on the guard during that period," wrote Colonel Rice, their commander. Its members most dreaded being assigned to an especially bleak sector at the extreme south end of the park below the Agriculture Building. They called it Siberia. Colonel Rice used their dread to his advantage: "any Guard ordered to the post along the South fence would realize that he had been guilty of some minor breach of discipline, or that his personal appearance rendered him too unsightly for the more public parts of the grounds."

George Ferris fought the cold with dynamite, the only efficient way to penetrate the three-foot crust of frozen earth that now covered Jackson Park. Once opened, the ground still posed problems. Just beneath the crust lay a twenty-foot stratum of the same quicksand Chicago builders always confronted, only now it was ice cold and a torment to workers. The men used jets of live steam to thaw dirt and prevent newly poured cement from freezing. They drove timber piles to hard-pan thirty-two feet underground. On top of these they laid a *grillage* of steel, then filled it with cement. To keep the excavated chambers as dry as possible, they ran pumps twenty-four hours a day. They repeated the process for each of the eight 140-foot towers that would support the Ferris Wheel's giant axle.

At first, Ferris's main worry was whether he could acquire enough steel to build his machine. He realized, however, that he had an advantage over anyone else trying to place a new order. Through his steel-inspection company he knew most of the nation's steel executives and the products they made. He was able to pull in favors and spread his orders among many different companies. "No one shop could begin to do all the work, therefore contracts were let to a dozen different firms, each being chosen because of some peculiar fitness for the work entrusted to it," according to an account by Ferris's company. Ferris also commanded a legion of inspectors who evaluated the quality of each component as it emerged from each mill. This proved to be a vital benefit since the wheel was a complex assemblage of 100,000 parts that ranged in size from small bolts to the giant axle, which at the time of its manufacture by Bethlehem Steel was the largest one-piece casting ever made. "Absolute precision was necessary, as few of the parts could be put together until they were upon the ground and an error of the smallest fraction of an inch might be fatal."

The wheel Ferris envisioned actually consisted of two wheels spaced thirty feet apart on the axle. What had frightened Burnham, at first, was the apparent insubstantiality of the design. Each wheel was essentially a gigantic bicycle wheel. Slender iron rods just two and a half inches thick and eighty feet long linked the rim, or felloe, of each wheel to a "spider" affixed to the axle. Struts and diagonal rods ran between the two wheels to stiffen the assembly and give it the strength of a railroad bridge. A chain weighing twenty thousand pounds connected a sprocket on the axle to sprockets driven by twin thousand-horsepower steam engines. For aesthetic reasons the boilers were to be located seven hundred feet outside the Midway, the steam shunted to the engines through ten-inch underground pipes.

This, at least, is how it looked on paper. Just digging and installing the foundation, however, had proven more difficult than Ferris and Rice had expected, and they knew that far greater hurdles lay ahead, foremost among them the challenge of raising that huge axle to its mount atop the eight towers. Together with its fittings, the axle weighed 142,031 pounds. Nothing that heavy had ever been lifted before, let alone to such a height.

Olmsted, in Brookline, got the news by telegram: Harry Codman was dead. Codman, his protégé, whom he loved like a son. He was twenty-nine. "You will have heard of our great calamity," Olmsted wrote to his friend Gifford Pinchot. "As yet, I am as one standing on a wreck and can hardly see when we shall be afloat again."

Olmsted recognized that now he himself would have to take over direct supervision of the exposition work, but he felt less up to the duty than ever. He and Phil, Harry's brother, arrived in Chicago at the beginning of February to find the city locked in brutal cold, the temperature eight degrees below zero. On February 4 he sat down at Codman's desk for the first time and found it awash with stacks of invoices and memoranda. Olmsted's head raged with noise and pain. He had a sore throat. He was deeply sad. The task of sorting through Codman's accumulated papers and of taking over the exposition work now seemed beyond him. He asked a former assistant, Charles Eliot, now one of Boston's best landscape architects, if he would come to help. After some hesitation Eliot agreed. On arrival Eliot saw immediately that Olmsted was ill. By the evening of February 17, 1893, as a blizzard bore down on Chicago, Olmsted was under a doctor's care, confined to his hotel.

The same night Olmsted wrote to John in Brookline. Weariness and sorrow freighted each page of his letter. "It looks as if the time has come when it is necessary for you to count me out," he wrote. The work in Chicago had begun to look hopeless. "It is very plain that as things are, we are not going to be able to do our duty here."

By early March Olmsted and Eliot were back in Brookline, Eliot now a full-fledged partner, the firm newly renamed Olmsted, Olmsted & Eliot. The exposition work was still far behind schedule and a major source of worry, but Olmsted's health and the pressure of other work had forced him from Chicago. With deep misgivings Olmsted had left the work in the care of his superintendent, Rudolf Ulrich, whom he had come to distrust. On March 11 Olmsted dispatched a long letter to Ulrich full of instructions.

"I have never before, in all the numerous works for which I have been broadly responsible, trusted as much to the discretion of an assistant or co-operator," Olmsted wrote. "And the results have been such that in the straights in which we are placed by the death of Mr. Codman and my ill health, and the consequent excessive pressure of other duties, I am more than ever disposed to pursue this policy, and to carry it further. But I must confess that I can not do so without much anxiety."

He made it clear that this anxiety was due to Ulrich, specifically, Ulrich's "constitutional propensity" to lose sight of the broad scheme and throw himself into minute tasks better handled by subordinates, a trait that Olmsted feared had left Ulrich vulnerable to demands by other officials, in particular Burnham. "Never lose sight of the fact that our special responsibility as *landscape* artists applies primarily to the broad, comprehensive *scenery* of the Exposition," Olmsted wrote. (The emphases were his.) "This duty is not to make a garden, or to produce garden effects, but relates to the scenery of the Exposition as a whole; first of all and most essentially the scenery, in a broad and comprehensive way. . . . If, for lack of time and means, or of good weather, we come short in matters of detailed decoration, our failure will be excusable. If we fall short in matters affecting broad landscape effects we shall fail in our primary and essential duty."

He went on to identify for Ulrich the things that most worried him about the fair, among them the color scheme chosen by Burnham and the architects. "Let me remind you that the whole field of the Exposition has already come to be popularly called 'THE WHITE CITY'. . . . I fear that against the clear blue sky and the blue lake, great towering masses of white, glistening in the clear, hot, Summer sunlight of Chicago, with the glare of the water that we are to have both within and without the Exposition grounds, will be overpowering." This, he wrote, made it more important than ever to provide a counterbalance of "dense, broad, luxuriant green bodies of foliage."

Clearly the possibility of failure at the exposition had occurred to Olmsted and troubled him. Time was short, the weather terrible. The spring planting season would be brief. Olmsted had begun to think in terms of fallback arrangements. He warned Ulrich, "Do not lay out to do anything in the way of decorative planting that you shall not be quite certain that you will have ample time and means to perfect of its kind. There can be little fault found with simple, neat turf. Do not be afraid of plain, undecorated, smooth surfaces."

It was far better, Olmsted lectured, to underdecorate than to overdecorate. "Let us be thought over-much plain and simple, even bare, rather than gaudy, flashy, cheap and meretricious. Let us manifest the taste of gentlemen."

Snow fell, bales of it. It fell day after day until hundreds of tons of it lay upon the rooftops at Jackson Park. The exposition was to be a warm-weather affair, set to run from May through October. No one had thought to design the roofs to resist such extreme loading from snow.

Men working at the Manufactures and Liberal Arts Building heard the shriek of failed steel and ran for cover. In a great blur of snow and silvery glass the building's roof—that marvel of late nineteenth-century hubris,

enclosing the greatest volume of unobstructed space in history—
collapsed to the floor below.

———

Soon afterward, a reporter from San Francisco made his way to Jackson Park. He had come prepared to admire the grand achievement of Burnham's army of workers but instead found himself troubled by what he saw in the stark frozen landscape.

"This seems to be an impossibility," he wrote. "To be sure, those in charge claim that they will be ready on time. Still the cold-blooded fact stares one in the face that only the Woman's Building is anywhere near completion inside and out."

Yet the fair was to open in little more than two months.

Acquiring Minnie

For Holmes, despite the persistent deep cold of the first two months of 1893, things never looked better. With Emeline gone and neatly disposed of, he now was able to concentrate on his growing web of enterprises. He savored its scope: He owned a portion of a legitimate company that produced a machine for duplicating documents; he sold mail-order ointments and elixirs and by now had established his own alcohol-treatment company, the Silver Ash Institute, his answer to Keeley's gold cure; he collected rents from the Lawrences and his other tenants and owned two houses, one on Honoré Street, the other the new house in Wilmette now occupied by his wife Myrta and daughter Lucy, which he himself had designed and then built with the help of as many as seventy-five largely unpaid workers. And soon he would begin receiving his first world's fair guests.

He spent much of his time outfitting his hotel. He acquired high-grade furnishings from the Tobey Furniture Company, and crystal and ceramics from the French, Potter Crockery Company, and did so without paying a dime, though he recognized that soon the companies would attempt to collect on the promissory notes he had given them. This did not worry him. He had learned through experience that delay and heartfelt remorse were powerful tools with which he could fend off creditors for months and years, sometimes forever. Such prolonged standoffs would not be necessary, however, for he sensed that his time in Chicago was nearing an end. Mrs. Lawrence's questioning had become more pointed, almost accusing. And lately some of his creditors had begun exhibiting an extraordinary hardening of resolve. One firm, Merchant & Co., which had supplied the iron for his kiln and vault, had gone so far as to secure a writ of replevin to take the iron back. In an inspection of the building, however, its agents had been unable to find anything they could identify conclusively as a Merchant product.

Far more annoying were the letters from parents of missing daughters and the private detectives who had begun showing up at his door. Independently of each other, the Cigrand and Conner families had hired "eyes" to search for their missing daughters. Although at first these inquiries troubled Holmes, he realized quickly that neither family believed he had anything to do with the disappearances. The detectives made no mention of suspecting foul play. They wanted information—the names of friends, forwarding addresses, suggestions on where to look next.

He was, of course, happy to oblige. Holmes told his visitors how much it grieved him, truly deeply grieved him, that he was unable to provide any new information to ease the worry of the parents. If he heard from the women, he of course would notify the detectives at once. Upon parting, he shook each detective's hand and told him that if his work should happen to bring him back to Englewood anytime in the future, by all means stop in. Holmes and the detectives parted as cheerily as if they had known each other all their lives.

At the moment—March 1893—the greatest inconvenience confronting Holmes was his lack of help. He needed a new secretary. There was no shortage of women seeking work, for the fair had drawn legions of them to Chicago. At the nearby Normal School, for example, the number of women applying to become teacher trainees was said to be many times the usual. Rather, the trick lay in choosing a woman of the correct sensibility. Candidates would need a degree of stenographic and typewriting skill, but what he most looked for and was so very adept at sensing was that alluring amalgam of isolation, weakness, and need. Jack the Ripper had found it in the impoverished whores of Whitechapel; Holmes saw it in transitional women, fresh clean young things free for the first time in history but unsure of what that freedom meant and of the risks it entailed. What he craved was possession and the power it gave him; what he adored was anticipation—the slow acquisition of love, then life, and finally the secrets within. The ultimate disposition of the material was irrelevant, a recreation. That he happened to have found a way to make disposal both efficient and profitable was simply a testament to his power.

In March fortune brought him the perfect acquisition. Her name was Minnie R. Williams. He had met her several years earlier during a stay in Boston and had considered acquiring her even then, but the distance was too great, the timing awkward. Now she had moved to Chicago. Holmes guessed that he himself might be part of the reason.

She would be twenty-five years old by now. Unlike his usual selections, she was plain, short, and plump, her weight somewhere between 140 and 150. She had a masculine nose, thick dark eyebrows, and virtually no neck. Her expression was bland, her cheeks full—"a baby face," as one witness put it. "She didn't seem to know a great deal."

In Boston, however, Holmes had discovered that she possessed other winning attributes.

⌐⚊⚊᠎

Born in Mississippi, Minnie Williams and her younger sister, Anna, were orphaned at an early age and sent to live with different uncles. Anna's new guardian was the Reverend Dr. W. C. Black, of Jackson, Mississippi, editor of the Methodist *Christian Advocate*. Minnie went to Texas, where her guardian-uncle was a successful businessman. He treated her well and in 1886 enrolled her at the Boston Academy of Elocution. He died in the midst of her three-year program and bequeathed to her an estate valued at between $50,000 and $100,000, (about $1.5 to $3 million in twenty-first-century dollars).

Anna, meanwhile, became a schoolteacher. She taught in Midlothian, Texas, at the Midlothian Academy.

When Holmes met Minnie, he was traveling on business under the alias Henry Gordon and found himself invited to a gathering at the home of one of Boston's leading families. Through various inquiries Holmes learned of Minnie's inheritance and of the fact that it consisted largely of a parcel of property in the heart of Fort Worth, Texas.

Holmes extended his Boston stay. Minnie called him Harry. He took her to plays and concerts and bought her flowers and books and sweets. Wooing her was pathetically easy. Each time he told her he had to return to Chicago, she seemed crushed, delightfully so. Throughout 1889 he traveled regularly to Boston and always swept Minnie into a whirl of shows and dinners, although what he looked forward to most were the days before his departure when her need flared like fire in a dry forest.

After a time, however, he tired of the game. The distance was too great, Minnie's reticence too profound. His visits to Boston became fewer, though he still responded to her letters with the ardor of a lover.

Holmes's absence broke Minnie's heart. She had fallen in love. His visits had thrilled her, his departures destroyed her. She was perplexed—he had seemed to be conducting a courtship and even urged her to abandon her studies and run with him to Chicago, but now he was gone and his letters came only rarely. She gladly would have left Boston under the flag of marriage, but not under the reckless terms he proposed. He would have made an excellent husband. He was affectionate in ways she rarely encountered in men, and he was adept at business. She missed his warmth and touch.

Soon there were no letters at all.

Upon graduation from the Academy of Elocution, Minnie moved to Denver, where she tried to establish her own theatrical company, and in the process lost $15,000. She still dreamed about Harry Gordon. As her theater company collapsed, she thought of him more and more. She dreamed also of Chicago, a city everyone seemed to be talking about and to which everyone seemed to be moving. Between Harry and the soon-to-begin World's Columbian Exposition, the city became irresistible to her.

202 • ERIK LARSON

She moved to Chicago in February 1893 and took a job as a stenographer for a law firm. She wrote to Harry to tell him of her arrival.

Harry Gordon called on her almost immediately and greeted her with tears in his eyes. He was so warm and affectionate. It was as if they had never parted. He suggested she come work for him as his personal stenographer. They could see each other every day, without having to worry about the interventions of Minnie's landlady, who watched them as if she were Minnie's own mother.

The prospect thrilled her. He still said nothing about marriage, but she could tell he loved her. And this was Chicago. Things were different here, less rigid and formal. Everywhere she went she found women her own age, unescorted, holding jobs, living their own lives. She accepted Harry's offer. He seemed delighted.

But he imposed a curious stipulation. Minnie was to refer to him in public as Henry Howard Holmes, an alias, he explained, that he had adopted for business reasons. She was never to call him Gordon, nor act surprised when people referred to him as Dr. Holmes. She could call him "Harry" at any time, however.

She managed his correspondence and kept his books, while he concentrated on getting his building ready for the world's fair. They dined together in his office, on meals brought in from the restaurant below. Minnie showed "a remarkable aptitude for the work," Holmes wrote in his memoir. "During the first weeks she boarded at a distance, but later, from about the 1st of March until the 15th of May, 1893, she occupied rooms in the same building and adjoining my offices."

Harry touched her and caressed her and let his eyes fill with tears of adoration. At last he asked her to marry him. She felt very lucky. Her Harry was so handsome and dynamic, she knew that once married they would share a wonderful life full of travel and fine possessions. She wrote of her hopes to her sister Anna.

In recent years the sisters had become very close, overcoming an earlier estrangement. They wrote to each other often. Minnie filled her letters with news of her fast-intensifying romance and expressed wonder that such a handsome man had chosen her to be his wife.

Anna was skeptical. The romance was advancing too quickly and with a degree of intimacy that violated all the intricate rules of courtship. Minnie was sweet, Anna knew, but certainly no beauty.

If Harry Gordon was such a paragon of looks and enterprise, why had he selected her?

In mid-March Holmes received a letter from Peter Cigrand, Emeline's father, asking yet again for help in finding his daughter. The letter was dated March 16. Holmes responded promptly, on March 18, with a typed letter in which he told Cigrand that Emeline had left his employ on December 1, 1892. It is possible that Minnie in her role as Holmes's personal secretary did the typing.

"I received her wedding cards about Dec. 10," he wrote. She had come to see him twice since her marriage, the last time being January 1, 1893, "at which point she was disappointed at not finding any mail here for her, and my impression is that she spoke of having written to you previous to that time. Before going away in December she told me personally that the intention was that she and her husband should go to England on business with which he was connected, but when she called here the last time she spoke as though the trip had been given up. Please let me know within a few days if you did not hear from her and give me her uncle's address here in the city and I will see him personally and ask if she has been there, as I know she was in the habit of calling upon him quite often."

He added a postscript in ink: "Have you written her Lafayette friends asking them if they have heard from her? If not I should think it well to do so. Let me hear from you at all events."

Holmes promised Minnie a voyage to Europe, art lessons, a fine home, and of course children—he adored children—but first there were certain financial matters that required their mutual attention. Assuring her that he had come up with a plan from which only great profit would result,

Holmes persuaded her to transfer the deed to her Fort Worth land to a man named Alexander Bond. She did so on April 18, 1893, with Holmes himself serving as notary. Bond in turn signed the deed over to another man, Benton T. Lyman. Holmes notarized this transfer as well.

Minnie loved her husband-to-be and trusted him, but she did not know that Alexander Bond was an alias for Holmes himself, or that Benton Lyman actually was Holmes's assistant Benjamin Pitezel—and that with a few strokes of his pen her beloved Harry had taken possession of the bulk of her dead uncle's bequest. Nor did she know that on paper Harry was still married to two other women, Clara Lovering and Myrta Belknap, and that in each marriage he had fathered a child.

As Minnie's adoration deepened, Holmes executed a second financial maneuver. He established the Campbell-Yates Manufacturing Company, which he billed as a firm that bought and sold everything. When he filed its papers of incorporation, he listed five officers: H. H. Holmes, M. R. Williams, A. S. Yates, Hiram S. Campbell, and Henry Owens. Owens was a porter employed by Holmes. Hiram S. Campbell was the fictive owner of Holmes's Englewood building. Yates was supposed to be a businessman living in New York City but in reality was as much a fiction as Campbell. And M. R. Williams was Minnie. The company made nothing and sold nothing: It existed to hold assets and provide a reference for anyone who became skeptical of Holmes's promissory notes.

Later, when questions arose as to the accuracy of the corporation papers, Holmes persuaded Henry Owens, the porter, to sign an affidavit swearing not only that he was secretary of the company but that he had met both Yates and Campbell and that Yates personally had handed him the stock certificates representing his share of the company. Owens later said of Holmes: "He induced me to make these statements by promising me my back wages and by his hypnotizing ways, and I candidly believe that he had a certain amount of influence over me. While I was with him I was always under his control."

He added, "I never received my back wages."

Holmes—Harry—wanted the wedding done quickly and quietly, just him, Minnie, and a preacher. He arranged everything. To Minnie the little ceremony appeared to be legal and in its quiet way very romantic, but in fact no record of their union was entered into the marriage registry of Cook County, Illinois.

Dreadful Things
Done by Girls

THROUGHOUT THE SPRING OF 1893 the streets of Chicago filled with unemployed men from elsewhere, but otherwise the city seemed immune to the nation's financial troubles. Preparations for the fair kept its economy robust, if artificially so. Construction of the Alley L extension to Jackson Park still provided work for hundreds of men. In the company town of Pullman, just south of Chicago, workers labored around the clock to fill backlogged orders for more cars to carry visitors to the fair, though the rate of new orders had fallen off sharply. The Union Stock Yards commissioned Burnham's firm to build a new passenger depot at its entrance, to manage the expected crush of fairgoers seeking a crimson break from the White City. Downtown, Montgomery Ward installed a new Customer's Parlor, where excursive fair visitors could loiter on soft couches while browsing the company's five-hundred-page catalog. New hotels rose everywhere. One entrepreneur, Charles Kiler, believed that once his hotel opened, "money would be so plentiful it would come a runnin' up hill to get into our coffers."

At Jackson Park exhibits arrived daily, in ever-mounting volume. There was smoke, clatter, mud, and confusion, as if an army were massing for an assault on Chicago. Caravans of Wells-Fargo and Adams Express wagons moved slowly through the park, drawn by gigantic horses. Throughout the night freight trains huffed into the park. Switching locomotives nudged individual boxcars over the skein of temporary tracks to their destinations. Lake freighters disgorged pale wooden crates emblazoned with phrases in strange alphabets. George Ferris's steel arrived, on five trains of thirty cars each. The Inman steamship line delivered a full-sized section of one of its ocean liners. Bethlehem Steel brought giant ingots and great slabs of military armor, including a curved plate seventeen inches thick meant for the gun turret of the dreadnought *Indiana.* Great Britain delivered locomotives and ship models, including an exquisite thirty-foot replica of Britain's latest warship, *Victoria,* so detailed that even the links of chain in its handrails were to scale.

From Baltimore came a long dark train that chilled the hearts of the men and women who monitored its passage across the prairie but delighted the innumerable small boys who raced open-jawed to the railbed. The train carried weapons made by the Essen Works of Fritz Krupp, the German arms baron, including the largest artillery piece until then constructed, capable of firing a one-ton shell with enough force to penetrate three feet of wrought-iron plate. The barrel had to be carried on a specially made car consisting of a steel cradle straddling two extra-long flatcars. An ordinary car had eight wheels; this combination had thirty-two. To ensure that the Pennsylvania Railroad's bridges could support the gun's 250,000-pound weight, two Krupp engineers had traveled to America the previous July to inspect the entire route. The gun quickly acquired the nickname "Krupp's Baby," although one writer preferred to think of it as Krupp's "pet monster."

A train with a more lighthearted cargo also headed for Chicago, this one leased by Buffalo Bill for his Wild West show. It carried a small army: one hundred former U.S. Cavalry soldiers, ninety-seven Cheyenne, Kiowa, Pawnee, and Sioux Indians, another fifty Cossacks and Hussars, 180 horses, eighteen buffalo, ten elk, ten mules, and a dozen other animals. It also carried Phoebe Anne Moses of Tiffin, Ohio, a young woman with a penchant for guns and an excellent sense of distance. Bill called her Annie, the press called her Miss Oakley.

At night the Indians and soldiers played cards.

Ships began converging on U.S. ports from all over the world bearing exposition cargoes of the most exotic kind. Sphinxes. Mummies. Coffee trees and ostriches. By far the most exotic cargo, however, was human. Alleged cannibals from Dahomey. Lapps from Lapland. Syrian horsemen. On March 9 a steamer named *Guildhall* set sail for New York from Alexandria, Egypt, carrying 175 bona-fide residents of Cairo recruited by an entrepreneur named George Pangalos to inhabit his Street in Cairo in the Midway Plaisance. In the *Guildhall*'s holds he stashed twenty donkeys, seven camels, and an assortment of monkeys and deadly snakes. His passenger list included one of Egypt's foremost practitioners of the *danse du ventre,* the young and lushly feminine Farida Mazhar, destined to become a legend in America. Pangalos had secured choice ground at the middle of the Midway, adjacent to the Ferris Wheel, in a Muslim diaspora that included a Persian concession, a Moorish palace, and Sol Bloom's Algerian Village, where Bloom had converted the Algerians' premature arrival into a financial windfall.

Bloom had been able to open his village as early as August 1892, well before Dedication Day, and within a month had covered his costs and begun reaping a generous profit. The Algerian version of the *danse du ventre* had proven a particularly powerful draw, once people realized the phrase meant "belly dance." Rumors spread of half-clad women jiggling away, when in fact the dance was elegant, stylized, and rather chaste. "The crowds poured in," Bloom said. "I had a gold mine."

With his usual flare for improvisation, Bloom contributed something else that would forever color America's perception of the Middle East. The Press Club of Chicago invited him to present a preview of the *danse du ventre* to its members. Never one to shun free publicity, Bloom accepted instantly and traveled to the club with a dozen of his dancers. On arrival, however, he learned that all the club had provided for music was a lone pianist who had no idea what kind of piece might accompany such an exotic dance.

Bloom thought a moment, hummed a tune, then plinked it out on the keyboard one note at a time:

Over the next century this tune and its variations would be deployed in a succession of mostly cheesy movies, typically as an accompaniment to the sinuous emergence of a cobra from a basket. It would also drive the schoolyard lyric, "And they wear no pants in the southern part of France."

Bloom regretted his failure to copyright the tune. The royalties would have run into the millions.

⌁

Sad news arrived from Zanzibar: There would be no Pygmies. Lieutenant Schufeldt was dead, of unclear causes.

⌁

There was advice, much of it of course from New York. The advice that rankled most came from Ward McAllister, factotum and chief slipperlick to Mrs. William Astor, empress of New York society. Appalled by the vision conjured by Chicago's Dedication Day, of crème and rabble mixing in such volume and with such indecorous propinquity, McCallister in a column in the *New York World* advised "it is not quantity but quality that the society people here want. Hospitality which includes the whole human race is not desirable."

He urged Chicago hostesses to hire some French chefs to improve their culinary diction. "In these modern days, society cannot get along without French chefs," he wrote. "The man who has been accustomed to delicate fillets of beef, terrapin pâté de foie gras, truffled turkey and things of that sort would not care to sit down to a boiled leg of mutton dinner with turnips." The thing is, McAllister was serious.

And there was more. "I should also advise that they do not frappé their wine too much. Let them put the bottle in the tub and be careful to keep the neck free from ice. For, the quantity of wine in the neck of the bottle being small, it will be acted upon by the ice first. In twenty-five minutes from the time of being placed in the tub it will be in a perfect condition to be served immediately. What I mean by a perfect condition is that when the wine is poured from the bottle it should contain little flakes of ice. That is a real frappé."

To which the *Chicago Journal* replied, "The mayor will not frappé his wine too much. He will frappé it just enough so the guests can blow the foam off the tops of the glasses without a vulgar exhibition of lung and lip power. His ham sandwiches, sinkers and Irish quail, better known in the Bridgeport vernacular as pigs' feet, will be triumphs of the gastronomic art." One Chicago newspaper called McAllister "A Mouse Colored Ass."

Chicago delighted in such repartee—for the most part. On some level, however, McAllister's remarks stung. McAllister was one particularly snooty voice, but it was clear to everyone that he spoke with the sanction of New York's blue bloods. Among Chicago's leading citizens there was always a deep fear of being second class. No one topped Chicago in terms of business drive and acumen, but within the city's upper echelons there was a veiled anxiety that the city in its commercial advance may indeed have failed to cultivate the finer traits of man and woman. The exposition was to be a giant white banner waved in Mrs. Astor's face. With its gorgeous classical buildings packed with art, its clean water and electric lights, and its overstaffed police department, the exposition was Chicago's conscience, the city it wanted to become.

Burnham in particular embodied this insecurity. Denied admission to Harvard and Yale and the "right" beginning, he had become a self-conscious connoisseur of fine things. He arranged recitals at his home and office and joined the best clubs and collected the best wines and was now leading the greatest nonmilitary campaign in the nation's history. Even so, the social columnists still did not write about his wife's dresses when he and she attended the opera, the way they described the nightly couture of *mesdames* Palmer, Pullman, and Armour. The fair was to be Burnham's redemption, and Chicago's. "Outside peoples already concede our material greatness and that we are well nigh supreme in manufactures and commerce," he wrote. "They do, however, claim that we are not cultivated and refined to the same extent. To remove this impression, the thought and work of this bureau has been mostly bent from the start."

Advice arrived also by the bookful. An author named Adelaide Hollingsworth chose to honor the fair with more than seven hundred pages of it, which she published early in the year under the title *The Columbia Cook Book*. Although her book did include compelling recipes for scrapple, ox cheek, and baked calf's head and tips for the preparation of raccoon, possum, snipe, plovers, and blackbirds (for blackbird pie) and "how to broil, fricassee, stew or fry a squirrel," it was much more than just a cookbook. Hollingsworth billed it as an overall guide to helping modern young housewives create a peaceful, optimistic, and sanitary household. The wife was to set the tenor of the day. "The breakfast table should not be a bulletin-board for the curing of horrible dreams and depressing symptoms, but the place where a bright key-note of the day is struck." In places Hollingsworth's advice revealed, by refraction, a certain Victorian raciness. In a segment on how best to wash silk underwear, she advised, "If the article is black, add a little ammonia, instead of acid to the rinsing water."

One of the most persistent problems of the day was "offensive feet," caused by the prevailing habit of washing feet only once a week. To combat this, Hollingsworth wrote, "Take one part muriatic acid to ten parts of water; rub the feet every night with this mixture before retiring to bed." To rid your mouth of the odor of onions, drink strong coffee. Oysters made the best rat-bait. To induce cream to whip, add a grain of salt. To keep milk sweet longer, add horseradish.

Hollingsworth offered sage medical advice—"Don't sit between a fever patient and a fire"—and provided various techniques for dealing with medical emergencies, such as accidental poisoning. Among a list of measures effective for inducing vomiting, she included: "Injections of tobacco into the anus through a pipe stem."

———

Jacob Riis, the New York journalist who had devoted himself to revealing the squalid housing of America's poor, came to Chicago bearing counsel of a graver sort. In March he gave a talk at Hull House, a reform settlement founded by Jane Addams, "Saint Jane." Hull House had become a bastion of progressive thought inhabited by strong-willed young women, "interspersed," as one visitor put it, "with earnest-faced, self-subordinating and mild-mannered men who slide from room to room apologetically." Clarence Darrow regularly walked the short distance from his office in the Rookery to Hull House, where he was admired for his intellect and social empathy but disparaged, privately, for his slovenly dress and less-than-exemplary hygiene.

At the time of Riis's talk, Riis and Addams were two of the best known people in America. Riis had toured Chicago's foulest districts and pronounced them worse than anything he had seen in New York. In his talk he noted the fast approach of the exposition and warned his audience, "You ought to begin house cleaning, so to speak, and get your alleys and streets in better condition; never in our worst season have we had so much filth in New York City."

In fact, Chicago had been trying to tidy itself for some time and had found the challenge monumental. The city stepped up its efforts to remove garbage and began repaving alleys and streets. It deployed smoke inspectors to enforce a new antismoke ordinance. Newspapers launched crusades against pestilent alleys and excess smoke and identified the worst offenders in print—among them Burnham's newly opened Masonic Temple, which the *Chicago Tribune* likened to Mount Vesuvius.

Carrie Watson, Chicago's foremost madam, decided her own operation merited a little sprucing up. Her place already was luxurious, with a bowling alley where the pins were bottles of chilled champagne, but now she resolved to increase the number of bedrooms and double her staff. She and other brothel owners anticipated a big spike in demand. They would not be disappointed. Nor, apparently, would their clients. Later, a madam named Chicago May recalled the boisterous year of the fair with a cringe: "What dreadful things were done by some of the girls! It always made me sick even to think of them. The mere mention of the details of some of the 'circuses' is unprintable. I think Rome at its worst had nothing on Chicago during those lurid days."

The man who helped make Chicago so hospitable to Carrie Watson and Chicago May, as well as to Mickey Finn and Bathhouse John Cough-

lin and a few thousand other operators of saloons and gambling dens, was
Carter Henry Harrison, whose four terms as mayor had gone a long way
to establish Chicago as a place that tolerated human frailty even as it nurtured grand ambition. After his failed run for the office in 1891, Harrison
had acquired a newspaper, the *Chicago Times,* and settled into the job of
editor. By the end of 1892, however, he had made it clear that he would
love to be the "Fair Mayor" and lead the city through its most glorious
time, but insisted that only a clear signal of popular demand could make
him actually enter the campaign. He got it. Carter H. Harrison Associations sprang up all over town, and now, at the start of 1893, Carter was
one of two candidates for the Democratic nomination, the other being
Washington Hesing, editor of the powerful German daily *Staats-Zeitung.*

Every newspaper in the city, other than his own *Times,* opposed
Harrison, as did Burnham and most of Chicago's leading citizens. To
Burnham and the others the new Chicago, as symbolized by the White
City rising in Jackson Park, required new leadership—certainly not
Harrison.

The city's legions of working men disagreed. They always had counted
Harrison as one of their own, "Our Carter," even though he was a plan-
tation-reared Kentucky man who had gone to Yale, spoke fluent French
and German, and recited lengthy passages from Shakespeare. He had
served four terms; that he should serve a fifth in the year of the fair
seemed fitting, and a wave of nostalgia swept the city's wards.

Even his opponents recognized that Harrison, despite his privileged
roots, made an intensely appealing candidate for the city's lesser tier. He
was magnetic. He was able and willing to talk to anyone about anything
and had a way of making himself the center of any conversation. "His
friends all noticed it," said Joseph Medill, once an ally but later Harrison's
most ardent opponent, "they would laugh or smile about it, and called it
'Carter Harrisonia.' " Even at sixty-eight Harrison exuded strength and
energy, and women generally agreed that he was more handsome now
than he had been in his fifties. Widowed twice, he was rumored to be
involved with a much younger woman. He had deep blue eyes with large
pupils and an unwrinkled face. He attributed his youthful aspect to a

heavy dose of morning coffee. His quirks made him endearing. He loved watermelon; when it was in season, he ate it at all three meals. He had a passion for shoes—a different pair each day of the week—and for silk underwear. Almost everyone had seen Harrison riding the streets on his white Kentucky mare, in his black slouch hat, trailing a plume of cigar smoke. At his campaign talks he often addressed his remarks to a stuffed eagle that he carried with him as a prop. Medill accused him of nurturing the city's basest instincts but also called him "the most remarkable man that our city has ever produced."

To the astonishment of the city's ruling class, 78 percent of the 681 delegates to the Democratic convention voted for Harrison on the first ballot. The Democratic elite implored the Republicans to come up with a candidate whom they too could support, anything to keep Harrison from returning to office. The Republicans chose Samuel W. Allerton, a rich packer from Prairie Avenue. The biggest and most powerful newspapers formed an explicit combine to back Allerton and undermine Harrison.

The ex-mayor countered their attacks with humor. During a talk before a large group of supporters at the Auditorium, Harrison called Allerton "a most admirable pig sticker and pig slaughterer. I admit it, and I don't arraign him because he slaughters the queen's English; he can't help it."

Harrison rapidly gained ground.

Patrick Prendergast, the young mad Irish immigrant, took pride in Harrison's renewed popularity and believed his own efforts at promoting the ex-mayor for reelection had had a lot do with the campaign's new momentum. An idea came to Prendergast. Just when it entered his brain he could not say, but it was there, and it gave him satisfaction. He had read extensively into law and politics and understood that political machines operated on a first principle of power: If you worked to advance the interests of the machine, the machine paid you back. Harrison was in his debt.

This notion came to Prendergast initially as a glimmer, like the first sunlight to strike the Masonic tower each morning, but now he thought of it a thousand times a day. It was his treasure and made him square his shoulders and raise his chin. When Harrison won, things would change. And Harrison *would* win. The great upwelling of enthusiasm in the wards seemed to assure Harrison's victory. Once elected, Prendergast believed, Harrison would offer him an appointment. He would have to. It was the law of the machine, as immutable as the forces that propelled the Chicago Limited across the prairie. Prendergast wanted to be corporation counsel. No more dealing with newsboys who did not know their place; no more walking in the yellow stew that bubbled between pavers; no more having to breathe the awful perfume of mortified horses left in the middle of the street. When Harrison took office, salvation would come to Patrick Prendergast.

The idea caused moments of exultation. Prendergast bought more postcards and sent exuberant notes to the men who soon would be his associates and clubmates—the judges, lawyers, and merchant princes of Chicago. He of course sent another card to his good friend Alfred S. Trude, the defense attorney.

"My Dear Mr. Trude," he began. He intended the next word to be "Hallelujah!" but certain words gave him trouble. In his fever to write, he plunged ahead.

"Allielliuia!" he wrote. "The attempt of the Herald gang to prevent the manifestation of the popular will has been checked—& Carter H. Harrison the popular choice will be our next mayor. The newspaper trust has been ingloriously sat down upon. What do I know about the candidacy of a Washington Hesing poor fellow—he has the 'tail end' of my sympathy. In his present trouble I hope it will not overcome him—& the noble newspaper trust. Glory to The Father Son & Holy Ghost!" He rambled on for a few more lines, then closed, "Friendship is the true test of character after all Sincerely,

"P. E. J. Prendergast."

Again something in the card drew Trude's attention. Many other recipients of Prendergast's cards also took note, despite the crush of mail each received from his true peers, this being a time when everyone who knew how to write did so and at length. In that glacier of words grinding toward the twentieth century, Prendergast's card was a single fragment of mica glinting with lunacy, pleading to be picked up and pocketed.

Once again Trude kept the letter.

In April 1893 the citizens of Chicago elected Carter Henry Harrison to his fifth term. In preparation for the fair, he ordered two hundred barrels of whiskey, to be used by his office in the entertainment of dignitaries.

He gave no thought whatsoever to Patrick Eugene Joseph Prendergast.

The Invitation

FOR THE MOMENT HOLMES held off on doing anything more with Minnie's property. Minnie had told her sister, Anna, of the transfer of the Fort Worth land, and now Holmes sensed that Anna was becoming suspicious of his true intentions. This did not trouble him, however. The solution was really quite simple.

One bright and fragrant spring day—as if on a wild equinoctial whim—Holmes suggested that Minnie invite her sister to Chicago to see the world's fair, at his expense.

Minnie was delighted and sent the good news to Anna, who immediately accepted. Holmes knew she would, for how could she have done otherwise? The chance to see Minnie was compelling in itself. Add Chicago and the great fair, and the combination became too alluring to turn down, no matter what Anna suspected about his and Minnie's relationship.

Minnie could hardly wait for the end of the school year, when her sister at last would be able to extricate herself from her duties at the Midlothian Academy. Minnie planned to show Anna all the wonders of Chicago—the skyscrapers, Marshall Field's store, the Auditorium, and of course the world's fair—but above all she looked forward to introducing Anna to her own personal wonder, Mr. Henry Gordon. Her Harry.

At last Anna would see that she could put her suspicions to rest.

Final Preparations

In THE FIRST TWO WEEKS of April 1893 the weather was gorgeous, but other cruelties abounded. Four exposition workers lost their lives, two from fractured skulls, two electrocuted. The deaths brought the year's total to seven. The exposition's union carpenters, aware of their great value in this final phase of construction, seized the moment and walked off the job, demanding a minimum union wage and other long-sought concessions. Only one of the eight towers of the Ferris Wheel was in place and workers had not yet completed repairs to the Manufactures and Liberal Arts Building. Each morning hundreds of men climbed to its roof; each evening they picked their way gingerly back down in a long dense line that from a distance resembled a column of ants. Frank Millet's "Whitewash Gang" worked furiously to paint the buildings of the Court of Honor. In places the staff coating already had begun to crack and chip. Patch crews patrolled the grounds. The air of "anxious effort" that suffused the park reminded Candace Wheeler, the designer hired to decorate the Woman's Building, "of an insufficiently equipped household preparing for visitors."

Despite the carpenters' strike and all the work yet to be done, Burnham felt optimistic, his mood bolstered by the fine weather. The winter had been deep and long, but now the air was scented with first blossoms and thawed earth. And he felt loved. In late March he had been feted at a grand banquet arranged largely by Charles McKim and held in New York at Madison Square Garden—the *old* Garden, an elegant Moorish structure designed by McKim's partner, Stanford White. McKim assigned Frank Millet to secure the attendance of the nation's finest painters, and these took their seats beside the most prominent writers and architects and the patrons who supported them all, men like Marshall Field and Henry Villard, and together they spent the night lauding Burnham—prematurely—for achieving the impossible. Of course, they ate like gods. The menu:

Blue Points à l'Alaska.

Sauternes.

POTAGES.

Consommé printanier. Crème de Celeri.

Amontillado.

HORS D'OEUVRES.

Rissoles Chateaubriand. Amandes salées. Olives, etc.

POISSON.

Bass rayée, sauce hollandaise. Pommes parisiennes.

Miersfeiner. Moet et Chandon. Perrier Jouet, Extra Dry Special.

REFEVE.

Filet de Boeuf aux champignons. Haricots verts. Pommes duchesse.

ENTRÉE.

Ris de Veau en cotelette. Petits Pois.

SORBET.

Romaine fantaisie. Cigarettes.

ROTI.

Canard de Tête Rouge. Salade de Laitue.

Pontet Canet.

DESSERT.

Petits Moules fantaisies. Gateaux assortis. Bonbons. Petits-fours.

Fruits assortis.

FROMAGES.

Roquefort et Camembert.

Café.

Apollinaris.

Cognac. Cordials. Cigars.

Newspapers reported that Olmsted also was present, but in fact he was in Asheville, North Carolina, continuing his work on Vanderbilt's estate. His absence prompted speculation that he had stayed away out of pique at not being invited to share the podium and because the invitation had identified the major arts only as painting, architecture, and sculpture, with no reference to landscape architecture. While it is true that Olmsted had struggled throughout his career to build respect for landscape architecture as a distinct branch of the fine arts, for him to shun the banquet because of hurt feelings would have been out of character. The simplest explanation seems best: Olmsted was ill, his work everywhere was behind schedule, he disliked ceremonies, and above all he loathed long-distance train travel, especially in transitional months when railcars, even the finest Pullman Palaces, were likely to be too hot or too cold. Had he attended, he would have heard Burnham tell the guests, "Each of you knows the name and genius of him who stands first in the heart and confidence of American artists, the creator of your own and many other city parks. He it is who has been our best advisor and our constant mentor. In the highest sense he is the planner of the Exposition, Frederick Law Olmsted. . . . An artist, he paints with lakes and wooded slopes; with lawns and banks and forest-covered hills; with mountain sides and ocean views. He should stand where I do tonight. . . ."

Which is not to say that Burnham wanted to sit down. He reveled in the attention and adored the engraved silver "loving cup" that was filled with wine and held to the lips of every man at the table—despite the prevalence in the city outside of typhoid, diphtheria, tuberculosis, and pneumonia. He knew the praise was premature, but the banquet hinted at the greater glory that would accrue to him at fair's end, provided of course the exposition met the world's elaborate expectations.

Without doubt huge progress had been made. The six grandest buildings of the exposition towered over the central court with an effect more dramatic and imposing than even he had imagined. Daniel Chester French's "Statue of the Republic"—nicknamed "Big Mary"—stood in the basin complete and gleaming, its entire surface gilded. Including plinth, the Republic was 111 feet tall. More than two hundred other buildings erected by states, corporations, and foreign governments stippled the surrounding acreage. The White Star Line had built a charming little temple at the northwest bank of the lagoon opposite the Wooded Island, with steps to the water. The monstrous guns of Krupp were in place in their pavilion on the lake south of the Court of Honor.

"The scale of the whole thing is more and more tremendous as the work proceeds," McKim wrote to Richard Hunt. A bit too tremendous, he noted cattily, at least in the case of the Manufactures and Liberal Arts Building. His own Agriculture Building, he wrote, "must suffer by comparison with its huge neighbor opposite, whose volume—215 feet high—off the main axis, is bound to swamp us and everything else around it." He told Hunt he had just spent two days with Burnham, including two nights at the shanty. "He is keeping up under his responsibilities and looking well, and we all owe him a great debt for his constant watchfulness and attention to our slightest wishes."

Even the carpenters' strike did not trouble Burnham. There seemed to be plenty of unemployed nonunion carpenters willing to step in for the absent strikers. "I fear nothing at all from this source," he wrote on April 6 in a letter to Margaret. The day was cold "but clear, bright and beautiful, a splendid day to live and work in." Workers were putting in "the embellishments," he wrote. "A lot of ducks were put in the lagoons yesterday, and they are floating around contentedly and quite like life this morning." Olmsted had ordered more than eight hundred ducks and geese, seven thousand pigeons, and for the sake of accent a number of exotic birds, including four snowy egrets, four storks, two brown pelicans, and two flamingoes. So far only the common white ducks had been introduced into the waters. "In two or three days," Burnham wrote, "all the birds will be in the water, which already commences to be still more beautiful than last year." The weather remained lovely: crisp, clear, and dry. On Monday, April 10, he told Margaret, "I am very happy."

Over the next few days his mood changed. There was talk that other unions might join the carpenters' strike and bring all work in Jackson Park to a halt. Suddenly the exposition seemed dangerously far from ready. Construction of the sheds for the stock exhibits at the south end of the grounds had yet to begin. Everywhere Burnham looked he saw rail tracks and temporary roads, empty boxcars and packing crates. Tumbleweeds of excelsior roved the grounds. He was disappointed with the unfinished appearance of the park, and he was peeved at his wife.

"Why do you not write me every day?" he asked on Thursday. "I look in vain for your letters."

He kept a photograph of Margaret in his office. Every time he walked by it, he picked it up and stared at it with longing. So far that day, he told her, he had looked at it ten times. He had counted on a rest after May 1 but realized now that the intensity would persist until long afterward. "The public will regard the work as entirely done, and I wish it were, so far as I am concerned. I presume anyone running a race has moments of half despair, along toward the end; but they must never be yielded to."

Margaret sent him a four-leafed clover.

⌐———————,

There was disarray in the fairgrounds, but not next door on the fifteen acres of ground leased by Buffalo Bill for his show, which now bore the official title "Buffalo Bill's Wild West and Congress of Rough Riders of the World." He was able to open his show on April 3 and immediately filled his eighteen-thousand-seat arena. Visitors entered through a gate that featured Columbus on one side, under the banner "PILOT OF THE OCEAN, THE FIRST PIONEER," and Buffalo Bill on the other, identified as "PILOT OF THE PRAIRIE, THE LAST PIONEER."

His show and camp covered fifteen acres. Its hundreds of Indians, soldiers, and workers slept in tents. Annie Oakley always made hers very homey, with a garden outside of primrose, geranium, and hollyhock. Inside she placed her couch, cougar skins, an Axminister carpet, rocking chairs, and assorted other artifacts of domestic life. And of course a diverse collection of guns.

Buffalo Bill always began his show with his Cowboy Band playing "The Star-Spangled Banner." Next came the "Grand Review," during which soldiers from America, England, France, Germany, and Russia paraded on horseback around his arena. Annie Oakley came next, blasting away at an array of impossible targets. She hit them. Another of the show's staples was an Indian attack on an old stagecoach, the Deadwood Mail Coach, with Buffalo Bill and his men coming to the rescue. (During the show's earlier engagement in London, the Indians attacked the coach as it raced across the grounds of Windsor Castle carrying four kings and the prince of Wales. Buffalo Bill drove.) Late in the program Cody himself demonstrated some fancy marksmanship, dashing around the arena on horseback while firing his Winchester at glass balls hurled into the air by his assistants. The climax of the show was the "Attack on a Settler's Cabin," during which Indians who once had slaughtered soldiers and civilians alike staged a mock attack on a cabin full of white settlers, only to be vanquished yet again by Buffalo Bill and a company of cowboys firing blanks. As the season advanced, Cody replaced the attack with the even more dramatic "Battle of the Little Big Horn . . . showing with historical accuracy the scene of Custer's Last Charge."

The fair was hard on Colonel Cody's marriage. The show always kept him away from his home in North Platte, Nebraska, but his absence wasn't the main problem. Bill liked women, and women liked Bill. One day his wife, Louisa—"Lulu"—traveled to Chicago for a surprise conjugal visit. She found that Bill's wife already had arrived. At the hotel's front desk a clerk told her she would now be escorted up to "Mr. and Mrs. Cody's suite."

Fearful that a wider strike could hobble the fair, even destroy it, Burnham began negotiations with the carpenters and ironworkers and agreed at last to establish a minimum wage and to pay time and a half for extra hours and double time for Sundays and key holidays, including, significantly, Labor Day. The union men, in turn, signed a contract to work until the end of the fair. Burnham's clear relief suggests that his earlier bravado might have been just for show. "You can imagine though tired I go to bed happy," he wrote to his wife. One measure of his exhaustion was the fact that the contorted syntax he usually worked so hard to suppress had now resurfaced. "We sat from early in the afternoon to nine o'clock. Till the fair is over this trial will not recur I believe, so your picture before me is unusually lovely as it looks up from the desk."

Burnham claimed the agreement was a victory for the exposition, but in fact the fair's concessions were a breakthrough for organized labor, and the resulting contracts became models for other unions to emulate. The fair's capitulation pumped steam into America's—and Chicago's—already-boiling labor movement.

—◦———◦—

Olmsted returned to Chicago accompanied by his usual troika of affliction and found the place galvanized, Burnham everywhere at once. On Thursday, April 13, Olmsted wrote to his son John, "Every body here in a keen rush, the greatest in imaginable outward confusion." Winds raced over the park's barren stretches and raised blizzards of dust. Train after train arrived bearing exhibits that should have been installed long before. The delayed installations meant that temporary tracks and roads had to remain in place. Two days later Olmsted wrote: "We shall have to bear the blame of everyone else's tardiness, as their operations are now everywhere in our way. At best the most important part of all our work will have to be done at night after the opening of the Exposition. I cannot see any way through the confusion but there are thousands of men at work under various chiefs & I suppose by & by the great labor will begin to tell together."

He assigned some of the blame for the incomplete landscape to himself, for failing to install a trustworthy overseer in Chicago after the death of Harry Codman. On April 15, 1893, he wrote to John, "I am afraid that we were wrong in leaving the business so much to Ulrich & Phil. Ulrich is not I hope intentionally dishonest but he is perverse to the point of deceiving & misleading us & cannot be depended on. His energy is largely exhausted on matters that he sh'd not be concerned with. . . . I cannot trust him from day to day."

His frustration with Ulrich grew, his distrust deepened. Later, in another note to John, he said, "Ulrich is unwittingly faithless to us. The difficulty is that he is ambitious of honors out of his proper line; cares more to be more extraordinarily active, industrious, zealous & generally useful, than to achieve fine results in L.A. [Landscape Architecture]." Olmsted grew especially leery of Ulrich's slavish attentiveness to Burnham. "He is all over the grounds, about all sorts of business, and Mr. Burnham & every head of Department is constantly calling for 'Ulrich!' In going over the works with Burnham I find him constantly repeating to his Secretary: 'Tell Ulrich to'—do this & that. I remonstrate, but it does little good. I can never find him at the work except by special appointment and then he is impatient to get away."

At heart what Olmsted feared was that Burnham had transferred his loyalty to Ulrich. "I suppose that our time is out—our engagement ended, and I fear that Burnham is disposed to let us go and depend on Ulrich—for Burnham is not competent to see the incompetency of Ulrich & the need of deliberate thought. I have to be cautious not to bore Burnham, who is, of course, enormously overloaded."

Other obstacles quickly appeared. An important shipment of plants from California failed to arrive, worsening an already critical shortage of all plants. Even the fine weather that prevailed in the first couple of weeks of April caused delays. The lack of rain and the fact that the park's water-works were not yet completed meant Olmsted could not plant exposed portions of the grounds. The wind-blown dust—"frightful dust," he said, "regular sandstorms of the desert"—continued and stung his eyes and propelled grit into his inflamed mouth. "I am trying to suggest why I seem to be accomplishing so little. . . ." he wrote. "I think the public for a time will be awfully disappointed with our work—dissatisfied & a strong hand will be required here for weeks to come to prevent Ulrich's energies from being wrongly directed."

By April 21 Olmsted was again confined to bed "with sore throat, an ulcerating tooth, and much pain preventing sleep."

Despite all this his spirits began slowly to improve. When he looked past the immediate delays and Ulrich's duplicity, he saw progress. The shore of the Wooded Island was just now beginning to burst forth in a dense profusion of new leaves and blossoms, and the Japanese temple, the Hoo-den, crafted in Japan and assembled by Japanese artisans, detracted little from the sylvan effect. The electric boats had arrived and were lovely, exactly what Olmsted had hoped for, and the waterfowl on the lagoons provided enchanting sparks of energy in counterpoint to the static white immensity of the Court of Honor. Olmsted recognized that Burnham's forces could not possibly finish patching and painting by May 1 and that his own work would be far from complete, but he saw clear improvement. "A larger force is employed," he wrote, "and every day's work tells."

Even this flicker of optimism was about to disappear, however, for a powerful weather front was moving across the prairie, toward Chicago.

During this period, the exact date unclear, a milk peddler named Joseph McCarthy stopped his cart near Chicago's Humboldt Park. It was morning, about eleven o'clock. A man in the park had caught his attention. He realized he knew the man: Patrick Prendergast, a newspaper distributor employed by the *Inter Ocean*.

The odd thing was, Prendergast was walking in circles. Odder still, he walked with his head tipped back and his hat pulled so low it covered his eyes.

As McCarthy watched, Prendergast walked face-first into a tree.

Rain began to fall. At first it did not trouble Burnham. It suppressed the dust that rose from the unplanted portions of the grounds—of which, he was disappointed to see, there were far too many—and by now all the roofs were finished, even the roof of the Manufactures and Liberal Arts Building.

"It rains," Burnham wrote to Margaret, on Tuesday, April 18, "and for the first time I say, let it. My roofs are in such good order at last, as to leaks we care little."

But the rain continued and grew heavier. At night it fell past the electric lights in sheets so thick they were nearly opaque. It turned the dust to mud, which caused horses to stagger and wagons to stall. And it found leaks. On Wednesday night a particularly heavy rain came pounding through Jackson Park, and soon a series of two-hundred-foot cataracts began tumbling from the glass ceiling of the Manufactures and Liberal Arts Building onto the exhibits below. Burnham and an army of workers and guards converged on the building and together spent the night fighting the leaks.

"Last night turned out the most terrible storm we have had in Jackson Park," Burnham wrote Margaret on Thursday. "No damage was done to the buildings on grounds except that the roofs of the Manufactures Building leaked on the east side, and we stayed there until midnight covering up goods. One of the papers says that Genl Davis was on hand and attending to things & that he never left the building till all was safe. Of course Mr. D had nothing whatever to do with it."

The rain seemed to bring into focus just how much work remained. That same Thursday Burnham wrote another letter to Margaret. "The weather is very bad here and has so continued since last Tuesday, but I keep right along although the most gigantic work lies before us. . . . The intensity of this last month is very great indeed. You can little imagine it. I am surprised at my own calmness under it all." But the challenge, he said, had tested his lieutenants. "The strain on them shows who is made of good metal and who is not. I can tell you that very few come right up to the mark under these conditions, but there are some who can be depended on. The rest have to be pounded every hour of the day, and they are the ones who make me tired."

As always, he longed for Margaret. She was out of the city but due back for the opening. "I will be on the look out for you, my dear girl," he wrote. "You must expect to give yourself up when you come."

For this buttoned-up age, for Burnham, it was a letter that could have steamed itself open.

Day after day the same thing: fogged windows, paper curled from ambient moisture, the demonic applause of rain on rooftops, and everywhere the stench of sweat and moist wool, especially in the workers' mess at lunch hour. Rain filled electrical conduits and shorted circuits. At the Ferris Wheel the pumps meant to drain the tower excavations ran twenty-four hours but could not conquer the volume of water. Rain poured through the ceiling of the Woman's Building and halted the installation of exhibits. In the Midway the Egyptians and Algerians and half-clothed Dahomans suffered. Only the Irish, in Mrs. Hart's Irish Village, seemed to take it in stride.

For Olmsted the rain was particularly disheartening. It fell on ground already saturated, and it filled every dip in every path. Puddles became lakes. The wheels of heavily loaded wagons sank deep into the mud and left gaping lacerations, adding to the list of wounds to be filled, smoothed, and sodded.

Despite the rain the pace of work increased. Olmsted was awed by the sheer numbers of workers involved. On April 27, three days before the opening, he reported to his firm, "I wrote you that there were 2,000 men employed—*foolishly.* There have been 2,000 men employed *directly* by Mr. Burnham. This week there are more than twice that number, *exclusive* of contractors forces. Including contractors and concessionaires' forces, there are now 10,000 men at work on the ground, and would be more if more of certain classes could be obtained. Our work is badly delayed because teams cannot be hired in sufficient numbers." (His estimate was low: In these closing weeks the total number of workers in the park was almost twenty thousand.) He was still desperately short of plants, he complained. "All resources for these seem to have failed and the want of them will be serious in its result."

His ulcerated tooth, at least, had improved, and he was no longer confined to bed. "My ulcer has shrunk," he wrote. "I still have to live on bread & milk but am going about in the rain today and getting better."

That same day, however, he wrote John a private and far bleaker letter. "We are having bad luck. Heavy rain again today." Burnham was pressuring him to take all manner of shortcuts to get the Court of Honor into presentable shape, such as having his men fill pots with rhododendrons and palms to decorate terraces, precisely the kind of showy transient measures that Olmsted disdained. "I don't like it at all," he wrote. He resented having "to resort to temporary expedients merely to make a poor show for the opening." He knew that immediately after the opening all such work would have to be redone. His ailments, his frustration, and the mounting intensity of the work taxed his spirits and caused him to feel older than his age. "The diet of the provisional mess table, the noise & scurry and the puddles and rain do not leave a dilapidated old man much comfort & my throat & mouth are still in such condition that I have to keep slopping victuals."

He did not give up, however. Despite the rain he jolted around the grounds to direct planting and sodding and every morning at dawn attended Burnham's mandatory muster of key men. The exertion and weather reversed the improvement in his health. "I took cold & was up all night with bone trouble and am living on toast & tea," he wrote on Friday, April 28. "Nearly constant heavy rain all the day, checking our work sadly." Yet the frenzy of preparations for Monday's opening continued unabated. "It is queer to see the painters at work on ladders & scaffolds in this heavy rain," Olmsted wrote. "Many are completely drenched and I should think their painting must be streaky." He noticed that the big Columbia Fountain at the western end of the central basin still was not finished, even though it was to be a key feature of the opening ceremony. A test was scheduled for the following day, Saturday. "It does not look ready by any means," Olmsted wrote, "but it is expected that it will play before the President next Monday."

As for the work under his own department, Olmsted was disappointed. He had hoped to accomplish far more by now. He knew, also, that others shared his disappointment. "I get wind of much misplaced criticism, by men as clever even as Burnham, because of impressions from incomplete work and undeveloped compositions," he wrote. He knew that in many places the grounds did look sparse and unkempt and that much work remained—anyone could see the gaps—but to hear about it from others, especially from a man whom he admired and respected, was profoundly depressing.

The deadline was immutable. Too much had been set in motion for anyone even to consider postponement. The opening ceremony was scheduled to begin, *would* begin, on Monday morning with a parade from the Loop to Jackson Park, led by the new president of the United States, Grover Cleveland. Train after train now entered Chicago bringing statesmen, princes, and tycoons from all over the world. President Cleveland arrived with his vice president and a retinue of cabinet officials, senators, and military leaders and their wives, children, and friends. The rain steamed off black locomotives. Porters hauled great trunks from the baggage cars. Caravans of water-slicked black carriages lined the streets outside the city's train stations, their red waiting lights haloed by the rain. The hours slipped past.

On the evening of April 30, the night before Opening Day, a British reporter named F. Herbert Stead visited the fairgrounds. The name Stead was well known in America because of Herbert's more famous brother, William, the former editor of London's *Pall Mall Gazette* and recent founder of *The Review of Reviews*. Assigned to cover the opening ceremony, Herbert decided to scout the grounds ahead of time to get a more detailed sense of the fair's topography.

It was raining hard when he exited his carriage and entered Jackson Park. Lights blazed everywhere as shawls of rain unfurled around them. The ponds that had replaced Olmsted's elegant paths shuddered under the impact of a billion falling droplets. Hundreds of empty freight cars stood black against the lights. Lumber and empty crates and the remains of workers' lunches lay everywhere.

The whole scene was heartbreaking but also perplexing: The fair's Opening Day celebration was set to begin the next morning, yet the grounds were clotted with litter and debris—in a state, Stead wrote, of "gross incompleteness."

The rain continued through the night.

Later that Sunday night, as rain thumped their windowsills, editors of Chicago's morning dailies laid out bold and elaborate headlines for Monday's historic editions. Not since the Chicago Fire of 1871 had the city's newspapers been so galvanized by a single event. But there was more quotidian work to be done as well. The more junior typesetters leaded and shimmed the classifieds and personals and all the other advertisements that filled the inside pages. Some that night worked on a small notice announcing the opening of a new hotel, clearly another hastily built affair meant to capitalize on the expected crush of exposition visitors. This hotel at least seemed to be well located—at Sixty-third and Wallace in Englewood, a short ride on the new Alley L from the fair's Sixty-third Street gate.

The owner called it the World's Fair Hotel.

PART III

In the White City

(May–October 1893)

The Court of Honor.

Opening Day

TWENTY-THREE GLEAMING BLACK CARRIAGES stood in the yellow mud of Michigan Avenue in front of the Lexington Hotel. President Cleveland boarded the seventh carriage, a landau. Burnham and Davis shared the sixth. Both men behaved, although they still had not shed their mutual distrust nor resolved their struggle for supreme control of the fair. The duke of Veragua, a direct descendent of Columbus, sat in the fourteenth carriage; the duchess occupied the fifteenth with Bertha Palmer, whose diamonds radiated an almost palpable heat. Mayor Harrison took the very last carriage and drew the loudest cheers. Assorted other dignitaries filled the remaining carriages. As the procession rumbled south along Michigan Avenue toward Jackson Park, the street behind became a following sea of 200,000 Chicagoans on foot and horseback, in phaetons, victorias, and stanhopes, and packed into omnibuses and streetcars. Many thousands of others boarded trains and jammed the bright yellow cars, dubbed "cattle cars," built by the Illinois Central to haul as many people as possible to the fair. Anyone with a white handkerchief waved it, and white flags hung from every lamppost. Damp bunting swelled from building façades. Fifteen hundred members of the Columbian Guard in their new uniforms of light blue sackcloth, white gloves, and yellow-lined black capes met the throng and cordially directed everyone to the Administration Building, recognizable by its lofty gold dome.

The procession approached the fair from the west, through the Midway Plaisance. Just as the president's carriage turned into the Avenue of Nations, which ran the thirteen-block length of the Midway, the sun emerged, igniting a roar of approval from spectators as it lit the forty concessions that lined the avenue, some the size of small towns. The carriages rolled past Sitting Bull's Cabin, the Lapland Village, the compound of the allegedly cannibalistic Dahomans, and, directly opposite, the California Ostrich Farm, redolent of simmering butter and eggs. The farm offered omelets made from ostrich eggs, though in fact the eggs came from domestic chickens. The procession passed the Austrian Village and Captive Balloon Park, where a hydrogen balloon tethered to the ground took visitors aloft. At the center of the Midway, the procession veered around the woefully incomplete Ferris Wheel, which Burnham eyed with displeasure. It was a half-moon of steel encased in a skyscraper of wooden falsework.

When President Cleveland's carriage came to Sol Bloom's Algerian Village, at the Muslim core of the Midway, Bloom gave a nod, and the women of the village dropped their veils. Bloom swore it was a customary gesture of respect, but of course with Bloom one could never be sure. The carriages skirted the Street in Cairo—not yet open, another disappointment—and passed the Turkish Village and the Java Lunch Room. Outside Hagenback's Animal Show, the most famous traveling zoo of the day, handlers prodded four trained lions into full roar. To the right, in the smoky distance, the president saw the banners of Buffalo Bill's Wild West flying over the arena Colonel Cody had built at Sixty-second Street.

At last the carriages entered Jackson Park.

There would be miracles at the fair—the chocolate Venus de Milo would not melt, the 22,000-pound cheese in the Wisconsin Pavilion would not mold—but the greatest miracle was the transformation of the grounds during the long soggy night that had preceded Cleveland's arrival. When Herbert Stead returned the next morning, a plain of wind-rippled water still covered portions of the park, but the empty boxcars and packing debris were gone. Ten thousand men working through the night had touched up the paint and staff and planted pansies and laid sod as a thousand scrubwomen washed, waxed, and polished the floors of the great buildings. As the morning advanced, the sun emerged more fully. In the bright rain-scrubbed air those portions of the landscape not still submerged looked cheerful, trim, and neat. "When the Fair opened," said Paul Starrett, one of Burnham's men, "Olmsted's lawns were the first amazement."

At eleven o'clock President Cleveland ascended the stairs to the speakers' platform, erected outside at the east end of the Administration Building, and took his seat, the signal for the ceremony to begin. The crowd surged forward. Twenty women fainted. Reporters lucky enough to be in the front rows rescued one elderly woman by hauling her over a railing and laying her out on a press table. Members of the Guard waded in with swords drawn. Mayhem reigned until Director-General Davis signaled the orchestra to begin playing the introductory "Columbian March."

Chastened by criticism of the stupefying length of October's Dedication Day ceremony, the fair's officers had kept the Opening Day program short and pledged to honor the timetable at all costs. First came a blessing, given by a blind chaplain to an audience made deaf by size and distance. Next came a poetic ode to Columbus that was as long and difficult to endure as the admiral's voyage itself: "Then from the *Pinta*'s foretop fell a cry, a trumpet song, 'Light ho! Light ho! Light!' "

That kind of thing.

Director-General Davis spoke next and offered a meaty helping of distorted reality, praising the way the National Commission, the Exposition Company, and the Board of Lady Managers had worked together without strife to produce such a brilliant exposition. Those privy to the warfare within and between these agencies watched Burnham closely but saw no change in his expression. Davis offered the podium to the president.

Cleveland, immense in black, paused a moment in sober examination of the crowd before him. Nearby stood a table draped in an American flag, on top of which lay a blue and red velvet pillow supporting a telegraph key made of gold.

Every bit of terrace, lawn, and railing in the Court of Honor was occupied, the men in black and gray, many of the women in gowns of extravagant hues—violet, scarlet, emerald—and wearing hats with ribbons, sprigs, and feathers. A tall man in a huge white hat and a white buckskin coat heavily trimmed in silver stood a full head above the men around him: Buffalo Bill. Women watched him. Sunlight fell between tufts of fast-shredding cloud and lit the white Panamas that flecked the audience. From the president's vantage point the scene was festive and crisp, but at ground level there was water and mud and the mucid sucking that accompanied any shift in position. The only human form with dry feet was that of Daniel Chester French's Statue of the Republic—Big Mary—which stood hidden under a silo of canvas.

Cleveland's speech was the shortest of all. As he concluded, he moved to the flag-draped table. "As by a touch the machinery that gives light to this vast Exposition is set in motion," he said, "so at the same instant let our hopes and aspirations awaken forces which in all time to come shall influence the welfare, the dignity, and the freedom of mankind."

At precisely 12:08 he touched the gold key. A roar radiated outward as successive strata of the crowd learned that the key had been pressed. Workmen on rooftops immediately signaled to peers stationed throughout the park and to sailors aboard the warship *Michigan* anchored in the lake. The key closed an electric circuit that activated the Electro-Automatic Engine Stop and Starter attached to the giant three-thousand-horsepower Allis steam engine at the Machinery Building. The starter's silver-plated gong rang, a sprocket turned, a valve opened, and the engine whooshed to life on exquisitely machined shafts and bearings. Immediately thirty other engines in the building began to thrum. At the fair's waterworks three huge Worthington pumps began stretching their shafts and pistons, like praying mantises shaking off the cold. Millions of gallons of water began surging through the fair's mains. Engines everywhere took steam until the ground trembled. An American flag the size of a mainsail unfurled from the tallest flagpole in the Court of Honor, and immediately two more like-sized flags tumbled from flanking poles, one representing Spain, the other Columbus. Water pressurized by the Worthington pumps exploded from the MacMonnies Fountain and soared a hundred feet into the sky, casting a sheet rainbow across the sun and driving visitors to raise their umbrellas against the spray. Banners and flags and gonfalons suddenly bellied from every cornice, a huge red banner unscrolled along the full length of the Machinery Building, and the canvas slipped from Big Mary's gold-leaf shoulders. Sunlight clattering from her skin caused men and women to shield their eyes. Two hundred white doves leaped for the sky. The guns of the *Michigan* fired. Steam whistles shrieked. Spontaneously the throng began to sing "My Country 'Tis of Thee," which many thought of as the national anthem although no song had yet received that designation. As the crowd thundered, a man eased up beside a thin, pale woman with a bent neck. In the next instant Jane Addams realized her purse was gone.

The great fair had begun.

Although Burnham recognized that much work lay ahead—that Olmsted had to redouble his efforts and Ferris needed to finish that damned wheel—the success of the exposition now seemed assured. Congratulations arrived by telegraph and post. A friend told Burnham, "The scene burst on me with the beauty of a full blown rose." The official history of the fair estimated that a quarter of a million people packed Jackson Park on Opening Day. Two other estimates put the total at 500,000 and 620,000. By day's end there was every indication that Chicago's fair would become the most heavily attended entertainment in the history of the world.

This optimism lasted all of twenty-four hours.

On Tuesday, May 2, only ten thousand people came to Jackson Park, a rate of attendance that, if continued, would guarantee the fair a place in history as one of the greatest failures of all time. The yellow cattle cars were mostly empty, as were the cars of the Alley L that ran along Sixty-third Street. All hope that this was merely an anomaly disappeared the next day, when the forces that had been battering the nation's economy erupted in a panic on Wall Street that caused stock prices to plummet. Over the next week the news grew steadily more disturbing.

On the night of Thursday, May 5, officials of the National Cordage Company, a trust that controlled 80 percent of America's rope production, placed itself in receivership. Next Chicago's Chemical National Bank ceased operation, a closure that seemed particularly ominous to fair officials because Chemical alone had won congressional approval to open a branch at the world's fair, in no less central a location than the Administration Building. Three days later another large Chicago bank failed, and soon after that a third, the Evanston National Bank, in Burnham's town. Dozens of other failures occurred around the country. In Brunswick, Georgia, the presidents of two national banks held a meeting. One president calmly excused himself, entered his private office, and shot himself through the head. Both banks failed. In Lincoln, Nebraska, the Nebraska Savings Bank had become the favorite bank of schoolchildren. The town's teachers served as agents of the bank and every week collected money from the children for deposit in each child's passbook account. Word that the bank was near failure caused the street out front to fill with children pleading for their money. Other banks came to Nebraska Savings' rescue, and the so-called "children's run" was quelled.

People who otherwise might have traveled to Chicago to see the fair now stayed home. The terrifying economy was discouraging enough, but so too were reports of the unfinished character of the fair. If people had only one chance to go, they wanted to do it when all the exhibits were in place and every attraction was in operation, especially the Ferris Wheel, said to be a marvel of engineering that would make the Eiffel Tower seem like a child's sculpture—provided it ever actually worked and did not collapse in the first brisk wind.

Too many features of the fair remained unfinished, Burnham acknowledged. He and his brigade of architects, draftsmen, engineers, and contractors had accomplished so much in an impossibly short time, but apparently not enough to overcome the damping effect of the fast-degrading economy. The elevators in the Manufactures and Liberal Arts Building, touted as one of the wonders of the fair, still had not begun operation. The Ferris Wheel looked only half finished. Olmsted had yet to complete grading and planting the grounds around the Krupp Pavilion, the Leather

Building, and the Cold Storage Building; he had not yet laid the brick pavement at the fair's train station or sodded the New York Central exhibit, the Pennsylvania Railroad exhibit, Choral Hall, and the Illinois State Building, which to many Chicagoans was the single most important building at the fair. The installation of exhibits and company pavilions within the Electricity Building was woefully behind schedule. Westinghouse only began building its pavilion on Tuesday, May 2.

Burnham issued stern directives to Olmsted and Ferris and to every contractor still at work. Olmsted in particular felt the pressure but also felt hobbled by the persistent delays in installation of exhibits and the damage done by the repeated comings and goings of drays and freight cars. General Electric alone had fifteen carloads of exhibit materials stored on the grounds. Preparations for the Opening Day ceremony had cost Olmsted's department valuable time, as did the planting and grading required to repair the damage the day's crowd had inflicted throughout the park. Many of the fair's fifty-seven miles of roadway were still either submerged or coated with mud, and others had been gouged and trenched by vehicles that had used the roads while they were still sodden. Olmsted's road contractor deployed a force of eight hundred men and one hundred teams of horses to begin regrading the roads and laying new gravel. "I remain fairly well," Olmsted wrote to his son, on May 15, "but get horribly tired every day. It is hard to get things done; my body is so overworked, and I constantly fail to accomplish what I expect to do."

First and foremost, Burnham knew, the fair had to be *finished,* but in the meantime lures had to be cast to encourage people to shed their fears of financial ruin and come to Chicago. He created the new post of director of functions and assigned Frank Millet to the job, giving him wide latitude to do what he could to boost attendance. Millet orchestrated fireworks shows and parades. He set aside special days to honor individual states and nations and to fete distinct groups of workers, including cobblers, millers, confectioners, and stenographers. The Knights of Pythias got their own day, as did the Catholic Knights of America. Millet set August 25 as Colored People Fete Day, and October 9 as Chicago Day. Attendance began to increase, but not by much. By the end of May the daily average of paying visitors was only thirty-three thousand, still far below what Burnham and everyone else had expected and, more to the point, far below the level required to make the fair profitable. Worse yet, Congress and the National Commission, bowing to pressure from the Sabbatarian movement, had ordered the fair closed on Sundays, thus withdrawing its wonders from a few million wage-earners for whom Sunday was the only day off.

Burnham hoped for an early cure to the nation's financial malaise, but the economy did not oblige. More banks failed, layoffs increased, industrial production sagged, and strikes grew more violent. On June 5 worried depositors staged runs on eight Chicago banks. Burnham's own firm saw the flow of new commissions come to a halt.

The World's Fair Hotel

THE FIRST GUESTS BEGAN ARRIVING at Holmes's World's Fair Hotel, though not in the volume he and every other South Side hotelier had expected. The guests were drawn mainly by the hotel's location, with Jackson Park a short trip east on the Sixty-third Street leg of the Alley L. Even though the rooms on Holmes's second and third floors were largely empty, when male visitors asked about accommodations Holmes told them with a look of sincere regret that he had no vacancies and kindly referred them to other hotels nearby. His guest rooms began to fill with women, most quite young and apparently unused to living alone. Holmes found them intoxicating.

Minnie Williams's continual presence became increasingly awkward. With the arrival of each dewy new guest, she became more jealous, more inclined to stay close to him. Her jealousy did not particularly annoy him. It simply became inconvenient. Minnie was an asset now, an acquisition to be warehoused until needed, like cocooned prey.

Holmes checked newspaper advertisements for a rental flat far enough from his building to make impromptu visits unlikely. He found a place on the North Side at 1220 Wrightwood Avenue, a dozen or so blocks west of Lincoln Park, near Halsted. It was a pretty, shaded portion of the city, though its prettiness was to Holmes merely an element to be entered into his calculations. The flat occupied the top floor of a large private house owned by a man named John Oker, whose daughters managed its rental. They first advertised the flat in April 1893.

Holmes went alone to examine the apartment and met John Oker. He introduced himself as Henry Gordon and told Oker he was in the real estate business.

Oker was impressed with this prospective tenant. He was neat—maybe fastidious was the better word—and his clothing and behavior suggested financial well-being. Oker was delighted when Henry Gordon said he would take the apartment; even more delighted when Gordon paid him forty dollars, cash, in advance. Gordon told Oker he and his wife would arrive in a few weeks.

Holmes explained the move to Minnie as a long-overdue necessity. Now that they were married, they needed a bigger, nicer place than what they currently occupied in the castle. Soon the building would be bustling with visitors to the fair. Even without the guests, however, it was no place to raise a family.

The idea of a large, sunny flat did appeal to Minnie. Truth was, the castle could be gloomy. Was always gloomy. And Minnie wanted everything as perfect as possible for Anna's visit. She was a bit perplexed, however, as to why Harry would choose a place so far away, on the North Side, when there were so many lovely homes in Englewood. She reasoned, perhaps, that he did not want to pay the exorbitant rents that everyone was charging now that the world's fair was under way.

Holmes and Minnie moved into the new flat on June 1, 1893. Lora Oker, the owner's daughter, said Gordon "seemed to be very attentive to his wife." The couple went on bicycle rides and for a time kept a hired girl. "I can only say that his behavior was all that could be wished during his sojourn with us," Miss Oker said. "Minnie Williams he introduced as his wife and we always addressed her as 'Mrs. Gordon.' She called him 'Henry.' "

With Minnie housed on Wrightwood Avenue, Holmes found himself free to enjoy his World's Fair Hotel.

His guests spent most of their time at Jackson Park or on the Midway and often did not return until after midnight. While present in the hotel they tended to stay in their rooms, since Holmes provided none of the common areas—the libraries, game parlors, and writing rooms—that the big hotels like the Richelieu and Metropole and the nearby New Julien offered as a matter of routine. Nor did he supply the darkroom facilities that hotels closest to Jackson Park had begun installing to serve the growing number of amateur photographers, so-called "Kodak fiends," who carried the newest portable cameras.

The women found the hotel rather dreary, especially at night, but the presence of its handsome and clearly wealthy owner helped dispel some of its bleakness. Unlike the men they knew back in Minneapolis or Des Moines or Sioux Falls, Holmes was warm and charming and talkative and touched them with a familiarity that, while perhaps offensive back home, somehow seemed all right in this new world of Chicago—just another aspect of the great adventure on which these women had embarked. And what good was an adventure if it did not feel a little dangerous?

As best anyone could tell, the owner also was a forgiving soul. He did not seem at all concerned when now and then a guest checked out without advance notice, leaving her bills unpaid. That he often smelled vaguely of chemicals—that in fact the building as a whole often had a medicinal odor—bothered no one. He was, after all, a physician, and his building had a pharmacy on the ground floor.

Prendergast

PATRICK PRENDERGAST BELIEVED HIS APPOINTMENT as corporation counsel was about to occur. He wanted to be ready and began making plans for how to staff his office once the appointment came through. On May 9, 1893, he got out another of his postcards and addressed it to a man named W. F. Cooling, in the *Staats-Zeitung* Building. Prendergast lectured Cooling on the fact that Jesus was the ultimate legal authority, then gave him the good news.

"I am candidate for corporation counsel," he wrote. "If I become corporation counsel you shall be my assistant."

Night Is the Magician

DESPITE ITS INCOMPLETE EXHIBITS, rutted paths, and stretches of unplanted ground, the exposition revealed to its early visitors a vision of what a city could be and ought to be. The Black City to the north lay steeped in smoke and garbage, but here in the White City of the fair visitors found clean public bathrooms, pure water, an ambulance service, electric streetlights, and a sewage-processing system that yielded acres of manure for farmers. There was daycare for the children of visitors, and much fun was made of the fact that when you left your child at the Children's Building, you received a claim check in return. Chicago's small but vocal censorians feared that impoverished parents would turn the building into a depository for unwanted children. Only one child, poor Charlie Johnson, was ever thus abandoned, and not a single child was lost, although anxiety invested the closing moments of each day.

Within the fair's buildings visitors encountered devices and concepts new to them and to the world. They heard live music played by an orchestra in New York and transmitted to the fair by long-distance telephone. They saw the first moving pictures on Edison's Kinetoscope, and they watched, stunned, as lightning chattered from Nikola Tesla's body. They saw even more ungodly things—the first zipper; the first-ever all-electric kitchen, which included an automatic dishwasher; and a box purporting to contain everything a cook would need to make pancakes, under the brand name Aunt Jemima's. They sampled a new, oddly flavored gum called Juicy Fruit, and caramel-coated popcorn called Cracker Jack. A new cereal, Shredded Wheat, seemed unlikely to succeed— "shredded doormat," some called it—but a new beer did well, winning the exposition's top beer award. Forever afterward, its brewer called it

Pabst Blue Ribbon. Visitors also encountered the latest and arguably most important organizational invention of the century, the vertical file, created by Melvil Dewey, inventor of the Dewey Decimal System. Sprinkled among these exhibits were novelties of all kinds. A locomotive made of spooled silk. A suspension bridge built out of Kirk's Soap. A giant map of the United States made of pickles. Prune makers sent along a full-scale knight on horseback sculpted out of prunes, and the Avery Salt Mines of Louisiana displayed a copy of the Statue of Liberty carved from a block of salt. Visitors dubbed it "Lot's Wife."

One of the most compelling, and chilling, exhibits was the Krupp Pavilion, where Fritz Krupp's "pet monster" stood at the center of an array of heavy guns. A popular guide to the fair, called the Time-Saver, rated every exhibit on a scale of one to three, with one being merely "interesting" and three being "remarkably interesting," and gave the Krupp Pavilion a three. For many visitors, however, the weapons were a disturbing presence. Mrs. D. C. Taylor, a frequent visitor to the fair, called Krupp's biggest gun "a fearful hideous thing, breathing of blood and carnage, a triumph of barbarism crouching amid the world's triumphs of civilization."

Mrs. Taylor adored the Court of Honor and was struck by the oddly sober manner people adopted as they walked among its palaces. "Every one about us moved softly and spoke gently. No one seemed hurried or impatient, all were under a spell, a spell that held us from the opening of the fair until its close."

In the Midway she found a very different atmosphere. Here Mrs. Taylor ventured into the Street in Cairo, open at last, and witnessed her first belly dance. She watched the dancer carefully. "She takes a few light steps to one side, pauses, strikes the castanets, then the same to the other side; advances a few steps, pauses, and causes her abdomen to rise and fall several times in exact time to the music, without moving a muscle in any other part of her body, with incredible rapidity, at the same time holding her head and feet perfectly rigid."

As Mrs. Taylor and her companions left the Street, she sang quietly to herself, "My Country 'Tis of Thee," like a frightened child easing past a graveyard.

The fair was so big, so beyond grasp, that the Columbian Guards found themselves hammered with questions. It was a disease, rhetorical smallpox, and every visitor exhibited it in some degree. The Guards answered the same questions over and over, and the questions came fast, often with an accusatory edge. Some questions were just odd.

"In which building is the pope?" one woman asked. She was overheard by writer Teresa Dean, who wrote a daily column from the fair.

"The pope is not here, madame," the guard said.

"Where is he?"

"In Italy, Europe, madame."

The woman frowned. "Which way is that?"

Convinced now that the woman was joking, the guard cheerfully quipped, "Three blocks under the lagoon."

She said, "How do I get there?"

Another visitor, hunting for an exhibit of wax figures, asked a guard, "Can you tell me where the building is that has the artificial human beings?"

He began telling her he did not know, when another visitor jumped in. "I have heard of them," he said. "They are over in the Woman's Building. Just ask for the Lady Managers."

One male visitor, who had lost both his legs and made his way around the fair on false limbs and crutches, must have looked particularly knowledgeable, because another visitor peppered him incessantly with questions, until finally the amputee complained that the strain of answering so many questions was wearing him out.

"There's just one more thing I'd like to know," his questioner said, "and I'll not trouble ye anymore."

"Well, what is it?"

"I'd like to know how you lost your legs."

The amputee said he would answer only on strict condition that this was indeed the last question. He would allow no others. Was that clear?

His persecutor agreed.

The amputee, fully aware that his answer would raise an immediate corollary question, said, "They were bit off."

"*Bit off.* How—"

But a deal was a deal. Chuckling, the amputee hobbled away.

—◦—

As the fair fought for attendance, Buffalo Bill's Wild West drew crowds by the tens of thousands. If Cody had gotten the fair concession he had asked for, these crowds first would have had to pay admission to Jackson Park and would have boosted the fair's attendance and revenue to a welcome degree. Cody also was able to hold performances on Sundays and, being outside the fairgrounds, did not have to contribute half his revenue to the Exposition Company. Over the six months of the fair an average of twelve thousand people would attend each of Cody's 318 performances, for a total attendance of nearly four million.

Often Cody upstaged the fair. His main entrance was so close to one of the busiest exposition gates that some visitors thought his show *was* the world's fair, and were said to have gone home happy. In June a group of cowboys organized a thousand-mile race from Chadron, Nebraska, to Chicago, in honor of the fair and planned to end it in Jackson Park. The prize was a rich one, $1,000. Cody contributed another $500 and a fancy saddle on condition the race end in his own arena. The organizers accepted.

Ten riders, including "Rattlesnake" Pete and a presumably reformed Nebraska bandit named Doc Middleton, set out from the Baline Hotel in Chadron on the morning of June 14, 1893. The rules of the race allowed each rider to start with two horses and required that he stop at various checkpoints along the way. The most important rule held that when he crossed the finish line, he had to be riding one of the original horses.

The race was wild, replete with broken rules and injured animals. Middleton dropped out soon after reaching Illinois. Four others likewise failed to finish. The first rider across the line was a railroad man named John Berry, riding Poison, who galloped into the Wild West arena on

June 27 at nine-thirty in the morning. Buffalo Bill, resplendent in white buckskin and silver, was there to greet him, along with the rest of the Wild West company and ten thousand or so residents of Chicago. John Berry had to settle for the saddle alone, however, for subsequent investigation revealed that shortly after the start of the race he had loaded his horses on an eastbound train and climbed aboard himself to take the first hundred miles in comfort.

Cody upstaged the fair again in July, when exposition officials rejected a request from Mayor Carter Harrison that the fair dedicate one day to the poor children of Chicago and admit them at no charge. The directors thought this was too much to ask, given their struggle to boost the rate of paid admission. Every ticket, even half-price children's tickets, mattered. Buffalo Bill promptly declared Waif's Day at the Wild West and offered any kid in Chicago a free train ticket, free admission to the show, and free access to the whole Wild West encampment, plus all the candy and ice cream the children could eat.

Fifteen thousand showed up.

Buffalo Bill's Wild West may indeed have been an "incongruity," as the directors had declared in rejecting his request for a concession within Jackson Park, but the citizens of Chicago had fallen in love.

The skies cleared and stayed clear. Roadways dried, and newly opened flowers perfumed the air. Exhibitors gradually completed their installations, and electricians removed the last misconnects from the elaborate circuits that linked the fair's nearly 200,000 incandescent bulbs. Throughout the fairgrounds, on Burnham's orders, clean-up efforts intensified. On June 1, 1893, workers removed temporary railroad tracks that had scarred the lawns near the lagoon and just south of the Electricity and Mines buildings. "A strikingly noticeable change in the general condition of things is the absence of large piles of boxes stacked up in the exterior courts around Manufactures, Agriculture, Machinery, and other large buildings," the *Tribune* reported on June 2. Unopened crates and rubbish that just one week earlier had cluttered the interior of the

Manufactures and Liberal Arts Building, particularly at the pavilions erected by Russia, Norway, Denmark, and Canada, likewise had been removed, and now these spaces presented "an entirely different and vastly improved appearance."

Although such interior exhibits were compelling, the earliest visitors to Jackson Park saw immediately that the fair's greatest power lay in the strange gravity of the buildings themselves. The Court of Honor produced an effect of majesty and beauty that was far greater than even the dream conjured in the Rookery library. Some visitors found themselves so moved by the Court of Honor that immediately upon entering they began to weep.

No single element accounted for this phenomenon. Each building was huge to begin with, but the impression of mass was amplified by the fact that all the buildings were neoclassical in design, all had cornices set at the same height, all had been painted the same soft white, and all were so shockingly, beautifully unlike anything the majority of visitors ever had seen in their own dusty hometowns. "No other scene of man's creation seemed to me so perfect as this Court of Honor," wrote James Fullerton Muirhead, an author and guidebook editor. The court, he wrote, "was practically blameless; the aesthetic sense of the beholder was as fully and unreservedly satisfied as in looking at a masterpiece of painting or sculpture, and at the same time was soothed and elevated by a sense of amplitude and grandeur such as no single work of art could produce." Edgar Lee Masters, Chicago attorney and emerging poet, called the Court "an inexhaustible dream of beauty."

The shared color, or more accurately the shared absence of color, produced an especially alluring range of effects as the sun traveled the sky. In the early morning, when Burnham conducted his inspections, the buildings were a pale blue and seemed to float on a ghostly cushion of ground mist. Each evening the sun colored the buildings ochre and lit the motes of dust raised by the breeze until the air itself became a soft orange veil.

One such evening Burnham led a tour of the fair aboard an electric launch for a group that included John Root's widow, Dora, and a number of foreign emissaries. Burnham loved escorting friends and dignitaries through the grounds but sought always to orchestrate the journeys so that his friends saw the fair the way he believed it should be seen, with the buildings presented from a certain perspective, in a particular order, as if he were still back in his library showing drawings instead of real structures. He had tried to impose his aesthetic will on all the fair's visitors by insisting during the first year of planning that the number of entrances to Jackson Park be limited to a few and that these be situated so that people had to enter first through the Court of Honor, either through a large portal at the rail station on the west side of the park or an entry on the east from the exposition wharf. His quest to create a powerful first impression was good showmanship, but it also exposed the aesthetic despot residing within. He did not get his way. The directors insisted on many gates, and the railroads refused to channel their exposition traffic through a single depot. Burnham never quite surrendered. Throughout the fair, he said, "we insisted on sending our *own* guests whose opinions we specially valued into the Grand Court first."

The electric launch carrying Burnham, Dora Root, and the foreign dignitaries cut silently through the lagoon, scattering the white city reflected upon its surface. The setting sun gilded the terraces on the east bank but cast the west bank into dark blue shadow. Women in dresses of crimson and aquamarine walked slowly along the embankments. Voices drifted across the water, laced now and then with laughter that rang like crystal touched in a toast.

The next day, after what surely had been a difficult night, Dora Root wrote to Burnham to thank him for the tour and to attempt to convey the complexity of her feelings.

"Our hour on the lagoon last evening proved the crown of a charming day," she wrote. "Indeed I fear we would have lingered on indefinitely had not our foreign friends prepared a more highly spiced entertainment. I think I should never willingly cease drifting in that dreamland." The scenes elicited conflicting emotions. "I find it all infinitely sad," she wrote, "but at the same time so entrancing, that I often feel as if it would be the part of wisdom to fly at once to the woods or mountains where one can always find peace. There is much I long to say to you about your work of the past two years—which has brought about this superb realization of John's vision of beauty—but I cannot trust myself. It means too much to me and I think, I hope, you understand. For years his hopes and ambitions were mine, and in spite of my efforts the old interests still go on. It is a relief to me to write this. I trust you will not mind."

<hr />

If evenings at the fair were seductive, the nights were ravishing. The lamps that laced every building and walkway produced the most elaborate demonstration of electric illumination ever attempted and the first large-scale test of alternating current. The fair alone consumed three times as much electricity as the entire city of Chicago. These were important engineering milestones, but what visitors adored was the sheer beauty of seeing so many lights ignited in one place, at one time. Every building, including the Manufactures and Liberal Arts Building, was outlined in white bulbs. Giant searchlights—the largest ever made and said to be visible sixty miles away—had been mounted on the Manufactures' roof and swept the grounds and surrounding neighborhoods. Large colored bulbs lit the hundred-foot plumes of water that burst from the MacMonnies Fountain.

For many visitors these nightly illuminations were their first encounter with electricity. Hilda Satt, a girl newly arrived from Poland, went to the fair with her father. "As the light was fading in the sky, millions of lights were suddenly flashed on, all at one time," she recalled, years later. "Having seen nothing but kerosene lamps for illumination, this was like getting a sudden vision of Heaven."

Her father told her the lights were activated by electric switches.

"Without matches?" she asked.

Between the lights and the ever-present blue ghosts of the Columbian Guard, the fair achieved another milestone: For the first time Chicagoans could stroll at night in perfect safety. This alone began to draw an increased number of visitors, especially young couples locked in the rictus of Victorian courtship and needful of quiet dark places.

At night the lights and the infilling darkness served to mask the exposition's many flaws—among them, wrote John Ingalls in *Cosmopolitan,* the "unspeakable debris of innumerable luncheons"—and to create for a few hours the perfect city of Daniel Burnham's dreams.

"Night," Ingalls wrote, "is the magician of the fair."

The early visitors returned to their homes and reported to friends and family that the fair, though incomplete, was far grander and more powerful than they had been led to expect. Montgomery Schuyler, the leading architectural critic of Burnham's day, wrote, "It was a common remark among visitors who saw the Fair for the first time that nothing they had read or seen pictured had given them an idea of it, or prepared them for what they saw." Reporters from far-flung cities wired the same observation back to their editors, and stories of delight and awe began to percolate through the most remote towns. In fields, dells, and hollows, families terrified by what they read in the papers each day about the collapsing national economy nonetheless now began to think about Chicago. The trip would be expensive, but it was starting to look more and more worthwhile. Even necessary.

If only Mr. Ferris would get busy and finish that big wheel.

Modus Operandi

AND SO IT BEGAN. A waitress disappeared from Holmes's restaurant, where his guests ate their meals. One day she was at work, the next gone, with no clear explanation for her abrupt departure. Holmes seemed as stumped as anyone. A stenographer named Jennie Thompson disappeared, as did a woman named Evelyn Stewart, who either worked for Holmes or merely stayed in his hotel as a guest. A male physician who for a time had rented an office in the castle and who had befriended Holmes—they were seen together often—also had decamped, with no word to anyone.

Within the hotel chemical odors ebbed and flowed like an atmospheric tide. Some days the halls were suffused with a caustic scent, as of a cleanser applied too liberally, other days with a silvery medicinal odor, as if a dentist were at work somewhere in the building easing a customer into a deep sleep. There seemed to be a problem with the gas lines that fed the building, for periodically the scent of uncombusted gas permeated the halls.

There were inquiries from family and friends. As always Holmes was sympathetic and helpful. The police still did not become involved. Apparently there was too much else for them to do, as wealthy visitors and foreign dignitaries began arriving in ever-greater numbers, shadowed by a swarm of pickpockets, thugs, and petty swindlers.

Holmes did not kill face to face, as Jack the Ripper had done, gorging himself on warmth and viscera, but he did like proximity. He liked being near enough to hear the approach of death in the rising panic of his victims. This was when his quest for possession entered its most satisfying phase. The vault deadened most of the cries and pounding but not all. When the hotel was full of guests, he settled for more silent means. He filled a room with gas and let the guest expire in her sleep, or he crept in with his passkey and pressed a chloroform-soaked rag to her face. The choice was his, a measure of his power.

No matter what the approach, the act always left him in possession of a fresh supply of material, which he could then explore at will.

The subsequent articulation by his very talented friend Chappell constituted the final phase of acquisition, the triumphal phase, though he used Chappell's services only sparingly. He disposed of other spent material in his kiln or in pits filled with quicklime. He dared not keep Chappell's frames for too long a time. Early on he had made it a rule not to retain trophies. The possession he craved was a transient thing, like the scent of a fresh-cut hyacinth. Once it was gone, only another acquisition could restore it.

One Good Turn

In the first week of June 1893 Ferris's men began prying the last timbers and planks from the falsework that had encased and supported the big wheel during its assembly. The rim arced through the sky at a height of 264 feet, as high as the topmost occupied floor in Burnham's Masonic Temple, the city's tallest skyscraper. None of the thirty-six cars had been hung—they stood on the ground like the coaches of a derailed train—but the wheel itself was ready for its first rotation. Standing by itself, unbraced, Ferris's wheel looked dangerously fragile. "It is impossible for the non-mechanical mind to understand how such a Brobdingnag continues to keep itself erect," wrote Julian Hawthorne, son of Nathaniel; "it has no visible means of support—none that appear adequate. The spokes look like cobwebs; they are after the fashion of those on the newest make of bicycles."

On Thursday, June 8, Luther Rice signaled the firemen at the big steam boilers seven hundred feet away on Lexington Avenue, outside the Midway, to build steam and fill the ten-inch underground mains. Once the boilers reached suitable pressure, Rice nodded to an engineer in the pit under the wheel, and steam whooshed into the pistons of its twin thousand-horsepower engines. The drive sprockets turned smoothly and quietly. Rice ordered the engine stopped. Next workers attached the ten-ton chain to the sprockets and to a receiving sprocket at the wheel. Rice sent a telegram to Ferris at his office in the Hamilton Building in Pittsburgh: "Engines have steam on and are working satisfactorily. Sprocket chain connected up and are ready to turn wheel."

Ferris was unable to go to Chicago himself but sent his partner W. F. Gronau to supervise the first turn. In the early morning of Friday, June 9, as his train passed through the South Side, Gronau saw how the great wheel towered over everything in its vicinity, just as Eiffel's creation did in Paris. The exclamations of fellow passengers as to the wheel's size and apparent fragility filled him with a mixture of pride and anxiety. Ferris, himself fed up with construction delays and Burnham's pestering, had told Gronau to turn the wheel or tear it off the tower.

Last-minute adjustments and inspections took up most of Friday, but just before dusk Rice told Gronau that everything appeared to be ready.

"I did not trust myself to speak," Gronau said, "so merely nodded to start." He was anxious to see if the wheel worked, but at the same time "would gladly have assented to postpone the trial."

Nothing remained but to admit steam and see what happened. Never had anyone built such a gigantic wheel. That it would turn without crushing its bearings and rotate smoothly and true were engineering hopes supported only by calculations that reflected known qualities of iron and steel. No structure ever had been subjected to the unique stresses that would come to bear upon and within the wheel once in motion.

Ferris's pretty wife, Margaret, stood nearby, flushed with excitement. Gronau believed she was experiencing the same magnitude of mental strain as he.

"Suddenly I was aroused from these thoughts by a most horrible noise," he said. A growl tore through the sky and caused everyone in the vicinity—the Algerians of Bloom's village, the Egyptians and Persians and every visitor within one hundred yards—to halt and stare at the wheel.

"Looking up," Gronau said, "I saw the wheel move slowly. What can be the matter! What is this horrible noise!"

Gronau ran to Rice, who stood in the engine pit monitoring pressures and the play of shafts and shunts. Gronau expected to see Rice hurriedly trying to shut down the engine, but Rice looked unconcerned.

Rice explained that he had merely tested the wheel's braking system, which consisted of a band of steel wrapped around the axle. The test alone had caused the wheel to move one eighth of its circumference. The noise, Rice said, was only the sound of rust being scraped off the band.

The engineer in the pit released the brake and engaged the drive gears. The sprockets began to turn, the chain to advance.

By now many of the Algerians, Egyptians, and Persians—possibly even a few belly dancers—had gathered on the wheel's loading platforms, which were staged like steps so that once the wheel opened six cars could be loaded at a time. Everyone was silent.

As the wheel began to turn, loose nuts and bolts and a couple of wrenches rained from its hub and spokes. The wheel had consumed 28,416 pounds of bolts in its assembly; someone was bound to forget something.

Unmindful of this steel downpour, the villagers cheered and began dancing on the platforms. Some played instruments. The workmen who had risked their lives building the wheel now risked them again and climbed aboard the moving frame. "No carriages were as yet placed in position," Gronau said, "but this did not deter the men, for they clambered among the spokes and sat upon the crown of the wheel as easy as I am sitting in this chair."

The wheel needed twenty minutes for a single revolution. Only when it had completed its first full turn did Gronau feel the test had been successful, at which point he said, "I could have yelled out loud for joy."

Mrs. Ferris shook his hand. The crowd cheered. Rice telegraphed Ferris, who had been waiting all day for word of the test, his anxiety rising with each hour. The Pittsburgh office of Western Union received the cable at 9:10 P.M., and a blue-suited messenger raced through the cool spring night to bring it to Ferris. Rice had written: "The last coupling and final adjustment was made and steam turned on at six o'clock this evening one complete revolution of the big wheel was made everything working satisfactory twenty minutes time was taken for the revolution—I congratulate you upon it complete success midway is wildly enthusiastic."

The next day, Saturday, June 10, Ferris cabled Rice, "Your telegram stating that first revolution of wheel had been made last night at six o'clock and that same was successful in every way has caused great joy in this entire camp. I wish to congratulate you in all respects in this matter and ask that you rush the putting in of cars working day and night—

if you can't put the cars in at night, babbitt the car bearings at night so as to keep ahead." By "babbitt" he no doubt meant that Rice should install the metal casings in which the bearings were to sit.

The wheel had worked, but Ferris, Gronau, and Rice all knew that far more important tests lay ahead. Beginning that Saturday workers would begin hanging cars, thus placing upon the wheel its first serious stresses. Each of the thirty-six cars weighed thirteen tons, for a total of just under one million pounds. And that did not include the 200,000 pounds of additional live load that would be added as passengers filled the cars.

On Saturday, soon after receiving Ferris's congratulatory telegram, Rice cabled back that in fact the first car already had been hung.

Beyond Jackson Park the first turn of Ferris's wheel drew surprisingly little attention. The city, especially its *frappé* set, had focused its interest on another event unfolding in Jackson Park—the first visit by Spain's official emissary to the fair, the Infanta Eulalia, the youngest sister of Spain's dead King Alfonso XII and daughter of exiled Queen Isabel II.

The visit wasn't going very well.

The infanta was twenty-nine and, in the words of a State Department official, "rather handsome, graceful and bright." She had arrived two days earlier by train from New York, been transported immediately to the Palmer House, and lodged there in its most lavish suite. Chicago's boosters saw her visit as the first real opportunity to demonstrate the city's new refinement and to prove to the world, or at least to New York, that Chicago was as adept at receiving royalty as it was at turning pig bristles into paintbrushes. The first warning that things might not go as planned should perhaps have been evident in a wire-service report cabled from New York alerting the nation to the scandalous news that the young woman smoked cigarettes.

In the afternoon of her first day in Chicago, Tuesday, June 6, the infanta had slipped out of her hotel incognito, accompanied by her lady-in-waiting and an aide appointed by President Cleveland. She delighted in moving about the city unrecognized by Chicago's residents. "Nothing could be more entertaining, in fact, than to walk among the moving crowds of people who were engaged in reading about me in the newspapers, looking at a picture which looked more or less like me," she wrote.

She visited Jackson Park for the first time on Thursday, June 8, the day Ferris's wheel turned. Mayor Harrison was her escort. Crowds of strangers applauded her as she passed, for no other reason than her royal heritage. Newspapers called her the Queen of the Fair and put her visit on the front page. To her, however, it was all very tiresome. She envied the freedom she saw exhibited by Chicago's women. "I realize with some bitterness," she wrote to her mother, "that if this progress ever reaches Spain it will be too late for me to enjoy it."

By the next morning, Friday, she felt she had completed her official duties and was ready to begin enjoying herself. For example, she rejected an invitation from the Committee on Ceremonies and instead, on a whim, went to lunch at the German Village.

Chicago society, however, was just getting warmed up. The infanta was royalty, and by God she would get the royal treatment. That night the infanta was scheduled to attend a reception hosted by Bertha Palmer at the Palmer mansion on Lake Shore Drive. In preparation, Mrs. Palmer had ordered a throne built on a raised platform.

Struck by the similarity between her hostess's name and the name of the hotel in which she was staying, the infanta made inquiries. Upon discovering that Bertha Palmer was the wife of the hotel's owner, she inflicted a social laceration that Chicago would never forget or forgive. She declared that under no circumstances would she be received by an "innkeeper's wife."

Diplomacy prevailed, however, and she agreed to attend. Her mood only worsened. With nightfall the day's heat had given way to heavy rain. By the time Eulalia made it to Mrs. Palmer's front door, her white satin slippers were soaked and her patience for ceremony had been extinguished. She stayed at the function for all of one hour, then bolted.

The next day she skipped an official lunch at the Administration Building and again dined unannounced at the German Village. That night she arrived one hour late for a concert at the fair's Festival Hall that had been arranged solely in her honor. The hall was filled to capacity with members of Chicago's leading families. She stayed five minutes.

Resentment began to stain the continuing news coverage of her visit. On Saturday, June 10, the *Tribune* sniffed, "Her Highness . . . has a way of discarding programs and following independently the bent of her inclination." The city's papers made repeated reference to her penchant for acting in accord with "her own sweet will."

In fact, the infanta was coming to like Chicago. She had loved her time at the fair and seemed especially to like Carter Harrison. She gave him a gold cigarette case inlaid with diamonds. Shortly before her departure, set for Wednesday, June 14, she wrote to her mother, "I am going to leave Chicago with real regret."

Chicago did not regret her leaving. If she had happened to pick up a copy of the *Chicago Tribune* that Wednesday morning, she would have found an embittered editorial that stated, in part, "Royalty at best is a troublesome customer for republicans to deal with and royalty of the Spanish sort is the most troublesome of all. . . . It was their custom to come late and go away early, leaving behind them the general regret that they had not come still later and gone away still earlier, or, better still perhaps, that they had not come at all."

Such prose, however, bore the unmistakable whiff of hurt feelings. Chicago had set its table with the finest linen and crystal—not out of any great respect for royalty but to show the world how fine a table it could set—only to have the guest of honor shun the feast for a lunch of sausage, sauerkraut, and beer.

Nannie

ANNA WILLIAMS—"NANNIE"—ARRIVED from Midlothian, Texas, in mid-June 1893. While Texas had been hot and dusty, Chicago was cool and smoky, full of trains and noise. The sisters hugged tearfully and congratulated each other on how fine they looked, and Minnie introduced her husband, Henry Gordon. Harry. He was shorter than Minnie's letters had led Anna to expect, and not as handsome, but there was something about him that even Minnie's glowing letters had not captured. He exuded warmth and charm. He spoke softly. He touched her in ways that made her glance apologetically at Minnie. Harry listened to the story of her journey from Texas with an attentiveness that made her feel as if she were alone with him in the carriage. Anna kept looking at his eyes.

His warmth and smile and obvious affection for Minnie caused Anna's suspicions quickly to recede. He did seem to be in love with her. He was cordial and tireless in his efforts to please her and, indeed, to please Anna as well. He brought gifts of jewelry. He gave Minnie a gold watch and chain specially made by the jeweler in the pharmacy downstairs. Without even thinking about it, Anna began calling him "Brother Harry."

First Minnie and Harry took her on a tour of Chicago. The city's great buildings and lavish homes awed her, but its smoke and darkness and the ever-present scent of rotting garbage repulsed her. Holmes took the sisters to the Union Stock Yards, where a tour guide led them into the heart of the slaughter. The guide cautioned that they should watch their feet lest they slip in blood. They watched as hog after hog was upended and whisked screaming down the cable into the butchering chambers below, where men with blood-caked knifes expertly cut their throats. The hogs, some still alive, were dipped next in a vat of boiling water, then scraped clean of bristle—the bristle saved in bins below the scraping tables. Each steaming hog then passed from station to station, where knifemen drenched in blood made the same few incisions time after time until, as the hog advanced, slabs of meat began thudding wetly onto the tables. Holmes was unmoved; Minnie and Anna were horrified but also strangely thrilled by the efficiency of the carnage. The yards embodied everything Anna had heard about Chicago and its irresistible, even savage drive toward wealth and power.

The great fair came next. They rode the Alley L along Sixty-third Street. Just before the train entered the fairgrounds, it passed the arena of Buffalo Bill's Wild West. From the elevated trestle they saw the earthen floor of the arena and the amphitheater seating that surrounded it. They saw his horses and buffalo and an authentic stagecoach. The train passed over the fair's fence, then descended to the terminal at the rear of the Transportation Building. Brother Harry paid the fifty-cent admission for each of them. At the fair's turnstiles even Holmes could not escape paying cash.

Naturally they first toured the Transportation Building. They saw the Pullman Company's "Ideal of Industry" exhibit, with its detailed model of Pullman's company town, which the company extolled as a workers' paradise. In the building's annex, packed with trains and locomotives, they walked the full length of an exact duplicate of the all-Pullman New York & Chicago Limited, with its plush chairs and carpeting, crystal glassware, and polished wood walls. At the pavilion of the Inman line a full-sized slice of an ocean liner towered above them. They exited the building through the great Golden Door, which arced across the light-red face of the building like a gilt rainbow.

Now, for the first time, Anna got a sense of the true, vast scale of the fair. Ahead lay a broad boulevard that skirted on the left the lagoon and the Wooded Island, on the right the tall facades of the Mines and Electricity buildings. In the distance she saw a train whooshing over the fair's all-electric elevated railway along the park's perimeter. Closer at hand, silent electric launches glided through the lagoon. At the far end of the boulevard, looming like an escarpment in the Rockies, stood the

Manufactures and Liberal Arts Building. White gulls slid across its face. The building was irresistibly huge. Holmes and Minnie took her there next. Once inside she saw that the building was even more vast than its exterior had led her to believe.

A blue haze of human breath and dust blurred the intricate bracing of the ceiling 246 feet above. Halfway to the ceiling, seemingly in midair, were five gigantic electric chandeliers, the largest ever built, each seventy-five feet in diameter and generating 828,000 candlepower. Below the chandeliers spread an indoor city of "gilded domes and glittering minarets, mosques, palaces, kiosks, and brilliant pavilions," according to the popular Rand, McNally & Co. *Handbook to the World's Columbian Exposition*. At the center stood a clock tower, the tallest of the interior structures, rising to a height of 120 feet. Its self-winding clock told the time in days, hours, minutes, and seconds, from a face seven feet in diameter. As tall as the tower was, the ceiling was yet another 126 feet above.

Minnie stood beaming and proud as Anna's gaze moved over the interior city and upward to its steel sky. There had to be thousands of exhibits. The prospect of seeing even a fraction of them was daunting. They saw Gobelin tapestries at the French Pavilion and the life-mask of Abraham Lincoln among the exhibits of the American Bronze Company. Other U.S. companies exhibited toys, weapons, canes, trunks, every conceivable manufactured product—and a large display of burial hardware, including marble and stone monuments, mausoleums, mantels, caskets, coffins, and miscellaneous other tools and furnishings of the undertaker's trade.

Minnie and Anna rapidly grew tired. They exited, with relief, onto the terrace over the North Canal and walked into the Court of Honor. Here once again Anna found herself nearly overwhelmed. It was noon by now, the sun directly overhead. The gold form of the Statue of the Republic, Big Mary, stood like a torch aflame. The basin in which the statue's plinth was set glittered with ripples of diamond. At the far end stood thirteen tall white columns, the Peristyle, with slashes of the blue lake visible between them. The light suffusing the Court was so plentiful and intense, it hurt their eyes. Many of the people around them donned spectacles with blue lenses.

They retreated for lunch. They had innumerable choices. There were lunch counters in most of the main buildings. The Manufactures and Liberal Arts Building alone had ten, plus two large restaurants, one German, the other French. The café in the Transportation Building, on a terrace over the Golden Door, was always popular and offered a spectacular view of the lagoon district. As the day wore on, Holmes bought them chocolate and lemonade and root beer at one of the Hires Root Beer Oases that dotted the grounds.

They returned to the fair almost daily, two weeks being widely considered the minimum needed to cover it adequately. One of the most compelling buildings, given the nature of the age, was the Electricity Building. In its "theatorium" they listened to an orchestra playing at that very moment in New York. They watched the moving pictures in Edison's Kinetoscope. Edison also displayed a strange metal cylinder that could store voices. "A man in Europe talks to his wife in America by boxing up a cylinder full of conversation and sending it by express," the Rand, McNally guidebook said; "a lover talks by the hour into a cylinder, and his sweetheart hears as though the thousand leagues were but a yard."

And they saw the first electric chair.

They reserved a separate day for the Midway. Nothing in Mississippi or Texas had prepared Anna for what she now experienced. Belly dancers. Camels. A balloon full of hydrogen that carried visitors more than a thousand feet into the sky. "Persuaders" called to her from raised platforms, seeking to entice her into the Moorish Palace with its room of mirrors, its optical illusions, and its eclectic wax museum, where visitors saw figures as diverse as Little Red Riding Hood and Marie Antoinette about to be guillotined. There was color everywhere. The Street in Cairo glowed with soft yellows, pinks, and purples. Even the concession tickets provided a splash of color—brilliant blue for the Turkish Theater, pink for the Lapland Village, and mauve for the Venetian gondolas.

Sadly, the Ferris Wheel was not quite ready.

They exited the Midway and strolled slowly south back to Sixty-third Street and the Alley L. They were tired, happy, and sated, but Harry promised to bring them back one more time—on July 4, for a fireworks display that everyone expected would be the greatest the city had ever witnessed.

Brother Harry seemed delighted with Anna and invited her to stay for the summer. Flattered, she wrote home to request that her big trunk be shipped to the Wrightwood address.

Clearly she had hoped something like this would happen, for she had packed the trunk already.

Holmes's assistant Benjamin Pitezel also went to the fair. He bought a souvenir for his son Howard—a tin man mounted on a spinning top. It quickly became the boy's favorite possession.

Vertigo

As FERRIS'S MEN BECAME accustomed to handling the big cars, the process of attaching them to the wheel accelerated. By Sunday evening, June 11, six cars had been hung—an average of two a day since the first turn of the wheel. Now it was time for the first test with passengers, and the weather could not have been better. The sun was gold, the sky a darkling blue in the east.

Mrs. Ferris insisted on being aboard for the first ride, despite Gronau's attempts to dissuade her. Gronau inspected the wheel to make sure the car would swing without obstruction. The engineer in the pit started the engines and rotated the wheel to bring the test car to one of the platforms. "I did not enter the carriage with the easiest feeling at heart," Gronau said. "I felt squeamish; yet I could not refuse to take the trip. So I put on a bold face and walked into the car."

Luther Rice joined them, as did two draftsmen and the city of Chicago's former bridge engineer, W. C. Hughes. His wife and daughter also stepped aboard.

The car swung gently as the passengers took positions within the car. Glass had not yet been installed in its generous windows, nor the iron grill that would cover the glass. As soon as the last passenger had entered, Rice casually nodded to the engineer, and the wheel began to move. Instinctively everyone reached for posts and sills to keep themselves steady.

As the wheel turned, the car pivoted on the trunnions that both connected it to the frame and kept it level. "Owing to our car not having made a trip," Gronau said, "the trunnions stuck slightly in their bearings and a crunching noise resulted, which in the condition of our nerves was not pleasant to hear."

The car traveled a bit higher, then unexpectedly stopped, raising the question of how everyone aboard would get down if the wheel could not be restarted. Rice and Gronau stepped to the unglazed windows to investigate. They looked down over the sill and discovered the problem: The fast-growing crowd of spectators, emboldened by seeing passengers in the first car, had leaped into the next car, ignoring shouts to stay back. Fearful that someone would be hurt or killed, the engineer had stopped the wheel and allowed the passengers to board.

Gronau estimated that one hundred people now occupied the car below. No one sought to kick them out. The wheel again began to move.

Ferris had created more than simply an engineering novelty. Like the inventors of the elevator, he had conjured an entirely new physical sensation. Gronau's first reaction—soon to change—was disappointment. He had expected to feel something like what he felt when riding a fast elevator, but here he found that if he looked straight ahead he felt almost nothing.

Gronau stationed himself at one end of the car to better observe its behavior and the movement of the wheel. When he looked out the side of the car into the passing web of spokes, the car's rapid ascent became apparent: ". . . it seemed as if every thing was dropping away from us, and the car was still. Standing at the side of the car and looking into the network of iron rods multiplied the peculiar sensation. . . ." He advised the others that if they had weak stomachs, they should not do likewise.

When the car reached its highest point, 264 feet above the ground, Mrs. Ferris climbed onto a chair and cheered, raising a roar in the following car and on the ground.

Soon, however, the passengers became silent. The novelty of the sensation wore off, and the true power of the experience became apparent.

"It was a most beautiful sight one obtains in the descent of the car, for then the whole fair grounds is laid before you," Gronau said. "The view is so grand that all timidity left me and my watch on the movement of the car was abandoned." The sun had begun its own descent and now cast an orange light over the shorescape. "The harbor was dotted with vessels of every description, which appeared mere specks from our exalted position, and the reflected rays of the beautiful sunset cast a gleam upon the surrounding scenery, making a picture lovely to behold." The entire park came into view as an intricate landscape of color, texture, and motion. Lapis lagoons. Electric launches trailing veils of diamond. Carmine blossoms winking from bulrush and flag. "The sight is so inspiring that all conversation stopped, and all were lost in admiration of this grand sight. The equal of it I have never seen, and I doubt very much if I shall again."

This reverie was broken as more bolts and nuts bounded down the superstructure onto the car's roof.

———

Spectators still managed to get past the guards and into the following cars, but now Gronau and Rice shrugged it off. The engineer in the pit kept the wheel running until the failing light made continued operation a danger, but even then thrill-seekers clamored for a chance. Finally Rice informed those who had shoved their way into the cars that if they remained he would run them to the top of the wheel and leave them there overnight. "This," Gronau said, "had the desired effect."

Immediately after leaving the car, Mrs. Ferris telegraphed her husband details of the success. He cabled back, "God bless you my dear."

The next day, Monday, June 12, Rice cabled Ferris, "Six more cars hung today. People are wild to ride on wheel & extra force of guards is required to keep them out." On Tuesday the total of cars hung reached twenty-one, with only fifteen more to add.

———

Burnham, obsessing as always over details, sought to decree the style and location of a fence for the wheel. He wanted an open, perforated fence, Ferris wanted it closed.

Ferris was fed up with Burnham's pressure and aesthetic interference. He cabled Luther Rice, ". . . Burnham nor anyone else has any right to dictate whether we shall have a closed or open fence, any more than from an artistic standpoint."

Ferris prevailed. The eventual fence was a closed one.

At last all the cars were hung and the wheel was ready for its first paying passengers. Rice wanted to begin accepting riders on Sunday, June 18, two days earlier than planned, but now with the wheel about to experience its greatest test—a full load of paying passengers, including entire families—Ferris's board of directors urged him to hold off one more day. They cabled Ferris, "Unwise to open wheel to public until opening day because of incompleteness and danger of accidents."

Ferris accepted their directive but with reluctance. Shortly before he left for Chicago, he cabled Rice, "If the board of directors have decided not to run until Wednesday you may carry out their wishes."

It's likely the board had been influenced by an accident that had occurred the previous Wednesday, June 14, at the Midway's Ice Railway, a descending elliptical track of ice over which two coupled bobsleds full of passengers could reach speeds of forty miles an hour. The owners had just completed the attraction and begun conducting their first tests with passengers, employees only, when a group of spectators pushed their way into the sleds, eight in the first, six in the second. The interlopers included three of Bloom's Algerians, who had come to the railway, one explained, because "none of us had ever seen ice," a doubtful story given that the Algerians had just endured one of Chicago's coldest winters.

At about six forty-five P.M. the operator released the sleds, and soon they were rocketing along the ice at maximum speed. "It was about sundown when I heard the sleds coming around the curve," said a Columbian Guard who witnessed the run. "They seemed to be flying. The first went around the curve. It struck the angle near the west end of the road, but went along all right. The second struck the same point, but it jumped the track. The top of the car, with the people holding tightly to the seats, broke the railing and fell to the ground. As it fell, the sled turned over and the people fell under it."

The sled plummeted fifteen feet to the ground. One passenger was killed; another, a woman, suffered fractures of her jaw and both wrists. Four other men, including two of the Algerians, sustained contusions.

The accident had been tragic and was a black mark for the fair, but everyone understood that the Ferris Wheel, with thirty-six cars carrying more than two thousand passengers, embodied the potential for a catastrophe of almost unimaginable scale.

Heathen Wanted

DESPITE HIS MISGIVINGS OLMSTED LEFT the completion of the exposition landscape in the hands of Ulrich and adopted a punishing schedule of work and travel that took him through sixteen states. By mid-June he was back at Vanderbilt's North Carolina estate. Along the way, in rail-cars, stations, and hotels, he solicited the views of strangers about the fair while keeping his own identity a secret. The fair's lackluster attendance troubled and perplexed him. He asked travelers if they had visited the fair yet, and if so what they had thought of it, but he was especially interested in the opinions of people who had not yet gone—what had they heard, did they plan to go, what was holding them back?

"Everywhere there is growing interest in the Exposition," he told Burnham in a June 20 letter from Biltmore. "Everywhere I have found indications that people are planning to go to it." Firsthand accounts of the fair were sparking heightened interest. Clergymen who had seen it were working the fair into sermons and lectures. He was delighted to find that what visitors liked best were not the exhibits but the buildings, waterways, and scenery and that the fair had surprised them. "People who have gone to the Fair have, in the main, found more than the news-papers . . . had led them to expect." He concluded, "There is a rising tidal wave of enthusiasm over the land."

But he saw that other factors were exerting a countervailing force. While personal accounts of the fair were enthusiastic, Olmsted wrote, "nearly always incompletenesses are referred to, favoring the idea that much remains to be done, and that the show will be better later." Farm-ers planned to wait until after harvest. Many people had put off their vis-its in the expectation that the nation's worsening economic crisis and pressure from Congress eventually would compel the railroads to reduce their Chicago fares. Weather was also an issue. Convinced that Chicago was too hot in July and August, people were postponing their visits until the fall.

One of the most pernicious factors, Olmsted found, was the widespread fear that anyone who ventured to Chicago would be "fleeced unmercifully," especially in the fair's many restaurants, with their "extortionate" prices. "This complaint is universal, and stronger than you in Chicago are aware of, I am sure," he told Burnham. "It comes from rich and poor alike. . . . I think that I have myself paid ten times as much for lunch at the Exposition as I did a few days ago, for an equally good one in Knoxville, Tenn. The frugal farming class yet to come to the Fair will feel this greatly."

Olmsted had another reason to worry about high meal prices. "The effect," he wrote, "will be to induce people more and more to bring their food with them, and more and more to scatter papers and offal on the ground."

It was critical now, Olmsted argued, to concentrate on making improvements of a kind most likely to increase the gleam in the stories people took back to their hometowns. "This is the advertising now most important to be developed; that of high-strung, contagious enthusiasm, growing from actual excellence: the question being not whether people shall be satisfied, but how much they shall be carried away with admiration, and infect others by their unexpected enjoyment of what they found."

Toward this end, he wrote, certain obvious flaws needed immediate attention. The exposition's gravel paths, for example. "There is not a square rod of admirable, hardly one of passable, gravel-walk in all of the Exposition Ground," he wrote. "It appears probable to me that neither the contractor, nor the inspector, whose business it is to keep the contractor up to his duty, can ever have seen a decently good gravel walk, or that they have any idea of what good gravel walks are. What are the defects of your walks?"—*Your* walks, he says here, not *mine* or *ours*, even though the walks were the responsibility of his own landscape department—"In some places there are cobbles or small boulders pro-truding from the surface, upon which no lady, with Summer shoes, can step without pain. In other places, the surface material is such that when damp enough to make it coherent it becomes slimy, and thus unpleasant to walk upon; also, without care, the slime is apt to smear shoes and dresses, which materially lessens the comfort of ladies." His voyage to Europe had shown him that a really good gravel path "should be as even and clean as a drawing room floor."

The cleanliness of the grounds also fell short of European standards, as he had feared it would. Litter was everywhere, with too few men assigned to clean it up. The fair needed twice as many, he said, and greater scrutiny of their work. "I have seen papers that had been appar-ently swept off the terraces upon the shrubbery between them and the lagoons," Olmsted wrote. "Such a shirking trick in a workman employed to keep the terraces clean should be a criminal offence."

He was bothered, too, by the noise of the few steam vessels that Burnham, over his repeated objections, had authorized to travel the exposition's waters alongside the electric launches. "The boats are cheap, graceless, clumsy affairs, as much out of place in what people are calling the 'Court of Honor' of the Exposition as a cow in a flower garden."

Olmsted's greatest concern, however, was that the main, Jackson Park portion of the exposition simply was not fun. "There is too much appearance of an impatient and tired doing of sight-seeing duty. A stint to be got through before it is time to go home. The crowd has a melan-choly air in this respect, and strenuous measures should be taken to over-come it."

Just as Olmsted sought to conjure an aura of mystery in his landscape, so here he urged the engineering of seemingly accidental moments of charm. The concerts and parades were helpful but were of too "stated or programmed" a nature. What Olmsted wanted were "minor incidents . . . of a less evidently prepared character; less formal, more apparently spon-taneous and incidental." He envisioned French horn players on the Wooded Island, their music drifting across the waters. He wanted Chinese lanterns strung from boats and bridges alike. "Why not skipping and dancing masqueraders with tambourines, such as one sees in Italy? Even lemonade peddlers would help if moving about in picturesque dresses; or cake-sellers, appearing as cooks, with flat cap, and in spotless white from top to toe?" On nights when big events in Jackson Park drew visitors away from the Midway, "could not several of the many varieties of 'heathen,' black, white and yellow, be cheaply hired to mingle, unobtrusively, but in full native costume, with the crowd on the Main Court?"

When Burnham read Olmsted's letter, he must have thought Olmsted had lost his mind. Burnham had devoted the last two years of his life to creating an impression of monumental beauty, and now Olmsted wanted to make visitors laugh. Burnham wanted them struck dumb with awe. There would be no skipping and dancing. No heathen.

The exposition was a dream city, but it was Burnham's dream. Everywhere it reflected the authoritarian spandrels of his character, from its surfeit of policemen to its strict rules against picking flowers. Nowhere was this as clearly evident as in the fair's restrictions on unauthorized photography.

Burnham had given a single photographer, Charles Dudley Arnold, a monopoly over the sale of official photographs of the fair, which arrangement also had the effect of giving Burnham control over the kinds of images that got distributed throughout the country and explains why neat, well-dressed, upper-class people tended to populate each frame. A second contractor received the exclusive right to rent Kodaks to fair visitors, the Kodak being a new kind of portable camera that eliminated the need for lens and shutter adjustments. In honor of the fair Kodak called the folding version of its popular model No. 4 box camera the Columbus. The photographs these new cameras created were fast becoming known as "snap-shots," a term originally used by English hunters to describe a quick shot with a gun. Anyone wishing to bring his own Kodak to the fair had to buy a permit for two dollars, an amount beyond the reach of most visitors; the Midway's Street in Cairo imposed an additional one-dollar fee. An amateur photographer bringing a conventional large camera and the necessary tripod had to pay ten dollars, about what many out-of-town visitors paid for a full day at the fair, including lodging, meals, and admission.

For all Burnham's obsession with detail and control, one event at the fair escaped his attention. On June 17 a small fire occurred in the Cold Storage Building, a castlelike structure at the southwest corner of the grounds built by Hercules Iron Works. Its function was to produce ice, store the perishable goods of exhibitors and restaurants, and operate an ice rink for visitors wishing to experience the novelty of skating in July. The building was a private venture: Burnham had nothing to do with its construction beyond approving its design. Oddly enough, its architect was named Frank P. Burnham, no relation.

The fire broke out in the cupola at the top of the central tower but was controlled quickly and caused only a hundred dollars in damage. Even so, the fire prompted insurance underwriters to take a closer look at the building, and what they saw frightened them. A key element of the design had never been installed. Seven insurers canceled their policies. Fire Marshal Edward W. Murphy, acting chief of the World's Fair Fire Department, told a committee of underwriters, "That building gives us more trouble than any structure on the grounds. It is a miserable firetrap and will go up in smoke before long."

No one told Burnham about the fire, no one told him of the cancellations, and no one told him of Murphy's forecast.

At Last

AT THREE-THIRTY P.M. on Wednesday, June 21, 1893, fifty-one days late, George Washington Gale Ferris took a seat on the speakers' platform built at the base of his wheel. The forty-piece Iowa State Marching Band already had boarded one of the cars and now played "My Country 'Tis of Thee." Mayor Harrison joined Ferris on the platform, as did Bertha Palmer, the entire Chicago city council, and an assortment of fair officials. Burnham apparently was not present.

The cars were fully glazed, and wire grills had been placed over all the windows so that, as one reporter put it, "No crank will have an opportunity to commit suicide from this wheel, no hysterical woman shall jump from a window." Conductors trained to soothe riders who were afraid of heights stood in handsome uniforms at each car's door.

The band quieted, the wheel stopped. Speeches followed. Ferris was last to take the podium and happily assured the audience that the man condemned for having "wheels in his head" had gotten them out of his head and into the heart of the Midway Plaisance. He attributed the success of the enterprise to his wife, Margaret, who stood behind him on the platform. He dedicated the wheel to the engineers of America.

Mrs. Ferris gave him a gold whistle, then she and Ferris and the other dignitaries climbed into the first car. Harrison wore his black slouch hat.

When Ferris blew the whistle, the Iowa State band launched into "America," and the wheel again began to turn. The group made several circuits, sipping champagne and smoking cigars, then exited the wheel to the cheers of the crowd that now thronged its base. The first paying passengers stepped aboard.

The wheel continued rolling with stops only for loading and unloading until eleven o'clock that night. Even with every car full, the wheel never faltered, its bearings never groaned.

The Ferris Company was not shy about promoting its founder's accomplishment. In an illustrated pamphlet called the "Ferris Wheel Souvenir" the company wrote: "Built in the face of every obstacle, it is an achievement which reflects so much credit upon the inventor, that were Mr. Ferris the subject of a Monarchy, instead of a citizen of a great Republic, his honest heart would throb beneath a breast laden with the decorations of royalty." Ferris could not resist tweaking the Exposition Company for not granting him a concession sooner than it did. "Its failure to appreciate its importance," the souvenir said, "has cost the Exposition Company many thousands of dollars."

This was an understatement. Had the Exposition Company stood by its original June 1892 concession rather than waiting until nearly six months later, the wheel would have been ready for the fair's May 1 opening. Not only did the exposition lose its 50 percent share of the wheel's revenue for those fifty-one days—it lost the boost in overall admission that the wheel likely would have generated and that Burnham so desperately wanted. Instead it had stood for that month and a half as a vivid advertisement of the fair's incomplete condition.

⌁

Safety fears lingered, and Ferris did what he could to ease them. The souvenir pamphlet noted that even a full load of passengers had "no more effect on the movements or the speed than if they were so many flies"—an oddly ungracious allusion. The pamphlet added, "In the construction of this great wheel, every conceivable danger has been calculated and provided for."

But Ferris and Gronau had done their jobs too well. The design was so elegant, so adept at exploiting the strength of thin strands of steel, that the wheel appeared incapable of withstanding the stresses placed upon it. The wheel may not have been unsafe, but it looked unsafe.

"In truth, it seems too light," a reporter observed. "One fears the slender rods which must support the whole enormous weight are too puny to fulfill their office. One cannot avoid the thought of what would happen if a high wind should come sweeping across the prairie and attack the structure broadside. Would the thin rods be sufficient to sustain not only the enormous weight of the structure and that of the 2,000 passengers who might chance to be in the cars, but the pressure of the wind as well?"

In three weeks that question would find an answer.

Rising Wave

AND SUDDENLY THEY BEGAN to come. The enthusiasm Olmsted had identified during his travels, though still far from constituting a tidal wave, at last seemed to begin propelling visitors to Jackson Park. By the end of June, even though the railroads still had not dropped their fares, paid attendance at the exposition had more than doubled, the average for the month rising to 89,170 from May's dismal 37,501. It was still far below the 200,000 daily visitors the fair's planners originally had dreamed of, but the trend was encouraging. From Englewood to the Loop, hotels at last began to fill. The Roof Garden Café of the Woman's Building now served two thousand people a day, ten times the number it had served on Opening Day. The resulting volume of garbage overwhelmed its disposal system, which consisted of janitors bumping large barrels of fetid garbage down the same three flights of stairs used by customers. The janitors could not use the elevators because Burnham had ordered them turned off after dark to conserve power for the fair's nightly illuminations. As stains and stench accumulated, the restaurant's manager built a chute on the roof and threatened to jettison the garbage directly onto Olmsted's precious lawns.

Burnham retracted his order.

The fair had become so intensely compelling that one woman, Mrs. Lucille Rodney of Galveston, Texas, walked thirteen hundred miles along railroad tracks to reach it. "Call it no more the White City on the Lake," wrote Sir Walter Besant, the English historian and novelist, in *Cosmopolitan,* "it is Dreamland."

Even Olmsted now seemed happy with it, although of course he had his criticisms. He too had wanted to manage the first impressions of visitors by having a central entry point. The failure of this idea, he wrote in a formal critique for *The Inland Architect,* "deducted much" from the fair's value, although he hastened to add that he was making this criticism "not in the least in a complaining way" but as a professional offering guidance to others who might confront a similar problem. He still wished the Wooded Island had been left alone, and he decried the unplanned proliferation of concession buildings that "intercepted vistas and disturbed spaces intended to serve for the relief of the eye from the too nearly constant demands upon attention of the Exposition Buildings." The effect, he wrote, "has been bad."

Overall, however, he was pleased, especially with the process of construction. "Really," he wrote, "I think that it is a most satisfactory and encouraging circumstance that it could be found feasible for so many men of technical education and ability to be recruited and suitably organized so quickly and made to work together so well in so short a time. I think it a notable circumstance that there should have been so little friction, so little display of jealousy, envy and combativeness, as has appeared in the progress of this enterprise."

He attributed this circumstance to Burnham: "too high an estimate cannot be placed on the industry, skill and tact with which this result was secured by the master of us all."

Visitors wore their best clothes, as if going to church, and were surprisingly well behaved. In the six months of the fair the Columbian Guard made only 2,929 arrests, about sixteen per day, typically for disorderly conduct, petty theft, and pickpocketing, with pickpockets most favoring the fair's always-crowded aquarium. The guard identified 135 ex-convicts and removed them from the grounds. It issued thirty fines for carrying Kodaks without a permit, thirty-seven for taking unauthorized photographs. It investigated the discovery on the grounds of three fetuses; a Pinkerton detective "assaulting visitors" at the Tiffany Pavilion; and a "Zulu acting improperly." In his official report to Burnham Colonel Rice, commander of the Guard, wrote, "With the tens of thousands of employees and the millions of visitors, it must be admitted that our success was phenomenal."

With so many people packed among steam engines, giant rotating wheels, horse-drawn fire trucks, and rocketing bobsleds, the fair's ambulances superintended by a doctor named Gentles were constantly delivering bruised, bloody, and overheated visitors to the exposition hospital. Over the life of the fair the hospital treated 11,602 patients, sixty-four a day, for injuries and ailments that suggest that the mundane sufferings of people have not changed very much over the ages. The list included:

820 cases of diarrhea;

154, constipation;

21, hemorrhoids;

434, indigestion;

365, foreign bodies in the eyes;

364, severe headaches;

594 episodes of fainting, syncope, and exhaustion;

1 case of extreme flatulence;

and 169 involving teeth that hurt like hell.

One of the delights of the fair was never knowing who might turn up beside you at the chocolate Venus de Milo or at the hearse exhibit or under the barrel of Krupp's monster, or who might sit at the table next to yours at the Big Tree Restaurant or the Philadelphia Café or the Great White Horse Inn, a reproduction of the public house described by Dickens in *The Pickwick Papers*; or who might suddenly clutch your arm aboard the Ferris Wheel as your car began its ascent. Archduke Francis Ferdinand, described by an escort as being "half-boor, half-tightwad," roamed the grounds incognito—but much preferred the vice districts of Chicago. Indians who had once used hatchets to bare the skulls of white men drifted over from Buffalo Bill's compound, as did Annie Oakley and assorted Cossacks, Hussars, Lancers, and members of the U.S. Sixth Cavalry on temporary furlough to become actors in Colonel Cody's show. Chief Standing Bear rode the Ferris Wheel in full ceremonial headdress, his two hundred feathers unruffled. Other Indians rode the enameled wooden horses of the Midway carousel.

There were Paderewski, Houdini, Tesla, Edison, Joplin, Darrow, a Princeton professor named Woodrow Wilson, and a sweet old lady in black summer silk flowered with forget-me-not-blue named Susan B. Anthony. Burnham met Teddy Roosevelt for lunch. For years after the fair Burnham used the exclamation, "Bully!" Diamond Jim Brady dined with Lillian Russell and indulged his passion for sweet corn.

No one saw Twain. He came to Chicago to see the fair but got sick and spent eleven days in his hotel room, then left without ever seeing the White City.

Of all people.

———

Chance encounters led to magic.

Frank Haven Hall, superintendent of the Illinois Institution for the Education of the Blind, unveiled a new device that made plates for printing books in Braille. Previously Hall had invented a machine capable of typing in Braille, the Hall Braille Writer, which he never patented because he felt profit should not sully the cause of serving the blind. As he stood by his newest machine, a blind girl and her escort approached him. Upon learning that Hall was the man who had invented the typewriter she used so often, the girl put her arms around his neck and gave him a huge hug and kiss.

Forever afterward, whenever Hall told this story of how he met Helen Keller, tears would fill his eyes.

———

One day as the Board of Lady Managers debated whether to support or oppose opening the fair on Sunday, an angry male Sabbatarian confronted Susan B. Anthony in the hall of the Woman's Building to challenge her contention that the fair should remain open. (Anthony was not a lady manager and therefore despite her national stature could not participate in the board's meeting.) Deploying the most shocking analogy he could muster, the clergyman asked Anthony if she'd prefer having a son of hers attend Buffalo Bill's show on Sunday instead of church.

Yes, she replied, "he would learn far more. . . ."

To the pious this exchange confirmed the fundamental wickedness of Anthony's suffragist movement. When Cody learned of it, he was tickled, so much so that he immediately sent Anthony a thank-you note and invited her to attend his show. He offered her a box at any performance she chose.

At the start of the performance Cody entered the ring on horseback, his long gray hair streaming from under his white hat, the silver trim of his white jacket glinting in the sun. He kicked his horse into a gallop and raced toward Anthony's box. The audience went quiet.

He halted his horse in a burst of dirt and dust, removed his hat, and with a great sweeping gesture bowed until his head nearly touched the horn of his saddle.

Anthony stood and returned the bow and—"as enthusiastic as a girl," a friend said—waved her handkerchief at Cody.

The significance of the moment escaped no one. Here was one of the greatest heroes of America's past saluting one of the foremost heroes of its future. The encounter brought the audience to its feet in a thunder of applause and cheers.

The frontier may indeed have closed at last, as Frederick Jackson Turner proclaimed in his history-making speech at the fair, but for that moment it stood there glittering in the sun like the track of a spent tear.

•══════•

There was tragedy. The British draped their elaborate ship model of the H.M.S. *Victoria* in black bunting. On June 22, 1893, during maneuvers off Tripoli, this marvel of naval technology had been struck by the H.M.S. *Camperdown*. The *Victoria*'s commander ordered the ship to proceed full speed toward shore, intending to ground her there in accord with standing fleet orders meant to make it easier to raise a sunken ship. Ten minutes later, her engines still at full steam, the cruiser heeled and sank with many of her crew still trapped belowdecks. Others lucky enough to have jumped free now found themselves mauled by her whirling propellers or burned to death when her boilers exploded. "Screams and shrieks arose, and in the white foam appeared reddened arms and legs and wrenched and torn bodies," a reporter said. "Headless trunks were tossed out of the vortex to linger a moment on the surface and sink out of sight."

The accident cost four hundred lives.

The Ferris Wheel quickly became the most popular attraction of the exposition. Thousands rode it every day. In the week beginning July 3 Ferris sold 61,395 tickets for a gross return of $30,697.50. The Exposition Company took about half, leaving Ferris an operating profit for that one week of $13,948 (equivalent today to about $400,000).

There were still questions about the wheel's safety, and unfounded stories circulated about suicides and accidents, including one that alleged that a frightened pug had leaped to its death from one of the car's windows. Not true, the Ferris Company said; the story was the concoction of a reporter "short on news and long on invention." If not for the wheel's windows and iron grates, however, its record might have been different. On one ride a latent terror of heights suddenly overwhelmed an otherwise peaceful man named Wherritt. He was fine until the car began to move. As it rose, he began to feel ill and nearly fainted. There was no way to signal the engineer below to stop the wheel.

Wherritt staggered in panic from one end of the car to the other, driving passengers before him "like scared sheep," according to one account. He began throwing himself at the walls of the car with such power that he managed to bend some of the protective iron. The conductor and several male passengers tried to subdue him, but he shook them off and raced for the door. In accord with the wheel's operating procedures, the conductor had locked the door at the start of the ride. Wherritt shook it and broke its glass but could not get it open.

As the car entered its descent, Wherritt became calmer and laughed and sobbed with relief—until he realized the wheel was not going to stop.

It always made two full revolutions. Wherritt again went wild, and again the conductor and his allies subdued him, but they were growing tired. They feared what might happen if Wherritt escaped them. Structurally the car was sound, but its walls, windows, and doors had been designed merely to discourage attempts at self-destruction, not to resist a human pile driver. Already Wherritt had broken glass and bent iron.

A woman stepped up and unfastened her skirt. To the astonishment of all aboard, she slipped the skirt off and threw it over Wherritt's head, then held it in place while murmuring gentle assurances. The effect was immediate. Wherritt became "as quiet as an ostrich."

A woman disrobing in public, a man with a skirt over his head—the marvels of the fair seemed endless.

○━━━○

The exposition was Chicago's great pride. Thanks mainly to Daniel Burnham the city had proved it could accomplish something marvelous against obstacles that by any measure should have humbled the builders. The sense of ownership was everywhere, not just among the tens of thousands of citizens who had bought exposition stock. Hilda Satt noticed it in the change that came over her father as he showed her the grounds. "He seemed to take a personal pride in the fair, as if he had helped in the planning," she said. "As I look back on those days, most people in Chicago felt that way. Chicago was host to the world at that time and we were part of it all."

But the fair did more than simply stoke pride. It gave Chicago a light to hold against the gathering dark of economic calamity. The Erie Railroad wobbled, then collapsed. Next went the Northern Pacific. In Denver three national banks failed in one day and pulled down an array of other businesses. Fearing a bread riot, city authorities called out the militia. In Chicago the editors of *The Inland Architect* tried to be reassuring: "Existing conditions are only an accident. Capital is only hidden. Enterprise is only frightened, not beaten." The editors were wrong.

In June two businessmen committed suicide on the same day in the same Chicago hotel, the Metropole. One slit his throat with a razor at ten-thirty in the morning. The other learned of the suicide from the hotel barber. That night in his own room he tied one end of the silk sash of his smoking jacket around his neck, then stretched out on the bed and tied the other end to the bedstead. He rolled off.

"Everyone is in a blue fit of terror," wrote Henry Adams, "and each individual thinks himself more ruined than his neighbor."

Long before the fair's end, people began mourning its inevitable passage. Mary Hartwell Catherwood wrote, "What shall we do when this Wonderland is closed?—when it disappears—when the enchantment comes to an end?" One lady manager, Sallie Cotton of North Carolina, a mother of six children staying in Chicago for the summer, captured in her diary a common worry: that after seeing the fair, "everything will seem small and insignificant."

The fair was so perfect, its grace and beauty like an assurance that for as long as it lasted nothing truly bad could happen to anyone, anywhere.

Independence Day

THE MORNING OF JULY 4, 1893, broke gray and squally. The weather threatened to dull the elaborate fireworks display that Frank Millet had planned as a further boost for the exposition's attendance, which despite steady week-to-week increases still lagged behind expectations. The sun emerged late in the morning, though squalls continued to sweep Jackson Park through much of the day. By late afternoon a soft gold light bathed the Court of Honor and storm clouds walled the northern sky. The storms came no closer. The crowds built quickly. Holmes, Minnie, and Anna found themselves locked within an immense throng of humid men and women. Many people carried blankets and hampers of food but quickly found that no room remained to spread a picnic. There were few children. The entire Columbian Guard seemed to be present, their pale blue uniforms standing out like crocuses against black loam. Gradually the gold light cooled to lavender. Everyone began walking toward the lake. "For half a mile along the splendid sweep of the Lake-Front men were massed a hundred deep," the *Tribune* reported. This "black sea" of people was restless. "For hours they sat and waited, filling the air with a strange, uneasy uproar." One man began singing "Nearer My God to Thee," and immediately a few thousand people joined in.

As darkness fell, everyone watched the sky for the first rockets of the night's display. Thousands of Chinese lanterns hung from trees and railings. Red lights glowed from each car of the Ferris Wheel. On the lake a hundred or more ships, yachts, and launches lay at anchor with colored lights on their bows and booms and strung along their rigging.

The crowd was ready to cheer for anything. It cheered when the exposition orchestra played "Home Sweet Home," a song that never failed to

reduce grown men and women to tears, especially the newest arrivals to
the city. It cheered when the lights came on within the Court of Honor
and all the palaces became outlined in gold. It cheered when the big
searchlights atop the Manufactures and Liberal Arts Building began
sweeping the crowd, and when colorful plumes of water—"peacock
feathers," the *Tribune* called them—began erupting from the
MacMonnies Fountain.

At nine o'clock, however, the crowd hushed. A small bright light had
arisen in the sky to the north and appeared to be drifting along the
lakeshore toward the wharf. One of the searchlights found it and
revealed it to be a large manned balloon. A light flared well below its basket. In the next instant bursts of sparks in red, white, and blue formed a
huge American flag against the black sky. The balloon and flag drifted
overhead. The searchlight followed, its beam clearly outlined in the sulphur cloud that trailed the balloon. Seconds later rockets began arcing
over the lakeshore. Men with flares raced along the beach lighting mor-
tars, as other men aboard barges set off large rotating flares and hurled
bombs into the lake, causing the water to explode in extravagant geysers
of red, white, and blue. Bombs and rockets followed in intensifying numbers until the climax of the show, when an elaborate wire network
erected at Festival Hall, on the lakeshore, abruptly flared into a giant
explosive portrait of George Washington.

The crowd cheered.

Everyone began moving at the same time, and soon a great black tide
was moving toward the exits and the stations of the Alley L and Illinois
Central. Holmes and the Williams sisters waited hours for their turn to
board one of the northbound trains, but the wait did nothing to dampen
their spirits. That night the Oker family heard joking and laughter coming from the upstairs flat at 1220 Wrightwood.

There was good reason for the merriment within. Holmes had further
sweetened the night with an astonishingly generous offer to Minnie
and Anna.

Before bed Anna wrote home to her aunt in Texas to tell her the excellent news.

"Sister, brother Harry, and myself will go to Milwaukee tomorrow, and will go to Old Orchard Beach, Maine, by way of the St. Lawrence River. We'll visit two weeks in Maine, then on to New York. Brother Harry thinks I am talented; he wants me to look around about studying art. Then we will sail for Germany, by way of London and Paris. If I like it, I will stay and study art. Brother Harry says you need never trouble any more about me, financially or otherwise; he and sister will see to me."

"Write me right away," she added, "and address to Chicago, and the letter will be forwarded to me."

She said nothing about her trunk, which was still in Midlothian awaiting shipment to Chicago. She would have to get along without it for now. Once it arrived, she could arrange by telegraph to have it forwarded as well, perhaps to Maine or New York, so that she could have all her things in hand for the voyage to Europe.

Anna went to bed that night with her heart still racing from the excitement of the fair and Holmes's surprise. Later William Capp, an attorney with the Texas firm of Capp & Canty, said, "Anna had no property of her own, and such a change as described in her letter meant everything for her."

The next morning promised to be pleasant as well, for Holmes had announced he would take Anna—just her—to Englewood for a brief tour of his World's Fair Hotel. He had to attend to a few last-minute business matters before the departure for Milwaukee. In the meantime Minnie would ready the Wrightwood flat for whatever tenant happened to rent it next.

Holmes was such a charming man. And now that Anna knew him, she saw that he really was quite handsome. When his marvelous blue eyes caught hers, they seemed to warm her entire body. Minnie had done well indeed.

Worry

AT THE FAIRGROUNDS LATER that night the ticketmen counted their sales and found that for that single day, July 4, paid attendance had totaled 283,273—far greater than the entire first week of the fair.

It was the first clear evidence that Chicago might have created something extraordinary after all, and it renewed Burnham's hopes that the fair at last would achieve the level of attendance he had hoped for.

But the next day, only 79,034 paying visitors came to see the fair. Three days later the number sagged to 44,537. The bankers carrying the fair's debt grew anxious. The fair's auditor already had discovered that Burnham's department had spent over $22 million to build the fair (roughly $660 million in twenty-first-century dollars), more than twice the amount originally planned. The bankers were pressuring the exposition's directors to appoint a Retrenchment Committee empowered not just to seek out ways of reducing the fair's expenses but to execute whatever cost-saving measures it deemed necessary, including layoffs and the elimination of departments and committees.

Burnham knew that placing the future of the fair in the hands of bankers would mean its certain failure. The only way to ease the pressure was to boost the total of paid admissions to far higher levels. Estimates held that to avoid financial failure—a humiliation for Chicago's prideful leading men who counted themselves lords of the dollar—the fair would have to sell a minimum of 100,000 tickets a day for the rest of its run.

To have even a hope of achieving this, the railroads would have to reduce their fares, and Frank Millet would have to intensify his efforts to attract people from all corners of the country.

With the nation's economic depression growing ever more profound—banks failing, suicides multiplying—it seemed an impossibility.

Claustrophobia

HOLMES KNEW THAT MOST if not all of his hotel guests would be at the fair. He showed Anna the drugstore, restaurant, and barbershop and took her up to the roof to give her a broader view of Englewood and the pretty, tree-shaded neighborhood that surrounded his corner. He ended the tour at his office, where he offered Anna a seat and excused himself. He picked up a sheaf of papers and began reading.

Distractedly, he asked Anna if she would mind going into the adjacent room, the walk-in vault, to retrieve for him a document he had left inside.

Cheerfully, she complied.

Holmes followed quietly.

⌒────⌒

At first it seemed as though the door had closed by accident. The room was utterly without light. Anna pounded on the door and called for Harry. She listened, then pounded again. She was not frightened, just embarrassed. She did not like the darkness, which was more complete than anything she had ever experienced—far darker, certainly, than any moonless night in Texas. She rapped the door with her knuckles and listened again.

The air grew stale.

⌒────⌒

Holmes listened. He sat peacefully in a chair by the wall that separated his office and the vault. Time passed. It was really very peaceful. A soft breeze drifted through the room, cross-ventilation being one of the benefits of a corner office. The breeze, still cool, carried the morning scent of prairie grasses and moist soil.

⌐────⌐

Anna removed her shoe and beat the heel against the door. The room was growing warmer. Sweat filmed her face and arms. She guessed that Harry, unaware of her plight, had gone elsewhere in the building. That would explain why he still had not come despite her pounding. Perhaps he had gone to check on something in the shops below. As she considered this, she became a bit frightened. The room had grown substantially warmer. Catching a clean breath was difficult. And she needed a bathroom.

He would be so apologetic. She could not show him how afraid she was. She tried shifting her thoughts to the journey they would begin that afternoon. That she, a Texas schoolmarm, soon would be walking the streets of London and Paris still seemed an impossibility, yet Harry had promised it and made all the arrangements. In just a few hours she would board a train for the short trip to Milwaukee, and soon afterward she, Minnie, and Harry would be on their way to the lovely, cool valley of the St. Lawrence River, between New York and Canada. She saw herself sitting on the spacious porch of some fine riverside hotel, sipping tea and watching the sun descend.

She hammered the door again and now also the wall between the vault and Harry's breeze-filled office.

⌐────⌐

The panic came, as it always did. Holmes imagined Anna crumpled in a corner. If he chose, he could rush to the door, throw it open, hold her in his arms, and weep with her at the tragedy just barely averted. He could do it at the last minute, in the last few seconds. He could do that.

Or he could open the door and look in on Anna and give her a big smile—just to let her know that this was no accident—then close the door again, slam it, and return to his chair to see what might happen next. Or he could flood the vault, right now, with gas. The hiss and repulsive odor would tell her just as clearly as a smile that something extraordinary was under way.

He could do any of these things.

He had to concentrate to hear the sobs from within. The airtight fittings, the iron walls, and the mineral-wool insulation deadened most of the sound, but he had found with experience that if he listened at the gas pipe, he heard everything much more clearly.

This was the time he most craved. It brought him a period of sexual release that seemed to last for hours, even though in fact the screams and pleading faded rather quickly.

He filled the vault with gas, just to be sure.

⁂

Holmes returned to the Wrightwood apartment and told Minnie to get ready—Anna was waiting for them at the castle. He held Minnie and kissed her and told her how lucky he was and how much he liked her sister.

During the train ride to Englewood, he seemed well rested and at peace, as if he had just ridden his bicycle for miles and miles.

⁂

Two days later, on July 7, the Oker family received a letter from Henry Gordon stating that he no longer needed the apartment. The letter came as a surprise. The Okers believed Gordon and the two sisters still occupied the flat. Lora Oker went upstairs to check. She knocked, heard nothing, then entered.

"I do not know how they got out of the house," she said, "but there were evidences of hasty packing, a few books and odds and ends being left lying about. If there had been any writing in the books all traces were removed, for the fly leaves had been torn out."

Also on July 7 the Wells-Fargo agent in Midlothian, Texas, loaded a large trunk into the baggage car of a northbound train. The trunk—Anna's trunk—was addressed to "Miss Nannie Williams, c/o H. Gordon, 1220 Wrightwood Ave., Chicago."

The trunk reached the city several days later. A Wells-Fargo drayman tried to deliver it to the Wrightwood address but could not locate anyone named Williams or Gordon. He returned the trunk to the Wells-Fargo office. No one came to claim it.

———

Holmes called upon an Englewood resident named Cephas Humphrey, who owned his own team and dray and made a living transporting furniture, crates, and other large objects from place to place. Holmes asked him to pick up a box and a trunk. "I want you to come after the stuff about dark," Holmes said, "as I do not care to have the neighbors see it go away."

Humphrey showed up as requested. Holmes led him into the castle and upstairs to a windowless room with a heavy door.

"It was an awful looking place," Humphrey said. "There were no windows in it at all and only a heavy door opening into it. It made my flesh creep to go in there. I felt as if something was wrong, but Mr. Holmes did not give me much time to think about that."

The box was a long rectangle made of wood, roughly the dimensions of a coffin. Humphrey carried it down first. Out on the sidewalk, he stood it on end. Holmes, watching from above, rapped hard on the window and called down, "Don't do that. Lay it down flat."

Humphrey did so, then walked back upstairs to retrieve the trunk. It was heavy, but its weight gave him no trouble.

Holmes instructed him to take the long box to the Union Depot and told him where on the platform to place it. Apparently Holmes had made prior arrangements with an express agent to pick up the box and load it on a train. He did not disclose its destination.

As for the trunk, Humphrey could not recall where he took it, but later evidence suggests he drove it to the home of Charles Chappell, near Cook County Hospital.

———

Soon afterward Holmes brought an unexpected but welcome gift to the family of his assistant, Benjamin Pitezel. He gave Pitezel's wife,

Carrie, a collection of dresses, several pairs of shoes, and some hats that had belonged to his cousin, a Miss Minnie Williams, who had gotten married and moved east and no longer needed her old things. He recommended that Carrie cut up the dresses and use the material to make clothing for her three daughters. Carrie was very grateful.

Holmes also surprised his caretaker, Pat Quinlan, with a gift: two sturdy trunks, each bearing the initials MRW.

Storm and Fire

BURNHAM'S WORK DID NOT CEASE, the pace at his office did not slow. The fair buildings were complete and all exhibits were in place, but just as surely as silver tarnishes, the fair became subject to the inevitable forces of degradation and decline—and tragedy.

On Sunday, July 9, a day of heat and stillness, the Ferris Wheel became one of the most sought-after places to be, as did the basket of the Midway's captive balloon. The balloon, named *Chicago,* was filled with 100,000 cubic feet of hydrogen and controlled by a tether connected to a winch. By three o'clock that afternoon it had made thirty-five trips aloft, to an altitude of one thousand feet. As far as the concession's German aerialist was concerned, the day had been a perfect one for ascensions, so still, he estimated, that a plumb line dropped from the basket would have touched the winch directly below.

At three o'clock, however, the manager of the concession, G. F. Morgan, checked his instruments and noted a sudden decline in barometric pressure, evidence that a storm was forming. He halted the sale of new tickets and ordered his men to reel in the balloon. The operators of the Ferris Wheel, he saw, did not take equivalent precautions. The wheel continued to turn.

Clouds gathered, the sky purpled, and a breeze rose from the northwest. The sky sagged toward the ground and a small funnel cloud appeared, which began wobbling south along the lakeshore, toward the fair.

The Ferris Wheel was full of passengers, who watched with mounting concern as the funnel did its own *danse du ventre* across Jackson Park directly toward the Midway.

At the base of the captive balloon, Manager Morgan ordered his men to grab mooring ropes and hang on tight.

⸻

Within Jackson Park the sudden shift from sunlight to darkness drew Burnham outside. A powerful wind reared from all directions. Lunch wraps took flight and wheeled in the air like gulls. The sky seemed to reach into the exposition, and somewhere glass shattered, not the gentle tinkling of a window extinguished by a stone but the hurt-dog yelp of large sheets falling to the ground.

In the Agriculture Building a giant pane of glass fell from the roof and shattered the table at which, just a few seconds earlier, a young woman had been selling candy. Six roof panes blew from the Manufactures and Liberal Arts Building. Exhibitors raced to cover their displays with duckcloth.

The wind tore a forty-square-foot segment from the dome of the Machinery Building and lifted the roof off the fair's Hungarian Café. The crew of one of Olmsted's electric launches made a hasty landing to evacuate all passengers and had just begun motoring toward shelter when a burst of wind caught the boat's awning and whipped the five-ton craft onto its side. The pilot and conductor swam to safety.

Giant feathers rocked in the air. The twenty-eight ostriches of the Midway ostrich farm bore the loss with their usual aplomb.

⸻

In the wheel, riders braced themselves. One woman fainted. A passenger later wrote to *Engineering News*, "It took the combined effort of two of us to close the doors tight. The wind blew so hard the rain drops appeared to be flowing almost horizontal instead of vertical." The wheel continued to turn, however, as if no wind were blowing. Passengers felt only a slight vibration. The letter-writer, apparently an engineer, estimated the wind deflected the wheel to one side by only an inch and a half.

The riders watched as the wind gripped the adjacent captive balloon and tore it from the men holding it down and briefly yanked Manager

Morgan into the sky. The wind pummeled the balloon as if it were an inverted punching bag, then tore it to pieces and cast shreds of its nine thousand yards of silk as far as half a mile away.

Morgan took the disaster calmly. "I got some pleasure out of watching the storm come up," he said, "and it was a sight of a lifetime to see the balloon go to pieces, even if it was a costly bit of sightseeing for the people who own stock in the company."

Whether the storm had anything to do with the events of the next day, Monday, July 10, can't be known, but the timing was suspicious.

On Monday, shortly after one o'clock, as Burnham supervised repairs and crews removed storm debris from the grounds, smoke began to rise from the cupola of the Cold Storage tower, where the fire of June 17 also had taken light.

The tower was made of wood and housed a large iron smokestack, which vented three boilers located in the main building below. Paradoxically, heat was required to produce cold. The stack rose to a point thirty inches short of the top of the tower, where an additional iron assembly, called a thimble, was to have been placed to extend the stack so that it cleared the top completely. The thimble was a crucial part of architect Frank Burnham's design, meant to shield the surrounding wooden walls from the superheated gases exiting the stack. For some reason, however, the contractor had not installed it. The building was like a house whose chimney ended not above the roof but inside the attic.

The first alarm reached the fire department at 1:32 P.M. Engines thundered to the building. Twenty firemen led by Captain James Fitzpatrick entered the main structure and climbed to its roof. From there they made their way to the tower and climbed stairs another seventy feet to the tower's exterior balcony. Using ropes they hauled up a line of hose and a twenty-five-foot ladder. They secured the hose firmly to the tower.

Fitzpatrick and his men didn't realize it, but the fire at the top of the tower had set a lethal trap. Fragments of burning debris had fallen into the space between the iron stack and the inner walls of the tower, made of smooth white pine. These flaming brands ignited a fire that, in those narrow confines, soon depleted the available air and extinguished its own flames, leaving in their place a superheated plasma that needed only a fresh supply of oxygen to become explosive.

As the firemen on the tower balcony concentrated on the fire above them, a small plume of white smoke appeared at their feet.

The Fire Department rang a second alarm at 1:41 P.M. and activated the big siren at the exposition's Machinery Building. Thousands of visitors now moved toward the smoke and packed the lawns and paths surrounding the building. Some brought lunch. Burnham came, as did Davis. The Columbian Guard arrived in force to clear the way for additional engines and ladder wagons. Riders on the Ferris Wheel got the clearest, most horrific view of what happened next.

"Never," the Fire Department reported, "was so terrible a tragedy witnessed by such a sea of agonized faces."

Suddenly flames erupted from the tower at a point about fifty feet *below* Fitzpatrick and his men. Fresh air rushed into the tower. An explosion followed. To the firemen, according to the department's official report, it appeared "as though the gaseous contents of the air-shaft surrounding the smokestack had become ignited, and the entire interior of the tower at once became a seething furnace."

Fireman John Davis was standing on the balcony with Captain Fitzpatrick and the other men. "I saw there was only one chance, and I made up my mind to take it," Davis said. "I made a leap for the hose and had the good luck to catch it. The rest of the boys seemed transfixed with horror and unable to move."

Davis and one other man rode the hose to the ground. The firemen still on the balcony knew their situation was deadly and began to tell each other good-bye. Witnesses watched them hug and shake hands. Captain Fitzpatrick grabbed a rope and swung down through the fire to the main roof below, where he lay with a fractured leg and internal injuries, half his huge mustache burned away. Other men jumped to their deaths, in some cases penetrating the main roof.

Fire Marshal Murphy and two other firemen on the ground climbed a ladder to retrieve Fitzpatrick. They lowered him by rope to colleagues waiting below. He was alive but fading.

In all, the blaze killed twelve firemen and three workers. Fitzpatrick died at nine o'clock that night.

The next day attendance exceeded 100,000. The still-smoking rubble of the Cold Storage Building had proved irresistible.

The coroner immediately convened an inquest, during which a jury heard testimony from Daniel Burnham; Frank Burnham; officials of Hercules Iron Works; and various firemen. Daniel Burnham testified he had not known of the previous fire or the omitted thimble and claimed that since the building was a private concession he had no authority over its construction beyond approving its design. On Tuesday, July 18, the jury charged him, Fire Marshal Murphy, and two Hercules officers with criminal negligence and referred the charges to a grand jury.

Burnham was stunned but kept his silence. "The attempt to hold you in any degree responsible or censurable for the loss of life is an outrage," wrote Dion Geraldine, his construction superintendent at the fair. "The men who gave this verdict must have been very stupid, or sadly misinformed."

Under customary procedures, Burnham and the others would have been placed under arrest pending bail, but in this instance even the coroner's office seemed taken aback. The sheriff made no move to arrest the director of works. Burnham posted bond the next morning.

With the stink of charred wood still heavy in the air, Burnham closed the roof walks of the Transportation and Manufactures and Liberal Arts buildings and the balconies and upper galleries of the Administration Building, fearing that a fire in the buildings or among their exhibits could start a panic and cause a tragedy of even greater magnitude. Hundreds of people had crowded the roof walk of the Manufactures Building each day, but their only way down was by elevator. Burnham imagined terrified men, women, and children trying to slide down the glass flanks of the roof and breaking through, then falling two hundred feet to the exhibit floor.

As if things could not get any blacker, on the same day that the coroner's jury ordered Burnham's arrest, July 18, the directors of the exposition bowed to bank pressure and voted to establish a Retrenchment Committee with nearly unrestricted powers to cut costs throughout the fair, and appointed three cold-eyed men to staff it. A subsequent resolution approved by the Exposition Company's directors stated that as of August 1, "no expenditures whatever connected with the construction, maintenance or conduct of the Exposition shall be incurred unless authorized by said committee." It was clear from the start that the committee's primary target was Burnham's Department of Works.

Equally clear, at least to Burnham, was that the last thing the fair needed right now, as he and Millet continued their fight to boost the rate of paid admissions—a campaign with its own necessary costs—was a troika of penny-pinchers sitting in judgment on every new expense. Millet had some extraordinary ideas for events in August, including an elaborate Midway ball during which fair officials, including Burnham, would dance with Dahoman women and Algerian belly dancers. That the committee would view the expense of this ball and other Millet events as frivolous seemed certain. Yet Burnham knew that such expenditures, as well as continued spending on police, garbage removal, and maintenance of roads and lawns, was vital.

He feared that the Retrenchment Committee would cripple the fair for once and for all.

Love

THE REMAINS OF THE Cold Storage fire were still visible as a party of schoolteachers arrived from St. Louis, accompanied by a young reporter. The twenty-four teachers had won a contest held by the *St. Louis Republic* that entitled them to a free stay at the fair at the newspaper's expense. Along with assorted friends and family members—for a total of forty travelers—they had piled into a luxurious sleeper car, named *Benares,* provided by the Chicago & Alton Railroad. They arrived at Chicago's Union Depot on Monday, July 17, at eight o'clock in the morning and went immediately by carriage to their hotel, the Varsity, located close enough to the fair that from its second-floor balcony the teachers could see the Ferris Wheel, the top of the Manufactures and Liberal Arts Building, and Big Mary's gilded head.

The reporter—Theodore Dreiser—was young and suffused with a garish self-confidence that drew the attention of the young women. He flirted with all but of course was drawn most to the one woman who seemed least interested, a small, pretty, and reserved woman named Sara Osborne White, whom a past suitor had nicknamed "Jug" for her tendency to wear brown. She was hardly Dreiser's type: By now he was sexually experienced and in the middle of an entirely physical affair with his landlady. To him Sara White exuded "an intense something concealed by an air of supreme innocence and maidenly reserve."

Dreiser joined the teachers on the Ferris Wheel and accompanied them on a visit to Buffalo Bill's show, where Colonel Cody himself greeted the women and shook hands with each. Dreiser followed the ladies through the Manufactures and Liberal Arts Building where, he said, a man "could trail round from place to place for a year and not get tired." In the

Midway Dreiser persuaded James J. Corbett to meet the women. Corbett was the boxer who had downed John L. Sullivan in the great fight of September 1892, a battle that had consumed the entire front page of the next morning's *Chicago Tribune*. Corbett too shook the women's hands, although one teacher declined the opportunity. Her name was Sullivan.

Every chance he got, Dreiser tried to separate Sara White from the *Republic*'s entourage, which Dreiser called the "Forty Odd," but Sara had brought along her sister Rose, which complicated things. On at least one occasion Dreiser tried to kiss Sara. She told him not to be "sentimental."

He failed at seduction, but was himself successfully seduced—by the fair. It had swept him, he said, "into a dream from which I did not recover for months." Most captivating were the nights, "when the long shadows have all merged into one and the stars begin to gleam out over the lake and the domes of the palaces of the White City."

Sara White remained on his mind long after he and the Forty Odd departed the fair. In St. Louis he wrote to her and courted her and in the process resolved to make more of himself as a writer. He left St. Louis for a job editing a rural Michigan newspaper but found that the realities of being a small-town editor did not live up to the fantasy. After a few other stops he reached Pittsburgh. He wrote to Sara White and visited her whenever he returned to St. Louis. He asked her to sit in his lap. She refused.

She did, however, accept his proposal of marriage. Dreiser showed a friend, John Maxwell of the *St. Louis Globe-Democrat,* her photograph. Where Dreiser saw an enticing woman of mystery, Maxwell saw a schoolmarm of drab demeanor. He tried to warn Dreiser: "If you marry now—and a conventional and narrow woman at that, one older than you, you're gone."

It was good advice for a man like Dreiser. But Dreiser did not take it.

✦━━━╸

The Ferris Wheel became a vector for love. Couples asked permission to be married at the highest point on the wheel. Luther Rice never allowed it, but in two cases where the couples already had mailed invitations, he did permit weddings in his office.

Despite the wheel's inherent romantic potential, however, rides at night never became popular. The favorite hour was the golding time between five and six in the evening.

⌐━━━┐

Holmes, newly free and land rich, brought a new woman to the fair, Georgiana Yoke, whom he had met earlier in the year at a department store, Schlesinger & Meyer, where she worked as a saleswoman. She had grown up in Franklin, Indiana, and lived there with her parents until 1891, when she set out for a bigger, more glamorous life in Chicago. She was only twenty-three when she met Holmes, but her small size and sun-blond hair made her look much younger, almost like a child—save for the sharp features of her face and the intelligence that inhabited her very large blue eyes.

She had never met anyone like him. He was handsome, articulate, and clearly well off. He even possessed property in Europe. She felt a certain sadness for him, however. He was so alone—all his family was dead, save one aunt living in Africa. His last uncle had just died and left him a large fortune consisting of property in the South and in Fort Worth, Texas.

Holmes gave her many presents, among them a Bible, diamond earrings, and a locket—"a little heart," she said, "with pearls."

At the fair he took her on the Ferris Wheel and hired a gondola and walked with her on the dark fragrant paths of the Wooded Island, in the soft glow of Chinese lanterns.

He asked her to be his wife. She agreed.

He cautioned, however, that for the marriage he would have to use a different name, Henry Mansfield Howard. It was his dead uncle's name, he said. The uncle was blood proud and had bequeathed Holmes his estate on condition he first adopt the uncle's name in full. Holmes had obliged, out of respect for his uncle's memory.

⌐━━━┐

Mayor Harrison too believed he was in love, with a New Orleans woman named Annie Howard. He was sixty-eight and a widower twice over; she was in her twenties—no one knew exactly where in her twenties, but estimates put her between twenty-one and twenty-seven years old. She was "very plump," by one account, and "full of life." She had come to Chicago for the duration of the fair and was renting a mansion near the mayor's. She spent her days at the fair buying art.

Harrison and Miss Howard had some news for the city, but the mayor had no plans to reveal it until October 28, when the exposition would host American Cities Day. *His* day, really—two days before the official close, but the day when he would get to stand before several thousand mayors from around the country and revel in his stature as mayor of Chicago, the city that built the greatest fair of all time.

Freaks

On July 31, 1893, after two investigative hearings, the Retrenchment Committee gave its report to the exposition's Board of Directors. The report stated that the financial management of the fair "can only be characterized as shamefully extravagant." Drastic cuts in spending and staff were necessary, immediately. "As to the Construction Department, we hardly know what to say," the report continued. "We had no time to go into details, but have formed the decided impression that this is being run now, as in the past, upon the general theory that money is no object."

The Retrenchment Committee made it clear that, at least for its three members, the financial success of the fair was as important as its obvious aesthetic success. The honor of Chicago's leading men, who prided themselves on their unsentimental—some might say ruthless—pursuit of maximum profit, was in peril. The report closed, "If we are not to be disgraced before the public as business-men, this matter must be followed up sharply and decisively."

In separate statements, the Retrenchment Committee urged the directors to make the committee permanent and invest it with the power to approve or deny every expenditure at the exposition, no matter how small.

This was too much, even for the equally hardened businessmen of the exposition board. President Higinbotham said he would resign before he would cede such power to anyone. Other directors felt likewise. Stung by this rejection, the three men of the Retrenchment Committee themselves resigned. One told a reporter, "If the directory had seen fit to continue the committee with power as originally intended, it would have dropped heads enough to fill the grand court basin. . . ."

The retrenchers' report had been too harsh, too much a rebuke, at a time when the mood throughout Chicago was one of sustained exultation at the fact that the fair had gotten built at all and that it had proven more beautiful than anyone had imagined. Even New York had apologized—well, at least one editor from New York had done so. Charles T. Root, editor of the *New York Dry Goods Reporter* and no relation to Burnham's dead partner, published an editorial on Thursday, August 10, 1893, in which he cited the ridicule and hostility that New York editors had expressed ever since Chicago won the right to build the exposition. "Hundreds of newspapers, among them scores of the strongest Eastern dailies, held their sides with merriment over the exquisite humor of the idea of this crude, upstart, pork-packing city undertaking to conceive and carry out a true World's Fair. . . ." The carping had subsided, he wrote, but few of the carpers had as yet made the *"amende honorable"* that now clearly was due Chicago. He compounded his heresy by adding that if New York had won the fair, it would not have done as fine a job. "So far as I have been able to observe New York never gets behind any enterprise as Chicago got behind this, and without that splendid pulling together, prestige, financial supremacy, and all that sort of thing would not go far toward paralleling the White City." It was time, he said, to acknowledge the truth: "Chicago has disappointed her enemies and astonished the world."

None of the exposition directors or officers had any illusions, however. The rate of paid admissions, though rising steadily, had to be increased still more, and soon. Only three months remained until the closing ceremony on October 30. (The closure was supposed to happen at the end of October, meaning October 31, but some unidentified crafter of the federal legislation erred in thinking October only had thirty days.)

The directors pressured the railroads to lower fares. The *Chicago Tribune* made fare reductions a crusade and openly attacked the railroads. "They are unpatriotic, for this is a national not a local fair," an editorial charged on August 11, 1893. "They are also desperately and utterly selfish." The next day the newspaper singled out Chauncey Depew, president of the New York Central, for a particularly caustic appraisal. "Mr.

Depew all along has posed as the special friend of the World's Fair and has been lavish in his declarations that his roads would do the fair thing and would enable tens of thousands to come here beyond Niagara Falls. . . ." Yet Depew had failed to do what he promised, the *Tribune* said. "It is in order for Chauncey M. Depew to hand in his resignation as Chicago's adopted son. Chicago wants no more of him."

Frank Millet, director of functions, meanwhile stepped up his own efforts to promote the fair and arranged an increasingly exotic series of events. He organized boat races in the basin of the Court of Honor that pitted inhabitants of the Midway villages against one another. They did battle every Tuesday evening in vessels native to their homelands. "We want to do something to liven up the lagoons and basin," Millet told an interviewer. "People are getting tired of looking at the electric launches. If we can get the Turks, the South Sea Islanders, the Singalese, the Esquimos, and the American Indians to float about the grand basin in their native barks, it will certainly add some novelty as well as interest to the scene."

Millet also organized swim meets between the Midway "types," as the press called them. He scheduled these for Fridays. The first race took place August 11 in the lagoon, with Zulus swimming against South American Indians. The Dahomans also competed, as did the Turks, "some of them as hairy as gorillas," the *Tribune* said, with the anthropological abandon common to the age. "The races were notable for the lack of clothing worn by the contestants and the serious way in which they went at the task of winning five-dollar gold pieces."

Millet's big coup was the great Midway ball, held on the night of Wednesday, August 16. The *Tribune* called it "The Ball of the Midway Freaks" and sought to whet the nation's appetite with an editorial that first noted a rising furor within the Board of Lady Managers over the belly dancers of the Midway. "Whether the apprehensions of the good ladies . . . were due to infringements of morality or to the anticipation that the performers may bring on an attack of peritonitis if they persist in their contortions is not clear, but all the same they have taken the position that what is not considered very much out of the way on the banks of the Nile or in the market places of Syria is entirely improper on the Midway between Jackson and Washington Parks."

But now, the *Tribune* continued, the belly dancers and every other depraved jiggling half-dressed woman of the Midway had been invited to the great ball, where they were expected to dance with the senior officers of the fair, including Burnham and Davis. "The situation therefore, as will be seen, is full of horrifying possibilities," the *Tribune* said. "It should cause a shiver in the composite breast of the Board of Lady Managers when they consider what may happen if Director-General Davis should lead out some fascinating Fatima at the head of the grand procession and she should be taken with peritonitis in the midst of the dance; or if [Potter] Palmer should escort a votary of the Temple of Luxor only to find her with the same ailment; or if Mayor Harrison, who belongs to all nations, should dance with the whole lot. Will they suppress their partners' contortions by protest or by force, or, following the fashion of the country, will they, too, attempt Oriental contortions? Suppose that President Higinbotham finds as his vis-à-vis an anointed, bare-backed Fiji beauty or a Dahomeyite amazon bent upon the extraordinary antics of the cannibal dance, is he to join in and imitate her or risk his head in an effort to restrain her?"

Further enriching the affair was the presence at Jackson Park of George Francis Train—known universally as "Citizen Train"—in his white suit, red belt, and red Turkish fez, invited by Millet to host the ball and the boat and swim races and anything else that Millet could devise. Train was one of the most famous men of the day, though no one knew quite why. He was said to have been the model for Phileas Fogg, the globe-trotter in *Around the World in Eighty Days*. Train claimed the real reason he was invited to the exposition was to save it by using his psychic powers to increase attendance. These powers resided in his body in the form of electrical energy. He walked about the fairgrounds rubbing his palms to husband that energy and refused to shake hands with anyone lest the act discharge his potency. "Chicago built the fair," he said.

"Everybody else tried to kill it. Chicago built it. I am here to save it and I'll be hanged if I haven't."

The ball took place in the fair's Natatorium, a large building on the Midway devoted to swimming and bathing and equipped with a ballroom and banquet rooms. Bunting of yellow and red hung from the ceiling. The galleries that overlooked the ballroom were outfitted with opera boxes for fair officials and socially prominent families. Burnham had a box, as did Davis and Higinbotham and of course the Palmers. The galleries also had seats and standing room for other paying guests. From railings in front of the boxes hung triangles of silk embroidered with gold arabesques, all glowing with the light of adjacent incandescent bulbs. The effect was one of indescribable opulence. The Retrenchment Committee would not have approved.

At nine-fifteen that night Citizen Train—dressed in his usual white, but now for some reason carrying an armful of blooming sweet pea—led the procession of exotics, many barefoot, down the stairway of the Natatorium to the ballroom below. He held the hand of a ten-year-old Mexican ballerina and was followed by scores of men and women in the customary clothing of their native cultures. Sol Bloom kept order on the ballroom floor.

The official program dedicated dances to particular officials and guests. Director-General Davis was to lead a quadrille, Burnham a "Berlin," Mayor Harrison a polka. Once the dances were completed, the crowd was to sing "Home Sweet Home."

It was hot. Chief Rain-in-the-Face, the Sioux chief who had killed Custer's brother and now occupied Sitting Bull's cabin in the Midway, wore green paint that streamed down his face. A Laplander wore a fur shirt; Eskimo women wore blouses of walrus skin. The maharajah of Kapurthala, visiting that week from India, sat in a makeshift throne on the ballroom stage fanned by three servants.

The ballroom burst with color and energy: Japanese in red silk, Bedouins in red and black, Romanians in red, blue, and yellow. Women who ordinarily would have come wearing almost nothing—like Aheze,

314 • ERIK LARSON

an Amazon, and Zahtoobe, a Dahoman—were given short skirts constructed of small American flags. The *Tribune,* in an unintended parody of its own penchant for describing the gowns of the rich, noted that Lola, a South Sea Islander, wore her "native costume of bark cloth covering about half the body, with low cut and sleeveless bodice." As the night wore on and the wine flowed, the line to dance with Lola grew long. Sadly, the belly dancers came in robes and turbans. Men in black dress suits circled the floor, "swinging black Amazons with bushy hair and teeth necklaces." Chicago—and perhaps the world—had never seen anything like it. The *Tribune* called the ball "the strangest gathering since the destruction of the Tower of Babel."

There was food, of course. The official menu:

———

RELISHES.
Hard boiled potatoes, à la Irish Village.
International hash, à la Midway Plaisance

COLD DISHES.
Roast Missionary, à la Dahomey, west coast of Africa.
Jerked buffalo, à la Indian Village.
Stuffed ostrich, à la Ostrich Farm.
Boiled camel humps, à la Cairo street.
Monkey stew, à la Hagenbeck.

ENTREES.
Fricassee of reindeer, à la Lapland.
Fried snowballs, à la Ice Railway.
Crystallized frappé, from Libby glass exhibit.

PASTRY.
Wind doughnuts, à la Captive Balloon.
Sandwiches (assorted), especially prepared by the
Leather Exhibit.

———

And for dessert, the program said, "Twenty-five percent of gross receipts."

The ball ended at four-thirty A.M. The exotics walked slowly back to the Midway. The guests climbed into their carriages and slept or softly sang "After the Ball"—the hit song of the day—as their liverymen drove them home over empty streets that echoed with the plosive rhythm of hooves on granite.

⌐━━━⌐

The ball and Frank Millet's other inventions imparted to the exposition a wilder, happier air. The exposition by day might wear a chaste gown of white staff, but at night it danced barefoot and guzzled champagne.

Attendance rose. The daily average of paid admissions for August was 113,403—at last topping the vital 100,000 threshold. The margin was slim, however. And the nation's economic depression was growing steadily worse, its labor situation more volatile.

On August 3 a big Chicago bank, Lazarus Silverman, failed. Burnham's firm had long been a client. On the night of August 10 Charles J. Eddy, a former top official of the bankrupt Reading Railroad, one of the first casualties of the panic, walked into Washington Park just north of the Midway and shot himself. Of course he had been staying at the Metropole. He was the hotel's third suicide that summer. Mayor Harrison warned that the ranks of the unemployed had swollen to an alarming degree. "If Congress does not give us money we will have riots that will shake this country," he said. Two weeks later workers scuffled with police outside City Hall. It was a minor confrontation, but the *Tribune* called it a riot. A few days after that, 25,000 unemployed workers converged on the downtown lakefront and heard Samuel Gompers, standing at the back of speaker's wagon No. 5, ask, "Why should the wealth of the country be stored in banks and elevators while the idle workman wanders homeless about the streets and the idle loafers who hoard the gold only to spend it in riotous living are rolling about in fine carriages from which they look out on peaceful meetings and call them riots?"

For the city's industrialists and merchant princes who learned of

Gompers's speech in their Sunday morning newspapers, this was a particularly unsettling question, for it seemed to embody a demand for much more than simply work. Gompers was calling for fundamental change in the relationship between workers and their overseers.

This was dangerous talk, to be suppressed at all costs.

Prendergast

IT WAS EXCITING, THIS PROSPECT of becoming one of the city's most important officials. At last Prendergast could leave behind the cold mornings and filthy streets and the angry newsboys who disobeyed and taunted him. He was growing impatient, however. His appointment as corporation counsel should have occurred by now.

One afternoon in the first week of October Prendergast took a grip-car to City Hall to see his future office. He found a clerk and introduced himself.

Incredibly, the clerk did not recognize his name. When Prendergast explained that Mayor Harrison planned to make him the city's new corporation counsel, the clerk laughed.

Prendergast insisted on seeing the current counsel, a man named Kraus. Certainly Kraus would recognize his name.

The clerk went to get him.

Kraus emerged from his office and extended his hand. He introduced Prendergast to the other men on his staff as his "successor." Suddenly everyone was smiling.

At first Prendergast thought the smiling was an acknowledgment that soon he would be in charge, but now he saw it as something else.

Kraus asked if he'd like the position immediately.

"No," Prendergast said. "I am in no hurry about it."

Which was not true, but the question had thrown Prendergast. He did not like the way Kraus asked it. Not at all.

Toward Triumph

By TEN O'CLOCK IN THE MORNING on Monday, October 9, 1893, the day Frank Millet had designated as Chicago Day, ticket-takers at the fair's Sixty-fourth Street gate made an informal count of the morning's sales thus far and found that this one gate had recorded 60,000 paid admissions. The men knew from experience that on any ordinary day sales at this gate accounted for about one-fifth of the total admissions to the fair for any given time, and so came up with an estimate that some 300,000 paid visitors already had entered Jackson Park—more than any other full day's total and close to the world's record of 397,000 held by the Paris exposition. Yet the morning had barely begun. The ticket-takers sensed that something odd was happening. The pace of admissions seemed to be multiplying by the hour. In some ticket booths the volume grew so great, so quickly, that silver coins began piling on the floors and burying the ticket-takers' shoes.

Millet and other fair officials had expected high attendance. Chicago was proud of its fair, and everyone knew that only three weeks remained before it would close forever. To assure maximum attendance, Mayor Harrison had signed an official proclamation that urged every business to suspend operation for the day. The courts closed, as did the Board of Trade. The weather helped, too. Monday was an apple-crisp day with temperatures that never exceeded sixty-two degrees, under vivid cerulean skies. Every hotel had filled to capacity, even beyond capacity, with some managers finding themselves compelled to install cots in lobbies and halls. The Wellington Catering Company, which operated eight restaurants and forty lunch counters in Jackson Park, had braced for the day by shipping in two traincar loads of potatoes, 4,000 half-barrels of beer,

15,000 gallons of ice cream, and 40,000 pounds of meat. Its cooks built 200,000 ham sandwiches and brewed 400,000 cups of coffee.

No one, however, expected the sheer crush of visitors that actually did arrive. By noon the chief of admissions, Horace Tucker, wired a message to fair headquarters, "The Paris record is broken to smithereens, and the people are still coming." A single ticket-seller, L. E. Decker, a nephew of Buffalo Bill who had sold tickets for Bill's Wild West for eight years, sold 17,843 tickets during his shift, the most by any one man, and won Horace Tucker's prize of a box of cigars. Lost children filled every chair at the headquarters of the Columbian Guard; nineteen spent the night and were claimed by their parents the next day. Five people were killed in or near the fair, including a worker obliterated while helping prepare the night's fireworks and a visitor who stepped from one grip-car into the path of another. A woman lost her foot when a surging crowd knocked her from a train platform. George Ferris, riding his wheel that day, looked down and gasped, "There must be a million people down there."

The fireworks began at eight o'clock sharp. Millet had planned an elaborate series of explosive "set pieces," fireworks affixed to large metal frames shaped to depict various portraits and tableaus. The first featured the Great Fire of 1871, including an image of Mrs. O'Leary's cow kicking over a lantern. The night boomed and hissed. For the finale the fair's pyrotechnicians launched five thousand rockets all at once into the black sky over the lake.

The true climax occurred after the grounds closed, however. In the silence, with the air still scented with exploded powder, collectors accompanied by armed guards went to each ticket booth and collected the accumulated silver, three tons of it. They counted the money under heavy guard. By one forty-five A.M., they had an exact total.

Ferris had nearly gotten it right. In that single day 713,646 people had paid to enter Jackson Park. (Only 31,059—four percent—were children.) Another 37,380 visitors had entered using passes, bringing the total admission for the day to 751,026, more people than had attended any single day of any peaceable event in history. The *Tribune* argued that the only greater gathering was the massing of Xerxes' army of over five million souls in the fifth century B.C. The Paris record of 397,000 had indeed been shattered.

When the news reached Burnham's shanty, there were cheers and champagne and stories through the night. But the best news came the next day, when officials of the World's Columbian Exposition Company, whose boasts had been ridiculed far and wide, presented a check for $1.5 million to the Illinois Trust and Savings Company and thereby extinguished the last of the exposition's debts.

The Windy City had prevailed.

⌐━━━⌐

Now Burnham and Millet made final arrangements for Burnham's own great day, the grand closing ceremony of October 30 that would recognize once and for all that Burnham really had done it and that his work was now complete—that for once there was nothing left to do. At this point, Burnham believed, nothing could tarnish the fair's triumph or his own place in architectural history.

Departures

FRANK MILLET HOPED THE closing ceremony would attract even more people than the fair's Chicago Day. While Millet did his planning, many of the other men who had helped Burnham construct the fair began the return to ordinary life.

Charles McKim disengaged reluctantly. For him the fair had been a brilliant light that for a time dispelled the shadows that had accumulated around his life. He left Jackson Park abruptly on the morning of October 23 and later that day wrote to Burnham, "You know my dislike for saying 'Good-bye' and were prepared to find that I had skipped this morning. To say that I was sorry to leave you all is to put it only one half as strongly as I feel.

"You gave me a beautiful time and the last days of the Fair will always remain in my mind, as were the first, especially identified with yourself. It will be pleasant for the rest of our natural lives to be able to look back to it and talk it over and over and over again, and it goes without saying that you can depend upon me in every way as often hereafter as you may have need of me."

The next day McKim wrote to a friend in Paris of the deepening consensus among himself, Burnham, and most of Chicago that the fair was too wonderful a thing to be allowed simply to fall into disrepair after its official closure on October 30, just six days thence: "indeed it is the ambition of all concerned to have it swept away in the same magical manner in which it appeared, and with the utmost despatch. For economy, as well as for obvious reasons, it has been proposed that the most glorious way would be to blow up the buildings with dynamite. Another scheme is to destroy them with fire. This last would be the easiest and grandest spectacle except for the danger of flying embers in the event of a change of wind from the lake."

Neither McKim nor Burnham truly believed the fair should be set aflame. The buildings, in fact, had been designed to maximize the salvage value of their components. Rather, this talk of conflagration was a way of easing the despair of watching the dream come to an end. No one could bear the idea of the White City lying empty and desolate. A *Cosmopolitan* writer said, "Better to have it vanish suddenly, in a blaze of glory, than fall into gradual disrepair and dilapidation. There is no more melancholy spectacle than a festal hall, the morning after the banquet, when the guests have departed and the lights are extinguished."

Later, these musings about fire would come to seem like prophecy.

⚬━━━⚬

Olmsted too severed his connection. Toward the end of summer his busy schedule and the stifling heat caused his health to fail once again and reactivated his insomnia. He had many projects under way, chief among them Biltmore, but he felt himself nearing the end of his career. He was seventy-one years old. On September 6, 1893, he wrote to a friend, Fred Kingsbury, "I can't come to you and often dream of a ride through our old haunts and meeting you and others but have pretty well surrendered to Fate. I must flounder along my way to the end." Olmsted did, however, allow himself a rare expression of satisfaction. "I enjoy my children," he told Kingsbury. "They are one of the centers of my life, the other being the improvement of scenery and making the enjoyment of it available. Spite of my infirmities which do drag me cruelly, I am not to be thought of as an unhappy old man."

Louis Sullivan, engorged with praise and awards for his Transportation Building—especially its Golden Door—again took up his work with Dankmar Adler but under changed circumstances. The deepening depression and missteps by the two partners had left the firm with few projects. For all of 1893 they would complete only two buildings. Sullivan, never easy on his peers, became furious with one of the firm's junior architects when he discovered the man had been using his free time to design houses for clients of his own. Sullivan fired him.

The junior man was Frank Lloyd Wright.

Ten thousand construction workers also left the fair's employ and returned to a world without jobs, already crowded with unemployed men. Once the fair closed, many thousands more would join them on Chicago's streets. The threat of violence was as palpable as the deepening cold of autumn. Mayor Harrison was sympathetic and did what he could. He hired thousands of men to clean streets and ordered police stations opened at night for men seeking a place to sleep. Chicago's *Commercial and Financial Chronicle* reported, "Never before has there been such a sudden and striking cessation of industrial activity." Pig iron production fell by half, and new rail construction shrank almost to nothing. Demand for railcars to carry visitors to the exposition had spared the Pullman Works, but by the end of the fair George Pullman too began cutting wages and workers. He did not, however, reduce the rents in his company town.

The White City had drawn men and protected them; the Black City now welcomed them back, on the eve of winter, with filth, starvation, and violence.

Holmes too sensed it was time to leave Chicago. The pressure from creditors and families was growing too great.

First he set fire to the top floor of his castle. The blaze did minimal damage, but he filed a claim for $6,000 on a policy acquired by his fictional alter ego, Hiram S. Campbell. An investigator for one of the insurance companies, F. G. Cowie, became suspicious and began a detailed investigation. Though he found no concrete evidence of arson, Cowie believed Holmes or an accomplice had started the fire. He advised the insurers to pay the claim, but only to Hiram S. Campbell and only if Campbell presented himself in person.

Holmes could not claim the money himself, for by now Cowie knew him. Ordinarily he simply would have recruited someone else to masquerade as Campbell and claim the money, but of late he had become increasingly wary. The guardians of Minnie Williams had dispatched an attorney, William Capp, to look for Minnie and to protect the assets of her estate. Anna's guardian, the Reverend Dr. Black, had hired a private detective who had come to Holmes's building. And letters continued to arrive from the Cigrands and Smythes and other parents. No one yet had accused Holmes of foul play, but the intensity of this new wave of inquiry was greater, more obliquely accusatory, than anything he previously had experienced. Hiram S. Campbell never claimed the money.

But Holmes found that Cowie's investigation had a secondary, more damaging effect. In the course of digging up information about Holmes, he had succeeded in stirring up and uniting Holmes's creditors, the furniture dealers and iron suppliers and bicycle manufacturers and contractors whom Holmes had cheated over the previous five years. The creditors now hired an attorney named George B. Chamberlin, counsel for Chicago's Lafayette Collection Agency, who had been pestering Holmes ever since he failed to pay the furnace company for improving his kiln. Later Chamberlin would claim to be the first man in Chicago to suspect Holmes of being a criminal.

In the fall of 1893 Chamberlin contacted Holmes and requested he come to a meeting at his office. Holmes believed he and Chamberlin would be meeting alone, one on one, but when Holmes arrived at the office, he found it occupied by two dozen creditors and their attorneys and one police detective.

This surprised Holmes but did not faze him. He shook hands and met the angry gazes of his creditors head on. Tempers immediately cooled a few degrees. He had that effect.

Chamberlin had planned the meeting as a trap to try to shatter Holmes's imperturbable façade, and was impressed with Holmes's ability to maintain his insouciance despite the rancor in the room. Chamberlin told Holmes that all together he owed the creditors at least $50,000.

Holmes adopted his most sober expression. He understood their concerns. He explained his lapses. His ambition had gotten ahead of his ability to pay his debts. Things would have been fine, all the debts resolved, if not for the Panic of 1893, which had ruined him and destroyed his hopes, just as it had for countless others in Chicago and the nation at large.

Incredibly, Chamberlin saw, some of the creditors nodded in sympathy.

Tears filled Holmes's eyes. He offered his deepest, most heartfelt apologies. And he suggested a solution. He proposed to settle his debts by giving the group a mortgage secured by his various properties.

This nearly made Chamberlin laugh, yet one of the attorneys present in the room actually advised the group to accept Holmes's offer. Chamberlin was startled to see that Holmes's false warmth seemed to be mollifying the creditors. A few moments earlier the group had wanted the detective to arrest Holmes the moment he entered the room. Now they wanted to talk about what to do next.

Chamberlin told Holmes to wait in an adjacent room.

Holmes did so. He waited peacefully.

As the meeting progressed—and grew heated—the attorney who previously had wanted to accept Holmes's mortgage stepped out of Chamberlin's office and entered the room where Holmes waited, ostensibly for a drink of water. He and Holmes talked. Exactly what happened next is unclear. Chamberlin claimed later that this attorney had been so angry at having his recommendation rebuffed that he tipped Holmes to the fact the creditors were again leaning toward arrest. It is possible, too, that Holmes simply offered the attorney cash for the information, or deployed his false warmth and teary regret to seduce the attorney into revealing the group's mounting consensus.

The attorney returned to the meeting.

Holmes fled.

Soon afterward Holmes set out for Fort Worth, Texas, to take better advantage of Minnie Williams's land. He had plans for the property. He would sell some of it and on the rest build a three-story structure exactly like the one in Englewood. Meanwhile he would use the land to secure loans and to float notes. He expected to lead a very prosperous and satisfying life, at least until the time came to move on to the next city. He brought along his assistant, Benjamin Pitezel, and his new fiancée, the small and pretty Miss Georgiana Yoke. Just before leaving Chicago Holmes acquired a life insurance policy, from the Fidelity Mutual Life Association of Philadelphia, to insure Pitezel's life for $10,000.

Nightfall

THROUGHOUT OCTOBER ATTENDANCE AT the fair rose sharply as more and more people realized that the time left to see the White City was running short. On October 22 paid attendance totaled 138,011. Just two days later it reached 244,127. Twenty thousand people a day now rode the Ferris Wheel, 80 percent more than at the start of the month. Everyone hoped attendance would continue rising and that the number of people drawn to the closing ceremony of October 30 would break the record set on Chicago Day.

To attract visitors for the close, Frank Millet planned a day-long celebration with music, speeches, fireworks, and a landing by "Columbus" himself from the exposition's full-sized replicas of the *Niña, Pinta,* and *Santa María,* built in Spain for the fair. Millet hired actors to play Columbus and his captains; the crew would consist of the men who had sailed the ships to Chicago. Millet arranged to borrow tropical plants and trees from the Horticulture Building and have them moved to the lakeshore. He planned also to coat the beach with fallen oak and maple leaves to signify the fact that Columbus landed in autumn, even though live palms and dead deciduous leaves were not precisely compatible. Upon landing, Columbus was to thrust his sword into the ground and claim the New World for Spain, while his men assumed positions that mimicked those depicted on a two-cent postage stamp commemorating Columbus's discovery. Meanwhile, according to the *Tribune,* Indians recruited from Buffalo Bill's show and from various fair exhibits would "peer cautiously" at the landing party while shouting incoherently and running "to and fro." With this enactment Millet hoped to carry visitors "back 400 years"—despite the steam tugboats that would nudge the Spanish ships toward shore.

First, however, came Mayor Harrison's big day, American Cities Day, on Saturday, October 28. Five thousand mayors and city councilmen had accepted Harrison's invitation to the fair, among them the mayors of San Francisco, New Orleans and Philadelphia. The record is silent as to whether New York's mayor attended or not.

That morning Harrison delighted reporters by announcing that yes, the rumors about him and the very young Miss Annie Howard were true, and not only that, the two planned to marry on November 16.

The glory time came in the afternoon, when he rose to speak to the assembled mayors. Friends said he had never looked so handsome, so full of life.

He praised the remarkable transformation of Jackson Park. "Look at it now!" he said. "These buildings, this hall, this dream of poets of centuries is the wild aspiration of crazy architects alone." He told his audience, "I myself have taken a new lease of life"—an allusion perhaps to Miss Howard—"and I believe I shall see the day when Chicago will be the biggest city in America, and the third city on the face of the globe." He was sixty-eight years old but announced, "I intend to live for more than half a century, and at the end of that half-century London will be trembling lest Chicago shall surpass it. . . ."

With a glance at the mayor of Omaha, he graciously offered to accept Omaha as a suburb.

He changed course. "It sickens me when I look at this great Exposition to think that it will be allowed to crumble to dust," he said. He hoped the demolition would be quick, and he quoted a recent remark by Burnham: " 'Let it go; it has to go, so let it go. Let us put the torch to it and burn it down.' I believe with him. If we cannot preserve it for another year I would be in favor of putting a torch to it and burning it down and let it go up into the bright sky to eternal heaven."

⌐⎯⎯⎯⌐

Prendergast could stand it no longer. His visit to the corporation counsel's office—by rights *his* office—had been humiliating. They had humored him. Smirked. Yet Harrison had promised him the job. What did he have to do to get the mayor's attention? All his postcards had achieved nothing. No one wrote to him, no one took him seriously.

At two o'clock on American Cities Day Prendergast left his mother's house and walked to a shoe dealer on Milwaukee Avenue. He paid the dealer four dollars for a used six-chamber revolver. He knew that revolvers of this particular model had a penchant for accidental discharge when bumped or dropped, so he loaded it with only five cartridges and kept the empty chamber under the hammer.

Later, much would be made of this precaution.

At three o'clock, about the time Harrison was giving his speech, Prendergast walked into the Unity Building in central Chicago where Governor John P. Altgeld had an office.

Prendergast looked pale and strangely excited. An official of the building found his demeanor troubling and told him he could not enter.

Prendergast returned to the street.

It was nearly dark when Harrison left Jackson Park and drove north through the cold smoky evening toward his mansion on Ashland Avenue. Temperatures had fallen sharply over the week, down to the thirties at night, and the sky seemed perpetually overcast. Harrison reached his home by seven o'clock. He tinkered with a first-floor window, then sat down to supper with two of his children, Sophie and Preston. He had other children, but they were grown and gone. The meal, of course, included watermelon.

In the midst of supper, at approximately seven-thirty, someone rang the bell at the front door. Mary Hanson, the parlor maid, answered and found a gaunt young man with a smooth-shaven face and close-cut black hair. He looked ill. He asked to see the mayor.

By itself, there was nothing peculiar about the request. Evening visits by strangers were a regular occurrence at the Ashland house, for Harrison prided himself on being available to any citizen of Chicago, regardless of social stature. Tonight's visitor seemed seedier than most, however, and behaved oddly. Nonetheless, Mary Hanson told him to come back in half an hour.

⌐⎯⎯⌐

The day had been an exciting one for the mayor but also exhausting. He fell asleep at the table. Shortly before eight o'clock his son left the dining room to go up to his room and dress for an engagement in the city later that night. Sophie also went upstairs, to write a letter. The house was cozy and well lit. Mary Hanson and the other servants gathered in the kitchen for their own supper.

At precisely eight o'clock the front bell again rang, and again Hanson answered it.

The same young man stood at the threshold. Hanson asked him to wait in the hall and went to get the mayor.

"It must have been about eight o'clock when I heard a noise," Harrison's son Preston said. "I was startled; it sounded like a picture falling." Sophie heard it, too, and heard her father cry out. "I thought nothing of it," she said, "because I thought it was some screens falling on the floor near the back hall. Father's voice I took to be a yawn. He had a way of yawning very loud."

Preston left his room and saw smoke drifting up from the entry hall. As he came down the steps, he heard two more reports. "The last shot was clear and penetrating," he said. "I knew it to be a revolver shot." It sounded "like a manhole explosion."

He ran to the hall and found Harrison lying on his back surrounded by servants, the air silvered with gunsmoke. There was very little blood. Preston shouted, "Father is not hurt, is he?"

The mayor himself answered. "Yes," he said. "I am shot. I will die."

Three more shots sounded from the street. The coachman had fired his own revolver once in the air to alert police, once at Prendergast, and Prendergast had returned the shot.

The commotion brought a neighbor, William J. Chalmers, who folded his coat under Harrison's head. Harrison told him he had been shot over the heart, but Chalmers did not believe it. There was too little blood.

They argued.

Chalmers told Harrison he had *not* been shot over the heart.

Harrison snapped, "I tell you I am; this is death."

A few moments later his heart stopped.

"He died angry," Chalmers said, "because I didn't believe him. Even in death he is emphatic and imperious."

⌐━━━╸

Prendergast walked to the nearby Desplaines Street police station and calmly told desk sergeant O. Z. Barber, "Lock me up; I am the man who shot the mayor." The sergeant was incredulous, until Prendergast gave him the revolver, which smelled strongly of blown powder. Barber found that its cylinder contained four spent cartridges and a single live one. The sixth chamber was empty.

Barber asked Prendergast why he had shot the mayor.

"Because he betrayed my confidence. I supported him through his campaign and he promised to appoint me corporation counsel. He didn't live up to his word."

⌐━━━╸

The Exposition Company canceled the closing ceremony. There would be no Jubilee March, no landing by Columbus, no address by Harlow Higinbotham, George Davis, or Bertha Palmer; no presentation of awards, no praise for Burnham and Olmsted; no "Hail Columbia"; no mass rendition of "Auld Lang Syne." The closing became instead a memorial assembly in the fair's Festival Hall. As the audience entered, an organist played Chopin's "Funeral March" on the hall's giant pipe organ. The hall was so cold, the presiding officer announced that men could keep their hats on.

Reverend Dr. J. H. Barrows read a blessing and benediction and then, at the request of exposition officials, read a speech that Higinbotham had prepared for the originally planned ceremony. The remarks still seemed appropriate, especially one passage. "We are turning our backs upon the fairest dream of civilization and are about to consign it to the dust," Barrows read. "It is like the death of a dear friend."

The audience exited slowly into the cold gray afternoon.

At exactly four forty-five, sunset, the warship *Michigan* fired one of its cannon and continued to fire twenty times more as one thousand men quietly took up positions at each of the exposition's flags. With the last boom of the *Michigan*'s gun, the great flag at the Administration Building fell to the ground. Simultaneously, the thousand other flags also fell, as massed trumpeters and bassoonists in the Court of Honor played "The Star-Spangled Banner" and "America." Two hundred thousand visitors, many in tears, joined in.

The fair was over.

The six hundred carriages in Carter Harrison's cortege stretched for miles. The procession moved slowly and quietly through a black sea of men and women dressed for mourning. A catafalque carrying Harrison's black casket led the cortege and was followed immediately by Harrison's beloved Kentucky mare, stirrups crossed on its empty saddle. Everywhere the white flags that had symbolized the White City hung at half mast. Thousands of men and women wore buttons that said "Our Carter" and watched in silence as, carriage by carriage, the city's greatest men drove past. Armour, Pullman, Schwab, Field, McCormick, Ward.

And Burnham.

It was a difficult ride for him. He had passed this way before, to bury John Root. The fair had begun with death, and now it had ended with death.

So grand was the procession, it needed two hours to pass any one point. By the time it reached Graceland Cemetery, north of the city, darkness had fallen and a soft mist hugged the ground. Long lines of policemen flanked the path to the cemetery's brownstone chapel. Off to the side stood fifty members of the United German Singing Societies.

Harrison had heard them sing at a picnic and, joking, had asked them to sing at his funeral.

⚯

Harrison's murder fell upon the city like a heavy curtain. There was the time before, there was the time after. Where once the city's newspapers would have run an endless series of stories about the aftereffects of the fair, now there was mostly silence. The fair remained open, informally, on October 31, and many men and women came to the grounds for one last visit, as if paying their respects to a lost relative. A tearful woman told columnist Teresa Dean, "The good-by is as sad as any I have known in all the years that I have lived." William Stead, the British editor whose brother Herbert had covered the fair's opening, arrived in Chicago from New York on the night of its official close but made his first visit to the grounds the next day. He claimed that nothing he had seen in Paris, Rome, or London was as perfect as the Court of Honor.

That night the exposition illuminated the fairgrounds one last time. "Beneath the stars the lake lay dark and sombre," Stead wrote, "but on its shores gleamed and glowed in golden radiance the ivory city, beautiful as a poet's dream, silent as a city of the dead."

The Black City

THE EXPOSITION PROVED UNABLE to hold the Black City at bay for very long. With its formal closure thousands more workers joined the swelling army of the unemployed, and homeless men took up residence among the great abandoned palaces of the fair. "The poor had come lean and hungry out of the terrible winter that followed the World's Fair," wrote novelist Robert Herrick in *The Web of Life*. "In that beautiful enterprise the prodigal city had put forth her utmost strength and, having shown the world the supreme flower of her energy, had collapsed. . . . The city's huge garment was too large for it; miles of empty stores, hotels, flat-buildings, showed its shrunken state. Tens of thousands of human beings, lured to the festive city by abnormal wages, had been left stranded, without food or a right to shelter in its tenant-less buildings." It was the contrast that was so wrenching. "What a spectacle!" wrote Ray Stannard Baker in his *American Chronicle.* "What a human downfall after the magnificence and prodigality of the World's Fair which had so recently closed its doors! Heights of splendor, pride, exaltation in one month: depths of wretchedness, suffering, hunger, cold, in the next."

In that first, brutal winter Burnham's photographer, Charles Arnold, took a very different series of photographs. One shows the Machinery Building soiled by smoke and litter. A dark liquid had been thrown against one wall. At the base of a column was a large box, apparently the home of an out-of-work squatter. "It is desolation," wrote Teresa Dean, the columnist, about a visit she made to Jackson Park on January 2, 1894. "You wish you had not come. If there were not so many around, you would reach out your arms, with the prayer on your lips for it all to come back to you. It seems cruel, cruel, to give us such a vision; to let us dream and drift through heaven for six months, and then to take it out of our lives."

Six days after her visit the first fires occurred and destroyed several structures, among them the famous Peristyle. The following morning Big Mary, chipped and soiled, stood over a landscape of twisted and blackened steel.

The winter became a crucible for American labor. To workers, Eugene Debs and Samuel Gompers came increasingly to seem like saviors, Chicago's merchant princes like devils. George Pullman continued to cut jobs and wages without reducing rents, even though his company's treasury was flush with over $60 million in cash. Pullman's friends cautioned that he was being pigheaded and had underestimated the anger of his workers. He moved his family out of Chicago and hid his best china. On May 11, 1894, two thousand Pullman workers went on strike with the support of Debs's American Railway Union. Other strikes broke out around the country, and Debs began planning a nationwide general strike to begin in July. President Cleveland ordered federal troops to Chicago and placed them under the command of General Nelson A. Miles, previously the grand marshal of the exposition. Miles was uneasy about his new command. He sensed in the spreading unrest something unprecedented, "more threatening and far-reaching than anything that had occurred before." He followed orders, however, and the former grand marshal of the fair wound up fighting the men who had built it.

Strikers blocked trains and burned railcars. On July 5, 1894, arsonists set fire to the seven greatest palaces of the exposition—Post's immense Manufactures and Liberal Arts Building, Hunt's dome, Sullivan's Golden Door, all of them. In the Loop men and women gathered on rooftops and in the highest offices of the Rookery, the Masonic Temple, the Temperance Building, and every other high place to watch the distant conflagration. Flames rose a hundred feet into the night sky and cast their gleam far out onto the lake.

Belatedly, Burnham had gotten his wish. "There was no regret," observed the *Chicago Tribune,* "rather a feeling of pleasure that the elements and not the wrecker should wipe out the spectacle of the Columbian season."

Later, in the next year, came the wonder:

"There are hundreds of people who went to Chicago to see the Fair and were never heard from again," said the *New York World.* "The list of the 'missing' when the Fair closed was a long one, and in the greater number foul play suspected. Did these visitors to the Fair, strangers to Chicago, find their way to Holmes' Castle in answer to delusive advertisements sent out by him, never to return again? Did he erect his Castle close to the Fair grounds so as to gather in these victims by the wholesale . . . ?"

Initially the Chicago police had no answers, other than the obvious: That in Chicago in the time of the fair, it was so very easy to disappear.

The secrets of Holmes's castle eventually did come to light, but only because of the persistence of a lone detective from a far-off city, grieving his own terrible loss.

Part IV

Cruelty Revealed

1895

Dr. H. H. Holmes.

"Property of H. H. Holmes"

DETECTIVE FRANK GEYER WAS A big man with a pleasant, earnest face, a large walrus mustache, and a new gravity in his gaze and demeanor. He was one of Philadelphia's top detectives and had been a member of the force for twenty years, during which time he had investigated some two hundred killings. He knew murder and its unchanging templates. Husbands killed wives, wives killed husbands, and the poor killed one another, always for the usual motives of money, jealousy, passion, and love. Rarely did a murder involve the mysterious elements of dime novels or the stories of Sir Arthur Conan Doyle. From the start, however, Geyer's current assignment—it was now June 1895—had veered from the ordinary. One unusual aspect was that the suspect already was in custody, arrested seven months earlier for insurance fraud and now incarcerated in Philadelphia's Moyamensing Prison.

The suspect was a physician whose given name was Mudgett but was known more commonly by the alias H. H. Holmes. He once had lived in Chicago where he and an associate, Benjamin Pitezel, had run a hotel during the World's Columbian Exposition of 1893. They had moved next to Fort Worth, Texas, then to St. Louis, and on to Philadelphia, committing frauds along the way. In Philadelphia Holmes had swindled the Fidelity Mutual Life Association of nearly $10,000 by apparently faking the death of a policyholder, Ben Pitezel. Holmes had bought the insurance in 1893 from Fidelity's Chicago office, just before the close of the exposition. As evidence of fraud accumulated, Fidelity had hired the Pinkerton National Detective Agency—"The Eye That Never Sleeps"— to search for Holmes. The agency's operatives picked up his trail in Burlington, Vermont, and followed him to Boston, where they arranged to have him arrested by police. Holmes confessed to the fraud and agreed to be extradited to Philadelphia for trial. At that point the case appeared to be closed. But now in June 1895 it was becoming increasingly apparent that Holmes had not *faked* the death of Ben Pitezel, he had killed him and then arranged the scene to make the death seem accidental. Now three of Pitezel's five children—Alice, Nellie, and Howard—were missing, last seen in Holmes's company.

Geyer's assignment was to find the children. He was invited to join the case by Philadelphia district attorney George S. Graham, who over the years had come to rely on Geyer for the city's most sensitive investigations. Graham had thought twice this time, however, for he knew that just a few months earlier Geyer had lost his wife, Martha, and his twelve-year-old daughter, Esther, in a house fire.

Geyer interviewed Holmes in his cell but learned nothing new. Holmes insisted that when he had last seen the Pitezel children, they were alive and traveling with a woman named Minnie Williams, en route to the place where their father was hiding out.

Geyer found Holmes to be smooth and glib, a social chameleon. "Holmes is greatly given to lying with a sort of florid ornamentation," Geyer wrote, "and all of his stories are decorated with flamboyant draperies, intended by him to strengthen the plausibility of his statements. In talking, he has the appearance of candor, becomes pathetic at times when pathos will serve him best, uttering his words with a quaver in his voice, often accompanied by a moistened eye, then turning quickly with a determined and forceful method of speech, as if indignation or resolution had sprung out of tender memories that had touched his heart."

Holmes claimed to have secured a cadaver that resembled Ben Pitezel and to have placed it on the second floor of a house rented especially for the fraud. By coincidence or out of some malignant expression of humor, the house was located right behind the city morgue, a few blocks north of City Hall. Holmes admitted arranging the cadaver to suggest that Pitezel had died in an accidental explosion. He poured a solvent on the cadaver's upper body and set it on fire, then positioned the body on the floor in direct sunlight. By the time the body was discovered, its features had been distorted well beyond recognition. Holmes volunteered to assist the coroner in making an identification. At the morgue he not only helped locate a distinctive wart on the dead man's neck, he pulled out his own lancet and removed the wart himself, then matter-of-factly handed it to the coroner.

The coroner had wanted a member of the Pitezel family also to be present at the identification. Pitezel's wife, Carrie, was ill and could not come. Instead she sent her second-eldest daughter, Alice, fifteen years old. The coroner's men draped the body so as to allow Alice to see only Pitezel's teeth. She seemed confident that the corpse was her father. Fidelity paid the death benefit. Next Holmes traveled to St. Louis, where the Pitezel family now lived. Still in possession of Alice, he persuaded Carrie to let him pick up two more of her children, explaining that their father, in hiding, was desperate to see them. He took Nellie, eleven, and Howard, eight, and embarked with all three children on a strange and sad journey.

Geyer knew from Alice's letters that initially she found the trip to be something of an adventure. In a letter to her mother, dated September 20, 1894, Alice wrote, "I wish you could see what I have seen." In the same letter she expressed her distaste for Holmes's treacly manner. "I don't like him to call me babe and child and dear and all such trash." The next day she wrote again, "Mamma have you ever seen or tasted a red banana? I have had three. They are so big that I can just reach around it and have my thumb and next finger just tutch." Since leaving St. Louis, Alice had heard nothing from home and feared her mother's illness might have gotten much worse. "Have you gotten 4 letters from me besides this?" Alice wrote. "Are you sick in bed yet or are you up? I wish that I could hear from you."

One of the few things that Detective Geyer knew with certainty was that neither of these letters ever reached Carrie Pitezel. Alice and Nellie had written to their mother repeatedly while in Holmes's custody and had given the letters to Holmes with the expectation that he would mail them. He never did. Shortly after his arrest police discovered a tin box, marked "Property of H. H. Holmes," containing various documents and a dozen letters from the girls. He had stored them in the box as if they were seashells collected from a beach.

Now Mrs. Pitezel was nearly crushed with anxiety and grief, despite Holmes's latest assurances that Alice, Nellie, and Howard were in London, England, under the able care of Minnie Williams. A search by Scotland Yard had found no trace of any of them. Geyer had little hope that his own search would fare any better. With more than half a year having elapsed since anyone had heard from the children, Geyer wrote, "it did not look like a very encouraging task to undertake, and it was the general belief of all interested, that the children would never be found. The District Attorney believed, however, that another final effort to find the children should be made, for the sake of the stricken mother, if for nothing else. I was not placed under any restrictions, but was told to go and exercise my own judgment in the matter, and to follow wherever the clues led me."

Geyer set out on his search on the evening of June 26, 1895, a hot night in a hot summer. Earlier in June a zone of high pressure, the "permanent high," had settled over the middle Atlantic states and driven temperatures in Philadelphia well into the nineties. A humid stillness held the countryside. Even at night the air inside Geyer's train was stagnant and moist. Leftover cigar smoke drifted from men's suits, and at each stop the roar of frogs and crickets filled the car. Geyer slept in jagged stretches.

The next day, as the train sped west through the heat-steamed hollows of Pennsylvania and Ohio, Geyer reread his copies of the children's letters to look for anything he might have missed that could help direct his search. The letters not only provided irrefutable proof that the children had been with Holmes but contained geographic references that allowed Geyer to plot the broad contours of the route Holmes and the children had followed. Their first stop appeared to have been Cincinnati.

Detective Geyer reached Cincinnati at seven-thirty P.M. on Thursday,

June 27. He checked into the Palace Hotel. The next morning he went to police headquarters to brief the city's police superintendent on his mission. The superintendent assigned a detective to assist him, Detective John Schnooks, an old friend of Geyer's.

Geyer hoped to reconstruct the children's travels from Cincinnati onward. There was no easy way to achieve his goal. He had few tools other than his wits, his notebook, a handful of photographs, and the children's letters. He and Detective Schnooks made a list of all the hotels in Cincinnati located near railroad stations, then set out on foot to visit each one and check its registrations for some sign of the children and Holmes. That Holmes would use an alias seemed beyond doubt, so Geyer brought along his photographs, even a depiction of the children's distinctive "flat-top" trunk. Many months had passed since the children had written their letters, however. Geyer had little hope that anyone would remember one man and three children.

On that point, as it happens, he was wrong.

The detectives trudged from one hotel to the next. The day got hotter and hotter. The detectives were courteous and never showed impatience, despite having to make the same introductions and tell the same story over and over again.

On Central Avenue they came to a small inexpensive hotel, the Atlantic House. As they had done at all the other hotels, they asked the clerk if they could see his registration book. They turned first to Friday, September 28, 1894, the day that Holmes, while already in possession of Alice, had picked up Nellie and Howard from their St. Louis home. Geyer guessed Holmes and the children had reached Cincinnati later that same day. Geyer ran his finger down the page and stopped at an entry for "Alex E. Cook," a guest who according to the register was traveling with three children.

The entry jogged Geyer's memory. Holmes had used the name before, to rent a house in Burlington, Vermont. Also, Geyer by now had seen a lot of Holmes's handwriting. The writing in the ledger looked familiar.

The "Cook" party stayed only one night, the register showed. But Geyer knew from the girls' letters that they had remained in Cincinnati an additional night. It seemed odd that Holmes would go to the trouble of moving to a second hotel, but Geyer knew from experience that making assumptions about the behavior of criminals was always a dangerous thing. He and Schnooks thanked the clerk for his kind attention, then set out to canvass more hotels.

The sun was high, the streets steamed. Cicadas scratched off messages from every tree. At Sixth and Vine the detectives came to a hotel called the Bristol and discovered that on Saturday, September 29, 1894, a party identified as "A. E. Cook" had checked in, with three children. When the clerk saw Geyer's photographs, he confirmed that the guests were Holmes, Alice, Nellie, and Howard. They checked out the next morning, Sunday, September 30. The date fit the likely chronology of events: Geyer knew from the children's letters that on that Sunday morning they had left Cincinnati and by evening had arrived in Indianapolis.

Geyer was not yet ready to leave Cincinnati, however. Now he played a hunch. The Pinkertons had found that Holmes sometimes rented houses in the cities through which he traveled, as he had done in Burlington. Geyer and Schnooks turned their attention to Cincinnati's real estate agents.

Their search eventually took them to the realty office of J. C. Thomas, on East Third Street.

Something about Holmes must have caused people to take notice, because both Thomas and his clerk remembered him. Holmes had rented a house at 305 Poplar Street, under the name "A. C. Hayes," and had made a substantial advance payment.

The date of the agreement, Thomas said, was September 28, 1894, the Friday when Holmes and the children had arrived in Cincinnati. Holmes held the house only two days.

Thomas could offer no further details but referred the detectives to a woman named Henrietta Hill, who lived next door to the house.

Geyer and Schnooks immediately set out for Miss Hill's residence and found her to be an acute observer and a willing gossip. "There is really very little to tell," she said—then told them a lot.

—————

She first had noticed the new tenant on Saturday, September 29, when a furniture wagon stopped in front of the rental house. A man and a boy descended. What most caught Miss Hill's attention was the fact that the furniture wagon was empty save for an iron stove that seemed much too large for a private residence.

Miss Hill found the stove sufficiently strange that she mentioned it to her neighbors. The next morning Holmes came to her front door and told her he was not going to stay in the house after all. If she wanted the stove, he said, she could have it.

Detective Geyer theorized that Holmes must have sensed an excess of neighborly scrutiny and changed his plans. But what were those plans? At the time, Geyer wrote, "I was not able to appreciate the intense significance of the renting of the Poplar Street house and the delivery of a stove of such immense size." He was certain, however, that he had "taken firm hold of the end of the string" that would lead to the children.

Based on the girls' letters, Geyer's next stop was obvious. He thanked Detective Schnooks for his companionship and caught a train to Indianapolis.

—————

It was even hotter in Indianapolis. Leaves hung in the stillness like hands of the newly dead.

Early Sunday morning Geyer went to the police station and picked up a new local partner, Detective David Richards.

One part of the trail was easy to find. In Nellie Pitezel's letter from Indianapolis, she had written "we are at the English H." Detective Richards knew the place: The Hotel English.

In the hotel's register Geyer found an entry on September 30 for "three Canning children." Canning, he knew, was Carrie Pitezel's maiden name.

Nothing was simple, however. According to the register, the Canning children had checked out the next day, Monday, October 1. Yet Geyer knew, again from their letters, that the children had remained in Indianapolis for at least another week. Holmes seemed to be repeating the pattern he had established in Cincinnati.

Geyer began the same methodical canvass he had conducted in Cincinnati. He and Detective Richards checked hotel after hotel but found no further reference to the children.

They did, however, find something else.

At a hotel called the Circle Park they discovered an entry for a "Mrs. Georgia Howard." Howard was one of Holmes's more common aliases, Geyer now knew. He believed this woman could be Holmes's latest wife, Georgiana Yoke. The register showed that "Mrs. Howard" had checked in on Sunday, September 30, 1894, and stayed four nights.

Geyer showed his photographs to the hotel's proprietor, a Mrs. Rodius, who recognized Holmes and Yoke but not the children. Mrs. Rodius explained that she and Yoke had become friends. In one conversation Yoke had told her that her husband was "a very wealthy man, and that he owned real estate and cattle ranches in Texas; also had considerable real estate in Berlin, Germany, where they intended to go as soon as her husband could get his business affairs into shape to leave."

The timing of all these hotel stays was perplexing. As best Geyer could tell, on that one Sunday, September 30, Holmes somehow had managed to maneuver the three children and his own wife into different hotels in the same city, without revealing their existence to one another.

But where had the children gone next?

Geyer and Richards examined the registers of every hotel and boardinghouse in Indianapolis but found no further trace of the children.

The Indianapolis leg of Geyer's search seemed to have reached a dead end, when Richards remembered that a hotel called the Circle House had been open during the fall of 1894 but had since closed. He and Geyer checked with other hotels to find out who had run the Circle House, and learned from its former clerk that the registration records were in the possession of a downtown attorney.

The records had been poorly kept, but among the guests who had arrived on Monday, October 1, Geyer found a familiar entry: "Three Canning children." The register showed the children were from Galva, Illinois—the town where Mrs. Pitezel had grown up. Geyer now felt a pressing need to talk to the hotel's past manager and found him running a saloon in West Indianapolis. His name was Herman Ackelow.

Geyer explained his mission and immediately showed Ackelow his photographs of Holmes and the Pitezel children. Ackelow was silent a moment. Yes, he said, he was sure of it: The man in the photograph had come to his hotel.

It was the children, however, that he remembered most clearly, and now he told the detectives why.

Until this point all Geyer knew about the children's stay in Indianapolis was what he had read in the letters from the tin box. Between October 6 and 8 Alice and Nellie had written at least three letters that Holmes had intercepted. The letters were brief and poorly written, but they offered small bright glimpses into the daily lives of the children and the state of near-captivity in which Holmes held them. "We are all well here," Nellie wrote on Saturday, October 6. "It is a little warmer to-day. There is so many buggies go by that you can't hear yourself think. I first wrote you a letter with a crystal pen. . . . It is all glass so I hafto be careful or else it will break, it was only five cents."

Alice wrote a letter the same day. She had been away from her mother the longest, and for her the trip had become wearisome and sad. It was Saturday, raining hard. She had a cold and was reading *Uncle Tom's Cabin* so much that her eyes had begun to hurt. "And I expect this Sunday will pass away slower than I don't know what. . . . Why don't you write to me. I have not got a letter from you since I have been away and it will be three weeks day after tomorrow."

On Monday Holmes allowed a letter from Mrs. Pitezel to reach the children, which prompted Alice to write an immediate reply, observing, "It seems as though you are awful homesick." In this letter, which

Holmes never mailed, Alice reported that little Howard was being difficult. "One morning Mr. H. told me to tell him to stay in the next morning that he wanted him and he would come and get him and take him
out." But Howard had not obeyed, and when Holmes came for him, the
boy was nowhere to be found. Holmes had gotten angry.

Despite her sorrow and boredom, Alice found a few cheery moments
worth celebrating. "Yesterday we had mashed potatoes, grapes, chicken
glass of milk each ice cream each a big sauce dish full awful good too
lemon pie cake don't you think that is pretty good."

The fact that the children were so well fed might have comforted Mrs.
Pitezel, had she ever received the letter. Not so, however, the story the
former hotel manager now told Geyer.

Each day Ackelow would send his eldest son up to the children's room
to call them for their meals. Often the boy reported back that the children were crying, "evidently heartbroken and homesick to see their
mother, or hear from her," Geyer wrote. A German chambermaid named
Caroline Klausmann had tended the children's room and observed the
same wrenching scenes. She had moved to Chicago, Ackelow said. Geyer
wrote her name in his notebook.

"Holmes said that Howard was a very bad boy," Ackelow recalled,
"and that he was trying to place him in some institution, or bind him out
to some farmer, as he wanted to get rid of the responsibility of looking
after him."

Geyer still nurtured a small hope that the children really were alive, as
Holmes insisted. Despite his twenty years on the police force, Geyer found
it difficult to believe that anyone could kill three children for absolutely
no reason. Why had Holmes gone to the trouble and expense of moving
the children from city to city, hotel to hotel, if only to kill them? Why had
he bought each of them a crystal pen and taken them to the zoo in Cincinnati and made sure they received lemon pie and ice cream?

Geyer set out for Chicago but felt deep reluctance about leaving
Indianapolis—"something seemed to tell me that Howard had never left

there alive." In Chicago he found, to his surprise, that the city's police department knew nothing about Holmes. He tracked down Caroline Klausmann, who was now working at the Swiss Hotel on Clark Street. When he showed her his photographs of the children, tears welled in her eyes.

Geyer caught a train to Detroit, the city where Alice had written the last of the letters in the tin box.

Geyer was getting a feel for his quarry. There was nothing rational about Holmes, but his behavior seemed to follow a pattern. Geyer knew what to look for in Detroit and, with the assistance of another police detective, once again began a patient canvass of hotels and boarding-houses. Though he told his story and showed his photographs a hundred times, he never tired and was always patient and polite. These were his strengths. His weakness was his belief that evil had boundaries.

Once again he picked up the children's trail and the parallel registrations of Holmes and Yoke, but now he discovered something even stranger—that during this same period Carrie Pitezel and her two other children, Dessie and baby Wharton, had also checked into a Detroit hotel, this one called Geis's Hotel. Geyer realized to his astonishment that Holmes now was moving *three* different parties of travelers from place to place, shoving them across the landscape as if they were toys.

And he discovered something else.

In walking from lodging to lodging, he saw that Holmes had not only kept Carrie away from Alice, Nellie, and Howard: He had placed them in establishments only three blocks apart. Suddenly the true implication of what Holmes had done became clear to him.

He reread Alice's final letter. She had written it to her grandparents on Sunday, October 14, the same day her mother, along with Dessie and the baby, had checked into Geis's Hotel. This was the saddest letter of them all. Alice and Nellie both had colds, and the weather had turned wintry. "Tell Mama that I have to have a coat," Alice wrote. "I nearly freeze in that thin jacket." The children's lack of warm clothing forced them to stay in their room day after day. "All that Nell and I can do is to draw and I get so tired sitting that I could get up and fly almost. I wish I could see you all. I am getting so homesick that I don't know what to do. I suppose Wharton walks by this time don't he I would like to have him here he would pass away the time a goodeal."

Geyer was appalled. "So when this poor child Alice was writing to her grandparents in Galva, Illinois, complaining of the cold, sending a message to her mother, asking for heavier and more comfortable clothing, wishing for little Wharton, the baby who would help them pass away the time—while this wearied, lonely, homesick child was writing this letter, her mother and her sister and the much wished for Wharton, were within ten minutes walk of her, and continued there for the next five days."

It was a game for Holmes, Geyer realized. He possessed them all and reveled in his possession.

One additional phrase of Alice's letter kept running through Geyer's brain.

"Howard," she had written, "is not with us now."

Moyamensing Prison

HOLMES SAT IN HIS CELL at Moyamensing Prison, a large turreted and crenellated building at Tenth and Reed streets, in south Philadelphia. He did not seem terribly troubled by his incarceration, although he complained of its injustice. "The great humiliation of feeling that I am a prisoner is killing me far more than any other discomforts I have to endure," he wrote—though in fact he felt no humiliation whatsoever. If he felt anything, it was a smug satisfaction that so far no one had been able to produce any concrete evidence that he had killed Ben Pitezel or the missing children.

He occupied a cell that measured nine by fourteen feet, with a narrow barred window high in its outer wall and a single electric lamp, which guards extinguished at nine o'clock each night. The walls were whitewashed. The stone construction of the prison helped blunt the extreme heat that had settled on the city and much of the country, but nothing could keep out the humidity for which Philadelphia was notorious. It clung to Holmes and his fellow prisoners like a cloak of moist wool, yet this too he seemed not to mind. Holmes became a model prisoner— became in fact the *model* of a model prisoner. He made a game of using his charm to gain concessions from his keepers. He was allowed to wear his own clothes "and to keep my watch and other small belongings." He discovered also that he could pay to have food, newspapers, and magazines brought in from outside. He read of his increasing national notoriety. He read too that Frank Geyer, a Philadelphia police detective who had interviewed him in June, was now in the Midwest searching for Pitezel's children. The search delighted Holmes. It satisfied his profound need for attention and gave him a sense of power over the detective. He knew that Geyer's search would be in vain.

Holmes's cell was furnished with a bed, a stool, and a writing table, upon which he composed his memoir. He had begun it, he said, the preceding winter—to be exact, on December 3, 1894.

He opened the memoir as if it were a fable: "Come with me, if you will, to a tiny quiet New England village, nestling among the picturesquely rugged hills of New Hampshire. . . . Here, in the year 1861, I, Herman W. Mudgett, the author of these pages, was born. That the first years of my life were different from those of any other ordinary country-bred boy, I have no reason to think." The dates and places were correct; his description of his boyhood as a typical country idyll was most certainly a fabrication. It is one of the defining characteristics of psychopaths that as children they lied at will, exhibited unusual cruelty to animals and other children, and often engaged in acts of vandalism, with arson an especially favored act.

Holmes inserted into his memoir a "prison diary" that he claimed to have kept since the day he arrived at Moyamensing. It is more likely that he invented the diary expressly for the memoir, intending it as a vehicle for reinforcing his claims of innocence by fostering the impression that he was a man of warmth and piety. He claimed in the diary to have established a daily schedule aimed at personal betterment. He would wake at six-thirty each day and take his "usual sponge bath," then clean his cell. He would breakfast at seven. "I shall eat no more meat of any kind while I am so closely confined." He planned to exercise and read the morning newspapers until ten o'clock. "From 10 to 12 and 2 to 4 six days in the week, I shall confine myself to my old medical works and other college studies including stenography, French and German." The rest of the day he would devote to reading various periodicals and library books.

At one point in his diary he notes that he was reading *Trilby*, the 1894 best seller by George Du Maurier about a young singer, Trilby O'Farrell, and her possession by the mesmerist Svengali. Holmes wrote that he "was much pleased with parts of it."

Elsewhere in the diary Holmes went for the heart.

One entry, for May 16, 1895: "My birthday. Am 34 years old. I wonder if, as in former years, mother will write me. . . ."

In another entry he described a visit from his latest wife, Georgiana Yoke. "She has suffered, and though she tried heroically to keep me from seeing it, it was of no avail: and in a few minutes to again bid her good-bye and know she was going out into the world with so heavy a load to bear, caused me more suffering than any death struggles can ever do. Each day until I know she is safe from harm and annoyance will be a living death to me."

From his cell Holmes also wrote a long letter to Carrie Pitezel, which he composed in a manner that shows he was aware the police were reading his mail. He insisted that Alice, Nellie, and Howard were with "Miss W." in London, and that if the police would only check his story in detail, the mystery of the children would be solved. "I was as careful of the children as if they were my own, and you know me well enough to judge me better than strangers here can do. Ben would not have done anything against me, or I against him, any quicker than brothers. We *never* quarrelled. Again, he was worth too much to me for me to have killed him, if I had no other reason not to. As to the children, I never will believe, until you tell me so yourself, that you think they are dead or that I did anything to put them out of the way. Knowing me as you do, can you imagine me killing little and innocent children, especially without any motive?"

He explained the lack of mail from the children. "They have no doubt written letters which Miss W., for her own safety, has withheld."

Holmes read the daily papers closely. Clearly the detective's search had borne little fruit. Holmes had no doubt that Geyer soon would be forced to end his hunt and return to Philadelphia.

The prospect of this was pleasing in the extreme.

The Tenant

ON SUNDAY, JULY 7, 1895, Detective Geyer took his search to Toronto, where the city's police department assigned Detective Alf Cuddy to assist him. Together Geyer and Cuddy scoured the hotels and boardinghouses of Toronto and after days of searching found that here, too, Holmes had been moving three parties of travelers simultaneously.

Holmes and Yoke had stayed at the Walker House: "G. Howe and wife, Columbus."

Mrs. Pitezel at the Union House: "Mrs. C. A. Adams and daughter, Columbus."

The girls at the Albion: "Alice and Nellie Canning, Detroit."

No one remembered seeing Howard.

Now Geyer and Cuddy began searching the records of real estate agencies and contacting the owners of rental homes, but Toronto was far larger than any other city Geyer had searched. The task seemed impossible. On Monday morning, July 15, he awoke facing the prospect of yet another day of mind-numbing routine, but when he arrived at headquarters, he found Detective Cuddy in an unusually good mood. A tip had come in that Cuddy found promising. A resident named Thomas Ryves had read a description of Holmes in one of the city's newspapers and thought it sounded like a man who in October 1894 had rented the house next door to his, at 16 St. Vincent Street.

Geyer was leery. The intensive press coverage of his mission and his arrival in Toronto had generated thousands of tips, all useless.

Cuddy agreed that the latest tip was probably another wild goose chase, but at least it offered a change of pace.

By now Geyer was a national fascination, America's Sherlock Holmes. Reports of his travels appeared in newspapers throughout the country. In that day the possibility that a man had killed three young children was still considered a horror well beyond the norm. There was something about Detective Geyer's lone search through the sweltering heat of that summer that captured everyone's imagination. He had become the living representation of how men liked to think of themselves: one man doing an awful duty and doing it well, against the odds. Millions of people woke each morning hoping to read in their newspapers that this staunch detective at last had found the missing children.

Geyer paid little attention to his new celebrity. Nearly a month had passed since the start of his search, but what had he accomplished? Each new phase seemed only to raise new questions: Why had Holmes taken the children? Why had he engineered that contorted journey from city to city? What power did Holmes possess that gave him such control?

There was something about Holmes that Geyer just did not understand. Every crime had a motive. But the force that propelled Holmes seemed to exist outside the world of Geyer's experience.

He kept coming back to the same conclusion: Holmes was enjoying himself. He had arranged the insurance fraud for the money, but the rest of it was for fun. Holmes was testing his power to bend the lives of people.

What irked Geyer most was that the central question was still unanswered: Where were the children now?

The detectives found Thomas Ryves to be a charming Scotsman of considerable age, who welcomed them with enthusiasm. Ryves explained why the renter next door had caught his attention. For one thing, he had arrived with little furniture—a mattress, an old bed, and an unusually large trunk. One afternoon the tenant came to Ryves's house to borrow a shovel, explaining that he wanted to dig a hole in the cellar for the storage of potatoes. He returned the shovel the next morning and the following day removed the trunk from the house. Ryves never saw him again.

Detective Geyer, now galvanized, told Ryves to meet him in front of the neighboring house in exactly one hour; then he and Cuddy sped to the home of the realtor who had arranged the rental. With little preamble Geyer showed her a photograph of Holmes. She recognized him instantly. He had been very handsome, with amazing blue eyes.

"This seemed too good to be true," Geyer wrote. He and Cuddy offered quick thanks and rushed back to St. Vincent Street. Ryves was waiting outside.

Now Geyer asked to borrow a shovel, and Ryves returned with the same one he had lent the tenant.

The house was charming, with a steeply pitched central gable and scalloped trim like the gingerbread house in a fairy tale, except this house sat not alone in a deep wood, but in the heart of Toronto on a fine street closely lined with elegant homes and yards fenced with fleur-de-lis pickets. Clematis in full bloom climbed one post of the veranda.

The current tenant, a Mrs. J. Armbrust, answered the door. Ryves introduced the detectives. Mrs. Armbrust led them inside. They entered a central hall that divided the house into halves of three rooms each. A stairwell led to the second floor. Geyer asked to see the cellar.

Mrs. Armbrust led the detectives into the kitchen, where she lifted a sheet of oilcloth from the floor. A square trap door lay underneath. As the detectives opened it, the scent of moist earth drifted upward into the kitchen. The cellar was shallow but very dark. Mrs. Armbrust brought lamps.

Geyer and Cuddy descended a steep set of steps, more ladder than stairway, into a small chamber about ten feet long by ten feet wide and only four feet high. The lamps shed a shifting orange light that exaggerated the detectives' shadows. Hunched over, wary of the overhead beams,

Geyer and Cuddy tested the ground with the spade. In the southwest corner Geyer found a soft spot. The spade entered with disconcerting ease.

"Only a slight hole had been made," Geyer said, "when the gases burst forth and the stench was frightful."

At three feet they uncovered human bone.

———

They summoned an undertaker named B. D. Humphrey to help recover the remains. Geyer and Cuddy gingerly climbed back down into the cellar. Humphrey leaped down.

The stench now suffused the entire house. Mrs. Armbrust looked stricken.

Then the coffins arrived.

The undertaker's men put them in the kitchen.

———

The children had been buried nude. Alice lay on her side, her head at the west end of the grave. Nellie lay face-down, partially covering Alice. Her rich black hair, nicely plaited, lay along her back as neatly as if she had just combed it. The men spread a sheet on the cellar floor.

They began with Nellie.

"We lifted her as gently as possible," Geyer said, "but owing to the decomposed state of the body, the weight of her plaited hair hanging down her back pulled the scalp from her head."

They discovered something else: Nellie's feet had been amputated. During the search of the residence that followed, police found no trace of them. At first this seemed a mystery, until Geyer recalled that Nellie was clubfooted. Holmes had disposed of her feet to remove this distinctive clue to her identity.

———

Mrs. Pitezel learned of the discovery of her girls by reading a morning newspaper. She had been visiting friends back in Chicago and thus Geyer had been unable to telegraph the news to her directly. She caught a train to Toronto. Geyer met her at the station and took her to his hotel, the Rossin House. She was exhausted and sad and seemed perpetually near fainting. Geyer roused her with smelling salts.

Geyer and Cuddy came for her the next afternoon to bring her to the morgue. They carried brandy and smelling salts. Geyer wrote, "I told her that it would be absolutely impossible for her to see anything but Alice's teeth and hair, and only the hair belonging to Nellie. This had a paralyzing effect upon her and she almost fainted."

The coroner's men did what they could to make the viewing as endurable as possible. They cleaned the flesh from Alice's skull and carefully polished her teeth, then covered her body with canvas. They laid paper over her face, and cut a hole in the paper to expose only her teeth, just as the Philadelphia coroner had done for her father.

They washed Nellie's hair and laid it carefully on the canvas that covered Alice's body.

Cuddy and Geyer took positions on opposite sides of Mrs. Pitezel and led her into the dead house. She recognized Alice's teeth immediately. She turned to Geyer and asked, "Where is Nellie?" Only then did she notice Nellie's long black hair.

⸺

The coroner, unable to find any marks of violence, theorized that Holmes had locked the girls in the big trunk, then filled it with gas from a lamp valve. Indeed, when police found the trunk they discovered a hole drilled through one side, covered with a makeshift patch.

"Nothing could be more surprising," Geyer wrote, "than the apparent ease with which Holmes murdered the two little girls in the very center of the city of Toronto, without arousing the least suspicion of a single person there." If not for Graham's decision to send him on his search, he believed, "these murders would never have been discovered, and Mrs. Pitezel would have gone to her grave without knowing whether her children were alive or dead."

For Geyer, finding the girls was "one of the most satisfactory events of my life," but his satisfaction was tempered by the fact that Howard remained missing. Mrs. Pitezel refused to believe Howard was dead; she "clung fondly to the hope that he would ultimately be found alive."

Even Geyer found himself hoping that in this one case Holmes had not lied and had done exactly what he had told the clerk in Indianapolis. "Had [Howard] been placed in some institution, as Holmes had intimated his intention of doing, or was he hidden in some obscure place beyond reach or discovery? Was he alive or dead? I was puzzled, nonplussed, and groping in the dark."

A Lively Corpse

IN PHILADELPHIA, ON THE MORNING of Tuesday, July 16, 1895—the day Geyer's Toronto discoveries were reported in the nation's newspapers—the district attorney's office telephoned an urgent message to the warden at Moyamensing Prison, instructing him to keep all the morning's newspapers away from Holmes. The order came from Assistant District Attorney Thomas W. Barlow. He wanted to surprise Holmes with the news, hoping it would rattle him so thoroughly that he would confess.

Barlow's order came too late. The guard sent to intercept the morning papers found Holmes sitting at his table reading the news as calmly as if reading about the weather.

In his memoir Holmes contended that the news did shock him. His newspaper came that morning at eight-thirty as it always did, he wrote, "and I had hardly opened it before I saw in large headlines the announcement of the finding of the children in Toronto. For the moment it seemed so impossible, that I was inclined to think it one of the frequent newspaper excitements that had attended the earlier part of the case. . . ." But suddenly, he wrote, he realized what must have happened. Minnie Williams had killed them or had ordered them killed. Holmes knew she had an unsavory associate named "Hatch." He guessed that Williams had suggested the killings and Hatch had carried them out. It was all too horrible to comprehend: "I gave up trying to read the article, and saw instead the two little faces as they had looked when I hurriedly left them—felt the innocent child's kiss so timidly given and heard again their earnest words of farewell, and I realized that I had received another burden to carry to my grave. . . . I think at this time I should have lost my senses utterly had I not been hurriedly called to prepare to be taken to the District Attorney's office."

The morning was hot. Holmes was driven north on Broad Street to City Hall through air as sticky as taffy. In the DA's office he was questioned by Barlow. The *Philadelphia Public Ledger* reported that Holmes's "genius for explanation had deserted him. For two hours he sat under a shower of questions and refused to talk. He was not cowed by any means, but he would give absolutely no satisfaction."

Holmes wrote, "I was in no condition to bear his accusations, nor disposed to answer many of his questions." He told Barlow that Miss Williams and Hatch apparently had killed Howard as well.

Holmes was driven back to Moyamensing. He began earnestly trying to find a publisher for his memoir, hoping to get it quickly into print to help turn public opinion to his favor. If he could not exert his great powers of persuasion directly, he could at least attempt to do so indirectly. He struck a deal with a journalist named John King to arrange publication and market the book.

He wrote to King, "My ideas are that you should get from the New York *Herald* and the Philadelphia *Press* all the cuts they have and turn those we want over to the printer, to have them electroplated at his expense." In particular he wanted a *Herald* picture of himself in a full beard. He also wanted to have "the autographs of my two names (Holmes and Mudgett) engraved and electroplated at the same time to go under the picture." He wanted this done quickly so that as soon as the manuscript was set in type, all components of the book would be in hand, ready for the presses.

He offered King some marketing advice: "As soon as the book is published, get it onto the Philadelphia and New York newsstands. Then get reliable canvassers who will work *afternoons* here in Philadelphia. Take one good street at a time, leave the book, then return about a half hour later for the money. No use to do this in the forenoon when people are busy. I canvassed when a student in this way and found the method successful.

"Then, if you have any liking for the road, go over the ground covered by the book, spending a few days in Chicago, Detroit, and Indianapolis. Give copies to the newspapers in these cities to comment upon, it will assist the sale. . . ."

Aware that this letter, too, would be read by the authorities, Holmes used it to reinforce, obliquely, his claims of innocence. He urged King that when his sales effort took him to Chicago, he should to go a particular hotel and look for evidence in the register, and collect affidavits from clerks, proving that Minnie Williams had stayed there with Holmes long after she was supposed to have been murdered.

"If she was a corpse then," Holmes wrote to King, "she was a very lively corpse indeed."

"All the Weary Days"

IT WAS A STRANGE MOMENT for Geyer. He had examined every lead, checked every hotel, visited every boardinghouse and real estate agent, and yet now he had to begin his search anew. Where? What path was left? The weather remained stifling, as if taunting him.

His instincts kept telling him that Holmes had killed Howard in Indianapolis. He returned there on July 24 and again received the assistance of Detective David Richards, but now Geyer also called in the press. The next day every newspaper in the city reported his arrival. Dozens of people visited him at his hotel to make suggestions about where he ought to look for Howard. "The number of mysterious persons who had rented houses in and about Indianapolis multiplied from day to day," Geyer wrote. He and Richards trudged through the heat from office to office, house to house, and found nothing. "Days came and passed, but I continued to be as much in the dark as ever, and it began to look as though the bold but clever criminal had outwitted the detectives . . . and that the disappearance of Howard Pitezel would pass into history as an unsolved mystery."

Meanwhile the mystery of Holmes himself grew deeper and darker.

Geyer's discovery of the girls prompted Chicago police to enter Holmes's building in Englewood. Each day they delved more deeply into the secrets of the "castle," and each day turned up additional evidence that Holmes was something far worse than even Geyer's macabre discoveries indicated. There was speculation that during the world's fair he might have killed dozens of people, most of them young women. One estimate, certainly an exaggeration, put the toll at two hundred. To most people, it seemed impossible that Holmes could have done so much killing without detection. Geyer would have agreed, except that his own search had revealed again and again Holmes's talent for deflecting scrutiny.

Chicago detectives began their exploration of the castle on the night of Friday, July 19. First they made a broad survey of the building. The third floor contained small hotel rooms. The second floor had thirty-five rooms that were harder to classify. Some were ordinary bedrooms; others had no windows and were fitted with doors that made the rooms airtight. One room contained a walk-in vault, with iron walls. Police found a gas jet with no apparent function other than to admit gas into the vault. Its cut-off valve was located in Holmes's personal apartment. In Holmes's office they found a bank book belonging to a woman named Lucy Burbank. It listed a balance of $23,000. The woman could not be located.

The eeriest phase of the investigation began when the police, holding their flickering lanterns high, entered the hotel basement, a cavern of brick and timber measuring 50 by 165 feet. The discoveries came quickly: a vat of acid with eight ribs and part of a skull settled at the bottom; mounds of quicklime; a large kiln; a dissection table stained with what seemed to be blood. They found surgical tools and charred high-heeled shoes.

And more bones:

Eighteen ribs from the torso of a child.

Several vertebrae.

A bone from a foot.

One shoulder blade.

One hip socket.

Articles of clothing emerged from walls and from pits of ash and quicklime, including a girl's dress and bloodstained overalls. Human hair clotted a stovepipe. The searchers unearthed two buried vaults full of quicklime and human remains. They theorized the remains might be the last traces of two Texas women, Minnie and Anna Williams, whom Chicago police had only recently learned were missing. In the ash of a large stove they found a length of chain that the jeweler in Holmes's pharmacy recognized as part of a watch chain Holmes had given Minnie as a gift. They also found a letter Holmes had written to the pharmacist in his drugstore. "Do you ever see anything of the ghost of the Williams sisters," Holmes wrote, "and do they trouble you much now?"

The next day the police discovered another hidden chamber, this one at the cellar's southwest corner. They were led to it by a man named Charles Chappell, alleged to have helped Holmes reduce corpses to bone. He was very cooperative, and soon the police recovered three fully articulated skeletons from their owners. A fourth was expected from Chicago's Hahneman Medical College.

One of the most striking discoveries came on the second floor, in the walk-in vault. The inside of the door showed the unmistakable imprint of a woman's bare foot. Police theorized the print had been made by a woman suffocating within. Her name, they believed, was Emeline Cigrand.

———

Chicago police telegraphed District Attorney Graham that their search of the Holmes building had uncovered the skeleton of a child. Graham ordered Geyer to Chicago to see if the remains might be those of Howard Pitezel.

Geyer found the city transfixed by the revelations emerging from the castle. Press coverage had been exhaustive, taking up most of the front page of the daily newspapers. One *Tribune* headline had cried VICTIMS OF A FIEND, and reported that the remains of Howard Pitezel had been found in the building. The story took up six of the seven columns of the front page.

Geyer met with the lead police inspector and learned that a physician who had just examined the child's skeleton had ruled it to be that of a little girl. The inspector thought he knew the girl's identity and mentioned a name, Pearl Conner. The name meant nothing to Geyer.

Geyer telegraphed his disappointment to Graham, who ordered him back to Philadelphia for consultation and rest.

On Wednesday evening, August 7, with temperatures in the nineties and traincars like ovens, Geyer set out again, this time accompanied by Fidelity Mutual's top insurance investigator, Inspector W. E. Gary. Geyer was glad for the company.

They went to Chicago, then to Indiana, where they stopped in Logansport and Peru, then to Montpelier Junction, Ohio, and Adrian, Michigan. They spent days searching the records of every hotel, boardinghouse, and real estate office they could find, "all," Geyer said, "to no purpose."

Although Geyer's brief rest in Philadelphia had recharged his hopes, he now found them "fast dwindling away." He still believed his original instinct was correct, that Howard was in Indianapolis or somewhere nearby. He went there next, his third visit of the summer.

"I must confess I returned to Indianapolis in no cheerful frame of mind," Geyer wrote. He and Inspector Gary checked into Geyer's old hotel, the Spencer House. The failure to find Howard after so much effort was frustrating and puzzling. "The mystery," Geyer wrote, "seemed to be impenetrable."

On Thursday, August 19, Geyer learned that during the preceding night Holmes's castle in Englewood, his own dark dreamland, had burned to the ground. Front-page headlines in the *Chicago Tribune* shouted, "Holmes' Den Burned; Fire Demolishes the Place of Murder and Mystery." The fire department suspected arson; police theorized that whoever set the fire had wanted to destroy the secrets still embedded within. They arrested no one.

Together Detective Geyer and Inspector Gary investigated nine hundred leads. They expanded their search to include small towns outside Indianapolis. "By Monday," Geyer wrote in a report to headquarters, "we will have searched every outlying town, except Irvington, and another day will conclude that. After Irvington, I scarcely know where we shall go."

They went to Irvington on Tuesday morning, August 27, 1895, aboard an electric trolley, a new kind of streetcar that drew its power through a wheeled conducting apparatus on the roof called a troller. Just before the trolley reached its final stop, Geyer spotted a sign for a real estate office. He and Gary resolved to begin their search there.

The proprietor was a Mr. Brown. He offered the detectives each a chair, but they remained standing. They did not think the visit would last long, and there were many other offices to touch before nightfall. Geyer opened his now-soiled parcel of photographs.

Brown adjusted his glasses and examined the picture of Holmes. After a long pause he said, "I did not have the renting of the house, but I had the keys, and one day last fall, this man came into my office and in a very abrupt way said I want the keys for that house." Geyer and Gary stood very still. Brown continued: "I remember the man very well, because I did not like his manner, and I felt that he should have had more respect for my gray hairs."

The detectives looked at each other. Both sat down at the same time. "All the toil," Geyer said, "all the weary days and weeks of travel—toil and travel in the hottest months of the year, alternating between faith and hope, and discouragement and despair, all were recompensed in that one moment, when I saw the veil about to lift."

◦———◦

At the inquest that followed a young man named Elvet Moorman testified he had helped Holmes set up a large woodstove in the house. He recalled asking Holmes why he didn't install a gas stove instead. Holmes answered "that he did not think gas was healthy for children."

The owner of an Indianapolis repair shop testified that Holmes had come into his shop on October 3, 1894, with two cases of surgical instruments and asked to have them sharpened. Holmes picked them up three days later.

Detective Geyer testified how during his search of the house he had opened the base of a chimney flue that extended from roof to cellar. While sifting the accumulated ash through a fly screen, he found human teeth and a fragment of jaw. He also retrieved "a large charred mass, which upon being cut, disclosed a portion of the stomach, liver and spleen, baked quite hard." The organs had been packed too tightly into the chimney and thus never had burned.

And of course Mrs. Pitezel was summoned. She identified Howard's overcoat and his scarf pin, and a crochet needle that belonged to Alice.

Finally the coroner showed her a toy that Geyer himself had found in the house. It consisted of a tin man mounted on a spinning top. She recognized it. How could she not? It was Howard's most important possession. Mrs. Pitezel herself had put it in the children's trunk just before she sent them off with Holmes. His father had bought it for him at the Chicago world's fair.

Malice Aforethought

On September 12, 1895, a Philadelphia grand jury voted to indict Holmes for the murder of Benjamin Pitezel. Only two witnesses presented evidence, L. G. Fouse, president of Fidelity Mutual Life, and Detective Frank Geyer. Holmes stuck to his claim that Minnie Williams and the mysterious Hatch had killed the children. Grand juries in Indianapolis and Toronto found this unconvincing. Indianapolis indicted Holmes for the murder of Howard Pitezel, Toronto for the murders of Alice and Nellie. If Philadelphia failed to convict him, there would be two more chances; if the city succeeded, the other indictments would be moot, for given the nature of the Pitezel murder, a conviction in Philadelphia would bring a death sentence.

Holmes's memoir reached newsstands. In its final pages he stated, "In conclusion, I wish to say that I am but a very ordinary man, even below average in physical strength and mental ability, and to have planned and executed the stupendous amount of wrong-doing that has been attributed to me would have been wholly beyond my power. . . ."

He asked the public to suspend judgment while he worked to disprove the charges against him, "a task which I feel able to satisfactorily and expeditiously accomplish. And here I cannot say finis—it is not the end—for besides doing this there is also the work of bringing to justice those for whose wrong-doings I am to-day suffering, and this not to prolong or save my own life, for since the day I heard of the Toronto horror I have not cared to live; but that to those who have looked up to and honored me in the past it shall not in the future be said that I suffered the ignominious death of a murderer."

The thing editors could not understand was how Holmes had been able to escape serious investigation by the Chicago police. The *Chicago Inter Ocean* said, "It is humiliating to think that had it not been for the exertions of the insurance companies which Holmes swindled, or attempted to swindle, he might yet be at large, preying upon society, so well did he cover up the traces of his crime." Chicago's "feeling of humiliation" was not surprising, the *New York Times* said; anyone familiar with the saga "must be amazed at the failure of the municipal police department and the local prosecuting officers not only to prevent those awful crimes, but even to procure any knowledge of them."

One of the most surprising and perhaps dismaying revelations was that Chicago's chief of police, in his prior legal career, had represented Holmes in a dozen routine commercial lawsuits.

The *Chicago Times-Herald* took the broad view and said of Holmes: "He is a prodigy of wickedness, a human demon, a being so unthinkable that no novelist would dare to invent such a character. The story, too, tends to illustrate the end of the century."

EPILOGUE

The Last Crossing

Statue of the Republic, after the Peristyle fire, 1894.

The Fair

THE FAIR HAD A POWERFUL and lasting impact on the nation's psyche, in ways both large and small. Walt Disney's father, Elias, helped build the White City; Walt's Magic Kingdom may well be a descendant. Certainly the fair made a powerful impression on the Disney family. It proved such a financial boon that when the family's third son was born that year, Elias in gratitude wanted to name him Columbus. His wife, Flora, intervened; the baby became Roy. Walt came next, on December 5, 1901. The writer L. Frank Baum and his artist-partner William Wallace Denslow visited the fair; its grandeur informed their creation of Oz. The Japanese temple on the Wooded Island charmed Frank Lloyd Wright, and may have influenced the evolution of his "Prairie" residential designs. The fair prompted President Harrison to designate October 12 a national holiday, Columbus Day, which today serves to anchor a few thousand parades and a three-day weekend. Every carnival since 1893 has included a Midway and a Ferris Wheel, and every grocery store contains products born at the exposition. Shredded Wheat did survive. Every house has scores of incandescent bulbs powered by alternating current, both of which first proved themselves worthy of large-scale use at the fair; and nearly every town of any size has its little bit of ancient Rome, some beloved and becolumned bank, library or post office. Covered with graffiti, perhaps, or even an ill-conceived coat of paint, but underneath it all the glow of the White City persists. Even the Lincoln Memorial in Washington can trace its heritage to the fair.

The fair's greatest impact lay in how it changed the way Americans perceived their cities and their architects. It primed the whole of America—not just a few rich architectural patrons—to think of cities in a way they never had before. Elihu Root said the fair led "our people out of the wilderness of the commonplace to new ideas of architectural beauty and nobility." Henry Demarest Lloyd saw it as revealing to the great mass of Americans "possibilities of social beauty, utility, and harmony of which they had not been able even to dream. No such vision could otherwise have entered into the prosaic drudgery of their lives, and it will be felt in their development into the third and fourth generation." The fair taught men and women steeped only in the necessary to see that cities did not have to be dark, soiled, and unsafe bastions of the strictly pragmatic. They could also be beautiful.

William Stead recognized the power of the fair immediately. The vision of the White City and its profound contrast to the Black City drove him to write *If Christ Came to Chicago,* a book often credited with launching the City Beautiful movement, which sought to elevate American cities to the level of the great cities of Europe. Like Stead, civic authorities throughout the world saw the fair as a model of what to strive for. They asked Burnham to apply the same citywide thinking that had gone into the White City to their own cities. He became a pioneer in modern urban planning. He created citywide plans for Cleveland, San Francisco, and Manila and led the turn-of-the-century effort to resuscitate and expand L'Enfant's vision of Washington, D.C. In each case he worked without a fee.

While helping design the new Washington plan, Burnham persuaded the head of the Pennsylvania Railroad, Alexander Cassatt, to remove his freight tracks and depot from the center of the federal mall, thus creating the unobstructed green that extends today from the Capitol to the Lincoln Memorial. Other cities came to Daniel Burnham for citywide plans, among them Fort Worth, Atlantic City, and St. Louis, but he turned them down to concentrate on his last plan, for the city of Chicago. Over the years many aspects of his Chicago plan were adopted, among them the creation of the city's lovely ribbon of lakefront parks and Michigan Avenue's "Miracle Mile." One portion of the lakefront, named Burnham Park in his honor, contains Soldier Field and the Field Museum, which he designed. The park runs south in a narrow green border along the lakeshore all the way to Jackson Park, where the fair's Palace of Fine Arts, transformed into a permanent structure, now houses the Museum of Science and Industry. It looks out over the lagoons and the Wooded Island, now a wild and tangled place that perhaps would make Olmsted smile—though no doubt he would find features to criticize.

Early in the twentieth century the fair became a source of heated debate among architects. Critics claimed the fair extinguished the Chicago School of architecture, an indigenous vernacular, and replaced it with a renewed devotion to obsolete classical styles. Parroted from thesis to thesis, this view first gained prominence through a curiously personal dynamic that made it difficult and—as is often the case in the cramped and stuffy rooms of academic debate—even dangerous to resist.

It was Louis Sullivan who first and most loudly condemned the fair's influence on architecture, but only late in his life and long after Burnham's death.

Things had not gone well for Sullivan after the fair. During the first year of the postfair depression the firm of Adler & Sullivan received only two commissions; in 1895, none. In July 1895 Adler quit the firm. Sullivan was thirty-eight and incapable of cultivating the relationships that might have generated enough new commissions to keep him solvent. He was a loner and intellectually intolerant. When a fellow architect asked Sullivan for suggestions on how to improve one of his designs, Sullivan replied, "If I told you, you wouldn't know what I was talking about."

As his practice faltered, Sullivan found himself forced to leave his office in the Auditorium and to sell his personal belongings. He drank heavily and took mood-altering drugs called bromides. Between 1895 and 1922 Sullivan built only twenty-five new structures, roughly one a year. From time to time he came to Burnham for money, although whether he sought outright loans or sold Burnham artwork from his personal collection is unclear. An entry in Burnham's diary for 1911 states, "Louis Sullivan called to get more money of DHB." That same year Sullivan inscribed a set of drawings, "To Daniel H. Burnham, with the best wishes of his friend Louis H. Sullivan."

But Sullivan laced his 1924 autobiography with hyperbolic attacks on

Burnham and the fair's impact on the masses who came through its gates. The classical architecture of the White City made such a profound impression, Sullivan claimed, that it doomed America to another half-century of imitation. The fair was a "contagion," a "virus," a form of "progressive cerebral meningitis." In his view it had fatal consequences. "Thus Architecture died in the land of the free and the home of the brave—in a land declaring its fervid democracy, its inventiveness, its resourcefulness, its unique daring, enterprise and progress."

Sullivan's low opinion of Burnham and the fair was counterbalanced only by his own exalted view of himself and what he saw as his role in attempting to bring to architecture something fresh and distinctly American. Frank Lloyd Wright took up Sullivan's banner. Sullivan had fired him in 1893, but later Wright and Sullivan became friends. As Wright's academic star rose, so too did Sullivan's. Burnham's fell from the sky. It became de rigueur among architecture critics and historians to argue that Burnham in his insecurity and slavish devotion to the classical yearnings of the eastern architects had indeed killed American architecture.

But that view was too simplistic, as some architecture historians and critics have more recently acknowledged. The fair awakened America to beauty and as such was a necessary passage that laid the foundation for men like Frank Lloyd Wright and Ludwig Mies van der Rohe.

For Burnham personally the fair had been an unqualified triumph. It allowed him to fulfill his pledge to his parents to become the greatest architect in America, for certainly in his day he had become so. During the fair an event occurred whose significance to Burnham was missed by all but his closest friends: Both Harvard and Yale granted him honorary master's degrees in recognition of his achievement in building the fair. The ceremonies occurred on the same day. He attended Harvard's. For him the awards were a form of redemption. His past failure to gain admission to both universities—the denial of his "right beginning"—had haunted him throughout his life. Even years after receiving the awards, as he lobbied Harvard to grant provisional admission to his son Daniel, whose own performance on the entry exams was far from stellar, Burnham wrote, "He needs to know that he is a winner, and, as soon as he does, he will show his real quality, as I have been able to do. It is the keenest regret of my life that someone did not follow me up at Cambridge . . . and let the authorities know what I could do."

Burnham had shown them himself, in Chicago, through the hardest sort of work. He bristled at the persistent belief that John Root deserved most of the credit for the beauty of the fair. "What was done up to the time of his death was the faintest suggestion of a plan," he said. "The impression concerning his part has been gradually built up by a few people, close friends of his and mostly women, who naturally after the Fair proved beautiful desired to more broadly identify his memory with it."

Root's death had crushed Burnham, but it also freed him to become a broader, better architect. "It was questioned by many if the loss of Mr. Root was not irreparable," wrote James Ellsworth in a letter to Burnham's biographer, Charles Moore. Ellsworth concluded that Root's death "brought out qualities in Mr. Burnham which might not have developed, as early anyway, had Mr. Root lived." The common perception had always been that Burnham managed the business side of the firm, while Root did all the designs. Burnham did seem to "lean more or less" on Root's artistic abilities, Ellsworth said, but added that after Root's death "one would never realize anything of this kind . . . or ever know from his actions that he ever possessed a partner or did not always command in *both* directions."

In 1901 Burnham built the Fuller Building at the triangular intersection of Twenty-third and Broadway in New York, but neighborhood residents found an uncanny resemblance to a common domestic tool and called it the Flatiron Building. Burnham and his firm went on to build scores of other structures, among them the Gimbel's department store in New York, Filene's in Boston, and the Mount Wilson Observatory in Pasadena, California. Of the twenty-seven buildings he and John Root built in Chicago's Loop, only three remain today, among them the Rookery, its top-floor library much as it was during that magical meeting in

February 1891, and the Reliance Building, beautifully transformed into the Hotel Burnham. Its restaurant is called the Atwood, after Charles Atwood, who replaced Root as Burnham's chief designer.

Burnham became an early environmentalist. "Up to our time," he said, "strict economy in the use of natural resources has not been practiced, but it must be henceforth unless we are immoral enough to impair conditions in which our children are to live." He had great, if misplaced, faith in the automobile. The passing of the horse would "end a plague of barbarism," he said. "When this change comes, a real step in civilization will have been taken. With no smoke, no gases, no litter of horses, your air and streets will be clean and pure. This means, does it not, that the health and spirits of men will be better?"

On winter nights in Evanston he and his wife went sleigh-riding with Mr. and Mrs. Frank Lloyd Wright. Burnham became an avid player of bridge, though he was known widely for being utterly inept at the game. He had promised his wife that after the exposition the pace of his work would ease. But this did not happen. He told Margaret, "I thought the fair was an intense life, but I find the pressing forward of all these important interests gives me quite as full a day, week or year."

Burnham's health began to decline early in the twentieth century, when he was in his fifties. He developed colitis and in 1909 learned he had diabetes. Both conditions forced him to adopt a more healthful diet. His diabetes damaged his circulatory system and fostered a foot infection that bedeviled him for the rest of his life. As the years passed, he revealed an interest in the supernatural. One night in San Francisco, in a bungalow he had built at the fog-licked summit of Twin Peaks, his planning shanty, he told a friend, "If I were able to take the time, I believe that I could prove the continuation of life beyond the grave, reasoning from the necessity, philosophically speaking, of a belief in an absolute and universal power."

He knew that his day was coming to an end. On July 4, 1909, as he stood with friends on the roof of the Reliance Building, looking out over the city he adored, he said, "You'll see it lovely. I never will. But it *will* be lovely."

Recessional

THE ROARING IN OLMSTED'S EARS, the pain in his mouth, and the sleeplessness never eased, and soon an emptiness began to appear in his gaze. He became forgetful. On May 10, 1895, two weeks after his seventy-third birthday, he wrote to his son John, "It has today, for the first time, become evident to me that my memory for recent occurrences is no longer to be trusted." He was seventy-three years old. That summer, on his last day in the Brookline office, he wrote three letters to George Vanderbilt, each saying pretty much the same thing.

During a period in September 1895 that he described as "the bitterest week of my life," he confessed to his friend Charles Eliot his terror that his condition soon would require that he be placed in an asylum. "You cannot think how I have been dreading that it would be thought expedient that I should be sent to an 'institution,'" he wrote on September 26. "Anything but that. My father was a director of an Insane Retreat, and first and last, having been professionally employed and behind the scenes in several, my dread of such places is intense."

His loss of memory accelerated. He became depressed and paranoid and accused son John of orchestrating a "coup" to remove him from the firm. Olmsted's wife, Mary, took Olmsted to the family's island home in Maine, where his depression deepened and he at times became violent. He beat the family horse.

Mary and her sons realized there was little they could do for Olmsted. He had become unmanageable, his dementia profound. With deep sorrow and perhaps a good deal of relief, Rick lodged his father in the McLean Asylum in Waverly, Massachusetts. Olmsted's memory was not so destroyed that he did not realize he himself had designed McLean's grounds. This fact gave him no solace, for he saw immediately that the same phenomenon that had diminished nearly every one of his works—Central Park, Biltmore, the world's fair, and so many others—had occurred yet again. "They didn't carry out my plan," he wrote, "confound them!"

Olmsted died at two in the morning on August 28, 1903. His funeral was spare, family only. His wife, who had seen this great man disappear before her eyes, did not attend.

The Ferris Wheel cleared $200,000 at the fair and remained in place until the spring of 1894, when George Ferris dismantled it and reassembled it on Chicago's North Side. By then, however, it had lost both its novelty and the volume of ridership that the Midway had guaranteed. The wheel began losing money. These losses, added to the $150,000 cost of moving it and the financial damage done to Ferris's steel-inspection company by the continuing depression, caused Ferris to sell most of his ownership of the wheel.

In the autumn of 1896 Ferris and his wife separated. She went home to her parents; he moved into the Duquesne Hotel in downtown Pittsburgh. On November 17, 1896, he was taken to Mercy Hospital, where he died five days later, apparently of typhoid fever. He was thirty-seven years old. One year later his ashes were still in the possession of the undertaker who had received his body. "The request of Mrs. Ferris for the ashes was refused," the undertaker said, "because the dead man left closer relatives." In a eulogy two friends said Ferris had "miscalculated his powers of endurance, and he died a martyr to his ambition for fame and prominence."

In 1903 the Chicago House Wrecking Company bought the wheel at auction for $8,150, then reassembled it at the Louisiana Purchase Exposition of 1904. There the wheel again became profitable and earned its new owners $215,000. On May 11, 1906, the wrecking company dynamited the wheel, for scrap. The first hundred-pound charge was supposed to cut the wheel loose from its supports and topple it onto its side.

Instead the wheel began a slow turn, as if seeking one last roll through the sky. It crumpled under its own weight into a mountain of bent steel.

———

Sol Bloom, chief of the Midway, emerged from the fair a rich young man. He invested heavily in a company that bought perishable foods and shipped them in the latest refrigerated cars to far-off cities. It was a fine, forward-looking business. But the Pullman strike halted all train traffic through Chicago, and the perishable foods rotted in their train-cars. He was ruined. He was still young, however, and still Bloom. He used his remaining funds to buy two expensive suits, on the theory that whatever he did next, he had to look convincing. "But one thing was quite clear. . . ." he wrote. "[B]eing broke didn't disturb me in the least. I had started with nothing, and if I now found myself with nothing, I was at least even. Actually, I was much better than even: I had had a wonderful time."

Bloom went on to become a congressman and one of the crafters of the charter that founded the United Nations.

———

The fair made Buffalo Bill a million dollars (about $30 million today), which he used to found the town of Cody, Wyoming, build a cemetery and fairground for North Platte, Nebraska, pay the debts of five North Platte churches, acquire a Wisconsin newspaper, and further the theatri-cal fortunes of a lovely young actress named Katherine Clemmons, thereby deepening the already pronounced alienation of his wife. At one point he accused his wife of trying to poison him.

The Panic of 1907 destroyed his Wild West and forced him to hire himself out to circuses. He was over seventy years old but still rode the ring under his big white hat trimmed in silver. He died in Denver at his sister's house on January 10, 1917, without the money even to pay for his burial.

———

Theodore Dreiser married Sara Osborne White. In 1898, two years before publishing *Sister Carrie,* he wrote to Sara, "I went to Jackson Park and saw what is left of the dear old World's Fair where I learned to love you."

He cheated on her repeatedly.

For Dora Root life with John had been like living upon a comet. Their marriage had brought her into a world of art and money where everything seemed energized and alive. Her husband's wit, his musical talent, those exquisite long fingers so evident in any photograph imparted a gleam to her days that she was never able to recapture after his death. Toward the end of the first decade of the twentieth century, she wrote a long letter to Burnham. "It means so much to me that you think I have done well all these years," she wrote. "I have such grave doubts about myself whenever I stop to think about the subject, that a word of encouragement from one who has so wonderfully sounded out his life, gives me a new impetus. If absorbing myself before the coming generation, and humbly passing on the torch, is the whole duty of women, I believe I have earned a word of praise."

But she knew that with John's death the doors to a brighter kingdom had softly but firmly closed. "If John had lived," she told Burnham, "all would have been different. Under the stimulus of his exhilarating life, I would have been his wife as well as the mother of his children. And it would have been interesting!"

Patrick Eugene Joseph Prendergast stood trial in December 1893. The prosecutor was a criminal attorney hired by the state just for this case.

His name was Alfred S. Trude.

Prendergast's lawyers tried to prove Prendergast was insane, but a jury of angry, grieving Chicagoans believed otherwise. One important piece of evidence tending to support the prosecution's case for sanity was the care Prendergast had taken to keep an empty chamber under the hammer of his revolver as he carried it in his pocket. At 2:28 P.M. on December 29, after conferring for an hour and three minutes, the jury found him guilty. The judge sentenced him to death. Throughout his trial and subsequent appeal, he continued to send Trude postcards. He wrote on February 21, 1894, "No one should be put to death no matter who it is, if it can be avoided, it is demoralizing to society to be barbarous."

Clarence Darrow entered the case and in a novel maneuver won for Prendergast a sanity inquest. This too failed, however, and Prendergast was executed. Darrow called him "a poor demented imbecile." The execution intensified Darrow's already deep hatred of the death penalty. "I am sorry for all fathers and all mothers," he said, years later, during his defense of Nathan Leopold and Richard Loeb, accused of killing a Chicago boy for the thrill of it. "The mother who looks into the blue eyes of her little babe cannot help musing over the end of the child, whether it will be crowned with the greatest promises which her mind can image or whether he may meet death upon the scaffold."

Leopold and Loeb, as they became known worldwide, had stripped their victim to mask his identity. They dumped some of his clothes in Olmsted's lagoons at Jackson Park.

In New York at the Waldorf-Astoria a few years into the new century, several dozen young men in evening clothes gathered around a gigantic pie. The whipped-cream topping began to move. A woman emerged. She was stunning, with olive skin and long black hair. Her name was Farida Mazhar. The men were too young to remember, but once, a long while before, she had done the *danse du ventre* at the greatest fair in history.

What the men noticed now was that she wore nothing at all.

Holmes

In the fall of 1895 Holmes stood trial in Philadelphia for the murder of Benjamin F. Pitezel. District Attorney George Graham brought thirty-five witnesses to Philadelphia from Cincinnati, Indianapolis, Irvington, Detroit, Toronto, Boston, Burlington, and Fort Worth, but they never were called. The judge ruled that Graham could present only evidence tied directly to the Pitezel murder and thus eliminated from the historical record a rich seam of detail on the murders of Dr. Herman W. Mudgett, alias Holmes.

Graham also brought to the courtroom the wart Holmes had removed from Benjamin Pitezel's corpse and a wooden box containing Pitezel's skull. There was a good deal of macabre testimony about decomposition and body fluids and the effects of chloroform. "There was a red fluid issuing from his mouth," testified Dr. William Scott, a pharmacist who had accompanied police to the house where Pitezel's body had been discovered, "and any little pressure on the stomach or over the chest here would cause this fluid to flow more rapidly. . . ."

After one particularly grisly stretch of Dr. Scott's testimony, Holmes stood and said, "I would ask that the Court be adjourned for sufficient time for lunch."

There were sorrowful moments, especially when Mrs. Pitezel took the stand. She wore a black dress, black hat, and black cape and looked pale and sad. Often she paused in midsentence and rested her head on her hands. Graham showed her the letters from Alice and Nellie and asked her to identify the handwriting. These were a surprise to her. She broke down. Holmes showed no emotion. "It was an expression of utmost indifference," a reporter for the *Philadelphia Public Ledger* said. "He made his notes with a manner as unconcerned as if he were sitting in his own office writing a business letter."

Graham asked Mrs. Pitezel whether she had seen the children since the time in 1894 when Holmes took them away. She answered in a voice almost too soft to hear, "I saw them at Toronto in the morgue, side by side."

So many handkerchiefs appeared among the men and women in the gallery that the courtroom looked as if it had just experienced a sudden snowfall.

Graham called Holmes "the most dangerous man in the world." The jury found him guilty; the judge sentenced him to death by hanging. Holmes's attorneys appealed the conviction and lost.

As Holmes awaited execution, he prepared a long confession, his third, in which he admitted killing twenty-seven people. As with two previous confessions, this one was a mixture of truth and falsehood. A few of the people he claimed to have murdered turned out to be alive. Exactly how many people he killed will never be known. At the very least he killed nine: Julia and Pearl Conner, Emeline Cigrand, the Williams sisters, and Pitezel and his children. No one doubted that he had killed many others. Estimates ranged as high as two hundred, though such extravagance seems implausible even for a man of his appetite. Detective Geyer believed that if the Pinkertons had not caught up with Holmes and arranged his arrest in Boston, he would have killed the rest of the Pitezel family. "That he fully intended to murder Mrs. Pitezel and Dessie and the baby, Wharton, is too evident for contradiction."

Holmes, in his confession, also clearly lied, or at least was deeply deluded, when he wrote, "I am convinced that since my imprisonment I have changed woefully and gruesomely from what I was formerly in feature and figure. . . . My head and face are gradually assuming an elongated shape. I believe fully that I am growing to resemble the devil—that the similitude is almost completed."

His description of killing Alice and Nellie rang true, however. He said he placed the girls in a large trunk and made an opening in its top. "Here I left them until I could return and at my leisure kill them. At 5 P.M. I borrowed a spade of a neighbor and at the same time called on Mrs. Pitezel at her hotel. I then returned to my hotel and ate my dinner, and at 7:00 P.M. I again returned to the house where the children were imprisoned, and ended their lives by connecting the gas with the trunk, then came the opening of the trunk and the viewing of their little blackened and distorted faces, then the digging of their shallow graves in the basement of the house."

He said of Pitezel, "It will be understood that from the first hour of our acquaintance, even before I knew he had a family who would later afford me additional victims for the gratification of my blood-thirstiness, I intended to kill him."

Afraid that someone would steal his own body after his execution, Holmes left instructions with his lawyers for how he was to be buried. He refused to allow an autopsy. His lawyers turned down an offer of $5,000 for his body. The Wistar Institute in Philadelphia wanted his brain. This request, too, the lawyers refused, much to the regret of Milton Greeman, curator of Wistar's renowned collection of medical specimens. "The man was something more than a mere criminal who acted on impulse," Greeman said. "He was a man who studied crime and planned his career. His brain might have given science valuable aid."

Shortly before ten A.M. on May 7, 1896, after a breakfast of boiled eggs, dry toast, and coffee, Holmes was escorted to the gallows at Moyamensing Prison. This was a difficult moment for his guards. They liked Holmes. They knew he was a killer, but he was a charming killer. The assistant superintendent, a man named Richardson, seemed nervous as he readied the noose. Holmes turned to him and smiled, and said, "Take your time, old man." At 10:13 Richardson released the trap and hanged him.

Using Holmes's instructions, workmen in the employ of undertaker John J. O'Rourke filled a coffin with cement, then placed Holmes's body inside and covered it with more cement. They hauled him south through the countryside to Holy Cross Cemetery, a Catholic burial ground in Delaware County, just south of Philadelphia. With great effort they transferred the heavy coffin to the cemetery's central vault, where two Pinkerton detectives guarded the body overnight. They took turns sleeping in a white pine coffin. The next day workers opened a double grave and filled this too with cement, then inserted Holmes's coffin. They placed more cement on top and closed the grave. "Holmes' idea was evidently to guard his remains in every way from scientific enterprise, from the pickling vat and the knife," the *Public Ledger* reported.

Strange things began to happen that made Holmes's claims about being the devil seem almost plausible. Detective Geyer became seriously ill. The warden of Moyamensing prison committed suicide. The jury foreman was electrocuted in a freak accident. The priest who delivered Holmes's last rites was found dead on the grounds of his church of mysterious causes. The father of Emeline Cigrand was grotesquely burned in a boiler explosion. And a fire destroyed the office of District Attorney George Graham, leaving only a photograph of Holmes unscathed.

No stone or tomb marks the grave of Herman Webster Mudgett, alias H. H. Holmes. His presence in Holy Cross Cemetery is something of a secret, recorded only in an ancient registry volume that lists his location as section 15, range 10, lot 41, at the center of graves 3 and 4, just off a lane that the cemetery calls Lazarus Avenue, after the biblical character who died and was restored to life. The entry also notes "ten feet of cement." At the gravesite there is only an open lawn in the midst of other old graves. There are children and a World War I pilot.

No one ever left flowers here for Holmes, but as it happens, he was not entirely forgotten.

In 1997 police in Chicago arrested a physician named Michael Swango at O'Hare Airport. The initial charge was fraud, but Swango was suspected of being a serial killer who murdered hospital patients through the administration of lethal doses of drugs. Eventually Dr. Swango pled guilty to four murders, but investigators believed he had committed many more. During the airport arrest police found in Swango's possession a notebook in which he had copied passages from certain books, either for the inspiration they provided or because of some affirming resonance. One passage was from a book about H. H. Holmes called *The Torture Doctor* by David Franke. The copied passage sought to put the reader into Holmes's mind.

" 'He could look at himself in a mirror and tell himself that he was one of the most powerful and dangerous men in the world,' " Swango's notebook read. " 'He could feel that he was a god in disguise.' "

Aboard the *Olympic*

ABOARD THE *OLYMPIC* BURNHAM waited for more news of Frank Millet and his ship. Just before sailing he had written, in longhand, a nineteen-page letter to Millet urging him to attend the next meeting of the Lincoln Commission, which was then on the verge of picking a designer for the Lincoln Memorial. Burnham and Millet had lobbied strongly for Henry Bacon of New York, and Burnham believed that his earlier talk to the Lincoln Commission had been persuasive. "But—I know and you know, dear Frank, that . . . the rats swarm back and begin to gnaw at the same old spot, the moment the dog's back is turned." He stressed how important it was for Millet to attend. "Be there and reiterate the real argument, which is that they should select a man in whom we have confidence. I leave this thing confidently in your hands." He addressed the envelope himself, certain that the United States Post Office would know exactly what to do:

Hon. F. D. Millet
To arrive on
Steamship Titanic.
New York

Burnham hoped that once the *Olympic* reached the site of the *Titanic*'s sinking, he would find Millet alive and hear him tell some outrageous story about the voyage, but during the night the *Olympic* returned to its original course for England. Another vessel already had reached the *Titanic*.

But there was a second reason for the *Olympic*'s return to course. The builder of both ships, J. Bruce Ismay, himself a *Titanic* passenger but one of the few male passengers to survive, was adamant that none of the other survivors see this duplicate of their own lost liner coming to their aid. The shock, he feared, would be too great, and too humiliating to the White Star Line.

The magnitude of the *Titanic* disaster quickly became apparent. Burnham lost his friend. The steward lost his son. William Stead had also been aboard and was drowned. In 1886 in the *Pall Mall Gazette* Stead had warned of the disasters likely to occur if shipping companies continued operating liners with too few lifeboats. A *Titanic* survivor reported hearing him say, "I think it is nothing serious so I shall turn in again."

That night, in the silence of Burnham's stateroom, as somewhere to the north the body of his last good friend drifted frozen in the strangely peaceful seas of the North Atlantic, Burnham opened his diary and began to write. He felt an acute loneliness. He wrote, "Frank Millet, whom I loved, was aboard her . . . thus cutting off my connection with one of the best fellows of the Fair."

Burnham lived only forty-seven more days. As he and his family traveled through Heidelberg, he slipped into a coma, the result apparently of a combined assault of diabetes, colitis, and his foot infection, all worsened by a bout of food poisoning. He died June 1, 1912. Margaret eventually moved to Pasadena, California, where she lived through time of war and epidemic and crushing financial depression, and then war again. She died December 23, 1945. Both are buried in Chicago, in Graceland, on a tiny island in the cemetery's only pond. John Root lies nearby, as do the Palmers, Louis Sullivan, Mayor Harrison, Marshall Field, Philip Armour, and so many others, in vaults and tombs that vary from the simple to the grand. Potter and Bertha still dominate things, as if stature mattered even in death. They occupy a massive acropolis with fifteen giant columns atop the only high ground, overlooking the pond. The others cluster around. On a crystalline fall day you can almost hear the tinkle of fine crystal, the rustle of silk and wool, almost smell the expensive cigars.

NOTES AND SOURCES

The White City, viewed from Lake Michigan.

THE THING THAT ENTRANCED ME about Chicago in the Gilded Age was the city's willingness to take on the impossible in the name of civic honor, a concept so removed from the modern psyche that two wise readers of early drafts of this book wondered why Chicago was so avid to win the world's fair in the first place. The juxtaposition of pride and unfathomed evil struck me as offering powerful insights into the nature of men and their ambitions. The more I read about the fair, the more entranced I became. That George Ferris would attempt to build something so big and novel—and that he would succeed on his first try—seems, in this day of liability lawsuits, almost beyond comprehension.

A rich seam of information exists about the fair and about Daniel Burnham in the beautifully run archives of the Chicago Historical Society and the Ryerson and Burnham libraries of the Art Institute of Chicago. I acquired a nice base of information from the University of Washington's Suzallo Library, one of the finest and most efficient libraries I have encountered. I also visited the Library of Congress in Washington, where I spent a good many happy hours immersed in the papers of Frederick Law Olmsted, though my happiness was at times strained by trying to decipher Olmsted's execrable handwriting.

I read—and mined—dozens of books about Burnham, Chicago, the exposition, and the late Victorian era. Several proved consistently valuable: Thomas Hines's *Burnham of Chicago* (1974); Laura Wood Roper's *FLO: A Biography of Frederick Law Olmsted* (1973); and Witold Rybczynski's *A Clearing in the Distance* (1999). One book in particular, *City of the Century* by Donald L. Miller (1996), became an invaluable companion in my journey through old Chicago. I found four guidebooks to be especially useful: Alice Sinkevitch's *AIA Guide to Chicago* (1993); Matt Hucke and Ursula Bielski's *Graveyards of Chicago* (1999); John Flinn's *Official Guide to the World's Columbian Exposition* (1893); and *Rand, McNally & Co.'s Handbook to the World's Columbian Exposition* (1893). Hucke and Bielski's guide led me to pay a visit to Graceland Cemetery, an utterly charming haven where, paradoxically, history comes alive.

Holmes proved an elusive character, owing in large part to the Philadelphia judge's unfortunate decision to bar District Attorney Graham's three dozen witnesses from giving testimony. Several books have been written about Holmes, but none tells quite the same story. Two of them, Harold Schechter's *Depraved* and David Franke's *The Torture Doctor* (the work quoted by the modern serial killer Dr. Swango), seem the most trustworthy. Two other works exist that provide a concrete foundation of facts. One is Detective Frank Geyer's memoir, *The Holmes-Pitezel Case*, a detailed account of events from the time of Holmes's arrest onward, in which Geyer presents excerpts of primary documents that no longer exist. I was lucky enough to acquire a copy from an online seller of antique books. The second is *The Trial of Herman W. Mudgett, Alias, H. H. Holmes*, published in 1897, a complete transcript of the trial. I found a copy in the law library of the University of Washington.

Holmes left a memoir, *Holmes' Own Story*, which I found in the Library of Congress's rare book collection. He also made at least three confessions. The first two appear in Geyer's book. The third and most sensational appeared in the *Philadelphia Inquirer*, which paid him a rich fee to write it. Though mostly untrue, his memoir and confessions were nuggeted with details that jibed with facts established in court or unearthed by Geyer and by the legions of reporters who covered Holmes's story after his arrest in Boston. I relied heavily on newspaper articles published in the *Chicago Tribune* and in two Philadelphia newspapers, the *Inquirer* and the *Public Ledger*. Many of these articles were full of inaccuracies and, I suspect, embellishments. I mined them for bits of apparent fact and for reproductions of original documents, such as letters, telegrams, interviews, and other primary materials uncovered by police or produced by witnesses who stepped forward once the nature of Holmes's "Castle of Horrors" became front-page news. One of the most striking, and rather charming, aspects of criminal investigation in the 1890s is the extent to which the police gave reporters direct access to crime scenes, even while investigations were in progress. At one point during the Holmes investigation Chicago's chief of police told a *Tribune* reporter he'd just as soon have a squad of reporters under his command as detectives.

Exactly what motivated Holmes may never be known. In focusing on his quest for possession and dominance, I present only one possibility, though I recognize that any number of other motives might well be posited. I base my account on known details of his history and behavior and on what forensic psychiatrists have come to understand about psychopathic serial killers and the forces that drive them. Dr. James O. Raney, a Seattle psychiatrist who now and then provides forensic evaluations, read the manuscript and gave me his observations about the nature of psychopaths, known more tediously in today's psychiatric handbooks as people afflicted with "antisocial personality disorder." It is a good thing Alfred Hitchcock died before the change was made.

Clearly no one other than Holmes was present during his murders—no one, that is, who survived—yet in my book I re-create two of his killings. I agonized over exactly how to do this and spent a good deal of time rereading Truman Capote's *In Cold Blood* for insights into how Capote achieved his dark and still deeply troubling account. Sadly, Capote left no footnotes. To build my murder scenes, I used threads of known detail to weave a plausible account, as would a prosecutor in his closing arguments to a jury. My description of Julia Conner's death by chloroform is based on expert testimony presented at Holmes's trial about the character of chloroform and what was known at the time about its effect on the human body.

I do not employ researchers, nor did I conduct any primary research using the Internet. I need physical contact with my sources, and there's only one way to get it. To me every trip to a library or archive is like a small detective story. There are always little moments on such trips when the past flares to life, like a match in the darkness. On one visit to the Chicago Historical Society, I found the actual notes that Prendergast sent to Alfred Trude. I saw how deeply the pencil dug into the paper.

I have tried to keep my citations as concise as possible. I cite all quoted or controversial material but omit citations for facts that are widely known and accepted. For the two murder scenes I document my reasoning and my approach and cite the facts upon which I relied. The citations that follow constitute a map. Anyone retracing my steps ought to reach the same conclusions as I.

PROLOGUE

Aboard the *Olympic*

3. *The date was*: Burnham identified the suite numbers in a diary entry dated April 3, 1912; Burnham Archives, Diary, Roll 2. For information about the *Olympic* and *Titanic* see Brinnin; Lynch; Eaton and Haas; and *White Star*. The last, which reprints articles published in 1911 from *Shipping World and Shipbuilder*, includes detailed specifications of both ships as well as maps and schematics of the *Olympic*'s decks and accommodations.

3. *"This prolonging*: Moore, *Burnham, Architect*, 2:172.

5. *"the greatest event*: Miller, 488.

PART I: FROZEN MUSIC

The Black City

11. *"Never before*: Miller, 511.

11. *"The parlors and bedrooms*: Ibid., 516.

11. *"a human being*: Ibid., 193.

"The Trouble Is Just Begun"

14. *It was this big talk*: Dedmon, 221.

16. *"the hawks, buzzards*: *Chicago Tribune*, July 24, 1889.

16. *"The men who have helped*: *Chicago Tribune*, August 2, 1889.

17. *"The gloom*: *Chicago Tribune*, February 24, 1890.

17. *"Gentlemen. I am prepared*: Ibid.

19. *"the records of the Old Central*: Hines, 402.

19. *"I went to Harvard*: Ibid., 11.

19. *"greatest architect*: Ibid., 12.

19. *"There is a family tendency*: Miller, 315.

21. *"My idea*: Sullivan, Louis, 285.

21. *"There is a black sheep*: Letter, Daniel Hudson Burnham, Jr., to Charles Moore, February 21, 1918, Burnham Archives, Charles Moore Correspondence, Box 27, File 3.

22. *"A long wait frightened us*: Monroe, *Poet's Life*, 59.

22. *"so completely happy*: Ibid., 60.

23. *"probably not equaled*: Miller, 321.

24. *"our originality*: Moore, *Burnham, Architect*, 1:24.

24. *"if," he said, "the earth*: Ibid., 1:321.

24. *"The building throughout*: Ibid.

25. *"What Chartres was*: Hines, 53.

26. *"who will not have an office*: Miller, 326.

26. *"Daniel Burnham Hudson was*: Starrett, 29.

26. *"Make no little plans*: Ibid., 311.

26. *"I've never seen*: Miller, 319.

27. *"His conversational powers*: Ibid., 316.

27. *"I used always to think*: Ibid., 317

27. *"The office was full*: Starrett, 32.

27. *"The work of each man*: Miller, 318.

28. *"that Gordian city*: Lewis, 19.

28. *"a gigantic peepshow*: Ibid., 136.

28. *"I did it*: Burnham to mother, undated, Burnham Archives, Burnham Family Correspondence, Box 25, File 2.

29. *"You must not worry*: Burnham to Margaret, February 29, 1888, Burnham Archives, Burnham Family Correspondence, Box 25, File 3.

29. *"The coroner*: Burnham to Margaret, March 3, 1888, ibid.

30. *"Burnham was not pleased*: Sullivan, Louis, 294.

30. *"smear another façade*: Morrison, 64.

30. *"an innocent*: Sullivan, Louis, 291.

30. *"He was elephantine*: Ibid., 288.

32. *"When may we see you*: ChicagoTribune, February 25, 1890.

32. *"The most marvelous exhibit*: Ibid.

34. *"Chicago is like*: Chicago Tribune, February 27, 1890.

The Necessary Supply

35. *His height was*: Franke, 24. Franke reproduces an image of a "Rogue's Gallery" file card with details of Holmes's weight, height, and so forth as entered by Boston police upon his arrest.

35. *"The eyes are very big*: Schechter, 282.

36. *A telegraph pole*: Englewood Directory, 37.

36. *"While at times*: Sullivan, Gerald, 49.

36. *Holmes entered the store*: Mudgett, 22–23; Schechter, 13–17; Boswell and Thompson, 81. See also *Town of Lake Directory*, 217.

37. *"an elemental odor*: Sinclair, 25.

37. *"river of death*: Ibid., 34.

37. *"I had daily*: Mudgett, 6.

38. *"Nor did they desist*: Ibid., 6

39. *"mother's boy*: Ibid., 199

39. *"twelve-year-old sweetheart*: Ibid., 200.

39. *Mudgett's only close friend*: Schechter, 12.

40. *"itinerant photographer*: Mudgett, 7.

40. *"Had he next proceeded*: Ibid., 8.

40. *"I kept it for many years*: Ibid., 8.

41. *He enrolled*: Ibid., 14.

41. *"the first really dishonest*: Ibid.,15.

41. *"I could hardly count*: Ibid.,16.

42. *Eventually he came to Mooers Forks*: Ibid., 16; *Chicago Tribune*, July 31, 1895; *New York Times*, July 31, 1895.

42. *"Some of the professors*: Franke, 118.

42. *"In the fall of 1885*: Mudgett, 17.

43. *"This scheme called for*: Ibid.,19.

43. *"the necessary supply*: Ibid.

43. *"This," he said, "necessitated*: Ibid., 20.

43. *"and for the first time*: Ibid.

44. *The owner of the house*: *Chicago Tribune*, July 31, 1895.

44. *"This," he wrote, "was my first*: Mudgett, 21.

45. *"The city had laid*: Dreiser, *Sister Carrie*, 16.

45. *"there was such a rush*: Sullivan, Gerald, 14.

45. *In 1868 a Mrs. H. B. Lewis*: Ibid.

46. *"To the business men*: Catalogue, 3.

46. *"My trade was good*: Mudgett, 23.

46. *He put up a new sign*: Franke, 210.

"Becomingness"

48. *A friend of Burnham's*: Ellsworth to Olmsted, July 26, 1890, Burnham Archives, Box 58, File 13.

49. *"I have all my life*: Rybczynski, *Clearing*, 385–86.

50. *"flecks of white or red*: Olmsted, "Landscape Architecture," 18.

50. *"I design with a view*: Rybczynski, *Clearing*, 396.

50. *"Suppose," he wrote*: Olmsted to Van Brunt, January 22, 1891, Olmsted Papers, Reel 22.

51. *"we are always personally*: Roper, 421.

51. *He was prone*: Rybczynski, *Clearing*, 247–48, 341

51. *"My position is this*: Ellsworth to Olmsted, July 26, 1890.

52. *Certainly that seemed*: Articles of Agreement, 1890, Olmsted Papers, Reel 41; Rybczynski, *Clearing*, 387.

52. *"When can you be here?*: Telegram quoted in Olmsted to Butterworth, August 6, 1890, Burnham Archives, Box 58, File 13.

52. *"Having seen it*: *Chicago Tribune*, July 7, 1890.

53. *a man they could work with*: Codman to Olmsted, October 25, 1890, Olmsted Papers, Reel 57.

54. *"It is to be desired*: Olmsted, *Report*, 51.

57. *"a man of the world*: Sullivan, Louis, 287.

57. *"she patted the mortar*: *Chicago Tribune*, November 2, 1890.

58. *Root, according to a witness*: Miller, 316.

58. *"While in school*: *Chicago Record*, December 16, 1893, McGoorty Papers.

59. *"He got smart*: *Chicago Record*, December 15, 1893, Ibid.

60. *"murky pall*: *Chicago Tribune*, November 16, 1890.

"Don't Be Afraid"

64. *"Ambition has been the curse*: Schechter, 238.

65. *"His presence*: Franke, 112.

65. *"It is said that babies*: Ibid., 112.

66. *The building's broad design*: *Philadelphia Public Ledger*, July 22, 25, 26, 27, 29, 30, 1895; *Chicago Tribune*, July 17, 21, 23, 25, 27, 28, 29, August 18, 1895; *New York Times*, July 25, 26, 29, 31, 1895.

67. *"There is an uneven settlement*: *Chicago Tribune*, July 25, 1895.

67. *The high rate of turnover*: Ibid.; Schechter, 28–29.

68. *"I don't know*: Franke, 95–96.

69. *At first, Latimer said*: Ibid., 43.

69. *"In a general way*: Geyer, 26–27.

69. *"fine physique*: Trial, 145.

69. *"Come with me*: Schechter, 25.

70. *"Pitezel was his tool*: Trial, 449.

71. *Captain Horace Elliot*: Englewood Directory, 36.

71. *To the buyer's chagrin*: Schechter, 36.

71. *City directories*: Englewood Directory, 179, 399; Franke, 40.

72. *"He was the smoothest man*: Franke, 42–43.

72. *"I sometimes sold him*: Ibid., 111.

73. *"Don't be afraid*: *Chicago Tribune*, July 31, 1895; *New York Times*, July 31, 1895; Franke, 110.

73. *Unlike most Americans*: *Chicago Tribune*, July 26, 1895.

74. *An advertisement*: Hoyt, 177.

Pilgrimage

75. *Immediately the directors*: Burnham and Millet, 14–17; Burnham, *Design*, 7–9; Monroe, *Root*, 222–23.

76. *"at once cheap wooden quarters*: Burnham to Committee on Buildings and Grounds, December 1, 1890, Burnham Archives, Box 58, File 3.

77. *"It may not occur to you*: Burnham to Davis, December 8, 1890, Burnham Archives, Business Correspondence, vol. 1.

77. *"cut to the quick*: Monroe, *Root*, 235.

77. *"feeling confident*: Moore, Burnham interview, 3.

79. *"McKim, damn your preambles*: Moore, *McKim*, 113.

80. *"To himself*: Monroe, *Poet's Life*, 115.

81. *"They all approved*: Burnham to Olmsted, December 23, 1890, Olmsted Papers, Reel 57.

82. *"they said*: Moore, Burnham interview, 3.

82. *"Burnham had believed*: Sullivan, Louis, 319.

83. *"I think he, Adler*: Moore, Burnham interview, 4.

83. *"He said he was tired: Inland Architect and News Record,* vol. 16, no. 8 (January 1891), 88.

84. *He was depressed:* Monroe, *Root,* 249.

84. *"He felt that this:* Ibid., 249.

A Hotel for the Fair

86. *In a parody:* Boswell and Thompson, 81.

86. *When Myrta's great-uncle:* Ibid., 80; Schechter, 235; *Chicago Tribune,* July 27, 1895; *New York Times,* July 29, 1895; *Philadelphia Public Ledger,* July 29, 1895.

87. *Holmes returned to Englewood:* Boswell and Thompson, 80.

87. *"Beside his own person:* See *Oxford English Dictionary,* 2nd ed.

88. *Half a century later:* Cleckley, 369.

88. *People exhibiting:* Millon et al., 124.

89. *"When I went to bed:* Schechter, 235.

89. *"Presently," Belknap said:* Ibid.

89. *"I refused to open:* Ibid.

89. *"If I'd gone:* Boswell and Thompson, 80.

90. *He planned to install:* *Chicago Tribune,* July 30, 1895.

91. *The manager of the furnace company:* Franke, 94–95

91. *"the necessary amount of heat:* Ibid., 94.

92. *"In fact," he said:* Ibid.

92. *These clerks:* *Philadelphia Public Ledger,* July 27, 1895.

The Landscape of Regret

94. *The eastern architects left:* Hunt to Olmsted, January 6, 1891, Olmsted Papers, Reel 58.

94. *Two hours before:* Moore, *McKim,* 113; *Chicago Tribune,* January 11, 1891.

94. *"It was one:* Moore, Burnham Interview, 3.

95. *"they gazed:* Burnham, *Design,* 24.

95. *"remote and repulsive:* Ingalls, 142.

95. *"sandy waste:* Bancroft, 46.

95. *"If a search had been made:* "A Report Upon the Landscape," 8, Olmsted Papers, Reel 41.

95. *"it became almost:* Burnham and Millet, 45.

96. *The park's gravest flaw:* "A Report Upon the Landscape," 7, Olmsted Papers, Reel 41.

96. *"a feeling of discouragement:* Burnham and Millet, 5.

96. *"Do you mean to say:* Hines, 82; Moore, Burnham interview, 4;

96. *"He went down to the office:* Monroe, *Root,* 259.

96. *"looking ill:* Starrett, 47.

97. *"ill almost unto death:* Monroe, *Poet's Life,* 113.

97. *"After the 15th:* Ibid., 260.

98. *"Oysters:* *Chicago Tribune,* January 11, 1891.

98. *"Gentlemen," he said:* Poole, 184; Moore, *Burnham, Architect,* 43.

99. *"The men left:* Burnham, *Design,* 26.

99. *"In talking with them:* Monroe, *Root,* 249; Monroe, *Poet's Life,* 113.

Vanishing Point

100. *After years spent*: Chicago Tribune, July 21, 23, 24, 26, 28, 29, 1895; *Philadelphia Public Ledger*, July 22, 23, 27, 1895; Boswell and Thompson, 83–84; Franke, 98–101; Schechter, 39–44.

102. *"I shut the door*: Chicago Tribune, July 28, 1895.

102. *"a mysterious disappearances*: Chicago Tribune, November 1, 1892.

102. *Fannie Moore*: Ibid.

102. *J. W. Highleyman left*: Ibid.

103. *Cheyenne*: Ibid.

Alone

104. *"Himself not especially*: Sullivan, Louis, 288.

104. *"It soon became noticeable*: Ibid., 320.

104. *"Hell," he snapped*: Ibid.

105. *"Burnham came out*: Ibid.

105. *"The natural dominance*: Baker, *Hunt*, 398.

105. *"the function created*: Sullivan, Louis, 290.

105. *"In each firm*: Ibid., 288.

105. *"John Root was*: Ibid.

106. *"I haven't escaped sickness*: Monroe, *Root*, 261.

106. *"Mr. Root is quite low*: Burnham to Boyington, January 14, 1891, Burnham Archives, Business Correspondence, Vol. 1.

106. *"am able this morning*: Burnham to Boyington, January 15, 1891, ibid.

107. *"You won't leave me*: Moore, Burnham interview, 5.

107. *"Do you hear that?*: Ibid.

107. *"I have worked*: Monroe, *Poet's Life*, 114.

108. *"most distinguished architect*: Chicago Tribune, January 16, 1891.

108. *"There is no man*: Chicago Tribune, January 17, 1891.

108. *"It's all nonsense*: Chicago Tribune, January 25, 1891.

108. *"I was born*: Philadelphia Inquirer, April 12, 1896.

PART II: AN AWFUL FIGHT

Convocation

113. *His gout*: Moore, Burnham interview, 6.

113. *"almost in whispers*: "The Organization, Design and Construction of the Fair," January 7, 1895, 56, Moore Papers.

113. *Its center was an octagon*: Rand, McNally, 49–57.

114. *"a panorama*: Ibid., 126.

114. *"I don't think I shall advocate*: Moore, *Burnham, Architect*, 47 (In Moore, Burnham interview, 4, the phrasing is slightly different: "I do not think I will advocate that dome, I will probably modify the building.")

114. *"one grand entrance*: Burnham to Sullivan, February 11, 1891, Burnham Archives, Business Correspondence, Vol. 1.

115. *"the tension of feeling*: Burnham and Millet, 29.
115. *"quiet intentness*: "The Organization, Design and Construction of the Fair," January 7, 1895, 56, Moore Papers.
115. *"Drawing after drawing*: Burnham and Millet, 29.
115. *"The room was still as death*: Moore, *Burnham, Architect,* 47.
115. *"You are dreaming*: "The Organization, Design and Construction of the Fair," January 7, 1895, 58, Moore Papers.
115. *"I never expected*: Different versions of St. Gaudens's remark appear in the literature. I've combined elements of two. See Burnham, *Design,* 39, and Hines, 90.
116. *"We should try to make*: Olmsted to Burnham, January 26, 1891, Olmsted Papers, Reel 41.
116. *"What we shall want*: Ibid.
116. *"I mean such as Malay proas*: Ibid.
117. *"mysterious poetic effect*: "Memorandum as to What is to be Aimed at in the Planting of the Lagoon District of the Chicago Exposition," Olmsted Papers, Reel 59.
117. *"through the mingling intricately together*: Ibid.
118. *"a display of flowers*: Ibid.
118. *"to slightly screen*: Ibid.
118. *The overall effect*: Ibid.
119. *"that army our hundreds*: Olmsted to "Fred" (most likely Federick J. Kingsbury, a friend), January 20, 1891, Olmsted Papers, Reel 22.
119. *"How is it possible*: Lewis, 172.
120. *"We must push this now*: *Chicago Tribune,* February 20, 1891.
120. *"Examination of the facts*: Director of Works Report, October 24, 1892, Burnham Archives, Box 58, File 12.
120. *"There will not be a brick*: *Chicago Tribune,* March 20, 1891.
120. *Atwood stood him up*: Moore, Burnham interview, 7.
121. *He was an opium addict*: Ibid.
121. RUSH: *Chicago Tribune,* May 16, 1891.
121. *"a family of twelve*: *Chicago Tribune,* February 20, 1891.
121. *"That un-American institution*: *Inland Architect and News Record,* vol. 17, no. 5 (June 1891), 54.
122. *P. T. Barnum died*: *Chicago Tribune,* May 30, 1891.
122. *"I think it quite necessary*: *Chicago Tribune,* February 14, 1891.

Cuckoldry
123. *Lovely, dark Gertrude*: *Chicago Tribune,* July 26, 1895.
124. *"of an easy-going innocent*: *Chicago Tribune,* July 21, 1895.
124. *"Some of my friends*: *Chicago Tribune,* July 26, 1895.
124. *Holmes proposed to sell*: *Chicago Tribune,* July 21, 1895.
125. *Holmes even wanted Ned*: *Chicago Tribune,* July 26, 28, 1895.
126. *"Separation couldn't come*: *Chicago Tribune,* July 26, 1895.
126. *He heard her footsteps*: Ibid.
126. *"I told her after I left*: Ibid.
126. *At night, after the first-floor stores*: This is speculation, but I base it on the following: In

Mooers Holmes was known to pace at midnight, suggesting he was not a restful sleeper. Psychopaths need stimulation. The kiln would have been an irresistible attraction. Admiring it and igniting its flames would have reinforced his sense of power and control over the occupants above.

Vexed

128. *"You must not think*: Burnham to Margaret, March 15, 1892, Burnham Archives, Family Correspondence, File 4.

128. *"Among the trees*: Burnham and Millet, 36.

129. *"practically an unknown*: Inland Architect and News Record, vol. 22, no. 1 (August 1893), 8.

129. *They laid a platform*: Ibid.

131. *Edison suggested*: Chicago Tribune, May 12, 13, 1891.

131. *General Electric offered*: Baker, Life, 158–59.

131. *"We are at a dead standstill*: Burnham to Hunt, June 2, 1891, Burnham Archives, Business Correspondence, Vol. 2.

132. *"The delay you are causing us*: Burnham to Hunt, June 6, 1891, ibid.

132. *He ordered*: "List of bedding plants to be ordered either in this country, or from Europe," July 13, 1891, Olmsted Papers, Reel 59.

132. *"It was bad enough*: Ulrich, 11.

133. *"He is the arbiter*: Chicago Tribune, May 14, 1891.

133. *"incongruity*: World's Fair, 851.

134. *"President Baker wants*: Chicago Tribune, July 21, 1891.

134. *C. F. Ritchel of Bridgeport*: Chicago Tribune, October 12, 1889.

134. *"As the cost*: McComber's tower idea: Chicago Tribune, November 2, 1889.

135. *The engineer urged*: Chicago Tribune, November 9, 1889.

135. *In August 1891*: Chicago Tribune, August 5, 1891.

135. *The engineers were outraged*: Chicago Tribune, August 16, 1891.

137. *"How soon*: Bloom, 117.

140. *"The more I thought*: Ibid.

141. *"I could not*: Burnham to Dredge, November 18, 1891, Burnham Archives, Business Correspondence, vol. 4.

141. *"The criticism now*: Burnham to Dredge, November 24, 1891, ibid.

141. *"was about as intelligent*: Bloom, 119.

141. *"anxious to get*: Sandweiss, 14.

141. *"You are a very young man*: Bloom, 120.

142. *"I do hope*: Allen to Palmer, October 21, 1891, Chicago Historical Society, World's Columbian Exhibition–Board of Lady Managers Archive, Folder 3.

142. *"When I think of the days*: Weimann, 176.

143. *" 'I think it would be better*: Ibid.

143. *"A severe breakdown*: Ibid.,177.

144. *"I suspect that even Codman*: Olmsted to Burnham, December 23, 1891, Olmsted Papers, Reel 22.

145. *In December*: Burnham, Final Official Report, 78.

145. *"A few questions of design*: Interim Report on Construction, "To the Editor of the Chicago *Herald*," December 28, 1891, Burnham Archives, Box 58, File 9.

145. *"the failure of the fair*: Lewis, 175.

Remains of the Day

Holmes left no firsthand account of the method he used to kill Julia and Pearl Conner; nor did he describe how he managed to subdue both victims, although he did at one point state that Julia had died of a "criminal operation," meaning an abortion. I constructed the murder scenes in this chapter using a combination of sources: fragments of known evidence (for example, the fact that he possessed two cases of surgical instruments, equipped his building with dissection tables, and favored chloroform as a weapon and bought large quantities of it); the detective work of other investigators of the Holmes saga (Schechter, Franke, and Boswell and Thompson); statements made by Holmes after the murders; psychiatric research into the character, motives, and needs of criminal psychopaths; and testimony at Holmes's trial as to how a person would react to an overdose of chloroform. The Conner case and the anatomical moonlighting of Charles Chappell received extensive news coverage. In addition to the specific sources cited below, see *Chicago Tribune*, July 21, 23, 24, 25, 26, 28, 29, 30, 1895; *New York Times*, July 29, 1895; *Philadelphia Public Ledger*, July 23, 27, 29, 30, 1895; Boswell and Thompson, 81–86; Franke, 98–101; Schechter, 39–44.

146. *In November 1891*: Schechter, 43–44.

147. *Julia and Mrs. Crowe*: Chicago Tribune, July 29, 1895.

148. *dark amber bottle*: Merck's Manual, 28.

148. *She gripped his hand*: Trial, 166, 420–422.

149. *On Christmas morning*: Chicago Tribune, July 29, 1895.

150. *"The gentlemen were acting*: Chicago Tribune, February 27, 1890. See also March 2, 1890, for a tantalizing but likely apocryphal story of a St. Louis man buried alive—allegedly in a deep coma—only to have his body stolen by medical students. The students discovered his true condition with the first incision and quickly deposited him on the steps of the St. Louis courthouse, where he awoke with a painful and inexplicable cut across his abdomen. Or so the story went.

150. *"Yes, the party*: Chicago Tribune, March 24, 1890.

151. *"The body," he said*: Philadelphia Public Ledger, July 29, 1895. The article also cites the $36 price.

151. *They found dishes*: Franke, 101.

152. *"I last saw her*: Mudgett, 33.

A Gauntlet Dropped

153. *The ranks included*: Hines, 74–75.

153. *A rising union man*: Burnham to Geraldine, February 24, 1892, Burnham Archives, Business Correspondence, vol. 6.

154. *"inaccurate or 'slouchy' work*: Burnham to Cloyes, January 6, 1892, ibid., vol. 5.

154. *"it seems to me*: Burnham to Ulrich, January 6, 1892, ibid.

154. *"You will please dismiss*: Burnham to Geraldine, January 6, 1892, ibid.

154. *"Guarded by sentries*: Wyckoff, 248.

155. *"ho, boy*: Oxford English Dictionary, 2nd ed., 278; Wyckoff, 11.

155. *He "was eminently engaging*: Anderson, 53.

155. "*the architects of America*: Untitled typescript, Ferris Papers, 1.

156. "*cut to the quick*: Ibid.

157. *superintendent of sheep*: Chicago Tribune, July 14, 1892.

157. "*We are now organizing*: Burnham to Davis, November 12, 1891, Burnham Archives, Business Correspondence, vol. 4.

157. "*I think it is pretty well understood*: Chicago Tribune, January 5, 1892.

157. "*The time was well spent*: Burnham to Margaret, March 15, 1892, Burnham Archives, Family Correspondence, Box 25, File 4.

158. *Late in March*: Burnham to Margaret, March 31, 1892, ibid.

159. "*Mr. Davis has not been to see me*: Chicago Tribune, April 9, 1892.

159. *The congressmen, Burnham wrote*: Burnham to Margaret, March 31, 1892.

160. "*spectacular advertising*: Bloom, 120.

160. "*I could tell*: Ibid.

The Angel from Dwight

In addition to the specific citations below, for this chapter I relied on detailed coverage of the Cigrand case in the *Chicago Tribune* and *Philadelphia Public Ledger,* as well as broader accounts of the case in Boswell and Thompson, Franke, and Schechter.

H. Wayne Morgan's detailed historical essay on Leslie Enraught Keeley's alcohol-treatment empire, "'No, Thank You, I've Been to Dwight,'" in the *Illinois Historical Journal,* offers a charming look at a bygone rage.

See *Chicago Tribune,* July 26, 27, 29, 30, 31, 1895; *Philadelphia Public Ledger,* July 27, 29, 31, 1895; Boswell and Thompson, 86–87; Franke, 102–105; Schechter, 48–51.

161. *In the spring of 1892*: Schechter, 48.

161. *Gold was the most famous*: Morgan, 149.

161. *the Chicago post office*: Ibid., 159–160.

161. "*he was too valuable*: Mudgett, 122.

162. *Thousands of people*: Morgan, 157.

162. "*passing through the line*: Ibid., 154.

162. "*No, thank you*: Ibid., 158.

162. *the story Pitezel now told*: Schechter, 48, 49.

162. "*a flattering offer*: Chicago Tribune, July 30, 1895.

162. *Emeline accepted*: Ibid.

163 "*White pique hats*: Chicago Tribune, August 7, 1895.

164. "*got to talking*: Chicago Tribune, July 28, 1895.

164. "*a handsome blonde*: Ibid.

164. "*I told her*: Ibid.

164. "*She was one*: Franke, 102.

165. "*It was not long*: Ibid.

165. *son of an English lord*: Schechter, 49.

165. "*I was charmed*: Chicago Tribune, July 30, 1895.

Dedication Day

167. "*All over its surroundings*: Ulrich, 19.

168. "*Would you object*: Burnham to Olmsted, November 20, 1891, Burnham Archives, Business Correspondence, vol. 4.

168. *"a few tents, some horses*: Burnham to Buchanan, December 19, 1891, ibid.

168. *"They propose*: Burnham to Olmsted, February 5, 1892, ibid.

169. *"unreasonable, unjust*: Roper, 434.

169. *"When Olmsted is blue*: Rybczynski, *Clearing,* 247–48.

170. *"They had picked*: Bloom, 122.

170. *"a tolerable idea*: Olmsted, "Report by F.L.O.," April 1892, Olmsted Papers, Reel 41.

170. *"It seemed to me*: Olmsted to John, May 15, 1892, Olmsted Papers, Reel 22.

170. *The Paris buildings*: Olmsted, "Report by F.L.O."

171. *"I am having*: Rybczynski, *Clearing,* 391.

171. *"I can only conclude*: Olmsted to Codman, May 25, 1892, Olmsted Papers, Reel 22.

171. *A doctor, Henry Rayner*: Roper, 439.

171. *"You know that I am*: Olmsted to Codman, June 16, 1892, Olmsted Papers, Reel 22.

171. *"every day more or less*: Olmsted to "Partners," July 21, 1892, ibid.

171. *"childish, vulgar, flaunting*: Ibid.

171. *"there is nothing in America*: Olmsted to Codman, July 30, 1892, ibid.

171. *"The finest combination*: Olmsted to John, May 15, 1892, ibid.

172. *"Everywhere the best ornamental grounds*: Olmsted to John Olmsted, May 19, 1892, ibid., Reel 41.

172. *"Let us as much as possible*: Olmsted to "Partners," July 17, 1892, ibid.

172. *"I think more than ever*: Olmsted to Codman, April 20, 1892, ibid.

172. *"The standard of an English laborer*: Olmsted to Codman, April 21, 1892, ibid., Reel 22.

172. *"The only cloud*: Olmsted to "Partners," July 21, 1892, ibid.

173. *"I could see them*: Bloom, 122.

173. *"I suggest you be more civil*: Ibid.

173. *"At present," he said*: Ibid.

174. *"Too fragile*: Barnes, 177.

174. *"The wind*: *Chicago Tribune,* April 28, 1892.

174. *"largely on account*: Moore, Burnham interview, 8.

174. *"His genius was betrayed*: Monroe, *Poet's Life,* 103.

174. *"I was urging*: Hines, 101.

175. *"I don't see it that way*: Moore, Burnham interview, 8.

175. *"ordinary white lead*: Millet, 708.

175. *"the Whitewash Gang*: Hall, 213.

175. *"with the utmost vigor*: Burnham to Geraldine, March (illegible) 1892, Burnham Archives, Business Correspondence, vol. 6.

176. *On Saturday evening*: McCarthy, "Should We Drink," 8–12; *Chicago Tribune,* March 1, May 8, 9, 13, 20, 1892; Burnham, *Final Official Report,* 69–70.

176. *"You had better write a letter*: Moore, *McKim,* 120.

177. *On Wednesday, June 1*: Photograph, Manufactures and Liberal Arts Building, June 1, 1892, Burnham Archives, Box 64, File 34.

177. *Two weeks later*: Photograph, Manufactures and Liberal Arts Building, June 13, 1892, Burnham Archives, Oversize Portfolio 13.

178. *The contractor*: *Chicago Tribune,* June 15, 1892.

178. *"I have assumed personal control*: Burnham to Olmsted, September 14, 1892, Olmsted Papers, Reel 59.

179. *"I had no precedent*: Anderson, 53.

179. *"monstrosity*: Barnes, 177.

179. *"I was more disabled*: Rybczynski, *Clearing*, 391.

179. *"I am still tortured*: Olmsted to John, October 11, 1892, Olmsted Papers, Reel 22.

180. *"Of course the main work suffers*: Olmsted to John, undated but received in Brookline, Mass., October 10, 1892, ibid.

181. *The dedication had been anticipated*: Schlereth, 174.

181. *"Ninety thousand people*: Wheeler, 846.

182. *"both orators waving*: Monroe, *Poet's Life*, 130.

182. *That winter she burned*: Ibid., 131.

Prendergast

183. *On November 28, 1892*: Prendergast to Alfred Trude, Trude Papers; *Chicago Record*, December 15 and 16, 1893, in McGoorty Papers; *Chicago Tribune*, December 15, 16, 17, 21, 22, 1893.

183. *"My Dear Mr. Trude*: Prendergast to Alfred Trude, Trude Papers.

"I Want You at Once"

185. *"I have on hand*: Ferris to Rice, December 12, 1892, Ferris Correspondence, Miscellaneous, Ferris Papers.

185. *that this wheel*: Anderson, 55; Miller, 497.

Chappell Redux

186. *The gift delighted*: Franke, 102.

186. *"She seemed delighted*: Ibid.

187. *"It had seemed to me*: Ibid., 103.

187. *Later there was speculation*: *Chicago Tribune*, July 30, 1895.

187. *"Oh, she's gone away*: Franke, 104.

188. *"This will tell you*: Ibid.

188. *The announcement read*: Ibid., 105.

189. *"Some days after going*: Mudgett, 247; see also Mudgett, 246–249.

189. *"Oh, he is a fellow*: Franke, 105.

189. *"lady of refinement*: *Chicago Tribune*, July 28, 1895.

189. *"The day after*: Franke, 104.

190. *Soon afterward*: *Chicago Tribune*, July 31, 1895; *Philadelphia Public Ledger*, July 31, 1895.

190. *"This," said Dr. B. J. Cigrand*: *Philadelphia Public Ledger*, July 27, 1895.

190. *"I had at last*: *Chicago Tribune*, July 31, 1895.

190. *That the name Phelps*: *Chicago Tribune*, August 7, 1895.

190. *That on January 2, 1893*: *Chicago Tribune*, July 28, 1895.

190. *That a few weeks later*: Schechter, 51.

190. *Somehow a footprint*: *Chicago Tribune*, July 28, August 1, 1895.

191. *To explain the print's permanence*: *Chicago Tribune*, August 1, 1895.

"The Cold-Blooded Fact"

192. *"The winter of 1892–3*: Rice, 10, 12.

193. *George Ferris fought the cold*: Anderson, 58; Untitled typescript, Ferris Papers, 4; regarding use of dynamite, see Ulrich, 24.

193. *"No one shop*: Untitled typescript, Ferris Papers, 3; Anderson, 55, 57; Meehan, 30.

194. *Together with its fittings*: "Report of Classified and Comparative Weights of Material Furnished by Detroit Bridge & Iron Works for the 'Ferris Wheel,' " Ferris Papers.

194. *"You will have heard*: Stevenson, 416.

195. *"It looks as if*: Olmsted to John, February 17, 1893, Olmsted Papers, Reel 22.

195. *"I have never before*: Olmsted to Ulrich, March 3, 1893, ibid., Reel 41.

197. *"This seems to be an impossibility*: Bancroft, 67.

Acquiring Minnie

I base my conclusions about Holmes's motivation on studies of psychopaths conducted throughout the twentieth century. Holmes's behavior—his swindles, his multiple marriages, his extraordinary charm, his lack of regard for the difference between right and wrong, and his almost eerie ability to detect weakness and vulnerability in others—fits with uncanny precision descriptions of the most extreme sorts of psychopaths. (In the late twentieth century psychiatrists officially abandoned the term *psychopath* and its immediate successor term *sociopath* in favor of *antisocial personality disorder,* though the term *psychopath* remains the favored everyday description.)

For an especially lucid discussion of psychopaths see Dr. Hervey Cleckley's pioneering *The Mask of Sanity,* published in 1976. On page 198 he cites "the astonishing power that nearly all psychopaths and part-psychopaths have to win and to bind forever the devotion of woman." See also *Diagnostic and Statistical Manual of Mental Disorders,* 4th ed., 645–60; Wolman, 362–68; Millon et al., throughout but especially 155, which quotes Philippe Pinel's appraisal of psychopathic serial killers: "Though their crimes may be sickening, they are not sick in either a medical or a legal sense. Instead, the serial killer is typically a sociopathic personality who lacks internal control—guilt or conscience—to guide his own behavior, but has an excessive need to control and dominate others. He definitely knows right from wrong, definitely realizes he has committed a sinful act, but simply doesn't care about his human prey. The sociopath has never internalized a moral code that prohibits murder. Having fun is all that counts."

Also in Millon et al., at page 353, a contributing author describes a particular patient named Paul as having "an uncanny ability to identify naïve, passive and vulnerable women—women who were ripe for being manipulated and exploited."

For details of the Williams case I relied, once again, on an array of newspaper articles, and on Boswell and Thompson, Franke, and Schechter. See *Chicago Tribune,* July 20, 21, 27, 31, August 4, 7, 1895; *New York Times,* July 31, 1895; *Philadelphia Public Ledger,* November 21, 23, 26, 1894, December 22, 1894, July 22, 24, 27, 29, 1895: Boswell and Thompson, 86–90; Franke, 106–109; Schechter, 58–63.

198. *Silver Ash Institute*: *Chicago Tribune,* July 27, 1895.

198. *as many as seventy-five*: *Chicago Tribune,* July 25, 1895.

198. *Tobey Furniture Company*: *Chicago Tribune,* July 27, 1895.

198. *French, Potter Crockery Company*: Ibid.

198. *Merchant & Co.*: *Chicago Tribune,* July 30, 1895.

199. *At the nearby Normal School*: *Chicago Tribune,* June 26, 1892.

200. *"a baby face*: Boswell and Thompson, 87.

200. *Born in Mississippi*: For various details about Minnie and Anna Williams's backgrounds, I relied heavily on the *Chicago Tribune* of July 31, 1895.

201. *Throughout 1889*: Exactly how and when Holmes courted Minnie is unclear, but it's certain he traveled to Boston to see her and that he did so often enough to have won her adoration. The *Chicago Tribune* of July 29, 1895, describes Minnie's first meeting with Holmes. See the *Tribune* of July 20, for other details, such as the date Minnie went to Boston for her education in elocution and a sketch of her subsequent travels, including her loss of $15,000 in an ill-starred attempt to establish a theatrical group. See also *Philadelphia Public Ledger,* November 22, 1894, July 27, 29, 1895.

202. *"a remarkable aptitude*: Mudgett, 45.

203. *Anna was skeptical*: Schechter, 61.

203. *"I received her wedding cards*: *Chicago Tribune,* July 28, 1895.

204. *She did so on*: *Chicago Tribune,* July 27, 31, 1895.

204. *He established'*: *Philadelphia Public Ledger,* November 21, 23, 1894.

204. *"He induced me*: *Philadelphia Public Ledger,* July 25, 1895.

205. *no record of their union*: *Philadelphia Public Ledger,* November 26, 1894.

Dreadful Things Done by Girls

206. *"money would be so plentiful*: Kiler, 61.

208. *"The crowds poured in*: Bloom, 135.

208. *Bloom thought a moment*: Ibid., 135–36.

209. *Bloom regretted*: Ibid., 135.

209. *"it is not quantity*: Dedmon, 223–24.

209. *"the mayor will not frappé*: Ibid., 224.

210. *"A Mouse Colored Ass*: Ibid.

210. *"Outside peoples already concede*: Hines, 108.

211. *"how to broil*: Hollingsworth, 155.

211. *"The breakfast table*: Ibid., 12.

211. *"If the article is black*: Ibid., 581.

211. *"Take one part muriatic acid*: Ibid., 612.

211. *"Don't sit between*: Ibid., 701.

211. *"Injections of tobacco*: Ibid., 749.

211. *"interspersed," as one visitor put it*: Miller, 420.

212. *Clarence Darrow regularly*: Tierney, 140.

212. *"You ought to begin*: Lewis, 36.

212. *"What dreadful things*: Tierney, 84.

213. *"His friends all noticed it*: Miller, 440.

214 *His quirks*: Johnson, 81–88; Poole, 158, 160, 163, 169.

214. *"the most remarkable man*: Miller, 438.

214. *"a most admirable pig*: Abbot, 212.

215. *"My Dear Mr. Trude*: Prendergast to Trude, Daniel P. Trude Papers.

The Invitation

217. *Holmes suggested*: Schechter, 61.

217. *Minnie planned to show*: I've inserted here a few of the attractions that Gilded Age visitors to Chicago found especially compelling. That Minnie planned to take her sister on such a tour is likely but not certain, as unfortunately she left no journal detailing the minutiae of her days.

Final Preparations

218. *"anxious effort*: Wheeler, 832.

219. *The menu*: Program, "Banquet to Daniel Hudson Burnham," Burnham Archives, Box 59.

220. *"Each of you knows*: Moore, *Burnham, Architect*, 74.

221. *"The scale of the whole thing*: Moore, *McKim*, 122.

221. *"I fear nothing*: Burnham to Margaret, April 6, 1893, Burnham Archives, Family Correspondence, Box 25.

221. *"I am very happy*: Burnham to Margaret, April 10, 1893, ibid.

222. *"Why do you not write*: Burnham to Margaret, April 13, 1893, ibid.

222. *"The public will regard*: Ibid.

222. *Margaret sent him*: Burnham to Margaret, April 18, 1893, ibid.

222. PILOT OF THE OCEAN: Carter, 368.

223. *At the hotel's front desk*: Ibid., 374.

223. *"You can imagine*: Burnham to Margaret, April 10, 1893, Burnham Archives, Family Correspondence, Box 25.

224. *"Every body here*: Olmsted to John, April 13, 1893, Olmsted Papers, Reel 22.

224. *"We shall have to bear*: Olmsted to John, April 15, 1893, ibid.

224. *"I am afraid*: Ibid.

224. *"Ulrich is unwittingly faithless*: Olmsted to John, May 3, 1893, ibid.

225. *"I suppose that our time is out*: Ibid.

225. *"frightful dust*: Olmsted to John, April 13, 1893, Olmsted Papers, Reel 22.

225. *"with sore throat*: Olmsted to John, April 23, 1893, ibid.

226. *"A larger force is employed*: Ibid.

226. *The odd thing was*: *Chicago Record,* December 16, 1893, in McGoorty Papers.

226. *"It rains*: Burnham to Margaret, April 18, 1893, Burnham Archives, Family Correspondence, Box 25.

227. *"Last night turned out*: Burnham to Margaret, April 20, 1893, ibid.

227. *"The weather is very bad*: Ibid.

228. *"I wrote you*: Olmsted to unidentified recipient (stamped as received and read by his firm), April 27, 1893, Olmsted Papers, Reel 22.

228. *"My ulcer has shrunk*: Ibid.

228. *"We are having bad luck*: Olmsted to John, April 27, 1893, ibid.

229. *"I don't like it at all*: Ibid.

229. *"The diet of the provisional mess*: Ibid.

229. *"I took cold*: Olmsted to unidentified recipient, April 28, 1893, ibid.

229. *"It is queer*: Ibid.

229. *"It does not look ready*: Ibid.

229. *"I get wind*: Ibid.

230. *"gross incompleteness*: Miller, 489.

231. *the World's Fair Hotel*: Schechter, 56.

PART III: IN THE WHITE CITY

Opening Day

235. *Twenty-three gleaming*: For details of the Opening Day procession: Badger, xi, xii; Burg, 111; *Chicago Tribune*, May 2, 1893; Miller, 490; Muccigrosso, 78–80; Weimann, 141–46; *The World's Fair*, 13–16, 253–63.

235. *Burnham and Davis*: *The World's Fair*, 254.

235. *the sun emerged*: Ibid.

236. *The farm offered omelets*: Bloom, 137.

236. *Bloom gave a nod*: *The World's Fair*, 255.

237. *"When the fair opened*: Starrett, 50.

237. *Twenty women fainted*: Burg, 111.

237. *Reporters lucky enough*: Ibid., 23.

237. *"Then from the Pinta's foretop*: *The World's Fair*, 257–58.

237. *Director-General Davis spoke*: Ibid., 259.

237. *Nearby stood a table*: Weimann, 241.

238. *A tall man*: Miller, 490.

238. *"As by a touch*: Badger, xii.

238. *At precisely 12:08*: *Chicago Tribune*, May 2, 1893.

239. *Jane Addams realized*: Badger, xi; Miller, 490.

239. *"The scene burst on me*: Frank Collier to Burnham, May 1, 1893, Burnham Archives, Box 1, File 13.

239. *The official history*: For crowd estimates, see Badger, xii; Dedmon, 226; Weimann, 242.

239. *On Tuesday, May 2*: Weimann, 556.

240. *On the night of Thursday*: *Chicago Tribune*, May 5, 1893.

240. *Next Chicago's Chemical National Bank*: *Chicago Tribune*, May 9, 1893.

240. *Three days later*: *Chicago Tribune*, May 19, 1893.

240. *In Brunswick, Georgia*: Ibid.

240. *In Lincoln, Nebraska*: Ibid.

240. *Olmsted had yet to complete*: Ulrich, 46–48.

241. *General Electric alone*: *Chicago Tribune*, May 3, 1893.

241. *"I remain fairly well*: Olmsted to John, May 15, 1893, Olmsted Papers, Reel 22.

242. *On June 5 worried depositors*: Bogart and Mathews, 395.

The World's Fair Hotel

243. *The first guests began arriving*: Boswell and Thompson write, "Every night the rooms on the two upper floors of the Castle were filled to overflowing. Holmes reluctantly accommodated a few men as paying guests, but catered primarily to women—preferably young and pretty ones of apparent means, whose homes were distant from Chicago and who had no one close to them who might make inquiry if they did not soon return. Many never went home. Many, indeed, never emerged from the castle, having once entered it" (87). Franke writes, "We do know that Holmes advertised his 'hotel' as a suitable lodging for visitors to the world's fair; that no fewer than fifty persons, reported to the police as

missing, were traced to the Castle; and that there their trail ended" (109). Schechter: "No one can say exactly how many fairgoers Holmes lured to the Castle between May and October 1893, though he appears to have filled the place to capacity on most nights" (56).

243. *He found a place*: *Chicago Tribune*, July 21, 1895.

243. *They first advertised*: Ibid.

243. *Holmes went alone*: Ibid.

244. *Holmes explained the move*: That Holmes wanted Minnie as far from the hotel as reasonably possible seems certain, given his choice of an apartment on the North Side, though exactly what he told her about the move can't be known. I propose one likely possibility.

244. *Holmes and Minnie moved*: *Chicago Tribune*, July 21, 1895.

244. *"seemed to be very attentive*: Ibid.

245. *That he often smelled*: A barber who worked in Holmes's building reported the many "queer" smells generated within. *Chicago Tribune*, July 30, 1895. In *Tribune*, July 28, 1895, a police detective states, "We have always heard of Holmes' castle as being the abode of bad odors."

Prendergast

246. *"I am a candidate*: *Chicago Record*, December 16, 1893, McGoorty Papers.

"Night Is the Magician"

247. *Only one child*: Weimann, 352. For broader discussion of daycare at the fair, see Weimann, 254–333, 349–52.

247. *Within the fair's buildings*: Burg, 206; Gladwell, 95; Miller, 494; Muccigrosso, 93, 163; Schlereth, 174, 220; Shaw, 28, 42, 49.

248. *A popular guide*: Burg, 199.

248. *"a fearful hideous thing*: Taylor, 9.

248. *"Every one about us*: Ibid., 7.

248. *"She takes a few*: Ibid., 22–23.

249. *"My Country 'Tis of Thee*: Ibid., 23.

249. *"In which building*: Dean, 335.

249. *One male visitor*: Ibid., 378.

250. *Over the six months*: Muccigrosso, 150; *The World's Fair*, 851.

250. *Often Cody upstaged*: Carter, 372–73; Downey, 168–69

251. *"A strikingly noticeable change*: *Chicago Tribune*, June 2, 1893.

252. *"No other scene*: Pierce, *As Others See Chicago*, 352.

252. *"an inexhaustible dream*: Masters, 7.

253. *"we insisted on sending*: Untitled manuscript beginning: "To him who has taken part," Burnham Archives, Box 59, File 37.

253. *"Our hour on the lagoon*: Dora Root to Burnham, undated, Burnham Archives, Box 3, File 63.

254. *The fair alone*: Hines, 117.

254. *"As the light was fading*: Polacheck, 40.

255. *"unspeakable debris*: Ingalls, 141.

255. *"Night," Ingalls wrote*: Ibid.

255. *"It was a common remark*: Schuyler, 574.

Modus Operandi

256. *And so it began*: Chicago Tribune, July 30, 1895, August 1, 1895. In the *Tribune*, July 26, 1895, Chicago's police chief states, "There is no telling how many people this man Holmes has made away with." See also *Philadelphia Inquirer*, April 12, 1896.

256. *chemical odors*: Chicago Tribune, July 30, 1895.

256. *There were inquiries*: Philadelphia Public Ledger, November 21, 1894, July 22, 1895; Franke, 106; Schechter, 233. Also see Eckert, 209–10: Eckert quotes a letter from Julia Conner's mother, dated December 22, 1892. Eckert's book, *The Scarlet Mansion,* is a novel; the letter, Eckert told me in e-mail correspondence, is real.

256. *Holmes did not kill face to face*: Chicago Tribune, July 28, 1895, where a Chicago police inspector states, "While I believe that Holmes would not dispatch a victim with an ax or other deadly weapon, I fully believe him capable of sneaking into a dark room where his victim was asleep and turning on the gas."

257. *The subsequent articulation*: Regarding the work of the "articulator," Charles Chappell, see *Chicago Tribune*, July 21, 23, 24, 25, 26, 28, 29, 30, 1895; *New York Times*, July 29, 1895; *Philadelphia Public Ledger,* July 23, 27, 29, 30, 1895; Boswell and Thompson, 81–86; Franke, 98–101; and Schechter, 39–44.

257. *He disposed of other*: Chicago Tribune, July 20, 23, 24, 25, 26, August 18, 1895; *Philadelphia Public Ledger,* July 22, 24, 25, 26, 27, 29, 30, 1895.

One Good Turn

258. *The rim arced*: The Ferris Wheel had a diameter of 250 feet but a maximum height of 264 feet because of the necessary gap between the bottom of the wheel and the ground. The Masonic Temple was 302 feet tall, but that height included a cavernous roof that rose high above the building's last rentable floor.

258. *"It is impossible*: Hawthorne, 569.

258. *"Engines have steam*: Rice to Ferris, June 8, 1893, Ferris Papers, Ferris Correspondence: Miscellaneous.

259. *"I did not trust myself to speak*: Anderson, 58.

259. *"Suddenly I was aroused*: Ibid.

260. *As the wheel began to turn*: Ibid., 60.

260. *"No carriages were as yet placed*: Ibid.

260. *"I could have yelled out*: Ibid.

260. *"The last coupling*: Rice to Ferris, June 9, 1893, Ferris Papers, Ferris Correspondence: Miscellaneous.

260. *"Your telegram stating*: Ferris to Rice, June 10, 1893, Ferris Papers, Ferris Correspondence: Miscellaneous.

261. *"rather handsome*: Weimann, 560.

262. *"Nothing could be more entertaining*: Ibid.

262. *"I realize with some bitterness*: Ibid., 262.

262. *In preparation*: Weimann, 560.

262. *She declared*: Ibid.

263. *"Her Highness*: Quoted in Wilson, 264.

263. *"I am going to leave*: Ibid., 267.

263. *"Royalty at best*: Ibid., 269.

Nannie

264. *Without even thinking*: *Chicago Tribune*, July 20, 1895.

264. *First Minnie and Harry*: Despite the stench and pools of blood, the Union Stock Yards were Chicago's single most compelling attraction for visitors, and tour guides did indeed lead men and women into the heart of the operation. It seems likely that Holmes would have brought Minnie and Nannie there, partly because of the yards' status, partly because he would have derived a certain satisfaction from subjecting the women to its horrors. In *The Jungle* Upton Sinclair wrote, "It was too much for some of the visitors—the men would look at each other, laughing nervously, and the women would stand with hands clenched and the blood rushing to their faces, and the tears starting in their eyes" (35). For details on the stockyards and the operation of the overhead hog-butchering line, see Sinclair, especially 34–38; all of Jablonsky; and all of Wade. Wade notes that in the year of the fair more than one million people visited the stockyards (xiv). Rudyard Kipling, in his essay "Chicago," writes, "Turning a corner, and not noting an overhead arrangement of greased rail, wheel and pulley, I ran into the arms of four eviscerated carcasses, all pure white and of a human aspect, pushed by a man clad in vehement red" (341–44, especially 342).

265. *The great fair*: I've presented one likely path, based on guidebooks from the era, maps of the fairgrounds, and reports that described the features that exposition visitors found most attractive. For details of fair exhibits, see Flinn, 96–99, 104, 113–14; *Rand McNally*, 34–36, 71, 119–20, 126.

266. *Below the chandeliers*: *Rand, McNally*, 119–20.

266. *Minnie and Nannie rapidly grew tired*: Tours of the Manufactures and Liberal Arts Building were said to be exhausting. One common maxim of the day held that a boy entering the building at one end would emerge from the other as an old man. *Rand, McNally & Co's. Handbook to the World's Columbian Exposition* observes, "The standing army of Russia could be mobilized under its roof" (116).

267. *"A man in Europe talks*: Flinn, 71.

267. *the Moorish Palace*: Flinn, 25; Gilbert, 114.

267. *Even the concession tickets*: For a collection of the actual tickets see Burnham Archives, Oversize Portfolio 4, Sheets 16 and 17.

268. *He bought a souvenir*: Geyer, 300.

Vertigo

269. *By Sunday evening*: Anderson, 60.

269. *"I did not enter*: Ibid.

269. *"Owing to our car*: Ibid.

270. *The car traveled*: Ibid.

270. *Gronau's first reaction*: Ibid.

270. *". . : it seemed as if*: Ibid., 62.

270. *"It was a most beautiful sight*: Ibid.

271. *"This," Gronau said*: Ibid.

271. *"God bless you*: Untitled typescript, Ferris Papers, 6.

271. *"Six more cars*: Rice to Ferris, June 12, 1893, Ferris Papers, Ferris Correspondence: Miscellaneous.

272. *"Burnham nor anyone*: Ferris to Rice, June 14, 1893, ibid.

272. *"Unwise to open*: Robert W. Hunt to Ferris, June 17, 1893, ibid.

272. *"If the directors*: Ferris to Rice, June 17, 1893, ibid.

272. *"It was about sundown*: Chicago Tribune, June 15, 1893.

Heathen Wanted

274. *He traveled through*: Olmsted to Burnham, June 20, 1893, Olmsted Papers, Reel 41.

274. *"Everywhere there is*: Ibid.

278. *On June 17*: Chicago Tribune, July 11,19, 1893.

278. *"That building gives us*: Chicago Tribune, July 11, 1893.

At Last

279. *At three-thirty P.M.*: Anderson, 62; Barnes, 180.

279. *"No crank will have*: Alleghenian, July 1, 1893.

279. *"wheels in his head*: Untitled typescript, Ferris Papers, 6.

280. *"Built in the face*: "The Ferris Wheel Souvenir," Ferris Papers, 1.

280. *"In truth, it seems too light*: Alleghenian, July 1, 1893.

Rising Wave

282. *By the end of June*: Chicago Tribune, August 1, 1893.

282. *The Roof Garden Café*: Weimann, 267.

282. *Mrs. Lucille Rodney*: Badger, 162.

282. *"Call it no more*: Besant, 533.

283. *The failure of this*: Olmsted, "Landscape Architecture."

283. *In the six months*: Rice, 85.

283. *In his official report*: Ibid., Appendix I, 2.

284. *Over the life of the fair*: Burnham, Final Official Report, 77–80.

284. *"half-boor, half-tightwad*: Dedmon, 232; May, 334–35, 340–41.

285. *Frank Haven Hall*: Hendrickson, 282.

286. *"he would learn far more*: Weimann, 566.

286. *When Cody learned of it*: Badger, 163–64; Weimann, 565–66.

286. *"as enthusiastic as a girl*: Weimann, 566.

286. *There was tragedy*: Chicago Tribune, June 27, 1893.

287. *In the week beginning*: "Ferris Wheel, Statement of Business by the Week," Ferris Papers.

287. *"short on news*: Untitled typescript, Ferris Papers, 7.

287. *Wherritt staggered*: Anderson, 66.

288. *"He seemed to take*: Polacheck, 40.

288. *"Existing conditions*: Inland Architect and News Record, vol. 22, no. 2 (September 1893), 24.

416 · Erik Larson

288. *In June two businessmen*: *Chicago Tribune*, June 4, 1893.
289. *"Everyone is in a blue fit*: Steeples and Whitten, 1.
289. *"What shall we do*: Muccigrosso, 183.
289. *"everything will seem small*: Weimann, 577.

Independence Day
290. *"For half a mile*: *Chicago Tribune*, July 5, 1895.
290. *One man began singing*: Ibid.
290. *Red lights glowed*: Ibid.
290. *"Home Sweet Home*: Ibid.
291. *At nine o'clock*: For details about the night's fireworks displays see *Chicago Tribune*, July 5, 1895; Burg, 43; Gilbert, 40.
291. *That night the Oker family*: Franke, 108.
292. *"Sister, brother Harry and myself*: Boswell and Thompson, 88. This letter is quoted also in Franke, 106, and Schechter, 62.
292. *"Anna had no property*: *Chicago Tribune*, July 30, 1895.
292. *Holmes had announced*: Schechter proposes the scenario wherein Holmes invites Anna, alone, to accompany him on a tour of the hotel. It seems likely. Another possibility is that Holmes asked for Anna's help with some last-minute clerical work at his office and recommended that Minnie stay behind in the apartment to handle final preparations for their mutual journey. Certainly Holmes would have wanted to separate the women, for he was not physically strong. His power lay in persuasion and cunning. Schechter, 62.

Worry
293. *At the fairgrounds*: See daily attendance statistics in *Chicago Tribune*, August 1, 1893.
293. *But the next day*: Ibid.
293. *The fair's auditor*: *Chicago Tribune*, August 16, 1893.
293. *The bankers were pressuring*: *Chicago Tribune*, August 2, 3, 1893.
293. *Estimates held*: *Chicago Tribune*, August 1, 1893.

Claustrophobia
Police speculated that Holmes killed Nannie and Minnie Williams in his vault. Schechter proposes this scenario: "As they got ready to leave, Holmes paused abruptly, as though struck by a sudden realization. He needed to fetch something from his vault, he explained—an important business document that he kept stored inside a safe-deposit box. It would only take a moment.

"Grasping Nannie by the hand, he led her toward the vault" (62).

Something like this must have occurred, although I think my proposal that Holmes sent her into the vault on a false errand, then followed her and shut the door, would have suited more closely his temperament. He was a killer but a cowardly one. See note above from p. 292.

That Holmes killed the women on July 5 is supported by a March 14, 1895, letter from an attorney, E. T. Johnson, who had been dispatched to hunt for the missing women. He states they left the Wrightwood house "about July 5, 1893, and none of us have ever heard from them any more" (*Chicago Tribune*, July 21, 1895). Taken together, this letter and Anna's happy letter to her aunt written on the evening of July 4, cited above from page 292, provide evidence that the murders did indeed occur on July 5.

296. *Two days later*: Franke, 108.

296. *"I do not know how*: *Chicago Tribune*, July 21, 1895.

296. *Also on July 7*: The *Chicago Tribune* of July 20, 1895, identifies the express company as Wells-Fargo. The *Philadelphia Public Ledger* of November 23, 1894, states that the trunk was shipped from Midlothian, Texas, on July 7, 1893.

296. *The trunk was addressed*: *Chicago Tribune*, July 20, 1895; *Philadelphia Public Ledger*, November 23, 1894.

296. *A Wells-Fargo drayman tried*: Ibid.

297. *"I want you to come*: *Chicago Tribune*, July 28, 1895; *Philadelphia Public Ledger*, July 29, 1895.

297. *"It was an awful looking place*: *Chicago Tribune*, July 28, 1895; *Philadelphia Public Ledger*, July 29, 1895.

297. *"Don't do that*: *Chicago Tribune*, July 28, 1895; *Philadelphia Public Ledger*, July 29, 1895.

297. *He gave Pitezel's wife*: *Chicago Tribune*, August 1, 1895.

298. *Holmes also surprised*: Ibid.

Storm and Fire

299. *The balloon*: *Chicago Tribune*, July 10, 1893.

300. *The sky seemed to reach*: Ibid.

300. *In the Agriculture Building*: Ibid.

300. *"It took the combined effort*: Anderson, 66.

301. *"I got some pleasure*: *Chicago Tribune*, July 10, 1893.

301. *The tower*: *Chicago Tribune*, July 11, 12, 1893.

301. *The first alarm*: Burnham, *Final Official Report*, 61, 74; *Chicago Tribune*, July 11, 1893; *Graphic*, July 15, 1893, Chicago Historical Society; *Synoptical History*, 74–77.

302. *"Never," the Fire Department reported*: *Synoptical History*, 75.

302. *"as though the gaseous*: Burnham, *Final Official Report*, 61.

302. *"I saw there was*: *Chicago Tribune*, July 11, 1893.

303. *Daniel Burnham testified*: *Chicago Tribune*, July 12, 1893

303. *On Tuesday, July 18*: *Chicago Tribune*, July 19, 1893.

303. *"The attempt to hold you*: Geraldine to Burnham, July 19, 1893, Burnham Archives, Business Correspondence, Box 1, File 32.

303. *With the stink*: *Chicago Tribune*, July 14, 1893.

304. *As if things*: *Chicago Tribune*, August 3, 1893.

304. *"no expenditures whatever*: Ibid.

Love

305. *The twenty-four teachers*: Dreiser, *Journalism*, 121.

305. *"an intense something*: Lingeman, 118.

305. *Dreiser followed the ladies*: For details about the teachers' visit to the fair, see Dreiser, *Journalism*, 121–38.

306. *"sentimental*: Lingeman, 121.

306. *"into a dream*: Ibid., 119.

306. *"If you marry now*: Ibid., 122.

306. *Couples asked permission*: Untitled typescript, Ferris Papers, 9.

307. *Georgiana Yoke*: Trial, 364.

307. *He was so alone*: Ibid., 436.
307. *"a little heart*: Ibid., 364.
307. *He cautioned, however*: Ibid., 436.
308. *Mayor Harrison too*: Abbot, 233; *Chicago Tribune*, August 24, 1893; Muccigrosso, 181.

Freaks
309. *"can only be characterized*: *Chicago Tribune*, August 3, 1893.
309. *"If the directory had seen fit*: *Chicago Tribune*, August 2, 1893.
310. *"Hundreds of newspapers*: *Chicago Tribune*, August 13, 1893.
311. *"We want to do something*: *Chicago Tribune*, August 9, 1893.
311. *Millet also organized*: *Chicago Tribune*, August 12, 1893.
311. *"Whether the apprehensions*: *Chicago Tribune*, August 11, 1893.
312. *Further enriching the affair*: *Chicago Tribune*, August 17, 1893; Downey, 168.
312. *"Chicago built the fair*: *Chicago Tribune*, August 16, 1893.
313. *At nine-fifteen that night*: *Chicago Tribune*, August 17, 1893.
313. *It was hot*: Ibid.
314. *"native costume of bark*: Ibid.
314. *The official menu*: Ibid.
315. *Attendance rose*: *Chicago Tribune*, October 10, 1893.
315. *"If Congress does not give*: *Chicago Tribune*, August 9, 1893.
315. *"Why should the wealth*: *Chicago Tribune*, August 31, 1893.

Prendergast
316. *One afternoon*: *Chicago Record*, December 16, 1893, McGoorty Papers.
316. *"No," Prendergast said*: Ibid.

Toward Triumph
317. *By ten o'clock*: Dybwad and Bliss, 38–40.
318. *"The Paris record*: Ibid., 38.
318. *"There must be a million*: Ibid., 39.
318. *The fireworks*: Ibid., 64–68.
318. *In that single day*: *Chicago Tribune*, October 10, 1893.
318. *The Tribune argued*: Ibid.
319. *But the best news*: Badger, 109.

Departures
320. *"You know my dislike*: Moore, *McKim*, 127.
321 *"indeed it is the ambition*: Ibid., 126.
322 *"better to have it vanish*: Boyesen, 186.
322. *"I can't come to you*: Stevenson, 415.
322. *For all of 1893*: Crook, 102.
323. *"Never before*: Bogart and Mathews, 398.
323. *The pressure*: *Philadelphia Public Ledger*, November 21, 1894.
323. *First he set fire*: *Philadelphia Public Ledger*, November 23, 1894; Boswell and Thompson, 89; Franke, 41; Schechter, 64–65.
323. *He advised the insurers*: Ibid.

324. *The guardians of Minnie*: Philadelphia *Public Ledger*, November 21, 1894; July 27, 1895; Franke, 106.

324. *In the fall of 1893*: Philadelphia *Inquirer*, May 8, 1896.

325. *Holmes fled*: Ibid.

325. *Soon afterward Holmes set out*: Geyer, 346; *Trial*, 302, 608; Franke, 213.

326. *Just before leaving*: Geyer, 346; *Trial*, 210.

Nightfall

327. *Throughout October*: *Chicago Tribune*, October 29, 1893.

327. *Twenty thousand people*: "Ferris Wheel, Statement of Business by the Week," Ferris Papers.

327. *"peer cautiously*: *Chicago Tribune*, October 25, 1893.

328. *"Look at it now*: Abbot, 228.

329. *At two o'clock*: *Chicago Tribune*, October 29, 1893.

329. *At three o'clock*: *Chicago Tribute*, December 20, 1893.

329. *In the midst of supper*: *Chicago Times*, December 14, 1893, McGoorty Papers.

330. *"It must have been*: Ibid.

331. *They argued*: *Chicago Record*, December 15, 1893, and *Chicago Daily News*, October 23, 1943, McGoorty Papers.

331. *"Lock me up*: *Chicago Record*, December 15, 1893, McGoorty Papers.

332. *"We are turning our backs*: *Chicago Tribune*, October 31, 1893.

332. *At exactly four-forty-five*: Ibid.

332. *The six hundred carriages*: *Chicago Tribune*, November 2, 1893; Miller, 101.

333. *Harrison had heard them*: *Chicago Tribune*, November 2, 1893.

333. *"The good-by*: Dean, 418.

333. *"Beneath the stars*: Pierce, *As Others See Chicago*, 357.

The Black City

334. *"The poor had come*: Herrick, 135.

334. *"What a spectacle!*: Gilbert, 211.

334. *One shows*: Hales, 47.

334. *"It is desolation*: Dean, 424.

335. *George Pullman continued*: Wish, 290.

335. *"more threatening*: Papke, 29.

335. *On July 5, 1894*: Gilbert, 210; Miller, 550.

335. *"There was no regret*: Miller, 550.

336. *"There are hundreds*: Quoted in *Chicago Tribune*, August 18, 1895.

PART IV: CRUELTY REVEALED

"Property of H. H. Holmes"

339. *Detective Frank Geyer*: For details about Geyer, I relied heavily on his book, *The Holmes-Pitezel Case*, a detailed, dispassionate, and above all accurate account of the murder of Benjamin Pitezel, and Geyer's search for Benjamin Pitezel's children. Salted throughout are copies of letters written by the children and excerpts of other valuable documents, such as interrogations and confessions. I found additional material about Geyer at the Free

Library of Philadelphia in annual reports from the city's superintendent of police included in the "Annual Message" of the city's mayor. (See City of Philadelphia, below.) These reports contain valuable bits of information, for example, the fact that for routine detective work Geyer was paired with another top detective, Thomas G. Crawford, the man who escorted Holmes to Philadelphia from Boston. On that trip Holmes asked permission to hypnotize Crawford. The detective refused. Holmes asked again, this time offering to pay $500 for the privilege—a thinly veiled bribe. Geyer and Crawford consistently ranked first or second among the city's two-man teams of detectives for the dollar value of stolen goods they recovered.

I also mined details from *The Trial of Herman W. Mudgett, Alias, H. H. Holmes,* a word-for-word transcript of the trial, with closing arguments and the appellate court's opinion. See also Franke, 61–81 and Schechter, 195–205.

340. *Geyer's assignment:* Geyer, 158–61, 171–74.
340. *Graham had thought twice:* Schechter states, "In March 1895 a fire had consumed Geyer's home, killing his beloved wife, Martha, and their only child, a blossoming twelve-year-old girl name Esther" (202).
340. *"Holmes is greatly given:* Geyer, 54.
340. *Holmes claimed:* Ibid., 53–57. The first half of Geyer's book (13–172) provides a richly detailed portrait of the insurance fraud and the murder of Benjamin Pitezel. For still more detail, see *The Trial.*
341. *The coroner:* Geyer, 33–40.
341. *"I wish you could see:* Ibid., 353–54.
341. *"Mamma have you:* Ibid., 355.
342. *"Property of H. H. Holmes:* Ibid., 158.
342. *"it did not look like:* Ibid., 173.
342. *Geyer reached Cincinnati:* Ibid., 174. Geyer devotes pages 173–298 to a nearly day-by-day account of his search.
345. *"There is really:* Ibid., 174.
345. *"I was not able:* Ibid., 180.
346. *"a very wealthy man:* Ibid., 188.
347. *"We are all well here:* Ibid., 269–70.
347. *"And I expect:* Ibid., 271.
347. *"It seems as though:* Ibid., 272.
348. *"evidently heartbroken:* Ibid., 190.
348. *"Holmes said that Howard:* Ibid., 189.
348. *"something seemed to tell me:* Ibid., 190.
349. *Geyer realized:* Ibid., 213–14.
349. *"Tell mama:* Reprinted in Franke, 223–24.
350. *"So when this poor child:* Geyer, 258.
350. *"Howard," she had written:* Franke, 224.

Moyamensing Prison
351. *"The great humiliation:* Mudgett, 215.
351. *"and to keep my watch:* Ibid., 216.

352. *"Come with me*: Ibid., 5.

352. *It is one of the defining*: Diagnostic, 646; Karpman, 499; Silverman, 21, 28, 32–33.

352. *"prison diary*: Mudgett, 210. His supposed diary appears on 211–21.

353. *"I was as careful*: Letter reprinted in Geyer, 163–71.

The Tenant

354. *On Sunday, July 7, 1895*: Geyer, 214.

356. *"This seemed too good*: Ibid., 230.

357. *"Only a slight hole*: Philadelphia Public Ledger, August 5, 1895.

357. *"We lifted her*: Geyer, 233.

357. *Nellie's feet*: Schechter, 224.

358. *"I told her*: Geyer, 244.

358. *"Where is Nellie?*: Ibid., 245.

358. *"Nothing could be more*: Ibid., 250.

358. *"one of the most satisfactory*: Philadelphia Public Ledger, August 5, 1895.

359. *"Had he been placed*: Geyer, 251–52.

A Lively Corpse

360. *In Philadelphia*: Barlow's attempt to catch Holmes by surprise is detailed in *Philadelphia Public Ledger*, July 17, 1895.

360. *"and I hardly opened it*: Mudgett, 226.

361. *"genius for explanation*: Philadelphia Public Ledger, July 17, 1895.

361. *"I was in no condition*: Mudgett, 227.

361. *"My ideas are*: Boswell and Thompson, 112–13.

"All the Weary Days"

363. *"The number of mysterious persons*: Geyer, 268.

363. *"Days came and passed*: Ibid., 269.

364. *at two hundred*: Boswell and Thompson, 87; Franke, 109.

364. *Chicago detectives*: The search of Holmes's castle conducted by Chicago police was heavily reported in the nation's newspapers. See *Philadelphia Public Ledger*, July 22, 25, 26, 27, 29, 30, 1895; *Chicago Tribune*, July 17, 21, 23, 25, 27, 28, 29, August 18, 1895; and *New York Times*, July 25, 26, 29, 31, 1895.

365. *"Do you ever see*: Chicago Tribune, July 26, 1895.

365. *One Tribune headline*: Chicago Tribune, July 20, 1895.

366. *"all," Geyer said*: Geyer, 283.

366. *"I must confess*: Ibid., 283–84.

366. *"The mystery*: Ibid., 284.

366. *"Holmes' Den Burned*: Chicago Tribune, August 19, 1895.

366. *"By Monday*: Geyer, 285.

367. *"I did not have the renting*: Ibid., 286.

367. *"All the toil*: Ibid., 287.

367. *"that he did not think*: Ibid., 301.

368. *"a large charred mass*: Ibid., 297.

368. *It was Howard's*: Ibid., 300.

Malice Aforethought

369. *On September 12, 1895*: For news reports on the Philadelphia, Indianapolis, and Toronto indictments, see *Philadelphia Public Ledger,* September 13, 1895.

369. *"In conclusion*: Mudgett, 255–56.

370. *"It is humiliating*: Quoted in *Literary Digest,* vol. 11, no. 15 (1896) 429.

370. *Chicago's "feeling of humiliation*: Ibid.

370. *One of the most surprising*: *Chicago Tribune,* July 30, 1895.

370. *"He is a prodigy*: Schechter, 228.

EPILOGUE: THE LAST CROSSING

The Fair

373. *Walt Disney's father*: Mosley, 25–26; Schickel, 46.

373. *The writer L. Frank Baum*: Adams, 115; Updike, 84–85.

373. *The Japanese temple*: Miller, 549.

373. *The fair prompted*: Jahn, 22.

373. *Even the Lincoln Memorial*: The fair's success boosted Burnham's prestige and helped get him appointed to the federal commission charged with building the monument. His own devotion to classical styles then held sway. See page 389 and corresponding note below. Also see Hines, 154–57.

374. *"our people out*: Moore, McKim, 245.

374. *"possibilities of social beauty*: Hines, 120.

374. *William Stead recognized*: Whyte, 53.

374. *They asked Burnham*: Hines, 140, 180–83, 188–89, 190–91. See also Burnham and Bennett, *Plan*; Burnham and Bennett, *Report*; McCarthy, "Chicago Businessmen."

374. *While helping design*: Hines, 148–49.

374. *Other cities came to Daniel Burnham*: Hines, 347.

375. *"If I told you*: Crook, 112. See Crook throughout for an excellent if dry account of Sullivan's decline after the world's fair—dry because the work is a doctoral thesis.

375. *"Louis Sullivan called*: Hines, 232.

375. *"To Daniel H. Burnham*: Ibid.

376. *"contagion*: Sullivan, Louis, 321, 324.

376. *"virus*: Ibid., 324

376. *"progressive cerebral meningitis*: Ibid.

376. *"Thus Architecture died*: Ibid., 325.

376. *Both Harvard and Yale*: Hines, 125.

377. *"He needs to know*: Ibid., 254, 263.

377. *"What was done*: Daniel Burnham, "Biography of Daniel Hudson Burnham of Chicago," Moore Papers, Speech, Article and Book File, Burnham 1921, Proofs and Biographical Sketches.

377. *"It was questioned by many*: Ellsworth to Moore, February 8, 1918, Moore Papers, Speech, Article and Book File, Burnham Correspondence, 1848–1927, Box 13, File 2.

377. *In 1901 Burnham built*: Hines, 288.

377. *Of the twenty-seven buildings*: Lowe, 122.

378. *"Up to our time*: Hines, 351.

378. "*I thought the fair*: Burnham to Margaret, April 7, 1894, Burnham Archives, Family Correspondence, Box 25, File 5.

378. "*If I were able*: Edward H. Bennett, "Opening of New Room for the Burnham Library of Architecture," October 8, 1929, Burnham Archives, Box 76.

378. "*You'll see it lovely*: Undated biography, Burnham Archives, Box 28, File 2.

Recessional

379. "*It has today*: Olmsted, May 10, 1895, memory no longer to be trusted.

379. *That summer*: Stevenson, 424.

379. "*the bitterest week*: Rybczynski, *Clearing*, 407.

379. "*You cannot think*: Ibid.

379. *He beat the family horse*: Roper, 474.

379. "*They didn't carry out*: Ibid.

379. *His wife*: Rybczynski, *Clearing*, 411.

380. *In the autumn of 1896*: Anderson, 75.

380. *On November 17*: Ibid., 75.

380. "*The request of Mrs. Ferris*: Ibid., 77.

380. "*miscalculated his powers*: Ibid., 75.

380. *In 1903*: For details on the fate of Ferris's wheel, see Anderson, 77–81.

381. "*But one thing*: Bloom, 143.

381. *The fair made Buffalo Bill*: Carter, 376; Monaghan, 422.

381. *He died in Denver*: Monaghan, 423.

382. "*I went to Jackson Park*: Lingeman, 114.

382. "*It means so much*: Hines, 266–67.

383. "*No one should be*: Prendergast to Alfred Trude (the letter is dated February 21, 1893, but the date is clearly incorrect, as the letter was written after his conviction; the return address is the Cook County Jail), Trude Papers.

383. "*a poor demented imbecile*: Darrow, 425.

383. "*I am sorry for all fathers*: Weinberg, 38.

383. *They dumped*: Darrow, 228.

383. *In New York*: Legend holds that a notorious belly dancer named Little Egypt made her debut at the world's fair. Sol Bloom says she was never there (Bloom, 137). Donna Carlton, in *Looking for Little Egypt*, says it's possible a dancer named Little Egypt was indeed at the fair but that many dancers adopted the name. Some sources also claim that Little Egypt's name was Farida Mazhar. (Half a dozen spellings exist; I've chosen this one.) About all that can be said with certainty is that a dancer named Farida Mazhar likely did appear at the fair. Carlton says she "probably performed" (74) on the Midway and cites a source who contends that Farida believed "'the title of Little Egypt belonged to her.'" George Pangalos, the impresario who brought the Street in Cairo to the Midway, stated publicly that he hired Mazhar to dance at his concession in the Midway and that she was considered one of the finest dancers in Cairo. And columnist Teresa Dean describes a visit to the theater in the Street in Cairo where she saw "Farida, the pretty girl who goes through her contortions" (157). In any event a young woman using the name Little Egypt apparently did pop out of a whipped-cream pie in New York several years after the fair, at a stag party that became so notorious it was called the Awful Seeley Dinner. Its host was

Herbert Barnum Seeley, a nephew of the late P. T. Barnum, who threw the party on behalf of his brother, Clinton Barnum Seeley, who was about to be married (Carlton, 65).

Holmes

384. *"There was a red fluid*: Trial, 117.

384. *"I would ask*: Ibid., 124.

384. *"It was an expression*: Philadelphia Public Ledger, October 31, 1895.

385. *"I saw them at Toronto*: Trial, 297.

385. *"the most dangerous man*: Schechter, 315.

385. *"That he fully intended*: Geyer, 317.

385. *"I am convinced*: Philadelphia Inquirer, April 12, 1896.

385. *"Here I left them*: Ibid.

386. *"It will be understood*: Ibid.

386. *His lawyers turned down*: Franke, 189.

386. *The Wistar Institute*: Philadelphia Inquirer, May 10, 1896.

386. *"The man was something*: Ibid.

386. *"Take your time, old man*: Philadelphia Inquirer, May 8, 1896. The *Philadelphia Public Ledger* of the same date offers a slightly different version: "Don't be in a hurry, Aleck. Take your time."

387. *"Holmes' idea*: Philadelphia Inquirer, May 8, 1896.

387. *Strange things*: I derived this account mainly from news clippings gathered as an appendix in Holmes's memoir. See Mudgett, after page 256. Schechter offers a nice distillation of these strange events on 333–37.

387. *No stone*: My observations.

387. *In 1997*: Stewart, 70.

Aboard the *Olympic*

389. *"But—I know*: Burnham to Millet, April 12, 1912, Moore Papers, Speech, Article and Book File, Burnham Correspondence, 1848–1927. Box 13, File 1.

389. *Hon. F. D. Millet*: Envelope, April 11, 1912, ibid.

390. *The builder of both ships*: Lynch, 159.

390. *"I think it is nothing serious*: Whyte, 314.

390. *"Frank Millet, whom I loved*: Hines, 359.

390. *As he and his family traveled*: Hines, 360, 433.

390. *Both are buried*: My observations. See also Hucke and Bielski, 13–30.

BIBLIOGRAPHY

Abbot, Willis John. *Carter Henry Harrison: A Memoir.* Dodd, Mead, 1895.

Adams, Henry. *The Education of Henry Adams.* Modern Library, 1999 (1918).

Adams, Rosemary. *What George Wore and Sally Didn't.* Chicago Historical Society, 1998.

Anderson, Norman D. *Ferris Wheels: An Illustrated History.* Bowling Green State University Popular Press, 1992. Chicago Historical Society.

Badger, Reid. *The Great American Fair.* Nelson Hall, 1979.

Baker, Charles. *Life and Character of William Taylor Baker, President of the World's Columbian Exposition and of the Chicago Board of Trade.* Premier Press, 1908.

Baker, Paul R. *Richard Morris Hunt.* MIT Press, 1980.

Bancroft, Hubert Howe. *The Book of the Fair.* Bancroft Co., 1893.

Barnes, Sisley. "George Ferris' Wheel, The Great Attraction of the Midway Plaisance," *Chicago History,* vol. 6, no. 3 (Fall 1977). Chicago Historical Society.

Besant, Walter. "A First Impression." *Cosmopolitan,* vol. 15, no. 5 (September 1893).

Bloom, Sol. *The Autobiography of Sol Bloom.* G. P. Putnam's Sons, 1948.

Bogart, Ernest Ludlow, and John Mabry Mathews. *The Modern Commonwealth, 1893–1918.* Illinois Centennial Commission, 1920.

Boswell, Charles, and Lewis Thompson. *The Girls in Nightmare House.* Fawcett, 1955.

Boyesen, Hjalmar Hjorth. "A New World Fable." *Cosmopolitan,* vol. 16, no. 2 (December 1893).

Brinnin, John Malcolm. *The Sway of the Grand Saloon.* Delacorte Press, 1971.

Burg, David F. *Chicago's White City of 1893.* University of Kentucky Press, 1976.

Burnham, Daniel H. Archives, 1943.1, Series I–IX, Art Institute of Chicago.

———. *The Design of the Fair.* Report. Burnham Archives, Box 58.

———. *The Final Official Report of the Director of Works of the World's Columbian Exposition.* Garland, 1989.

Burnham, Daniel H., and Edward H. Bennett. *Plan of Chicago.* Da Capo Press, 1970 (1909).

———. *Report on a Plan for San Francisco.* Urban Books, 1971 (1906).

Burnham, Daniel H., and Francis Davis Millet. *The Book of the Builders.* Columbian Memorial Publication Society, 1894.

Carlton, Donna. *Looking for Little Egypt.* IDD Books, undated.

Carter, Robert A. *Buffalo Bill Cody: The Man Behind the Legend.* John Wiley & Sons, 2000.

Catalogue of 200 Residence Lots. Chicago Real Estate Exchange, 1881. Chicago Historical Society.

City of Philadelphia. "Report of the Superintendent of Police," in *First Annual Message of Charles F. Warwick, Mayor of the City of Philadelphia*. (For the year ended December 31, 1895.) Free Library of Philadelphia.

———."Report of the Superintendent of Police," in *Fourth Annual Message of Edwin S. Stuart, Mayor of the City of Philadelphia*. (For the year ended December 31, 1894.) Free Library of Philadelphia.

Cleckley, Hervey. *The Mask of Sanity*. C. V. Mosby, 1976.

Commager, Henry Steele. *The American Mind*. Yale University Press, 1950.

Crook, David Heathcote. *Louis Sullivan, The World's Columbian Exposition and American Life*. Unpublished thesis, Harvard University, 1963.

Darrow, Clarence. *The Story of My Life*. Charles Scribner's Sons, 1934.

Dean, Teresa. *White City Chips*. Warren Publishing Co., 1895. Chicago Historical Society.

Dedmon, Emmett. *Fabulous Chicago*. Atheneum, 1981.

Diagnostic and Statistical Manual of Mental Disorders, 4th ed. American Psychiatric Association.

Douglas, John, and Mark Olshaker. *The Anatomy of Motive*. Pocket Books, 1999.

———. *The Cases That Haunt Us*. Scribner, 2000.

Downey, Dennis B. *A Season of Renewal: The Columbian Exposition and Victorian America*. Praeger, 2002.

Dreiser, Theodore. *Journalism*. Edited by T. D. Nostwich. Vol. 1. University of Pennsylvania Press, 1988.

———. *Sister Carrie*. Penguin, 1994 (1900).

Dybwad, G. L., and Joy V. Bliss. *Chicago Day at the World's Columbian Exposition*. The Book Stops Here (Albuquerque), 1997.

Eaton, John P., and Charles A. Haas. *Falling Star*. W. W. Norton, 1990.

Eckert, Alan W. *The Scarlet Mansion*. Little, Brown, 1985.

The Englewood Directory. George Amberg & Co, 1890. Chicago Historical Society.

Ferris, George Washington Gale. Papers. Chicago Historical Society.

Flinn, John. *Official Guide to the World's Columbian Exposition*. Columbian Guide Co., 1893.

Franke, David. *The Torture Doctor*. Hawthorn Books, 1975.

Geyer, Frank P. *The Holmes-Pitezel Case*. Frank P. Geyer, 1896.

Gilbert, James. *Perfect Cities: Chicago's Utopias of 1893*. University of Chicago Press, 1991.

Gladwell, Malcolm. "The Social Life of Paper." *New Yorker*. March 25, 2002.

Hales, Peter. *Constructing the Fair. Platinum Photographs by C. D. Arnold*. Art Institute of Chicago, 1993.

Hall, Lee. *Olmsted's America*. Little, Brown, 1995.

Hawthorne, Julian. "Foreign Folk at the Fair." *Cosmopolitan*, vol. 15, no. 5 (September 1893).

Hendrickson, Walter B. "The Three Lives of Frank H. Hall." *Journal of the Illinois State Historical Society*, vol. 49, no. 3 (Autumn 1956).

Herrick, Robert. *The Web of Life*. Grosset & Dunlap, 1900.

Hines, Thomas S. *Burnham of Chicago*. Oxford University Press, 1974.

Hollingsworth, Adelaide. *The Columbia Cook Book*. Columbia Publishing Co., c.1893.

Hoyt, Homer. *One Hundred Years of Land Values in Chicago*. University of Chicago Press, 1933.

Hucke, Matt, and Ursula Bielski. *Graveyards of Chicago*. Lake Claremont Press, 1999.

Ingalls, John J. "Lessons of the Fair." *Cosmopolitan,* vol. 16, no. 2 (December 1893).

Jablonsky, Thomas J. *Pride in the Jungle: Community and Everyday Life in Back of the Yards Chicago.* Johns Hopkins University Press, 1993.

Jahn, Raymond. *Concise Dictionary of Holidays.* Philosophical Library, 1958.

Johnson, Claudius O. *Carter Henry Harrison I: Political Leader.* University of Chicago Press, 1928.

Karpman, Ben. "The Problem of Psychopathies." *Psychiatric Quarterly,* vol. 3 (1929).

Kiler, Charles Albert. *On the Banks of the Boneyard.* Illinois Industrial University, 1942.

Kipling, Rudyard. "Chicago." *Kipling's Works.* "Sahib Edition." Vol. 6 (undated). Author's collection.

Lewis, Arnold. *An Early Encounter with Tomorrow.* University of Illinois, 1997.

Lingeman, Richard. *Theodore Dreiser.* G. P. Putnam's Sons, 1986.

Lowe, David. *Lost Chicago.* Houghton Mifflin, 1975.

Lynch, Don. *Titanic: An Illustrated History.* Hyperion, 1992.

Masters, Edgar Lee. *The Tale of Chicago.* G. P. Putnam's Sons, 1933.

May, Arthur J. "The Archduke Francis Ferdinand in the United States." *Journal of the Illinois State Historical Society,* vol. 39, no. 3 (September 1946).

McCarthy, Michael P. "Chicago Businessmen and the Burnham Plan." *Journal of the Illinois State Historical Society,* vol. 63, no. 3 (Autumn 1970).

———. "Should We Drink the Water? Typhoid Fever Worries at the Columbian Exposition." *Illinois Historical Journal,* vol. 86, no. 1 (Spring 1993).

McGoorty, John P. Papers. Chicago Historical Society.

Meehan, Pat. "The Big Wheel." *University of British Columbia Engineer,* vol. 5 (1965).

Merck's Manual of the Materia Medica. Merck & Co., 1899.

Miller, Donald L. *City of the Century.* Simon & Schuster, 1996.

Millet, F. D. "The Decoration of the Exposition." *Harper's,* vol. 12, no. 6 (December 1892).

Millon, Theodore, et al. *Psychopathy: Antisocial, Criminal, and Violent Behavior.* Guilford Press, 1998.

Monaghan, James. "The Stage Career of Buffalo Bill." *Journal of the Illinois State Historical Society,* vol. 31, no. 4 (December 1938).

Monroe, Harriet. *A Poet's Life.* Macmillan, 1938.

———. *John Wellborn Root: A Study of His Life and Work.* Prairie School Press, 1896.

Moore, Charles. Burnham interview, Burnham Archives, 1943.1, World's Columbian Exposition, Box 59.

———. *Daniel H. Burnham, Architect, Planner of Cities.* Vols. 1 and 2. Houghton Mifflin, 1921.

———. *The Life and Times of Charles Follen McKim.* Da Capo, 1970 (1929).

———. Papers. Library of Congress.

Morgan, H. Wayne. " 'No, Thank You, I've Been to Dwight': Reflections on the Keeley Cure for Alcoholism." *Illinois Historical Journal,* vol. 82, no. 3 (Autumn 1989).

Morrison, Hugh. *Louis Sullivan: Prophet of Modern Architecture.* W.W. Norton, 1998.

Mosley, Leonard. *Disney's World.* Scarborough House, 1990.

Muccigrosso, Robert. *Celebrating the New World: Chicago's Columbian Exposition of 1893.* Ivan R. Dee, 1993.

Mudgett, Herman W. *Holmes' Own Story.* Burk & McFetridge, 1895. Library of Congress.

Olmsted, Frederick Law. "The Landscape Architecture of the World's Columbian Exposition." *Inland Architect and News Record,* vol. 22, no. 2 (September 1893).

———. Papers. Library of Congress.

———. *Report on Choice of Site of the World's Columbian Exposition.* Reprinted in Jack Tager and Park Dixon Goist, *The Urban Vision.* Dorsey Press, 1970.

Papke, David Ray. *The Pullman Case.* University Press of Kansas, 1999.

Pierce, Bessie Louise. *A History of Chicago,* vol. 3. Alfred A. Knopf, 1957.

Pierce, Bessie Louise, ed. *As Others See Chicago: Impressions of Visitors, 1673–1933.* University of Chicago Press, 1933.

Polacheck, Hilda Satt. *I Came a Stranger: The Story of a Hull-House Girl.* Edited by Dena J. Polacheck Epstein. University of Illinois Press, 1991.

Poole, Ernest. *Giants Gone: Men Who Made Chicago.* Whittlesey/McGraw-Hill, 1943.

Rand, McNally & Co.'s Handbook to the World's Columbian Exposition. Rand, McNally, 1893.

Rice, Edmund. *Report of the Columbian Guard.* World's Columbian Exposition, Chicago. 1894. Chicago Historical Society.

Roper, Laura Wood. *FLO: A Biography of Frederick Law Olmsted.* Johns Hopkins, 1973.

Rybczynski, Witold. *A Clearing in the Distance: Frederick Law Olmsted and America in the 19th Century.* Touchstone/Simon & Schuster, 1999.

———. *The Look of Architecture.* New York Public Library/Oxford University Press, 2001.

Sandweiss, Eric. "Around the World in a Day." *Illinois Historical Journal,* vol. 84, no. 1 (Spring 1991).

Schechter, Harold. *Depraved.* Pocket Books, 1994.

Schickel, Richard. *The Disney Version.* Simon & Schuster, 1968.

Schlereth, Thomas J. *Victorian America: Transformations in Everyday Life, 1876–1915.* HarperCollins, 1991.

Schuyler, Montgomery. *American Architecture and Other Writings,* vol. 2. Belknap Press/Harvard University Press, 1961.

Shaw, Marian. *World's Fair Notes: A Woman Journalist Views Chicago's 1893 Columbian Exposition.* Pogo Press, 1992. Chicago Historical Society.

Silverman, Daniel. "Clinical and Electroencephalographic Studies on Criminal Psychopaths." *Archives of Neurology and Psychiatry.* vol. 30, no. 1 (July 1943).

Sinclair, Upton. *The Jungle.* University of Illinois, 1988 (1906).

Sinkevitch, Alice, ed. *AIA Guide to Chicago.* Harvest/Harcourt Brace, 1993.

Smith, F. Hopkinson. "A White Umbrella at the Fair." *Cosmopolitan,* vol. 16, no. 2 (December 1893).

Starrett, Paul. *Changing the Skyline.* Whittlesey House, 1938.

Steeples, Douglas, and David O. Whitten. *Democracy in Desperation: The Depression of 1893.* Greenwood Press, 1998.

Stevenson, Elizabeth. *Park Maker: A Life of Frederick Law Olmsted.* Macmillan, 1977.

Stewart, James. "The Bench: A Murderer's Plea." *New Yorker.* September 18, 2000.

Sullivan, Gerald E., ed. *The Story of Englewood, 1835–1923.* Englewood Business Men's Association, 1924.

Sullivan, Louis H. *The Autobiography of an Idea.* Dover Publications, 1956 (1924).

A Synoptical History of the Chicago Fire Department. Benevolent Association of the Paid Fire Department, Chicago, 1908. Chicago Historical Society.

Taylor, D. C. *Halcyon Days in the Dream City,* 1894. Chicago Historical Society.

Tierney, Kevin. *Darrow: A Biography.* Thomas Y. Crowell, 1979.

Town of Lake Directory. George Amberg and Co., 1886. Chicago Historical Society.

The Trial of Herman W. Mudgett, Alias, H. H. Holmes. George T. Bisel, 1897.

Trude, Daniel P. Papers. Chicago Historical Society.

Ulrich, Rudolf. *Report of Superintendent. Landscape, Road and Miscellaneous Departments.* Burnham Archives, 1943.1, Box 58.

Updike, John. "Oz Is Us." *New Yorker.* September 25, 2000.

Wade, Louise Carroll. *Chicago's Pride: The Stockyards, Packingtown, and the Environs in the Nineteenth Century.* University of Illinois Press, 1987.

Weimann, Jeanne Madeline. *The Fair Women.* Academy Chicago, 1981.

Weinberg, Arthur, ed. *Attorney for the Damned.* Simon & Schuster, 1957.

Wheeler, Candace. "A Dream City." *Harper's,* vol. 86, no. 516 (May 1893).

The White Star Triple Screw Atlantic Liners, Olympic and Titanic. Ocean Liners of the Past. Patrick Stephens, Cambridge, 1983.

Whyte, Frederic. *The Life of W. T. Stead,* vol. 2. Houghton Mifflin, 1925.

Wilson, Robert E. "The Infanta at the Fair." *Journal of the Illinois State Historical Society,* vol. 59, no. 3 (Autumn 1966).

Wish, Harvey. "The Pullman Strike: A Study in Industrial Warfare." *Journal of the Illinois State Historical Society,* vol. 32, no. 3 (September 1939).

Wolman, Benjamin B., ed. *International Encyclopedia of Psychiatry, Psychology, Psychoanalysis, and Neurology,* vol. 10. Aesculapius Publishers/Van Nostrand, 1977.

The World's Fair, Being a Pictorial History of the Columbian Exposition. Chicago Publication and Lithograph, 1893. Chicago Historical Society.

Wyckoff, Walter A. *The Workers: An Experiment in Reality.* Charles Scribner's Sons, 1899.

ACKNOWLEDGMENTS

THIS IS MY THIRD BOOK with Crown Publishers and with my editor, Betty Prashker, who once again proved herself to be one of New York's supreme editors—confident, obliquely forceful, always reassuring. Every writer needs support, and she gave it unstintingly. Every book also needs support, and once again Crown marshaled a team of committed men and women to help the book find its way to as many readers as possible. Thanks, here, to Steve Ross, publisher; Andrew Martin, Joan DeMayo, and Tina Constable, marketing wizards; and Penny Simon, the kind of veteran publicist most writers wish they had but seldom get.

I have been blessed as well with one hell of an agent, David Black, a man whose instinct for narrative drive—and excellent wine—is unparalleled. He also happens to be an excellent human being.

On the homefront my family kept me sane. I could not have written this book without the help of my wife, Christine Gleason, a doctor by profession but also one of the best natural editors I've encountered. Her confidence was a beacon. My three daughters showed me what really matters. My dog showed me that nothing matters but dinner.

Two friends, both writers, generously agreed to read the entire manuscript and offered their wise critiques. Robin Marantz Henig sent me a dozen pages of pinpoint suggestions, most of which I adopted. Carrie Dolan, one of the best and funniest writers I know, offered her criticisms in a way that made them seem like compliments. Hers is a knack that few editors possess.

Thanks also to Dr. James Raney, Seattle psychiatrist and forensic consultant, who read the manuscript and offered his diagnosis of the psychic malaise that likely drove Holmes's behavior. Gunny Harboe, the Chicago architect who led the restoration of two of Burnham & Root's remaining buildings—the Reliance and the Rookery—gave me a tour of both and showed me Burnham's library, restored to its original warmth.

Finally, a word about Chicago: I knew little about the city until I began work on this book. Place has always been important to me, and one thing today's Chicago exudes, as it did in 1893, is a sense of place. I fell in love with the city, the people I encountered, and above all the lake and its moods, which shift so readily from season to season, day to day, even hour to hour.

I must confess a shameful secret: I love Chicago best in the cold.

ILLUSTRATION CREDITS

Page vii: Rascher Publishing Company. Chicago Historical Society (ICHi–31608).

Page 1: *World's Columbian Exposition Photographs by C. D. Arnold,* Ryerson and Burnham Archives, The Art Institute of Chicago. Photograph courtesy of the Art Institute of Chicago.

Page 9: Chicago Historical Society. ICHi–21795.

Page 111: *World's Columbian Exposition Photographs by C. D. Arnold,* Ryerson and Burnham Archives, The Art Institute of Chicago. Photograph courtesy of the Art Institute of Chicago.

Page 233: Photograph by William Henry Jackson. Chicago Historical Society. ICHi–17132.

Page 337: © Bettman/CORBIS

Page 371: Chicago Historical Society. ICHi–25106.

Page 391: Chicago Historical Society. ICHi–17124.

INDEX

Note: Page numbers in *italic* type refer to illustrations.

DATE DUE

DEMCO 38-297

S0-BAQ-577

PHYSICS OF THE EARTH

A SERIES of related monographs prepared under the direction of various committees of the National Research Council.

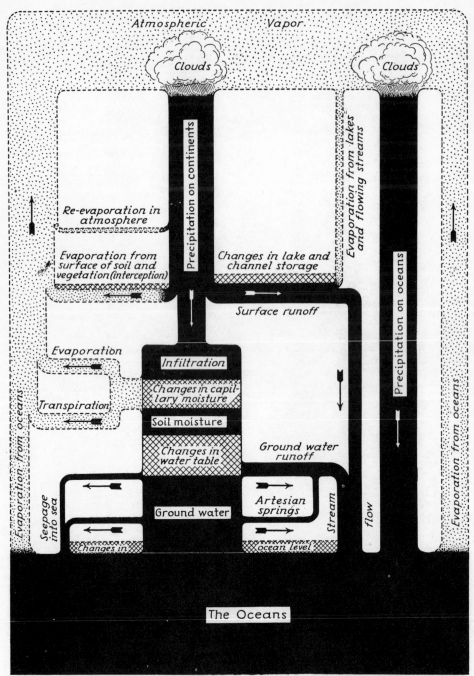

(Prepared by Adolph F. Meyer)

The Hydrologic Cycle.

PHYSICS OF THE EARTH—IX

HYDROLOGY

EDITED BY OSCAR E. MEINZER

Contributors

LEONARD D. BAVER	FRANÇOIS E. MATTHES
MERRILL BERNARD	OSCAR E. MEINZER
JAMES E. CHURCH	ADOLPH F. MEYER
ROYAL W. DAVENPORT	GEORGE W. MUSGRAVE
MARGARET D. FOSTER	CHARLES H. PIERCE
SIDNEY T. HARDING	LE ROY K. SHERMAN
CHARLES S. HOWARD	HAROLD T. STEARNS
WILLIAM G. HOYT	LORENZ G. STRAUB
CLARENCE S. JARVIS	ALLYN C. SWINNERTON
WALTER B. LANGBEIN	KARL V. TERZAGHI
HARRY R. LEACH	WILLIAM H. TWENHOFEL
CHARLES H. LEE	LELAND K. WENZEL

DOVER PUBLICATIONS, INC.

NEW YORK,

Library of Congress Catalog Card Number: 49-50117

Manufactured in the United States of America
Dover Publications, Inc.
180 Varick Street
New York, N.Y. 10014

FOREWORD

It is generally agreed that more attention should be given to research in the middle ground between the sciences. Geophysics—the study by physical methods of the planet on which we live—is a conspicuous example of such a middle-ground science, as it shades off imperceptibly in one direction or another into the fields of physics, astronomy, and geology, to say nothing of biology, with which the subject of oceanography is closely connected. Some branches of geophysics, such as meteorology, terrestrial magnetism, geodesy, and oceanography, have long been studied more or less independently, but it has become increasingly clear that these subjects and many others are all parts of geophysics. For various reasons there has lately been a considerable development of interest in geophysics, but this development has not been matched by the publication in English of systematic treatises on the subject. With these ideas in mind Dr. Joseph S. Ames, during his term as chairman of the Division of Physical Sciences of the National Research Council, was instrumental in organizing in 1926 a large committee to prepare a series of volumes on the physics of the earth, the purpose being "to give to the reader, presumably a scientist but not a specialist in the subject, an idea of its present status, together with a forward-looking summary of its outstanding problems.".

In due course subcommittees were formed to carry out this comprehensive project. As a result of their work the following volumes, including the present one, have been published:

That this project, as ambitious as it is important, has now come to fruition with the publication of this series of nine volumes is due partly to the skill and farsightedness with which Dr. Ames selected the committee and assisted in outlining its program; partly to the care and interest with which Dr. Ames's successor, Prof. Dayton C. Miller, directed the committee's activities during his term as chairman of the Division of Physical Sciences; and particularly to the devotion with which the chairmen and members of the several subcommittees have carried out their respective assignments. The hearty thanks of the National Research Council and of the readers of these volumes are due to the several authors for their efforts.

In 1936, upon a recommendation from the American Geophysical Union, Dr. Robert A. Millikan, as chairman of the Division of Physical Sciences, appointed a subcommittee on hydrology, with O. E. Meinzer as chairman, and R. W. Davenport as vice-chairman. It was planned to have each member of the subcommittee contribute to the volume on Hydrology, but for various reasons it became necessary to make several changes. In addition to the arduous and painstaking work done by the chairman, vice-chairman, and other joint authors, valuable help of one kind or another has been given by many other investigators in the different fields of hydrology. Special mention should be made of the specific services rendered by the following members of the United States Geological Survey: Bernard H. Lane, chief editor, recently retired, who edited the volume with respect to style and expression; Rodney Hart, who drafted most of the illustrations; V. C. Fishel and C. L. McGuinness, who assisted the chairman in technical editing; and R. G. Kazmann, who assisted especially in the preparation of the outline of the history of hydrology. Mr. Lane's systematic and expert work, based on many years of experience, was his last major task before his death Jan. 12, 1942. Acknowledgment should also be made of the cooperation of the following scientific organizations, chiefly through the contributions made by members of their staffs: The Geological Survey, the Soil Conservation Service, and the Weather Bureau; the Universities of California, Minnesota, Nevada, and Wisconsin; and Antioch College and the North Carolina State College of Agriculture and Engineering. Furthermore, special appreciation is due to the joint authors who, as consulting engineers, have contributed much of their valuable time without remuneration, namely, Messrs. Lee, Meyer, Sherman, and Terzaghi, and also to Walter J. Parsons, Jr., of the U. S. Army Engineers Office, whose previously published discussion of ice in streams is a valuable contribution to this volume.

Some of the statements in the preface of volume VIII of this series are equally applicable to this volume, as follows: The various authors have approached their subjects from many viewpoints. Naturally there will be some overlapping in the treatments and some differences of opinion. Repetition has been eliminated so far as has been possible without interfering with the continuity of thought. Many features in the rapid developments of theory and experiment in the field and in the laboratory of more recent years pave the way for different interpretations by investigators. It is increasingly apparent, however, that, although such differences of interpretation may seem great, they tend toward a harmonious integration in the solution of moot questions.

The arrangement of the present volume is based on the principle of following the hydrologic cycle as nearly as practicable, but it is recognized that different arrangements could be made under the same principle. After the introduction the two basic processes, precipitation and evaporation, are described. Then the numerous and complicated processes of storage and transfer of the water are covered more or less systematically, leading ultimately to a discussion of the residual process, which is essentially the flow of the water back into the sea. The extended treatment of the processes of storage and transfer are followed by the chapter on the physical and chemical work done by the natural waters in the course of their circulation. Finally, somewhat as appendices, are the last two chapters, which describe the distinctive hydrology of the limestone and lava-rock terranes.

Citations to literature are indicated by figures in brackets referring to the bibliography at the end of the particular chapter.

CONTENTS

CHAPTER I

INTRODUCTION

Oscar E. Meinzer[1]

DEFINITION OF HYDROLOGY

HYDROLOGY AN EARTH SCIENCE

Hydrology is, etymologically, the science that relates to water. It is, however, an earth science. It is concerned with the occurrence of water in the earth, its physical and chemical reactions with the rest of the earth, and its relation to the life of the earth. It includes the description of the earth with respect to its waters. It is not concerned primarily with the physical and chemical properties of the substance known as water. Like geology and the other earth sciences, it uses the basic sciences as its tools, but in doing so, it has developed a technique and subject matter that are distinct from those of the basic sciences.

THE CENTRAL CONCEPT

The central concept in the science of hydrology is the so-called hydrologic cycle—a convenient term to denote the circulation of the water from the sea, through the atmosphere, to the land; and thence, with numerous delays, back to the sea by overland and subterranean routes, and in part, by way of the atmosphere; also the many short circuits of the water that is returned to the atmosphere without reaching the sea. See the diagram of the hydrologic cycle by Adolph Meyer that is given in the frontispiece.

The science of hydrology is especially concerned with the second phase of this cycle—that is, with the water in its course from the time it is precipitated upon the land until it is discharged into the sea or returned to the atmosphere. It involves the measurement of the quantities and rates of movement of water at all times and at every stage of its course—rain and snow gaging to determine both the quantities and rates of rainfall and snowfall in all parts of the earth; snow surveying to determine the quantities of water stored as snow on the surface and the rates of its accumula-

---

[1] Geologist in charge, Division of Ground Water, Geological Survey, United States Department of the Interior, Washington, D. C.

1

tion and disappearance; observations of the advance and retreat of glaciers and surveys of the glaciers to determine the quantities of water that they contain and their rates of gain or loss; the gaging of streams, both large and small, to obtain continuous records of their flow at many points and during long periods; the gaging of lake levels to compute the gains and losses in their storage; measurements of the rates and quantities of infiltration into the soil and the movement of the soil moisture; periodic or continuous measurements of the water levels in wells to compute the gains and losses in underground storage; determinations of the permeability of the water-bearing formations and of the rates at which they are transmitting water; measurements of the discharge of springs and of total effluent seepage; determinations of the loads of dissolved and suspended matter which the waters contain in every position and the rates at which they carry it from one position to another; the quantities of water lost by evaporation and the rates of loss from the lakes, ponds, swamps, and streams, from the land surface, from objects on the surface and from the soil, and the quantities lost by transpiration from the leaves of growing plants, including native and cultivated trees, shrubs, and herbs. Hydrology is concerned with the development of accurate and feasible methods of making these measurements of diverse kinds, and with the accumulation and compilation of the great mass of resulting quantitative data. Finally, it is concerned with the great task of making rigorous studies of all the base data to determine the principles and laws involved in the occurrence, movement, and work of the waters in the hydrologic cycle.

KINDS OF WATER INCLUDED

Until recently hydrology has not had much recognition as a distinctive science, and therefore it is essential at the beginning of this volume to discuss somewhat critically its field and its relation to sciences that have been better recognized. In its broadest sense, hydrology relates to all the waters of the earth, but for practical reasons it has been limited in several respects.

The greatest reservoir of water on the earth is the ocean, which contains most of the earth's total supply. The science relating to the ocean is, however, called oceanography or, more properly, oceanology, and is not generally included in hydrology except as to the relations of the ocean to the waters of the land.

The study of the water in the interstices of the rocks—even the water at comparatively great depths below the land surface—belongs unquestionably to the science of hydrology. In most of the earth, however, the pressure of the overlying rock materials is so great that interstices cannot exist. There is abundant evidence that water or the dissociated elements of water occur in this internal part of the earth in some sort of solution with the other rock material and that from time to time some of this internal water reaches the surface or the rock interstices near the surface. This juvenile water comprises additions to the tangible water supply of the earth. It is also at one of the fringes of the science of hydrology. The critical studies of the water of internal origin have been made chiefly in connection with volcanology and metalliferous geology and belong most properly to those branches of geology. The study of springs, however, belongs definitely to hydrology, whether their water is hot or cold, and whether it is of internal origin or is derived from rain and snow.

A very small but very active and important part of the water of the earth occurs in the atmosphere, either as a constituent of the gaseous envelope or as liquid or solid particles suspended in it. The study of the earth's atmosphere is primarily a part of the science of meteorology, but hydrology deals almost entirely with water of atmospheric origin. Hence, it is concerned with the geographic distribution of the precipitated water, whether as rain or snow, with the quantities precipitated at each place, with the rates of precipitation, and with the whole complex subject of variations in quantity and rate. It is concerned with the source of the atmospheric water, whether from the sea or the land, and with its movements from the points of origin to the points of precipitation. It is also concerned with the return of the water to the atmosphere—that is, the modes of evaporation, as from water and land surfaces or by transpiration, and with the rates of evaporation under many different conditions.

The supply of water in the earth is not a fixed and immutable quantity, but is decreased by hydration and increased by dehydration of the rocks. These chemical reactions are at the fringe of hydrology. They belong more properly to one of the branches of geology. Hydrology is concerned essentially with the chemically free or uncombined water of the earth.

In both Europe and the United States there has been a tendency to restrict the term "hydrology" to the study of the water below the land surface and to use terms such as "hydrography" and "hydrometry" to denote the study of the surface water. Thus in the United States Geological Survey prior to 1906 there was a Division of Hydrography, which investigated the surface water, and a Division of Hydrology, which investigated the ground water. Thus also the German treatise "Hydrologie" [42], published in 1919, relates to the ground water and defines the term "hydrology" as that branch of the general science of water which relates specifically to the water below the surface ("unterirdisches Wasser"). This tendency probably resulted from a conception that the scientific study of ground water was essentially distinct from the scientific study of surface water and that the maintenance of such a distinction through the application of independent terms would be desirable.

The International Association of Scientific Hydrology, organized in 1924 as a member of the International Union of Geodesy and Geophysics, covers the study of all land waters as above defined and recognizes the approximate boundaries between its field and those of its sister associations of oceanography, volcanology, and meteorology. The Section of Hydrology of the American Geophysical Union, organized in 1930, recognizes the same boundaries.

At a meeting of the Executive Committee of the International Association of Scientific Hydrology in Zurich, in March 1938, four subdivisions of hydrology were recognized—(a) potamology, (b) limnology, (c) hydrology (eaux souterraines) and (d) cryology. Potamology relates to surface streams, limnology to lakes, and cryology to snow and ice. The use of the term "hydrology" for the study of the water that occurs below the surface shows that this restrictive use has not been entirely outgrown and also that the committee lacked a distinctive term for the branch of hydrology relating to the subsurface or subterranean water. To correct this deficiency the recommendation was made by the writer at the meeting of the International Association of Scientific Hydrology in Washington in September 1939 that the term "geohydrology" be adopted to denote the branch of hydrology relating to the subsurface or subterranean waters —that is, to all the waters below the surface [33].

With the physical fringes of hydrology thus defined, the science may be said to relate, in its restricted sense, essentially to the waters of the land—the atmospheric water so far as precipitation and evaporation are concerned; the water occurring on the land surface, as snow or ice or as liquid water that is flowing or impounded; and the water occurring below the surface in the interstices of the soil and the underlying rocks.

FACTORS DETERMINING THE HYDROLOGIC CYCLE

The hydrologic cycle may be said to be determined by conditions of three kinds—(1) the nature and application of the energy that keeps up the circulation; (2) the inherent properties of the medium of circulation —that is, of the water itself; and (3) the structure of the natural reservoirs and conduits—that is, of the atmosphere, the land surface, and the soil and rocks, which hold water or conduct it in its course.

SOURCE OF ENERGY

The principal source of energy for operating the great natural system of waterworks is the sun. Some movements are produced by forces that are wholly or in part of terrestrial origin, such as the tides, the emanation of juvenile water, and the movements of water caused by earthquakes. These are, however, relatively incidental. The energy that keeps up the main circulation of the natural waters and enables them to do most of the mechanical and chemical work is derived by radiation from the sun. The solar energy is applied in raising the temperature of air, soil and water, which results in the evaporation of some of the water and its transportation to land surfaces at higher altitudes. Thus potential energy is acquired whereby, in response to the force of the earth's gravity, the water moves in devious ways over the land and through the soil and rocks, not always downward, but sometimes upward in a part of its course, as in any gravity system of waterworks. As the water moves it does a great amount of work in pushing or rolling the rocks, carrying materials in suspension and solution, and bringing together elements that cause chemical reactions. The solar energy, however, also operates on the water in processes that are not parts of the main circulation just outlined, as, for example, frost action in the weathering of the rocks and the circulation of the water in lakes as a result of temperature changes.

Evaporation of water from the soil, directly or through the agency of the plants, sets in operation another force—namely, that of the molecular attraction of the soil particles for water. Thus in the soil there are two principal forces, gravity and molecular attraction, that produce movement in the water, and often these two forces oppose and counteract each other.

Properties of the Water

The circulation of the water in the earth is conditioned in many ways by the properties of the water itself. The pressure relation between the waters in the liquid and the gaseous state and its variation with temperature determine the amounts of evaporation and precipitation and hence the degree of activity in the hydrologic cycle. In general the activity increases with the average atmospheric temperature. Presumably if the earth's atmosphere were much warmer, the hydrologic activity would be greatly increased, up to the critical temperature.

The freezing temperature of the water falls within the narrow range of temperatures of the earth's atmosphere near the surface, and hence there is a variety and variation as between frozen and unfrozen conditions. Even slight lowering in average temperature has produced the radically different hydrologic conditions of the glacial stages, and any pronounced lowering that would congeal the waters over the entire surface of the earth would produce a condition of almost complete stagnation in hydrologic processes. The high specific heat and the latent heat of melting and vaporization have great effects in retarding the otherwise more rapid changes in the hydrologic processes. The density or specific gravity of the water determines the force that it exerts. The changes in density with changes in temperature, the expansion when freezing, with greatest density slightly above the melting point, all have marked consequences, especially in the hydrology of the lakes. The viscosity determines the rate of flow of both surface and subterranean water and the relation between turbulent and laminar flow. It also determines the capacity of the water to carry material in suspension. The solvent properties give the water its capacity to disintegrate and dissolve the rocks, to carry the mineral substances in solution, and to precipitate them, cementing and altering the rocks and forming rock and ore deposits.

STRUCTURE OF THE NATURAL RESERVOIRS AND CONDUITS

The lower part of the earth's atmosphere serves as a vehicle in which water vapor is transported in all directions, but with a net movement from the sea to the land, where it is precipitated and in general starts on its return course—partly through the flow of surface streams, partly through re-evaporation and wind movement, and partly through subterranean flow. The complicated influences of latitude and of the shape and size of the land bodies over which the atmosphere moves produce a great variation in the precipitation of the water vapor. This variation in precipitation is the primary cause of variations in stream flow and in other processes of the hydrologic cycle.

The character and shape of the land surface determine to a great extent the disposal of the precipitated water. The geomorphology, geology, soil, and vegetation of a drainage basin all influence profoundly its stream regimen and, indeed, every phase of its hydrology. Striking contrasts at once come to mind—rugged mountain areas with their swift torrential streams, contrasted with aggrading deltas and sluggish waters; maturely dissected areas with their prompt and complete drainage, contrasted with areas of recent glacial drift in which lakes and swamps abound; well-forested lands that tend to hold the rain and snow, contrasted with denuded lands that allow quick runoff; areas of cavernous limestone with their extensive subterranean drainage and big springs, contrasted with areas of relatively impermeable granitic rock that have well-developed systems of surface streams and numerous small springs. The evaluation of these different conditions and of the results of their complex combinations affords a large field for hydrologic study, on which only a beginning has been made.

The hydrology of the ground water is everywhere controlled by the geology. The head and movement of the ground water, its recharge and discharge, its quantity and quality are all controlled by the character and structure of the rock formations. Some of the water from the rain and snow that passes beneath the surface is stored only temporarily as perched ground water or as bank storage, or it flows through the surficial interstices quickly enough to augment the floods or to maintain high stages of the streams immediately after the floods; some of the water sinks to the main water table and furnishes the principal flow of the streams during the dry or frozen seasons; some percolates through artesian aquifers for hundreds or thousands of years before it is returned to the surface or discharged into the sea; and some apparently remains entrapped in deep-seated formations through a whole era of geologic time.

THE HYDROLOGIC CYCLE IN RELATION TO LIFE

The chief practical significance of the hydrologic cycle lies in the fact that it is the process by which water supplies are furnished to the land plants and animals and to man for his consumption and many other uses, and the related fact that water has the solvent, evaporative, and other properties which make it essential to the life processes of all plants and animals and adapt it for many domestic and industrial uses [32, pp. 86–87].

As all life depends upon water, hydrology is intricately related to biology, especially to the physiology and ecology of the plant kingdom. Thus in the United States about two-thirds of the water that falls as rain or snow passes by evaporation into the atmosphere, a large part of it being discharged through the life processes of the plants. The vegetative cover of the land, the root systems, and the plant and animal organisms in the soil greatly affect different important hydrologic processes, including not only evaporation in its different forms, but also infiltration, groundwater recharge, runoff, and the mechanical and chemical work of the water.

The Cambrian strata contain the record of abundant marine life. In the half billion years that have elapsed since the Cambrian period both plant and animal kingdoms have undergone vast evolution, with extensive and effective adaptation for life on the land, even in the most arid regions. However, in this long process of adaptation to different environments no species of plant or animal has escaped from the fundamental requirement of a water supply in order to carry on its life processes.

As the plant and animal kingdoms moved in large part from the sea to the land, radical adaptations to their changed water supply resulted. Thus it became necessary for both the land plants and the land animals to adapt themselves to the use of fresh water instead of salt water, and this adaptation has become so thorough that now salt water means death to nearly all land life.

With advancing civilization the human race has found water to be a most convenient substance for a large and ever-enlarging list of uses. Indeed, its several properties, such as its solvent ability, its high specific heat, and its occurrence in the solid, liquid, and gaseous states within convenient temperature intervals and with high latent heat in passing from one state to another, lend themselves so remarkably to the needs of civilized man in his multitudinous domestic and industrial operations, recreational activities, and therapeutic applications that it seems as if these properties were providentially designed for his benefit. It is an interesting exercise to make a list of the uses to which water is put by man, many of which are analogous to the physiologic functions of water in living organisms, as for example, the conveyance and storage of material and energy, often with resultant chemical changes, the regulation of temperature, and the elimination of waste [32, pp. 86, 87].

As water is essential to all life and as it is the earth's leading vehicle for mechanical and chemical transportation, it is not surprising that many practical applications are made of all phases of the science of hydrology. Conservation of the soil and soil moisture, river, shore, and harbor improvements to promote navigation and flood control, reservoir construction, well construction, water-supply developments, irrigation, water treatment, sewage disposal—all these human activities depend upon the principles and data of hydrology. This condition gives impetus to the study of hydrology, but it may be detrimental in diverting the attention of hydrologists too much from the development of the science to its application.

The works of man have produced many changes in the regimen of the natural waters. To the hydrologists these are large-scale experiments by means of which the principles and laws of hydrology may be tested. The study of these artifically modified conditions, therefore, forms an important part of hydrologic research, which should not be confused with the engineering work of planning and building the structures that produce the changes.

HISTORICAL DEVELOPMENT OF HYDROLOGY

ANCIENT AND MEDIEVAL CONCEPTS

The concept of the hydrologic cycle has become so generally accepted that it is difficult to appreciate the long history that lies back of its development and demonstration. From the dawn of history until comparatively recent times the source of the water of the springs and streams has constituted a puzzling problem that has been the subject of much speculation and controversy. Prior to the later part of the seventeenth century it was generally assumed that the water discharged by the springs could not be derived from the rain—first, because the rainfall was believed to be inadequate in quantity, and second, because the earth was believed to be too impervious to permit penetration of the rain water far below the surface. With these two erroneous postulates lightly assumed, the philosophers devoted their thought to devising ingenious hypotheses to account in some other way for the spring and stream water. Some of the early writers were apparently satisfied with the postulate that the water is derived from huge inexhaustible subterranean reservoirs, but others recognized that there must be replenishment of the reservoirs which supply the springs. Thus arose the concept of a hydrologic cycle in which water was supposed to be returned from the ocean to the springs, not by way of the atmosphere but by way of subterranean channels.

In Book 21 of the Iliad is the statement "With Jove neither does King Achelous fight nor the mighty strength of the deep-flowing Oceanus, from which flow all rivers and every sea and all springs and deep wells." This statement suggests the concept of the hydrologic cycle. Homer, who lived nearly 1,000 years before Christ, is generally regarded as the author of the Iliad, but the critical studies of Robinson Smith have shown that large parts of the present Iliad, including the above quotation, were not in the original Iliad by Homer but were added at some later date. The writings of Thales (about 650 B.C.) likewise state that the springs and streams are supplied from the ocean, and the explanation is made that the sea water is driven into the rocks by the winds and is then elevated in the mountains by the pressure of the rocks [21, p. 74]. Plato (427–347 B.C.), in his dialogue entitled Phaedon, makes a statement to the effect that the waters that form the seas, lakes, rivers, and springs come from a vast cavern, called Tartarus, and that all these waters return through various routes to Tartarus [37, p. 65].

The hypothesis that the springs are fed by sea water through subterranean channels gave rise in ancient and medieval times to subsidiary hypotheses to explain how the sea water is freed from its salt and how it is elevated to the altitude of the springs. The removal of the salt was vaguely ascribed to various processes of either filtration or distillation. The elevation of the water was ascribed by different writers to processes of vaporization and subsequent condensation, to rock pressure, to suction of the wind, to a vacuum produced by the flow of springs, to pressure exerted on the sea by the wind and waves, to "the virtue of the heavens", to capillary action, and to the curvature of the surface of the sea whereby the sea was believed to stand higher than the springs and hence to furnish the necessary head.

Aristotle (384–322 B.C.) developed a theory of subterranean condensation, suggested by the condensation of atmospheric water vapor [1, p. 4; 2, pp. 426–431]. In his treatise entitled Meteorologica he recognized the processes of evaporation and condensation. He had the concept that through the sun's rays the water is changed into air, and that when the air becomes cold it is changed back into water and falls as rain. He recognized that some of the rain is discharged by the streams and apparently also that some percolates into the earth and reappears in the springs. He placed the greatest emphasis, however, upon his theory that subterranean condensation produces the major part of the water that flows from the springs and supplies the rivers. He was apparently not much concerned with the problem of the hydrologic cycle.

Two main replenishment theories were thus developed by the philosophers of ancient Greece—one to the effect that sea water is conducted through subterranean channels below the mountains and is then purified and raised to the springs, and the other to the effect that in the cold dark caverns under the mountains the subterranean atmosphere and perhaps the earth itself are changed into the moisture that feeds the springs [31]. These philosophers were pioneering in vast untrodden fields of thought. Although both theories were erroneous, each was in some respects close to the truth. The Greeks were familiar with cavernous limestone terranes, and hence they conceived the subterranean regions to have great open spaces with natural processes comparable to those on the surface.

The Roman philosophers in general followed the Greek ideas. Lucretius (about 95–52 B.C.) and Pliny (23–79 A.D.) adopted the sea-water concept, but Seneca (3 B.C.–65A.D.) accepted Aristotle's condensation theory. Lucretius recognized that water is evaporated from the sea and the land and that it is eventually returned as rain. In his De Rerum Natura (Book 6) as abbreviated from the translation by Munro, he stated, "The clouds imbibe much sea water. In like manner moisture is taken up out of all rivers into the clouds; and when the particles of water have met in them the close-packed clouds endeavor to discharge their moisture, from two causes: the force of the wind drives them together and the very abundance of the rain clouds pushes down, presses from above and forces the rain to stream out." His explanation of the origin of the rivers is, however, based mainly on the theory of subterranean return of the sea water, as is shown by the following language (Book 5): "That the sea, rivers, and springs always stream over with new moisture and that waters well up without ceasing, it needs no words to prove. But the water on the surface is always taken off, and thus it is that on the whole there is no overflow, partly because the seas are lessened by the strong winds sweeping over them and by the ethereal sun decomposing them with his rays; partly because the water is diffused below the surface over all lands, for the salt is strained off and the liquid streams back again to the source and all meets together at the river heads and then flows over the lands in a fresh current."

The two books on the water supply of Rome by Julius Frontinus, water commissioner of the city in 97 A.D., were translated by Clemens Herschel [18], who also made enlightening comments which indicate the lack of knowledge at that time of anything that might be called hydrology of either surface or ground water. Although the Romans had a great appreciation of the value of water and built remarkable aqueducts to supply water to the capital city, their methods of measuring or estimating the flow of water were very crude, based on cross-section areas, with only vague recognition of the effects of head and velocity. Herschel points out that Hero of Alexandria, who may be considered the teacher of Frontinus, had a clearer understanding of what is involved in measuring flowing water and recommended better practice than was anywhere shown in Roman water law. He translated a statement by Hero as follows: "Observe always that it does not suffice to determine the section of flow in order to know the quantity of water furnished by the spring. It is necessary to find the velocity of its current, because the more rapid the flow the more water the spring will furnish, and the slower it is the less it will produce. For this reason, after having dug a reservoir under the stream, examine by means of a sundial how much water flows into it in an hour, and from that deduce the quantity of water furnished in a day."

During the Middle Ages, according to Adams [1, pp. 8 and 9; 2, p. 432], all the philosophers and interpreters of Holy Scripture, from St. Jerome (340–420 A.D.) down, taught that the springs have their origin in the sea. The writers stated that the water escapes through holes in the bottom of the sea, flows through subterranean channels, and thence is elevated to the springs. They generally based this assumption on passages in the Bible, such as Ecclesiastes 1:7, the King James version of which reads as follows: "All the rivers run into the sea, yet the sea is not full; unto the place from whence the rivers come thither they return again." The traditional author of this book is King Solomon, who, like Homer, lived nearly 1,000 years before Christ. Critical studies have, however, shown that the book was written in a later period by some other Hebrew author. It should be noted that it is not this verse in Ecclesiastes but the medieval misinterpretation of it that is in conflict with the modern concept of the hydrologic cycle, for it does not express any theory as to the operation of the landward phase of the cycle. Nevertheless, it became heresy to doubt the subterranean sea-water theory.

The following comment on Ecclesiastes 1:7 is made by James Moffatt in a personal communication: "The Hebrew idiom is that the rivers continue to flow. It is possible that the hydrological idea [hydrologic cycle] was present to the writer's mind, as it appearently was to the mind of another Hebrew in touch with Greek thought, the author of Job 36: 27 and 28, but in any case it is not the point of his argument. All he means to indicate, as Aristophanes does in the Clouds, is the strange fact that 'the sea grows no bigger though rivers flow into it.' Lucretius at a later period discusses the scientific explanations, but our Hebrew writer is simply illustrating what is to him the unending and vain course of things in nature, and there is no clear suggestion that he alludes to evaporation or to subterranean channels."

The Moffatt translation of the verse reads as follows:

> The streams all flow into the sea,
> But the sea they never fill,
> Though the streams are flowing still.

The King James version and also Luther's German translation accord with St. Jerome's Latin translation and were probably derived from it rather than from the original Hebrew. St. Jerome was familiar with the Greek literature and also with the writings of Lucretius. Thus it appears that he, rather than the Hebrew author, may have placed the hydrologic cycle into the book of Ecclesiastes and also that the medieval defenders of the faith were defending Greek philosophy and not the authentic teachings of the Holy Scriptures.

The theory now generally accepted—that the ground water is for the most part derived from rain and snow by infiltration from the surface—was briefly but clearly stated by Marcus Vitruvius, who lived about the time of Christ. Vitruvius was not a philosopher but an architect. He produced a work on architecture in ten books, and in conformity with the importance given by the Romans to water supplies, he devoted one of the ten books to that subject. At the beginning of Book 8, as quoted from the English translation by Givilt [46, pp. 177–200], he stated: "As it is the opinion of physiologists, philosophers, and priests that all things proceed from water, I thought it necessary, as in the preceding seven books rules are laid down for buildings, to describe in this the method of finding water, its different properties according to the varied nature of places, how it ought to be conducted, and in what manner it should be judged of; inasmuch as it is of infinite importance for the purposes of life, for pleasure, and for our daily use." The mountains, he explained, receive a large amount of rain and snow, the water from which percolates through the rock strata to the foot of the mountains and there, issuing forth, gives rise to streams.

Vitruvius gave a list of plants that indicate the occurrence of ground water, and he endeavored to specify the conditions under which they may be regarded as reliable indicators. He also explained the process of alkali accumulated by evaporation of ground water. Similar statements in regard to plant indicators are found in the writings of Pliny, who apparently quoted Vitruvius, and in those of Cassiodorus, in the sixth century, who obtained his ideas largely from an "aquilege", or professional water finder, who came to Rome from the arid regions of Africa. "Because of the great aridity of the terranes of his country," wrote Cassiodorus, "the art of discovering springs is there cultivated with the greatest care."

Vitruvius and the other Roman writers who have been mentioned discussed also less tangible methods of locating ground water, such as color and dampness of the soil, mists rising from the ground early in the morning, and sponges becoming moist when placed in shallow holes in the ground. Obviously these methods border closely on divining, or water-witching, and it is greatly to the credit of Vitruvius, Pliny, and Cassiodorus that none of them apparently recognized divining or any other magical method for locating water. Although the means suggested by Vitruvius as aids in finding water may not have had much value, yet they were serious efforts to discover practicable methods at a time when the science of geology was still a complete blank.

THE FOUNDERS OF HYDROLOGY

Until near the end of the seventeenth century the two old Greek hypotheses chiefly occupied the field, with many fantastic adornments, but the infiltration theory was advocated by a few writers, notably by Leonardo da Vinci (1452–1519) and Bernard Palissy (about 1509–89).

Leonardo da Vinci was a man of exceptional genius and versatility, and he had the habit of making accurate observations of nature and basing his conclusions on such observations. In charge of the canals in the Milan area, his attention was directed to the occurrence and behavior of the natural waters. He had a correct understanding of the hydrologic cycle, including infiltration of rain and return of the water through springs, as is shown by the following excerpts from his writings, as translated by Richter (Oxford University Press, 1939):

Whence we may conclude that the water goes from the rivers to the sea and from the sea to the rivers, thus constantly circulating and returning, and that all the sea and rivers have passed through the mouth of the Nile an infinite number of times. . . . The conclusion is that the saltness of the sea must proceed from the many springs of water which, as they penetrate the earth, find mines of salt, and these they dissolve in part and carry with them to the ocean and other seas, whence the clouds, the begetters of rivers, never carry it up.

Palissy was a French Huguenot, the inventor of enameled pottery, and a pioneer paleontologist [36]. He was reared in poverty and was not educated in Greek or Latin. He began early to observe nature, and he based his theories on his own observations. "I have had no other books," he wrote, "than Heaven and Earth, which are open to all." His discourse on water and springs was written in French, whereas the philosophic treatises of that period were generally in Latin. This discourse is in the form of a fascinating dialogue between "Theory" and "Practice." It was translated into English by E. E. Willett in 1876 (W. J. Smith, Brighton).

"When for a long time," says Practice, "I had closely considered the cause of the sources of natural fountains and the place whence they might proceed, at length I became plainly assured that they could proceed from or be engendered by nothing but the rains." Theory replies: "After having heard your opinion I am compelled to say that you are a great fool. Do you think me so ignorant that I should put more faith in what you say than in so large a number of philosophers who tell us that all waters come from the sea and return thither? There are none, even to the old men, who do not hold this theory, and from all time we have believed it. It is a great presumption in you to wish to make us believe a doctrine altogether new, as if you were the cleverest philosopher." To which Practice replies: "If I were not well assured in my opinion, you would put me to great shame, but I am not alarmed at your abuse or your fine language; for I am quite certain that I shall win against you and against all those who are of your opinion, though they be Aristotle and the best philosophers that ever lived; for I am quite assured that my opinion is trustworthy."

Thus the argument is developed. Theory defends first the seawater and then the condensation hypothesis, while Practice, with clear and valid arguments, shows the absurdities of these hypotheses and then presents simple but convincing evidence that all the water of the springs is derived from rain. In positive language he explains that the rain water seeps into the earth and sinks to impervious rock, over which it flows until it reaches an outlet and discharges as a spring.

The science of hydrology may be considered to have begun with the work of Pierre Perrault (1608–80), Edmé Mariotté (1620–84), and other French physicists and of the English astronomer Edmund Halley (1656–1742). These men put hydrology for the first time on a quantitative basis.

Perrault made measurements of the rainfall during 3 years, and he roughly estimated the area of the drainage basin of the Seine River above a point in Burgundy and of the runoff from this same basin. Thus he computed that the quantity of water that fell on the basin as rain or snow was about six times the quantity discharged by the river. Crude as was his work, he nevertheless demonstrated the fallacy of the age-old assumption that the rainfall is inadequate to account for the discharge of springs and streams. Perrault also exposed water and other liquids to evaporation and made observations on the relative amount of water thus lost. He also made investigations of capillarity, established the approximate limits of capillarity in sand, and showed that water absorbed by capillarity cannot form accumulations of free water at higher levels.

Mariotté computed the discharge of the Seine at Paris by measuring its width, depth, and velocity at approximately its mean stage, making the velocity measurements by the float method. He essentially verified Perrault's results. In his publications, which appeared after his death in 1684, he defended vigorously the infiltration theory and created some of the modern thought on the subject [27]. According to the brief digest of his work by Keilhack [21, pp. 80–81], he maintained that the water derived from rain and snow penetrates into the pores of the earth and accumulates in wells; that this water percolates downward till it reaches impermeable rock and thence percolates laterally; and that it is sufficient in quantity to supply the springs. He demonstrated that the rain water penetrates into the earth and used for this purpose the cellar of the Paris Observatory, the percolation through the cover of which was comparable with the amount of rainfall. He also showed that the flow of springs increases in rainy weather and diminishes in times of drought, and explained that the more constant springs are supplied from the larger underground reservoirs.

The relative credit that should be given to Perrault and Mariotté has been a question of considerable disagreement. Several writers have stated that Perrault opposed the infiltration theory. Fortunately there is in the United States Geological Survey library a copy of the 1678 edition of his treatise on the origin of springs [38], first published in 1674. In this treatise Perrault did not argue against the infiltration theory, but rather explained that, while Vitruvius and Palissy believed that ground-water recharge occurs chiefly from rain and snow on the mountains, he himself held that the rain feeds the streams directly and that the seepage from the streams on the lower slopes supplies the ground water, which eventually returns to the surface in the lowlands [31, pp. 11–12].

Soon after Perrault and Mariotté measured the flow of the Seine River and demonstrated that the rainfall is sufficient to supply the stream flow, Halley made observations on the rate of evaporation and demonstrated that the evaporation from the Mediterranean Sea is ample to supply the quantity of water returned to that sea by the rivers flowing into it. His tests of evaporation were made with much care on a salt solution having the concentration of sea water, but his estimates of stream discharge were very crude. He described his work on this subject in papers published in 1687, 1690, and 1694 [24].

Vitruvius, da Vinci, and Palissy were discoverers and pioneer advocates of correct hydrologic principles, but their contributions were not effectively followed up. Perrault, Mariotté, and Halley, however, undertook hydrologic research of the modern scientific type, and they may well be regarded as the founders of hydrology.

EARLY DEVELOPMENT OF THE SCIENCE

The study of artesian water naturally came next in historical development to that of the origin of springs. Even before the emergence of geology, the basic principles of artesian pressure were understood. Pioneers in the development of the hydrostatic theory of artesian pressure were the Italian astronomer and geographer Giovanni Cassini (1625–1712) and the Italian physician Bernardini Ramazzini, whose best-known publication appeared in 1691. In 1715 Antonio Vallisnieri, president of the University of Padua, Italy, published a book based on his personal observations in northern Italy, which gave a correct explanation of the source of artesian water and the mechanism of artesian systems. His theory was illustrated with geologic sections by Scheuchzer, which, according to Adams [2, p. 454], were among the earliest geologic sections ever drawn.

The origin and early development of hydraulic science was outlined by Herschel [18, pp. 216–219] as follows:

"To appreciate Frontinus' position with regard to a proper knowledge of the velocity of efflux and generally of the velocity of running water, it is instructive to follow the development of the art from his time until we arrive at the formula $v = \sqrt{2gh}$, now known to every beginner in hydraulic science, and the very foundation stone of that science as it is known at the present day. This formula and the numerical values it gives to velocities of efflux were not discovered until about the year 1738, when Daniel Bernouilli and John Bernouilli, his father, each published a different mathematical demonstration of this law.

"Castelli (1577–1644), a Benedictine monk, the pupil of Galileo, first showed that the quantity of efflux in a given time depended by law on, or was a function of, the depth of water in a bowl—that is, was a function of the head. It was his pupil Torricelli (1608–47), the inventor of the barometer, the grandson, in a professional sense, of Galileo, who first proved, in 1644, or only 2 years after Galileo's death, that the velocities of efflux are as the square roots of the head. But this still furnished no numerical value for the velocity of efflux. Huygens (1629–95), the inventor of pendulum clocks, first found the numerical value of the acceleration of gravity, commonly represented by the letter g, in 1673. Sixty-five more years had to elapse, until the genius of the two Bernouillis, father and son, in 1738, finally laid the foundation of modern determinate hydraulics, by writing the equation of $v = \sqrt{2gh}$."

Quantitative hydrology also received impetus from the work of Henri Pitot in 1732 when he described a series of experiments designed to measure the velocity in different parts of the cross section of a river. Among other things he told of a curved tube which he had invented to measure the velocity of water at any point. This instrument, with little refinement, is still widely used to measure the velocities of fluids. With it engineers were able to obtain much more accurate measurements than previously of the quantity of water flowing past a given point during a given time.

Other workers contributed to the development of the science of hydrology during the first half of the eighteenth century. Thus Bernard Forest Belidor (1697–1761) devised apparatus to utilize tidal power and wrote books on hydraulics; Rev. J. T. Desaguliers (1683–1744) proposed the siphon theory of ebbing and flowing springs; and James Jurin (1684–1750) and Jean D'Alembert (1717–76) contributed to the mathematics of hydraulic theory.

In 1762 Paul Frisi published a "Treatise on rivers and torrents" [14], which gave some quantitative data and refuted some incorrect hydrologic theories while introducing new theories equally incorrect.

Frisi's most important contribution, however, was in pointing out the limitations of the theoretical approach to formulas for measuring the flow of water. His empirical attitude toward hydrodynamics, still widely held by engineers, is illustrated by the following quotation from his treatise [14, p. 57]:

"One single reflection is sufficient to show that all hydraulic problems are beyond the reach of geometry and calculus. The difficulty of all problems is increased in proportion to the number of conditions (variables) . . . Thus, mechanical problems become so much more complicated as the number of bodies whose motions are sought and which act in any way on each other is augmented. . . . In a fluid mass which moves in a tube or in a canal the number of bodies acting together is infinite; whence it follows that to determine the motion of each body is a problem depending on an infinity of equations, which it is, of course, beyond all the powers of algebra to reach."

In 1775 Antoine de Chézy [7] announced that the velocity of a river varies with its surface slope, and he expressed the relation between slope and velocity in a formula that is still known as the Chézy formula [17, pp. 117–127]. This formula gave hydrologists a new basis for estimating the flow of water in streams, and, with minor changes, it is still in use. In 1779 Dubat, in a study financed by the French Government, established the principle that the motive force of each particle of water is due entirely to the surface slope of the water and that the resistances are due to the viscosity of the water and friction on the bed.

In 1791 hydrology received impetus from the work of La Métherie, who extended the researches of Mariotté and placed them on a broader basis while simultaneously bringing them to the attention of meteorologists. He investigated the permeability of different kinds of rocks and explained that a part of the water from rain and snow flows off directly, a second part moistens the soil and evaporates or feeds the plants, and a third part penetrates to reservoirs at greater depths, from which it gradually issues as springs [21, p. 81].

In 1798 Giovanni Venturi made a contribution on the flow of water in his treatise giving the results of his experiments upon the contraction of the fluid vein. This treatise formed the basis for the work of Clemens Herschel, who in 1886 invented the device that he named the venturi meter.

HYDROLOGY IN THE FIRST PART OF THE NINETEENTH CENTURY

The science of hydrology, so far as it relates to ground water, could not be greatly developed until the fundamental principles of geology were established, near the end of the eighteenth century. In the early part of the nineteenth century William Smith, who has been called the father of English geology, did pioneer work in applying the newly developed science of geology to the problems of hydrology [43]. The most systematic and effective early work in developing geohydrology, however, was done by French scientists. Largely through their work the principles of the geologic occurrence of ground water and the hydrostatic theory of artesian flow became established by the middle of the nineteenth century.

During the first part of the nineteenth century the French hydrologists were especially active. Among them Poncelet and Lesbros, Belanger, de Thury, Laval, Deschamps, de Buffon, and Mulot may be mentioned. These men improved river-velocity formulas, investigated artesian flow, drilled the first deep wells, discussed the theory and practice of river improvement, fought incorrect hydrologic hypotheses, and did the first work on some problems that remained unsolved until more recently. Thus there is an interesting parallel between Laval's observations and conclusions on the effects of bridge piers in increasing flood stages, and the work of the United States Waterways Experiment Station in Vicksburg, nearly 100 years later, in conducting model studies on a specific problem of the same nature.

Among the Italian hydrologists in this period were Venturoli and Lombardini. Venturoli analyzed the flow of the Tiber River over a period of years; Lombardini wrote many papers in which he discussed the effects of lakes in equalizing flow and of levees in increasing flood heights and analyzed by statistical methods the monthly discharges of several Italian rivers.

Among German investigators were Julius Weisbach, who contributed to hydraulic theory; Johann Eytelwein, who made experiments for the determination of coefficients for the Chézy formula; O. E. Meyer, who preceded Darcy in discovering the law of the flow of ground water; and Karl Bischof, the results of whose work in ground water were given in his textbook on chemical and physical geology.

The art of measuring systematically the flow of streams to determine their daily discharge progressed slowly during the nineteenth century. The earliest records were computed by means of various slope formulas. The next step was to make a few determinations of velocity to check or modify existing formulas or to serve as the basis for new ones. The third step was the measurement of velocity by current meters.

During the first half of the nineteenth century considerable pioneer work was done in the measurement of the discharge of streams. Escher de la Linth computed the annual discharge of the upper Rhine near Basel during the years 1809 to 1821. Defontaine made a series of measurements of the Rhine and its tributaries during the years 1820 to 1833. Venturoli computed the daily discharge of the Tiber at Rome for the years 1825 to

1836. Baumgarten made a series of measurements and observations of the Garonne River between 1837 and 1846. These discharges were computed by means of slope formulas, a few of them modified by measurements of velocity, probably by means of floats.

In 1813 Baron Cornelius Krayenhoff [23], a Dutch hydrologist, published a comprehensive collection of tables of observations upon the topography and hydrography of Holland. Included in this publication were detailed records of discharge, based on records of slopes of the water surfaces of the rivers, gage heights, velocity profiles, and similar hydrologic data.

Toward the end of the eighteenth century the English scientist John Dalton had conducted notable experiments on evaporation, and in 1801 he discovered the law of partial pressures that bears his name. He was interested in infiltration, and in 1802 he published the results of experiments that he made with lysimeters to determine the quantities of water that percolate through soils of different types. He made experiments and observations to determine whether the quantity of rain and dew in England and Wales is equal to the quantity of water carried off by rivers and raised by evaporation, with an inquiry into the origin of springs. He reached the conclusion that they are equivalent [24].

In the first half of the nineteenth century the development of hydrology in the United States was stimulated not only by the needs for water supply but also by the needs for river and canal transportation. About 1817 to 1820 extensive studies of the hydrology of lakes, canals, and rivers were undertaken by DeWitt Clinton [8], who was a president of the New York Philosophical Society but is better known as a governor of New York and the builder of the Erie Canal. He made no important original contributions but he promoted public interest in hydrology and set a wholesome example by applying all existing knowledge to the problems in planning the Erie Canal. He made a study of lake levels and estimated the losses to be expected in a canal through evaporation and percolation. His knowledge of hydrologic theory was used to achieve his dream of a canal connecting the granaries of the newly opened Midwest with the European markets. His arguments for the building of the canal were so well founded and so ably stated that he convinced the public that his plan was hydrologically feasible. Consequently when he was elected governor of New York public support of the project was insured and the canal was built.

In 1822 Gen. Simon Bernard and Col. Joseph Totten made a report to the commandant of the United States Engineers on the condition of the Ohio and Mississippi Rivers, giving exact details concerning the falls of the Ohio. This report was the forerunner of the elaborate hydrologic studies that have been made on these river systems in the last 100 years.

In 1843, on the completion of the Croton Aqueduct for the public water supply of New York City, a commemorative volume was issued which dealt fully with the hydrology and construction of the city's water-supply system [22].

HYDROLOGY IN THE MIDDLE PART OF THE NINETEENTH CENTURY

In 1850 appeared the "Manual of hydrology" by the English civil engineer Nathaniel Beardmore [3], which remained a source book for hydrologists and hydraulic engineers for almost 50 years. The book was twice revised and was published in second and third editions. In the third edition, published in 1862, the author made the following remarks:

"The refined but practical questions of surface slope and velocity of water and, above all, of the volume accompanying a given fall and velocity or certain known rainfall, were subjects almost untouched [until publication of the first edition of this volume]; the source or supply of water in reference to the amount of rain was a subject which only a few canal and waterworks engineers had investigated; and they were not much disposed in olden times to communicate the practical experience acquired by the hard labor of years.

"Hydrological science embraces the widest conditions; not only has climate to be considered, but the elevation, inclination, and geological formation of the substratum. Practical construction requires great previous experience, when the science has to be applied;—for instance, in drainage and waterworks. . . .

"The treatise being designed to form a practical manual for every day use, it would be out of place to have entered at any length upon theory."

Beardmore attempted to compile and correlate all the existing applicable hydrologic and hydraulic data and to place them in accessible form for the engineer and engineering student. His manual had an important effect in removing hydrology and hydraulics from the sphere of secrecy into the field of open scientific research and discussion.

The manual contained four divisions. The first division related primarily to hydraulic engineering. The discharges of weirs, sluices, pipes, culverts, and rivers were computed and put into accessible form. There were many tables of conversions and a few mathematical tables to facilitate computation. Although in general the tables are now out of date, they were a great improvement over reliance upon the individual judgments of isolated engineers. The second part related to the hydrology of surface waters—the flow from land areas and the recorded flow of several large rivers, together with a description of their drainage basins and remarks on springs, percolation, and wells. The third division dealt primarily with a favorite British topic—namely, the tides at different ports and their strength, direction, and height in the different estuaries. The fourth division related to rainfall and evaporation. It included a few records of evaporation and about 80 pages of rainfall records pertaining to all parts of the world.

In 1849 John Fletcher Miller [35] sent to the Royal Society of London the records of a systematic attempt to correlate rainfall with altitude and the effects of elevating rain gages above the land surface. The investigation was financed by several engineers and others who needed the basic information given by the study. This work illustrates a trend, which was becoming more noticeable, to collect basic hydrologic data rather than to formulate and reformulate mathematical expressions from laboratory experiments or restricted field observations.

In 1857 Lorin Blodget published his book entitled "Climatology of the United States" [5], which contributed notably to the hydrology of the United States in its discussion of the distribution of the rain and its presentation of a series of rainfall maps of the country.

Between 1848 and 1850 several notable publications on the Mississippi River system appeared. Andrew Brown published a paper in which he presented the results of a series of discharge and sediment measurements on the Mississippi River at Natchez. Lt. Robert A. Marr, of the United States Navy, published the results of certain observations at Memphis, Tenn., which included precipitation, mean temperature, weekly evaporation, gage heights, and daily discharge of the Mississippi River. Charles Ellett, Jr., published a memoir on the physical geography of the Mississippi Valley and did pioneer work in developing the rating-curve method of stream gaging. Caleb G. Forshey published some observations on the regimen of the Mississippi in Louisiana.

In 1850 the Congress of the United States authorized the study of hydrology on a rather large scale when it directed that a "topographical and hydrographical survey of the delta of the Mississippi River" be made to determine "the most practicable plan to secure it from inundation." Capt. A. A. Humphreys, of the United States Topographical Engineers, was put in charge of the work, and in 1854 he received the assistance of Lt. H. L. Abbot [19, p. 21]. Until 1860 this notable team labored on measurements, maps, research, theory of flow, and estimates of discharge. Their observations were numerous and very painstaking, and their conclusions were carefully drawn and well supported. Their work has stood the test of time, and to a large extent it has blazed the trail for modern hydrology both in this country and in Europe. Their comprehensive report, published in 1861, includes a history of the hydraulics of rivers [19, pp. 184–197], together with a critical estimate of the work done on this subject prior to that time.

In 1855 J. B. Francis [13] published the results of numerous experiments, made in his pioneer hydraulic laboratory in Lowell, Mass., on the discharge of water over weirs. So highly regarded were these experiments that in 1895 Herschel [17, p. 108] said that "if weirs are to be looked on as devices for measuring water, we have in Francis' Lowell hydraulic experiments nearly all that will ever be needed upon that subject. . . . As is well known, no expense was spared in the conduct of the Lowell experiments to insure extreme accuracy, and as a consequence the boon of exact knowledge on the cases of weir discharge treated in the book named has been conferred, by these experiments, on succeeding generations."

In a different attempt to measure flowing water, the quest for a satisfactory coefficient for Chézy's formula has been continued since the publication of that formula. Probably the most complicated formula ever devised for determining that elusive coefficient was published by the Swiss engineers Ganguillet and Kutter, in 1869 [15]. In 1890 another formula to find Chézy's coefficient was proposed by an American, Robert Manning [26], and this formula has been used considerably in American practice [41, p. 138].

About the middle of the nineteenth century there appeared several publications, chiefly in France, based on extensive research in different phases of the subject of ground water. Eugène Belgrand, in the first of his many works [4], published in 1846, made the fundamental distinction between permeable and impermeable formations as applied to ground water; the Abbé Paramelle, whose treatise on ground water [37] was published in 1856; and the hydraulic engineer Henri Darcy, whose painstaking work [9], also published in 1856, established the law of the flow of ground water. Others were Jules Dupuit [11], Jean Dumas, Gustave Dumont, and Henri Bazin, who was associated with Darcy, although he remained active into the present century and made his most important contribution on the flow of water in open channels.

HYDROLOGY IN THE LAST PART OF THE NINETEENTH CENTURY AND IN THE
TWENTIETH CENTURY TO THE WORLD WAR

In the last two or three decades of the nineteenth century many engineers and geologists in Europe devoted much time to the study of hydrology in connection with the development of water supplies for public waterworks and other uses, and this activity continued into the twentieth century. Much of the work was done by members of scientific establishments of the several governments. Some idea of the extent of work that was done on the hydrology of ground water is afforded by the bibliography in the second edition of the textbook by E. Prinz [42], published in 1923, which lists 398 publications relating to the subject, all except a few of which are European, and the bibliography by Michele Gortani [16], which lists about 1,000 publications on the ground-water hydrology of Italy between 1870 and 1923.

Outstanding in France was the work of the geologist Gabriel Daubrée [10], who made a large and valuable contribution to the subject of the relation of geologic structure to the occurrence and movement of ground water, the principal results of which were published in three large volumes in 1887. Mention may also be made of Léon Pochet [39] and Edmond Maillet [25], both of whom published treatises in 1905 relating to the hydraulics of ground water; Edouard Martel [28], who devoted much work to the occurrence and movement of water in cavernous limestone; and Edouard Imbeaux [20], who since 1886 has published extensively on the subject of ground water.

The pioneer of intensive ground-water investigations in Germany was Adolph Thiem [44], who introduced field methods for making tests of the flow of ground water and applied the laws of flow in developing water supplies. Under his influence Germany became the leading country in supplying the cities with ground water, as is shown by the recent estimate that 86 percent of the water supply of Germany is derived from wells or springs. The results of his work appeared in several papers, the first in 1870. Mention may also be made of Konrad Keilhack and E. Prinz, whose comprehensive treatises on ground water appeared in 1912 and 1919, respectively; E. Ebermayer, who studied the relation of forests to water supply; A. Herzberg, who was one of the discoverers of the law of the balance between sea water and fresh ground water; and Günther Thiem [45], who developed the pumping method of determining premeability that has come into general use in this country.

In Austria notable work was done by Edouard Suess, who developed the theory of juvenile water, and by Phillip Forchheimer. In a personal communication, Karl Terzaghi makes the following comment: "It was my privilege to be intimately associated with Forchheimer for a period of more than 30 years. . . . In my opinion his contributions accomplished more in the line of clarifying our ideas concerning the movement of ground water than those of all the other contemporaneous hydrologists of Europe combined."

In nearly every European country there were during this period scientists who made contributions to ground-water hydrology, among whom the following may be mentioned: In England, William Whittaker and Horace B. Woodward; in Holland, W. Badon Ghyben, who is generally regarded as the first discoverer of the law of salt-water balance [6], Eugene Dubois, J. Pennink, and J. Versluys; in Belgium, René D'Andrimont, who also made studies of the relations of salt and fresh water; in Sweden, Johan G. Richert, who developed successful methods of artificial recharge; in Russia, P. Ototzky and Alexander Lebedeff, who studied chiefly the distribution and movement of soil moisture; in Switzerland, Albert Heim and Arnold Engler, who studied the relation of forests to water supply; in Italy, D. Spataro, G. Cuppari, and M. Canavari; and in Spain, G. Garcia. The ground-water work in the United States is briefly described on a following page. Much ground-water work has also been done in Australia, India, and Japan, and some work has been done in other parts of Asia, in Africa, and in the Latin American countries.

In the United States no regular records of stream discharge were obtained after the end of the Mississippi River work, in 1858, until 1871, when the Army Engineers began their survey of the Connecticut River. During that work T. G. Ellis devised the Ellis current meter and used it in making measurements of velocity from which rating tables were constructed. By means of these tables applied to records of daily gage heights, computations were made of the daily discharge during the years 1871 to 1874. A current meter had been devised about 1790 by Woltmann, and other meters had been devised at later dates, but the early meters were so delicate that they were not practicable for continuous or extensive use. It was not until Ellis devised his meter that the practicability of meters for stream gaging was demonstrated. Thereafter other meters were devised, and the current meter gradually became the standard means of measuring the velocity for the determination of discharge. In 1878 the State Engineer of California began a stream-gaging program by establishing 12 gaging stations, which were rated by the use of current meters. This work was discontinued about 1884. In 1881 the State Engineer of Colorado established a gaging station and rated it by a current meter. This station is still being maintained. The foregoing outline of the early history of stream gaging in Europe and America is based on information furnished by Robert Follansbee.

The United States Geological Survey was established in 1879; Maj. John W. Powell, who was intensely interested in the water resources and irrigation possibilities of the West, became its director in 1881; the first appropriation for the study of the water resources was made in 1888; and systematic stream gaging was begun the next year. The history of the hydrologic work of the Geological Survey has been recorded in detail by Follansbee [12].

Follansbee states that during the seventies there was a growing appreciation, especially by Powell, of the importance of reliable records of the water resources in connection with the development of the West, but that little quantitative information on stream flow was obtained—chiefly a few miscellaneous measurements of discharge made by means of floats. Although Powell realized the importance of knowledge of the water supply, he had no idea of the proper methods for acquiring this knowledge. He decided, however, that whatever the methods, "it will be necessary also to gage a certain number of streams at all seasons of the year, so as to ascertain their total discharge and its seasonal distribution, and also to gage a greater number of streams at certain seasons determined to be critical."

A stream-gaging camp was established at Embudo, N. Mex., on the Rio Grande, in 1888. The purpose of the camp was to teach a selected group of members of the Geological Survey the theory and practice of stream gaging. It was decided not to use either Kutter's formula or Humphreys' and Abbot's float method for measuring velocity, but instead to use a current meter. In January 1889 the first regular gaging station of the Geological Survey went into operation at Embudo. This was the beginning of the systematic work which, through many vicissitudes, has been gradually developed into the present nation-wide program of exact stream gaging. Outstanding in the early development of this program was Frederick H. Newell, who has been called the "father of systematic stream gaging." The program was developed chiefly under Nathan C. Grover, who was the chief of the Water Resources Branch of the Geological Survey from 1913 to 1939.

Prior to 1870 some general studies of ground water were made, chiefly by State geological surveys and western expeditions. During the last three decades of the nineteenth century there was great activity throughout the country in developing ground-water supplies for domestic and stock use and for railroads and public waterworks, and many of the artesian basins of the country were discovered during this period. From 1873 to 1879, in connection with the Geological Survey of Wisconsin, Thomas C. Chamberlin made a thorough study of artesian conditions in that state. His principal report on the artesian wells was published by the State Survey in 1877; his well-known paper "The requisite and qualifying conditions of artesian flow" was published by the United States Geological Survey in 1885. In 1890 Major Powell [40] presented before a committee of Congress a remarkably interesting and informative statement on the artesian conditions and prospects in the arid regions of the United States. This statement shows that considerable ground-water work had already been done and that some of the main features of the ground-water conditions of the country were already understood.

In the last decade of the nineteenth century a group of eminent American geologists directed their attention to ground water and published comprehensive and sound areal reports on the subject. Among these men were Robert T. Hill, Israel C. Russell, Nelson H. Darton, Frank Leverett, and William H. Norton. Near the end of the century notable work was done on the hydraulic phases of the subject of ground water by Allen Hazen, Franklin H. King, and Charles S. Slichter. In the early years of the present century a group of younger geologists became active in ground-water studies, among them Walter C. Mendenhall and Arthur C. Veatch.

A few observations of rainfall have been made since colonial days, and organized meteorologic observations have been made by governmental agencies since 1817, when such work was undertaken by the General Land Office. In 1870 a national weather service was established in the Signal Corps of the United States Army, and meteorologic observations were made, especially at the military stations in the interior and western parts of the country. In 1891 the United States Weather Bureau was organized in the Department of Agriculture. It developed the meteorologic program until in 1922 observations were being made at about 6,000 places in the country, river stages were observed at many points in connection with flood forecasts, records of evaporation were obtained at 38 well-distributed stations, and several hundred stations were maintained in the mountain regions of the Western States at which precise measurements were made of the depth and water contents of the snow [47].

Numerous studies of the occurrence and movement of soil moisture were made during this period in the United States as well as in Europe, most of them in the present century. A large part of this work was done by members of the United States Department of Agriculture and the State agricultural experiment stations. Special mention may be made of Eugene W. Hilgard, a pioneer in this field, whose first important publication on the subject appeared in 1860, and Lyman J. Briggs, a leader among the able workers of more recent times.

Much hydrologic work was also done by other agencies, such as the Miami Conservancy District, the Pittsburgh Flood Commission, and the hydraulic laboratories established in some of the leading universities and technical schools.

In 1904 appeared a textbook by Daniel W. Mead entitled "Notes on hydrology" [29], and in 1919 his larger and more thorough treatise entitled "Hydrology" [30]. In 1917 another very good textbook on the subject was published, "The elements of hydrology," by Adolph F. Meyer [34]. These comprehensive and systematic presentations have contributed greatly toward the development of hydrology as a distinct science.

RECENT DEVELOPMENTS

After the war of 1914–18 many large projects involving the water resources were undertaken in the different countries, and hydrologic research bearing on these projects was liberally supported by governmental funds. In connection with this increased activity in hydrology several international organizations were formed to coordinate the research in this and related subjects.

In 1919 the International Union of Geodesy and Geophysics was organized in Brussels. In the assembly of the Union in Rome in 1922 steps were taken to organize the Section of Scientific Hydrology, which was later called the International Association of Scientific Hydrology, the expression "scientific hydrology" being used to distinguish its field from that of applied hydrology. Subsequently regular meetings of this association were held as a part of the triennial assembly of the Union in Madrid, 1924; Prague, 1927; Stockholm, 1930; Lisbon, 1933; Edinburgh, 1936; and Washington, 1939.

The first All-Russian Hydrologic Congress was held in Leningrad in 1924, and the second in the same city in 1928. The first Baltic Hydrologic Conference was held in Riga in 1926 and subsequent conferences were held in Reval, 1928; Warsaw, 1930; Leningrad, 1933; Helsingfors, 1936; and Berlin, 1938. Other international organizations that relate in part to hydrology are the International Society of Soil Science, the International Congress of Oceanography, the World Power Conference, the International Congress on Large Dams, and the International Association for Hydraulic Structures Research.

The scientific work of the International Association of Scientific Hydrology is conducted chiefly through commissions, of which the principal ones at present are the Commissions on Potamology, Limnology, Subterranean Water, and Snow and Glaciers. The Commission on Glaciers was organized at the International Geological Congress in Zürich, Switzerland, in 1894, and was concerned chiefly in obtaining records of the advance and retreat of glacier fronts. After the war of 1914–18 this commission became a part of the International Association of Scientific Hydrology. On the recommendation of the American Geophysical Union, an International Commission on Snow was organized at the Lisbon assembly in 1933. James E. Church, the American authority on snow surveying, was placed at the head of the commission. At the Washington assembly in 1939 steps were taken to merge the glacier and snow commissions.

Until recently the activities of the International Association of Scientific Hydrology were conducted chiefly by hydrologists from several of the European countries, with only meager and irregular help from other countries. Beginning with the Edinburgh assembly in 1936, however, the United States has taken a very active part, and there has been a strong and wholesome movement to include every country and colonial territory of the world in the work of the association. This movement was started by Church and has the support of Otto Lütschg, of Switzerland, the president of the association, and of other leading European and American hydrologists. The most prominent feature of the Edinburgh meeting was a symposium on snow and ice at which about 80 papers were presented,

representing five continents and 18 countries or colonial territories.   For
the Washington meeting about 60 papers were presented on subterranean
water in printed, mimeographed, or typewritten form, representing all six
of the continents and 27 countries or colonial territories.

In the United States there has been a great increase in the quantity
and intensiveness of hydrologic investigations along a wide front, largely
through governmental agencies.   The investigations of these agencies
have many points of common interest but may be classified roughly according to dominant aspects—surface- and ground-water hydrology by the
Geological Survey; precipitation and related features by the Weather
Bureau; snow surveying by several agencies, coordinated through the
Western Interstate Snow Survey conferences; stream dynamics and river-
system hydrology by the Army Engineers; infiltration, erosion, and trans-
spiration by the Forest Service and Soil Conservation Service; and various
phases of hydrology by other bureaus of the Department of Agriculture,
the National Hydraulic Laboratory of the Bureau of Standards, the
Bureau of Reclamation, the Tennessee Valley Authority, and others.
Much work has also been done by hydrologists in State organizations, in
universities and technical schools, and in private practice.   This work
has been coordinated to some extent by the Water Resources Committee
of the National Resources Planning Board and its predecessors, beginning
with the Mississippi Valley Committee in 1933.

A notable development in recent years has been the establishment of
many hydraulic and hydrologic laboratories, some of which are very well
equipped.   An incomplete compilation by the Hydraulics Research Center
of the United States Waterways Experiment Station at Vicksburg, supplemented by other information, shows that there were, in 1939, about
238 such laboratories in the world, of which 109 were in the United States,
35 in Russia, 15 in Germany, 11 in Great Britain, 7 each in India, Italy,
and Sweden, and 6 each in Canada and France.   According to this compilation, 114 of these laboratories were connected with universities, technical schools, or research institutions, 91 were governmental establishments,
29 were independent, and 4 had connections that were not determined;
65 were in existence before 1920, 126 were established since 1920, and in
regard to 47 information was lacking.   At the Washington assembly a
round-table discussion was held on the utilization of these laboratories
for scientific research.

The American Geophysical Union was organized as a member of the
International Union of Geodesy and Geophysics in 1919, and the Section
of Hydrology was organized in 1930 as a constituent unit of the American
Geophysical Union and as the American representative in the International Association of Scientific Hydrology.   Hitherto there had been no
national organization representing hydrology, and consequently the Sec-

tion of Hydrology at once attracted the interest of many workers in this field throughout the country. As a result of this interest and the very generous and helpful attitude of the officers and executive committee of the Union, the new section became very active and soon gained general recognition as the national center for the science of hydrology. In 1940 it had 741 members, and including that year it has published in the Annual Transactions of the American Geophysical Union about 600 technical papers and reports, covering about 3,000 pages of printed matter.

Two effective policies were adopted by the Section of Hydrology at the beginning—the appointment of permanent research committees and the movement to hold scientific meetings in different regions of the West in addition to the annual meetings in Washington. About 115 prominent scientists and engineers accepted appointment and began to work on the nine original research committees, namely the Committees on Snow; Glaciers; Evaporation; Absorption and Transpiration; Runoff; Physics of Soil Moisture; Underground water; Dynamics of Streams; and Chemistry of Natural Waters. Subsequently the third and fourth of these committees were reorganized as the Committee on Evaporation and Transpiration and the Committee on Infiltration, and two new committees were created, namely, the Committee on Rainfall and the Committee on Physical Limnology.

Successful regional meetings of the Section of Hydrology have been held as follows: 1934: Berkeley, Calif.; 1936: Pasadena, Calif.; 1937: Denver, Colo.; Spokane, Wash.; 1938: Davis, Calif., Los Angeles, Calif., Spokane, Wash.; 1939: Columbus, Ohio; 1940: Stanford University, Calif., Seattle, Wash.; 1941: Sacramento, Calif.; State College, Pa.; Dallas, Texas. Some of the regional meetings were in cooperation with other scientific and engineering societies.

The Mississïppi Valley Committee has pertinently stated: "Land, water, and people go together. The people cannot reach the highest standard of well-being unless there is the wisest use of land and water. . . Flood control, low-water control, navigation, power, water supply, sanitation, and erosion are integral parts of the picture. All of them may be encountered in the treatment of a single stream" [48, p. 3]. As civilization has advanced the per capita use of water has increased. It increased in the time of Vitruvius and Frontinus but greatly decreased in the Middle Ages and has again greatly increased in modern times; indeed, there has been a great increase in per capita consumption in this country during the last decade. Human well-being also demands the fuller control of the natural waters.

The science of hydrology is thus intimately connected with the development of human society. Frisi studied river discharge to make lasting improvements; Clinton studied hydrology to construct a great useful canal; Humphreys and Abbot investigated the Mississippi River to regulate it for human good; the Germans and the French studied ground water because their cities needed public water supplies; Blodget studied rainfall to give the pioneers information as to rain for their crops in many sections of the virgin continent; the Miami Conservancy District made hydrologic studies to plan a system of flood control; and the Russians studied certain phases of hydrology to determine whether projects such as the Dnieperstroy dam or the Greater Volga Scheme would be feasible. In each project advance in hydrology has come in response to the needs of the people, and each advance in the science has made possible more effective service.

REFERENCES

1. Adams, F. D., The origin of springs and rivers—an historical review: Fennia 50, No. 1, Helsingfors, Finland, 1928.

2. Adams, F. D., The birth and development of the geological sciences, Baltimore, 1938.

3. Beardmore, Nathaniel, Manual of hydrology, London, 1850.

4. Belgrand, Eugène, Étude hydrologique de la partie supérieure du bassin de la Seine, 1846. For an estimate of Belgrand's work see Pochet, Léon, Études sur les sources, vol. 1, pp. 3–5, 1905.

5. Blodget, Lorin, Climatology of the United States, Philadelphia, 1857.

6. Brown, J. S., A study of coastal ground water, with special reference to Connecticut: U. S. Geol. Survey Water-Supply Paper 537, 1925. Contains bibliography and digest of American and foreign literature on coastal ground water.

7. Chézy, Antoine de, Manuscript report on the Canal de l'Yvette, 1775. Part containing formula translated into English by Clemens Herschel, One hundred fifteen experiments on the carrying capacity of large riveted metal conduits, note D, pp. 117–127, John Wiley & Sons, 1897.

8. Clinton, DeWitt, Letters on the natural history and internal resources of the State of New York [By Hibernicas (pseudonym)], New York, 1822.

9. Darcy, Henri, Les fontaines publiques de la ville de Dijon, Paris, 1856.

10. Daubrée, A., Les eaux souterraines à l'époque actuelle et aux epoques anciennes, 3 vols., Paris, 1887. For an estimate of Daubrée's work see Zittel, K. A., Geschichte der Geologie und Palaeontologie bis Ende des 19 Jahrhunderts, p. 304, 1899. (English translation by M. M. Ogilvie-Gordon, pp. 200–202, 1901.)

11. Dupuit, Jules, Études théoriques et pratiques sur le mouvement des eaux courantes, Paris, 1848; also Traité de la conduite et de la distribution des eaux, Paris, 1854.

12. Follansbee, Robert, A history of the Water-Resources Branch of the United States Geological Survey to June 30, 1919 [processed], Washington, 1939. The history of later periods is in preparation.

13. Francis, J. B., Lowell hydraulic experiments, 1855.

14. Frisi, Paul, Treatise on rivers and torrents, 1762. Translated by J. Garstin in 1861.

15. Ganguillet, E., and Kutter, W. R., A general formula for the uniform flow of water in rivers and other channels, 1869. Translated into English by Rudolph Hering and John C. Trautwine, 1888.

16. Gortani, Michele, Saggio bibliografico dell'idrologia sotteranea d'Italia dal 1870 al 1923: Giorn. geologia Pratica, vol. 19, 1924. Contains also introduction concerning Italian ground-water work.

17. Herschel, Clemens, One hundred fifteen experiments on the carrying capacity of large riveted metal conduits, note D, John Wiley & Sons, 1897.

18. Herschel, Clemens, The two books on the water supply of the city of Rome of Sextus Julius Frontinus, Boston, Dana Estes & Co., 1899.

19. Humphreys, A. A., and Abbot, H. L., Report on the physics and hydraulics of the Mississippi River: Corps of Top. Engineers Prof. Paper 4, Lippincott & Co., 1861.

20. Imbeaux, Ed., Essai d'hydrogéologie, Paris, 1930.

21. Keilhack, Konrad, Grundwasser und Quellenkunde, 1st ed., Berlin, 1912.

22. King, Charles, A memoir on the cost, construction and capacity of the Croton Aqueduct, compiled from official documents, New York, 1843.

23. Krayenhoff, Cornelius, Recueil de observations hydrauliques et topographiques faites en Hollande, 1813.

24. Livingston, G. J., An annotated bibliography of evaporation: Monthly Weather Rev., June, September, November, 1908; February, March, April, May, June, 1909. Also reprint.

25. Maillet, Edmond, Essais d'hydraulique souterraine et fluviale, Paris, 1905.

26. Manning, Robert, Flow of water in open channels and pipes, Inst. Civil Eng. Ireland Trans., vol. 20, 1890.

27. Mariotté, Edmé, Traités du mouvement des eaux et des autres corps fluides, 1686. According to Keilhack [21] the complete works of Mariotté were published in Leyden in 1717.

28. Martel, E. A., Nouveau traité des eaux souterraines, Paris, 1921.

29. Mead, D. W., Notes on hydrology, Chicago, 1904.

30. Mead, D. W., Hydrology, New York, 1919.

31. Meinzer, O. E., The history and development of ground-water hydrology: Washington Acad. Sci. Jour., vol. 24, pp. 6–32, 1934.

32. Meinzer, O. E., Our water supply: Washington Acad. Sci. Jour., vol. 27, pp. 85–101, 1937.

33. Meinzer, O. E., Discussion of question No. 2 of the International Commission on Subterranean Water: Definitions of the different kinds of subterranean water: Am. Geophs. Union Trans., 1939, vol. 4, pp. 674–677, 1939.

34. Meyer, A. F., The elements of hydrology, 1st ed., New York, 1917.

35. Miller, J. F., On the meteorology of the lake district of Cumberland and Westmoreland: Royal Soc. London Philos. Trans., 1849, pt. 2.

36. Palissy, Bernard, Discours admirable de la nature des eaux et fontaines tant naturelles qu'artificielles, Paris, 1580. Morley, Henry, The Life of Bernard Palissy of Saintes, 2 vols., Boston, 1853.

37. Paramelle, L'Abbé, L'art de découvrir les sources, 1856; 4th ed., pp. 64–112, 1896.

38. [Perrault, Pierre], De l'origine des fontaines, Paris, 1678. The name of the author does not appear in this volume, but it is evidently Perrault's treatise.

39. Pochet, Léon, Études sur les sources; Hydraulique des nappes aquifères et des sources et applications pratiques, 2 vols., Paris, 1905.

40. Powell, J. W., U. S. Geol. Survey 11th Ann. Rept., pt. 2, pp. 260–278, 1891.

41. Powell, R. W., Mechanics of liquids, New York, Macmillan Co., 1940.

42. Prinz, E., Handbuch der Hydrologie, Berlin, 1st ed., 1919; 2d ed., 1923.

43. Sheppard, Thomas, William Smith, his maps and memoirs, Hull, 1920.

44. Thiem, Adolph, Über die Ergiebigkeit artesische Bohrlöcher, Schachtbrunnen, u.s.w., 1870. For a list of some of Thiem's later publications see Slichter, C. S., Theoretical investigations of the motion of ground water: U. S. Geol. Survey 19th Ann. Rept., pt. 2, p. 384, 1898.

45. Thiem, Günther, Hydrologische Methoden, Leipzig, 1906.

46. Vitruvius, Marcus Pollio, Architecture, book 8, translated from the Latin by Joseph Givilt, London, John Weale, 1860.

47. Weber, G. A., The Weather Bureau: Inst. Govt. Research Service Monographs of the United States Govt., No. 9, Washington, 1922.

48. Report of the Mississippi Valley Committee of the Public Works Administration, Washington, 1934.

CHAPTER II

PRECIPITATION

MERRILL BERNARD[1]

The march of events that marks the progress of an elemental particle of water from the sea surface into the atmosphere, to the land, and back to the sea is known as the hydrologic cycle. In its passage two major influences are exerted—heat and the gravitational pull of the earth.

Heat emanating from the sun is absorbed by the earth's surface and radiated back into the masses of free air moving over this surface. Heat

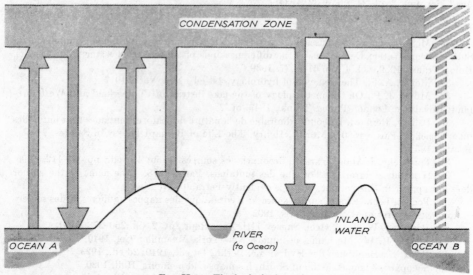

FIG. II-1.—The hydrologic cycle.

then becomes the basic cause of turbulence in the air layers coming into contact with ground, vegetal, and water surfaces. Thus, through displacement, repeated opportunity is provided for the absorption and removal of evaporated moisture.

The hydrologic cycle is not completely represented in the usually accepted sequence—from sea to land to sea. The graphic presentation of the cycle in Figure II-1 shows that a particle of water evaporated from an ocean surface may very shortly be deposited at sea as part of a raindrop and so may never reach the land. Another particle may be taken into an

[1] Principal hydrologist, Weather Bureau, United States Department of Commerce, Washington, D. C.

air mass that moves to and over an extensive land area and out to sea again before meeting the influences necessary to convert it from the vapor to the liquid state [4, 9, 1]. Still another representative element in the train of moving water vapor may be deposited as rain or snow on the land, taken into the atmosphere by evaporation, and transported back to the sea by air.

Much of the transitional water of the earth follows the more typical cycle that deposits the raindrop on the land surface, where it joins runoff in overland flow, and enters a stream that ultimately flows into the sea. A modified cycle is that in which the raindrop enters the ground and reaches the stream later through orifices below the flow line of its channel, while still another drop may continue downward under the action of gravity to some deep ground-water reservoir from which it may ultimately reach a stream or percolate into the sea.

If all the moisture in the atmosphere were suddenly precipitated there would be only enough to produce an average depth of about 1 inch of water over the total surface of the earth. What, then, accounts for the fact that rainfalls of more than 20 inches in 24 hours are experienced in many parts of the world? The answer is given by the meteorologist who observes and analyzes the factors known to bring about the convergence of vast air masses heavily burdened with moisture.

MOISTURE IN THE ATMOSPHERE

The meteorologist has taken advantage of modern development in radio engineering to improve his observational technique. Daily observations of atmospheric pressure, humidity, and temperature are now made to a height of more than 10 miles, enabling him to determine characteristics of air masses unrevealed in surface observations.

Moisture exists in the atmosphere in three states—(1) as an invisible gas in the form of water vapor, (2) as a liquid in the form of minute particles of water held in a suspended cloud mass and as fully developed raindrops, and (3) as a solid in the form of snow or hail.

Moisture in the form of water vapor acts as any other independent gas and mixes freely with the other constituent gases of the atmosphere. Like other gases, it can absorb, retain, or release heat and exert pressure.

The heterogeneous character of the atmosphere makes it difficult to express the relation between its elements. The fairly simple relations between the volume, pressure, and temperature of a small confined unit of air become complicated when applied to the free atmosphere. Particularly do complications arise when an element of the air is moved upward as the result of convection or orographic and frontal lifting. Because of these complexities it is necessary to identify the more conservative properties of air masses and make use of them in comparing and expressing

their characteristics.   Although the moisture in the atmosphere can be
conceived of in terms of the pressure exerted by the water vapor, its
nature is better understood if expressed as specific humidity, which is the
ratio of the weight of water, in grams (or some other unit of weight) to
the weight of the humid air containing the water, in kilograms (or a corresponding unit).

The temperature of the air shows the least effect of changes in pressure and humidity when stated in terms of "potential temperature."
As dry air moves upward it expands and in so doing cools at the rate of
about $5\frac{1}{2}°$F. for each 1,000 feet of rise.   This ascent is known as the
"adiabatic process," and the rate of decrease in temperature, or "lapse
rate," is called the "adiabatic lapse rate."   Potential temperature is that
temperature which an element of air will attain if brought to standard
pressure under adiabatic conditions.   If the absolute temperature and
the pressure of the air are represented by T and p respectively, and the
standard pressure by P, the potential temperature, Θ, is derived by the
equation:

$$\Theta = T \left(\frac{P}{p}\right)^{0.29}$$

The moisture content of the air on any surface of constant potential
temperature can now be expressed in terms of specific humidity.   Such
a surface is shown in Figure II-2, b, which is called an "isentropic chart."
It shows the atmospheric pressure, in millibars (and therefore altitude in
feet above the earth), on a surface in which the potential temperature was
found to be 295° Abs. on March 17, 1936.   The chart shows also the
specific humidity at this potential-temperature level; the condensation
pressure, in millibars, which is specific humidity expressed in terms of
pressure; and the position of the dry and moist "tongues" as they prevailed on that day.

Figure II-2, c, shows a cross section A-A of the isentropic chart, and
gives the vertical position of the potential-temperature surfaces, the lines
of equal specific humidity, the position of the cold front in the vertical
plane represented by the cross section, and the data on potential temperature and specific humidity obtained through radio-sonde observations
taken at San Antonio, Shreveport, Murfreesboro, and Lakehurst.

Figure II-2, a, is the "synoptic" weather map of March 17, 1936.
It shows the areas of high and low pressure as recorded on the earth's
surface, the general movement of the surface winds, the positions of the
warm front (warm air moving forward and over cold air), the cold front
(cold air moving forward and under warm air), and the area that received
rainfall during the period from 8 p.m. March 16 to 8 a.m., March 17.

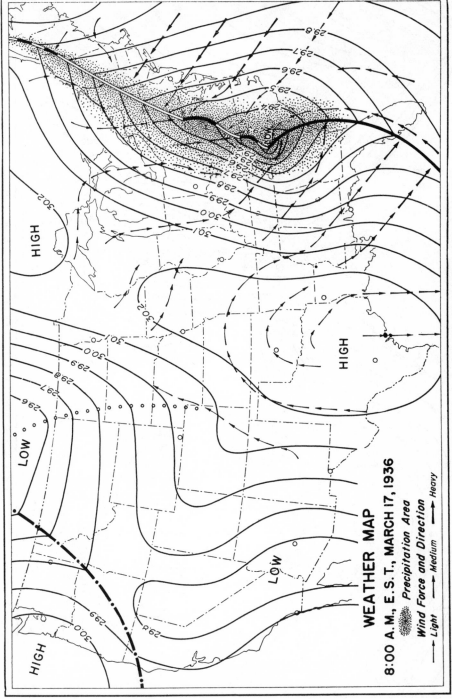

WEATHER MAP
8:00 A.M., E.S.T., MARCH 17, 1936

░ Precipitation Area

Wind Force and Direction

→ Light   → Medium   → Heavy

Fig. II-2a.—Weather map of the United States, March 17, 1936.

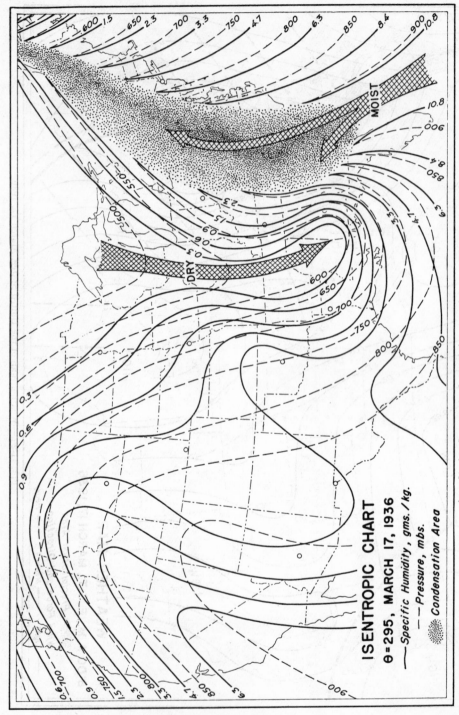

ISENTROPIC CHART
Θ = 295, MARCH 17, 1936

—— Specific Humidity , gms. / kg.
— — Pressure, mbs.
⣿⣿ Condensation Area

FIG. 11-2b.—Isentropic chart of the United States, March 17, 1936.

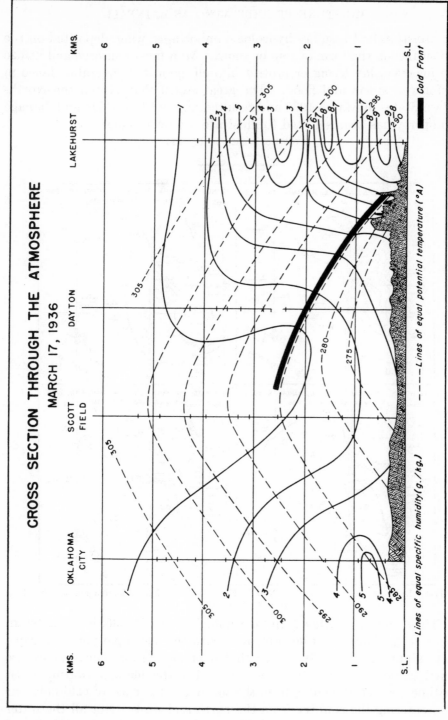

CROSS SECTION THROUGH THE ATMOSPHERE
MARCH 17, 1936

——— Lines of equal specific humidity(g./kg.)

-------- Lines of equal potential temperature (°A)

▬ Cold Front

FIG. II-2c.—Cross section through the atmosphere, March 17, 1936.

MOISTURE PRECIPITATED AS RAINFALL

Moisture first assumes hydrologic importance when deposited on the land surface in the form of rain or snow.   Man must conserve and utilize it in his everyday living or protect himself against its overabundance in the form of storm and flood.   The great storm that visited the Northeastern States in March 1936 and resulted in great loss of life and damage to property has been selected to illustrate the overabundance.

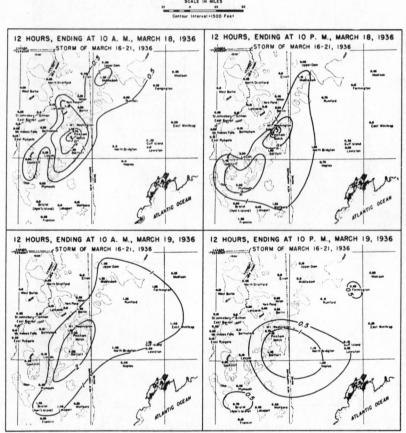

FIG. II-3.—Isohyetal maps of northern New England showing 12-hour increments of rainfall for March 18-19, 1936.

The synoptic weather map for 8 a.m. March 17, 1936, is presented in Figure II-2, *a*, and is to be compared with the accompanying isentropic chart, Figure II-2, *b*.   It is seen that overrunning and convergence are occurring along the frontal zone separating the mass of warm, moist maritime air (*mTw*) coming from the south and the mass of cold polar air (*cPw*) entering the country from the north and west.   Not all the water contained in the moist tongue was deposited as rain, although it is believed

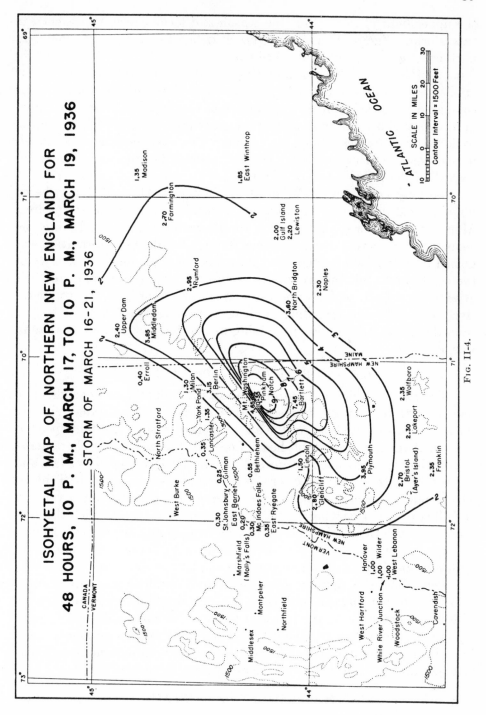

ISOHYETAL MAP OF NORTHERN NEW ENGLAND FOR
48 HOURS, 10 P. M., MARCH 17, TO 10 P. M., MARCH 19, 1936
STORM OF MARCH 16-21, 1936

Fig. II-4.

the upper limit of rainfall for the season and locality was approached in this storm. Figure II-3 shows the distribution of precipitation over northern New England in the 12-hour periods ending at 10 a.m. and 10 p.m. March 18 and 10 a.m. and 10 p.m. March 19, 1936. The erratic application of rain throughout the progressive phases of the storm is to be compared with the symmetrical pattern of total rainfall shown in Figure II-4. As puddles first appear when a garden hose is played over a lawn, so do "wave impulses" along the extended front between the opposing air masses tend to bring about the concentrations that appear as centers or "eyes" of the isohyetal maps of rainfall.

The maps of storm rainfall displayed in Figures II-3 and II-4 are based upon plotted depths of rain observed at stations within the storm area. Many of the records contributing to the data were received from the cooperative observers of the Weather Bureau. Valuable information was gained from individuals who were impressed with the unusual severity of the storm and took the trouble to record the amounts coming to their attention. Of particular importance were the records of the comparatively few automatic recording rain gages in the region, for it was largely from these that information pertaining to the time distribution of rainfall was obtained.

SIZE AND RATE OF FALL OF RAINDROPS

The rate at which a raindrop can fall through still air depends upon its size. Its velocity will increase until equilibrium between the weight of the drop and the resistance of the air is reached, when a constant speed or "terminal velocity" is established. Lenard [7] measured the characteristics of raindrops suspended by upward currents of air produced by a fan, and the results with some corrections in computations, are given in Table 1. The results of Lenard's experiments in determining the terminal velocity of falling drops of varying diameter appear in Table 2, in which they are compared with the results obtained by Laws [6] in measuring the velocities of drops of water falling through still air. Velocities of raindrops in nature probably lie somewhere between the two sets of values.

For drops with diameters greater than 5.5 millimeters the terminal velocity does not increase with the size of the drop but tends to decrease. This is accounted for by the fact that the drop becomes deformed, spreading out horizontally, with the result that the air resistance is increased. For diameters greater than 5.5 millimeters the deformation is sufficient to break up the drops before terminal velocity is reached.

MEASUREMENT OF RAINFALL

Automatic recording rain gages are, in general, of two types. One registers increments of fall as a small bucket fills, tips, and records; the other, known as the weighing type, makes an autographic record of accumulative precipitation as it falls. A weighing rain gage is shown in figure II-5. This particular gage is equipped with a flexible shield, the effect of which is to minimize the influence of wind on the "catch" of the gage. A typical autographic record for a rain gage of this type is shown in figure II-6. Besides the total amount of rainfall, the time distribution and rate of fall can be determined from such a record.

TABLE 1.—*Characteristics of falling raindrops*

Drops			Number of drops per square meter per second								
Diameter		Volume (cubic millimeters)	Rain "looking very ordinary"	Rain with breaks during which the sun shone	Beginning of a short fall like a thundershower	Sudden rain from a small cloud	Violent rain like a cloudburst, with some hail	Period of heaviest cloudburst	Period of less heavy cloudburst	Ending period of continuous fall
Millimeters	Inch		1	2	3	4	5	6	7	8	9
0.5	0.019	0.065	1,000	1,600	129	60	0	100	514	679	7
1.0	0.039	0.524	200	120	100	280	50	1,300	423	524	233
1.5	0.059	1.77	140	60	73	160	50	500	359	347	113
2.0	0.079	4.19	140	200	100	20	150	200	138	295	46
2.5	0.098	8.18	0	0	29	20	0	0	156	205	7
3.0	0.118	14.1	0	0	57	0	200	0	138	81	0
3.5	0.138	22.4	0	0	0	0	0	0	0	28	32
4.0	0.157	33.5	0	0	0	0	50	0	0	20	39
4.5	0.177	47.7	0	0	0	0	0	200	101	0	0
5.0	0.196	65.4	0	0	0	0	0	0	0	0	25
Total...............			1,480	1,980	488	540	500	2,300	1,829	2,179	502
Rate of rainfall:											
Millimeters per minute			0.06	0.07	0.10	0.04	0.31	0.72	0.57	0.38	0.25
Inches per hour.......			0.14	0.16	0.23	0.10	0.74	1.69	1.35	0.89	0.60

TABLE 2.—*Velocity of falling raindrops*

Diameter (millimeters)	Maximum falling velocity (meters per second)	
	Lenard	Laws
1.0	4.4	
2.0	5.9	6.6
3.0	7.0	8.0
4.0	7.7	8.8
5.0	7.9	9.2
5.5	8.0	9.3
6.5	7.8	

The record of the weighing rain gage is in the form of a "mass curve," whereas the data from a nonrecording gage are usually limited to depth

Fig. II-5.—Recording weighing rain gage.

Table 3.—*Unusual rainfalls in the United States*

Station	Amount (inches)	Duration		Intensity inches per hour	Date
		Hr.	Min.		
Opids Camp, Calif.	1.03		1	61.80	Apr. 5, 1926
St. Louis, Mo.	5.05		15	20.20	Aug. 15, 1848
Guinea, Va.	9.25		30	18.50	Aug. 24, 1906
Galveston, Tex.	3.95		14	16.93	June 14, 1871
Buffalo, N. Y.	0.79		3	15.80	Mar. 20, 1897
Augusta, Ga.	1.24		5	14.88	June 18, 1911
Norfolk, Va.	2.48		10	14.88	Aug. 20, 1888
Taylor, Tex.	8.02		40	12.03	Sept. 9, 1921
Brownsville, Tex.	1.20		6	12.00	Oct. 23, 1884
Catskill, N. Y.	10.00	1		10.00	July 26, 1819
Sandusky, Ohio	2.25		15	9.00	July 11, 1879
Erie, Pa.	2.02		15	8.08	June 17, 1886
D'Hanis, Tex.	21.84	3 −		7.28+	May 31, 1935
Springbrook, Mont.	6.94	1	5	6.41	June 20, 1921
Catskill, N. Y.	18.00	7	30	2.40	July 26, 1819
Hearne, Tex.	24.00	24		1.00	June 28, 1899
Kaplan, La.	23.00+	24		.96+	Aug. 9, 1940
Taylor, Tex.	23.11	24		.96	Sept. 9–10, 1921
Alta Pass, N. C.	22.22	24 −		.92+	July 15–16, 1916
Springbrook, Mont.	11.50	14 −		.82+	June 19–20, 1921
Beaulieu, Minn.	10.75	24		.45	July 20, 1909

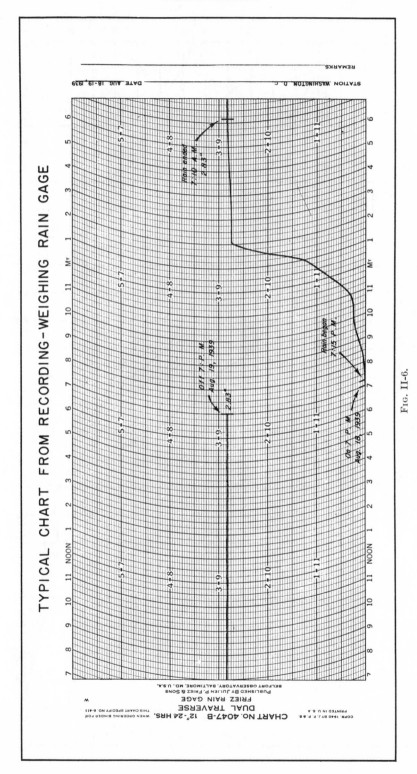

TYPICAL CHART FROM RECORDING-WEIGHING RAIN GAGE

Fig. II-6.

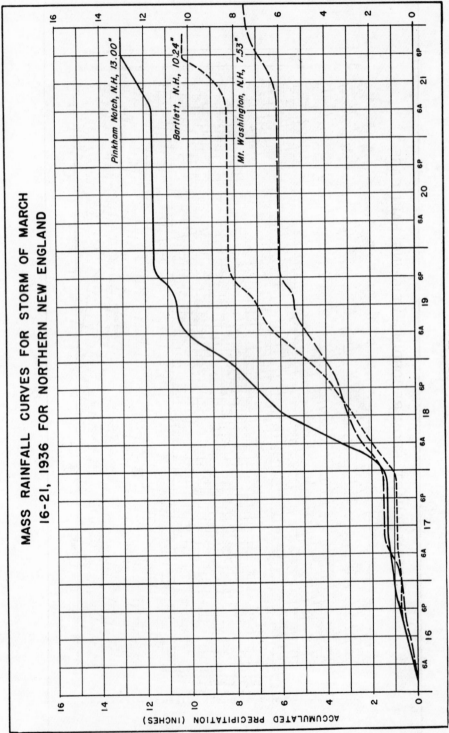

MASS RAINFALL CURVES FOR STORM OF MARCH
16-21, 1936 FOR NORTHERN NEW ENGLAND

Pinkham Notch, N.H., 13.00"

Bartlett, N.H., 10.24"

Mt. Washington, N.H., 7.53"

ACCUMULATED PRECIPITATION (INCHES)

Fig. II-7.

measurements taken at infrequent intervals and require a high degree of ingenuity on the part of the analyst for effective utilization. Mass curves for three stations within the area covered by the storm of March 16–21, 1936, are shown in figure II-7. The relation between the cumulative depth of rainfall and its duration at Pinkham Notch, N. H., and in selected areas is shown in figure II-8.

EXCESSIVE RATES OF RAINFALL

In general, the intensity of rainfall is inversely proportioned to the length of the period throughout which it can sustain itself. This is true because the dynamic meteorologic forces that cause heavy rainfall are also the means of shifting it with relative rapidity from one area to another, so that no point within the area of an intensive storm is subjected to a heavy downpour for any great length of time.

TABLE 4.—*Intensity-duration-frequency formulas*

Locality	Formula	Reference
Boston	$i = \dfrac{16F^{0.27}}{(t + 7)^{0.7}}$	Sherman [8]
Boston	$i = \dfrac{15.6(1.6F - 0.6)^{0.22}}{(t + 6)^{0.7}}$	Kennison [5]
New York	$i = \dfrac{42.5F^{0.3}}{(t + 12)^{0.85}}$	Bleich [3]
New York	$i = \dfrac{28F^{0.22}}{\left(t + \dfrac{9}{F^{0.20}}\right)^{0.75}}$	Bernard [3]
Detroit	$i = \dfrac{37.6F^{0.263}}{(t + 8)^{0.855}}$	Wagnitz and Wilcoxen [3]
Kansas City	$i = \dfrac{10F^{0.183}}{t^{0.444}}$	Bernard [2] and Yarnell [10] (5 to 60 minutes)
Kansas City	$i = \dfrac{44F^{0.183}}{t^{0.79}}$	Bernard [2] and Yarnell [10] (60 to 1,440 minutes)

Table 3 contains examples of unusual rainfall intensities experienced in the United States.

The relations among the intensity, duration, and frequency of rainfall play a particularly important part in the solution of many engineering problems. It is in this form that statistical relations are usually expressed. Intensity is understood to be the average rate at which rain falls throughout a given period of time. Presented as intensity-duration-frequency curves the results are understood to be average rates of rainfall, i, for durations of t minutes, reached or exceeded once on the average in F years.

A general expression for rainfall intensity is

$$i = \frac{KF^x}{(t + b)^n}$$

in which K, b, x, and n are coefficients and exponents varying in value with geographic location and F is the frequency in years with which average intensities are reached or exceeded.

Table 4 compares various intensity-duration-frequency formulas.

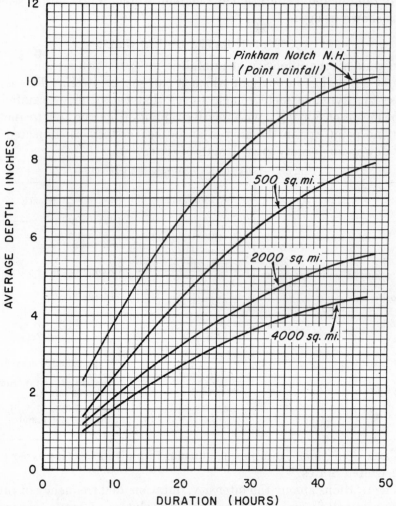

FIG. II-8.—Relation between cumulative depth and duration of rainfall in storm of March 16–21, 1936, in northern New England.

RAINFALL RELATED TO AREA

The foregoing discussion has considered only the relations between intensity, depth, time, and frequency at a single locality. These relations are much more complex when given areal application. In general, the depth of rainfall varies inversely with the area covered, as indicated in the isohyetal maps of the storm of March 16–21, 1936 (Figs. II-3 and II-4). Typical area-depth curves for this storm are shown in figure II-9.

EVOLUTION OF THE NATIONAL NETWORK OF PRECIPITATION STATIONS

Our knowledge of storm rainfall, as for all phenomena associated with vast quantities beyond the possibility of direct measurement, must be gained through a procedure of sampling. The dimensional ratio between the sample, the 8-inch rain gage, and that portion of the storm area repre-

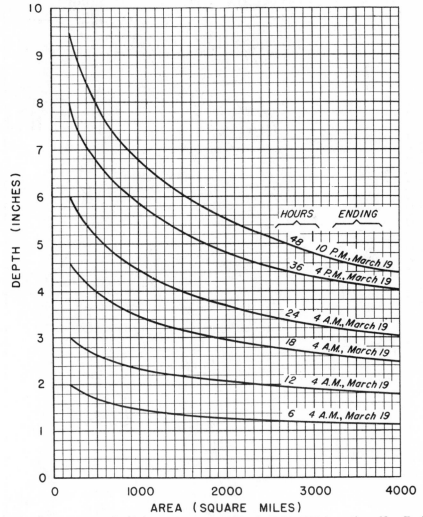

HOURS   ENDING

48   10 P.M., March 19
36   4 P.M., March 19
24   4 A.M., March 19
18   4 A.M., March 19
12   4 A.M., March 19
6   4 A.M., March 19

FIG. II-9.—Maximum area-depth curves for storm of March 16–21, 1936, in northern New England.

sented by the gage (which for most gages in use at the present time is several hundred square miles) is at first thought somewhat difficult to accept with confidence. However, an experience of many years indicates a consistent reliability and accounts for the general acceptance of the 8-inch gage as a rainfall sampler.

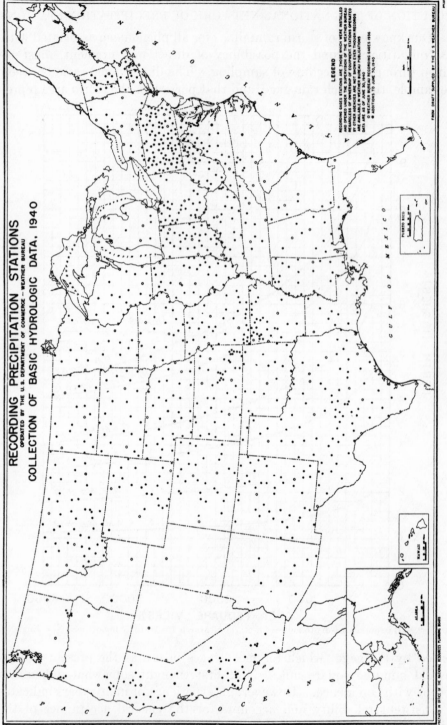

FIG. II-10a.

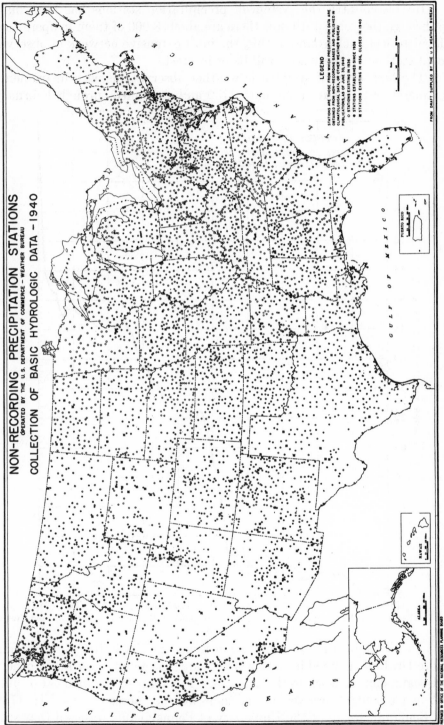

Fig. II-10b

In this country the system of precipitation stations has been built up through the years until now there are about 8,000 of them in operation. The historical background of this, the most extensive network of observational stations in the world, will be of interest.

The first series of systematic weather observations with instruments in America was begun in January 1730 and continued through February

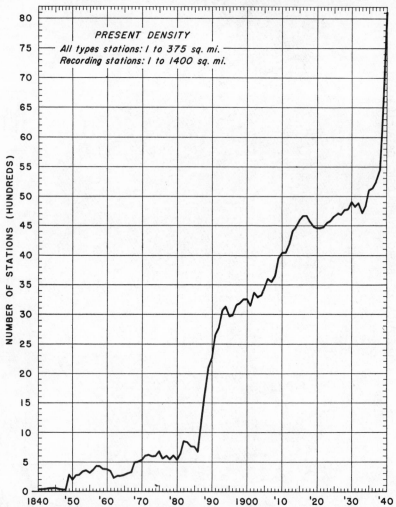

FIG. II-11.—Historical development of the network of precipitation stations in the United States, 1840–1940.

1753 by Dr. John Lining, a physician living in Charleston, S. C. Long before Dr. Lining ended his noteworthy career as an observer many others had begun similar work in the colonies. Members of the medical profession in particular were zealous in their weather observations. In 1789 Dr. Benjamin Rush, at the University of Pennsylvania, insisted that students in his graduating classes "preserve a register of the weather and its influence upon the vegetable production of the year. Above all, the record of epidemics of every season, their times of appearing and disappearing, and the connection of the weather with each of them."

Official recognition of the general need for a network of stations to take weather observations came in 1814, when John C. Calhoun, then Secretary of War, issued orders for all surgeons on duty at Army posts to keep records of precipitation and temperature. This activity did not get under way until 1819 and was not organized as a service until 1825. By this time all sizable communities had become "weather-conscious," boards of health were encouraging public-spirited citizens to obtain instru-

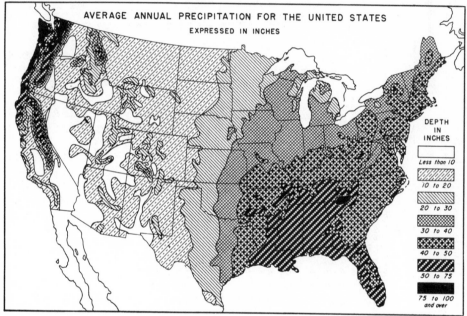

FIG. II-12.

ments and make observations, and most newspapers were publishing weekly reports on weather. About 1847 the Smithsonian Institution began to coordinate the activities of the individual observers, and within a few years the network of climatologic stations had spread over the entire United States. Records of the United States Patent Office and the United States Signal Corps were added to the collection, and on July 1, 1891, all were turned over to the newly organized United States Weather Bureau.

Many prominent names are to be found in early weather history. Washington's diary, the simultaneous observations of Jefferson and Madison, Benjamin Franklin's records, and the diary of Oliver Wendell Holmes are contributions to the early climatologic record.

In Figure II-10*a* and *b* are shown the networks of recording and non-recording gages, respectively. Figure II-11 is a graph showing the pro-

TABLE 5.—*Precipitation, in inches, at Weather Bureau stations*
[All records to 1940 inclusive]

Station	Years of record	Short periods			Daily			Monthly		Yearly		
		Maximum 5 minutes	Maximum 15 minutes	Maximum 60 minutes	Maximum	Date	Average	Maximum	Month and year	Average	Maximum	Year
Boston, Mass	70	0.55	1.12	1.80	6.04	July 9, 1921	3.74	11.7	July, 1921	41.1	65.5	1878
New Haven, Conn	68	.84	1.96	2.38	8.73	Aug. 8–9, 1874	4.41	17.1	July, 1889	46.1	60.3	1888
Albany, N.Y.	115	.60	1.17	2.97	4.75	Oct. 9, 1903	3.87	8.9	Sept., 1890	37.1	49.8	1827
Philadelphia, Pa.	121	.65	1.34	3.81	5.89	Aug. 4, 1898	4.48	12.1	Aug., 1911	42.3	58.1	1859
Baltimore, Md.	70	.80	1.92	2.87	7.62	Aug. 23, 1933	4.64	12.3	Aug., 1911	42.7	62.4	1889
Washington, D. C.	70	.77	1.51	3.42	7.31	Sept. 12, 1934	4.41	17.5	Sept., 1934	42.2	61.3	1889
Norfolk, Va.	70	.66	1.36	3.34	6.64	Aug. 20, 1933	5.73	12.4	July, 1939	45.1	70.7	1889
Columbia, S. C.	67	.74	1.39	2.34	5.50	Sept. 6, 1928	5.61	14.6	Sept., 1928	43.5	63.3	1873
Atlanta, Ga.	75	.88	1.57	3.23	7.36	Mar. 29, 1886	5.38	15.8	Jan., 1883	48.5	67.7	1929
Jacksonville, Fla.	76	.78	1.65	3.22	9.86	Sept. 26, 1894	7.13	21.8	Sept., 1908	50.5	82.0	1885
Meridian, Miss.	51	.71	1.58	3.66	9.50	Apr. 17, 1906	5.30	20.1	June, 1900	52.8	71.9	1900
Nashville, Tenn.	70	.75	1.33	2.09	6.05	Nov. 21, 1900	5.16	14.8	Jan., 1937	46.8	67.2	1880
Louisville, Ky.	68	.74	1.37	2.70	5.50	July 4, 1896	4.25	19.2	Jan., 1937	42.8	56.5	1882
Cleveland, Ohio	85	.78	1.46	1.88	4.97	Sept. 2, 1901	3.43	10.6	July, 1910	34.1	53.5	1878
Detroit, Mich.	70	.86	1.86	3.09	4.75	Aug. 1, 1925	3.46	8.8	July, 1878	31.8	47.7	1880
Indianapolis, Ind.	76	.83	1.30	2.68	6.80	Sept. 4, 1895	3.94	13.1	July, 1875	40.0	56.5	1862
Springfield, Ill.	61	.61	1.41	2.75	5.94	June 5, 1917	4.34	15.2	Sept., 1926	35.9	58.2	1882
Minneapolis, Minn.	104	.81	1.17	2.29	6.35	July 27, 1892	4.07	11.9	July, 1892	27.0	49.7	1849
Des Moines, Iowa	64	.66	1.36	2.65	5.14	June 20, 1881	4.76	15.8	June, 1881	31.5	56.8	1881
St. Louis, Mo.	103	.59	1.39	3.47	7.02	Aug. 19, 1915	4.47	17.1	June, 1848	39.2	68.8	1858
Little Rock, Ark.	63	.63	1.35	2.42	9.58	Apr. 9, 1913	4.98	18.0	Jan., 1937	47.8	75.5	1882
El Paso, Tex.	72	.43	.90	1.57	6.50	July 9, 1881	1.75	8.2	July, 1881	8.7	21.8	1856
Oklahoma City, Okla.	50	.60	1.49	3.10	7.87	Oct. 1, 1927	4.93	14.1	June, 1932	31.1	52.0	1901
Lincoln, Nebr.	63	.69	1.70	3.11	8.38	Aug. 29, 1910	4.12	14.2	Aug., 1910	27.3	40.0	1914
Helena, Mont.	59	.46	.76	1.06	3.69	June 5, 1908	2.19	6.7	May, 1927	12.9	20.0	1881
Cheyenne, Wyo.	68	.59	1.36	2.51	4.70	July 15, 1896	2.43	7.7	Apr., 1900	14.6	22.7	1905
Salt Lake City, Utah	76	.35	.76	1.17	2.72	May 3, 1901	1.94	5.8	Nov., 1875	16.4	27.6	1866
Seattle, Wash.	63	.29	.52	.80	3.52	Dec. 12, 1921	5.68	15.3	Dec., 1933	33.8	56.4	1879
Portland, Oreg.	69	.40	.83	1.31	7.66	Dec. 13, 1904	7.13	20.1	Dec., 1882	42.3	67.2	1882
Reno, Nev.	70	.32	.69	.93	2.71	Jan. 27–28, 1903	1.44	6.8	Jan., 1916	7.1	13.7	1890
San Francisco, Calif.	91	.33	.65	1.07	4.67	Jan. 29, 1881	4.73	24.4	Jan., 1862	21.8	38.8	1884
Los Angeles, Calif.	63	.44	.81	1.51	5.42	Sept. 24–25, 1939	3.10	15.8	Dec., 1890	15.1	40.3	1884

gressive expansion of the network of climatologic stations, at all of which precipitation has been or is being measured. The number has steadily increased except for minor reductions at times of such national disturbances as the war with Mexico (when the Army posts were preoccupied

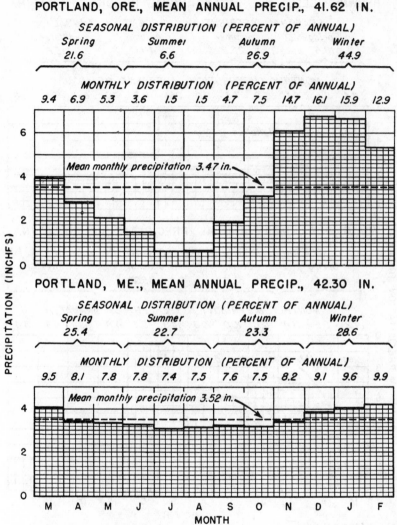

Fig. II-13.—Distribution of average monthly and seasonal precipitation at Portland, Ore., and Portland, Me.

with weightier matters), the Civil War, the World War of 1914–18, and the usual retrenchment that follows periods of business depression.

RAINFALL REGIMEN OF THE UNITED STATES

It would be difficult to isolate a phase of our national life that does not in some degree reflect the influence of precipitation. In the humid

East the principal concern is that of conducting the runoff from excessive rainfall back to the sea with minimum damage to the property occupying the flood plains of the rivers. In the arid West attention is directed to the conservation of all the rain that falls. Maps showing the geographic

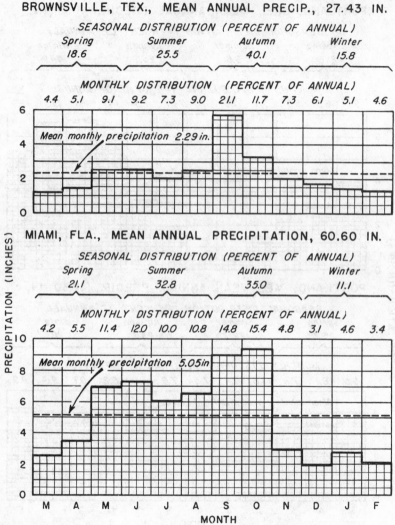

Fig. II-14.—Distribution of average monthly and seasonal precipitation at Brownsville, Tex., and Miami, Fla.

distribution of various vegetal covers, crop types, land-use practices, population, electric-power development, and stream-system density all conform in general to the pattern of average annual precipitation shown in Figure II-12. Resort to the smoothing process in determining averages has masked the degree of variation in rainfall and snowfall from month to month, season to season, and year to year. As the apparently unrelated patterns of rainfall increments in Figure II-2 combined to produce the fairly symmetrical pattern of the total storm, so the patterns of the hundreds of storms occurring within the period of record have combined to give the picture of the country's precipitation regimen shown in Figure II-12.

Table 5 gives summarized precipitation data gathered at selected Weather Bureau stations throughout the country. Marked differences from station to station reflect the regionalization of climate and emphasize the degree of variation in rainfall characteristics known to exist throughout the country.

SEASONAL DISTRIBUTION OF RAINFALL

The precipitation regimen of a region is controlled by many factors, among which are (1) position relative to source regions of moisture; (2) proximity to a "battle ground" upon which the aggressive cold air meets the masses of warm moist air and subjects them to conditions under which they can no longer retain their moisture; (3) presence of mountain ranges, which may in one place minimize the occurrence and intensity of rain and in another add an influence conducive to greater and more frequent rainfall; and (4) altitude of the region, which determines to a great extent whether the greater proportion of the total precipitation will be in the form of rain or of snow. Two widely separated localities may have the same average annual precipitation but a distinctly different seasonal distribution. Both Portland, Oreg., and Portland, Maine, have an average annual precipitation of about 42 inches. The marked contrast in the distribution of this amount throughout the year at the two places is shown in Figure II-13. On the other hand, Miama, Fla., and Brownsville, Tex., have strikingly similar patterns but quite different amounts of mean annual rainfall (Figure II-14), owing to differences in the positions of these cities with respect to source of moisture and prevailing movement of air masses.

REFERENCES

1. Bernard, Merrill, Hydrometeorology—a coordination of meteorology and hydrology: Am. Geophys. Union Trans., 1938, pt. 2, pp. 598–602.

2. Bernard, Merrill, Modified rational method of estimating flood flows, in Low dams, app. A, Nat. Resources Comm., 1938.

3. Bleich, S. D., Rainfall studies from New York, N. Y.: Am. Soc. Civil Eng. Trans., vol. 100, 1935.

4. Holzman, Benjamin, Sources of moisture for precipitation in the United States: U. S. Dept. Agr. Tech. Bull. 589, 1937.

5. Kennison, H. F., Sixty-year rainfall record analyzed: Civil Eng., Nov. 1940.

6. Laws, J. O., Measurements of the fall-velocities of water drops and raindrops (to be published in Am. Geophys. Union Trans., 1941).

7. Lenard, P., Über Regen: Meteorol. Zeitschr., Band 21, Braunschweig, 1904.

8. Sherman, C. W., Frequency and intensity of rainfall, Boston, Mass.: Am. Soc. Civil Eng. Trans., vol. 95, p. 951, 1931.

9. Thornthwaite, C. W., The hydrologic cycle reexamined: Soil Conservation, vol. 3, No. 4, 1937.

10. Yarnell, D. L., Rainfall intensity—frequency data: U. S. Dept. Agr. Misc. Pub. 204. 1935.

CHAPTER III

EVAPORATION FROM FREE WATER SURFACES

Sidney T. Harding[1]

INTRODUCTION

Evaporation is the process by which a liquid is changed to a vapor or gas. This chapter is limited to evaporation from free water surfaces; evaporation from soil surfaces is treated in chapter VIII. This chapter has been prepared with the assistance of the Evaporation Committee of the Section on Hydrology of the American Geophysical Union, although individual members of the committee may not agree with all statements made. Those who have assisted include H. F. Blaney, N. W. Cummings, Robert Follansbee, J. A. Folse, R. E. Horton, I. E. Houk, R. E. Kennedy, Carl Rohwer, and C. M. Saville.

The measurement of the evaporation from water surfaces is obviously the most direct means for its determination. However, there are few natural water surfaces of large extent for which records can be obtained. A direct determination of the evaporation from a large natural water surface requires the measurement of all elements of inflow and draft, with the unaccounted for difference assigned to evaporation. This places all the errors of measurement in the resulting evaporation. Where evaporation is a small percentage of the total supply, small errors in the main items represent a large difference in the resulting estimate of evaporation.

There are some lakes for which conditions are sufficiently favorable to permit such direct measurements, but they represent only a small proportion of the areas for which evaporation needs to be known.

Evaporation from an exposed water surface is subject to the effect of all the varying factors that result from such exposure. The resulting evaporation is a complex process, difficult to analyze and difficult to correlate with measurements of individual factors that affect its amount. Even if the relation of evaporation to all the factors that affect it could be determined quantitatively, full and accurate observations necessary for application of these relations would be difficult to make, as these factors vary over the surface of any large water area and change rapidly.

Although much theoretical study and experimental work has been directed toward determining the laws controlling evaporation and the

[1] Professor of irrigation, University of California, Berkeley, Calif.

quantitative effect of the factors involved, there is still much difference of opinion regarding this subject. Several lines of approach have been used. Some have undertaken theoretical analyses of rates of diffusion and character of air movement in contact with and above the water surface, from which they have derived formulas for evaporation based on such elements. Others have analyzed the disposal of solar radiation received by a water surface and have undertaken to determine evaporation from the amount of water that the net solar radiation could convert to vapor. Those more directly concerned with quantitative results on large water surfaces have attempted to correlate measured evaporation with recorded items of climate, in an attempt to derive formulas for application where climatic records were available but where evaporation had not been directly measured. Many, impatient with the inability of any of these methods to give a complete basis from which local rates of evaporation could be estimated with the closeness needed in many water supply matters, have attempted to measure evaporation from small sample areas, using direct observations from various forms of pans, tanks, or atmometers.

None of these methods have yet produced a complete answer that meets the standards of the physicist in the expression of the principles governing the process of evaporation and also meets the needs of engineers and others requiring quantitative results. To meet theoretical requirements any expression for evaporation must include correctly all factors that affect its amount; to meet the needs of those seeking to determine the amount of evaporation any law or formula must include only those items which are measurable and for which adequate records exist or can be obtained.

In view of this situation it is not surprising that there is no general agreement regarding the best method of determining evaporation or formulas for its expression. Similarly no general agreement can be expected regarding the scope and content of a chapter that attempts to present a general review of this subject. An effort has been made in this chapter to describe the different points of view regarding evaporation from free water surfaces, but the treatment emphasizes those phases of the subject with which the author's work has been most closely concerned. These are, in general, the engineering uses of quantitative results.

This chapter is further limited to evaporation from water surfaces that are fully exposed to all local climatic factors. Evaporation from small water areas under controlled exposure that can be maintained under constant conditions depends on the same physical principles that control evaporation from large fully exposed water areas. Experiments on evaporation under controlled conditions are useful in determining the principles governing evaporation and the quantitative effect of changes in the controlling factors. Such controlled experiments may have only partial application to fully exposed areas if the observations required for their application are difficult to make or if conditions affecting the exposed water area vary over its different parts or change rapidly with small intervals of time. This accounts for the difficulty of applying results obtained in work relating to heating or ventilating practice to the conditions of large exposed water areas.

Evaporation from the ocean is important in meteorology and oceanography as an element in climate. The conditions affecting evaporation differ on water surfaces of relatively small area surrounded by land and on water areas, such as oceans, which may be too large to be materially affected by marginal conditions.

PROCESS OF EVAPORATION

The rate at which water particles may leave the water and enter the adjacent air depends upon the heat supply of the water and the condition of the air. Such particles are continually leaving the surface of the water. If the air above the water is still and saturated, it cannot retain additional moisture and the water particles return to the water surface. If the air in contact with the water is not saturated or is replaced as it approaches its vapor-holding capacity, the rate of evaporation is determined by the heat supply available to produce evaporation.

Vapor may be removed from a water surface by diffusion, by convection, or by wind action. Diffusion is continuous whenever the vapor pressure of the air over the water is below that corresponding to the temperature of the water at its surface. Convection occurs when the water is warmer than the air; the heating of the air in contact with the water causes upward air movement. Such removal of vapor by convection would occur in still air; but as still air seldom occurs on fully exposed water surfaces, vapor removal by convection is usually combined with removal by wind action. Vapor removal by wind action is most active when wind movement is turbulent. Fully laminar wind movement over large water areas would not change the character of air in contact with the water.

FACTORS AFFECTING EVAPORATION

Attempts have been made to correlate evaporation with temperature of the air and water, differences in vapor pressure, humidity of the air, solar radiation, wind movement both in amount and in character, altitude or barometric pressure, and the chemical quality of the water. Some of these factors are themselves interrelated.

DIFFERENCES IN VAPOR PRESSURE

The effect of differences in the vapor pressure at the temperatures of the water and of the air has been recognized as a factor in the rate of evaporation since Dalton [7] published his laws in 1802. If other factors remain constant, evaporation is proportional to the deficit in vapor pressure, which is the difference between the pressure of saturated vapor at the temperature of the water and the vapor pressure of the air. The combined effect of the vapor pressure at the temperature of the water and of the dew point of the air is generally expressed in terms of their difference. Their determination requires the measurement of the temperatures of the air and water and of the moisture content of the air. The moisture content of the air is usually measured by a sling psychrometer consisting of wet-and dry-bulb thermometers. The pressure of the aqueous vapor corresponding to the observed temperatures t and t' is computed from the formula

$$e = e' - 0.000367P(t - t')\left(1 + \frac{t' - 32}{1571}\right)$$

in which t and t' are the temperatures recorded by the wet- and dry-bulb thermometers in degrees Fahrenheit; P is the barometric pressure of the air in inches, all corrections having been applied; and e' is the maximum or saturation pressure of aqueous vapor at the temperature recorded by the wet bulb. The United States Weather Bureau has published tables [24] giving the numerical values for the items needed in using this formula.

Difference in vapor pressure includes any effects of absolute or relative humidity. Absolute humidity represents the moisture present in the air; relative humidity represents the moisture present in the air in terms of the percentage of the moisture that would be present in fully saturated air of the same temperature.

TEMPERATURE

Evaporation is affected by the temperature of both the air and the water. The rate of vapor emission is dependent upon the water temperature. The rate of vapor removal is affected by the temperature of the air. The vapor-holding capacity of the air varies with its temperature; the difference in vapor pressure between the water and the air is directly affected by the temperature of the air.

That evaporation is not dependent upon mean air temperatures alone is illustrated by the results plotted in Figure III-1. These all represent records of evaporation from large water areas based on measurements of inflow and outflow [11 and later records]. For lakes 200 feet in depth, such as Walker and Pyramid Lakes, for the same mean monthly air temperatures the evaporation in the later months of the year is larger than that in the earlier months. Eagle Lake, with depths of 30 to 50 feet, shows a temperature loop of similar type with smaller differences. For lakes having depths of 10 to 20 feet, such as Tulare and Elsinore Lakes, the temperature loop is reversed, with larger amounts of evaporation in some of the early months.

HEAT SUPPLY

Heat is the source of energy that causes evaporation. The primary source of heat on the earth's surface is the sun, and the amount of evapora-

MONTHLY EVAPORATION, IN INCHES

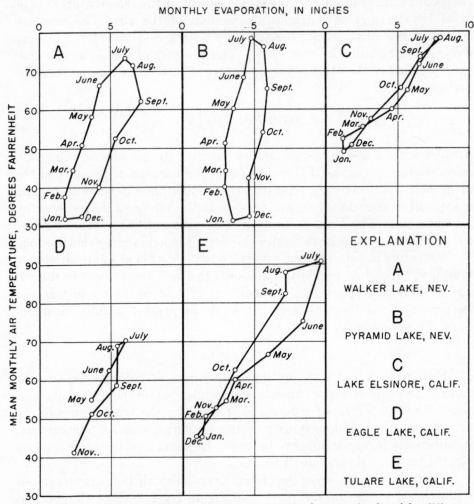

FIG. III-1.—Relation of mean monthly air temperature and evaporation from lakes (11).

tion that may occur from a water surface is primarily dependent upon the amount of solar radiation received and retained. For small areas heat may be gained or lost by movement from or to adjacent areas, and the evaporation may be either more or less than the evaporation that would result from the net solar radiation reaching the water surface. Such heat exchanges may occur either by convection or conduction in both the air and the water. For large water areas such gains or losses of heat are small in relation to the heat received directly from the sun. There will be time lags between the receipt of heat and the resulting evaporation where the heat received raises the temperature of the water to depths below the influence of surface conditions. Such absorbed heat returns later to the surface in the cycle of temperature changes within the water, so that for periods as long as years there is little difference in the heat content of the water. Such gains or losses in deep bodies of water affect evaporation for shorter periods.

Heat storage

The variable relation between monthly rates of evaporation and the mean air temperature is discussed above and is illustrated in figure 1.

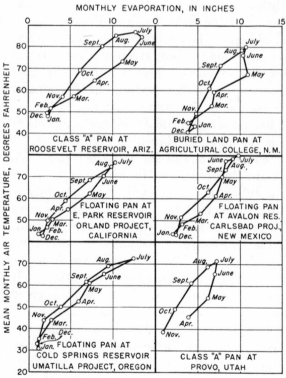

Fig. III-2.—Relation of mean monthly air temperature and evaporation from pans of different types.

A part of this variation is the result of heat storage within the volume of the water exposed to evaporation. In deep bodies of water temperature changes extend to considerable depths. The warming of such depths of water in the spring and early summer utilizes some of the heat supply that would otherwise be available for evaporation. Similarly the release of such stored heat in the fall and winter makes available a heat supply in excess of that received at such times through the atmosphere. As a result the evaporation from deep waters is reduced relatively to the heat supply in the spring and early summer and increased in the fall and winter.

Records of the amounts of such heat storage have not been sufficient to furnish adequate data on its amount. It has been reported to extend to depths of 180 feet [26] on Lake Superior.

That such heat storage may be a material item is shown by the results plotted in Figure III-2 [13]. For small bodies of water, such as tanks and pans, the volume of water is not enough for such heat storage to be significant. For example, in the United States Weather Bureau class A pan at Roosevelt Dam the evaporation in the later part of the summer was less for equivalent air temperatures than in the earlier months, thus reversing the form of the temperature loop for deep lakes shown in Figure III-1. The same conditions are shown for the buried land pan at the Agricultural College, N. Mex., and the class A pan at Provo, Utah. The three other records plotted in Figure III-2 represent floating pans and show less spread in the temperature loop. They resemble the form of loop shown in Figure III-1 for shallow lakes. This was to be expected, as these floating pans were in reservoirs in shallow water or in areas drawn down by the use of the reservoir storage in the later summer.

Houk [14] has reported vertical temperature profiles for the Elephant Butte Reservoir for 1935, as shown in Figure III-3. The variations in temperature extended to the full depth of the water. The seasonal march from the minimum temperatures in January to the maximum surface temperatures in July was fairly regular. From July to September surface temperatures decreased but heat moving downward increased the deeper temperatures. After September general cooling extended to the full depth and the temperatures decreased steadily toward the minimum of the preceding January. The heat increase from January to August was sufficient, if available and used for evaporation, to have evaporated a depth of water equal to more than 2 feet; the average evaporation from a class A pan during the same months is more than 6 feet [13].

Houk [14] has also reported the similar temperature profiles for the Owyhee Reservoir from June to November 1936. This reservoir was less affected by inflow and draft at that time than the Elephant Butte Reservoir. The variations in temperature were practically confined to the upper 100 feet of depth. The amounts of heat stored from June 13 to August 31 would have been sufficient to evaporate a depth of about 5 inches of water; the reduction in heat from August 31 to November 30 was sufficient to evaporate a depth of more than 1½ feet of water.

Such amounts of heat storage are important in relation to the heat represented by the depths of water evaporated and account for much of the difference in the form of the temperature loops for deep and shallow bodies of water. Such heat storage also explains why late fall and winter evaporation on deep water may be greater and spring and early summer evaporation may be less than would be expected for shallow water. The annual evaporation from deep and shallow water should not differ materially, as the annual variations in the water temperature are relatively small, but the monthly distribution may be materially different.

WIND

Wind movement replaces the air in contact with the water by air which may have a different temperature or moisture content. Some

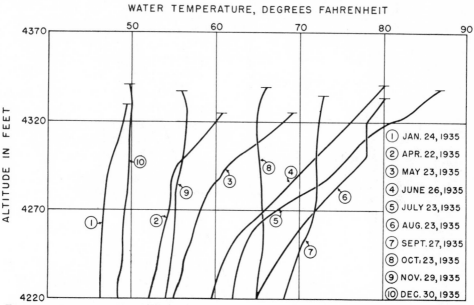

Fig. III-3.—Vertical distribution of temperature in Elephant Butte Reservoir in 1935. [*After I. E. Houk* (14).]

investigators have considered wind to be a secondary factor whose effect is reflected in the measurements of temperature, humidity, or differences in vapor pressure.

Wind above some limiting velocity may have no additional effect on evaporation. For winds sufficiently strong to remove all vapor as rapidly as it may be formed, additional wind velocity may produce no further effect. Such limiting velocities will vary with the other factors affecting evaporation.

Wind movement may be turbulent or laminar. Turbulent movement will remove water vapor from contact with the water surface and increase evaporation. Laminar movement may not materially affect evaporation on large water areas if the lower air strata have uniform temperature and vapor content.

Evaporation into still air in contact with the water surface will be controlled by the rate at which diffusion takes place between the air and the water. Water surfaces under natural exposures are seldom in contact with still air.

The wind velocities that affect evaporation are those of the wind in contact with the water surface. The observations of wind velocity by the United States Weather Bureau are made at stations that may be at considerable heights above the ground surface. The rate of increase of

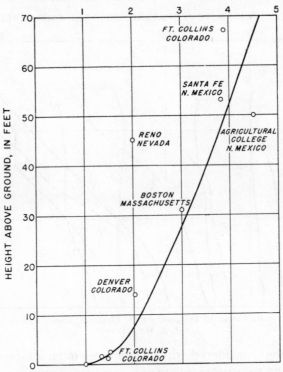

RATIO OF OBSERVED WIND TO GROUND WIND

FIG. III-4.—Ratios of observed wind velocity at different heights above the ground to wind velocity at the ground. [*After C. Rohwer* (28).]

wind velocity with height above the ground as derived by Rohwer [28] is shown in Figure III-4.

BAROMETRIC PRESSURE

Evaporation increases with a decrease of barometric pressure if all other factors remain unchanged. For freely exposed water surfaces changes in barometric pressure are accompanied by changes in other factors affecting evaporation, so that the evaporation from any water surface cannot be correlated with local changes in pressure alone.

Differences in barometric pressure may be a measure of the difference in evaporation at different altitudes. Evaporation should increase with increase in altitude if other climatic factors did not also change. The usual effect of the decrease in temperature and the changes in other climatic factors with increasing altitude is greater than the effect of the reduction in barometric pressure, so that increases in altitude in similar latitudes result in a net reduction in the evaporation.

The rate of change due to differences in altitude found in two series of records is shown in Figure III-5. One of these curves is based on observations with pans on Mount Whitney [10], and the other on direct records of lakes in the western part of the Great Basin [11]. These records do not

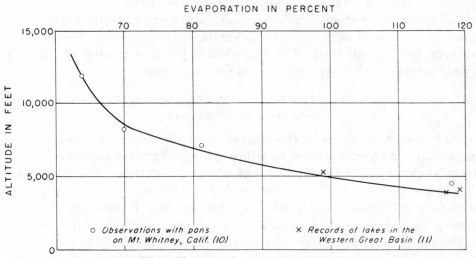

FIG. III-5.—Variation of evaporation with altitude.

include observations at altitudes below 3,800 feet. The rate of variation shown by these results is not necessarily applicable to other areas.

QUALITY OF WATER

The rate of evaporation decreases with increase in salt content of the water until a salt content of about 30 percent is reached. At this content crusts tend to form on the water surface unless the water is subject to wave action. The rate of variation is generally linear, evaporation decreasing about 1 percent for each 1 percent increase in salt content. Rohwer [29] found reductions for water containing sodium chloride similar to those found by Lee [17] for water of Owens Lake and by Adams [2] for water of Great Salt Lake. For sodium sulphate solution there was little difference in the evaporation for contents up to 10 percent. Sea water would be expected to have a rate of evaporation about 2 to 3 percent less than that of similarly exposed fresh water.

METHODS OF DETERMINING EVAPORATION

Methods of determining evaporation may be divided into five classes, as follows: (1) Theoretical analyses; (2) computation from formulas based on atmospheric elements; (3) computation from formulas based on the transformation of energy; (4) observations with various types of pans or atmometers; (5) direct records from large water areas.

Computations based on atmospheric elements would permit existing climatic records to be used if satisfactory formulas based on such elements could be derived. Formulas based on the transformation of energy have sound theoretical support and will be useful if the items necessary for their application can be economically and effectively observed. The difficulties in deriving the relations between evaporation and the climatic or energy items necessary in formulas of either of these types have led to the general use of direct observations from controlled water surfaces. Results of such observations require adjustment to obtain the evaporation from large water surfaces, so that this method is intermediate between the use of general formulas and direct observations on large water areas.

THEORETICAL STUDIES OF ATMOSPHERIC CONDITIONS AFFECTING EVAPORATION

Theoretical analyses of the conditions of air movement over water surfaces and the distribution of moisture in the air have been used to derive formulas expressing the conditions that affect evaporation. These include the studies by Jeffreys [15] and Sutton [33] in England. Similar analyses in the United States include those by Rossby [30], Rossby and Montgomery [31], Leighly [19], Sverdrup [34], and McEwen [22]. These methods include consideration of atmospheric turbulence and of the existence of a thin boundary layer in contact with the water surface in which air movement is laminar. In this boundary layer vapor moves by diffusion; in the turbulent air above the boundary layer vapor is distributed through the mixing that results from the turbulence.

Leighly's analysis [19] is based on conditions within the laminar boundary layer, in which the gradient in vapor pressure is linear. His results are not applicable to large areas, and instruments are not available for the measurement of differences in vapor pressure within the very small distances involved. Sverdrup [34] and McEwen [22] have applied their results in estimating the evaporation from the oceans.

Thornwaite and Holzman [35] have developed equations and observational procedures for the measurement of evaporation from land surfaces. These are based on the vertical distribution of moisture in the air and the intensity of turbulent mixing. The observations required are the moisture concentrations at two levels within the turbulent layer; the heights of the two observations, so that moisture gradients may be obtained; and the wind velocity at two or more levels, to give the intensity of turbulent mixing. The moisture concentration in the air has been measured as specific humidity by means of recording hair hygrometers.

Within the heights used above the ground surface air pressure is essentially constant and the specific humidity is proportional to the vapor pressure.

The formula utilizing these observational data is as follows:

$$E = \frac{17.1(e_1 - e_2)(v_2 - v_1)}{T + 459.4}$$

in which E = evaporation, in inches per hour.

e_1 and e_2 = vapor pressure at the two levels, in inches of mercury.

v_1 and v_2 = wind velocity at the two levels, in miles per hour.

T = temperature.

Two experimental stations for this method have been in operation at the Muskingum Climatic Research Center, in Ohio, and Arlington Farm, in Virginia. By means of a tower an instrument shelter large enough to contain a hydrothermograph may be raised to any height up to 28 feet. Such observations supply records of the moisture gradient at the site of the tower, which can be used to compute the upward rate of moisture movement. The upward moisture movement will have its source in the supply from which the moisture is obtained. This may be the area under the tower for conditions of still air or the area to the windward from which the air and moisture come during wind movements. For areas of uniform vegetation or for water surfaces that are large in relation to the area of wind movement such observations represent the loss from such surfaces. For areas of mixed crop and moisture conditions the results represent the mean rate of loss of moisture for the area contributing to the air whose moisture gradient is measured at the tower.

This method represents an added approach in the efforts to measure evaporation under field conditions. It was developed to measure moisture losses from areas of cropped lands but, if found applicable, will be equally suitable for measurement of evaporation from water surfaces. Comparisons of this method for water surfaces with other methods by which evaporation can be measured are needed.

FORMULAS BASED ON ATMOSPHERIC ELEMENTS

Formulas based on atmospheric elements have generally been derived from a consideration of the factors affecting evaporation with the empirical coefficients necessary to reduce the results to losses from large areas determined by comparisons with observations of losses from water surfaces. Such formulas began with that of Dalton [7] in 1802. Among other formulas more frequently quoted are those of Fitzgerald [8], Russell [1], Bigelow [3], Horton [12], Meyer [25], Hayford-Folse [9], and Rohwer [28]. These formulas have been expressed, so far as it is practicable, in the following nomenclature:

E = evaporation in inches per 24 hours unless otherwise stated.
a and c = constant coefficients
e_s = mean pressure of saturated vapor at the temperature of the water surface, in inches of mercury.
e_d = mean pressure of saturated vapor at the temperature of the dew point, in inches of mercury.
d = relative humidity of the air.
B = mean barometer reading, in inches of mercury at 32° Fahrenheit.
w = mean velocity of wind at surface of ground or water, in miles per hour.
t_s = mean temperature of the water surface, in degrees Fahrenheit.
t_a = mean temperature of the air 1 inch above the water surface, in degrees Fahrenheit.
e_w = vapor pressure at the mean wet-bulb temperature, in inches of mercury.
$\dfrac{d_e}{d_s}$ = rate of change in the maximum vapor pressure with temperature.

Dalton's statement [7, 28] of the principles controlling evaporation has been expressed as

$$E = c(e_s - e_d)$$

In some statements of this formula [23] the factor $1 + aw$ has been added to include the effect of the wind. The term $e_s - e_d$ represents Dalton's conclusions regarding the effect of the temperature of the air and water and the relative humidity of the air.

Fitzgerald's formula [8] is

$$E = (0.40 + 0.199w)(e_s - e_d)$$

This formula was published in 1886 as the result of observation on small pans.

Russell's formula [1] was based on observations with Piche atmometers at many localities in 1886. It is

$$E = \left[\frac{(1.96e_w + 43.88)(e_w - e_d)}{B} \right]$$

On the basis of these observations Russell prepared a map showing lines of equal evaporation in the United States, which has been frequently copied, although there is much uncertainty regarding the reduction of such records to the equivalent evaporation from large water areas.

Bigelow's formula [3] is the result of extensive work for the United States Weather Bureau. It is

$$E = 0.00236 \frac{e_s}{e_d} \frac{d_e}{d_s} (23 + 0.62w)$$

Horton's formula [12] for standard Weather Bureau pans with water and air temperatures equal is

$$E = 0.40[\psi e_s - e_d] \qquad \text{with} \qquad \psi = 2.0 - e^{-0.2w},$$

in which e is the base of Naperian or natural logarithms. For large areas the calculated evaporation is to be multiplied by an area factor

$$F = (1 - P) + P\frac{\psi - 1}{\psi - h},$$

in which h is the relative humidity (decimal) and P is the fraction of the time during which the wind is turbulent.

Meyer's formula [25] is

$$E \text{ in inches per 30 days} = C(V - v)(1 + w/10)$$

in which V is the maximum vapor pressure in inches of mercury corresponding to the monthly mean air temperature observed by the Weather Bureau at nearby stations, v is the pressure of vapor in the air based on Weather Bureau determinations of monthly mean air temperature and relative humidity at nearby stations, and w is the monthly mean wind velocity, also from Weather Bureau stations where the velocities are measured at considerable heights above the ground. For small shallow ponds and for moisture on grass, leaves, etc., $C = 15$. For large or deep bodies of water, V is the maximum vapor pressure corresponding to water temperature instead of air temperature, v is the pressure of vapor in air about 30 feet above the water surface, and $C = 11$.

The Hayford-Folse formula [9] was derived from an extensive study of records on the three upper Great Lakes. It is

$$E = (e_s - e_d)[(0.319 + 0.358)(w - 10.8)]$$

In obtaining this formula the meteorologic records of the United States Weather Bureau were used, including the records for wind velocity. Only positive values of $(w - 10.8)$ were used, as winds of less than 10.8 miles an hour at the heights above ground at which the Weather Bureau records were obtained are considered to have no effect on the evaporation at the ground level. Folse has computed the probable error resulting from the application of this formula on any day when the wind velocity is less than 10.8 miles an hour as 11.6 percent, assuming that there are no systematic errors.

Rohwer's formula [28] is the result of extensive investigational work by the Bureau of Agricultural Engineering of the United States Department of Agriculture. His general formula is

$$E = 0.771(1.465 - 0.0186B)(0.44 + 0.118W)(e_s - e_d)$$

The work from which this formula was derived included both indoor and outdoor pan observations and comparisons with an 85-foot reservoir at Fort Collins, Colo., and observations with pans at several other localities covering a wide range in altitude. It includes factors representing altitude, wind movement, and differences on vapor pressure. The use of this formula requires records of wind movement and air and water temperatures and readings of wet- and dry-bulb thermometers. These items, except the water temperatures, are observed at regular Weather Bureau stations. Wet- and dry-bulb readings are not made by voluntary observers.

Rohwer applied this formula to local observations at 19 stations for which records of mean monthly evaporation from pans were also available. The algebraic mean for all computed results differed less than 2 percent from the pan observations for the full period of record. For different months the differences of the computed evaporation from the observed evaporation ranged from −15 to +12 percent. For individual stations the mean differences ranged from −18.5 to +34 percent.

Few comparisons of the results obtained by the use of these evaporation formulas with the evaporation from large water areas can be made, owing to the lack of records of all the items required. Comparisons with the evaporation from small pans are subject to the uncertainties regarding the relations between such pans and large areas.

Formulas based on atmospheric elements are useful where direct local observations of evaporation are not available. To give accurate results a formula that correctly represents the factors controlling evaporation would need to be applied to short periods, such as hours, within which there is slight variation in the factors involved. A correct formula of this sort cannot be expected to give accurate results when applied to monthly or annual means of its factors. Detailed applications to short periods are burdensome, however, and such formulas have usually been applied to the means for monthly or annual periods. For such long periods only general agreement between the computed and the actual evaporation should be expected, even where the formula may correctly represent the relations of the factors involved.

FORMULAS BASED ON TRANSFORMATION OF ENERGY

The total amount of evaporation that may occur is limited by the total amount of heat that is available to convert water into vapor. The main source of such heat for natural bodies of water is the sun. Such heat may reach a water surface directly as solar radiation, or it may be brought to the water indirectly by air movement.

The amount of solar radiation received at any point on the earth's surface varies with the inclination of the sun's rays, the duration of sunshine, the amount of cloudiness, and the atmospheric depletion of the solar radiation received at the exterior of the earth's atmosphere. The solar constant represented by the radiation received by a surface exposed vertically to the sun's rays at the upper limit of the atmosphere varies within a relatively narrow range and averages 1.93 calories per minute per square centimeter of surface. The mean monthly solar radiation received on the earth's surface ranges from 36 to 65 percent of that at the exterior of the atmosphere; for different latitudes the mean monthly values range from less than 100 to about 700 calories per square centimeter per day [27].

Solar radiation is measured by various forms of pyrheliometers [37]. Records of 16 stations are now published by the United States Weather Bureau. The amount differs widely at different stations and at different times of the year.

Evaporation may be computed by accounting for all of the solar radiation received from the sun and assigning to evaporation the heat not otherwise used. This method is an application of the law of the conservation of energy. It has been used by Cummings [6], Bowen [4], Richardson [27] and McEwen [21]. Evaporation in these terms is generally stated as follows:

$$E = \frac{(I - B - S - C)}{L(1 + R)} \tag{1}$$

in which

$$R = \frac{0.46(t_1 - t_2)}{P_1 - P_2} \frac{P}{760} \tag{2}$$

In metric units these terms are:

E = evaporation, in centimeters of depth.
I = incoming radiation per square centimeter of horizontal surface.
B = back radiation to the sky, in the same units as I.
S = heat storage in the water for unit cross section to the full depth of water.
C = combined correction for heat leakage through the walls of the container or the heat received or lost in a lake from running water.

The quantities in the numerator are expressed in calories per square centimeter of open water surface for the time period corresponding to that used for E.

L = heat of vaporization of water, in calories per cubic centimeter at ordinary temperatures; for the units defined in the formula this is about 585; for E in inches it is about 1,500.
R = Bowen's ratio [4] = ratio of sensible heat to latent heat, computed by equation 2. Water loses heat by vaporization and as sensible heat. Sensible heat may be a gain or a loss; it is a gain when the air is warmer than the water.

In equation 2

t_1 = water surface temperature, in degrees centigrade.
t_2 = air temperature, in degrees centigrade.
P_1 = vapor pressure of saturated vapor at t_1, in millimeters of mercury.
P_2 = partial pressure of actual vapor in the air, in millimeters of mercury.
P = barometric pressure, in millimeters of mercury.

Back radiation to the sky, B, is always positive. For hourly periods it ranges from 0 to about 10 calories per square centimeter [6]. The heat stored in the water, S, is generally small over long periods, but for short periods it may range from -10 to $+10$ calories per hour per square centimeter [6].

Bowen's ratio, R, may vary widely for short periods; its 24-hour values seldom exceed 0.30 and frequently fall below 0.20 [6].

The method of determining evaporation by computing heat energy is a correct accounting for the solar radiation received by a body of water and the proportion of such energy available for evaporation. However, there are fewer records of solar radiation now available than of the other climatic factors affecting evaporation, so that for many areas this method cannot now be applied to compute local evaporation. When used with available general data its results will be representative of general evaporation rather than of evaporation for local areas or for short periods.

The method based on heat energy may also be used to obtain evaporation by making the observations necessary for insertion in the formula. Observations of water and air temperatures, records of wet- and dry-bulb thermometers, and in addition local observations of solar radiation and back radiation would be essential. Solar radiation can be measured with some form of pyrheliometer, but suitable direct methods of measuring with high precision back radiation to the sky have not yet been worked out. Though the method based on heat energy is helpful to an understanding of the processes of evaporation, it is difficult, for the present at least, to measure the items required for the use of this method. Such measurements may be simplified by the use of an insulated pan for which S and C would be reduced to zero.

Instruments for the Direct Measurement of Evaporation

The difficulty of making direct measurements of evaporation from large water surfaces has led to the use of many types of small water areas in tanks or pans and special surfaces, such as those used in atmometers. All these instruments attempt to integrate the effect of the various climatic factors affecting evaporation and to record a directly measurable loss that is proportional to that from an adjacent large water area. Pans of several types are shown in Figure III-6.

Records with all these instruments require the use of coefficients or other adjustments to reduce the observed loss to that from large water areas. It has generally been assumed that the relation between the evaporation from such pans and from a large water surface is constant, and a uniform coefficient has been applied.

If pans are to be used for the measurement of evaporation it is essential that the relation of their evaporation to that from large areas should be sufficiently constant to permit a mean value of the coefficient to be used or that the coefficient should vary by some simple relation dependent

(a)

(b)

Fig. III-6.—Pans for the measurement of evaporation by C. Rohwer (28). (a) left to right, U. S. Weather Bureau Class A land pan, four-foot circular sunken pan, and Colorado pan. (b) U. S. Weather Bureau Class A land pan used as a floating pan.

on easily measured factors. If the factors causing variations in such coefficients are complex and result in material differences in the coefficient, the usefulness of the pan method of observation will be materially reduced. If such pans do not reflect the effect of the factors controlling evaporation from large areas, direct observations of such factors and their use in a formula based on the factors would be as direct as the use of such pans.

The evaporation from the pans now in use has, in general, a fairly uniform relation to the evaporation from large water surfaces for annual periods, for which the variations in climatic factors are usually small. Less close agreement is usually shown for shorter periods. Further investigation is needed on the value and variation of the coefficients of the pans now more generally used and also on the development of additional types of pans having a more nearly constant relation to large areas. Until such results are obtained records with pans are subject to uncertainties when applied to short periods or at times of small rates of loss.

Tanks or pans of all types represent shallow depths of water having small capacity for heat storage. Land pans, whether set on or in the ground, have conditions of water temperature different from those in deep bodies of water. Such conditions are only partly corrected with floating pans of practicable types. The character and extent of the effect of heat storage in deep water and in shallow pans is discussed above and illustrated in Figures III-1, III-2, and III-3. The evaporation from no form of shallow pan can be expected to have a constant ratio or coefficient to the evaporation from an adjacent large water surface of material depth. Heat storage can only be a minor item in any shallow tank, as it is in a shallow lake. Though tanks or pans may have a fairly consistent coefficient for annual periods, similar consistency cannot be expected for shorter periods, such as months.

Effect of size of pan.—Pans have been found to have larger rates of evaporation than adjacent large water areas. The coefficients which it is necessary to apply to pan results vary with the size of the pan and approach unity for the larger pans. Sleight [32] at Denver derived a relation of the annual evaporation from sunken pans, based on differences in diameter. The relations which he found were consistent when applied to annual periods but were variable when applied by months, as indicated in the table shown on page 75. The relations found by Sleight for pans of this type under the conditions at Denver may not be applicable to pans of other types or at other localities.

Sleight also found that the evaporation from the 12-foot pan was closely similar to that from a larger area. Observations with pans adjacent to large water surfaces have been too few to enable the limits of the relations of the evaporation from pans to that from large water areas or for short periods of time to be fully determined.

Comparison of evaporation from tanks of different diameter
Observations by R. B. Sleight [32] at Denver, for 12 months in 1915–16, using sunken round
tanks 3 feet deep]

Diameter of tank (feet)	Mean coefficient to be applied to each size of tank to obtain evaporation from 12-foot tank	Deviation of coefficient from annual mean (per cent)			
		Weekly		Monthly	
		Range	Mean	Range	Mean
9	99.0	−8 to +15.0	3.8	−5.5 to +4.5	2.2
6	91.3	−10.5 to +18.0	4.2	−10.7 to +4.6	3.8
3.39	82.9	−15.6 to +17.0	4.7	−19.8 to +7.8	5.3
2	77.9	−15.9 to +9.6	4.1	−13.0 to +5.3	4.2
1	64.5	−19.5 to +28.6	8.6	−14.0 to +13.0	5.6

Effect of depth of pan.—Evaporation from shallow pans may be greater or less than that from deeper ones, depending on the relative temperature of the air and water. Working with tanks from 0.25 to 5.75 feet deep, Sleight [32] found little difference for tanks more than 3 feet deep and recommended depths of at least 2 feet. The total evaporation for a period of several months did not vary widely with the depth, but the weekly variations were larger with the shallower pans, which showed a larger relative loss during the part of the period having higher temperatures.

Class A land pan of the United States Weather Bureau.—The class A land pan is the standard pan of the United States Weather Bureau [16, 38]. It is 4 feet in diameter and 10 inches deep, and the water is maintained within 2 and 3 inches of the top. It is set on timbers so that the bottom of the pan is 6 inches above the adjacent ground; this reduces the difficulties with drifting soil or snow sometimes found with sunken pans. Earth is banked within an inch of the top of the timbers, leaving some air circulation under the pan. The temperature of the water in the pan fluctuates closely with the air temperature.

This pan has been used in the United States more extensively than any other. The coefficient now more generally recommended to reduce observed losses from the pan to the loss from large water areas is 0.70 [38]. Annual coefficients of 0.66 to 0.70 were found under Colorado climatic conditions; for individual weeks the variations ranged from +19 percent to −14 percent of the mean [32]. Rohwer [28], in comparisons with an 85-foot reservoir, found a mean of 0.70 and a range from 0.91 to 0.57 in different months. Young [36], in comparisons with a 12-foot sunken pan for one year's record at Fullerton, Calif., found an annual coefficient of 0.77 for the standard pan.

On the basis of the present available records a general coefficient of 0.70 is recommended for reducing observed evaporation from this pan to evaporation from large water areas where there are no records indicating the value of the coefficient for the local conditions. The coefficient may vary widely for short periods, but available data are inadequate to establish values for such periods under variable climatic conditions and depths of water.

Colorado sunken pan.—The Colorado sunken pan, which has been used in the Western States, is 3 feet square and from $1\frac{1}{2}$ to 3 feet deep [38]. Its rim projects about 4 inches above the ground to avoid splashing rain, drifting snow, dust, and trash, without giving too great an obstruction to the wind. Water in the pan is maintained at the ground level. The temperature of the water does not fluctuate as rapidly as the temperature of the air, so that conditions approach those in large lakes.

The general coefficient for this pan, now more generally recommended, is 0.78 [38], different results range from 0.75 to 0.86 for annual periods. Rohwer [28] found monthly values ranging from 0.69 to 0.92. He also found that the average variation of the monthly records from the mean annual value of the coefficient was 7 percent.

Six-foot sunken pans.—Sunken pans 6 feet in diameter and 3 feet deep have been used by the Bureau of Agricultural Engineering; similar pans 2 feet deep have been used by the Bureau of Plant Industry. Few determinations of the coefficient for these pans have been made. Colorado results [28, 32] have indicated annual values of 0.90 to 0.94; California results at East Park Reservoir [28] indicated a value of 0.78 for a pan 4 feet in diameter.

Floating pans.—Floating pans have been used in an attempt to establish conditions similar to those of the surrounding water. Such pans are subject to splashing during winds, even when surrounded by a raft and are less accessible for measurement than land pans. Coefficients are also required to reduce results with floating pans to the evaporation from large water surfaces. Floating pans are not now generally used; when used it is advisable to install a land pan also, to supply data for missing periods in the records of the floating pan.

For floating pans, the type known as the United States Geological Survey pan [38] has been generally used. This is 3 feet square and 18 inches deep and is supported by drum floats. Diagonal baffles in the pan are used to reduce wave action. A coefficient of 0.80 is generally recommended for this pan [38]; different comparisons have indicated a range from 0.70 to 0.91.

Insulated pans.—In order to avoid heat losses or gains through the sides and bottom of evaporation pans, insulated pans have been proposed, and some observations with such pans have been made. The Bureau of Agricultural Engineering has used a pan at Fullerton, Calif., designed by Cummings [5], set above the ground, 2.54 feet square and 8.5 inches deep, insulated with a 0.5-inch layer of celotex. Unpublished results for one year's work show evaporation about 20 percent larger than that from a 12-foot sunken pan from March to October and about 40 percent larger from November to February. The evaporation from the insulated pan was generally similar to that from a 2-foot sunken pan.

A completely insulated pan would be a form of pyrheliometer, in which the evaporation would be a measure of the difference between the solar radiation and the back radiation to the sky. The effect of wind on the evaporation from such a pan would be included and would be representative of the wind effects on the adjacent lake area if the exposures were similar. The insulated pan would receive the same solar radiation as the lake area and would be subject to the same back radiation. Differences in heat storage in the pan would be relatively small compared to those in the deep lake areas, and vertical temperature profiles would need to be observed in the lake at the frequency for which the evaporation was to be computed. To apply the results with such insulated pans to adjacent large water areas quantitatively, temperature records of the air and water with wet- and dry-bulb thermometers for the large water area would be needed. From these records Bowen's ratio could be computed for the application of the heat-energy formula. Cummings [6a] has made observations of this type at Bear Lake, in Utah. This method may be used if the observations and their computations can be made at reasonable cost. Present data do not permit determination of the coefficients that may need to be used with such pans.

Atmometers.—Atmometers are instruments having special surfaces which are kept moist and from which the water loss is recorded. The Piche atmometer consists of a paper disk [1]. The porous-cup atmometer as developed by Livingston [20] uses either black or white spherical porous cups.

Such small surfaces do not have the same exposure as large water areas. They represent more nearly the conditions affecting loss of moisture from plants and have been used in plant studies. Records of such atmometers are not directly applicable to the evaporation from a water surface.

Evaporation from large areas

Conditions are seldom favorable for the direct determination of evaporation from large water areas. Such evaporation has to be obtained as the residual item from records of all other items of inflow and outflow. Evaporation cannot be determined for lakes or reservoirs having unmeasurable seepage gains or losses.

Records on western lakes [11] indicate a mean annual evaporation of 4.2 feet on Walker Lake and 4.15 feet on Pyramid Lake, in Nevada, and of 3.5 feet on Eagle Lake, 4.6 feet on Tulare Lake, and 4.6 feet on

Lake Elsinore, in California. Lee [18] computed an annual evaporation of 5.07 feet from Owens Lake, Calif., from 1906 to 1914; for fresh water this is equivalent to about 5.6 feet.

VARIATIONS IN AMOUNT OF EVAPORATION IN ANY LOCALITY

The annual evaporation at any locality varies within a narrower range than other water-supply items. Where direct local observations for any year are not available it is customary to use the mean annual evaporation for all years of record. The small range in the annual evaporation is illustrated by the records for Lake Elsinore [11], in California, where for 19 years the annual evaporation ranged from 93 to 105 percent of the mean.

Variations for shorter periods are larger. The same month may show large differences in different years, owing to variations in the climatic factors. For 12 years of pan records at East Park Reservoir [13], in California, monthly records in different years ranged from about 50 to 150 percent of the mean in the months of smaller loss and from about 75 to 120 percent of the mean in the summer months of larger evaporation.

EVAPORATION FROM ICE AND SNOW

Records of the evaporation from ice and snow are meager, although it is generally recognized that such evaporation occurs. Observations with pans have frequently been discontinued when the pans freeze. The relative evaporation from a frozen pan and an adjacent lake would differ from that at higher temperatures, as such pans will freeze before an adjacent open water surface that is subject to wind and wave action. Large lakes may not freeze at temperatures materially below 32°F.

Snow is subject to some evaporation while temperatures are near 32°F. There is also considerable loss by evaporation from banked snow during the melting period.

ANNUAL EVAPORATION IN THE UNITED STATES

The most extensive available tabulation of evaporation records is that assembled by Follansbee [38]. This includes about 300 records reduced to the equivalent evaporation from a large water surface. Follansbee has summarized these records as follows:

"Most of the records of evaporation were taken in the western part of the United States, comparatively few being available east of the Mississippi River. These records indicate in a general way, however, the variation in the United States.

"The area of lowest evaporation is the Great Lakes region, where it ranges from 15 to 20 inches per year. East of the Mississippi River the evaporation increases from 20 inches in Maine to 43 inches at Birmingham,

Ala., and then decreases slightly toward the Gulf coast, with its greater humidity.

"West of the Great Lakes the evaporation increases to 40 inches in the upper Missouri River Basin. Southwest of the Missouri River it gradually increases to 70 inches in southwestern Texas and southeastern New Mexico.

"In the Rocky Mountain region the evaporation depends largely upon temperature, which decreases with an increase in elevation.

"As few records are available at the higher elevations, it is impossible to estimate the variation in evaporation in the Rocky Mountain region.

"In the inter-mountain region, between the Rockies and the Sierra Nevada, the evaporation ranges from 38 inches in northern Nevada to 60 inches in southern Nevada and Arizona.

"In the arid section of Washington and Oregon, comprising chiefly the region east of the Coast Range, evaporation ranges from 40 to 50 inches. In the western half of Washington the evaporation is generally less than 25 inches, the lowest being at Lake Kachess, with a rate of 20.15 inches. In western Oregon it is between 30 and 40 inches.

"In California the rate of evaporation depends largely upon the elevation of the station. In the Sierra Nevada it ranges from 32 inches at Lake Tahoe to 62 inches in the southern part of the State. Throughout the remainder of California it ranges from 38 to 57 inches, except in Imperial Valley, where an extreme of 97.10 inches has been recorded near Salton Sea, in the center of the valley."

EVAPORATION FROM THE OCEAN

Sverdrup [34] has computed the evaporation from the sea on the assumptions that (1) a boundary layer exists next to the surface within which transport of water vapor takes place by ordinary diffusion; (2) above the boundary layer the transport of water vapor takes place by eddy conductivity; (3) laboratory results show that the eddy conductivity is a linear function of altitude above the sea and depends upon the roughness of the surface.

The layer of diffusion was found to have a probable thickness of $4.12/w$, where w = wind velocity in centimeters per second. The sea surface is considered to be rough, having a roughness parameter of 0.6 centimeter. Using these assumptions and available data, Sverdrup computed the evaporation from the Atlantic Ocean in millimeters per 24 hours for latitudes of 50° N. to 55° S., and his results show a good agreement with those of Wust in 1920 based on observations to which a correction factor of 1.22 had been applied, and with a later revision by Wust and separate results by Mosby in 1936.

The results are as follows:

Evaporation from the Atlantic Ocean in regions of different latitude

Region	Evaporation per 24 hours (millimeters)		Evaporation per year (feet)	
	Sverdrup	Wust × 1.22	Sverdrup	Wust × 1.22
50° to 40° N	2.3	2.2	2.76	2.64
40° to 30° N	3.3	3.2	3.96	3.84
30° to 8° N	5.2	4.3	6.25	5.16
8° to 3° N	1.9	3.0	2.28	3.60
3° N to 20° S	4.1	4.0	4.92	4.80
20° S to 40° S	3.2	3.2	3.84	3.84
40° S to 45° S	2.2	1.6	2.64	1.92

McEwen [22] has computed the evaporation from the Pacific Ocean from latitude 20° to 50° North, using surface temperatures observed and published by the Imperial Japanese Observatory at Kobe, the average daily solar radiation reaching the sea surface as prepared by H. H. Kimball, of the United States Weather Bureau, and measurements of solar radiation at various depths.   Equating the rate of change of heat in an elementary volume of water with the heat furnished by the absorption of penetrating solar radiation less the rate of loss enabled him to formulate an equation expressing the theoretical sea temperature in terms of time, latitude, and depth for depths less than 35 meters.   Using 0.2 for Bowen's ratio, McEwen derived the following ratio:

Computed rates of evaporation from the Pacific Ocean

Latitude N	Computed evaporation	
	Meters per month	Equivalent feet per year
20°	0.106	4.27
25°	.102	4.00
30°	.094	3.70
35°	.084	3.30
40°	.072	2.83
45°	.055	2.16
50°	.047	1.85

REFERENCES

1. Abbe, Cleveland, Piche evaporimeter: Monthly Weather Rev., vol. 33, pp. 253–255, 1905.

2. Adams, T. C., Evaporation from Great Salt Lake: Am. Meteorol. Soc. Bull., vol. 15, No. 2, pp. 35–39, 1934.

3. Bigelow, F. H., Studies in the phenomena of the evaporation of water over lakes and reservoirs: Monthly Weather Rev., vol. 38, pp. 1133–1135, 1910.

4. Bowen, I. S., The ratio of heat losses by conduction and by evaporation from any water surface: Phys. Rev., vol. 27, pp. 779–787, 1926.

5. Cummings, N. W., Use of the Burt phototube as an integrating pryheliometer: Am. Geophys. Union. Trans., 1935, pt. 2, pp. 515–519.

6. Cummings, N. W., Evaporation from water surfaces: Am. Geophys. Union Trans., 16th Ann. Meeting, pt. 2, pp. 507–509, 1936.

6a. Cummings, N. W., The evaporation-energy equations and their practical application: Am. Geophys. Union Trans., 21st Ann. Meeting, pt. 2, pp. 512–522, 1940.

7. Dalton, J., Experimental essays on the constitution of mixed gases; on the force of steam or vapor from waters and other liquids in different temperatures, both in a Torricellian vacuum and in air; on evaporation; and on the expansion of gases by heat: Manchester Lit. and Philos. Soc. Mem. 5, pp. 535–602, 1802.

8. Fitzgerald, D., Evaporation: Am. Soc. Civil Eng. Trans., vol. 15, pp. 581–646, 1886.

9. Folse, J. A., A new method of estimating stream flow based upon a new evaporation formula: Carnegie Inst. Washington Publ. 400, pp. 1–237, 1929.

10. Fortier, S., Evaporation losses in irrigation: Eng. News, vol. 58, pp. 304–307, 1907.

11. Harding, S. T., Evaporation from large water surfaces based on records in California and Nevada: Am. Geophys. Union Trans. 15th Ann. Meeting, pt. 2, pp. 507–511, 1935.

12. Horton, R. E., A new evaporation formula developed: Eng. News-Record, vol. 78, pp. 196–199, 1917, and correspondence.

13. Houk, I. E., Evaporation on United States reclamation projects: Am. Soc. Civil Eng. Trans., vol. 90, pp. 266–286, 1927.

14. Houk, I. E., Water temperatures in reservoirs: Am. Geophys. Union Trans., 1937, pt. 2, pp. 523–527.

15. Jeffreys, H., Some problems of evaporation: Philos. Mag., 6th ser., vol. 35, p. 270, 1918.

16. Kadel, B. C., Instructions for the installation and operation of class A evaporation stations: U. S. Weather Bur., Instrument Div., Circ. L, pp. 1–30, 1919.

17. Lee, C. E., Discussion of evaporation on United States reclamation projects: Am. Soc. Civil Eng. Trans., vol. 90, pp. 330–343, 1927.

18. Lee, C. H., Discussion of evaporation from large water surfaces: Am. Geophys. Union Trans., 1935, pt. 2, pp. 511–512.

19. Leighly, John, A note on evaporation: Ecology, vol. 18, No. 2, pp. 180–198, 1937.

20. Livingston, B. E., Atmometers of porous porcelain and paper and their use in physiological ecology: Ecology, vol. 16, p. 438, 1935.

21. McEwen, G. F., Results of evaporation studies: Scripps Inst. Oceanography Tech. ser., vol. 2, No. 11, pp. 401–415, 1930.

22. McEwen, G. F., Some energy relations between the sea surface and the atmosphere: Sears Foundation Jour. Marine Research, vol. 1, No. 3, pp. 217–238, 1938.

23. Marvin, C. F., A proposed new formula for evaporation: Monthly Weather Rev., vol. 37, pp. 57–61, 1909.

24. Marvin, C. F., Psychrometric tables for obtaining the vapor pressure, relative humidity and temperature of the dew point: U. S. Weather Bur. 235, pp. 1–87, 1936.

25. Meyer, A. F., and Levens, A. S., Determining evaporation losses from Weather Bureau data: Eng. News-Record, vol. 118, pp. 481–483, 1937.

26. Pettis, C. R., and Hickman, H. C., Hydrology of the Great Lakes—a symposium: Am. Soc. Civil Eng. Proc., vol. 65, No. 4, pp. 584–606, 1939.

27. Richardson, B., Evaporation as a function of insolation: Am. Soc. Civil Eng. Trans., vol. 95, pp. 996–1019, 1931.

28. Rohwer, C., Evaporation from free water surfaces: U. S. Dept. Agr. Tech. Bull. 271, pp. 1–96, 1931.

29. Rohwer, C., Evaporation from salt solutions and from oil-covered water surfaces: Jour. Agr. Research, vol. 46, pp. 715–729, 1933.

30. Rossby, C. G., Generalization of the theory of the mixing length with applications to atmospheric and oceanic turbulence: Massachusetts Inst. Technology Meteor. Papers, vol. 1, No. 4, p. 1–36, 1936.

31. Rossby, C. G., and Montgomery, R. B., The layer of frictional influence in wind and ocean current: Massachusetts Inst. Technology and Woods Hole Oceanog. Inst. Papers in Physical Oceanography and Meteorology, vol. 3, No. 3, 1935.

32. Sleight, R. B., Evaporation from the surfaces of water and riverbed materials: Jour. Agr. Research vol. 10, No. 5, pp. 209–262, 1917.

33. Sutton, O. G., Wind structure and evaporation in a turbulent atmosphere: Roy. Soc. London Proc., ser. A., Math. Phys. Sciences, vol. 146, p. 701, 1934.

34. Sverdrup, H. V., On the evaporation from the oceans: Sears Foundation Jour. Marine Research, vol. 1, No. 1, pp. 3–14, 1937.

35. Thornwaite, C. W., and Holzman, Benjamin ,The determination of evaporation from land and water surfaces: Monthly Weather Rev., vol. 67, pp. 4–11, 1939.

36. Young, A. A., Evaporation from water surfaces: Am. Geophys. Union. Trans., 1936, pt. 2, pp. 509–512.

37. Pyrhelimometers and pyrheliometer measurements: U. S. Weather Bur. Circ. Q, pp. 1–28, 1931.

38. Evaporation from water surfaces, a symposium: Am. Soc. Civil Eng. Trans., vol. 99, pp. 671–747, 1934.

CHAPTER IV

SNOW AND SNOW SURVEYING; ICE

James E. Church[1]

The subject of snow and snow surveying, like its companion glaciers and ice sheets, belongs to the field of cryology.   This field and its relations are represented in the accompanying chart, figure IV-1.   However, so elementary is the progress in all these applications that any reference to them must be in the nature of ideals rather than achievements.   To keep within the limits of the definition of hydrology and the space limitations of this volume, discussion will be confined so far as possible to the hydrologic characteristics of snow and ice.

FORMS OF SNOW AND ICE

Among the elements of nature obvious to primitive man were earth, fire, air, and water.   All fascinated him, but the moods of the fire, air, and water must have caused him reflection.   Even now the whence and the whither of the water are not fully comprehended.

Water vapor in its distribution in the atmosphere is, in a general way, controlled by cold.   The precipitates of water vapor—rain and snow, dew and frost, water and ice—are chemically kindred, but physically they are variants.   Moreover, the transition from invisible vapor to ice and return is not necessarily effected through water, although evaporation of ice is accelerated by passing through the water stage.   This is demonstrated by the appearance of cirrus clouds, composed entirely of ice crystals, and by the evaporation of ice and snow.

Snow or ice crystals range in form from the simple columns and plates to complex aggregates.   The column frequently appears as a needle and the plate as a star, especially to the unaided senses.   The forms are all variants of the triangle or more probably the hexagon.   The apparent divergence between the column and the plate is merely the result of differences in proportional growth, that of the column being in length rather than in width.   Crystalographically they are one.

The simpler forms occur most commonly at great altitudes, where the temperature is very low, the amount of water vapor therefore small, and the growth of the crystals relatively slow.   This accounts for the ice-crystal halos at high altitudes in the warmer zones and at the surface in

---

[1] Meteorologist, Nevada Agricultural Experiment Station, Reno, Nev.

the polar region.   The perfection of the forms is probably due to their small size from lack of moisture and their consequent wide separation, which permits uniform growth.

By use of a hair to provide a nucleus and support for snow crystals Nakaya [35] has been able to direct and observe their formation and

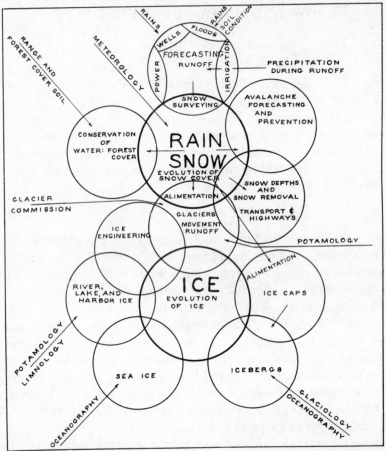

Fig. IV-1.—Relations of rain, snow, and ice to the various scientific and technical activities in the fields of cryology.   Precipitation is at the center of hydrologic interest, and wherever snow cover exists the precipitation in the form of snow becomes dominant in the study of water.

growth.   In natural snow a hexagonal plate with fernlike extensions at the corners is frequently observed.   This type of crystal he produced artificially by abruptly raising the temperature of the vapor-supplying water in the course of the crystal's development.   Thus he simulated the fall of the crystal from the relatively cold dry upper layers of the atmosphere into the warmer more humid layer nearer the earth's surface.

The numerous variety of crystals is attributed by Nakaya to the complexity of atmospheric conditions encountered by the crystal in its descent. Heavy snow usually consists of formless particles or agglomerates of crystals more or less deformed. He hopes ultimately to determine the conditions of the formation of all types of snow. There is here a rich field for free-air study and laboratory confirmation.

A similar study of the variation in snow crystals with variation in weather-elements has been conducted by V. I. Arnold-Alabiev [10] at the Central Geophysical Observatory, Leningrad, since 1936. In each storm the snow crystals are caught and their types and the frequency of each are determined. Temperature, humidity, and wind, preferably of the upper air, are recorded. This method lacks the selectivity and creative process of Nakaya's. It must await the slow chance combinations of nature.

This Soviet study could well be extended to the Arctic region, where the natives have several distinct terms for snow, descriptive of its relative value for sledging. There is also a field, particularly in Canada, where the cause of ski friction for airplanes is being studied, and in Washington State, where diverse weather and snow texture require specialized technique in removal of snow from the highways. Closely associated with this problem is the forecasting of ice on airplanes and sleet on highways. Prevention and avoidance should outweigh the cost of removal.

DEFINITIONS

Definitions, like names, are essential to identification. The condensation forms of water vapor include fogs and clouds with their active derivatives, rain and snow. When the temperature of the air is below freezing up to a considerable altitude, rain falling into it from above is likely to reach the ground only as frozen pellets, known as sleet. In England and in some places in North America the term "sleet" refers to rain and snow mixed.

Rain drops frozen at higher altitudes and frequently built up in layered balls to large size are known as hail.

Kindred to hail is the snow pellet (known as "graupel" or "tapioca snow"), a "tiny ball of softish ice or snow that looks as if it might have begun as a snow crystal and by capture of under-cooled cloud droplets ended as a wad of rime" [12, p. 21].

Glaze is the result of rain falling on exposed objects when either the rain is supercooled or the surface temperature is at or appreciably below the freezing point and turning to "slick and clearish" ice. Such objects may be airplanes flying far above the surface of the earth. The phenomenon is under study in connection with both air and land transport.

Other derivatives of water vapor are dew, Beschlag, frost, and rime, known as condensation deposits rather than precipitates, because not so visibly falling from heaven.

Dew results from the cooling of the immediately adjacent air by exposed objects and the deposition by the saturated air upon them of moisture in delicate droplets if the air is above the freezing point.   Strictly this is the case only where the ground cools by radiation; where warm moist air succeeds a cold spell, there may be a similar deposit, which is called "Beschlag."

If the temperature is below freezing, the deposit of dew is called frost.   It may be simply frozen dewdrops but is usually hoar, a product of sublimation.   "The forms are columnar when deposited rapidly at temperatures not far below the freezing point and tabular when deposited slowly in very low temperatures" [12, p. 21].   The tabular form when appearing on the surface of snow fields is known as "surface hoar" and is welcomed for its soft yet reliable texture.

Rime ("frozen-fog deposit") is a "tufty deposit of (granular) ice caused by the sudden freezing at the time and place of impact of undercooled fog or cloud droplets" [12, p. 21].   Unlike graupel, it builds up continuously and into the wind and attains its greatest size on mountain tops where cloudcaps persist and high winds accelerate deposition.   It has scant relation to icicles, which represent the gravity flow of water under conditions of glaze.

DISTRIBUTION OF RAIN AND SNOW

The snow varies in quantity and duration directly in relation to temperature.   This is also true in a broader sense of the water-vapor constituent of the atmosphere from which it is derived.   "At and above the height of 5 miles the amount of water vapor is always small, even when saturation obtains, owing to the very low temperatures at these levels. That is why water vapor (in appreciable amounts) is confined almost wholly to the lower atmosphere" [25, p. 11].

In the distribution of rain and snow over the earth the coldest places should therefore be the driest.   This means that the highest peaks and the polar regions should have the least precipitation.   On the other hand, because of the cold and consequent slowness of melting and evaporation they retain precipitation longest, and this is in the form of snow and ice. The increase in wind velocity with altitude offsets somewhat the retarding effect of cold, however.

As condensation of water vapor is due chiefly to cooling, maximum precipitation should be expected where moist air is forced upward by colder air, by converging currents, or by the slopes of mountains athwart its course.   Such processes are more effective near the ocean, the great source of evaporating moisture.   Conversely, the minimum precipitation should be sought in the lee of high mountains or progressively northward and away from the sea sources.

The counteracting influences of altitude and latitude on precipitation are shown by the climatic maps of the United States and Canada (Figs.

II-12 and IV-2; 45 and 45a). Through the center of the continent the isohyets decrease northward from 40 to 10 inches of water (normal annual precipitation), while on the Atlantic coast the isohyets continue at 40 inches or higher as far north as Greenland and on the Pacific coast they rise from 40 inches in Mexico or even 10 inches in southern California to as high as 160 inches on the coast of Alaska.

East of the barrier range isohyets of 10 inches are found in the Great Basin, as in the Arctic region, and east of the barrier range of southwestern

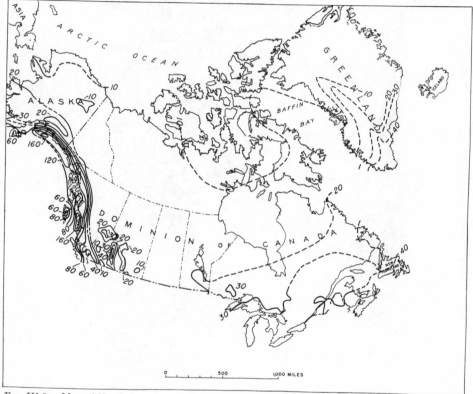

Fig. IV-2.—Map of North America, north of the United States, showing mean annual precipitation, in inches. By Charles F. Brooks and others. (*Courtesy of Blue Hill Meteorological Observatory.*)

Greenland the Michigan-Greenland Expedition found the annual precipitation in 1927–28 to have a water content of less than 3 inches.

Figure IV-3 shows the relative amount of precipitation that falls in the form of snow. The isopleths range from 0 percent at the Gulf of Mexico to 50 percent in the Arctic region. The effect of mountain ranges in distorting these curves northward is shown on the east and the west. Even so, the curves fail to show the preponderance of snowfall over rainfall in the higher mountains of the West. Furthermore, snow falls throughout the year on the back of the inland ice of Greenland above 8,800 feet (2,700 meters) and its accumulation apparently exceeds melting above

Fig. IV-3.—Map of North America, showing percentage of annual precipitation that falls in the form of snow.   See Fig. II-12, page 51, and Fig. IV-2, page 87; see also references 45 and 45a, on page 144.   By Charles F. Brooks and R. G. Stone.   (*Courtesy of Blue Hill Meteorological Observatory.*)

7,200 feet (2,200 meters). This failure is doubtless due to the lack of continuous records either of precipitation or of snow cover at high altitudes. It is this very accumulation in the American Far West that has built up its civilization on irrigation and hydroelectric power.

There is need of maps showing snow accumulation, preferably by April 1, the approximate beginning of the major runoff from snowfall watersheds. These maps can be based upon snow surveys that are now being made in most of the mountain areas as far north as southern Canada and Newfoundland. Maps of snow cover are preferable to those of annual precipitation, for, owing to the single soil priming attending the melting of the snow, runoff is the direct reflection of accumulated snow rather than of individual and scattered rains. For the same reason, the water tolerance of forest trees should be studied in terms of the more water-efficient snow cover. In any case the snow cover marks a seasonal hydrologic and cultural period.

In addition to the map showing annual snowfall in North America [45] there are maps of snow depth for various months of the winter in Sweden, with snow-depth measurements in Finland, Latvia, Czechoslovakia, and Australia. No complete continental maps have been attempted, but such a plan has been inaugurated by the International Commission of Snow and Glaciers through a committee directed by Dr. Charles F. Brooks. The only partial equivalent is a climatic map of E. Alt (Köppen-Geiger, vol. 3, p. M94), giving the days with snowfall in Europe. Isopleths up to 70 days are shown. Records are being kept in China of the mean annual and maximum monthly snowfall. Great Britain and others record the number of days snow lies on the ground. New England, Wisconsin, and Washington have regional and state snow depth maps.

ALTITUDE OF MAXIMUM SNOWFALL

A distinction must be maintained between the altitudes of maximum snowfall and maximum accumulation of snow. The latter should lie above the former and is associated with the alimentation zone of glaciers. The governing factor is again temperature.

Other things being equal, maximum snowfall follows the isohyets of maximum rainfall and deviates only as continuous cold affords opportunity for accumulation. Thus on the western slope of the central Sierra Nevada the zone of maximum precipitation is at an altitude of about 4,500 to 6,500 feet (average altitude of Grass Valley, Blue Canyon, Lake Spaulding, and Bowman Dam, 4,466 feet; average normal annual precipitation 69.0 inches of water. Altitude Fordyce Dam 6,500 feet; normal annual precipitation 67.1 inches of water), but the altitude of maximum snow cover is 8,000 feet or higher (water content of normal snow cover April 1 at Soda Springs Station, altitude 6,752 feet, 38.9 inches; Donner Summit, altitude 7,017 feet, 41.3 inches; Webber Peak, altitude 8,000 feet, 42.8 inches). At Soda Springs Station the normal annual precipitation and snow cover April 1 are nearly identical (precipitation 44.93 inches, snow cover 38.9 inches water). However, despite similarity of altitude, the normal annual precipitation at Soda Springs Station is far less than at Fordyce Dam, the figures for altitude and water content being 6,752 feet (44.93 inches) and 6,500 feet (67.1 inches) respectively. This barrier range offers an attractive opportunity for studying the variations in altitude of maximum precipitation both in summer and in winter.

On the eastern slope of the range, where the precipitation diminishes immediately with increase of distance to the leeward, the maximum precipitation, whether of snow or of rain, is at the crest. It is of course possible that summer convectional rains or thunderstorms may exceed the high-mountain storms in volume and intensity.

The perennial snow line, as indicated by occasional residual snow banks and glaciers, descends from 9,500 feet in the high or southern Sierra to 7,500 feet in the Cascade Range. Owing to the long summer insolation and light precipitation in the Arctic region, the snow line there retreats upward, although the glaciers themselves attain sea level. The snow line in Greenland is at 2,200 meters (7,200 feet), the altitude found far south in the Cascade Range. On the Equator, where mountains provide the requisite altitude, the snow line should be highest.

In the Antarctic region the climatic snow line, except at the northernmost point of Graham Land, lies outside the Antarctic coast and is therefore at sea level. At Laurie Island (S. 61°), at the outer edge of the Antarctic area, the mean temperature of the warmest months, January and February (1903–34), is +0.1° C. Only small bare spots occur, and most of the sun's rays are reflected. Local melt water where rocks protrude is absorbed by the snow. There is no runoff.

Despite the meager precipitation, estimated at 0.20 inch (5 millimeters) at the South Pole (altitude 3,000 meters) and 12 inches (300 millimeters) at the border of Antarctica, the persistence of the snow line is shown in East Antarctica by the buried buildings of Little America and Mawson's camp at Cape Denison and the alimentation of the pack ice surrounding the continent.

The equilibrium of precipitation, evaporation, and movement of the ice cap is a compelling problem, as is also the ultimate effect of wind—often foehn in character—on the distribution and wastage of snow. Is the ice cap now flowing from alimentation or from its previously accumulated mass? The annual growth of the snow cover at Cape Denison, despite exposure to wind, indicates the former.

Wagner [41, p. 114] has suggested that a reason for the higher altitude of the zone of maximum snowfall than of rainfall is the lighter weight of the snow flakes and their lesser ability to withstand the vertical component of the up-slope wind. Steinhauser [41, p. 113] has found the zone of maximum snowfall uniformly higher on Sonnblick Peak, in Austria, as observed on three available sides during a 5-year period. The altitude of maximum summer rainfall on the three sides was about 8,400 to 9,400 feet, but that of maximum winter precipitation was at the summit, at 3,080 meters (10,102 feet). The altitude of maximum rainfall on the southern or windward flank of the Himalayas is given by Wagner [41, p. 115] as about 1,300 meters (4,260 feet), and that of accumulated snow is set by Gorrie [5, p. 775] at about 13,000 to 16,000 feet.

The drifting of snow after it reaches the ground cannot be considered a basic element in this phenomenon, for the divergence occurs even where forested slopes prevent such drifting.

Also it is difficult to segregate snow from rain. In the central Sierra Nevada when the winter season has been sufficiently cold the altitude of maximum snowfall is identical with that of maximum precipitation. Unfortunately snow cover represents the residue and not the total precipitation and therefore fails as a dependable criterion in the transitional zone.

REGION OF GREATEST SNOWFALL

Owing to the lack of sufficient measurements at points of possible maximum snowfall, it is difficult to bring other areas, such as the Himalayas, into comparison with the United States. The estimate by Professor Heske, director of the Forest School at Tharandt, Germany, of a depth of 30 meters in the higher Himalayas is regarded as "fantastic." According to Dr. R. MacLaglan Gorrie [5, p. 775], of the Forest Research Division of the Punjab, "the actual average depth of snow accumulated at the end of the snowfall season is about 3 meters at 3,000 meters and certainly not more than 5 meters at 4,000+ to 5,000 meters, about 13,000 to 16,000 feet, above which precipitation does not increase perceptibly with increase in height."

However, this reasonable depth of 16 feet is still impressive and compares closely with the average depth of snow of 184 inches (15.3 feet) at Paradise Inn (altitude 5,550 feet), on the flank of Mount Rainier, Washington, regarded as probably the point of greatest snowfall in North America, unless perchance heavier snowfall may result in the mountains of Alaska opposite the coast center of rainfall of about 160 inches.

Lassen Peak, California, at Lake Helen (altitude 8,400 feet), had a snow depth of 233.2 inches (19.4 feet) in 1940, but this represents only the face of the mountain that is exposed to the direct impact of the moisture-laden southwest wind. The normal precipitation at Mount Rainier for the winter season of November to March is 64.28 inches, as compared with a normal snow cover at Lassen Peak having a water content of at least 92.2 inches. However, at the density of 47.6 percent found on Lassen Peak the normal water content on Mount Rainier should be 87.6 inches, an amount considerably in excess of the measured precipitation. Further-more, the snow depth should increase with the altitude. Fortunately, snow sampling conducted by William Pruitt, Jr., during the winter of 1940–41 has revealed a depth of snow of 141 inches on Mount Rainier at Edith Creek Basin (altitude 5,000 feet) as compared with a depth of 71 inches on Lassen Peak at Paradise Inn. The density of the snow at both places was between 49 and 50 percent, indicating water contents of about 62 and 35.5 inches, respectively. Unfortunately, however, the seasonal snow cover was only 38.6 percent of normal on Mount Rainier as compared with 134 percent on Lassen Peak. If the measurements on both moun-tains are reduced to normal, the water content of the snow cover is 100 inches on Lassen Peak and 161 inches on Mount Rainier. Mr. Pruitt reports that there is little likelihood of deeper snow on Mount Rainier. Because Edith Creek Basin is at timber line it would be difficult to find places at higher altitudes where the measurements would not be greatly distorted by drifting. The honor of greatest depth definitely seems to have passed from Blue Lakes and Donner Pass.[1]

The probability of finding a region of maximum snowfall north of Mount Rainier is rendered doubtful by the fact that the season of maxi-mum precipitation in Alaska is a month later than in Washington State and 3 months later than in the central Sierra Nevada, where maximum precipitation occurs in midwinter, thus reducing the proportion of annual precipitation that falls in the form of snow. The nearest known com-petitor to Mount Lassen and Mount Rainier is the Jumbo mine, on Prince of Wales Island.

The following table gives the available basic data:

Relation of snowfall to total precipitation

Station	Altitude (feet)	Water content of annual precipitation (inches)	Period of maximum precipitation	Water content of accumulated snowfall on basis of 1:10 (inches)	Proportion of snow to total precipitation
Blue Lakes, Central Sierra, Calif.........	8,000	50.63	Dec.–Mar.	45.91	0.91
Mount Rainier, Washington State......	5,550	99.23	Oct.–Jan.	59.13	.60
Ketchikan, Southern Alaska............	Sea level	157.67	Sept.–Dec.	4.62	.03
Jumbo mine (near Ketchikan)..........	1,500	195	Sept.–Dec.	45	.23
Fort Liscum (Prince William Sound)....	30	73.12	Sept.–Dec.	36.88	.50

[1] Blue Lakes (altitude 8,000 feet), 40.8 inches of water; Lake Lucile (8,400 feet), 61.9 inches; Donner Pass (7,017 feet), 41.3 inches; Webber Peak (8,000 feet), 42.8 inches; Lassen Peak (8,400 feet), 92.2 inches; Crater Lake (6,018 feet), 46.73 inches; Mount Rainier (5,550 feet), 64.28 inches. The figures for all but Crater Lake and Mount Rainier represent snow cover.

Unfortunately this comparison is based on accumulated snowfall rather than on residual snow cover at the end of the season of accumulation.

The final decision must depend upon high-level snow surveys on Mount Rainier and the mountains, such as Mount Fairweather, of the southern Alaskan area.

A striking fact is the very small snowfall at the South Pole, where latitude and altitude offer minimum temperature and the air currents have lost most of their force. As already mentioned, the total annual precipitation is estimated at only 0.20 inch, with evaporation probably correspondingly small. This might aptly be called "the land of cirrus deposit." A year's sojourn would provide fruitful solitude.

DENSITY OF SNOW COVER

The most obvious characteristic of the snow cover is its variation in density, which stems directly from the varying density of the snowflakes that form it. These may be almost impalpable, like the vaporous moonbeams of the polar regions, or heavy as hail or rime. The lightest snow ever recorded on the ground at the time of fall is 0.4 of 1 percent (0.004) water content, in Sodankylä, Finland, during the winter of 1917–18. A fall of 0.5 percent water content was recorded at Charles City, Iowa, during the winter of 1904–05. Rime, though filled with air cells, has the power to accumulate on a $3/16$-inch guy rod in sufficient diameter to tear out the eyes of the sections and break the T couplings of the one-inch tubular supports through the resulting unbalancing of strains (See Fig. IV-15.). The weight of a linear foot of the accumulation was 13 pounds. However, it is difficult to determine with precision the density of either fluffy snow or feathery rime, because of the irregularity of the surface. [5, pp. 571–585. See also Am. Meteorol. Soc. Bull., vol. 20, pp. 53–54, 225, 1939.]

The relation of snow density to altitude should be primarily its relation to cold and wind. The simpler crystals, whether columns or plates, are formed where the air is cold and therefore at high altitudes, whereas the complex star-shaped crystals are formed in relative warmth. Furthermore, because of difference in absolute humidity in the two zones, the columns and plates are sparse and the stars dense. On the other hand, because of simplicity of form the columns and plates will pack together under movement more readily than the stars, thus simulating water-laid sand.

Paradoxically, the cold-born snow, though initially lighter, soon becomes denser than the warm-born snow and quickly approaches maximum density. The transition was noticed during the winter observations on the inland ice of Greenland. The measurements were made by Helge Bangsted (unpublished report). In no case did the depth of "new-born" snow exceed 1.4 inches, so small was the quantity. Therefore gravity had

little or no part in the increase in density.   The temperature ranged from
−17.2° to −15.0° C. (+0.4 to +5.0° F.).   The air was still.   The snow
density at the two temperature extremes was 3.6 percent, or about one-
third of the formular density of 10 percent.   During the night at a temperature of −18.1° C. (−1.0° F.) but during wind the density increased
to 11.5 percent (average of four measurements), but where the snow was
less exposed to the wind the density increased to only 5.6 percent.

New snow after apparently only a day or a night of drifting attained
an average density of 17.6 percent.   Later in the same period snow only
2.9 inches in average depth attained a density of 24.3 percent.   The
density of old snow (depth 5.8 inches) was found to be as high as 28.0
percent.   Drift snow (depth 7.2 inches) after sufficient movement to cover
the sled had a density of 35.4 percent.

Unfortunately identical records are not available for mountain peaks,
but the following comparison several days after a storm indicates that
density at high altitudes is due mainly to wind.

Density of snow at high altitudes

Cornice on Mount Rose, Nevada (10,800 feet), exposed			San Francisco Peaks, spruce forest, Flagstaff, Ariz. (10,000 ft.), sheltered		
Date, 1911	Depth of snow (inches)	Density (percent)	Date, 1917	Depth of snow (inches)	Density (percent)
Feb. 2.................	115.5	44.2[a]	Mar. 7.................	24.0	16.3
May 2.................	100.6	49.7	May 1.................	44.0	29.8
June 8–9..............	71.8	47.7	May 30...............	39.0	34.9
Maximum increase......	.....	5.5	Maximum increase.....	....	18.6

[a] 7 days after storm.

Soft snow was found by Whymper at 20,000 feet, in the Andes.   He
wrote, "Louis Carrel could not touch bottom with a twelve-foot pole that
he was carrying.   It would have continued to descend by its own weight
if he had left hold of it. . . . as the slope steepened the snow became firmer
again."[1]   FitzGerald encountered at 18,700 feet on Aconcagua, Chile, in
the Andes, "high clouds of driven snow, fine as sand, which nearly suffocated them," and "fell into a huge drift of soft snow."[2]   The minimum temperature was −28° C. (−18.4° F.).   Of the Himalayas, Odell
writes, "Our soft snow on Nanda Devi up to 25,000 feet was in a
more or less sheltered reentrant of the mountain, while the exposed
summit calotte (25,645 feet) had on the whole a harder compacted surface,
although not uniformly so.   The more sheltered parts of the flanks of

[1] Travels Amongst the Great Andes of the Equator by Edward Whymper, pp. 68, 71
(ascent of Mount Chimborazo, Ecuador).

[2] The Highest Andes by E. A. FitzGerald, pp. 89, 92, 114.

Everest's north face are of soft floury snow, and there is on the whole only restricted windslab on the more salient portions."[1]

However, wind-blown snow quickly acquires a high density, which is only slightly increased during the season. The firmness of this snow under foot usually makes mountain ascents easier in winter than in summer.

MEASUREMENT OF SNOW

Because of its unstable character and various phases, snow is extremely difficult to measure by any method and requires several. In this respect it differs from rain, which is both relatively heavy and inelastic. Rain also disappears quickly except when stored. The depth and duration of snow are the simplest standards for measuring it. Its water content is another, and its surface and structure constitute still others.

Snow depth on the ground, if measured 10 days after a storm or long enough to allow the snow to settle, is satisfactory as an approximate method. It is visual and vivid also. However, because of drifting, a series of measurements should be employed rather than the record of a single or isolated snow stake. Snow courses are preferable even to several stakes or measurements at random. On the basis of 10,000 individual measurements under various conditions, sufficient uniformity has been discovered to prepare a table of water content based on altitude, depth, and season.

Accumulated depth of snowfall is an attempt to measure the total seasonal precipitation by adding up the depth of snowfall as it occurs day by day or storm by storm. To make it comparable to rainfall for purposes of statistics, 10 inches of snowfall is rated as equivalent to 1 inch of rain. However, the average ratio for four winter seasons (January to March) at Tahoe City, Calif. (altitude 6,230 feet), has ranged from 1:5.23 to 1:10.32. As representative of depth of snow on the ground the accumulated depth is utterly confusing, because of the rapid shrinkage in depth of newly fallen snow and the apparently fantastic total. A classic example is successful snow removal at Crater Lake, Oregon, with a reported official snowfall record of 59 feet 11 inches. On the basis of 45 percent probable density the depth of the snow cover removed was 16 feet.

Precipitation-gage measurements are gradually increasing in accuracy. The tendency of snow flakes to ride buoyantly on wind currents created by the gage itself makes them very elusive as compared with the heavier raindrops. On the summit of Mount Rose (altitude 10,800 feet), where strong up drafts occur, it would have been necessary to turn the gage upside down to get the snow to enter. (See Fig. IV-15.)

[1] Unpublished correspondence, International Commission of Snow, Washington Meeting, 1939.

Shielded gages have now been developed by J. Cecil Alter (Fig. IV-4) which neutralize the air currents and clear themselves of accumulating snow. These gages give results comparable to those of snow surveys in the vicinity. A network of mountain snowfall stations equipped with these gages is now being spread by the United States Weather Bureau over the Western States. The average altitude of the 92 stations erected

is 7,643 feet. Five stations are above 10,000 feet. The immediate program comprises 6,000 nonrecording and 2,500 recording precipitation stations. "The purpose is to provide data of rainfall and snowfall for all purposes involved in the control and utilization of water." The catch of all gages is determined by weight, and evaporation is restrained by the use of a film of oil.

Recording gages are superior in indicating the date and rate of accumulation and loss by evaporation or otherwise. The Fergusson and Stevens gages represent the present development in the United States of recorders for rain and snow combined. Further tests of these instruments under severe snow conditions seem desirable. A Fergusson gage with an Alter screen is shown in Fig. IV-4. Figure IV-5 shows the Fergusson weighing recording rain and snow gage.

FIG. IV-4.—Alter screen for protecting orifice of rain and snow gages, shown with a Fergusson gage. (*Courtesy of United States Weather Bureau.*)

The Mougin totalizator (Fig. IV-6), now in general use in the Alps, was developed to catch the total winter precipitation, or even the total annual precipitation, in places inaccessible for long periods of time. The catch is determined by the dilution of the chemical contents placed in the reservoir at the beginning of the period to melt the snow as it enters. Because of the location of these instruments in rough country, a check of their accuracy, as by snow surveying, is difficult. Such a check is very desirable because of the presence of heavy wind currents.

There are several devices for neutralizing air currents at the orifice of a precipitation gage. The original Nipher screen has passed through many variations, although the principle remains unchanged. This type is now undergoing a supreme test in Antarctica, where a gage developed on Mount Washington under the supervision of Dr. C. F. Brooks has been taken in an attempt to measure precipitation under wild conditions of wind. Spindrift must be eliminated by raising the gage on a tower, if possible, above the zone of drifting snow, 50 to perhaps 100 feet.[1]

FIG. IV-5.—Fergusson weighing recording rain and snow gage. (*Courtesy of Julian P. Friez & Sons, Inc.*)

Snow sampling supplements and extends the measurement of snowfall by gages. By its means both depth and water content of snowfall or snow cover can be determined wherever desired. By the use of snow courses, distortion in measurements due to wind can be avoided. The variation in snowfall can be determined in areas where gages would not be feasible because of situation or number required. Furthermore, the evolution of the snow cover can be traced, and its residue, upon which the snow runoff is chiefly based, can be determined.

[1] H. G. Dorsey, Jr., Meteorologist at the East Base, Antarctica, has since reported that his station was so situated as to favor unusually low wind velocities during precipitation and that the gage was elevated above all drift. Owing to scarcity of precipitation gages, no comparison of the catch in shielded and unshielded gages was made. (*Am. Geophys. Union Trans.*, 1941.)

The snow sampler is built on the principle of cutting cores from the snow and determining their water content by weighing. Thus an inelastic standard for comparison with rain is established. The snow depth is measured by the sampler tube. The density of the snow is computed from the relation of water content to depth and varies throughout the season.

Fig. IV-6.—Mougin totalizator. It contains saline solution to melt the snow immediately upon entry into the can. It also has a Nipher screen to break the wind currents at the orifice. Summit of the Diablerets, Alpes Vaudoises, Switzerland, 1915. (*Courtesy of P.-L. Mercanton.*)

Practically all types of snow samplers are based on the Mount Rose snow sampler (fig. IV-7), developed by the Nevada Agricultural Experiment Station in the winter of 1908–9 for studies of the relation of forests and mountains to the conservation of snow. Its chief feature is a tube of usable size containing a special cutter and vertical slots through which to determine the length of the core and reach the interior of the instrument, if necessary. Sections can be added to any feasible length. Snow to

Fig. IV-7.—Mount Rose snow sampler, showing cutter and couplings. The stamped graduations and numbers should be filled with pigment to make them more visible in dim light. The slots are used for observing the rise of the core within the tube and also for dislodging snow if it adheres. The sampler can be lengthened to 20 or 30 feet by the addition of extra sections. The slots are staggered in each section so that the rise of the snow can be seen at every point in the tube, except at the couplings.

depths of more than 20 feet has been measured, and the equipment is being developed for depths of 30 feet or more. The cutter contains a shoulder to lift the core when the sampler is raised from the snow. The core after being weighed is discharged by inverting the tube.

A spring balance, adjustable to zero to eliminate the weight of the sampler, directly indicates the net weight of the core in inches of water—that is the amount of water in the snow at the point of sampling. A driving wrench is employed where the density or depth of the snow requires. A coat of shellac or paraffin reduces the sticking of snow to the tube.

(a)   (b)

Fig. IV-8.—(a) Refuge hut in the Cascade Range, Ore., with "Santa Claus" entrance tower. (b) Winter view, showing the usual depth of the snow. (*Courtesy of R. A. Work, Div. of Irrigation, United States Soil Conservation Service.*)

Three changes have been made in this sampler by the Utah Agricultural Experiment Station to reduce cost and weight. A tubular spring balance has been substituted for the adjustable dial balance, and the diameter of the cutter has been decreased slightly so that ounces are equivalent to inches of water. However, this balance lacks the extremes in capacity and also the adjustability that the original possesses. Duralumin has been substituted for steel, with a diminution of 60 percent in weight. This metal is more rigid than steel but bends and tears more readily. Its durability is still under test. It is also a rapid conductor of heat and cold and therefore promotes the melting and subsequent freezing of snow to the surface. A coating such as shellac checks this tendency somewhat. Can a material of low wetting or conduction coefficient be found as a coating or even as a substitute?

Tubes 2.65 inches in diameter are used in the Eastern States and other regions where the snow is coarse but shallow, in order to obtain more nearly complete cores by increasing the size of the orifice. In "tapioca snow" the Kadel sampler is sometimes employed. This consists of a tube 5.94 inches in diameter to confine the snow column from spreading and a snow auger to close the lower end of the tube while the tube is being drawn to the surface. The larger diameters are feasible only where the snow is shallow, for only man power is available to do the driving.

A typical shelter used in snow surveying is shown in Figure IV-8.

SNOW SURVEYING AND FORECASTING STREAM FLOW

Two systems of snow surveying have been developed—the percentage system and the quantitative system. The percentage system was developed in Nevada and is also known as the Nevada system. Its purpose is to determine at the end of the winter season the relative water content of the snow cover in entire basins and to apply this percentage as a forecast of the ensuing stream flow that is due mainly to the melting of the snow. This runoff, known as major flow, lasts about four months (April through July).

The quantitative system determines the cubical water content of the snow cover over the basin and forecasts what residue from it will appear as runoff.

Both systems must be distinguished from the precipitation system, which records the total annual precipitation for the water year, October to September, and seeks from it an index of runoff. The percentage and quantitative systems deal with snow residue in its most effective form for producing maximum runoff; the precipitation system deals with total precipitation, which may include a portion of ineffective rain. The total accumulated precipitation, unless carefully analyzed and weighted, must therefore fail to attain the precision of the others as a method of forecast. However, it serves as a background in determining soil wetting and concurrent runoff.

PERCENTAGE SYSTEM

The Percentage System came into being through the obvious impossibility of determining the quantitative water content of the snow on the rugged and high watersheds of the West, where the snow cover attains maximum depth.

SNOW COURSES

The use of snow courses as a tool originated in the running of straight-line courses through typical areas of mountain slopes and forests to determine the effect of each upon the gathering and dissipation of snow. The snow sampler became an essential adjunct to reduce all types of snow to the common standard of water content. The seasonal harmony of the snow-course averages throughout a watershed led to the conclusion that two or three key courses in a basin, if averaged, would indicate usually within 10 percent of normal the ensuing runoff from it.

The first forecast of snow resources, issued on Mount Rose in the spring of 1910–11, was the result of averaging snow courses laid out for the study of the relation of mountains and forests to the conservation of snow and read as follows: "On Mount Rose the amount of moisture in the form of snow available for irrigation the present season was 44.4 inches, or almost double the amount (23.5 inches) available last season. Furthermore, on account of the lateness of the spring, 38.3 inches of moisture were available a year ago." Thus it was indicated that the snow cover of 1910–11 should furnish 189.4 percent of that provided by the cover of 1909–10, and it was only necessary to apply this percentage to the measured stream flow in the basin in 1909–10 to determine the acre-feet of water to be expected in 1910–11. Normals or averages for both snow courses and runoff would yield even closer forecasts.

The length and shape of courses should be such as to neutralize the irregularities due to drifting of the snow. A cross course will detect and neutralize drifting caused by change in seasonal wind direction. The indispensable condition is unvarying identity in the position of the individual points of sampling. Therefore, points of sight and exact distance between measurements are rigidly maintained. Standard maps, descriptions, and markers are now provided.

The only areas still unfavorable for snow courses are gentle treeless slopes where the sweep of the wind is unhindered. Such are the deserts, the polar areas, and the highland of Sweden. Aspen or birch trees if sufficiently high to remain unburied, are ideal deadeners of wind and anchors for snow. Courses of unusual length might provide an accurate cross section of wind-blown snow.

WIDE-AREA FORECASTING

The application of seasonal percentage in one basin to adjacent basins, even on opposite sides of the range, was made possible by the fact that the snow cover is the result of general storms of wide uniformity as compared with convectional summer rains, upon the diversity of which the belief in the diversity of all precipitation, even over small basins, had previously been based.

Fortunately the long range of the Sierra Nevada, lying at right angles to the prevailing storm track, provided ideal conditions for observing this uniformity and determining its limits. It was found by snow surveys that the maximum divergence between individual basins along the central Sierra Nevada did not exceed 25 percent in terms of the normal, even for distances of approximately 100 miles. In the series including the South

Maximum variation in runoff in individual basins of the Sierra Nevada, April–July, 1909–20, by areas and slopes
[Percent of normal]

Side of range and area	Basins included	1909–10	1910–11	1911–12	1912–13	1913–14	1914–15	1915–16	1916–17	1917–18	1918–19	1919–20
East side (175 miles):												
Central Sierra area (110 miles)	Tahoe to West Walker (3 basins)	32.4	26.1	13.8	16.7	11.4	4.6	14.5	21.8	20.6	15.4	46.6[a]
East side entire......	Including Owens	32.4	34.9	19.1	16.7	19.3	7.3	26.4	21.8	20.6		
West side (505 miles):												
Northern Sierra area (120 miles)	Upper Klamath to Pit (4 basins)	.....	16.7	8.6	28.5	27.4	91.4	11.3	73.0	10.8	17.7	
	Omitting upper Sacramento and McCloud	.....	16.7	6.1	17.2	27.4	26.0	7.4	16.6	10.8		
Central Sierra area (210 miles)	Feather to Tuolumne (6 basins)	19.3	38.0[b]	13.6	25.1	18.3	34.0[c]	13.4	9.2	25.5[c]	15.8	
Southern Sierra area (175 mi)	Merced to Kern (5 basins)	37.6	57.0	9.7	11.2	72.0	22.9	259.0	41.9	28.0	16.4	
	Omitting Kern	32.4	57.9	2.0	11.2	38.6	14.1	23.9	8.6	22.6	11.1	
West side entire......	.....	53.6	74.9	42.5	65.7	72.0	91.4	299.4	80.0	35.4	24.9	

[a] Probably due to diversions above point of gaging.
[b] Divergence between adjoining streams.
[c] Extreme ends of area.

Yuba, Tahoe, Carson, and Walker Basins the maximum divergence for the 7 years 1915–22, in percent, was as follows:

1915–16	1916–17	1917–18	1918–19	1919–20	1920–21	1921–22
9.8	5.1	11.0	12.8	13.0	14.0	24.7

In the succeeding years it has been even less.

In the absence of other snow-survey courses, a comparison of the runoff during the period April to July (representing the probable effect of the snow cover) was immediately made for all basins along the range, with the result that for purposes of forecasting the region was divided into three areas with uniformity of conditions similar to that in the central Sierra, except where the topography is erratic (Table page 102).

The upper Sacramento and McCloud Basins are possibly erratic because of their source on the flanks of Mount Shasta. The Kern Basin, being situated in the semidesert area at the south end of the Sierra Nevada, has a tendency to show flash records despite its source in the highest part of the range, and must therefore be treated as a separate unit. The foothill streams, fed only to a minor extent by snow, have been omitted from the table. The primary peak of their flow occurs in midwinter, and only occasionally does their April to July runoff correspond closely with that of the crest streams.

The variation between the runoff of adjacent streams on opposite slopes of the Sierra Nevada indicates a close correspondence in their seasonal percentage of snow cover, although the quantities are necessarily different because of the greater snowfall on the windward side of the range. However, occasional aberrations are apparent. The table on page 104 presents details.

Within the individual areas the variation between opposite slopes occurs by years rather than by basins. During the years of comparison only two seasons showed excessive variation. In the central Sierra area in 1913–14 the snowfall on the eastern or lee slope was far more intense than that on the western slope; in 1914–15 the reverse was true.

The evidence of snow surveys now established in all the Sierra Nevada basins corroborates the foregoing exploratory comparison. Furthermore, the following variations for 1939 indicate the harmony that can occur over the entire length of 500 miles: North area, 2 percent; central area, 25 percent; southern area, 15 percent; the three areas combined, 25 percent. The Yuba is the discordant basin; without it, the maximum variation would be only 17 percent.

Courses along the crest with outpost courses for each slope provide the basic data for detecting oscillation in the seasonal snow cover and thus afford abundant opportunity to arrange for routing electric power from the more favored to the less favored areas served. This interlocking

Maximum variation between runoff of streams on opposite slopes of the Sierra Nevada but having a common crest, 1909-20

[Percentage of normal]

Group and basins	1909-10	1910-11	1911-12	1912-13	1913-14	1914-15	1915-16	1916-17	1917-18	1918-19	1919-20
Central Sierra area:											
Truckee (exclusive of Tahoe) and Yuba (cross axis 70 miles)	22.8	15.3	5.9	15.5	28.5	36.1	11.7	18.3	5.5	6.3	3.7
Tahoe and American (cross axis 78 miles)	3.7	11.8	.8	7.6	42.4	35.2	0.3	17.3	9.1	5.1	
Carson and Mokelumne (cross axis 103 miles)	15.9	8.5	10.8	5.4	49.2	15.7	2.4	15.2	2.3	8.7	
West Walker and Tuolumne (cross axis 81 miles)	20.1	.1	3.6	8.5	....	....	6.7	1.1	8.8	3.1	
Southern Sierra area:											
Owens (at Round Valley) and San Joaquin	10.4	34.3	6.4	19.2	6.8	18.2	32.0	20.3	3.3		

system has long reached even across the range. In pooling water supplies and power for southern California, the Continental Divide is closely linked with the Sierra Nevada through the Boulder Dam and the Metropolitan water system from the Parker Dam, on the Colorado.

Snow surveys at key stations during the winter will keep the public in sympathetic touch with the seasonal growth of the snow cover and forestall wild estimates. For this purpose the surveys should preferably be made the first of each month and the report given in percentage of normal to date and normal for the entire season of accumulation, which ends usually April 1 or later at high altitudes and latitudes.

Altitude zoning

Occasionally premature melting of the snow cover at the lower altitudes disturbs the balance upon which the accuracy of the survey depends and causes the apparent snow cover to exceed the runoff. To avoid this possibility each basin was divided into zones of 1,000 feet or more in altitude from the stream-gaging station to the crest, and the area of each zone was computed from topographic maps if available. One or more snow-survey courses were maintained in each zone, and the seasonal percentage of each group was weighted according to the relative area of its zone as compared with the others.

The application of the zoning system in the Tahoe Basin will illustrate the procedure. This basin rises from an altitude of 6,225 to 10,900 feet at its highest point. It was divided naturally into four zones, two representing oscillation in intensity of precipitation from the crest of the basin eastward and two representing zones of premature melting. The altitude of horizontal division was placed at 7,000 feet. The resulting areas, in square miles, were as follows:

	East side	West side	Total
Above 7,000 feet	89.3	87.3	176.6
Below 7,000 feet	47.5	82.8	130.3
	136.8	170.1	306.9

In 1931 the snow-survey results April 1, in percent of normal, were as follows:

	East side	West side	Total
Above 7,000 feet	39.3	42.0	40.7
Below 7,000 feet	34.0	18.4	26.2
Average	36.7	30.2	33.5

The average of the high-level percentages is 40.7; of the high and low combined, 33.5; and the weighted percentage of the four zones is 33.6. The rise of Lake Tahoe from April 1 to the maximum was 30.3 percent, or 10 percent below the percentage of snow at the crest. The loss had occurred in the lower zones, particularly on the west side. Quantitatively, a large divergence normally exists between the four zones because of the diminishing of the precipitation from west to east and from the crest downward—a phenomenon native to the lee side of mountains. This is eliminated by the use of percentage of normal.

Normals

By comparing a snow survey with that of a previous season whose runoff has been measured, it is possible at once to forecast in terms of the former season, providing its resultant runoff occurred under approximately normal conditions of precipitation during the runoff period. Or a system of parallel normals either of snow cover or of runoff can be built up from an adjoining area where longer measurements of snow cover or streams have been made. The two should be interchangeable, but the comparison should be limited to the same period of time.

A weighted normal can be produced by adapting it to a longer adjacent series. Thus the normal water content of the snow cover at Donner Summit has been weighted at 47.8 inches for use in forecasting the runoff of the Truckee River to the east and at 41.3 inches for forecasting the runoff of the Yuba River to the west. The lesser weight for the Yuba was made possible by the longer record of stream flow of that river, which covered a leaner period of years.

The fact that snow cover and stream flow have occasionally reached more than 200 percent of normal and never can fall below 0 is leading toward the adoption of medians in place of averages or normals. In flashy streams like the Kern, where within 10 years seasonal variations from 52.6 to 390.3 percent occurred, with two years reaching 174.1 and 170.3 percent, it became necessary for purposes of adapting forecasts to needs for irrigation to eliminate the abnormal seasons from the practical normal, at least until the series absorbed the flood peaks. Therefore it is sometimes best to recompute normals only after periods of drought and excess have somewhat counterbalanced each other.

Some engineers have suggested that normals be confined to 10-year periods, so that the forecasts will conform to man's present impressions of the usual or current water supply. In the Humboldt Basin, Nevada, water users have requested that the normal March-July runoff of the river be retained at 255,000 acre-feet, which represents the amount necessary to satisfy or give a 100 percent water supply to the irrigated lands of the basin.

However, in actuality all forecasts are reduced to total acre-feet or under special conditions to latest date at which flow is available. On this basis the water master apportions the water according to the terms of allocation, which are often complex.

Factors affecting forecasts

That the snow cover is basic in forecasting is indicated by the accompanying graph (Fig. IV-9), showing the general harmony between the seasonal percentage of the snow cover at even a single station at the crest of the Truckee River Basin, Nevada, and the April-July runoff of the stream. The divergencies are caused by other factors mentioned below. Views of the Lake Tahoe and Truckee River Basins are shown in Figure IV-10.

Therefore, the basic formula in forecasting by the percentage system is "the seasonal percentage of the accumulated snow cover represents the percentage of the major seasonal runoff from it. Since the runoff can be measured with fair precision the percentage can be translated immediately into total acre-feet of flow. This major runoff usually covers 4 months, April to July, but in extreme cases may cover March to June or May to August."

The factors affecting the forecasts—that is, causing shrinkage or expansion in the expected flow—are still under investigation. Those that can be estimated at the time of the snow survey are (a) priming of the soil, (b) the influence of stream channel, and (c) the effect of diversions above gaging stations. The unpredictable factors, in the order of importance, are (a) precipitation during the period of major runoff, (b) temperature, (c) wind, and (d) evaporation. As these factors are absorbed or negligible when conditions are normal—that is, 100 percent in the percentage system of forecasting—only the variations need be considered, and these are relatively small.

Priming of the soil.—The factor of soil priming naturally depends on the amount of saturation locally required to produce runoff. In the semiarid, mountainous West the amount of moisture required to prime the soil at the beginning of the runoff season is practically fixed irrespective of previous precipitation or temperature. Indeed, the effect of the heaviest

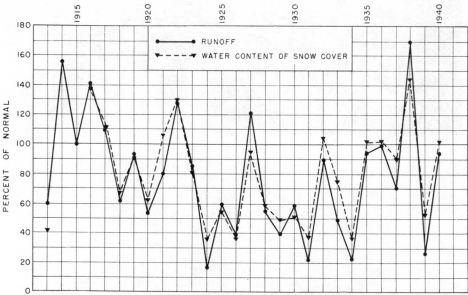

Fig. IV-9.—Comparison of the April-July runoff of the Truckee River, Calif.-Nev. (exclusive of Lake Tahoe), with water content of the snow cover determined from measurements at a single station. Normal runoff is average for 24-year period ending in 1927. Normal water content of snow cover is based on comparison with runoff for corresponding years. (*Data from Nevada Cooperative Snow Surveys, after H. P. Boardman.*)

snow cover in the central Sierra Nevada, which is cumulative far in excess of the effect of rain, does not persist beyond October, or 4 months after its peak flow. This is due to the steep mountain slopes and a surface material sufficiently porous to permit rapid runoff. Even the heavier autumn rains are drained off before the winter has arrived. Moreover, the freezing of the surface soil, so effective on priming in the East, is entirely lacking except for small meadow areas, for the surface has been drained dry before the freezing temperatures of winter occur.

In the Pacific Northwest, however, where the autumn rains are more abundant and the soil remains moist into the winter, the relative moisture of the soil at the beginning of the spring runoff becomes a vital factor, as it is in the far East, where the precipitation is distributed more evenly

(a)

(b)

Fig. IV-10.—For descriptive legend see opposite page.

throughout the year and frost occurs before snowfall or where the snow cover is relatively shallow.

Where the variants of soil moisture and frost are eliminated, as in the Sierra Nevada, the factor of soil priming becomes a simple ratio between the water content of the snow cover and the moisture capacity of the underlying soil. As the soil here is shallow and the underlying rock is impervious, the total loss in priming the soil does not exceed an estimated 8.25 inches, a low amount compared with the normal snow cover of 40 to 60 inches water content. For the entire South Yuba Basin the loss has been computed at one-third of the winter precipitation of 45 inches, measured at the center of the basin, at Fordyce Dam.

Although this factor is theoretically potent, actually it has been detected only in the South Yuba Basin, where small area and a zoning system have made close measurements possible. Here a correction factor of 3 percent in the runoff has been found applicable for a 60 percent diminution of the normal snow cover (water content 44.12 inches).

Strangely, in the Great Basin and the Wasatch Basin, where the snow cover is approximately one-fourth and one-half respectively of that in the South Yuba Basin, no trace of the soil-priming factor has been found. Here the factor may be eclipsed by depth and porosity of the soil.

Dams.—The relative effect of obstructions, such as tight dams in the streams, and of floods depends upon the height of the water in the channel and the amount of overflow onto lands from which the water cannot return.

Diversions.—The effect of diversions above points of gaging is similar to that of subnormal snow and can be readily computed if the diversions represent fixed withdrawals irrespective of seasonal flow. Dried-out meadows can produce a similar but irregular effect because of irregularity in soil moisture.

The solution of these problems is essential to forecasting both seasonal runoff and floods.

Unpredictable factors

Precipitation during runoff period.—The chief distorting factor, which unfortunately is unpredictable, is the divergence from normal of precipitation during the runoff period, for normal precipitation during runoff is essential in keeping the snow fields up to the percentage set by the snow survey. Theoretically, if precipitation is entirely lacking, the runoff will fall below the forecast to an amount depending upon the ratio of the nor-

Fig. IV-10.—Views of Lake Tahoe and Truckee River Basins, where snow surveying was developed. (*a*) Lake Tahoe from altitude of 9,000 feet, showing State Line Point and snow-survey stations in the northwest quadrant of the basin. The lake never freezes, thus affording a coast line 72 miles long that is accessible to a cabin cruiser for a variety of snow studies. (*b*) Upper Truckee Basin from Mount Rose (altitude 10,800 feet). Donner Lake is in the middle distance. Unlike Lake Tahoe, Donner Lake nearly always freezes, and here appears like a meadow. Donner Pass (Summit) is immediately above Snow courses at Summit and the gaging station at Iceland are indicated.

mal precipitation during runoff to the water content of the normal snow cover. The ratio is smallest in the Sierra Nevada and gradually increases eastward to the Continental Divide, where the summer rains nearly equal the winter precipitation representing the snow fields. East of the Continental Divide the precipitation during runoff is in the ascendancy.

Practically, however, the snow cover is far more effective, for the percolation from the snow cover is practically continuous and thus simulates a continuous downpour of rain, whereas the precipitation during the runoff season often falls upon dry soil and, like intermittent rain, is wasted in priming the soil.[1]

For this reason the April and May precipitation is far more effective than that of June and July, for the snow cover should at that time be continuous and extend farther down the slopes, thus catching the rain without loss. Furthermore, west of the Continental Divide the precipitation during April and May is normally far heavier than during June and July and thus permits an early estimate of possible deficiency in precipitation during runoff and close revision of the original forecast.

The ratio of summer (April-July) to winter (November-March) precipitation in the Western States and Provinces and the estimated loss in runoff due to 100 percent deficiency in summer precipitation are shown in the following table:

Winter and summer precipitation in Western States and Provinces

Region	Precipitation (inches)		Ratio of summer to winter precipitation (percent)	Estimated percent of runoff for 100 percent deficiency in summer precipitation
	Winter	Summer		
Sierra Nevada: Colfax, 1870–1923.....	37.52	6.89	18.2	16.2
Humboldt Basin: 6 stations, 1918–30...	6.31	3.83	60.7	22.7
Logan Basin: 5 stations..............	7.06	6.72	95.2	35.6
Continental Divide: Durango, Telluride, and Leadville, Colo...........	7.78	6.67	85.7	30[a]
East of Continental Divide:				
Denver, Colo.....................	3.22	7.67	238.2	75–90
Calgary, Alberta.................	2.99	8.52	284.9	75–90

[a] Approximate.

Water surfaces are far more responsive to direct precipitation and evaporation than land surfaces. In large lakes such as Tahoe, where the water area bears a ratio of 2:3 to the land area of the basin, the shrinkage

[1] A difference in effectiveness between continuous and intermittent rains of about 30 percent has been found in Hawaii (Rice, R. C., Relation between rainfall and runoff in Hillebrand Glen, Nuuanu Valley, Oahu, Hawaii: Monthly Weather Rev., vol. 45, pp. 178–181, 1917). A similar divergence has been found by the author in sand-box studies.

in expected rise is double that in rivers. These estimates are subject to still further increase owing to increased evaporation attending lack of precipitation, especially when prolonged.

For rivers that flow eastward from the Continental Divide an attempt is being made to forecast the trend in the summer precipitation, but without uniform success. However, owing to the fact that summer rains in this area are mainly of the thunder-storm type and scattered, their effect on runoff is doubtless much less than represented above. At worst, the snow cover should indicate the minimum runoff that can possibly occur. In the upper Columbia Basin, on the opposite side of the Continental Divide, the problem of deficiency in summer precipitation has failed thus far to appear.

Temperature.—Contrary to the usual belief, changes in temperature within normal limits merely accelerate or retard the rate of runoff without noticeably changing the total amount. This is because dripping from the snow fields, once started in the spring, does not cease sufficiently to allow the soil to dry out and require a second priming. Furthermore, the snow descends into the soil in the form of what may be called restrained rain rather than a deluge. This is especially true at the higher altitudes, where the depth of the snow gives it additional capillarity.

In four seasons of abnormal shrinkage in runoff the seasonal temperature during the runoff period was from 0.7° to 4.2° F. in excess of normal, suggesting that high temperatures are relatively ineffective in increasing the total flow. However, low temperatures of 3.3°, 3.1°, and 7.0° F. below normal persisting during March, April, and May, 1933, in the Humboldt Basin were associated with a loss of 50 percent of normal in the forecast of runoff. The loss may have occurred in the alluvial floor of the basin. It was evidently due to excessively low temperatures, which caused repriming of the soil or reduced the rate of flow to absorptive proportions. Fortunately, such low temperatures after melting has begun are of rare occurrence. They have been recorded in the Humboldt Basin only four times in 38 years.

As the monthly departure from normal temperature is usually far less than the normal monthly shift, the phase of expected flow likewise varies within narrow limits. Seldom is an expected flow accelerated or retarded as much as a month. How rarely this should happen is illustrated by the temperature departures at Elko, Nev., in the Humboldt Basin, during 1922–31. The normal monthly shift in temperature ranges from 3.6° to 9.0° F. Out of 81 months (November to July), only six departures in excess of 7.0° F. occurred, and these were all confined to the period November to February, when melting could not be greatly affected. The extremes were +10.1° and −12.0°F. During the months March to July only nine times was the temperature departure more than 4.0° F.

Because of the resulting general uniformity of phase with similar snow covers, basins where storage is scant are having fair success in making forecasts of the probable date when the stream flow will become deficient.

That the water from late mountain snows of light density has a tendency to run off prematurely is not proved by data so far gathered. The fact is rather that these snows pass through a process of accelerated ripening as a result of the alternation of thawing and freezing that occurs normally in April above the altitude of 7,000 feet. It is true that snow of light density at the beginning of the time of melting, before losing its water, fails to attain the density of snow of higher initial density, but the maximum seasonal variation in density for the Tahoe Basin as a whole is under 13 percent, and no marked effect from light densities appears in the runoff.

On the other hand, deep snow of high density may melt prematurely, even under normal temperature, unless protected by new snow whose greater reflectivity reduces absorption of insolation and whose capillarity temporarily prevents the downward movement of melt water. Such protection is essential at the end of the season of accumulation, when the temperature is rising.[1] During March 1923, under practically normal temperature and depth of snow, the snow cover in the central Sierra Nevada, of 4.1 to 8.5 percent density above normal, lost from 7.4 to 23.4 percent of normal water content. The cause of the superdensity evidently lay in the almost complete lack of new snow after Feb. 12. Measurable snow fell on only 3 days out of 47, with a maximum total water content of 1.60 inches.

Evaporation.—The rate of evaporation from snow under average conditions has been estimated at 1 to 2 inches of water monthly. Wet snow and wet ice will evaporate more rapidly. Under foehn conditions on the inland ice in Greenland the daily evaporation of snow has ranged from 0.045 to 1.40 inches water content, and that of ice from 0.056 to 1.01 inches or in one instance possibly more since the pan was found dry. Fortunately the various periods were short.

The monthly evaporation of snow on a watershed in the semi-arid West is illustrated by the series of measurements shown on page 113. The averages are based upon evaporation from November through June, though the evaporation that affects the forecast of runoff is confined to the months of April, May, and June.

On the basis of the extremes for any single month, as shown by measurements of evaporation in the open at an altitude of 6,230 feet, the maximum monthly variation in evaporation to be expected from variation in the weather is about 1 inch, or 6 percent of the normal snow cover at that altitude. As the increase in evaporation with altitude will be offset by

[1] Eng. News-Record, vol. 92, No. 6, p. 234, Feb. 7, 1924.

the increase in depth of the snow cover, this percentage may well be representative for the entire watershed.

Monthly evaporation of snow in the Sierra Nevada, 1910–11 to 1916–17, in inches

Altitude 6,230 feet:

Typical fir forest	0.46
Small fir glade	.36
Pine and fir forest typical of snow courses	.52
Medium pine forest	.59
Openings in forest	.68
Semiopen forest	.78
Small meadow	.84
Open meadow	1.26
Deforested south slope	1.17

Altitude 8,000 feet:

Semiopen forest	1.40

Altitude 9,500 feet:

Timber line	5.52[a]

[a] A single measurement, undoubtedly much to large because of wind effect.

Above the altitude of 10,000 feet, where sun cups and sun pits are found, evaporation may exceed melting, but this phenomenon, being included in the normal runoff, does not materially affect the seasonal percentage of runoff.

Adjusting snow surveys to major, complex basins

Forming the sides of a gigantic **A**, of which the Sierra Nevada-Cascade range with its local drainage systems, forms the cross bar, the Columbia River system shares almost equally with the Colorado River system the western side of the Continental Divide from southern British Columbia to northern New Mexico, a distance of about 1,300 miles. However, the Columbia lies in the storm track and drains a region of increasing precipitation toward its mouth, and its normal annual runoff at The Dalles (computed in 1922) is 151,710,000 acre-feet, as compared with 17,449,000 acre-feet in the Colorado at Yuma, or a ratio of 9 to 1.

The tremendous flow of the Columbia is furnished by three principal tributaries—the upper Columbia with the Kootenay (52,521,000 acre-feet), the Clark Fork-Pend Oreille (19,180,000 acre-feet), and the Snake (45,518,000 acre-feet). The combined system covers with a more or less complete net the entire arid region of Idaho, Oregon, and Washington and thus guarantees to these States a permanent foundation for agricultural and power development. The chief problem, especially downstream, will be the lifting of water to the high lands, and its solution may be the power potential of the stream itself.

The three tributaries supply 77 percent, barring losses enroute, or about 117,000,000 acre-feet, of the annual flow of the Columbia at The Dalles, and their basins are so large and their flow so abundant that at least two of them have become centers for a series of great reclamation projects. Of the other tributaries, the Spokane has long been the source of interstate power.

The problem of forecasting the summer (April-July) runoff of the Columbia is virtually the problem of forecasting the runoff of its individual feeders, for the interests served are on the tributaries rather than on the main stream. However, the collective forecast for the feeders would represent the forecast for the main stream. This is shown by the record of 1913–21, during which the maximum annual variation between the collective runoff of the major feeders and the runoff of the main stream at The Dalles was 7 percent and the maximum variation for April to July was within 11 percent, although divergences of 20 to 35 percent frequently occur between the tributaries themselves. Furthermore, fragmentary records indicate that a similar closeness of agreement prevailed throughout the preceding decade.

However, forecasting for even the individual feeders is far more complex than in the Sierra Nevada. Precipitation during April to July grows relatively heavier with increase in distance from the Pacific coast, and the snow cover on the upper Columbia Basin melts slowly during this period, thus catching and ultimately transmitting to the stream the bulk of the precipitation.

The lower Columbia drains the Cascade and Coast Ranges, which are here of low altitude and transmit the bulk of their snow immediately to the streams. For instance, 57.0 percent of the runoff of the Willamette comes in December to March and 27.4 percent in April to July. Furthermore, the precipitation on this basin is relatively light during April to July and adds little to the summer flow in the lower stream. On the other hand, the Columbia above The Dalles flows only 16.8 percent in December to March and 61.0 percent in April to July.

Consequently the upper and lower Columbia are complementary to each other, and whatever late spring and summer rise occurs in the Columbia will be due to the snow on the Continental Divide. On the other hand, except for the influence of the chinook, the high water in winter should be due to heavy precipitation in the Cascade and Coast Ranges and should occur mainly in the lower Columbia and its immediate tributaries, for the bed of the upper Columbia is too capacious to be overflowed in its low-water season except under abnormal conditions.

Unlike the Columbia, the Colorado River, with the negligible exception of its tributary the Gila, rises entirely in the highlands of the Continental Divide and receives practically no accretions toward its mouth. Thus the area of 225,000 square miles above Yuma is reduced for forecast purposes by about one-half, and the crest line of 760 miles is reduced to 330 miles. Furthermore, three tributaries, the Green (5,797,760 acre-

feet), the Grand or upper Colorado (6,650,200 acre-feet), and the San
Juan (2,745,270 acre-feet) furnish 87.1 percent of the mean annual runoff
at Yuma.

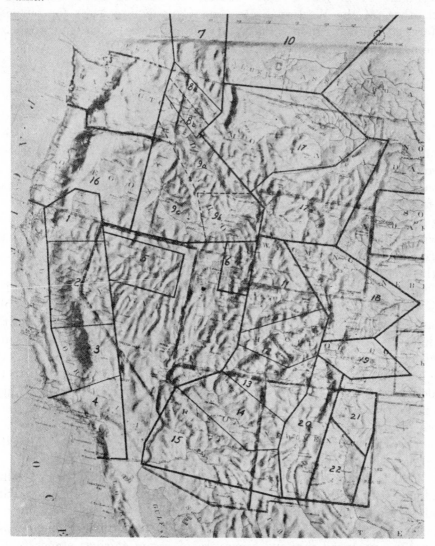

Fig. IV-11.—Western snow survey system, showing areas used in forecasting the runoff of the
basins and sub-basins of the Western States and Provinces: (1) Northern Sierra, (2) Central Sierra,
(3) Southern Sierra, (4) Southern California, (5) Humboldt, Nevada, (6) Wasatch-Uinta, (7) Upper
Columbia, (8) Clark Fork-Pend Oreille-Spokane (*a*, Clark Fork-Pend Oreille Basin; *b*, Spokane
Basin), (9) Snake (*a*, Salmon Basin; *b*, upper Snake Basin; *c*, lower Snake-Boise Basin), (10) Sas-
katchewan, (11) Green River, (12) Grand River (upper Colorado), (13) San Juan, (14) Little Colorado, (15) Gila, (16) Oregon State, (17) Upper Missouri (*a*, Yellowstone), (18) Platte, (19) Arkansas, (20) Rio Grande, (21) Canadian, (22) Pecos.

The purpose of a snow survey in this basin will be the efficient control
of Boulder Dam to store the maximum water possible without flood

strain on the structure.   Unlike the Columbia, the Colorado has far more irrigable land tributary to it than it can serve.

Figure IV-11 indicates the feasible division of these two systems and others of the Western States and Canada into areas for purposes of forecasting their runoff.   Snow surveys and forecasts are now regularly conducted throughout the entire area.

QUANTITATIVE SYSTEM

Application

The quantitative system of snow surveying is native to the Eastern States, where the snow is shallow and may melt during the winter season. Here the cubic content of the water in the snow cover is determined by circuit surveys representing the various altitudes and areas of each basin. In the Androscoggin Basin, Maine, where the first attempt at snow surveying in America was made by Charles A. Mixer, in 1902, a snow-sampling circuit of more than 300 miles is now maintained at frequent time intervals during the winter, to determine the snow-water storage and correlate it with the winter and summer flow.

Snow surveys are continued until the snow cover has melted.   For this reason the variant factors affecting forecasts, though now wholly quantitative, cover intervals so short that they have little effect on the estimates.   Moisture and frost in the soil, rain on the snow, and the tendency of the snow to melt constitute the forecaster's uncertainties.   On the basis of 12 inches of water in the snow cover, 3 inches, or 25 percent, is deducted for soil priming and evaporation, leaving 75 percent (a high proportion compared with that in the West) for the replenishing of reservoirs, which are abundant in this glaciated region.   This percentage is based provisionally on ground-water studies made by observing the water level in wells and the yield of certain drainage areas in dry periods.

Paul L. Bean, who developed the Androscoggin system, is expanding his forecast of bank storage and possible minimum flow to the succeeding year to afford the lumbermen information regarding the possibility of fluming their hardwood logs to market.   As the crop is perishable, cutting cannot be ventured without assurance of essential river stages in the following spring.

A short-cut method of quantitative snow surveying is now being developed in the Merrimack Basin, New Hampshire, by John V. Salo. It seeks to determine the water content of the snow cover of the various feeders of the basin by weighting the snow surveys at the mean altitude of the snow cover of each feeder.   The altitude of the basin as a whole ranges from 250 to 5,250 feet.

Floods

The quantitative system of snow surveying is particularly valuable in forecasting the imminence of floods wherever shallow snow is subject to sudden melting. Its success was remarkably demonstrated by the timely warning by Paul L. Bean of the disastrous flood of March, 1936, in the Androscoggin and other adjoining basins in the Northeast.

To paraphrase the report by Mr. Bean, on March 1, 1936, a very thorough snow survey of the Androscoggin Basin indicated about 10 inches of water in the snow at the lower levels and 12 to 18 inches at the higher levels—an unprecedented condition, indicating a potential volume of flood water to pass Lewiston of not less than 60 billion cubic feet. The basin embraced slightly less than 3,500 square miles, of which two-thirds was entirely uncontrolled except for natural storage. As high altitudes predominate in the uncontrolled drainage area, it was clearly evident that if heavy precipitation, accompanied by high temperature, should occur, a flood of major magnitude could be expected. Moreover, the snow cover extended far to the south, was heavy, and showed little sign of melting. This condition clearly pointed to a sudden break, which actually occurred March 13, when the other necessary elements were provided to produce the greatest flood in this area within the memory of man.

In the White Mountains area of the basin 20.3 inches of rain fell on a snow cover with a water content of 18 inches. Practically the entire basin received a rainfall approximating 10 inches or more on a snow cover containing nowhere less than 10 inches of water. These severe conditions continued for nearly a week. Considerably more than 40 billion cubic feet of water passed Lewiston. The river rose close to 40 feet at the peak flow. It was the supreme experience of life to see a flow greater than normally passes Niagara Falls hurtling down a channel with a normal average flow of 1,800 cubic feet per second. Damage ran into millions of dollars, but there was no loss of life due directly to the flood, though several persons were so frightened that they died of heart failure.

This can be a recurrent experience in the Northeastern States, which because of their situation between the warm moist air of the Atlantic and the cold continental air from Canada are subject to snow accumulation and heavy midwinter rainstorms that may melt the snow and add this store of latent water to its own. The shallow soil underlain by impervious slate or frozen in its lower unforested areas transmits its overburden of water with little retention.

The Susquehanna Basin, apparently the flood center of this area, is described as having "approximately 10 percent of the total flood damage of the entire country in a drainage area that is not much more than 1 percent of the total." Carroll F. Merriam, manager of the Pennsylvania Water & Power Co., suggests that investigations be made of the critical density and temperature of snow at which it may abruptly release its water content. Cooperation in this study is being arranged.

In New York State Dr. Robert E. Horton has noticed that major floods seldom occur when the snow is deep. This observation is substantiated by the fact that rain even at 50° F. melts only one-eighth of its weight of snow. In Michigan and Wisconsin floods are reported as rare because of the depth of glacial covering and the undersoil pockets and lakes of the region, assisted by increasing remoteness from the rain belt. This should be true to a lesser degree over most of the Great Lakes and St. Lawrence drainage area because of the natural storage provided by the glaciated topography.

In the West torrential rains appear to be the chief cause of floods. Maximum floods, however, would probably be the result of the melting of large areas of shallow snow in the vicinity of the snow line or covering the valley floor below. Such was the destructive flood of early March, 1910, in the Humboldt Basin, Nevada, caused wholly by the slow accumulation of snow during a cold winter and its sudden melting by an abrupt rise in temperature. The total average precipitation for the basin during December to February was only slightly above normal and only 0.07 inch of precipitation was reported at the lower end of the stream throughout the progress of the flood.

The great snow fields at higher altitudes are probably impregnable to all but the heaviest rains and highest temperatures. However, the threat of these two elements is shown in the tendency of the snow cover at 8,400 feet (Lake Lucile) in the Tahoe Basin, California, to drip at the end of the abnormally open winter of 1939–40. The average depth of the snow was 184.6 inches, and its water content 69.3 inches. Snow densities at higher altitudes in the basin were 37 to 45 percent. On this experience is based the formula, the deeper the snow the smaller the flood. The capacity of flood-detention reservoirs need not be based upon the total snow storage of the mountains.

THE REGIME OF GLACIER STREAMS

The regime of glacier streams can be best presented against the background of rain and snow-fed streams. Secondo Alfieri has done pioneer work in this field [127]. In the Italian Alps and Appenines he has selected five basins, ranging in area from 30.4 to 88.5 square kilometers, three of which have snow and glaciers, one snow, and one mostly rain. The areas covered by glaciers in the three glacier basins range from 28 to 47 percent of the total areas of the basins. The heavy melting of the glaciers that had been in regression for several years naturally increased the ratio of runoff to precipitation. Thus, in the seven years, 1931 to 1937, covered by the comparison, the runoff from the three glacier basins substantially exceeded the precipitation. However, Alfieri's data apparently gave too high percentages of runoff in at least some of the basins, because he used only a few precipitation stations and these without regard to altitude.

The regimen of the glacier and snow-fed streams is determined not so much by the seasonal distribution of the precipitation as by the temperature, which reduces the accumulation. The glacier basins are somewhat higher than those of the central Sierra Nevada, and are slightly farther north. Their peak flow should therefore be later. The glacier basins, because of the low temperature at their high altitude and reserves of ice, have their major runoff from June to September. The lower snow-fed basin has its major runoff from March to June, when the seasonal storage of snow becomes exhausted. In the basin in which the precipitation is chiefly rain the runoff lags less behind the precipitation, but its season of minimum runoff, in July, August, and September, synchronizes with the three months of minimum precipitation.

The forecasting of the runoff of snow and glacier streams requires merely a normal or standard of comparison of the annual snow cover and the ablation of the ice. As early as 1914 Dr. Alfred de Quervain and Dr. R. Billwiller began sampling the annual reserve of snow in the névé of glaciers.[1] This system should be extended to the entire watershed, both non-glacier and glacier, in the same manner as applied to snow basins. Because of the ruggedness of the terrain the percentage method should preferably be used. Where possible, gaging stations should be established, particularly in the non-glacier areas, as a check on the accuracy of the snow surveys. Precipitation stations would also be valuable if numerous enough to represent the effects of altitude. Since fluctuations in temperature can not be forecast, estimates should be confined to the total major runoff rather than to peak flows.

Through the pioneer efforts of Dr. Otto Lütschg-Lötscher, photogrammetric surveys of the fluctuation of glaciers in volume now provide an accurate method of determining the seasonal water content of the ice as of a reservoir. The net relationship between annual accumulation and dissipation can thus be determined. Charts of the Upper Saas Valley, Monte Rosa Massif, and Upper Grindelwald Glacier, in the Jungfrau Group, make these areas highly desirable initial areas for the development of snow surveys in the Alps.

CONSERVATION OF SNOW

The problem of snow conservation by mountains and forests is complex. Mountains, if very high, may waste snow by sublimation, as the

[1] Present Methods of Glacier Study in the Swiss Alps (Mo. Weather Rev., vol. 52, pp. 264–266, 1924) by J. E. Church.

evaporation on ordinary peaks appears to be fully four times that in the wooded mountain valleys at their base. (See Fig. IV-12.) If directly facing the sun and wind the slopes may accelerate melting and evaporation. On the whole, however, they serve as reservoirs, holding the snow cover far above the heat of the valleys and releasing its moisture slowly, in general harmony with the advancing growth of vegetation below. If sufficiently rugged, they concentrate the drifting snow in their lee with little loss of altitude but great increase in depth (Figs. IV-13 and IV-14),

Fig. IV-12.—Sun cups at an altitude of 10,000 feet on Mount Rose, Nev., showing tendency of snow to evaporate rather than melt at high altitudes. At higher altitudes the cups enlarge into pits, whose walls finally wear into leaning fins called by the Spaniards "Nieve penitente" because of their mass resemblance to a band of penitent monks.

thus assuring shelter from wind and possibly from sun and retardation in melting due to its greater depth. This applies, however, to exposed ridges and peaks.

Such conservation can be still further increased by timber screens, especially on the lips of canyons, where they accentuate the shelter afforded by the slopes. In strong contrast to this protection are the far transport of the snow in the mountains of Sweden, where the slopes are gentle and the timber is low, and the seemingly endless sweep of the snow over the open tundra of the Arctic regions.

The efficiency of mountain forests as gatherers and retainers of snow is plainly evident from a comparison of measurements made on the lee

(a)

(b)

Fig. IV-13.—Conservation of snow by Mount Rose, Nev. (a) Windward side. Snow is swept away except where caught or protected by timber screens. (b) Leeward side. The snow is caused to accumulate by the mountain barrier, forming an incipient glacier. The timber line breaks the wind currents and brings the snow to rest.

side of the rocky summit of Mount Rose and in the timber-line forests beneath at 47 stations in April, 1910.   Below is given the depth of snow, in inches, with the water content in parentheses.

Unforested talus slope.. 40.8 (18.4)
Cornice included in above.................................... 52.5 (25.1)
Forested slope... 88.6 (41.1)
Protected slope... 78.1 (35.1)

The influence of scrub of varying heights is shown by measurements made at 52 stations:

Talus slope covered with low scrub............................ 32.4 (13.4)
Slightly steeper talus dotted with timber screens 10 to 20 feet high. . 61.4 (26.5)

In a season of normal or heavy precipitation the snow on the first slope rises as high as the tips of the scrub, but no higher, for the slope is then exposed to the unobstructed sweep of the wind.

Fig. IV-14.—Depth of snow caught by timber-line forest.   The snow is as deep as the sampler is tall (21 feet).

Area for area on mountains of gentler contour—and such mountains are the rule rather than the exception—the talus slopes are less efficient than forests as conservers of snow.   It is true that some of the snow above timber line outlasts the snow in the forest below.   This difference is confined, however, to the deeper cornices of small area.   The use of timber screens instead of a forest cover evenly distributed would create drifts but little inferior in size and lasting power to those of the cornices on the talus slopes.   Furthermore, the number of such drifts can be multiplied by planting trees, whereas the cornices on the rocks not only cannot be increased in number, but they place too large an area under contribution and the water supplied by them is released late.

Forests, however, are wasters as well as protectors of snow in proportion to their density and shade and their climatic situation. In the East the hardwood and softwood forests possess diverse and in some respects opposite qualities. The softwoods or conifers tend to intercept the snow and expoes it, if wet and clinging, to long and accelerated evaporation

FIG. IV-15.—The problem of combating rime on Mount Rose, Nev. The "frost feathers" (rime) are 4 feet long. Because of the weight of ice festoons on the guy lines it was found necessary to use timber or pipe supports instead of the usual rods. The precipitation intake pipe at the left indicates an effort made to obtain a record of precipitation on the mountain top. However, the tendency of the snow to blow upward instead of downward at the crest made this effort futile. In repairing the station the masts were made much heavier, and guy lines were shortened or eliminated in favor of timber braces. The arrow of the wind vane was made short and the tail long to keep the vane in the eye of the wind.

in the branches. However, the snow that reaches the ground is afforded abundant shade from the sun. On the other hand, the hardwood or deciduous trees offer little interception to falling snow but provide scanty shelter against the sun. In forests of both types the snow is protected against drifting. The deciduous forest, because of accumulation of fallen leaves, affords greater protection against frost in the soil and resulting impervious runoff surface but permits early melting.

In the West the forests are mainly conifers. The snow also is drier in its fall and consequently is blown more readily from the branches. Thus it escapes excessive evaporation. The forests, where not too dense, appear even to collect more snow than the open, as shown by the following comparison of the net gathering power of open and forested areas in the Tahoe Basin, California, March, 1910 (Tables (a) and (b)).

(a) Tahoe City (6,230 ft.)	Net gathering power (snow cover and water content March 11, 1910, in inches)	Net retention in spring April 20, 1910
Treeless meadow............	39.8 (11.7)	Gone April 10–13
Forest of pine and fir........	31.4 (12.1)	1.3 (0.6)
Fir forest.................	30.4 (11.0)	7.1 (2.7)

A further comparison (b) of various types of forest at Blackwood Creek, indicates that the dense forest with glades has a maximum gathering and retaining power:

(b) Blackwood Creek (6,230 ft.)	March 13–14	April 25
Open forest of pine and cedar.................	34.9 (13.5)	0.5 (0.2)
Very dense fir forest.........................	31.0 (10.9)	2.1 (0.9)
Dense fir forest with glades...................	42.7 (16.5)	7.8 (3.2)

The index of protection capacity is confirmed in the figures for total evaporation, in inches of water, December to May, 1913–14, at Tahoe City, Calif.; Small fir glades, 1.5; large forest opening, 2.2; open meadow, 4.8; deforested southern slope, 5.9.

The ideal forest for the conservation of snow is one honeycombed with glades whose extent is so related to the height of the trees that the sun cannot reach the surface of the snow. Such a forest will permit far more snow to reach the ground than a forest of great and uniform density and yet will protect the snow from the effect of sun and wind. A fir forest having a maximum number of glades or a forest of mountain hemlock meets these requirements. However, glades can be produced in any dense forest by the simple operation of cutting. Such a forest, when viewed from above, would resemble a gigantic honeycomb, the glades of the forest being equivalent to the cells of the comb. Fortunately, this method, proposed by the author in 1912,[1] has now been found compatible with modern forest cutting, which seeks to develop the area for water as well as for timber.

An attempt has been made to obtain exact measurements of the evaporation of snow in tree crowns. A drip pan provided with a mezza-

[1] Sci. Am. Suppl., vol. 74, No. 1914 (Sept. 7, 1912) p. 155; Am. Geophys. Union Trans., 1940, p. 925.

nine story of wire screen to expose snow from both above and below after the manner of branches was hung in the trees, and a few measurements were obtained. That the factor is small is suggested by the table of collecting power given above. Further measurements should be made, particularly in the East.

Likewise, further investigation should be conducted regarding the power of deep snow to prevent frost from penetrating the soil or to aid the earth warmth to remove it before the period of seasonal flood runoff occurs.

SNOW-SURVEY POSSIBILITIES

The limitations of snow surveys, originally felt to be narrow, have been gradually pushed back with unfolding knowledge of the potency of snow.

Snow surveys were extended into the shallow snows of the East to determine the auxiliary water supply in the Black River, N.Y., stored in the seasonal snow cover. They were also made in the St. Maurice Basin, Quebec, but the percentage method there has failed to yield close forecasts in some years.

In the Susquehanna Basin, although the snow constitutes only one-third of the annual precipitation, it is far more effective than the remaining two-thirds. C. F. Merriam writes that "for a period of the year the runoff normally exceeds the rainfall by about 2 inches." This is due to the fact that in spring the snow melts continuously and therefore with little loss in priming the shallow soil, whereas during the summer the deciduous trees, putting out leaves, intercept the rain, as do also the conifers, and use it in transpiration. As the rain falls in showers, much is wasted in rewetting the soil. The snow provides the excess runoff.

Thus the snow cover in the East, as in the West, is the basic factor in forecasting runoff. The satisfactory results by the quantitative method in Maine, New Hampshire, and Newfoundland are reassuring. A study should be made of the snow cover, probably scant, in the Tennessee Basin, now under hydrologic development, to determine the relative effectiveness of snow and rain at their extreme ratio.

Snow-cover conditions in wild-life refuges have been requested by the United States Fish and Wildlife Service to plan more exactly for winter feeding and summer water supplies.

The latest advance is the use of snow surveys in Utah to estimate and apportion ground-water supplies. One of the earliest advances in snow surveying was also made in Utah, where in 1934 the first drought conference in history was held before the drought occurred. A project is also under way in Nevada to seek a relation between the snow cover in the Charleston Range and the artesian flow in its neighborhood.

THE MELTING OF SNOW

With rare exceptions snow melts only from above and active melting is at or near the surface. Percolation is possible only when the snow is at the point of melting and is dependent upon excess of gravity pull over lift by capillarity.

Although the heat of the sun is the ultimate cause of melting, the immediate causes in probable order of effectiveness are radiation from sun and sky, convection and condensation from the air, and the warmth of rain. The penetration of the snow cover by the radiant energy of the sun and its refraction from beneath and the residual warmth of the earth from the previous season are minor factors.

The present section deals with the complete melting of snow within a single season. The evolution of snow to perennial firn and glacial ice is discussed in the chapter on Glaciers. The data have largely been obtained from field rather than laboratory measurements and should thus be freer from possible exaggerations. To permit percolation, snow must become ripe, and in the process it tends to become homogeneous in density.

RIPE AND OVERRIPE SNOW

When snow has attained its maximum power of water suspension it is "ripe," and when this point has been exceeded and it begins to lose

Density of ripe and overripe snow in relation to depth of snow and its exposure to wind, Central Sierra Nevada
(average of many measurements)

Locality, elevation, and exposure	Year and precipitation	Depth of snow (inches)	Density (percent)	
			Ripe	Overripe
Tahoe City, 6,230 feet, forested, wind light......	1911–1912 light	31.4	30.1	35.4
	1913–1914 heavy	68.8	34.6·	38.6
	1915–1916 heavy	57.1	36.2	42.2
Marlette Lake, 8000 feet, semi-forested, wind strong.	1915–1916(?)	81.3	44.4	49.6
Summit Station, 7,017 feet, semi-forested, wind strong.	1915–1916 heavy	133.5	48.4	51.6
	1909–1910 normal	50.7	47.2	53.1
	1910–1911 heavy	94.8	47.4	56.5
Mt. Rose, 9,000–10,800 feet, wind-swept.........	1912–1913 light	38.0	38.2	46.4
	1915–1916 heavy	73.9	47.2	53.4

its water content it is "overripe." The density of ripeness and, over-ripeness varies with the initial density of the snow. This in turn is dependent on the character of the snow crystal.

Apparently snow crystals do not consolidate under melting as closely as under wind or compression but rather tend to become coarsely granular. Some increase in compactness results from melting, but this is followed by a slight diminution in density as the water begins to drain from the snow.

In all types of snow the difference in density between ripeness and over-ripeness does not exceed about 10 percent, whatever the density of ripeness may be. Consequently the snow that is protected from the wind and so is initially light will rarely attain the density or capillarity of its wind-blown neighbor. Herein lies the greater value of high mountain snow. The divergence between various types of snow is shown in the table on page 126.

TENDENCY OF THE SNOW TO BECOME HOMOGENEOUS

The second trait to be noted is the tendency of ripening snow to become homogeneous in density, a development doubtless accelerated by water permeating the mass. This is not a wholly ideal trait, for when the entire depth has attained ripeness the capillarity reserve of the snow cover has ceased to exist and all further water from melting passes directly through and into the soil, if not impermeable.

Solid pack snow lacks the spongy or suspensive character of snow of lighter density and even under normal temperature may lose some of its water prematurely. This is particularly true in March, when winter is passing into spring and nature is delicately balanced. At this crisis in water supplies an overlay of newly fallen snow with its abundant capillarity is needed to insulate the old snow against melting. For instance during March, 1923, under virtually normal conditions of temperature and depth of snow, the snow cover in the central Sierra having a density of 4.1 to 8.5 percent above normal lost from 7.4 to 23.4 percent of normal of its water content, though melting usually does not begin until April 1.

The belief that early snow will pack better and therefore last longer in the spring is apparently based on observations of spring snowfall which necessarily disappears quickly because of its scant water content. In the mountains late-fallen snow being assisted by advancing spring will quickly attain the density of the earlier snow.

The accompanying cross-section of snow cover strata at Donner Summit in 1917 gives a picture of this evolution in detail.

Tendency of snow to become homogeneous in density, Donner Summit Station (7,017 feet), 1917
(Depth of snow in inches; density in percent)
A—Timbered flat

Stratum	April 1		April 23		May 6		May 20		June 3	
Numbered from surface down	In.	Per-cent	In.	Per-cent	In.	Per-cent	In.	Per-cent	In.	Per-cent
1	6.5	24.6	4.3	41.9						
2	7.0	38.6	6.9	40.6						
3	12.3	40.7	7.5	50.7						
4	10.6	46.2	11.0	49.1	3.8	52.6				
5	27.8	46.8	24.7	51.8	25.0	52.8	[a]1.8	[a]22.2		
6	59.9	48.1	54.9	49.0	56.0	50.2	59.6	52.2	29.6	53.0
Total Snow Cover	124.1	45.1	109.3	48.9	84.8	51.1	61.4	51.3	29.6	53.0

B—Wind-swept hilltop continuous with preceding

Stratum	May 6		May 20		June 3	
Numbered from surface downward	Inches	Percent	Inches	Percent	Inches	Percent
4–5	29.3	57.7	[b]8.5	[b]43.5		
6	56.8	57.4	53.9	59.6	17.4	57.5
Total snow cover	86.1	57.5	62.4	57.4	17.4	57.5

[a] New snow.   [b] Partly new snow.

LAG

Owing to initial capillarity or adhesiveness of the water in the snow crystals there is a natural lag between the beginning of melting at the top of the snow cover and the appearance of the water at the base of the snow. This necessarily pre-supposes the temperature of 32°F. or 0°C. (the temperature of melting) throughout. Otherwise the percolating water will freeze and form crusts en route. Likewise when percolation has become established, it will continue temporarily after melting at the surface has ceased. While this does not prevent oscillation in the runoff, it usually assures sufficient moisture to maintain percolation in the snow and underlying soil and avoid the repriming losses common in the case of intermittent rains. Thus only a single priming is necessary to deliver a season's snow cover to the streams. In only one or two instances during the three decades of snow-surveying has the cold been continued sufficiently long to dry out the snow and the soil and thereby cause less runoff than was expected.

CHANGE IN DENSITY DURING MELTING

Clyde (18) has noticed that the density of the snow cover increases until runoff occurs and then falls to a lower density which is maintained with only slight variation during the completion of the melting. This is apparently due to the breaking down of the capillarity of the snow by the melting of some of the crystals. If freezing and consolidation should occur, the density at least locally would increase.

The decrease from 49.4 percent to 37.0 percent cited is unusual. At Donner Summit the density of stratum 6, representing the water-worn bottom of the snow cover, has suffered a fall below that of stratum 5 on April 23 and May 6 but the fall is less than 3 percent. On April 1 percolation had obviously not yet occurred. If the density of the total snow cover is used as a standard, the density increases from beginning to end of the melting period though the increase toward the end is slight.

The saturation zone sometimes found at the base of the snow cover is apparently caused by underlying impervious earth or ice-crust which blocks the pull of gravity. Such is slush which will drain rapidly when the barrier has been perforated. The maximum capillary height at the base of a snow prism of 44.8 percent density resting on a solid surface has been observed by Horton (22) to be 2 inches or 1.1 inch of water, without the capillary downward pull of unsaturated underlying soil. In general, he estimates the capillary height in inches at 3 to 5 times the density of the snow. Above this capillary zone the snow is drained white to the surface tension of the crystals at which the original percolation occurred.

RATES OF MELTING

The rate or intensity of melting will necessarily depend upon the degree of heat above freezing.

The average rate of melting of a snow field in the Central Sierra Nevada mountains is shown in the following table, which covers six consecutive years and affords a striking example of uniformity in rate.

Rates of melting of the snow cover at Soda Springs Station (6,752 ft.), Central Sierra Nevada in the month of April 1936–1941

	1936	1937	1938	1939	1940	1941	Average
Depth of snow cover April 1 (inches of snow)	94.8	110.5	153.7	52.8	101.3	83.0	99.4
Density, April 1 (percent)	46.2	40.0	40.7	40.7	42.2	49.8	43.3
Mean of temperatures above freezing during month* (°F.)	9.4	7.4	7.7	12.5	8.8	8.1	9.0
Total melting adjusted for precipitation during April (inches of water)	14.61	10.85	10.15	21.84	13.86	10.62	13.65
Average daily melting (inches of water)	0.487	0.362	0.338	0.728	0.462	0.354	0.455
Average daily melting per degree F. (inches of water)	0.052	0.049	0.044	0.058	0.053	0.044	0.051*

* Mean monthly temperature above freezing = ½ (Mean maximum temperature −32°F). Wet-bulb temperatures are preferable, and near the snow surface. Probable wet-bulb average daily rate of melting at Soda Springs approximates 0.61 in. per degree F.

Confirming the average daily rate of melting of 0.455 inch at Soda Springs Station is the average daily rate of 0.42 inch (corrected for precipitation of 2.40 inches) at adjacent Donner Summit from April 1 to May 6, 1917, at a mean temperature of 5.9°F. above freezing for the period, or 3.1°F. below the average temperature for April at Soda Springs Station.

The temperature above freezing is plainly the controlling factor as shown by the uniformity of the average daily melting per degree F. High density as in 1941 is apparently ineffective at 6.5 percent above the mean. But excess temperature of 3.5°F. above average may account for the high daily melting rate of 0.728 inch or 0.058 inch per degree F. in 1939.

The high daily melting rate of 1.08 inches reported by Clyde (18) for Gooseberry Creek, Utah, April 23-May 9, 1928, with a temperature of 19.9°F. above freezing, or 0.054[1] per degree F. can best be accounted for by the fact that during the 16 days of melting the temperature fell below freezing on only 6 nights, an unusual occurrence in April and May above 8,500 feet altitude. The daily melting, instead of being interrupted for several hours, was practically continuous nearly half of the time. To provide for such exceptional cases or to attain greater precision the hourly rather than the daily melting rate per degree F. above freezing should be computed as a standard of comparison.

The rates of melting for various periods during April have been determined for all of Finland, including all types of open country and forests (26). Melting in spring time is the principal cause of the runoff maximum in all parts of Finland, although, owing to lakes, the annual high water in many basins is observed as late as in June or July. The snow is relatively shallow.

The daily melting rate of 0.528 inch for 30 days in Finland corresponds fairly well with the rate of 0.455 inch in the central Sierra Nevada. The rate of melting per degree F. in Finland is 0.108 inch; at Soda Springs Station 0.051 inch. The mean degree above freezing in Finland during April is 4.9°F. (2.7°C.)[2] as compared with 9.0°F. for the central Sierra Nevada. Finland lies at 60–70°N. latitude and the central Sierra Nevada at 38°N. The daily insolation at the Arctic Circle, or average latitude of Finland, is far longer than at 38° but the angle of incidence of the sun is much lower. Thus the daily cycle of melting at this latitude on the Greenland inland ice at 1,500 feet altitude in August has been found to last only from 9 A.M. to 4 P.M.

In the laboratory Clyde has observed a melting rate of .054 to .076 inch per degree F. daily (24 hrs.) and Horton a corresponding rate of

---

[1] The estimate 0.091 given by Clyde applies to Centigrade scale.

[2] Estimated by Ralph W. Burhoe from Köppen-Geiger, Handbuch der Meteorologie on basis of 14 stations representing a cross section of the latitude extremes of Finland.

0.04 to 0.06 inch. The mean room-temperature above freezing during Clyde's experiment was 48.0°F. and during Horton's 40.1 and 42.1°F. Owing to the moderate size of the snow cores[1] the tests lasted only from 5½ to 10½ hours.

At Soda Springs Station the average temperature above freezing was only 9.0°F. and interruption in melting occurred during approximately 12 hours or probably longer in 24. If the assumed 24 hours of daily melting in the laboratory are reduced by half in approximate conformity with the length of the melting period at Soda Springs Station, the daily laboratory rate would be 0.027 to 0.038 inch (Clyde) and 0.02 to 0.03 inch (Horton) as compared with the field rate of 0.051 inch (Soda Springs).

The laboratory experiments are admittedly crude because of the constant variation in the surface area and contour of the snow prisms. The field experiments are affected by insolation, fluctuating temperature, and particularly by diurnal cessation of melting. Much remains to be done in developing a standard unit of melting.

ATMOSPHERIC HEAT

The main sources of heat are insolation and the warm, turbulent atmosphere which establishes direct thermal contact with the snow.

The diurnal penetration of névé at 14,000 feet has been found by J. Vallot (20, p. 493) to be within one meter. It seems far deeper at lower elevations if the diurnal change from freezing to melting is considered. Furthermore, this change is almost sudden on or near the surface at sunset. The temperature, however, within the snow never rises appreciably above 32°F. because of the resulting occurrence of melt water.

Dryness in a warm wind should accelerate evaporation while moistness should increase melting. A rainless flood in the Humboldt Basin, Nevada, February 21 to March 12, 1910, was occasioned by a mean daily maximum temperature of 25.3°F. above freezing and a minimum of 0.8°F. above freezing, causing practically continuous melting during the period. The snow, accumulated by a uniformly cold winter, had 3 to 4 inches of water content on the floor of the basin but 7.75 inches at 6,000 feet, where the mountain slopes rise. The average relative humidity as recorded at Winnemucca in the center of the basin was 69 percent. The phenomenon was characterized as a "sudden thaw accompanied by chinook wind," and its effects were the most severe experienced there in a quarter century.

That chinooks cause sudden floods despite their low relative humidity is shown by the following experience recorded by Hoover (74) in Alberta,

---

[1] Clyde: 25 in. high × 8 in. diam.; 8 in. high × 6 in. diam. Horton: 20 in. high × 8 in. diam.; 9.3 in. high × 7.8 in. diam.

Canada, March 18 to 23, 1939. With a mean temperature at Calgary of 16.7°F. above freezing and a mean relative humidity of approximately 50 percent, 10 inches of snow (water content probably 2½ inches) nearly disappeared during the first two days, and four prairie streams from 160 to 370 miles east of the Rocky Mountains, although completely dry during the winter, attained peak flows of 1,000 to 3,500 second-feet. The runoff in terms of the total area of the watersheds was 0.11 inch to 0.16 inch. No measurement of evaporation was obtained, but a daily evaporation loss of 0.492 inch (water content) has been measured on the Greenland inland ice during a foehn period. The mean daily temperature there was 26.3°F. above freezing, the wind velocity was 7.2 miles per hour, and the relative humidity was 62 percent. On the lee of the hummock the daily evaporation of snow was 0.206 inch or slightly less than half that on the windward. The evaporation of ice fully exposed was likewise 0.206 inch. The moistening of the snow crystals and the surface of the ice accelerates the evaporation rate. The chinook problem is still young.

Effect of rain

Another factor in melting potency is rain. Max Oechslin has found that rain at 4°C. (39.2°F.) will percolate through snow at a decreasing rate as the density of the snow increases. For example, in snow 50 centimeters deep the time of percolation is as follows: for 10 percent density, 90 seconds; 20 percent, 115; 30 percent, 145; 40 percent, 175; 50 percent, 255. Horton (21 and 22) has computed the transmission constant for water overlying packed new snow of 64 percent density at 2.28 inches depth per minute or approximately one-half of Oechslin's rate of 50 centimeters in 255 seconds, or 4.63 inches per minute for snow at the density of 50 percent. However, Horton feels "that the transmission capacity of mature snow at the base of a snow layer, where the crystals have become more or less cubical in form, will in general be much greater." Oechslin also has found that if the snow is compact and wind-carried, the time of percolation may decrease as the density increases, for the reason that open channels are formed through which the percolating water is discharged.

As the points of the crystals are melted and smaller crystals are dissolved the amount of surface tension area or capillarity is diminished and the size of free channels is increased. Thus when the snow has become saturated, that is, when its limit of suspension has been reached, it can exercise no further restraint against gravity unless, as mentioned above, the grains are consolidated by freezing.

A striking example of percolation caused by rain is offered by Horton (22). During December 17 and 18, 1915, 1.35 inches of rain fell on a snow cover 23.5 inches deep, with an original water content of 3.34

inches, an initial density of 14.1 percent, and a final density of 24.1 percent. This rain produced a gain in the water content of the snow cover of only 0.15 inch but caused the ground water level to rise. The rain had been insufficiently warm and copious to melt the snow although it had broken down its crystals considerably.

According to B. S. Barnes,[1] rain of 40°F., which is the ordinary rain of spring when the precipitation oscillates from rain to snow, will melt only 5.5 percent of its weight of snow. Even at 60°F. the rain would melt only 20 percent of its weight of snow. Consequently, if the snow cover is heavy, the rain must be very heavy to remove it entirely. If the snow has not attained full ripeness, some of the rain will be held in suspension.

EFFECT OF INSOLATION AND RADIATION

Owing to direct insolation the surface of the snow near midday in sunlight may melt although the air temperature is −10°C. (18°F. below freezing). This effect is greatly limited, however, by the albedo, or reflectivity of the surface of the snow, depending on the latter's form and state. Thus dry, new snow has greater albedo than moist or packed soiled snow. However, the cumulative seasonal effect is large.

Kalitin (27, 20) has found the reflective value of dazzling, fresh, soft snow to be 87 percent and that of the soiled turf after the disappearance of the snow to be as low as 18 percent. Maximum values found by others have varied from 70 to 89 percent.

The depth of penetration of the sun's rays into snow has been found by Kalitin to be 15 centimeters (5.9 inches) for wet snow and 60 centimeters (23.6 inches) for dry snow. On the Greenland inland ice, 1926–1928, the writer found that opaque bodies sank only pencil deep (6 to 7 inches) into the ice, where they remained inert. The diameter of the holes was proportionate to the area of the opaque material, tiny objects producing a hole having the diameter of a lead pencil. Most holes were crescent-shaped and tilted toward the sun, as in the case of the pinnacles of the nieve penitente. The shallowness of the holes was probably due to the presence of melt water that could not escape.

In the Sierra Nevada, black-bulb thermometers recorded no higher than the others beyond depths of 16 to 18 inches. Since the thermometers were in sealed tubes and thus were dry, these measurements should be representative of dry snow. In preliminary measurements in the Wasatch Mountains, Irving F. Hand and Roy E. Lundquist have found the sun's penetration in wet snow of 50 percent density and in ice to be far less.

The power of the sun to penetrate to the opaque earth beneath the snow and cause melting from below is therefore limited to extremely shallow snow particularly when wet.

[1] Amer. Meteorol. Soc. Bull. 21.3 (March, 1940) pp. 99–100.

Effect of earth warmth

The effect of the residual warmth of the earth from the previous season appears to be small in the light of dry cores of snow formed throughout the winter and the relatively small winter runoff of the streams. Even wet meadows are limited in area and effectiveness.

A quantitative comparison of mid-winter and maximum runoff on snow-fed streams is provided by the West Walker River, in California and Nevada, the February runoff of which is 2.1 percent of the annual runoff, whereas the maximum, in June, is 28.9 percent. Bishop Creek and the South Yuba and Truckee Rivers flow 3.4, 4.7, and 4.9 percent, respectively, in February as compared with maximum flows of 22.9 percent (July) and 29.2 and 25.8 percent (May) respectively.

The effect of earth warmth in removing frost from the soil with the aid of insulating snow should be maximum where the summers are warm and the conductivity of the ground is high.

AVALANCHES

Avalanches, or "valleyward" snow, are a mountain phenomenon born from the instability of the snow and early named from their spectacular descent into the valleys. Their latent peril to travelers and habitations has spurred detailed study of the evolution of avalanche snow until, under the leadership of Paulcke, followed by Welzenbach, Seligman, and the Swiss Avalanche Commission, a science of snow structure has arisen.

Among the factors in the occurrence of avalanches are density, porosity, and friction, and these are directly affected by temperature, humidity, pressure, and wind.

The gradient of the slope at which snow deposits are stable depends upon the friction or coherence of the snow crystals and snow strata. Snow slopes steeper than 22° must be regarded with suspicion, says Seligman (116), though old firn snow will be stable at 50°. But this is to be regarded only as a general rule, for wet snow avalanches have come down on slopes of only 15°.

The high cohesion of moist earth is evidently due to the slight film of water surrounding the grains and the loss of cohesion in wet earth to excessive water causing lubrication or floating of the grains. Likewise moist snow should be most cohesive and wet and watersoaked snow least. Wild snow, being almost impalpable, should lack cohesion entirely, while new powder snow, because of the interlocking of the plumes of the crystals, will be strongly coherent. Sand snow, whose facets are angular, should also be stable because of internal friction.

In the early winter the ground and trees may provide sufficient anchorage to prevent movement of the snow. But unless the points of control are sufficiently high to extend through the increasing snow cover, snow crusts may be formed above them and produce slip planes upon which newer snow may become very unstable. Only when the snow falls sufficiently moist to be consolidated with the crust is the anchorage extended upward.

However, melt water later in the season may be caught by the crust and cause it to become a plane of discontinuity, lubricated for the descent of the overlying snow. Frozen ground, long grass, and flattened brush may act in the same way. Sometimes melt water from steeper slopes exposed to the more direct rays of the sun may accumulate on gentler slopes below and cause avalanches where less expected.

Types of avalanches

In their most obvious forms avalanches fall into three main classes: (1) Loose-snow avalanches, (2) wind-slab avalanches, and (3) ice avalanches. But in the order of their seasonal appearance they are (1) dry soft-snow avalanches, (2) wind-slab avalanches, and (3) wet-snow avalanches. However, avalanche types are frequently complex and the season varies with elevation.

Loose-snow avalanches are less dependent on slide-strata than wet-snow avalanches and may result merely from overburden of new snow. However, a hard-frozen under-stratum will greatly increase their occurrence. The most spectacular but rare of winter avalanches is the wild-snow avalanche that flows even through forests and by its snow-dust may suffocate at a distance or penetrate tightly closed rooms out of the immediate path of the avalanche. If the slope is steep, it may float in the air. Snow cushions, of loose powder snow, slip readily on the crust on which they are originally deposited. Steep slopes may make whole fields of loose snow unstable. Sun-balls caused by the moistening of cold new snow by the sun are often the forerunners of dry avalanches. The wind-slab avalanche is provided not only with a slip crust but also frequently with depth hoar to accelerate its movement. But wet-snow avalanches are usually caused by warm moist winds that increase the density of the snow, break down the cohesion of the snow crystals, and provide melt-water lubrication. Ice avalanches, akin to glacier cascades, occur above cliffs or steep rocks, and are usually a glacier product.

Blasts and speed

The blasts that sometimes accompany avalanches and break off trees far above the ground and on either side of their course are caused both by the frontal thrust of the snow and the vacuum created by its passage. The prerequisite for blasts is a large cross-section of dense swiftly traveling snow. As the velocity of the snow decreases at the foot of its slope, the blast may overtake it and travel far ahead, even to the opposite slope and cause an additional avalanche there.

The speed of avalanches is dependent upon type and volume of snow and smoothness and gradient of underlayer. Dry powder snow is fastest, damp snow is slowest. Owing to friction the speed of the sides and bottom is slower than that of the center. Hence the surf-like movement of the mass and the danger of being drawn under and compacted. J. Coaz gives a mean speed of 350 kilometers (217 miles) per hour for the great Glärnisch powder-snow avalanche of March 6, 1898, on an average slope of 44°. In a total distance of 7 kilometers the avalanche crossed a valley 2 kilometers wide and climbed several hundred meters up the opposite wall and then flowed back. It started as a wind-slab avalanche. The descent lasted only 1.2 minutes but 7 more minutes elapsed before the snow dust had settled. Mougin and C. Bernard estimate the speed of a wet-snow avalanche at 17 miles per hour on a slope of 45°.

A volume of one million cubic meters, says Seligman, is not uncommon for both powder and wet-snow avalanches.

PREVENTION AND AVOIDANCE

Avalanches can often be stayed at their source by creating an anchorage of contour trenches, terraces, walls, and screens of trees. Farther down their course, deflecting walls can be constructed to detour the avalanches or split them if buildings are in the path. Where avalanche danger is cumulative, incipient avalanches can be brought down while still ineffective by cutting or explosives.

The avoidance of avalanches can often be accomplished by noting the nature of the snow and the character of the weather. Avalanches are most abundant in winter when the snow is unstable and storms frequent and changeable. At normal winter temperatures dry-snow avalanches come down only six to twenty-four hours after snowfall, when the snowflakes are losing cohesion and one to two hours after the reappearance of the sun. In spring, during periods of sunshine, wet snow avalanches will occur in the afternoon after the cohesion of the snow has been lessened. At night, falling temperature accelerated by radiation, will cement the snow again. But during storms, avalanches may occur at any hour. However, no fixed rule can be given, for impulse to avalanche movement is complex and may be slight and difficult to foresee.

TESTING AND FORECASTING

Tests of the tendencies of suspected snow fields can be made by perforating the snow to determine the cohesiveness of its crystals and crusts. Paulcke inaugurated the use of a snow sampler one meter long with windows (113). The Swiss Avalanche Commission has installed meters to determine the pressure or creep of the snow and uses a field ram to determine snow resistance or cohesiveness. Tests of both tensile strength and compressibility are also made in the laboratory. Time profiles of the changing snow cover are kept (114, 115). On the foundation of such profiles, providing they can be used to interpret snow conditions at other elevations in the region, forecasts can be made of avalanche tendencies under prevailing or impending weather.

ICE

To round out this general chapter on snow and ice, the reader is referred to the chapter on Ice in the Sea by Commander Edward H. Smith in "Oceanography" (volume V of this series) and to the following section on the Evolution of Ice in Streams. Both sea and river ice are socially and economically of far greater present importance than glaciers and ice caps but, with the exception of icebergs, lack their fascination. However, glacier ice has had its world influence in the past and may exert it again.

THE EVOLUTION OF ICE IN STREAMS[1]

WALTER J. PARSONS, JR.[2]

Much has been observed and written about the open summer phase of river behavior; but little about the winter phase. This section will attempt to describe objectively some of the less well-known phenomena of the winter phase of a river's annual cycle.

The freeze-up.—With the coming of cold weather the water in a stream is gradually cooled, its temperature being intermediate between that of the cold air on the surface and that of the warm rock of the river bed, which still retains the heat of the summer. Within the mass of the water temperatures tend to be uniform, the water being continually stirred by turbulent currents. This uniformity is further aided by the sinking of the cold, dense surface layers and the welling up of the warm, lighter bottom layer. Occasionally temperature stratification occurs in deep, quiet pools. The water cools degree by degree until the entire mass is close to the freezing point. Finally the surface film of water is cooled below the freezing point and suddenly changed into needlelike crystals of ice that are slightly lighter than water.

The degree of turbulence compared with the rapidity of freezing now causes the ice formation to follow one of three general courses. In case 1, when turbulence is large, the crystals are carried below the surface and the entire body of water is converted into a milky mixture of ice and water. This is called "frazil ice" and causes considerable trouble at power plants

---

[1] Ice in the northern streams of the United States (Western Interstate Snow-Survey Conf. Trans.): Am. Geophys. Union Trans., 1940, pt. 3, pp. 970–973.

[2] Hydraulic Engineer, United States Engineers Office.

and control gates. When the floating crystals touch any surface that has a temperature even a fraction of a degree below the freezing point, such as a submerged portion of a steel rack or a mass of sheet ice, the crystals instantly adhere and form a spongy, rapidly growing mass than can quickly choke even large waterway openings.

In case 2, when turbulence is less, the crystals remain floating on the surface, touch, interlock into a loose network, form little floating islands that join, are crushed together, and grow larger. Within the open meshes of the network the liquid water is trapped and cannot easily mix with warmer subsurface water. It therefore freezes rapidly and unites the network into solid pans of ice. These pans are carried downstream until they touch the cold shore, freeze tight, catch other pans, and so jam from shore to shore. This is the end of free flow in the river. Floating pans strike the jam and rapidly extend it upstream, submerged crystals of frazil ice are carried under the ice bridge and, floating upward, adhere to the bottom surface and thicken it. Soon the whole reach of river is solidly covered.

In case 3, with still less turbulence, the floating nets of crystals unite without crushing, and crystal growth in the interstitial water unites the mass into a clear sheet of "rubber ice."

Upon the creation of a continuous ice cover the freezing process enters a new phase. Heat can no longer be lost by radiation directly from the free water surface to the cold air but must be carried by conduction through the ice layer. As ice is a poor conductor of heat, the temperature gradient is steep, and the rate of freezing from the bottom surface of the ice rapidly decreases as an inverse exponential function. Normal winter temperatures in the Northern States rarely can freeze single sheets of river ice more than 30 inches thick. When there is a snow blanket on top of the sheet ice, the conduction of heat is still further reduced and the rate of freezing correspondingly decreased. The end result of the process is a dense, watertight sheet of floating ice with its temperature ranging from a fraction of a degree below freezing at the bottom surface to temperatures of from freezing to as low as 60° F. below zero at the top surface.

An abnormal type of ice formation called "anchor ice" occurs in clear swift streams with dark rock bottoms. On cold, clear nights the dark rocks of the bottom lose heat so rapidly by radiation up through the water into the air that they cool below the freezing point of the water above them. The adjacent water is frozen into transparent "skull caps" as much as 2 inches in thickness, firmly attached to the rocks. The effect on the river flow is the same as if the bottom had suddenly risen 1 or 2 inches throughout. When daylight comes the sunshine penetrates through the clear water and transparent anchor ice to the dark rocks and warms them up. The anchor ice is melted loose and floats up to the surface. The result is that shortly after sunrise there is a sudden increase in the amount of floating ice, and trouble due to clogging of gates and racks becomes acute.

Another abnormal phenomenon is associated with the thickening of the original ice cover. It has been observed that during a prolonged cold spell, when the air temperature remains continuously below 0° F., the thickening of the original ice cover decreases at an abnormally rapid rate. When, on the contrary, the low temperature fluctuates enough to approach the freezing point, the ice thickens at a normal rate. A possible explanation of this phenomenon lies in the theory that liquid water is a mixture of several molecular forms of H_2O, only one of which can change into solid ice. At temperatures well above freezing the several forms maintain their normal proportions by continuous interchange. As the freezing point is approached the speed of interchange is greatly slowed down. During a prolonged cold spell the ice-making form is soon exhausted, and further ice making is delayed until this form can be replenished from the other forms. Fluctuating temperatures permit the maintenance of normal proportion of the different forms.

Effect of ice on river-flow characteristics.—Although the viscosity of water increases with decreasing temperature, the effect on the normal turbulent flow of water in natural rivers is rarely large enough to be observed by current-meter measurements. The retarding effect of suspended frazil ice or floating pan or slush ice is likewise small. With the formation of a complete ice cover solidly anchored to the banks flow conditions change radically. The depth of the ice below the free water surface has been subtracted from the area available for flow, and in addition the under surface of the ice acts as an additional friction surface. The free water surface (which is what is ordinarily measured by river gages) may have to rise as much as 4 feet, under extreme conditions, to pass the same flow as before the formation of the ice cover. At first the under surface of the ice is rough, with many projections formed by the protruding edges of pans of ice that were turned on edge as they jammed together. Rough porous masses of frazil ice are caught under the ice sheet and greatly obstruct flow. The sudden increase in stage throughout the channel requires the storage of large volumes of water. As a result the river flow temporarily decreases. When the additional storage has been satisfied the flow returns to normal. This sudden decrease and recovery is a sure indication that the upstream reaches of a stream have changed to the winter phase. Within 1 or 2 weeks the reduction in heat loss due to the insulating effect of the ice cover permits the temperature of the water to rise sufficiently to melt the masses of frazil ice and the projecting slabs of ice below the solid ice cover. The under surface of the ice becomes smooth as glass and almost plane. Flow conditions are improved and stages slowly drop, releasing part of the stored water. Near stable conditions now exist, with the only change the slow increase in stage as the ice cover gradually thickens.

Behavior of ice in midwinter.—The ice cover is normally in a state of almost complete flotation. The edges of the ice sheet are frozen solidly to the banks and to projecting boulders and bridge piers, but the stiffness of the ice against cross bending is so small that within a distance equal to about ten times the ice thickness, the ice is at the normal flotation level. Rising stages lift the center of the ice sheet but leave a depression along the shore that may be below the free water surface. Such a depression soon fills with water from melting snow or through cracks in the ice, and the next cold spell freezes the water, restoring the level upper surface of the ice. Rarely a stream bed is so narrow between projecting boulders that a sudden decrease in flow will cause the water to drop completely below the ice, leaving the ice temporarily suspended and the water flowing freely inside a tunnel. This condition does not last long before the ice cracks and falls back to normal flotation level.

Ice expands and contracts with temperature changes in the same way as rocks, although the presence of water in contact with the under side reduces the range of temperature. Rising temperatures cause expansion that exerts outward pressure toward the banks. Normally there are enough weak points in the ice sheet to permit the release of this pressure by buckling of the sheet or crumbling of its edges. Occasionally the temperature rise is so rapid that enormous expansive pressures are developed at the edges of the ice and, exposed piers, bulkheads, or sea walls are overturned or shoved bodily. When the expansion is less rapid the ice has time to adjust itself at weak points by crumbling and internal shear, so that little damage is done. Sometimes the entire frozen surface of the river bank, including rocks, earth, and sand, is sheared free from the unfrozen subsoil and piled up in characteristic long ridges parallel to the stream channel. This action on midchannel sand bars piles them up above water level.

Similarly, dropping temperatures cause contraction of the ice sheet. As ice is very weak in tension, the stress is easily released by numerous tension cracks. The ice sheet already shoved up on the bank is not retracted but remains perched on the bank. Contraction of ice is usually harmless to engineering structures. However, the combination of alternate expansion and contraction causes a ratchet action that is more severe than either action separately. As contraction takes place at colder temperatures, the water that rises in the tension cracks freezes at once, filling and sealing the cracks. When temperatures rise again the cracks cannot close, and the entire expansion must take place at the edges of the sheet. Similarly, compression cracks due to buckling freeze solid and are stronger than before. Each cycle of contraction and expansion shoves the edges of the sheet farther up the bank.

Piers or walls exposed to the full force of ice expansion are usually protected by maintaining a belt of open water in front of them. As new ice freezes in the open lane of water, or as ice expansion closes it, this protective belt must be reopened and the ice cakes removed. A clever use can be made of the residual heat of the water under the ice. A perforated air pipe is placed along the bottom of the river in front of the wall or gate. The rising air bubbles drag warm bottom water upward and cause active circulation that prevents surface freezing and even melts heavy sheet ice that has been shoved into the protecting lane.

Thawing of river ice.—When winter comes to an end and air temperatures rise, the ice sheet begins to melt. The water beneath the ice has always been warmer than the ice, but now the insulating snow blanket is melted away and the sun beats down on the bare upper surface. Solid clear ice melts very slowly. Massive cakes of ice 3 feet thick that were solidly frozen to the face of steel gates remained frozen in place for as long as 48 hours after they had been deeply submerged by lowering of the gate, although the ice was surrounded by swiftly moving water passing through the open gate. However, in favorable localities, the snow melt water on top of the ice carries heat down every crack in the ice, and the once solid, watertight mass is transformed into a honeycomb structure of long crystals normal to the surface, which occupies the same total volume but which is structurally weak and has its pores filled with water. To the casual eye the ice looks as solid as it did in January, but actually it has changed radically. Then comes the first spring rise in the river. The snow-melt water from the hillsides enters the stream, the flow increases and the stage rises, the ice sheet is broken loose from the banks, and the cracks are not resealed with fresh ice. Then one day comes that ever-fascinating sight, the ice run. A weak section of ice floats free of its anchorage and releases the water stored above it. This extra water floats the next section free, releasing more stored water. All at once the whole river begins to move, the apparently solid cakes crumbling into slush as they strike the bank and against each other. A few ice cakes from shaded locations are still hard and strong. Armed with gravel and boulders frozen into their bottom, they crash on bridge piers and grind timber cribbing to match sticks. However, the greater part of the ice disintegrates into slush that melts while one watches it. The next day the river is running clear from bank to bank, with only a solitary ice cake piled up here and there on a sand bar.

REFERENCES

The following individual references merely indicate the general development of snow and ice studies. Of equal importance are the transactions of the Western Interstate Snow-Survey Conference and of the International Commissions of Snow and Glaciers, which form a library of research reports on every phase of the subject. To these should be added the annual reports of the Research Committee on the Hydrology of Snow (American Geophysical Union) and the minutes of the Association for the Study of Snow and Ice.

General

1. Church, J. E., International snow: Am. Meteorol. Soc. Bull 18, March, 1937.
2. Research Committee on the Hydrology of Snow (Am. Geophys. Union), Annual reports, 1931, Am. Geophys. Union Trans., Washington, D. C.
3. Connaughton, C. A., Research on snow by the Forest Service: Western Interstate Snow-Survey Conf. Trans. (Am. Geophys. Union Trans.), 1940.
4. Dobrowolski, A. B., Sur la nécessité de la fondation d'une institution internationale pour l'étude de la glace: IV. Conf. hydro.. états baltiques, No. 97, Leningrad, September 1933.
5. International Commissions of Snow and Glaciers Trans., (Edinburgh), 1936: Assoc. internat. d'hydrologie scientifique Bull. 23 (Union internat. géodesie et géophysique); Trans., Washington, 1939 (awaiting publication).
6. Association for the Study of Snow and Ice Minutes, London, 1937--——.
7. American Geophysical Union (Section of Hydrology) Trans. 1931-——, Washington.
8. Western Interstate Snow-Survey Conference, Proc., 1933, Reno; Trans. (Am. Geophys. Union Trans.), 1934-——, Washington.

Physics of snow and ice

9. Ahlman, H. W., Die Fähigkeit des Schnees, Wasser durch zu lassen und aufzuspeichern: Internat. Comm. Snow and Glaciers Trans., Washington, 1939 (awaiting publication).
10. Arnold-Alabiev, V. I., On the investigation of snow crystals: Internat. Comm. Snow and Glaciers Trans., Washington, 1939 (awaiting publication).
11. Barrera, Humberto. A study of the "nieve penitente" of the Chilean Andes: Internat. Comm. Snow and Glaciers Trans., Edinburgh, 1936 (Internat. Assoc. Bull. 23).
12. Bentley, W. A., and Humphreys, W. J., Snow crystals, McGraw-Hill Book Co., 1931.
13. Bergeron, Tor, Hydrometeorbeschreibungen mit den vom Internationalen Meteorologischen Komitee in Salzburg, 1937, angenommenen Anderungen: Weddelanden, Serien Uppsatser No. 22, Statens Meteorologisk-Hydrografiske Anstalt.
14. Catalano, L. R., Los penitentes de nieve y observaciones geofísicas atmosféricas: Asoc. cultural conferencia Rosario, Cien. natur., 1935, No. 3.
15. Church, J. E., Climate and evaporation in Alpine and Arctic zones; temperatures of Arctic soil and water (reports of Greenland expeditions, vol. 2): Michigan Univ. Studies, 1941.
16. Church, J. E., Evaporation at high altitudes and latitudes: Am. Geophys. Union Trans., 1934.
17. Clyde, G. D., The effect of rain on the snow cover, Utah Agr. Exper. Sta., July 11, 1929; Monthly Weather Rev., vol. 57, August 1929.
18. Clyde, G. D., Snow-melting characteristics: Utah Agr. Exper. Stat. Tech. Bull. 231.
19. Clyde, G. D., Change in density of snow cover with melting: Monthly Weather Rev., vol. 57, August 1929.
20. Dorsey, N. E., Properties of ordinary water substance in all its phases—water-vapor, water, and all the ices, Reinhold Pub. Corp., 1940.
21. Horton, R. E., Phenomena of the contact zone between the ground surface and a layer of melting snow: Internat. Comm. Snow and Glaciers, Edinburgh, 1936 (Internat. Assoc. Bull. 23).
22. Horton, R. E., The melting of snow: Monthly Weather Rev., vol. 43, December 1915
23. Horton, R. E., Water losses in high latitudes and at high elevations: Am. Geophys Union Trans., 1934.

24. Hughes, T. P., and Seligman, Gerald, The bearing of snow permeability and retentivity on the density increase of firn and ice-band formation in glaciers: Jungfrau Research Party. Pub. 3, 1938.

25. Humphreys, W. J., The atmosphere—origin and composition: Meteorology, Physics of the Earth, vol. III (Nat. Research Council Bull. 79), 1931.

26. Kaitera, Pentti, Snow melting in springtime: Internat. Comm. Snow and Glaciers, Washington, 1939 (awaiting publication).

27. Kalitin, N. N., Die Radiationseigenschaften des Schnees und des Eises: IV. Hydrol. Konf. Baltischen Staaten, Leningrad, 1933; (a) The measurements of the albedo of a snow cover, Monthly Weather Rev., vol. 58, February, 1930.

28. Kennedy, R. E., The melting of snow computed by the energy equation: Internat. Comm. Snow and Glaciers, Washington, 1939 (awaiting publication).

29. Light, Phillip, Analysis of high rates of snow melting: Western Interstate Snow-Survey Conf. Trans. (Am. Geophys. Union Trans.), 1941.

30. Matthes, F. E., Ablation of snow fields at high altitudes by radiant solar heat: Am. Geophys. Union Trans., 1934.

31. Oechslin, Max, Wasserdurchsicherung und Wasserrückhaltvermögen der Schneedecke: Internat. Comm. Snow and Glaciers, Washington, 1939 (awaiting publication).

32. Meinardus, W., Klimakunde der Antarktis: Köppen-Geiger, Handbuch der Klimatologie, Bd 4, Teil U., Gebrüder Borntraeger, Berlin, 1938.

33. Nakaya, Ukitiro, and others, Investigations on snow, Hokkaido Imperial Univ., Sapporo, Japan, 1934:
No. 1. Physical investigations on snow, pt. 1, Snow crystals observed in 1933 at Sapporo and some relations with meteorological conditions.
No. 2. Physical investigations on snow, pt. 2, Classification and explanation of snow crystals observed in the winter of 1933–34 at Mount Tokati and at Sapporo.
No. 3. On the electrical nature of snow particles.
No. 4. Simultaneous observations of the mass, falling velocity, and form of individual snow crystals.
No. 5. On the correspondence of snow and rime crystals.
No. 7. Notes on irregular snow crystals and snow pellets.
No. 8. General classification of snow crystals and their frequency of occurrence.
No. 10. Preliminary experiments on the artificial production of snow crystals.
No. 11. Further experiment on the production of snow crystals.
No. 12. Experimental researches on window hoar crystals, a general survey.

34. Nakaya, Ukitiro, and others, Investigations on snow, The physics of skiing, the preliminary and general survey, Hokkaido Imperial Univ., Sapporo, Japan, 1936.

35. Nakaya, Ukitiro, Formation of snow crystals in the mountains and in the laboratory in Japan (accompanying a sound film): Western Interstate Snow-Survey Conf. Trans. (Am. Geophys. Union Trans.), 1940.

36. Pagliuca, Salvatore, On the methods of estimating the contribution to runoff of frozen fog deposits on mountains: Internat. Comm. Snow and Glaciers, Edinburgh, 1936 (Internat. Assoc. Bull. 23).

37. Palmer, A. H., The region of greatest snowfall in the United States: Monthly Weather Rev., vol. 43, May 1915.

38a. Rugen, Otto N., The snow-melt problem as affecting the design of flood control-works: Am. Geophys. Union Trans., 1940.

38b. Sokolovsky, D. L., Effect of intensity of snow melt on the creation of maximum discharges: Internat. Comm. Snow and Glaciers, Washington, 1939 (awaiting publication).

39. Thams, Chr., Über die Strahlungseigenschaften der Schneedecke: Gerlands Beitr. Geophysik, Band 53, 1938.

40. Tutton, A. E. H., The high Alps: a natural history of ice and snow, Kegan Paul, Trench, Trubner & Co., 1927.

41. Wagner, A., Gibt es im Gebirge eine Hohenzone maximalen Niederschlages: Internat. Comm. Snow and Glaciers, Edinburgh, 1936 (Internat. Assoc. Bull. 23).

42. Wegener, Kurt, Wissenschaftliche Ergebnisse der Deutschen Grönland-Expedition

Alfred Wegener, 1929 und 1930, Band 1, Geschichte der Expedition mit Beiträgen über Einzelergebnisse von den Mitgliedern der Expedition, Brockhaus, 1933; Band III, Glaciologie.

43. Wilson, W. T., An outline of the thermodynamics of snow melt. Western Interstate Snow-Survey Conf. Trans. (Am. Geophys. Union Trans.), 1941.

Precipitation measurements

44. Bernard, Merrill, The expanded program of the United States Weather Bureau in snow work: Western Interstate Snow-Survey Conf. Trans. (Am. Geophys. Union Trans.), 1938.

45. Brooks, C. F., Need for universal standards for measuring precipitation, snowfall, and snow cover: Internat. Comm. Snow and Glaciers, Edinburgh, 1936 (Internat. Assoc. Bull. 23). Annotated Bibl.

45a. Brooks, C. F., Connot, A. J., and others, Climatic Maps of North America, Harvard Univ., Cambridge, Mass., 1936.

46. Recording rain and snow gages: Western Interstate Snow-Survey Conf. Proc., 1933 Univ. Nevada. (Ferguson and Mougin gages.)

47. Rinker, L. E., The Stevens seasonal snow-rain recorder: Western Interstate Snow-Survey Conf. Trans (Am. Geophys. Trans. Union), 1938.

48. Mercanton, P. L., and Billwiller, R., MZA indication pour l'emploi des totalisateurs de precipitations (Mougins): Internat. Comm. Snow and Glaciers, Edinburgh, 1936 (Internat. Assoc. Bull. 23).

49. Mercanton, P. L., and Lugeon, Jean, L'ectrosonde MZA pour la mesure du contenu des totalisateurs de précipitations (Mougins): Internat. Comm. Snow and Glaciers, Edinburgh, 1936 (Internat. Assoc. Bull. 23).

Snow surveying

50. Bean, P. L., A quantitative forecast system for power and flood warning in the Androscoggin River Basin, Maine: Western Interstate Snow-Survey Conf. Trans. (Am. Geophys. Union Trans.), 1940.

51. Bernard, Merrill, Progress toward a rational program of snow-melt forecasting: Western Interstate Snow-Survey Conf. Trans. (Am. Geophys. Union Trans.), 1941.

52. Church, J. E., Principles of snow surveying as applied to forecasting stream flow: Jour. Agr. Research, vol. 51, No. 2, 1935.

53. Church, J. E., Snow surveying—its principles and possibilities. Geog. Rev., vol. 23, October 1933.

54. Church, J. E., Snow surveying—its problems and their present phases with reference to Mount Rose, Nev., and vicinity: Pan Am. Sci. Cong. Proc. Sec. 2, vol. 2, 1915–16.

55. Church, J. E., Jones, E. H., and Boardman, H. P., Precipitations and runoff at the Continental Divide: Eng. News-Record, vol. 94, No. 5, January 29, 1925.

56. Church, J. E., Smith, A. L., and Boardman, H. P., Snow surveying in relation to forecasting stream flow—its principles and problems (The evolution of measuring snow and snow surveying): Nevada Agr. Exper. Sta., 1935 (awaiting publication).

57. Clyde, G. D., Establishing snow courses for representativeness, permanence, and continuity of record. Western Interstate Snow-Survey Conf. Trans. (Am. Geophys. Union Trans.), 1937.

58. Devore, G. G., Phillips, J. E., and Clyde, G. D., Symposium on economic aspects of snow surveying. Western Interstate Snow-Survey Conf. Trans. (Am. Geophys. Union Trans.), 1938.

59. Horton, R. E., Snowfalls, freshets, and the winter flows of streams in the State of New York: Monthly Weather Rev., vol. 33, May 1905.

60. Leaver, Robert, and Boardman, H. P., Winter precipitation versus snow survey for forecasting on Skagit River, Washington: Western Interstate Snow-Survey Conf. Trans. (Am. Geophys. Union Trans.), 1938.

61. Lowdermilk, W. C., Considerations in measurement of yield of snow packs in percolation water: Western Interstate Snow-Survey Conf. Proc., 1933.

62. Mixer, C. A., River floods and melting snow. Monthly Weather Rev., vol. 31, April 1903.

63. Paget, F. H., Development of snow surveying in California (the direct method): Western Interstate Snow-Survey Conf. Trans. (Am. Geophys. Union Trans.), 1938.

64. Salo, J. V., A quantitative forecast system of runoff based on snow surveys at the mean elevation of the snow cover: Western Interstate Snow-Survey Conf. Trans (Am. Geophys. Union Trans.), 1940.

65. Siren, Allan, Bestimmung des Wasserwertes der Schneedecke: V. Hydrol. Konf. der Baltischen Staaten, Finland, 1936, No. 18 B.

Factors in forecasting runoff

66. Atkinson, H. B., and Bay, C. E., Some factors affecting frost penetration. Western Interstate Snow-Survey Conf. Trans. (Am. Geophys. Union Trans.), 1940.

67. Belotelkin, K. T., Soil freezing and forest cover: Western Interstate Snow-Survey Conf. Trans. (Am. Geophys. Union Trans.), 1941.

68. Boardman, H. P., Normals of the eastern slope of the central Sierra Nevada: Western Interstate Snow-Survey Conf. Proc., 1933.

69. Church, J. E., High density of snow accelerates its melting and runoff: Eng. News-Record, vol. 99, No. 14, Oct. 6, 1927.

70. Church, J. E., Snow density in relation to runoff: Eng. News-Record, vol. 92, No. 6, Feb. 7, 1924.

71. Church, J. E., The snow survey and summer precipitation: Geog. Rev., vol. 25, October 1935.

72. Church, P. E., Boardman, H. P., and Wells, E. L., Report of committee on median vs. arithmetical average: Am. Geophys. Union Trans., 1941.

73. Clyde, G. D., Soil-moisture studies as an aid in forecasting runoff from snow cover: Western Interstate Snow-Survey Conf. Trans. (Am. Geophys. Union Trans.), 1940.

74. Hoover, O. H., Effects of chinook (foehn) winds on snow cover and runoff: Internat. Comm. Snow and Glaciers, Washington, 1939 (awaiting publication).

75. Horton, R. E., Relation of soil moisture and antecedent rainfall to runoff and runoff prediction: Internat. Comm. Snow and Glaciers, Washington, 1939 (awaiting publication).

76. Keranen, J., Über den Bodenfrost in Finland: Met. Zentralanstalt des finnischen Staates Mitt. Nr. 12, Helsinki, 1923.

77. Keranen, J., Über die Temperatur des Bodens und der Schneedecke in Sodankylä, Univ. Helsingfors, 1920.

78. Keso, Lauri, Beobachtungen über den Dranabfluss in Tonboden und in gefrorenen Boden: V. Hydrol. Konf. der Baltischen Staaten, Finnland, 1936, No. 4 B.

79. Lee, C. H., Calculations of normals for use with snow-survey data: Am. Geophys. Union Trans. 1936.

80. McLaughlin, W. W., Factors affecting run off forecasts based on snow surveys: Internat. Comm. Snow and Glaciers, Washington 1939 (awaiting publication); Soil Conservation, vol. 6, December 1939.

81. Mindling, G. W., Do climatological averages serve adequately as normals? Am. Meteorol. Soc. Bull. 21.1 (January 1940). Discussion by Clarence Pedersen: Am. Geophys. Union Trans., 1940.

82. Velner, August, Frostwirkung auf die Abflussverteilung eines Flussgebietes: Internat. Comm. Snow and Glaciers, Edinburg, 1936 (Internat. Assoc. Bull. 23).

Conservation

83. Church, J. E., Das Verhältniss des Waldes und des Gebirges zur Erhaltung des Schnees: Meteorol. Zeitschr., Band 30.1, 1913.

84. Church, J. E., Restraining effect of forests on sudden melting of snows: Eng. Record, vol. 69, June 1914.

85. Church, J. E., The conservation of snow—its dependence on forests and mountains: Sci. Am. Suppl., vol. 74, No. 1914 (Sept. 7, 1912).

86. Horton, R. E., Rainfall interception: Monthly Weather Rev., vol. 47, September 1919.

87. Korhonen, W. W., Der mittlere Wassergehalt der Schneedecke in Finnland am 15. März in den Jahren 1919–34: V. Hydrol. Konf. der Baltischen Staaten, Finland, 1936, Nr. 18 A.

88. Korhonen, W. W., Untersuchungen der Schneedecke und der Schneeniederschlage in Finnland: V. Hydrol. Konf. der Baltischen Staaten, Finland, 1936, Nr. 18 C.

Floods

89. Baldwin, H. I., and Brooks, C. F., Forests and floods in New Hampshire, New England: Regional Planning Commission, Boston, Publ. No. 47, 28 pp. (Mimeo.), December, 1936.

89a. Baldwin, Henry I., Forests, snow cover, and floods in New Hampshire: Internat. Comm. Snow and Glaciers, Washington, 1939 (awaiting publication).

90. Brooks, C. F., and Thiessen, A. H., The meteorology of great floods in the eastern United States: Geog. Rev., vol. 27, No. 2, April 1937.

91. Church, J. E., Snow surveys as an aid to flood forecast and control: Eng. News-Record, vol. 114, June 20, 1935.

92. Church, J. E., The relation of snow to maximum flood peaks—a discussion: Western Interstate Snow-Survey Conf. Trans. (Am. Geophys. Union Trans.), 1940.

93. Hoyt, W. G., Snow and ice—a flood hazard: Internat. Comm. Snow and Glaciers, Washington, 1939 (awaiting publication).

94. Matthes, G. H., Relation of snow and ice to floods: Internat. Comm. Snow and Glaciers, Washington, 1939 (awaiting publication).

95. Parsons, W. J., Jr., The relation of snow to maximum flood peaks: Western Interstate Snow-Survey Conf. Trans. (Am. Geophys. Union Trans.), 1940.

Avalanches, transport, winter sports

96. Arenberg, D. L., and Harney, P. J., The Mount Washington icing research program: Am. Meteorol. Soc. Bull. 22.2, February 1941.

97. Drane, B. S., Report on an informal exploration toward improved nomenclature for general use in classifying forms and conditions of snow: Am. Geophys. Union Trans., 1939.

98. Golovkov, M., Investigation of ice formed on the airplanes: Acad. sci. Union Répub. soviét, Bull. sociol. No. 1, 1940.

98a. Lacey, J. K., A study of meteorological and physical factors affecting the formation of ice on airplanes: Amer. Met. Soc. Bull., v. 21, pp. 357–367, Nov., 1940.

98b. McNeal, D., Ice formation in the atmosphere: J. Aero. Sci., N. Y., v. 4, no. 3, pp. 117–123, Jan., 1937.

99. Haefeli, R., A contribution to the study of snow mechanics: Internat. Comm. Snow and Glaciers, Washington, 1939 (awaiting publication); Summary, Am. Geophys. Union Trans., 1940, pp. 394–395.

100. Klein, G. J., Interim report on the snow characteristics of aircraft skis, Nat. Research Council of Canada, 1936.

101. Klein, G. J., The snow performance of aircraft skis, Nat. Research Council of Canada, 1938.

102. Klein, G. J., The snow resistance of aircraft skis: Internat. Comm. Snow and Glaciers, Washington, 1939 (awaiting publication).

103. Lund, Arnold, Alpine skiing at all heights and seasons, Methuen & Co. 1926.

104. MacVicar, J. D., Snow types met in highway snow removal: Western Interstate Snow-Survey Conf. Trans. (Am. Geophys. Union Trans.), 1940; Roads and Streets, September, 1940 (article prepared by V. J. Brown).

105. Morikofer, W., The physical properties of the snow cover: Internat. Comm. Snow and Glaciers, Washington, 1939 (awaiting publication).

106. National Water Resources Committee, Uniform nomenclature of snow cover: Internat. Comm. Snow and Glaciers, Washington, 1939 (awaiting publication).

107. Niggli, P., Changes in snow during and after deposition: Internat. Comm. Snow and Glaciers: Washington, 1939 (awaiting publication); Summary, Am. Geophys. Union Trans., 1940, pp. 393–394.

108. Oechslin, Max, Lawinengeschwindigkeiten und Lawinenluftdruck: Schweiz. Zeitsch. Forstwesen. No. 6, 1938.

109. Paulcke, Wilhelm, und Welzenbach, Willi, Schnee, Wächten, Lawinen: Zeitschr. Gletscherkunde, Band 16, Nr. 1–2, 1928.

110. Paulcke, Wilhelm, Eisbildungen—I, Der Schnee und seine Diagenese: Zeitschr. Gletscherkunde, Band 21, Nr. 4–5, 1934; summary by R. G. Stone, Am. Meteorol. Soc. Bull., 19.2, February 1938.

111. Paulcke, Wilhelm, Schnee-Wächten und Lawinen: Zeitschr. deutsch. und österreich. Alpenverein, 1934.

112. Paulcke, Wilhelm, Praktische Schnee- und Lawinenkunde, Julius Springer, 1938.

113. Paulcke, Wilhelm, Über die wichtigsten Ergebnisse meiner Schnee- und Lawinen-forschungen: Internat. Comm. Snow and Glaciers Trans., Edinburgh, 1936 (Internat. Assoc. Bull. 23).

114. Schweiz, Schnee- und Lawinenforschungs-kommission, Der Schnee und seine Meta-morphose: erste Ergebnisse und Anwendungen einer systematischen Untersuchung der alpinen Winterschneedecke von H. Bader, R. Haefeli, E. Bucher, J. Neher, O. Eckel, Chr. Thams, mit einer Einführung von P. Niggli, durchgeführt von der Station Weissfluhjoch-Davos 1934–38, Kümmerly & Frey, 1939.

115. Die Schweiz. Schnee- und Lawinenforschuug und der Parsenndienst. Lawinen—die Gefahr für den Skifahrer. 1940.

116. Seligman, Gerald, Snow structure and ski fields (snow and ice, avalanches and snow-craft), Macmillan, 1936.

117. Simpson, G. C., Ice accretion on aircraft: Meteorol. Office Prof. Notes No. 82, London, 1937; Am. Meteorol. Soc. Bull. 19.8, October 1938.

118. Welzenbach, W., Untersuchungen über die Stratigraphie der Schneeablagerungen und die Mechanik der Schneebewegungen nebst Schlussfolgerungen auf die Methoden der Ver-bauung: Wiss. Veröff. deutsch. u. öst. Alpen-Verein, 1930, Nr. 9.

119. Zsigmondy, Emil, und Paulcke, Wilhelm, Die Gefahren der Alpen, Rudolf Rother, 1933.

Glacial snow and runoff

120. Ahlmann, H. W., and others, Scientific results of the Swedish-Norwegian Arctic Expedition in the summer of 1931, vol. 1, pt. 1–9; Geog. Annaler, 1933.

121. Ahlmann, H. W., Contribution to the physics of glaciers: Geog. Jour. vol. 86, No. 2, August 1935.

122. Ahlmann, H. W., Determination of the ablation of snow and ice. Meddelande Geog. Instit. Vid Stockholms Hogskola No. 21 (Geog. Annaler, 1935, Sven Hedin).

123. Ahlmann, H. W., Sverdrup, H. U., and others, Scientific results of the Norwegian-Swedish Spitsbergen Expedition in 1934, pt. 1–8: Geog. Annaler, 1935, 1936.

124. Ahlmann, H. W., The Swedish-Icelandic Vatnajökull Expedition, 1936: Internat. Comm. Snow and Glaciers, Edinburgh, 1936 (Internat. Assoc. Bull. 23).

125. Ahlmann, H. W., and Thorarinsson, Sigurdur, Vatnajökull, Scientific results of the Swedish-Icelandic investigations, 1936–38: Geog. Annaler, 1937, 1938.

126. Ahlmann, H. W., and Thorarinsson, Sigurdur, The Vatnajökull Glacier (prelimi-nary report of the Swedish-Icelandic investigation, 1936–37): Geog. Rev., July 1938.

127. Alfieri, Secondo, Influenza della neve e del ghiaccio sulla portata dei corsi d'aqua: Internat. Comm. Snow and Glaciers. Washington, 1939 (awaiting publication).

128. Coutagne, Aimé, Influence de la neige et de la glace sur le debit des cours d'eau: Internat. Comm. Snow and Glaciers. Washington, 1939 (awaiting publication).

129. Loewe, Fritz, The amount of rime and snowdrift as factors in the mass balance of glaciers: Internat. Comm. Snow and Glaciers Trans., Edinburgh, 1936 (Internat. Assoc. Bull. 23).

130. Lütschg, Otto, Über Niederschlag und Abfluss im Hochgebirge; Sonderdarstellung des Mattmarkgebietes; ein Beitrag zur Fluss- und Gletscherkunde der Schweiz, mit Beiträgen von R. Eichenberger, H. Christ, P. Huber und M. Petitmermet, 1926.

131. Lütschg, Otto, Zum Wasserhaushalt der schweizer Hochgebirges: Internat. Assoc. Scientific Hydrology, Washington, 1939 (awaiting publication).

132. Seligman, Gerald, The structure of a temperate glacier: Geog. Rev., vol. 97, No. 5, May 1941.

133. Sorge, Ernst, Glaziologische Untersuchungen in Eismitte: Wissenschaftliche Ergebnisse der Deutschen Grönland-Expedition Alfred Wegener, 1929 und 1930–31, Band 3, Brockhaus, Leipzig.

134. Tyler, R. G., Flow characteristics of glacier-fed and snow-fed streams. Western Interstate Snow-Survey Conf. Trans. (Am. Geophys. Union Trans.), 1934.

135. Wegener, Kurt, Die Temperatur am Boden des grönlandischen Inlandeises: Zeitschr. Geophysik, Band 12.4, 1936.

136. Wegener, Kurt, Zusammenfassung der Wissenschaftlichen Ergebnisse der Deutschen Grönland-Expedition Alfred Wegener, 1939 und 1930–31, Brockhaus, Leipzig, 1940.

Ice

137. Altberg, W. J., Flusseis und Winterregime: V. Hydrol. Konf. der Baltischen Staaten, Finnland, 1936, No. 7 D.

138. Altberg, V. J., Twenty years of work in the domain of underwater ice formation: Internat. Comm. Snow and Glaciers Trans., Edinburgh, 1936 (Internat. Assoc. Bull. 23).

139. Barnes, H. T., Ice engineering, Montreal, Renouf Pub. Co., 1928.

140. Barnes, H. T., Ice formation (especially anchor ice and frazil), John Wiley & Sons, 1906.

141. Bragg, Sir William, Ice: Royal Inst. Great Britain Proc. vol. 30, pt. 2, No. 141.

142. Kennedy, R. E., The melting of snow computed by the energy equation: Internat. Comm. Snow and Glaciers, Washington, 1939 (awaiting publication).

143. Koch, Harry, Swedish air photos of the ice in the Gulf of Bothnia in the spring of 1936: V. Hydrol. Conf. Baltic States, Finland, 1936, No. 13 C.

144. Stakle, P., Die Eisverhältnisse der Ostsee und ihre Erforschung: V. Hydrol. Konf. der Baltischen Staaten, Finnland, 1936, No. 13 A.

145. Stevens, J. C., Winter overflow from ice gorging on shallow streams: Western Interstate Snow-Survey Conf. Trans. (Am. Geophys. Union Trans.), 1940.

146. Timonoff, V. E., On the establishment of a working hypothesis of ice phenomena in lakes and rivers: Internat. Comm. Snow and Glaciers Trans., Edinburgh, 1936 (Internat. Assoc. Bull. 23).

147. Weinberg, Boris, Latest investigation on snow and ice of the Soviet cryologists: Internat. Comm. Snow and Glaciers, Washington, 1939 (awaiting publication); List of latest publications. Am. Geophys. Union Trans., 1940, pp. 757–779.

148. Weinberg, Boris, (a) The role of regelation in the condensation of the snow cover; (b) Mechanical properties of ice, (c) An attempt at a program of theoretical and experimental investigation of the properties of snow and ice: Internat. Comm. Snow and Glaciers Trans., Edinburgh, 1936 (Internat. Assoc. Bull. 23).

Icebergs

149. Schell, I. I., Foreshadowing the severity of the iceberg season south of Newfoundland: Internat. Comm. Snow and Glaciers, Washington, 1939 (awaiting publication); Am. Meteorol. Soc. Bull. 21.1, January 1940.

150. Smith, E. H., Icebergs—their drift into the North Atlantic and protective measures: Internat. Comm. Snow and Glaciers, Washington, 1939 (awaiting publication).

151. Smith, E. H., Ice in the sea: Oceanography (Physics of the Earth, vol. V (Nat. Research Council Bull. 85), 1932 (With classification of natural ice and a list of standard terms).

152. Smith, E. H., Recent movements of North Atlantic ice and a proposed Coast Guard expedition to the West Greenland glaciers, Am. Geophys. Union Trans., 1940.

153. Zukriegel, Josef, Cryologia Maris, Geog. Inst. Charles IV Univ., Praha, 1935.

CHAPTER V

GLACIERS

François E. Matthes[1]

INTRODUCTION

A large proportion of the total volume of water that is distributed over the land areas of the Earth at the present time is locked up in the crystalline state in glaciers, ice caps, and ice sheets. So enormous is the aggregate volume of ice—about 11,374,000 cubic miles—that, if it were all released by melting and returned to the oceans, the oceans would rise, according to different authorities, 130 to 190 feet above their present level [27, p. 12], and all the great seaports of the world and large areas of fertile valley land would be submerged. Yet hydrologists have thus far paid little attention to these vast masses of crystalline water substance, leaving them to be studied chiefly by glaciologists and geologists. The reason is, of course, that the bulk of this land ice is contained in the ice sheets of Antarctica and Greenland and in the ice caps of circumpolar islands, all of which are so far from the principal centers of civilization that the possibility of utilizing the stores of ice on them for practical purposes seems almost nil, for the present at least. The hydrologic interest that attaches to these remote masses of land ice is therefore largely academic.

Quite different is the situation in regard to mountain glaciers, for many of these, notably in central Europe and in the northwestern United States, lie sufficiently close to urban, industrial, and agricultural districts to constitute important sources of water supply. Already the runoff from a considerable number of such glaciers is being utilized for power production, irrigation, and municipal consumption, and as a consequence hydrologic investigations have been made or are being made in connection with these supplies. In most places these investigations have been prompted by the realization that glaciers are inherently variable masses, being extremely sensitive to cyclic climatic changes. They often react strongly to climatic changes that are so gradual and so subtle as to be hardly noticeable in other ways. The present time, moreover, happens to be a period of pronounced and almost universal glacier shrinkage, and as a consequence it is felt by some that the runoff from glaciers may continue to diminish until it reaches a catastrophic end in the near future.

[1] Geologist, Section of Glacial Geology, Geological Survey, United States Department of the Interior, Washington, D. C.

This feeling of apprehension, furthermore, is founded in no small measure upon the belief, still widely held, that the present recession of the glaciers is part and parcel of the gradual waning of glacial conditions all over the Earth that has been in progress more or less constantly ever since the end of the great ice age. Apparently little attention has been paid, at least in this country, to the considerable body of data on recent glacier oscillations, mostly of European observation, that utterly refutes that prevailing belief. It seems in order, therefore, to present here a synopsis of these neglected data and thereby to afford American hydrologists a perspective of the sequence of recent glacial events, of which the present recession is but the latest episode.

Before doing this, however, it is desirable to epitomize also, in compact form, the new factual knowledge concerning the physical character of glaciers, their alimentation, regimen, and motion, that has been gathered during the last few decades and in part even during the last few years. Little of this new knowledge has yet found its way into the textbooks, but it is no exaggeration to say that some of the recent contributions are among the most momentous that have been made in the entire history of glaciology. They dispel many misconceptions of long standing and bid fair to settle controversies that have been carried on for more than a century by generations of glaciologists.

PRINCIPAL TYPES OF GLACIERS

The general term *glacier* is applied to all bodies of land ice that consist of recrystallized snow accumulated on the surface of the ground. There are, however, many different types of glaciers owing, primarily, to the fact that glacier ice in sufficiently large masses behaves as a plastic substance and under its own weight—that is, in response to the force of gravity—seeks by slow flowage to assume a form of equilibrium adapted to the configuration of its base. Whatever doubt there may have been in the past in regard to the reality of plastic flow in glaciers, there is, as a result of recent researches, none left today. Indeed, plastic flow may be said to be the distinctive characteristic of glaciers which sets them apart from all stationary bodies of accumulated snow.

Several different systems of classification have been proposed for the many diverse types of glaciers that are now known, but all of these systems, it is to be observed, were devised before plastic flow had been definitely established as the primary element in glacier motion. They were not founded on a recognition of the fundamental fact that the external form of a glacier of any type is the resultant of adaptation of the mass to the topography of its base by flowage and other subordinate types of motion. It is therefore in order now to set up a new classification based upon the newly gained insight into the mobility of glacier ice. A complete classification, including all of the subordinate types and varieties of glaciers, will not be attempted here; only the major classes will be outlined, the purpose being to put the reader at the outset in possession of the modern point of view.

Fundamentally, all glacier types fall into two broad classes—*ice streams* and *ice caps*. That division does not differ appreciably from that which has already been proposed by several glaciologists, but it now rests upon an understanding of the mechanics of glacier motion as well as upon morphologic distinctions. The term *ice stream*, which has long been used

FIG. V-1.—The crest of the Chugach Mountains, in Alaska, showing typical alpine, or mountain glaciers tributary to the Harvard Glacier below. The altitudes range from 13,250 feet on Mount Marcus Baker, the highest summit, to about 2,000 feet on the Harvard Glacier. Each mountain glacier originates in a separate cirque that constitutes an effective basin for the catchment, concentration, and conservation of snow. The snow collects in them not merely by direct precipitation but also in large measure by drifting and avalanching. (*Aerial photo by Bradford Washburn.*)

loosely, and mostly in a figurative sense, is now seen to be entirely legitimate and highly appropriate for those glaciers which because of the steepness of their beds flow chiefly under the direct pull of gravity and, owing to secondary topographic controls, tend to assume elongate, stream-like forms. Typical of this class are the *mountain glaciers* (Figure 1) which have their sources near the crests of lofty mountains and thence descend as narrow, gradually tapering tongues, following valleys, much as streams of water follow channels. To this class belong also the *valley glaciers* (figure 2) which, fed by many converging mountain tributaries, flow like broad, majestic rivers of ice for tens and even scores of miles down the main valleys of a mountain system. Still larger, but often less typical, are the great *intermontane* glaciers (Figure 2) that are produced by the confluence of numerous mountain and valley glaciers, and that occupy spacious troughlike depressions between separate mountain ranges or mountain groups.   To the ice streams, finally, belong also the *outlet glaciers* that issue from the margins of ice caps and carry the surplus ice out through deep-cut valleys and fiords.   Among them are the longest and mightiest ice streams in existence.   Several of the great outlet glaciers on the western margin of the Antarctic ice sheet, notably, attain lengths

Fig. V-2.—The Geikie Glacier, one of the lesser ice streams on the west side of Glacier Bay, Alaska.   It has its sources on the relatively-low mountain range in the middle distance (altitudes 4,000 to 5,000 feet), which is separated from the lofty Fairweather Range, in the background (altitudes 10,000 to over 12,000 feet) by the broad intermontane ice mass known as the Brady Glacier. The smooth surface of that ice mass, sloping gently toward the left, is just visible above the summits of the lower range.   The Geikie Glacier is a typical example of a compound valley glacier formed by the coalescence of several tributary ice streams.   That each of these ice streams maintains its identity after coalescence is shown by the parallel courses of the medial moraines that form the "sutures" between them; yet the main glacier has but one central current or line of maximum velocity.   The terminus of the Geikie Glacier reaches down to sea-level at the head of Geikie Inlet, an arm of Glacier Bay.   (*Photograph by Naval Alaskan Aerial Survey Expedition.*)

of well over 100 miles [Gould 44, p. 727], and certain outlet glaciers in northern Greenland are reported to be equally long.

The term *ice cap* is applied generically to all those broad cakelike ice masses, whether of continental or more restricted extent, that cover land areas of relatively moderate relief, or, to put it in more general terms, of such configuration that direct gravitational flow of the ice can not take place on them, save locally.   Such ice masses have as a rule radially divergent flow systems actuated primarily by differential pressures within themselves and only partially controlled by the underlying topography. They therefore tend to spread out in all directions and typically have lobate borders.

To the ice cap class belong the small plateau glaciers of Norway and the larger ice masses of the Spitsbergen and Franz Josef archipelagos, of Novaya Zemlya, and Iceland, all of which lie in the main on uplands of subdued relief. Some of these ice masses, however, are so thin that the configuration of the land underneath is reflected in some measure in the undulations of their surfaces. Their motion is probably in part directly gravitational, and they are therefore on the borderline between true ice caps and ice streams. The vast ice sheets of Antarctica and Greenland, on the other hand, are so thick that they literally bury entire mountain systems and over large parts of their interiors have gently domed surfaces that do not betray the topography of the land beneath. In them flowage due to differential pressure is clearly dominant.

GENERAL CHARACTERISTICS OF GLACIERS

Glaciers, like all other bodies of water-substance associated with the lands of the Earth, are creatures of regional climatic conditions. They can originate only in areas where annually more snow accumulates (not merely falls) than wastes away, by melting, evaporation, or other dissipating processes. There is required, in general, a combination of abundant snow precipitation, either in winter or throughout the year, and sufficiently low temperatures, especially in summer, to conserve a part of the fallen snow. However, so infinitely varied are the geographic conditions in different parts of the Earth, that there are many different combinations of this kind. Representative of one extreme—that of aridity combined with freezing temperatures the year round—are the climatic conditions in Antarctica. The total annual snow fall, as measured at Little America by the First Byrd Antarctic Expedition, amounts to only 7½ inches of water, and in the interior of Antarctica it is doubtless scantier still, owing to the continentality of the climate and the persistence of anticyclonic winds. Representative of the opposite extreme are the conditions that prevail in the wet southern part of Iceland. The climate there is decidedly maritime and influenced, in the bargain, by the proximity of a regular path of cyclonic storms. The precipitation consequently is heavy, the temperatures, in winter as well as in summer, are moderate, and ice wastage is correspondingly great. The measurements by Ahlmann and Thorarinsson [6, p. 423] show that on the south side of the ice cap, at an altitude of about 3,600 feet, the precipitation (snow and rain) in 1935–1936 averaged 118 inches of water, and in 1936–1937, a relatively wet year, it amounted to 197 inches of water. On the other hand, the lower parts of the outlet glaciers are annually stripped of about 6 feet of ice by ablation, and even the central portion of the ice sheet, at altitudes of 3,500 feet and higher, is covered with slush and pools of water in mid-summer [Roberts 81, pp. 293–294].

The prime condition requisite for the formation of a glacier is that a residual layer of snow, representing the excess of accumulation over wastage, shall remain in place each year and become incorporated in the ice mass. In the temperate regions this new snow is transformed in the course of a few months into a fairly hard, granular substance called *névé* or *firn* (French and German terms, respectively, that originated in Switzerland and now are used by glaciologists the world over); and this substance, again, is transformed in the course of many years, by processes and under conditions to be described farther on, into compact, glassy, crystalline glacier ice. In the polar regions, where the firn remains frozen the year round, the transformation is much slower.

The continued addition of annual layers of firn, however, does not cause the thickness of a glacier to increase indefinitely, for, when the mass attains a certain minimum thickness, its own weight suffices to overcome its rigidity as well as the frictional resistance of its base and to initiate a sluggish flowlike motion whereby a continuous transfer of excess ice is set up from the area of accumulation to areas of predominant wastage. Thus a mountain glacier originating in the frigid Alpine Zone of a mountain range will gravitate, streamwise, down slope into successively lower and warmer zones, where the ice is finally converted into runoff. If the excess of ice is sufficiently great, the ice stream may reach down even to levels where the climate is warm enough to support a luxuriant vegetation. The Nisqually Glacier, on Mount Rainier, Washington, for instance, makes a total descent of about 10,000 feet in altitude. In 1940 its terminus lay at an altitude of 4,250 feet—nearly 3,000 feet below the timber line. An ice cap, on the other hand, tends to spread out laterally, in all directions permitted by the terrain, by reason of the differential pressures existing within its mass, and its margins advance over the land until they reach either warmer regions, where they melt, or the sea board, where they break off in icebergs.

The minimum thickness that is required for the inception of plastic flow in a glacier is, in the temperate regions, quite moderate—a matter of only 100 to 150 feet. That fact became evident to the writer when he was mapping the higher peaks of the Bighorn Mountains of Wyoming, in 1898–1899 [65]. Of the numerous valleys carved in the flanks of those peaks (by preglacial stream erosion) only those well over 100 feet in depth showed definite signs of glaciation—that is, of erosion by moving glaciers during the Pleistocene epoch; the shallower valleys had remained unglaciated and were only nivated—that is, subjected to frost action associated with annual snow drifts. Moreover, certain valleys that had contained glaciers several miles in length proved to be unglaciated at their heads, the latter being too shallow, only 100 feet or less deep. It was thus clear that in these fairly steep mountain valleys glacier motion did not set in until a point was reached where the firn attained a minimum thickness of 100 to 150 feet.

Closely similar estimates were arrived at by another method by Demorest [29] in Glacier National Park, Montana. He reconstructed, with all data available, the longitudinal profile of the little Clements Glacier, from the top of its last terminal moraine up to the cliff at its head, and thus found that when the ice surface was flush with the top of the moraine that glacier was at most only 200 feet thick. There was ample reason, furthermore, for believing that plastic flow occurred when it was somewhat thinner. Demorest therefore concluded that a thickness of "probably more than 100 feet but certainly less than 200 feet" had been sufficient to initiate flowage in the Clements Glacier. He further calculated, on this basis, the minimum pressure that was required to cause flowage. Assuming a thickness of ice of 150 feet, he found that the pressure exerted on the basal layers would amount to 4 kilograms per square centimeter (57 pounds per square inch). In the polar regions, where negative temperatures penetrate into the ice to depths of several hundred feet, the initiation of glacier motion doubtless requires much greater pressures.

By virtue of the inherent mobility of glacier ice under pressure, which prevents it from accumulating indefinitely, glaciers of all types function as links in the endless chain of water circulation, from ocean to atmosphere, from atmosphere to land, and from land back to ocean. At the same time, because of the exceeding slowness of their motion, they act as reservoirs, retaining for long periods the water-substance received before again releasing it. That statement is as true of the smallest glacieret ensconced in a mountain recess as of a trunk glacier many miles in length, or of an ice sheet of continental extent. In a glacieret 3,000 feet long, situated in a shady cirque in the Ural Mountains, Aleschkow [7] counted 220 annual layers of ice. The oldest of these therefore had been "in storage" for fully two centuries. To American hydrologists this instance may be of especial interest, as the small cirque glaciers on the western mountains of the continental United States are comparable in size to Aleschkow's glacieret and probably have had a somewhat similar history.

In a trunk glacier many miles in length a full count of the annual ice layers can rarely be had, because in the course of such a glacier's descent over its irregular bed these layers become distorted and broken and, in addition, obscured by the development of shear planes in the ice, some of which are difficult to distinguish from bedding planes between depositional layers. However, if the rate at which the ice in such a glacier moves forward from day to day and from year to year is known, an estimate can be made of the length of time that it takes a particle of ice to travel from the head of the glacier down to its terminus.

A particularly favorable subject for such a calculation is the Unteraar Glacier in Switzerland, for observations have been made over a period of 82 years—from 1840 to 1922—on the progress of a large boulder that lay on its surface, close to the line of maximum velocity. (That boulder was originally the caprock of a colossal "glacier table" in whose ice pedestal Louis Agassiz and his companions had hewn a chamber that served them as an abode for three successive summers while they were studying the motion of the glacier.) In 82 years that boulder traveled a distance of 2.858 miles. The mean rate of movement of the ice therefore was about 184 feet per year. If that rate were constant throughout the entire length of the glacier, which is close to 10 miles, it would take a particle of ice 287 years to travel from its head to the terminus. However, the stretch covered by the boulder comprised the middle third of the glacier, in which movement is much faster than in either the upper or the lower third. Especially toward the terminus, where the glacier becomes progressively thinner, the movement slows down to a mere fraction of the rate observed in the middle portion. It follows that the time of transit of a particle of ice down the whole length of the glacier may readily be 500 years or more. The ice which one beholds at the terminus of the Unteraar Glacier is therefore probably not less than five centuries old.

The length of time that ice may remain stored in an ice sheet of continental proportions is to be reckoned, undoubtedly, in thousands of years rather than in hundreds. Inasmuch as the movement in an ice sheet takes place chiefly in the mobile lower layers, under the pressure exerted by the less plastic upper ones, it can not be measured at the surface and must perforce remain a matter of conjecture. Nevertheless, conservative minimum estimates can be based on reasonable assumptions. Thus, by taking such data as are now available regarding the thickness of the ice sheet of Greenland, the nature of its internal motion, and the topography of the land surface upon which it lies, the writer has made rough calculations that show that a particle of ice would require probably not less than 10,000 years to travel from the top of the main ice dome to the west coast of Greenland. If that estimate is anywhere near the truth, then it appears that some of the ice in the icebergs that break off from the great fiord glaciers may date from the end of the glacial epoch.

Much older, even, must be some of the ice that reaches the coasts of Antarctica—more especially the coast facing the Indian Ocean. If any of that ice has come all the way from the "ice divide" back of the Queen Maude Range, it must have traveled air-line distances of 1,400 to 1,800 miles, with a mean surface gradient of only 6 or 7 feet per mile. Assuming a mean rate of movement of one foot per day—which is probably excessive —that ice would have been in transit fully 20,000 years. It would date from the time of the last climax of the Wisconsin stage of the Pleistocene ice age.

Not all ice caps, however, contain such ancient ice. There are good reasons to believe, as will be explained farther on, that the little secondary ice caps that surround the main ice cap of Iceland, and many of the small independent ice caps on the otherwise ice-free fringe of land around the inland ice of Greenland (Figure 6) contain ice that is at most a few hundred years old.

REGIONS OF SNOW ACCUMULATION, AND THE SNOW LINE

Regions where the climatic conditions permit continual accumulation of snow in excess of wastage are commonly referred to as regions of perpetual snow, and their lower limit of altitude is known as the snow line. Unfortunately, both terms are misleading and represent vague concepts that presumably were based largely on observations made from afar, for, as every alpine climber and arctic explorer knows, there is really no such thing as perpetual—that is, permanent, snow. If any considerable part of a mountain range or a polar land is perennially mantled with snow, then snow is accumulating there and forming glacier ice. It seems preferable, therefore, to employ the term *region of snow accumulation*. As for the snow line, it would perhaps more logically be termed the ice line, but that term, too, is open to objection, as all of the major mountain glaciers and the fringes of most ice caps descend below the lower limit of snow accumulation, and many minor glaciers even originate below it, as will be shown presently. The term snow line therefore will be retained here, but in the sense of the level above which snow accumulates from year to year to generate ice bodies over a large part or all of the land, depending upon latitude, altitude, and topography. It will be called the *regional snow line*.

It might be thought that the regional snow line, as thus defined, would coincide with the highest level to which the snow cover retreats at the end of the melting season—the autumnal snow line—but actually the two lines coincide only on the smooth, broadly curving surfaces of ice caps. On boldly sculptured mountains the accumulation and conservation of snow are controlled by so many local factors—chiefly by wind direction, insolation, and angle of slope—that the autumnal snow line is not a line at all but a broad, patchy zone in which small isolated ice bodies lie in sheltered places at many different levels. The regional snow line therefore must lie at the upper limit of that patchy, transitional zone. It corresponds in some measure, though not exactly, with the *climatic snow line* of the European glaciologists, which is the level above which snow accumulates indefinitely on flat surfaces fully exposed to sun and wind. As such surfaces are absent in most mountain regions, however, the climatic snow line is little more than a theoretical concept.   The regional snow line, on the other hand, is an observable thing, though, of .course, more clearly defined in some areas than in others.

Lack of definite criteria for its determination has resulted in large discrepancies between the altitude figures which different explorers have reported for the snow line in certain mountain regions, and there is reason to suspect that in some instances the observers, misled by the nature of the term snow line, have looked for snow when they should have looked for ice.   Making due allowance for inconsistencies of this kind, and relying chiefly on the data of the more recent observers, one may pursue the regional snow line over the entire Earth as follows:

At the Poles the snow line is, according to Bonacina [12, pp. 81–82], not at sea level but somewhat above it.   Thence it rises, subject to sundry local climatic influences, toward the equatorial regions, where it attains altitudes well over 16,000 and, in places, close to 19,000 feet.   The land areas that lie within the zone of snow accumulation consequently have their greatest extent at and about the Poles, and it is there that all of the ice sheets and ice caps now extant are situated.   In the middle latitudes the snow line rises to such great altitudes that only the higher mountains can bear glaciers, and with further approach toward the Equator the areas of permanent land ice contract until at last they are restricted to the tops of the highest peaks.

Antarctica is almost completely mantled with ice.   Only the higher peaks of its mountain backbone (11,000 to 12,000 feet in altitude) rise above the surface of its ice sheet, and some of the coastal cliffs are bare. So superabundant is the supply of ice—in spite of the fact that the ice sheet at present is in a distinctly depleted state—that it literally flows off the continent on all sides and spreads out upon the sea for hundreds of miles as floating shelf ice.   Including the shelf ice, indeed, the ice sheet is several thousand square miles larger than the continent.   Its total area is estimated at about 5 million square miles, and that is, as has been pointed out by Gould [43, p. 836], "a much larger area than was occupied by any of the great ice sheets which covered parts of North America and Eurasia at the culmination of the Pleistocene."   It is noteworthy, further, that each of the numerous islands off the coast of Antarctica bears an individual ice cap and that even the shelf ice receives an annual increment of firn and is largely composed of it.

No such wholesale glacierization—to use the term introduced by Wright and Priestley [104, p. 134]—is to be found anywhere in the northern hemisphere.   Even in the Franz Josef Archipelago, in latitudes 80° to 82° N., the snow line lies 150 to 250 feet above sea level and the ice does not cover the land completely.   In the Spitsbergen Archipelago, in latitudes 76°-30′ to 80°-30′ N., the snow line rises to altitudes above 1,000 feet and sufficient land is ice-free to permit the maintenance of permanent settlements and the mining of coal. The Vatnajökull, the famous ice cap of Iceland, in latitudes 64° to 64°-40′ N., covers but one-tenth of the surface of that island. Its area measures about 3,400 square miles, and the snow line rises from 3,000 feet at the southern margin to 4,600 feet in the central portion.

In Greenland (Figure 6), which extends from about latitude 84° N southward to latitude 60° N, a distance of about 1,650 miles, the snow line, as a result of varying climatic influences, ranges from less than 1,000 feet up to 4,500 feet. Partly owing to the great height of the snow line, and partly because it is hemmed in by coastal ranges, the ice sheet of Greenland, though the second-largest, and probably the thickest in the world, covers only about 85 per cent of the entire land surface. Throughout the greater part of its extent it leaves untouched a marginal strip of land, 10 to 100 miles in width. That marginal strip, nevertheless, is not entirely ice-free, for it bears many local ice caps and glaciers. The total area of the *inland ice*, as it is commonly called, is variously estimated at 700,000 to 715,000 square miles.

In Norway, whose high plateaus, in latitude 61°-40′ N, are covered with small ice caps, the snow line rises to 6,000 feet. In the European Alps it attains 8,000 feet, and locally, even, 9,500 feet. In the Caucasus the snow line ranges up to 11,000 and even 12,000 feet.

In North America the snow line rises slowly along the moist west coast from 5,000 feet in Alaska to 6,000 feet on Mount Olympus, which overlooks Puget Sound. Farther south, owing to increasing dryness, it rises rapidly to 10,000 feet on Mount Hood, in Oregon, and to nearly 14,000 feet on Mount Shasta, in northern California. Thence southward no other peak in the United States, not even Mount Whitney (14,495 feet), is high enough to have a snow line. In Ecuador the great volcanoes Cotopaxi (19,613 feet) and Chimborazo (20,498 feet), which stand just south of the Equator, bear permanent ice at altitudes well above 16,000 feet.

These figures, however, do not form part of a steadily ascending series, for solar radiation, which varies inversely with the latitude, is but one of several factors that control the altitude of the snow line. Abundant snow precipitation in winter, coupled with cloudy and humid summers, such as are characteristic of a maritime climate, tends to depress the snow line, and scanty snowfall and dry, sunny summers such as are characteristic of a continental climate, combine to raise it. Therefore the snow line rises from the humid coast of a continent toward its relatively arid interior. In Alaska, for instance, the snow line rises from 5,000 feet on the Chugach Mountains. which face the coast, to 7,000 feet on the Wrangell Range, which stands 75 miles farther inland, and to about 7,500 feet on the Alaska Range, which is situated still farther in the interior.

The movement of cyclonic storms along certain habitual paths, and the predominance of anticyclonic winds in other areas, also determine in large measure the distribution of glaciers and account for some apparently anomalous contrasts in their distribution. The ice sheet of Greenland, which is nourished chiefly by snow-bearing cyclones coming from the southwest, attains a thickness of probably over 6,000 feet, but parts of the North Canadian Archipelago and of northern Alaska, which lie in the same latitudes as Greenland, are devoid of glaciers because of extreme aridity due to anticyclonic winds.

Closely similar are the conditions in northern Siberia. Although situated in part to the north of the Arctic Circle, and afflicted with an intensely cold winter climate, it bears no ice sheet but only small cirque glaciers on its higher mountains. Nor was it completely covered by an ice sheet during glacial times. Over large areas the soil has never been protected from the cold by a glacial mantle, and, according to Nikiforoff (68), that circumstance accounts for the great depth to which the ground in northern Siberia is permanently frozen. The present climatic conditions, nevertheless, he believes to be responsible in some measure for the perpetuation of that remarkable condition. At Yakutsk, in latitude 62°-30′ N, a well dug for water reached a depth of 382 feet without disclosing anything but frozen ground. At the bottom the temperature of the ground was 26.6°F, and from the temperature gradient observed it has been calculated that the ground may be frozen to a total depth of 550 to 650 feet. The ground at Yakutsk consists of alluvial sediments.

To return to the Equatorial regions, one would hardly expect to find any glaciers on a tropical island in the Pacific Ocean, yet there is a notable occurrence of that kind. The Nassau or Snow Mountains, in the Dutch part of New Guinea, though only 4 degrees south of the Equator, are so bountifully supplied with snow that they bear several small glaciers in spite of their tropical environment. One of those ice-bodies is a miniature ice cap covering a slanting plateau. On these mountains the snow line is at an altitude of about 16,000 feet (von Dosy, 98). In contrast, on the Himalayas, which stand 27° to 30° north of the Equator, but relatively far from the sea, the snow line ascends to 17,000 feet on the wet south side and to 18,000 feet on the dry north side. On the Kuenlun Mountains, to the north of desiccated Tibet, the snow line is said to range up to 19,000 feet. On the Kilimanjaro group, in central Africa, the snow line reaches about the same altitude, but nowhere in the world does it attain so great a height as in the Maritime Cordillera of southern Peru. According to Bowman (13, p. 284) the Chachani Range there bears perennial ice only at altitudes above 20,000 feet, and the great volcano El Misti bears none at all, though 20,013 feet high.

THE FIRN LINE ON GLACIERS

The highest level to which the fresh snow cover on a glacier's surface retreats during the melting season is properly termed the *firn line.* Above it accumulation normally continues from year to year, and the residual snow remains as firn; below it the glacier's body is annually divested of snow, so that the old granular ice is left exposed and subject to wastage. The firn line therefore is really the snow line on the glacier's surface, but European glaciologists prefer to call it the firn line, and it is well that it should have a separate name, for on glaciers that originate in recesses carved deep in the flanks of mountains—and the vast majority of glaciers so originate—the firn line is independent of the regional snow line and lies at a considerably lower level.

One reason is that such glaciers are alimented not by direct precipitation alone but also in large measure by the wind. The violent gales that are prevalent on lofty mountains do not permit the snow to lie in a layer of uniform thickness on all features of the landscape but sweep it while still in a powdery state from the windward slopes, up and over the crests of the mountains, to let it swirl down in the "wind shadows" on their lee sides. From the cliffs and steep rock slopes, moreover, the snow is discharged in avalanches and so is added to that which has settled directly in the sheltered hollows. The combined action of the two processes results in the concentration of snow in the hollows at the expense of surrounding areas of mountain land.

Another reason is that the hollows, which originally were narrow valley-heads incised between spurs, have acquired through long-continued glacial erosion capacious amphitheaterlike forms—they have been transformed into *glacial cirques* (figure 1), and hollows of that type are particularly well adapted for the conservation of snow. The masses of snow that accumulate in them are of fairly compact form and have less area of exposed surface per unit of volume than equal masses of elongated form; and in addition they are protected from the sun's rays for many hours daily by the high walls of the cirques. Naturally the most favorable combination of circumstances, for both concentration and conservation of snow occurs when the lee side of a mountain is also its shady side. Then the wind shadows and sun shadows largely coincide in the cirques.

That cirque glaciers under such favorable conditions can exist at altitudes far below the snow line was first observed in Norway. The ice caps of Norway are confined to plateaus at altitudes close to 6,000 feet, and their margins in some places indicate rather closely the altitude of the regional snow line. Yet 1,000 to 1,500 feet lower down small independent glaciers lie ensconced in steep-walled cirques carved in the flanks of the plateaus. These cirque glaciers are nourished very largely by snow blown down from the ice caps and, in addition, they are effectively conserved by the cool shadows of the cliffs about them.

Analogous *drift glaciers* occur on the promontories that rise between the fiords of Greenland. Their true nature was first recognized by T. C. Chamberlin [20, pp. 207–209] on the west coast of Greenland. Pedersen [70, pp. 259–260] has reported the existence of such glaciers on south-facing bluffs near Scoresby Sound, on the east coast. In that latitude (70° N), evidently, the sun's radiant heat does not suffice to offset the accumulating power of the northerly winds, and shadows are not essential for the conservation of ice bodies below the snow line.

In each of the examples cited the country above the drift glaciers was high enough to have a regional snow line and, even, to bear ice caps, but drift glaciers can exist also on mountain ranges that are too low to have a snow line. The great majority of the glaciers of the western United States are, in fact, precisely so situated. Only the main ice streams on Mount Rainier, Mount Baker, Mount Olympus, Glacier Peak, Mount Adams, Mount Hood, and Mount Shasta originate definitely above the regional snow line, but all of the numerous cirque glaciers and glacierets in Glacier National Park, on the Wind River Range, the Cascade Mountains, and the Sierra Nevada are of the drift type and lie on mountains that have no regional snow line at all. In late summer they are usually the only white patches that remain in the landscape.

TRANSFORMATION OF SNOW INTO GLACIER ICE

The freshly fallen snow on the surface of a glacier has a density ranging from about 0.06 to 0.16, depending upon its consistency; it is full of air and transmits water readily. On the other hand, the ice into which it is ultimately transformed in the lower parts of the glacier has a density not far from 0.9; it is a compact, coarsely crystalline, glassy ice that contains no air spaces between its tightly interlocked crystals and is impervious to water. By what processes the change is effected has long been a matter of conjecture, quite naturally so as there is involved not merely mechanical compaction but also recrystallization and crystal growth—molecular readjustments that cannot be studied save under a polarizing microscope. Within the last few years, however, such microscopic studies have been made successfully, and as a result considerable factual knowledge is now at hand concerning the successive stages in the metamorphosis of snow into glacier ice.

The first change takes place fairly rapidly. Chiefly by sublimation and the migration of individual molecules, in part also by melting and refreezing, promoted by the infiltration of melt water, the feathery snow-flakes lose their delicate plumes and the tabular ones their sharp edges, and so they are all transformed into polygonal and approximately equi-dimensional granules 0.1 to 0.2 millimeter in diameter. Each of these is a single crystal of the hexagonal system and lies with its optical axis oriented normal to the surface of the glacier—that is, in the direction of the temperature gradient, the same as the crystals of pond ice. In the course of the summer the granules grow in size to about one millimeter; they settle closer together, and the entire mass of the preceding winter's snow attains a density averaging 0.45. It then has a firm, granular consistency halfway between snow and ice and is properly called *névé* or *firn*. Our knowledge of the details of this first transition is due chiefly to the studies of Gerald Seligman [84] and of members of the Swiss Snow and Avalanche Commission [10; 45].

Although in a temperate region such as Switzerland infiltration and refreezing of melt water undoubtedly play a part in the transformation of snow into firn, it is to be noted, nevertheless, that the transformation takes place without their aid, but mainly by sublimation, in the polar regions, where the upper layers of glaciers and ice caps have negative temperatures the year round. Firn one year old there is, however, not nearly so hard as in temperate regions.

The transition from firn to glacier ice was investigated in 1938 by a party of British physicists and crystallographers working under the leadership of Seligman [85] in a low-temperature laboratory hewn in a stationary ice apron at the head of the Great Aletsch Glacier, in Switzerland. Proximity to the International Research Station built on the Jungfraujoch enabled them to continue their studies at the altitude of 11,350 feet for three consecutive months. They made thin sections of firn and ice obtained from different parts of the glacier and examined them with a polarizing microscope, applying the standard methods of optical crystallography. In short, they analyzed the crystal fabric of firn and of glacier ice in the same way that petrologists analyze the crystal fabric of rocks. From the petrologist's point of view, firn and glacier ice are, indeed, crystalline rocks in different stages of metamorphism.

The results obtained by the Jungfraujoch research party may be summarized as follows: As the firn grows older and becomes subjected to greater and greater superincumbent loads, its density increases at progressively slower rates. The granules grow but little in size, but they settle closer and closer together, as more and more air is expelled from the interstices between them. The firn portion of a glacier is in a constant state of shrinkage, and it is readily understandable why more than one alpinist has noted hissing sounds at certain points on a glacier where the air was rushing out under pressure.

When the firn of the Great Aletsch Glacier is three years old and has become buried to a depth of 46 feet it attains a density of 0.72, but not until it is six years old and buried to a depth of 75 feet does it attain a density of 0.80. At that stage the air passages between the granules cease to intercommunicate, and the remaining air is held imprisoned. When a density of about 0.84 has been reached, at a depth of fully 100 feet (age not stated), the transition to glacier ice begins. The granules are still only a few millimeters in diameter, and the texture of the mass differs vastly from that of old glacier ice such as is to be found at the lower end of a glacier, where the ice is made up of intricately intergrown and tightly fitting crystals ranging in diameter from one centimeter to more than 10 centimeters (¼ inch to over 4 inches).

The air that is contained in such ice occurs in bubbles entrapped within the crystals. It is under strong compression and often causes blocks of ice to burst into fragments when released from their confinement within a glacier. J. P. Koch [59, p. 12], on his expedition across northern Greenland, in 1912–13, found that the air bubbles in ice taken from a shaft 24 feet deep exerted a pressure of 10 atmospheres. As Koch put it, glacier ice is literally charged with an explosive, and the presence of the compressed air in it accounts for the disconcerting habit that icebergs have of occasionally exploding to bits with a terrific roar.

There is, however, another and highly significant difference between old firn and typical glacier ice. As was revealed by the microscopic examinations of the Jungfraujoch research party, the firn granules, as a result of their progressive settling, independently of one another or in small clusters, come to lie with their optical axes in haphazard positions; but the crystals in the glacier ice lie with their axes more or less definitely oriented at right angles to the direction of the glacier's motion. Where differential movement is concentrated in shear zones—blue bands, as they are commonly called—the oriented arrangement of the crystals is particularly uniform. Inasmuch, however, as they are too tightly interlocked to turn individually, it can only be inferred that they have been recrystallized so as to lie in the proper orientation with reference to the shearing stress. This is an extremely important point in connection with the moot question of the intimate nature of glacier motion, for it implies that the characteristic crystal fabric of glacier ice develops in response to the deforming stresses that are active in the basal parts of a glacier, and, further, that it facilitates the plastic deformation—the flow—of the ice.

That ice, in spite of its well-known brittleness, is capable of plastic deformation under properly prolonged and directed pressure has long been known, chiefly through the classic experiments of J. C. McConnell and D. A. Kidd, in 1888 (63, 64). Ice crystals, being of the hexagonal system, are composed of extremely thin plates arranged in a parallel series at right angles to the optical axis. In the experiments mentioned a single ice crystal supported at the two ends of its axis was subjected to pressure normal to the edges of its plates. These, it was found, then glided over one another, causing the crystal to be permanently deformed. Pressure applied in the direction of the axis, on the other hand, merely resulted in a slight elastic bending of the crystal followed by rupture when the pressure was increased beyond the elastic limit. It follows, then, that glacier ice is capable of progressive plastic deformation if its crystals are properly oriented with reference to the direction of the pressure.

More recently Bader [10] has found that when a block of ice composed of variously oriented crystals is subjected to shearing stress most of its crystals become reoriented with respect to the plane of shearing. It may then be properly inferred that the characteristic tendency of the crystals in old glacier ice to assume a uniform orientation is due to recrystallization induced by the stresses to which they are subjected, and there is good reason to suppose, also, that their remarkable increase in size is due to the growth of the favorably oriented crystals at the expense of those of their neighbors that are unfavorably oriented. It is a fact of observation that glacier ice becomes coarser with increasing age. At the terminus of a glacier crystals the size of a fist are not uncommon, and crystals "the size of melons" have been reported from the long glaciers of Greenland, in which the ice must be extremely old (Perutz and Seligman, 71, p. 355).

The latest experimental researches on the recrystallization of glacier ice under deforming stresses have been made in this country by Demorest. In 1939 and 1940 he studied the structure of certain glaciers on Mount Rainier, cut from them selected blocks of ice, shipped these, packed in "dry ice," to Yale University, and in a low-temperature laboratory there examined thin sections of them under a specially adapted polarizing microscope. He also succeeded in recording on motion-picture film the process of recrystallization as it takes place under moderate but prolonged stresses. These researches are still in progress at the time of this writing, and only two abstracts of preliminary reports on the results obtained have been published thus far [30, p. 525], but the following statements are here set down with Demorest's consent:

In the first place, his experiments confirm, in general, the tentative conclusions of the Jungfraujoch research party, that the transformation of the small equidimensional firn granules to the large, intricately intergrown crystals of glacier ice is effected by recrystallization induced by the deforming stresses that are active in the basal parts of a glacier.

As to the precise nature of such recrystallization, his researches suggest as probably most important a sudden reorientation of the crystal axis and reorganization of the lattice structure of the parallel plates in a new position that will permit their gliding under the existing pressure. This he would term "instantaneous recrystallization." Next in importance he would place the process of "regelation," involving partial melting of the crystals at points of contact where they are subjected to the most intense pressure, followed by prompt refreezing when the pressure is relieved. This process naturally would be most effective in temperate regions where the temperature in the basal portion of a glacier is at or near the pressure-melting point throughout the year. In the polar regions, where the temperature of the ice is below the melting point for long periods, regelation doubtless is subordinate to sublimation. A third possible process is "recrystallization as a result of nuclear development and growth" at separate centers, after the manner in which new crystals originate in metals in the process of annealing.

Although, manifestly, further research of this type needs to be made before we shall have a complete understanding of these molecular processes it is clear that enough has already been done to leave no doubt that the apparently plastic deformation and the flowlike motion of a glacier are rendered possible by the recrystallization of the ice under the stresses that are active in the basal layers. There can be no question, therefore, that there exists in the basal layers of every glacier, beneath the superincumbent firn, a zone of pronounced recrystallization and consequent flowage.

THE RIDDLE OF GLACIER MOTION

To review here, even in briefest form, all of the different hypotheses that have been advanced in explanation of the flowlike motion of glaciers would extend this chapter far beyond its proper limits. Nor is there, in the writer's opinion, real need of such a review, now that we have gained a fair insight into the intimate nature of the molecular processes that enable glacier-ice to yield to prolonged stresses like a plastic substance. Nevertheless, it will be worthwhile, before outlining the principal types of movement that occur in glaciers, to set forth briefly the arguments of the two main schools of thought that have been locked in controversy with each other on the subject of glacier motion for nearly a hundred years, for, as is so often true in prolonged scientific discussions, so in this instance, both sides prove to be right to a certain extent; and, with the new factual knowledge at hand we are today in a better position than before to evaluate their respective contributions and to harmonize their apparently contradictory claims.

That the motion of the ice in a mountain glacier occupying a valley with approximately parallel sides is in many respects comparable with the flow of water in a stream occupying a channel with parallel sides became manifest as far back as the early 1840's, when Agassiz, Forbes, and

Tyndall instituted systematic measurements on certain glaciers in the European Alps. Agassiz selected for his studies the Unteraar Glacier as a representative example of a mountain glacier. He set stakes in the ice in a straight line at right angles to the glacier's axis, and by accurate measurements from time to time, over a period of six years, determined their displacement by the movement of the ice. Thus he established the fact that the movement is fastest at the middle of the section and thence decreases differentially toward the sides. The velocity curve across the breadth of the glacier, as indicated by the stakes, proved to be closely analogous to the velocity curve across the breadth of a river, the only difference being that the ice in the glacier moved at an extremely slow rate as compared with the water in a river.

A glacier, it was thus apparent, has a central "current," like a stream of water, and the differential decrease of the velocities toward the sides is obviously due to the same causes as in a stream, namely, to the frictional resistance of the channel walls, on the one hand, and to internal friction, on the other hand. Agassiz' figures for the surface velocities are given in the table below, converted into English units. They represent the mean rate of movement per year for each stake during a three-year period.

Description of point	Distance from left margin (in feet)	Mean velocity per year (in feet)
Left margin	0.0	9.8
	98.4	18.4
	246.0	67.9
	492.0	159.7
	735.0	181.4
	1,230.3	206.0
	1,722.4	211.1
Central current	2,313.0	231.0
	3,198.8	210.3
	3,572.8	156.2
	3,986.2	130.6
	4,281.5	39.0
Right margin	4,478.3	5.2

While Agassiz was engaged in these studies on the Unteraar Glacier, Forbes was making similar studies on the Mer de Glace, one of the main glaciers of the Mont Blanc chain in Savoy. His findings accorded closely with those of Agassiz and tended further to strengthen the analogy between glacier motion and stream flow. Indeed, without going into details, it may be said that the various facts disclosed by these early pioneer investigations, taken together, demonstrated fully the appropriateness of the appellation "ice stream" (fleuve de glace) which Bishop

Rendu [78] had previously applied to mountain glaciers, largely on the basis of his intuitive understanding of their mode of movement. So deeply impressed was Forbes with the analogy between glaciers and streams that he finally announced it as his conviction that a glacier is essentially a stream of imperfectly fluid, or highly viscous material.

Forbes' "viscosity theory," however, soon met with strong objections from Tyndall. The latter pointed to the crevasses in glaciers, which afford proof of the limited tensile strength of glacier ice, and he pointed to the manner in which glaciers break into a chaos of blocks and séracs where they descend over abrupt breaks in their beds. These facts, he declared, afford evidence of rigidity and brittleness, the opposites of viscosity and toughness. Though in some places the motion of a glacier simulates the flow of a fluid, therefore, he insisted that it is not flow

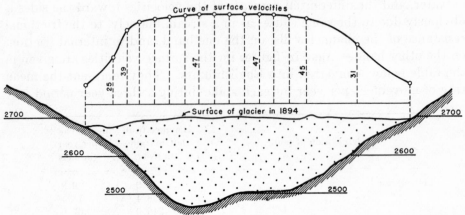

Fig. V-3.—Cross section of Hintereisferner and curve of surface velocities as determined by Blümke and Hess. The curve bears a definite relation to the configuration of the glacier channel. Elevation figures on cross section are in meters above sea level. Velocities are expressed in meters per year.

properly speaking, and that, after all, a glacier is and remains a mass of solid, crystalline ice throughout.

In order to account for a glacier's ability to mold itself progressively to the curves and irregularities of a narrow, winding mountain valley, he appealed to the action of a process which Faraday's experiments with ice as well as his own had demonstrated in the laboratory and which he termed "regelation." Two pieces of ice, when placed in contact with each other, at a temperature near the melting point, soon freeze together; and likewise, when ice is broken into miscellaneous fragments, these fragments under moderate pressure again unite. Ice, he found, can be given any desired shape by breaking it into fragments and letting the fragments freeze together in an appropriate mold. Thus, he supposed, the brittle ice of a glacier, as it moves down through its irregular channel, cracks and shears in innumerable places, only to freeze together again. Its temperature being near the melting point throughout, there would be momentary melting at the fracture and shearing planes due to pressure, promptly followed by regelation when the pressure is relieved. In this connection Tyndall pointed to the "blue bands" that characteristically traverse the lower end of a glacier in parallel series. These bands he interpreted to be shear planes on which slipping movements had taken place, the ice having been momentarily liquefied and then refrozen. He likened them to the cleavage planes in slate, which geologists interpret as shear planes produced by slippage under powerful differential stresses.

Thus originated the two opposing conceptions of the nature of glacier motion—the conception of flow by continuous, plastic yield, and the conception of spasmodic fracture and shear followed by regelation. During the ensuing decades the proponents of the flow theory found plenty of support in the results of elaborate and refined measurements on the movement of the Rhône Glacier, instituted in 1874 by the Swiss Alpine Club, and on the movement of the Vernagtferner and Hintereisferner in the Tyrol by Blümke and Hess [11] in 1896 and 1898. Of no little interest were Albert Heim's experiments on the Rhône and Hüfi Glaciers. Across each of those glaciers he laid a row of small dark stones touching each other. The straight row was gradually transformed into a smooth curve bowed downstreamward, and it was a notable fact that at no point was this curve broken by any angular offsets such as would have been produced by localized shearing movements.

Strong confirmation was found also in the results of the various laboratory experiments in which crushed ice placed in a pressure chamber was made to flow out through an orifice, much like water from a spigot. The ice in such experiments extruded completely recrystallized in the form of a clear, glassy rod. It flowed out more slowly at low temperatures than at 32° F, but the fact of prime importance was that it did flow even at temperatures so low that there could not possibly have been any pressure-melting followed by regelation. Elaborate experiments of this kind were made notably by Tammann [91] and by Hess [50, p. 17]. The latest were made by Tarr and von Engeln at Cornell University in 1911–12 [94].

All these experimenters, it should be understood, realized that they were dealing, not with "viscous flow" in the true sense of the term, but with the plastic deformation of a crystalline substance, which process is, in many respects, analogous to the "solid flow" of cold-rolled metals. However, to von Engeln it seemed hardly possible that the limited capacity for plastic deformation that ice crystals have (by the gliding of their basal plates) could adequately account for the ease with which the ice in the experiments flowed out, and he therefore appealed to an auxiliary agency in the form of a lubricating film of saline solution between the ice crystals. In this he followed Quincke's conception [75] that the crystals

in glacier ice are of the nature of "foam cells" separated from one another
by oily films having a slightly lower melting point than pure ice.   In
Europe, it is true, traces of Na, Cl, NH₄, SO₄, and particles of dust have
been found in newly fallen snow, and it is well known that some impurities,
organic as well as inorganic, are brought down out of the atmosphere by
snowfalls and rain in all parts of the world.   But the percentage quantity
of such foreign matter that becomes incorporated in glacier ice is likely to
be minute, except, of course, on stratification planes in glaciers that were
exposed to the weather for a considerable time before being covered by
fresh snowfalls.   Whether interstitial impurities in the form of lubricating
films can, intrinsically, be important agents in promoting the flow of glacier

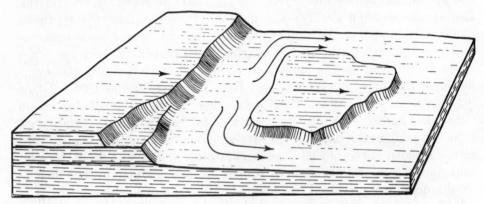

Fig. V-4.—Sketch showing lines of flow of a glacier deflected by an obstruction.   The straight
arrows indicate the direction of the ice movement as a whole.   The curving arrows follow striae
indicating local deflection of the flow.   There is no evidence of shearing.   The obstructing slab is
about 4 inches high.   (*After Demorest.*)

ice, moreover, seems doubtful from another point of view.   Whereas
they may conceivably facilitate differential movement among the equidimensional granules of the firn, they can hardly do the same among the
irregularly shaped and tightly interlocked crystals of true glacier ice—
and it is to be borne in mind that the bulk of a glacier is made up of such
crystals.   It seems justifiable, then, to conclude, in the light of present
knowledge, that the plastic flow of ice, as observed in laboratory experiments and as occurring in glaciers, is rendered possible chiefly by recrystallization and the inherent capacity of the individual ice crystals for
deformation under steadily applied forces.

Particularly convincing proofs of flowage in the basal layers of a
glacier were found recently by Demorest [29] in Glacier National Park,
Montana, in the form of glacial striae graved in a rock floor that was
freshly exposed to view as a result of the recession of a small glacier.
The rock floor was composed of thin, flat-lying beds of argillite cut by
two sets of vertical joints extending at right angles to each other.   The

glacier's principal eroding action had consisted of quarrying out rectangular slabs of this rock, thereby producing a series of square-cut steps, a foot to two feet high, in the floor. Down over these steps the debris-laden ice had moved, leaving distinct striae in the fine-grained argillite to indicate exactly the paths it had followed. Curving around obstacles and winding sinuously in and out of small transverse trenches due to the removal of individual slabs, these striae revealed deflections of the flow-lines of the ice that were of precisely the same pattern as the deflections of the flow-lines in a sheet of water descending over such a rock floor (figure 4). So complete was the analogy, even as to eddying currents in pockets and recesses, that Demorest felt justified in declaring that the flow of the ice in the basal layers of the glacier had apparently taken place "in response to the laws of fluid mechanics."

The courses of the striae shown in Figure 4 speak for themselves. Obviously, if shearing were the principal element of glacier motion, the ice of the glacier would have sheared on meeting the obstructing slab, and the striae would have had angular, more or less broken courses instead of smoothly curving ones.

The advocates of the shear-and-regelation theory, on their side, have ever pointed to the actual existence of shear planes and overthrusts in glaciers. T. C. Chamberlin [19, pp. 205–210)] on his explorations in Greenland discovered in the terminal portions of many glaciers unmistakable evidence of both small differential movements on shear planes and of large-scale thrusting on what may properly be termed fault planes. Such movements, he rightly insisted, indicate rigidity of the ice rather than plasticity. In Europe H. Philipp [72] has made particularly detailed studies of the thin "blue bands" of clear ice that occur in glacier tongues, forming concentrically curving series separated by broader bands of whitish ice containing air bubbles. These blue bands, he maintained, are slippage planes along which the ice had been crushed and liquefied and then refrozen. In his diagrams he pictured them arranged in concentric boatlike forms, roughly paralleling the outlines of the glacier's terminus and dipping inward toward its axis.

The rate at which localized shearing movements take place in glaciers is not readily measured because it is extremely slow, yet a few successful measurements have actually been made. Sherzer [86] in 1905 observed in the sloping ice front of the Victoria Glacier, in Canada, certain small overhangs that, he surmised, were produced by overthrusting movements along discrete shear, or fault planes. Driving a set of spikes into the ice immediately above one of these overhangs, and another set immediately below it, he found that in the course of 7 days the upper ice layer had advanced 6.9 inches over the lower, in spite of the fact that its exposed surface had melted back at a mean rate of 1.75 inches per day, while the surface of the lower layer had melted back at a mean rate of only 1.53 inches per day.   The net mean rate of the overthrusting movement was 1.2 inches per day.

More refined measurements, with an automatically recording "shear-meter" have been made by Rollin T. Chamberlin [16].   Though not successful in detecting differential movement in blue bands, he did obtain good continuous records of thrusting movements on a discrete shear plane in the terminus of the Brenva Glacier, on the Italian side of the Mont Blanc chain.   These records revealed slow, steady shearing alternating with spasmodic instantaneous slips of small amplitude.   There were also brief intervals when the movement ceased altogether, but in the main it was continuous, during the night as well as during the day.

To Seligman's Jungfraujoch research party belongs the credit of having first demonstrated that shearing movements occur in the blue bands [Perutz and Seligman 71].   In the wall of an ice grotto in the lower part of the Eiger Glacier, in Switzerland, they placed a series of screws exactly along a plumb line crossing one of these blue bands.   In the course of 14 days an offset of 3.5 mm (0.2 inch) had been produced in the line of screws at the point where it crossed the blue band, showing that the upper mass had been shoved bodily over the lower one.   The screws in the upper mass remained in a vertical line, that mass having behaved as a rigid body; but the line of screws in the lower mass had become bent, the ice there having suffered plastic deformation as a result of the "drag" exerted by the upper mass.   Within the blue band itself there was no discrete parting or crack, but the ice crystals were much larger than in the adjacent ice, and the air had been expelled from them and segregated into a series of large, flattened bubbles lying in a plane at the upper boundary of the band.   Microscopic examination of a thin section cut from the band, furthermore, disclosed that on an average five out of six crystals in it lay with their basal plates parallel to the plane of the band.   It was therefore concluded that they had been recrystallized with this predominant orientation as a result of the shearing stresses to which they had been subjected.

Demorest's recent studies of blue bands in the glaciers of Mount Rainier have since confirmed the essential correctness of these observations.   He also noted that such blue bands are not clean cut fault fractures in the ice but consist, as viewed in cross section, of a line of large crystals whose predominant orientation, with their basal plates parallel to the plane of each band, appears to be due chiefly to recrystallization induced by differential movement [30].

During the past decade, however, it has become increasingly clear to a number of glaciologists that neither plastic flow alone nor rigid shearing alone accounts for all of the different phases of glacier motion that have been observed.   It has come to be realized that both types of motion occur in association with each other. That realization is evident from the more recent writings of Rollin T. Chamberlin (17, 18), although his special interest has ever been in the study of shearing movements in glaciers. It is evident likewise from the writings of von Engeln [100] and Demorest [29], although they are interested primarily in demonstrating the reality of plastic flow. It stands out clearly from Washburn's interpretation of the sinuous morainic bandings of the Malaspina Glacier and the thrusting phenomena displayed in certain other glaciers in Alaska [101].

How, then, it may be asked, is this paradoxical combination of plastic flow and rigid shearing in glaciers to be explained? Why, if glacier ice is capable of flowing in smooth curves around obstacles, following "the laws of fluid mechanics," as exemplified in Figure 4, should it shear at all? The reason, which has been set forth only quite recently by Demorest (in manuscript still unpublished at the time of this writing) is really a simple one, but before it can be stated it is necessary first to explain the two different modes of flow that occur in glaciers and each of which under appropriate circumstances may be accompanied by shearing movements.

THE MOTION OF ICE STREAMS

It is an orthodox belief that in a mountain glacier movement is fastest at the surface and thence decreases differentially downward to a minimum at the bottom. The original basis for that belief is found, doubtless, in the velocity measurements which Forbes, Martins, and Tyndall in succession made on pegs driven at different heights in vertical ice walls in certain Swiss glaciers. Those pioneer observations of the 1840's and 1850's actually disclosed a progressive decrease in the velocities from the surface downward, but, it is to be noted, they were all made on glacier tongues descending fairly steep gradients under the direct pull of gravity. It was not suspected by those early observers that in those parts of their courses where mountain glaciers move over nearly level stretches, or through basins—and all geomorphologists now know that mountain glaciers do excavate basins in valley floors—the velocities are distributed quite differently, the line of maximum velocity being near the bottom instead of at the top of the section. (See Figure 5.) That such is a fact is now definitely established by a number of independent observations. There are, then, two distinct and contrasting types of flow structure in mountain glaciers. The reality of these two types will be evident from the following brief review:

Blümke and Hess [52, pp. 241–242], in connection with their systematic and prolonged studies of the motion and variations of the Hintereisferner, in the Tyrol, made a number of borings in that glacier in order to determine its thickness. One of these borings, in 1901, for some reason was abandoned after it had reached a depth of 118 feet, and the iron pipe used for the boring was left in the ice. Thirty-two years later that pipe was discovered some distance farther down the glacier, projecting several feet above the surface as the result of the stripping away of ice by ablation. It was no longer vertical but leaning forward at an angle of 23½ degrees, thereby showing that its lower end had traveled more slowly than its upper end, owing to a decrease in the velocity of the ice from the surface downward.

The pipe in this experiment, it is to be noted, was not long enough to penetrate below the zone of crevassing—the so-called "brittle upper crust" of the glacier—hence its slanting position revealed that even in that upper crust there is appreciable differential movement. It does not merely ride passively on the actively flowing basal layers, as is commonly believed, but has a slow flowage of its own. Hess does not stress that point, but it deserves to be brought out.

In 1904 Blümke and Hess made another boring, this time reaching bedrock at a depth of 702 feet. The iron pipe used for that boring was purposely left in place, and during succeeding years observations were made on its progressively increasing departure from the vertical, as it moved downvalleyward with the ice. At the end of 29 years it was leaning at an angle of 24½ degrees, the angle having increased differentially at a mean rate of 51 minutes per year. Hess calculated that the upper end of the pipe (including the lengths that had to be unscrewed as the ice surface was lowered by ablation) had traveled a total distance of 3,084 feet during the 29-year interval. Assuming that the pipe had remained straight throughout its length, its lower end would have traveled only 2,756 feet during the same interval, and the bottom velocity would be about 90 percent of the surface velocity (in the particular part of the glacier where the measurements were made).

Hess at first [51, pp. 42–43] assumed that the pipe had remained straight because he supposed the coefficient of internal friction in a glacier to be uniform throughout the entire depth of its section; but later [52], on the basis of Bridgman's experiments on the compressibility of ice [14], he took the position that the internal friction increases with the depth in the section and that therefore the ice in the basal layers of a glacier has less plasticity than at the surface. Neither of these conceptions, however, harmonizes with the fact definitely established by the experiments that have been made on the plastic flow of ice under slowly applied pressure— namely, that the plasticity of ice increases with the pressure. On the strength of that fact it is probably safe to say that the pipe in the Hinter- eisferner did not remain straight but became bent in a curve convex toward the terminus of the glacier. By inference the bottom velocity must have been considerably less than 90 percent of the surface velocity. The curve of the pipe presumably was roughly indicative of the vertical velocity curve of the ice mass. The latter curve may be imagined to be somewhat similar to the vertical velocity curve in a stream of water, differing, however, in that its curvature becomes progressively sharper toward the bottom, the internal friction in the ice decreasing with depth instead of remaining constant as in water. The velocity curve marked A in Figure 5 has therefore been drawn in accordance with that conception.

That the motion in a firn basin at the head of a glacier may under certain conditions increase, instead of decrease, from the surface downward, was first pointed out by Agassiz [1, p. 270]. He observed that the firn strata, which at the head of the basin slope gently downvalleyward, become gradually deformed during their passage through the basin, so that they reappear at the lower end steeply uptilted—that is, with reversed slope. And he therefore inferred that in such a basin the ice moves more rapidly at some depth below the surface than at the surface itself. Unfortunately, that extremely valuable observation and the inference which Agassiz drew from it made little impression upon the other glaciologists of his time and remained neglected for several decades. As late as 1885 Albert Heim in his Handbuch der Gletscherkunde [49, pp. 163–164] expressed the nebulous state of ideas on the subject as follows: "We do not know definitely whether under certain conditions the squeezing out of the lower portions [of the ice] by the overlying load does not result in the acceleration of the motion below; nor do we know whether the relative velocities from surface down to bottom are affected by the seasons in a similar way as the relative velocities at the surface of a glacier, from the middle out toward the margins, or whether, possibly, they are affected in a different way."

Reid [77] was the first to grapple with the problem by making actual measurements of the vertical components of the movement within a glacier. He selected a simple tongue-shaped ice stream, the Forno Glacier, in the Upper Engadine, in Switzerland. Five rows of stakes he planted in the ice—two across the firn basin, one in the vicinity of the firn line, two across the glacier tongue, and one across the terminal portion. The locations and elevations of all the stakes were carefully determined in 1896 and checked in 1897. In addition the thickness of firn added during the year above the firn line, and the thickness of ice removed by ablation below the firn line were measured.

The result was that in the firn basin the movement of the ice was found to have an appreciable downward component, the highest stakes having shifted their positions obliquely downward at an angle of 4°-30' to the surface slope of the glacier. The vertical component decreased gradually to zero in the vicinity of the firn line, and in the glacier tongue below that line there was found to be an upward component that steadily increased toward the terminus. The stakes there had shifted their positions obliquely upward with reference to the ice surface, at angles ranging from 2° up to 13°-30′ near the terminus. These measurements harmonized with the observed fact that the firn strata at the head of the glacier slope downvalleyward, whereas the ice strata in the glacier tongue dip upvalleyward, their inclination becoming steeper and steeper toward the terminus.

Reid therefore drew an idealized longitudinal section of a glacier in which the stratification lines run in curves, concave upward, from the head of the glacier to its terminus, and in which the lines of flow run in still more strongly concave curves. That diagram has for many years been the basis of prevailing conceptions of the general structure and the flow lines in a glacier. It is now realized, however, that while it fits approximately the conditions in a short, simple ice stream descending a fairly continuous, unaccidented slope, it is not representative of the much more complex conditions in a glacier descending a valley with a roughly stairlike longitudinal profile such as is shown in Figure 5. Yet that kind of profile is the characteristic product of vigorous and prolonged glacial erosion and predominates in practically all glaciated mountain regions.

Three other observers have since recognized that the depositional strata of ice in a mountain glacier have concave, spoon-shaped forms, so that their upturned edges crop out at the surface of the glacier at the lower end of the cirque and farther down in the glacier tongue; and all three have explained this structure as being due to the fact that the line of maximum velocity plunges to the bottom of the cirque and there becomes what for convenience will here be termed a *bottom current*. Streiff-Becker [90], who for twenty consecutive years (1915–1935) made systematic measurements on the Clariden Firn on the Tödi group, in Switzerland, probably was the first; Aleschkow [7] in 1929 observed the phenomenon in a cirque glacier in the Ural Mountains and depicted it in longitudinal profile; and Gibson and Dyson [40] rediscovered it in 1937, in the strongly depleted Grinnell Glacier, in Glacier National Park, Montana. To Streiff-Becker, however, belongs the credit for having demonstrated the existence of a bottom current in a firn basin by a quantitative, though approximate, method, and in addition, for having shown that such a bottom current is restricted to the firn basin, being replaced by a *top current* wherever the glacier flows over a sill or down an inclined bed.

The Clariden Firn is a broad mass of firn and ice occupying a gently sloping, in part probably concave, rock-shelf situated on the Tödi group, at altitudes ranging from 8,500 to 10,300 feet. At two definitely located points he measured annually, at the end of the melting season, the thickness of new firn added to the mass. He also obtained velocity measurements at different times of the year. By taking sights to reference points of known altitude, moreover, he determined the amount by which the surface-level was being raised or lowered. That surface-level, he found, fluctuates up and down, as the firn moves forward in waves, but it is remarkably constant in the long run. In 20 years it was lowered but slightly. He felt justified, therefore, in concluding that, on the whole, the annual increment of firn is counterbalanced by the annual outflow from the basin. Having an excellent topographic map of the Tödi group he was able to determine with a fair degree of accuracy the area of the firn basin that drains through a certain section. Then, knowing the average thickness of new firn that is added annually (2.85 meters), he computed the total quantity of firn that passes annually through the section, making due allowance for the progressive compaction of the firn. The total amounted to about 3,100,000 cubic meters.

The velocities measured at the surface, however, proved to be altogether too small to account for the annual transport of so large a mass. Even if the maximum velocity measured at the middle of the section (14.2 meters per year on an average) were effective over its entire width, retardation by friction at the flanking rock walls being neglected, only 952,000 cubic meters, or less than one-third of the total annual increment of new firn, would be accounted for. He therefore concluded that in a basin of this kind velocities much greater than those measured at the surface must occur at some depth in the section. Corroborative evidence he found, not only in the deformation and uptilting of the depositional layers, but also in two other facts: 1. The crevasses in the firn basin are not V-shaped, like those in a glacier tongue, but widen downward to a considerable depth before closing up; and 2. boreholes several years old, when exposed to view again by the stripping away of the newer firn layers during an excessively warm summer, are still vertical, thereby showing that the firn has little or no differential motion of its own, but rides passively on the more actively flowing glacier ice beneath it.

Assuming the firn basin to be 110 meters deep, as seemed indicated by its general configuration, Streiff-Becker drew successive concentric velocity zones in its cross-section, measured the areas thereof by planimeter, and calculated velocities for them that would together suffice to carry off the 3,100,000 cubic meters of firn and ice per year. He thus obtained a vertical velocity-curve of the type marked B in Figure 5, the maximum velocity in the lower half of the section being 115 meters per year, or about eight times the maximum velocity measured at the surface. Assuming an excessive depth of 200 meters for the section, he obtained a maximum velocity of only 38 meters per year, but the vertical velocity-curve was still decidedly of the B-type. His conception of this kind of glacier motion therefore was that the more mobile ice near the bottom of the basin is squeezed out, so to speak, from beneath the relatively inert overlying firn.

In reaching that conclusion Streiff-Becker was merely guided by his "sense of mechanics," as he expressed it; he was unable to present a rigorous analysis in terms of mechanics. Moreover, not being a geomorphologist, he missed the point that, fundamentally, the two contrasting types of glacier flow, characterized by a bottom current and a top current, respectively, are organized in response to topographic controls. But he did perceive that glacial erosion must be particularly effective in a basin because there the line of maximum velocity is close to the rock bed. And that certainly is an extremely important point. The longitudinal section of a glacier which he drew to show ideally the manner in which the depositional strata are pushed up into tilted altitudes in the firn basin

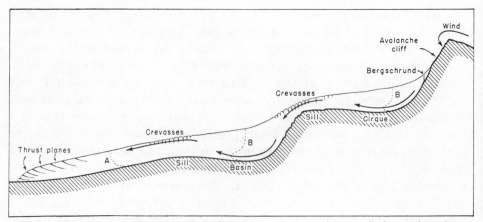

FIG. V-5.—Longitudinal section of an ideal mountain glacier showing the locus of maximum velocity in its different parts. Over the sills and the straight slopes the locus of maximum velocity is at the surface, but in the basins it is near the bottom of the glacier. The vertical velocity curves consequently are of two contrasting types, *A* and *B*. The *A* type is representative of simple gravity flow; the *B* type is representative of pressure-controlled flow.

Shear and thrust planes develop where either of these two types of flow is obstructed by slower-moving masses. Only those thrust planes are shown which occur in the terminal portion of the ice tongue, where the movement slows down because of decreasing thickness (in this case also because of flattening bed slope).

and then flatten out again over the sill at the lower end of the basin and in the glacier tongue, is not altogether free from inconsistencies, but it doubtless presents a truer picture of the progressively changing internal structure of a mountain glacier, apart from shear planes and other accessory features, than any diagram that had been previously drawn.

No attempt has been made to show in our Figure 5 the successive changes that take place in the attitude of the depositional strata in a glacier, but the line of maximum velocity passing from a bottom current in the basins to a top current over the sills and the slopes of sufficient gradient, is indicated by arrows, and the velocity-curves characteristic of the two modes of flow, A and B, are conventionally sketched in with dotted lines.

The first well-reasoned exposition, in terms of mechanics, of the two modes of glacier flow outlined above has been given by Demorest. Although his paper on this subject is still unpublished at the time of this writing, the gist of it is presented here with his consent. Where the gradient of the bed is sufficient to permit the force of gravity to overcome the frictional resistance of the bed, but not so high as to cause the ice to break into a cascade, a mountain glacier flows much like a stream of water, with a central current, or line of maximum velocity, at or near the surface, the vertical velocity-curve being of the type marked A in Figure 5. Where, on the other hand, the bed is basin-shaped, or has a gradient too low to enable the force of gravity to overcome the frictional resistance of the channel, flow is induced by differential pressure within the ice mass itself, provided it has attained sufficient thickness and a sufficiently steep surface-slope. Under those conditions outflow is most rapid in the basal portion of the section, where the ice has the greatest mobility, and the vertical velocity-curve consequently is of the type marked B in Figure 5.

For the first mode of glacier flow Demorest has proposed the term *gravity flow*, for the second the term *extrusion flow* [31]. The former is *drainage-controlled* and invariably downslope; the latter is *pressure-controlled* and therefore can take place on a level surface or even upslope, provided the ice mass is thick enough and has a sufficiently steep surface gradient.

As is evident from Figure 5, a mountain glacier can have gravity flow in one part of its course and extrusion flow in another, depending upon the irregularities in the longitudinal profile of its bed. If the bed descends by successive stairlike steps, as is commonly the case in strongly glaciated valleys, the two types of flow will alternate with each other. They are, in fact, the authors of the stairlike valley profile, and tend to accentuate it whenever the glacier has a large volume and correspondingly great kinetic energy. While in a depleted state, on the other hand, the glacier merely finds its way down the best it can over those boldly hewn features without modifying them materially, just as a stream of water at low stage flows with relative impotence over the broad bed which it has fashioned while in flood.

It remains to explain the cause of shearing movements in mountain glaciers and their relation to the plastic flow. Demorest's explanation, reduced to its simplest terms, is: Wherever a part of a glacier flowing with a certain speed finds its progress blocked by another, more slowly moving, or wholly stagnant part, it tends to crowd upon and override the latter. Shear planes then develop in the ice, curving forward and upward, in the manner shown ideally in Figure 5. All shearing and thrusting movements in glaciers occur where the normal flow is impeded in such a way that the ice can not pass over or around the obstruction by continuous plastic flow. As there are two modes of plastic flow in glaciers, so there are also two modes of obstructed flow that give rise to shearing movements. These Demorest proposes to call *obstructed gravity flow* and *obstructed extrusion flow*.

The only shear planes shown in Figure 5 are those caused by obstructed gravity flow. Such planes are a normal feature of the terminal portion of a mountain glacier because there the thickness of the ice decreases progressively by ablation, and any decrease in thickness lessens the pressure upon the basal layers and consequently lessens the mobility of the ice in them. At the terminus itself, where the surface slope becomes more and more abrupt, shear planes are especially numerous and closely spaced, and the ice consequently appears sheared into thin slices. They are the so-called "blue bands" to which Philipp, in Europe, and Rollin T. Chamberlin, in this country, have repeatedly called attention. They intersect the surface of the glacier at high angles, as a rule, but at the terminus outcrop at progressively lower angles, the lowest being nearly parallel to the glacier's bed.

These blue bands are not discrete partings in the ice; neither do they traverse the entire thickness of the ice mass. They are merely narrow zones of localized differential movement and consequent recrystallization of the ice granules; and they originate in the plastic lower layers of the glacier, where differential movement and recrystallization are most active and most generally distributed. In addition to the blue bands, however, there occur, probably as the result of sudden or complete blocking of the flow, thrusting movements along discrete fault planes. Many of these extend down to the base of the glacier, and along them rock débris from the bed is often dragged up to the surface. There, as ablation continues through the years, this débris accumulates and forms a protective mantle that retards the melting of the ice. What was originally ground moraine thus becomes, as the result of upthrusting and ablation, a surficial veneer. The dirty aspect of the terminal portions of many glaciers is due largely to the combined action of these two processes, in less measure to the concentration of englacial débris.

Shear planes and thrust planes may occur in other parts of glaciers besides the terminus. They are formed notably wherever the slope of a glacier's bed flattens downvalleyward, for there, inevitably, the flow slows down. If this happens at several places in a glacier's course the ice becomes criss-crossed by several sets of blue bands. The older sets may become non-functional but they remain recognizable. On the other hand, wherever a glacier passes from a relatively gentle slope to a steeper one, the flow is accelerated and, the upper layers, being subjected to strong tension, become rent by V-shaped crevasses. These, however, do not extend down to the bed, but only down to the plastic lower layers, which adapt themselves by flowage to the inequalities of the bed.

No attempt has been made to show in Figure 5 some of the shear and thrust planes that are formed wherever the extrusion flow active in the cirques and valley basins is obstructed. Indeed, so little observational material is at hand concerning them that a diagrammatic representation of them is not yet justified. On purely deductive grounds, however, it seems probable that shearing and thrusting occur at the lower ends of the basins, where the transition from bottom current to top current sets in.

The different types of motion that have been set forth occur not merely in mountain glaciers but in all glaciers of the ice stream class— in valley glaciers, intermontane glaciers, and the outlet glaciers at the margins of ice caps—for they all follow valleys as channels and have essentially unidirectional flow organized around a central current, or medial line of maximum velocity, generated by the direct pull of gravity.

MOTION IN ICE CAPS

The mode of movement of the ice in glaciers of the ice cap class is today still to some extent a matter of conjecture—necessarily so, as it is not so readily apprehended as the motion in ice streams, either by direct observation or by inference from the erosional and depositional effects produced by former ice caps. Opinions are still divided, and by some, even, it is maintained that ice caps inherently are motionless save in their marginal portions. Although it is not desired to enter here into a controversial discussion of that doctrine, it is in order, nevertheless, for the sake of clear thinking, to point out that no belief that an ice mass thousands of feet thick and free to expand laterally will remain immobile, save at its margins, is consistent with the laws of mechanics applying to plastic solids.

That glacier ice in large masses behaves as a plastic solid under its own weight—that is, under the influence of gravity—is now a definitely established fact, as has been shown in the foregoing pages. Differential movement has actually been measured by Seligman's Jungfraujoch research party, both in the firn at the head of a glacier and in the compact ice in the terminal portion; and the crystallographic studies of that party have revealed that in the transformation of firn into glacier ice recrystallization takes place, the new crystals being reoriented predominantly into positions favorable to their deformation by the differential pressures [Perutz and Seligman 71]. Geomorphologic studies, furthermore, have shown that only a moderate thickness of ice is required to initiate plastic flow. On a suitably inclined base a glacier need be only 100 to 150 feet thick in order to develop flowage. (See pp. 154–155.) To be sure, both Demorest's observations on the site of the Clements Glacier [29] and the

writer's observations on the minimum depth of the glaciated valleys of
the Bighorn Mountains [65] dealt with the initiation of glacier motion
by the direct pull of gravity, but the sites investigated were not steep
enough to permit the ice to slide down bodily in rigid cakes.   It *flowed*
down with differential motion adapted to the configuration of the rock
bed as was demonstrated by the striae.

That on a nearly level base, where the direct pull of gravity is not
operative, an ice mass must have greater thickness in order to develop
flowage, seems a reasonable inference.   Yet there is plenty of observational evidence to show that even there only a moderate thickness suffices.
The small ice caps, or "plateau glaciers," of Norway, which lie on gently
undulating uplands, are only a few hundred feet thick, yet they clearly
have plastic flow, for they feed a number of ice streams that descend
steeply into the valleys that are cut into the flanks of the uplands.   The
lesser ice caps on Iceland, Spitsbergen, and the partly ice-free borders of
Greenland likewise are only hundreds—not thousands—of feet thick,
yet from many of them issue sizable ice streams that flow down to lower
levels.

The examples just cited are from temperate, or at least cool-temperate
regions, where the summer temperatures are high enough to cause considerable melting at the surface of an ice cap, and where melt water plays
an important part in the recrystallization of the firn and in raising its
temperature to the melting point.   In such regions ice caps are at pressure-melting temperature throughout their entire thickness during the
summer months, and that circumstance adds to their mobility.   For
them Ahlmann [4] has proposed the term *temperate glaciers*.   In contrast
to them stand the *high polar glaciers*, which are situated in regions of such
intense and persistent cold that negative temperatures prevail in them the
year round to depths of several hundred feet.   Their mobility is thereby
greatly diminished and as a consequence much greater thicknesses are
required to produce plastic flow.   Typical examples are the ice sheets of
Greenland and Antarctica   At their surfaces, above the firn line, no
melting ever takes place, and the dry snow changes to firn, and the firn
increases in density, only with extreme slowness, chiefly by sublimation.
Intermediate between the *high polar* 'and the *temperate glaciers* are the
subpolar glaciers.

In the shaft which they dug at their station Eismitte, near the top
of the Greenland ice sheet, the Alfred Wegener Expedition of 1930–31 [32]
found a practically constant temperature of $-30°$ C at a depth of 52 feet.
Computations by Brockamp based on the observable temperature gradient
in the shaft showed that at a depth of 591 feet the temperature is still
$-16°$ C.   Tentative extrapolation of the temperature curve indicated
that negative temperatures may extend several thousand feet down into

the mass (whose total thickness below Eismitte is probably not less than 6,000 feet, as is to be inferred from the not altogether reliable seismic depth measurements made by the expedition). Pressure-melting temperatures, accordingly, would be restricted to the basal layers. If active flowage also is restricted to them, it may be presumed that the firn is not transformed into coarsely crystalline glacier ice until it is lowered to that low level. At Eismitte the seismic waves did not indicate conclusively where that level lies, but at a station 38.5 miles from the western margin of the ice sheet they did indicate a fairly abrupt increase in density, presumably marking the change from firn to glacier ice, at depths ranging from 984 to 1,150 feet. The underlying ice appeared to be about 3,280 feet thick. (On purely theoretical grounds, of course, it is to be expected that the thickness of the firn would decrease from the middle of the ice sheet out towards its margins.)

That perpetually frozen firn has a high degree of rigidity appears to be evident from the behavior of the Antarctic shelf ice, which, especially in its seaward portion, is composed wholly of fine-grained firn, at least, as far as it is exposed above tide-level. Its sea cliff, 100 to 150 feet high, shows no signs of plastic deformation, and the huge tabular icebergs, 20 to 60 and even 70 miles in length [Wordie and Kemp, 103, pp. 431–433] that detach from it float away as essentially rigid masses. They show no tendency to spread out radially by flowage. It may be presumed, therefore, that the thick mass of frozen firn that forms the upper layers of an ice sheet such as that of Greenland or Antarctica is on the whole susceptible of but little plastic deformation and rests on the more plastic lower layers of glacier ice largely as an immense dead weight. The general absence of signs of movement at the surface of the central portions of an ice sheet would be thus accounted for. It does not, however, imply complete immobility of the mass all the way down to its base.

That motion actually exists in ice caps of the *high polar* class is abundantly attested by the fact that enormous quantities of ice flow radially out from them. The inland ice of Greenland, over a long stretch of coast facing Melville Bay, where it is not obstructed by mountains, literally flows in a broad sheet down to the sea. Along the greater part of its extent, however, it is hemmed in by coastal ranges, and there outflow takes place through the gaps in the form of tongue-shaped ice streams. The speed with which some of these ice streams flow out into the fiords, and the large number of icebergs which they produce annually, are among the most remarkable glaciologic phenomena that are known. Rates of movement at the ice fronts of 30 to 60 feet per 24 hours are not uncommon. The Jakobshavn Glacier by several observers has been found to advance 65 to 92 feet per day; the Upernivik Glacier, according to Ryder's [83] measurements, advances at times as much as 100 to 124 feet per day at certain points of its broad front—that is, about 100 times as fast as the average mountain glacier in the Alps.

These exceedingly rapid rates of movement, it is to be understood, occur only in the fiords where the friction of the ice masses on their beds

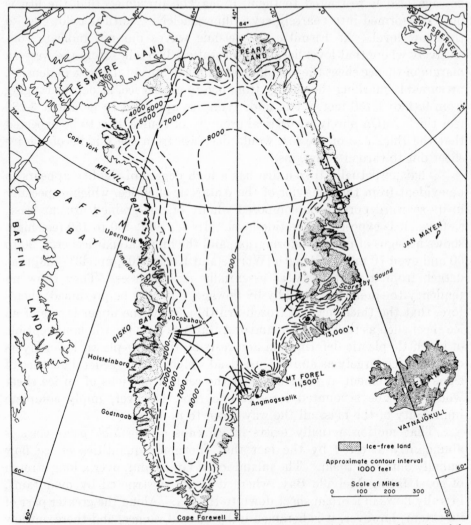

Fig. V-6.—Map of Greenland showing the approximate outlines and surface configuration of the ice cap. No accuracy is claimed for the contour lines. They are really form lines serving to bring out the fact that there are two ice domes separated by a broad saddle. The arrows indicate conventionally the convergence of flow lines in the embayments in the ice cap which accounts for the extraordinarily rapid outflow of certain glaciers on the west and east coasts. The Vatnajökull of Iceland is shown on the same scale for comparison. The ice on Spitsbergen and other islands is not shown.

is reduced by the buoyant effect of the water. Farther inland the glaciers move at considerably slower rates, yet still faster than ordinary mountain glaciers. It is, however, the output in the form of icebergs at their fronts that is really the most impressive phenomenon. Loewe [62] estimated that the Rink Glacier, in the northern part of Umanak Bay, discharges about 18,000 million cubic feet of ice in a few minutes during each of its biweekly debacles. Rink [80] calculated from his measurements on its front that the Karajak Glacier produces annually icebergs having an aggregate volume of 5 cubic miles. As there are in Greenland 25 fiords containing glaciers of similar magnitude, he estimated that their combined output of icebergs might well amount to 128 cubic miles per year.

According to Hobbs' theory of the motion in ice caps [55], all of this ice discharged by the outlet glaciers, and all that which gravitates to the sea in broad sheets, as on the coast of Melville Bay, would be derived from a marginal belt about 50 miles in breadth, the vast interior mass of ice behind that belt remaining entirely inert. As a matter of fact, however, the outlet glaciers head largely below the firn line—that is, in the zone where ablation exceeds precipitation: it is therefore clear that they draw their sustenance chiefly from the great interior mass, and that there is movement within that mass. What is more, it is evident from the configuration of the spoon-shaped depressions at their heads—the "dimples" or "exudation basins," as they have been called—that each of these outlet glaciers is fed by a system of converging ice currents that extends far back into the interior of the ice sheet, in the manner indicated, conventionally, by the arrows in Figure 6.

For simple mechanical reasons, it may be added, it would be impossible for the great interior mass of an ice sheet to remain motionless while the marginal portions are moving forward and away from it, for any such movement at the margins would tend to leave the interior mass unsupported at the sides, and, as it is plastic in its basal layers, it would at once tend to flow out after the marginal portions. And so the movement would be propagated farther and farther inward towards the center.

Hobbs [55] apparently regarded crevassing as the one sure evidence of motion, and because crevassing is confined to the marginal belt of the Greenland ice sheet he assumed that there was no motion back of it. Crevasses, however, are evidences of gravity flow only, and those in the marginal belt occur where the ice overrides the coastal ranges and moves down their slopes under the direct pull of gravity. The absence of crevasses farther back in the ice sheet merely indicates the absence of gravity flow, but does not necessarily indicate lack of motion of any kind. As is evident from the strong flow of ice in the outlet glaciers, there is deep down in the ice sheet active extrusion flow that feeds them.

Hobbs' doctrine of the immobility of ice sheets hangs together with another doctrine of his, according to which the meteorological conditions over an ice sheet of large extent are dominated by a more or less permanent anticyclone called forth by the intense cold of the ice expanse itself [53, 54].

The air chilled by contact with the surface of the ice tends to flow down in gravity currents in all directions from the central dome, and thus a system of centrifugal winds is created which in turn is replenished at the center by air descending from the upper atmosphere. Nourishment of the ice sheet by such a *glacial anticyclone* would necessarily be scanty, consisting largely of ice spicules due to condensation of moisture close to the chilling surface; and of this scanty precipitation the bulk would be swept out towards the margins of the ice sheet by the radially blowing winds. The central dome therefore would receive the least nourishment, but, as its losses by evaporation are very small, owing to the intense cold, and as the ice in it has no motion, according to the immobility theory, a practically static condition would result.

Meteorological observations designed to test the theory of the glacial anticyclone have been made during the period 1926 to 1933 by four successive expeditions sponsored by the University of Michigan and led by Prof. Hobbs, and by a fifth under the auspices of the University with support by Pan American Airways, led by Prof. Belknap. Other observations for the same purpose have been made in 1929 and 1930–1931 by the Alfred Wegener Greenland Expedition sent out by Germany. The latter expedition maintained for an entire year a station, which they named Eismitte, near the top of the Greenland ice sheet at an altitude of somewhat less than 10,000 feet, and at a distance of 245 miles from the west coast; also a station near the west coast and another on the east coast. In their interpretations of the results obtained the meteorologists of the American expeditions, on the one hand, and of the German expedition on the other hand, are not entirely agreed on all the aspects of the problem, but from their findings, nevertheless, several facts of major importance stand out clearly:

1. Gravity currents of chilled air flowing down in various directions from the central dome of the Greenland ice sheet do predominate, in accordance with Hobbs' theory, but they are frequently disorganized by cyclonic depressions that come from the southwest and travel northward along either the west coast or the east coast of Greenland, and sometimes far into the interior.

2. The radially diverging air currents constitute in effect a local anticyclone associated with the ice sheet, but these air currents have but moderate depth and volume. As a consequence Greenland's anticyclone makes itself felt but a few miles beyond the coast lines and is distinctly subordinate in its geographic range to the powerful winter anticyclones of Siberia and northern Canada, which are keeping large areas of land in northern latitudes from being covered by ice sheets. Greenland therefore is not the wind pole of the northern hemisphere, as Hobbs believed it to be.

3. Rime in the form of ice spicules does occur at times, but in the main the Greenland ice sheet is nourished by snow blizzards brought on by cyclonic depressions. Although much snow is swept away by the wind, on an average 33.9 inches of firn, representing 12.2 inches of water, is annually added to the top of the ice sheet. That fact was determined by the Wegener Expedition in its 49-foot shaft at Eismitte. At a point 87 miles from the west coast (about one-third of the distance to Eismitte), and at an altitude of 7,380 feet, the average annual increment of firn amounted to 19.7 inches of water. That figure accords in a general way with those obtained by previous expeditions.

It is thus manifest that the ice sheet of Greenland is nourished, not by the glacial anticyclone, as Hobbs supposed, but in spite of it, by ordinary cyclonic storms. It receives at its surface accretions of snow aggregating, according to Hess' estimate [51, p. 116], on an average about 272 cubic miles of water per year; and, on the other hand, it loses annually an enormous volume at its margins, through the outflowing glaciers and by ablation in the zone below the firn line. According to Sorge [87, p. 336], 13 to 16 feet of ice are annually stripped away by ablation at the western margin. It follows that the ice sheet is not in a static condition, but has a continuous internal circulation—unless, indeed, it be supposed that its height is being increased from year to year by a net 33.9 inches, while its margins are actively melting back under present climatic conditions, a supposition that seems hardly logical. Far more probable is it that the surface of the ice sheet subsides annually by a small amount as the result of outflow of ice through the plastic lower layers. Under conditions of perfect equilibrium the annual outflow would be compensated exactly by the annual accretions at the surface, and the height of the ice sheet would remain unchanged. Whether such a state of equilibrium exists at the present time is, of course, unknown, but it seems unlikely, in view of the present trend of climatic conditions, which is causing all glaciers in the arctic and subarctic regions to shrink in volume.

That an ice sheet such as that of Greenland has internal motion, and that the ice of its plastic basal layers is squeezed out, so to speak, by the pressure exerted by the more rigid upper layers, is a concept that has long been in the minds of glaciologists. Rink [80] probably was the first to express it tentatively; von Drygalski, as the result of his explorations in Greenland, became convinced of the truth of it [99, p. 283]; and Hess undertook to state the mechanics involved [51, p. 113], but erred in supposing the pressure within the basal layers to be transmitted hydrostatically by interstitial water—forgetting that glacier ice long ago was proved to be impervious to water. Demorest [31], it seems to the writer, is the first to present a sound mechanical analysis of the mode of movement of the ice in an ice sheet, basing it upon the inherent plasticity of glacier ice under differential pressure, as demonstrated by the crystallographic studies of Seligman's Jungfraujoch research party and as confirmed by his own studies. Motion in an ice sheet, accordingly, is seen to be primarily what Demorest terms *extrusion flow* generated by differential pressure. As it takes place in the direction of diminishing pressure, it naturally tends to follow lines radiating from the central and highest part of an ice sheet out towards the thinner margins. The rate of movement from point to point varies, in general, with the pressure gradient, which is controlled primarily by the angle of the surface slope. As that angle is practically zero at the center of the mass and thence increases at first at an almost imperceptible rate, the extrusion flow in the basal layers, directly beneath the center is, theoretically, nil and thence proceeds for long distances outward at infinitesimally slow yet gradually increasing rates. Only in the marginal portions, where the surface slope becomes appreciably steeper, is there an appreciable gain in speed. The actual movement within the central portions of an ice sheet therefore does not differ much from the state of utter immobility postulated by Hobbs, yet there is some slight motion, increasing differentially from the center outward, that compensates for the increments of new firn that are constantly being received at the top of the ice sheet.

The basal outflow doubtless does not actually take place along simple radiating lines, as stated for the ideal case, but in some places is deflected, or even wholly blocked, by the major topographic features of the land surface beneath the ice. As a result the extrusion flow is locally obstructed and shearing takes place along planes that curve upward, presumably in much the same manner as in a case of obstructed gravity flow. (See Figure 5.) This, however, is a matter that can for the present be stated only on a basis of deductive reasoning. Though shear planes have been observed in abundance at the margins of ice sheets, they have not, so far as the writer knows, been studied with special reference to the mechanics of obstructed extrusion flow in the interior.

The general laws governing the motion in high polar ice sheets, as just set forth, hold for the ice sheet of Antarctica as well as for that of Greenland. From the Antarctic continent the ice flows off in all directions and on an immense scale, yet the surface throughout the main— eastern—portion of the ice sheet slopes so gently (5 to 7 feet per mile on an average) that in all probability gravity flow there is largely excluded, no matter what the topography of the land surface underneath may be. Except in the outlet glaciers and in its crevassed marginal portions, therefore, the Antarctic ice is to be conceived as moving predominantly by extrusion flow.

In regard to nourishment by precipitation, the Antarctic ice sheet offers a much better exemplification of Hobbs' theory than the Greenland ice sheet, for the meteorological conditions over central Antarctica are clearly dominated by the south polar anticyclone, which is intensified by the chilling effect of the ice sheet itself. The result, however, appears to be not a static condition of the ice sheet, as Hobbs' theory demands, but an undernourished, "starved" condition, to use the term employed by antarctic explorers. As is definitely indicated by the high level at which glacial boulders lie stranded on rocky heights overlooking the great outlet glaciers, the ice sheet of Antarctica today is fully 1,000 feet thinner than it has been in the past. For a long time, evidently, it has been in a state of hydrologic unbalance, its outgo of water substance exceeding its income—not because of increased warmth but because of the intense frigidity of the climate. The situation raises several questions—as to the inherent adequacy of a strong anticyclone as a source of nourishment for a large ice sheet, and as to the nature of the former meteorological conditions under which the Antarctic ice sheet was built up to the great thickness indicated by the erratic boulders. These are questions that are still under discussion at the present time and for which there is as yet no definite answer.

Summary

1. Recent researches have demonstrated that glacier ice in large masses behaves under its own weight as a plastic solid. It does so because when subjected to prolonged differential pressure the ice granules recrystallize and the new crystals tend to assume positions favorable to their deformation by the gliding of their basal plates.

2. Because glacier ice has this inherent capacity for plastic deformation glaciers of all types have a slow flowlike motion initiated by the force of gravity and adapted to the configuration of their beds.

3. Those glaciers that have beds of sufficiently high gradient to flow under the direct pull of gravity, flow much as streams of water do, the differential movement being typically *unidirectional*, organized around a central current, or line of maximum velocity, at or near the middle of the surface, and decreasing both laterally towards the sides and downward to the bottom. For that reason and because they tend to assume elongate, streamlike forms in following valleys as channels, glaciers of this class are appropriately termed *ice streams*.

4. Those ice masses that lie spread out broadly over land areas of such configuration that direct *gravity flow* cannot take place, develop flowage by reason of differential pressures within themselves. Such flowage is most active in the basal layers and therefore is termed *extrusion flow*. It is typically *multidirectional*, proceeding from the central area of greatest height radially out towards the thinning margins. Ice masses of this class are appropriately termed *ice caps*.

5. Wherever the plastic flow of glacier ice, whether actuated by the direct pull of gravity or by differential pressure, is obstructed by slower-moving, or wholly motionless masses, shearing movements occur, along narrow zones of recrystallization and along discrete fault planes.

RECENT VARIATIONS OF GLACIERS VIEWED IN THEIR RELATION TO THE PLEISTOCENE ICE AGE

INTRODUCTION

The present is a time of marked glacier recession throughout the world. In the southern hemisphere as well as in the northern all the glaciers, a small number excepted, are gradually shrinking in size. In the United States such shrinkage has not been observed methodically for a sufficiently long period to indicate the time when it began, and as a consequence the belief still prevails in some quarters that it is part of the process of deglaciation that set in toward the end of the Pleistocene ice age, some 25,000 years ago, and has been steadily going on ever since. European data, on the other hand, are so full and extend so far back in time as to leave no doubt that the present recession comprises but a brief episode, that it was preceded by repeated ice advances during the period of modern history, and, what is most significant, that those ice advances were the greatest that have occurred since the Pleistocene epoch—that is, during the last 10,000 years. A perspective of these matters should be helpful to the hydrologist as a background for his interpretation of current variations of glaciers, and accordingly a brief synopsis of recent glacier history, as it is now known, is presented in the following pages.

THE PRESENT RECESSION

The present recession is the only one of the successive glacier oscillations of historic times that has been recorded in any detail. In the European Alps it began shortly after the middle of the nineteenth century. It followed upon one of the most notable ice advances of the historic period—the advance of the 1850's, as it is now generally called. At that time many glaciers in the Alps overrode the terminal moraines which they had deposited during previous centuries, and others approached closely to their earlier moraines. So well attested is this advance of the 1850's that on some of the Swiss topographic maps and on many detailed maps of individual glaciers the moraines of that decade are marked with their respective dates. There was no perfect synchronism in the climax of the numerous glaciers in the Alps (about 1,150 in Switzerland alone); neither did they all begin to recede simultaneously. During the 1860's, however, recession was general, and during the early 1870's some of the glaciers shrank to smaller sizes than they had had at any time during the nineteenth century.

It was this recession, which caused alarm lest it continue and impair important water supplies, that led to the inception of systematic measurements to record the secular variations of glaciers. In 1874, at the urging of Prof. F. A. Forel, the Swiss Alpine Club instituted the first annual measurements of the variations in length, thickness, and rate of movement of the Rhône Glacier, which is the principal source of the Rhône River. During the ensuing decades such measurements were continued on an elaborate scale, under the auspices of the Swiss government, and as a result the Rhône Glacier has come to be one of the most thoroughly investigated glaciers in the world.

The recession, however, soon came to a halt and, about 1875, one glacier after another began to readvance. During the 1880's practically all the glaciers in the Alps were gaining in length. For most of them the climax came during the 1890's, but some lagged until the end of the century. This was only a minor advance as compared with the greater one of the 1850's, but it stimulated the interest of scientists throughout the world, and as a result the Sixth International Geological Congress, meeting at Zurich in 1894, created, upon the joint recommendation of Prof. Forel and Captain Marshall Hall, of England, an International Glacier Commission. On that commission were represented Switzerland, Great Britain, Austria, Germany, France, Denmark, Sweden, Norway, Russia, and the United States of America. Italy joined soon afterwards.

The members of this commission succeeded in securing the active cooperation of governmental agencies, scientific societies, and mountaineering clubs in their respective countries, and so the systematic measuring of glacier oscillations became a regular routine in Europe. The statistical results were published annually by the International Glacier Commission, first in the Archives des Sciences Physiques et Naturelles, in Geneva, and, beginning in 1906, in the Zeitschrift für Gletscherkunde.

The world war which began in 1914 disrupted international coordination of action along these lines, but glacier measurements nevertheless were made in some countries. In 1927, chiefly through the efforts of its devoted secretary, P. L. Mercanton, of Switzerland, the international organization was revived. This time, however, it was set up as a commission of the International Association of Scientific Hydrology, a component unit of the International Union of Geodesy and Geophysics. Under these new auspices the International Commission of Glaciers carried on its work on an ever increasing scale, many hundreds of glaciers in different parts of Europe being listed in its annual reports. At the Washington Assembly of the International Association of Scientific Hydrology in 1939, the International Commission of Glaciers was consolidated with the International Commission of Snow. The dislocation of international relations caused by the second world war naturally has seriously interfered with the world-wide program which the newly formed International Commission of Snow and Glaciers has set itself, but considerable glacier research has nevertheless been carried on, and is being carried on in the neutral countries.

Since 1931 the United States has taken an increasingly active part in the recording of glacier oscillations. Prior to that year only occasional observations on the state of American glaciers had been made by scientists and interested mountaineers; only one glacier, the Nisqually, on Mount Rainier, was systematically measured from year to year, beginning in 1918. In 1931, however, the Section of Hydrology of the American Geophysical Union appointed a Committee on Glaciers charged with the duty of obtaining and interpreting systematic records of the variations of glaciers in the continental United States and Alaska, with especial reference to their hydrologic significance. That committee, enlisting the cooperation of the National Park Service, within whose reservations many of the more important glaciers are situated, and of a number of western mountaineering clubs, inaugurated a comprehensive program of glacier measurements patterned in a general way after that of the European organizations. The results are published annually in the Transactions of the American Geophysical Union and triennially in the Transactions of the International Association of Scientific Hydrology.

Of the vast mass of data concerning the present recession of glaciers that has been brought together by the organizations mentioned only the briefest sort of abstract can be given here. For a more comprehensive survey of the material the reader is referred to Thorarinsson's excellent paper on "Present glacier shrinkage, and eustatic changes of sea level" [96].

Statistics for the glaciers of the European Alps show that after the readvance of the 1890's recession again set in and since then has continued through the 1930's, though interrupted at intervals by short-lived advances in which not all of the glaciers took part. Such readvances occurred in 1910–13, in 1916–20, and in 1926. Plotted graphically they appear merely as small peaks on a generally descending curve. The readvance of 1916–20, nevertheless, is outstanding, for immediately afterwards recession was distinctly accelerated, and the curve bends more sharply downward.

A few figures will serve to give some conception of the rates at which European glaciers have been receding during the 1930's. Of the 100 glaciers that are annually measured in Switzerland the majority receded 30 feet or less per year; a number of them receded as much as 50 to 100 feet in certain years; an occasional one as much as 150 feet. In no year did all the glaciers recede in unison. On an average only 84 percent of them receded, while 10 percent made small, short-lived advances, and 6 percent remained unchanged. Similar conditions obtained in the Austrian and Italian Alps, but among the 275 glaciers reported on by the Comitato Glaciologico Italiano the percentage that were in recession annually was greater and the rate of recession somewhat slower. The Scandinavian glaciers, on the other hand, receded more rapidly, recessions of 100 feet per year being frequent among them. A few receded as much as 400 feet in certain years; one receded over 800 feet in one year, another over 1,800 feet.

The glaciers that form the southern fringe of the Vatnajökull of Iceland receded at comparable rates. Thanks to the close watch that some of the Iceland farmers have kept on the glaciers that menace their lands, it is definitely known that there was a general advance about 1850 and another that culminated about 1890. The oscillations of the Iceland glaciers therefore appear to have synchronized closely with those of the European glaciers, but the advance in 1890 in many instances exceeded that of the 1850's. Since 1890 nearly all the glaciers in Iceland have been in recession, and since about 1930 their recession has been accelerated, in some districts to "an almost catastrophic" rate, as Thorarinsson [96, p. 144] terms it. The Hoffellsjökull, one of the more easterly outlet glaciers of the ice cap, by 1936 had retreated a distance of 4,265 feet from the moraine it had deposited in 1890. Other glaciers had retreated anywhere from 3,000 to 10,000 feet during the same interval.

For the Hoffellsjökull, however, there are at hand other data of far greater hydrologic significance than mere recession figures. The regimen of that glacier—that is, its annual income of water in the form of snow, rain, and rime, on the one hand, and its outgo by melting and evaporation, on the other hand, have been the subject of painstaking investigations by Ahlmann and Thorarinsson [5 and 6] during the years 1936, 1937, and 1938, and as a result quantitative estimates can be made of its loss in volume during those years. From Thorarinsson's latest summary [96, pp. 133–134] it appears that the ablation area below the firn line comprises about 44 square miles and the loss of water over that area averaged about 32 inches per year. The mean annual loss in volume during the three-year period therefore amounted to about 94 million cubic meters (76,000 acre-feet) of water.

From the height of the old strand lines of lakes in side valleys that are dammed by the Hoffellsjökull, Thorarinsson has determined that from 1890 to 1936 the part of the glacier that lies below the firn line was reduced 130 to 160 feet in thickness, the corresponding mean annual loss of water being 39 inches. During this period of 46 years, that part of the glacier lost 6 billion cubic meters (nearly 5 million acre-feet) of water. To this is to be added a loss of 400 million cubic meters (about 325,000 acre-feet) of water due to the recession of the ice front.

As the other four outlet glaciers on the south side of the Vatnajökull appear to have sustained comparable reductions in thickness during the same period, Thorarinsson estimates that from 1890 to 1936 the five glaciers together lost a total of 50 billion cubic meters (about 40 million acre-feet) of water. These figures gain additional interest from the fact that the glaciers in question are situated in a district that has a pronounced maritime climate characterised by very heavy precipitation. In 1935–36 the total accretion of water substance (snow, rain, and rime) averaged 118 inches. At the altitude of 3,600 feet the firn deposited in 1936–37 contained on an average 197 inches of water [Ahlmann and Thorarinsson 6, p. 423], but this was an unusually large quantity that resulted in a temporary gain in the glacier's volume.

The ice caps and glaciers on the Spitsbergen Archipelago also are in recession. Ahlmann's measurements on the Fourteenth of July Glacier [3, p. 194] show that in 1933–34 its losses by ablation exceeded the accretions of snow and rime by 34 million cubic meters (27,500 acre-feet) of water; they were 43 per cent larger than the glacier's income. Glen [41, p. 6] describes the West Ice, on North East Land, as being in process of "degenerating into what may become small domes."

On Novaya Zemlya some of the glaciers are receding and others appear to be stagnant. Even on the Franz Josef Archipelago the glaciers are gradually shrinking. On Jan Mayen Island some of the glaciers have recently receded from fresh-looking moraines that still contain cores of ice.

Relatively few data are at hand concerning the variations of the glaciers of Greenland. Carlson [15] in 1931 found that since 1887 the Upernivik Glacier, on the west coast, had receded on an average 3,000 feet, in some parts of its front as much as 5,000 feet. The great Jakobshavn Glacier is known to have made a notable advance in 1851 and another in 1888. From 1888 to 1925, on the other hand, it receded not less than 6 miles. According to Lauge Koch [60, p. 107], most of the glaciers in the vicinity of Cape York made a small advance in 1920 but since then have been in recession. Demorest [28, p. 53] in 1932–33 found the local glaciers on the Upper Nugssuak Peninsula completely divested of snow and "dying from excessive ablation." All ice fronts, including those of the main ice sheet, were bordered by a strip of freshly exposed rock floor, 10 to 50 yards in width, that was unweathered and devoid of lichens, showing that recession had set in rather recently. To judge from Tarr's observations in 1896 [92, p. 262], it began presumably around 1890. In northeast Greenland and at a number of points on the east coast glaciers were reported to be in recession during the 1930's. According to Sorge [87, p. 336], measurements by the Alfred Wegener Expedition of 1931–32 show that the surface of the Greenland ice sheet at its western margin at that time was being reduced by ablation at rates of 13 to 16 feet per year.

For the glaciers of the continental United States recession data are available as a rule only since 1931—the year when annual measurements were begun at the request of the Committee on Glaciers of the American Geophysical Union. In a number of instances, however, the record can be extended back several decades by comparison with dated maps and photographs. On one glacier, the Nisqually, on Mount Rainier, annual measurements were instituted as early as 1918 by the National Park Service, and on this glacier too, it happens, reliable observations were made at intervals as far back as 1857.

Recession, it is evident from all these data, has been universal among American glaciers at least as far back as the 1880's, though interrupted at times by feeble readvances, notably about 1920. The record of the Nisqually Glacier follows.

Year	Recession (in feet)	Year	Recession (in feet)
1857–1885	760	1927–1928	89
1885–1892	140	1928–1929	52
1892–1910	900	1929–1930	118
1910–1918	410	1930–1931	49
1918–1919	59	1931–1932	50
1919–1920	46	1932–1933	44
1920–1921	106	1933–1934	155
1921–1922	67	1934–1935	54
1922–1923	44	1935–1936	65
1923–1924	83	1936–1937	55
1924–1925	73	1937–1938	90
1925–1926	86	1938–1939	85
1926–1927	43	1939–1940	70

The Nisqually's total recession from 1857 to 1940 amounted to 3,793 feet. The rate of recession, however, was by no means uniform throughout that period. From 1857 to 1885 the mean annual rate was 27 feet; from 1885 to 1892 it was 20 feet (there may even have been a brief readvance during that interval); from 1892 to 1918 it was 50 feet; and from 1918 to 1940 it was 72 feet. Since 1892, therefore, the rate has doubled and trebled.

That the recession of other glaciers in the United States has been similarly accelerated can not be stated positively, as the records do not extend sufficiently far back, but from both personal observations and comparisons of dated photographs it is evident that in many districts the annual losses of ice have been much greater during the 1920's and

1930's than during the decades immediately preceding. Thus a comparison of aerial photographs of Mount Shasta, in California, taken in 1935, with similar photographs taken in 1920, reveals that that peak lost considerably more than 50 per cent of its glacial mantle in those 15 years. Still earlier photographs, taken from the ground, suggest no diminution of the glaciers at any comparable rate.

Authentic data collected by Phillips [73, 74] show that the peaks of the Cascade Range in Oregon are being rapidly divested of ice.   Already three small glaciers that are mentioned in the earlier literature—one on Mount Jefferson, one on Diamond Peak, and one on Mount McLoughlin— have vanished during the past 25 years.

Of peculiar interest is the fact that the glaciers in the northern districts, close to the Canadian boundary, are melting away faster than the glaciers farther south. The glaciers in Glacier National Park, Montana, (latitudes 48°-35' to 49°-00') are wasting away at a rate which, if continued, will result in their total extinction within the next few decades. On the other hand, recession is appreciably slower in the Wind River Range, in Wyoming (latitudes 42°-45' to 43°-20') ; and in Rocky Mountain National Park, Colorado (latitude 40°-15') vestigial glacierets such as the Andrews and Tyndall are suffering but slight reduction.

The Easton Glacier, on Mount Baker, in Washington (latitude 48°-45'), in 1936 had receded 4,900 feet since it was mapped in 1908. This implies a mean rate of 176 feet per year. The Nisqually Glacier, on Mount Rainier, in Washington (latitude 46°-50'), which like the Easton has a southerly exposure, from 1910 to 1936 receded only 1,692 feet, or at a mean rate of 65 feet per year. And the Eliot Glacier, on Mount Hood, in Oregon (latitude 45°-22'), from 1901 to 1940 receded only 505 feet, or at a mean rate of 13 feet per year. During the 1930's, however, its rate was accelerated to a mean of 28 feet per year. Still farther south the East Lyell Glacier, in the Sierra Nevada of California (latitude 37°-45'), from 1931 to 1939 receded only 87 feet, or at a mean rate of less than 11 feet per year.

This remarkable diminution in the rate of recession from north to south is accounted for in part by certain climatic factors, quantitative data for which can not be presented here; in large part, however, also by the fact that the northern glaciers reach down to much lower altitudes than the southern and consequently are exposed in their lower portions to greater atmospheric warmth and for longer periods annually. The Easton Glacier in 1908 reached down to an altitude of 4,200 feet; the Nisqually in 1910 reached down to about 4,000 feet. The Eliot Glacier, on the other hand, terminates at an altitude between 5,900 and 6,000 feet, and the East Lyell Glacier, which is little more than a cirque glacier, terminates at an altitude of about 11,400 feet.

Recent observations by the writer in the Sierra Nevada have impressed him with the fact that many of the cirque glaciers on that range are fronted by massive morainal embankments that are extremely fresh looking and out of proportion to the size of the small ice bodies that produced them. These embankments are covered with loose and unstable blocks and slabs of unweathered rock and are manifestly much younger than the youngest of the Pleistocene moraines that lie farther down in the canyons. Within the last three years, moreover, it has been discovered that several of these fresh looking embankments consist really of glacier ice thinly mantled with rock débris. They are the termini of the glaciers themselves and have remained standing, 50 to 100 feet in height, because of the protection from ablation furnished by the mantling rock débris, while the cleaner ice behind them has wasted away. These embankments are therefore clearly of very recent origin and comparable to the moraines of the historic period in the European Alps. As they had much the same appearance as now in 1883, when Russell [82, p. 325] observed them, they must have originated at an earlier date, but it does not seem probable that they date back more than a century, in view of the fact that the mantling rock débris is only a few feet thick and does not prevent slight losses by melting in midsummer. If the last glacier advance on our western mountains synchronized with the last one in the Alps, as may reasonably be supposed, in view of the synchronism of the present recession, it seems quite probable that the embankments with ice cores in the Sierra Nevada date from the middle of the nineteenth century.

The Nisqually Glacier, on Mount Rainier, not only has the longest recession record of any glacier in the United States, but is also the one most extensively studied for progressive loss of volume. The reason is that the city of Tacoma is dependent for hydroelectric power upon the Nisqually River, which derives most of its water from the glacier. Concern lest the discharge of the river might be appreciably reduced in the near future as the result of the continued shrinking of the glacier, led to a cooperative agreement between the city of Tacoma and the United States Geological Survey providing for plane table surveys of the lower portion of the Nisqually Glacier, to be repeated at intervals of five years for the purpose of obtaining comparative data from which losses in the volume of ice might be computed.

The first of these plane table surveys, covering the lower two miles of the glacier's course (entire length 4½ miles) was made in 1931 on a scale of 1:4,800 and with a contour interval of 20 feet. The second survey was made in 1936, and the third, originally scheduled for 1941, was made in 1940, because of the evident acceleration of the glacier's reduction in volume. There is available also for at least an approximate comparison the topographic map of Mount Rainier National Park on the scale of

1:48,000 and with a contour interval of 100 feet, which was made by the Geological Survey in 1910–11.

The latest report on these surveys, by Fred F. Lawrence, of the Geological Survey, includes longitudinal profiles which show that from 1931 to 1936 the glacier over a stretch of 3,000 feet suffered a reduction in thickness of 30 to 60 feet, and from 1936 to 1940 a reduction of 40 to 60 feet. Toward the terminus these losses increased to as much as 150 feet in each period. Since 1910 the vertical losses over the 3,000-foot stretch have averaged about 200 feet, the maximum near the middle of the stretch being 240 feet. During this 30-year period, therefore, this part of the glacier was being reduced at a mean rate of 6.6 feet per year, the maximum being 8 feet. That ablation is proceeding at an accelerated rate is evident from the fact that from 1931 to 1936 the rate ranged from 6 to 12 feet per year, and from 1936 to 1940 it ranged from 10 to 15 feet per year.

These figures are only for the portion of the glacier that lies below the altitude of about 5,200 feet. Above that level the glacier during the period 1931–1936 increased in thickness as much as 40 feet, only to decrease again 50 to 60 feet between 1936 and 1940. Unfortunately no temperature measurements above and below the 5,200-foot level are available, and consequently no correlations between ablation and temperature can be made.

The losses in volume sustained by the Nisqually Glacier in the portion covered by the surveys are, during 1910–1931, about 500 acre-feet per year; during 1931–1936, about 750 acre-feet per year; and during 1936–1940, fully 3,400 acre-feet per year. The tremendous increase in the losses sustained by ablation from 1936 to 1941 is not reflected in the linear recession of the ice front, as may be seen in the table given above. That fact once more emphasizes the unreliability of recession data as an index of volume changes in glaciers.

In the Rocky Mountains, the Selkirks, and the Coast Range of Canada, observations by members of the Canadian Alpine Club and others show that most of the glaciers have been more or less constantly in recession during the last two or three decades. In several instances a decided acceleration of the recession was noted, beginning in or after 1920. The situation is in general comparable to that which prevails in the northwestern United States.

An adequate discussion of the recent variations of Alaskan glaciers would require a whole chapter in itself. No complex of mountain glaciers elsewhere in the world has shown greater diversity of behavior nor more sudden and rapid changes among its component members. Since 1880, in every year that scientific observations have been made, some glaciers were advancing while others were receding; and such opposite phases occurred not only between glaciers in widely separated districts but often also between glaciers occupying adjoining valleys. For instance, the Muir Glacier, in Glacier Bay, between 1899 and 1935 receded 13½ miles, while the Columbia Glacier, in Prince William Sound, 440 miles farther up the coast, during the same period merely oscillated back and forth between limits 1,000 feet apart on the west side of its 7-mile front and ¾ mile apart on the east side. Whereas the ice in Glacier Bay by 1935 had receded a total distance of over 60 miles since Vancouver viewed it in 1794, the Columbia Glacier in 1935 was still within a few hundred feet of the moraine which it deposited on Heather Island, around 1920, and at one point it had transgressed that moraine, thus attaining' greater length than it has had "in more than four centuries" [Field 35, p. 70]. A notable example of two adjoining glaciers that are in opposite phase is that of the Taku and Mendenhall, near Juneau. The Taku between 1909 and 1933 advanced 7,600 feet, while the less extensive Mendenhall between 1906 and 1933 receded 3,375 feet.

Interpretation of such striking and apparently anomalous differences in the behavior of Alaskan glaciers can for the present be hardly more than a matter of conjecture, chiefly because of the paucity of meteorologic records. In some instances, moreover, it is rendered doubly uncertain because the effects of earthquakes or of changes in the height of the land with respect to sea-level may be superimposed upon variations due to climatic causes.

Tarr and Martin [93] by their studies in and around Yakutat Bay were led to ascribe the spasmodic and short-lived advances of certain glaciers in that district during the first decade of this century to the shaking down of huge quantities of snow and firn into the gathering basins of those glaciers by the sharp earthquakes that occurred in 1899. But those authors nevertheless realized that, though earthquakes may account for some of the sudden and swift glacier advances that have taken place in different parts of Alaska at one time or' another, they cannot be invoked as a general cause of such advances.

It is, moreover, often difficult, if not impossible, to correlate a given glacier advance with an earthquake of a certain date, because of the lag that inevitably occurs between the shaking down of the snow in the cirques and the initiation of the advance of the terminus. The time in which the suddenly accumulated mass of snow is translated as a "wave" from the head of a glacier to its terminus depends upon the length of the glacier, upon its general conformation, and upon its slope, and necessarily varies considerably between different glaciers. In ice streams a dozen or a score of miles in length the lag may easily amount to several years.

The case of the Black Rapids Glacier—the "runaway glacier," as it was popularly called—whose phenomenal forward rush of 3 miles in

1936–37 at one time threatened to block the Richardson Highway to Fairbanks, well illustrates the difficulties that may attend the discovery of the true cause of such a catastrophic advance. Hance [47] was inclined to attribute the cause to excessive snowfall during a period of several years in the mountains at the head of the glacier, but earthquake action nevertheless is not wholly excluded as a possible cause, inasmuch as fairly severe earthquakes did occur in that part of Alaska during the preceding years.

The lack of synchronism between the advances of different groups of glaciers, and even of glaciers in adjoining valleys, may in some instances find its explanation in unequal distribution of snow precipitation or in other purely meteorologic causes; but there can be no doubt that in other cases differences in the configuration of the glacier basins, in the arrangement of the tributary glacier channels within those basins, and in their capacity relative to the size of the outflow channel together determine in large measure the timing, the magnitude, and the speed of the oscillation of the respective outflowing trunk glaciers. In a region of such marked topographic diversity as Alaska, therefore, it is to be expected that some glacier basins will respond more quickly than others, and on a different scale, to a given change in climatic conditions. It is, indeed, quite probable, as Cooper [23, pp. 58–60] has pointed out, that the prodigious recession of the ice in Glacier Bay, and the equally prodigious advance that preceded it, were rendered possible in large part by the general configuration and, especially, the "palmate" arrangement of the converging glacier channels in the vast basin that drains into the bay.

The height at which glaciers have their sources manifestly is also an important factor. It will readily be seen that a moderate shift upward of the zone of maximum snowfall may result in the decline and recession of the lesser glaciers in a given district that originate on low mountains and simultaneously in the upbuilding and advance of the larger glaciers that head on lofty peaks. Meteorologic data to prove it are lacking, but it may well be supposed that an upward shift of the zone of maximum snowfall has actually taken place in some sections of Alaska, as in the northern part of Prince William Sound, where the glaciers with low firn basins are shrinking and the glaciers with high firn basins are expanding.

A summary statement of the climatically caused glacier variations along the entire coast and in the interior of Alaska being beyond the scope of this chapter, only a few generalizations will be offered here. These are based largely on recent reports by Field [35], Cooper [21, 22, 23, 24], and Wentworth and Ray [102].

1. Throughout probably all of Alaska the past 50 or 60 years (reckoning back from 1940) have been a period of predominant glacier recession, though in several districts great and rapid readvances have taken place.

2. The net recession during the last 50 or 60 years has been moderate on the whole. The majority of the glaciers today reach to within less than a mile of the farthest limits which they had previously attained.

3. The period of greatest glacier extension fell probably within the last 150 to 200 years.

4. At the time of their greatest extension many of the large trunk glaciers invaded forests containing trees several hundred years old. These maximal advances therefore were the greatest that have occurred in many centuries, and probably in more than a thousand years.

5. As late as 1935 a number of large glaciers in the coastal districts were still readvancing and approaching the farthest limits which they had previously attained. The majority of these glaciers were in the northwestern fiords of Prince William Sound; the others were distributed over a 750-mile stretch of coast (air-line) all the way to southeastern Alaska.

6. In 1935 five large glaciers—the Harvard and the Yale, in College Fiord, the Columbia, in Prince William Sound, the South Crillon, on the coastal side of the Fairweather Range, and the Taku, near Juneau—were farther advanced than they had been in many centuries, and all of them, except the Columbia, were invading mature forests or old alder thickets.

7. On the other hand, most of the lesser glaciers, even those in the immediate vicinity of the advancing trunk glaciers, were receding or growing thinner.

8. In two districts—around Yakutat Bay and Glacier Bay—the greatest ice expansions appear to have occurred during the middle or the second half of the eighteenth century, and recession, interrupted by occasional periods of stagnation or readvance, has prevailed ever since. In Glacier Bay recession has assumed the proportions of partial deglaciation, the main fiord having become ice-free over a length of about 60 miles.

9. The mountain fastnesses that lie to the northeast of the St. Elias Range—chiefly in Yukon Territory—together with the adjoining Alaskan ranges, comprise today the most extensively and most completely glacierized section of North America, and probably have retained that aspect essentially unchanged ever since Pleistocene times.

Data concerning the recession of glaciers in other parts of the world are relatively scanty. From the reports of explorers and mountain climbers it is clear that throughout the length of South America, from the Andes of Venezuela and the Sierre de Santa Marta of Colombia south to Patagonia, the glaciers are now generally in recession and have been for several decades. Many of them, it is apparent from published photographs, have retreated only a short distance from the moraines which they laid down during the last advance. Their relations to these moraines are closely analogous to those characteristic of the glaciers in the western United States.

The small glaciers in Africa—on the Kilimanjaro group, Mount Kenia, and Mount Ruwenzori—are likewise in recession, and some of them are on the verge of extinction.

Among the glaciers of the numerous Asiatic ranges those of the Caucasus are perhaps the most frequently observed. Kalesnik [57] lists 96 of them and notes that recession is general among them, but that advances have taken place in 1877–87, 1907–14, and 1927–33. A general advance apparently occurred in 1850–60, and the record as a whole corresponds closely with that of the European Alps. In Turkey, Iran, and Turkestan recession has been particularly rapid since the end of the nineteenth century, but some glaciers advanced during the period 1906–15. The Fedtchenko Glacier, which is probably the greatest in Asia, and measures 48 miles in length, made notable advances in 1870 and 1914 but is now receding. Kalesnik [57, p. 686] stresses the point that "during the recession periods all glaciers retreat, and during the periods of advance some of them advance, whereas others continue to retreat." That statement expresses the conditions that prevail throughout central Asia— in the Altai, Tianschan, Pamir, Hindukush, Karakorum, Kuenlun, and Himalayan ranges. Particularly significant, as coming from a glaciologist of the modern school, is Finsterwalder's [36, pp. 103–106] dictum that the glaciers in the Nanga-Parbat district (Kashmir) are retreating slowly from moraines of an advance that "with certainty" can be correlated with that of the 1850's in Europe. The certainty is based on a remarkably accurate portrayal of the Chungphar Glacier in a painting of the Nanga Parbat group which A. Schlagintweit made in 1856.

The small glaciers in the Nassau Mountains of New Guinea, according to von Dosy [98] also have receded recently, leaving fresh terminal moraines that are still devoid of vegetation. Even within 4 degrees of the Equator, therefore, the climatic change that is causing glaciers to shrink throughout the world has made itself felt.

Appreciable recession of the glaciers of New Zealand has recently been reported by Speight [88, 89]. Observations on several of the major ice streams have been made at intervals as far back as 1865 and indicate in the main recession interrupted by repeated brief readvances. Definite measurements show that from 1909 to 1921 the Franz Josef Glacier was receding; from 1926 to 1934 it advanced somewhat; from 1934 to 1938 it receded slowly; and since 1938 its recession has been phenomenal. Recent terminal moraines are lacking in many valleys, owing to the destructive action of the rivers, but freshly abandoned lateral moraines indicate both recession and reduction in the thickness of the glaciers.

The Tasman and Fox Glaciers have changed but little in length in several decades, but their bodies in the same interval have lost fully 150 feet in thickness.

Diminution of the ice cover of Antarctica is attested by only a few observations, but these are quite definite. Particularly convincing is Fleming's [37] report that certain glaciers near Marguerite Bay, on Palmer Land, are now so depleted that they are stagnant and their lower portions are mantled with morainal and talus material. He also describes "fringing glaciers" that are situated on narrow rock platforms at the base of coastal cliffs, which are probably relics of once extensive shelf ice "that must have broken away from the coast quite recently" [38]. These relict masses in his opinion are evanescent features that will not endure long if present climatic conditions persist. It is evident, further, that some of the tabular ice masses that lie on small coastal islands are remnants of recently vanished shelf ice that once had considerable extent. According

Areas covered by glacier ice (after Thorarinsson)

Region		Areas of Glacier Ice (Square Miles)
Continental Europe:		
Alps	1,930	
Pyrenees	20	
Scandinavia	1,930	
Total:		3,880
Continental Asia:		
Caucasus	770	
Turkestan	3,500	
Karakorum	5,300	
Other Asiatic ranges	33,700	
Total		43,270
Africa		8
New Guinea		6
New Zealand		386
Continental North America		30,900
Continental South America		9,600
South Polar regions:		
Antarctica	5,019,300	
Sub-antarctic islands	1,150	
Total		5,020,450
North Polar regions:		
Iceland	4,830	
Jan Mayen Island	40	
Spitsbergen Archipelago	22,400	
Franz Josef Archipelago	6,560	
Novaya Zemlya	5,790	
Zevernaya Zemlya	5,830	
Greenland	637,100	
North Canadian Archipelago	38,600	
Total		721,150
Grand total for the world		5,829,670

to Gould [42, p. 1392] even the Ross Shelf Ice, which lies in a sheltered embayment, is gradually diminishing in area.

It is to be noted, however, that all these reported evidences of ice-shrinkage are from the coastal fringes of Antarctica, which have a maritime climate. In the interior of the continent, very probably, the ice sheet is in a nearly static condition owing to the continentality of the climate, which is intensified by the great altitude, by the extremely low temperatures, and by the persistent anticyclone. The prevailing view among antarctic explorers is that the ice sheet in the interior is in a depleted state, not as a result of increased ablation but owing to diminished precipitation. Whereas practically all other bodies of land ice on the globe are perceptibly shrinking as a result of increasing warmth, the antarctic ice sheet is wasting very slowly under exceptionally frigid and arid conditions.

The areas of glacier ice now in existence in different parts of the Earth are indicated in the table at the bottom of page 203 which is based upon figures published by Thorarinsson (96, pp. 136, 140).

Earlier glacier oscillations of the historic period and their relation to the Pleistocene ice age

The general advance of the glaciers in the Alps that culminated during the 1850's was preceded by several other advances of approximately the same magnitude during the seventeenth, eighteenth, and nineteenth centuries. Naturally those earlier oscillations are less fully recorded than the one of the 1850's, yet the data suffice to establish their sequence quite definitely. Particularly significant is the fact that the major advances were essentially synchronous in all parts of the Alps. Each advance and each recession evidently was called forth by one and the same climatic pulsation that made itself felt throughout the mountain system. As a rule, however, the oscillations were more accentuated in the western Alps than in the eastern.

The earlier records, of course, are not based on scientific observations. They are found chiefly in legal documents relating to the havoc that was wrought to human habitations and privately owned lands by catastrophic glacier advances or by the torrential streams that accompanied them. Little or no mention is made of the uneventful intervals when the glaciers were in a state of stagnation or slow recession.

In Switzerland the Upper and Lower Grindelwald glaciers, which are situated in close proximity to the village of Grindelwald, have ever been among the most assiduously watched. About 1595 both of those glaciers began to issue from the rugged mountain valleys in which they had been previously ensconced, and about 1620 they attained their farthest limits on the lowland—the farthermost limits they have reached during historic times. In 1719 they again came forward, and so rapidly, that the terrified villagers appealed to the authorities to take measures to drive the glaciers back. Whereupon, it is related, the glaciers did go back. Other notable advances occurred in 1743 and 1770. The 1770 advance lasted nine years. It is evident that those were times of harsh climatic conditions. The first half of the nineteenth century was little better, for a strong advance which started in 1814 and culminated in 1819 to 1822 nearly equalled the one of the early 1600's. In 1838 began the slower and more protracted advance whose climax, about 1850, marked the turning point in the modern glacial history of central Europe.

Closely comparable is the record of the Vernagtferner, in the Tyrolese Alps. It is based chiefly on the inundations of a side valley that were caused each time the glacier advanced far enough to block its mouth. The dates of those inundations are 1599–1601, 1678–1681, 1771, 1820, and 1848. Many other glaciers in the eastern Alps made advances in approximately the same years.

Most dramatic are the accounts, written in quaint old French, of the devastations that have been caused in the valley of Chamonix by advances of the glaciers on the Mont Blanc chain. Rabot [76] has brought these accounts together from documents found in the archives of Chamonix. They show that in the closing years of the sixteenth century and the opening years of the seventeenth the glaciers descended from their hanging valleys and, spreading out upon the floor of the main valley, partially overwhelmed several villages and damaged much land. A second, somewhat greater advance in 1609 to 1611 completed the destruction of the villages, and a third in 1640 to 1644 caused additional ruin.

There ensued a prolonged period of prevailing stagnation and recession, interrupted by occasional minor advances. Then, in 1770, a new, sharp advance took place, and with the turn of the century a more gradual advance set in that culminated between 1818 and 1825. Some of the glaciers then reached nearly as far as they had in the seventeenth century. The final advance of the 1850's fell but little short of that of the 1820's.

At least 14 major and minor glacier advances appear to have occurred in the Alps between 1595 and 1939. Attempts to discover a rhythmic periodicity in them and to correlate them with definite climatic cycles have met with only partial success. Richter [79] endeavored to correlate the first 9 advances (up to 1891) with Brückner's 35-year climatic cycle, but found no consistent correspondence. The periods between successive glacial maxima ranged actually from 20 to 45 years. Faith in the Brückner cycle is not as strong now as it was in the nineteenth century. Neither has any distinct 11-year period that might be linked with the sunspot cycle been discovered in the record of glacier oscillations.

These matters cannot be discussed here at any length, as that would require a detailed analysis of all the European glacier records, but it is pertinent to point out that those records, as they now stand, are necessarily incomplete, especially for the seventeenth and eighteenth centuries. Only the more prominent glacier advances that attracted popular attention were then recorded. The lesser ones often escaped notice or were forgotten. The recorded advances, moreover, were chiefly those of the longer valley glaciers whose response to climatic pulsations usually lagged considerably, and in varying degrees, behind their occurrences; and it is quite probable that the effects of some of the weaker climatic pulsations died out before they reached the termini. It is a noteworthy fact that since systematic annual measurements to the termini of glaciers have been instituted, and supplementary observations have been made on increases or decreases in the thickness of glaciers, the statistics indicate a greater frequency of oscillations than was previously recorded. The advances now appear to recur at intervals of only 6 or 8 years.

The most significant fact that stands out from the glacial records of the entire historic period is, in the writer's opinion, that toward the end of the sixteenth century the climate of central Europe grew distinctly more severe than it had been before. The destruction of the villages by advancing glaciers at the beginning of the seventeenth century implies, unquestionably, that milder conditions had previously prevailed in the Alps for at least several hundred years. As Rabot has pointed out, the mountain folk would hardly have built their settlements in places which they thought might possibly be menaced by glaciers. It may reasonably be concluded, therefore, that throughout the Middle Ages, and perhaps even during still earlier times, the glaciers in the Alps were relatively small and sufficiently remote from the main valleys to cause no apprehension about a possible invasion from them.

That the more severe climatic conditions that set in toward the end of the sixteenth century have in the main persisted until the present time is evident from the fact that, in spite of the recent recession, many glaciers in the Alps are still larger today than they were in the Middle Ages. The silver mine from which the village of Argentière, in the valley of Chamonix, takes its name, and which was being worked during the Middle Ages, is still buried under the ice. The village of St. Jean de Perthuis, in the Veni valley, south of the Mont Blanc chain, which about 1600 was overwhelmed—church and all—by the Brenva Glacier, also remains under the ice. Ditches dug to supply communities in the valley below the Great Aletsch Glacier with potable water remain abandoned because their intakes still are covered by that glacier. Many other bits of evidence of a like nature might be cited.

Kinzl [58], from a comprehensive survey of the moraines of the historic period in the Alps and of their relations to the youngest moraines of the Pleistocene ice age, has concluded that the historic moraines date, in general, from three main epochs of glacier expansion—those of the early 1600's, the 1820's, and the 1850's. He finds no evidence of the occurrence of glacier expansions of like magnitude prior to the end of the sixteenth century. The next older moraines in the valleys of the Alps he holds to be those of the "Daun stadium"—the last notable readvance of the declining Pleistocene glaciers. Accordingly, he feels justified in declaring that the glacier advances of the last 300 years are the greatest that have occurred since the Pleistocene ice age. Those 300 years therefore comprise really a separate epoch of glacier expansion, a lesser ice age, that was preceded by a warm period of considerable duration.

The occurrence of that warm period, in the middle of the Post-Pleistocene interval, is abundantly and conclusively attested in the Alps by peat deposits and forest remains at high altitudes that show that the timber line then reached 1,000 to 1,300 feet higher on the mountains than it does today. The regional snow line, it follows, must have lain correspondingly higher, and the glaciers must have been much smaller than they now are. Some of the lesser ones probably vanished altogether but were regenerated later, when cooler and moister conditions brought the snow line down again.

In Scandinavia the glacier oscillations of historic times are less fully recorded than in the Alps, but there is definite information that the last quarter of the seventeenth century and the first half of the eighteenth were times of general glacier expansion and increasingly severe weather conditions, causing farms in the upper valleys of the Jostedal district to be abandoned. The climax came about 1748 to 1750. Øyen [69] discovered that the moraines of that period overlap lands that had previously borne vegetation for a long time during the Post-Pleistocene interval. Hamberg [46], as early as 1896, felt reasonably certain that in the Kvikkjokk district some of the Pleistocene glaciers had disappeared entirely during the warm period and that some of the present small ice bodies there had been formed anew in relatively recent times.

The glaciers of Iceland, it is evident from the scattered historic data which Eythorsson [33] and Thorarinsson [95] have gathered, have in general synchronized rather closely in their major oscillations with the Scandinavian glaciers. There is little doubt that at the time of its colonization by the Norsemen, about the end of the ninth century, and for several hundred years thereafter, Iceland had a milder climate and less extensive glaciers than it has today. But already in the fifteenth century farms situated near glaciers were being abandoned, and such instances became more frequent during the stressful period that lasted from the end of the seventeenth century to the middle of the eighteenth. New cirque glaciers even came into existence at that time—cirque glaciers that have not vanished since. From the 1750's on, however, the glaciers have been generally smaller, though their recession was interrupted by the readvances of 1850 and 1890.

It has been observed repeatedly that the outlet glaciers of Iceland's Vatnajökull bring forth fragments of peat and trunks of birch trees, thereby showing that they have overridden land that once was covered with fairly dense vegetation. Only scrubby birches a few feet high now manage to survive the Iceland winters, but the trunks that are being washed out from the glaciers, according to Ahlmann [5, p. 182], attest the former existence of "a birch forest which must have been luxuriant for Iceland." There is good reason to believe that the relatively genial conditions thus indicated date back to the time of the Post-Pleistocene "climatic optimum." It is, moreover, entirely probable, in the opinion of Ahlmann [3, pp. 205–206] that the ice caps and glaciers of Iceland, Spitsbergen, and Scandinavia are to be regarded as "manifestations of a recurrent glaciation after the postglacial warm period."

Some of the small independent ice caps and glaciers situated in the coastal fringe of partly bare land that surrounds the inland ice of Greenland are probably also of Recent origin. On the upper Nugssuak Peninsula, Demorest [28] found small firn masses that apparently had not been in existence long enough to be recrystallized into true glacier ice in their basal layers. These he believes to be Post-Pleistocene accumulations rather than remnants of the main ice sheet. It is not impossible, in the present writer's opinion, that, like the new cirque glaciers in Iceland, they date from the eighteenth century. On climatological grounds alone it might be expected that in Greenland as in Iceland the last three centuries were a time of general ice expansion. It is significant, in any event, that in several coastal districts the natives maintain that not long ago certain glaciers advanced and buried old Norse ruins [Carlson 15].

Another region where glaciers have overwhelmed ancient forests during late Post-Pleistocene time is Glacier Bay, in southeastern Alaska. The phenomenal recession of the ice during the past 150 to 200 years there has uncovered extensive deposits of glacial outwash gravel, and, buried beneath those deposits, as is revealed at many points by the eroding action of streams and the waves of the Bay, stand the stumps of an old forest, still erect and rooted where the trees grew. The wood of these stumps and, in some places, the bark and the moss on them, are well preserved. There is no sign of petrifaction.

The gravel is manifestly of very recent origin and in all probability was laid down by the waters that flowed from the ice during the last great advance, not many centuries ago. It was overridden by the ice during the culminating phases of the advance and partly eroded away; as a consequence in some places the buried trees are found all decapitated at about the same level. In other places the gravel deposits are over 200 feet thick and contain occasional layers of soil with plant remains and even stumps of trees. It is thus evident that the advance was not a brief, transient episode but really a fairly long period of prevailing glacier expansion during which the ice front oscillated back and forth repeatedly and the outflowing streams often shifted their courses.

The remnants of the ancient forests buried beneath the gravels have been viewed and described by the scientists of several successive expeditions, but it has remained for a plant ecologist—William S. Cooper [21, 22, 23, 24]—to make the intensive studies that have given us a general insight into the history of the great glacier advance that overrode the forests and of the long period of deglaciation that preceded it. The following data therefore are based chiefly upon his writings.

The ancient forest was composed of hemlock and Sitka spruce—the same tree species that make up the climax forest of the Glacier Bay region at the present time. No appreciable climatic change is therefore indicated by the ancient forest, but the fact that it was composed predominantly of hemlock, which is normally the last species to gain ascendency in the plant succession in the Glacier Bay region, shows that the ancient forest had been in existence for a long time. Ring counts indicate that many of the trees in it were over 200 years old. One had 383 rings and showed evidence of suppression during its youth by trees of an older generation. Some trees clasp in their roots decayed logs of considerable age. There is thus abundant reason to believe that the forest had been fully established in climax phase for a thousand years or more.

Again, it is evident from Cooper's investigations in 1935, that the climax phase of the forest extends undiminished as far up Muir Inlet as the ice has withdrawn. It is therefore probable, in his opinion, that it ranged much farther over the relatively low lands to the east of the Bay, and even up the mountain sides, to the height of the present timber line, which is at about 2,000 to 2,500 feet. That the climax forest could have covered so large an area, however, implies widespread and prolonged deglaciation.

All of these considerations, it seems to the present writer, preclude the possibility that the buried forest of the Glacier Bay region dates back to some period less remote than the middle of Post-Pleistocene time, for, so far as our present knowledge goes, the cool climate of the last 4,000 years, though it has fluctuated frequently, has never been interrupted by any warm interval of the order of a thousand years or more.

Abundant confirmatory evidence of a "climatic optimum" in the middle of the Post-Pleistocene interval has recently come from microscopic studies of pollen grains found entombed in peat bogs. Such studies, designed to identify the different types of vegetation that have succeeded one another during Post-Pleistocene times, were initiated in Sweden by L. von Post and G. Erdtman, and have since been carried on by a number of plant ecologists in different parts of Europe and North America. They reveal, most clearly in the northern districts, that during the first few thousand years after the withdrawal of the continental ice sheets the hardy spruce and fir forests advanced northward and were gradually replaced by pines; that the pines later made way for oak, hickory, beech, and maple forests, which require a fairly warm climate; and that, finally, within the last few thousand years the deciduous trees were again crowded back to some extent by southward retreating conifers [Cooper 25].

Similar evidences of a gradual amelioration of the climate in early Post-Pleistocene time, of a succeeding period of relatively mild climate, and a final return of somewhat cooler conditions in late Post-Pleistocene time, are indicated also for the southern hemisphere by the "pollen analyses" which Cranwell and von Post [26] have made from samples of peat collected in New Zealand by Caldenius. The types of vegetation identified by these analyses differ greatly from those that are found in the peat deposits of the northern hemisphere, yet they tell essentially the same story. Corroborative evidence from other parts of the southern hemisphere is needed before definite conclusions can be based upon these initial studies by Cranwell and von Post, but the expert character of their research meanwhile warrants at least provisional acceptance of their findings as indicating that the major climatic changes that have occurred in the southern hemisphere during the Post-Pleistocene interval have been essentially synchronous with those in the northern hemisphere.

There remains the question, how long ago, in terms of years or centuries, the cool and moist period began that brought with it the mild recrudescence of glacial conditions of historic times? The figures indicated by the pollen analyses vary considerably and in themselves afford no really conclusive answer. They range all the way from 1,000 to 4,000 years. Some of the analyses do not show any definite evidence of a return to cooler conditions. Naturally, much depends in each case upon the latitude of the locality, the regional climatic conditions, and a variety of local factors that can for the most part only be surmised. However, other clues such as have been obtained from remains of animal life preserved in lake silts, ancient beaches, and calcareous tufa deposits, point in general to figures close to 4,000 years. According to Antevs [8] European students of Post-Pleistocene plant and animal remains now generally regard 4,000 years as a rough measure of the time that has elapsed since the warm period came to an end. The year 2,000 B. C. therefore commonly appears in their writings as the approximate date of the transition.

However insecure these figures for the duration of the cool period may seem, it is probably no mere coincidence that closely accordant figures are indicated by calculations based upon entirely different classes of data— chiefly geologic, geomorphologic, and hydrologic data. Among these calculations are several from American sources, and of these the more significant deserve mention.

1. At the head of Portland Canal, the narrow fiord that separates the southernmost tip of Alaska from British Columbia (latitude 56°), the Bear River has built a small delta. That delta, according to Hanson [48], is composed very largely of glacial silt derived from several small glaciers situated at the head of the Bear River. From his measurements of the rate at which the frontal margin of the delta advances from year to year, as the result of continued deposition of sediment, Hanson calculates that the entire delta was built in about 3,600 years. The glaciers at the head of the river, he therefore concludes, can not have been in existence more than 3,600 or possibly 4,000 years. They are not shrunken remnants of the large glaciers that filled the valley during the Pleistocene epoch, but modern glaciers that were formed when cooler and moister conditions returned after the prolonged warm period that caused the Pleistocene glaciers to melt away.

2. Abert Lake and Summer Lake, in southern Oregon (approximate latitude 42°-40'), are two shallow saline desert lakes that occupy the lowest portions of a broad depression which in Pleistocene times contained one large and deep saline lake that had no outflow. They have long been regarded as remnants of that ancient lake, but examinations by Van Winkle [97] leave no doubt that their salt content is much too small to represent a concentrate due to the progressive evaporation of that large body of water. He therefore interprets them to be pools of relatively recent origin that were formed after a prolonged period of desiccation during which the salts precipitated from the ancient lake had become buried under alluvial material or absorbed by the underlying lacustrine silts. From their present salt content, the quantity and quality of the inflowing waters, and the probable rate of evaporation, Van Winkle estimates that Abert Lake and Summer Lake both originated in round numbers 4,000 years ago.

3. Closely similar is Antevs' [9] interpretation of the Post-Pleistocene history of Owens Lake, in California (latitude 36°-25'). That lake was formerly regarded as a remnant of the much larger and deeper body of water that occupied the lower end of Owens Valley during late Pleistocene time, but it is now seen to be a new pool that came into existence after the

lake basin had been desiccated during the warm middle part of the Post-Pleistocene interval. During that period of desiccation the salt left from the Pleistocene lake was gradually buried under alluvium brought in by short-lived freshets and presumably also in part under wind-blown sand. As a result the basin was "freshened," so that, when the new lake was formed with the advent of cooler and moister conditions, it started its life as a body of essentially fresh water and concentration of salt began anew. Gale [39] had previously calculated that the amount of salt which Owens Lake contained in 1912, before water was diverted from Owens River into the Los Angeles Aqueduct, had required approximately 4,000 years to accumulate. It may reasonably be supposed, therefore, that the cooler and moister conditions that regenerated the lake set in about 4,000 years ago.

It is the present writer's belief that the history of the drying up of the large Pleistocene Owens Lake and the subsequent birth of the small modern Owens Lake furnishes the key also to the Post-Pleistocene history of the glaciers of the Sierra Nevada [Matthes 66, 67]. The modern lake is fed largely—in many years almost exclusively—by melt water from the abundant winter snows on that range. Direct precipitation in the form of rain is normally insignificant on the east flank of the range and in Owens Valley, which has justly earned the name of "the land of little rain." The same abundant snows that feed the lake also maintain the fifty-odd small glaciers on the range. It can hardly be doubted that the large ancient Owens Lake was contemporaneous with the great Pleistocene glaciers of the Sierra Nevada, some of which attained lengths of 30 to 60 miles; neither can it be reasonably doubted that when the temperature rose and the snow on the range was so reduced that it failed to maintain the ancient lake in existence, it likewise failed to maintain the glaciers. The present small glaciers are losing annually 3 to 6 feet of ice from their surfaces by ablation, and, as they are only 200 to 300 feet thick, are at that rate likely to vanish in less than a century. Several of them already have vanished during the last 50 years. It does not seem likely, therefore, that these small ice bodies, which evidently were delicately adjusted to the climatic conditions of the past centuries, could have survived the long warm period that caused the complete desiccation of Owens Lake.

The testimony of the moraines points to the same conclusion. There is a notable absence of any gradational series of successively younger moraines leading up from the Wisconsin moraines in the canyons below to the fresh-looking modern moraines that lie close to the ice fronts, and there is nothing to suggest that those modern moraines were formed merely by the last of a long series of recessional stages of the glaciers. They form an entirely separate group of very recent origin. Their volume of rock waste, moreover, is too small to represent an accumulation of 10,000 years or more. There is thus, on this score also, good reason to believe that the present glaciers of the Sierra Nevada, like the modern Owens Lake, are creatures of the cooler and more snowy period that followed the Post-Pleistocene "climatic optimum." They are successors to, rather than remnants of, the large glaciers of the Pleistocene epoch, and their age is presumably about the same as that of the present Owens Lake—that is, about 4,000 years.

The history of the Sierra glaciers, it will be seen, is essentially analogous to that of the glaciers at the head of the Bear River, and that fact implies that hundreds of other small glaciers on the Cordilleran ranges of North America, between latitudes 37° and 56°—and doubtless still others farther north—were reborn during the last 4,000 years. To the writer it seems entirely probable from his observations on Post-Pleistocene moraines that the great majority, perhaps all, of the cirque glaciers on the Sierra-Cascade chain and on the various ranges of the Rocky Mountains within the continental United States belong to the modern generation. Only the main glaciers, several miles in length, that are situated on such peaks as Mount Olympus, Mount Baker, Mount Rainier, and Glacier Peak, are probably survivors from the Pleistocene ice age. If so, however, they must have shrunk greatly during the Post-Pleistocene "climatic optimum" and reexpanded during the last 4,000 years.

That the Cordilleran ranges of North America today bear a far greater load of glacier ice than they bore some 5,000 years ago is no longer open to question. The same is true of Iceland, Scandinavia, and the Alps. In each of these regions there is indubitable evidence of a general reexpansion of the glaciers that took place during the last few thousand years; in each of them, also, there exist small glaciers that clearly have been formed since the Post-Pleistocene "climatic optimum." Particularly convincing examples from different parts of the Alps have recently been described by Lichtenecker [61]. The photographs published by him show small glaciers of precisely the same type as the reborn glacierets on the mountains of the western United States, and fronted by precisely the same kind of modern moraines as the latter. It is to be noted, however, that although the small European glaciers in question are confidently stated to have originated within the last 4,000 years, no tangible data are adduced from which their age might be calculated, or even roughly estimated. Only in North America has it been found possible, thus far, to estimate the approximate age of certain glaciers of the reborn, modern kind from the age of contemporaneous physiographic features that exist in their vicinity. These are the glaciers at the head of Bear River, in British Columbia, and the glaciers of the Sierra Nevada, in California. Significantly, the estimates for the two groups yield closely accordant figures.

In conclusion it may be remarked that the present period of glacier recession, which is already threatening the extinction of many of the lesser ice bodies—notably those of the reborn class—does not necessarily presage the end of this latest chapter of glacial history, which has lasted some 4,000 years thus far. It may merely mark the beginning of a brief interlude of moderate glacier shrinkage that will be followed ere long— possibly within a few decades from now—by another period favorable to glacier growth. That the "little ice age" of the last 4,000 years has been interrupted frequently by such interludes of glacier shrinkage is evident from the disposition of the modern moraines at the fronts of many reborn glacierets in closely spaced, concentric series. It is evident also from the arrangement of the laminae of ice in the glacierets themselves, in groups divided from one another by planes of discontinuity—unconformities, as geologists would call them. Should, however, the present period of increasing warmth and glacier recession continue indefinitely, it would surely result in widespread deglaciation and in increasing aridity over large areas. Conditions such as prevailed during mid-Post-Pleistocene time might then return, the deciduous forests would again extend them-selves northward at the expense of the conifers, and hydrologists in some parts of the world might face an era of water scarcity to which modern civilization might find it difficult to adjust itself.

SUMMARY

1. The period of modern history, from about the year 1600 on, has been a time of moderate but on the whole persistent glacier expansion over the entire Earth. That fact is definitely established by observational records in the Alps, in Scandinavia, and in Iceland. In the continental United States it is to be inferred from the character and disposition of the modern moraines of the glaciers on the western ranges, which moraines are closely analogous to those of the historic period in Europe. In New Zealand, likewise, it may be inferred from the modern moraines.

2. The glaciers of the Alps, Scandinavia, and Iceland made repeated advances and attained their greatest extension since the Pleistocene epoch during the seventeenth, eighteenth and nineteenth centuries. In Alaska many glaciers have recently invaded forests that contain trees several centuries old and may have been in existence more than a thousand years.

3. There is abundant evidence in the Alps, in Scandinavia, and in Iceland that the climate was milder during the Middle Ages than it is at present and permitted communities to exist and farming to be carried on in places that have been since invaded by advancing glaciers or devastated by glacial streams.

4. There is, further, abundant evidence, especially in the form of vegetal remains at high altitudes in the Alps, of tree trunks washed out of

glaciers in Iceland, and of pollen of deciduous trees entombed in northern bogs, that the moderate recrudescence of glacial conditions during historic times was preceded during the middle part of the Post-Pleistocene interval by a long period of climate warmer than the present. The sequence of pollen types in New Zealand bogs indicates a similar story for the southern hemisphere.

5. Circumstantial evidence in British Columbia and the Sierra Nevada, in California, warrants the inference that many of the lesser glaciers on the Cordilleran ranges of North America are, not remnants of Pleistocene glaciers, but "modern" glaciers that came into existence during the cooler period that followed the "climatic optimum" of Post-Pleistocene time. The age of those "modern" glaciers, as indicated by the calculated age of the Bear River delta on the one hand, and that of Owens Lake, in California, on the other hand, is probably between 3,600 and 4,000 years.

6. The present recession of the glaciers, which began in the 1850's and which since 1920 has proceeded at an accelerated rate, is merely the latest episode in this "little ice age." It may mark the end, or it may not.

References

1. Agassiz, Louis, Nouvelles études et expériences sur les glaciers actuels, leur structure, leur progression, et leur action physique sur le sol: Paris, 1847.

2. Ahlmann, Hans W:son, Scientific results of the Swedish-Norwegian Arctic Expedition in the summer of 1931, Part 8, Glaciology: Geografiska Annaler, vol. 15, pp. 161–216, 1933.

3. Ahlmann, Hans W:son, Scientific results of the Norwegian-Swedish Spitsbergen Expedition in 1934, Part 5, the Fourteenth of July Glacier: Geografiska Annaler, vol. 17, pp. 22–218, 1935.

4. Ahlmann, Hans W:son, Contribution to the physics of glaciers: Geogr. Jour., vol. 86, pp. 97–113, 1935.

5. Ahlmann, Hans W:son, and Thorarinsson, Sigurdur, Vatnajökull, Scientific results of the Swedish-Icelandic Investigations 1936–37: Geografiska Annaler, vol. 19, pp. 146–229, 1937.

6. Ahlmann, Hans W:son, and Thorarinsson, Sigurdur, The Vatnajökull Glacier. Preliminary report on the work of the Swedish-Icelandic investigations of 1936–37: Geograph. Review, vol. 28, pp. 412–438, 1938.

7. Aleschkow, A., Ein rezenter Gletscher im nördlichen Ural: Zeitschrift für Gletscherkunde, vol. 18, pp. 58–62, 1930.

8. Antevs, Ernst, Review of Rolf Nordhagen's paper on De senkvartäre klimavekslinger i Nordeuropa og deres betydning for kulturforskningen (Late-Quaternary climatic changes in northern Europe and their significance in archeologic research): Instit. for Sammenlignende Kulturforskning, Ser. A, no. 12, 1933. Geogr. Review, vol. 25, pp. 699–700, 1935.

9. Antevs, Ernst, Post-pluvial climatic variations in the Southwest: Am. Meteor. Soc. Bull., vol. 19, pp. 190–193, 1938.

10. Bader, H., Der Schnee und seine Metamorphose: Beiträge zur Geologie der Schweiz, Series Hydrologie, part 3, 1939.

11. Blümke, A., and Hess, Hans, Untersuchungen am Hintereisferner: Zeitschrift des Deutschen und Oesterreichischen Alpenvereins, Wissenschaftliche Ergänzungsheft no. 2, 1899.

12. Bonacina, L. C. W., Snow as a form of precipitation and factors controlling distribution over the globe: Internat. Assoc. of Scientific Hydrology, Bull. 23, Sixth General Assembly at Edinburgh, 1936, pp. 79–90, 1938.

13. Bowman, Isaiah, The Andes of southern Peru: Am. Geogr. Soc., New York, 1916.

14. Bridgman, P. W., Water in the liquid and five solid forms, under pressure: Am. Acad. of Arts and Sciences, vol. 47, pp. 441–558, 1912.

15. Carlson, William S., Movement of some Greenland glaciers: Geol. Soc. America, Bull., vol. 50, no. 2, pp. 239–256, 1939.

16. Chamberlin, Rollin T., Instrumental work on the nature of glacial motion: Jour. Geol., vol. 36, pp. 1–30, 1928.

17. Chamberlin, Rollin T., Glacier motion as typical rock deformation: Jour. Geol., vol. 44, pp. 93–104, 1936.

18. Chamberlin, Rollin T., Glacier mechanics: Am. Alpine Journal, vol. 4, no. 1, pp. 40–52, 1940.

19. Chamberlin, Thos. C., Recent glacial studies in Greenland: Geol. Soc. America, Bull., vol. 6, pp. 199–220, 1894.

20. Chamberlin, Thos. C., Glacial studies in Greenland: Jour. Geol., vol. 3, pp. 198–218, 1895.

21. Cooper, William S., The recent ecological history of Glacier Bay, Alaska: Ecology, vol. 4, pp. 93–128, 1923.

22. Cooper, William S., A third expedition to Glacier Bay, Alaska: Ecology, vol. 12, pp. 88–95, 1931.

23. Cooper, William S., The problem of Glacier Bay, Alaska: Geograph. Review, vol. 27, pp. 37–62, 1937.

24. Cooper, William S., A fourth expedition to Glacier Bay, Alaska: Ecology, vol. 20, pp. 130–155, 1939.

25. Cooper, William S., Contributions of botanical science to the knowledge of post-glacial climates (Abstract): Geol. Soc. America, Bull., vol. 52, no. 12, p. 2023, 1941.

26. Cranwell, Lucy, and von Post, Lennart, Post-Pleistocene pollen diagrams from the southern hemisphere: Geografiska Annaler, vol. 18, pp. 308–347, 1936.

27. Daly, Reginald A., The changing world of the Ice Age: New Haven, Yale Univ. Press, 1934.

28. Demorest, Max, Glaciation of the Upper Nugssuak Peninsula, West Greenland: Zeitschrift für Gletscherkunde, vol. 25, pp. 35–56, 1937.

29. Demorest, Max, Ice flowage as revealed by glacial striae: Jour. Geol., vol. 46, pp. 700–725, 1938.

30. Demorest, Max, Ice deformation in the flow of glaciers: Am. Geophys. Union, Trans. of 1941, Part II, p. 525, 1941.

31. Demorest, Max, Glacier flow and its bearing on the classification of glaciers: Geol. Soc. America, vol. 52, no. 12, part 2, p. 2025, 1941.

32. Deutsche Grönland Expedition Alfred Wegener, 1929 und 1930–31. Wissenschaftliche Ergebnisse, vol. 3, Glaziologie, 1935.

33. Eythorsson, Jon, On the variations of glaciers in Iceland. Some studies made in 1931: Geografiska Annaler, vol. 17, pp. 121–137, 1935.

34. Faegri, Knut, Uber die Längenvariationen einiger Gletscher des Jostedalsbrae und die dadurch bedingten Pflanzensukzessionen: Bergens Museums Årbok, 1933, Naturv. rekke, no. 7, 1934.

35. Field, Wm. Osgood, Jr., Observations on Alaskan coastal glaciers in 1935: Geograph. Review, vol. 27, pp. 63–81, 1937.

36. Finsterwalder, R., Die Gletscher des Nanga Parbat: Zeitschrift für Gletscherkunde, vol. 25, pp. 57–108, 1937.

37. Fleming, W. L. S. Notes on the scientific work of the British Graham Land Expedition 1934–37: Geogr. Jour., vol. 91, pp. 508–512, 1938.

38. Fleming, W. L. S., Relic glacial forms on the western seaboard of Graham Land: Geogr. Jour., vol. 96, pp. 93–100, 1940.

39. Gale, Hoyt S., Salines in the Owens, Searles, and Panamint basins, southeastern California: U. S. Geol. Survey Bull. 580-L, pp. 251–323, 1914.

40. Gibson, Geo. R. and Dyson, James L., Grinnell Glacier, Glacier National Park, Montana: Geol. Soc. America, Bull., vol. 50, pp. 681–696, 1939.

41. Glen, A. R., The glaciology of North East Land: Geografiska Annaler, vol. 21, pp. 1–38, 1939.

42. Gould, Laurence M., The Ross Shelf Ice: Geol. Soc. America, Bull., vol. 46, pp. 1367–1394, 1935.

43. Gould, Laurence M., Glaciers of Antarctica: Am. Philos. Soc., Proc., vol. 82, no. 5, pp. 835–876, 1940.

44. Gould, Laurence M., The glacial geology of the Pacific Antarctic: Sixth Pacific Science Congress, Proc., pp. 723–740, 1939.

45. Haefeli, R., Der Schnee und seine Metamorphose: Beiträge zur Geologie der Schweiz, Ser. Hydrologie, vol. 3, Bern, 1939.

46. Hamberg, Axel, Om Kvikkjokksfjällens glaciärer: Geol. Föreningen Förhandl., vol. 18, no. 175, 1896.

47. Hance, James H., The recent advance of Black Rapids Glacier, Alaska: Jour. Geol., vol. 45, pp. 775–783, 1937.

48. Hanson, George, The Bear River Delta, British Columbia, and its significance regarding Pleistocene and Recent Glaciation: Roy. Soc. of Canada, Trans., 3d ser., vol. 28, pp. 179–185, 1934.

49. Heim, Albert, Handbuch der Gletscherkunde, Stuttgart, 1885.

50. Hess, Hans, Die Gletscher, Braunschweig, Friedrich Vieweg und Sohn, 1904.

51. Hess, Hans, Das Eis der Erde: Handbuch der Geophysik, vol. 8, pp. 1–121, 1933.

52. Hess, Hans, Zur Physik des Gletschers: Petermanns Geogr. Mitteil, pp. 241–244, 1939.

53. Hobbs, William H., The fixed glacial anticyclone compared to the migrating anticyclone: Am. Philos. Soc., Proc., vol. 60, no. 1, pp. 34–42, 1921.

54. Hobbs, William H., The glacial anticyclones, the poles of the atmospheric circulation: Michigan Univ. Studies, Sci. ser., vol. 4, New York, MacMillan Co., 1926.

55. Hobbs, William H., The glaciers of mountain and continent: Science N. S., vol. 79, pp. 419–422, 1934; Zeitsch. für Gletsch., vol. 22, pp. 1–19, 1935.

56. Hughes, T. P., and Seligman, Gerald, The temperature, meltwater movement and density increase in the névé of an Alpine glacier: Monthly notices of the Roy. Astron. Soc., Geophysical Supplement, vol. 4, no. 8, pp. 616–647, 1939.

57. Kalesnik, S. V., Fluctuation of glaciers in U.S.S.R. and measurement of their ablation: Association Internationale d'Hydrologie Scientifique, Bull. 23, pp. 669–689, 1938.

58. Kinzl, H., Die grössten nacheiszeitlichen Gletschervorstosse in den Schweizer Alpen und in der Mont Blanc-Gruppe: Zeitschrift für Gletscherkunde, vol. 20, nos. 4–5, pp. 269–397, 1932.

59. Koch, J. P., Vorläufiger Bericht über die wichtigsten glaziologischen Beobachtungen auf der dänische Forschungsreise quer durch Nordgrönland, 1912–13: Zeitschrift für Gletscherkunde, vol. 10, no. 1, pp. 1–43, 1916.

60. Koch, Lauge, Ice cap and sea-ice in North Greenland: Geogr. Review, vol. 16, pp. 98–107, 1926.

61. Lichtenecker, Norbert, Die tiefstgelegenen Gletscher der Alpen. Ein morphologischer Beweis für die postglaziale Wärmezeit in den Alpen: Zeitschrift für Gletscherkunde, vol. 27, nos. 1–2, pp. 29–35, 1940.

62. Loewe, Fritz, Central western Greenland, the country and its inhabitants: Geogr. Jour., vol. 86, no. 3, pp. 263–275, 1935.

63. McConnel, J. C., and Kidd, D. A., On the plasticity of glacier and other ice: Roy. Soc. London, Proc., vol. 44, pp. 331–367, 1888.

64. McConnel, J. C., On the plasticity of an ice crystal: Roy. Soc. London, Proc., vol. 48, pp. 256–260, 1890; vol. 49, pp. 323–343, 1891.

65. Matthes, François E., Glacial sculpture of the Bighorn Mountains, Wyoming: U. S. Geol. Survey, 21st Ann. Report, Part 2, pp. 167–190, 1900.

66. Matthes, François E., Report of Committee on Glaciers, April 1939: Am. Geophys. Union, Trans. pp. 518–523, 1939.

67. Matthes, François E., Committee on Glaciers 1939–1940, Am. Geophys. Union, pp. 396–406, 1940.

68. Nikiforoff, Constantin, The perpetually frozen ground of Siberia: Soil Science, vol. 26, pp. 61–81, 1928.

69. Øyen, P. A., Klima und Gletscherschwankungen in Norwegen: Zeitschrift für Gletscherkunde, vol. 1, pp. 46–61, 1906.

70. Pedersen, Alwin, Einiges über Gletscher und glaziologische Erscheinungen an der Ostküste Grönlands, insbesondere im Bereich des Scoresbysund: Zeitschrift für Gletscherkunde, vol. 15, nos, 4–5, pp. 253–260, 1897.

71. Perutz, M. F., and Seligman, Gerald, A crystallographic investigation of glacier structure and the mechanism of glacier flow: Roy. Soc. London, Proc., Ser. A., no. 950, vol. 172, pp. 335–360, 1939.

72. Philipp, H., Geologische Untersuchungen über den Mechanismus der Gletscherbewegung und die Entstehung der Gletscherstruktur: Neues Jahrbuch für Mineralogie, Geologie und Paleontologie, vol. 43, pp. 439–556, 1920.

73. Phillips, Kenneth N., Our vanishing glaciers: Mazama, pp. 24–41, 1938.

74. Phillips, Kenneth N., Farewell to Sholes Glacier, Mazama, pp. 37–40, 1939.

75. Quincke, G., The formation of ice and the grained structure of glaciers: Nature, vol. 72, pp. 543–545, 1905.

76. Rabot, Charles, Récents travaux glaciaires dans les Alpes françaises: La Géographie, vol. 30, pp. 257–268, 1915.

77. Reid, Harry F., De la progression des glaciers, leur stratification, et leur veines bleues: Congrès Géologique International 8, Paris, 1900, Comptes Rendus, pp. 749–755, 1901.

78. Rendu, Mgr. L., Theory of the glaciers of Savoy: MacMillan Co., 1874.

79. Richter, Eduard, Geschichte der Schwankungen der Alpengletscher: Zeitschrift des Deutschen und Oesterreichischen Alpenvereins, vol. 22, pp. 1–74, 1891.

80. Rink, H., Nogle Bemaerkningen om Inlandsisen og Isfjeldenes Oprindelse: Meddelelser om Grönland, vol. 8, pp. 271–279, 1889.

81. Roberts, Brian, The Cambridge Expedition to Vatnajökull, 1932: Geogr. Jour., vol. 81, no. 4, pp. 289–313, 1933.

82. Russell, Israel C., Quaternary history of Mono Valley, California: U. S. Geol. Survey, 8th Ann. Report 1886–87, pp. 261–394, publ. 1889.

83. Ryder, C. H., Undersögelse af Grönlands Vestkyst fra 72° til 74° 35′ N.B.: Meddelelser om Grönland, vol. 8, pp. 215–270, 1889.

84. Seligman, Gerald, Snow structure and ski fields: New York, MacMillan Co., 1936.

85. Seligman, Gerald, The structure of a temperate glacier: Geogr. Jour., vol. 97, pp. 295–317, 1941.

86. Sherzer, W. H., Glacial studies in the Canadian Rockies and Selkirks: Smithson. Miscell. Collection, vol. 47, pp. 453–496, 1905.

87. Sorge, Ernst, The scientific results of the Wegener Expedition to Greenland: Geogr. Jour., vol. 81, pp. 333–344, 1933.

88. Speight, R., Some aspects of glaciation in New Zealand: Report of the Australian and New Zealand Assoc. for the Advancement of Science, vol. 24, Canberra Meeting, pp. 49–71, 1939.

89. Speight, R., Ice wasting and glacier retreat in New Zealand: Jour Geomorph., vol. 3, pp. 131–143, 1940.

90. Streiff-Becker, R., Zur Dynamik des Firneises: Zeitsch. für Gletsch., vol. 26, nos. 1–2, pp. 1–21, 1938.

91. Tammann, G., Uber die Ausflussgeschwindigkeit kristallizierter Stoffe: Annalen der Physik, vol. 7, pp. 198–224, 1902.

92. Tarr, Ralph S., Valley glaciers of the Upper Nugssuak Peninsula, Greenland: American Geologist, vol. 19, pp. 262–267, 1897.

93. Tarr, Ralph S., and Martin, Lawrence, Alaskan Glacier studies: National Geogr. Soc., Washington, 1914.

94. Tarr, Ralph S., and von Engeln, O. D., Experimental studies of ice with reference to glacier structure and motion: Zeitsch. für Gletsch., vol. 9, no. 2, pp. 81–139, 1915.

95. Thorarinsson, Sigurdur, Grössenschwankungen der Gletscher in Island: Internat. Assoc. of Scientific Hydrology, Trans. of Washington Assembly 1939 (preprint).

96. Thorarinsson, Sigurdur, Recent glacier shrinkage and eustatic changes of sea-level. Geograf. Annaler, vol. 22, nos. 3–4, pp. 131–159, 1940.

97. Van Winkle, Walton, Quality of the surface waters of Oregon: U. S. Geol. Survey Water-Supply Paper 363, pp. 117–123, 1914.

98. Von Dosy, J. J., Eine Gletscherwelt in Niederländisch Neuguinea: Zeitschrift für Gletscherkunde, vol. 26, pp. 45–51, 1938.

99. Von Drygalski, Erich, Die Bewegung von Gletschern und Inlandeis: Mitteil. der Geogr. Gesellsch. in Wien, vol. 81, nos. 9–10, pp. 273–283, 1938.

100. Von Engeln, O. D., The motion of glaciers: Science N.S., vol. 81, no. 2106, pp. 459–461, 1935.

101. Washburn, Bradford, Morainic bandings of Malaspina and other Alaskan glaciers: Geol. Soc. America, Bull., Vol. 46, no. 12, pp. 1879–1890, 1935.

102. Wentworth, C. K., and Ray, L. L., Studies of certain Alaskan glaciers in 1931: Geol. Soc. America, Bull., vol. 43, pp. 879–934, 1936.

103. Wordie, J. M., and Kemp, Stanley, Observations on certain antarctic icebergs: Geogr. Jour., vol. 81, no. 5, pp. 428–434, 1933.

104. Wright, C. S., and Priestley, R. E., British (Terra Nova) Antarctic Expedition, 1910–1913; Glaciology, London, 1922.

CHAPTER VI

LAKES

Sidney T. Harding[1]

INTRODUCTION

Lakes are bodies of water filling depressions in the earth's surface. They range in area from small ponds to inland seas and in depth from a few feet to 2,000 feet. Although lakes are usually continuous during their geologic life, many are temporary, becoming alternately filled and dry, owing to fluctuations in their water supply and to evaporation.

Lakes are important in the topography and water supply of many drainage areas. They occur more abundantly in areas of some types of geologic formation than in areas of other types but are widely distributed. Among the larger groups of lakes in the United States are the Great Lakes, the Florida lake areas, and the enclosed lakes of the Great Basin. In addition there are large numbers of small lakes, such as those in the glaciated portions of the States adjacent to the Great Lakes, which, though not individually large, cover a considerable total area.

Lakes represent a natural form of storage, which usually is beneficial in regulating stream flow, although lakes of large area and shallow depth may lose a large proportion of their inflow by evaporation. Lakes are used for water supply for municipal use, power, and irrigation, for navigation, for recreation, and for wild life. Many lakes have been converted into artificial reservoirs by raising their surface by dams or by lowering and controlling their outlets.

The proportion of a drainage area that may be maintained as water surface varies widely. In arid regions the runoff is insufficient to support more than a minor percentage of the drainage area as a water surface. In some humid areas rainfall exceeds evaporation and the entire drainage area could be supported as a lake if the basin had no outlet. There are drainage areas with large outflows in which over one-third of the total area consists of lakes.

Lakes have a very slight range in level where their area and outlet capacity are large. Some lakes fluctuate through a wide range both within the year and over longer periods. Lakes that exist only after brief periods of inflow and soon evaporate to dryness are called playas; these are of wide occurrence in desert areas. Some lakes that cover large areas

[1] Professor of Irrigation, University of California, Berkeley, Calif.

and may attain considerable depth during a series of years of more than average precipitation become depleted or entirely dry during periods of deficient supply.

Any lake may pass through all these conditions. It may be formed by any one of the agencies that create depressed basins. As soon as it is formed it is subject to filling by the material eroded from its drainage area. It may be divided into two or more lakes by local deposits of alluvium, or its whole area may be gradually filled. It may be destroyed by the lowering of its outlet by erosion of its outflow or by movements of the earth's crust.

Swamps include lakes so shallow that aquatic vegetation grows within the lake area. Swamps also occur on sloping lands where vegetation grows rankly enough to restrict drainage. Many swamps and shallow lakes have been drained in order that the reclaimed areas may be used for agriculture.

The variations in size, climatic conditions, character of origin, and uses for different lakes make it difficult to generalize in regard to their characteristics and functions. Although generally beneficial in their effects, lakes may be wasteful of water and land.

ORIGIN OF LAKES

Classifications of lakes based on their origin are presented in several texts [16, 18, 22, 24, 26]. These are generally similar and include the following:

1. Lakes on new land areas.
2. Lakes resulting from glacial action.
3. Lakes resulting from aqueous agencies.
4. Lakes resulting from volcanic agencies.
5. Lakes resulting from movements of the earth's crust.
6. Lakes resulting from atmospheric agencies.
7. Lakes resulting from landslides.
8. Lakes resulting from miscellaneous causes, such as chemical action, organic agencies, and meteors.

Individual lakes may be formed as a result of the combination of more than one of these causes.

Lakes on new land areas.—The emergence of land from the sea results in the preservation in the land forms of the depressions that may have existed on the sea floor. These depressions frequently become lakes. Such lakes resulting from relatively recent emergence are well illustrated by the lakes of Florida, of generally low altitude and small depth. Many lakes occur in areas which were formerly covered by the sea but in which the topography has undergone major changes during the geologic periods since emergence. Such lakes are not now properly placed in this class.

Emergence lakes may be short-lived, as rapid erosion of their outlets may drain them dry or erosion on their drainage areas may result in rapid filling.

Some of the lakes now occupying parts of the areas formerly covered by ancient lakes that have disappeared or shrunk as a result of climatic changes may be classified in this group if no major topographic change has occurred. Present lakes within the former areas of Lakes Bonneville and Lahontan, such as Utah Lake and Walker Lake, come within this class.

Lakes resulting from glacial action.—The most extensive lakes resulting from glacial action, both in number and distribution, are those formed by glacial debris. Birge and Juday [1] have classified glacial lakes as follows, on the basis of their study of large numbers of such lakes in Wisconsin:

1. Pits resulting from the melting of buried ice blocks that were embedded in glacial debris. Such lakes generally have steep sides. Many lakes in the Oconomowoc-Waukesha area are of this type.

2. Lakes formed by the damming of preglacial valleys. These are illustrated by Green Lake and Lake Mendota.

3. Lakes formed in depressions between parallel glacial ridges. These are less numerous; Big Cedar Lake was mainly formed by such action.

4. Lakes resulting from inequalities in ground moraine. These are shallow with gentle slopes.

Morainal material may be sufficiently impervious to retain the waters of a lake and may also contain sufficient coarse material to prevent draining of the lake by erosion of its outlet. Lake George, in New York, is formed by a dam of glacial drift deposited across the course of the stream. Lake Como, in Montana, and Grant Lake, in California, were formed by terminal moraines.

In addition to the lakes formed by moraines, glacial erosion may result in depressions in the rock, which become lakes. Many such lakes occur in the higher portions of the Sierra Nevada, but most of them are small.

Lakes may be formed during glacial periods by the ice of the glaciers. Such lakes cease to exist with the melting of the ice. Lake Agassiz [27] was formed during the glacial retreat. It covered a large area in Canada and extended into the United States. Smaller lakes may be formed by ice moving down the main stream channel and blocking the tributaries; such lakes have an outlet through or under the ice and are subject to relatively large fluctuations as their outlet conditions change.

Lakes resulting from aqueous agencies.—Lakes may be due to stream action or to waves and currents.

Tributary streams may deposit alluvial material across the valley of the main stream, forming lakes above the alluvial ridge. Lake Pepin, on the Mississippi River, was formed by the deposit of alluvial material brought in by the Chippewa River. This lake in turn has been partly filled by silt carried by the Mississippi River. The Mississippi River has formed Lake St. Croix by depositing material across the mouth of the St. Croix River. Tulare Lake, in California, was formed in the San Joaquin Valley by an alluvial ridge deposited across the valley by the Kings River.

The overflow of streams having flat gradients results in raising the stream banks by the deposit of the coarser sediments carried by the stream. Such action in turn results in the formation of low trough areas between the stream and the valley sides, in which water may collect, either at times of flood or permanently. Such lakes occur along the lower Mississippi and Sacramento Rivers. Similar lakes may occur between the distributary channels in flat delta areas. Meandering streams may change the location of their channels so as to leave disconnected sections or oxbows in which water remains, forming long, narrow lakes. Stream action may erode basins large enough to be classified as lakes at the base of waterfalls; lakes of this type occupy part of the channel of Grand Coulee in Washington [21].

Lakes resulting from waves and currents are represented by those formed by bars across or along the margins of larger lakes or of the ocean. These may be temporary, with the bar broken at times of larger outflow, or they may be permanent, with the outflow occurring as seepage through the bar. Humboldt Lake, in Nevada, was formed separately from the adjacent and slightly lower area of Carson Sink by a gravel bar across its south end. This bar is now broken, and water is retained in Humboldt Lake only temporarily at times of larger inflow.

Lakes resulting from volcanic agencies.—Lakes may be formed by lava streams crossing or closing natural drainage channels. Such lakes occur in Lassen National Park [2]. Crater lakes occur within the craters of extinct volcanoes. Soda Lake, in Nevada, is of this type. Lakes are also formed in the depression resulting from the destruction of volcanoes by further eruption. Crater Lake, in Oregon, has been placed in this classification. Lakes may also fill depressions in the surface of lava sheets.

Lakes resulting from movement of the earth's crust.—Basins may result from earthquake movement and general faulting. Lakes were formed in Missouri and Arkansas by general movement of the surface in the New Madrid earthquakes of 1811 to 1813 [5]. Lakes may form along fault lines where the upheaval on one side of the fault forms an escarpment across the former direction of drainage. Lake Abert, in Oregon [22], is the result of such action. General tilting of the earth's surface may form basins; such movement accounts in part for the formation of the Great Lakes.

Lakes resulting from atmospheric agencies.—Wind is the principal atmospheric agency forming lakes. Drifting sands may form dunes or bars, ponding water behind them to create lakes. Such lakes may represent the division of larger lake areas or the separation of beach areas from the ocean. The bars may be temporary or intermittent. Moses Lake [21], in Washington, is an example of a lake formed in an old stream channel by wind action. Shore bars resulting from the combined effect of wind, waves, and ice occur along the shores of many lakes and beaches and form lagoons or lakes separated from the main lake area.

Wind erosion in dry periods may deepen depressions, which later become filled with water, forming lakes. Drifting sand may form both mounds and depressions. Where the depressions extend below the present local ground-water level lakes are formed. Many such lakes occur in the sand-hill areas of western Nebraska.

Lakes resulting from landslides.—Slips of the material on the sides of a valley may result in filling the stream channel and forming lakes. Such lakes may be temporary, such as that formed on the Gros Ventre River, in Wyoming, in 1925, in which the erosion of the overflow quickly cut through the slide material [3]. The material forming the lake may resist erosion, so that the lake remains; such lakes occur in the northwestern part of the Great Basin [23, pp. 231–254] and in Kern Lake, on the North Fork of the Kern River, in California [15, pp. 291–381]. The lakes of this class in the northwestern part of the Great Basin are the result of the undermining of capping strata of basaltic rim rocks by stream action, the rock material in the slide being sufficiently heavy to resist erosion by the overflow of the stream, so that permanent lakes are formed. Some valleys in this area are the result of the complete filling of such lakes.

Lakes resulting from miscellaneous causes.—Some basins are due to chemical action, organic agencies, and meteors. In general such basins are relatively small. Chemical action is represented by limestone sinks resulting from the removal of the rock in solution by water. Lakes due to organic agencies include those formed by the building up of coral reefs. Depressions in peat or tundra areas may become filled with water to form lakes. Dams built by beavers may form pools large enough to be considered lakes. Depressions may be formed by the impact of meteors.

COMPARISON OF PRESENT AND PLEISTOCENE LAKES IN THE GREAT BASIN

Many changes in lakes have occurred since Pleistocene time. Such changes are most significant in the areas containing enclosed lakes, as their fluctuations furnish an index of the climatic changes that have occurred. Changes in lakes in humid areas represent mainly topographic changes in the lake basins as a result of all the geologic factors that may affect them.

In the Great Basin Pleistocene lakes occupied much of the lower drainage area and have left their records with sufficient clearness to enable their history to be determined. A comparison of the present lakes and the climatic conditions that support them enables some estimates to be made of the climate necessary for the support of the former large lakes.

The work of Gilbert [6] on Lake Bonneville and of Russell [19] on Lake Lahontan, together with later work by others, has made available the record of these lakes. Gilbert found that Lake Bonneville occupied an area equal to 37 percent of its total drainage basin, or 58 percent of its tributary area. At its highest stages Lake Bonneville overflowed to the Snake River drainage basin; its inflow was more than sufficient to meet the evaporation losses of this area.

Russell reported that Lake Lahontan occupied 21 percent of its total basin, equivalent to 26 percent of its tributary drainage area. Jones [14] gives 16 and 18 percent respectively for these two areas. The drainage area of Lake Lahontan included more land having sparse runoff than was included in the Lake Bonneville area, so that Lake Lahontan supported a relatively smaller area than Lake Bonneville. Lake Lahontan did not overflow.

The recent areas of Great Salt Lake and Utah Lake represent about 14 percent of their tributary areas. This is about one-fourth as much as the corresponding area supported by Lake Bonneville.

Russell found that the present lake areas in the Lahontan Basin are only about 18 percent of that of Lake Lahontan; this is equivalent to less than 5 percent of their tributary area. Walker Lake has has a recent area equal to 3 percent of its drainage area. Honey Lake has had an area equal to 6 percent of its tributary area and has also been dry several times since 1850. Eagle Lake, in Lassen County, Calif., has supported a lake area of 12 percent of its tributary area. The Humboldt River, draining 15,000 square miles representing the eastern one-third of the Lahontan Basin, has supplied little surplus runoff to Humboldt Lake and Carson Sink from the annual precipitation of 5 to 10 inches over much of its drainage area.

The runoff of the upper Truckee River passes through Lake Tahoe. The lower river ends in Pyramid Lake, which overflows at its higher stages into Winnemucca Lake. Lake Tahoe has an area of 59 percent of its tributary area and maintains an outflow except in some periods of less than average precipitation. Its drainage area is high and mountainous and represents the most productive portion of the basin. Prior to extensive diversion of their inflow for irrigation, the area of Pyramid and Winnemucca Lakes has been as much as 9 percent of their tributary area. The area of Winnemucca Lake has varied widely, and it is now practically dry.

In 34 years of record the drainage area of the Truckee River between Lake Tahoe and the California-Nevada line has had a runoff ranging from 25 to 200 percent of the mean. If the evaporation when Lake Lahontan was at its high stage was only two-thirds of that at present, runoff similar to that in the years of maximum record would have maintained a lake area equivalent to that of the Lahontan high stage. As the high stage of Lake Lahontan is generally dated at the end of the last glacial period, lower temperatures and reduced evaporation represent a reasonable assumption.

Mono Lake, though not a part of the Lahontan Basin, is adjacent to it. Russell [20, pp. 261–394] has described the former lakes in the Mono Basin. At maximum stage the area of Mono Lake was about four times the present area. Mono Lake has been the least disturbed of the present Great Basin lakes, as there have been only small diversions of its inflow. The present lake area is 15 percent of its tributary drainage area. Conditions on the entire Lahontan drainage area would not need to have been much more humid than the present conditions in the Mono Basin in order to maintain the former Lahontan maximum stages. Mono Lake receives its main supply from the higher mountains to the west, but its basin also includes nonproductive desert areas to the east. Its high altitude results in lower temperature and evaporation than in the Lahontan Basin. There are still remnants of glaciers on the higher peaks in the Mono Basin, and probably there were at least equivalent glaciers in the Lahontan Basin at its higher stages.

Goose Lake in California, has occasionally overflowed to the Pit River; at such stages its area was about 17 percent of its tributary drainage area. Goose Lake has had much smaller areas within its recorded period and has been dry in recent years, mainly as a result of the diversion of its inflow for irrigation. During the more favorable recent periods Goose Lake has maintained nearly as large a percentage of its drainage area in lake surface as Lake Lahontan maintained at its high stage. The annual precipitation on the different parts of the Goose Lake drainage area ranges from 10 to 30 inches. As the drainage area of Goose Lake does not include extensive deserts, the average rainfall on the productive portions of the Lahontan drainage area would need to have been larger than these amounts in order to maintain an equivalent lake area.

Some comparisons may be made with present humid areas. The present Great Lake system above the Niagara River [11] has an area of 56 percent of its tributary drainage area and an annual outflow equal to nearly 1 foot in depth from the total drainage area. The average annual rainfall is about 33 inches, and the average evaporation about 25 inches— that is, the rainfall more than offsets the evaporation. Without outflow this drainage system could maintain its entire area in water surface, even with a 25 percent reduction in rainfall. Such a drainage area will fill its basins until they overflow. From this it might be reasoned that the climate when Lakes Bonneville and Lahontan were at their maximum stages was less humid than the present climate of the Great Lakes area. However, the evaporation rate in the Great Basin is now about twice as large as in the Great Lakes area and was probably greater also in Pleistocene time. Precipitation is also more uniformly distributed in the Great Lakes area than in the Great Basin—a difference that also detracts from the reliability of comparisons between these areas.

Jones [14] has suggested that Lake Lahontan might be restored to its high stages with a rainfall about $2\frac{1}{2}$ times that at present. Antevs [14] concluded that summer temperatures at former high stages were sufficiently lower than at present to result in less evaporation, so that Lake Lahontan could be restored with less rainfall than would be required with present rates of evaporation.

Although present water areas in the Lahontan Basin are from one-fifth to one-third of that of the former high stages, a similar ratio of increase in precipitation would not be required to restore Lake Lahontan. Runoff increases more rapidly than precipitation, and inflow would be much more than doubled by doubling the rainfall. The comparisons with present conditions indicate that an increase of 100 percent in the present mean annual precipitation, with its probable accompanying decrease in temperature and evaporation, would restore Lake Lahontan with an area approaching or equaling its former high stage. Under such conditions the average precipitation would be similar to that of the wettest recent years of record. Then, as now, much of the drainage area was probably relatively arid, the increased inflow from increased precipitation coming mainly from the western mountainous areas. The last high stage of Lake Lahontan is placed at about 25,000 years ago by the larger number of the geologists who have studied its history. Similar general topography existed at that time, and the relative distribution of rainfall and run-off was also probably similar to the present conditions.

RECORDS OF LAKE LEVELS

Observations of lake levels are made by various public agencies. In the United States observations are made by the United States Geological Survey as a part of its stream-gaging work. Records on some navigable lakes are maintained by the agencies concerned with such navigation, such as the United States Army Engineers and the United States Lake Survey. Many local organizations maintain records on lakes in which they are interested.

The records obtained by public agencies are published where the extent of public interest justifies it and are public records available for examination if not published. Other records are generally available. Records of the United States Geological Survey are included in its annual publications on surface-water supply. Records of other public agencies are included in their annual reports or other publications.

Present records in the United States are fairly adequate on the larger lakes involving navigation or other public uses where public interest has called for such observations. There is room for a greater extent and frequency of observation on many smaller lakes whose fluctuations reflect local climatic variations, conditions affecting wild life or other less extensive use. Such records should be maintained continuously and systematically if they are to be of maximum usefulness.

The observation of lake levels requires only the measurement of water altitudes, and their record is much easier to obtain than similar records of stream flow. Adequate instruments for continuous records of lake levels are now available.

On small lakes a single point of observation is adequate. On larger lakes subject to wind effects records at any one point may be distorted by storm conditions, and additional points of record are needed in order to obtain the mean altitude. Observations of altitude on open staff gages are unsatisfactory, and adequate installations require enclosed stilling wells for both staff gages and the floats of recording gages.

TIDES

Lakes are subject to tidal influence similarly to oceans, but few lakes are large enough for tidal effects to be noticeable. Tides of about 3 inches occur at the south end of Lake Michigan and the west end of Lake Superior [11].

SEICHES

A seiche is defined by Hayford [10] as "an oscillation in the water of a lake under the influence of inertia. It is a free oscillation as distinguished from a forced oscillation. It is a wave motion involving both horizontal transfer of water back and forth and a vertical oscillation of the water surface."

Seiches are pulsations in the level of the water surface in lakes represented by the synchronous rising in one portion and lowering in others. They are caused by winds, changes in barometric pressure, or any other factors that disturb the level of the lake. Such pulsations continue until the surface of the lake again becomes level or until new conditions start other pulsations.

Winds blowing across a lake drive water toward the leeward side and lower the windward side. The surface water is generally estimated to move with a velocity of about 5 percent of that of the wind. The gradient established by the wind results in a reverse flow, which may continue until the pulsations die out. Fluctuations of several feet due to wind action have occurred on Lake Erie at Buffalo [11]. Similar changes of as much as 2 feet have occurred on Lakes Michigan and Huron.

In seiches caused by differences in barometric pressure, the lake surface lowers in areas of high pressure and water flows toward areas of low pressure. A difference of an inch in a mercurial barometer is equivalent to 13.5 inches in depth of water. Barometric differences of as much as 1 inch seldom occur within the area of a lake, but smaller differences are common.

Seiches have been extensively studied by Forel [4] in Switzerland and by Murray and Pullar [17] in Scotland. Whipple [28] quotes the following formula:

$$t = \frac{2L}{3,600 \sqrt{dg}}$$

in which t = time, in hours.

L = length of the lake (or width if there are transverse seiches), in feet.

d = mean depth of lake along the axis of observation, in feet.

g = acceleration of gravity (32.16).

Whipple states that the application of this formula to Lake Erie gives a computed seiche period of 14.4 hours and that the observed periods have ranged from 14 to 16 hours.

ICE ON LAKES

Wind and wave action may prevent the complete freezing of large lakes when the air temperature falls below 32°F. On small lakes or in the sheltered portions of large lakes ice forms when air temperatures fall below 32°F.

When ice has formed a further decrease in temperature causes shrinkage cracks in the ice or breaks the shore contact, and additional water freezes in the cracks and around the shore. The later expansion when the temperature rises causes buckling of the ice or crowds the ice up the shore slopes. Such shore crowding exerts sufficient force to affect structures along the shore (Figure VI-1) and to push lake-bed

FIG. VI-1.—Concrete bench mark on shore of Utah Lake, Utah, overturned by action of shore ice.

materials shoreward, forming ridges or bars above the water line composed of materials from the shallower part of the lake bed. Such ice ramparts may be several feet in height and may contain large boulders.

STRATIFICATION IN LAKES

Stratification of the water in deep lakes may occur whenever there are differences in density at different depths.   Such differences in density may be caused by differences in temperature, suspended silt, or dissolved salts.   They may be transient or permanent, depending upon the depth of the lake, wind movement, or temperature changes.   They may be caused by differences in the quality of the inflowing water or by changes in the water while stored in the lake.   The factors governing stratification in lakes and in reservoirs are similar, and observations from either source are useful in determining the principles involved.   The depth of water and the annual change in volume of water usually vary more widely in reservoirs than in lakes.

EFFECT OF TEMPERATURE

The temperature of the surface water in lakes fluctuates with the temperature of the air with which it is in contact and follows the seasonal cycle of the air temperature.   Water is a slow conductor of heat, and heat received from the air penetrates slowly and only to moderate depths by conduction.   Greater circulation of heat occurs from convection, resulting from differences in density caused by differences in temperature. Wave action causes a mixing of water and distribution of heat to the depths affected by the waves.   The temperature of lakes is also affected by the temperature of inflowing water.

As pointed out by Humphreys [13, pp. 586–587] temperature changes in lakes vary with the minimum air temperatures reached during the year. Where the temperature of the surface water does not fall to 39.2°F., the temperature of maximum density, less turnover occurs than where the temperature falls below 39.2°.

Surface temperature falling below 39.2°F.—When lakes whose surface temperature has been above 39.2°F. during the summer begin to become cool in the fall, the density of the surface water increases, and it sinks through the lighter lower water, causing a turnover to the depth to which the water has been warmed above 39.2° during the summer.   Water below this depth will remain closely at 39.2° continuously.   With further cooling of the surface water below 39.2° expansion occurs and the cooler surface water remains on top, where it may freeze if temperatures fall below 32°. Continued lowering below the freezing point results in increased thickness of ice without further temperature changes in the deeper water.   Water just below ice remains closely at 32°.

In the spring, as the temperature of the surface water rises to 39.2°, the increased density causes another turnover, the surface water sinking through the cooler deeper water and the cooler water rising.   When the

time during which the temperature of the surface water rises from 32°
to 39.2° is short, a full vertical turnover may not take place before the
surface water rises above 39.2° and, becoming lighter than the cooler underlying water, remains on the surface.

These two annual temperature changes are generally called the fall
and spring turnover. The movement due to changes in temperature
and density is further complicated by wave action. Shallow lakes generally show fairly uniform temperatures throughout their depth; in deep
lakes the principal variations are usually confined to the upper 200 feet.
Below this depth water remains at 39.2° in areas where air temperatures
fall to or below this temperature.

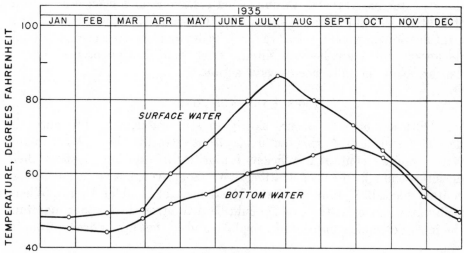

Fig. VI-2.—Variations in the temperature of water in the Elephant Butte Reservoir in 1935. The
depth of water ranged from 105 to 120 feet. (*After I. E. Houk* [12].)

These seasonal turnovers are important in connection with water
supplies obtained from lakes. Oxidation of organic matter proceeds at
different rates at different depths. These vertical currents may result
in water drawn from some levels being, at times, less desirable than water
drawn from other levels.

Surface temperatures remaining above 39.2°F.—Where the temperature
of the surface water does not fall to 39.2°F., the temperature of the deep
water should be equal to the minimum air temperatures, as such temperatures give the maximum density water will have for the particular locality.
There will be no spring turnover, because the surface water becomes lighter
as it becomes warmer. Changes in temperature of the water will be
limited to the depths to which conduction and wave action cause a rise
above the minimum winter temperature. This type of variation is illustrated by the results of observations in the Elephant Butte Reservoir
shown in Fig. VI-2 [12, pp. 523–527]. These results may be affected also

by the temperature of the inflowing water, which contains silt and tends to remain on the bottom. They show a seasonal change of about 20° at a depth of 100 feet.

EFFECT OF SILT

Water containing suspended silt has a higher density and tends to flow along the bottom of a lake that it may enter. Such muddy water has passed through reservoirs with only slight mixing with the previously stored clear water. The heavily silted water tends to remain in the bottom of the reservoir. Such heavily silted water or mud occupied a depth of 50 feet against the face of Bouler Dam within 2 years of its use for storage. Silted water has traveled through long reservoirs and been drawn from the outlets without material dilution by the ponded clear water [7]. Such stratification may enable clear water to be drawn from a reservoir, although its lower depths are heavily silted. Such stratification occurs only at depths below the influence of wave action.

EFFECT OF SALT CONTENT

Diffusion of salts occurs slowly in still water, and differences in density resulting from this factor may cause stratification. Most inland water supplies contain insufficient impurities in solution to affect their densities enough to cause stratification. Some vertical variations in salt content have been found in Lake Mead back of Boulder Dam. Where such variations exist the draft should be made from levels that maintain the most desirable conditions in the lake and in the supply drawn from it.

CHANGES IN LAKE LEVELS

Lakes with outlets fluctuate with variations in their inflow as it is regulated by the capacity of the outlets. Lakes on streams act as equalizers of the runoff; pondage in the lake reduces the peak stream flows. Such pondage may also increase the low flow of the stream unless the evaporation from the lake exceeds the effect of the pondage. The effects of pondage depend on the constrictions of the outlet as well as on the variations in inflow. Pondage in a large number of small lakes well distributed over the drainage area may be as effective as pondage in a large lake.

Many lakes are a part of the general water table of the area in which they occur. Such lakes occupy depressions below the ground water level, and their outflow and evaporation are supplied in whole or in part by movement of ground water into the lake. These lakes reflect the variations in level of the adjacent ground water. Many lakes of this type occur in the Middle West and rise and fall with the variations in the local rainfall.

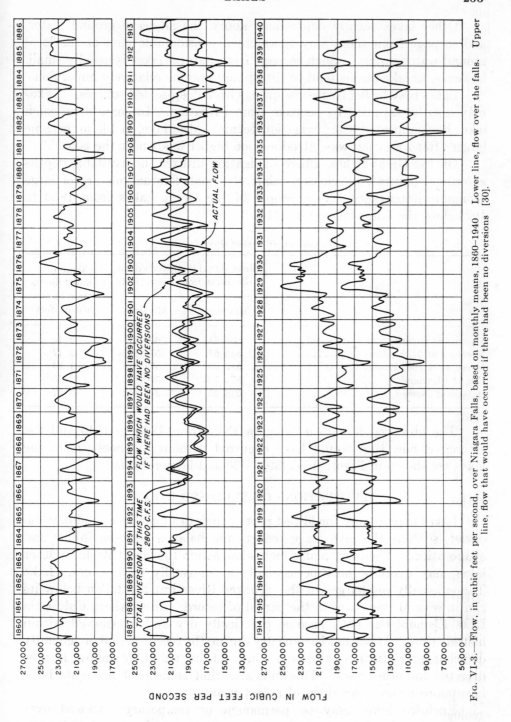

FLOW IN CUBIC FEET PER SECOND

FIG. VI-3.—Flow, in cubic feet per second, over Niagara Falls, based on monthly means, 1860–1940 Lower line, flow over the falls. Upper line, flow that would have occurred if there had been no diversions [30].

Other lakes occupy depressions above the adjacent ground water, and seepage from them may represent a considerable part of the local ground-water supply. Such seepage from natural lakes is usually small, however, as lake basins tend to silt up and become relatively impervious.

Lakes may be fed by fissure springs from deep-seated sources. Lakes may also be supplied by seepage from irrigation. In some areas such lakes have appeared after irrigation began. Mud lake, in Idaho, became larger after irrigation was introduced on higher lands near the lake.

On the Great Lakes, where navigation utilizes the available depths at critical points very closely, relatively small fluctuations are of large economic importance. The records of the Great Lakes from 1860 to 1924 show the following results [11]:

Fluctuations in level of Great Lakes

Lake and locality	Mean monthly altitude during the navigation season (feet)		Maximum annual fluctuation in one year in (feet)
	Maximum	Minimum	
Superior at Superior and Marquette........	603.81	600.57	2.15
Michigan at Milwaukee...................	583.57	578.54	2.17
Huron at Harbor Beach..................	583.66	578.62	1.94
Erie at Cleveland......................	574.52	570.63	2.50
Ontario at Oswego.....................	248.95	243.41	3.47

The observed flow over Niagara Falls from 1860 to 1940 and the estimated flow that would have occurred without diversions from the lakes are shown in Figure VI-3 [30]. [30 and later records.]

FLUCTUATIONS OF ENCLOSED LAKES

Lakes may occupy the lowest part of their drainage areas and have no outlet, so that the lake stage reflects the balance between inflow and evaporation. There are many such lakes within the Great Basin. Other lakes may overflow only occasionally at unusually high stages. Lake Tahoe usually discharges to the Truckee River but has fallen below its rim in several years within the period of record. In southern California Lake Elsinore has both become practically dry and overflowed within historic time. It has not become dry during the recent period of generally deficient precipitation, although much of its tributary inflow is now diverted for other uses. This indicates that some past droughts have been more severe than those of recent years.

Enclosed lakes may be permanent or temporary. Viewed over geologic time few lakes have been permanent or without major changes in their volume. Even within historic time much fluctuation has occurred.

Some depressions receiving adjacent runoff are broad, flat areas on which the tributary inflow spreads thinly and evaporates quickly. Such lakes may form during the months of larger runoff and become entirely dry later in the season, leaving bare clay flats, frequently crusted with alkali. These occur mainly in desert areas that have small amounts of widely variable precipitation. In occasional years the runoff may be sufficient to carry the lake through the entire season; in others practically no inflow may be received. Silver Lake, in the lower Mojave River drainage basin, has contained water at infrequent intervals. Records of the presence of such a lake are found in some early reports [29]. It was

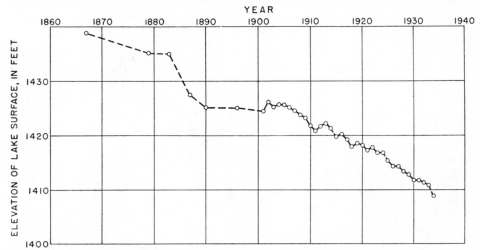

Fig. VI-4.—Fluctuations of Devils Lake, N. D. From U. S. Geol. Survey water-supply papers. Graph based on the highest stage for each year of record.

continuously dry for a long period prior to 1916, when it filled again, but it disappeared shortly and has remained dry to date.

Devils Lake, in North Dakota, is an enclosed lake that has shrunk from an area of nearly 75,000 acres in 1883 to about 6,000 acres. Its fluctuations since 1867 are shown in Figure VI-4. The lowering of this lake is the result of the smaller rainfall on its drainage area in recent years and of cultivation of its tributary lands.

ENCLOSED LAKES OF THE GREAT BASIN AS CLIMATIC INDICATORS

The fluctuations of enclosed lakes afford a good index of climatic variations. In periods of more than average inflow the lakes rise until the evaporation from the increased area equals the inflow. In periods of less than average inflow evaporation is supplied from the accumulated water in the lake, and the lake lowers. Some lakes, such as Great Salt Lake, have generally flat shore slopes, and the lake area changes rapidly with changes in level. Such lakes equalize variations in inflow with small variations in level.   Other lakes have steeper side slopes, and variations in inflow are absorbed mainly in variations in storage in the lake.   In such a lake the fluctuations are larger and the lake is a more sensitive index of inflow.   Mono Lake is an illustration of this type.

Nearly all the enclosed lakes in the Great Basin are now affected by the diversion of their inflow for irrigation or other uses.   Present fluctuations of these lakes are not directly comparable with those of the period prior to such diversions.   In some of the lakes allowance can be made for the effect of such diversions.

Although systematic records of the fluctuation of these lakes were not begun in the early years of western settlement, some direct and indirect

Fig. VI-5.—Trees at south end of Eagle Lake, Calif., submerged prior to 1917 as a result of a rise in lake level.

records are available from which the general fluctuations can be determined.   There are some records prior to 1860.   Fairly continuous observations have been made on Great Salt Lake since 1850.   For more recent periods, when diversion of the inflow has affected these lakes, other climatic records are available.

In addition to direct records of lake level there are many comments in early diaries or reports on the conditions of enclosed lakes which enable their levels at those times to be determined.   Such indirect records are much more tangible in regard to lake stages than similar records on stream flow.

The climate of the localities of many enclosed lakes in the Great Basin is too arid to permit the growth of trees on their margins, such tree growth surrounds some of these lakes at higher altitudes.   During the period of generally larger runoff in the later part of the nineteenth century

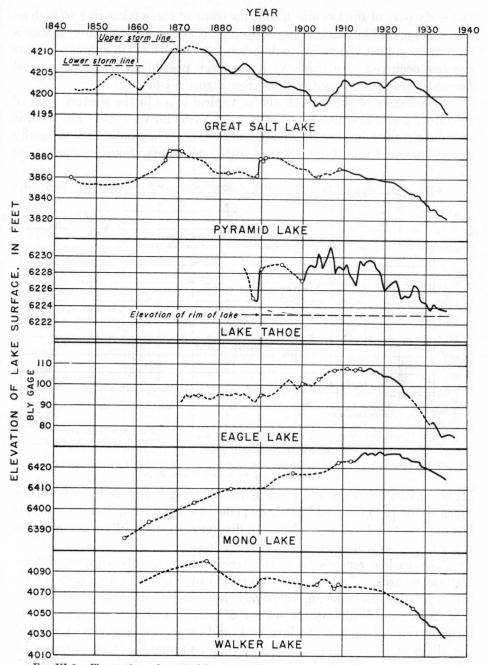

Fig. VI-6.—Fluctuations of certain lakes in the Great Basin, based on historical records. Only seasonal high stages are plotted, even where detailed records are available. Periods for which records are incomplete are shown by a dashed line; individual records during these periods are shown by circles. In recent years the levels of all lakes shown except Tahoe and Mono Lakes have been affected by diversions of their inflow [8].

and early part of the twentieth century some of these lakes rose so high as to submerge and kill such trees. From their age and the altitude at which these trees grew it is possible to determine the length of time since a similar rise has occurred. In this way it has been possible to estimate general fluctuations for 200 to 300 years. See Figure VI-5.

The results of these methods for typical lakes in the western part of the Great Basin are illustrated in Figures VI-6 and VI-7 [8]. The records of the different lakes are relatively consistent. They indicate a generally upward trend from about 1860 to 1915, when the stages reached were

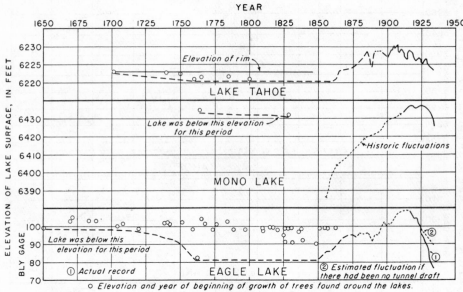

FIG. VI-7.—Fluctuations of Tahoe, Mono, and Eagle Lakes, as indicated by age and location of submerged trees and by historical records [8].

higher than those that had been reached during the preceding 200 years. Since about 1915 the trend has been generally downward, and the lowering has occurred on lakes not subject to diversion of their inflow as well as on those now affected by such use.

The earlier records from the trees can be partly supported from historic records. Surveys and comments in the 1840's and early 1850's are consistent in showing relatively low stages of these lakes. Such records include Williamson's survey of part of Goose Lake in 1849, the location of roads across the lake bed, and comments in diaries regarding the alkali conditions surrounding the lake; Frémont's diary covering his trip along Pyramid Lake in 1844; surveys on Mono Lake in 1856 and 1857; and comments in various diaries on the conditions surrounding Humboldt Lake.

These results are of interest in regard to the fluctuations of the lakes themselves. They are of greater importance as an index of the variations in water supply to which this area is subject. The average runoff necessary to support the generally rising stages from 1860 to 1915 was materially larger than the runoff that has occurred since 1915 [9, pp. 572–574]. As these periods are relatively very long in relation to the equalization of stream flow by constructed storage, irrigation here will need to be limited to the area that can be maintained during periods similar to 1916–1935 if severe shortages in supply are to be avoided. Expansion of use on the basis of the supply during the more favorable periods can be expected to result only in severe shortage in the deficient periods. As direct stream records were largely begun during the later part of this favorable period, some early estimates of water supply were more liberal than recent years could support, and some reductions in the areas irrigated have been required with resulting hardships. The longer record of fluctuations on these lakes furnishes a basis on which future similar losses can be avoided or reduced.

SWAMPS

Swamps may be regarded as shallow lakes where the small depth of water and the slight range of fluctuation permits the growth of aquatic vegetation. Swamps occur mainly in areas of flat gradient and narrow stream channels. On steeper slopes vegetation may be sufficiently dense to retard runoff and prevent channel erosion, resulting in swamp conditions. Swamps tend to become filled from the growth of vegetation and from silting. Many swamps are old lakes in the later stages of filling.

Swamps are generally divided into inland or fresh-water swamps and coastal or sea-water swamps [18]. The inland swamps include lake swamps resulting from the filling of lakes and growth of aquatic vegetation; river swamps along flood plains and deltas subject to frequent overflow; spring swamps formed by the discharge of springs; flat-land swamps on poorly drained land, such as the Great Dismal Swamp in Virginia and North Carolina and swamps in the Everglades of Florida; and raised bogs on flat lands of small runoff where precipitation exceeds the evaporation. Coastal swamps are frequently formed between high and low tides.

There is no close demarcation between lakes, swamps, and marshes. Shaler [25, pp. 261–346] has made the following classification between marine marshes and fresh-water swamps:

Marine marshes......................
Above mean tide:
  Grass marshes.
  Mangrove marshes.
Below mean tide:
  Mud banks.
  Eel-grass areas.

Fresh-water swamps..................... $\begin{cases} \text{River swamps:} \\ \quad \text{Terrace.} \\ \quad \text{Estuarine.} \\ \text{Lake swamps:} \\ \quad \text{Lake margins.} \\ \quad \text{Quaking bogs.} \\ \text{Upland swamps:} \\ \quad \text{Wet woods.} \\ \quad \text{Climbing bogs.} \\ \text{Ablation swamps.} \end{cases}$

Shaler applies the term "marsh" to marine or salt-water inundated areas and "swamps" to similar fresh-water areas.

In 1850 Congress passed the Swamp and Overflow Land Act, providing a special procedure for the acquirement of title to public lands of these types. Under this act about 65,000,000 acres has been transferred to 15 States and in turn transferred by the States to private owners. There is little present activity under this act; only 1,100 acres was patented in 1935–36.

The 15th Census reports for 1929 that 23,000,000 acres of swamp land not previously in farms had been drained at a cost of $210,000,000. This represented 27 percent of all the lands drained in the United States, the remaining areas having been drained for the improvement of lands already in farms, the removal of seepage and alkali resulting from irrigation, or protection against overflow. Enterprises reporting the reclamation of swamp land as their principal purpose were located mainly in the coastal region between Virginia and Texas, in the Mississippi Delta, in Wisconsin, and in northern Minnesota.

EFFECTS OF REDUCTION IN LAKE LEVELS

There has been a general reduction in the areas of lakes, both from natural causes during years of less than average precipitation and from artificial causes, such as the deepening of outlets and drainage of lake areas. Such changes affect the water-supply conditions of the streams supplied by the lakes. Reduction in lake levels due to deficiencies in precipitation cannot be controlled and will be adjusted when periods of larger rainfall occur. Such lake lowering may make available a larger storage capacity near the level of the lake outlet and have a beneficial effect on the control of flood flows. The low-water flow is reduced as the lakes lower.

Artificial lowering of lakes to make their areas available for agriculture reduces the lake capacity and its equalizing effect on floods. Lowering of lake outlets with control structures changes the lake into a controlled reservoir, so that its water supply can be conserved for use. On many lakes topographic conditions are such that storage can be obtained more economically by lowering in this way than by raising the lake. The reservoir constructed on Lake Cle Elum, in Washington, was formed partly by lowering the outlet and partly by a dam.

Lakes are favorable sites for recreation and are extensively used for summer homes and pleasure resorts. A small range of fluctuation is essential for beach and dock purposes. Lowering of some lakes has resulted in depreciation of the value of their recreational facilities.

Reduction in lake areas has affected wild fowl, both for breeding areas and in migration. Substitute water areas have been constructed in some places to provide for wild-fowl needs.

EFFECT OF LAKES AND SWAMPS ON CLIMATE

Lakes and swamps return moisture to the air by evaporation. Changes in their areas affect the amount of evaporation and runoff and may change the amount of precipitation. Large lakes or swamps affect some elements of the climate of adjacent areas. Air passing over water areas is cooled in summer and warmed in winter. Fruit crops can be successfully grown on some areas around the Great Lakes toward which the wind blows from the lakes; where the wind blows from the land such crops may not be practicable.

Drainage of swamps makes additional land available for agriculture and aids in malaria and pest control but may destroy areas used by fish and water fowl. Agricultural and public-health interests in swamp reclamation may be opposed to wild-life interests in swamp preservation. Drainage of lakes and swamps may increase the rate of flood runoff and decrease the later low-water flow by removing or reducing the retarding areas.

Reduction in lake and swamp areas reduces evaporation from water surfaces but does not entirely eliminate it, as the exposed drained areas supply moisture to the air by evaporation of soil moisture and transpiration by plants. Although drainage of such areas may affect the total runoff from a drainage basin, the factors affecting runoff are so numerous and complex that very careful records would be required to show differences resulting from any one factor. Drainage of water areas has usually been accompanied by other changes in use in the drainage basin, and any changes in runoff have been the composite result of all the factors involved.

Increasing lake areas may increase evaporation and in turn increase precipitation. In the general rainfall cycle all moisture reaching the surface of the earth is returned to the air as vapor or eventually reaches the ocean as surface or underground flow. It is only by changing the moisture entering the air over land surfaces that the total moisture received by the air can be changed, as runoff reaching the ocean does not essentially affect its evaporating area or rate of evaporation. It has been estimated that the moisture capacity of the air under usual conditions is equivalent to a depth of water of about 1 inch.   Consequently any material change in the quantity of vapor discharged into the air must be reflected relatively soon in a change in the moisture returning to the earth as precipitation.   Even with such slight storage capacity for moisture in the atmosphere, the effect of changes in the evaporation from lakes and swamps cannot be definitely traced to changes in precipitation on specific areas.   Such increased moisture from the land may be precipitated on the ocean.

Runoff generally represents less than one-half of the precipitation. In humid areas it may exceed this proportion; in arid areas it is much less. If only 20 percent of the precipitation on a drainage area has been leaving that area as runoff, no increase in water areas can increase the evaporation from the area by more than 25 percent.   As water areas can seldom be increased to control all runoff fully, the practicable increase on such areas cannot result in a major increase in the moisture entering the air or in a major change in rainfall.   The irrigation of about 500,000 acres and the increased area of Salton Sea resulting from the diversions of Colorado River water to the Imperial Valley have not materially modified the local rainfall, which has remained at 2 or 4 inches a year.

Changes in lake areas or uses of water in an area having no outlet do not affect the total moisture entering the air in such a basin.   In the Great Basin all precipitation has been returned to the air since the last overflow of Lake Bonneville.   Diversions of the inflow of Great Basin lakes have reduced the amount of water reaching the lake areas and changed the localities at which the moisture enters the air but have not changed the total amount.   Such diversions result in lower average lake stages.   The lake fluctuations equalize variations in inflow.   In any year all precipitation in the Great Basin has been returned to the air except the relatively small amounts represented by differences in lake and ground-water storage.   There have been no consistent variations in rainfall in the Great Basin traceable to the increased use of water.

REFERENCES

1. Birge, E. A., and Juday, C., Inland lakes of Wisconsin: Wisconsin Geol. and Nat. Hist. Survey Bull. 27, 137 pp., 1914.

2. Diller, J. S., A late volcanic eruption in northern California and its peculiar lava: U. S. Geol. Survey Bull. 79, 33 pp., 1891.

3. Emerson, F. C., Gros Ventre landslide dam: Eng. News-Record, vol. 98, No. 21, p. 878, 1927.

4. Forel, F. A., Le Léman, Monographie limnologique, 3 vols., 539, 646, 675 pp., 1892, 1895, 1904.

5. Fuller, M. L., The New Madrid earthquake: U. S. Geol. Survey Bull. 494, 119 pp., 1912.

6. Gilbert, G. K., Lake Bonneville: U. S. Geol. Survey Mon. 1, 438 pp., 1890.

7. Grover, N. C., and Howard, C. S., The passage of turbid water through Lake Mead: Am. Soc. Civil Eng. Proc., April 1937, pp. 643–655.

8. Harding, S. T., Changes in lake levels in Great Basin area: Civil Eng., vol. 5, No. 2, pp. 87–90, 1935.

9. Harding, S. T., Variations in runoff of California streams: Civil Eng., vol. 5, No. 9, 1935.

10. Hayford, J. F:, Effect of winds and of barometric pressure on the Great Lakes: Carnegie Inst. Washington Pub. 317, 133 pp., 1922.

11. Horton, R. E., Report of Engineering Board of Review of Sanitary District of Chicago on lake-lowering controversy and a program of remedial measures, pt. 3, app. 2, Hydrology of the Great Lakes, 415 pp., 1927.

12. Houk, I. E., Water temperatures in reservoirs: Am. Geophys. Union Trans. 1937, pt. 2, pp. 523–527.

13. Humphreys, W. J., Temperature of deep water: Monthly Weather Rev.. vol. 42. December 1924.

14. Jones, J. C., Antevs, Ernst, and Huntington, Ellsworth, Quaternary climates: Carnegie Inst. Washington Pub. 352, 212 pp., 1925.

15. Lawson, A. C., Geomorphogeny of the upper Kern Basin: California Univ. Pub. in Geology, vol. 3, No. 15, 1904.

16. Mead, D. W., Hydrology: 626 pp., 1919.

17. Murray, J., and Pullar, L., Bathymetrical survey of the Scottish fresh-water lochs 6 vols., 1910.

18. Ries, H., and Watson, T. L., Elements of engineering geology, 354 pp., 1921.

19. Russell, I. C., Geological history of Lake Lahonton, a Quaternary lake of northwestern Nevada: U. S. Geol. Survey Mon. 11, 288 pp., 1885.

20. Russell, I. C., The Quaternary history of Mono Valley, Calif.: U. S. Geol. Survey 8th Ann. Rept., pt. 1, pp. 261–394, 1889.

21. Russell, I. C., Geological Reconnaissance in central Washington: U. S. Geol. Survey Bull. 108, 108 pp., 1893.

22. Russell, I. C., Lakes of North America, 120 pp., 1895.

23. Russell, R. J., Landslide lakes of the northwest Great Basin: California Univ. Publ. in Geography, vol. 2, No. 7, 1927.

24. Salisbury, R. D., Physiography, 3d ed., 665 pp., 1929.

25. Shaler, N. S., General account of the fresh-water morasses of the United States: U. S. Geol. Survey 10th Ann. Rept., pt. 1, pp. 255–339, 1890.

26. Tarr, R. S., College physiography, 812 pp., 1915.

27. Upham, Warren, The glacial Lake Agassiz: U. S. Geol. Survey, Mon. 25, 658 pp., 1895.

28. Whipple, G. E., The microscopy of drinking water, revised by G. M. Fair and M. C. Whipple, 563 pp., 1927.

29. Williamson, R. S., Explorations and surveys for railroad route-explorations in California: vol. 5, 370 pp., 1853.

30. Preservation and improvement of the scenic beauty of the Niagara Falls and rapids: 71st Cong., 2d sess., S. Doc. 128, 355 pp., 1931.

CHAPTER VII

INFILTRATION

Leroy K. Sherman[1] and George W. Musgrave[2]

Infiltration is the movement of water from the surface of the ground into the soil. In a rainstorm the infiltration normally begins at a high rate and decreases to a minimum (designated f_c) as the rain continues. During the storm the precipitation may be disposed of in several ways: (1) interception by the canopy of vegetal cover; (2) retention in the depressions upon the land surface; (3) infiltration; (4) evaporation, which is, however, very small during the course of a storm; (5) precipitation directly upon the watercourses; and (6) surface runoff from the land. Therefore, when snow storage or melting is not involved, the infiltration is equal to the precipitation minus the other five losses.

Infiltration is often viewed by the hydraulic engineer as a loss and by the agriculturist as a gain. It is the process that provides water for nearly all terrestrial plants and for much of the animal life; it furnishes the ground water for wells and most of the stream flow in periods of fair weather; it reduces floods and soil erosion. Infiltration is therefore a process of vital economic importance.

METHODS OF MEASURING INFILTRATION

Various methods have been used in attempts to measure infiltration. These methods have differed in accord with differing purposes and available facilities. Inasmuch as soil structure largely controls the rate of infiltration, it is usually necessary to conduct measurements upon soil in place. Laboratory or other determinations of infiltration of soil of modified structure are likely to give results differing widely from those that occur in the field.

Among the various methods that have been used to obtain comparative results are: (1) measurement of the rate of intake of water on areas defined by concentric rings of various sizes; (2) measurement of the rate of intake of water on areas defined by tubes with differing technique by different workers; (3) measurement of the rate of intake of water on areas defined by irrigation practices, particularly flooding; (4) measurement of

---

[1] Consulting engineer, Chicago, Ill.

[2] Soil conservationist, Head, Infiltration Studies, Soil Conservation Service, United States Department of Agriculture, Washington, D. C.

runoff of water applied to small sample areas by rainfall simulators of various kinds; (5) measurement of precipitation compared with surface runoff.

In the use of concentric rings a series of rings of suitable size (usually ranging from 9 to 36 inches in diameter) are pressed a few inches into the selected soil profile, and water is added at such a rate that a constant depth is maintained on all units. The purpose of the outer ring is primarily to provide a buffer or wetted area around the inner ring which is the critical or test area. Several replicates (15 or more) are usually required to sample soil variability properly on a given site, and enough sites are used to represent the entire area of soil or land-use condition on which information is desired. The rate of application necessary to maintain the predetermined depth of water within the rings (preferably 1 centimeter or less) is the rate which is taken as infiltration.

Tubes, which have been employed by various workers such as Auten [1], Müntz [18], and Musgrave [19], are used in an essentially similar manner to rings, differing only in the greater depth to which they are inserted in the soil. As they may penetrate the less permeable subsoil, exterior buffer or wetted areas are unnecessary. A constant head of water is maintained upon the soil surface, and its rate of replenishment indicates the rate of intake by the soil. Because of variability of soils from point to point, a number of replicates are necessary.

Flood irrigation has been used to measure or compare different areas with respect to their infiltration rates. Where the amount of water used is definitely known, and particularly where its rate of application can be measured, the time required for a given quantity to enter the profile may be determined.

Rainfall simulators of various types have recently been used to determine infiltration rates on sample areas lying within and representing larger areas about which information is desired. Various sizes of plots have been tested, ranging from 1 square foot to 435.6 square feet (0.01 acre) in area. Artificial rainfall is applied under a standardized procedure, so that in addition to a known rate of application there is some control of the pattern of distribution, the drop size and its distance of fall, and similar essential items. The rate of rainfall and runoff is then determined and the hydrograph plotted and analyzed. Equipment of this kind has undergone frequent revision of design in recent years, and neither equipment nor technique is yet completely standardized.

Although the percolation phenomenon differs from that of infiltration comparative studies have been made in which samples of soil have been placed in suitable containers, usually at known densities, and the rates of percolation determined. Also lysimeters have been used to obtain comparative information on rates of percolation for different soils and soils of different treatment. In most of the early lysimeter work the soils were added to the container after screening and mixing and hence had an artificial structural arrangement. Though quantitative data from these studies cannot be regarded as precisely representing rates of infiltration under natural conditions, they nevertheless frequently give information of much comparative value.

On a drainage basin the rate of infiltration can be approximately determined for various storms if stream-gaging stations have been installed, and if there are adequate records of both the amount and intensity of rainfall on the various subdivisions of the basin. The precision of the determination depends largely upon the adequacy of the records. Frequently the limiting factor is that of an adequate rainfall record, because rain gages are seldom distributed in a manner to sample fairly the precipitation of a large drainage basin. Some difficulties also arise in the measurement of such other factors as the amount of canopy interception, the amount of evaporation, and the amount of surface detention. Inasmuch, however, as these amounts are usually small, it is believed that no great error is introduced by their omission or approximation.

FACTORS THAT AFFECT INFILTRATION

The factors that affect both the amount and the rate of infiltration are primarily those which characterize the pore sizes of the soil and their relative permanency. The soil may be regarded as a porous medium, the passages and pores of which cover a wide range of sizes and fluctuate from time to time within certain limits according to its chemical and physical properties. However, different soils, each varying in porosity from day to day, may be distinctly different with respect to the range through which the fluctuations occur. In general, the distribution of pore sizes of a soil is dependent upon (1) the sizes of particles or single grains that make up the body of the soil; (2) the arrangement of the particles with reference to their position; and (3) the degree of aggregation of the individual particles and the extent to which the aggregates behave like large individual particles.

Soil particles, commonly ranging in size from coarse sand to fine sand, to silt, and to clay, are usually found in various combinations and mixtures of these sizes in any given profile. As porous media soils are highly complex and have correspondingly complex effects upon the movement of internal water. Other things being equal, soils composed solely of large single grains will have pores of greater diameter than soils made up of fine particles only. Thus it is to be expected that the infiltration of water into sands may be greater than into clays. However, this is not true except where the only difference between the soils is that of particle size. A soil composed of single grains of uniform size obviously is different in porosity characteristics from a soil having a mixture of two or more sizes. As has been well demonstrated by Slichter and many others, the arrangement of the particles may be such as to provide either comparatively large spaces between grains or much smaller ones. In a medium that is composed of both large and small particles there may be an intermingling of particles of differing size and an arrangement such that a very dense and compact structure exists. In many soils something of this kind is found in the upper portion of the subsoil, where compact zones usually occur. The discussion of grain size and its influence upon the height and rate of capillary rise in chapter IX is pertinent to a consideration of these effects upon porosity.

Where individual particles are well aggregated an entirely different situation is found. A single aggregate may behave very much like a single grain of similar size. Many soils, a mechanical analysis of which would disclose that they are comprised largely of silt and clay—that is, particles of small size—may be aggregated to such an extent as to permit many comparatively large spaces between the aggregates. This condition is particularly true of virgin soils and soils that have been subjected to good management practices. It accounts for the fact that many forest and pasture soils have comparatively high infiltration rates.

It is clear, therefore, that the rate of infiltration is not conditioned upon the total porosity so much as it is upon the numbers of large pores that exist throughout the medium. The total porosity of the soil may well serve to indicate the potential capacity for water, but it does not necessarily indicate the rate at which the water may move into the soil.

DYNAMIC CHARACTERISTICS OF SOIL STRUCTURE AND POROSITY

The structure of the soil does not represent a permanent or fixed condition. Soils which in a dry state may have a favorable structure often undergo a marked reduction in effective size of pores during the course of a storm or from the effects of antecedent storms.

Such reductions in pore sizes are due primarily to (1) the swelling of colloids, (2) the infiltration of soil particles, (3) the slaking of aggregates by water, and (4) the occupancy of space by water.

Nearly all soils except pure sands contain some colloids. The hydration of colloids results in a marked swelling, the converse of which is the common cause for the shrinkage and cracking often observed in the field. Varying amounts of time are required by different soils and colloids to reach maximum expansion. One of the reasons why moisture in soils reduces the rate of infiltration is undoubtedly the swelling that occurs as a result of the hydration of the colloids.

Another cause of the reduction of effective size of pores by rains is the infiltration of soil particles. As water moves downward through the orifices it frequently carries small particles of silt and sediment of various sizes, which lodge at a point of constriction, tending thus to affect greatly the rate of infiltration. Lowdermilk [16] has shown that this action is very effective in reducing infiltration.

The slaking of aggregates during the course of the storm, causing their disintegration, likewise is effective in reducing the effective sizes of pores. The stability of aggregates in water has been shown by many workers to vary widely. In some soils the aggregates are very stable, and comparatively few of them are disintegrated during a storm. In other soils most of the aggregates are unstable and readily disintegrate during a storm, contributing thus to the formation of a dense soil profile.

The water of antecedent rains or that of the early part of a storm may gradually fill the voids between the particles and reduce the capacity for further additions of water. Much depends upon the natural provision in the soil profile for the movement of water to lower levels. In some soils a compact, dense zone may greatly limit the rate of downward movement of water, and under this condition the voids above the dense zone may be rather quickly filled. Under other conditions there may be opportunity for downward movement to considerable depths, and a comparatively small proportion of the voids may become filled with water. Inasmuch as a soil profile 3 feet in depth may have a capacity for nearly 18 inches of water, which is very much more than occurs in ordinary storms, it may be assumed that the moisture-holding capacity alone is seldom the chief factor in limiting infiltration but that the other factors above mentioned are the more common causes.

The entire soil profile in its several zones has various characteristics so that any one zone may differ widely from another in particle size, degree of aggregation, and pore size. Although commonly the surface soil is more permeable than the subsoil, this is by no means universally true, and successive zones may represent any order of permeability. Inasmuch as the least permeable zone controls the final infiltration rate (f_c) it may be considered to be the critical one, and its depth to be primarily determinative of the average infiltration rate (f_{av}). Thus where the least permeable zone occurs at the surface f_c and f_{av} may be closely similar. Where it occurs at considerable depth (3 feet or more) the average infiltration rate may greatly exceed the final minimum rate.

TIME IN RELATION TO THE AMOUNT OF INFILTRATION

A still further factor that doubtless affects the amount of infiltration is the time element. The time available for the infiltration of surface water is contingent largely upon surface and topographic conditions. On uneven surfaces—for example, land that is contoured or bears tillage marks—there may be considerable surface storage of water. Likewise,

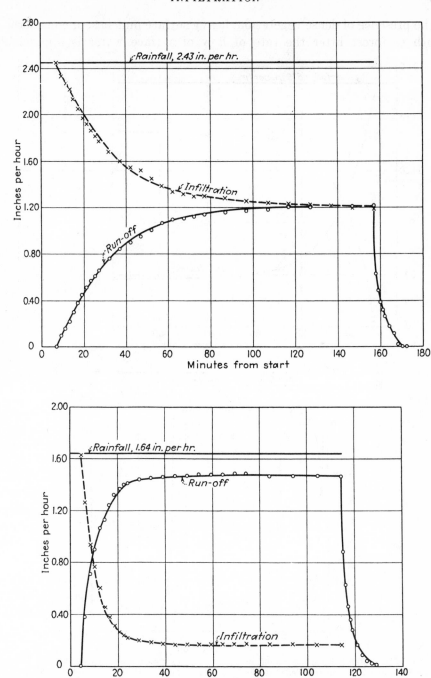

Fig. VII-1.—Rainfall, surface runoff, and infiltration on lands subjected to poor and good grazing management in the Concho River Basin, Tex. (Data from infiltrometer tests by G. W. Musgrave.)

in the presence of dense vegetation, heavy surface mulches, or considerable depth of forest litter the rate of flow of surface water is appreciably

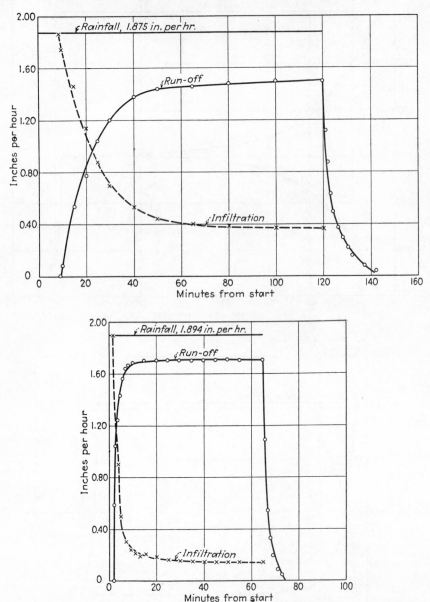

Fig. VII-2.—Rainfall, surface runoff, and infiltration on forested land (pine 55 years old) and on bare abandoned land in the Tallahatchie River Basin, Miss.   (Data from infiltrometer tests by G. W. Musgrave.)

retarded.   A similar condition, although not as marked in effect, is found in the degree of slope of the land surface.   On level land or very gentle slopes the rate of discharge is appreciably below the rate on steep slopes.

Existing evidence on the effect of slope is rather meager, as systematic studies of its effect have not been recorded in the literature. It is clear, however, that other things being equal an increase in the time available for infiltration results in an increase in its total amount, and the evidence available (see Figures VII-1 and VII-2) shows that on different land surfaces the effect may be appreciable.

TYPE OF LAND USAGE IN RELATION TO INFILTRATION

The type of land usage in its effect upon infiltration has received considerable attention in recent years, with the result that, particularly for small areas and average storms, a considerable body of experimental evidence has been accumulated [7, 8, 12, 20]. For large areas less information is available, it being more difficult to segregate the single factor of land usage on drainage basins of considerable size on which variations in slope, soil, and other factors also prevail.

The commonly observed higher infiltration and lower runoff for virgin soils, native grass, forest, or rotated-crop land, in contrast to low infiltration and high runoff for intensively cultivated land, is fully in harmony with the known effects of these practices upon soil structure. The Ohio Agricultural Experiment Station [21], reporting upon tests covering 32 years, showed the tremendous loss in organic matter that has occurred as a result of the continuous growing of corn. Bradfield [4] has shown the effect of cultivation in destroying organic residues and natural structural aggregates, and the tendency under these conditions for soil particles to assume gradually a position of closer packing. He states that "in many cases from 25 to 30 percent more soil is crammed into a cubic foot than was present in the virgin soil."

Jenny [13] has shown the effect of cultivation on reducing the size of soil aggregates as in the following table:

Change in size of soil granules due to cultivation

Soil granules	Prairie (percent)	Cultivated field (percent)	Difference (percent)
Large ("sand" size)......................	39	28	−28
Fine ("clay" size)........................	14	19.5	+39

Virgin soil usually embodies structural relations that are most favorable in promoting infiltration. Higher content of organic matter, better state of aggregation, and larger size of pores definitely favor rapid movement of soil water. Other things being equal, the more nearly land usage approaches these conditions the more favorable is it for the infiltration process.

Houk [12] concluded on the basis of his studies in the Miami (Ohio) Conservancy District that the amount of water absorbed by the upper 2 feet of soil during a given storm is greater under sod surfaces than under surfaces of bare soil, also that for extremely small areas the occurrence and amount of runoff are affected much less by surface slope than by surface cover.

Similar effects have been shown by the University of Missouri [17], by the Texas Agricultural Experiment Station [5], and by the various experiment stations of the Soil Conservation Service [2].

The effect of land usage upon infiltration is also exemplified by a series of direct measurements made in 1939 in the South Concho drainage basin, Texas and in 1940 in the Tallahatchie Basin, Mississippi (see table below.) In the Texas area measurements were made in pairs upon like soils and slopes both for good and for poor grazing histories. During the season several hundred measurements of this kind were made at points well distributed over the major soil types. Significantly higher infiltration was found on the land that had had better management. Studies of associated soil characteristics showed that such land also had a higher content of organic matter and a greater degree of aggregation, with accompanying greater porosity of the large noncapillary dimensions. (Figure VII-1)

Effect of land use on infiltration
[Inches per hour]

Tallahatchie River Basin, Mississippi[1]		Concho River Basin, Texas		
Pine[2]	Bare	Good grazing management		Poor grazing management
0.38	0.18	Abilene silty clay loam {	0.22	0.10
.11	.19		.57	.13
.56	.13		.53	.09
.06	.10		1.02	
.85				
.53	.10	Reagan silty clay loam {	2.64	.09
.17	.11		2.09	.13
.15	.17		1.20	.25
.32	.14			.21
Total 3.13	1.12			
Average .35	.14	Mereta clay loam {	0.29	.15
			1.81	.16
			1.36	.15
		Total	11.73	1.46
		Average	1.17	.15

[1] Comparisons made in pairs for similar soils and slopes; data summarized from manuscript by G. W. Musgrave "Effects of land use on infiltration," to be published by Soil Conservation Service, U. S. Dept. Agr.

[2] Minimum (f_c) rates of infiltration during second or "wet" runs by infiltrometers.

shows hydrographs and (Figure VII-3) photographs of soil structure, typical of these contrasting conditions.

Comparisons of 55-year old stands of pine and of formerly cultivated but now abandoned land in Mississippi were also arranged in pairs upon similar soils and slopes. On the forested land runoff was less and infiltration higher to a statistically significant degree. Composite hydrographs for these two types of land use are shown in (Figure VII-2).

Free, Browning, and Musgrave [6] in a field and laboratory study of 68 soils of the United States from New York to New Mexico and from Oregon to Georgia have shown that the rate of infiltration was significantly associated with the content of organic matter, the degree of aggregation of the soil particles, and the amount of large (noncapillary) pores.

FIG. VII-3.—(a) Permeable soil structure of Reagan silty clay loam having a fair to good grazing history. Infiltration 1.95 inches per hour. (b) Dense soil structure of Reagan silty clay loam having a history of overgrazing. Infiltration 0.14 inch per hour. Note how aggregation of particles differs from that of soil shown in a. The soil profile of b is also lower in quantity of organic matter than that of a.

It is not intended to imply, however, that high infiltration is invariably associated with low runoff. In some localities a highly permeable profile may contribute to a high rate of sub-surface storm flow. Possibly something of this kind occurred at San Dimas, Calif., in the storm of February 28 to March 2, 1938, when flood flows and infiltration were both of large magnitude.

Other factors probably also affect the rate and amount of infiltration of water into soil, although in the present state of knowledge we have little experimental evidence concerning them. The temperature and viscosity of water probably affect its rate of movement, particularly through a medium having very fine pores. These effects may account in part for the reductions in infiltration which frequently occur during the fall, winter, and spring. Most probably also the temperature and specific heat of the soil exert effects upon the viscosity of water. As the specific heat of a soil varies in accord with its differing structural conditions and as the structure itself varies from season to season, it may be supposed that for this reason also there is a seasonal fluctuation in infiltration.

The quality of water also affects the rate of infiltration, and in irrigation practice particularly the importance of this factor is well recognized. Where artificial applications of water are made in field tests for the determination of infiltration rates saline waters should be avoided. Scofield [22] cited tests in which the rate of water penetration was six to eight times as fast in samples that had not been subjected to the action of alkaline salts as in samples that had. The effects are variable both in direction and in magnitude, depending upon the base-exchange reactions of the constituents of the soil and of the water.

Seasonal variations in infiltration accompany seasonal variations in temperature of air, soil, and water, variations in soil moisture and in vegetal cover, and other factors. Houk [12], Horton [11], and Horner and Lloyd [9] have shown variations in infiltration on a single drainage basin, in which during the summer rates are commonly higher than in the spring or fall. Numerous unpublished data show similar results. In looking upon the soil as a porous medium, therefore, it must be regarded as dynamic rather than static.

APPLICATION TO SURFACE RUNOFF

In considering the practical application of the infiltration concept to the prediction of runoff it is well to recall that storm waters may be disposed of in several different ways, as shown above.

During later stages of a storm subsurface storm flow is likely to develop, and its amount is dependent upon the characteristics of the soils and other features of the drainage area. In these later stages the capacities of the canopy to intercept additional rainfall, of the surface depressions to retain further quantities, and of the soil to infiltrate storm waters gradually become satisfied and approach zero.

Because infiltration and surface runoff ordinarily constitute the greatest proportion of the total volume of heavy rainfall, a simple subtraction of recorded runoff from recorded rainfall often gives a close approximation of total infiltration. However, as upon occasion other factors may exert considerable influence and as such factors as subsurface storm flow, particularly, are not readily susceptible of precise measurement, it is clearly not practicable to depend entirely upon infiltration as a basis of estimating runoff.

It has been customary to estimate runoff by using a coefficient derived primarily from the average relation of rainfall and runoff for a given drainage basin. Houk [12] as early as 1921 presented not only the concept of the variable effects of the different phases of the hydrologic cycle but also considerable experimental evidence upon them; nevertheless practical engineering design continued to depend upon "runoff coefficients" for more than a decade.

The presentation of the unit hydrograph by Sherman [23] gave considerable stimulus to research in this field. This research has from time to time led to certain modifications and refinements of procedure in the development of a unit hydrograph. In 1934 Bernard [3] developed certain factors of the unit hydrograph leading to the distribution graph and the pluviagraph. In 1938 Langbein [14] presented methods for a more precise allocation between sub-surface and surface storm flow, the essentials of which were used in Water-Supply Paper 838 of the United States Geological Survey [27]. He has also pointed out [15] the recent trend toward treatment of the rainfall and runoff relations in two parts— (1) the ground phase, which includes such processes as infiltration and evaporation, and (2) the channel phase, which includes the flow of water in the channel system. Snyder [26] states that it cannot be repeated too often that the unit graph procedure is a means of determining the time distribution of surface runoff but does not solve the problem of determining how much runoff will occur under any given set of conditions.

The entire concept of the relation between rainfall and runoff was clarified considerably when Horton [10] pointed out the possibilities of both analysis and synthesis of the hydrograph. Recent progress in the overall study of rainfall and runoff relations may be attributed largely to these various steps toward improved hydrograph analysis.

In analyzing the record of the New England flood of September 1938 the authors of Water-Supply Paper 867 [28] made use of an infiltration index. For this purpose the difference between precipitation and runoff was divided by the duration in hours of significant rainfall, in a manner similar to that followed in Water-Supply Paper 838. Significant rainfall for their purposes was defined as rain that falls at a rate approximately equal to or greater than one-half the maximum rate of infiltration. It was not implied that this infiltration index corresponds to any limiting rate of absorption. It was used rather as a statistical measure of the absorbtive capacity that is more nearly independent of the amount of rainfall. The detailed calculations led to the development of a map showing the infiltration index in inches per hour for the storm period. It was found that during the periods of most intense rainfall water was apparently absorbed at rates considerably in excess of the average and that after the beginning of active runoff nearly all rates of rainfall were productive of runoff. Along the sandy areas of the Coastal Plain there is a predominance of higher rates of infiltration and in general a tendency for an increase of infiltration in a downstream direction. The data presented correspond to a general average rate of 0.10 inch per hour. In the calculations in this paper the amount of water in transit to stream channels,

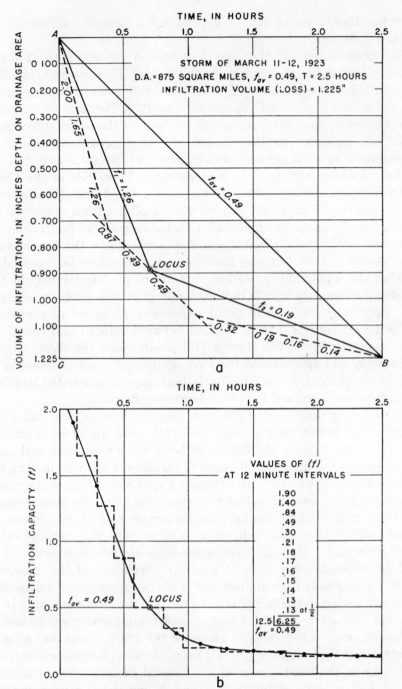

FIG. VII-4.—Derivation of infiltration capacities from average loss rates, Macoupin Creek Basin above Kane, Ill. (*After L. K. Sherman* [25].)

termed the "surface detention," was computed essentially by the methods of Sherman [24].

Horner and Lloyd [9] analyzed a large number of hydrographs of two small drainage basins, achieving considerable success in the preparation of infiltration rate curves and not only testing certain of these theories but also showing seasonal variations in infiltration throughout the period of observation.

In a study of large natural basins Sherman [25] presented the example of the Macoupin Basin, Illinois. He derived the infiltration rate curve (f) (Figure VII-4) from average rates of infiltration (fav), which may be determined on basins of any size. This rate is calculated for periods during the storm when the rain intensity exceeds infiltration capacity. Sherman calls this condensation of time "equivalent duration time (T)." He gives a procedure called the 10-point method for deriving the f curve and points out that the average or combination of several f curves is desirable.

The f curves thus derived for large natural basins are materially less concave than those derived by infiltrometers on small plots and probably less concave than those derived on very small drainage basins. This is to be expected, as on a small area surface runoff reaches recording instruments much sooner than it does on large areas.

Obviously, to ascertain the range of fluctuation for any large area requires numerous records. The analyst is commonly confronted by such conditions as lack of homogeneity in the basin, partial-area and partial-time storms, and partial records. The meagerness of existing records has been pointed out [29], and in order to emphasize the deficiencies it is only necessary to recall that many large drainage basins have in their entire area not more than one or two recording rain gages. Because of these deficiencies in basic information, methods of estimating runoff or of deriving infiltration rate curves for large areas have been directed toward procedures that are adaptable to meeting existing needs, through the use of such information as is commonly available.

For flood forecasting, for estimating flood stages or flood frequencies from rainfall, the concept of infiltration on large areas is of major importance. This field has not yet had the attention it deserves. The real test of a method for deriving infiltration on natural basins will be reached when the predicted runoff matches the observed runoff.

REFERENCES

1. Auten, J. T., Porosity and water absorption of forest soils: Jour. Agr. Research, vol. 46, pp. 997–1014, 1933.

2. Bennett, H. H., Soil conservation, New York and London, McGraw-Hill Book Co., Inc., 1939.

3. Bernard, M. M., Approach to determinate stream flow: Am. Soc. Civil Eng. Proc., vol. 60, pp. 3–18, 1934.

4. Bradfield, Richard, Soil conservation from the viewpoint of soil physics: Am. Soc. Agronomists Jour., vol. 29, pp. 85–92, 1937.

5. Conner, A. B., Dixon, R. E. and Scoates, D., Factors influencing runoff and soil erosion: Texas Agr. Exper. Sta. Bull. 411, 1930.

6. Free, G. R., Browning, G. M., and Musgrave, G. W., Relative infiltration and related physical characteristics of certain soils: U. S. Dept. Agr. Tech. Bull. 729, 1940.

7. Hays, O. E., and Palmer, V. J., Progress report of the Upper Mississippi Valley Soil and Water Conservation Experiment Station, La Crosse, Wisc., 1932–35: U. S. Soil Conserv. Service ESR-1, 1937.

8. Hill, H. O., Elwell, H. M., and Slosser, J. W., Progress report of the Red Plains Soil Conservation Experiment Station, Guthrie, Okla., 1930–35: U. S. Soil Conserv. Service ESR-3, 1937.

9. Horner and Lloyd, Infiltration capacity values as determined from a study of an 18-month record at Edwardsville, Ill.: Am. Geophys. Union Trans., 1940.

10. Horton, R. E., Surface runoff phenomena, pt. 1, Analysis of the hydrograph: Horton Hydrol. Laboratory Pub. 101, 1935.

11. Horton, R. E., Determination of infiltration capacity for large drainage basins: Am. Geophys. Union Trans., 1937, pt. 2.

12. Houk, I. E., Rainfall and runoff in Miami Valley: Miami Conservancy Dist. Tech. Repts., pt. 8, 1921.

13. Jenny, Hans, Soil-fertility losses under Missouri conditions: Missouri Univ., Coll. Agr., Agr. Exper. Sta. Bull. 324.

14. Langbein, W. B., Some channel-storage studies and their application to the determination of infiltration: Am. Geophys. Union Trans., 1938.

15. Langbein, W. B., Channel-storage and unit-hydrograph studies: Am. Geophys. Union Trans., 1940.

16. Lowdermilk, W. C., Influence of forest litter on runoff, percolation, and erosion: Jour. Forestry, vol. 28, No. 4, pp. 474–491, 1940.

17. Miller, M. F., and Krusekopf, H. H., The influence of systems of cropping and methods of culture on surface runoff and soil erosion: Missouri Univ., Coll. Agr., Agr. Exper. Sta. Research Bull. 177, 1932.

18. Muntz, A., Faure, L., and Lainé, E., Études sur la permeabilité des terres faites en vue de l'arrosage: France, Min. de l'agr., Dir. gén. Eaux et Forêts Ann., Forêts-Hydraul., 33.

19. Musgrave, G. W., The infiltration capacity of soils in relation to the control of surface runoff and erosion: Am. Soc. Agronomists Jour., vol. 27, No. 5, 1935.

20. Musgrave, G. W., and Norton, R. A., Soil Conservation Exper. Sta. Missouri Valley, Loess Reg., Clarinda, Iowa, Tech. Bull. 558, 1937.

21. Ohio Agr. Exper. Sta. 45th Ann. Rept., Bull. 402, 156 pp., 1927.

22. Scofield, C. S., The movement of water in irrigated soils: Jour. Agr. Research, vol. 27, No. 9, 1924.

23. Sherman, L. K., Stream flow from rainfall by the unit-hydrograph record: Eng. News-Record, vol. 108, 1932.

24. Sherman, L. K., Determination of infiltration rates from surface runoff: Am. Geophys. Union Trans., 1938.

25. Sherman, L. K., Derivation of infiltration capacity (f) from average loss rates (f_{av}): Am. Geophys. Union Trans., 1940.

26. Snyder, F. F., Synthetic unit graphs: Am. Geophys. Union Trans., 1938.

27. Floods of Ohio and Mississippi Rivers, January-February 1937: U. S. Geol. Survey, Water-Supply Paper 838, 1938.

28. Hurricane floods of September 1938: U. S. Geol. Survey, Water-Supply Paper 867, 1940.

29. Deficiencies in hydrologic research, National Resources Plannng Board, 1940.

CHAPTER VIII

TRANSPIRATION AND TOTAL EVAPORATION

CHARLES H. LEE[1]

INTRODUCTION

Total evaporation is the relatively fixed charge which precipitation upon the land surface of the earth must pay before it returns as runoff to the ocean. Transpiration is often the largest component of total evaporation and represents the cost of maintaining plant life upon the earth. Interception is a minor component, which must also be charged up against plant life. Direct evaporation from water and snow surfaces and from moist soil constitutes the remainder of total evaporation. Snow and soil evaporation would be greater were it not for the shade afforded by plant life. Thus plant life is intimately connected with total evaporation, and its characteristics and processes must be given major consideration in any discussion of total evaporation.

The physiology and ecology of plants both involve the interrelations of water and plant life. In the following discussion of the physical process of transpiration, the writings of three leading authorities on these subjects have been freely consulted, and any facts not specifically supported by references may be found in their published works [50, 58, 79].

USES OF WATER BY PLANT LIFE

Water is as necessary to plant life as it is to animal life. Without a continuous water supply plant functions cease and the plant dies. Next to temperature, water is the most important single factor in controlling the distribution of vegetation over the surface of the earth. Plants use water for the following purposes:

1. For the proper functioning of protoplasm, which includes all the chemical reactions occurring within the cell, in which water either enters directly or is the solvent.

2. For the maintenance of turgor in the living cells, essential for the growth of cells and erectness of the plant.

3. As a transportation medium for the inorganic salts absorbed from the soil and supplied as raw material to the leaves for conversion into organic foods. These and other plant foods manufactured in the leaves must, in turn, be transported in water solution to various parts of the plant organism for cell growth and tissue building or for temporary storage.

4. For chemical combination with carbon dioxide from the air to form the carbohydrates, principally cellulose, which compose the dry matter of the plant.

5. To replace losses, principally by transpiration and guttation.

[1] Consulting engineer, San Francisco, Calif.

The maximum amount of water held in storage in the plant at any time for the use of protoplasm, in maintaining turgor, and in translocation, plus that chemically combined, is less than 1 percent of that lost from the plant during the growing season.   The principal need of plants for water is therefore to replace that continuously lost through stems and leaves by transpiration and guttation.

TRANSPIRATION

DEFINITIONS

Transpiration is the process by which water vapor escapes from the living plant, principally the leaves, and enters the atmosphere.   It includes *cuticular transpiration*, or direct evaporation from moist membranes into the atmosphere through the cuticle, and *stomatal transpiration*, or outward diffusion into the atmosphere, through the pores of stomata and lenticula, of water vapor previously evaporated from imbibed membranes into gas spaces within the plant leaf.   As considered practically, transpiration also includes guttation.

Guttation is the loss of water in liquid form from the uninjured leaf or stem of the plant, principally through "water stomata" or hydathodes.

PHYSICAL PROCESS OF TRANSPIRATION

Plant classification with respect to water supply

Plants are of differing types with respect to the water environment and transpiration [79].   Hydrophytes live wholly or partly submerged in water, or with roots in saturated soil that is intermittently submerged. Mesophytes grow in habitats that usually have neither excess nor deficiency of water.   Xerophytes are plants that have adapted themselves to high evaporation rate and deficient water supply.

Hydrophytes are of three types—submerged, floating and amphibious. *Submerged hydrophytes* absorb gases and nutrients directly from the water and lack structural adaptations for protection against water loss.   *Floating hydrophytes* have poorly developed root systems but greatly expanded foliage.   The foliage has ample facilities for absorbing gases from the air but only rudimentary protection from water loss.   The water lily is a typical example.   *Amphibious plants* are adapted to live with roots in the water and stem and foliage mostly in air, the stem having large air chambers crossed by pervious diaphragms, which afford aeration to submerged portions.   Structural adaptations for protection against water loss are poorly developed.   Common examples are the tule, papyrus, and cattail.

For a fourth type of plants the term *phreatophytes* has been proposed by Meinzer [46] to include plants that habitually obtain their water supply either directly from the zone of saturation or through the capillary fringe.   Such plants form a distinct ecologic group in desert regions where, in contrast to xerophytes, they have an arid environment for their transpiration organs but a humid environment for their roots.   They are virtually natural wells, with pumping equipment raising water from the zone of saturation.   In addition to rushes, reeds, and sedges, phreatophytes include salt grass, pickleweed, alkali saccaton, rabbit brush, greasewood (*Sarcobatus*), mesquite, willows, palms, and other trees.

In contrast to hydrophytes, mesophytes and xerophytes grow with root systems in well-drained aerated soil and stems and foliage in air. They have well-developed structural protection against water loss.   Their roots require oxygen, and a rise of water table with saturation of the soil will cause death of submerged roots by drowning and possibly death of the plant itself.

Sources of water supply

The principal source of water supply for mesophytic, xerophytic, and phreatophytic plants is soil moisture absorbed through the root system. Although leaves and stem may under certain circumstances absorb moisture, the conditions for such absorption seldom occur in nature, and the amount so absorbed is so small compared with the loss by transpiration from leaves that it has no significance in the water economy of the plant. Humid atmosphere, light showers, or dew are often of value, however, because they reduce the evaporation rate to a point less than the rate of absorption by roots, thus permitting leaves to become turgid and normal functioning of the plant to proceed.

The range of soil moisture favorable for mesophytic and xerophytic types of vegetation lies between the two limits of specific retention (or field capacity) and wilting coefficient.   Plant roots are unable to remove all moisture from the soil, and when permanent wilting occurs there remains a residuum of moisture unavailable to the plant.   The term "wilting coefficient" is in general use, defining the moisture content of the soil (expressed as percentage of dry weight) at the time of permanent wilting of plants growing in it.   A plant is described as permanently wilted when its leaves have become so flaccid as a result of deficiency in soil moisture that they will not recover normal turgidity when placed in an approximately saturated atmosphere without the addition of water to the soil [7].   The numerical value of the wilting coefficient depends principally upon the type of soil.   The smaller the soil particles the greater is the amount of water remaining in the soil when wilting occurs.   For the ordinary types of soil the coefficient ranges from 1 percent or less for coarse sand to 15 percent for clay loams and as high as 30 percent for heavy clay soils.

Experimental work with seedling plants and those in an early stage of development has indicated that plants differ but little in their ability to reduce the moisture content of the soil [1].　For larger plants it is difficult to determine the wilting point, because of the progressive shedding of leaves from lower to higher levels.　It is probable, however, that even in soils of similar types well-developed plants under field conditions differ in their wilting points.

The wilting coefficient has been determined either directly, by growing plants in sealed containers and measuring the soil moisture after allowing it to decrease to the point of permanent wilting, or indirectly, by calculation.　Indirect methods, although furnishing only approximate results, are more practical for application to plants growing under field conditions [7].　They are based upon the relation, established by laboratory tests, of wilting point to moisture retentiveness as measured by certain physical factors of the soil such as moisture equivalent, hygroscopic coefficient, or moisture-holding capacity.

The principal environmental conditions that control the relation of plants to soil moisture are (1) the capacity of the soil to deliver water to the plant roots and (2) the capacity of the atmosphere to induce water loss by transpiration.　Experimental evidence indicates that the absorbing power of root cells exceeds the back pull of the soil for water even at the wilting point [65].　The rate of movement of adhesive water through the soil is very slow [78] and controls the capacity of the soil to deliver water.　If, owing to high humidity, low temperature, or some other cause, the rate of transpiration is low, as the critical stage is approached the roots may continue to obtain moisture for a considerable time and so, without injury to the plant, may deplete soil moisture to a point lower than if the transpiration rate were high.　If, on the other hand, the rate of loss by evaporation into the air is high, owing to hot, dry atmospheric conditions, the soil may fail to supply water with sufficient rapidity and the plant may wilt and even die.　The ability of the plant to obtain water at the time wilting begins is therefore controlled, on the one hand, by the rate of movement of soil moisture, which depends upon the soil temperature and the gradient and the degree of soil moisture; and, on the other hand, by the rate of transpiration, which depends upon climatic conditions and variety of plant.

Pathway of water movement

It has long been known that water enters the plant through the roots, traverses the stem, and escapes from the leaves.　More recently its course through the plant tissue has also been definitely established.　This course is essentially as follows:

Water enters the plant through the outer layer of epidermal cells of the younger portions of the root system, principally through the root hairs. From the epidermal cells it moves through the cells of the cortex and the endodermis, passing thence into the cavities (lumina) of the long cells known as tracheids and tracheae. These form the conducting tissue of the vascular system, which traverses roots, stem, and leaves as part of the xylem. Water ascending through these tubes finally reaches the vascular system of the leaves. Thence it moves through the chlorenchyma (green) cells to those bordering upon the intercellular air spaces at the base of the stomata. Here it leaves the cell walls as vapor and escapes through the stomata into the external atmosphere. In certain plants water may also travel upward through the cortex and pith of the root and stem, but the amount is apparently very small except in young plants.

Root system.—The root system of each plant species is distinctive, but single specimens may vary with the conditions of growth as to structure, extent, weight, number, and direction. The behavior of roots in the soil is influenced by many factors, important among which are age, soil moisture, nutrients, oxygen supply, temperature, soil texture, and gravity.

The direction of root growth is toward soil with greater available moisture content. Roots will not penetrate dry soil to reach a moister soil beyond, but when in contact or close proximity to moisture will turn toward or follow it. Roots will avoid waterlogged or poorly aerated soil.

With respect to extent of the root system, plants may be classified as annuals, close-growing perennials, shrubs, and trees. The root systems of annuals range from 10 to 100 inches vertically and 4 to 70 inches horizontally. Close-growing perennials such as alfalfa reach much greater depths, extremes of 40 feet in soil and more than 100 feet in fissured rock being reported. Shrubs and trees that form tap roots, such as the pine and oak, reach to depths of 10 to 20 feet in fine-textured soil, but shallow-rooted varieties such as spruce and cottonwood seldom exceed 5 feet. The lateral spread of the roots of shrubs and trees is from two to seven times that of the branches. The working depth of root systems seldom exceeds 6 feet and lies principally in the first 3 feet. For this reason root competition between herbaceous cover and trees is keen.

The absorptive area of the root is confined to the part near the end of the growing tip of each rootlet, beginning usually 1 to 3 millimeters from the apex. It is here that the root hairs occur. They are in contact with films of soil water and increase the absorbing surface of the epidermal cells manyfold. They are not roots but tubular outgrowths of the exterior walls of certain superficial epidermal cells and are to be distinguished from the small fibrous hair roots often mentioned in agricultural literature. They range in length from a fraction of a millimeter to 10 millimeters depending upon soil conditions. The formation of root hairs is affected by available water, temperature, obstructions, hydrogen ion concentration, and toxic substances. Saturated soil tends to suppress the production of root hairs. Their longevity depends upon species of plant and moisture conditions of soil. In some species it is only a few days or weeks; in others they last for several years but do not function that long.

Stem.—The stem of a plant includes the root crown and main stalk or trunk, with all branches, twigs, and slender supports of leaves, flowers, or fruit. In section it is made up of cortex (bark), endodermis, cambium, xylem (wood), phloem, fibrovascular bundles, medulla (pith), etc. The fibrovascular system of the xylem is the channel for the transpiration stream from roots to leaves; the phloem is the channel for transmission of food from the leaves to all parts of the plant. In herbaceous plants these elements are arranged more or less concentrically about the medulla. In shrubs and trees the living tissue with its function of conduction is confined to the soft sap wood and cortex composed of the current and immediately adjacent annual rings. The main trunk is composed of dead tissue or heartwood, in which the lumina have been blocked up and hardened by tyloses. The water content of the stem of herbaceous plants constitutes from 70 to 90 percent of the green weight, that of trees 40 to 60 percent.

Leaves.—Leaves are the green expanded organs (foliage) which make up most of the external covering of a plant. Their function is the manufacture of plant food from sap and gases absorbed from the atmosphere, utilizing the energy of the sun operating through chlorophyll. They are relatively broad, flat, and thin, with a large surface area in proportion to mass. The total leaf surface of most plants is manyfold larger than the ground area covered by the plant.

The ordinary leaf is composed largely of thin-walled cells (mesophyll) permeated with numerous finely divided vascular bundles (veins) with open ends. Of the veins there may be as many as 6,000 per square centimeter of leaf surface. The entire leaf is covered by a layer of cells, generally one cell thick, known as the epidermis, which is more or less impervious to moisture and gases, particularly when the exposed surface is well cutinized. The epidermis is perforated with numerous pores called stomata. The mesophyll is loosely constructed, with many air spaces between cells. The intercellular spaces join and finally unite with one of the relatively large air spaces beneath each pore or stoma. These intercellular spaces form from 3 to 70 percent of the total volume of the leaf.

The thin-walled cells of mesophyll are in direct contact with the lumina or tubes of the fibrovascular bundles, which in turn are directly connected through the roots with the water supply of the soil. A portion of the moist surface of the mesophyll cells is also exposed to the intercellular air cavities, which are connected to the atmosphere through the stomata. The area of moist cell surfaces exposed to the intercellular air spaces is manyfold greater than the external leaf surface. Leaf structure, although well adapted to the absorption of gases from the atmosphere or the excretion of waste gases from metabolism, is poorly arranged for the retention of water and is a constant menace to the life of the plant by excessive evaporation.

Controlling forces

In living plants there is a continuous column of water, derived from soil moisture and ascending, first, through epidermal cells, cortex, and endodermis of the root, and second, through the fibrovascular systems of the root, stem, and leaves, finally reaching the walls of mesophyll cells facing the intercellular spaces of the leaf. Thence it escapes into the atmosphere through the stomata. This moving column or transpiration stream is made up of many minute threads, each terminating at menisci, one in the submicroscopical cavities in cell walls of epidermal cells of the root, and the other in the outer walls of mesophyll cells of the leaves. These columns are of widely differing size and length in different types of plants. In large trees the height of the water column may exceed 300 feet and the aggregate rate of flow in the conducting channels of the xylem may amount to many hundred gallons per day. The forces involved in this hydrodynamic system, which feed it at the base, which hold the water column in place, and which cause upward flow to replace water lost by evaporation at the leaves, are many and complicated and although given much study are not fully understood. For detailed consideration these forces may be divided into groups associated with the three processes of absorption, ascent, and discharge.

Absorption by roots.—Absorption of the soil water by the roots includes the entrance of water into the root system and its movement across it to the endodermis cells. Three forces are recognized in this process—imbibition, osmotic forces, and passive absorption.

Imbibition is the attraction of solid substances for water and is especially characteristic of colloidal material in a gel condition. Both the cell wall and the protoplasm of epidermal cells of young root tissue are colloidal in nature, and both have strong affinity for water of soil particles with which they are in contact. Water is drawn into the cell wall of epidermal cells by imbibition and thence by the same force into the adjacent protoplasm within the cell. Imbibed water arranges itself around solid particles as films, which cause separation of the particles and swelling of the mass. The limit of separation depends upon the cohesive forces between the particles. In wood the limit is soon reached, but in gelatin the amount of imbibed water may increase until the particles go into colloidal solution. The force of imbibition exerted by dry cell walls and protoplasm amounts to hundreds of atmospheres and is very strong, even within the plant, where cell walls and protoplasm contain considerable water. The imbibition of water by cell walls and protoplasm produces water contact between the vacuole or cell sap of adjacent cells and thus provides a continuous waterway by which water and water-soluble substances may move from cell to cell. Imbibition of water is thus a necessary preliminary to the operation of osmotic forces.

Osmosis is broadly defined as the diffusion of watery solutions through membranes, the direction of major movement being from the region of high concentration to that of low concentration of the diffusing material either as solvent or as solute. Plant cell walls and protoplasm constitute membranes. Some of these membranes are permeable—that is, they allow both solvent and solute to pass through; many others are semipermeable, allowing the solvent to pass but not the solute.

Osmosis in living plant tissue produces a pressure in cell sap termed "osmotic pressure," which may be viewed from two aspects—(1) as the pressure that dissolved materials in cell sap would be capable of exerting upon the protoplasm and cell wall if the cell were placed in pure water, it being assumed that the cell wall is absolutely rigid and that the protoplasm allows water to enter freely, but that neither protoplasm nor cell wall will allow dissolved materials to escape from the cell sap; (2) as the pull that the water of cell sap is capable of exerting upon pure water from which it is separated by a perfectly semipermeable membrane. The osmotic pressure or pull of cell sap varies directly with the concentration of the solute and results from the relations of membranes and solutions.

Osmotic pressure of cell sap in a living cell may be regarded as exerting a hydrostatic pressure against the protoplasm and cell wall. This causes the protoplasm to maintain close contact with the cell wall and the cell to be more or less expanded. An expanded cell is rigid and is described as turgid. The hydrostatic pressure of cell sap against the cell wall is termed the "turgor pressure" of the cell, and the opposing pressure of the cell wall against the protoplasm and cell sap is termed "wall pressure" of the cell. If deficiency of water is brought about in cell sap by higher concentration of the external solution or by excessive evaporation, the hydrostatic pressure is destroyed, and the cell wall contracts to its minimum limit. Protoplasm is more elastic, however, and will continue to contract as water is withdrawn until it becomes loosened from the cell wall. This condition is termed "plasmolysis." It is an abnormal condition, which, if continued, will cause death. The condition when the cell wall has reached its limit of contraction but when the protoplasm has not yet receded from the wall is known as incipient plasmolysis. Wall pressure and turgor pressure are both zero at incipient plasmolysis. Wall pressure is at its maximum when a cell has reached its limit of expansion and is equal to the osmotic or turgor pressure at that time.

The osmotic value of cell sap is the degree of concentration of the osmotically active substance in the sap. It is the potential or latent osmotic pressure of the cell sap and expressed in terms of osmotic pressure in atmospheres. In a living plant it is greatest at incipient plasmolysis and least when the cell is in equilibrium with distilled water.

The absorbing power or suction pressure of the plant cell is the force that causes water to enter the cell. It varies with the relative osmotic value of the cell sap and external solutions. The osmotic value of the cell sap of epidermal root cells is always greater than that of the external soil solution, and this superiority is maintained as concentration of the external solution increases. The relation of the absorbing power of epidermal root cells and the osmotic value may be expressed by the following equation:

Absorbing power = osmotic value of cell sap − (osmotic value of external solution + wall pressure)

If the cell sap is in equilibrium with pure water, the absorbing power is zero; if the cell is at incipient plasmolysis, the absorbing power is at its maximum. For normal plant-cell conditions the absorbing power lies between these extremes.

The absorbing power of the epidermal root cell has been observed to be one or more atmospheres. Under the force of osmotic action soil water enters the root provided there is an increasing gradient of absorbing power from cell to cell across the cortex to the endodermis cells.

In the absorption of water by the root system and movement of water across it, osmotic forces always act jointly with imbibitional forces, with a tendency for the two forces to equalize. Whenever imbibitional forces exceed osmotic forces water will move into imbibing matter such as protoplasm or cell wall. If, on the other hand, osmotic forces are the greater, water will move from imbibing matter into cell sap.

Under conditions of little or no transpiration and abundant water supply, the absorption of water and its movement across the root system can be explained by osmotic and imbibitional forces in the root system, provided that a saturation deficit is created in the endodermal cells. This deficit, however, must be created by other than imbibitional or osmotic forces. Under conditions of high transpiration, on the other hand, absorption by these forces is too slow to replace the water transpired. Under such conditions stronger forces pulling from the region above the endodermal cells are controlling, the root cells being passive and their principal function then being to prevent the entrance of air through the absorbing surface.

It is thus apparent that the absorption of water by the root system and movement across it is complex, involving the forces of imbibition, osmotic pressure, and passive absorption, acting either separately or jointly. It is doubtful, however, whether these forces supply the plant with sufficient water to replace losses during periods of active transpiration.

Ascent through stem.—That water or sap of plants ascends from the endodermal cells through the fibrovascular system of the stem to the leaves has been fully established. The forces involved in this process, however, are not fully understood, largely because of the lack of external evidence and the difficulty of measuring and interpreting the available manifestations. To be valid, any explanation of the process must include the extreme case of the tall leafy tree. Among the forces that have been suggested are atmospheric pressure, capillarity, imbibition, "root pressure," and the vital forces of protoplasm. Logical reasoning and experiment have shown that none of these are adequate to explain the phenomenon.

There being no pumping mechanism in plant tissue itself, water must either be pushed up from below or pulled up from above. The evidence is in favor of the latter, the cohesion theory affording the best explanation known at present. This theory is based upon the observed fact that a column of fluid, such as water, if free from air bubbles and enclosed in a rigid tube to the wall of which it adheres, can transmit a very considerable tension owing to the attraction or cohesion of fluid particles for one another. The fluid, being unable to change its shape and by virtue of its cohesion, transmits a pull like a steel wire. The tensile strength of a column of water with small diameter exceeds 300 atmospheres at rupture.

In the ascent of sap the tubes of the fibrovascular system contain water columns which are free from air bubbles and which adhere to the walls of the lumina, thus fulfilling the requirements for transmission of tension in fluids. Cross walls at the end of the lumina do not interfere with the continuity of the water column, for they are fully soaked with water. Transpiration from cell walls exposed to intercellular air spaces in the leaves induces tension in these water columns. According to the cohesion theory, this tension is transmitted throughout the fibrovascular system of the stem to the endodermal cells of the root, where it creates a water deficit. If the rate of transpiration is low this deficit is supplied from soil moisture in contact with root hairs by the forces of imbibition and osmotic pressure. If the rate is high the tension extends through the endodermis and cortex of the root to the epidermal cells. Here the root hairs absorb water from soil moisture by increased condensation induced by the greater concavity of the menisci.

The flow of water up the highest tree is thus caused by the difference between the vapor pressure at the surface of the epidermal cells of the root system and that at the walls of mesophyll cells exposed to the atmosphere in the intercellular cavities of the leaves. It is possible that the energy required for raising water in this manner is provided by plant respiration.

Discharge.—Discharge of water from plants by transpiration is accomplished through the ordinary process of atmospheric evaporation as modified by the structure and functions of the plant. It takes the place in the air-filled intercellular cavities of leaves. Water moistening the walls of mesophyll cells surrounding these cavities vaporizes and escapes from the leaf into the outside atmosphere through the stomata. The same basic factors of solar radiation, temperature, relative humidity, and wind that control evaporation thus also control transpiration. There are environmental factors, however, that cause the rate of transpiration per unit area to be less than evaporation and that also modify somewhat the time variations.

Influencing factors

The rate of loss of water from plants by transpiration varies greatly with the species of plant, the conditions under which it grows, and the time of the day, month, or year, and from year to year. The factors that influence the rate of transpiration can be classified as physiologic and environmental.

Physiologic factors.—The physiologic factors that control transpiration include the density and behavior of stomata, the extent and character of protective coverings, the leaf structure, and plant diseases.

The stomata are minute more or less elongated openings through the epidermis. Each stoma lies between two specialized cells known as guard cells, which in turn are bordered by subsidiary cells; the whole group is termed the stomatal apparatus. The structure of the apparatus differs in different plants but is generally similar.

The number of stomata per unit area of leaf, or density, is characteristic of the plant species and is also influenced by environmental conditions such as humidity, light intensity, and soil moisture. Density in various types of plants ranges from 50,000 to nearly 800,000 stomata per square inch. It is greater on the lower than the upper side of the leaf, the ratio ordinarily being about 3 to 1. A few observations have been reported in which no stomata were formed on the upper side. Density varies in different portions of the same leaf and in different leaves on the same plant. In general there is an inverse relation between the number and the size of the stomata, which are smallest where density is greatest. Stomatal dimensions vary widely, but the area is of the order of 100 square microns. The aggregate area of stomatal openings is from 1 to 3 percent of the total leaf surface.

The opening and closing of stomata is produced by changes in turgor of guard cells and results from uneven thickening of the walls of the guard cells. The osmotic value of cell sap in guard cells differs from that of sap in the epidermal cells of the leaf and varies during the day somewhat in accord with the opening and closing of stomata. The important factors affecting opening and closing are as follows:

1. Light intensity. Stomata usually open in the light and close in darkness. This is true of all plants.
2. Moisture supply of leaves. Stomata close regardless of other influences when guard cells loose turgor. True of all plants.
3. Temperature of air. Affects speed of opening.
4. Humidity. High humidity permits stomata to open wider and remain open longer.

There are various types of daily movement of stomata. The following are typical of agricultural field crops:

Alfalfa. Open from 2 to 6 hours after daylight, remaining open 3 to 6 hours, then slowly closing, remaining closed for period twice as long as open. Typical of thin-leaved mesophytes.
Potatoes. Open continuously except for 3 hours after sundown.
Barley. None opening at night. Many closed in day and when open only for an hour or two. Typical of cereals.

The capacity of stomata for diffusion of gases is ordinarily three to six times that needed for discharge of water evaporated from the interior of intercellular air cavities, even at the maximum rate. Stomata may therefore close to a considerable degree and still provide ample capacity for escaping vapor.

Contrary to general belief, the control exercised by the stomata upon the rate of transpiration is limited [43, 50]. Stomata do not close in anticipation of wilting but after the leaf has wilted to a sufficient degree for turgor to decrease in the guard cells. Changes may occur in the rate of transpiration without corresponding changes in the size of stomatal openings. When the stomata are fully open, the transpiration rate is determined by the factors that control evaporation alone. As they close, the influence of evaporation factors decreases, but even at a closure of 50 percent atmospheric influence is superior to stomatal regulation. When stomata are almost closed (2 percent) they begin to exert a controlling influence upon water loss. It is not known how completely transpiration is prevented by complete closure of stomata. Cuticular transpiration, although differing in various plant species, accounts for about 10 percent of the total water loss from leaves and stem.

Many textbooks state that protective coverings of leaves, such as hairs, reduce transpiration, but experimental investigations made in recent years do not substantiate this statement. Although they may have slight protective effect in wind, their influence upon transpiration is relatively very small in comparison with their abundant development.

Waxy coverings are much more effective in reducing transpiration, and certain nontoxic oils when applied as sprays are effective in retarding transpiration from transplanted nursery stock of coniferous trees.

Leaf structure has also been considered as having an effect upon transpiration. It has been found, for example, that the typical leaf structure of xerophytic plants, characterized by development of dense palisade and sponge tissue with small intercellular space and deep-set stomata, is very effective in reducing transpiration. Many exceptions to the rule have been found, however, and Shreve [64] concludes that the differences in anatomical structure of mesophytic and xerophytic leaves do not account for the difference in resistance to water loss by plants in arid regions.

Another feature of leaf structure that affects transpiration is the water content of the leaf, as related to incipient drying—that is, the drying out of cell walls surrounding the intercellular air spaces of the leaves with temporary decrease in transpiration rate that may accompany increase in evaporating power of the air. The reduction in transpiration is apparently due to the retreat of water films into the pores of the cell walls with increase of surface tension in the water surfaces. If the water content of the leaves is high, increased power of evaporation does not produce incipient drying, and transpiration increases. If, on the other hand, the water content of the leaves is low, incipient drying occurs and the rate of transpiration tends to decrease. This phenomenon is illustrated by the higher transpiration rate observed in plants with relatively small leaf surface, which are able to maintain a higher water content of exterior cell walls than plants with larger leaf surface.

Environmental factors.—The principal environmental factors that influence transpiration are solar radiation, atmospheric and soil conditions, chemicals, and fungus diseases.

Solar radiation is a source of daylight energy from the sun which, impinging upon leaf surface, has a positive effect upon evaporation of water and hence upon transpiration. Study of the effect of solar radiation upon transpiration has been confined principally to light intensity. It has been found that light has a direct accelerating influence upon transpiration, in addition to any secondary effect upon stomatal movement. In two varieties of plants investigated it was found to average 4 percent [22]. Increased transpiration due to increase of light has been attributed to its action in producing higher temperature of the leaves and greater permeability of protoplasm and cell wall colloids.

Atmospheric conditions also affect the evaporation rate. The term "evaporating power of the air," or "evaporativity," is used to designate the combined influence of air temperature, humidity, and wind movement. The evaporating power of the air, unlike solar radiation, acts both day and night. It is usually positive in action but may be negative, as when the plant absorbs moisture from the air or when dew is formed upon its surfaces. Air temperature is the most influential factor in transpiration, tests indicating that it causes about 60 percent of the loss. Relative humidity is the factor next in importance [52], but there are few quantitative data available as to its relative influence upon transpiration. Although wind may have considerable momentary influence, its aggregate effect upon the transpiration loss during the growing season has been found to be less than 5 percent.

Evaporation and transpiration are largely controlled by the same factors, but they respond in different manner and different degree. Expressed numerically, approximately 90 percent of transpiration loss is determined by the factors that control evaporation. Evaporation rates are thus indicative of transpiration rates and are useful in studies in which approximate rates of transpiration are required. For botanical and horticultural research small portable instruments known as atmometers are in use for measuring the rate of evaporation. These are of two types, those with a small tank with free water surface and those with moist porous surface. The latter are most widely used, especially the porous clay-cup type [41]. Evaporation as measured by atmometers differs greatly from evaporation from a large free water surface, which is the standard used by engineers and hydrologists.

The ratio of transpiration, as the measured rate of water loss from a plant, to evaporation, as measured by an atmometer, has been termed "relative transpiration" or "transpiration coefficient." This ratio, if plotted for short periods such as a day, reflects the influences that are peculiar to transpiration. If plant and atmometer responded alike to changes in environment, the values of relative transpiration would lie in a straight line. Actually the line is periodic in form, with a pronounced minimum during the night. This fluctuation is assumed to represent the departure of transpiration from that which would occur if the plant responded freely to its environment. It thus represents the physiologic departure of transpiration rate from the normal due to closure of stomata or other changes within the plant. It has been found that all atmometers do not respond similarly to environment, so that this method is not as definite an indicator of plant changes as was formerly supposed [50].

Soil conditions influence transpiration from two aspects—the texture of the soil and the degree of soil moisture. The influence of texture is exercised principally through its relation to the rapidity of movement of soil water. If the movement is very slow, as in clayey soils, the momentary supply available to the roots at a time of increasing evaporation power may be so small that incipient drying of leaves will occur, with decrease in transpiration. Abundant water supply, on the other hand, such as may be available in loam soils in which the movement is more rapid, will permit transpiration to increase with increase in evaporating power. Experimental evidence relative to the effect of soil moisture upon transpiration indicates that a plant will transpire at maximum rate when the soil has sufficient moisture for good tilth, and that increase above this amount does not increase the rate. Decrease of soil moisture below this amount, on the other hand, will lower the rate of transpiration until the water content has reached the wilting coefficient and the plant is badly wilted. At that point the rate of transpiration may be only 2 to 3 percent of that with ideal soil moisture.

Chemicals applied either to the soil in which the plant is growing or to the leaves in the form of spray may increase or decrease the transpiration rate. Fungus diseases of plant leaves produce similar effects.

Relative advantages and disadvantages

The relative advantages and disadvantages of transpiration have been the subject of much debate, the extreme positions being (1) that the process is an unavoidable evil and (2) that it is vitally important to the normal functioning of the plant organism. Among the arguments in support of the second position is that transpiration cools the leaves and prevents injury or death by high temperatures. Experimental work has shown that the degree of cooling rarely exceeds 2° to 5° C., which, in view of the present state of knowledge of protoplasm, could be of little aid in preventing injury from heat [50]. The death of leaves in hot weather is apparently due to excessive loss of water from protoplasm rather than excessive increase in temperature.

Another argument is that transpiration increases the rate of absorption from the soil of inorganic salts that are required for plant food. It has been proved conclusively, however, that there is no relation between rate of transpiration and absorption of mineral salts from the soil [50]. It is also seriously questioned whether the transpiration stream aids materially in transporting absorbed salts from roots to leaves, leading authorities stating that transpiration can have little or no effect upon the movement of nutrients [50]. Viewed in all its aspects, transpiration is unquestionably a very wasteful process, and its harmful effects upon plant life appear to exceed by far its beneficial effects. The benefits, if any, do not compensate for the elements of danger.

It has been pointed out [3] that the explanation of this anomalous condition may be found in the origin and development of the transpiration process. Probably in the primitive state plants lived in water and derived the carbon dioxide and oxygen needed in the process of photosynthesis and respiration directly from this source. As development took place plants have not materially changed their method of obtaining these gases. As at present organized, with foliage exposed to the atmosphere instead of to water, wet cell walls are exposed to drying by evaporation as well as absorption of carbon dioxide, and except under special conditions have developed no effective means of protection against loss of water. Transpiration, although a constant source of danger to plant life, is thus unavoidable and must be recognized in any study of the hydrologic balance.

Guttation

The loss of water by guttation occurs under conditions favorable for root absorption but unfavorable for transpiration. It is essentially a rapid process of plant relief for the disposal of water absorbed by the roots in excess of transpiration. It occurs principally at night but may also take place in the daytime if proper conditions prevail. Cool nights following warm days or high humidity during warm weather are both favorable. The water of guttation escapes through specialized organs termed "hydrothodes." They are of two types, with reference to the vascular or water-conducting system of the plant. One type has no connection with this system, consisting of modified epidermal cells that form specialized hairs or conical protrusions. The other type, known as epithem hydrothodes, are directly connected to the ends of the fibrovascular bundles and open to the atmosphere through water stomata whose guard cells have lost their power of adjustment. The water of guttation ordinarily collects at the edges and tips of leaves, but under extreme conditions it may appear over the entire leaf surface. The escape of water by guttation is produced by pressure in the fibrovascular system known as root pressure, because of its supposed origin in certain root cells. The same force produces exudation from cut stems or holes bored in the stem, although the loss from holes may also be caused by forces of local origin. Water lost by guttation is appreciable in quantity and may often be felt as a fine mist under trees of certain types. A common example is that of willow and cottonwood trees during warm, humid summer days in semiarid or arid regions.

Methods of measuring transpiration

The measurement of transpiration has been approached from differing standpoints by research workers in various fields. The botanist, investigating transpiration as a physiologic process, is interested in relative rates as controlled by physiologic or environmental conditions. Such data can be most conveniently obtained by tests of a few hours or days made upon detached parts of plants. Investigators interested in the application of transpiration data to problems of silviculture, agriculture, and engineering, on the other hand, require information for longer periods, ranging from a few weeks to the full growing season. They also are interested in transpiration from the whole plant or extensive stands rather than from a part of a plant. The principal methods used in measurement of transpiration, as described below, reflect the purpose and background of the investigator.

Measurement of water vapor transpired

Hygroscopic absorption.—In the Freeman method special apparatus is used consisting of a large glass cylinder as a transpiration chamber for a growing twig or portion of a plant, two U tubes containing phosphoric anhydride for absorption of moisture, and a water aspirator of known capacity, all connected by rubber tubing. Air is drawn through the system by opening the aspirator valve, and the amount of moisture absorbed by the U tubes is measured and corrected for atmospheric moisture. The leaf area in the cylinder is then determined and the rate of transpiration calculated. This method can be used for plants too large to be grown in containers, or when the whole plant cannot be sacrificed for the test. It gives quantitative data on the comparative rates of transpiration for different plants. Objectionable features of the method are the abnormal conditions of temperature and humidity in the transpiration cylinder and the tendency of moisture to condense on the walls of the cylinder. These difficulties can be partly overcome by the use of more active drying agents, such as anhydrous magnesium perchlorate and barium perchlorate, as attempted by Minckler [51]. The method has been used in botanical and silvicultural research.

Hygrometer.—The hygrometer method consists of measuring changes in humidity in a closed container in which is placed a small growing plant or twig. It is open to the objection that the humidity is abnormally high and constantly increasing.

Indicators applied to leaf.—The most commonly used indicator applied to a leaf is cobalt chloride, which changes in color with change in moisture content. Strips of filter paper dipped in a solution of the salt are placed against the growing leaf, and the time required for color change, called leaf test time, is obtained. This is compared with the water test time for a standard evaporating surface, to obtain the index of transpiration power. This method is very sensitive to change or difference in transpiration rate and furnishes quantitative information relative thereto. It has been improved and standardized by Livingston and Shreve [42] and is now used by a large number of botanical research workers.

Measurement of change in weight due to loss of water

Potometer.—The potometer (poton, drink; meter, measure) consists of a vessel containing water into which can be inserted the cut end of a severed leaf, twig, branch, or plant. After proper sealing, measurements are made of the amount of water removed from the vessel. The period of test is limited to a few hours or days. This method was formerly used extensively by botanists and silviculturists for theoretical laboratory study of transpiration. The apparatus is simple and easy to manipulate and is fairly satisfactory for determining relative rates under differing conditions, provided losses are determined by periodic weighing of container and specimen, thus eliminating the error due to water going into storage or upbuilding of plant tissue. The method is not adapted, however, to obtaining reliable quantitative results applicable to plants normally rooted in the soil. This has been clearly shown by comparative tests and study of the relative behavior of stomata for plants in potometers and growing in the soil [50].

Weighing freshly cut parts of plants.—Another method consists of weighing freshly cut leaves, twigs, or stalks of growing plants, immediately after cutting and at short intervals thereafter, during a period of hours or days or until wilting commences. The accuracy of the method is based on the assumption that transpiration continues at approximately the same rate immediately before and after cutting. Cutting and weighing is done either in air or in water. If cut in air, the rate of loss is determined from the rate of change in weight during intervals of a few minutes for the first hour, the weighing being done at the site of the growing plant and under the same atmospheric conditions. If cut in water, a great change in transpiration rate occurs, usually an increase, due to ample water supply and reduction of plant tissue between leaf and water. In time, however, the rate is reduced to what it was previously. Changes at the cut surface, in the size of stomatal openings, and in suction forces are all involved, but they need study to be fully understood.

Results have been used quantitatively to determine 24-hour loss where the ratio of transpiration rate at the time of cutting to the average 24-hour rate is known. For application to the whole growing period the relation of leaf area at the time of cutting to the average leaf area during the growing period is also required. The method has been applied both to single plants and to close-growing field crops such as alfalfa or meadow grass. It has been tried in silvicultural and engineering investigations but is not in general use [16, 34, 38].

Phytometer.—Phytometers (phyton, plant; meter, measure) are of various types and are in general use by botanists for registering the effect upon growing plants of differing environmental conditions. They differ from potometers by containing soil in which the whole plant is grown, thus reproducing more nearly the natural conditions for rooted plants. The period of test may be varied, as desired, from a few hours up to the full length of the growing season.

For measuring transpiration the closed phytometer has been extensively used by silvicultural, agricultural, and engineering experimenters.

This consists of a water-tight container, either pot or tank, which can be sealed after the plant is well established, so as to exclude precipitation and to prevent the escape of water except through the plant. Soil is placed in as near the original natural condition as possible and brought to the desired moisture content, which is maintained by adding water from time to time in amount necessary to bring the container and specimen back to the initial weight. For long-time experiments provision is made for aeration.

Pots or tanks are used as containers. The tanks are usually cylindrical galvanized-iron cans holding from 250 to 1,000 pounds of soil. Successive weights are obtained either by automatic balances in the laboratory, or for large containers in the field by means of block and tackle and suspended balances or platform scales. Results are expressed either in depth of water loss over area of soil surface during the period of observation, or in weight of water required to produce a unit weight of dry matter.

By use of the closed phytometer both the progressive rates of transpiration during the growing season and the total amount of water used in producing the fully grown plant can be determined. It is the most satisfactory and convenient method for theoretical study of transpiration losses, although its application is limited to plants with small root systems. Difficulties experienced by early experimenters in obtaining accurate results were as follows:

1. Obtaining sufficient soil to attain normal transpiration relations and root development of the plant.

2. Obtaining the same atmospheric and light exposure as under natural field conditions.

3. Obtaining the same leaf development or density of planting as under field conditions.

4. Preventing disturbance of the soil during excavation and replacement in the container, especially with respect to aeration and permeability.

Transpiration ratio (water requirement).—A modification of the phytometer method is widely used in agricultural research, and to a moderate extent by silviculturists, to determine the total amount of water lost by transpiration in relation to dry matter produced. Water requirement is defined as the ratio of the weight of water absorbed by, conveyed through, and transpired from a plant during the growing season to the weight of dry matter produced exclusive of roots. The term "water requirement" is misleading, however, as the results merely indicate the amount of water transpired from the plant stem and leaves under certain more or less artificial conditions of climate, soil fertility, soil moisture, and physical conditions of the plant. The terms "transpiration ratio" or "water-use ratio" for certain described conditions are more appropriate and do not conflict with the term "water requirement" as used by irrigation engineers to represent the total quantity of water, regardless of its source, required by crops for normal growth under field conditions.

The transpiration ratio serves primarily as a measure of relative efficiency of plants in the use of water, but in some places where data on crop production are available it can be applied to determine transpiration loss from large areas of cropped land. The method consists of growing plants to maturity in sealed tanks containing about 300 pounds of soil and weighing the amount of aerial dry matter produced after drying at a temperature between 100° and 110° C. The container is weighed at frequent intervals during the growing season, and measured quantities of water are regularly added to the soil to replace losses. The amount of water consumed by the plant is computed from the sum of the quantities of water added during the season corrected for the difference in weight of the container with contents at the beginning and end of the test. The amount of water retained within the plant at harvesting is negligible in comparison with the amount transpired. Results for a single plant variety may vary 100 percent or more with varying conditions of climate, soil, soil moisture, and fertilizer.

In order to use the transpiration ratio in determining water losses from large areas of growing crops, experimenters sometimes dry and weigh only that portion of the plant which is harvested and for which figures on harvested yields per acre are available. Published results may thus be based upon differing portions of the plant, such as aerial dry matter in hay and alfalfa; grain in cereals, beans, and corn; or tubers in potatoes and sugar beets. Few of the early investigators determined total dry weight, even of matter above ground, and the conditions under which their experiments were carried on were seldom fully described. In some experiments the tanks were not sealed, so that soil evaporation was included with transpiration. As a result, it is difficult to correlate the work of early investigators, or to determine the applicability of published data to field conditions in any given area. Beginning with the work of Briggs and Shantz in 1910 [8, 9, 63], followed by Kisselbach and Montgomery [52], Dillman [12], and Miller [50], the experimental methods have been more systematic, and published descriptions of conditions more nearly complete.

Application of results

Measurements by the potometer, Freeman, and cobalt chloride methods and also the weighing of freshly cut parts are all useful for intensive study of transpiration. They furnish during short periods of time a quantitative basis for comparing the relative rates of transpiration from detached specimens under differing environmental conditions. Grossly erroneous results may be obtained, however, if such data are used to determine the transpiration from whole plants or stands or for long periods of time. An attempt made by Pfaff [58, p. 76], for example, to determine total transpiration from a large oak tree during the growing season, by periodic measurements of leaf area and water loss from cut twigs, applied to computed leaf area of the tree, gave a result equivalent to nearly ten times the annual precipitation upon the projected area covered by crown and roots. On the other hand, Lee [34] obtained reasonable results by applying the measured rate at which water was lost from a known area of freshly cut alfalfa during the first 15 minutes after cutting, but even here considerable assumptions were involved in applying data from 15 minute observational periods to a 7-month growing season.

The phytometer method, in contrast to those listed above, furnishes quantitative results for whole plants that are cumulative over long periods of time. It is not very applicable to large shrubs and trees or to close-growing stands. Silviculturists have attempted to bridge this gap in two ways—first, by determining transpiration per unit leaf area of a specimen of a given species during a given period of time and multiplying this by the estimated leaf area in the whole tree or forest area; second, by obtaining the dry weight of mature leaves per unit area for the particular species and locality by cutting and stripping a known area and applying to this result the transpiration ratio as experimentally determined for the same species in a similar environment. The first method involves greater assumptions and is the less reliable. The second method is more costly but has practical utility. Both are subject to the limitations of the phytometer method.

Data on transpiration ratio have been used principally by agriculturists and engineers, in determining water loss from field crops. If crop yields are known the data for similar crops can be applied directly to larger areas on an acreage basis. Where the harvested crop includes only a portion of the aerial dry matter, the relative weights of harvested and entire dry matter must be determined. As the transpiration ratio varies considerably with climatic conditions, these conditions must be taken into consideration in selecting ratios for purposes of estimation. Final results are subject to inaccuracies from differences in the growing conditions that surround the plant in the tank and in the field.

Agriculturists and engineers have extensively utilized the results of phytometer tank experiments made on low, close-growing vegetation, in which water loss for a given period is expressed as depth over the area of soil surface in the tank covered by the vertical projection of the plants. This figure is then applied to field areas of cultivated crops or close-growing natural vegetation, either directly or after application of a correction factor. The correction is essential where tanks are isolated or have abnormal exposure. The numerical value of the factor to be used must depend upon the experience and judgment of the user and may range from 0.30 to 1.0, depending upon conditions [6].

QUANTITATIVE EXPERIMENTAL DATA

Availability

The quantitative results of measurements by the phytometer, Freeman, cobalt chloride, and similar methods are the basis of the various conclusions at which botanical investigators have arrived concerning the process of transpiration. They are voluminous, and their complete reproduction is beyond the scope of this paper. The only data of this type presented herein are those pertaining to diurnal variation in transpiration.

Quantitative measurements by the phytometer method furnish data of total water loss by transpiration over long periods of time and are of interest to hydrologic, agricultural, and silvicultural workers. Unfortunately the available information is scanty, most of it being in the form of data on transpiration ratio. Where soil evaporation is negligible, data derived from tank measurements of consumptive use approximately represent transpiration loss.

Variations of rate with time

Diurnal variations.—The variations of transpiration within the diurnal and seasonal cycles and also from year to year are of practical interest. Diurnal variations reflect the daily cycle of environmental influences such as temperature, humidity, and especially light intensity. The details are well illustrated by (Fig. VIII-1) prepared by Lee [34] from potometer observations made under the direction of F. E. Clements at the University of Minnesota on a cloudy day, February 17, 1907 [60]. It is evident from this chart that light intensity is the primary factor controlling diurnal variations in transpiration. A similar chart (Fig. VIII-2), prepared from the experimental work of Miller and Coffman [50], shows the relation of hourly transpiration from corn and milo to evaporation from a porous-cup atmometer at Garden City, Kans., July 26 and 27, 1916. Evaporation can be considered as representing the composite effect of solar radiation and atmospheric conditions during daylight hours, and this portion of the curve shows a striking resemblance to that of transpiration. The closure of stomata with darkness, however, abruptly terminates the similarity of the two curves. In general 94 to 97 percent of daily transpiration occurs during daylight hours, the maximum rate occurring between 11 a.m. and 3 p.m. Variations from day to day due to changing weather conditions may be large.

Seasonal variations.—Seasonal variations in transpiration are primarily controlled by plant activity but can be correlated with evaporation. This is illustrated by (Figure VIII-3), prepared from data obtained by Lee in Owens Valley near Independence, Calif., during 1911 [35]. Observations of transpiration from second-year growth of salt grass were made

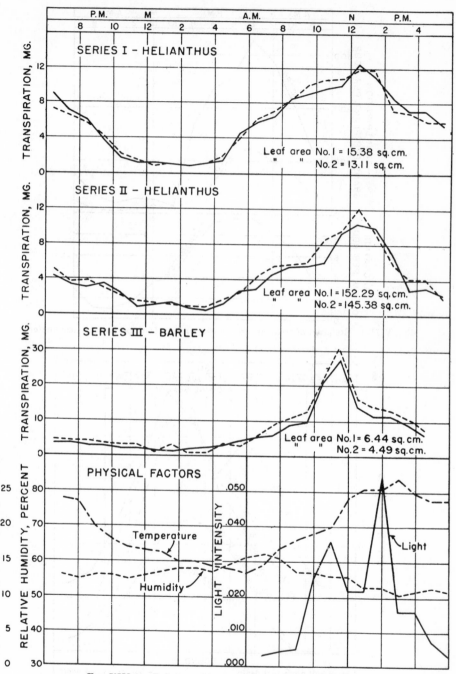

Fɪɢ. VIII-1.—Relation of transpiration to light intensity.

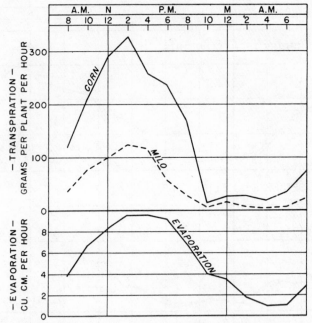

Fig. VIII-2.—Relation of transpiration to evaporation from porous-cup atmometer.

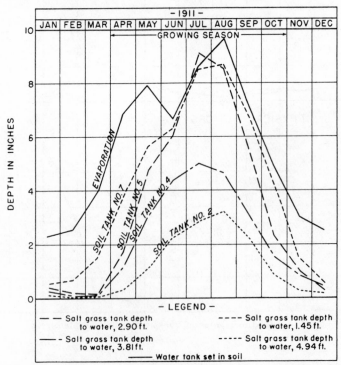

Fig. VIII-3.—Mean monthly depth of transpiration and evaporation near Independence, Calif., for the year 1911.

by the phytometer method in tanks 7 feet 6 inches in diameter and 6 feet 6 inches deep, set flush with the ground surface and surrounded by similar growth. Although the tops of the tanks were not sealed, loss by soil evaporation was nominal, owing to the cover afforded by the close and luxuriant growth of salt grass. Water losses from salt-grass tanks during the growing season, extending from March 15 to October 15, averaged 91 percent of the total for the year, while that from the free water surface was 77 percent. Measurements of water evaporation were made in a circular tank 3 feet 6 inches by 4 feet, set with the top flush with the surface of the ground. The persistence of water evaporation during the nongrowing season differentiates the evaporation curve from the transpiration curve (Fig. VIII-3).

TABLE 1.—*Transpiration ratio in pounds of water per pound of dry leaf matter and evaporation, in inches from free water surface at Akron, Col., season April 1 to September 30, 1911–17*
[Data from reference 63, table 27]

Plant	1911	1912	1913	1914	1915	1916	1917	Average
Alfalfa.....................	1,068	657	834	890	695	1,047	822	859
Oats, Swedish select...........	615	423	617	599	448	876	635	602
Oats, Burt..................	639	449	617	615	445	809	636	601
Barley, Hannchen...........	527	443	513	501	404	664	522	511
Wheat, Kubanka.............	468	394	496	518	405	639	471	484
Corn, Northwest Dent........	368	280	399	368	253	495	346	358
Millet, Kursk................	287	187	286	295	202	367	284	273
Sorghum, Red Amber.........	298	239	298	284	303	296	272	270
Average transpiration ratio.....	534	384	508	509	382	649	499	495
Evaporation[1]................	48.8	37.7	43.0	41.8	33.4	47.1	42.7	42.1
Transpiration ratio, percent of average..................	107	78	104	103	77	131	101	100
Evaporation, percent of average	116	90	102	99	79	112	101	100

[1] Observed in sunken land pan 8 feet in diameter, 24 inches deep, 1911–15 and similar pan 6 feet in diameter, 1916–17; evaporation about 80 percent of that for 12 months.

Secular variations.—Transpiration varies greatly from year to year as the result of climatic differences, just as evaporation from a free water surface varies. This fact is well illustrated by data on transpiration ratio for standard crops obtained at Akron, Colo., for the years 1911 to 1917 (see table 1, above), and at Newell, S. Dak., 1912 to 1918, and Mandan, N. Dak., 1919 to 1922 (see table 2). The close agreement each year in the percentage departures from average transpiration ratio and evaporation at these three stations shows conclusively that annual variations in transpiration ratio are controlled by the same climatic factors that control evaporation. This relation apparently applies not only to annual variations at the same locality but to differences in average transpiration ratio at localities with differing climatic conditions. These relations make it possible to correct a single year's observations of transpiration ratio to the average for a period of years, and to convert an average at one locality to that at another, provided the annual evaporation is known for a period of years. The accompanying Figure VIII-4 expresses the relation of

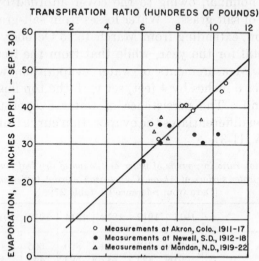

Fig. VIII-4.—Relation between evaporation for reservoir surface and transpiration ratio of alfalfa. (Evaporation from reservoir surface computed from evaporation from 8-foot sunken land pan by use of a coefficient of 0.94.)

TABLE 2.—*Transpiration ratio, in pounds of water per pound of dry leaf matter, and evaporation, in inches, from free water surface season April 1 to August 31, at Newell, S. Dak., 1912–18, and Mandan, N. Dak., 1919–22*
[Data from reference 12, table 32]

Plant	1912	1913	1914	1915	1916	1917	1918	1919	1920	1921	1922	Average
Alfalfa, all varieties.........	701	759	1,036	602	694	898	947	706	670	936	742	802
Wheat, Kubanka C. I. 1440..	463	436	528	333	352	487	415	520	340	531	372	434
Millet, all varieties..........	261	316	307	177	232	278	239	303	186	....	....	255
Sorgo, Dakota Amber.......	....	....	....	210	239	275	284	273	229	....	....	252
Sudan grass.................	....	....	....	272	314	344	333	347	274	....	....	314
Evaporation:[a]												
April–September..........	37.7	37.1	35.1	27.4	32.5	34.8	32.5	39.6	35.3	39.3	33.9	35.0
June–August.............	22.7	23.4	22.4	15.1	18.1	22.8	20.2	24.5	21.9	24.7	20.3	21.5
Transpiration ratio, percent of average...............	100	105	112	76	90	108	98	110	88	118	95	100
Evaporation, percent of average.....................	106	109	105	70	84	106	94	114	102	115	95	100

[a] Observed in sunken land pan 8 feet in diameter, 24 inches deep.

evaporation to transpiration ratio as indicated by the data for alfalfa in tables 1 and 2 and is regarded as having general application for this crop in localities where data on evaporation from a reservoir surface or equivalent are available.

It was also found at Akron that changes in weather conditions may cause the loss of water from plants to vary as much as 600 percent on successive days, so that the conditions prevailing during periods of a month or even 10 days may determine whether the water requirement for the year will be high or low [63].

Total plant discharge

Total plant discharge includes the total loss from plants by transpiration and guttation throughout the growing season. For practical use in hydrology the data must apply in extended stands, either for a single variety or for a group of naturally associated varieties. The various types of vegetation growing in North America may be broadly classified as follows:

Natural vegetation:
    Evergreen forests.
    Deciduous forests.
    Grassland.
    Woodland.
    Sagebrush.
    Desert scrub.
    Weeds.

Cultivated vegetation:
    Field crops:
        Grains.
        Legumes.
        Cucurbits.
        Crucifers.
        Miscellaneous.
    Orchard.
    Vineyard.

The broad groups of natural vegetation are subdivided into groups technically termed formations or climaxes, which are controlled by climatic conditions, such as arid, semiarid, humid, and tropical. Locally there are further subdivisions controlled by surface- or ground-water conditions. Such subdivisions are of special importance in arid and semiarid regions. Among them are the types of vegetation characteristic of stream borders, river-bottom lands, meadows, swamps, and marshes.

Experimental determinations of transpiration in America have been largely confined to cultivated crops and associated native vegetation. In Europe some work has been done upon forest trees, the phytometer method being used and the results expressed as transpiration ratio for leaves. In a few experiments the method of weighing freshly cut parts of plants has been attempted. Lee [34] found by this method that the total transpiration loss from a stand of alfalfa at Independence, Calif., averaged 3.4 feet in depth, and Hammatt [16] found an average loss from sugar grass at Chewaucan Marsh, near Paisley, Oreg., of 1.2 feet. The results of the most reliable and comparable tests of transpiration ratio for agricultural crops are assembled in table 3, and for forest trees in table 4.

Agricultural crops.—The most complete and reliable series of tests on agricultural crops are those made by Briggs and Shantz [8, 9, 63] at Akron, Colo., during the years 1911 to 1917, and by Dillman at Newell, S. Dak.,

TABLE 3.—*Transpiration ratio, in pounds of water per pound of dry leaf matter, for agricultural crops*
[Data from references 8, 12, 13, and 63]

Plants	Lawes, 1850, Rothamsted, England	Wollny, 1886, Munich, Germany	Hellriegel, 1883, Dahme, Germany	King, 1892–95, Madison, Wis.	Von Seelhorst, 1896–98, Göttingen, Germany	Leather, 1910–11, Pusa, India	Fortier and Beckett, Davis, Calif.	Fortier and Gieseker, Bozeman, Mont.	Fortier and Peterson, Reno, Nev.	Briggs and Shantz, 1911–17, Akron, Colo.[a]	Dillman, 1912–22, Newell, S. Dak.; Mandan, N. Dak.[a]
Grain crops:											
Proso	...	...	...	...	...	...	...	...	...	267	254
Millet	...	...	...	...	...	...	...	...	...	268	260
Sorghum	...	233	...	...	...	...	...	...	...	296	
Corn	...	...	...	348	...	...	...	...	...	349	
Teosinte	...	...	...	...	...	337	...	...	...	368	
Millet (Turkestan)	...	...	...	...	...	...	...	...	...	368	
Sudan grass	...	...	...	...	...	...	...	...	...	380	335
Barley	260	774	297	388	365	468	...	...	...	518	
Wheat	235	...	339	...	333	544	326	271	360	538	430
Buckwheat	...	...	...	...	...	...	...	...	...	540	
Oats	...	665	401	514	469	469	...	...	...	583	536
Rye	...	...	377	...	...	...	...	...	...	634	
Rice	...	...	...	...	...	811	...	...	...	682	668
Flax	...	...	...	...	...	...	...	...	...	783	
Other crops:											
Beet sugar	...	...	...	423	281	...	...	...	...	377	304
Potato	...	...	...	...	...	...	...	...	...	575	
Crucifers:											
Cabbage	...	...	...	...	...	...	...	...	...	518	
Turnip	...	...	...	...	...	...	...	...	...	614	
Rape	...	...	...	...	...	...	...	...	...	714	
Cotton	...	...	...	...	...	...	...	...	...	568	
Cucurbits:											
Watermelon	...	...	...	...	...	...	...	...	...	577	
Canteloupe	...	...	...	...	...	...	...	...	...	597	
Cucumber	...	...	...	...	...	...	...	...	...	686	
Squash	...	...	...	...	...	...	...	...	...	719	
Pumpkin	...	...	...	...	...	...	...	...	...	802	
Legumes:											
Guar	...	...	...	...	...	...	...	...	...	523	
Cowpea	...	...	...	...	...	...	...	...	...	569	
Alfalfa (Peruvian)	...	...	...	...	...	...	...	...	...	626	

TABLE 3.—*Transpiration ratio, in pounds of water per pound of dry leaf matter, for agricultural crops.*—(*Continued*)

Plants	Lawes, 1850, Rothamsted, England	Wollny, 1886, Munich, Germany	Hellriegel, 1883, Dahme, Germany	King, 1892–95, Madison, Wis.	Von Seelhorst, 1896–98, Göttingen, Germany	Leather, 1910–11, Pusa, India	Fortier and Beckett, Davis, Calif.	Fortier and Gieseker, Bozeman, Mont.	Fortier and Peterson, Reno, Nev.	Briggs and Shantz, 1911–17, Akron, Colo.[a]	Dillman, 1912–22, Newell, S. Dak.; Mandan, N. Dak.[a]
Legumes:—(*Continued*)											
Chick pea	251									638	
Clover, red			330	481						698	
Bean (navy, Mexican)										700	
Vetch										708	
Bean (soy)										715	
Clover (sweet)										731	
Pea	235	416	292	477		563				747	
Lupine										837	
Alfalfa							930	823[b]		868	809
Grasses:											
Wheat grass										678	1018
Brome										977	784
Native plants:											
Purslane										281	288
Tumbleweed and Pigweed										283	261
Grass, buffalo										308	
Thistle, Russian										314	224
Grass, buffalo and grama										336	
Cocklebur										415	
Clammyweed										483	
Nightshade										487	
Iva										534	
Buffalo Bur										536	
Sunflower, annual										577	
Gumweed										585	
Sage, mountain										654	
Lambsquarters										658	435
Polygonum										678	
Verbena										702	
Marigold, fetid										847	
Wheat grass (western)										857	
Ragweed										912	
Franseria										1131	

[a] Weighted means.   [b] State College. N. Mex.

and Mandan, N. Dak., from 1912 to 1922 (table 3).   Akron is 100 miles
east of Denver, and its climatic conditions are representative of the central
Great Plains.   The climatic conditions at Newell and Mandan are typical
of the northern Great Plains.   The tests at Akron embraced 59 varieties
of plants, 14 grain crops, 25 other crops, and 20 native varieties.   Plants
were grown to maturity in large galvanized pots holding 250 pounds of

TABLE 4.—*Transpiration ratio, in pounds of water per pound of dry leaf matter, for forest trees*
[Data from reference 23, tables 1 and 15]

Variety	Botanical name	Transpiration ratio
1. Larch (tamarack)............	Larix europea	1,165
2. Beech......................	Fagus sylvatica	1,043
3. Linden (basswood)..........	Tilia grandifolia	1,038
4. Ash.......................	Fraxinus excelsior	981
5. Aspen.....................	Populus tremuloides	873
6. White birch................	Betula alba	849
7. Black alder................	Alnus glutinosa	840
8. Hornbeam (ironwood)........	Carpinus betulus	787
9. Field elm..................	Ulmus campestris	738
10. Gray alder.................	Alnus incana	678
11. Stiel oak..................	Quercus pedunculus	
12. Trauben oak...............	Quercus sessilifolia	616
13. Zerr oak...................	Quercus cerris	
14. Sycamore maple............	Acer platanoides	
15. Mountain maple............	Acer pseudoplatanus	578
16. Field maple............	Acer campestre	
17. Norway spruce.............	Abies excelsa	242
18. Austrian pine..............	Pinus austriaca	123
19. Scotch pine................	Pinus sylvestris	110
20. Fir.......................	Abies pectinata	86
Average for deciduous and associated evergreen trees with normal habitat on stream borders or continually moist soil, Nos. 1 to 7.............................		970
Average for deciduous trees with normal habitat in well-drained soils and on slopes, Nos. 8 to 16..............		680
Average for evergreen trees, Nos. 17 to 20..............		140

soil.   Each pot was provided with a tight-fitting cover sealed with wax
around stem plants.   To protect the plants from birds and the elements,
experiments were conducted in screened enclosures.   A long series of
observations was made to compare results from tanks in shelter, in the
open, and set into the ground in the field and surrounded by an extensive
stand of the same crop.   Although the results showed wide variations,
the general conclusion was reached that plants in the field had a transpiration ratio 10 percent greater than those in shelter, and plants in freely

exposed tanks a ratio 13 percent greater. Dillman's work was similar to that at Akron and included 14 varieties of agricultural plants and weeds. The results of other reliable measurements of transpiration ratio shown in table 3 agree reasonably well with those made in the Great Plains region, if correction is made for climatic and other differing conditions. Tests by Sleight [66] at Denver in the 12-foot and 9-foot ground pans indicate that evaporation from April 1 to September 30 in the locality of Akron is 80 percent of the annual evaporation.

Forest trees.—The most systematic and extensive set of experiments to determine transpiration ratios for forest trees is that of Franz von Höhnel at the Austrian Forest Experiment Station at Maraibrunn from 1878 to 1880. Although using methods of doubtful value, Höhnel's results agree fairly well with those of other workers and are as reliable as any others available [58]. He transplanted 5-year old seedlings to pots equipped with conical covers, containing about 10 pounds of soil. Various pots were given sun, shade, and half-shade exposures. Water was systematically added during the growing season, and at the end of each season the leaves were gathered and dried. The results were expressed as weight of water per unit weight of dry leaf matter. Twenty varieties of trees were used, including both evergreen and deciduous trees. Observations during the year 1878 were made to determine minimum requirements under local conditions, and those in 1880 maximum requirements. The conditions during 1879 were probably more nearly average, and the results have been compiled from Höhnel's original reports by Horton [23] and are reproduced in table 4.

Application of transpiration ratio.—The practical use of the transpiration ratio in hydrologic studies is limited. Hay is the only agricultural crop for which harvest yields are stated in terms of total aerial dry matter. Briggs and Shantz [9] made tests in 1913 on 20 varieties of plants to determine the transpiration ratio in terms of dry seed tubers, roots, or fruit produced. The data thus obtained indicated that the ratio in terms of dry harvested crop is two to four times greater than that for the whole plant, but the tests were insufficient to produce usable results. For applying Höhnel's data to stands of deciduous forest trees, Horton [23] proposes the formula

$$T = \frac{dhN}{10,000} \times \frac{E}{45},$$

in which T = transpiration rate, in inches of depth per acre.
      d = breast-height diameter of tree, in inches.
      h = height of tree, in feet.
      N = number of trees per acre.
      E = annual evaporation, in inches.

Lee has cut and stripped close-growing sapling willow trees 10 feet in height within a measured area and obtained an oven dry weight per acre of 2,367 pounds.

Broadly considered, data on transpiration ratio although of general interest and of specific value in agriculture and silviculture because they indicate the wide range in transpiration that may be expected with different plant varieties and environments, are of little practical use to the engineer and hydrologist. In fact, losses by soil evaporation and interception are so intimately associated with transpiration that for any areal studies experimental data should represent the natural integrated value of all three of these elements of water loss, rather than a synthetic combination. For this reason, data on consumptive use and total evaporation are of greater practical utility than data on transpiration ratio.

SOIL EVAPORATION

Physical process

Soil evaporation is the loss of water by evaporation into the atmosphere from water films adhering to moist soil grains. It usually occurs at or near the surface of the ground, but if the upper zones of the soil are sufficiently open for atmospheric circulation, it may also occur as interior evaporation. Evaporation from bare soil is much greater than that from soil shaded by vegetation.

In order for soil evaporation to occur, soil grains must be enveloped by film water in excess of hygroscopic moisture. Film water is most abundant within the capillary fringe immediately above the water table, where it is termed "fringe water." Soil moisture above the capillary fringe may be termed *"adhesive water"* and varies in degree from field capacity to *hygroscopic* moisture. At the hygroscopic condition soil moisture is in equilibrium with atmospheric moisture, and evaporation ceases. The rate of soil evaporation varies with the abundance of film water, and the aggregate evaporation within any period of time depends upon the continuity of the film at a given state of soil moisture. The ratio of evaporation from the soil to the potential evaporation from a free water surface at any instant is termed the "evaporation opportunity."

For maintenance of evaporation opportunity there must be a continuing replenishment of film water to replace that lost by evaporation. If the evaporating zone is within the capillary fringe the water table serves as a constant source of supply, and the rate of capillary flow is usually great enough to maintain a film. Under such conditions the maximum rate of soil evaporation occurs with a very shallow water table and a condition of saturation at or near the ground surface. The rate decreases as the water table declines and the water film decreases in thickness, becoming nominal or zero soon after the water table drops below the limit of capillary rise. In sand the capillary rise is from 1 to 2 feet. In sandy loam it may exceed 4 feet, and in clayey soils it may be as great as 10 feet.

Above the capillary fringe the movement of adhesive film water from areas of greater to areas of lesser moisture content is so slow that the flow is practically negligible [78]. The replenishment of film water above the capillary fringe is therefore intermittent, the water being derived from precipitation, surface flooding, or irrigation. The evaporation opportunity under such conditions is extremely variable, changing rapidly from unity to zero as the top soil passes through the cycle from dryness at hygroscopic moisture, to saturation, to field capacity, and finally back to dryness.

QUANTITATIVE DATA

Soil moistened from water table

Measurement of evaporation from bare soil moistened from a water table has been undertaken in western America by several investigators during the last 25 years, using the tank method. Lee's work in Owens Valley, Calif., 1909 to 1911 [34, 35], was an early attempt. Sleight's work on evaporation at Denver, Colo., 1915 to 1917 [66], included tests of evaporation from moist river bed materials. Parshall made an exhaustive study at Fort Collins, Colo., 1925 to 1927 [54], of evaporation from saturated soil and river-bed sands, the water table being maintained at a depth of less than 12 inches by Mariotté tank control. Similar work, with the water table ranging in depth from a few inches to 4 feet was carried on by the United States Reclamation Service in 1926 to 1928, as reported by Houk [54]. White [80] also made tests in Escalante Valley, Utah, during 1926 and 1927, and Tipton and Hart [84] made tests at Garnett in San Luis Valley, Colo., during 1927, 1928, 1930, and 1931.

Conclusions drawn from the results of these various tests may be summarized as follows:

1. Evaporation from sand saturated at the surface is equal to or slightly in excess of that from a free water surface. For loams and clayey soils such as adobe it is less, ranging from 75 to over 90 percent. A working ratio for the relation of evaporation from a saturated bare soil surface to that from a free water surface, applicable to sand, is 100 percent, and to average loamy soil 90 percent. Lower ratios should be used for heavy soils.

2. Evaporation from the soil of water derived from the water table ceases when the water table reaches a depth exceeding the limit of capillary rise for the soil. For heavy soils, including clay loams and adobes, soil evaporation practically ceases when the water table reaches a depth of 4 feet, even though the capillary limit may exceed this figure. Soil losses

with the water table below this depth occur by plant transpiration rather than by soil evaporation.

3. Soil evaporation varies between these maximum and minimum limits, depending upon the depth of the water table. The rate of variation is generally proportional to the depth, although the available data are not entirely conclusive on this point.

Freely draining soil

The evaporation from freely draining soil above the capillary fringe has been frequently investigated, both in the United States and abroad.

TABLE 5.—*Evaporation from bare well-drained soil*

Locality	Years of work	Type of soil	Size of tank	Average annual precipitation (inches)[a]	Average soil evaporation (inches)	Authority
LYSIMETER METHOD						
Geneva, Switzerland....	2	....	....	26.0	15.2	Maurice [75].
Orange, southern France	2	....	....	28.0	21.0	Gasparin [75].
Ferrybridge, Yorkshire, England.	5	Magnesian limestone	1 × 1 × 3 ft.	24.6	19.8	Charnock [75].
Lee Bridge, London, England.................	14	Fine sand	3 × 3 × ? ft.	25.7	4.1	Greaves [75].
Görlitz, Silesia, Germany	4	Clay	? × 1.25 m.	25.6	18.4	Von Möllendorff [75].
Do.................	4	Loam	Do.	25.6	15.1	Do.
Do.................	4	Sandy Loam	Do.	25.6	15.2	Do.
Munich, Bavaria........	3	Sand	? × 1.20 m.	42.3	13.9	Wollny [75].
Do.................	3	Loam	Do.	42.3	31.1	Do.
Do.................	3	Peat	Do.	42.3	15.2	Do.
Rothamsted, Hertfordshire, England.	32	Heavy loam	6.5 × 6.5 × 1.7 ft.	28.1	14.4	Laws and Gilbert [75].
Do.................	32	Do.	6.5 × 6.5 × 3.3 ft.	28.1	13.6	Do.
Do.................	32	Do.	6.5 × 6.5 × 5 ft.	28.1	14.6	Do.
FIELD-PLOT METHOD						
Anaheim, Calif........	1[b]	Fine sandy loam	10 × 10 ft.	12.39	6.0	Blaney and Taylor [5][c].
Ontario, Calif..........	1[b]	Sand over silt loam	Do.	11.52	4.7	Do.
Do.................	1[b]	Sand	Do.	12.79	6.8	Do.
Glen Avon Heights, Calif.	1[b]	Loam	Do.	12.18	8.1	Do.

[a] For period of observation.

[b] Oct. 1 to Apr. 15, including practically all of the annual rainy season.

[c] Concluded that average soil evaporation during a winter storm does not exceed 0.5 inch.

The favorite method of measurement in England and in continental Europe has been by means of the lysimeter, soil evaporation being computed as the difference of precipitation and measured percolation through the soil column. Many observations by this method have been made upon bare soil, and some of them extended over long periods of years. Data regarding those made prior to 1905 have been comprehensively compiled by Veatch [75] and are reproduced in table 5.

The lysimeter method has been said to give results for percolation which are (1) too high because the soil is not in a natural state of consolidation and the runoff factor is suppressed, or (2) too low because the method of underdrainage is unnatural [75]. For soil evaporation, however, these errors tend to compensate or do not apply, and the method should give fairly accurate results. Lysimeter data in table 6 (p. 298), although somewhat erratic, indicate a higher loss from clay and loam soils than from sandy soils, and a greater loss with greater precipitation. The mean soil evaporation for all tanks listed in the table is 52 percent of the mean precipitation.

Measurements of soil evaporation from well-drained soil in America have been made in connection with irrigation practice in the West and with conservation of water in southern California. The measurements on irrigated areas have been productive of very few quantitative data useful in hydrologic work but have demonstrated that losses by direct evaporation from the soil are negligible below a depth of 1 foot [76]. Blaney's work in the Santa Ana River valley of southern California [5] included tests by the field-plot method on clean bare soil, with systematic measurements of precipitation, runoff, and soil moisture. His results are also included in table 6 and tend to confirm the conclusions derived from lysimeter tests regarding the effect of soil texture. The mean soil evaporation from all field plots was 54 percent of the mean precipitation.

In the foregoing discussion soil evaporation has been considered as occurring from bare soil without shading from the direct rays of the sun. Where shade is provided by growing vegetation water losses by soil evaporation are far less than indicated and under some conditions may be nominal. The total losses from soil covered with vegetation are greater, however, owing to the activity of roots, which penetrate the soil to depths of at least 10 feet in search of water.

INTERCEPTION

Interception is the process by which precipitation is caught and held by foliage, twigs, and branches of trees, shrubs, and other vegetation and evaporated from their exposed surfaces.

Interception is probably greatest in forested areas. It has been found to exceed 40 percent of the summer precipitation in well-developed stands of Douglas fir in the Pacific Northwest, and similar percentages of winter snowfall are reported for dense stands of white fir in the Sierra Nevada [32]. Kittredge [32] states that for average forest conditions over large areas the seasonal interception may range between 10 and 25 percent of the precipitation, but for cut or burned areas or heavily grazed range it may approach zero. Horton [23] states that the loss by interception is roughly 15 percent of the rainfall. Interception unquestionably represents a major item of loss in shrub and forest areas.

TABLE 6.—*Consumptive use*

Locality or river system	Mean annual temperature (°F.)	Average annual precipitation (inches)	Average growing season (days between frosts)	Years of work	Size of tank or area of moist land[a]	Vegetation	Consumptive use (acre-feet per year per acre of moist land)	Authority[b]	Remarks
VOLUMETRIC METHOD—TANKS									
Santa Ana River at Santa Ana, Calif.	61.7	12.3	304	1½ 2½ 1 1½ 1½	Circular 2 × 6 ft.	Salt grass	3.5 3.0 2.1 1.1 1.6	6 6 6 6 6	Set in ground in native vegetation; depths to water 1, 2, 3, 4, and 5 feet
Santa Ana River at San Bernardino, Calif.	62.9	16.0	262	2⅜ 2½ 2 2	Circular, 2 × 3½ ft.	Bermuda grass / Do. / Tules / Do.	3.1 2.6 5.2 5.3	72,6 72,6 6 6	Same; depths to water 2 and 3 feet. Set in ground, roots submerged; isolation factors used, 0.388, 0.337, 0.542.
Santa Ana River at Santa Ana, Calif.	61.7	12.3	304	2 1½	Circular, 6 × 3 ft.	Cattails / Willow	5.3 4.0	6 6	Depth to water 2 feet: isolation factor, 0.85.
Santa Ana River at Prado, Calif.	63±	13.2	285	2⅜	Circular, 2 × ? ft.	Tules	6.1	6	Roots submerged. Isolation factor 0.293.
					Circular, 6 × 3 ft.	Do.	6.5	6	In swamp, roots submerged.
Mojave River at Victorville, Calif.	63.5	5.4	255	2	Circular, 2 × 6 ft. / Do.	Do. / Do.	7.0 22.6	6 6	On bank, roots submerged. Isolated exposure.
Sacramento and San Joaquin delta, Calif.	59.5	16.0	290	6	Circular, 2 × 5 ft.	Asparagus	2.69	44	Do.
						Beans	2.12	44	Do.
						Beets	2.30	44	Do.
						Celery	1.50	44	Do.
						Corn	2.90	44	Do.
						Grain and hay	2.62	44	Do.
						Onions	2.14	44	Do.
						Potatoes	2.09	44	Do.
						Bare land	1.02	44	
						Cattails	16.53	72	Exposed to wind and sun, roots submerged.
						Tules	18.48	72	
						Cattails	7.50	72	Protected by surrounding natural tule growth, roots submerged.
						Tules	8.63	72	
Do.	59.5	16.0	290	1	Do.	Cattails	4.56	72	Protected by surrounding natural tule growth, water level in tank at ground surface.
						Tules	4.05	72	

Location					Plot size	Crop	Evaporation	Days	Remarks
Owens River, Independence region, Calif.	57.6	5.26	197	2	Circular, 7.4 × 5.5 ft.	Salt grass	4.05	34	Field exposure; depth to water 1.45 feet.
							3.73	34	Same; depth 1.86 feet.
							3.35	34	Same; depth 2.90 feet.
							2.05	34	Same; depth 3.81 feet.
							2.64	34	Same; depth 4.46 feet.
							1.12	34	Same; depth 4.94 feet.
San Luis Valley near Garnett, Colo.	41.0	6.7	100	2	Circular, 3 × 3 ft.	Salt grass	2.28[c]	84	Depth to water 4 inches.
							2.19[c]	84	Depth to water 13 inches.
							1.76[c]	84	Depth to water 24.5 inches.
Upper Nile River, Sudd region, Egypt.	76.3	35	365	6	10 m. sq., 2 m. deep	Papyrus	4.33	[d]	Exposed in papyrus swamp.
Snake River, Twin Falls project, Idaho.	48	10.7	183	2	90,000 acres	Forage and grain crops	2.65[c]	19	
Mud Lake basin, Idaho.	40±	9.6±	150	2	Circular, 4 × 4 ft.	Tule	4.78[c]	68	Exposed in tule swamp.
Middle Rio Grande valley; N. Mex.:									
Near Los Griegos.	55.6	8.5	196	2	Circular, 4 × 4 ft.	Salt grass	1.70	84	Depth to water 2.1 feet.
				2	Circular, 4 × 3 ft.	Do.	2.85	84	Depth to water 1.25 feet.
				2	Circular, 4 × 2 ft.	Do.	3.95	84	Depth to water 0.42 foot.
Isleta-Belan area.	57	9.0	195	1	21,074 acres	Alfalfa, grass, etc.	2.70	84	
M.R.G.V. Conservancy District:									
Cochiti division.	55	9.0	190	1	19,439 acres	Miscellaneous crops and native grass	3.19	84	Entire valley by integration method.
Albuquerque division.	56	9.0	195	1	58,127 acres	Alfalfa, miscellaneous crops and native grass	3.08	84	
Belen division.	57	9.0	195	1	77,044 acres	Do.	2.92	84	
Socorro division.	58	10.0	200	1	33,072 acres	Do.	3.54	84	
Cochiti division.	55	9.0	190	1	5,208 acres	Native hay and miscellaneous crops	2.41	84	
Albuquerque division.	56	9.0	195	1	22,819 acres	Alfalfa and miscellaneous crops	2.70	84	Irrigated land only by integration method.
Belen division.	57	9.0	195	1	23,895 acres	Do.	2.73	84	
Socorro division.	58	10.0	200	1	7,237 acres	Do.	2.50	84	
Wickes field, near Burns, Oreg.	45.6	12	95	1915	Circular, 3 × 4 ft.	Sugar and mixed meadow grass	1.48[c]	16	Pans set 3 feet deep in growing field. Water at surface of ground, as in field.
			127	1916		Do.	2.04[c]	16	
Frye field, near Burns, Oreg.	45.6	12	55	1915		Mixed meadow grass	1.08[c]	16	
			115	1916		Do.	1.60[c]	16	
Verdo field, near Burns, Oreg.	45.6	12	67	1915		Sugar grass	1.34[c]	16	
			130	1916		Do.	1.86[c]	16	
Escalante Valley, near Milford, Utah.	....	9.2	150	2	Circular 4 × 4½ ft.	Alfalfa	2.26[c]	80	Depth to water 1.75 feet.
		9.2	150	2		Salt grass	1.42[c]	80	Depth to water 1.75 to 2.6 feet.
		9.2	150	2		Greasewood	.22[c]	80	
		9.2	150	2		Shad scale and greasewood	.26[c]	80	
VOLUMETRIC METHOD—FIELD PLOTS									
Devil Canyon shaft, near San Bernardino, Calif.	63	16	260	2	1 plot	Native brush	1.6	5	Some rainfall penetration below root zone.

TABLE 6.—*Consumptive use.*—(*Continued*)

Locality or river system	Mean annual temperature (°F.)	Average annual precipitation (inches)	Average growing season (days between frosts)	Years of work	Size of tank or area of moist land [a]	Vegetation	Consumptive use (acre-feet per year per acre of moist land)	Authority [b]	Remarks
Muscovy, near San Bernardino, Calif.	63	16	260	2	Ave. 2 plots	Native brush	1.5	5	All precipitation consumed.
Claremont tunnel, near Ontario, Calif.	61	18	270	3	1 plot	Native brush	1.2	5	
Palmer Canyon near Ontario, Calif.	61	18	270	1	1 plot	Native weeds, grass and brush	1.6	5	
Stations 75 and 76, near San Bernardino, Calif.	63	16	260	2	Ave. 2 plots	Native brush	1.4	5	
Station A, near Anaheim, Calif.	62	12.0	300	1	10 × 10 ft.	Native grass and weeds	1.05	5	
Station D, near Ontario, Calif.	62	18.0	270	1	....	Native grass	1.06	5	
Station E, near Ontario, Calif.	62	18.0	270	1	....	Native grass	1.17	5	
Station F, near Cucamonga, Calif.	62	18.0	260	1	....	Native grass and weeds	1.15	5	
Station H, near Redlands, Calif.	63	14.7	260	1	....	Barley	1.03	5	
Cache Valley near Logan, Utah	47.1	15.5	125	17	30 × 60 ft.	Sugar beets	2.4c	20	For most profitable yield.
				17	....	Potatoes	2.2c	20	
				17	....	Alfalfa	4.6c	20	
				17	....	Corn	2.2c	20	
				17	....	Wheat	2.5c	20	
				17	....	Oats	3.1c	20	
VOLUMETRIC METHOD—IRRIGATED FARMS									
Cache la Poudre Valley, Colo.	48	14	135	2	....	Sugar beets	3.0c	21	For average yield per acre; possibly some deep percolation.
						Potatoes	3.3c	21	
						Alfalfa	3.7c	21	
						Barley	2.3c	21	
						Wheat	2.1c	21	
						Oats	1.4c	21	
Snake River Plain, Idaho	48	11.6	150	4	....	Diversified field crops	2.1c	2	
Snake River at Twin Falls, Idaho	48	10.7	150	3	....	Wheat	1.18c	40	Plots of average production.
						Oats	1.45c	40	
						Barley	1.58c	40	
						Peas	1.36c	40	
						Beans	1.20c	40	
						Corn	1.29c	40	
						Potatoes	1.60c	40	
						Clover	1.54c	40	
						Alfalfa	2.55c	40	

Sevier Valley, Utah........	48	8	110	7	....	{ Sugar beets Potatoes Alfalfa	3.1[c] 2.6[c] 3.4[c]	19 19 19	} Possibly some deep percolation.
VOLUMETRIC METHOD—IRRIGATION PROJECTS									
Boise Valley, Idaho:									
Pioneer drainage district....	50	11	155	2	13,500	General field crops	2.1[c,e]	71	
Nampa, Meridian drainage district.	50	11	155	1	50,000	Do	1.9[c,e]	19	
Snake River, Twin Falls project, Idaho	48	10.7	150	2	95,000	Do	2.7[c,e]	10	
VOLUMETRIC METHOD—VALLEYS									
San Gabriel Valley, Calif.......	62.5	19.5	365	4	132,840 acres	Principally citrus and deciduous orchard	1.7	19	
Owens River, Calif.:									
Independence region........	57.6	5	197	3	34,940 acres	Meadow grass, salt grass, and moist bare soil	2.33	19	
Bishop-Big Pine region........	54.2	6	152	6	55,780 acres	Alfalfa, pasture and seeped land	3.00	19	
San Luis Rey Valley, Calif	60	13	260	4	6,640	Willow and other water-loving trees	2.15	19	River dry in summer 6 to 8 months.
Santa Ana River valley, Riverside Narrows to Prado, Calif.	63	13	285	2	4,040 acres	River-bottom vegetation, trees, grass, etc.	4.18	6	Continuously flowing river.
Cache la Poudre Valley, Colo......	48	14	135	2	220,000	Diversified field crops	1.8[c,e]	19	
South Platte River and tributary valleys, Colo.	49	14	145	10	1,100,000 acres	Diversified field crops and natural grasses	1.8[c,e]	19	
San Luis Valley, Colo........	41.7	7.6	108	11	400,000	Diversified field crops and native vegetation	1.66	84	
North Platte River at North Park, Colo........	38	10	80	...	120,000 acres	Chiefly meadows	1.8[c,e]	19	
Lower South Platte River, Colo......	48	14	145	2	229,000 acres	Diversified field crops	1.9[c,e]	19	
Middle Rio Grande Valley-Isleta-Belen area, N. Mex...	57	9.0	195	1	17,500 acres	Alfalfa, grass, etc.	2.7	84	
Mesilla Valley, N. Mex.-Tex......	61	9	220	17	109,000 acres	Diversified field crops	2.73	84	
Truckee River valley, Nev........	49	8	140	18	27,000 acres	Alfalfa and native grass	3.00[c,e]	19	
Sevier Valley, Utah.......	48	8	110	7	65,000 acres	Alfalfa, sugar beets, and potatoes	1.9[c,f]	19	
Yakima River basin, Wash........	...	...	160±	3	103,000 acres	Chiefly meadows	2.8[c,g]	19	
Little Laramie River, Wyo........	40	14	95	12	28,000 acres	Chiefly meadows	1.2[c,e]	19	
VOLUMETRIC METHOD—CANYON STREAM CHANNEL									
Coldwater Canyon, upper section, Calif.	64	23	240	1	5.89 acres	Alder, bay, and maple trees	4.16	6	
Coldwater Canyon, lower section, Calif.	64	23	240	1	2.36 acres	Alder, sycamore, and bay trees	5.33	6	

TABLE 6.—Consumptive use.—(Continued)

Locality or river system	Mean annual temperature (°F.)	Average annual precipitation (inches)	Average growing season (days between frosts)	Years of work	Size of tank or area of moist land[a]	Vegetation	Consumptive use (acre-feet per year per acre of moist land)	Authority[b]	Remarks
LYSIMETER METHOD									
Idaho Falls, Idaho	44	14.2	180	2	Circular, 2 × 6 ft.	Alfalfa	2.0[c]	2	Computed, from automatic water-stage records and specific yield by formula $q = y(24r \pm s)$
WATER-TABLE METHOD—DIURNAL FLUCTUATION									
Escalante Valley near Milford, Utah		9.2	150	2		Alfalfa	2.26[c]	80	
						Salt grass and greasewood	1.24[c]	80	
						Shadscale	.38[c]	80	
						Greasewood	.22[c]	80	
WATER-TABLE METHOD—SEASONAL FLUCTUATIONS									
San Joaquin Valley, Calif.:									
Madera area	63	9.8	280	8	69,000	Vineyard; deciduous orchard and alfalfa	2.50	30	
Fresno area	63	9.8	280	8	195,700	Do.	1.95	30	
Consolidated area	63	9.5	280	8	124,200	Do.	1.90	30	
Alta area	63	9.1	280	8	79,000	Do.	1.90	30	
Kaweah-Lindsay area	62	9.0	250	8	124,000	Citrus, deciduous crops, and cotton	2.17	30	
Tule-Deer Creek area	62	8.5	280	8	67,200	Deciduous crops, alfalfa, and cotton	2.20	30	
McFarland-Shafter area	62	7.0	250	8	50,000	Field crops, alfalfa, and cotton	2.00	30	
AVAILABLE-HEAT METHOD									
Middle Rio Grande Valley, N. Mex	56	9	198				2.50[c]	84	Crop consumptive use per cropped acre.
							4.10[c]	84	Valley consumptive use per irrigated acre.

a Includes irrigated agricultural crops, natural phreatophytic vegetation, water surface, and bare moist soil.
b See Bibliography, pp. 327–330.
c For crop year or irrigation season.
d Data from Physical Department, Egyptian Ministry of Public Works.
e Stream-flow depletion plus rainfall during growing season.
f Stream-flow depletion plus rainfall during growing season plus draft upon soil moisture.
g Stream-flow depletion.

CONSUMPTIVE USE
DEFINITIONS

The term *consumptive use of water* has been in growing use since about 1910 among engineers and others interested in the technical phases of irrigated agriculture in western America. It was first used by John E. Field, State engineer of Colorado, to describe waters completely consumed in irrigation and has since appeared extensively in unpublished engineering reports, in court proceedings, and in records pertaining to the Colorado River Compact. The extensive use of the term, although local, and the availability of a large amount of valuable published data on the subject entitle it to a place in any discussion of transpiration and total evaporation.

The first basic definition in published literature was the following as proposed by the Duty of Water Committee, Irrigation Division, American Society of Civil Engineers [19]—namely, "The quantity of water in acre-feet per cropped acre per year absorbed by a crop and transpired or used directly in the building of plant tissue, together with that evaporated from the crop-producing land."

Recognizing the impracticability of confining water loss to crop-producing areas, the Committee on Absorption and Transpiration, Section of Hydrology, American Geophysical Union, later proposed a similar definition, adding natural to cropped vegetation and including "intercepted precipitation" [39].

Amplified definitions, applicable to large irrigated areas and to entire valleys with interspersed areas of natural vegetation and bare moist land, have since been adopted by the Bureau of Agricultural Engineering, United States Department of Agriculture, in connection with investigations in the upper Rio Grande Basin [84]. These definitions as set forth below are comprehensive and fully representative of current thought on the subject.

Consumptive use (evapo-transpiration) is the sum of the water used by the vegetative growth of a given area in transpiration or building of plant tissue and that evaporated from adjacent soil, snow, or intercepted precipitation on the area in any specified time. It is expressed in acre-inches per acre or depth in inches for short periods of time, and in acre-feet per acre or depth in feet for long periods such as a growing season or a 12-month year.

Valley consumptive use is the sum of the water absorbed by and transpired from crops and native vegetation and lands upon which they grow and that evaporated from bare land and water surfaces in the valley. All amounts are measured in acre-feet per 12-month year on the respective areas within the exterior boundaries of the valley.

Stream-flow depletion is the amount of water that annually flows into a valley or onto a particular land area minus the amount that flows out of the valley or away from the particular land area. It is usually less than consumptive use, which in addition includes water derived from precipitation and ground water.

These more complete and specific definitions are very useful in coordinating the work of early investigators, some of whom, approaching the problem with reference only to irrigation, failed to segregate losses from noncrop areas, later termed "nonbeneficial consumptive use," or to include all sources of water supply. The water loss from valleys as determined by most of the early investigators was stream-flow depletion rather than valley consumptive use.

METHODS OF MEASUREMENT

Numerous methods have been devised to measure consumptive use. They can be classified under the four headings volumetric, lysimeter, water table, and available heat. A comprehensive discussion of methods was presented by the Duty of Water Committee, American Society of Civil Engineers in 1927 [19], and an instructive application of methods to a particular area appears in the report of Rio Grande Joint Investigation in the upper Rio Grande Basin dated February 1938 [84].

Volumetric methods

The volumetric methods are based upon measurements of inflow, outflow, and change in storage volume in a water-tight container during a specified period of time, using the equation

Consumptive use = inflow − outflow ± change in storage

Containers vary in type and size from small metal tanks containing soil with growing plants to large alluvium-filled rock basins whose surfaces constitute fertile valleys with cultivated farms, towns, and the conveniences of modern community life.

Tanks.—The use of unsealed tanks sunk into the ground with top almost flush with the surface for determination of consumptive use, although somewhat questionable as to accurate reproduction of growing conditions in the field, is simple and inexpensive and has been widely adopted by investigators. There has been a marked tendency to overcome the principal objections to this method and to eliminate the errors of earlier experiments. The present practice is to use large tanks permitting a more normal root development, the dimensions as now adopted by investigators ranging from 27 inches in diameter to 10 meters square and from 30 inches to 9 feet 9 inches in depth. Filling tanks with undisturbed soil, burying tanks in the field closely surrounded by the natural growth, limiting the number of plants to average density, preventing spread of foliage beyond tank boundaries, and providing replacements for lost or diseased plants are all included in the best recent practice.

For plants growing in freely draining soil it is also necessary to limit the amount of water added to the tank at each application, in order to prevent percolation to the bottom of the tank, with the building up of capillary storage either with or without a water table. For plants normally drawing their supply from the capillary fringe a water table must be maintained in the tank at a constant level. This has been satisfactorily accomplished with the Mariotté tank, water being supplied to the soil tank through a connecting pipe [55]. As pointed out by Rohwer [54] and others, however, to obtain reliable results by this device, especial care must be exercised to eliminate leaks from the supply system and to keep the supply tank at constant temperature.

The results of tank measurements, where they have been checked by independent methods, appear to be reasonably reliable, if the tanks are properly designed and exposed and systematically observed. The conditions surrounding tank experiments, especially the exposure, should be thoroughly investigated, however, before placing dependence upon results as applied to field conditions. If tank exposures are abnormal correction factors should be applied to the measurements.

The results of tank experiments are applied to large areas such as irrigation projects or valleys by the "integration method." This consists of the summation of products of consumptive use for each crop or stand of native vegatation times its respective area, plus water-surface evaporation times its area, plus bare-soil evaporation times its area [84].

There are five classes of modern investigational work in which tanks have been employed for measuring consumptive use—namely, use of water in irrigation, discharge of ground water, salvage of water consumed by natural vegetation, prospective losses from vegetation in backwater areas, and conservation of water.

Study of the use of water in irrigation by the integration or analytical method employs results of tank measurements, both of consumptive use and of transpiration and soil evaporation. The work of Hammatt [16] in eastern Oregon, that of Crandall [10] in Idaho, and that of the Bureau of Agricultural Engineering, United States Department of Agriculture [84], in the upper Rio Grande Valley, are excellent examples of this method. Hammatt used tanks for measuring the transpiration ratio of growing meadow grasses and the soil evaporation, adding these to change in soil moisture and deep percolation to obtain total use of water in irrigation. Crandall measured consumptive use from an irrigated area of 100,000 acres of mixed field crops in the lower Snake River Valley during a 2-year period, obtaining very close agreement by the following three independent methods:

1. Measurement of annual increase in spring flow below the project as augmented by percolation losses from irrigated land gave a result of 2.7 acre-feet per acre.

2. Determinations of soil moisture before and after irrigation gave a result of 2.6 acre-feet per acre.

3. Computations based on transpiration ratio for each crop, as obtained by tank experiment under somewhat similar climatic and soil conditions and applied to classified crop areas plus similarly applied rates of soil and water evaporation, gave a result of 2.65 acre-feet per acre.

The determination of ground-water discharge from underground reservoirs by either the inventory or the discharge method involves consumptive use as measured by the tank method. The inventory method was first applied by Lee [34] in the Independence region of Owens Valley, Calif., and consisted of a detailed accounting for a period of 3 years of all elements of ground-water intake, storage, and discharge, for a closed geologic basin of 232 square miles, with its tributary high-mountain drainage area of 125 square miles. One element of discharge consisted of transpiration and soil evaporation from 52 square miles of moist valley land. Large tanks (7.5 by 5.5 feet) were used to measure consumptive use from salt grass for various depths to water table and also soil evaporation. A close balance was obtained between inflow and outflow, 90 percent of the outflow being consumptive use. Lee also [36] made an intensive study of San Luis Rey Valley, San Diego County, Calif., involving large losses by transpiration from willow trees, and obtained very close agreement between ground-water replenishment and draft, principally by consumptive use, over a 20 year period. White [80], employing the discharge method for determining ground water discharge from Escalante Valley, Utah, made tank measurements of consumptive use for alfalfa, salt grass, and greasewood as a check against the water-table method.

Salvage water as represented by consumptive use of native vegetation in a proposed reservoir site was volumetrically determined by Stearns and Bryan [68] at Mud Lake, Idaho, where the tank method was used to measure transpiration and evaporation from partly submerged tule growth. Similar work on papyrus by the Physical Department of the Egyptian Ministry of Public Works in the Sudd region of the upper Nile is especially interesting. Fully 50 percent of the water supplied by Lakes Victoria, Albert, and Edward and other sources never reaches the main stream of the Nile, being consumed in the papyrus swamps of the Sudd region, covering over 3,200 square miles. Consumptive use by papyrus was measured over a period of years by growing it in a water-tight concrete basin 10 meters square and 2 meters deep, closely surrounded by natural growth, water in the tank being kept at a constant level submerging the roots.[1] It is now planned to by-pass the swamps by detouring the upper Nile in canals for a distance of 400 miles.

[1] Information by letter from H. E. Hurst, Director General, Physical Department, Egyptian Ministry of Public Works, Cairo, Egypt.

A notable determination of prospective losses from vegetation in backwater areas by tank measurement of consumptive use was that made by the California Division of Water Resources in connection with studies to determine the feasibility of constructing a barrier across upper San Francisco Bay to prevent salt-water encroachment into the delta of the Sacramento and San Joaquin Rivers. The total backwater area above the lowest proposed barrier embraced 1,140 square miles, of which 1,085 square miles supported vegetation, 550 square miles cultivated field crops, and 195 square miles tules, salt grass, willows, and other natural vegetation. Tank measurements were made by the United States Department of Agriculture, Division of Agricultural Engineering, under the immediate supervision of O. V. P. Stout, on 14 varieties of local field crops and on tule, of which there are large areas [44]. Supplemental studies for the salt grass, tule, and willow were made by Lee [38]. The results of these investigations were an important factor in preparation of plans for the Central Valley project now under construction in California causing the abandonment of the idea of a salt-water barrier in favor of release of water from mountain storage to push back the salt water entering the delta from San Francisco Bay.

In water-conservation work in southern California Blaney [5, 6] has measured consumptive use by several varieties of natural vegetation whose roots are submerged or are supplied from the capillary fringe. Varieties included Bermuda grass, salt grass, tules, willow, and wire rush, and tests were also made on bare soil. The water surface in the soil tanks was maintained at constant level by use of the Mariotté equipped supply tank.

Field plots.—The direct measurement of consumptive use in field plots is generally considered to give more reliable results than tests with tanks. The practice has been to use plots of leveled ground, usually less than 1 acre in area, in which mesophytic and xerophytic plants are grown as in the field or naturally. Water input is derived from precipitation and, if necessary, from irrigation in small amounts, not to exceed 5 inches in depth in a single application. Any runoff or waste is measured at the border of the plot. Water input minus outflow is corrected for storage as soil moisture in computing consumptive use. An important feature of this type of measurement is the location of the plot in an area where the water table lies too deep for roots to reach the capillary fringe, thus limiting the water supply available to growing vegetation to that applied at the surface. The accuracy of the method depends largely upon the elimination of deep percolation. The practice of small and frequent irrigation is depended upon to minimize deep percolation, but it is open to doubt whether such percolation has always been negligible in amount. Another element of uncertainty is the practice of including total precipitation as input, whereas, during the summer especially, much of this is lost by interception and immediate soil evaporation and never penetrates into the soil. Investigators in this field include Widstowe and Harris in Utah [20, 81, 82], Snelson in Alberta [67], and Powers in Oregon [56, 57].

A modification of the plot method has been developed by Blaney [5] in southern California, primarily for the determination of deep percolation from winter rainfall but including consumptive use as an essential element. Extensive measurements were made during 1927 to 1930 upon native brush consisting chiefly of chamisal, sage, wild olive, and native grass followed by weeds. Systematic measurements of soil moisture were made at each field plot, with an improved soil tube [77]. Soil samples were taken in 1-foot sections to depths of 12 to 18 feet, reaching well below the principal root zone. Sampling was done in the fall before the winter rains commenced, at intervals during the rainy season, and finally at the end of the growing season. A rain gage and runoff plot were installed with each soil-moisture plot. From the data thus obtained volumetric calculations were made of consumptive use and of rainfall penetrating beyond the root zone. By this procedure all uncertainty regarding deep percolation is eliminated from the field-plot method.

Irrigated farms.—The farm represents the next larger unit employed in the measurement of consumptive use. The crops include one or more varieties of garden, field, or orchard crops. The methods are the same as for field plots, but the results are more open to question because less attention has been given to the possibility of unmeasured loss by deep percolation. Significant work has been done by Bark [2] and Lewis [40] in Idaho, Hemphill [21] in Colorado, and Israelson and Winsor [28] in Utah. The results obtained from farm plots are of more value as a record of irrigation-water use than of consumptive use.

Irrigation projects.—Under this heading project areas irrigated from complete canal systems are considered the units. Lands are classified as to crop, natural vegetation, or moist bare soil, and the area of each is determined. During the irrigation season measurements are made of inflow into the project area as canal diversions from streams and precipitation. Measurements are also made of outflow as surface waste and runoff, evaporation from bare land, transpiration from natural vegetation, and deep percolation appearing in natural or artificial channels at the project boundary. Consumptive use is computed as water inflow minus outflow corrected for storage as soil moisture and ground water. Possible sources of error are inadequate determination of changes in soil moisture, time lag in the appearance of percolating water in surface streams, and lack of knowledge of ground-water inflow and outflow. In general, the project area is not a natural hydrologic unit, and the irrigation season is not a complete climatic cycle. As a consequence, the measurement of project consumptive use is seldom as satisfactory as that of valley consumptive use. Work in this field has been done by Steward [71] in Boise Valley, Idaho, and by Crandall [10] in the Snake River Valley, Idaho.

Alluvium-filled valleys.—Valleys filled with alluvium constitute the largest unit for the volumetric measurement of consumptive use. The container is the bedrock basin that underlies and surrounds the valley. These basins are of two general types—(1) the "closed basin," in which the alluvial fill is for practical purposes completely enclosed by impermeable bedrock bottom and sides continuous with the surrounding hills or mountains; (2) the "open basin," in which the bedrock is leaky or the alluvial fill has one or more areas of direct contact with similar formations outside of the valley that are sufficiently permeable to transmit ground water. The open-basin type presents difficulties of measurement that are in some valleys insurmountable, but most alluvium-filled valleys can be utilized for a reasonably accurate determination of consumptive use by either the volumetric or some other method.

Valley consumptive use is computed as the difference between valley inflow, consisting of flow of streams entering the valley, both surface and subsurface, plus precipitation upon the surface, and valley outflow in surface streams or underflow, with appropriate adjustments for changes in the storage of water underground as soil moisture and water of saturation.

Investigators have approached the problem with two differing backgrounds and purposes. First, the irrigation or drainage engineer seeks to determine consumptive use as a basis for project planning or for maximum economic utilization of the visible supply; second, the ground-water hydrologist endeavors to ascertain the permanent quantitative ground-water yield of the entire basin, of which one element is the consumptive use. For reliable results the method used requires an analysis of all elements of inflow and outflow, both surface and subsurface, as well as ground storage. Gross error in the final results can easily arise by the omission of hidden elements whose importance is not fully realized, or by the omission of measurements for which funds are not available. In general the most reliable result is obtained where the approach is the broadest and all elements are considered with attention given to the technical aspects of ground-water hydrology, geology, botany, and water chemistry, as well as irrigation practice and hydrography. The climatic year is the most desirable unit of time, and a minimum period of 3 years should be allowed for observation. More reliable results are obtainable for a valley in which irrigation has been practiced for many years and ground-water conditions have become stabilized than for a newly irrigated valley where ground storage is still accumulating.

Published reports were made by Parshall [19] on the lower South Platte Valley, Colo.; Hemphill [21] on the Cache la Poudre Valley, Colo.; Ullrich [74] on the Sevier Valley, Utah; Harding [17] on the Truckee River Valley, Nev., and Parker [53] on eastern Washington. Investigators interested in ground-water supply who have volumetrically determined valley consumptive use as one of the involved elements have been Lee in Owens Valley [19, 34, 35] and San Luis Rey Valley [19], Conkling in San Gabriel Valley [19]; and Troxell in Santa Ana River Valley [6], all in California.

Most of the early investigations of valley consumptive use by the volumetric method are represented by unpublished reports. Among the more active workers were R. I. Meeker and R. J. Tipton, engineers for the State of Colorado; Charles R. Hedke, R. J. Hosea, Herbert W. Yeo, and R. F. Black, engineers for the State of New Mexico; and E. B. Debler, Harold Conkling, and C. C. Elder, engineers of the United States Bureau of Reclamation [84, 19].

Canyon stream channel.—Throughout the Southwest the principal sources of surface-water supply are streams from mountain canyons tributary to the main valleys. These streams, after gathering from upper tributaries, flow through long stretches of canyon between precipitous rocky slopes where the channel is lined with vigorously growing native vegetation. Large losses occur by evaporation and transpiration from such channels. The native vegetation consists largely of water-loving trees, such as alder, willow, and sycamore, and also grasses, tule, etc. Determination of consumptive use by the volumetric method is possible in many canyons by selecting bedrock control stations and measuring inflow and outflow for the section of channel between the controls. Blaney [5, 6] has made such determinations in Temescal and Coldwater Canyons, in southern California. The results of such observations are useful in planning for maximum utilization of the available water supply.

Lysimeter

In the lysimeter method of measuring consumptive use, the water absorbed from rain or irrigation upon the surface exposed under field conditions percolates downward through an enclosed soil column. The equipment usually consists of an open cylinder with impervious sides and pervious bottom filled with soil and buried so that the top is flush with the surrounding ground surface. Water passing through the soil column is collected at the bottom and conducted through a small tube to a measuring gage in an adjacent pit. Consumptive use is computed as the difference between water absorbed at the surface and measured at the bottom.

Losses by plant transpiration and soil evaporation can be measured by the lysimeter with the same accuracy as by the volumetric tank method, if all precautions found necessary in that method are taken. In addition, uniform distribution of the downward-percolating water throughout the soil column should be insured. The soil column should also be of sufficient length for the zone of capillary storage to be below the reach of plant roots. The necessity for this precaution lies in the tendency for capillary storage to accumulate in the lower portion of a soil column in the absence of a water table, owing to surface tension at the bottom of the column.

The lysimeter method was employed by Bark [2] in connection with experimental work in Idaho on the duty of water in irrigation. To prevent percolation between the soil and the inside of the cylinder Bark painted bands of hot asphalt around the inside just prior to filling. The method has also been employed by several European investigators [75] for the purpose of measuring infiltration. Although this method has possibilities for the measurement of evaporation from bare soil, it has not been found satisfactory for measuring infiltration.

Water-table fluctuation

Diurnal fluctuations.—It was first demonstrated by Smith [80] in San Pedro Valley, Ariz., that the daily decline in the water table was due to withdrawal of ground water by trees from the capillary fringe and zone of saturation. His observations were made from 1916 to 1922 by means of continuous graphs of water-level fluctuations in shallow wells adjacent to cottonwood and mesquite trees. In 1925 and 1926 White [80] made an intensive investigation of the subject in Escalante Valley, Utah, obtaining continuous automatic records of shallow water-level fluctuation in wells located in fields of subirrigated crops and natural vegetation. Separate tests were made on alfalfa, salt grass, greasewood, rabbit brush, pickle-weed, willows, meadow grasses, and sagebrush. Special tests were also made on cleared fields, on cropped fields before and after cutting plants, and during rainstorms. This work proved conclusively that diurnal fluctuations of the water table can be caused by growing vegetation drawing its supply from shallow ground water and suggested a new method for determination of consumptive use. White, after analysis of daily graphs and study of results from simultaneous tank experiments with the same plant varieties, developed the formula

$$q = y(24r + s)$$

in which q = depth of water withdrawn from ground water by plant transpiration and soil evaporation during a 24-hour period, in inches

y = specific yield of the soil in which the daily fluctuation of the water table occurs,

r = hourly-rate of rise of the water table, in inches, from midnight to 4 A.M. when there is no discharge from the zone of saturation.

s = net fall or rise of the water table during the 24-hour period, in inches.

The terms r and s can be readily determined from automatic daily records of water-table fluctuations in wells within the area covered by each plant variety (Fig. VIII-5). Tests of specific yield involve extended measurements on isolated columns of undisturbed soil showing the rise or fall of water level with addition or withdrawal of measured quantities of water. Such tests should be made for distinctive types of soil within the area of observed water-table fluctuation. Consumptive use for long periods of time such as the growing season are obtained by summation of amounts for each day.

The method has application in areas of shallow water table where vegetation depends entirely upon ground water. In some areas it might be applied at less cost than other volumetric methods. Its greatest value is in areas where inflow and outflow are at scattered or inaccessible points and not susceptible of accurate measurement.

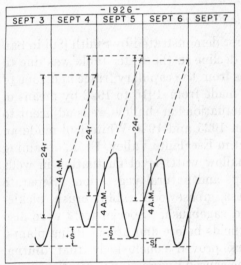

Fig. VIII-5.—Daily water table fluctuations in salt-grass meadow, Escalante Valley, Utah, September 4-6, 1926.

Seasonal fluctuations.—In regions where the average annual rainfall is less than 10 inches and occurs during the winter very little water is available to growing plant life from direct precipitation. Under such conditions surface supply from canals and ground-water supply from wells must be depended upon for irrigation. For regions of this character, where irrigation is well established and where topography and subsurface formations are uniform and slopes moderate to flat, Harding [18] has developed a method for computing consumptive use, utilizing seasonal fluctuations of the water table.

The method is based on the fact that for a complete climatic cycle the balance between the annual supply to the area by surface and underground flow from higher levels and depletion of the supply by draft, waste, and subsurface-flow to lower levels is reflected in the rise or fall of the water table within the area. When the elements of supply exceed those of depletion, an accumulation of ground water will occur, with rise in the water table. Conversely, when depletion exceeds supply the water table will drop. For equality of supply and depletion there will be no change in water level. In practical application of the method, Harding selects unit areas embracing one or more canal systems, in order to simplify the assembling of data.

The essence of the method is a simple graph, the vertical axis of which represents the annual change, in feet, of average ground-water level within the area, and the horizontal axis represents annual inflow, in feet of depth per net acre irrigated (Fig. VIII-6). Experience in applying the method to areas in the upper San Joaquin Valley, Calif., where records are available covering several years with both ample and short supply, indicates a straight-line relation among the plotted points. The point at which this line crosses the line of zero change in water level is assumed to represent consumptive use for the area. For validity, this assumption requires the following conditions:

1. No appreciable ground-water increment from rainfall within the area.
2. Substantial equality or inappreciable amount of underground inflow and outflow for the area.
3. Substantial equality throughout the area of average specific yield at different levels within the range of fluctuation of the water level.
4. Adequate supply of water for crop uses every year either from canal or from pumped sources.

Consumptive use per acre irrigated as determined by this method includes water consumed on nonirrigated land as transpiration from natural vegetation and evaporation from bare moist soil. It is greater than if computed upon the gross area served by the canal. Results for different canal systems are thus not strictly comparable, if the percentages of waste land differ greatly. Analyses made for the

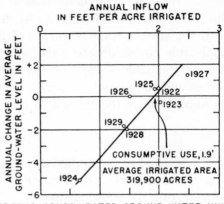

FRESNO-CONSOLIDATED GROUND WATER UNIT

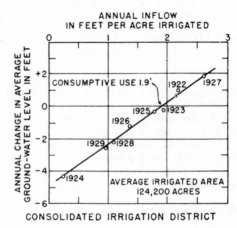

CONSOLIDATED IRRIGATION DISTRICT

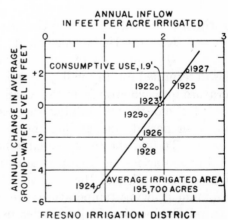

FRESNO IRRIGATION DISTRICT

Fig. VIII-6.—Relation of inflow to change in level of ground water in vicinity of Fresno Calif.

period 1921–29 in several areas in the upper San Joaquin Valley have disclosed consistent variations in the annual fluctuations of water table with the surface-water supply and indicate that the method is generally applicable to conditions existing in these areas [30]. The method is probably capable of application in other areas where conditions are similar and should be especially useful in valleys that are too large to treat as units for application of the volumetric method.

Available heat

A method of computation developed by Hedke [19] utilizes the relation of consumptive use of water to the number of heat units available to crops during the growing season. This method is based upon the partly substantiated fact that under favorable agricultural conditions the use of water by growing crops is directly proportional to the use of available heat. The application of this method to a valley in which agriculture is of a high standard necessitates the following assumptions as stated by the Duty of Water Committee, American Society of Civil Engineers [19]:

1. That the heat consumed by a particular crop during any day or other time period is determined by the amount of heat available to the crop above the germinating or minimum growing temperature.
2. That under favorable agricultural practices each crop consumes water in direct relation to the heat available as defined.
3. That the soils considered are abundantly supplied with moisture and plant food, so that the yield of a crop will be limited only by the amount of heat available.
4. That the influence of variations in wind velocity relative humidity, and vapor pressure on consumptive use of water are relatively small compared to the influence of available heat.

With these assumptions fulfilled

$$U = KQ$$

in which U = valley consumptive use.
K = the Hedke coefficient.
Q = quantity of available heat, in day degrees.

Q is determined for any valley by subtracting the minimum growing temperature for each crop from the mean temperature for each month or portion of a month, multiplying the result by the number of days in the month or period, and adding the results for all months in the growing season. To find the total available heat units for a project or valley the total available for each crop is multiplied by the percentage of the crop area to the total, and the sum of the products is taken. The following minimum growing temperatures were assumed by the Bureau of Agricultural Engineering in its studies using this method in Mesilla Valley, N. M. [84]: Alfalfa 33° F., cotton 48° forage 44°, fruits 46°, grains 44°, pasture 38°, vegetables 40°, miscellaneous 38°.

The evaluation of the coefficient K involves complications due to differing standards of agricultural practice in different valleys. As determined by Hedke for Cache la Poudre Valley, Colo., where there is a relatively high standard of agriculture, $K = 0.000423$. For valleys with a lower standard the coefficient would be less. It would also differ in valleys with differing areal percentages of native vegetation or bare moist soil, depending upon whether it was computed for consumptive use in the entire valley per irrigated acre or for crop consumptive use per acre. Thus the Bureau of Agricultural Engineering in evaluating K for Mesilla Valley found 0.00073 for valley consumptive use per irrigated acre and 0.00044 for crop consumptive use per cropped acre. The determination of K, therefore, involves considerable judgment on the part of the engineer.

The available-heat method will require much research before it can be applied with the accuracy and reliability of the volumetric method or that based on water-table fluctuation. Its best field of application would appear to be in valleys with high standard of agriculture and small percentage of wet waste land.

QUANTITATIVE DATA

Availability

The mass of quantitative data on consumptive use which has become available during the last 25 years far exceeds that on pure transpiration. Careful but far from exhaustive review of published literature has yielded the data compiled in table 6, with classification by method and plant variety. Within certain limitations these data are directly applicable to hydrologic uses and constitute a valuable aid to the hydrologist and hydraulic engineer.

Results

Examination of table 6 reveals a general similarity in results for similar types of vegetation, regardless of the method of measurement. The plant varieties that are greatest consumers of water are shown to be hydrophytes, such as tule, cattail, and papyrus, and phreatophytes, such as willow, cottonwood, alder, and sycamore trees, all of which use more than 4 feet a year. Tule and cattail are the greatest consumers, tank measurement with natural exposures indicating 5 to 8 feet a year. Records from tanks with abnormal exposures give 16.5 to 22.6 feet a year, but these figures are obviously far in excess of field losses.

The group next in order includes phreatophytic grasses such as salt grass, bermuda grass, native hay and meadow grasses, and in some localities alfalfa, growing under conditions of shallow water table and warm summers, for which annual losses range from 3.0 to 4.0 feet.

Exclusive of the method of measurement by farm plots, for which the consumptive use may include an item of deep percolation, alfalfa and native hay and grass follow next, with annual losses ranging from 2.0 to

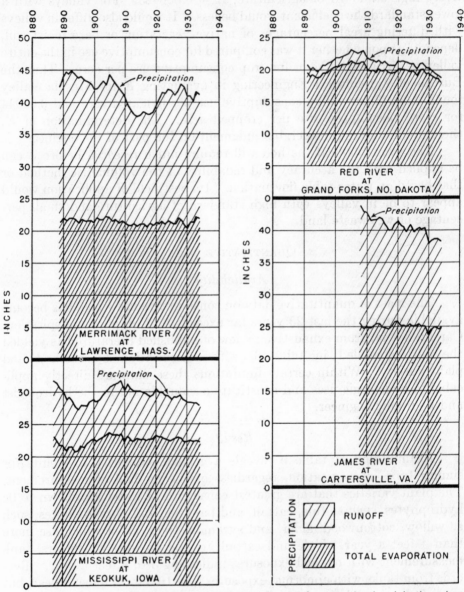

Fig. VIII-7.—Relation of annual precipitation to total evaporation (precipitation minus

3.0 feet. Below this come general field crops, orchards, and vineyards, which consume annually between 2.5 and 1.5 feet, except in the delta of the Sacramento and San Joaquin Rivers, where results ranging from 2.0

to 3.0 feet a year were obtained by the tank method. It is possible that the last-mentioned figures are a little high, owing to unnatural exposure of the tanks.

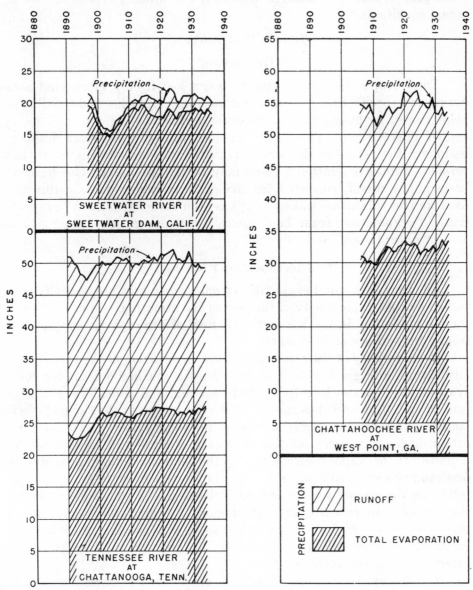

runoff), by 10-year averages, for typical stream drainage basins in the United States.

Varieties with annual losses of 1.5 feet or less include (a) salt grass where the depth to water table is greater than 3 to 5 feet; (b) field crops, native hay, and meadow grasses in cold regions with a short growing season; and (c) native grasses and brush growing in well-drained soil in arid and semiarid regions.

The figures given above appear reasonable as applying to the different plant groups, and it is believed that they are broadly representative of actual conditions.

TOTAL EVAPORATION

DEFINITION

Total evaporation is the sum of water lost from a given land area during any specific time by transpiration from vegetation and building of plant tissue; by evaporation from water surfaces, moist soil, and snow; and by interception. The term is applied primarily to stream drainage basins for the period of the annual climatic cycle or subdivision of that period. Total evaporation is essentially precipitation upon the drainage basin minus runoff, corrected for change in storage volume within the basin and for subsurface leakage. It has been variously termed "evaporation," "evaporation from land areas," "evapo-transpiration," "total loss," "water losses," and "fly-off."

CONTROLLING FACTORS

All elements in total evaporation from a given area are basically controlled by the evaporativity of the part of the atmosphere in contact with the surface—that is, by the potential rate of atmospheric evaporation from a free surface of fresh water.

Evaporativity of the atmosphere over any portion of the earth's surface during any given period of time fixes a maximum limit for total evaporation. It also broadly controls seasonal and annual variations in total evaporation and thus relates total evaporation to the same climatic factors that control evaporation from a free water surface. Total evaporation during any period of time, however, is limited in amount by the opportunity for evaporation afforded by the particular area. Evaporation opportunity varies with the aerial extent of water, snow, or growing vegetation on the ground surface and with the degree of soil moisture below the surface. In semiarid and arid regions the precipitation in certain years may be insufficient to supply the needs of vegetation. Under such conditions the annual precipitation is the limit of total evaporation, except where irrigation is practiced.

Specifically, for transpiration, the factors that control evaporation opportunity are (1) the annual amount and monthly distribution of precipitation; (2) the texture and depth of the soil as it influences infiltration and retention of water from precipitation; (3) the area within which the water table or permanent bodies of surface water are within reach of plant roots; and (4) the area, character, and type of growing vegetation.

Opportunity for evaporation from water depends upon the exposed area of permanent water bodies, such as streams, lakes and swamps, and that for evaporation from snow depends upon the area and permanence of snow upon the ground.

Opportunity for evaporation from soil depends upon (1) storm frequency and seasonal distribution, (2) rainfall intensity, (3) soil texture, depth, and drainage facilities, (4) the area and character of soil cover that affords protection from evaporation, such as growing vegetation or humus, (5) the extent to which the soil is frozen, and (6) the slope of the ground surface.

Evaporation opportunity for interception depends upon (1) storm frequency and seasonal distribution, (2) the area and character of vegetation, and (3) the occurrence of forest litter.

A recognized characteristic of total evaporation is its constancy in amount during long periods of time and its relatively narrow range of fluctuations from year to year in comparison with precipitation and run-off [59]. This is illustrated by data covering many years for typical catchment basins, as assembled in Figure VIII-7. The reason for this characteristic is apparent in the stability of the factors that control it. Evaporativity is the basic factor and changes little from year to year, largely because of the small fluctuation in annual air temperature over any particular area. Another factor is the relatively constant demand for water by growing vegetation. The factors that control evaporation opportunity are also constant, or at least subject to very slow change, the only exceptions being precipitation and the frequency and duration of storms. Even storms are minor factors where precipitation is sufficient for the needs of vegetation and occurs principally during the winter, when evaporativity is low.

The constancy of total evaporation has an important bearing upon the relation between precipitation and runoff, for it makes runoff the residual of precipitation, after deduction of water losses. This fact has been recognized by hydraulic engineers for many years and has been utilized in computations of water supply available from stream flow [15, 27, 37, 59]. Much information is at hand in engineering literature as a basis for the quantitative determination of total evaporation by difference. The essential relation for such determinations for a given drainage basin and period of time is the equation $E = P - R \pm S - L$, in which E = total evaporation, P = precipitation, R = runoff, S = storage correction, and L = leakage from the basin, all expressed in inches of depth upon the area of the drainage basin.

Methods of measurement

The essential quantitative elements in determining total evaporation for the annual climatic cycle are mean annual precipitation upon the drainage basin and run-off from it. Over-year storage accumulation or depletion may be large in any one year but is ordinarily equalized over a period of 3 to 5 years. Leakage from the basin is generally inappreciable, exceptions occurring where the bedrock is composed of permeable sandstone or soluble limestone or gypsum.

Precipitation is easily measured, and numerous records, many of which cover long periods, are available except for inaccessible mountain areas. The mean annual precipitation for a given area is computed most accurately by preparation of an isohyetal map and more approximately by the "weighted method" [24]. For large stream drainage basins, it is desirable to determine mean precipitation for the principal tributaries as well as for the basin as a whole.

The ideal method of determining runoff consists of systematic measurement of stream discharge for a period of years. This is now being done on an increasing scale by both public and private agencies, but because of the far-reaching ramification of stream systems it is and probably always will be economically impossible to measure the runoff from all basins the use of whose yield may be contemplated. For this reason various methods have been devised for determining runoff from precipitation where no measurements of stream flow are available. Several of these are included among the methods described below for determining total evaporation.

By formula

Various attempts have been made to develop a formula for computing runoff from rainfall. These attempts have assumed either that total evaporation is more or less constant, having minor variations with temperature [Vermeule, 59], or that total evaporation is proportional to rainfall [Justin, 31]. As pointed out by Rafter [59], however, stream runoff is the product of many complex factors, and each stream is a law unto itself. Although an empirical formula may be devised that will appear to give fairly close results for a certain period of years on a group of local streams, no formula can be devised that can be generally applied to basins in precipitation years of all types.

Rainfall percentage

One method assumes that the percentage of runoff to rainfall as determined from gagings in one area can be applied to other drainage areas with similar physical and meteorologic conditions. Its weaknesses lie in the facts, (1) that few drainage basins are exactly similar, and (2) that runoff is not proportional to rainfall but is a residue from rainfall after deduction of losses. In regions where in certain years rainfall may be insufficient for the needs of transpiration absurd results may be obtained by this method. The use of data on either runoff or total evaporation as obtained by percentage is hazardous unless full information regarding the drainage basin is available.

Rational method

Meyer [49] has developed a rational method of determining total evaporation from a drainage basin by computing separately the various losses from the basin by evaporation, transpiration, and leakage. This method involves detailed knowledge of climatic conditions and physical characteristics of the drainage basin, as well as of controlling factors and local rates of evaporation from water, snow, soil, of transpiration, and of interception. It is laborious in application and of necessity must contain many assumptions. It is applicable only by a trained and experienced hydrologist. For these reasons it has not been extensively used.

Graphic method

The graphic method of determining runoff from precipitation has often been used, the amounts in inches of depth for the catchment area for a given period being plotted as ordinates and abscissas upon standard coordinate paper, and a curve being drawn to represent the average relation of runoff to precipitation [59]. The characteristics of the runoff curve and some of its typical forms with differing relative amounts of precipitation and total evaporation have been pointed out both by Grunsky [15] and by Lee [37]. To illustrate these characteristics, typical runoff curves for widely differing basins and precipitation conditions are assembled in Figure VIII-8. Examination of these curves shows them to be of three types, which may be described as follows:

1. Annual precipitation small (less than 30 inches) with reference to total evaporation. This type is illustrated by the Sweetwater River, Calif., and the Red River, Minn. For this condition a minimum annual precipitation of 10 to 15 inches is required for priming the basin before runoff occurs, except with unusual conditions such as frozen ground or high intensity of rain. For precipitation exceeding the minimum the percentage of runoff increases more rapidly than that of precipitation. The typical runoff curve for this condition commences from zero at the minimum precipitation and rises with sharp curvature. If the range in annual precipitation is great enough, the curve may ultimately approach a straight line of one of the two types described below. This type of curve is typical of coastal streams in the Pacific coast region south of San Francisco, in southern California, at lower levels in the Great Basin, and in the Mississippi Valley west of the 95th meridian.

2. Annual precipitation large (more than 30 inches) with reference to total evaporation, and a considerable portion occurring during the summer. This type is illustrated by the Merrimac River, Mass.; the Mississippi

River above Keokuk, Iowa; the James River, Va., the Tennessee River; the Chattahoochee River, Ga.; and the Neosho River, Kans. For this condition the relation between precipitation and runoff is represented by a straight line whose slope is slightly flatter than that of the line of 100 percent runoff. The vertical intervals between the two lines represent total evaporation for the respective amounts of precipitation. For the streams studied the differences in slope are similar and represent 0.15 inch

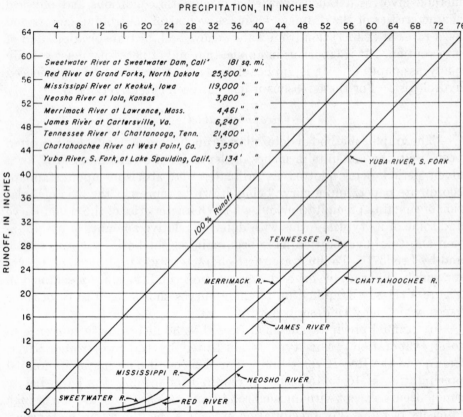

FIG. VIII-8.—Relation of precipitation and runoff for typical stream drainage basins in the United States. Data from U. S. Geol. Survey water-supply papers and from Lee O. Murphy Chief Hydrographer, Pacific Gas and Electric Company.

of increased evaporation per inch of greater precipitation. For a maximum variation from a normal precipitation of 15 to 25 inches, which is characteristic of the areas represented by these streams [83], the corresponding annual variation from mean total evaporation is from 2.25 to 3.75 inches. Runoff curves of this kind are typical of the United States east of the 95th meridian and at higher levels in the Rocky Mountain and Great Basin regions.

    3. Annual precipitation large (exceeding 30 inches) with reference to total evaporation and occurring principally during the winter. This type

is illustrated by the South Fork of Yuba River, Calif. For this condition the relation between precipitation and runoff is a straight line parallel to the line of 100 percent runoff, the vertical interval between the two lines representing average total evaporation. This type is characteristic of Pacific slope streams north of San Francisco and the mountain basins of the Cascade Range and Sierra Nevada.

The graphic method affords a simple and effective means for study of total evaporation. A frequent weakness is the wide spread in plotted points that is caused by variations in influencing factors other than precipitation, such as temperature and storage within the drainage basin. The effect of storage can be largely overcome, however, by plotting averages for periods of 3 to 5 years so as to iron out the annual inequalities.

Differences between precipitation and runoff

Another method of determining total evaporation during an annual climatic cycle is based upon the use of measurements of precipitation and runoff for a given drainage basin. Total evaporation is computed as average precipitation over the area minus measured runoff. Corrections are necessary under certain conditions, as follows:

1. Precipitation on certain basins in occasional years may be less than normal plant requirements plus evaporation and interception losses. Predominant vegetational types in such catchment areas are usually tolerant, and plants will adjust themselves to moisture deficiency, with losses by death limited to minor varieties of perennials. Normal total evaporation can be approximately determined from years of greatest precipitation if the runoff curve, by measuring the intercept between the extreme upper end of the curve and the 100 percent runoff line, approaches a straight line in its upper portion. Otherwise total evaporation can be determined only as a statistical average, subject to wide variations for short periods of years.

2. Leakage may occur from the catchment basin. Examination of geologic formations may disclose the specific areas or points of leakage. The amount of leakage from runoff can then be determined by stream-flow measurements above and below the leaky formation. Annual losses of 2.7 and 3.7 inches into limestone have been reported by Foster [14] for Wisconsin streams. In certain streams tributary to Pecos Valley, N. Mex., from the west, local strata of gypsum exposed in stream channels absorb large percentages of the runoff. In other localities complete disappearance of streams into limestone formations has been observed.

3. Storage regulation may occur either in lakes or reservoirs or as snow, soil moisture, or ground water. Correction can be made for individual years where volumetric measurement is possible, as in lake, reservoir, or snow storage. Under some conditions soil moisture and ground-

water accretion and depletion are capable of measurement. Otherwise the effects of storage can be eliminated by use of 3 to 5 year averages, the length of period depending upon the magnitude of storage and the rapidity of adjustment.

The recent availability of maps showing lines of equal mean annual precipitation and runoff for the whole of the United States [83] have made it possible to prepare a map showing by contours distribution of annual

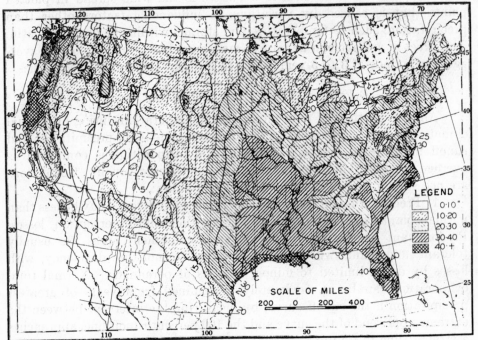

Fig. VIII-9.—Map showing the distribution of annual water losses in the United States, in inches of depth.

water losses in inches of depth over areas larger than stream drainage basins. Kittredge [33] made the first comprehensive attempt to prepare such a map and his map is reproduced herewith by permission as Figure VIII-9. Study of this map is very illuminating, and as future editions are prepared, using more accurate base maps of precipitation and runoff, they will assume a place of great value in hydrologic practice.[1] In England and Sweden, for example, it has been found possible to determine annual runoff very closely by subtracting a constant value for water losses. It may be possible to extend this procedure to other regions and to shorter time periods.

[1] Since writing the above, U.S.G.S. Water Supply Paper 846 has been published containing a more detailed map of mean annual water loss for the United States and also a suggestive graphical comparison of mean annual water loss and mean annual temperature.

TABLE 7.—*Water losses from stream drainage basins*

Stream	Locality	Drainage area square miles	Period of observation	Average annual precipitation (inches)	Average annual runoff (inches)	Precipitation minus runoff (inches)	Authority[b]
Kennebec River.........	Waterville, Maine	4,270	1893–1905	39.6	23.7	15.9	26
Cobbosseecontee River....	Gardiner, Maine	240	1891–1905	42.2	17.4	24.8	26
Sudbury River..........	Massachusetts	75	1875–1932	44.3	21.2	23.1	61
Wachusett River.........	Massachusetts	109	1897–1932	45.0	23.7	21.2	61
Merrimac River.........	Lawrence, Mass.	4,461	1880–1934	41.6	20.1	21.5	27
Lake Cochituate.........	Cochituate, Mass.	18.9	1863–1900	47.1	20.3	26.8	59
Mystic Lake............	Boston, Mass.	26.9	1878–95	44.1	20.0	24.1	59
Abbott Run............	Rhode Island	27	1908–32	42.9	21.1	21.8	61
Nepaug River...........	Hartford, Conn.	32	1929–35	42.4	17.3	25.1	62
Pomperaug River........	Bennetts Bridge, Conn.	89	1914–16	44.5	19.5[a]	23.2	48
Hudson River...........	Mechanicville, N. Y.	4,500	1888–1901	44.2	22.3	20.9	59
Croton River...........	Croton Dam, N. Y.	375	1868–1932	47.7	23.4	24.4	61
Delaware River.........	Port Jervis, N. Y.	3,070	1902–1930	42.8	25.9	16.9	29
Delaware River.........	Trenton, N. J.	6,800	1897–1930	44.7	24.9	19.8	29
Neshaminy Creek........	Forks, Pa.	139	1884–99	47.6	23.1	24.5	59
Perkiomen Creek........	Frederick, Pa.	152	1884–99	48.0	23.6	24.4	59
Tohickon Creek.........	Point Pleasant, Pa.	102	1888–1911	48.9	26.1	22.8	49
Susquehanna River......	Harrisburg, Pa.	28,030	1891–1905	39.4	21.1	18.3	26
Potomac River..........	Point of Rocks, Md.	9,650	1895–1905	36.8	14.2	22.6	26
James River............	Cartersville, Va.	6,240	1899–1934	40.8	15.6	25.2	27
Do.................	Buchanan, Va.	2,060	1895–1905	41.2	16.9	24.3	26
Roanoke River..........	Roanoke, Va.	390	1897–1905	42.7	17.7	25.0	26
Shenandoah River.......	Millville, W. Va.	3,000	1895–1905	38.3	13.6	24.7	26
Ohio River.............	Wheeling, W. Va.	23,820	1884–1905	41.7	22.7	19.0	26
Miami River............	Dayton, Ohio	2,525	25 yrs.	37.1	11.9	25.2	25
Muskingum River.......	Dresdon, Ohio	5,828	1888–95	39.7	13.1	26.6	59
Tennessee River.........	Chattanooga, Tenn.	21,400	1881–1934	50.3	24.2	26.1	27
Chattahoochee River.....	West Point, Ga.	3,550	1896–1934	54.6	22.3	32.3	27
Tombigbee River........	Columbus, Miss.	4,440	1901–9	49.2	17.1	32.1	49
Rock River.............	Rockton, Ill.	6,290	1904–8	33.9	10.0	23.9	49
Wisconsin River.........	Rhinelander, Wis.	1,110	1909–14	29.6	15.1	14.5	49
Mississippi River........	Minneapolis, Minn.	19,500	1897–1913	27.3	5.3	22.0	49
Little Fork River........	Little Fork, Minn.	1,720	1909–13	23.9	5.1	18.8	49
Root River.............	Houston, Minn.	1,560	1908–13	31.4	5.2	26.4	49
Ottertail River..........	Fergus Falls, Minn.	1,310	1908–13	23.0	2.6	20.4	49
St. Croix River.........	St. Croix Falls, Minn.	5,930	1902–12	30.0	9.6	20.4	49
Red River..............	Grand Forks, N. Dak.	25,500	1882–1934	20.9	1.2	19.7	27
Mississippi River........	Keokuk, Iowa	119,000	1878–1934	29.5	7.0	22.5	27
Ralston Creek..........	Iowa City, Iowa	3	1925–35	33.1	6.8	26.3	45
Drainage basin A........	Wagonwheel Gap, Colo.	.35[c]	1911–26	21.1	6.1	15.0	4
Drainage basin B........	Do.	.31[d]	1911–26	21.0	6.7	14.3	4
Colorado River..........	Austin, Tex.	37,000	1900–9	26.9	.7	26.2	49
South Fork of Coquille River..................	Powers, Oreg.	168	1917–26	96.0	63.5	32.5	37
Rogue River.............	Raygold, Oreg.	2,020	1906–28	43.6	22.6	21.0	37
Pilarcitos and San Andreas Creeks.	San Andreas Reservoir, Calif.	12[e]	1869–1903	45.0	18.0	27.0	15
South Fork of Yuba River.	Lake Spaulding, Calif.[e]	123.5[e]	1907–39	60.60	47.4	13.2	f

[a] Corrected for ground-water storage.
[b] See Bibliography, pp. 327–330.
[c] Mean altitude 11,200 feet; vegetation fir.
[d] Mean altitude 11,200 feet; vegetation pine, spruce, and grass; deforested in 1918 and grew up to poplars.
[e] Altitude 4,500 to 7,500 feet.
f Data furnished by Pacific Gas & Electric Co.

Quantitative data

Availability

The principal sources of quantitative data for total evaporation are the reports and published writings of hydraulic engineers interested in runoff as a source of developed water supply. Search of engineering literature has yielded information for 47 drainage basins well distributed throughout the United States and ranging in size from 3 to 119,000 square miles (table 7). Although the data as compiled represent precipitation minus runoff, it is believed that the records are sufficiently long to eliminate errors due to over-year storage. The Pomperaug River, in Connecticut, is an exception, but the results on this stream were here corrected for ground storage. The data in table 7 have been compared with those in Figure VIII-9 and found to be in essential agreement. Taken together, this table and map present a broad picture of total evaporation throughout the United States.

Quantitative results

In general, the average annual total evaporation as indicated by table 7 and Figure VIII-9 ranges from 3.3 feet along the Gulf of Mexico to less than 0.5 foot in the Great Basin region. Generally in the Southeastern States it ranges from 2.0 to 3.0 feet; in the Northern States east of the 100th meridian from 1.7 to 2.5 feet; and in the Mississippi Valley west of the 100th meridian from 1.75 to 1.25 feet. On the Pacific coast it varies widely; isolated areas with coastal exposure in northern California, Oregon, and Washington are shown in figure 8 as having total evaporation in excess of 3.3 feet. These areas receive very heavy precipitation, some of them more than 100 inches annually. Because of the cool temperature and humidity in these areas it is questioned whether the data are sufficient to establish definitely a total evaporation much, if any, greater than 3 feet a year.

With a knowledge of the distribution of forest vegetation, Kittredge [33] has prepared a tabulation of annual water losses in forest regions of the United States, reproduced herewith as table 8. This table indicates an average evaporation from 3 feet for the longleaf-loblolly-slash pine forests of the south Atlantic and Gulf coasts and the river-bottom hardwoods and cypress to 1.0 feet for the spruce-fir forests in the northern Rocky Mountain regions. The Douglas fir and redwood forests of the northwest coast are credited with an annual average of more than 3 feet and a maximum of 5 feet, but the maximum figures are probably too high and would bear further investigation. The sugar and ponderosa pine forests of the Sierra Nevada average over 2 feet. The figures for other types of forest are as low as 0.5 foot for desert-shrub areas. With the

TABLE 8.—*Annual water losses in forest regions of United States*
[Data from reference 33, table 1]

Type of vegetation	Annual water losses (depth)	
	Inches	Feet
EASTERN REGIONS		
Longleaf, loblolly, and slash pine....................	30–40	2.5–3.3
River bottom hardwoods and cypress................	30–40	2.5–3.3
Oak and pine..	25–35	2.1–2.9
Oak, chestnut, and yellow poplar....................	20–30	1.7–2.5
Oak and hickory....................................	20–30	1.7–2.5
Tall grass..	20–30	1.7–2.5
Birch, beech, maple, and hemlock...................	15–20	1.25–1.7
White, red, and jack pine...........................	15–20	1.25–1.7
Spruce and fir......................................	10–20	.8–1.7
WESTERN REGIONS		
Pacific Douglas fir..................................	25–60	2.1–5.0
Redwood...	25–55	2.1–4.6
Sugar and ponderosa pine...........................	15–40	1.25–3.3
Western larch and western white pine................	15–20	1.25–1.7
Spruce and fir......................................	10–20	.8–1.7
Ponderosa pine.....................................	10–20	.8–1.7
Short grass..	10–20	.8–1.7
Lodgepole pine.....................................	10–15	.8–1.25
Piñon and juniper..................................	5–15	.4–1.25
Chaparral..	5–15	.4–1.25
Sagebrush..	5–10	.4– .8
Desert shrub.......................................	4–10	.3– .8

exception noted, all the figures appear reasonable and show a remarkable quantitative similarity to those of consumptive use for vegetation growing under similar conditions of water supply. This method of studying total evaporation is a very promising field for future hydrologic research.

CONCLUSIONS

The foregoing review of transpiration and total evaporation sets forth the present status of research in these subjects, outlines the methods of measurement, and assembles the essential results of quantitative measurements. From this mass of information present deficiencies and trends can be determined and a program formulated for future investigational work.

PRESENT STATUS

Transpiration, soil evaporation, and interception

The research activities of botanists, silviculturists, and workers at agricultural experiment stations have extended to practically all phases of the physical process of transpiration, its controlling forces, and the influencing factors.   The essential facts regarding processes and influencing factors have been established, and present research is directed to confirming and rounding out these facts.   Little has been definitely established regarding the controlling forces, and this remains as an active field for future research.   Quantitative data on transpiration are largely in the form of transpiration ratio (water requirement).   This ratio has been determined for about 60 varieties of agricultural crops, native weeds, and grasses growing in the central and northern Great Plains region and for miscellaneous varieties in other scattered localities.   The transpiration ratio in any one locality has been shown to vary closely from year to year in proportion to evaporation from a free water surface.   The same relation appears to hold for differences in transpiration ratio at different localities. The practical utility of transpiration ratio in hydrologic work is very slight, however, because of the incomplete knowledge of the production of dry matter for crops grown in the field or in stands of natural vegetation, and the consequent inability to convert transpiration ratio into depth of water over land areas.

The research work of experiment-station workers, hydrologists, and engineers has established the relations of evaporation from continuously moistened soil and from a free water surface in the same locality and has made some progress in the determination of evaporation from soil intermittently wet and dry.

Sufficient study has been made by silviculturists and hydrologists to establish the fact that interception is an important element of loss from vegetation, especially in forested areas experiencing rains in summer or snow in winter.

Practically all hydrologic studies involving water losses from land areas include lands with more or less growing vegetation.   Losses by soil evaporation and often by interception occur from such areas, as well as loss by transpiration.   Owing to shading by the vegetation, it is impossible to determine the extent to which soil evaporation is operative in such areas, and the amount of interception is also indeterminate.   Transpiration data for such areas, if available, are of little value if soil evaporation and interception are unknown.   The most practical procedure for measurement is therefore to obtain all three items in natural combination as one total.   This is accomplished by measuring consumptive use in the irrigated areas of western America and more generally by measuring total evaporation from stream basins or large areas, especially those in humid or tropical regions.

Consumptive use

Attempts have been made to measure consumptive use by at least ten different methods.   Present practice includes six of these methods, some of which are applicable only under special conditions.

(*a*) The open-tank method as now perfected has the widest application. Results can be applied to large areas by use of exposure factors and the integration method.

(*b*) The field-plot method approaches natural conditions more nearly, but it can be effectively used only where a complete accounting of absorption can be made. This has been found possible in arid and semiarid regions by use of the improved soil auger for taking moisture samples to considerable depth.

(*c*) The volumetric method as applied to alluvium-filled valleys enclosed by impermeable rock basins is widely used. It requires the measurement of all elements of inflow and outflow plus precipitation upon the surface and appropriate adjustment for surface and ground storage.

(*d*) The volumetric method as applied to stream bottoms in canyons has a more limited application.

(*e*) For broad, gently sloping valley areas with small rainfall the method involving determination of the annual fluctuation in the water table is very satisfactory.

(*f*) The method involving determination of the available heat has possibilities but is still in the experimental stage.

A large body of information on consumptive use is available, and this method of approach to the study of water losses in arid and semiarid valleys has become a valuable addition to hydrologic practice.

Total evaporation

There are two general methods of measuring total evaporation—(1) the so-called rational method by integration of transpiration, soil evaporation, and interception for the area under consideration and (2) the method based on difference between precipitation and runoff. The latter method is the more practical and with the increasing availability of long runoff records is being increasingly studied. For stream drainage basins it may be applied graphically by development of diagrams showing rainfall and runoff or it may be calculated numerically. The graphic method automatically irons out annual eccentricities resulting from surface or ground storage. The numerical method requires correction for storage unless annual averages based upon periods of 3 to 5 years are available. For large areas the contour map showing annual water loss is useful, as prepared from contour maps of annual precipitation and runoff. The water loss from areas of distinctive types of vegetation can be determined from such a map by outlining on it the boundaries of the respective areas.

FUTURE PROGRESS

The determination of water losses will continue to be a major feature of practical hydrology, and suggestions for future research and the perfection of methods of measurement are pertinent.

The growing inadequacy of water supply in arid and semiarid regions as population increases creates a strong demand for reduction of water losses by transpiration, both from natural vegetation and from agricultural crops. By research, methods may be found to accomplish this end, either by modification of vegetational types and varieties or by control of the process of transpiration through the use of sprays or chemicals.

The close relation of water losses by transpiration, consumptive use, and total evaporation to the evaporation rate from a free water surface makes possible the wider use of quantitative data where the relative rates of evaporation are known. Further study is needed to correlate these various quantities definitely with evaporation from a free water surface, as measured under standard conditions. Evaporation records are already available in the United States at more than 60 class A evaporation stations of the United States Weather Bureau for periods averaging 10 years in length, at 27 United States Bureau of Plant Industry stations (6-foot pans 20 inches deep buried 16 inches in the ground) for periods averaging 19 years, and at many other stations. These records could be systematically correlated with each other and with available data on consumptive use and transpiration, to the end of standardizing the method of adjusting the evaporation data for use at other points.

The methods of measuring consumptive use by tank, field plot, valley, and canyon bottom should be further improved and standardized, and the available-heat method should be thoroughly investigated. An important point for improvement in the technique of tank measurement, for plants growing in freely draining soil, is elimination of the effect of capillary storage in the lower portion of the soil column resulting from surface tension at the bottom of the column. This tends to increase the water supply available to the plant and cause measured consumptive use to exceed that in the field. Improvement might result either by greater care in application of water at the surface so as to prevent percolation beyond the reach of plant roots, or by lengthening the soil column so that the roots will not penetrate to the zone of capillary storage.

The various methods of determining total evaporation by the difference between precipitation and runoff should be more thoroughly studied. The first step is a more systematic determination of average precipitation over drainage basins for which long records of runoff are available. The period required to eliminate the holdover effect of extremely wet and extremely dry years should also be studied. The preparation of more accurate contour maps of precipitation and runoff for large areas should be undertaken in order to further the determination of total evaporation by difference as a basis for determining total evaporation from distinctive vegetational types.

A most promising field of basic investigation is the relation of evaporation and transpiration to solar energy. The energy of the sun may be found to be a fundamental cause, of which air temperature, water temperature, evaporation, transpiration, and other factors are all effects. If so, the analysis of data on solar energy may lead to identification of a cause for variations in evaporation and transpiration that will clarify theory and be of practical value in applied hydrology. To facilitate such work many additional pyrheliometer installations are needed for measurement of solar radiation at points where observations on evaporation and transpiration are made. In this connection quantitative segregation of measured solar radiation into its visible light and ultraviolet components may assist in solving the problem. Ultraviolet radiation has now been definitely correlated with growths of algae in reservoirs [14a]. Preliminary experiments also indicate that there is a close relation between evaporation and ultraviolet radiation. This field of investigation is at present the most promising for progress in determination of the underlying causes of evaporation and transpiration.

REFERENCES

1. Alway, F. J., Studies of the relation of the nonavailable water of the soil to the hygroscopic coefficient: Nebraska Sta. Research Bull. 3, pp. 5–122, 1913.

2. Bark, D. H., Experiments on the economical use of irrigation water in Idaho: U.S. Dept. Agr. Bull. 339, 1916.

3. Barnes, C. R., The significance of transpiration: Science, new ser., vol. 15, p. 460, 1902.

4. Bates, C. G., and Harvy, A. J., Stream-flow experiment at Wagonwheel Gap, Colo.: Monthly Weather Rev. Suppl. 17, 1922; Suppl. 30, 1928.

5. Blaney, H. F., Rainfall penetration and consumptive use of water in Santa Ana River Valley and Coastal Plain, pt. 2: California Dept. Public Works, Div. Water Resources, Bull. 33, 1930.

6. Blaney, H. F., Water losses under natural conditions from wet areas in southern California, pt. 1: California Dept. Public Works, Div. Water Resources, Bull. 44, 1933.

7. Briggs, L. J., and Shantz, H. L., The wilting coefficient for different plants and its indirect determination: U.S. Dept. Agr., Bur. Plant Industry, Bull. 230, 1912.

8. Briggs, L. J., and Shantz, H. L., The water requirement of plants, pt. 2-A, Review of the literature: U.S. Dept. Agr., Bur. Plant Industry, Bull. 285, 1913.

9. Briggs, L. J., and Shantz, H. L., Relative water requirements of plants: Jour. Agr. Research, vol. 3, No. 1, pp. 1–165, 1914.

10. Crandall, Lynn, Report of use of water on Twin Falls North Side project (unpublished report, 1918. For summary see reference 19).

11. Debler, E. B., Valley consumptive use: Am. Geophys. Union Trans. 18th Ann. Meeting, pt. 2, p. 532, 1937.

12. Dillman, A. C., The water requirement of certain crop plants and weeds in northern Great Plains: Jour. Agr. Research, 42, pp. 187–238, 1931.

13. Fortier, Samuel, Use of water in irrigation, p. 151, McGraw-Hill Book Co., Inc., 1915.

14. Foster, E. E., The effects of bedrock on runoff of Wisconsin streams: Eng. Soc. Wisconsin Proc., 1926, p. 162.

14a. Goudey, R. F., Sun-ray counts save sulphate: Eng. News-Record, Apr. 11, 1940, p. 95.

15. Grunsky, C. E., Rain and runoff near San Francisco: Am. Soc. Civil Eng. Trans., vol. 61, p. 510, 1908.

16. Hammatt, W. C., Determination of the duty of water by analytical experiment: Am. Soc. Civil Eng. Trans., vol. 83, p. 200, 1920.

17. Harding, S. T., Irrigation studies on the Truckee River, Nev.: Data from testimony in Truckee River adjudication, 1918.

18. Harding, S. T., Ground-water resources of the southern San Joaquin Valley: California Dept. Public Works, Div. Engineering and Irrigation, Bull. 11, 1927.

19. Harding, S. T., and others, Consumptive use of water in irrigation; progress report of the Duty of Water Committee of Committee of the Irrigation Division: Am. Soc. Civil Eng. Trans., vol. 94, p. 1349, 1930.

20. Harris, F. S., The duty of water in Cache Valley, Utah: Utah Agr. Exper. Sta. Bull. 173, 1920.

21. Hemphill, R. G., Irrigation in northern Colorado: U.S. Dept. Agr. Bull. 1026, 1922.

22. Henderson, F. Y., On the effect of light and other conditions upon the rate of water loss from the mesophyll: Annals of Botany, vol. 40, pp. 507–535, 1926.

23. Horton, R. E., Transpiration of forest trees: Monthly Weather Rev., vol. 51, p. 569, 1923.

24. Horton, R. E., Determining the mean precipitation on a drainage basin: New England Water Works Assoc. Jour., vol. 38, No. 1, 1924.

25. Houk, I. E., Rainfall and runoff in the Miami Valley: Miami Conservancy Dist. Tech. Repts., pt. 8, 1921.

26. Hoyt, J. C., Comparison between rainfall and runoff in the northeastern United States: Am. Soc. Civil Eng. Trans., vol. 59, p. 431, 1907.

27. Hoyt, W. G., and others, Studies of relations of rainfall and runoff in the United States: U.S. Geol. Survey Water-Supply Paper 772, 1936.

28. Israelsen, O. W., and Winsor, L. M., Duty of water in Sevier Valley, Utah: Utah Agr. Exper. Sta. Bull. 182, 1922.

29. Jarvis, C. S., Rainfall and runoff characteristics of Delaware River Basin: Am. Geophys. Union Trans. 13th Ann. Meeting, p. 388, 1932.

30. Jones, J. H., and others, San Joaquin River Basin: California Dept. Public Works, Div. Water Resources, Bull. 29, 1934.

31. Justin, J. D., Determination of runoff from rainfall data: Am. Soc. Civil Eng. Trans., vol. 77, p. 346, 1914.

32. Kittredge, Joseph, Jr., Natural vegetation as a factor in the losses and yields of water: Jour. Forestry, vol. 35, No. 11, p. 1011, 1937.

33. Kittredge, Joseph, Jr., The magnitude and regional distribution of water losses influenced by vegetation: Jour. Forestry, vol. 36, No. 8, p. 775, 1938.

34. Lee, C. H., An intensive study of the water resources of a part of Owens Valley, Calif.: U. S. Geol. Survey Water-Supply Paper 294, 1912.

35. Lee, C. H., The determination of safe yield of underground reservoirs of the closed-basin type: Am. Soc. Civil Eng. Trans., vol. 78, p. 148, 1915.

36. Lee, C. H., Ground-water supply of the San Luis Rey Valley, Calif. (unpublished report, 1916).

37. Lee, C. H., Discussion of the paper "Water supply from rainfall on valley floors," by A. L. Sonderegger: Am. Soc. Civil Eng. Trans., vol. 94, p. 1920, 1930.

38. Lee, C. H., Economic aspects of a salt-water barrier below confluence of Sacramento and San Joaquin Rivers: California Dept. Public Works, Div. Water Resources Bull. 28, app. C, 1931.

39. Lee, C. H., and others, Report of the Committee on Absorption and Transpiration, app. A: Am. Geophys. Union Trans. 15th Ann. Meeting, pt. 2, p. 295, 1934.

40. Lewis, M. R., Experiments on the proper time and amount of irrigation, Twin Falls Experiment Station, 1914, 1915, and 1916, U. S. Dept. Agr., cooperating with Twin Falls County Commissioners, Twin Falls Canal Co., and Twin Falls Commercial Club, 1919.

41. Livingston, B. E., Operation of the porous-cup atomometer: Plant World, vol. 13, pp. 111–119, 1910.

42. Livingston, B. E., and Shreve, E. B., Improvements in the method for determining the transpiring power of plant surfaces by hygrometric paper: Plant World, vol. 19, pp. 287–309, 1916.

43. Loftfield, J. V. G., The behavior of stomata: Carnegie Inst. Washington Pub. 314, 1921.

44. Mathew, Raymond, and others, Variation and control of salinity in Sacramento-San Joaquin Delta and upper San Francisco Bay: California Dept. Public Works, Div. Water Resources Bull. 27, pp. 68–75, 1931.

45. Mavis, F. T., and Soucek, Edward, A summary of hydrologic data, Ralston Creek watershed, 1924–35: Iowa Univ. Engineering Studies, Bull. 9, 1936.

46. Meinzer, O. E., Plants as indicators of ground water: U. S. Geol. Survey Water-Supply Paper 577, 1927.

47. Meinzer, O. E., Outline of methods of estimating ground-water supplies: U. S. Geol. Survey Water-Supply Paper 638-C, 1931.

48. Meinzer, O. E., and Stearns, N. D., A study of ground water in the Pomperaug Basin, Conn.: U. S. Geol. Survey Water-Supply Paper 597-B, 1929.

49. Meyer, A. F., Computing runoff from rainfall and other physical data: Am. Soc. Civil Eng. Trans., vol. 79, pp. 1056–1224, 1915.

50. Miller, E. C., Plant physiology, New York, McGraw-Hill Book Co., Inc., 1938.

51. Minckler, L. S., A new method of measuring transpiration: Jour. Forestry, vol. 24, pp. 36–39, 1936.

52. Montgomery, E. G., and Kisselbach, T. A., Studies in water requirements of corn: Nebraska Agr. Exper. Sta. Bull. 128, 1912.

53. Parker, G. L., and Store, F. B., Water powers of the Cascade Range, pt. 3, Yakima River Basin: U. S. Geol. Survey Water-Supply Paper 369, 1916.

54. Parshall, R. L., Experiments to determine rate of evaporation from saturated soils and river-bed sands, with discussions by Fortier, Sonderegger, Blaney, Cummings, Rohwer, and Houk: Am. Soc. Civil Eng. Trans., vol. 94, p. 961, 1930.

55. Parshall, R. L., Laboratory measurement of evapo-transpiration losses: Jour. Forestry, vol. 35, No. 11, p. 1033, 1937.

56. Powers, W. L., Irrigation and soil-moisture investigations in western Oregon: Oregon Agr. Exper. Sta. Bull. 140, 1914.

57. Powers, W. L., The economical use of irrigation water: Oregon Agr. Exper. Sta. Bull. 140, 1917.

58. Raber, Oran, Water utilization by trees, with special reference to the economic forest species of the North Temperate Zone: U. S. Dept. Agr. Misc. Pub. 257, 1937.

59. Rafter, G. W., The relation of rainfall to runoff: U. S. Geol. Survey Water-Supply Paper 80, 1903.

60. Sampson, A. W., and Allen, L. M., Influence of physical factors on transpiration: Minnesota Bot. Studies, pt. 1, vol. 4, p. 33, Minnesota Univ., 1909.

61. Saville, C. M., Some relationships of runoff to rainfall: Am. Geophys. Union Trans. 15th Ann. Meeting, pt. 2, p. 444, 1934.

62. Saville, C. M., The underground water-index—its relation to surface runoff: Am. Geophys. Union Trans. 17th Ann. Meeting, pt. 2, p. 382, 1936.

63. Shantz, H. L., and Piemeisel, L. N., The water requirement of plants at Akron, Colo.: Jour. Agr. Research, vol. 34, No. 12, pp. 1093–1190, 1927.

64. Shreve, E. B., Factors governing seasonal changes in transpiration of *Encelia farinosa*: Bot. Gazette, vol. 77, pp. 432–439, 1924.

65. Shull, C. A., Measurement of the surface forces in soils: Bot. Gazette; vol. 62, pp. 1–29, 1916; Science, new ser., vol. 43, p. 1361, 1916.

66. Sleight, R. B., Evaporation from the surfaces of water and river-bed materials: Jour. Agr. Research, vol. 10, pp. 209–262, 1917.

67. Snelson, W. H., Irrigation practice and water requirements for crops in Alberta: Canada Dept. Interior Irrigation Series, Bull. 6, 1922.

68. Stearns, H. T., and Bryan, L. L., Preliminary report on the geology and water resources of the Mud Lake Basin, Idaho: U. S. Geol. Survey Water-Supply Paper 560-D, p. 101, 1925.

69. Stearns, H. T., Crandall, Lynn, and Steward, W. G., Geology and ground-water resources of the Snake River Plain in southeastern Idaho: U. S. Geol. Survey Water-Supply Paper 774, 1938.

70. Stevens, J. C., The duty of water in the Pacific Northwest: Am. Soc. Civil Eng. Trans., vol. 83, p. 2094, 1920.

71. Steward, W. G., Distribution and disposition of irrigation water: Joint Conference of the Irrigation, Engineering, and Agricultural Societies of Idaho Proc., pp. 171–182, 1919.

72. Stout, O. V. P., Transpiration and evaporation losses from areas of native vegetation: Am. Geophys. Union Trans. 15th Ann. Meeting, pt. 2, p. 559, 1934.

73. Taylor, G. H., Investigations relating to the absorption of precipitation and its penetration to the zone of saturation: Am. Geophys. Union Trans. 12th Ann. Meeting, pp. 206–211, 1931.

74. Ullrich, C. J., Testimony at hearing of the Colorado River Commission, Salt Lake City, Utah, March 27, 28, 1922.

75. Veatch, A. C., Fluctuation of the water level in wells, with special reference to Long Island, N. Y.: U. S. Geol. Survey Water-Supply Paper 155, pp. 44–48, 1906.

76. Viehmeyer, F. J., Some factors affecting irrigation requirements of deciduous orchards: Hilgardia, vol. 2, pp. 125–284, 1927.

77. Viehmeyer, F. J., An improved soil-sampling tube: Soil Science, vol. 27, No. 2, 1929.

78. Viehmeyer, F. J., Evaporation from soils and transpiration: Am. Geophys. Union Trans. 19th Ann. Meeting, pt. 2, p. 612, 1938.

79. Weaver, J. E., and Clements, F. E., Plant ecology, New York, McGraw Hill Book Co., Inc., 1938.

80. White, W. N., Method of estimating ground-water supplies based on discharge by plants and evaporation from soil—Results of investigations in Escalante Valley, Utah: U. S. Geol. Survey Water-Supply Paper 659-A, 1932.

81. Widtsoe, J. A., The production of dry matter with different quantities of irrigation water: Utah Agr. Exper. Sta. Bull. 166, 1912.

82. Widtsoe, J. A., The yields of crops with different quantities of water: Utah Agr. Exp. Sta. Bull. 117, 1912.

83. Nat. Resources Board, Report of Water Planning Committee, pt. 3, p. 294, 1934.

84. Nat. Resources Committee, Regional planning, pt. 6, The Rio Grande joint investigation in the upper Rio Grande Basin, vol. 1, 1938.

CHAPTER IX

SOIL MOISTURE

IXa. SOIL MOISTURE AND CAPILLARY PHENOMENA IN SOILS

Karl Terzaghi[1]

GROUND WATER AND SOIL MOISTURE[2]

If the ground water were subject to no force other than gravity there would be a sharp boundary between dry and saturated soil. This boundary would be located at the level to which the water rises in observation wells. Below this surface, which is called the water table or the phreatic surface, the water is acted upon solely by the force of gravity and behaves according to the laws of ground-water flow.

However, it is an empirical fact that the soil is capable of retaining permanently considerable quantities of water within the voids between the surface of the ground and the phreatic surface. The permanent presence of water within this zone can be accounted for only by the existence of forces that counteract the mechanical effect of the force of gravity. These are known as capillary forces, and the water which is retained in the soil above the phreatic surface by means of the capillary forces is called the soil moisture.

Soil moisture near the surface is subject to considerable seasonal variations due to evaporation and to the withdrawal of water through the roots of plants, and to rainfall. The present contribution is limited to a discussion of the moisture in the soil located below this top layer.

The principal symbols that will be used in connection with the theoretical discussion of the subject are listed below.

C_u = Allen Hazen's uniformity coefficient, or the ratio between the grain size that is finer than 40 percent of the material and the grain size that is finer than 90 percent of the material.

D_{10} = Allen Hazen's effective size [5], which is finer than 90 percent of the material and coarser than 10 percent of it.

d = diameter.

e_a = volume of air per unit of volume of solid.

e_w = volume of water per unit of volume of solid.

$e = e_a + e_w$ = void ratio, or the ratio between the volume occupied by the voids and the volume occupied by the solid.

---

[1] Consulting engineer, lecturer at Harvard University, Cambridge, Mass.

[2] The word "soil" is used in this section for the rock material above the water table. The section does not include the capillary phenomena in the uppermost zone, which supports rooted plants.

$G_a = \dfrac{e_a}{e}$ = degree of aeration.

$G_s = \dfrac{e_w}{e}$ = degree of saturation.

g = acceleration due to gravity.

h = height.

h_c = height of capillary rise of water in a tube or of soil moisture in a soil.

h_{cc} = height of zone of complete capillary saturation in a soil.

i = hydraulic gradient or the ratio between the hydraulic head and the distance between two points of a flow line, measured along the flow line. The hydraulic head represents the difference between the levels to which the water rises in piezometric tubes established at the two points.

k = coefficient of permeability, equal to the volume of water that percolates per unit of time through the unit of area of a section perpendicular to the direction of the flow at a hydraulic gradient equal to unity.

n = porosity, or ratio between the volume of voids and the total volume of the soil.

p_a = atmospheric pressure.

r = radius.

t = time.

T = temperature, in degrees centigrade.

T_{sT} = surface tension of the water in grams per centimeter at a temperature T.

T_s = approximate surface tension of water at room temperature, 0.073 gram per centimeter.

u_z = hydrostatic pressure in the water at a depth z below the reference level.

$v = ki$ = discharge velocity, or the quantity of water that percolates per unit of time through the unit of area of a section perpendicular to the direction of the flow.

v_s = seepage velocity, equal to the ratio between the discharge velocity v and the corresponding porosity n (average velocity at which the water percolates through a section perpendicular to the direction of the flow of water through the soil).

w = water content, or the ratio between the weight of the water contained in the soil and the dry weight of the soil.

z = variable height or depth.

α = contact angle, or angle between the vertical wall of a capillary tube and the adjoining free water surface.

γ_T = weight of water per unit of volume at a temperature T.

γ_w = approximate unit weight of water, equal to 1 gram per cubic centimeter or 62.4 pounds per cubic feet values sufficiently accurate for practical purposes.

CAPILLARY RISE AND CAPILLARY SATURATION

If the lower end of a cylindrical specimen of dry soil is dipped into water, the water penetrates the voids of the soil and rises in the voids to a level h_c above the free water level. This can easily be demonstrated by the following experiment. Take a glass cylinder with a perforated bottom, as shown in Fig. IXA-1, *a*, fill the cylinder with a fine, light-colored dry sand and dip the lower end of the cylinder into water. As soon as the sand comes into contact with the water, the water invades the voids of the sand, changing the color of the sand from light to dark. The rise of the upper boundary continues with decreasing speed until the boundary becomes stationary at a level h_c above the free water surface. The height h_c is called the height of capillary rise. In the lower section of the wetted part of the column the voids are completely filled with water; in the upper section, parts of the voids are occupied by air. In Fig. IXA-1, *b*, the width of the areas marked "water" (left) and "air" (right) represents for each level z the volume occupied by water and air per unit of volume of solid. To designate the degree to which the water and the air participate in the occupancy of the voids the following values are used:

$$G_s = \frac{e_w}{e} = \text{degree of saturation at level } z.$$

$$G_a = \frac{e_a}{e} = \text{degree of aeration at level } z.$$

Since $e_w + e_a = e$ we obtain $G_s + G_a = 1$.

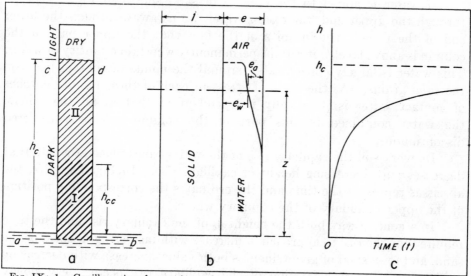

Fig. IXA-1.—Capillary rise of water in a column of dry sand. See text or explanation of a, b, c.

If γ_s is the unit weight of the solid particles and γ_w the unit weight of the water, the water content w of the soil is

$$w = e_w \frac{\gamma_w}{\gamma_s}, \qquad \text{or} \qquad e_w = w \frac{\gamma_s}{\gamma_w}$$

As an example let us assume $w = 0.19$, $\gamma_w = 1$ gram per cubic centimeter, and $\gamma_s = 2.65$ gram per cubic centimeter. Introducing these values into the preceding equation, we get

$$e_w = 0.19 \frac{2.65}{1.00} = 0.50$$

which means that the water occupies a space equal to one-half of that occupied by the solid particles. The degree of saturation is equal to e_w/e and the degree of aeration is $1 - e_w/e$.

In order to compute the degree of saturation or aeration, it is necessary to determine both the water content w and the void ratio e of the sample.

Up to level h_{cc} in Fig. IXA-1, b, the degree of saturation is equal to unity, and the corresponding part of the column of sand is said to be in a state of complete capillary saturation. The water contained in this zone represents continuous capillary water. Above the upper boundary of the continuous capillary water, at level h_{cc}, the wider capillary channels are filled with air. With increasing height above the zone of capillary saturation the number and the total cross section of the air-filled channels increase. As the water contained in this zone is continuous only in a vertical direction it is said to be in a semicontinuous state.

If water is added to the column of sand shown in Fig. IXA-1, a, through the upper end, the excess water drains away through the lower end of the tube. Yet in spite of the fact that the upper part of the column is above level h_c it retains permanently a certain quantity of water. This water is largely concentrated around the points of contact between the sand grains. As the state of stress in each of these minute patches of contact water is practically independent of that in all the others, the water contained in this part of the column can be considered discontinuous.

In every soil the capillary rise of the water takes place at a rate that decreases with increasing height of capillary rise. In Fig. IXA-1, c, the abscissas represent the time and the ordinates the corresponding position of the upper boundary of the capillary water.

In a general way both the height h_c of the capillary rise and the time required for the rise to approach h_c increase with increasing fineness of the sand, and for a sand of given fineness both values increase with decreasing void ratio. The last fraction of the capillary rise occurs very slowly and extends, even in coarse-grained soils, over periods of weeks or months. During the same period the upper boundary of the zone of capillary saturation rises slowly and the air content in the moistened part of the sand decreases without ever becoming equal to zero. In a sand with an effective size $D_{10} = 0.15$ millimeter, a uniformity coefficient $C_u = 1.44$, and a porosity $n = 0.41$, the water was found to rise within 10 minutes to a height of 25 centimeters, and the corresponding average degree of aeration was 0.30. During the following 9 days the upper boundary of the moist zone rose 2 centimeters more and the corresponding degree of aeration was 0.26. Yet the stationary state had not yet been reached.

The average degree of aeration for different stages of a test of capillary rise can be determined by simultaneous observation of the height of the capillary rise and of the corresponding quantity of water that has entered the sand. The degree of aeration is determined by the difference between the total volume of the voids within the moistened zone and the volume of water that has flowed into the voids [2].

Up to a height h_{cc} above the phreatic table the soil is in a state of complete capillary saturation. This height can be determined indirectly by means of the capillarimeter, which measures the excess air pressure required to produce the first continuous air channel from the top to the bottom of a saturated sample. The excess air pressure can be obtained either by raising the pressure of the air above the sample or by suction applied to the base of the sample [2]. For fine-grained soils the result of capillarimeter tests is likely to be strongly influenced by the rate at which the excess pressure is applied.

The distribution of the air content in a column of sand such as that shown in Figure IXA-1, *a*, has thus far been determined only by cutting the column of sand into several sections and determining the water content of each section individually.

SURFACE TENSION OF WATER AND THE RISE OF WATER IN CAPILLARIES

The rise of water into the voids of a dry sand represents the combined result of three physical causes—the molecular attraction between the sand grains and the water, the surface tension of the water, and the capacity of the water to resist hydrostatic tensile stresses of many atmospheres without losing its continuity. The existence of the surface tension of the water can best be

Fig. IXA-2.—Greased steel needle supported by surface tension of water.

demonstrated by carefully lowering a greased needle in a horizontal position onto a free water surface, as shown in Figure IXA-2. In spite of its high specific gravity the needle does not sink into the water. It merely produces a shallow, troughlike depression. This fact indicates that the uppermost film of water must have a definite tensile strength, similar to a rubber membrane. However, in contrast to the stress in a rubber membrane, the stress in the surface film of a liquid is independent of the strain. Young [22] and Laplace [8] showed that surface tension represents a necessary consequence of the attraction between the molecules of a liquid. For water the estimated intensity of the molecular attraction ranges between 10,700 and 25,000 atmospheres. As the tensile strength of a liquid is, at least theoretically, identical with the force of attraction of the molecules on both sides of a section, it is not surprising that water is capable of resisting very high hydrostatic tensile stresses without losing its continuity.

If the lower end of a tube having a very small diameter (capillary) is dipped into water, the surface of the water comes to rest within the tube either above or below the free water surface outside the tube, depending on the chemical composition of the walls of the tube or of the impurities that cover the surface in the interior of the tube. Figure IXA-3 illustrates the first case. Within the tube the column of water terminates in a cuplike depression, called the meniscus. The film of water covering the concave surface is in a state of tension similar to the tension of a stretched rubber membrane, and it is anchored to the walls of the tube by the molecular attraction between the molecules of the liquid and the adjoining molecules of the surface layer of the wall. It should be emphasized, however, that the attraction exerted by the molecules of the walls of the tube does not extend beyond an extremely small distance from the wall. Hence practically the entire liquid content of the capillary tube is in the same physical state as it is in a pipe line, and as a consequence it follows the same laws, called the laws of hydraulics.

FIG. IXA-3.—Meniscus at the upper end of a column of water in a capillary tube.

The equilibrium of the column of water requires that the surface tension of the water carries the weight of the water just as the surface tension of the water shown in Figure IXA-2 carries the weight of the needle. In general, the meniscus intersects the wall of the tube at an angle α, called the angle of contact. This angle varies with the chemical composition of the liquid and with the chemical composition of the walls of the tube or of the impurities that cover this wall. If the angle of contact is 0°, as it is between pure water and clean glass, a thin film of liquid is pulled up along the wall of the tube above the meniscus. For any value of the angle α the condition for the equilibrium of the column of water is

$$r^2 \pi \gamma_T h_c = T_{sT} \, 2r \, \pi \cos \alpha$$

wherein γ_T is the unit weight of the water and T_{sT} the surface tension, both at a temperature T. From this equation we obtain

$$h_c = \frac{2T_{sT}}{r\gamma_T} \cos \alpha \tag{1}$$

The value of the surface tension T_{sT} has been determined by several independent methods, whose results are practically identical. The following table [23] gives the magnitude of the surface tension of water in fractions of a gram per centimeter for different temperatures T in degrees centigrade.

$T =$	0°	10°	20°	30°	40°
$T_{sT} =$	0.0756	0.0742	0.0727	0.0711	0.0695

For room temperature we have approximately $T_{sT} = T_s = 0.073$ gram per centimeter and $\gamma_T = \gamma_w = 1$. With these numerical values we obtain from equation 1

$$h_c \text{ (centimeters)} = \frac{0.15}{r} \cos \alpha \tag{2}$$

The state of stress in the water contained in a capillary tube depends on the pressure, p_a, in the air above the water. If the test illustrated by Figure IXA-4, a, is made in a perfect vacuum, the entire column of water above the free water level is in a state of tension for the following reasons. Both the hydrostatic pressure in the water at the height of the free water level and the shearing resistance of the water are equal to zero. As a consequence, the vertical forces that act on a section of the column of

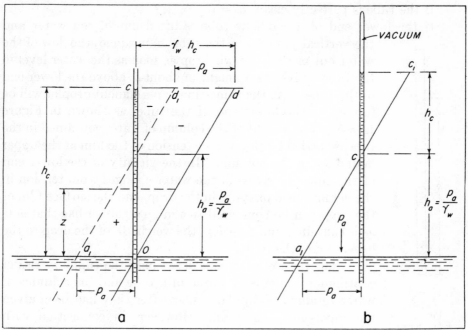

Fig. IXA-4.—State of stress in the water contained (a) in an open capillary tube and (b) in a closed and evacuated capillary tube.

water at a height z above the base consist solely of the weight of the water, $z\gamma_w$, per unit of area of a section through the column and the hydrostatic pressure (or tension), u_z, per unit of area of the section. Hence the equilibrium of the column of water requires that

$$u_z + z\gamma_w = 0$$

or

$$u_z = -z\gamma_w \tag{3}$$

In Figure IXA-4, a, the values of u_z are represented by the abscissas of the straight line od.

If the space above the water is invaded by air under a pressure p_a, the pressure in the water increases everywhere by p_a. Hence the pressure in the water will be as shown by the abscissa of the dotted line a_1d_1 in Figure

IXA-4, a. The height h_c of capillary rise remains unaltered. According to Figure IXA-4, a, no tension will exist in the water unless the height h_c of capillary rise is greater than $h_a = \dfrac{p_a}{\gamma_w}$, or approximately 10 meters. Finally, if the lower end of an evacuated capillary tube, Figure IXA-4, b, is dipped into water in contact with air under a pressure p_a, the water will rise in the tube to a height of

$$h_a + h_c = \frac{p_a}{\gamma_w} + \frac{0.15}{r} \cos \alpha \qquad (4)$$

If the tube is perfectly clean, $\alpha = 0$.

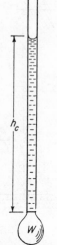

If the lower end of a capillary tube is lifted out of the water and the vertical position of the tube maintained, the flow of the water out of the tube will stop as soon as the water level in the tube arrives at a height of about h_c above the lower end of the tube. At the same time a permanent droplet will be formed at the lower end of the tube, as shown in Figure IXA-5. The weight of the column of water contained in the tube is carried by the surface tension of the film at the upper boundary of the column. In the vicinity of the lower end of the tube the stress in the water changes from tension in the column into pressure in the drop, and the surface film of the drop can be compared to a minute rubber bag that acts as a container and transfers the weight W of the drop to the lower end of the tube.

Fig. IXA-5. —Permanent droplet maintained by surface tension at the lower end of a capillary tube.

Thus far we have considered only the capillary rise of continuous columns of water in a tube and the columns of water retained in capillary tubes after they had been given an opportunity to drain. However, in connection with the origin of soil moisture we are also interested in the capillary rise of water in slits and grooves and in the droplets that are retained at the points of contact between uneven surfaces.

If the lower edges of two glass plates that are separated from each other by a very narrow air space are immersed, the water rises within this space as it does in a capillary tube, although the sides of the air space are open. If the position of the glass plates is adjusted in such a way that they touch each other along one of their vertical sides, the height of the capillary rise in the groove thus obtained decreases from the contact toward the open side. Very narrow grooves can even be used as capillary siphons for transporting water out of a container, provided they are given the shape of a hook whose outer end is below the surface of the water in the container, as shown in Figure IXA-6.

In an accumulation of solid particles such as sand every point of contact between two adjoining particles is surrounded by an annular, groove-like space having a V-shaped cross section. The width of this space increases from zero at the contact in every radial direction. When sand is drained by gravity or by centrifuging, each one of these grooves retains a minute quantity of water held in place by capillary forces, as shown in Figure IXA-7, in which the forces exerted by the solid on the surface film are indicated by arrows. As these forces tend to increase the diameter of the particle of water surrounding the point of contact, the water is maintained in a state of tension, and the solid particles on both sides of the point of contact are forced

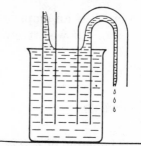

Fig. IXA-6.—Test arrangement for demonstrating capillary flow of water in a narrow open groove.

together with a pressure equal and opposite to the tension in the water.

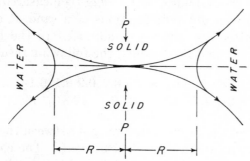

Fig. IXA-7.—Water held by capillary forces.

INFLUENCE OF GRAIN SIZE ON HEIGHT AND SPEED OF CAPILLARY RISE IN SOILS

Every soil consists of an accumulation of solid particles separated from each other by capillary passageways. The connections between these passageways and their variable width merely complicate the problem without eliminating the fundamental identity between the soil and a system of capillary tubes. Hence the capillary rise of the water into a column of sand, as shown in Figure IXA-1, can be compared to the capillary rise of the water into a system of vertical capillary tubes and grooves.

According to equation 2 the height h_c of capillary rise increases inversely as the diameter $2r$ of the tubes, and it also increases in direct proportion to the cosine of the angle of contact α. Laboratory experience regarding the influence of the porosity on the coefficient of permeability of sands shows that the effective average width, $2r$, of the capillary passages increases approximately in simple proportion to the void ratio e.

On the basis of this experience we obtain for the average radius of the capillaries in the soil the equation

$$r = BeD^2_{10}$$

wherein B is an empirical factor depending on the shape of the grains of the sand. If we introduce this value into equation 2 we get

$$h_c = \frac{0.15}{BeD_{10}} \cos \alpha = \frac{C}{eD_{10}} \tag{5}$$

in which
$$C = \frac{0.15 \cos \alpha}{B}$$

The value of the factor C depends on the shape of the grains and on the angle of contact α, which in turn depends on the amount and the kind of impurities that cover the surface of the grains. In a general way, the relation expressed by equation 5 is confirmed by experience. The following data will serve as examples. Atterberg [1] measured the height of the capillary rise in seven different fractions of a sand at a temperature of 17° C. 72 days after the water was admitted to the lower end of the cylindrical specimen, and he obtained the following results:

Grain size, mm...	5-2	2-1	1-0.5	0.5-0.2	0.2-0.1	0.1-0.05	0.05-0.02
h_c, cm..........	2.5	6.5	13.1	24.6	42.8	105.5	200 (still rising)

The porosity of the sands tested ranged between the narrow limits of 40.1 and 41.8 percent and averaged 41 percent. The corresponding void ratio is 0.69. The table shows that the height of capillary rise increased very nearly inversely to the first power of the grain size.

The present writer measured the height of the capillary rise of the water in a clean dune sand with an effective grain size of $D_{10} = 0.186$ millimeters and a uniformity coefficient of $C_u = 1.18$. In one set of tests the average void ratio was $e_1 = 0.85$ and the corresponding height of the capillary rise $h_c = 4.75$ centimeters. In the second set of tests the corresponding values were $e_2 = 0.65$ and $h = 6.5$ centimeters. Hence the ratio between the two values for h_c was equal to $6.5 \div 4.75 = 1.37$. According to equation 5 this ratio should be equal to

$$\frac{e_1}{e_2} = \frac{0.85}{0.65} = 1.31$$

This test result also agrees reasonably well with equation 5. However, available experimental data are not yet sufficient to permit a decision as to what extent the influence of porosity on capillary rise is correctly appraised.

The most uncertain part of equation 5 lies in the value of the factor C, because this factor was found to be far from a constant. The following examples may suffice to illustrate this point.

Assuming the validity of equation 5 we can express the results of the tests of Atterberg by the empirical formula

$$h_c = \frac{C}{eD_{10}} = \frac{0.45}{eD_{10}} \tag{6}$$

in which h_c and D_{10} are expressed in centimeters. On the other hand, from the results of the tests with the dune sand investigated by the present writer, we obtain for C in equation 5 the value 0.10, instead of 0.45 obtained from the Atterberg tests. Furthermore, in one of a series of tests made in the Soils Laboratory of Harvard University, during the years 1934 to 1938, under the direction of A. Casagrande, the drying of a sand in the desiccator sufficed to reduce the height of capillary rise in this sand to 10 percent of that in the same sand in a slightly moistened state. The difference was undoubtedly due to a difference in the angle of contact. This result also demonstrates the futility of the attempts to assign to the different constituents of natural sands numerical values for the angle of contact, such as the value of 36° postulated by A. Hochstetter for the angle of contact between water and quartz.

Equation 5 is only one of many that have been derived during the last 40 years by several investigators on the basis of various assumptions. In most of these equations the grain-size characteristics of the soil are expressed in terms of its specific inner surface. However, none of them can claim more than a theoretical interest, because according to the preceding discussion the height of the capillary rise in soils depends on many factors other than the grain size and the porosity. Foremost among these factors seems to be the nature of the impurities that cover the surface of the grains, a factor which always represents an unknown quantity.

As the height of capillary rise in soil cannot be calculated, we are compelled to determine this height by experimental methods. The method illustrated by Figure IXa-1 is as good as any other. Before the soil is introduced into the container it should be slightly moistened, because in nature soils never occur in a perfectly dry state. If the porosity of the soil is known, it is also possible to determine the corresponding average degree of capillary saturation for the different stages of the test. It is sufficient to measure the height of the capillary rise and determine the total weight of the moistened column of soil.

The finer the soil the longer it takes for the rising water level to arrive in the vicinity of its ultimate position, at a height h_c above the free water level. This is due to the fact that the permeability of the soil decreases with the square of the effective grain size. In order to evaluate the influence of permeability on the speed of the capillary rise we assume, as a first approximation, that the state of complete capillary saturation extends to the very top of the moistened zone of the soil. We also assume the validity of Darcy's law

$$v = ki \tag{7}$$

in which v = the discharge velocity.

i = the hydraulic gradient.

k = the coefficient of permeability, or the discharge velocity for $i = 1$.

If a water particle travels along a flow line through a distance l, the corresponding hydraulic gradient depends on the hydrostatic head at the two ends of the line of travel. The hydrostatic head for any point of the flow line is equal to the height to which the water level rises at that point in a piezometric tube above an arbitrarily chosen reference level—for instance, the level of the adjoining free water surface. The height of the rise is also equal to the algebraic sum of the height of the point above the reference level and the stress in the water at that point, expressed by the height of a column of water with a cross section equal to unity, whose weight is equal to the stress in the water. The height of a column of water equivalent to a pressure in the water is positive, and the height equivalent to a tension in the water is negative. If the hydrostatic head at the two ends of the path with the length l is equal to h_1 and h_2 respectively, the hydraulic gradient is equal to

$$i = \frac{h_1 - h_2}{l}$$

In the capillary rise of water into a column of soil, illustrated by Figure IXA-8, a, the flow lines start at the bottom of the column and rise in a vertical direction toward the top of the moistened zone. At the base of the wetted column the hydrostatic head is always equal to zero. After the process of capillary rise has come to an end, the water stands in the soil at a height h_c above the free water surface. At h_c the surface tension produces a tensile stress in the water with the intensity $\gamma_w h_c$. Otherwise the water could not remain in the sand at a height h_c above the free water level. Yet this tensile stress is fully compensated by the weight of the column of water that is suspended within the capillaries of the soil. Hence the corresponding hydrostatic head is equal to zero.

At the time t the surface film of the capillary water is at a level z above the free water surface. The stress in the water due to surface tension is independent of the position of the boundary between air and water. It is always equal to $\gamma_w h_c$. Yet the column of water that is suspended at the surface film has only the height z. Hence, at time t

the upper boundary of the moistened zone is the seat of an unbalanced tensile stress equivalent to the weight of a column of water with the height $h_c - z$. This "head" $h_c - z$ is negative, because the corresponding stress in the water is a tensile stress. The total loss of head of the water, on its flow from the lower boundary of the column, at level 0, through a

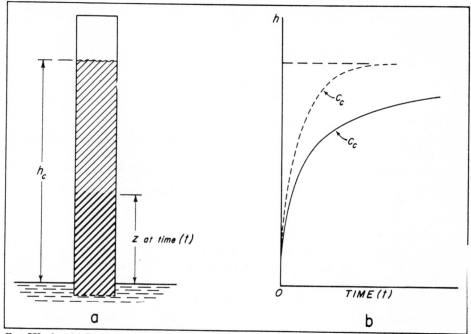

Fig. IXA-8.—(a) Rise of capillary water in a column of dry sand. (b) Observed (C_c) and computed (C'_c) relation between time and height of capillary rise of water in a column of dry sand.

distance z toward the upper boundary, is

$$h_1 - h_2 = 0 - [-(h_c - z)] = h_c - z$$

and the corresponding hydraulic gradient is

$$i = \frac{h_c - z}{z}$$

The rate $\dfrac{dz}{dt}$ at which the upper boundary of the moistened zone rises in a vertical direction is identical with the seepage velocity v_s, that is, with the average velocity of the water in the capillary passageways. According to the law of Delesse, the porosity of a plane section through an isotropic porous material is equal to the porosity n of this material. Hence the area of the openings per unit of area of a horizontal section through the soil in Figure IXA-8, a, is equal to n. As the discharge velocity v referred to in equation 7 represents the quantity of water that percolates per unit of time through the unit of area of a horizontal section through the soil sample, the seepage velocity v_s must be

$$v_s = \frac{v}{n} = \frac{dz}{dt}$$

If we introduce into this equation the values of v (equation 7) and of i, we obtain

$$\frac{dz}{dt} = \frac{k}{n} \frac{h_c - z}{z}$$

and, by integration,

$$t = \frac{n h_c}{k} \left[ln \frac{h_c}{h_c - z} - \frac{z}{h_c} \right] \tag{8}$$

In order to compare our theory with reality, we determine experimentally h_c and z at some convenient time t, and solve equation 8 for $\frac{n}{k}$. The curve that corresponds to equation 8 can then be plotted without previous experimental determination of $\frac{n}{k}$. When this is done, we always find that the theoretical curve, C'_c in Figure IXA-8, b, approaches the asymptote much more rapidly than the empirical curve, C_c. This obvious discrepancy between theory and reality seems to be due chiefly to the assumption that the coefficient of permeability is a constant. In reality, the value of k is bound to decrease with increasing height above the base of the sample, because as the upper boundary of the moistened zone is approached the flow of the water is more and more confined to the narrowest capillaries of the soil.

Equation 8 has also been used for the purpose of estimating the height h_t to which the water rises by capillarity within a definite time—for instance, 24 hours. This value, $h_t = h_{24}$ can be considered a measure of the readiness of a soil to pass from the dry state into a state of capillary saturation. In a coarse sand the water rises rapidly but the height of capillary rise is insignificant. On the other hand, in a clay soil the water is capable of rising to a very high level. Yet, on account of the low permeability of the soil, the rise is extremely slow. Hence there must be an optimum grain size, involving a maximum 24-hour rise.

In order to utilize equation 1 for making a theoretical estimate of the 24-hour rise h_{24}, we replace the value h_c in this equation by its equivalent as given by equation 5 and evaluate k according to Allen Hazen's equation [5]:

$$k = \text{constant} \times D^2_{10} \tag{9}$$

In this fashion we obtain for the relation between grain size and the 24-hour capillary rise the curve shown by the continuous line in Figure IXA-9 [13]. The curve shown by the dashed line in the same figure represents the results of tests made by Atterberg. According to both curves, the value h_{24} assumes a maximum for soils with an effective grain size of about 0.02 millimeter.

It should be noted, however, that the descending part of the empirical curve is very much steeper than the corresponding part of the theoretical curve. The writer believes that this discrepancy is due to a discrepancy between equation 9, on which the theory is based, and reality. According to this equation, the coefficient of permeability, k, decreases in direct proportion to the square of the effective grain size, D_{10}. However, below a grain size of about 0.02 millimeter the coefficient of permeability seems to decrease at a higher rate, because the width of the voids approaches the order of magnitude of the thickness of the zone of adsorbed water that surrounds the solid particles.

The author's theory that led to equation 8 is only one of many that have been published during the last decades. Some of them are very complicated. Yet thus far none of them can be considered fully satisfactory. (See also article on rate of drainage.)

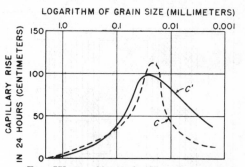

Fig. IXA-9.—Observed (C) and computed (C') relation between effective grain size and the height to which the capillary water rises in a column of dry sand in 24 hours.

SOIL MOISTURE UNDER FIELD CONDITIONS

Natural sediments and soils are never perfectly homogeneous, and the capillary moisture never enters them under conditions as simple as those shown in Figure IXA-1. Hence the theories concerning the capillary rise of water in dry soils are merely a means of elucidating some of the fundamental processes involved in the infinitely more complicated capillary phenomena that occur under field conditions. A knowledge of the states of capillary saturation in natural soil deposits under field conditions can be obtained only by observations and measurements in the field, for which theoretical knowledge of the subject serves as a guide.

Figure IXA-10 illustrates the most important processes which take place within the zone of soil moisture under field conditions. In this figure a and b represent systems of vertical capillary tubes whose lower ends are immersed in water. At the outset of the test the water stands in the tubes at a height h_c above the free water level. The value h_c is determined by equation 2. If water is allowed to enter the tubes through their upper ends, as shown in Figure IXA-10, a, it is drawn into the capillaries by the surface tension, and some air will be trapped between the upper and the lower capillary water. The pressure in the air at the boundary between air and water is equal to the algebraic sum of the stress in the water and the pressure exerted on the air by the surface tension. If water enters the tubes continuously from above, the air descends together with the water toward the lower ends of the tubes and escapes through the body of free water below the tubes. If the supply of water is cut off before the air has escaped, the water in the tubes comes to rest at a level $h_c + h_l$, in which h_l represents the height of the cushion of air, and the air remains permanently trapped between two layers of capillary water (Figure IXA-10, b).

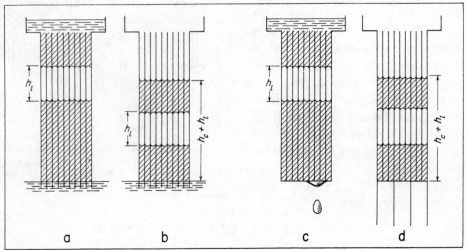

FIG. IXA-10.—Downward flow of water produced by flooding the upper ends of bundles of capillary tubes (a) with immersed lower ends and (c) with free lower ends. b and d show the body of capillary water that remains permanently in the tubes after drainage. h_l, height of layer of trapped air.

If the lower end of the bundle of capillary tubes is not immersed, as shown in Figure IXA-10, b, the water that flows out at that end emerges into a continuous layer of water, and the discharge occurs by a succession of big drops. As soon as the inflow of water through the upper end of the capillaries ceases, the discharge at the lower end also ceases as soon as the water level in the tubes arrives at a position $h_c + h_l$ above the discharge level. The water that ultimately remains in the capillaries is called suspended capillary water. It may contain layers of trapped air, as shown in Figure IXA-10, d. This figure represents a bundle of fine capillaries on top of a bundle of wider ones and illustrates the fact that the transition from fine to wide capillaries may give rise to the formation of a layer of suspended capillary water.

Figure IXA-11, illustrates several ways in which soil moisture may be distributed in sedimentary deposits. In this figure a and b show a bed of fine silty sand containing a lens-shaped pocket, *G*, of clean, coarse sand and gravel. Owing to the action of plant roots and to the seasonal variations in temperature and humidity, the top layer of fine-grained soil deposits is usually much more permeable than the material at greater depth. Within this top layer the state of the soil moisture is likely to vary among the continuous, semicontinuous and discontinuous states. Below the base of this layer the possibility for a temporary occurrence of almost discontinuous soil moisture is limited to the pocket of sand and gravel. Toward the end of a dry spell the distribution of the soil moisture may be as shown in Figure IXA-11, *a*. One zone of capillary

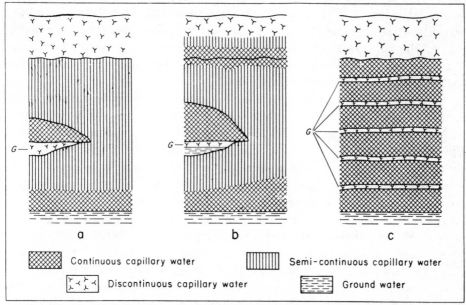

Fig. IXA-11.—(*a*) Soil moisture in a bed of fine silty sand containing a lens of clean sand and gravel *G*, after a dry spell; (*b*) soil moisture in the same deposit after a wet spell; (*c*) soil moisture in a laminated deposit consisting of layers of fine silty sand separated from each other by thin layers of clean sand and gravel. The water table is assumed to be stationary.

saturation lies above the water table. Another one lies above the top of the lens of gravel, *G*, whose voids are mostly filled with air. It corresponds to the suspended capillary water shown in Figure IXA-10, *d*. The rest of the deposit contains the soil moisture in a semicontinuous state. In a rainstorm additional water enters the soil through its top surface, with the consequences illustrated by Figure IXA-11, *b*. The upper boundary of each of the zones of capillary saturation rises, the percentage of semicontinuous moisture increases, and water accumulates above the base of the gravel pocket, which can be described as a temporary, perched ground-water table. After the rain has stopped the moisture conditions gradually approach again the state represented by Figure IXA-11, *a*.

If air has been trapped within the soil during the rainstorm, it gradually escapes toward the surface during the following dry period.

If the bed of silty sand shown in a and b, Figure IX$_A$-11, contains a series of thin layers of coarse sand and gravel, as shown in Figure IX$_A$-11, c, the presence of these layers increases the amount of soil moisture that can be permanently retained by the sand. This is due to the fact that each layer of gravel induces the formation of a superimposed layer of continuous soil moisture, comparable to the body of capillary water contained in the bundle shown in Figure IX$_A$-10, d. If the distance between the layers of gravel is smaller than the height to which the water could rise by capillarity in the strata between these layers, the entire mass of sand between the layers of gravel can remain permanently in a state of capillary saturation, to any height above the water table. On the other hand, part of the voids of the layers of gravel will periodically be filled with air. During a rainstorm each of the layers of gravel becomes temporarily the seat of a perched ground-water table.

The distribution and the seasonal variations of soil moisture under field conditions are illustrated by data obtained by the writer [14] in connection with a survey of soil moisture in the flood plain of the Connecticut River. The survey covered an area of about 50 square kilometers, and it was continued over a period of about 1 year. The first step consisted in exploring the ground water and the soil conditions by means of 15 drill holes. The results of these borings indicated that the water table was nowhere at a depth of more than 5 meters. From the land surface to a considerable depth below the water table the subsoil consisted of a fine, more or less silty sand with an average effective grain size of $D_{10} = 0.04$ to 0.01 millimeter. The coefficient of permeability ranged between 1.10^{-4} and 20.10^{-4} centimeter per second. Eight of the drill holes were transformed into observation wells for the purpose of recording the variations in the position of the water table. On the basis of the results of the test borings, eight representative sites were selected, covering the entire range of soil conditions disclosed by the borings. At each site and in different seasons of the year shafts were excavated, and in each shaft one undisturbed cylindrical sample was taken for each 45-centimeter section of the shaft. Each sample had a height of 7.5 centimeters. The total number of samples was 200. In the laboratory the degree of aeration, G_a, of each sample was determined. The following figures represent the extreme limits of the degree of aeration at eight different localities and at five different times during the year 1928:

1. After a wet month with rain and snow in February........... 0.140–0.178
2. Five days after a heavy rain in July......................... 0.127–0.162
3. Six days after a heavy rain in September..................... 0.089–0.111
4. After 3 weeks of dry weather in October..................... 0.200–0.207
5. After 2 months of dry weather in December.................. 0.230–0.251

The difference between the extreme values of the degree of aeration for the different localities at any given time of the year is by no means as great as the difference between the extreme values of the average effective grain size and the average permeability of the soils encountered in these localities would lead one to expect. It was also noticed at each of the localities investigated that the degree of aeration was practically independent of the height of the samples above the water table.

Thus far our knowledge of the degree of aeration of soils under field conditions is very fragmentary. Nevertheless, the available data suffice to indicate that the corresponding aeration curve for temperate climates cannot be far from the tentative curve E shown in Figure IXA-15 (p. 356). The boundaries of the shaded area in this figure represent the probable range of seasonal variation.

CAPILLARY SIPHON EFFECTS IN THE FIELD

The capillary propagation of water through grooves illustrated by Figure IXA-6 also occurs in natural sediments, whenever the surface of the ground water on both sides of a low, feebly permeable ridge lies at different levels. Haedicke [4] observed the migration of water across a ridge from one ground-water level 0.5 meter below the crest of the ridge to another one 3.5 meters below the crest. A similar migration of water also occurs out of the storage reservoir behind an earth dam with a clay core, as shown in Figure IXA-12. The water is drawn by capillarity out of the reservoir and flows over the crest of the core into the downstream portion of

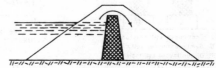

Fig. IXA-12.—Capillary siphon effect in the shell of an earth dam with a clay core.

the embankment. On a section of the Berlin-Ştettin Canal 20 kilometers long the loss of water due to this process amounted to 28 liters per second. The crest of the clay core was 30 centimeters above the level of the water in the canal. By adding 40 centimeters to the height of the core the loss of water was reduced to less than 7 liters per second [2]. Versluys [19] measured the discharge through a capillary siphon consisting of a hook-shaped pipe with a diameter of 5 centimeters, filled with dune sand. The height h_{cc} of complete capillary saturation for the sand was 29.3 centimeters. The discharge through the capillary siphon decreased rapidly with increasing height of the crest of the siphon above the free water level. Yet the capillary flow did not stop until this height became equal to 154 centimeters = $5.3h_{cc}$. Koženy [7], Weiland [21], and others have observed and photographed through a glass window the capillary flow of water across impermeable ridges, by injecting a solution of potassium permanganate or other colored liquids into the capillary current.

EXPERIMENTAL METHODS OF INVESTIGATING THE WATER-HOLDING POWER OF SOILS

All these methods involve the following procedure: A sample of the soil is introduced in a saturated condition into a container with a perforated bottom, and then the water is allowed to drain out through the bottom under the influence of simple gravity or of a centrifugal force. The water contained in the voids of the soil after the end of the test is considered a measure of the water-holding power of the soil, which in turn is supposed to stand in some definite relation to the soil moisture contained in the same soil under field conditions.

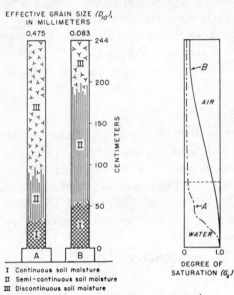

I   Continuous soil moisture
II Semi-continuous soil moisture
III Discontinuous soil moisture

a   b

Fig. IXA-13.—(a) State of capillary saturation in two columns of sand 2½ years after being completely saturated and allowed to drain; (b) relation between degree of saturation and height above the lower ends of the columns shown in a (tests by F. H. King, 1899).

If the expelled water is entirely replaced by air the process is called "drainage with air substitution" or briefly "drainage." On the other hand, if the loss of water is fully compensated by a corresponding decrease of the volume of the voids without entrance of air into the system, the process is called "drainage by consolidation" or briefly "consolidation." The drainage of coarse-grained soils always involves air substitution, but the drainage of typical clays always occurs by consolidation. In soils with intermediate grain size, such as silts, the mechanical expulsion of water involves a process of combined drainage by air substitution and consolidation.

According to the mechanical means that are used for driving the excess water out of the voids of a soil the methods for determining the water-holding power of soils can be divided into gravity, centrifuge and suction methods. Figure IXA-13, a represents the test arrangement used by King [6, pp. 86–91] for the purpose of investigating the water-holding power of sands with different grain size. The procedure belongs in the category of gravity methods. The sands were contained in galvanized iron tubes 2.44 meters high, with perforated bottoms. The effective sizes of the sands ranged between 0.475 and 0.083 millimeters. At the outset of the tests a state of saturation was established in the sands by gradually introducing the columns of sand in a vertical position into water until they were completely immersed. Then the tubes were taken out of the water and lined up in a vertical position, and the water was allowed to drain out of the samples through the lower ends of the tubes. The upper end of each tube was covered, so as to prevent a loss of water by evaporation. From time to time the weight of the columns was determined. At 2½ years after the beginning of the tests the observations were discontinued and the degree of saturation of successive sections of the columns of sand was determined. In Figure IXA-13 a shows the test arrangement, b shows the

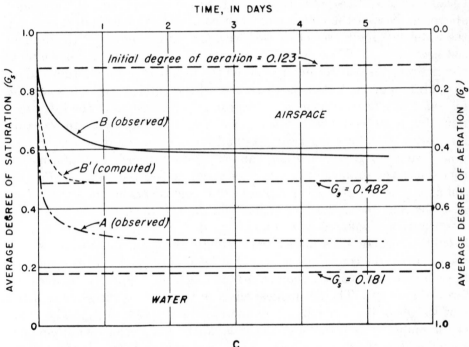

FIG IXA-13—(c) Observed and computed relation between time and average degree of saturation in the columns of sand shown in a.

change of the air space with height for the finest and the coarsest sand at the end of the period of observation, and c represents the relation between the time and the average degree of saturation for these two sands, for the first 5 days of the process of drainage.

At the end of the 2½-year period the lower part of each sample was occupied by continuous soil moisture (I, Figure IXA-13, a), the middle part by semicontinuous soil moisture (II), and the upper part by discontinuous soil moisture (III). However, in nature it seldom occurs that a soil is allowed to drain for a period of 2½ years, because the soil is frequently invaded by rain water through the top surface. Hence the state of drainage shown in Figure IXA-13, b, represents an extreme case which will hardly ever be approached under field conditions. According to equa-

tion 6 the height h_c of the capillary rise in the coarse sand should be equal
to 14 centimeters and in the fine sand 77 centimeters. However, according
to a and b, Figure IXA-13, neither of the two columns of sand exhibits
any abrupt change of the degree of saturation in the vicinity of the levels
that correspond to the theoretical values h_c.

According to the test results shown in b and c, Figure IXA-13, it is
obvious that neither the water content of the drained soil nor the degree
of saturation can be assigned a definite value characteristic of the soil,
because each of these quantities is a function of time and of the height
above the base of the column of moist soil. Some investigators identify
the water-holding power of the soil with the water content of the drained
soil near the top of the column; others with the average water content;
and in every test the results depend on the height H of the column and on
the duration of the test. Furthermore, all the gravity methods share the
following serious shortcoming. According to the results of the investigations by King and many others, the height of the saturated section
increases with decreasing grain size and for a given soil it decreases with
time. Hence a gravity method cannot possibly furnish any information
concerning the drainage properties of a soil, unless the value h_{cc} for this
soil at a time t after the beginning of drainage is smaller than the height
H of the container. For every finer soil the test furnishes for the degree
of saturation a value close to unity regardless of grain size. In order to
avoid this risk and to insure a more energetic expulsion of the water within
a short time, the centrifuge method has been developed. In this method
the soil moisture is acted upon by a centrifugal force equal to N times the
force of gravity. The mechanical effect of this force is the same as if the
unit weight of the water had been increased from γ_w to $N\gamma_w$. The value
of the multiplication factor N depends on the number of revolutions per
second and on the distance R between the sample and the axis of rotation.

In order to realize the physical meaning of the result of centrifuge
moisture tests, let us consider a saturated sample with a thickness H, a
coefficient of permeability k, and a volume of voids n. The height to
which the water can rise in this material by capillarity is h_c. If the force
of gravity that acts on the sample is increased from g to Ng, the unit
weight of the water increases from γ_w to $N\gamma_w$, while the surface tension
and the viscosity remain practically unaltered. According to the laws
of the hydraulics of capillary systems an increase of the unit weight of
the liquid from γ_w to $N\gamma_w$, unaccompanied by a change in the surface tension and the viscosity, reduces h_c to $\frac{1}{N} h_c$ and increases k to Nk. If we
apply to the process of drainage the reasoning that led to equation 8, we
obtain the following approximate equation for the time t required to
establish by simple gravity drainage a certain degree of drainage z_r

(ratio between the amount of water that has been expelled at the end of the test to the total amount of water that can be expelled by drainage)

$$t = \frac{h_c n G_a}{k} \left[ln \frac{1}{1 - z_r} + z_r \frac{h_c}{H - h_c} \right] = \frac{h_c n G_a}{k} \cdot f \left(z_r, \frac{h_c}{H} \right) \qquad (10)$$

wherein G_a is the degree of aeration of the sample after complete drainage. The term $f \left(z_r, \frac{h_c}{H} \right)$ is an abbreviation of the term in brackets. If the drainage of the sample described above is accomplished by centrifuging we must replace the values h_c and k in the preceding equation by h_c/N and Nk respectively whereupon we obtain

$$\bar{t} = \frac{h_c n G_a}{N^2 k} \cdot f \left(z_r, \frac{h_c}{NH} \right) \qquad (11)$$

On the other hand, if the thickness of the sample is equal to NH and the drainage takes place only under the influence of gravity we must replace the value H in equation 10 by NH while h_c and k remain unchanged. Thus we obtain for the time t_1 required to reach a degree of drainage z_r the value

$$t_1 = \frac{h_c n G_a}{k} \cdot f \left(z_r, \frac{h_c}{NH} \right)$$

By combining this equation with equation 11 we get

$$t_1 = N^2 \bar{t} \qquad (12)$$

According to this equation the degree of draingae after centrifuging the sample during a period $\bar{t}$ is equal to the degree of drainage in a bed of the same material with a thickness NH, at a time $N^2 t$ after drainage has been started. It should be emphasized, however, that the preceding interpretation is no longer valid when the water content of the sample has passed from the semicontinuous into the discontinuous state, for the reason that the expulsion of discontinuous water particles like those shown in Figure IXA-7 ceases as soon as the weight of each particle becomes small enough to be compensated by the surface tension along the rim of the particle. The force that tends to expel the isolated water particles in a soil subject to centrifuging is many times greater than the force that acts on the particles in a soil under the influence of simple gravity, but the surface tension is under both conditions the same. Hence a soil subject to drainage by simple gravity can hold permanently a higher percentage of discontinuous moisture than a sample subject to centrifuging.

Samples of very fine-grained soils consolidate in the centrifuge without any air entering the voids of the soil. Application of the theory of consolidation [18] to a soil of this kind led in first approximation to the conclusion that the degree of consolidation after centrifuging the sample during a period $\bar{t}$ is equal to the degree of consolidation in a bed of the same material with a thickness NH, at a time $N^2\bar{t}$ after consolidation has started. This conclusion is identical with the preceding one concerning drainable soils and it demonstrates the importance of the influence on the test results of the thickness H of the samples. It is also very important to make sure that the sample in its original state does not contain any air and to measure the porosity of the sample before and after the test.

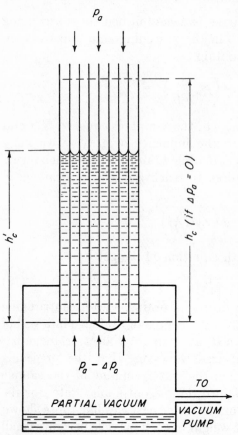

Fig. IXA-14.—Diagram showing how partial vacuum below lower end of a bundle of capillary tubes reduces height of layer of capillary water from h_c to h'_c.

In the moisture-equivalent test used by the Bureau of Public Roads [3] the multiplication factor N is equal to 1,000 and the duration $\bar{t}$ of the test is 1 hour. If the thickness of the sample is 1 centimeter, the sample represents the equivalent for a layer of soil with a thickness $H = 1,000$ centimeters subject to drainage by simple gravity for a period of about 100 years, provided that the initial state of the soil in the field was identical with that of the sample used in the test.

Lebedeff [9] increased the multiplication factor N up to 70,000 and concluded from his investigations that nothing can be gained by going beyond $N = 18,000$ and $t = 2$ minutes.

In a general way the results of the centrifuge test lead to the following conclusions: In sands and silts the process of centrifuging merely produces a replacement of water by air. In clay soils with an effective grain size of less than 0.001 millimeter the expulsion of water is due exclusively to consolidation whereby the soil remains in a saturated state. In accordance with the laws of consolidation [18] the excess moisture escapes in two opposite directions, through the top and the bottom of the sample. The accumulation of water on the top surface of the sample is termed "waterlogging." It is always an indication of drainage by consolidation and of a degree of saturation equal to unity.

The suction method was introduced by Zunker [2] in 1929 in connection with investigations of agricultural soils. It does not differ from the original gravity methods except that the perforated bottom of the soil container is located above another container in which a partial vacuum can be produced, involving a difference Δp_a between the air pressures acting on the top and the bottom surfaces of the sample. If the pressure in the air above the top of a bundle of capillary tubes (Figure IXA-14) is increased by Δp_a above the air pressure acting on the bottom of the bundle, the surface tension of the water has to carry the excess pressure Δp_a in addition to the weight $h\gamma_w$ of the water located below the surface film. Hence the excess pressure Δp_a lowers the upper boundary of the zone of capillary saturation from h_c to h'_c. The pressure Δp_a represents the equivalent of the weight of a column of water with the height $\dfrac{\Delta p_a}{\gamma_w}$. As a consequence the elevation of the boundary will be lowered from h_c to $h'_c = h_c - \dfrac{\Delta p_a}{\gamma_w}$. Zunker's soil containers have a height of 10 centimeters. Assuming a complete vacuum, $\Delta p_a = p_a$, we obtain $\dfrac{\Delta p_a}{\gamma_w} = 1{,}000$ centimeters. However, if h_c is smaller than 1,000 centimeters, the air will break through the soil and invade the vacuum, whereupon the air pressure in the vacuum chamber will rise. This increase depends on the width of the air channels, the height of the specimen, the capacity of the air pump, and other factors independent of the nature of the soil. This must be considered a serious disadvantage of the procedure, because the ultimate result of the process of drainage depends essentially on the vacuum pressure that existed after the first air channel was formed. Zunker evacuates his specimen for a period of 2 hours. In order to reduce the loss of water due to evaporation, the air is passed through a humidifier before it is admitted to the top surface of the sample.

Mining engineers have studied the problem of the water-holding power of sands in order to obtain information concerning the possibility of draining beds of sand above coal deposits. On the basis of general drainage experience in coal mining, Nahnsen [10] divides the sands that are likely to be encountered in coal mining into 20 classes and describes their properties as follows:

Classes	Properties	Degree of aeration after drainage
1–5	Very difficult to drain..........................	0–0.25
6–10	Can be drained under favorable conditions........	0.26–0.50
11–15	Can be drained easily............................	0.51–0.75
16–20	Cannot be classified as "quicksand" (Schwimmsand)...	0.76–1.00

The methods that have been used by mining engineers for the experimental determination of the air space that can be established by drainage belong in the category of gravity methods.

COMPARISON BETWEEN LABORATORY AND FIELD DATA

As the water-holding power of soils is far from being a quantity with a well-defined physical meaning, any set of values concerning soil moisture can be considered valid under certain conditions only. These conditions can be divided into two large groups—laboratory and field conditions. Figure IXA-15 summarizes the most significant facts concerning the values which the degree of saturation can assume under different conditions. The ordinates of the curves Z and L have been computed on the basis of the results of the tests by A. Zunker (curve Z, suction method, height

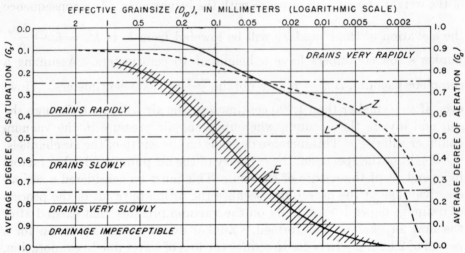

FIG. IXA-15.—Relation between effective grain size (D_{10}) and average degree of capillary saturation as determined by different experimental methods. L, centrifuge method, Z, suction method, E, from field observations.

of samples $H = 10$ centimeters, duration of drainage 2 hours) and by A. F. Lebedeff (curve L, centrifuge method, multiplication factor $N = 18,000$, $t = 2$ minutes). Neither of the lines Z and L exhibits any relation to the curve E representing the degree of saturation under field conditions. This statement also applies to the curves that have so far been obtained by means of all the other existing methods of investigating the water-holding power of the soil. The discrepancies between the field values and the test results are obviously due to the incompatibility between the field and the test conditions. The shortcomings of the suction method (curve Z) have been discussed on preceding pages. Hence attention may be concentrated on the centrifuge method represented by curve L.

By means of equations 11 and 12 we find that the data obtained by Lebedeff (curve L) approximately represent the relation between grain size and the average degree of saturation in a column of soil 180 meters high, 12,000 years after drainage by simple gravity has been started. These values are close to the minimum degree of saturation that can possibly be established in a soil by purely mechanical means. On the other hand, the ordinates of the curve E represent the average degree of saturation that was found to prevail under field conditions in humid climates in the C horizon of a number of sedimentary deposits up to a height of about 20 feet above the phreatic surface. The shaded area on both sides of the curve E (Figure IX$_A$-15) indicates the probable range of seasonal variations of the degree of saturation from the average.

In contrast to the curve L in Figure IX$_A$-15, the curve E, representing the average degree of saturation under field conditions, has the typical shape of an ordinary probability curve. The steepest part of this curve lies within the range of grain size 0.2 to 0.02 millimeter. Within this range both the degree of saturation and the rate of drainage decrease rapidly with decreasing grain size. Within the same range the ratio between the ordinates of the curves E and L also decreases very rapidly. This is due to the following facts: The ordinates of curve L represent the air-space equivalent for simple gravity drainage during a period of more than 10,000 years. At that stage the rate of drainage is practically equal to zero. On the other hand, under field conditions the degree of saturation ceases to decrease as soon as the rate of drainage becomes equal to the average recharge of the moistened zone by rain water invading the soil from above. With decreasing grain size the rate of drainage also decreases, whereas the average recharge by rain water is independent of grain size. Hence in fine-grained soils the equilibrium between discharge and recharge is reached in a far less advanced state of drainage than in coarse-grained soils. In Figure IX$_A$-15 this important fact is expressed by the relative position of the curves L and E, which has been emphasized above. It explains a fundamental difference between the laboratory and the field values for the degree of saturation. The laboratory determinations correspond to some arbitrarily chosen intermediate state or to the final state in a process of drainage that is never interrupted by recharge from above. On the other hand, the field value represents the degree of saturation at which discharge by drainage and recharge by rain water statistically balance each other. For this reason, no direct and simple relation between laboratory and field values can possibly exist, regardless of the method of drainage that is used in the laboratory. The periodic alimentation of natural sedimentary deposits with rain water from above also accounts for the conspicuous difference in the distribution of soil moisture under laboratory and field conditions. In the laboratory there is always a marked increase of the degree of saturation with the depth below the surface of the sample, as shown in Figure IX$_A$-13, b. In the field, below the top layers of the soil (A and B horizons) no such persistent decrease has thus far been observed.

In soils with an effective size of less than 0.002 millimeter (Figure IXA-15) the capillaries are narrow enough to prevent the penetration of air into the voids, even at a very considerable height above the ground-water level. Permanent lowering of the ground-water level merely produces consolidation not accompanied by entrance of air into the voids. No air can get into the voids of the soil unless the soil is subjected to as radical and unnatural a process of evacuation as those used by Zunker and Lebedeff. For this reason the empirical curve gradually merges into the horizontal axis in the vicinity of a point with an abscissa corresponding to an effective grain size of 0.002 millimeter, whereas the experimental curves descend steeply toward this axis on the right-hand side of this point.

The preceding analysis indicates that the field value for the degree of capillary saturation depends on the intensity and distribution of the annual rainfall. According to Figure IXA-11 it also depends on the details of the stratification and according to Figure IXA-13, b, on the thickness of the deposit subject to drainage. Hence even an empirical rule such as that represented by the curve E in Figure IXA-15 can be valid for only one well-defined set of field conditions. Moisture data pertaining to thin layers of soil subject to drainage in the humid Tropics would furnish a curve below E, and the corresponding data obtained by sampling thick deposits in a hot, arid country would lead to a curve high above E. In contrast to this, soil tests made in the laboratory furnish one set of values only, such as those represented by the curve L in Figure IXA-15. Hence a reliable interpretation of test results could be accomplished only by means of a set of empirical curves, similar to E, representing the relation between grain size and degree of saturation under different field conditions.

Pending the future accumulation of the field data required for plotting such curves, the following procedure could be used, provided the depth H of the layer subject to drainage and the average recharge are known. Representative samples of the soil are submitted to a process of centrifuging, the multiplication factor N being selected in such a fashion that the thickness $\overline{H}$ of the sample is equal to $\frac{1}{N} H$. During the test the loss of weight of the samples due to drainage is determined at regular intervals. From the data thus obtained, the corresponding average degree of saturation for the centrifuged sample and the time-discharge curve for the full-sized layer with depth H are computed. The degree of saturation for field conditions can be expected to be of the same order of magnitude as the degree of saturation at which the discharge from the full-sized layer with depth H is equal to the average recharge.

RATE OF DRAINAGE

Agronomists and civil and mining engineers are often compelled to drain a section of a sedimentary deposit by artificial means such as ditches, wells, or drainage galleries. In all such work it is of paramount importance to know in advance not only the degree of aeration of the sediment after drainage but also the time required to accomplish the desired result. In this connection, it is necessary to distinguish between the rate at which the water escapes into the drains and the rate at which the water level in observation wells descends. These two rates have nothing in common except that both approach zero. All the theoretical attempts that have been made thus far to compute either of these two rates are based on the assumptions that the soil subject to drainage is perfectly incompressible and that there is no zone of transition between the saturated and the drained part of this layer of soil. The degree of aeration of the drained part is assumed to be equal to its ultimate value [20, 17, 12]. Each of these assumptions involves a radical departure from reality. The principal source of error lies in the assumption that the flow of the water is limited to the zone of complete capillary saturation. However the theories which take the flow in the zone of partial capillary saturation into consideration [24 and 25] are so involved that they cannot yet be applied to current engineering problems of drainage. Hence, pending further developments in this field, the older theories have to be used. The difference between reality and the results furnished by the older theories is illustrated by Fig. IXA. 13, *c*. In this figure the dotted line B' shows the results of a theoretical computation of the process of drainage represented by the empirical curve B. Like the theoretical curve C'_c in Figure IXA-8, *b*, representing the rate of capillary rise of water in a column of sand, it approaches the asymptote much more rapidly than the corresponding empirical curve.

In 1929 the writer [16] measured the discharge during the drainage of two layers of soil, 1.8 meters deep, covering an area of about 18 square meters. In one of the tests the material consisted of clean, uniform sand, for which $D_{10} = 0.54$ millimeter and $h_c = 1.70$ centimeters, and in the other of modified redeposited glacial till, for which $D_e = 0.016$ millimeter and $h_c = 20$ centimeters. The materials were tested in an artificially compacted state. In both tests the relation between the theoretical and the empirical discharge curves was similar to that between the theoretical and empirical curves shown in Figure IXA-13, *c*—that is, the values obtained by theory for the rate of drainage were by far too high. However, from an analysis of the test results it was evident that the drainage of the coarse sand proceeded without appreciable consolidation. This fact justified at least one of the fundamental assumptions of the computation. On the other hand, the drainage of the fine-grained till had no resemblance whatsoever to that which the theory of drainage would lead us to expect. The discrepancy was chiefly due to the temporary expansion of gas bubbles contained in the till, associated with the change in the state of stress in the water [18]. Thus the theories concerning the rate of drainage are not yet satisfactory. In important cases pertinent information could be obtained by means of model tests in the centrifuge. The principle of this method is explained in the preceding section.

DRAINAGE BY EVAPORATION

In accordance with the prevalent concepts regarding capillary phenomena, every process of drainage by gravity should come to an end as soon as the weight of the water contained in the voids of the soil becomes equal to that which can be carried by the surface tension, regardless of the quantity of free water that is still contained in the voids. However, the existence of this state of equilibrium also requires that the relative humidity of the air in contact with the water should be equal to the relative vapor pressure of the liquid, which in turn depends not only on the chemical nature of the liquid but also on the curvature of the surface films. If this condition is not satisfied, a further loss of water occurs by evaporation along the surface of contact between air and water. The final result of this process depends on the conditions under which it takes place.

If a sample of moist soil is completely surrounded by air with a constant relative humidity smaller than unity, a state of permanent equilibrium is reached as soon as the water content reaches a definite quantity depending on the nature of the soil and the relative humidity of the air. For every soil under normal atmospheric conditions this equilibrium value represents only a small fraction of the quantity to which the water content of the soil can be reduced by purely mechanical means, such as energetic centrifuging. Nevertheless, for typical clay soils at room temperature it represents an appreciable percentage of the weight of the solid constituents.

If the lower end of a cylindrical sample of most soil is permanently immersed in water, the loss of water due to evaporation in the upper part of the sample becomes constant as soon as the rate of evaporation becomes equal to the rate of recharge by capillary rise through the lower end. Hence under this condition the drainage by evaporation tends to establish a stationary flow of water from the source of supply toward the zone of evaporation. For a given soil the distribution of soil moisture associated with the stationary state depends on the height of the sample above the source of supply and on the rate of evaporation. In the field the drainage due to evaporation occurs under similar conditions. However, owing to seasonal variations in the rate of evaporation and to the periodic feeding of the top layer by rain water through the top surface, the depth of the layer subject to seasonal drainage by evaporation depends essentially on climatic conditions. In humid climates it does not exceed a few feet. In the semiarid climate of Texas evidence has been found that the seasonal desiccation of stiff bentonite clays extends to a depth of more than 20 feet [11]. In hot, arid climates this depth may be still greater.

COMMON MISCONCEPTIONS CONCERNING CAPILLARY PHENOMENA

Certain misconceptions have found their way into publications dealing with capillary phenomena in soils.

Some engineers believe that the height of the capillary rise of water in soils cannot be greater than the height of about 9 meters to which water can rise in the suction tube of a pump. In order to realize the fallacy involved in this conception, it suffices to consider the group of facts illustrated by *a* and *b*, Figure IXA-4.

Many engineers and even some soil physicists maintain that all the water contained in the voids of a soil after centrifuging is kept within the voids of the soil by the attraction of the molecules of the solid particles. Closely related to this conception is the theory propagated in some publications on quicksand phenomena in coal mines, that the "sluggish water" does not participate in the movement of the ground water. The term "sluggish water" is applied to the water that drains out of the sand in an advanced state of the process of drainage, in contrast to the so-called active water, that drains out during the first period. These conceptions are incompatible with our present knowledge of the state of water in the voids of porous materials. A departure from the laws of hydraulics can be expected only of the water within the zones of adsorption or hydration. In soils with an effective grain size of more than about 0.005 millimeter this quantity does not exceed a small fraction of the water content of the soil after energetic centrifuging. Hence the major part of the water content of drained soils coarser than 0.005 millimeter must be considered free water, which is retained in the voids by surface tension only. Even the finest clays in a plastic state contain a certain amount of free water.

Finally, some have the conception, illustrated by Figure IXA-16, that the capillary forces are capable of resisting the flow through a porous material. This figure represents a section through a concrete gravity dam. The dotted lines indicate the lines of flow along which the water travels under the influence of gravity out of the reservoir toward the downstream face of the dam. According to the theory previously mentioned no such flow can occur, because the capillary forces are supposed to retain the water within the porous concrete. This erroneous conception seems to be due to the fact that the downstream face of a concrete dam is usually found to be dry. This, however, is merely due to the fact that the rate of surface evaporation is higher than the rate of flow, so that the surface of evaporation recedes into the interior of the concrete. Along the surface of evaporation the menisci are concave as viewed from a downstream direction. This causes an increase of the discharge over the quantity corresponding to a flow under the influence of gravity only [15]. Hence the capillary forces have an effect opposite to that corresponding to the conceptions previously mentioned. As soon as the surface tension on the downstream side is eliminated, for instance, by the wetting of this face during a rainstorm, the discharge through the concrete decreases until it

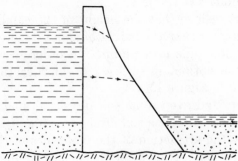

FIG. IXA-16.—Percolation of water through the voids of a concrete gravity dam toward the downstream face.

becomes equal to the quantity corresponding to a simple gravity flow through the dam.

REFERENCES

1. Atterberg, A., Studien auf dem Gebiet der Bodenkunde: Landw. Versuchstat., vol. 69, 1908.

2. Blanck, E., Handbuch der Bodenlehre, vol. 6, p. 114, Berlin, 1930.

3. Boyd, J. R., Procedure for testing subgrade soils: Public Roads, vol. 6, No. 2, April 1925.

4. Haedicke, H., Der Grundwasserspiegel: Zeitschr. prakt. Geologie, Jahrg. 19, p. 209, 1910.

5. Hazen, A., The filtration of public water supplies, New York, 1895.

6. King, F. H., Principles and conditions of the movements of ground water: U. S. Geol. Survey 19th Ann. Rept., pt. 2, pp. 59–294, 1899.

7. Koženy, J., Akad. Wiss. Wien Sitzungsber., Band 136, p. 284, 1927.

8. Laplace, P. S., Théorie de l'action capillaire; supplément au livre X de La mécanique céleste, pp. 1–65, Paris, 1806; Supplément à La théorie de l'action capillaire, Paris, 1807; Oeuvres, vol. 4, pp. 389–552.

9. Lebedeff, A. F., Determination of maximum molecular water capacity of soil by means of centrifuging: Pedology, vol. 4, Nos. 1–2, Rostov/Don, 1928.

10. Nahnsen, J., Die Praxis der planmässigen Entwässerung in Braunkohlenbergbau, Halle a. d. Saale, W. Knapp, 1929.

11. Simpson, W. E., Foundation experiences with clay in Texas: Civil Engineering, vol. 4, pp. 581–584, 1934.

12. Steinbrenner, W., Der zeitliche Verlauf der Grundwasserabsenkung: Wasserwirtschaft und Technik, H. 3 and 4, 1937.

13. Terzaghi, Karl, Erdbaumechanik, Vienna, 1925.

14. Terzaghi, Karl, Sickerverluste aus Kanälen: Wasserwirtschaft, H. 18–19, 1930.

15. Terzaghi, Karl, Auftrieb und Kapillardruck an betonierten Talsperren: Die Wasserwirtschaft, H. 31, 1933.

16. Terzaghi, Karl, Large retaining-wall tests: Eng. News-Record, Feb. 22 and Apr. 19, 1934.

17. Terzaghi, Karl, Retaining-wall design for Fifteenmile Falls Dam: Eng. News-Record, May 17, 1934.

18. Terzaghi, Karl, Soil Mechanics, vol. I, New York, 1942 (John Wiley and Sons).

19. Versluys, J., Internat. Mitt. Bodenkunde, vol. 7, p. 132, 1917.

20. Weber, H., Die Reichweite von Grundwasserabsenkungen mittels Rohrbrunnen, Berlin, 1928.

21. Weiland, H., Über Wasserbewegung im durchfeuchteten Boden mit besonderer Berücksichtigung der Heberwirkung des Sandes [Dissertation], Danzig, 1929.

22. Young, Th., Philos. Trans., vol. 1, p. 65, London, 1805.

23. Smithsonian Physical Tables, 1934.

24. Gardner, W., The role of the capillary potential in the dynamics of moisture: Journ. Agric. Research, vol. 53, 1936.

25. Wilson, B. D. and Richards, S. J.: Capillary conductivity of peat soils at different capillary tensions: Journ. Am. Soc. of Agronomy, vol. 30, 1938.

IXb. RETENTION AND MOVEMENT OF SOIL MOISTURE

Leonard D. Baver[1]

The soil contains pores of various sizes and shapes, whose amount and nature are determined by the arrangement of the soil particles. Air and water relations within the soil are determined primarily by the extent and character of the pore space. Water that enters the soil either is retained in the pores (a part of it later transpired or evaporated) or percolates through them to lower horizons. Air is found in the pores that are not filled with water. In general, the larger pores give soils their aeration and permeability; the smaller pores their water-holding capacity. Low water-holding capacity, high permeability, and high degree of aeration are characteristic of sands; high water-holding capacity, low degree of aeration, and low permeability are characteristic of clays.

The total porosity is not as important for determining moisture retention and movement as the relative distribution of the different-sized pores.

RETENTION OF SOIL MOISTURE

When a drop of water is brought into contact with a dry soil, it wets the surface of the particles with a moisture film. This film water is under the influence of the molecular forces operating between the soil particles and the water. As the thickness of the film increases, the water fills the wedges between the particles and air-water interfaces are set up within the soil. The addition of more water causes the smaller pores to become filled, with the possible inclusion of entrapped air spaces. Finally, when sufficient water has been added to fill all the pores in which water movement is extremely slow, further additions will result in rapid movement through the remainder of the pore space.

Earlier concepts of the retention of soil moisture emphasized primarily the capillary-tube nature of the soil pore space. Water retention was viewed as a function of the tension of the water films around the particles, and soil water was classified in three main categories—hygroscopic, capillary, and gravitational water. The classical contributions of Briggs [5], Bouyoucos [4], Lebedeff [15], and Zunker [31] are major examples of the capillary-tube point of view. It was recognized rather universally that there was no distinct demarcation between the various

[1] Director, Agricultural Experiment Station, North Carolina State College of Agriculture and Engineering, University of North Carolina, Raleigh, N. C.

forms of water suggested. Nevertheless, not much stress was placed upon the energy relations involved.

ENERGY RELATIONS IN RETENTION OF SOIL MOISTURE

The importance of the energy relations in soil-water phenomena was first recognized by Buckingham [8] in 1907. He assumed that the flow of water through the soil was analogous to the flow of electricity through a wire. The driving force for water movement originated in the difference in attraction for water between any two points within a homogeneous soil that did not have the same moisture content. The measure of the attraction of the soil for water at a given point was expressed by the term "capillary potential." "Potential" refers to the work that is necessary to bring a unit mass from an established reference point to some other point; it is the product of the force per unit mass and the distance of movement. Thus, if a given mass of water could be pulled away from a given mass of soil, a certain amount of work would be required. The work would be equivalent to the capillary potential times the mass of water, or the work required to overcome the force of attraction for the water at that point. As the capillary potential is the work required to pull a unit mass of water away from a unit mass of soil, it is defined as the work required to move a unit mass of water, against capillary forces in a column of soil, from a free water surface to a given point above that surface. Capillary pressures are negative because of the greater inward attraction of the water molecules at the air-water interface. Because the molecules within the liquid exert a greater attraction on the surface molecules than the air, a tension or negative pressure is exerted on the surface. Therefore, the capillary potential is negative in sign.[1]

The significance of the work required to remove water from the soil is well illustrated by the fact that it takes less work to pull a given amount of water from a nearly saturated soil than from one that is only slightly moist; hence the quantity of work required depends upon the soil and the moisture content. The greater the attractive forces, the higher is the capillary potential and the greater is the work required to extract water.

Recent investigations by Gardner [11, 12] and Richards [20, 21] have suggested that the capillary potential permits a new interpretation of the various constants that have been used rather widely in studies of soil moisture (moisture equivalent, field capacity, etc.). Gardner has pointed out that the capillary potential appears to be a linear function of the reciprocal of the moisture content over a considerable range of the tension-moisture curve.

---

[1] A detailed mathematical discussion of the capillary potential and its analogy to flow and thermal potentials may be found in Soil Physics, pp. 198–202, John Wiley & Sons, 1940.

Richards [20] studied the influence of texture on the relation of capillary potential to moisture content in soils (Fig. IX$_B$-1).   Sand has a very low moisture content at high negative potentials; clay contains six to seven times as much water as sand at the same potential; loam occupies an intermediate position between sand and clay.   In fine-textured soils there are a larger number of contacts between particles than in coarse-textured soils.   The amount of water at each point of contact is reduced, with a corresponding decrease in the radius of curvature of the water menisci in the pores.   These curves also show that the moisture content of the system tends to become constant at the more negative values of the capillary potential.   Lebedeff [15] has suggested that the forces of molec-

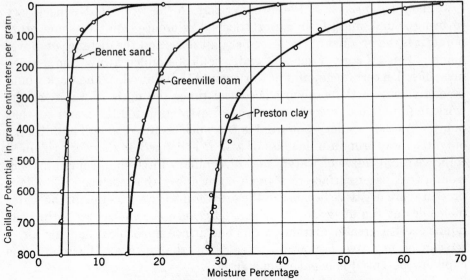

Fig. IX$_B$-1.—Tension-moisture curves of Richards [20].

ular cohesion as determined by the properties of the surface are the primary cause of water retention at these higher tensions.   Veihmeyer and Edlefsen [30] state that the accuracy of present methods may justify the assumption of a linear relation in the moisture-tension curve between the moisture contents of field capacity and permanent wilting.

The curves in Figure IX$_B$-1 were obtained by placing the soils in contact with a porous plate that was sealed to the top of a rectangular reservoir of water.   If these soils were placed in tubes that were in contact with a free water surface and enough time allowed for the water to come to equilibrium, the sand would have a moisture content of about 4 percent at a height of 800 centimeters; the clay would contain about 28 percent at the same height.

These curves indicate that the work necessary to remove water from the soil is a continuous function of soil moisture.   There is no distinct break in any of these curves. It does not necessarily follow, however, that there is no change in the nature of the factors that cause the attraction and retention of water somewhere along the curve. As Wadsworth [29] suggests, the tension-moisture curve may be a "composite of several curves in the same coordinates." Nevertheless, the apparent continuity of the tension-moisture curves places any classification of soil water upon a purely empirical basis. Even though it could be proved that the two ends of the curve represented two different phases so far as the nature of the forces involved was concerned, there could be no clear-cut differentiation between the two portions of the curve, because of overlapping effects.

Schofield [24] has attempted to simplify the usage of capillary potential in soil-water relations by introducing the term "*pF* of soil water" to express the energy with which water is held by soils. The term "*pF*" is simply the logarithm of the tension, when the tension is expressed in centimeters of water. This term has both advantages and disadvantages. Its chief merit lies in the fact that the use of the logarithmic scale permits the graphing of the relation of tension to moisture content on one simple scale. For example, the pF curves in Figure IXв-2 cover a range of tensions corresponding to 1 to 1,000,000 centimeters of water. Thus, it is possible to show the relations of the various soil-moisture constants to one another in terms of the energy with which the water is held. The main disadvantage in the use of pF is due to the fact that the logarithm of the tension as such cannot readily be used in developing the mathematical aspects of moisture retention and flow. The same objection holds true in using pH instead of hydrogen-ion concentration in acid-base relations. It is the writer's opinion that the convenience of the pF terminology has caused more individuals to grasp the significance of energy relations in soil-moisture problems than the use of potential functions. It is true, however, that the analysis of soil-water phenomena on the basis of potential functions should not be sacrificed for the sake of convenience. In many problems the use of the linear scale will prove more advantageous than that of the logarithmic scale.

The curves in Figure IXв-2 show that the moisture equivalent occurs at a pF of 2.7 to 3; the moisture content at field capacity corresponds to a pF of 3.2. If the hygroscopicity at 50 and 99 percent relative humidity, the moisture equivalent and the amount of water held at capillary saturation were known, an approximate pF curve for a soil could be drawn.

The capillary potential may be determined by calculations from freezing-point depression, by dilatometer and vapor-pressure measurements [25], by the use of seeds as osmometers [27], by determining the water distribution in long soil columns placed in contact with a water surface [8], by measuring the water distribution in a soil with porous clay cells, or by centrifugal force [20, 23]. Calculations from vapor-pressure measurements are used primarily to obtain data for the dry end of the curve; a centrifuge or a porous clay cell is used to obtain results for the wet end of the curve.

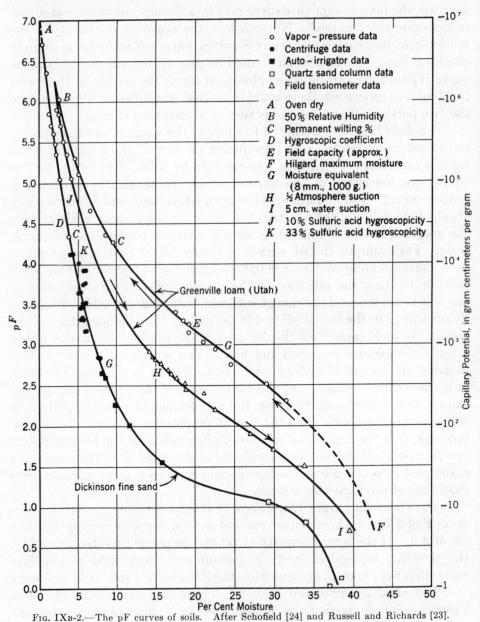

Fig. IXb-2.—The pF curves of soils. After Schofield [24] and Russell and Richards [23].

Lebedeff [15] has demonstrated that the moisture content of all soils decreases gradually as the centrifugal force increases from 400 to 18,000 times gravity. At still higher centrifugal forces the moisture content changes only slightly. Olmstead [19] centrifuged soils in an air-driven machine at a centrifugal force of 300,000 times that of gravity and reduced the moisture content to that of the hygroscopic coefficient. Russell and Richards [23], have developed a technique for determining the tension-moisture curve between the moisture equivalent and wilting point.

The most widely used method for measuring the moisture potential of soils depends upon the so-called suction force of the soil for water. A porous-clay cell, filled with water and connected to a mercury manometer, is placed in the soil, and the system is allowed to come to equilibrium. As the soil dries out, water moves from the cell into the soil and the mercury in the manometer rises. As the soil becomes wet, water enters the cup and the mercury in the manometer falls. When the water in the soil is in equilibrium with the water in the cup, the moisture potential of the soil at that moisture content is equal to that represented by the reading of the manometer. Such an instrument has been called a "tensiometer" [21, 22]. If the maximum tension exceeds 1 atmosphere, air enters the cup, and the tensiometer is no longer operative. There is a considerable hysteresis effect, and at the same reading of the manometer a soil that is drying out has a different moisture content from that of the same soil when it is being wetted. The reader is referred to the investigations of Richards and his associates [20, 21, 22, 23] for a discussion of various types of tensiometers.

PRESSURE DEFICIENCIES IN RELATION TO THE SOIL PORE SPACE

On the basis of the classical investigations of Slichter [28] and King [14], Haines [13] developed a concept of moisture retention and movement as related to the tension necessary to pull an air-water interface through the cell-like pores of the soil. The fundamental thesis of this concept was predicated on the assumption that the tension necessary to drain a pore is limited by the tension required to draw the meniscus through one of the narrow entries of the pore. The value of the pressure deficiency is determined by the narrow sections of the pores when the soil is drying and by the wider sections when the soil is being wetted. The individual cell-like pore does not fill or empty by smooth reversible changes but shows two unstable stages at which filling or emptying is completed quickly; these stages represent the entrance or removal of water through the pore opening.

It is interesting to prepare artificial systems of uniform sand separates and study the drainage of the pores as a function of the tension. The tension-moisture curves in Figure IXв-3 show that as the average size of the quartz particles decreases (which also reflects a decrease in pore size), the tension required to drain the pores of the system increases. These curves point out that it was necessary to bring each separate to a certain tension before any appreciable amount of water was withdrawn from the system.   The pores drained rapidly when this tension was reached.   In other words, drainage occurred only when the tension was high enough to pull the air-water interfaces through the pores.   The relatively flat section of the curve suggests that most of the pores had rather uniform sizes, which should be expected with fairly uniform separates.   Finally, after these pores were drained, the different separates came to approximately the same moisture content.   Apparently, the moisture films were discontinuous or very thin at this stage; probably most of the water was retained at the points of contact between particles.

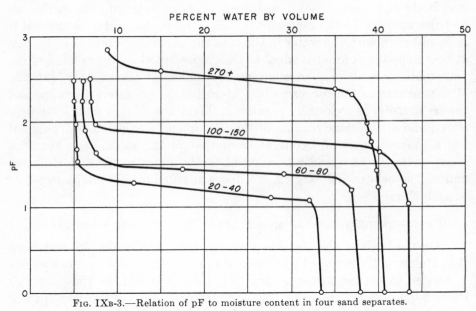

Fig. IXb-3.—Relation of pF to moisture content in four sand separates.

When four of these sand fractions are placed in contact with a porous plate at the same time (individually through the use of metal partitions), saturated with water and subjected to increasing tension, the tension-moisture curve A in Figure IXb-4 is obtained.   This curve is a composite of the four curves in Figure IXb-3.   The four breaks in the curve indicate that each separate drained at a tension characteristic for the size of pores of the separate.   The broken lines represent where each pure separate should drain, on the basis of the results shown in Figure IXb-3.   Slight differences in packing account for the minor variations between the tension-moisture curves in the two figures.   These results clearly demonstrate that a pore is not emptied until a certain tension is reached.   When the four separates are mixed together in equal volumes and placed on a porous plate, curve B in Figure IXb-4 is obtained.   The total porosity is greatly decreased, as the smaller particles fill the voids between the larger ones.   The system did not start to drain until a tension equivalent to that necessary to remove water from the 100- to 150-mesh[1] separate was reached. The curve is smooth but has a changing slope between the points where drainage began and ceased, and it is not as steep in its upper portion as the four curves in Figure IXв-3. This suggests the presence of variable-sized pores within the system. Such a curve represents in some degree those obtained with soils. Soils, although they vary widely in mechanical composition, are composed of particles ranging in size from those of colloidal dimensions

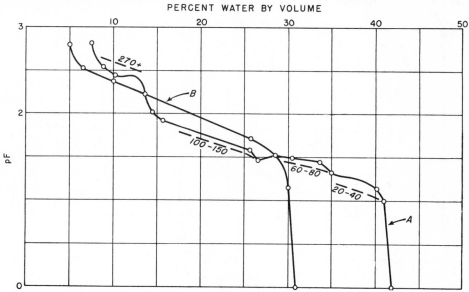

Fig. IXв-4.—Relation of pF to moisture content in four sand separates. (a) Four separates individually in contact with porous plate; (b) four separates mixed together.

to coarse sand and gravel. Various other factors, however, alter the nature of the pore spaces of soils in their natural structure.

If a layer of sand containing small pores (150- to 270-mesh sand) is placed over a layer composed of larger pores (40- to 60-mesh sand), no appreciable amount of water is removed from the system until a tension necessary to pull the air-water interfaces through the 150 to 270-mesh layer is reached, as shown in Figure IXв-5. However, when this point is reached, a large percentage of the water is removed from the system

[1] The following table shows the size of the sieve openings corresponding to the different mesh numbers:

Mesh No.	Sieve opening (millimeter)	Mesh No.	Sieve opening (millimeter)
20	0.84	100	0.15
40	.42	150	.10
60	.25	270	.053
80	.18		

with very little increase in tension. If this curve is compared with those in Figure IXв-3, it is evident that the final moisture content of the system is about 13 percent by volume in Figure IXв-5 as compared with about 7 percent in Figure IXв-3. The higher moisture content of the system in Figure IXв-5 is due to the high water content of the ⅛-inch layer of 150- to 270-mesh separate.

The following explanation apparently accounts for these differences in moisture content. As soon as the tension necessary to drain the larger pores in the surface layer is reached, the menisci are pulled through,

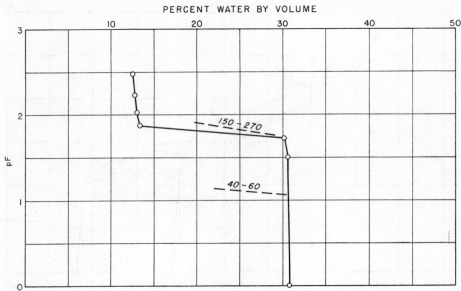

Fig. IXв-5.—Relation of pF to moisture content in a system consisting of 40- to 60-mesh sand overlain by 150- to 270-mesh sand.

thereby establishing an air passage down to the 40- to 60-mesh layer. When this occurs, the 40- to 60-mesh material drains immediately, leaving a nearly saturated system of fine sand above. After the coarser separates drain, no appreciable amount of water is further withdrawn. The 150- to 270-mesh layer does not have saturated contact with the porous plate. The water films in the 40- to 60-mesh layer are evidently so thin that capillary conductivity is zero and the system approaches a state of equilibrium.

This type of system is often simulated in lysimeter experiments where a core of soil is placed over a layer of sand. Also, subirrigation of plant beds in greenhouses, where fine-textured soils are placed over beds of gravel, often represents a similar situation.

If an artificial system is prepared where the fine-pored material is overlain by coarser fractions, the tension-moisture curve in Figure IXв-6 is obtained. In this system the 40- to 60-mesh layer drains at approximately its normal tension. When this layer is drained, it is necessary to raise the tension before the 150- to 270-mesh layer is drained. As this fine-textured layer is in contact with the porous plate, it drains to a moisture content of about 6 or 7 percent.

These experiments on the drainage of pores indicate that the tension at which a pore will drain is determined by the force necessary to pull the meniscus through the neck of the pore. If the pore has no constriction on top, it is drained down to the lower constriction at a tension character-

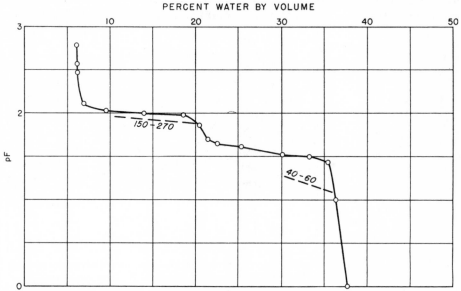

FIG. IXв-6.—Relation of pF to moisture content in a system consisting of 150- to 270-mesh sand overlain by 40- to 60-mesh sand.

istic for the wider section of the pore. The rate of drainage, of course, is affected.

If the experiment as shown by the results in Figure IXв-3 is repeated by using uniform aggregates of a soil instead of sand, similar curves are obtained. For example, the 40- to 60-mesh aggregates drain at approximately the same tension as 40- to 60-mesh sand. The tension-moisture curves of the 40- to 60-mesh separates of aggregates from four different soils, of zeolite, and of quartz sand are shown in Figure IXв-7. All these separates apparently drain at approximately the same tension. Quartz sand represents the only system in which the separates are not porous. The major differences between these curves are found in the total porosity and the moisture content to which the separates drain. The nonporous quartz sand has a total porosity of 36 percent and drains to a moisture content of about 6 percent after the major portion of the water is removed (as taken from the change in the slope of the curve). If the difference between these two values is considered air capacity, or "noncapillary" porosity at this tension, then sand has a "noncapillary" porosity of 30 percent. On the other extreme, Fe zeolite has a total porosity of 70 percent and drains to a moisture content of about 39 percent before the curve changes appreciably. This represents a "noncapillary" porosity of 31 percent.

If 30 percent represents the pore space between the particles in the quartz sand, about the same amount of pore space should be expected between the aggregates or zeolite particles. If 30 percent is subtracted from the saturation percentage, the point falls approximately at the flex

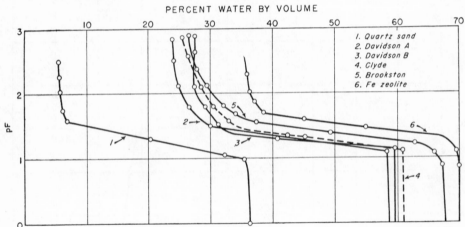

Fig. IXв-7.—Relation of pF to moisture content in 40- to 60-mesh separates of aggregates from four different soils, of zeolite, and of quartz sand.

for all the curves. Apparently, the pores that drain below this point represent those between the particles. Water that is withdrawn above this point comes primarily from the pores within the aggregates or zeolite. These curves indicate that the moisture equivalent of soils (pF 2.7) may measure the intragranular porosity. As the field capacity (pF 3.0 to 3.2) represents the amount of water that is retained after drainage has ceased, it seems as if the pores between the particles, especially in a granular soil, are those to which aeration is primarily due.

EQUILIBRIUM POINTS FOR CHARACTERIZING THE RETENTION OF SOIL
MOISTURE

Several so-called equilibrium points have been suggested to characterize moisture retention at different points on the tension-moisture curve.

The term "moisture equivalent" has been used rather widely to characterize the moisture-holding properties of soils. It refers to the amount of water which a saturated soil will retain after being centrifuged at a centrifugal force 1,000 times that of gravity. This term was first suggested by Briggs and McLane [6] in 1907 to represent the water that is held in the smaller pores. Fisher [10] suggested that the moisture equivalent not only measures the water held in the small pores but also the water imbibed by the soil colloids. He centrifuged soils saturated with xylene to obtain an index of the imbibed water. The amount of xylene retained is supposed to be equivalent to the pore-space water, and the difference between the moisture and xylene equivalents is considered an index of the imbibed water. This method has several possibilities for determining the relative hydration of different soils.

The curves in Figure IXb-2 show that the force with which water is held by a soil at the moisture equivalent corresponds to a pF of about 2.7. Capillary conductivity near this moisture content is very low, according to the investigations of Moore [18]. Figure IXb-7 indicates that most of the water retained by various aggregates at tensions above those corresponding to a pF of about 2.0 is held in the pores within the aggregates. Therefore, it seems that the moisture equivalent of an aggregated soil may be a fairly close measure of the water that is held within the pores of the aggregates.

The moisture equivalent has been used by several investigators as a means of expressing texture. Veihmeyer and Hendrickson [29] have observed that the moisture equivalent gives a fairly reliable measure of the field capacity of fine-textured soils.

The "field capacity," another commonly used moisture term, has been defined by Veihmeyer and Hendrickson [29] as "the amount of water held in the soil after the excess gravitational water has drained away and after the rate of downward movement of water has materially decreased." It has been called field-carrying capacity, normal field capacity, normal moisture capacity, and capillary capacity. Early studies by Alway and McDole [1] showed that when soils were wetted from above they drained to a uniform moisture content of about 2.5 times the hygroscopic coefficient (which was determined at a relative humidity of approximately 98 percent). These results have been confirmed by the work of later investigators. Alway and McDole, as well as Veihmeyer and Hendrickson, have observed that the field capacity of sands is higher than the moisture equivalent but that the field capacity of loams is about the same as the moisture equivalent. The curves in Figure IXb-2 show that water is held in these soils at a tension equivalent to a pF of about 3.0 to 3.2 at field capacity.

The "wilting point" is a term suggested by Briggs and Shantz [7] to denote the moisture content at which the soil cannot supply water at a rate sufficient to maintain the turgor of the plant; consequently, the plant wilts. All plants apparently reduce the moisture content of a given soil to about the same value before wilting occurs. Sunflowers are used most commonly for measuring the wilting point directly; all indirect methods are not satisfactory.

As noted in Figure IX$_B$-2, the wilting point corresponds to a tension equivalent to a pF of about 4.2. Water is probably held as a thin film around the individual soil particles at this tension. As capillary conductivity is practically zero at these low moisture contents, water movement takes place primarily in the vapor phase. It is possible, however, that plants may extract water from the soil at moisture contents lower than the wilting point, if the roots are in direct contact with the moisture films.

If plants wilt permanently at the wilting point, and if soils usually drain to the moisture content of the field capacity, it is obvious that the moisture difference between the field capacity and wilting point represents the amount of available water in the soil. Therefore, the nature of the tension-moisture curve is an index of water availability. A steep curve between these two points indicates that the water is held very tightly, a condition that corresponds to a low amount of available water. A gently sloping curve indicates fairly good availability of the soil water.

The "hygroscopic coefficient" is one of the oldest soil-moisture constants. It represents the adsorbed water on the surface of the soil particles. Various air humidities have been used to measure the hygroscopic coefficient or hygroscopicity of soils. Mitscherlich, in Germany, used a relative humidity of 94.3 percent, which is produced in air in contact with a 10 percent solution of sulphuric acid; the hygroscopic coefficient at this humidity is equivalent to a pF of 5. The Rothamsted investigators have used a relative humidity of 50 percent, and the hygroscopic coefficient obtained corresponds to a pF of 6. Workers in the United States Department of Agriculture have employed relative humidities of 98.2 and 74.9 percent, and the hygroscopic coefficients obtained correspond to pF values of 4.5 and 5.6, respectively. The normal definition of hygroscopic coefficient in the United States refers to the amount of water adsorbed by a soil in a saturated atmosphere.

All these values are found on the dry end of the tension-moisture curve. The individual values represent only certain equilibrium points on the vapor pressure-moisture curve. They provide an index of surface adsorption, for the attractive forces in the surface of the soil colloidal material cause the adsorption.

MOVEMENT OF SOIL MOISTURE

The movement of water through a given volume of soil must take place through the soil pore space. The type and rate of movement will be related to the properties affecting the nature of this pore space. Water movement may occur in the liquid or the vapor phase. Movement in the liquid phase is brought about either by the action of gravity or by capillary forces, alone or in combination. According to the dominance of the moving force, water movement may be considered with reference to unsaturated soils, where movement occurs in the presence of numerous air-water interfaces, or with reference to saturated soils, where the large pores are involved and movement occurs primarily under the influence of gravity.

Movement in the Liquid Phase in Unsaturated Soils

In an unsaturated soil the larger pores are filled with air, and numerous air-water interfaces exist. The distribution and movement of water may be in any direction, depending upon the forces involved. The dominant moving force is the capillary or moisture potential. Buckingham [8] defined the flow of water under these conditions as follows: "We must think of it as a current of water through the soil; and as a measure of the strength of the capillary current at any point we may take the amount of water which passes in one unit of time through a unit area of an imaginary plane surface perpendicular to the direction of motion." This definition is similar to those characterizing the flow of water through pipes, the flow of electricity, and the flow of heat.

In the flow of water through pipes, the rate of flow is proportional to the difference in pressure head times the conductance. The rate of flow across a given cross-sectional area of the pipe is proportional to the conductance times the potential gradient. In other words, the rate of flow is proportional to the fall in pressure head per unit length times the gravitational constant g. A potential gradient has both magnitude and direction (potential has only magnitude).

This means that the potential gradient is the change in potential per unit distance in the direction of the maximum rate of increase of the potential.

Inasmuch as flow always takes place from a higher to a lower potential, the rate of flow of water through a pipe can be expressed by the equation

$$\text{Rate of flow} = -K \text{ grad } \Pi \tag{1}$$

in which K is the conductance of the pipe and grad Π is the potential gradient. Similar analogies can be developed for the flow of heat or of electricity.

The capillary flow of water through soils can be analyzed in a comparable manner. The flow of capillary water may be expressed as follows:

$$Q = -K \text{ grad } \Psi \tag{2}$$

in which Q is the capillary current density, or the mass of water which in 1 second passes through 1 square centimeter of an imaginary plane perpendicular to the direction of flow, K is the capillary conductivity, and grad Ψ is the capillary potential gradient. Equation 2, however, applies only to horizontal flow. As the force of gravity enters into vertical flow, the gravitational potential gradient must be considered under these conditions

$$V = -K \text{ grad } \Phi \qquad (3)$$

in which V is the volume of flow, grad Φ is the change in the total water-moving force per unit distance, and K is the specific conductivity. Grad Φ in equation 3 is equal to grad Ψ + grad ϕ (the gravitational potential gradient).

Equation 3 indicates that the movement of moisture in soils is a function of a potential gradient or driving force and the conductivity of the system. Rapid flow takes place only when both conductivity and potential gradient are large. Slow water movement results if either or both of these factors are small. The greater the difference in moisture content between any two points in the soil, the greater will be the potential and the more rapid will be the movement of water, if capillary conductivity is not zero. If a dry soil is placed in contact with moist soils with different degrees of wetness, water will move into the dry soil faster from the wetter soils than from the drier. This is a case of difference in potential.

Capillary conductivity is related to the nature of the soil and its moisture content. The characteristics of the soil are evaluated in the constant K. Buckingham [8] recognized that capillary conductivity increased with the moisture content and with the size of the pores. Texture and structure affect capillary conductivity by influencing the number, size, and continuity of the pores. Gardner [11], using the term "capillary transmission constant" to characterize capillary conductivity, found that packing had a large influence on conductivity. The capillary transmission constants for extremely loose, well-packed, and natural soils were -1.8×10^{-3}, -5.4×10^{-3}, and -8.7×10^{-3}, respectively. The conductivity of the natural field soil included both gravitational and capillary flow. The pores in the extremely loose soil were evidently too large to provide adequate contacts of moisture films. Those in the well-packed soil apparently were so small that there was considerable resistance to flow.

Recent experiments by Moore [18] have indicated that capillary conductivity approaches zero at moisture contents below the moisture equivalent, owing, perhaps, to a discontinuity of moisture films. At a pF of 2 the capillary permeability of various soils was found to increase in the following order: Sand, fine sandy loam, light clay, and clay. Capillary conductivity was practically zero at the following moisture contents for the same soils: Sand, 5.0 percent at a pF of 1.9; fine sandy loam, 20.4 percent at a pF of 1.96; light clay, 24.6 percent at a pF of 2.08; and clay, 25.9 at a pF of 2.15. The water films that cause capillary movement apparently become discontinuous at much lower tensions in sands than in clays. Clays have a large number of small pores; sands have a smaller number of larger pores. These data discount the popular concept that there is considerable capillary movement in soils. If soils normally drain to a pF of about 3.0 at field capacity, and if capillary conductivity is practically zero at moisture contents less than field capacity, it is rather obvious that plant roots must permeate the soil rather thoroughly to make the most efficient use of soil moisture. The results obtained by Moore have not been confirmed completely by other investigators, and there are some data which suggest capillary movement at low moisture contents. Nevertheless, he has stimulated considerable interest in the nature and significance of moisture movement at low capillary conductivities.

The downward movement of water by capillarity occurs under the combined effects of the capillary potential gradient and the gravitational potential gradient. If evaporation is prevented at the surface, water will move downward until the soil is drained or until equilibrium is attained with an impermeable layer or a saturated layer. Alway and McDole [1] observed that water moved downward until the moisture retained in the soil at equilibrium was about 2.5 times that at the hygroscopic coefficient. This would correspond to a pF of about 3.0, as determined from the pF curves in Figure IXв-2, and is equivalent to "field capacity" or the moisture content of "zero capillary conductivity." Alway and McDole observed that each soil retained the same amount of water at equilibrium, irrespective of its place in a soil column containing six different soils.

Considerable difference of opinion exists concerning the height to which water will move by capillarity from the subsurface layers as the surface becomes dry. Alway and McDole came to the conclusion, on the basis of their experiments, that the deep subsoil contributes little water to the growth of annual plants. Upward movement below a depth of 12 inches was very slow at moisture contents approximating field capacity. These observations tend to confirm the laboratory data of Moore on the relation of tension to capillary conductivity. Rotmistrov, of Russia,, has also suggested that water does not move to the surface of soils by capillarity from depths greater than 16 to 20 inches. On the other hand, McGee [17] has estimated that 6 inches of water annually is brought to the surface by capillarity from depths as great as 10 feet. More recent results by Richards and his coworkers [22, 23], who used tensiometers, have indicated that there was an upward movement of capillary water in the Marshall silt loam from as great a depth as 24 inches.

Most of the experimental evidence, therefore, points out that the upward movement of water by capillarity is not as great as earlier investigators have led us to believe. The theory of the dust mulch as a conserver of soil moisture, which was originated from interpretations of some of the experiments by King, has been revised considerably in light of recent developments in the knowledge of capillary movement. The experiments of Call and Sewell in Kansas, Veihmeyer in California, and others have shown that a dust mulch is not necessary to conserve water. These experiments are easily interpreted when we consider that the movement of water in soils is very slow at moisture contents below the field capacity. When the soil dries out on the surface, a layer of zero capillary conductivity is automatically established. Unless the soil capillaries are in immediate contact with a free water surface or a water table, a dust mulch should not be expected to be necessary for the conservation of moisture.

The slow movement of water at moisture contents between field capacity and the wilting point raises the question as to the availability of soil water to plants. If the plant roots extract water from a given volume of soil and there is such slow movement from other portions of the soil in the vicinity of the roots, how can the plant remove water from the soil? The answer to this question seems to be associated with the fact that the complete utilization of soil moisture is dependent upon an extensive root system of the plant. In other words, the greater the contact between roots and soil the greater will be the number of water films that are in contact with growing roots. Hence, as a plant root removes water from a small volume of soil, the root grows and is brought into contact with more moist areas. This fact is well illustrated by the extensive root systems of plants in the semiarid regions.

By way of summary, the movement of water in unsaturated soils, where capillary forces are most dominant, is determined by the capillary conductivity of the soil and the magnitude of the driving force, as related to the difference in moisture content from one point to another. A proper evaluation of the conductivity and potential factors in the flow equation is necessary to understand the availability of water to plants and changes in soil-moisture content.

MOVEMENT IN SATURATED SOILS

The movement of water in saturated soils takes place through pores that contain little air, though it is realized that this condition is rarely attained. Darcy's law for the special case of horizontal flow states that the velocity of flow through a column of soil is directly proportional to the difference in pressure head and inversely proportional to the length of the column. In order to interpret Darcy's law in terms for flow in any direction the difference in "hydraulic head" rather than "pressure head" should be used. According to this terminology

$$V = k \frac{H}{l} \qquad (4)$$

in which V is the flow in cubic centimeters per square centimeter per second, l is the length of the column in centimeters, H is the difference in hydraulic head in centimeters, and k is the coefficient of permeability or permeability constant. This constant is a function of soil characteristics, particularly the amount and character of the soil pores.

The exact relation between soil porosity and permeability is not yet fully understood. A proper evaluation of the porosity factor in the permeability constant is desirable for a better understanding of flow equations under a variety of soils and soil conditions. Slichter [28], Zunker [31], Kozeny [31], and others have made concerted attempts to modify Darcy's law in order to include pore-space relations.

There is adequate evidence to show that the size, density of packing, and hydration of soil particles greatly influence permeability. Bodman [3] has shown that textural differences have no appreciable effect on permeability at very high apparent densities when the soil is of finer texture than fine sandy loams. Lutz [16] has demonstrated that the hydration of the clay particles determines the permeability of colloidal clays.

The use of total porosity, however, does not give the correct picture for understanding soil permeability. The size and distribution of the pores is of much greater importance. A soil with a high content of large pores is readily permeable to water. This fact was recognized as early as 1864, when Schumacher [26] developed the concept of capillary and noncapillary porosity. He observed that the amount of noncapillary pores (large enough not to hold water at relatively low tensions) usually determined the permeability of a soil. Burger [9] found that soils with low air capacities (small amount of noncapillary pores) usually had low percolation rates.

Although the use of noncapillary porosity to characterize pore sizes is rather advantageous as affording a simple explanation of the effect of porosity on soil-moisture relations, it leaves much to be desired from a purely technical sense. The tension at which a soil is drained to obtain information on the content of the so-called noncapillary pores will affect the amount of these pores. Recent experimental results [2] suggest that soil permeability is closely related to the shape of the tension-moisture curve (pF). In the first place, the amount of water that is withdrawn from zero tension to that of the flex point of the curve (this may be called the noncapillary porosity as measured at this tension) is closely associated with the percolation rate of the soil. This quantity is a measure of the number of large pores; the greater this quantity, the higher is the percolation rate.

In the second place, the tension at which the flex point of the curve occurs also is related to permeability. The higher the pF of the flex point, the slower is the rate of percolation. It seems that the height of the flex point is an index of the size of the pores. This fact is suggested by the curves in Figure IXв-3. The higher the tension necessary to drain these pores, the smaller will be the pores and consequently, the lower will be the permeability of the soil.

In the third place, there is a tendency toward greater permeability as the slope of the curve from zero tension to the flex point decreases. A steep curve signifies rather uniform pores of a given diameter; a sloping curve, on the other hand, suggests that pores of different sizes are present. Permeability will increase with an increase in the number of larger pores.

If a soil is compressed and the effect of this compression on the shape of the tension-moisture curve and on soil permeability is determined, several important changes are noted. There is a decrease in total porosity and in the content of large pores. There is an increase in the pF of the flex point and in the slope of the curve from zero tension to the flex point. These changes indicate that compression decreases the amount and size of the pores. The percentage decrease in the number of large pores is most significant.

Present information, therefore, indicates that the various portions of the tension-moisture curve, especially at the lower tensions, reflect certain characteristics of the soil pore space that are closely related to permeability. The amount, size, distribution, and perhaps continuity of the soil pores undoubtedly contribute to soil permeability. The continuity of the soil pores, although difficult to evaluate, probably plays a greater part in water movement through soils than is usually considered.

The question arises as to the possibility of suggesting some empirical tension for measuring the content of large pores (noncapillary porosity) that would have routine practical value. Numerous experiments by the writer and his associates have indicated that a pF of about 1.7 can be used to provide very useful information on soil porosity in relation to soil permeability. It is hoped that future researches will more adequately characterize the tension-moisture curve in terms of soil characteristics, so that the present empiricism can be avoided.

The downward movement of water in soils must take place through different zones that have varying physical characteristics. The porosity and permeability of each zone may also vary greatly. If a soil is saturated with water, the rate of downward movement is restricted by the permeability of the least pervious zone. An analogy to the rate of flow of water through a funnel with a constriction in the stem illustrates the situation that often occurs in soil.   An impermeable layer in the subsoil may determine the hydrology of the entire profile.

Finally, by way of summary, it can be stated that the downward movement of water by gravitational forces in natural soils is related (1) to the amount, size, and continuity of the larger pores as determined by soil structure, texture, volume changes, and biologic channels (root channels, worm holes, etc.); (2) to the hydration of the pores; and (3) to the resistance of entrapped air, if a rapid entrance of water into the soil does not permit the complete escape of the air in the soil pores.

REFERENCES

1. Alway, F. J., and McDole, G. R., Relation of the water-retaining capacity of a soil to its hygroscopic coefficient: Jour. Agr. Research, vol. 9, pp. 27–71, 1917.

2. Baver, L. D., Soil permeability in relation to non-capillary porosity: Soil Sci. Soc. America Proc., vol. 3, pp. 52–56, 1938.

3. Bodman, G. B., Factors affecting the downward movement of water in soils: American Soil Survey Assoc. Bull. 17, pp. 33–38, 1936.

4. Bouyoucos, G. J., A new classification of soil moisture: Soil Sci., vol. 11, pp. 33–48, 1921.

5. Briggs, L. J., The mechanics of soil moisture.   U. S. Dept. Agr., Bur. Soils, Bull. 10, 1897.

6. Briggs, L. J., and McLane, J. W., The moisture equivalent of soils: U. S. Dept. Agr., Bur. Soils, Bull. 45, 1907.

7. Briggs, L. J., and Shantz, H. L., The wilting coefficient for different plants and its indirect determination: U. S. Dept. Agr., Bur. Plant Industry, Bull. 230, 1912.

8. Buckingham, E., Studies on the movement of soil moisture: U. S. Dept. Agr., Bur. Soils, Bull. 38, 1907.

9. Burger, H., Die physikalische Bodenuntersuchung insbesondere die Methoden zur Bestimmung der Luftkapazität: 4th Internat. Conf. Soil Sci. (Rome) Proc., vol. 2, pp. 150–163, 1926.

10. Fisher, E. A., Some factors affecting the evaporation of water from soil: Jour. Agr. Sci., vol. 13, pp. 121–143, 1923.

11. Gardner, W., A capillary transmission constant and methods of determining it experimentally: Soil Sci., vol. 10, pp. 103–126, 1920.

12. Gardner, W., The capillary potential and its relation to soil-moisture constants: Soil Sci., vol. 10, pp. 357–359, 1920.

13. Haines, W. B., Studies in the physical properties of soils—IV, A further contribution to the theory of capillary phenomena in soils.   Jour. Agr. Sci., vol. 17, pp. 264–290, 1927; V, The hysteresis effect in capillary properties and the modes of moisture distribution associated therewith: Jour. Agr. Sci., vol. 20, pp. 97–116, 1930.

14. King, F. H., Principles and conditions of the movement of ground water: U. S. Geol. Survey 19th Ann. Rept., pt. 2, pp. 59–294, 1899.

15. Lebedeff, A. F., Methods of determining the maximum molecular moisture-holding capacity of soils: 1st Internat. Cong. Soil Sci. Proc., vol. 1, pp. 551–563, 1927.

16. Lutz, J. F., The physico-chemical properties of soils affecting soil erosion: Missouri Agr. Exper. Sta. Research Bull. 212, 1934.

17. McGee, W J, Field records relating to subsoil water: U. S. Dept. Agr., Bur. Soils, Bull. 93, 1913.

18. Moore, R. E., Water conduction from shallow water tables: Hilgardia, vol. 12, pp. 383–426, 1939.

19. Olmstead, L. B., Some moisture relations of the soils from the erosion experiment stations: U. S. Dept. Agr. Tech. Bull. 562, 1937.

20. Richards, L. A., The usefulness of capillary potential to soil-moisture and plant investigations: Jour. Agr. Research, vol. 37, pp. 719–742, 1928.

21. Richards, L. A., and Gardner, W., Tensiometers for measuring the capillary tension of soil water: Am. Soc. Agronomy Jour., vol. 28, pp. 352–358, 1936.

22. Richards, L. A., and Neal, O. R., Some field observations with tensiometers. Soil Sci. Soc. America Proc., vol. 1, pp. 71–91, 1936; vol. 2, pp. 35–44, 1937.

23. Russell, M. B., and Richards, L. A., The determination of soil-moisture energy relations by centrifugation: Soil Sci. Soc. America Proc., vol. 3, pp. 65–69, 1938; vol. 4, p. 53, 1939.

24. Schofield, R. K., The pF of the water in soil: 3d Internat. Soil. Cong. Trans., vol. 2, pp. 37–48, 1935.

25. Schofield, R. K., and DaCosta, J. V. B., The determination of the pF at permanent wilting and at the moisture equivalent by the freezing-point method: 3d Internat. Cong. Soil Sci., Trans., vol. 1, pp. 6–10, 1935.

26. Schumacher, Wilhelm, Die Physik—I, Die Physik des Bodens, pp. 81–102. Berlin, Wiegandt & Hempel, 1864.

27. Shull, C. A., Measurements of surface forces in soils: Bot. Gazette, vol. 62, pp. 1–29, 1916.

28. Slichter, C. S., Theoretical investigation of the motion of ground waters: U. S. Geol. Survey 19th Ann. Rept., pt. 2, pp. 295–384, 1899.

29. Veihmeyer, F. J., and Hendrickson, A. H., The moisture equivalent as a measure of the field capacity of soils: Soil Sci., vol. 32, pp. 181–193, 1931.

30. Veihmeyer, F. J., and Edlefsen, N. E., Interpretation of soil-moisture problems by means of energy changes: Am. Geophys. Union Trans. 18th Ann. Meeting, Hydrology, pp. 302–318, 1937.

31. Zunker, F., Die Durchlässigkeit des Bodens: 6th Com. Int. Soc. Sci. (Groningen) Trans., vol. B, pp. 18–43, 1933.

CHAPTER X

GROUND WATER

Xa. OCCURRENCE, ORIGIN, AND DISCHARGE OF GROUND WATER
Oscar E. Meinzer[1]

INTRODUCTION

The water that occurs below the surface of the land is invisible and relatively inaccessible and has consequently always possessed an aspect of mystery. What is the mode of its occurrence; what is its quantity; whither does it come; is it stationary or in motion? If in motion, what is its destination and its rate of movement, and what are the forces that propel it through the earth? What chemical work does it perform upon the rocks through which it moves? What causes it in some places to ooze almost imperceptibly from the ground and in other places to gush from the rocks in great volume—clear, cold, and pure, or boiling hot, or bubbling with various gases, or supercharged with dissolved minerals which it deposits upon the surface? These are some of the questions that confront the hydrologists who endeavor to look below the surface. They are questions of almost infinite complexity, involving a great amount of physics and chemistry and almost the whole field of geology.

The water that occurs beneath the land surface is called subsurface water, underground water, or subterranean water. It can be divided into two parts. The water that occurs in the zone of saturation, from which the springs and wells are supplied, is commonly called ground water, but the Greek term "plerotic water" has recently been suggested for it by the writer [23]. The water that occurs between the land surface and the zone of saturation has been called suspended water, but the Greek term "kremastic water" has been suggested for it as a companion to the term "plerotic water."

The springs and spring-fed streams attracted the attention of the ancient philosophers and caused the subject of ground water to be mentioned in many places in the early literature of different peoples. The very ancient practice of tapping the earth by means of wells to obtain water supplies, not only for domestic use and live stock but also for irrigation, resulted in the early development of a certain amount of practical

Geologist in charge, Division of Ground Water, Geological Survey, United States Department of the Interior, Washington, D. C. In the preparation of parts of this chapter the writer was effectively assisted by Vinton C. Fishel, of the Geological Survey.

knowledge concerning the occurrence of the ground water. The basic scientific concepts in regard to ground water owe their origin in part to the philosophic interest in springs but probably more to the practical interest in water supplies from wells.

Geology affords the framework on which ground-water hydrology is built; more accurately, it deals with the stratigraphy and structure of the rock formations that make up the great and intricate systems of natural waterworks the functioning of which forms the essential part of the subject of ground-water hydrology. Therefore, although earnest attempts were made by Vitruvius and others to give useful information as to the water-bearing properties of different rocks, the subject of ground-water hydrology could not be far developed until the fundamental principles of geology were established near the close of the eighteenth century.

FUNDAMENTAL CONCEPTS

ROCKS AS RECEPTACLES OF WATER

Perhaps the most fundamental concept in ground-water hydrology is that of the interstices of the rocks—the open spaces that form the receptacles and conduits of the ground water [24, p. 109].

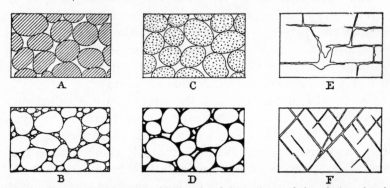

FIG. XA-1.—Diagram showing several types of rock interstices and the relation of rock texture to porosity. (A) Well-sorted sedimentary deposit having high porosity; (B) poorly sorted sedimentary deposit having low porosity; (C) well-sorted sedimentary deposit consisting of pebbles that are themselves porous, so that the deposit as a whole has a very high porosity; (D) well-sorted sedimentary deposit whose porosity has been diminished by the deposition of mineral matter in the interstices; (E) rock rendered porous by solution; (F) rock rendered porous by fracturing. (After U. S. Geol. Survey Water-Supply Paper 489.)

The rocks differ very widely in the size, shape, and arrangement of their interstices and in the aggregate volume of interstitial space, and these differences are of fundamental significance in hydrology. The openings range in size from the huge limestone caverns and lava tubes through all gradations to the minute pores that are too small to be seen with a microscope and that come within the obscure domain of molecular physics. (See Fig. XA-1.)

The interstices are generally irregular in shape, but different types of irregularities are characteristic of rocks of different kinds. In most rocks the interstices are connected, so that the water can move from one opening to another, but in some rocks they are largely isolated and there is little opportunity for the water to percolate. The stratification of most sedimentary rocks produces a laminar arrangement of the interstices that is of fundamental importance in the movement of the water.

Geology is concerned primarily with the solid parts of the rocks, and hydrology with their open spaces or interstices. However, the interstices are the products of the geologic agencies which through long ages have been at work on the materials of the earth, forming and altering the rocks and developing their structure.

The interstices of the rocks can be grouped in two great classes—the original interstices, which were formed when the rocks came into existence, and the secondary interstices, such as joints, fissures, and solution passages, which were developed later. Very generally the original interstices have undergone more or less radical change by solution, cementation, recrystallization, or other processes. The greatest amount of study has been devoted to the interstices of the granular sedimentary deposits, such as sand and sandstone.

Porosity

The porosity of a rock is its property of containing interstices. It is expressed quantitatively as the percentage of the total volume of the rock that is occupied by interstices or that is not occupied by solid rock material. A rock is said to be saturated when all its interstices are filled with water. In a saturated rock the porosity is practically the percentage of the total volume of the rock that is occupied by water.

The porosity of a sedimentary deposit depends chiefly on (1) the shape and arrangement of its constituent particles, (2) the degree of assortment of its particles, (3) the cementation and compacting to which it has been subjected since its deposition, (4) the removal of mineral matter through solution by percolating waters, and (5) the fracturing of the rock, resulting in joints and other openings. Well-assorted deposits of uncemented gravel, sand, and silt have high porosity, whether they consist of large or small grains. If the material is poorly sorted small particles occupy the spaces between the larger ones, still smaller ones occupy the spaces between these small particles, and so on, with the result that the porosity is greatly reduced. Boulder clay, which is an unassorted mixture of glacial drift containing particles of great variety in size, may have a very low porosity, whereas outwash gravel and sand, derived from the same source but assorted by running water, may be highly porous. The porosity of the different rock materials ranges through all gradations, from 80 or perhaps 90 percent in such jellylike substances as newly deposited delta material down to a fraction of 1 percent in the most compact rocks and perhaps to zero deep in the earth, where the weight of the overlying rocks is sufficient to close all the openings.

Mechanical composition

The determination of the mechanical composition of incoherent materials consists in separating into groups the grains of different sizes

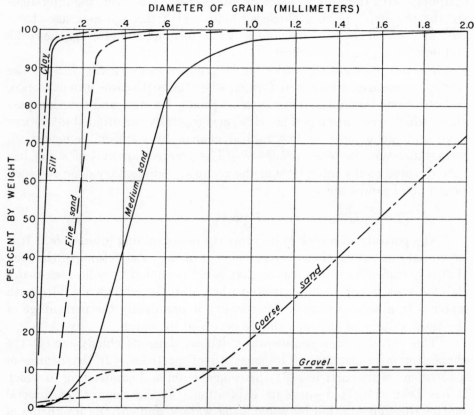

Fig. Xᴀ-2.—Accumulative curves of mechanical composition of typical materials.

and determining what percentage, by weight, each group constitutes. According to standard methods used by the United States Department of Agriculture, which has made thousands of mechanical analyses of soils, the following arbitrary limiting diameters, in millimeters, were adopted. However, hydrologists generally regard material as sand up to at least 2 millimeters.

> Fine gravel, 2 to 1.
> Coarse sand, 1 to 0.5.
> Medium sand, 0.5 to 0.25.

Fine sand, 0.25 to 0.1.
Very fine sand, 0.1 to 0.05.
Silt, 0.05 to 0.005.
Clay, less than 0.005.

The sizes of the interstices are determined largely by the mechanical composition—not only by the sizes of the grains but also by their assortment. Thus a sand with a small admixture of clayey material may be a much poorer water-bearing material than a clean sand of similar appearance because its interstices are in part filled with clay.

The mechanical composition of several representative materials is shown by means of the curves in Figure XA-2. Obviously the more nearly uniform the grains of the material the steeper is its curve. To give simple quantitative expression to the coarseness and degree of assortment of a material the terms "effective size" and "uniformity coefficient" were proposed by Allen Hazen. (See Chapter IXA.) In Figure XA-2 the 10 percent and 60 percent sizes can be determined by inspection. The 10 percent size is called the effective size and the 60 percent size divided by the 10 percent size gives the uniformity coefficient. Thus the uniformity coefficient is unity for a material whose grains are all of the same size, and it increases with variety in size.

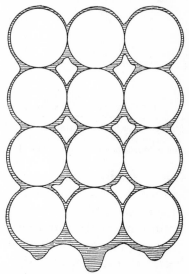

Fig. XA-3.—Diagram showing how a liquid clings to solid particles against the pull of gravity. Drawn from a photograph by L. J. Briggs in which oil and rubber balls about 1 inch in diameter were used to illustrate the principle involved.

FORCES CONTROLLING WATER IN ROCKS

In ground-water hydrology the force of molecular attraction is of fundamental significance. This is the attraction of the rock surfaces for the molecules of water near them and the attraction of the water molecules for one another [24, pp. 19–21]. The attraction of the rock surfaces for the water is illustrated by the film of water that adheres to a pebble after it has been immersed in a body of water. (See Figure XA-3.) Molecular attraction may be the controlling force in materials that have small interstices and a great aggregate area of rock surface that comes into contact with the water, as in the ordinary granular materials. (See Figure XA-4.) Thus a cubic foot of water-bearing sand may have several thousand square feet of rock surface forming the walls of its interstices, and a cubic foot of silty or clayey material may have an acre or even a few acres of rock surface. Although the wetted grain may not exert much molecular force and the quantity of water held by it may be negligible, the aggregate of thousands of square feet of rock surface within each cubic foot of rock material will exert a powerful force that may be the controlling factor in the behavior of the ground water. Thus ground-water hydrology is not merely the application of ordinary hydraulics to the water in the rock formations, but because of the powerful influence of the molecular forces it has its own basic principles and data and requires a distinctive technique.

A simple experiment is sometimes performed to illustrate the effects of molecular attraction in ground-water hydrology. A sample is taken

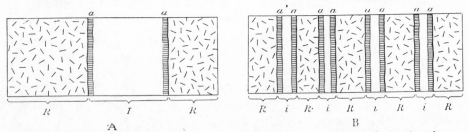

Fig. Xᴀ-4.—Diagram showing the relation between size of interstices and quantity of water controlled by molecular attraction. (*R*) Solid rock; (*I*) large interstice; (*i*) small interstices; (*a*) films of water held by attraction of rock walls. Speciman *B* has no more porosity than Speciman *A* but its total interstitial surface and hence the total quantity of water controlled by molecular attraction is four times as great. (*After U. S. Geol. Survey Water-Supply Paper 489.*)

from a sand formation that is known to yield water freely to wells. The sample is placed in a test tube, and water is added to it in measured quantities until it is saturated. When, however, an attempt is made to drain some of the water out of the sample of this productive sand, it may not surrender even a single drop. This little experiment serves as a warning that experiments with water-bearing materials may give wholly erroneous results unless the distinctive effects of molecular attraction are taken into account.

Hydrologic properties of rocks

It has been found that the ordinary geologic descriptions of rocks are entirely inadequate to indicate their hydrologic properties; moreover, a casual inspection of a material may lead to very erroneous conclusions as to its hydrologic properties. The two properties of a rock material that most largely determine the behavior of its contained water and its productiveness as a water-bearing formation are its specific yield and its permeability. Both of these properties are determined by the character of the interstices and the resultant effects of molecular attraction. The specific yield relates to the storage capacity of the rocks; the permeability relates to their capacity to transmit water. When the hydrologic laboratory of the Geological Survey was established in 1923 a plan was devised for setting up a quantitative hydrologic classification or definition of the granular rock materials, by determining their mechanical composition, porosity, moisture equivalent, and permeability [39]. The value of the first three of these determinations lies chiefly in the information that they give as to the specific yield but they also give indirect information as to the permeability of the material.

Specific yield

The total quantity of water stored in a saturated rock formation can be found by ascertaining its thickness and areal extent and determining its porosity. However, a part of the stored water can have no share in supplying springs or wells; it is held imprisoned in the rocks; in the language of hydraulic engineers it may be said to be in dead storage.

In cavernous limestones, broken and unweathered lava rocks, and clean gravel the amount of water thus held in dead storage is practically negligible; in coarse and well-assorted sands it is appreciable but still small; in fine sands the amount held may equal or exceed the amount that is free to move; and in silty and clayey materials all the water may be held, even though their porosity and hence their water content may be high.

Investigations pertaining to the effects of molecular attraction upon the water in the earth were made by Perrault about 250 years ago. Since his time the subject has been studied by many investigators in different countries, chiefly in the later part of the last century and in the present century. These investigations have pertained chiefly to the studies of soil, such as the work of Hilgard and later that of Briggs and many others. In part they related to studies of filter sands, such as the work of Hazen, and in part to ground-water studies, such as some of the work of King. In 1923 the terms "specific retention" and "specific yield" were proposed by the writer [25, p. 28] to designate respectively the water which is held and that which is free to drain out of a material under natural conditions, in percentages of the total volume of the rock. These terms have now become well established. In recent years much intensive work has been done in connection with the quantitative studies of ground water to differentiate between these two conditions and to develop laboratory and field methods of determining them. This work has produced some practicable methods of procedure but has also brought to light the great complexity of the subject [31, pp. 114–116; 32].

The moisture equivalent of a material is the ratio of (1) the weight of water which the material, after saturation, will retain against a centrifugal force 1,000 times the force of gravity to (2) the weight of the material when dry. This arbitrary device for expressing the hydrologic character of a material by means of a standardized laboratory test was used by Briggs and McLane [4] early in the present century as an aid in studying the hydrologic properties of soils in relation to the water supply of plants. In ground-water work the moisture equivalent, converted from percentage by weight to percentage by volume, has been found useful because it approximates the specific retention. Thus an estimate of the specific yield can be obtained by subtracting the moisture equivalent from the porosity, and a somewhat closer approximation can be obtained by first computing the specific retention from the moisture equivalent, by a method such as that devised by Piper [32], and then subtracting this computed quantity from the porosity.

Evidently these laboratory methods cannot be applied to consolidated rocks in which the principal water conduits are the joints, fissures, or solution passages. In recent work, however, much emphasis has been placed on field methods of determining specific yield, and these methods are more or less available for rocks of all types.

Permeability

A rock that is solid throughout is regarded by the hydrologist as having no capacity to hold or transmit water, although he recognizes the possibility of obscure processes of intermolecular movement that might conceivably have significant effects in the long course of geologic time. A rock that has isolated interstices may contain some water but is nevertheless also hydrologically inert. Materials such as the clays, which contain interconnecting interstices that are so small that their water is effectively held by molecular attraction, are apparently entirely impermeable under the pressures that normally occur in nature, but there is evidence that water or oil may migrate very slowly through them under pressure. The problem of movement in these dense materials has been attacked from different angles but is still obscure.

It is considered that the materials which contain interconnecting interstices of sufficient size that the molecular attraction of their walls does not extend entirely across them have more or less permeability. Saturated materials of this kind contain water that is free to move in response to any hydraulic gradient. The degree of permeability differs very widely with the porosity and especially with the size of the interstices. Recent studies are related largely to the development of reliable and practicable methods of determining the permeability of specific formations. (See Chapter XB.)

ZONES OF AERATION AND SATURATION

The permeable rocks that lie below a certain level are generally saturated with water under hydrostatic pressure, that is, under hydrostatic pressure in excess of the atmospheric pressure. Their interstices are filled with water that is called ground water or plerotic water. These saturated rocks are said to be in the zone of saturation. The water that enters from the surface into the rocks of the earth is drawn down by gravity to the zone of saturation except as it is held by the molecular attraction of the walls of the interstices through which it passes in its descent. The permeable rocks (including the soil) that lie above the zone of saturation may be said to be in the zone of aeration (a relatively new term that was proposed by the writer). Some of the interstices in this zone are also filled with water, but the water is either held in them by molecular attraction or is moving downward toward the zone of saturation [24, 25].

Impermeable rocks may be found within the zone of saturation, within the zone of aeration, or between these two zones, but they are in a sense not functional parts of either zone. They may contain minute interstices or larger isolated interstices that are filled with water, but these interstices will remain filled, whether they are in the zone of saturation or far above it. If impermeable rocks lie between the two zones they are rather arbitrarily classed as being in the zone of aeration. Oil-bearing and gas-bearing rocks generally lie deep within the zone of saturation.

In most places there is only one zone of saturation, but in certain localities the water may be hindered in its downward course by an impermeable or nearly impermeable bed to such an extent that it forms an upper zone of saturation, or perched water body, which is not associated with the lower zone of saturation. Water that saturates soil or subsoil immediately after a rain or before the deeper frost has disappeared in the spring forms a temporary perched water body.

The upper surface of the zone of saturation in ordinary permeable soil or rock is called the "ground-water table" or merely the water table. The term "phreatic surface" has also been applied to this surface. Where the upper surface of the zone of saturation is formed by impermeable rock the water table is absent. If a well is sunk it remains empty until it enters a saturated permeable bed—that is, until it enters the zone of saturation as defined above. Then water flows into the well. If all the rock through which the well passes is permeable the first water that is struck will stand in the well at the level of the top of the zone of saturation—that is, at the level of the water table. If the rock overlying the bed in which the first water is struck is impermeable the water is generally under pressure that will raise it in the well to some point above the level at which it was struck. In such a place there is no water table.

The zone of aeration has been divided, by the writer, with respect to the occurrence and circulation of its water into three belts—the belt of soil water, the intermediate belt, and the capillary fringe. The belt of soil water consists of soil and other materials that lie near enough to the surface to discharge water into the atmosphere in perceptible quantities by the transpiration of plants or by evaporation from the soil. The capillary fringe is the belt immediately above the water table that contains water held up above the zone of saturation by capillary action. Where the water table is so far below the surface that the belt of soil water does not extend down to the capillary fringe there is an intermediate belt. This threefold subdivision of the zone of aeration and the relations of the three belts to each other are illustrated in Figure XA-5.

In a paper by the author [23] the following terms of Greek origin were proposed for international use: "Kremastic water," for all the water in the zone of aeration; "rhizic water," for the water in the belt of soil water, or root zone; "argic water," for the water in the intermediate belt; and 'anastatic water," for the water in the capillary fringe.

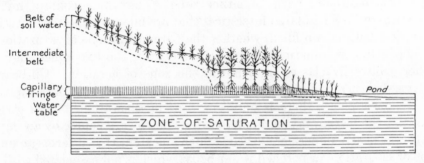

Fig. XA-5.—Diagram showing the zone of saturation and the three belts of the zone of aeration.

The domain of ground-water hydrology is the zone of saturation. The belt of soil moisture, which is essentially the same as what is often called the root zone, is of special interest to all scientists who are concerned with the water supply of the vegetable kingdom. It is the reservoir from which the plants ordinarily draw their water, and its capacity for holding water available to the plants is of primary importance. The capillary fringe is of interest to both ground-water hydrologists and botanical hydrologists where it touches the root zone, for in these places it may carry water upward from the zone of saturation to the roots of the plants. In the many places where the roots do not reach down to the capillary fringe the fringe is of concern chiefly as an agency which complicates all ground-water studies that involve the water table. The intermediate belt has been called the no man's land of hydrology. It contains water, but to a large extent its water is in dead storage—held by molecular attraction from seeping down to the zone of saturation and too far below the surface to be reached by the roots. However, this intermediate belt is not hydrologically entirely dormant, as water from the surface that replenishes the ground-water supplies passes through it.

The equilibrium distribution of water in the zone of aeration depends on the interaction of the forces of gravity, adhesive and cohesive molecular

attraction, and the vapor pressure [19, 35, 38].   The force of gravity tends
to withdraw all the water from the rock material, but the rock surfaces
exert an attractive force on a layer of water that is believed to be at
least a few molecules in thickness, and the water molecules at the outside
of this layer have an attraction for the nearby water molecules, which in
turn attract their neighbors, etc.

After an interstice in a granular material has been largely drained by
the force of gravity, the remaining water tends to be held by the adhesive
and cohesive forces.   The resultant effect of these molecular forces is to
develop rings of water around the contact points between the more or less
spherical grains of rock material [15, 38].   The air-water surfaces of these
rings are concave outward.   The convex rock surfaces between the rings
remain covered with films of water.   The cohesive force then tends to
draw water from the films into the rings, whereas the adhesion of the rock
surfaces doubtless prevents this action after the films have reached a certain minimum thickness.   Both evaporation and condensation of water
vapor may then occur in the same interstice, because a vapor that has
reached the saturation point or maximum vapor pressure with respect to
a concave water surface remains somewhat unsaturated with respect to a
convex water surface and also with respect to a concave surface of a lower
degree of concavity.   Hence water may be evaporating from a convex
water surface and at the same time condensing upon a concave water surface, or it may be evaporating from a concave surface and condensing
upon a surface having a greater degree of concavity.   In this manner the
curvatures of the water surfaces tend to adjust themselves so that they
will be in equilibrium with the vapor pressure.   It is possible that by this
process the films over the convex surfaces may eventually disappear
entirely, or the adhesive force may be effective in holding permanently
the molecules of water nearest to the rock surfaces.

Three conditions have been recognized by Versluys [48] for the moisture held in the zone of aeration by the adhesive and cohesive forces.
The term "pendular stage" was used by him to denote the condition in
which the rings of water around the contact points are isolated, the upper
limit of the pendular stage being reached when adjacent rings come into
contact with each other.   The opposite extreme that he recognized is the
condition, called the "capillary stage," in which the interstice is kept
entirely filled with water by the adhesive and cohesive forces.   The term
"funicular stage" was used for the intermediate condition.

As explained by Smith [38], if a high column of saturated material is
allowed to drain there will not be as thorough drainage as occurs in simple
capillary tubes, but a large quantity of water will at first be retained.
According to Smith, if complete equilibrium is ultimately attained the
distribution that finally prevails is dependent solely on the vapor pressure

of the liquid existing in the pore space during the last stages of the process, the final transfers of water presumably being effected by the process of evaporation and condensation.   According to his mathematical studies the upper part of the high column will ultimately contain only traces of moisture, while the lower parts will retain considerable amounts, the moisture conditions ranging from top to bottom through the pendular, funicular, and saturated (or capillary) stages, the zone in which the funicular stage occurs being a zone of hysteresis, in which all quantities of water between a normal minimum and complete saturation are usually possible.

CLASSIFICATION OF ROCKS WITH REFERENCE TO THEIR HYDROLOGIC PROPERTIES

The most productive unconsolidated water-bearing material is coarse, clean gravel.   Next to gravel comes coarse sand.   Unconsolidated water-bearing materials that yield smaller amounts but still supply many wells are the sediments of finer grain, such as fine sand and loess, and the mixtures of large and small grains, such as till, many alluvial deposits, and the products of rock decay that are still in place.

The consolidated rocks are of two kinds—those produced by the solidification of molten magma and those developed from unconsolidated sedimentary deposits through pressure, cementation, and recrystallization.   Both kinds are generally broken into blocks and yield most of their water from the cracks or joints between the blocks or from porous zones and open passages developed by the weathering and solution of the rocks where the water penetrates these joints.   The less thoroughly cemented sandstones yield most of their water from the original spaces between the grains, and they are on the whole the most valuable water bearers among the consolidated rocks.   Next to sandstones rank limestones, which yield most of their water from large open passages produced by the solution of the rock material, and lava rocks, which yield water from large openings produced when the lavas solidified and from open joints resulting from the rapid cooling of the solidified masses.   Most of the other hard rocks, such as granite, quartzite, shale, slate, and schist, yield small amounts from joints or zones of decayed rock.

Among rocks of all kinds the most productive and valuable water bearers are probably the deposits of gravel.   Next to gravel come sand, sandstone, limestone, and basalt.   Among the many kinds of rock material that do not yield water freely but are nevertheless drawn upon where first-class aquifers are lacking are the fine-grained and poorly assorted unconsolidated deposits and the hard rocks with only rather tight joints. The most completely unproductive of all materials are the true clays and fine silts, whose original interstices are too minute to yield water and which are too soft to have joints or other secondary openings [24, pp. 102–148].

The hydrology of both the limestones and the lava rocks is very different from that of other rocks, not only with respect to the ground water but also with respect to the surface water. For this reason, separate chapters are devoted to the hydrology of the terranes of these rocks (Chapters XIV and XV).

ORIGIN OF GROUND WATER

THE INFILTRATION THEORY

The infiltration theory postulates that the ground water is derived chiefly by the downward seepage of surface water, either directly from rain or melted snow or from streams and lakes supplied by rain and snow. This theory has now become firmly established. Its demonstration consists of well-substantiated and carefully analyzed data as to the downward penetration of the rain and snow water through the soil and subsoil; the seepage losses from streams; the rise of the water table in response to rainfall, melting snow, and the flow of influent streams; the slope of the water table from the demonstrated intake areas to the areas of ground-water discharge; the relation of the quantity of ground water discharged in a given area to the mean annual precipitation and to the permeability of the intake materials; and the fluctuation of discharge with fluctuations in precipitation.

The theory of juvenile water was developed chiefly by Suess [43] and the theory of connate water by Lane [18]. These theories supplement rather than conflict with the infiltration theory, and they cannot properly be regarded as having any real relation to the old condensation and sea-water hypotheses.

RECHARGE BY RAINFALL PENETRATION

Replenishment or recharge of the water supply in the zone of saturation from sources above the surface may be said to involve three steps (1) the infiltration of water from the surface into the soil and other rock materials that lie directly below the surface, (2) the downward movement of the water through the materials that comprise the zone of aeration, and (3) the delivery of a part of the water to the water table, where it enters the zone of saturation and becomes ground water or plerotic water. A part of the water that seeps into the zone of aeration is returned to the surface or into the atmosphere by evaporation and transpiration and consequently is lost so far as ground-water recharge is concerned.

Infiltration is produced by the joint action of two forces—molecular attraction and gravity. As has been explained by Buckingham [6], Haines [10], Veihmeyer [47], and others [35, 36], the molecular attraction is expressed as a potential gradient wherever the soil moisture is not in equilibrium.   When a drop of water touches the top of relatively dry soil a large potential gradient is established, and hence the water is pulled in rapidly, the mere weight of the water being of secondary importance in causing infiltration.   After the upper part of the soil has become moistened the molecular attraction becomes less effective, and infiltration is produced more largely by gravity.   The rate of infiltration then becomes more largely a function of the permeability of the soil.

The belt of soil moisture is of essential importance to the vegetable kingdom as the reservoir from which the plants draw their water supply. The storage is in moisture that is held by molecular attraction with relative effectiveness against the pull of gravity but only partly against the absorptive power of the roots of the plants.   Throughout the growing season the moisture supply in this soil reservoir is depleted by the constant draft made by the plants and is replenished from time to time by the rains or by irrigation.   Thus the belt of soil moisture functions as a formidable hindrance to ground-water recharge.   It is like an upstream reservoir that in general must be filled before water will pass through it to the downstream reservoirs, which in this case are the aquifers of the underlying terrane.

When the supply of soil moisture in a given place is fully replenished, any additional water received from the surface is carried downward by gravity from the belt of soil moisture, either directly to the water table or into the intermediate belt of the zone of aeration.   As this intermediate belt is not affected appreciably by evaporation or by absorption into the roots of the plants, it normally retains as much of the water as it can hold by molecular attraction, but most of the water tends to move downward in response to gravity.

Some water may escape through the belt of soil moisture even while there is still considerable deficiency in some parts, especially through tubular openings such as are provided by decaying roots and by the holes made by worms and larger animals.   On the other hand, the soil may temporarily be wetted far beyond the limit of what is regarded as its specific retention and indeed to the point of complete saturation.

As the subsoil is in many places less permeable than the soil proper, it is likely in times of abundant infiltration to retard downward percolation and to support above it a perched zone of saturation.   Such very shallow and ephemeral zones of saturation are found in many places at times of heavy and prolonged rain or melting snow, especially in the early spring.   They generally lose water by both downward percolation and effluent seepage, and in the growing season through absorption by the roots.   Although they disappear quickly, especially when plant growth gets under way, much of the recharge of the underlying permanent zone of saturation is likely to occur during the existence of these ephemeral perched water bodies.

In cold climates where the soil freezes to depths of a few feet the frozen soil may be quite impermeable. In the spring, as the frost leaves the soil progressively from the surface downward, the thawed soil becomes saturated with the water from the rains and melted snow. When the last of the frost disappears this perched water generally sinks rapidly and may in the course of a few days provide the principal crop of ground water for the year.

The precise manner in which the water moves downward to the water table is still only imperfectly understood, although the careful investigations of a number of physicists have made contributions to the solution of this problem [6, 10, 15, 35, 36, 47]. At times when rapid recharge occurs the water doubtless fills the network of interstices and moves downward as it would in any capillary or larger tube under sufficient head. However, when such a charge of water passes it leaves behind films of water adhering to the walls of the interstices, especially in the angular spaces, and also water in interstices or groups of interstices that remained full when the capillary columns of water broke below them on account of irregularities in the network of connecting interstices. All this water is held in some manner by molecular attraction, but a considerable part of it is held only temporarily. There is considerable evidence that draining continues at a diminishing rate for a long time.

RECHARGE BY INFLUENT SEEPAGE OF STREAMS

Streams can be classed in general as influent or effluent—influent if they flow above the water table and contribute water to it; effluent if they flow at a lower level than the water table and receive contributions of ground water.

In the relatively humid eastern part of the United States nearly all streams that flow perennially or for considerable periods are effluent. In this region the recharge occurs in the interstream areas, and the streams serve as natural drainage channels that discharge the overflow of the ground-water reservoirs. The recharge occurs largely by the downward penetration of rain and snow water in the locality where it has fallen. However, if the rain falls or the snow melts faster than it can pass downward through the surface, it will flow over the surface in the direction of the slope. First it may flow in a thin, irregular sheet of water, often called overland runoff, but soon the surface water will flow together in draws or ravines and will form ephemeral streams that lead into the system of perennial streams. Thus the lower parts of the slopes and the channels of the ephemeral streams carry water for a longer period and have a greater head of water than would be produced merely by the precipitation upon them, and therefore they generally have more than average infiltration and are especially effective in producing ground-water recharge. This is a rather important aspect of the subject that has commonly been neglected by those who have argued that there is little or no recharge from rain and snow.

In the western part of the United States most of the rain and snow falls upon the mountains, whereas the intervening valleys, many of which form extensive desert plains, are generally arid. In this region most of the streams rise in the mountains, where they are fed by springs and melted snow, and they become influent where they leave their mountain canyons and flow out upon the permeable gravelly alluvial slopes of their own construction. These streams are the principal sources of ground water in the western part of the country. In the valleys adjacent to lofty mountains with heavy rain and snowfall they supply very large quantities of ground water, as in many of the valleys of California.

In the most arid intermountain valleys there is little or no recharge from the precipitation on the valley floors, but in the less arid valleys of California, where the precipitation occurs chiefly in the winter, the recharge from local rainfall penetration is appreciable, and in the humid valleys of the far Northwest the recharge by rainfall penetration is large.

Considerable recharge also occurs in the ephemeral streams or dry washes of the arid regions, which carry freshets at infrequent intervals, but if the flood waters spread over extensive desert areas they may be consumed largely in supplying moisture to the dry desert soil, and their contribution to the ground-water supply may be small.

The ground-water supply of the Great Plains, in the central part of the United States, is derived chiefly from local precipitation. As the precipitation is not great and occurs chiefly in the growing season, the recharge is generally small and perennial streams are scarce. Hence the ephemeral tributaries of the stream systems—the draws or dry washes— are much longer than in the humid region and have a greater part in ground-water recharge. In parts of the region underlain by very permeable material, however, the recharge from precipitation is relatively great. A few streams that rise in the mountains to the west and flow across the Great Plains are influent in some places and effluent in others. Some of the deeper water-bearing beds have outcrops in or near the mountains, where they receive their water supplies.

CONDITIONS THAT INFLUENCE RECHARGE

The conditions that influence the rate and amount of ground-water recharge fall into two categories—those relating to precipitation, which is the source of supply, and those relating to the intake facilities, which determine the proportion of the rain and snow water that reaches the subterranean reservoirs.

Precipitation differs greatly in quantity from place to place and is notably variable in any one place. Ground-water recharge differs still more from place to place and from time to time—not only because of differing intake facilities but also because, with the same intake facilities, the ratio of recharge to precipitation differs greatly with the amount and distribution of the precipitation and its occurrence as rain or snow.

In general the proportion of the precipitation that becomes ground water increases with the precipitation, up to a certain limit. If the precipitation occurs in light, scattered rains, it may all be absorbed by the soil; the rains that occur after the deficiency of soil moisture has been satisfied are those that count for ground-water recharge. Over much of the humid eastern part of the United States more than one-third of the precipitation becomes ground water, but in the semiarid regions the recharge may be only a few percent of the precipitation, and in extensive arid areas the amount of recharge may be exceedingly small or there may be none.

The amount of recharge in any area depends largely upon the distribution of the precipitation. A given amount of precipitation during the growing season will produce the most recharge if it occurs in a period of persistent rain that falls about as fast as it can seep into the soil. If it is distributed as occasional rains over a longer period it may be of more benefit to the crops, but little or none of the water may get through the soil to the water table. On the other hand, if it occurs in a heavy downpour of short duration, only a small part may seep into the soil and a still smaller part may reach the water table, most of the water being discharged as direct runoff. In arid regions the scant precipitation is likely to occur in sudden downpours, but these cause freshets in dry washes, which may produce recharge.

In general a much larger part of the precipitation reaches the water table in the season of dormant vegetation than in the growing season. During the summer there may be no recharge or only moderate amounts during especially rainy periods. When the vegetation becomes dormant in the autumn there is generally a deficiency of soil moisture. Successive rains remove the deficiency, progressively from the surface downward to the bottom of the belt of soil moisture, after which each rain is likely to make a substantial contribution to the ground-water supply until spring, when the growing vegetation again becomes effective in diverting soil moisture. (See Figure Xa-6.)

In cold climates the winter is largely a dormant period in which the soil becomes impermeable because of frost and the precipitation is in the form of snow. The lowest water levels in wells for the year and the most

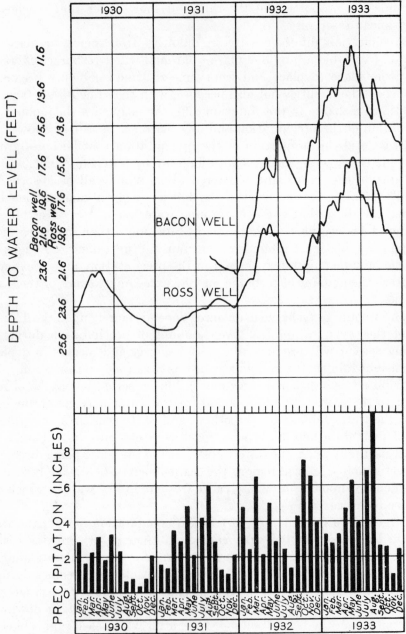

Fig. Xᴀ-6.—Graphs of water levels in two shallow wells in Virginia near Washington, D. C., showing fluctuations caused by precipitation and seasonal variations in evaporation and transpiration. The monthly precipitation is that recorded in Washington by the United States Weather Bureau. (*Data from U. S. Geol. Survey Water-Supply Paper 840.*)

trouble with failing water supplies is likely to occur about February. In the spring there is generally abundant recharge with a rather sudden rise in water levels. The amount of spring recharge depends not only on the amount of snow and of spring rain but also on the depth of frozen soil and the rate at which the snow melts. The depth of frozen soil is determined not only by the severity of the winter but also by the protection afforded by the snow cover. If the snow melts quickly before the frost has disappeared from the soil, most of the water runs off, forming a high spring freshet. On the other hand, if the soil has been largely protected from frost by deep snow and the snow melts gradually, most of the water may seep into the soil and the annual ground-water crop may be large.

The intake facilities are determined by several conditions that cause a very wide range in the percentage of precipitation that becomes ground water. The most effective of these conditions is the permeability of the terrane through which the water passes from the surface to the water table. Formations such as cavernous limestone, broken lava rock, clean gravel, or coarse sand may take in a large part of the precipitation and pass it to the water table, leaving little or no direct runoff. On the other hand, a clay formation may prevent water from going more than a few feet below the surface, except that it may sometimes receive water in large amounts through wide and deep cracks formed by drying of the clay. An impermeable formation generally has a surficial zone that has become somewhat permeable by weathering and that contains a small quantity of ground water which is supplied to shallow and unreliable wells.

The intake facilities of the soil are determined only in part by the character of the underlying formation from which the soil is derived. They are determined in part by the stage of development of the soil, the vegetation which it supports, and the kind of tillage it receives or the freedom from tillage. It appears that, as a rule, the soil which supports timber or sod has better intake facilities than similar soil which is tilled— partly because the leaf litter or grass keep the precipitated water clean, thereby preventing the puddling that may choke the interstices of tilled soil near the surface, and partly because the untilled soil preserves tubular openings formed by the roots and by worms and other burrowing animals.

The form of the land surface has a great influence on intake and hence also on ground-water recharge. In general intake is expedited in nearly level areas, such as parts of the Atlantic Coastal Plain and parts of the Great Valley of California, and in gently undulating areas with poorly developed drainage systems, such as the region covered by the most recent glacial drift. In such areas the precipitated water runs off more sluggishly than in rugged areas with well-developed drainage patterns, and consequently there is more opportunity for it to seep into the soil or rocks. There are, however, contrary tendencies if the water table is so near the surface that the underground reservoir does not have much capacity for additional storage at times of heavy and prolonged precipitation, or if the surface water moves so sluggishly that it silts up its channels.

The amount of recharge of a water-bearing formation depends largely on the extent of its intake area—that is, the area in which it lies at the surface or is covered only by permeable materials. A common fallacy is to underrate recharge from local precipitation and to look for some distant source of supply. In fact, the most productive aquifers are the permeable beds that are exposed over extensive areas, whereas artesian aquifers that lie below confining beds except along narrow belts of outcrop are obviously handicapped. The recharge is increased if the intake area receives not only the local precipitation but also the surface flow of a tributary catchment area, as is notably the case on alluvial slopes that receive surface water from large mountain areas with heavy precipitation.

The rate of recharge from influent streams is largely governed by the condition of the stream beds. Even though the underlying material is very permeable the stream may not lose much water, because its channel has been rendered impermeable by silting or by deposition of lime or other precipitate. The loss from surface reservoirs and irrigation canals generally diminishes with use as a result of silting. Natural streams, however, are subject to floods, which from time to time scour out the silt and precipitate and renew the recharge capacity of the streams. Surface reservoirs that regulate the flow of the streams may tend to prevent such rejuvenation. On the other hand, a prolonged flow of clear water may remove the silt and may thereby develop a permeable sandy bottom.

Artificial recharge

Wells have long been used in some localities to drain swampy land and unfortunately also to dispose of sewage and other waste water. The concept that the rock formations are reservoirs and that water can be stored for future use by discharging it into wells or letting it seep into the soil or gravelly valley floors has been regarded until recently as a novel idea, directly contrary to the usual idea that water which seeps into the earth is lost. It is, however, a fundamental concept in the conservation of the available water supplies and has been applied in various experiments in places where the supply of ground water has become depleted by heavy pumping—notably in Sweden, Germany, and other European countries to increase the water supplies for certain cities and in this country to increase the irrigation supplies. In recent years many experiments in artificial recharge by spreading surface water have been made in different areas in California and in other parts of this country, and the subject has received much popular attention and also considerable investigation. The best results have been obtained where the water is clear and is under control so that it can be applied in the most favorable localities and at the proper rate. Notably successful has been the underground storage of surplus water from the Owens Valley Aqueduct in the San Fernando Valley, California. In some of the European projects the conditions are so definitely controlled and the operations are so local that the artificial recharge approaches sand filtration in character. The subject has recently been treated thoroughly by Mitchelson and Muckel [30].

Recharge through wells is most successful in cavernous rocks, because formations with small interstices are likely to become clogged by particles carried in suspension or by algal or bacterial growths. On Long Island the attempt is being made to return the water pumped from beds of sand and gravel for air conditioning without giving it any access to the air, but even with this protection there is considerable clogging—probably for the most part by the particles of sand and silt that are pumped with the water out of the producing wells. Especially promising are projects for recharging aquifers from which water is pumped for air conditioning or other cooling purposes, by introducing clear, cold surface water during the winter—either through recharge wells or through producing wells that may be idle during the winter.

In many areas the physical conditions or economic limitations are such that it will not be practicable to augment the ground-water supply by artificial recharge. In certain localities, however, the water has relatively high value, and the conditions are favorable for conducting it in large quantities into the underground reservoirs at low unit cost, and in many of these localities artificial recharge will doubtless become established practice. Closely related are the questions as to the effects of different kinds of land use and soil conservation upon the amount of ground-water recharge and hence upon the water supplies from wells, springs, and streams.

METHODS OF DETERMINING RECHARGE

The principal methods of determining the amount of recharge are by (1) the use of lysimeters, (2) determining the amount of precipitation on a drainage basin and deducting the runoff and evaporation losses, (3) making periodic determinations of soil moisture at different depths, (4) observing the fluctuations of the water table and applying a factor for specific yield, and (5) determining the decrease in flow of influent streams between gaging stations. For convenience these may be called, respectively, the lysimeter, general inventory, soil-moisture inventory, water-table, and influent-seepage methods.

Many attempts have been made to measure directly the percolation from the surface to the water table. Mariotté, in the seventeenth century, observed the percolation of rain water into the cellar of the Paris Observatory. Measurements of percolation have been made with lysimeters, or vessels to catch the downward-percolating water, by several European and American investigators [46], and some very long records have been obtained in England [46, pp. 32–34, 44–49]. The first tests mentioned by Veatch were made by Dalton in Manchester, England, from 1796 to 1798, and by Maurice in Geneva, Switzerland, in 1796 and 1797. The longest record, that of Dickinson and Evans, in Hempel Hempstead, in England, extended over at least 49 years, from 1835 to 1884, and the records of Lawes and Gilbert and those of Greaves extended over 32 and 22 years, respectively.

Many of the lysimeter tests have been made with disturbed materials and under other artificial conditions, which may have produced results very different from those that would be found under natural conditions. Moreover, downward percolation is irregularly distributed, and it may be difficult to find a place for the test that is even approximately representative of average conditions. An extensive area may have little or no recharge except at a few places where water may be pouring into the zone of saturation in large volumes.

Tests by Blaney and C. A. Taylor [3] in California indicate that water percolating downward through unsaturated material tends to move around any vessel that is placed underground to catch it. If the material extends downward into the vessel, as in tests made by White [44] in Texas, the percolating water will accumulate in the capillary openings of the material in the vessel and can be detected by laboratory determination of the increase in moisture content of that material. However, unless the material lies within the vessel to a height exceeding the capillary range, no water may drain out of the material into the vessel even though recharge is occurring. These conditions have been explained in a paper by G. H. Taylor [44].

The earliest attempts to determine the rate of ground-water recharge were probably those of Perrault and Mariotté in the drainage basin of the Seine River in the seventeenth century. In the years that have elapsed since their work the most common method of estimating ground-water recharge has probably been to determine approximately the quantity of water that annually falls as rain or snow on a given area and to apply to this quantity the percentage that is assumed to reach the zone of saturation. Such procedure is of little value, however, except to give an idea of the maximum possibilities, unless there is a reliable basis for the assumed percentage. The method of deducting runoff and evaporation losses from precipitation may give fairly reliable results if the recharge is relatively large, as in some limestone and basalt terranes, but is inapplicable if the amount of recharge is of the order of magnitude of the probable errors in the other quantities. This method gave useful results as applied by McCombs [22, pp. 55–61] and Kunesh [17, pp. 85–92] in estimating the ground-water supply of the island of Oahu, where fairly accurate data as to precipitation and runoff are available and where the intake facilities are so good that a large proportion of the precipitation seeps into the rocks and percolates to the water table.

A detailed inventory was made by Blaney [34, pp. 152–157] of the water supply in certain intake areas in southern California. From the quantity of water produced by each rain during the winter rainy season were deducted the carefully estimated quantities of runoff produced by the rain and of evaporation and transpiration during the subsequent period of fair weather [3, pp. 87–104]. Borings and tests of soil moisture proved that the remaining water was stored in the soil to satisfy the deficiency of soil moisture in the root zone. After this deficiency had been completely supplied and the soil moisture had been brought up to the specific retention, any remaining surplus was assumed to percolate downward beyond the plant roots and ultimately to reach the water table. Where an impermeable bed intervened between the root zone and the water table, the downward-percolating water would necessarily form a body of perched ground water above the impermeable bed. Intensive inventory studies have also been made by Stearns, Robinson, Taylor, Piper, and others [31; 40, pp. 172–206] in the Mokelumne area, in California, in which the soil moisture was determined at intervals during the winter for each foot to depths below the root zone, and thus data were obtained as to replenishment of the soil moisture, evaporation from the soil, and deep percolation.

The most generally used and most widely applicable method of determining recharge is that based on the rise of the water levels in wells. Accurate records of water-level fluctuations are now obtained in the United States by means of automatic water-stage recorders in several hundred observation wells and periodic measurements in many thousands of wells. In order to use these records to compute recharge it is necessary (1) to know whether the rise in water level in the well represents a similar rise in the water table or is produced by some other cause, and (2) to have a fairly reliable factor of specific yield to apply. Artesian wells are likely to have large fluctuations that are due to pressure effects not related to replenishment from the surface. Even in the wells that extend only slightly below the water table and are called water-table wells, the fluctuations of the water levels do not always represent similar movements of the water table itself. In fine-grained materials of low specific yield the water table is likely to rise notably in wet periods, but the quantity of water that is taken into storage in such periods and is later available to sustain the stream flow may be surprisingly small.

A rise in the water table does not register the total recharge but rather the excess of recharge over discharge. Where the water table lies at considerable depth the water from the surface may arrive at the water table at a relatively constant rate and may be more or less continuously offset by the percolation out of the area. Under such conditions the slight fluctuations may register only a small part of the actual recharge.

The influent-seepage method consists of establishing gaging stations on influent streams and determining the quantities of water lost between successive stations. The quantity of water that reaches the water table consists of this loss minus the loss by evaporation and transpiration either directly from the stream or from soil moisture supplied by the stream. The method has been used in many ground-water investigations in the western mountain region. One of the most intensive studies of this method was made by Bailey [2, pp. 95–131] in his work on ground-water recharge in the Niles cone, California, by seepage from Alameda Creek. Bailey undertook to determine the daily recharge, which required accurate data on changes in channel storage with changes in gage heights. He also investigated the relation of rate of recharge to the temperature of the water and to the duration of high stages of the river. Ultimately he developed curves to show the relation of rate of seepage to rate of stream flow and produced an empirical formula by which the recharge in any day can be computed from the records of stream flow and temperature. Intensive use of the seepage method has been made by Conkling [8, pp. 52–72] in the drainage basin of the San Gabriel River, by Post [34] in the drainage basin of the Santa Ana River, and by Stearns, Robinson, Taylor, Piper and others [31, 40] on the Mokelumne River, all in California.

The most reliable results obtained by the influent-seepage method are those for streams with relatively constant flow and large losses in proportion to the total flow. The method is generally not applicable in times of flood, when the measurements of flow are relatively inaccurate and the percentage of loss is small. It is only difficultly applicable to perennial streams in which the loss is small in comparison to the total flow. As applied to ephemeral streams it presents two difficulties—the storm runoff is too flashy to be measured accurately, and a considerable part of the water lost by seepage may not reach the water table but may ultimately be returned to the atmosphere [49, pp. 77–80].

INFLOW AND CONDENSATION OF ATMOSPHERIC VAPOR

The openings in the soils and rock above the zone of saturation, whether consisting of small pores or great caverns, are largely filled with air that is in communication with the outside atmosphere. This interstitial air is more or less in motion, and interchange occurs between it and the outside atmosphere. The flow of air into or out from rock formations is most conspicuous in wind caves and in blowing or breathing wells, but it doubtless also occurs extensively in a less noticeable manner.

Blowing and breathing wells are found in many parts of the United States. They attract much attention because of their peculiar behavior and in the northern part of the country by the freezing that is caused in them through the inflow of cold air, sometimes at depths of more than 100 feet. They are described in numerous publications, as, for example, in a paper by Condra [7, pp. 41–42]. Practically all the writers who discuss the phenomena agree that, although various causes may be effective in certain wells, the principal cause of blowing or breathing consists of changes in the pressure of the atmosphere. As a rule such a well passes first through a cover of dense material and then into an underlying bed of limestone, gravel, sand or other permeable but unsaturated material that is not effectively cased off. Considerable movement of air into and out from the rocks may also be caused by fluctuations of the water table. Thus blowing has been reported in certain wells in Quincy Valley, Wash., during periods of rapid rise of the water table caused by ground-water recharge.

Whenever air flows into or out from the soil or rocks it carries with it some water in the form of invisible vapor. Whenever unsaturated air enters interstices that contain liquid water it acquires some of the water by evaporation until it becomes saturated or until the supply of liquid water has been reduced to the exceedingly thin film that constitutes the hygroscopic water. If the temperature of the interstitial air is increased, as commonly happens in the soil near the surface on hot, sunny days, its relative humidity is decreased and it is likely to acquire much additional water vapor. If later this interstitial air flows out of the interstices into the atmosphere, it is effective in removing water from the soil.

On the other hand, air flowing through interstices of soil or rocks may deposit water that is carried into them from the atmosphere. The interstices may be so dry that they will acquire hygroscopic moisture from the vapor in the air even when the air is not saturated, but this would in general occur only when the soil moisture is so greatly depleted that permanent wilting occurs in the plants. The air may enter at a temperature higher than that of the soil or rocks through which it subsequently flows and may become cooled below the dew point, when condensation and deposition of water may take place. This would in general occur only in the summer, when the air is warmer than the rocks. Moreover, the air may conceivably contain particles of liquid water when it enters, and these may adhere to the walls of the interstices as the air flows through them.

The processes of give and take that have been outlined occur at very different rates under the diverse conditions that are found in nature, and it is difficult to estimate their relative importance or their net result in contributing water to or removing it from the soil and rocks. That soil water is lost in great quantities by evaporation is a familiar fact. This loss is due largely to interstitial evaporation and subsequent ouflow of the water vapor. There is not much information as to the extent to which evaporation occurs at considerable depths in the zone of aeration. The movement of air involved in the blowing and breathing phenomena through natural openings in some terranes may well have a tendency to dry out the rocks at considerable depths, especially in arid regions, where the relative humidity of the atmosphere is generally low.

In the United States hydrologists have so completely accepted the theory that practically all available ground water is derived from infiltration of surface water that it is surprising to find that the condensation theory is still actively discussed in European countries and that it receives considerable support from some of the European hydrologists. According to this theory the ground water is derived, wholly or in large part, by subterranean condensation of water vapor in the air that circulates through the interstices of the soil and rocks. To strengthen the general theory, it has been suggested that the air which enters the rocks frequently carries fog with it, and that the droplets of liquid water constituting the fog are deposited in the interstices. The excellent textbook on ground water by Keilhack [16, pp. 74–82], gives serious consideration to this theory, states that some advocates of the theory maintain that ground water is derived exclusively from the condensation of water vapor in the subterranean atmosphere, cites a number of authorities who hold more or less fully to the theory, and describes briefly the observations and experiments that are believed to give evidence favorable to it. The principal lines of evidence are derived from (1) experiments purporting to show the process of subterranean condensation, (2) structurally and topographically isolated areas in which the discharge from springs is believed to be greater than can be explained by the precipitation upon the area, and (3) the rise of water levels in wells before rainfall occurs. The argument is also advanced that the ground water is clear, whereas the surface water is often turbid, and that the rocks through which the water percolates cannot be assumed to be eternally effective as a filter. Ice caves are also cited as an argument in favor of the theory. A sort of still was devised by Herman Haedicke in which water from the air was condensed as it passed through sand that was continuously refrigerated. He also found that some water collected in a vessel buried in gravel and sand above the water level in a shallow well [16, p. 447]. His results do not seem to be convincing. Evidence is presented that the water levels rise in wells prior to any rain at times of southerly winds and in warm cloudy weather. This evidence is regarded by Keilhack and others as indicating recharge by condensation, because the air at such times has high relative humidity and is warmer than the underlying soil and rocks. From studies in this country, however, it appears that such conclusions are not valid and that the rise in water levels is very probably due to low atmospheric pressure upon the water surfaces in the wells.

Several examples are cited of springs whose catchment areas appear too small to obtain the requisite amount of rainfall or are underlain by apparently impermeable beds. Keilhack points out, however, that these examples are not supported by adequate quantitative data as to precipitation and discharge. Springs have frequently been reported on the tops of hills or mountains in this country, but no such spring is known which, upon investigation, could not be adequately explained by precipitation at higher levels. An example is afforded by the springs in the Big Meadows, in the Shenandoah National Park, in Virginia. These springs are on the top of the Blue Ridge, and their source of supply was regarded as a mystery until an investigation by the United States Geological Survey demonstrated the existence of a drainage basin that is adequate to supply them.

A quantitative analysis of the possible rates of ground-water recharge by movement of water vapor in the zone of aeration was made by H. L. Penman and R. K. Schofield, of Great Britain, for the assembly of the International Association of Hydrology in Washington in 1939. The conclusion was reached that, except in the superficial layer from which evaporation into the atmosphere takes place, the diffusion of water vapor through the zone of aeration makes a negligible contribution to the water circulation, and also that the amount of water moved as vapor in the breathing action caused by changes in temperature and barometric pressure is quite negligible.

The evidence and arguments advanced for the condensation theory do not seem convincing, and the difficulties with respect to the volume of air that would have to circulate through the rocks and the amounts of cooling that would have to be performed by them seem to make the theory untenable. Moreover, except perhaps to an insignificant extent, the process has not been observed in caves, where it ought to be subject to observation. Although an open mind should be maintained regarding new theories, it seems unfortunate to continue to confuse the subject of ground-water recharge with a theory that has so little to support it and is inherently so improbable.

CONNATE WATER AND INFLOWING SEA WATER

Most sedimentary formations and some lavas were deposited in the sea or in some other body of water. If such a formation was later brought above the water level and so situated as to form a part of a circulatory system of ground water, its original water was gradually displaced by water from the surface. Otherwise the water may have moved very sluggishly, and some of the original water may still be in the formation even though the formation is very old. For such original water the term "connate water" was proposed by Lane [18, pp. 501–512], who advocated the theory that the deep-seated, highly mineralized water in the Lake Superior region is connate.

The Paleozoic formations between the Appalachian Mountains and the Great Plains probably afford as good evidence of the existence of connate water as is found in any other region. For the most part, where these formations contain salty water they lie nearly horizontal, far below the water table and largely below sea level, and the geologic history of the region indicates they have probably always lain at low levels, where effective ground-water circulation was not promoted. Salt water is commonly associated with natural oil and gas. Obviously the oil and gas must have been effectively entrapped, for otherwise they would have been dissipated long ago by natural processes. It is reasonable to suppose that the associated salty water has also been entrapped.

One of the apparent defects in the theory of connate water is that the dissolved solids do not generally occur in the ground water in even approximately the same proportions or concentrations as in ocean water. These differences have been explained by assuming (1) admixture of other ground waters, (2) dissolving of additional soluble substances from the rocks or chemical reactions between the matter in solution and the minerals composing the rocks, or (3) change in the composition of ocean water in the course of the long ages since the deposition of the formations that contain the salty water.

WATER OF DEHYDRATION

One of the common processes in the weathering of rocks is hydration, which is a chemical combination of water with mineral matter whereby new minerals are formed. A familiar example is the chemical combination of water and oxygen with iron to form iron rust. Van Hise [45, p. 162] stated that the amount of water which is thus fixed in the rocks by the process of hydration is very great. Under conditions of high temperature and pressure, such as are found at great depths, the hydrous minerals are likely to be dehydrated, thus liberating hydrogen and oxygen in the form of water. A familiar example of this process is the production of red bricks by burning yellow clay, the yellow hydrous iron compound disseminated through the clay being converted by the heat into a red anhydrous compound and water being driven off.

WATER OF INTERNAL ORIGIN

Water that occurs within the depths reached in wells and mines is found in the interstices or void spaces of the rocks. Farther in the interior of the earth the pressure due to the weight of the overlying rocks becomes so great that it is impossible for interstices to exist. The temperature also increases with increasing depth, and far in the interior it is doubtless very great. It is believed that under such conditions of temperature and pressure the mineral constituents form a sort of solution known as a rock magma and that, among the constituents in the solution is water or one or both of the elements of which water is composed. Thus, although there is doubtless a downward limit to the occurrence of liquid water in rock interstices, there may be no limit or only a much deeper limit to its occurrence in another form.

Before the laws of physics, chemistry, and geology were well understood vague theories were devised to account for ground water by mysterious emanations from the interior of the earth. When these sciences were developed, however, and when the principles set forth by Mariotté became well established and the intake of water from the surface came to be thoroughly understood, the theories as to internal sources of water were brushed aside and even the water ejected from volcanoes was regarded as water of external origin that had been entrapped or absorbed by the lava. More recently there has been a strong trend toward the theory that in part the water emitted by volcanoes is of internal origin in the same sense that the rest of the lava is of internal origin, and, moreover, that water is emitted by magmas which do not reach the surface, some of the water of hot springs being regarded as of such origin. The special exponent of the theory of juvenile water was Suess [43, pp. 133–150], whose principal paper on the subject was published in 1902. The question of the origin of ground water is closely related to that of the genesis of metalliferous deposits. Thus the students of ore deposits came from various vague theories to a clear understanding of the important functions of circulating ground water and later to a belief also in the importance of magmatic segregation, which involves the segregation of water from the magma.

Igneous rocks give evidence of the production of water of internal origin from structural features that record events of the past, whereas volcanoes and hot springs give evidence from processes that are now in progress. Many of the crystals of igneous rocks, especially the quartz crystals, contain minute hermetically sealed cavities containing water that was presumably present in the magma from which the crystals were formed. Quartz is known to be one of the last minerals to crystallize out of a magma, and water appears to be a residual product of the slow solidification of the magma. Hence the quartz crystals are likely to be formed in the presence of water, and it is not surprising that they should be especially rich in included water. Fossil evidence of another kind is afforded by the structure of some intrusive granitic rocks that are intimately related to and grade into quartz veins deposited by water. Evidence of this kind is set forth by Lindgren [20, p. 94] as follows:

"The best general evidence of the existence of juvenile waters is furnished, not by observation of the present springs but by the study of old intrusive regions. Here the granites merge into pegmatite dikes, the latter change into pegmatite quartz, and this into veins carrying quartz and metallic ores, such as cassiterite and wolframite. Here we have evidence difficult to controvert that dikes consolidated from magmas gradually turn into deposits the structure and minerals of which testify to purely aqueous deposition. This admitted, it is difficult to see what would prevent such waters from reaching the surface."

The work of Allen and Day [1, 9] has produced rather conclusive evidence that the water of some of the hot springs is in part juvenile water.

DISCHARGE OF GROUND WATER

GENERAL CONDITIONS

Water is discharged from the zone of saturation by the hydraulic process, or discharge through springs, and by the less conspicuous but equally effective process of evaporation, including both evaporation from the soil and transpiration of plants in areas having a shallow water table.

In most of the terranes in the eastern part of the United States, where the climate is relatively humid, the main streams receive water from numerous branches, which are fed by effluent seepage at many points and which gradually increase in flow downstream. In the limestone terranes, however, there are generally only a few spring-fed branches, and these rise in bold springs—that is, springs that flow freely from a few large openings. In the areas covered by the latest glacial drift the stream systems are only poorly developed, and hence the water table stands high and there are many swampy tracts except where they have been drained artificially. In these poorly drained areas the discharge of ground water by evaporation (including transpiration) is relatively large, whereas in most limestone areas it is relatively small.

In an approximate inventory of the water supply of the drainage basin of the Pomperaug River in Connecticut during a 3-year period [26, pp. 114–124] the average annual precipitation was computed to be about 44.5 inches and the average annual ground-water recharge about 15.6 inches, of which an average of about 8.7 inches was discharged as effluent seepage or ground-water runoff and 6.2 inches as ground-water evaporation (including transpiration), whereas an average of 0.6 inch was added to the ground-water storage during the period. From November to April the ground-water discharge was nearly all effected by effluent seepage, but from May to October less than one-third was due to effluent seepage, the rest being due to evaporation (including transpiration).

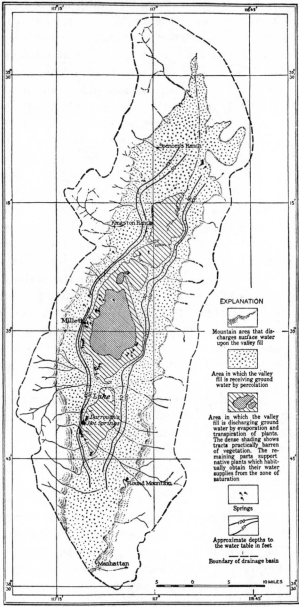

FIG. XA-7.—Map of the northern drainage basin of Big Smoky Valley, Nev., showing intake and discharge of ground water. (*After U. S. Geol. Survey Water-Supply Paper* 836-D.)

Toward the less humid parts of the country the rate of ground-water recharge and consequently also the rate of ground-water discharge decrease more rapidly than the precipitation, and the rate of ground-water runoff decreases still more rapidly, because the proportion of discharge by evaporation increases. Consequently in the Great Plains springs are scarce and small except in a few areas that have especially favorable geologic structure. In the drainage basin of the Tarkio River, in southwestern Iowa, during a period of 4 years, the average annual precipitation was computed to be 27 inches and the average annual ground-water runoff only 0.5 inch.

Over large plateau areas in the western mountain region springs and streams are lacking or very scarce. In the high mountains of that region however, there are many streams that are fed perennially or during large parts of each year by springs or by melted snow. The mountain springs are of many kinds, but they are largely seepage springs that discharge water from the surficial materials overlying relatively impermeable rock.

After the streams leave the mountains they flow down over their alluvial fans and lose all or a large part of their water by influent seepage. A large proportion of the intermountain valleys have closed drainage basins. With respect to ground-water discharge, these closed basins are of two kinds—(1) those which lose all their ground water by subterranean leakage out of the basin, the water table being at considerable depth even in the lowest places, and (2) those in which the water table is at or near the surface in the low central areas and in which ground water is discharged in part by springs but generally in much greater quantities through evaporation, including transpiration. (See Fig. XA-7.) Basins of the second class are the most numerous, and economically they are by far the most important. The playas, which occupy the lowest parts of the basins, are underlain by nearly impermeable clay that permits only a small amount of upward percolation. Near the margins of the playas there are commonly belts of springs that discharge the overflow of the underground reservoir. Surrounding the playas are broad belts of characteristic desert plants, called phreatophytes, which habitually obtain their water supplies by sending their roots down to the water table.

Springs

Springs have been of great interest and fascination for mankind since the beginning of human history and doubtless since the beginning of the human race. They occur in great variety, with many spectacular features. Their origin has appeared mysterious and indeed providential; they are generally surrounded with verdure; they give rise to the "living" streams; and for ages they have been the sources of the cleanest and most attractive water supplies available to man. The lore as to the healing properties of spring waters is of ancient origin and is deep-seated in human thought. Since the beginning of geology they have been of great scientific interest because of their close relation to rock stratigraphy and structure and to the changes that have taken place within the rocks. Thus it is not surprising that springs have been given scientific and pseudoscientific study from a number of viewpoints. The subject can here be covered only in brief outline.

Spring openings

Springs differ greatly in the size and number of the openings through which the water issues, the areas over which the openings are distributed, and the rate at which the water flows out of them. Springs that ooze or percolate out of many small openings are generally called seepage springs. They may discharge so little water that they are hardly noticeable. Their water may flow only a short distance or may scarcely wet the ground before it evaporates. They are true springs, however, if their water flows out upon the surface by hydrostatic pressure, as distinguished from moist areas in which the water reaches the surface by capillarity. A seepage spring may flow at night or on a cool cloudy day but may stop entirely on a hot sunny day, when evaporation is so great that the water table retreats below the surface. Effluent seepage occurs over extensive lowland tracts commonly called seepage areas. The amount of ground-water discharge of this kind is generally underestimated. The large springs that issue from definite openings naturally attract attention, but a great part of the total ground-water runoff comes from inconspicuous but widespread seepage.

If a seepage area is examined closely it is usually found, however, that most of the water comes from certain localities and that the intervening parts of the area contribute relatively little. This partial localization of the discharge is due in part to similar localization in the routes followed by the water through the formation and in part to the development of discharge conduits near the surface. The concept that ground water moves uniformly through the entire mass of a formation is somewhat inaccurate except for the best-assorted granular deposits. Near the surface these avenues of ground-water movement are further opened by weathering processes and to some extent by the work of the escaping water in carrying out the finer sediments, not unlike the process of developing a gravel screen around the intake of a well by vigorous pumping.

The hard and compact rocks generally give rise to springs that are more definite and more localized. These springs generally issue from joints or large fissures or fissure zones, which have been cleaned out and enlarged by the percolating water. They are commonly called fissure springs or fracture springs. In limestones and other soluble rocks the passages along which the water percolates are enlarged by the solvent action of the water, in some places forming great underground drainage systems, with huge springs issuing from great natural tunnels. Springs that issue from tubelike openings are commonly called tubular springs.

Forces producing springs

Springs have been divided by Bryan [5, pp. 557] into (1) springs due to gravitative pressure transmitted through a continuous body of ground water and (2) springs of deep origin flowing as the result of agencies other than gravity, operative deep within the earth, largely the expulsion of water during the crystallization of igneous rocks. The second class he divided into two subclasses—(1) springs associated with volcanism or volcanic rocks and (2) springs due to faults or fissures extending deep into the earth.

Altogether the following agencies are probably concerned in bringing water to the surface:

Gravity acting more or less directly on the water:
    Causing ground water to descend to the springs.
    Causing water in artesian systems to rise to the springs.
Nongravitative forces or forces only indirectly due to gravity:
    Due to the heat of the earth:
        Decreasing the specific gravity of the water that percolates to considerable depths
        in artesian systems.
        Producing steam.
    Due to gases associated with the ground water:
        Exerting pressure.
        Decreasing the specific gravity of the water and gas mixture.
    Due to the weight of overlying rocks, which compresses porous formations and expels
    water from them.
    Due to expulsion from solidifying magmas.

Rock structure in relation to springs

On account of the complicated structure of the rocks there is great irregularity in the distribution, size, and character of the springs. All that is known of the stratigraphy and structure of a region must be requisitioned to explain its springs, and at best the subject is likely to involve uncertainty because the details of the geology can be only imperfectly ascertained. The difficulties of determining the structure that produces springs are due in part to poor exposure of the rocks in the vicinity of many springs and in part to the tendency of the water in many places to percolate considerable distances through surficial deposits after it leaves the rock structure that is essential in bringing it near the surface. The poor exposures are due to unusual amounts of weathering and plant growth, to precipitates from the spring water, to accumulations of wind-blown dust and sand in the moist spring areas, and to accumulations of talus and alluvium in the low places where springs commonly emerge. Generally the cause of a spring is found by inference after studying the geology of the surrounding country rather than by direct observation of the rocks from which the water emerges.

Bryan divided the springs produced by gravity into the following four groups:

Depression springs, due to the land surface cutting the water table in permeable rocks.

Contact springs, due to permeable water-bearing rock overlying relatively impermeable rock.

Artesian springs, due to a permeable water-bearing bed between relatively impermeable confining beds.

Springs in impermeable rocks (tubular and fracture springs).

Each of these four groups is subdivided further, the subdivision of the large group called contact springs being especially detailed. Keilhack and other authors have made classifications that differ more or less from those of Bryan.

Topographic and geologic features produced by springs

The location of springs in any region is determined by the topography and structure of the region. On the other hand, when the springs come into existence they are likely to develop minor topographic and geologic features by their own activity. Ground water is ever active as an agent of erosion, deposition, or replacement, and its activity is greatly intensified at or near the points where it is discharged through springs. The features produced by springs are of two general types—the destructional features, or those produced by erosion, and the constructional features, or those produced by deposition.

As a rule, the streams issuing from springs are not so effective in erosion as those that carry more or less direct runoff, for the following reasons: (1) They are nearly devoid of suspended matter, whereas ordinary streams accomplish most of their erosion by means of the sand grains, pebbles, and boulders which they carry in suspension or roll along the stream beds; (2) they fluctuate less and hence do not exert the destructive energy characteristic of streams in flood; and (3) their water is commonly more mineralized and may tend to deposit mineral matter rather than to dissolve it. Erosion features are of two principal types—(1) channels or valleys eroded by the spring water at the point of discharge or as it flows over the surface after it has been discharged, and (2) deep pools that form the vents from which the ground water flows.

Many of the springs that are not depositing mineral matter issue from the heads of alcoves, channels, or ravines that have been excavated by the spring water. Springs in limestones or gypsum may issue from large and definite tunnels that were formed by the solvent action of the spring water. Remarkable alcoves, or "box canyons," in lava rock open into the canyon of the Snake River, in southern Idaho, and have very large springs at their heads. These features were described by I. C. Russell and have been studied more recently by Stearns [41, pp. 141–151], who believes that they were produced by gradual solution of the basalt by the spring water. Three of these—Blue Lake Canyon, Box Canyon, and Little Canyon—have no streams entering them from the adjacent uplands and can therefore not be accounted for except by the erosive work of their springs.

Many springs consist of deep pools that overflow and are perpetually replenished from beneath. The water in these pools is generally very clear, and the bottom of some of the pools is distinctly visible. In some pools the water has a beautiful bluish color due to effects produced by minute particles held in suspension. Hence the common name "Blue Springs." Some of the pools are inhabited by fish that can readily be seen in the clear water and have in some places given rise to the name "Fish Springs." Many pools are reported to be remarkably deep, but frequently the depth is greatly exaggerated. Spring pools are formed in different ways, and the origin of some is not fully understood. Some occupy the centers of spring-built mounds and thus are features of deposition rather than of erosion, but very commonly they are excavated out of the older formation. Some are found in limestone terranes and are generally due to the solvent action of ground water that rises through crevices from some deeper source or to sinkholes formed at a time when the water level was lower. Many of the distinctive spring pools, however, are not found in limestone or other indurated rocks but in relatively unconsolidated material. Thus, spring pools with a pronounced family resemblance occur in great numbers in some of the intermontane valleys in the western part of the United States.

Spring pools that do not have enough head to discharge water at the surface are, strictly, not springs at all. If they are associated with pools that discharge they are commonly regarded as springs; if they are not near true springs, are deep and steep-sided, and have relatively small water surfaces, they may be called natural wells; if their sides are less precipitous and they have relatively large water surfaces they are regarded merely as ponds or lakes.

Natural wells or spring pools that do not discharge are of two general types. One type consists of pools that formerly discharged and that may have been developed in the same manner as the pools that still discharge. They generally occupy more or less definite mounds, and the subsidence of their water levels is generally due to new avenues of escape which the spring water has found at a lower level. The other type consists of holes that extend down into the zone of saturation but were not developed by the discharge of ground water and never served as outlets for springs. The most common spring pools of this type are sinkholes in limestone or gypsum, such as the St. Jacobs well, in Kansas, but holes that expose the water table without giving a channel of escape to the ground water may also be produced by the wind, by streams, or by other surface agencies of erosion. Huge natural wells are also found in lava beds where lava tunnels extend into the zone of saturation.

Many springs are agents of deposition and have built mounds or terraces. The deposits consist largely of chemical precipitates from the spring water but partly of the remains of vegetation that flourished in the vicinity of the springs and of wind-borne material that has been arrested by the vegetation and held by the moisture in the spring localities. Spring mounds and terraces are abundant in the western part of the United States, where most of the thermal springs and other ascending springs that deposit such mineral matter are situated and where the climate is favorable to wind work.

When ground water emerges at the surface its environment is greatly changed, which results in disturbances in the chemical equilibrium of the substances in solution and frequently in the precipitation of chemical compounds. The principal changes that cause such precipitation are reduction in pressure, lowering of temperature, freedom to evaporate, contact with the oxygen of the atmosphere, contact with algae and other organisms, and contact with surface water of different chemical composition.

The deposits built by the precipitates from spring water assume various shapes that are controlled by the preexisting topography and other conditions. For the most part the deposits assume the shape of either terraces or mounds, the terraces being formed chiefly on sloping surfaces and the mounds on nearly level surfaces. Where springs that deposit calcium carbonate discharge into narrow valleys they may form travertine masses that dam the valley and produce rapids or falls. The travertine obstruction may be formed either at the spring or at some point farther downstream where there are preexisting riffles or rapids that expedite the deposition of calcium carbonate. Such rapids and falls, with the impounded reaches above them, are essentially modified spring terraces. Very beautiful and unusual features are formed by some of the springs that emerge below the surfaces of lakes and other bodies of water. Instead of building low, compact deposits, such as are formed by springs on land, these sublacustral springs tend to produce tall, graceful tubular deposits of various fantastic shapes. Such features in Mono Lake, Calif., and Pyramid Lake, Nev., have been described by Russell [35a].

On arid plains many spring deposits are built by the aid of the wind. In the vicinity of the spring the soil is moist and supports bushes or reeds that extend above the surrounding desert and break the wind, causing it to drop some of its load of sand or dust, where the material becomes moist and hence is not readily picked up again by the wind. Thus a spring on an arid plain is a veritable trap for wind-borne material.

Thermal springs

In 1937 the Geological Survey published a comprehensive report on the thermal springs in the United States by N. D. Stearns, H. T. Stearns, and G. A. Waring [42, pp. 59–190]. The following statements are largely digested from that paper. It appears that the earliest extensive studies of thermal springs in the United States were made by physicians. In 1831 Dr. John Bell issued a book entitled "Baths and mineral waters," in which he listed 21 spring localities. In the edition of this work published in 1855 the number was increased to 181. The earliest report on a geologic study of thermal springs was that of W. B. Rogers in 1840 on the thermal springs of Virginia. In 1875 G. K. Gilbert published a map and a table showing thermal springs in the United States and pointed out that they are present chiefly in the mountainous area of folded and faulted rocks. The first publication on thermal springs by A. C. Peale appeared in 1883, and others appeared in 1886 and 1894. Since that time a considerable number of papers dealing with thermal springs have appeared, some of them by geologists, such as Emmons, Lindgren, and Weed, who are interested in thermal springs in relation to ore deposits, and some by volcanologists, who are interested in the relations of thermal springs to problems of volcanic action. Especially valuable are the studies of Day and Allen in California and Yellowstone Park [1, 9].

The two main phases of the problem of the origin of thermal springs are the source of the water and the source of the heat. The water may be ordinary ground water that percolates downward, is heated, and then ascends to the surface; it may be juvenile—that is, a product from the magma itself which has reached the surface for the first time; or it may be a mixture of ordinary ground water and juvenile water in any proportion. The latest investigations indicate that the thermal springs in the eastern part of the United States discharge water that was originally derived from the surface and received its high temperature by deep percolation, but that the thermal springs in Yellowstone Park and other localities in the western part of the country derive a part of their water and much of their heat from magmatic sources.

Any statement as to the number of thermal springs in the United States depends upon the classification of springs that are only slightly warmer than the normal for their localities and upon the grouping of the recognized thermal springs. According to the report above cited, there are somewhat over 1,000 thermal springs in the western mountain region, 52 in the east-central region (of which 46 are in the Appalachian Highlands and 6 are in the Ouachita area in Arkansas), and 3 in the Great Plains region (in the Black Hills of South Dakota). (See Fig. XA-8.) The States having the largest number of thermal springs are Idaho 203, California

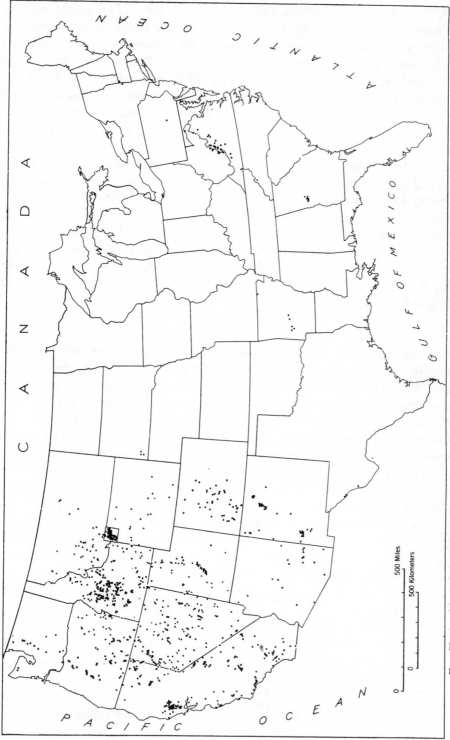

Fig. Xa-8.—Map of the United States showing thermal springs. (*After Norah D. Stearns, H. T. Stearns, and G. A. Waring.*)

184, Nevada 174, Wyoming 116, and Oregon 105. The geyser area of Yellowstone National Park, however, exceeds all others in the abundance of springs of high temperature. Indeed the number of thermal springs in that area might be given as several thousand if the individual springs were counted instead of being grouped. Nearly two-thirds of the recognized springs issue from igneous rocks—chiefly from the large masses of intrusive magma, such as the great batholith of Idaho, which still retain some of their original heat. Few if any, on the other hand, derive their heat from extrusive lavas.

In the paper above cited it is estimated that the total flow of all thermal springs in the United States is not more than 500,000 gallons a minute, which is equal to 720,000,000 gallons or about 2,700,000 cubic meters a day. The average discharge of 177 thermal springs in California on which data are available is 91 gallons a minute. The largest thermal spring in the United States is probably Warm Spring, in Montana, which has a temperature of only 68°F. (20°C.) but has a discharge of about 80,000 gallons a minute, which is equal to about 115,000,000 gallons or 440,000 cubic meters a day.

Size of springs

What is a large spring? This question will be answered very differently in different localities. In localities of small springs the designation "Big Spring" is doubtless borne by springs that yield no more than 10 gallons a minute, and in many parts of the United States a spring that discharges 1 second-foot—that is, 1 cubic foot a second, or 448 gallons a minute, would be regarded as a remarkable spring. On the other hand, in regions of truly large springs, springs yielding at the rate of several second-feet are sometimes called small springs.

In 1923 the writer [25, p. 53] called attention to the need for a classification of springs according to their rates of discharge and proposed two systems of classification—one based on the metric system and the other on the units commonly used in the United States. The second system, which has come into use, especially with respect to very large springs, is outlined in the following table:

Classification of springs with respect to size, based on units used in the United States

Magnitude	Discharge
First	100 second-feet or more.
Second	10 to 100 second-feet.
Third	1 to 10 second-feet.
Fourth	100 gallons a minute to 1 second-foot (448.8 gallons a minute)
Fifth	10 to 100 gallons a minute.
Sixth	1 to 10 gallons a minute.
Seventh	1 pint to 1 gallon a minute.
Eighth	Less than 1 pint a minute (less than 180 gallons or about 5 barrels a day).

In the United States there are doubtless thousands of springs of the third magnitude, as defined above, and hundreds of springs of the second magnitude. According to a study made by the writer [27, p. 47], there are in the entire country 65 springs of the first magnitude, of which 38 rise in volcanic rocks or associated gravel, 24 in limestone, and 3 in sandstone. Of the first-magnitude springs in volcanic rocks or associated gravel, 16 are in Oregon, 15 in Idaho, and 7 in California. Of the limestone springs, 9 rise in Paleozoic limestone (8 of them in the Ozark area of Missouri and Arkansas), 4 in Lower Cretaceous limestone (in the Balcones fault belt in Texas), and 11 in Tertiary limestone (in Florida or adjacent area). The 3 springs that issue from sandstone are in Montana. They are believed to owe their great discharge to faults or to other special features. With the additional data now available some revision of these figures could be made, but it would be of minor character.

The recorded discharge (generally the average of available measurements) of a few of the largest springs and groups of springs is given in the following table:

Recorded discharge of very large springs and groups of springs in the United States

	Cubic feet a second	Gallons a day	Cubic meters a day
Springs in volcanic rock or associated gravel:			
Sheep Bridge Spring, Oreg.	323	209,000,000	791,000
Springs along 10-mile stretch of Metrolius River, Oreg.	1,070	692,000,000	2,619,000
Springs along 10-mile stretch of Fall River, Calif.	1,400	905,000,000	3,425,000
Malade Springs, Idaho	1,133	732,000,000	2,761,000
Thousand Springs, Idaho	864	558,000,000	2,112,000
Springs along 50-mile stretch of Snake River, Idaho	5,085	3,787,000,000	14,334,000
Springs in limestone:			
Big Springs, Mo.	428	277,000,000	1,048,000
Comal Spring, Tex.	330	214,000,000	810,000
Silver Spring, Fla.	808	522,000,000	1,976,000
Spring in sandstone:			
Giant Springs, Mont.	600	388,000,000	1,447,000

Fluctuation of springs

Most springs fluctuate greatly in their rate of discharge but some are nearly constant. The fluctuations are produced chiefly by variations in the rate of recharge and in the rate of discharge by evaporation and transpiration, but other influences are also effective. The response to these variations differs greatly in different springs, according to the geologic and other conditions in the areas from which the springs are supplied. Some springs respond promptly and decisively to recharge, others only with much lag or with only very gradual increase in flow. Conversely some springs decline quickly or dry up in times of drought, but others are only slightly affected even by severe droughts.

Springs that obtain their supplies from surficial material of low specific yield generally fluctuate greatly, having strong flow in rainy seasons, especially during the winter, when the vegetation is dormant, and decreasing greatly in flow during long droughts, when the ground-water levels are lowered and the vegetation absorbs much of the shallow ground water before it reaches the spring openings. In the arid regions and during long droughts in the more humid regions springs of this type and streams fed by them show daily fluctuations, the flow generally being least in the afternoon, when the vegetation makes its heaviest demands, and greatest at night, when there is almost no transpiration.

Springs that obtain their supplies from surficial material with high specific yield may have relatively constant flow, because reservoirs of such material will take in and discharge large quantities of water with relatively small fluctuations of the water level. Thus streams issuing from the sand hills in Nebraska have well-sustained flow in dry seasons, because they are supplied at a fairly constant rate from the large quantity of water stored in the sand deposits.

Springs of the artesian type are relatively constant in flow, because they are supplied from the storage in deep reservoirs, which does not fluctuate greatly with the fluctuations in recharge and is protected from depletion by evaporation and transpiration, especially if the water is discharged through large definite openings. Springs of this type probably fluctuate with changes in atmospheric pressure and with changes in different agencies that produce pressure on the artesian aquifers that supply the springs, but not much definite information is as yet available on this subject. The water of the Warm Springs in Georgia is believed to come from surface sources, but it percolates to a considerable depth, where it obtains its relatively high température [11]. During the period from January 1, 1934, to June 30, 1935, the temperature of the water at the main source fluctuated less than 1°F. (between 87.6° and 88.2°F.); during this period the discharge of the springs was also relatively constant from day to day but nevertheless ranged between 595 and 678 gallons a minute. As shown in Figure XA-9, the fluctuations in discharge followed the variations in rainfall and ground-water level but with considerable lag.

Limestone springs differ in the amount of fluctuation according as they are fed by reservoirs having large storage or are the outlet of underground drainage systems with little storage. A striking example of great fluctuation in the discharge of a very large limestone spring is furnished by a 10-year record (1894–1903) of the Fontaine de Vaucluse, the largest spring in France. According to Pochet [33, p. 424], the discharge of this spring ranged during the 10-year period from 159 to 5,295 second-feet and averaged 808 second-feet.

The very large basalt springs on the Snake River in Idaho are relatively constant. The combined flow of Blue and Clear Lakes during the period from June 1, 1917, to December 31, 1930, ranged between about 660 and 760 second-feet, and the combined flow of all the large springs on the Snake River between Milner and King Hill during the period from

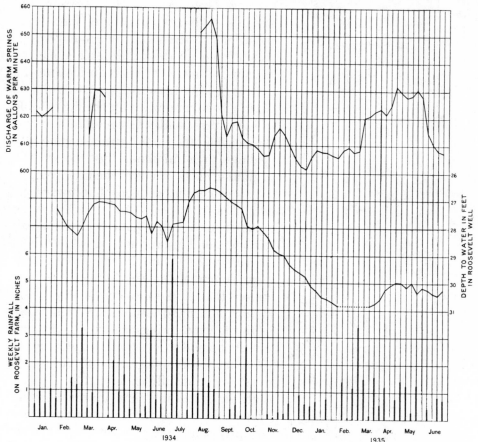

Fig. Xᴀ-9.—Relation of discharge of Warm Springs (Warm Springs, Ga.) to rainfall and ground-water level at Roosevelt Farm.

May 1, 1917, to December 31, 1918, ranged between 4,827 and 5,377 second-feet [27]. Figure Xᴀ-10 shows that the moderate fluctuations of these springs are due largely to irrigation and indicates that prior to irrigation their flow must have been even more nearly constant.

In many of the intermontane valleys of the West, where the ground-water recharge is derived chiefly from mountain streams that are largest in the spring, the valley springs reach their peak flows during the summer, soon after the season of greatest recharge. In Pahsimeroi Valley, Idaho,

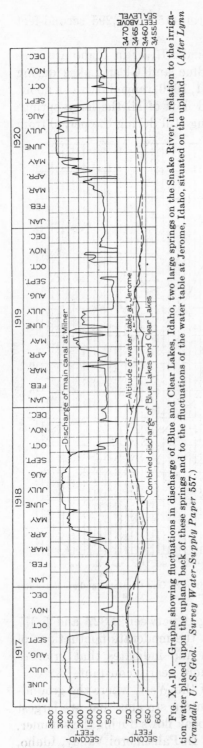

FIG. XA-10.—Graphs showing fluctuations in discharge of Blue and Clear Lakes, Idaho, two large springs on the Snake River, in relation to the irrigation water placed upon the upland back of these springs and to the fluctuations of the water table at Jerome, Idaho, situated on the upland. (*After Lynn Crandall, U. S. Geol. Survey Water-Supply Paper 557.*)

the maximum discharge of the springs occurs in August and September, when it may exceed 140 second-feet. This is perhaps 2½ or 3 months after the peak flow of the mountain streams. Thus the annual pulse advances as follows: First, the rapidly melting snow swells the streams, causing large seepage losses from the streams and correspondingly large contributions to the supply of ground water, which build up the water table along the streams; then the streams subside, but the discharge from the springs in the lowlands reaches a maximum; lastly, the water table becomes persistently flatter and lower and the discharge from springs gradually declines to a minimum just before the beginning of the floods of the next year.

It sometimes happens that toward the end of a long period of drought in the autumn springs that have been dry break out again and resume flowing, while others increase visibly in discharge. This occurs most commonly in California and other regions that have a pronounced dry season in the summer and autumn. Such increase in the flow of springs, coming before any rain that could relieve the drought, appears to casual observers as an anomalous occurrence but is readily explained by the fact that at a certain time in the autumn evaporation and transpiration decrease abruptly and their effects on springs become slight. In some places the rejuvenation of the springs before the end of a drought may be due to lag in the effects of the recharge during a rainy season prior to the drought.

Ebbing and flowing springs

Ebbing and flowing or periodic springs are distinctive features that are entirely different from the ordinary intermittent springs that flow in wet seasons and disappear in dry seasons. An ebbing and flowing spring has periods of flow, when it flows vigorously, and periods of ebb, when it ceases to flow or flows at a greatly reduced rate. The periods

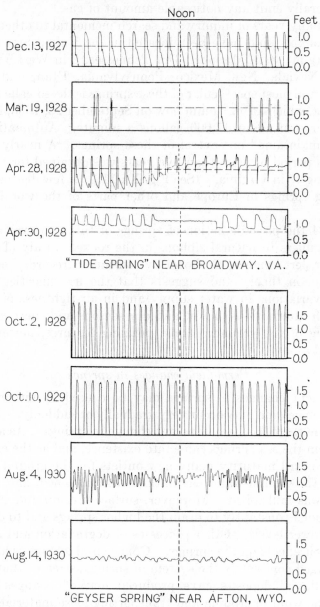

Fig. Xᴀ-11.—Hydrographs, for selected days, of the ebbing and flowing springs near Broadway, Va., and Afton, Wyo. (*After U. S. Geol. Survey Water-Supply Paper 836-D.*)

of flow may occur at nearly regular intervals or at very irregular intervals; they may occur at intervals of a few minutes or a few hours or even a few days or longer. All or nearly all the springs of this type issue from lime-

stone.   Nearly all are far from the ocean and they have no relation whatever to oceanic tides.   In their periodic action they resemble geysers, but
their water has the normal temperature of ordinary ground water, and they
do not generally emit any noticeable amount of gas.

After many years of inquiry and search incidental to other work, only
23 springs of this kind have been located in the United States, of which
9 are in Virginia, 4 in Missouri, 3 in Tennessee, 2 in West Virginia, and
1 each in Nevada, New Mexico, Pennsylvania, Utah, and Wyoming.
The largest and most spectacular of these springs is the so-called "Geyser,"
in Wyoming, which at maximum flow on September 29, 1933, had a measured discharge of about 17,000 gallons a minute.   Automatic recorders
have been maintained on several of these springs.   A nearly continuous
record for a period of more than five years was obtained for the so-called
"Tide Springs," in Virginia.   (See Fig. XA-11.)   A few distinctive ebbing
and flowing springs in Europe and other parts of the world have been
described.

In 1724 the periodic action of springs of this type was ascribed by
J. T. Desaguliers to natural siphons in the rocks.   Study of the springs
and of their performance, as shown by continuous records, seems to confirm the siphon theory and suggests that the irregularities are caused
chiefly by variations in water supply and in air-tightness of the siphon
system with alternations of wet and dry seasons and successive freezing
and thawing of the ground.   Some puzzling features, however, remain
unexplained.

Permanent changes in springs

Permanent changes in springs may be caused by either natural or
artificial agencies and may occur very gradually or suddenly.   Throughout
geologic time there has been constant change in springs.   As a region was
uplifted from the sea springs came into existence, and as the erosion cycle
advanced toward maturity many new outlets for the ground water were
developed, the ground-water circulation was quickened, and the number
of springs was multiplied.   Moreover, surface erosion and subterranean
solution tended constantly to drain the higher springs and to develop new
springs at lower levels.   Other processes of degradation and aggradation
also had their effects on the springs.   Continental ice sheets have in some
places changed completely the system of springs; streams that have built
up large alluvial deposits have produced marked changes in springs;
and even the wind in eroding and transporting loose materials has developed springs by exposing the water table or damming the surface water.
New springs may also be created or old ones permanently altered by such
sudden events as earthquakes, volcanic eruptions, landslides, and cave-ins.
In many places large deposits of travertine bear witness to the existence
of springs that have disappeared.

The changes made by man have greatly affected the discharge of springs in certain areas and have probably produced gradual changes in many others. It might be expected that in the United States such changes would be especially noticeable, because the country was so recently in its primeval condition and has been so rapidly and extensively settled and modified by human activity. Many springs have been dried up or their flow greatly reduced by the construction and operation of wells, mines, tunnels, drainage systems, and other excavations. On the other hand, irrigation has resulted in a large increase in the quantity of water that reaches the zone of saturation in some places and has been the cause of new springs and seepage areas.

The cutting of the timber and the development of agriculture are believed to have had the general effect in many parts of the country of reducing the flow of springs and spring-fed streams by reducing recharge. Such general changes have been difficult to establish, however, because of the lack of records of original conditions and because the changes are obscured by natural fluctuations from season to season and from year to year.

Sudden failure of springs is often reported, caused presumably by an explosion or by some catastrophic occurrence that either clogged a water-bearing crevice tributary to the spring or opened a new outlet. However, most springs that are regarded as failing on account of some mysterious subterranean cause are in fact merely feeling the effects of a drought or of some drainage or pumping development.

Effects of earthquakes on springs and wells

Disturbances in the water of springs and wells occur frequently in connection with earthquakes. The following changes produced by earthquakes have been reported: Rise or fall of the water levels in wells; roiling of the water of springs and wells; increase or decrease in the discharge of springs and flowing wells or complete cessation of flow; rise or fall in the temperature of the water of springs and wells; increase or decrease in the amount of gas emitted by springs and wells; emission of gas, such as hydrogen sulphide, that did not previously exist; changes in the mineral character of the water; breaking out of new springs; rise of ground water to the surface because of sinking of the land or opening of fissures; and forcible ejection of water, mud, or a mixture of sand and water from fissures or other openings in the earth. Many of these changes are only temporary, but some are permanent.

Rapid fluctuations in water level or artesian pressure caused by earthquakes are frequently registered by the automatic water-stage recorders on observation wells. Some of the earthquakes recorded in the United States have occurred in distant parts of the earth—for example, in such widely separated regions as Alaska, Chile, and Turkey. These fluctuations have been given considerable study by hydrologists and seismologists and have been the subject of several technical papers.

Methods of determining ground-water runoff

The flow of springs can be measured by several different devices, the method used depending on the size of the spring and the conditions of discharge. Small springs are often measured volumetrically, and larger ones by means of weirs, flumes, or current meters. A pigmy current meter has recently been developed by the Geological Survey for use in measuring small flows. Continuous records of discharge can be obtained, if the springs are not too small, by means of automatic water-stage recorders and rating curves, as in stream gaging. If the springs discharge into a stream under water it is necessary to measure the flow of the stream above and below the springs, the difference being the flow of the springs if there are no other complications. Thus the total flow of the Giant Springs, in Montana, has been determined to be about 600 second-feet by measuring the flow of the Missouri River above and below the springs.

Most perennial streams receive water from many small and widely distributed springs or from general seepage along the trunk streams and their many branches. These streams also carry water from rains and melted snow that enters the stream systems without first passing below the land surface. Thus the runoff consists of two components—called the surface runoff and the ground-water runoff or effluent seepage. Both of these components fluctuate, but the fluctuations of the surface runoff are very great and sudden and the fluctuations of the ground-water runoff relatively small and gradual. In the study of both surface water and ground water it is desirable to distinguish between these two components and to determine the quantity of each. The problem of making such a quantitative separation of the water that flows in a stream with respect to its origin has been given considerable study, but no wholly satisfactory solution has been found. The work done on the subject has been reviewed by W. G. Hoyt [14, pp. 111–119, 245–247], who analyzed carefully the available methods and published the computed average annual ground-water runoff from 22 stream systems in the eastern and central parts of the United States.

At the end of a long period of fair weather all the flow of a stream measured at the gaging station may be ground-water runoff. Soon after the beginning of a rather heavy rain, overland runoff begins to enter the stream system, and then some of the rain water begins to pass the gaging station, raising the stage of the stream and recording the passage of surface runoff. The effect of the rising stage is to check the effluent seepage, and under some conditions an effluent stream may become influent, or it may become influent in some places while still receiving ground water in other places. At some time during the flood the lowest ground-water runoff occurs, probably about at the peak of the flood. With falling stage the ground-water runoff increases rapidly and reaches a maximum at a time when the flood crest has passed but the flow of the stream is still large. At this time much water is entering the stream system from so-called bank storage and from shallow and temporary zones of saturation above the main water table. Indeed it is now known that much of the flood water of a stream may reach the stream system by a subsurface course. This water may be regarded as ground water, although it belongs

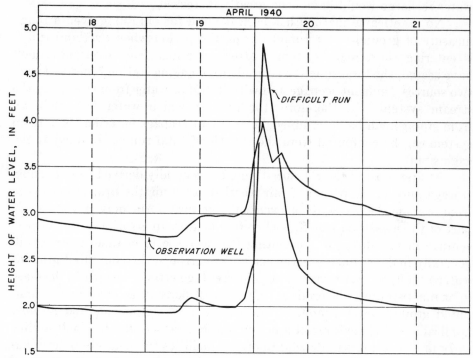

Fig. Xᴀ-12.—Graphs showing fluctuations in water level in Difficult Run near Fairfax, Va., and in an observation well five feet from the stream.

in a different category from the water in the formations below the permanent water table. It has been called subsurface storm flow.

Some relations of the stream flow to the water table are illustrated in figure Xᴀ-12, which shows the hydrographs of Difficult Run near Fairfax, Va., and of a well 5 feet from the stream gage. At noon on April 18, 1940, the water table at the well was about 0.9 foot higher than the stream level and there was presumably effluent seepage. Precipitation during the night of April 19 caused the water level in both the well and the stream to rise. At 1:15 a.m. April 20 the water had risen to the same level in the stream as in the well. The stream level continued to rise faster than the water level in the well and reached a peak considerably higher. After the peak the stream level declined faster than the water level in the well and passed it at about 5:30 a.m.   There is evidently not a wholly simple relation between the stream and the ground water at the well.   The water level in the well rose chiefly before it was eclipsed by the nearby stream level, indicating that the recharge occurred from farther upstream or from rainfall penetration or from some other source.   Likewise the decline in the well began while the water level was still below the nearby stream level, indicating percolation away from the well site.   If the stream had risen high enough to flood the lowland the influent seepage and ground-water recharge would have been greatly increased.

No practicable method has been devised for obtaining even a rough measure of ground-water runoff during the period when overland runoff is entering the stream system.   After accretions from overland runoff have ceased, the total runoff measured at the gaging station is derived from two sources—effluent seepage and withdrawal of water from storage in the stream system.   If, therefore, the rate at which water is withdrawn from storage can be determined, the effluent seepage entering the stream system can be computed from the records of total runoff obtained at the gaging station.

At first most of the measured runoff is generally derived from channel storage, but as the period of fair weather proceeds the proportion taken from storage decreases until eventually it may form only a very small part of the measured runoff.   Therefore at first an error of a certain percentage in measuring or estimating the decrease in channel storage will generally make a much greater percentage error in the computed ground-water runoff, but later even a large percentage error in regard to decrease in channel storage will produce only a small percentage error in the computed ground-water runoff.   Thus the channel-storage method is most applicable in the last part of a period of fair weather, and its applicability early in the period will depend upon the facilities for accurate determination of total runoff and decrease in storage.

In a study by the Geological Survey of the drainage basin of the Pomperaug River, in Connecticut [26], which has an area of 89 square miles, a gaging station was established near the mouth of the river.   It was determined, from considerations of channel storage, velocity of the water, and rate of movement of flood crests, that the direct runoff is nearly all delivered from the basin within a week of the time the water falls as rain, and that therefore the stream flow a week or more after the latest rain is virtually all derived from ground water.   A hydrograph was constructed of the total runoff for the years covered by the investigation, 1913 to 1916, and a hydrograph of the ground-water runoff was then made which coincided with that for total runoff in the long periods of fair weather and was interpolated by uncertain criteria between these periods.   The ground-water runoff was computed from this hydrograph. This general method was earlier used in the flood-control investigation of the drainage basin of the Miami River, in Ohio, by Houk [13], who prepared a hydrograph of the ground-water runoff of the Mad River for the period 1915 to 1919 by connecting the low points of the hydrograph for total runoff.

Recently a detailed study has been undertaken by the Geological Survey by the channel-storage method in a drainage basin of only about 1 square mile, consisting of the headwater area of Difficult Run, in Virginia [29], and such studies should be extended to larger basins. In a large basin the further complication is encountered that rain producing overland runoff occurs more frequently on at least some part of the basin.

The unit hydrograph, developed by L. K. Sherman and others, affords the means for determining the direct surface runoff from rainfall records and properly selected stream-flow records. (See Chapter XIᴇ.) It should accordingly afford the means for computing the ground-water runoff to the extent that it has been determined with sufficient accuracy independently of assumptions regarding ground-water runoff. This phase of the subject has also been discussed by Hoyt [14, p. 118].

Forecasting ground-water runoff

One of the principal uses of stream-flow records is to forecast, within limits, the quantity of water that the streams will carry in the future and the distribution of the flow. As streams that are otherwise comparable differ greatly in quantity and distribution of flow according to the geology and ground-water hydrology of their drainage basins, it appears that these branches of science could be put to effective use in forecasting stream flow. More systematic study of their use in this respect is much to be desired.

Fluctuations in the flow of springs and streams at low stages were critically studied about the beginning of this century by Maillet [21], with the purpose of developing methods of forecasting their flow. He mentions several investigations of this subject, dating back to 1863. The subject has been given considerable study in recent years, especially as to forecasting the low flow of streams in the summer and autumn from the ground-water runoff or the water levels in wells in the spring.

The history of the development of normal depletion curves has been discussed by R. E. Horton [12], who has presented formulas for such curves for drainage basins in which there is no direct abstraction from the water table by evaporation or transpiration. Starting at a time when all the flow is known to be derived from ground water, the formula permits computation of the ground-water flow at any subsequent time until there is further recharge. By projecting the curve backward, it can be used to some extent to separate ground-water runoff from surface runoff.

Some success has been attained in constructing rating curves for ground-water runoff from average water levels in observation wells of the water-table type, but the stage-discharge relation is radically changed by transpiration in the summer. Moreover, considerable increase in ground-water runoff may result from recharge near the streams and in perched reservoirs during moderate rains that do not affect observation wells that are at some distance from the streams and extend to the main water table. In the eastern part of the United States there is so much recharge in rainy periods during most summers that forecasts made from water levels in the spring have significance chiefly in dry summers.

Phreatophytes

Perhaps the most outstanding feature of the flora of the desert is its relation or lack of relation to the water table. On one hand are the true xerophytes, which are adapted to extreme economy of water, which depend on the rains that occur at long intervals for their scanty water supplies, and which during prolonged periods of drought maintain themselves in a nearly dormant condition. On the other hand are the phreatophytes, which habitually grow where they can send their roots down to the water table or to the capillary fringe immediately overlying the water table and are thus able to obtain a perennial and secure supply of water. The term phreatophyte is obtained from the Greek roots meaning a "well plant." Such a plant is literally a natural well with pumping equipment, lifting water from the zone of saturation.

In the most arid regions the plants that feed on ground water stand in sharp contrast to the desert plants that do not utilize water from the zone of saturation. However, in passing into less arid and then into more and more humid regions the control of the water table becomes progressively less rigid [28, p. 2].

The subject of plants as indicators of ground water was discussed by Vitruvius and Pliny and by Cassiodorus, who lived in the sixth century. The practical aspects of the subject were doubtless understood to some extent by Abraham, Isaac, and Moses and by inhabitants of arid regions from still more ancient times down to the present. Until recently, however, this subject and the entire related subject of ground-water discharge by plants received little attention and was not well understood by either botanists or hydrologists in Europe or the United States, whose training and work were chiefly under conditions of humid climate. In most of the older water-supply papers of the United States Geological Survey dealing with discharge of ground water no mention is made of discharge by plants or indeed by evaporation from the soil.

In France the subject received attention by Paramelle in 1856 and by Amy in 1861. The theory that plants in general, especially forest trees, draw upon the ground-water supply has been expressed by numerous authorities—for example, Ototsky in Russia and McGee in this country. The idea that plants of certain species more than others utilize water from the zone of saturation has been recognized by Warming and some other European botanists and by the botanists Coulter, Coville, Spalding, Shantz, Aldous, and Piemeisel in this country. Among hydrologists, G. E. P. Smith and Charles H. Lee are pioneers in this subject. In the later ground-water investigations by the Geological Survey, especially in the survey of desert watering places in 1917–18, the subject has been given much attention. It was treated rather comprehensively by the writer [28] in 1927.

The most widespread of the desert phreatophytes, at least in the United States, are salt grass (*Distichlis spicata*), greasewood (*Sarcobatus vermiculatus*), and mesquite (*Prosopis juliflora*, etc.). Salt grass shows the presence and approximate extent of hundreds of areas throughout the West where the water table is within about 12 feet of the surface. Greasewood and mesquite send their roots to much greater depths than salt grass and form conspicuous belts adjoining or surrounding the salt-grass areas— the greasewood in the northern part of the western arid region and the mesquite in the southern part. Greasewood grows luxuriantly where the depth to the water table is as much as 20 feet and in some places draws on ground water from depths of more than 30 feet. Mesquite sends its roots still deeper and in some places utilizes ground water from depths of more than 50 feet. Among the cultivated plants the most distinctive and aggressive phreatophyte is alfalfa, which readily utilizes ground water from rather great depths. Alfalfa was probably a true phreatophyte in the Old World long before it was introduced into this country. Among the many kinds of trees that depend more or less habitually on ground water may be mentioned the willow, cottonwood, and sycamore. The premier of all water indicators in the hot deserts of the Old World and in the Salton Sea region of this country is the palm tree (*Washingtonia filamentosa* in this country). As described by John S. Brown, it is an unfailing sign of a spring or of water that can be found by digging a few feet, and it stands up so conspicuously, with its green head high in the air, that it is visible for long distances and makes an excellent natural signpost.

In some localities the ground-water level has been observed to decline during the day and to rise at night with clocklike regularity, the decline beginning at about the same hour every morning and the rise at about the same hour every night. In 1888 F. H. King noted such fluctuations in certain shallow wells on low land adjoining the campus of Wisconsin University, which he attributed to changes in temperature. Daily fluctuations of the same character were noted by Prof. G. E. P. Smith, of the University of Arizona, in two wells in San Pedro Valley, Ariz., one in a forest of mesquite, the other in a grove of cottonwoods. Beginning in 1916 Professor Smith conducted a series of observations on these wells which demonstrated that the daily decline of the water table was due to withdrawal of ground water from the zone of saturation by the trees.

In 1925–27 a thorough study of the daily fluctuations of the water table caused by transpiration and of the quantities of ground water discharged by different species of phreatophytes was made by White [50] in the Escalante Desert, in Utah. About 75 shallow test wells were put down in this area of ground-water discharge in fields of many kinds of native phreatophytes and in fields of naturally subirrigated alfalfa. The records obtained from these observation wells show that during the growing season there is a marked daily fluctuation of the water table nearly everywhere in fields of ground-water plants. Usually the water starts down at 9 to 11 a.m. and reaches its lowest stage at 6 to 7 p.m. The water begins to rise at 7 to 9 p.m. and continues to rise until 7 to 9 a.m. the following morning. The maximum daily drawdown observed during the investigation amounted to about $1\frac{1}{2}$ inches in greasewood and shad scale, $2\frac{1}{2}$ inches in alfalfa, $3\frac{3}{4}$ inches in salt grass, and $4\frac{1}{2}$ inches in sedges and associated marsh grasses. The fluctuations do not occur in plowed fields, cleared lands, tracts of sagebrush, and tracts where the water table is far below the surface. In general they begin with the appearance of foliage in the spring and cease after killing frosts. They cease or are materially reduced after the plants are cut. The water table rises sharply almost immediately after a rain in fields of phreatophytes during the growing season, even though the rain is light and affords no ground-water recharge. There is little or no rise of the water table after rains in cleared lands at any time or in fields of ground-water plants when plant life is dormant.

The problem of interpreting the fluctuations of the water table in terms of water used by the plants was approached in three ways. (1) The amount of ground water discharged daily by the plants was computed by the formula $q = y(24r \pm s)$, in which q is the depth of ground water withdrawn, in inches, y is the specific yield of the soil in which the daily fluctuation of the water table takes place, r is the hourly rate of rise of the water table, in inches, from midnight to 4 a.m., and s is the net fall or rise of the water during the 24-hour period, in inches. In field experiments the quantities on the right-hand side of the formula except the specific yield can be readily determined from the automatic records of water-table fluctuations. Cylinders were driven near observation wells so as to enclose columns of undisturbed soil in the zone in which the fluctuations take place, and the rise and fall of the water table in the enclosed columns after the addition or subtraction of measured amounts of water were carefully noted. From these experiments the specific yield of the soils was determined. (2) Several phreatophytes were raised in tanks filled with soils of the types in which the plants were growing, provided with an automatic measured water supply, and otherwise equipped so as to duplicate as closely as possible conditions that exist in the field. Daily fluctuations of the water table similar to those that occur in the field were obtained in the tanks. These fluctuations were correlated with the daily ground-water discharge as indicated by the measured water supply delivered to the tanks. (3) The amount of water required to produce a unit weight of dry vegetable matter in the tanks was computed, and the coefficient of ground-water discharge thereby obtained was applied to the field on the basis of dry weight of vegetable matter produced per unit area.

WATER-BEARING FORMATIONS IN THE UNITED STATES AND THEIR DISTRIBUTION

The United States can be divided into four regions with respect to ground water—(1) the East-Central old-rock region, (2) the Atlantic and Gulf Coastal Plain region, (3) the Great Plains region, and (4) the Western Mountain region [24]. (See Fig. XA-13.)

The East-Central region includes about one-third of the area and two-thirds of the population of the country. Most of the region is underlain by Paleozoic rocks, including water-bearing sandstones and limestones and unproductive shales; the deep water from these rocks is highly mineralized. Parts of this region are underlain by Pre-Cambrian or Triassic rocks that yield small supplies. The glacial drift, in the northern part, and the glacial outwash sand and gravel beyond the drift border yield numerous large water supplies.

The wide and well-populated coastal plain bordering the Atlantic Ocean and Gulf of Mexico is underlain by Cretaceous, Tertiary, and Pleistocene formations, including many beds of sand and limestone that yield numerous supplies of water, many of which are large.

The semiarid or subhumid plains region lying east of the Rocky Mountains contains extensive Tertiary and Pleistocene deposits of water-bearing sand and gravel and Cretaceous sands that yield highly mineralized artesian water, especially in North Dakota and South Dakota; also water-bearing glacial drift in the north and productive Permian limestone in the Roswell artesian basin in New Mexico. In the areas of Cretaceous shale the water supplies are scarce.

The Western Mountain region, which occupies about one-third of the area of the country, is chiefly arid and contains extensive tracts in which water supplies are scarce. Its principal water-bearing beds are the sand and gravel in the Pleistocene or Tertiary valley fill, which in some parts, especially in California, yield very large supplies. In some places in the Northwest the Tertiary volcanic rocks yield much water to springs and wells.

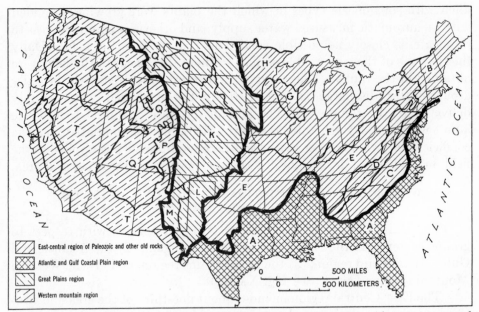

Fig. Xᴀ-13.—Map of the United States showing the four major regions with respect to ground water and their subdivision into ground-water provinces. (*After U. S. Geol. Survey Water-Supply Paper* 489, with some revision of provinces in the West, in part after C. F. Tolman. Reproduced from Water-Supply Paper 836-D. See explanation below.)

Explanation of figure Xᴀ-13

East-Central region of Paleozoic and other old rocks.—Province C is underlain by igneous and metamorphic rocks (chiefly pre-Cambrian) and Triassic sandstone. These rocks yield many small supplies of good water. Province D is mountainous and is underlain by folded and faulted Paleozoic strata, pre-Cambrian metamorphic rocks, and associated igneous rocks. These rocks supply water of good quality to numerous springs, spring-fed streams, and shallow wells. In province B the bedrocks (chiefly metamorphic) are overlain by glacial drift. The bedrock and boulder clay yield many small supplies of good water, and glacial sand and gravel yield large supplies in some places. Provinces E, F, and G are underlain by Paleozoic rocks. The sandstones and limestones yield good water to shallow wells, but deep wells strike mineralized water, much of which is unfit for use. The shales yield meager supplies. The glacial drift in province F yields many supplies, both large and small. The outwash sand and gravel in valleys in province G and the northern part of province E yield large supplies. In province H glacial drift yields many water supplies, but where the drift is thin only meager supplies are obtained from the underlying granite or other pre-Cambrian rocks. The water ranges in quality from soft and good in the eastern part of the province to highly mineralized and even unfit for use in the western part.

Atlantic and Gulf Coastal Plain region.—In province A Cretaceous, Tertiary, and younger strata of sand and limestone yield many small and many large water supplies. Much of the water is of good quality, but some is salty.

Great Plains region.—Provinces I, J, K, N, O, and Q′ are in general underlain by Cretaceous formations—chiefly unproductive shale with interbedded or underlying sandstone that yields highly mineralized artesian water. Flowing wells are especially abundant in province I. In large areas in province Q′ and in most of province J, except in the Black Hills, thick Cretaceous shales occur at the surface and are barren of water or yield only meager supplies of poor water. In province O and the eastern part of province N the Cretaceous strata are overlain by strata of early Tertiary and perhaps in part late Cretaceous age, which include sand, gravel, and coal that in most places yield small to moderate supplies. In provinces I and N the glacial drift generally yields supplies of hard but otherwise fairly good water. In provinces K and L Tertiary and Quaternary sand and gravel yield abundant supplies of somewhat hard but otherwise good water in most places. The underlying Cretaceous formations in province K and the underlying Permian or Triassic "Red Beds" in province L furnish water supplies in some places but generally are not of much value, and where they occur at or near the surface water may be scarce. In the Roswell artesian basin, in province M, Permian limestone yields large supplies of hard but usable water. Elsewhere the Carboniferous rocks underlying this province generally yield only meager supplies of poor quality, but in certain areas alluvial sand and gravel furnish abundant supplies.

Western Mountain region.—In the Rocky Mountains (provinces P and R) and the Sierra Nevada (part of province U) water supplies are furnished by springs, streams, and shallow wells. In province Q more or less flat-lying Paleozoic, Mesozoic, and younger strata form dissected plateaus with generally meager water supplies. In province S extensive lava beds and associated gravel give rise to very large springs and in some places yield large supplies of good water to wells. In provinces T, U, V, W, and X, sand and gravel in the broad valleys between mountain ranges yield numerous supplies of generally good water, at many places in large quantities. In parts of these provinces water supplies are obtained also from lava beds, glacial outwash, and other formations.

REFERENCES

1. Allen, E. T., and Day, A. L., Hot springs of the Yellowstone National Park: Carnegie Inst. Washington Pub. 466, 1935.

2. Bailey, Paul, Engineering investigation of percolation from Alameda Creek and ground-water studies on Niles cone: California Water Comm. 3d Bienn. Rept., pp. 95–131, 1921.

3. Blaney, H. F., Taylor, C. A., and Young, A. A., Rainfall penetration and consumptive use of water in Santa Ana River valley and coastal plain, California Dept. Public Works, Div. Water Resources, 1930.

4. Briggs, L. J., and McLane, J. W., The moisture equivalent of soils: U. S. Dept. Agr., Bur. Soils, Bull. 45, 1907.

5. Bryan, Kirk, Classification of springs: Jour. Geology, vol. 27, pp. 522–561, 1919.

6. Buckingham, Edgar, Studies on the movement of soil moisture: U. S. Dept. Agr., Bur. Soils, Bull. 38, 1907.

7. Condra, G. E., Geology and water resources of the Republican River Valley and adjacent areas, Nebr.: U. S. Geol. Survey Water-Supply Paper 216, 1907.

8. Conkling, Harold, San Gabriel investigation: California Dept. Public Works, Div. Water Rights, Bull. 5, 1927.

9. Day, A. L., and Allen, E. T., The volcanic activity and hot springs of Lassen Peak: Carnegie Inst. Washington Pub. 360, 1925.

10. Haines, W. B., Studies in the physical properties of soils: Jour. Agr. Sci., vol. 20, pp. 97–116, 1930.

11. Hewett, D. F., and Crickmay, G. W., The warm springs of Georgia: U. S. Geol. Survey Water-Supply Paper 819, 1937.

12. Horton, R. E., The role of infiltration in the hydrologic cycle: Am. Geophys. Union Trans., 1933, pp. 446–449.

13. Houk, I. E., Rainfall and runoff in Miami Valley, State of Ohio: Miami Conservancy District Tech. Repts., pt. 8, 1921.

14. Hoyt, W. G., and others, Studies of relations of rainfall and runoff in the United States: U. S. Geol. Survey Water-Supply Paper 772, 1936.

15. Keen, B. A., The physical properties of the soil, Longmans, Green and Co., 1931.

16. Keilhack, Konrad, Lehrbuch der Grundwasser und Quellekunde, 3d ed., Berlin, 1935.

17. Kunesh, J. F., Surface, spring, and tunnel investigations: Honolulu Sewer and Water Comm. Rept., 1929.

18. Lane, A. C., Mine waters and their field assay: Geol. Soc. America Bull., vol. 19, 1909. See also Mine waters: Lake Superior Min., Inst. Proc., vol. 13, pp. 63–152, 1908.

19. Leverett, M. C., Capillary behavior in porous solids: Am. Inst. Min. Met. Eng., Petroleum Div. Petroleum Tech. Paper 1223, 1940.

20. Lindgren, Waldemar, Mineral deposits, 3d ed., New York, McGraw-Hill Book Co., 1928.

21. Maillet, Edmond, Essais d'hydraulique souterraine et fluviale, Paris, Librairie scientifique A. Hermann, 1905.

22. McCombs, John, Methods of estimating safe yield of Honolulu artesian area: Honolulu Sewer and Water Comm. Rept., 1927.

23. Meinzer, O. E., Discussion of question No. 2 of the International Commission on Subterranean Water; definitions of the different kinds of subterranean water: Am. Geophys. Union Trans., 1939, pt. 4, pp. 674–677.

24. Meinzer, O. E., The occurrence of ground water in the United States: U. S. Geol. Survey Water-Supply Paper 489, 1923. See also Ground water in the United States, a summary: U. S. Geol. Survey Water-Supply Paper 836-D, 1939.

25. Meinzer, O. E., Outline of ground-water hydrology: U. S. Geol. Survey Water-Supply Paper 494, 1923.

26. Meinzer, O. E., and Stearns, N. D., A study of ground water in the Pomperaug Basin, Conn.: U. S. Geol. Survey Water-Supply Paper 597-B, 1929.

27. Meinzer, O. E., Large springs in the United States: U. S. Geol. Survey Water-Supply Paper 557, 1927.

28. Meinzer, O. E., Plants as indicators of ground water: U. S. Geol. Survey Water-Supply Paper 577, 1927.

29. Meinzer, O. E., Cady, R. C., Leggette, R. M., and Fishel, V. C., The channel-storage method of determining effluent seepage: Am. Geophys. Union Trans., 1936, pp. 415–418.

30. Mitchelson, A. T., and Muckel, D. C., Spreading water for storage underground: U. S. Dept. Agr. Tech, Bull. 578, 1937.

31. Piper, A. M., Gale, H. S., Thomas, H. E., and Robinson, T. W., Geology and ground-water hydrology of the Mokelumne area, California: U. S. Geol. Survey Water-Supply Paper 780, 1939.

32. Piper, A. M., Notes on the relation between the moisture equivalent and the specific retention of water-bearing materials: Am. Geophys. Union Trans., 1933, pp. 481–87.

33. Pochet, Léon, Études sur les sources, Paris, Ministère de l'Agriculture, 1895.

34. Post, W. S., Santa Ana investigation, flood control and conservation: California Dept. Public Works, Div. Engineering and Irrigation, Bull. 19, 1929.

35. Richards, L. A., Capillary conduction of liquids through porous mediums: Physics, vol. 1, No. 5, pp. 318–333, 1931.

35a. Russel, I. C., Geological history of Lake Lahontan, a Quaternary lake of northwestern Nevada: U. S. Geol. Survey Mon. 11, pp. 60–61, 221–222, 1885.

36. Schofield, R. K., The pF of the water in soil: 3d International Cong. Soil Sci. Trans., vol. 2, pp. 37–48, 1935.

37. Sheppard, Thomas, William Smith, his maps and memoirs, Hull, 1920.

38. Smith, W. O., The final distribution of retained liquid in an ideal uniform soil: Physics vol. 4, pp. 425–438, 1933.

39. Stearns, N. D., Laboratory tests on physical properties of water-bearing materials: U. S. Geol. Survey Water-Supply Paper 596, pp. 121–176, 1927.

40. Stearns, H. T., Robinson, T. W., and Taylor, G. H., Geology and water resources of the Mokelumne area, California: U. S. Geol. Survey Water-Supply Paper 619, 1930.

41. Stearns, H. T., Crandall, L., and Steward, W. G., Geology and ground-water resources of the Snake River Plain in southeastern Idaho: U. S. Geol. Survey Water-Supply Paper 774, 1938.

42. Stearns, N. D., Stearns, H. T., and Waring, G. A., Thermal springs in the United States: U. S. Geol. Survey Water-Supply Paper 679, 1935.

43. Suess, Edward, Über heisse Quellen, Leipzig, Gesell. Deutsche Naturforscher u. Artze Verhandlungen, 1902. Translated in part by D. H. Newland, Eng. and Min. Jour., vol. 76, pp. 52–53, July 11, 1903. See also Das Antlitz der Erde, vol. 3, pt. 2, pp. 630, 655, Vienna, 1909.

44. Taylor, G. H., Investigations relating to the absorption of precipitation and its penetration to the zone of saturation: Am. Geophys. Union Trans., 1931, pp. 206–211.

45. Van Hise, C. R., A treatise on metamorphism: U. S. Geol. Survey Mon. 47, 1904.

46. Veatch, A. C., Fluctuations of the water level in wells: U. S. Geol. Survey Water-Supply Paper 155, 1906. This paper summarizes the work that has been done with lysimeters in England and on the continent of Europe.

47. Veihmeyer, F. J., and Edlefsen, N. E., Interpretation of soil moisture problems by means of energy changes: Am. Geophys. Union Trans., 1939, pp. 543–545.

48. Versluys, J., Die Kapillarität der Boden: Internat. Mitt. Bodenkunde, vol. 7, pp. 117–140, 1917.

49. White, W. N., Preliminary report ón the ground-water supply of Mimbres Valley, N. Mex.: U. S. Geol. Survey Water-Supply Paper 637, 1931.

50. White, W. N., A method of estimating ground-water supplies based on discharge by plants and evaporation from soil: U. S. Geol. Survey Water-Supply Paper 659-A, 1932.

Xʙ. MOVEMENT OF GROUND WATER AND ITS RELATION TO HEAD, PERMEABILITY, AND STORAGE

Oscar E. Meinzer[1] and Leland K. Wenzel[2]

LAMINAR AND TURBULENT FLOW

The water in the interstices of the permeable rocks in the zone of saturation is, as a rule, moving very slowly and very steadily. This steady kind of movement is called laminar flow, also stream-line or viscous flow. In each thread of the laminar movement there is an endless procession of particles of water, following the same path, propelled by the differential head that overcomes the friction with the adjacent thread of more slowly moving particles nearer the wall of the opening. The different threads are not entirely parallel nor are they in straight lines, for they converge where they pass through narrow necks and diverge where they emerge into large interstices. The rate of movement is not the same in the different threads, those nearest the walls having the slowest rate and those in the middle the most rapid. Neither is the rate of movement of any particle constant, for it speeds up very gradually in approaching the necks and slows down where it enters the larger spaces. However, the whole process is conceived to be perfectly orderly, each water particle moving in a path that is predetermined by the irregular shapes of the interstices and the three-dimensional system of hydraulic gradients adjusted to these interstices—urged ever forward, gently but persistently.

In contrast to laminar flow is turbulent flow, in which eddies occur and the water particles move in irregular circuitous paths. It has been recognized for some time that the flow of water in pipes and open channels may be either laminar or turbulent. In general, laminar flow occurs at relatively low velocities and turbulent flow at higher velocities. The flow in rivers and creeks is generally turbulent, whereas the flow of ground water is laminar except under unusual conditions, as perhaps in some underground streams in cavernous limestone or where the ground water is entering a heavily pumped well [23].

The nature of the two modes of flow was demonstrated by Reynolds [25] in a series of experiments on parallel glass tubes of different diameters up to 2 inches. The velocity at which eddy formation is first noted in a long tube is termed the "higher critical velocity." There is also a lower

[1] Geologist in charge, Division of Ground Water, Geological Survey, United States Department of the Interior, Washington, D. C.

[2] Hydraulic engineer, Division of Ground Water, Geological Survey, United States Department of the Interior, Washington, D. C.

critical velocity, at which the eddies in originally turbulent flow die out. If the water is moving with laminar flow at a velocity between the two critical velocities, it is in an unstable state, and any slight disturbance may cause it to break down into turbulent motion. The critical velocity varies directly with the viscosity and hence is higher in cold than in warm water. It varies inversely with the diameter of the tube and with the roughness of the walls of the tube. The nature of the two types of flow was demonstrated visually by Reynolds and later by H. S. Hele-Shaw for openings of both regular and irregular shape [19]. (See Fig. XB-1.)

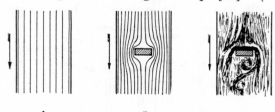

A   *B*   *C*

Fig. XB-1.—Diagrams showing laminar or stream-line flow (*A* and *B*) and turbulent flow (*C*). (*In general after H. S. Hele-Shaw.*)

DARCY'S LAW

The flow of water was first studied in open channels and pipes in which turbulent flow occurred, and it was found that the rate of flow varied approximately as the square root of the hydraulic gradient. The flow of water in capillary tubes was first studied by Hagen [9] and Poiseuille [24], who discovered that the rate of flow through very small tubes varies directly as the hydraulic gradient. Later Darcy [2] verified this law and demonstrated its application to water percolating through interstices of filter sand. He expressed the law by means of a formula essentially as follows:

$$v = \frac{Ph}{l},$$

in which v is the velocity of the water through a column of permeable material, h is the difference in head at the ends of the column, l is the length of the column, and P is a constant that depends on the character of the material, especially on the size and arrangement of the grains.

Since the results of Darcy's work were published there has been much discussion as to whether his formula expresses closely the law of flow of water through porous material, whether it is applicable only through a certain range of velocities, and if so, what are the lower and upper limits. Many laboratory investigations have been made on the flow of liquids and gases through permeable materials, and most of the early experiments were performed by French and German physicists and engineers [26]. A review of early investigations, including those of Ammon, Fleck, Hagen,

Renk, Sellheim, Trautivine, Welitschkowsky, and Woolny, was made by King [14]. He also made laboratory investigations of his own by observing the flow of liquids through wire gauze disks of perforated brass, sandstone, and sand [14, pp. 107–124] and the flow of air through sand, sandstone, and capillary tubes [14, pp. 157–178]. Included in his report is a review of the experiments of F. H. Newell, performed about 1885, on the flow of water and oil through rock [14, pp. 124–135]. King concluded that although the flow of fluids apparently was not directly proportional to the hydraulic gradient, the departures obtained were systematically either plus or minus, as might be expected if the departures were due to

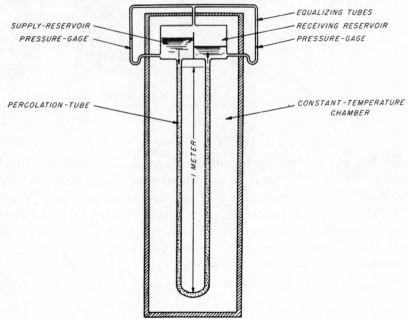

Fig. Xʙ-2.—Diagrams of apparatus of nondischarging U-tube type used in the hydrologic laboratory of the United States Geologic Survey in determining permeability under low hydraulic gradients.

imperfections in the apparatus and methods used. Laboratory experiments on the flow of water through tanks of sand and gravel were made later under the direction of Slichter [27, pp. 29–49], who concluded that "the law of direct variation of the flow of ground waters with head under which the flow takes place is verified by the experiments in the tank."

In 1923 the hydrologic laboratory of the United States Geological Survey was organized and systematic investigation was undertaken, under the direction of the senior author of this chapter, of the flow of water through permeable materials under the low gradients that occur naturally in ground water. In tests made in this laboratory on about 2,000 samples of material from many different water-bearing and non-water-bearing formations, the validity of Darcy's law has been thoroughly established. The first work on very low gradients was done by Mrs. Stearns [28], and later work on still lower gradients was done by Fishel [6, 19]. In 1933 Fishel and the senior author constructed an apparatus of the nondischarging U-tube type in which the temperature was kept constant and evaporation was prevented (Fig. XB-2). Tests made with this apparatus indicate that for the material tested the rate of flow varies directly with the hydraulic gradient down to a gradient of 2 or 3 inches to the mile and probably to indefinitely low gradients.

It is now clear that the simple law which states that the flow increases directly with the hydraulic gradient applies to laminar flow, in which essentially no energy is lost in producing eddies, whereas in turbulent flow the flow does not increase in proportion to the increase in hydraulic gradient, but, as has been empirically determined by many experiments, it increases more nearly in proportion to the square root of the hydraulic gradient. The failure of some of the early investigators to verify Darcy's law was probably due largely to the fact that they performed all or a part of their experiments with gradients so high that the flow through the porous media was of the turbulent type.

The results of Reynolds' work [25] were published in 1883, but the subject of the upper limit of Darcy's law was confused about the same time by Daniell [1, p. 293], who defined capillary tubes as those in which the flow of water follows Darcy's law and gave the limiting diameter of such tubes as one-fiftieth of an inch. It was further confused by Van Hise [36, pp. 134–146], who expressed one-fiftieth of an inch as 0.508 millimeter, thus giving an appearance of accuracy that was fictitious. The whole subject of the laminar and turbulent flow of water is effectively presented by Tolman [33, pp. 191–200] in his recent textbook. Tolman clears up the confusion by pointing out that the idea that there is a limiting size of tube which determines the type of flow is incorrect and that laminar flow takes place in tubes of any size provided the velocity is sufficiently low. On the basis of tests made by J. F. Poland and others, Tolman shows that under normal ground-water gradients turbulent flow in sand and gravel is virtually nonexistent.

It has long been recognized that Darcy's law is analogous to the fundamental laws of the conductivity of heat and electricity but that there are certain important differences in application. It seems remarkable that the application of so extremely simple a law to the flow of heat, electricity, or water should lead to complexities that can be expressed only by an array of formidable mathematical formulas if at all.

COURSE AND RATE OF MOVEMENT OF GROUND WATER

In general each water particle in the zone of saturation is moving from some point in an intake area where it first reached the water table toward

some point where water is being discharged through a subaerial, sublacu-
strine, or submarine spring or seep, or by evaporation or absorption by
the roots of plants.   The path through which the water particle threads
its way may be short and simple, never getting far below the water table,
or it may be many miles—indeed, as much as a few hundred miles—in
length and may follow a circuitous course, leading perhaps to depths of
hundreds or thousands of feet, as determined by the relief of the land, the
stratigraphy and structure of the rocks, and other conditions.   The time
consumed by the water particle in making the trip from source to exit
may be relatively brief, or it may be many years or many centuries.

The rate of movement of the ground water has been determined
directly or indirectly at many places.   The velocity of a surface stream is
generally measured with a current meter, but this instrument is obviously
not adaptable for measuring the velocity of ground water.   For this purpose use has been made of salts and dyes, which are introduced into the
ground water through an upstream well and later detected in one or more
downstream wells, the velocity being computed from the observed interval
of time and the measured distance between the wells.   Common salt
was first used by A. Thiem and other European hydrologists and was
detected in the downstream wells by chemical tests for chloride in successive samples taken from these wells.   Later the more convenient electro-
lytic method was devised in this country by Slichter [27].

Dyes have been used in many investigations in France and other
European countries and later in the United States [18, pp. 128, 129].
They have been used chiefly to trace the course of rather definite under-
ground streams, such as occur in limestone, and to determine whether
certain water supplies receive contributions from polluted sources.
Uranin dye was used successfully in 1921 and subsequent years by the
United States Public Health Service and the United States Geological
Survey near Fort Caswell, N. C., in a detailed three-dimensional survey
of the direction and rate of movement of the ground water in medium-
to fine-grained sand [29].

The flow of water through a formation can be computed by multiplying the average velocity by the average porosity and this product by the
cross-sectional area through which the flow occurs.   The cross-sectional
area can be determined approximately from the logs of wells, but there is
always considerable uncertainty as to the average velocity and the average
porosity.   In recent years the flow has generally been determined by ascertaining the permeability, hydraulic gradient, and cross-sectional area
and then applying Darcy's law.   The average velocity can then be computed if the average porosity can be determined.

A favorite question is, "How fast does ground water move?"   In
attempting to answer this question it may first be pointed out that among

about 2,000 natural earth materials tested in the hydrologic laboratory, the most permeable material carries water (under the same hydraulic gradient) at a rate about 450,000,000 times that of the least permeable. The range in ground-water velocities is probably even greater. In field tests rates of movement of several feet a day have been found, and in one place a rate of 420 feet a day was reported. The most permeable material that has been tested in the hydrologic laboratory is a gravel which under a hydraulic gradient of 10 feet to the mile will carry water at the rate of 60 feet a day. In nature rates of more than a few feet a day are exceptional. The lowest rate at which water has been observed to move through a natural material in the tests made in the hydrologic laboratory was about 1 foot in 10 years [28, 19]. Probably in nature, under lower gradients, even much slower rates of movement are common in dense and poorly permeable materials. In the recognized water-bearing formations, from which wells obtain their water supplies, the natural rate of movement of the ground water is generally not greater than 5 feet a day and not less than 5 feet a year. An example of a more or less average performance of a moderately productive water-bearing formation is afforded by the Carrizo sandstone in the Winter Garden region of Texas, in which the water was computed to be moving at an average rate of about 50 feet a year.

HEAD IN RELATION TO MOVEMENT

In formations through which ground water is percolating the water particles next to the walls of the interstices are doubtless held stationary, but those at even a minute distance from a wall are moving slowly as the friction between them and the fixed particles is overcome. With increasing distance from the walls there is increasing rate of movement, each thread of water particles moving against friction with the more slowly moving water particles on the outer side and offering resistance to the slightly more rapid movement of those on the inner side.

Thus as the water moves energy is expended in overcoming friction and is converted into heat or perhaps into some other form of energy. The movement is so slow that the energy consumed in overcoming the inertia of the water is relatively negligible. The energy that keeps the water in motion against the internal friction created by its own viscosity is provided by the difference in head between the place of intake and the place of discharge. The path followed by each thread of water particles may lead in varying directions, and in parts of its course it may have an upward trend, but the exit is at a lower level than the intake, and thus potential energy is lost. The difference in head is distributed throughout each thread of water as a hydraulic gradient, continuously but not at a constant rate, all the way from intake to exit. The viscosity of water decreases with increasing temperature, and therefore, other things being equal, the rate of movement increases with the temperature.

In the investigation of a given area, the ground-water hydrologist generally makes a contour map of the water table, because it throws much light on questions as to the intake and discharge areas and the direction of movement of the ground water. Strictly, however, even a perfect contour map of the water table would show only the horizontal direction of movement of the ground water at the water table. The hydraulic gradients are three-dimensional, however, and the water moves not only along the water table but also to depths below the water table and generally upward again to the water table at some other place. Obviously, where the water is moving downward there is a decrease in head with depth, and where it is moving upward there is an increase in head with depth. Thus even in a deposit of structureless sand the head at some depth is likely to be lower than the water table if it is in an intake area and higher if it is in a discharge area.

The sedimentary rocks are not structureless, however, but are generally composed of successive strata that differ greatly in permeability. Consequently the ground water moves chiefly along the stratification, through the most permeable strata, and much less freely through the less permeable strata. Some strata are believed to be entirely impermeable under the hydraulic gradients that exist in nature, but this is a moot question, as there is some evidence that water may move, with extreme slowness, even through strata that have been regarded as totally impermeable. The emphasis has so long been placed on lateral movement through the more permeable strata that the quantitative importance of movement at right angles to the strata has probably been underestimated. In applying Darcy's law, it is evident that although in movement at right angles to the strata the permeability factor is likely to be very small, the other two factors—hydraulic gradient and cross-sectional area—are likely to be relatively very great.

The principal movement of the ground water is nevertheless laterally through the permeable strata, and where these strata lie between relatively impermeable strata, the latter tend to form more or less effective confining beds. If the strata are tilted or deformed the water may be led from the intake areas of the permeable strata for long distances and to great depths through the conduits thus produced. It is a common fallacy to say that ground water always moves down the dip. In fact it generally moves down the dip for some distance from the intake area, but in its later course it may move down or up, according to the deformation of the strata, as, for example, in the Dakota sandstone and in the synclines that give rise to most of the thermal springs in the Appalachian area.

If the loss in head is less than the net descent of the water-bearing strata the water comes to be under artesian pressure in the sense that it will rise in wells to some level above the top of the aquifer; if the loss in head is less than the descent of the land surface the artesian pressure may be sufficient to cause the wells to overflow, thus producing an area of artesian flow. Many other structural features besides tilted or deformed strata may also produce artesian conditions, but the general principles are the same.

A piezometric surface of any aquifer is an imaginary surface that everywhere coincides with the head of the water in the aquifer. In areas of artesian flow it is above the land surface. Contour maps of piezometric surfaces are useful in much the same way as contour maps of the water table, in indicating the general direction of movement of the water and hence its approximate source and destination. Like water-table maps, they show only the horizontal direction of the movement, whereas if the confining beds are not entirely impermeable, there is generally upward or downward leakage through them. Thus if the water above the overlying confining bed is under greater head than the water in the confined aquifer there will be percolation into the aquifer, but if it is under less head there will be loss of water from the aquifer by upward escape. In many of the artesian systems the movement of water through the confining beds is an important factor in the recharge and discharge of the aquifer and in the building up or loss of head.

It has been recommended that for international purposes the following terms of Greek origin be used to designate the two kinds of plerotic water: "Phreatic water," for the water that occurs under water-table conditions, and "piestic water," for the water that occurs under artesian conditions in the sense that it is confined and is therefore under sufficient pressure to rise in wells above the bottom of the relatively impermeable formation or stratum that serves as the confining bed; further that three kinds of piestic water be recognized—hyperpiestic water, which will rise above the land surface; mesopiestic water, which will rise above the water table but not to the land surface; and hypopiestic water, which will rise above the bottom of the confining bed but not to the water table.

The water supplies of the springs and wells in the United States are largely derived from formations that have essentially water-table conditions. These are the surficial deposits of sand and gravel; the sandstones and limestones in their outcrop areas; the extrusive volcanic rocks of the Northwest; and the dense igneous and metamorphic rocks and clays and shales, which are commonly rendered somewhat permeable by weathering near the surface. As these formations are extensively exposed at the surface, their supplies are readily replenished by the water from rain and snow. The largest supplies of water come from the deposits of sand and gravel (in part artesian), and these may be grouped as follows: (1) Glacial outwash from the continental ice sheets occurring from the Atlantic to the Pacific, (2) valley fill in the western mountain region, (3) Tertiary and Quaternary deposits in the Great Plains region, and (4) Tertiary and Quaternary terrace and lowland deposits in the Atlantic and Gulf Coastal Plain.

The principal artesian systems in the United States are (1) the extensive Paleozoic artesian system, occupying a large part of the east-central region, in which the shales confine water under artesian pressure in the sandstones and limestones; (2) the small but productive Roswell artesian basin, in New Mexico, in which cavernous Permian limestone is the artesian formation; (3) the artesian system formed by the entire Atlantic and Gulf Coastal Plain, in which Cretaceous and Tertiary strata dip toward the sea, and the water in the sands and limestones is held under artesian pressure by the interbedded shales; (4) the Cretaceous artesian system of the northern and central parts of the Great Plains region, in which water is confined in the sandstones, under great artesian pressure, by the thick, dense overlying shales; (5) numerous small and imperfect artesian systems in the glacial drift; and (6) numerous artesian systems in the valley fill of the western mountain region, the largest of which are in the San Joaquin Valley, in California, and the San Luis Valley, in Colorado. In most areas of artesian flow the pressure has greatly diminished and where large supplies are obtained the wells are generally pumped.

PERMEABILITY OF WATER-BEARING MATERIALS

The hydraulic permeability of a porous material is its characteristic property of transmitting water through its interstices. The degree of this property has been designated by different names and has been expressed by various combinations of units of space and time. It is now rather widely called the coefficient of permeability.

The standard coefficient of permeability used in the hydrologic work of the United States Geological Survey (Fig. XB-3) is defined as the rate of flow of water at 60°F., in gallons a day, through a cross section of 1 square foot, under a hydraulic gradient of 100 percent. A related coefficient, which may be called the "field coefficient of permeability," is defined as the rate of flow of water, in gallons a day, under prevailing conditions, through each foot of thickness of a given aquifer in a width of 1 mile, for each foot per mile of hydraulic gradient. The standard coefficient is designated by P_m and the field coefficient by P_f. The standard coefficient of permeability can generally be computed very closely by multiplying the field coefficient by the ratio of (1) the viscosity of the water in the stratum to (2) the viscosity of water at 60°F.

Recently Theis [30, p. 520] introduced the very convenient term "coefficient of transmissibility," which is the "field coefficient of permeability" multiplied by the thickness, in feet, of the saturated part of the aquifer. Thus the coefficient of permeability denotes a characteristic of the water-bearing material, whereas the coefficient of transmissibility denotes the analogous characteristic of the aquifer as a whole.

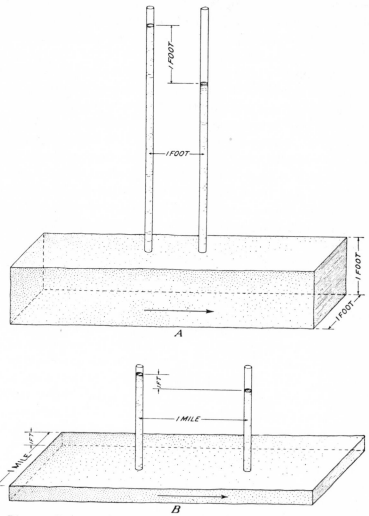

Fig. Xʙ-3.—Diagrams illustrating laboratory and field application of the coefficient of permeability used in the hydrologic work of the United States Geologic Survey.

Natural earth materials that have been tested in the hydrologic laboratory of the United States Geological Survey have been found to have coefficients of permeability ranging from about 0.0002 to about 90,000 —that is, the most permeable material carries water at a rate about 450,000,000 times that of the least permeable material. However, most water-bearing materials utilized by wells have coefficients that are whole numbers of two or more figures, generally between 10 and 5,000.

As the permeability of water-bearing materials is of fundamental importance in the study of ground water, it is not surprising that much work has been done in developing accurate and feasible methods of determining this property. The different methods may be grouped as (1) direct laboratory methods, (2) indirect laboratory methods, (3) field-velocity methods, and (4) field-discharge methods. The methods now chiefly used are the direct laboratory methods and the field-discharge methods [18, pp. 126–136].

The development of the direct laboratory methods has been discussed above. The permeability of a given sample can readily be determined with good accuracy in the laboratory, but it is often not practicable to obtain undisturbed samples, and the permeability of material that has been repacked after having its texture destroyed may be very different from that of the undisturbed material as it occurs in nature. Moreover, the permeability of most water-bearing formations differs so greatly, both stratigraphically and from place to place, that it is difficult to obtain a suite of even fairly representative samples.

In the ground-water work of the United States Geological Survey permeameters of several kinds are used, but they are all of the U-tube type, with the water generally percolating upward through the sample under low head. In the discharging type the water is discharged at a constant level, but the head may be kept constant by an overflow arrangement at the elevated intake, or, as in the apparatus used in the field for rapid work, the head is allowed to decrease as water passes through the sample and no new water is added. In the nondischarging type, which is especially adapted for tests with very low hydraulic gradients or very low permeability, no water is added and none is discharged from the U tube after the experiment has been started. Hence, as the water passes through the sample the water level in the supply limb of the tube declines and the water level in the receiving limb rises, the hydraulic gradient becoming less and less as the experiment proceeds.

In the indirect laboratory methods the permeability is computed from the mechanical composition and porosity. The work of Hazen, King, and Slichter in this respect has been concisely reviewed by Mrs. Stearns [28, pp. 170–176]. More recent work has been done by Fair and Hatch [5] and by Graton and Fraser [7]. Hazen [10, 11], in his work on filter sands in 1889 to 1893, used the term "effective size of grain," or size of grain that would give the permeability of a more or less heterogeneous material. He found that in the materials with which he was dealing the effective size was best shown by the "10 percent size"—that is, the size that is not exceeded by the grains in 10 percent of the material by weight [28]. These indirect methods of computing permeability are useful for some purposes but have not always given consistent results and are not in general to be recommended. Direct tests of permeability require no more work and are generally more satisfactory.

The field-velocity methods have also been mentioned above. They have been used chiefly to determine the underflow in stream valleys and are not generally feasible for investigations of aquifers that lie at considerable depths. Great uncertainties are generally involved in making computations of transmissibility from the data obtained by velocity methods, because of the difficulties in ascertaining the average velocity and the average effective porosity.

There are now in use in the United States Geological Survey several somewhat interrelated field-discharge methods or groups of methods that are expressed by formulas designated as the Thiem formula and associated limiting formula, the gradient formula, the non-equilibrium formula, and the recovery formula. These methods are described on pages 461–473.

STORAGE IN RELATION TO MOVEMENT

Another favorite question is, "How much water is there below the earth's surface?" This question was elaborately discussed by Fuller [8], who showed that several estimates have been made which, expressed as a layer of water over the entire earth, ranged from a thickness of a few thousand feet, according to some of the earlier estimates, down to Fuller's own estimate of only about 100 feet. It appears that while some of the older estimates are too large, that of Fuller is too small. Divergent though they are, these estimates all agree that the quantity of water in the rocks is much less than the quantity in the ocean but many times as great as the quantity in the lakes, streams, and atmosphere. These estimates considered only the water that occurs in the interstices of the rocks in the so-called zone of fracture and did not include the water in chemical combination nor the water that occurs, in molecular or dissociated form, in unknown quantities, in the interior of the earth. They included, however, the water in the rocks below the ocean. As the rocks below the land areas are more porous than those below the ocean, the estimates for the land areas alone would have been proportionately higher.

Of the water that occurs below the surface of the land probably less than half is free to flow out of the rocks into spring outlets or into wells, the rest being held by molecular attraction. Of the water that is not held by molecular attraction, only a part is fresh water with free circulation, most of the deep water being salty water that is apparently stationary or nearly so. Finally, of the fresh water that is free to flow, only a part is economically recoverable for human use. Nevertheless the quantities of fresh water available in storage in the most productive aquifers are very great—so great that in some places millions of gallons a day can be withdrawn from storage for a period of years before marked evidence of depletion occurs.

The slow movement of water through the permeable rock formations is comparable to the movement of water through a surface lake or reservoir from the mouths of the tributaries to the outlet. Some aquifers function chiefly as reservoirs and others chiefly as conduits, but all have some of the properties of both [18]. In all adequate ground-water studies these two functions must be recognized and differentiated.

It is generally considered that, for the most part, the formations or parts of formations that yield water with only moderate contents of dissolved mineral matter form parts of circulating systems in which water of meteoric origin flows from the intakes to the outlets of the formations, ultimately flushing out the salty connate water; and conversely to a great extent the formations or parts of formations that contain salty water have little or no circulation.

To a large extent the Paleozoic formations of the interior of the United States are below sea level and have perhaps never been above the present level of the sea. Over much of the region there are almost no means of escape for the deep water and almost no head to induce movement. Throughout most of the region the deep water is salty, though different in composition from the sea water. Thus there is reason to believe that, through the ages, there has been only very sluggish circulation through the deep-lying parts of the Paleozoic rocks and that the salty water is largely connate or at least very ancient [18, p. 224]. Within a few hundred feet of the surface there is more vigorous movement of the ground water from the upland areas of intake toward the stream valleys; consequently, the water in the Paleozoic rocks near the surface is generally fresh, and much of it is of excellent quality.

The fact that the deep artesian water is not so heavily mineralized in the areas adjacent to the Mississippi River as in most other parts of the interior region suggests that freshening may have been in progress ever since the valleys were cut, as a result of upward leakage of the artesian water in the valleys and its replacement by percolation of water from intake areas in northern Wisconsin and Minnesota, the Ozark area, and elsewhere.

It is believed that some of the artesian aquifers of the Atlantic and Gulf Coastal Plain have submarine outcrops that form potential outlets for the artesian water, whereas others pinch out or become impermeable at their seaward edge. In the aquifers that have outlets the fresh artesian water presses against the heavier sea water. If the head of the fresh water is relatively high and the submarine outlet is not too far below sea level, the fresh water discharges into the sea. Otherwise the sea water backs up into the aquifer and maintains a static condition, except as the fresh water may escape upward through the confining beds. In some places aquifers containing water of excellent quality occur below beds containing salt water. Flowing and pumped wells reduce the head and may thus cause the sea water to percolate toward them. To some extent the existing conditions may have been inherited from the Pleistocene epoch, when the sea stood at times higher and at other times lower than at present. This entire complex subject is receiving much critical study and will require much more [40, 41].

That salty water is definitely in circulation in some places is shown by the occurrence of large salt-water springs. Generally, as in the Tularosa Basin and the Malaga Bend area, in New Mexico, such springs derive their salt from salt deposits, but in some places, as at the salt spring in Florida, the source of the salt is still problematic.

If there were no intake or recharge the ground-water systems would gradually run down, somewhat like a clock that is not wound. But the ground-water systems form parts of the "hydrologic cycle." From time to time rain and snow descend upon the earth and a part of the water thus provided finds its way down to the water table. Whenever and wherever this occurs new water goes into storage in the aquifer, the water table is built up, the head is increased, new energy is supplied, and the movement of the ground water is quickened.

Recharge is never uniformly distributed but occurs chiefly in certain localities that are favorable for intake. Hence, the water table is built up irregularly, its shape is changed, and mounds are developed on it in the principal intake areas. Hence, the whole three-dimensional system of hydraulic gradients becomes disturbed, new lateral components of these gradients are developed, the direction of movement of the ground water is modified, and many of the water particles change their courses and head for new outlets. Whenever the water table is lowered in any discharge area—as at springs, in localities of ground-water evaporation and transpiration, or by pumping or artesian flow from wells—a series of changes occur which are the converse of those that result from recharge. It is these irregular changes in head that make the hydraulics of ground water complex.

The adjustments that result from disturbances in the head do not occur instantaneously, because they require the transfer of water from the localities of high head to those of low head. Moreover, the ground-water systems are not entirely like clocks, which run down at a uniform rate and come suddenly to a stop, but they approach an equilibrium condition with constantly diminishing speed. This fact has been recognized more or less for a long time so far as water-table conditions are concerned. Until rather recently it has been tacitly assumed that artesian systems are rigid. Under such conditions changes in head would be transmitted quickly, as no transfer of water would be involved except the small amount due to the slight volume elasticity of the water.

In studies of the Dakota artesian system by the senior author in 1923 and 1924 he recognized from several lines of evidence that the artesian system does not perform like a rigid system but like one having volume elasticity and hence variation in storage capacity with changes in the internal buoyant force due to artesian head. He found evidence that a large part of the water that had been discharged from the flowing wells was water taken from storage by compression of the water-bearing beds with loss of the artesian head. Consequently he stated the theory of the compressibility and elasticity of artesian aquifers [21, 17], which has since been verified by observations in many other areas. The phenomenon of compressibility has been found to be of great practical importance in the study of ground water and petroleum, it has caused the subsidence of the land surface in some heavily pumped localities [34], and it will probably be found to cause subsidence in many others. Presumably the compression and also re-expansion occur largely in the strata of relatively fine grain which feed into the strata of coarser grain that supply the wells [20, 34].

It has generally been considered that under artesian conditions there is very little lag in the surrender of the water due to compression. However, it now appears that if the principal compression occurs in fine-grained deposits that have low permeability and may be connected only rather indirectly with the most permeable part of the aquifer, there may be much more lag than has been assumed, and the quantities of artesian water removed from storage may be greater than is indicated by the coefficients of storage determined in tests of short duration.

The non-equilibrium method developed by Theis [30, 31] with the aid of C. I. Lubin attacks the problem of the hydraulics of ground water before equilibrium is reached, thereby involving time as a variable. It applies the mathematical theory of heat conduction to ground-water hydraulics. As Theis stated, this analogy between ground water and heat has been recognized at least since the work of Slichter, but apparently no previous successful attempt had been made to introduce the function of time into the mathematics of ground-water hydrology. With this formula it has become possible to use the hydrologic data in computing the long-term effects of pumping from wells, and it has led to new methods of determining permeability and storage coefficients. Recently Jacob [13] developed the non-equilibrium formula directly from hydrologic concepts without recourse to the analogy of heat.

HYDRAULICS OF WELLS

Works of man in relation to head and movement

Among the human projects that affect changes in the head and movement of the ground water are wells, dams, mines, tunnels, canals, railroad and highway cuts, and other structures and operations in connection with irrigation, drainage, river improvement, artificial recharge, flood control, deforestation and forestation, grazing, and agriculture. Whereas natural changes are generally gradual and lie within a moderate range, some of the changes produced by man are sudden and great, notably the heavy pumping from wells and the withdrawal of water by artesian flow.

Because of the importance of the development of water supplies from wells and of the other human activities that affect the ground-water regimen, the subject of the hydraulics of the ground water is of great practical significance and much attention is being given to it [12, 22]. The artificial disturbances, especially the withdrawal of water from wells, upset the approximate equilibrium of nature and create complicated conditions that make the hydraulics of the ground water complex. However, they also afford field laboratories in which the effects of definitely regulated changes can be observed and measured.

The Dupuit formula

The setting forth by Darcy [2] in 1856 of the law of ground-water movement made possible for the first time the mathematical treatment of the hydraulics of wells. Dupuit [4] apparently was the first to apply this treatment. He assumed the existence of a circular island (Fig. Xb-4) in the precise center of which is a well that extends through a permeable water-bearing formation of homogeneous character. The water-bearing formation rests on a horizontal impervious stratum. The water table extends horizontally beneath the entire island and is contiguous and level with the surface of a vast open reservoir whose supply is unlimited. Dupuit assumed further that the well was pumped at a constant rate for such a period that the cone of depression of the water table created by the pumping extended to the periphery of the island. A condition of hydraulic equilibrium then prevails—that is, the flow through each concentric cylindrical section around the well is equal to the flow through every other cylindrical section and is equal also to the discharge of the well.

According to Darcy's law the flow through each of the concentric cylindrical sections of water-bearing material is equal to PiA, where P is the coefficient of permeability, i is the hydraulic gradient and A is the cross-sectional area of the cylinder. If x is taken to be the radius of any cylinder and y the saturated thickness of material at the distance x from the well (Fig. Xb-4) the hydraulic gradient i is then equal to the rate of change of the coordinates—that is, $\dfrac{dy}{dx}$—and the cross-sectional area of the cylinder is equal to $2\pi xy$. The following formula can then be written to express the relation of the discharge of the well to the shape of the cone of depression:

$$Q = \int P \frac{dy}{dx} 2\pi xy$$

By integrating with respect to x and y

$$Q = \frac{\pi P y^2}{\log_e x} + c$$

At the periphery of the island the saturated thickness of water-bearing material is equal to H and at the wall of the well it is equal to h. The

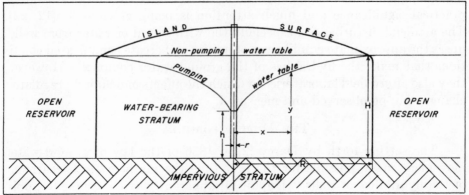

Fig. Xb-4.—Section showing ideal conditions assumed for the development of the Dupuit formula for water-table conditions.

radii of the two cylinders so delineated are R and r, respectively. By substituting these values for x and y the constant of integration is eliminated and the following equation is obtained:

$$Q = \frac{\pi P (H^2 - h^2)}{\log_e R - \log_e r}$$

This is the Dupuit formula for water-table conditions. The corresponding formula for artesian conditions is

$$Q = \frac{2\pi P m (H - h)}{\log_e R - \log_e r}$$

in which m is the thickness of the artesian stratum.

These formulas presumably were developed for the purpose of predicting the yield of wells in areas where estimates could be made of the permeability of the water-bearing material. It appears unlikely, however, that the formulas were ever used generally for this purpose, because the geologic and hydrologic conditions found in nature differ so widely from those on which the formulas are based. Wells are not situated in the centers of circular islands and therefore the cone of depression may expand almost indefinitely—that is, complete equilibrium probably will never be reached; some wells do not penetrate completely through the aquifer, and some are not screened in all parts of their extent through the aquifer; the strata on which the aquifers rest are not generally horizontal; the aquifer generally differs from place to place in both thickness and permeability; and the undisturbed water level is almost never horizontal. The Dupuit formula for water-table conditions is based on the erroneous assumption, moreover, that the water percolates to the pumped well in a horizontal direction, whereas, because of the drawdown of the water table, the movement is downward to some degree, and hence the cone of depression is altered somewhat from its theoretical form. Despite the obvious difficulties in applying the formulas, they have been included for years in the hydrologic literature with little or no discussion of their limitations.

The Thiem formula

In 1906 Günther Thiem [32], son of the German hydrologist Adolph Thiem, published the results of his work in connection with the determination of additional water supply for the city of Prague. In this investigation he determined the permeability of water-bearing material by means of pumping tests, using the following modified form of the Dupuit formula:

$$P = \frac{Q(\log_e r_2 - \log_e r_1)}{2\pi m(s_1 - s_2)}$$

in which P is the coefficient of permeability; Q is the rate of pumping, r_1 and r_2 are respective distances of two observation wells from the pumped well; m, for artesian conditions, is the vertical thickness of the water-bearing bed; m, for water-table conditions, is the average vertical thickness, at r_1 and r_2, of the saturated part of the water-bearing bed; and s_1 and s_2 are the drawdowns of the water level in two observation wells situated within the cone of depression. Thiem apparently was the first to employ the Dupuit formula for determining permeability and was also apparently the first to utilize the drawdowns in two observation wells. In recognition of these innovations the formula is generally called the Thiem formula in the United States.

The limiting formula

In 1930 the junior author made a study of the theoretical aspects of the development of the Thiem formula in an effort to evaluate at least qualitatively the effect of discrepancies between assumed and field conditions on computations of permeability. The study could not be carried

very far, however, because very little was known of the behavior of the
water level in the vicinity of discharging wells, and a search of the hydrologic literature disclosed practically no experimental data on the subject.
In order to obtain information of this kind a rather elaborate pumping

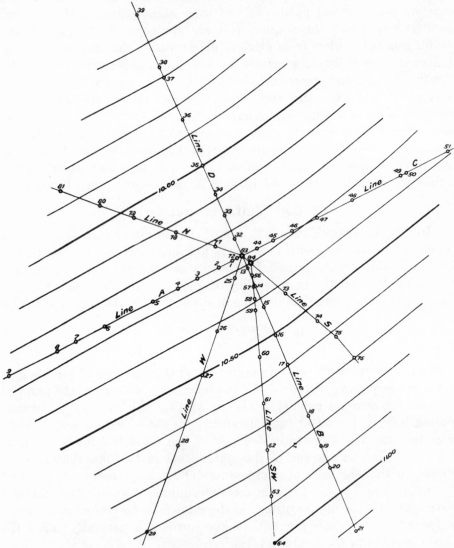

FIG. XB-5.—Map of a tract near Grand Island, Neb., showing contours on the water table before
pumping.   Scale, one inch equals about 190 feet.   Contour interval 0.1 foot.

test was made near Grand Island, Nebr., in the summer of 1931.   The
drawdown of the water table during the period of pumping and the recovery of the water table after the pumping was stopped were observed
through frequent measurements of the water levels in more than 80

observation wells situated out to about 1,200 feet on eight lines radiating from the pumped well [37]. Contours on the water table before pumping and 2 hours after pumping was begun are shown in Figures XB-5 and XB-6; profiles of the cone of depression are shown in Figure XB-7.

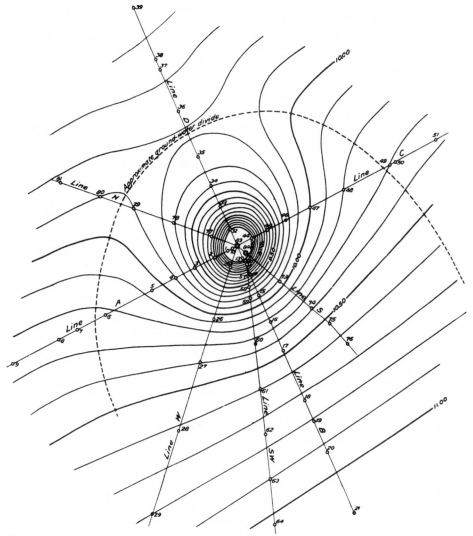

FIG. XB-6.—Map of the same tract near Grand Island, showing contours on the water table two hours after pumping was begun.

The data obtained in the Grand Island test were studied carefully, and a method of procedure was devised taking into account the limitations in applying the Thiem formula to field conditions [38]. It was found that consistent results for permeability can be obtained, providing the following procedure is observed: (1) Only those drawdowns are used that are

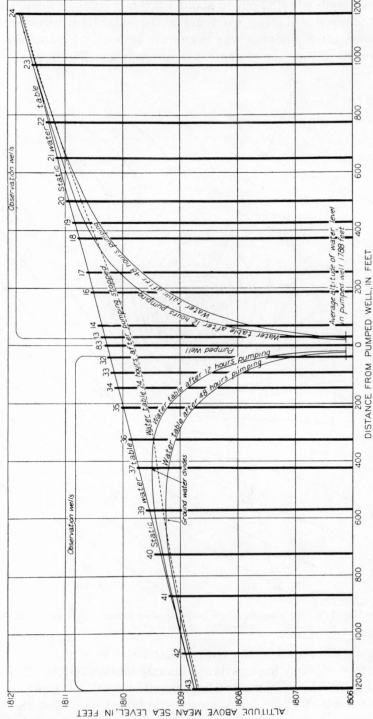

Fig. Xʙ-7.—Profiles of the water table in the vicinity of a pumped well.   Data obtained in pumping test near Grand Island, Neb.

obtained from observation wells situated on a straight line extending through the pumped well; (2) the drawdown of the water level s_1 is taken to be the average of the drawdowns on the opposite sides of the pumped well (preferably up gradient and down gradient) at the distance r_1 from the pumped well, and, similarly, s_2 is taken to be the average of the drawdowns on opposite sides of the pumped well at the distance r_2, etc.; (3) drawdowns are used only for wells within that part of the cone of depression that has reached approximate equilibrium in form by the end of the period of pumping; (4) drawdowns are used only for wells situated sufficiently far from the pumped well so that no appreciable effects on the slope of the water table are caused by the failure of the well to penetrate the entire thickness of the aquifer, or by changes in permeability of the water-bearing material produced by the development of the well; and (5) the drawdowns obtained at more than two distances from the pumped well are used.

Successful determinations of permeability have since been made in Nebraska [16, pp. 100–105], Kansas [39], and elsewhere by following this empirical procedure. The formula now is sometimes called the limiting formula and is written

$$P_f = 527.7qC$$

in which P_f is the field coefficient of permeability as defined previously in this paper, q is the discharge of the pumped well in gallons a minute, and C is a constant, equal to $\dfrac{A}{B}$, that is determined graphically. A is equal to

$$\frac{\log_{10}\dfrac{r_2}{r_1}}{0.25M}$$

and B is equal to

$$\tfrac{1}{2}(s_{1u} + s_{1d} - s_{2u} - s_{2d})$$

in which r_1 and r_2 are distances, in feet, to two points on the cone of depression that lie on a straight line through the pumped well; s_{1u} is the drawdown, in feet, on the line at the distance r_1 up gradient from the pumped well; s_{1d} is the drawdown, in feet, on the line at distance r_1 down gradient from the pumped well; s_{2u} is the drawdown, in feet, at the distance r_2 up gradient; s_{2d} is the drawdown, in feet, at the distance r_2 down-gradient; and M is the sum of the saturated thicknesses of water-bearing material, in feet, at the points of the four drawdowns.

To obtain C, all possible values of A are plotted against corresponding values of B and a straight line is drawn through the plotted points. More than one point is necessary, of course, to determine the plotted line and hence at least six observation wells—three up gradient and as many down gradient—are required. C is determined from the slope of the straight line. If most of the points do not fall approximately on a straight line through the origin, the differences between assumed conditions and field conditions are thus indicated to be great, and the method cannot be used.

BEHAVIOR OF GROUND WATER IN THE VICINITY OF DISCHARGING WELLS

The pumping test made near Grand Island, Nebr., in 1931 and the several tests made since then in other localities have provided much factual information on the behavior of the ground water in the vicinities of discharging wells under different conditions.

As soon as a pump begins discharging water from a well that penetrates an aquifer with a water table the water table is lowered around the well and a hydraulic gradient from all directions is established toward the well. The water table soon assumes a form that is comparable to an inverted cone, although it is not a true cone. Where the water-bearing material is homogeneous the base of this cone of depression, or area of influence, will be circular if the water table is initially horizontal, but somewhat elliptical if the water table has an initial slope. Some water-bearing material will be unwatered by the decline of the water table, and the water drained from this material will percolate toward the pumped well. Thus for a short time after pumping is begun most of the water that is pumped may be obtained from unwatered sediments comparatively close to the pumped well, and temporarily very little water may be drawn to the well from greater distances. However, as pumping is continued a hydraulic gradient that is nearly an equilibrium gradient will be established close to the well, and water will be transmitted through the water-bearing material close to the well at nearly the rate at which it is being pumped.

The decline of the water table and the resultant unwatering of material in this area will then proceed at a much slower rate. This necessitates the percolation of more water from greater distances, and hence the cone of depression will expand, gradually draining material farther away. Thus as the pumping of the well continues, more of the formation will gradually be unwatered, and an equilibrium gradient that will transmit to the well approximately the amount of water that is being pumped will be established at increasing distances from the well. Such an equilibrium gradient can be established only by an increase in drawdown. The water table near the well, in order to maintain an approximate equilibrium form, will therefore continue to lower indefinitely but at a decreasing rate.

If no water is added to the formation, the water table will continue to decline so long as the well is pumped, and the cone of depression will eventually extend to the limits of the formation. Recharge to the formation, however, may halt the development of the cone of depression by furnishing additional water that will become a supply for the pumped well.

The piezometric surface under artesian conditions behaves in a manner very similar to the behavior of a water table. Water is at first removed from storage, not by the unwatering of a part of the formation but rather by the compaction of the aquifer and of the included and associated beds of silt and clay as the head is reduced. The squeezing out of water by compaction delays the development of the cone of depression in much the same way as the development under water-table conditions is delayed by the unwatering of part of the formation. However, the quantity of water removed by compaction is generally much less than the quantity removed by the unwatering of a part of a formation, and consequently the drawdown of the water levels in the observation wells and the development of the cone of depression are usually more rapid.

One distinct difference exists between the removal of water from storage by the compaction of the aquifer and the removal of water from storage by the unwatering of a part of a formation in which a water table exists. The specific yield of a formation is not related to its thickness, hence lowering of the water table a given amount will release the same quantity of water to the pumped well regardless of the thickness of the formation. On the other hand, the volume of water released by the compaction of an aquifer and associated beds depends on their aggregate thickness, and hence a lowering of the water level of a given amount in a well discharging from an artesian aquifer will release more water to the well if the beds are thick than if they are thin.

It has been found by many investigators that a material after being saturated and allowed to drain will yield water for a considerable period. Although the material may yield a very large percentage of its water in a few hours or days, it may continue to yield small amounts for several years. The sand and gravel unwatered during the pumping test near Grand Island, Nebr., drained in such a manner that the computed specific yield of the material was 9.2 after 6 hours of pumping, 11.7 after 12 hours, 16.1 after 24 hours, 18.5 after 36 hours, and 20.1 after 48 hours [38, p. 55]. A much longer period of pumping would have been required before the true specific yield of the material was reached. The true specific yield was estimated to lie between 22 and 23.

Where the water table or piezometric surface initially is horizontal and the ideal conditions outlined by Dupuit exist, water percolates to a discharging well from all directions, moving on about straight lines from all directions to the well. Equal quantities of water percolate to the well through concentric cylindrical cross sections. In most places, however, the water level initially is not horizontal, and as a result water percolates to the discharging well in somewhat circuitous paths. Because the slope of the cone of depression is steeper up gradient from the discharging well than down gradient, more water percolates to the well from the up-gradient side. The slope of the cone down gradient becomes progressively less than the slope at the corresponding distance up gradient, until at some distance down gradient from the well the water table or piezometric surface is horizontal. This point lies on the ground-water divide. The ground-water divide extends up gradient in the general form of a parabola and separates the water that eventually percolates to the well from that which percolates down gradient past the well. All the water beyond the divide percolates away from the discharging well and all the water between the divide and the well percolates toward the well. If withdrawal of water from the well continues at a uniform rate, the cone of depression gradually becomes larger, and the ground-water divide gradually moves farther from the pumped well, but this movement occurs at a decreasing rate.

After the discharge of a well is stopped, water momentarily continues to percolate toward the well under the hydraulic gradient set up during the period that the well was operating, but instead of being discharged by the well it refills the well and the interstices of the material that were unwatered, or, under artesian conditions, it expands the aquifer and associated beds. As the formation near the well is gradually refilled, the hydraulic gradient toward the well is decreased and the recovery becomes progressively slower. At distances comparatively far from the well the water level may continue to lower for a considerable time after the discharge ceases, because at those distances water is still being taken from the interstices of the material to supply the water that refills the beds around the well. In time there is a general equalization of water levels over the entire region, and the water table or piezometric surface will assume a form similar to that it had under the original static conditions, although it may remain temporarily or permanently somewhat lower than before water was withdrawn.

In the Grand Island test [38, p. 35], as well as in other tests, the water table very close to the pumped well approximately regained its original slope very soon after pumping stopped. Even though the water table close to the pumped well initially had a greater amount to recover, the rate of rise after a certain time reduced to about the rate of rise of the water table at greater distances, and the remaining drawdown at both distances became approximately the same. Thus 12 hours after pumping stopped in the Grand Island test the remaining drawdown was 0.77 foot at 24.9 feet, 59.9 feet, and 114.4 feet from the pumped well, although at the time pumping stopped the drawdowns were respectively 4.03, 2.81 and 2.03 feet. Presumably, at some later time the rate of recovery out to a distance greater than 115 feet would become essentially the same.

The gradient formula

The flow of water through the ideal hydrologic system postulated by Dupuit is equal to PiA, where P is the coefficient of permeability, i is the hydraulic gradient, and A is the area of any one of a series of concentric cylindrical cross sections of water-bearing material around the pumped well. Therefore

$$P = \frac{Q}{iA} = \frac{Q}{2\pi ixy}$$

in which y is the thickness of saturated water-bearing material at the distance x from the pumped well. The equation can be solved directly for P by determining the hydraulic gradient graphically from a profile of the cone of depression.

The nonpumping water level in most formations has a slope, and therefore the flow of water toward a discharging well is not everywhere normal to cylindrical sections around the well. The flow is normal only along a line that extends directly up gradient and down gradient through the pumped well. The flow through a given cross-sectional area at a specified distance up gradient is greater than the flow through an equal cross-sectional area at the same distance down gradient. The data collected in the pumping tests at Grand Island indicates that the hydraulic gradient causing the flow is approximately equal to the average of the gradients at a given distance up gradient and down gradient from the pumped well. Thus, for water-table conditions

$$P = \frac{2Q}{\pi x(y_u + y_d)(i_u + i_d)}$$

in which i_u is the hydraulic gradient and y_u is the saturated thickness of the water-bearing material at the distance x up gradient, and i_d is the hydraulic gradient and y_d is the saturated thickness of water-bearing material at the distance x down gradient.

The hydraulic gradient at any distance r on one side of the pumped well can be determined approximately from a profile of the cone of depression by (1) ascertaining from the profile the altitude of the water table at the distances $(r + b)$ and $(r - b)$ from the pumped well and (2) dividing the difference in altitude of the water table at the two distances by $2b$. A study of the data collected in the pumping tests indicates that the hydraulic gradient can generally be determined satisfactorily from profiles of the cone of depression by taking the distance b as 10 feet. For water-table conditions

$$P_f = \frac{18{,}335q}{r(y_u + y_d)\left(f_{(r+10)u} + f_{(r+10)d} - f_{(r-10)u} - f_{(r-10)d}\right)}$$

and for artesian conditions

$$P_f = \frac{9{,}168q}{rm(f_{(r+10)u} + f_{(r+10)d} - f_{(r-10)u} - f_{(r-10)d})}$$

in which P_f is the field coefficient of permeability as defined previously, q is the discharge of the pumped well in gallons a minute, r is the distance, in feet, from the pumped well to any point on the part of the cone of depression that has reached an approximate equilibrium form, y_u and y_d are the respective thicknesses, in feet, of saturated water-bearing material at the distance r up-gradient and down-gradient from the pumped well, $f_{(r+10)u}$ and $f_{(r+10)d}$ are the respective altitudes, in feet, of the water level at the distance $r + 10$ up gradient and down gradient from the pumped well, $f_{(r-10)u}$ and $f_{(r-10)d}$ are the respective altitudes, in feet, of the water level at the distance $r - 10$ up gradient and down gradient from the pumped well, and m is the thickness, in feet, of the aquifer.

This formula is called the gradient formula. It has been used successfully to determine permeability from the data obtained in pumping tests in Nebraska, Kansas, and Arkansas.

THE NON-EQUILIBRIUM FORMULA

All the formulas so far described are based on the assumption that the hydraulic system can attain a state of equilibrium (steady-state of flow) —a condition that is reached only approximately near the discharging well. The factor of time is included in the formulas only in the sense that the well is assumed to have been operating for a sufficient period to produce a state of equilibrium.

In 1935 Theis [30] gave a formula for determining the drawdown of the water level in the vicinity of a discharging well, taking into account the removal of water from storage. This formula may be called a non-equilibrium formula because it does not depend on the hydraulic system reaching a state of equilibrium. The formula is based on the assumption that Darcy's law is analogous to the law of flow of heat by conduction and thus that the mathematical theory of heat conduction is largely applicable to hydraulic theory. The formula may be written

$$s = \frac{114.6q}{T} \int_{\frac{1.87r^2 S}{Tt}}^{\infty} \frac{e^{-u}}{u}\, du$$

in which s is the drawdown, in feet, at any point in the vicinity of a well pumped at a uniform rate; q is the discharge of the well, in gallons a minute; T is the coefficient of transmissibility of the aquifer (the field coefficient of permeability multiplied by the saturated thickness of the aquifer); r is the distance, in feet, of the pumped well to the point of observation; S is a coefficient of storage (cubic feet of water discharged from each vertical column of aquifer with base 1 foot square for each foot of lowering in head) as a decimal fraction; and t is the time, in days, that the well has been pumped.

The value of the integral

$$\int_{\frac{1.87r^2S}{Tt}}^{\infty} \frac{e^{-u}}{u} \, du$$

may be computed by the series

$$\int_{\frac{1.87r^2S}{Tt}}^{\infty} \frac{e^{-u}}{u} \, du = -0.577216 - \log_e u + u - \frac{u^2}{2 \cdot 2!} + \frac{u^3}{3 \cdot 3!} \cdots$$

in which

$$u = \frac{1.87r^2S}{Tt}$$

The formula is based on the assumptions that (1) the water-bearing formation is homogeneous and isotropic, (2) the formation has an indefinite areal extent, (3) the pumped well penetrates the entire thickness of water-bearing formation, (4) the coefficient of transmissibility is constant at all places and at all times, (5) the pumped well has an infinitesimal diameter, (6) the initial nonpumping piezometric surface is horizontal, (7) the impervious bed underlying the water-bearing bed is horizontal, and (8) water is taken from storage instantaneously by the decline in head.

Because the formula assumes that the transmissibility of the water-bearing material does not change during the period of pumping it can be applied strictly only to artesian conditions. Where the thickness of saturated material is great, however, it can probably be used also for water-table conditions without introducing serious error. For water-table conditions, the coefficient of storage is the specific yield of the water-bearing material.

As the coefficient of transmissibility appears on both sides of the equation, the formula cannot be solved directly for T (and therefore for the coefficient of permeability). However, T may be determined conveniently by the following graphic method suggested by Theis (personal communication, 1937). The formula may be written

$$s = \frac{114.6q}{T} \cdot W(u)$$

in which $W(u)$ may be read "well function of u" and the other terms are those previously defined. $W(u)$ is equal to

$$-0.577216 - \log_e u + u - \frac{u^2}{2 \cdot 2!} + \frac{u^3}{3 \cdot 3!} \cdots$$

and u is equal to

$$\frac{1.87\ r^2 S}{Tt}.$$

When T is to be determined from observations of the drawdown in one well, the logarithm of the drawdown is plotted against the logarithm of reciprocal of time since pumping began $\left(s \text{ against } \frac{1}{t}\right)$. When T is to be determined from the drawdowns in a line of wells, the logarithm of the drawdown is plotted against the logarithm of $\frac{r^2}{t}$. If the formation were entirely homogeneous and if water were discharged instantaneously with the fall in pressure, all plotted points (for all times and all wells) would fall on a smooth curve. The curve so determined is a segment of the type curve produced by plotting the logarithm of the value of the integral, $W(u)$, against the logarithm of the quantity u. If, therefore, (1) this type curve is plotted on logarithmic paper and (2) the observed drawdowns are plotted on transparent paper against $\frac{1}{t}$ (for one observation well) or $\frac{r^2}{t}$ (for a line of observation wells) to a logarithmic scale the same as that used for plotting the type curve, (3) the observed curve can be fitted to the type curve in only one place. Then (4) from this fit the value of $W(u)$ and the corresponding value of u may be determined from the type curve for any selected point on the curve of observed values, which (5) may be used in conjunction with the observed values for that point to determine T.

The coefficient of transmissibility is then computed by the formula

$$T = 114.6q\ \frac{W(u)}{s}$$

and the coefficient of permeability

$$P_f = \frac{114.6q}{m}\left(\frac{W(u)}{s}\right)$$

in which m is the saturated thickness of water-bearing material.

This method for determining permeability has been applied successfully to pumping tests made in Nebraska and elsewhere [39]. The coefficients of permeability determined from the drawdowns in wells located on a line through the pumped well (averaged in the same manner as for the limiting formula) checked very closely the permeabilities computed by both the limiting and the gradient formulas. However, the permeabilities computed by the non-equilibrium method, using the drawdowns in any one well, differed considerably from the permeabilities computed by the other methods and varied considerably, depending on which well was selected for the computation. This apparently was the result of the slow draining of the unwatered material, which altered the form of the drawdown curve from its theoretical form by making it relatively too steep for a time after pumping began and relatively too flat toward the end of the period of pumping. It is tentatively concluded, therefore, that at least for water-table conditions the coefficient of permeability should be determined by the non-equilibrium formula only from the drawdowns in observation wells situated on a line through the pumped well (from the shape of the cone of depression rather than from the shape of the drawdown curve).

The recovery formula

Theis [30] introduced also a formula for determining transmissibility from the recovery of the water level in a well after its discharge has stopped. It is based on the assumption that if a well is pumped or allowed to flow for a known period, the residual drawdown at any instant after the discharge of the well has stopped will be the same as if the discharge of the well had continued but a recharge well with the same flow had been introduced at the same point in the flow system at the instant the discharge stopped. Hydrologic and geologic assumptions are the same as for the non-equilibrium formula.

The formula may be written

$$T = \frac{264q}{s} \log_{10} \frac{t^1}{t}$$

in which T is the coefficient of transmissibility; q is the discharge of the well, in gallons a minute; s is the residual drawdown of the water level, in feet; t^1 is the time since pumping started, in any unit; and t is the time since pumping stopped, expressed in the same unit as t^1.

The value of $\dfrac{\log_{10} \dfrac{t^1}{t}}{s}$ should be determined graphically by plotting $\log_{10} \dfrac{t^1}{t}$ against s. If most of the points do not fall on a straight line the formula cannot be applied with assurance.

Application of permeability formulas to areas of heavy withdrawal

It is sometimes necessary to determine the permeability of water-bearing materials in areas where the withdrawal of water from wells must be almost continuous and therefore where the undistributed water level cannot be ascertained—for example, in cities where the operation of city wells cannot be stopped except for short periods. Neither the equilibrium nor the non-equilibrium formula can be directly applied under such conditions, because the drawdown of the water level resulting from the withdrawal cannot be determined. However, a modified application of the formulas can be made provided the withdrawal from the well or group of wells can be maintained at a constant rate for an appreciable time and then changed to another rate that can be maintained uniformly for a similar period. The permeability is computed by utilizing in the permeability formulas the change in the drawdown of the water level in observation wells caused by the change in rate of withdrawal from the discharging wells. Where water is withdrawn from only one well the center of pumping may, of course, be considered to be at that well, but where the water is withdrawn from a group of wells the effective center of pumping must be determined from the location of the wells and the relative discharge of each well.

Extent of cone of depression

Until very recently little attention was given to the effect of the length of the period of pumping or flow on hydrologic problems dealing with wells. The length of time that wells are pumped or allowed to flow necessarily enters almost all computations of ground-water flow, but it has often been included implicitly—usually in an assumption. A factor for time does not appear in any of the formulas of the equilibrium type, yet it is included in the assumption that the ground-water system has reached a condition of equilibrium. In the formulas of the equilibrium type only the ultimate condition of the ground-water system is considered; thus the period of pumping is infinite, and no consideration is given to the differing hydrologic conditions that exist prior to stability.

The disregard of the unstable conditions of ground-water flow probably has been due, at least in part, to the difficulties involved in mathematical treatment. The recent introduction of the non-equilibrium method by Theis has materially aided the formulation of correct concepts, but precise mathematical treatment of all factors involved in an unstable system has not yet been accomplished.

Observations on the behavior of the water table around pumped wells made in connection with pumping tests by the United States Geological Survey and cooperating parties show that the form of the cone of depression reaches essential stability in a small area around a pumped well in a relatively short time after pumping begins. However, the area of essential stability expands very slowly, and a considerable period of pumping is necessary for the cone to reach an approximate equilibrium form very far from the pumped well. The basic assumption of the formulas of the equilibrium type—that equilibrium is reached—is for practical purposes valid for only a small area around a pumped well. Beyond this small area the assumption is far from true.

There is, of course, an appreciable drawdown of the water level far beyond the area around a pumped well in which the cone of depression attains an essential equilibrium form. For example, a drawdown in water level of 0.06 foot occurred 1,050 feet from the pumped well in the Grand Island test after 48 hours of pumping, but the cone of depression had reached essential equilibrium only to about 200 feet. Doubtless a measurable drawdown existed at that time beyond 1,050 feet. The Nebraska pumping tests indicate that the cone of depression reached essential stability in form to a distance from the pumped well that is only a very small proportion of the distance to which the effect of the pumping is transmitted. This observed condition is significant, because it definitely limits the rigorous use of the formulas of the equilibrium type to a very small area around a pumped well and virtually invalidates the use of the formulas for larger areas unless the period of pumping is very long.

Many of the formulas of the equilibrium type given in the literature, including those of Dupuit [4], Slichter [26, p. 360], and Turneaure and Russell [35, p. 269], include the determination of R, the distance from the pumped well at which the drawdown of the water level is inappreciable. Such formulas also assume that a condition of equilibrium exists over the entire area of influence—that is, from the pumped well to the distance R. This, as has just been pointed out, is far from true. Several investigators have given arbitrary values to be used for R—Slichter [26, p. 360], 600 feet; Muskat [23, p. 95], 500 feet; and Tolman [33, p. 387], 1,000 feet. Slichter and Muskat give values for R in connection with discussions of artesian conditions, and Tolman gives his value for both water-table and artesian conditions. Turneaure and Russell determine R by a formula involving the initial slope of the water level.

Although it is obvious that the use of R in formulas of the equilibrium type will generally result in determinations that are more or less in error, criticism of its use is based probably more on the implication that R represents the distance from a discharging well at which the effect of the discharge is negligible. Leggette [15, p. 493] recently observed appreciable fluctuations of water level in wells caused by the shutting down of pumped wells 1 to 7.1 miles distant. The extent of the cone of depression is of very practical significance in determining the spacing of wells and in the solving of many quantitative problems. It also has been the crux of important legal controversies. Because empirical values for R, presumably intended chiefly for the solving of formulas for the discharge of wells in areas of known permeability, appear so persistently in the literature, it has generally been assumed that the extent of the cone of depression does not exceed these values. That the cone of depression may extend far beyond 500, 600, or 1,000 feet is a correct theoretical deduction and a field observation.

REFERENCES

1. Daniell, Alfred, A textbook of the principles of physics, 2d ed., Macmillan & Co., 1885.

2. Darcy, H. P. G., Les fontaines publique de la ville de Dijon, Paris, 1856.

3. Dole, R. B., Use of fluorescein in the study of underground water: U. S. Geol. Survey Water-Supply Paper 160, pp. 73–85, 1906.

4. Dupuit, J., Études théoriques et pratiques sur le mouvement des eaux, 1863.

5. Fair, G. M., and Hatch, L. P., Fundamental factors governing stream-line flow of water through sands: Am. Water Works Assoc. Jour., vol. 25, No. 11, pp. 1551–1565, 1933.

6. Fishel, V. C., Further tests of permeability with low hydraulic gradients: Am. Geophys. Union Trans., 1935, pt. 2, pp. 499–503; see also Meinzer, O. E , and Fishel, V. C., Tests of permeability with low hydraulic gradients: Am. Geophys. Union Trans., 1934, pt. 2, pp. 405–409.

7. Fraser, H. J., Experimental study of the porosity and permeability of clastic sediments: Jour. Geology, vol. 43, No. 8, pp. 910–1010, 1935. See also Graton, L. C., and Fraser, H. J., Systematic packing of spheres, with particular relation to porosity and permeability: Idem, pp. 785–909.

8. Fuller, M. L., Total amount of free water in the earth's crust: U. S. Geol. Survey Water-Supply Paper 160, pp. 59–72, 1906.

9. Hagen, G., Ueber die Bewegung des Wassers in engen cylindrischen Röhren: Poggendorff Annalen, Band 46, pp. 423–442, 1839.

10. Hazen, Allen, Experiments upon the purification of sewage and water at the Lawrence Experiment Station, Nov. 1, 1889, to Dec. 31, 1891: Massachusetts State Board of Health 23d Ann. Rept., 1892.

11. Hazen, Allen, Some physical properties of sands and gravels with special reference to their use in filtration: Massachusetts State Board of Health 24th Ann. Rept., 1893.

12. Hubbert, M. K., The theory of ground-water motion: Jour. Geology, vol. 48, No. 8, pp. 785–944, 1940.

13. Jacob, C. E., On the flow of water in an elastic artesian aquifer: Am. Geophys. Union Trans., 1940, pt. 2, pp. 574–586.

14. King, F. H., Principles and conditions of the movements of ground water: U. S. Geol. Survey 19th Ann. Rept., pt. 2, pp. 59–294, 1899.

15. Leggette, R. M., The mutual interference of artesian wells on Long Island, New York: Am. Geophys. Union Trans., 1937, pp. 490–494.

16. Lugn, A. L., and Wenzel, L. K., Geology and ground-water resources of south-central Nebraska: U. S. Geol. Survey Water-Supply Paper 779, pp. 100–105, 1938.

17. Meinzer, O. E., Compressibility and elasticity of artesian aquifers: Econ. Geology, vol. 23, No. 13, pp. 263–291, 1928.

18. Meinzer, O. E., Outline of methods for estimating ground-water supplies: U. S. Geol. Survey Water-Supply Paper 638, pp. 99–144, 1932.

19. Meinzer, O. E., Movements of ground water: Am. Assoc. Petroleum Geologists Bull., vol. 20, pp. 704–725, 1936.

20. Meinzer, O. E., Our water supply: Washington Acad. Sci. Jour., vol. 27, pp. 85–101, 1937; Smithsonian Rept. for 1937, pp. 291–305, 1938.

21. Meinzer, O. E., and Hard, H. A., The artesian-water supply of the Dakota sandstone in North Dakota, with special reference to the Edgeley quadrangle: U. S. Geol. Survey Water-Supply Paper 520, pp. 73–95, 1925.

22. Meinzer, O. E., and Wenzel, L. K., Present status of our knowledge regarding the hydraulics of ground water: Econ. Geology, vol. 35, No. 8, pp. 915–941, 1940.

23. Muskat, Morris, Flow of homogeneous fluids through porous media, New York, McGraw-Hill Book Co., 1937.

24. Poiseuille, J. M. L., Recherches expérimentales sur le mouvement des liquides dans les tubes de très petits diamètres: Acad. Sci. Paris Mém. sav. étrang., vol. 9, pp. 433–545, 1846. English translation by W. H. Herschel, Rheol. Mem., vol. 1, No. 1, January 1940. This publication also contains a brief biography of Poiseuille and a discussion of the work of Hagen and others on this subject.

25. Reynolds, Osborne, An experimental investigation of the circumstances which determine whether the motion of water shall be direct or sinuous and the law of resistance in parallel channels: Roy. Soc. London Trans., vol. A174, pp. 935–982, 1883; Sci. Papers, vol. 2, No. 51. See also Hele-Shaw, H. S., Experiments on the nature of the surface resistance in pipes and on ships: Inst. Naval Arch. Trans., 1897, pp. 145–156; Investigation of stream-line motion under certain experimental conditions: Inst. Naval Arch. Trans., 1898, pp. 21–46; Stream-line motion of a viscous fluid: British Assoc. Rept., 1898. An excellent discussion of the subject is given by W. C. Unwin under "Hydraulics" in the Encyclopedia Britannica, 11th ed.

26. Slichter, C. S., Theoretical investigation of the motion of ground waters: U. S. Geol. Survey 19th Ann. Rept., pt. 2, pp. 295–384, 1899.

27. Slichter, C. S., Field measurements of the rate of movement of underground water: U. S. Geol. Survey Water-Supply Paper 140, 1905.

28. Stearns, N. D., Laboratory tests on physical properties of water-bearing materials: U. S. Geol. Survey Water-Supply Paper 596, pp. 121–176, 1927.

29. Stiles, C. W., Crohurst, H. R., Thomson, G. E., and Stearns, N. D., Experimental bacterial and chemical pollution of wells via ground water, with a report on the geology and ground-water hydrology of the experimental area at Fort Caswell, N. C.: U. S. Pub. Health Service, Hygienic Lab., Bull. 147, 1927.

30. Theis, C. V., The relation between the lowering of the piezometric surface and the rate and duration of discharge of a well using ground-water storage: Am. Geophys. Union Trans., 1935, pp. 519–524.

31. Theis, C. V., The significance and nature of the cone of depression in ground-water bodies: Econ. Geology, vol. 33, pp. 889–902, 1938.

32. Thiem, Günther, Hydrologische Methoden, Leipzig, 1906.

33. Tolman, C. F., Ground Water, New York, McGraw-Hill Co., 1937.

34. Tolman, C. F., and Poland, J. F., Ground water, salt-water infiltration, and ground-surface recession in Santa Clara Valley, Santa Clara County, California: Am. Geophys. Union Trans., 1940, pt. 1, pp. 23–34.

35. Turneaure, F. E., and Russell, H. L., Public Water supplies, 1st ed., New York, John Wiley & Sons, Inc., 1901.

36. Van Hise, C. R., A treatise on metamorphism: U. S. Geol. Survey Mon. 47, 1904.

37. Wenzel, L. K., Recent investigations of Thiem's method for determining permeability of water-bearing materials: Am. Geophys. Union Trans., 1932, pp. 313–317.

38. Wenzel, L. K., The Thiem method for determining permeability of water-bearing materials: U. S. Geol. Survey Water-Supply Paper 679-A, pp. 1–57, 1936.

39. Wenzel, L. K., Methods for determining the permeability of water-bearing materials, with special reference to discharging well methods: U. S. Geol. Survey Water-Supply Paper 887, 1942.

40. Brown, J. S., A study of coastal ground water, with special reference to Connecticut: U. S. Geol. Survey Water-Supply Paper 537, 1925.

41. U. S. Geological Survey, Conference on salt-water conditions and problems, and methods of investigation; a series of papers by 30 authors, mimeographed, 1941.

CHAPTER XI

RUNOFF

XIa. INTRODUCTION

Adolph F. Meyer[1]

Runoff represents precipitation returning to the sea or to inland bodies of water. It is that portion of the precipitation that appears in surface streams. It consists, in ever varying proportions, of both surface runoff and ground-water runoff, or effluent seepage. There has been considerable difference in the use of terms relating to runoff, but it is suggested that the term "overland runoff" be used to designate the water flowing over the land surface before it reaches a definite stream channel; the term "surface runoff" to designate the water that reaches the stream as overland runoff, in contrast to the ground-water runoff; and the term "direct runoff" to designate the surface runoff that has not been retarded by storage on the surface as snow or ice or in a lake or other body of standing water.

Runoff from the land area of the earth represents the excess of evaporation from the ocean area over precipitation upon that area. Unless the two are equal, water vapor is continually escaping from the outer atmosphere, and the ocean level is progressively lowering. Temporarily excess evaporation from the ocean may be stored on the land area as snow and ice and as ground and surface storage. It can not be stored in the atmosphere, because the air can seldom hold more than 2 or 3 days' evaporation from a water surface in a given locality.

"All the rivers run into the sea, yet the sea is not full; unto the place from whence the rivers come thither they return again." Water evaporated from the ocean is in part precipitated on the ocean and in part carried inland by air currents, to be precipitated on the land.

Of the moisture precipitated on the land area, (a) some is evaporated and carried back over the ocean area by the winds to be reprecipitated or to be returned to the land area; (b) some returns to the sea as surface runoff; (c) some seeps into the ground to reappear in the streams as ground-water runoff; (d) some is evaporated from the ground surface and the surface of vegetation, only to be reprecipitated on the land area or carried out to sea; (e) some is temporarily stored in the soil to be reevaporated and reprecipitated; (f) some is absorbed by the roots of growing plants

[1] Consulting hydraulic engineer, Minneapolis, Minn.

and transpired into the atmosphere to be reprecipitated; (*g*) some enters into the plant fiber to remain until the plant is desiccated or destroyed.

The mean annual precipitation on the land area of the earth is about 40 inches. This represents about 35,000 cubic miles of water. Each year, on an average, the rivers return to the sea about 7,000 cubic miles of water, or about 20 percent of the annual precipitation. The remaining precipitation on the land area represents, in part, ocean-evaporated moisture carried inland by the larger mass movements of the air and, in part, land-evaporated moisture that is recirculated over the land area before it returns to the sea.

The proportion of the annual precipitation derived from land evaporation and transpiration varies greatly over the earth's surface. In general, it is greater over inland areas than along the seashore. It is normally greater in regions of moderate and low precipitation than in regions of heavy precipitation. The runoff water from such regions is usually returned inland step by step over regions of heavier precipitation. Frequently, however, there are great cyclonic movements that are sufficiently continuous to carry ocean-evaporated moisture directly into the interior of continents, and anticyclonic movements that return the land-evaporated moisture directly to the ocean.

The transportation systems by which man moves the produce of the earth and articles of his manufacture from place to place shrink into insignificance when compared with the system by which Nature transports thousands of millions of carloads of water back and forth across the surface of the earth. The investigations of recent years have emphasized the magnitude of the larger mass movements of the air and the amount of water vapor moved from place to place with these air masses. These recent investigations have seriously questioned the extent to which land precipitation is derived from land evaporation, even in areas lying far inland. An exact evaluation of land and sea as sources of precipitation for inland areas must await further observation and study, but of the existence of large exchanges of moisture between the ocean and the land there can be no doubt.

The hydrologic cycle is depicted in the frontispiece.

In the zone of cyclonic movements any changes on the earth's surface produced by man in areas of relatively high precipitation which result in returning the precipitated water as runoff to the sea more rapidly than under natural conditions must inevitably reduce the precipitation to some extent over the inland areas of lesser precipitation.

VEGETATION SUPPLIES A CONSIDERABLE AMOUNT OF ATMOSPHERIC MOISTURE

Vegetation supplies a considerable part of the atmospheric moisture that originates over the land area. Deep-rooted vegetation is exacting in its water requirements, but shallow-rooted vegetation is tolerant of changes in available moisture. Trees draw upon a great reservoir of ground water, gradually replenished during periods of heavy precipitation and depleted during periods of drought. Grains and grasses rely more upon current rainfall, the amount they need depending considerably upon the character of the soil. Although, to speak broadly, it is true that trees are the result of ample precipitation and not the cause, nevertheless, because all deep-rooted vegetation has a more constant supply of moisture

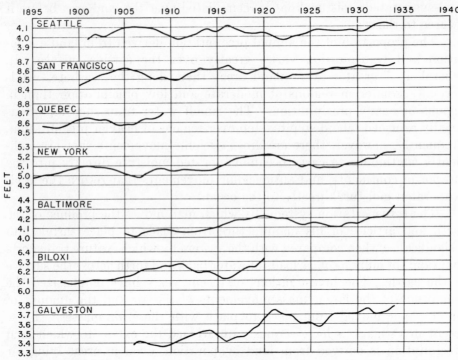

Fig. XIA-1.—Changes in annual mean sea level. Five-year moving average, plotted in center of period. (*From records of the U.S. Coast and Geodetic Survey, and the Canadian Department of Marine and Fisheries.*)

available to its root system, it must necessarily constitute a more constant source of atmospheric moisture and therefore tend in some measure to equalize rainfall from month to month and year to year.

CHANGES IN OCEAN LEVEL

Available records are not sufficient to show conclusively whether the ocean level is rising or falling with respect to the level of the adjacent land. The land around the Gulf of Mexico appears to be slowly sinking. Data furnished by the United States Coast and Geodetic Survey and the Canadian Department of Marine and Fisheries are summarized graphically in Figure XIA-1. Annual means of sea level are plotted as progressive 5-year mean values in the center of the period.

Pacific coast stations indicate a rising trend in ocean level of 0.1 foot in 35 to 50 years. Atlantic coast stations indicate a rising trend of 0.1 foot in 25 to 30 years. In general, the records of ocean levels also appear to reflect changes in continental storage of moisture, both annually and periodically. Along the Atlantic coast the level is low in winter and high in summer. Along the Pacific coast the reverse is true.

The ocean level also appears to follow, roughly, the sunspot cycle of 11.5 years. The Atlantic Ocean appears lower during sunspot maxima, and the Pacific appears higher. During great droughts the ocean level apparently has averaged higher than during periods of heavy land precipitation. Widespread depletion of surface-water and ground-water storage may have been reflected in high ocean levels.

PHYSIOGRAPHIC PROCESSES

Runoff is the primary agent continually engaged in carving a new face upon the earth. Wind, frost, ice, and vegetation are secondary agents. Runoff is, in general, tending to lower the land surface but the eroded material is building up some areas in the general down-cutting process. In a geologic sense the runoff will continue to be active until this down-cutting has been completed and diastrophism has ceased to produce new irregularities.

RIVER CHANNELS

Each river is tending to reduce its tributary drainage basin to a level from which there will be no further change. In general, streams in the upper portions of a drainage basin flow at relatively steep gradients. The gradients decrease as the streams approach the sea. Viewed as of today, each stream is continually changing. As the gradients in the swift portions become less, the stream begins to meander, attacking its banks and widening its valley. During periods of ordinary low flow the stream carries toward the sea some of the sediment brought into its channel by its tributaries during the preceding flood stage.

After rains have swollen a stream to a higher than bankfull stage the overflowing waters deposit sediment on the banks of the stream as they spread out over the flood plain with quickly reduced velocity. Gradually the stream builds its own levees until, refusing longer to be confined to its normal channel, it breaks through at some bend and selects a new floodwater channel in a lower portion of its valley. Streams like the lower Mississippi have built up their banks until, irrespective of the artificial levees that have been imposed upon those natural levees, the natural river banks are many feet higher than the lowest level of the flood plain miles away from the main channel.

RUNOFF IS RELATIVELY GRADUAL

Rain falling on the earth's surface with great irregularity in time and rate runs off from the land at a relatively uniform and steady rate, notwithstanding the existence of floods and droughts. There is a fundamental reason for this. The atmosphere can store only a few days' evaporation, but the earth's surface and the underlying soil and rock formations can store the accumulated precipitation of weeks and months. Ordinarily one foot of soil holds more water than the entire overlying atmosphere.

POWER OF RUNOFF WATER

The potential energy represented by the weight of the annual precipitation on the land area multiplied by its altitude above sea level is tremendous. A large portion of this energy is spent in overcoming frictional resistance to flow over the earth's surface. Where the obstacles in the path of the runoff have sufficient tenacity to withstand the attack, the energy is lost. Where the surface of the earth is granular and unprotected by vegetation, much of the available energy is spent in picking up the particles of earth and carrying them down the slopes into the valleys and, in part, onward to the sea, where great deltas of sediment are continually being formed, extending the continental areas.

In general, man's occupancy and cultivation of the earth's surface has greatly aided the force of degradation represented by the runoff. The consequent great waste of productive soil has recently come to be more fully appreciated, and soil conservation is everywhere receiving more attention. So far as runoff is retarded and soil is conserved by structures and methods of cultivation designed to oppose the forces of degradation, Nature's down-cutting processes are being retarded.

DIASTROPHISM

Diastrophism is still affecting drainage systems. Great changes have occurred in the shore lines of inland lakes in late geologic time. These changes have apparently progressed at a relatively uniform rate for several thousand years.

Gage readings around the Great Lakes point to a continuing deformation of the earth's surface. The north shore of Lake Superior and the east shore of Lake Ontario are still rising. Not very long ago the Ottawa River formed the outlet of the Great Lakes; then the St. Lawrence became the outlet; and in the future, the Great Lakes, if unrestrained, may drain into the Gulf of Mexico.

The uplift along the northerly shores of the Great Lakes apparently represents a slow recoil from the depression of the surface of the earth by the weight of the great ice sheet, which began its recession about 25,000 years ago.

The late Dr. John R. Freeman [1] concluded that earth tilting, or surface deformation, has been in progress in the Great Lakes region at the rate of 6 to 12 inches per 100 miles per century.

Earthquakes and volcanic eruptions continue to modify the earth's surface. The earthquake at New Madrid, Mo., of little more than a century ago, temporarily obstructed the Mississippi River and caused large areas of land in Arkansas and Tennessee to sink materially.

DEVELOPMENT OF SURFACE WATERCOURSES

At its source, while rain is falling, direct surface runoff moves in thin sheets over the surface of the earth and is largely governed by the laws of laminar flow, velocity being directly proportional to gradient. Soon, however, these sheets find surface depressions formed during previous rains. The depth of flow increases. It becomes turbulent and follows the laws of turbulent flow, velocity being approximately proportional to the square root of the gradient. While moving in thin sheets, surface runoff can not attack soil protected by vegetation. As the rills increase in size, however, the ground surface is attacked and, where the slopes are steep, gullies are formed. Unless the gullies are protected by the root systems of vegetation, they deepen rapidly, the sides cave, the water becomes heavily laden with sediment, and the forces of degradation are in active control.

The rate of progress toward the formation of surface watercourses is primarily dependent upon the character and condition of the surface of the earth and the rate and frequency of intense rainfall. Steep, unprotected slopes of fine, granular soils quickly become more gullied and produce rapid surface runoff. Relatively level land, particularly if the soil is granular, permits ready infiltration and ground-water recharge and produces well-sustained stream flow that tends to maintain well-defined watercourses.

In broad alluvial valleys surface watercourses generally follow meandering channels with gradients sufficient to permit the normal flow of the stream to maintain a well-defined channel. Although the meandering Mississippi River in its 1,047-mile course from Cairo to the sea has from time to time cut off bends aggregating 228 miles of channel in 165 years, yet its length from Cairo to the sea has not appreciably changed in that time [2]. Artificially reducing the channel length of a meandering stream may be a continuing undertaking unless the channel changes are made permanently effective by protecting the banks of the stream against the scouring effects of the increased velocity produced by shortening its course.

GROUND-WATER FLOW

In the more humid regions, particularly those of relatively flat topography and absorptive soil, the stream flow consists largely of ground-water runoff. The proportions vary greatly with the character of the soil, subsoil, and underlying rocks.

Although ground-water flow can not be directly measured until it has appeared in surface watercourses, yet a fair estimate of the portion of the flow of a given stream which at some point was ground-water flow can be made from the hydrograph of the stream and hydrologic data for its drainage basin. In general, it may be stated that at least one-third of the runoff reaches surface watercourses after some travel underground. Such underground movement of water is extremely slow and constitutes the principal factor in equalizing the runoff.

Changes in ground-water storage occur gradually through the year with changes in infiltration and ground-water outflow. In general, from 1 to 2 inches of infiltration is required to raise the ground-water table 1 foot in clayey soil; from 3 to 4 inches is required in sand. The gradients under which ground water moves toward surface-water channels vary with the character of the water-bearing material and necessarily change slowly.

Considerable information on the contribution of ground water to stream flow appears in United States Geological Survey Water-Supply Paper 772 [3]. The unweighted arithmetic average contribution given for nine basins in the United States is 40 percent of the total. The average annual precipitation on these basins is 38.9 inches, and the average annual runoff is 5.8 inches. Extremes of annual precipitation range from 18.5 inches for the Red River of the North at Grand Forks, N. Dak., to 59.7 inches for the Chattahoochee River in Georgia. Extremes of annual runoff range from 0.24 inch for the Red River of the North to 11.6 inches for the Chattahoochee.

In the same publication one minor basin, with relatively heavy soil and steep slopes, is shown with less than 20 percent of ground-water flow, and another, with relatively pervious soil and underlying rocks, with over 70 percent of ground-water flow. The portion of the total stream flow that appears as ground-water flow necessarily varies from year to year in each basin, depending upon the amount, character, and rate of precipitation.

SNOW RUNOFF

In the mountainous regions stream flow consists largely of water temporarily stored on the earth's surface as snow and ice. This surface storage tends to equalize the stream flow materially. Years of heavy precipitation may be years of relatively low summer temperature, with the result that the precipitation from one season is carried over into the next and stream flow is equalized. Perhaps the greatest equalization of stream flow is to be found in glacier-fed streams. The surface storage of precipitation in the great ice cap of Greenland is many times as large as the total surface storage in the mountain ranges of the earth, and the snow and ice storage in Antarctica dwarfs all other surface storage on the earth.

In the regions where a large portion of the annual precipitation occurs as snowfall winter evaporation is usually small. Winter precipitation, therefore, represents primarily moisture brought inland from the sea and from warmer inland areas. When the snowfall comes before the frost has deeply penetrated the ground, a large percentage is absorbed during the spring period of melting, to recharge the ground water and provide soil and subsoil storage for vegetation. On the other hand, when snow falls on saturated, frozen ground and later melts, most of it appears as surface runoff. The combination of heavy snowfall on frozen ground liquidated by warm rains is perhaps the greatest single flood-producing factor.

Streams fed primarily by direct surface runoff are always flashy. Streams fed largely by ground-water flow are well sustained throughout the year, although they may not escape floods produced by direct surface runoff during periods of intense precipitation.

REFERENCES

1. Freeman, J. R., Regulation of the Great Lakes, Sanitary District of Chicago, 1926.

2. The improvement of the lower Mississippi River for flood control and navigation, Corps of Engineers, U. S. Army, 1932.

3. Hoyt, W. G., and others, Studies of relations of rainfall and runoff in the United States: U. S. Geol. Survey Water-Supply Paper 772, 301 pp., 1936.

XIB. METHODS OF STREAM GAGING

CHARLES H. PIERCE[1]

The term "stream gaging" as ordinarily used in referring to measurements of river discharge relates to the process of determining the rate of flow, or the discharge, of a river. The average rate of flow for a period of time, such as an hour, day, month, or year, and the changes in the rate of flow from day to day, also the rate of flow corresponding to a given stage, regardless of time, are computed from observations and measurements made in the field. The average rate of flow for the 24 hours of a day, commonly called the daily discharge, is generally employed as the measure of the flow of a river. The units of discharge most commonly used are cubic feet per second, abbreviated to "second-feet," "sec.-ft.," or "c.f.s.," in English units; and cubic meters per second, or liters per second, in metric units.

The procedure used in gaging the flow of streams in open channels generally consists of individual measurements of discharge at various stages from low water to high water and the determination of the relations of stage to discharge, so that records of discharge may be derived from the records of stages by means of the stage-discharge relations. In order to arrive at a satisfactory determination of the stage-discharge relations at a gaging station and to insure that these relations when once established may be reasonably permanent, the hydraulic conditions controlling the relation of stage to discharge should be definite and stable. The hydraulic conditions that establish and control the stage-discharge relation at a gaging station are commonly referred to as the station control and include the reach of the river channel, with all its physical features, that hydraulically determines the stage of the river for a certain rate of flow at the gaging station. The station control may be either natural or constructed and may consist of a ledge of rock crossing the channel, a boulder-covered riffle, an indurated bed, an overflow dam, or any other physical feature capable of maintaining a fairly stable relation between the discharge of a stream and the water level at the selected point above it. The natural control for the gaging station on the Connecticut River at First Connecticut Lake, near Pittsburg, N. H., is shown in Fig. XIB-1.

Observations of stages and records of changes in stage from day to day are coordinate with the individual measurements of discharge as essen-

[1] Hydraulic engineer, Water-Resources Branch, Geological Survey, United States Department of the Interior, Washington, D. C.

tial requirements for the collection of records of river discharge at open-channel gaging stations. The stage-discharge relations expressed in the form of a rating curve or a rating table provide the means for converting records of stages into records of discharges.

Fig. XIb-1.—Natural control at gaging station on the Connecticut River at First Connecticut Lake, near Pittsburg, N. H. (*Photograph by C. H. Pierce.*)

CURRENT-METER MEASUREMENTS OF DISCHARGE

The individual determinations of discharge that are made at various stages from low water to high water and are used in the development of the rating curve are ordinarily made by the velocity-area method, a current meter being used for measuring the velocities. Under some circumstances other methods may be found desirable, especially for small streams and for conditions of low flow where volumetric measurements or determinations by weirs, flumes, or other devices may be practicable.

The current meter is an instrument used to measure the velocity of flowing water by means of a rotating element that is so constructed that when placed in the water the number of rotations in a unit of time will have a definite relation to the velocity of the water. By placing a current meter at a point in a stream and ascertaining the number of revolutions of the cups or vanes in a known interval of time, the velocity of the water at that point can be determined from the calibration of the meter. The equation of the meter rating ordinarily is obtained by calibration of the instrument in a rating flume where the meter is drawn through still water at a known speed and the number of rotations counted or automatically recorded. When used in measurements of river flow the number of rotations of the cups or vanes of the current meter under some conditions may be observed visually, although electrical devices are generally employed to transmit to the observer the contacts made at each revolution, or at every fifth or tenth revolution. The number of contacts are counted by the observer for an interval of time measured by a stop watch. Sometimes a recording mechanism is employed for indicating the revolutions and for measuring the time interval.

The current-meter equipment should provide means for placing and holding the instrument at any desired depth, so that velocity observations may be made at definite distances below the water surface. The number of points in a vertical section where observations are made depends upon the depth of water and the method used in making the measurement. Likewise, the number of places where velocities are measured in the horizontal distance across the stream depends somewhat upon the character of the stream bed and the uniformity in distribution of velocities. Satisfactory conditions for current-meter measurements require a fairly smooth stream bed without abrupt changes in depth and freedom from rocks or boulders that might cause excessive turbulence. This requirement applies to conditions upstream and downstream in the vicinity of the measuring section, as well as at the section used in the measurement.

It is often necessary to measure the discharge of a stream during a rising or a falling stage, and the method that is used should permit the measurement to be completed during a time interval in which the change in stage is not too great, otherwise the results of the measurement may be inconclusive with respect to the stage-discharge relation. An excessive number of observations might, because of the length of time required for the completion of the measurement, cause a measurement to be less reliable than one with fewer observations completed in a shorter time. The number of sections at which observations should be taken may range from 10 to 30 for small streams and from 20 to 50 for large rivers, including only that part of the river flowing in its usual channel. No definite rule can be given for the number and position across the stream of the points for the observations of depth and velocity except that the distance between the points should be so determined and the points so spaced as to disclose the true shape of the bed and the true mean velocity of the flowing water. The distance between the points of measurement may be as much as 15 or even 20 feet in a smooth channel 400 feet wide and perhaps as much as 40 feet in a channel 1,000 feet wide. The channel should be divided into 20 or more parts except for very small streams, where a somewhat smaller number may be sufficient if the distance between the points becomes less than 1 foot. The division is generally made so that there will be not more than 10 percent and preferably not more than 5 percent of the discharge between any two of the points. The number of measuring points would necessarily be increased at times of high water to include any additional channels due to overflow.

The distances between the points where the observations are made should be measured accurately, and markers should be placed on the bridge or cable so that the widths of the sections and the depth of the water at each point may be accurately determined, as the areas of the individual sections between the observation points are of equal importance with the mean velocities in those sections in determining the total discharge of the stream. When measurements are made by wading, a tag line should be stretched across the stream at the measuring section, so that the points of observation may be referred to an initial point on the bank for convenience in correlating the measurements of depth and velocity in the individual sections.

The position of the points where velocity determinations are made in a vertical section depends upon the depth of water and the method used in supporting the current meter. If the meter is supported by a hand line, with a weight suspended below the meter, observations ordinarily can be made at 0.2 of the depth and at 0.8 of the depth where the depth of water is 2.5 feet or more, and at 0.6 of the depth where the water is from 1.25 to 2.5 feet in depth. If the water is too shallow for obtaining observations at 0.6-depth with the hand-line suspension, a wading section where the meter can be supported by a rod should be used. With the rod suspension, observations at 0.2-depth and 0.8-depth can be made for depths of 1.5 to 2.5 feet, and at 0.6-depth for lesser depths. For depths less than 0.5 foot the meter may be placed at mid-depth [3]. The wading section need not necessarily be the same as the section used at higher stages when measurements are made from a bridge or a cableway.

Curves showing the distribution of velocities in a vertical section may be plotted from observations taken at a series of points in the vertical. Observations taken at intervals of one-tenth the total depth ordinarily are sufficient to determine the shape of the vertical velocity curve. The average velocity may be determined from the vertical velocity curve, and comparisons can be made with results obtained by the use of the average of the two observations made at 0.2-depth and 0.8-depth and with the results of the single-point observation made at 0.6-depth. It is generally found that the results by these different methods agree very closely, but the 0.2- and 0.8-depth method is somewhat more reliable than the 0.6-depth method for those depths where it can be used.

The stage of the river at beginning and end of the measurement, and at other times during the measurement if the stage is changing, should be observed and made an essential part of the record.

MEAN GAGE HEIGHT FOR A DISCHARGE MEASUREMENT

The mean gage height for a discharge measurement is one of the coordinates used in plotting the measurements that establish the discharge rating curve. An accurate determination of the mean gage height for a measurement is therefore as important as an accurate measurement of the discharge in providing the basic data for determination of the stage-discharge relation.

The gage height for a discharge measurement should always be referred to the gage that is used in obtaining the records of stage. At stations having auxiliary gages the stages indicated by those gages should also be recorded for purposes of comparison.

Before beginning a discharge measurement the gage height should be observed, and any available information as to changes in stage that are likely to occur before the completion of the measurement should be given proper consideration. On some streams subject to power operation the changes in stage may be so rapid that it would be inadvisable to attempt to make a discharge measurement under those conditions, and a time for making the measurement should be selected when the stage may be as nearly constant as can be obtained. Discharge measurements at times of high water must usually be made under conditions of rising or falling stages, and it then becomes necessary to determine the mean gage height for the measurement. The condition of a rising or a falling stage is a common occurrence on natural streams, although the amount of change during the time required for a measurement may not be so great as to cause serious difficulty in adjusting the results except for measurements of power-regulated streams and of streams during peaks caused by storm run off.

For discharge measurements made at constant or nearly constant stages there is ordinarily no difficulty in deciding upon the gage height that corresponds to the measured discharge. If the change in stage is small, such as 0.1 foot or less, and the measurement has progressed continuously from start to finish, the mean gage height can ordinarily be taken as the arithmetical average of the two observations. If a considerable change in stage has occurred, or if a major portion of the measured discharge corresponds more nearly to one than to the other of the two observations of stage, the proportional parts of the measured discharge and the observations of stage to which they more nearly relate should be taken into consideration by computing a weighted mean gage height. Additional observations of stage between the times of starting and finishing the measurement should be made if there is very much change in stage, and these observations should be used in computing a weighted mean gage height for the measurement.

RECORDS OF STAGE

Continuous records of stage obtained by water-stage recorders are generally desirable for use with the stage-discharge relations as the bases for computation of river discharge [1]. The water-stage recorders contain a time element and a height element, so arranged that a continuous graph of river stages is automatically produced on the record paper. The clock that controls the time element should be weight-driven, and the time and height scales should be on rectangular coordinates. The record of stage should be referred to the same gage that is used in the observations of stage at times of discharge measurements.

The water-stage recorder should be installed over a stilling well in the bank of the river, in a structure of sufficient height so that the instrument will be above maximum flood stages. The bottom of the well should

Fig. XIb-2.—Gaging station on the Potomac River at Hancock, Md. (*Photograph by C. H. Pierce.*)

be at a depth that is below minimum low water and should be connected with the river by an intake pipe at least $2\frac{1}{2}$ or 3 inches in diameter. The top of the well terminates in a shelter with a floor and support for the water-state recorder. The height element of the recorder has a direct connection to a float in the well by means of a stainless-steel or phosphor-bronze tape. The tape should be graduated for convenience in measuring the height of water in the well. Precise observations of stage may be made by means of the graduated tape or other reference gage inside the well. All gages used at the station should be set·to read to the same datum. Reinforced concrete is generally used in the construction of the gage well and shelter for permanent installations. The well should be at least 4 by 4 feet in inside dimensions, although in some places 36-inch corrugated steel-pipe wells have been found to be satisfactory. A typical reinforced-concrete structure at the gaging station on the Potomac River at Hancock, Md., is shown in Figure XIʙ-2.

EQUIPMENT FOR GAGING STATIONS

The basic principles involved in the collection of stream-flow records are fairly simple, and under favorable conditions good results may be obtained with a small amount of gaging-station equipment, but the importance of many of the records warrants the use of special equipment in order to facilitate the work and increase the accuracy of the records. On some streams the natural conditions of river channel at the section that controls the discharge relation may not be of a permanent nature, and it may be desirable to stabilize the stage-discharge relation by means of an artificial control. Bridges suitable for use in current-meter measurements of discharge are not always available at the places where measurements are desired; therefore, cableways may be needed for the use of the engineer when river stages are too high for wading. Suitable structures for housing water-stage recorders are generally necessary. Although comparatively small in size, the structures are of special design and construction, and careful attention to their position in or adjacent to the river channel is always desirable. Even the simple nonrecording gages require care in their installation in order to insure satisfactory records.

The following statement regarding installation of water-stage recorders is taken from a pamphlet issued by the United States Geological Survey for the use of its district engineers [4]:

The essential features of a water-stage recorder installation are listed below. The care with which the installations are designed and constructed to meet local conditions will, in a large measure, determine the successful operation of the recorder.

1. A stilling well connected by an intake pipe or other openings with the body of water whose stage is to be recorded.

2. A house over the stilling well to protect the recorder.

3. Staff or other nonrecording gages outside and inside the house and well for comparing the stage in the well with that outside and for use in setting and checking the recorder.

4. Permanent bench marks for use in maintaining the datum of the gage.

Unless the water flowing past the gage is clear and free from silt at all times, a flushing device for cleaning intake pipes is also essential and for streams with an unusually high silt content a silt trap may be desirable.

Detailed plans should be provided for the use of the field engineer, so that the structures may be built economically in accordance with the requirements of the work. Various articles of equipment for river measurements, including a water-stage recorder house and well built of reinforced concrete, are shown in Figure XIʙ-3.

A structure to support the engineer when making current-meter measurements is necessary for streams that are too deep and swift to permit measurements by wading. The principal types of structures used for this purpose are existing or specially constructed bridges, a boat held in place by a cable or guy line, and a cableway carrying a car.

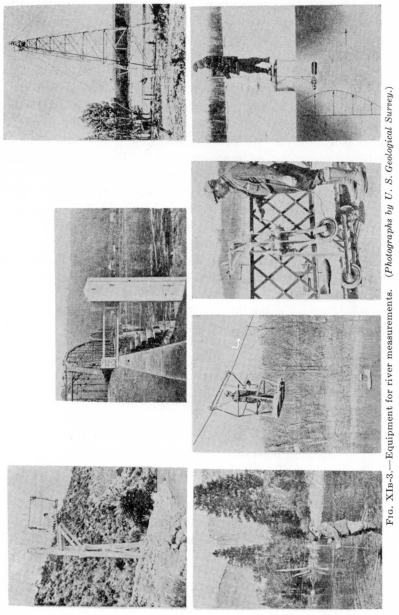

FIG. XIb-3.—Equipment for river measurements. (Photographs by U. S. Geological Survey.)

Bridges may in some localities provide the only practicable means for supporting the engineer in his use of the current meter, and for large streams like the Mississippi River, where heavy sounding weights and power-operated reels are needed, special equipment has been built for use in handling the current meter in making discharge measurements from bridges.   Boats are sometimes necessary, and their use is generally satisfactory if the velocity is not too great and suitable means are provided for keeping the boat in the desired position.   In making measurements from a boat, the current meter should be held upstream or far enough from the side so that the velocity at the place of observation may not be affected by any disturbed conditions of flow created by the boat.

The equipment and appurtenances for a cable installation consist of the cable and its accessories, the supports and anchorages for sustaining it, and a traveling car to carry the engineer across the stream while he is using the current meter.   A cable or wire rope consisting of six strands, seven wires to the strand, with the strands wound around a hemp center, has great flexibility and is frequently used.   The individual wires are galvanized before being built into the rope.   Rope of this type constructed from galvanized crucible-steel wire is sometimes called yacht-rigging rope and may be used for short spans, the size of the rope depending upon the span and the allowable sag.   Improved plow-steel rope of this type may be used for spans up to about 800 feet.   For long spans galvanized plow-steel tramway cable is preferable, and the greater strength of the tramway cable permits installations that would be impracticable or even impossible with yacht-rigging rope.

The following formulas [5] may be used in computing the stress in cables suspended between supports at the same height:

$$H = \frac{WS^2}{8D} + \frac{PS}{4D} = \frac{S(WS + 2P)}{8D}$$

$$T = H \sqrt{1 + \frac{16D^2}{S^2}} \text{ (approximate)}$$

in which H = horizontal tension in cable, in pounds.

T = maximum tension in cable, in pounds.

W = weight of cable, in pounds per foot.

S = span between supports, in feet.

D = deflection or sag, in feet.

P = concentrated load at center of span, in pounds.

To determine the deflection or loaded sag for a given tension the following formula, derived from the first formula given above, may be used:

$$D = \frac{S(WS + 2P)}{8H}$$

As cables erected for stream gaging have comparatively little sag, the secant of the angle of cable departure at the support is approximately unity.   The maximum tension is therefore practically the same as the horizontal tension and may be calculated directly by use of the first formula given above.

The length of cable required may be determined from the following formula for the curved length (L) between supports of an unloaded or uniformly loaded cable:

$$L = S\left(1 + \frac{8D^2}{3S^2}\right)$$

Where the cables are to have factory-installed sockets, the required length of cable should be carefully determined, with allowance for the maximum take-up that is to be provided.

Fig. XIb-4.— Artificial control at gaging station on the Olentangy River near Delaware, Ohio. (*Photograph by C. H. Pierce.*)

Artificial controls are structures built in the channel of a stream for stabilizing the stage-discharge relations, thereby simplifying the stream-gaging procedure and increasing the accuracy of the discharge records. Artificial controls may be of various types and may differ in design in accordance with the requirements of the individual gaging stations. For some streams where the bed is continually shifting and permanent foundations are not available, it may be desirable to stabilize the stream bed by means of a low structure that conforms to the general profile of the bed, but the artificial control is generally more effective if it is built to a height somewhat above the natural profile of the bed.

The transverse section of the control generally takes the form of a broad-crested weir, the downstream face having a slope flat enough to

cause the nappe of the flowing water to adhere to the crest. All corners
and changes in direction of the wetted surface of the cross section should
be of such shape that there may be no turbulence or irregularity in the
flow of water over the structure. The longitudinal profile of the control
should be so designed that at times of low flow the depth of water at the
lowest part of the control will be at least 0.3 foot. This requirement may
necessitate a profile having a comparatively short horizontal length in
the center of the stream, with upward slopes to each bank. For streams
where the low-water flow is very small the longitudinal profile of the

Fig. XIb-5.—Artificial control at gaging station on Devil Canyon Creek near San Bernardino, Calif.
(*Photograph by U. S. Geological Survey.*)

control may take the form of a notchlike depression in the center, with
the crest sloping upward toward the banks on each side. This type of
artificial control at the station on the Olentangy River near Delaware,
Ohio, is shown in Figure XIb-4. Another type of artificial control that is
used in some parts of California is shown in Figure XIb-5.

For rivers of flat slopes where changes in stage may be caused by
conditions other than changes in discharge, such as the regulation of the
height of the water by gates in a dam below the gage or the effects of
variations in the stages of a river to which the stream is tributary, it
may not always be possible to determine the discharge by means of a curve
of relation between stage and discharge. Under those circumstances the
slope or fall may be an important factor in the determination of discharge
by means of slope-stage-discharge relations.

COMPUTATION OF RECORDS

The discharge measurements and the records of stages are the basic
data for the computation of river discharge, but in addition to these data,

the results of field inspections of the gages generally provide information that is helpful in the interpretation and analysis of the records. After careful checking, the discharge measurements are plotted, and the discharge rating curve or curves are determined for the period under consideration. If the rating curve is found to differ from the curve previously used, new tables for the stage-discharge relation are computed and then applied to the records of stage to obtain the discharge.

As the discharge rating curve is a curvilinear function of the stage, the application of the rating curve or rating table to the mean gage height for a 24-hour period may not give the correct mean discharge for that period if there has been a large change in stage during the period. Therefore, for conditions of changing stage, the discharge should be ascertained for consecutive short intervals of time, and the mean discharge for the day computed as the average of the discharge determinations for the short intervals of time of equal length into which the 24 hours has been divided.

An instrument called the discharge integrator [2] has been developed by the United States Geological Survey for use in determining the mean daily discharge from records of stage obtained by water-stage recorders. This instrument contains a flexible steel curve that can be adjusted in accordance with the shape of the rating curve for the gaging station. When in use, the base plate of the instrument is placed on a specific gage-height division of the recorder chart, and a pointer is then drawn along the record in the direction of the time element. The mean discharge for the 24-hour period can be read directly on the instrument scale when the pointer has moved a distance corresponding to 24 hours on the time scale.

The method of arrangement of stream-flow records for publication and general use depends somewhat upon the conditions in the region where the records are obtained. Tabulations showing the mean daily discharge for each day of the year are generally desirable, and from these data the various hydraulic studies corresponding to the needs of individual problems can readily be made. Tabulations of mean, maximum, and minimum discharge for each month and for the year may give the essential facts in abbreviated form. Other data, such as figures showing monthly and yearly run off in second-feet per square mile, run off in depth in inches from the total drainage area, and run off in acre-feet, may be derived from the summary tables of mean monthly discharge. The records as published by the United States Geological Survey are expressed in English units but may be similarly computed for units used in the metric system. Tabulations showing the number of days or percentage of time when the flow was equal to or greater than certain indicated values are generally helpful in water power and water-storage investigations. Various other methods may be used in the arrangement and use of the data, and with the records of daily discharge available for each day of the year the user of the data can make his computations in accordance with the requirements of his individual problems.

REFERENCES

1. Pierce, C. H., Conditions requiring the use of automatic gages in obtaining records of stream flow: U. S. Geol. Survey Water-Supply Paper 375-F, pp. 131–139, 1916.

2. Pierce, C. H., The discharge integrator: Boston Soc. Civil Eng. Jour., vol. 4, pp. 289–291, 1917.

3. Pierce, C. H., Performance of current meters in water of shallow depths: U. S. Geol. Survey Water-Supply Paper 868-A, pp. 1–35, 1941.

4. Lee, Lasley, Equipment for river measurements, plans and specifications for reinforced-concrete house and well for water-stage recorders, U. S. Geol. Survey, 1933.

5. Lee, Lasley, Plans and specifications for structures from which discharge measurements are made, U. S. Geol. Survey, 1933

XIc. LONG RECORDS OF RIVER FLOW

ROYAL W. DAVENPORT[1]

By length of continuance, records of river-flow gain value and significance for practical and scientific applications. Thereby a more satisfactory basis is afforded for studying the stability and adequacy of water supply in relation to needs and uses, for analyzing the magnitude and frequency of floods as a basis for applying economic principles to provisions for flood control, for appraising the severity and frequency of droughts as a factor in the guidance of agricultural, industrial, and urban development, and for similar purposes. It is obvious that knowledge of hydrology and meteorology may be extended through the prolongation of observations of the processes treated by or related to these sciences. These observations appropriately include long records of river flow. Such records also afford opportunity for the examination of the natural phenomenon of the flow of water in rivers to discover significant evidence of occurrence of systematic sequences or cycles.

History from earliest times presents much evidence of the important part which rivers have played in human progress and experience. Usually, however, historical accounts contain only scanty references to river behavior, which have little quantitative scientific significance. Moreover, records of river flow, like and perhaps more than statistics of many other kinds pertaining to natural science, are of relatively recent origin.

For a few rivers of the United States authentic but incomplete information of floods and droughts extends back for 75 or 100 years and scantily for longer periods. The earliest determination of the daily discharge of a natural stream appears to have been made in 1821 by Escher de la Linth for the Rhine River at Basel, Switzerland, for the years 1809 to 1821. Marr, Ellet, and Humphreys and Abbot [2] did pioneer work on the determination of the discharge of the Mississippi and Ohio Rivers in the late 1840's and 1850's. Notable early contributions in this activity were made by others. However, the art of measuring the rate and volume of flow of natural streams has been developed essentially within the last 60 or 70 years. Systematic records of the stages of a few rivers extend back for longer periods than 60 or 70 years. Because of these and other reasons, as explained below, only a few reliable records of river flow in the United States exceed 50 years or even 40 years. The availability of long records of river flow is not materially greater in parts of the world

[1] Hydraulic engineer, Chief, Division of Water Utilization, Geological Survey, United States Department of the Interior, Washington, D. C.

where the progress of civilization and development of written records had been moving in advance of those in this country for hundreds and thousands of years.

The River Nile of Egypt is outstanding in respect to length of association with relatively advanced civilization, and by reason of its indispensable place in ancient and modern life it has perhaps been subject to discriminating observation for a longer time than any other river in the world. The crops of the Nile Valley are dependent on annual flooding by the river, and the height of flooding has determined the extent of the lands that could be tilled in any year and, therefore, the seasons of plentiful and deficient harvests. Jarvis [3] has compiled many interesting data concerning the flood records of the Nile. Known flood marks adjoining the river extends as far back as about 1800 B.C. Mention of the annual rises of the Nile is found in ancient inscriptions dating back to between 3000 and 3500 B.C. Jarvis has presented in graphic form maximum and minimum stages of the Roda gage at Cairo from all available records from 622 to 1926 A.D. Data for maximum stages are reasonably complete except for portions of the sixteenth and seventeenth centuries. The last 100 years of the record shows the influence of a diversion dam constructed in the river about 15 miles below the gage. Despite probable errors and inaccuracies in the records, a study of the trend of the stages through centuries discloses an apparent progressive sedimentation at a rate of considerable uniformity, averaging 10 to 15 centimeters per century. Information as to rates and volumes of discharge is available only since 1870.

In the article noted Jarvis refers briefly also to other long records of river flow in Europe and Asia as they bear upon great floods of the past. The Miami Conservancy District [6] has published information concerning storms and floods in European river basins. Both these sources give references to literature in English and other languages, which contains information regarding the floods and other features of river behavior for various foreign rivers over long periods in the past.

Through a report by the Government of Soviet Russia [5] interesting information is made available regarding a long record of the Memel River of Lithuania. Kolupaila states in this report that the Lithuanian Hydrometric Bureau published in its yearbook for 1930 the results of observations of the stages of the Memel River at Schmalleningken in 1812 to 1930. Kolupaila has undertaken to convert these stages into rates of discharge.

Measurements of discharge are said to be available for the reach of the Memel River at Schmalleningken since 1875. The Prussian, Russian, and Lithuanian discharge measurements for this reach vary but little from the averaged rating curves since 1890. However, study of the records seems to show an appreciable progressive change in the bed of the channel of the river or in other conditions that affect the hydraulic capacity of the channel. Consequently, Kolupaila has deduced and applied corrections to the stages from 31 centimeters to 0 before conversion to discharge. Application of special methods was also necessary for the determination of the discharge when the flow was affected by ice cover. The results seem still to show a progressive increase in discharge through the period of record, which Kolupaila apparently attributes to deficiencies in the methods of correction. The experience in reducing the Memel River stage record to a discharge record well illustrates the difficulties that are very common to the conversion of long records of stage into records of discharge.

Kolupaila's report also contains references to European literature pertinent to such difficulties. A notable reference is made to a similar study of a long record of stage of the Rhine River at Basel, Switzerland [1], where the progressive reduction of stages had led to a false theory that discharges were decreasing. Systematic corrections to the gage heights of +96 to −18 centimeters, based upon apparently sound reasoning, produced results that seem to invalidate this theory.

The process of determining the discharge of natural streams consists usually of the calibration of the discharge capacity of the channel at a certain place in relation to the stage of the water surface referred to a datum. Discharge measurements are made at a sufficient number of stages of the water surface and over a sufficient period of time to define the stage-discharge relation for the stream, so that the discharge may be determined if the stage is known.

It is an inherent characteristic of rivers to change their channels and beds as time passes, through natural agencies, including deposition and erosion. The effects of these natural agencies may be modified by artificial means, including the works of man. Consequently, a calibration of the discharge capacity of a natural channel in relation to altitude involves consideration of the variations in this relation, which approaches comparative stability only where the banks and bed of the stream remain essentially unchanged over a long period of time.

As indicated above, the extrapolation of a river-flow record into the past consists usually of the application of a calibration of discharge capacity, or a stage-discharge relation, to the river stages for a time antedating that for which such a relation was obtained. The difficulties referred to above in connection with the extrapolation of the records of flow of the Memel and Rhine Rivers are typical. Results so obtained are not reliable unless conditions are known to have been favorable for the maintenance of a stable stage-discharge relation, or unless there is some sound basis for determining the variable relations that existed.

As previously shown, records of notable floods were sometimes kept for many years prior to the initiation of systematic records of flow.   Per-

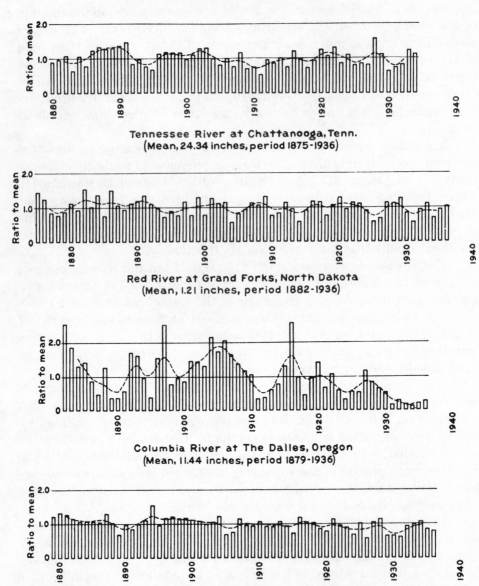

Fig. XIc-1.—Records of annual runoff, in depth in inches over the drainage areas above the river-measurement stations.

haps the longest record of flood heights in this country is that for the Connecticut River at Hartford, Conn. [4], which goes back continuously nearly 100 years and for some of the highest floods even longer.

References to or compilations of information regarding available past records of flood heights for many rivers are contained in several reports of recent floods published in the water-supply papers of the United States Geological Survey.

As the economic importance of surface streams has increased and as the sciences of hydrology and hydraulics have progressed, the applications of river-flow records have multiplied. Moreover, modern facilities for the measurement of flow make possible the collection of records that exceed materially in accuracy and detail those of 30 years ago and hence that are more widely usable—for example, in unit-hydrograph studies, in the determination of momentary peak flows, and in study of the behavior of flood waves. However, the earliest records in this country commonly furnish reliable records of annual volumes of runoff which serve to extend the present records into the past.

Figure XIc-1 is based on records of annual runoff above the sites of four of the longer-maintained river-measurement stations in the United States—the Merrimack River at Lawrence, Mass., the Tennessee River at Chattanooga, Tenn., the Red River at Grand Forks, N. Dak., and the Columbia River at The Dalles, Oreg. The stations have been selected with a view to illustrating some of the types of runoff occurrence as expressed in mean depths in inches over the tributary drainage areas. The types shown, although considerably different, represent only a few of the numerous types of runoff. Over much of the arid West the mean annual runoff is for most streams only a small fraction of an inch for the tributary drainage areas. The progressive influence of irrigation diversions above the older measurement stations materially impairs the value of many such records as a comparative index of annual runoff. Progressive development of storage regulation has also affected the value of runoff records as indexes of the operation of hydrologic factors. Many other long records are available for study, and more information concerning them may be obtained from the water-supply papers or by inquiry at district offices of the United States Geological Survey.

The data for the four rivers are presented graphically in the figure. The ratios of the annual runoff, in depth in inches, to the mean for the period of record are shown by the vertical columns. For the definition of a trend line to develop any uniformity of variation in periods longer than a year, smoothed values have been computed. The smoothed values are obtained by application of the formula

$$\frac{a + 4b + 6c + 4d + e}{16}$$

in which a, b, c, d, and e represent the runoff for the first, second, third, fourth and fifth years respectively. The values are determined progressively for each 5-year period and plotted for the third year of the group. A curve is drawn through the points so plotted.

The records at the four stations are given below.

MERRIMACK RIVER AT LAWRENCE, MASS.

Location.—At dam of the Essex Co.

Drainage area.—Total above Lawrence, 4,672 square miles. Net, exclusive of diverted parts of Nashua and Sudbury Rivers and Lake Cochituate Basins, 4,461 square miles.

Records available.—1879 to 1934.

Average annual runoff.—20.13 inches.

Remarks.—Records furnished by the Essex Co. and published in water-supply papers of the United States Geological Survey. Adjustments made to show runoff in depth in inches over the net contributing drainage area.

Runoff, in depth in inches, for the years ending September 30, 1880–1934

Year	Runoff	Year	Runoff	Year	Runoff	Year	Runoff
1880	17.60	1894	15.75	1908	23.07	1922	26.34
1881	18.90	1895	13.60	1909	14.09	1923	17.39
1882	21.63	1896	22.73	1910	14.98	1924	22.00
1883	12.76	1897	23.15	1911	10.65	1925	16.15
1884	20.90	1898	23.14	1912	19.11	1926	17.06
1885	15.72	1899	23.20	1913	17.10	1927	16.15
1886	24.58	1900	19.77	1914	20.09	1928	31.54
1887	26.27	1901	22.08	1915	15.06	1929	22.06
1888	25.08	1902	26.05	1916	24.15	1930	12.58
1889	25.76	1903	26.25	1917	19.71	1931	15.16
1890	27.42	1904	19.82	1918	14.49	1932	16.30
1891	28.96	1905	16.01	1919	19.37	1933	24.79
1892	16.42	1906	19.98	1920	25.19	1934	22.60
1893	19.19	1907	15.42	1921	21.60		

TENNESSEE RIVER AT CHATTANOOGA, TENN.

Location.—At Walnut Street Bridge, Chattanooga.

Drainage area.—21,400 square miles.

Records available.—1874–1936.

Average annual runoff.—24.34 inches.

Remarks.—Records published in Tennessee Division of Geology Bulletin 34 and in water-supply papers of United States Geological Survey. Some regulation by storage in Norris Reservoir beginning March 4, 1936.

Runoff, in depth in inches, for the years ending September 30, 1875–1936

Year	Runoff	Year	Runoff	Year	Runoff	Year	Runoff
1875	34.66	1891	32.45	1907	27.55	1922	27.79
1876	29.98	1892	26.45	1908	25.65	1923	26.94
1877	20.13	1893	23.98	1909	31.55	1924	21.82
1878	19.04	1894	17.27	1910	18.69	1925	14.14
1879	21.21	1895	21.10	1911	19.81	1926	16.61
1880	27.07	1896	18.24	1912	27.25	1927	27.41
1881	22.66	1897	27.96	1913	22.88	1928	27.19
1882	37.17	1898	18.92	1914	14.18	1929	30.71
1883	24.62	1899	30.98	1915	21.91	1930	20.24
1884	32.72	1900	18.96	1916	28.44	1931	13.89
1885	17.96	1901	30.59	1917	28.07	1932	22.55
1886	35.79	1902	26.86	1918	18.28	1933	26.87
1887	25.50	1903	27.66	1919	25.53	1934	16.56
1888	22.40	1904	13.91	1920	31.31	1935	22.71
1889	26.74	1905	19.57	1921	23.33	1936	24.59
1890	28.18	1906	23.94				

RED RIVER AT GRAND FORKS, N. DAK.

Location.—About 2 miles below the mouth of Red Lake River and earlier about half a mile below the mouth of Red Lake River.

Drainage area.—25,500 square miles.

Records available.—1882–1906.

Average annual runoff.—1.21 inches.

Remarks.—Records published in report of Minnesota State Drainage Commission, 1912, and in water-supply papers of the United States Geological Survey.

Runoff, in depth in inches, for the calendar years 1882–1936

Year	Runoff	Year	Runoff	Year	Runoff	Year	Runoff
1882	3.06	1896	1.85	1910	1.27	1924	0.38
1883	2.22	1897	3.05	1911	.39	1925	.71
1884	1.56	1898	.89	1912	.47	1926	.64
1885	1.70	1899	1.14	1913	.74	1927	1.41
1886	1.04	1900	1.02	1914	.93	1928	1.00
1887	.56	1901	1.74	1915	1.57	1929	.80
1888	1.50	1902	1.72	1916	3.12	1930	.63
1889	.42	1903	1.59	1917	1.19	1931	.18
1890	.44	1904	2.60	1918	.52	1932	.32
1891	.66	1905	2.09	1919	1.18	1933	.21
1892	2.04	1906	2.46	1920	1.69	1934	.13
1893	1.93	1907	1.89	1921	.80	1935	.24
1894	1.15	1908	1.64	1922	1.27	1936	.31
1895	.45	1909	1.41	1923	.70		

Location.—At The Dalles.

Drainage area.—237,000 square miles.

Records available.—1879–1936.

Average annual runoff.—11.44 inches.

Remarks.—Records published in water-supply papers of United States Geological Survey. Through the period of record there has been a progressive increase in utilization for irrigation and regulation by storage, but the net effect has been relatively small in relation to the total run-off.

Runoff, in depth in inches, for the years ending September 30, 1879–1936

Year	Runoff	Year	Runoff	Year	Runoff	Year	Runoff
1879	13.85	1894	17.77	1909	11.00	1924	7.87
1880	15.18	1895	11.13	1910	12.21	1925	11.51
1881	14.46	1896	13.15	1911	10.74	1926	6.77
1882	13.27	1897	13.87	1912	10.51	1927	11.79
1883	12.14	1898	13.19	1913	12.19	1928	13.28
1884	12.29	1899	13.47	1914	10.70	1929	7.61
1885	12.27	1900	12.85	1915	8.41	1930	7.60
1886	12.07	1901	12.53	1916	13.78	1931	7.00
1887	14.93	1902	11.30	1917	11.94	1932	10.64
1888	11.61	1903	12.09	1918	11.72	1933	11.34
1889	7.67	1904	13.89	1919	9.85	1934	12.11
1890	11.21	1905	8.02	1920	9.01	1935	9.76
1891	9.47	1906	8.98	1921	13.18	1936	9.13
1892	11.38	1907	13.12	1922	10.47		
1893	12.56	1908	11.27	1923	10.29		

REFERENCES

1. Ghezzi, C., Die Abflussverhältnisse des Rheins in Basel: Amt Wasserwirtschaft Mitt., Nr. 19, Bern, 1926.

2. Humphreys, A. A., and Abbot, H. L., Physics and hydraulics of the Mississippi River: U. S. Army, Bur. Topog. Eng., Paper 4, 1861.

3. Jarvis, C. S., Flood-stage records of the River Nile: Am. Soc. Civil Eng. Trans., vol. 62, pp. 1012–1071, 1936.

4. Kinnison, H. B., Conover, L. F., and Bigwood, B. L., Stages and flood discharges of the Connecticut River at Hartford, Conn.: U. S. Geol. Survey Water-Supply Paper 836-A, 1938.

5. Kolupaila, Steponas, Die Bestimmung des Abflusses des Memelstromes (Nemunas, 1812–1932): IV Hydrologishe Konferenz der Baltischen Staaten, Leningrad, September 1933.

6. Storm rainfall of eastern United States (revised)—Dayton, Ohio: Miami Conservancy Dist. Tech. Repts., pt. 1, pp. 314–328.

XId. THE RUNOFF CYCLE

WILLIAM G. HOYT[1]

The phenomena of runoff and the manner in which precipitation is translated into stream flow as described by various research workers (see references, p. 513) may be visualized as a cycle dependent on the nature of the supply.

FIRST PHASE

The first phase of the cycle relates to rainless periods, after natural surface storage and most channel storage have been depleted and when

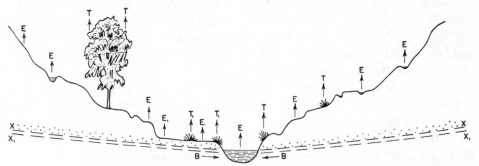

FIG. XId-1.—First phase of the runoff cycle—rainless period.

stream flow is maintained by outflow from natural subterranean storage. Figure XId-1 shows an idealized cross section of a stream valley in a humid area toward the end of a rainless period with no melting snow or ice or artificial storage.

During such a rainless period stream flow may be maintained for long periods by discharge of water (*B*) from the zone or zones of saturation into stream channels. Various terms such as "effluent seepage," "base flow," "sustained flow," or "ground-water flow" have been used to designate this outflow from subterranean storage. A ground-water table (*X*) as shown in Figure XId-1, is most commonly associated with valley-floor areas. In mountain areas or under steep slopes there may be no continuous water table, flow in stream clannels draining such areas being maintained from gravity water, either in perched layers with water tables at various levels or in rock interstices. In arid regions there may never be a water table or perched layers of water tributary to stream channels.

[1] Hydraulic engineer, Geological Survey, United States Department of the Interior, Washington, D. C.

Consequently, many of the streams are ephemeral and flow only during periods where there is runoff from surface sources.

The draining out of base flow at B with little or no replenishment results in a gradual lowering of the water table from X to X_1. When the water table drops below the channel or all the free gravity water has drained out of the rock interstices, stream flow ceases—a condition that is common in subhumid, subarid, and arid regions but occurs in humid regions only at the heads of the stream branches and after prolonged droughts. The gradual lowering of the water table results in an increase in subterranean storage capacity represented by the specific yield in the zone between X and X_1, and similarly the draining of the rock interstices results in an increase in storage represented by their total volume.

If there were no other discharge of ground water except by percolation toward the stream and discharge into the stream at B, the stream would continue to flow indefinitely at a constantly diminishing rate, but generally the ground water is also moving toward other outlets not in this cross section. Moreover, in addition to disposal of water by stream flow during rainless periods, evaporation is taking place from the surface of the stream at E; and from water in the zone of aeration E_1; and also from the zone of saturation where the ground water is near the surface, so that the capillary fringe (represented in the figure by dots above the water table) will lose water by evaporation.

In addition water is lost by transpiration from plants, the roots of which penetrate the zone of aeration T or, where depths are shallow, the zone of saturation or overlying capillary fringe T_1.

The reduction in the amount of water in the zone of aeration, from the land surface downward, through evaporation and transpiration and possibly by downward percolation to the zone of saturation, results in an increase in the amount of subterranean storage capacity represented by the volume of water required to bring the zone of aeration back to field moisture capacity.

If snow, ice, or frost is present and the air and ground temperatures are below freezing, the phenomena described remain essentially unchanged. If the temperatures are above freezing, there is a release of water from its storage in the form of snow, ice, or frost, and the water thus released will be disposed of in the second phase of the runoff cycle as described below.

If the first phase of the cycle were not interrupted, it would eventually lead to the drying up of all the surface streams. Generally, however, it is terminated by rainfall and melting of snow before the larger streams cease flowing, as is represented in Figure XI_D-2.

SECOND PHASE

The second phase of the runoff cycle marks the end of the rainless period and relates to an initial period of rain.

Figure XId-2 shows various hydrologic phenomena in the idealized cross section shortly after the beginning of a rain (P), assumed for the purpose of discussion as being of uniform light intensity. Part of the precipitation falls directly on streams and becomes an immediate increment to stream flow (C). Part of the rain is intercepted by vegetation (V). Part of the rain reaches the land surface (D) and infiltrates into the soil or is temporarily retained in surface depressions. The part that infiltrates (represented in Figure XId-2 by dots under the land surface) results in a gradual increase of water in the zone of aeration (A). If the natural storage (field moisture capacity) in the zone of aeration is not satisfied, there will generally be no appreciable increase in the amount of water in the zone of saturation.

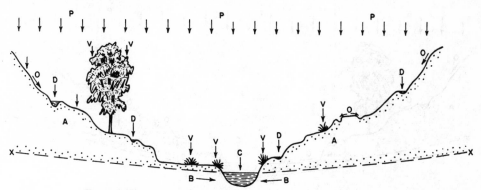

FIG. XId-2.—Second phase of the runoff cycle—initial rain period.

During the initial period of uniformly light rain interception and infiltration are functioning to such an extent that there is little if any surface or overland runoff (O) in the basin except from roads, buildings, impervious areas, and stream surfaces. Evaporation and transpiration take place to only a slight extent.

Movement of ground water into the stream channels (B) may or may not continue, depending on whether or not the first phase continued until stream flow ceased. Discharge of ground water by transpiration will be sharply decreased, because there is less transpiration during rainy or cloudy weather and because the recently acquired soil moisture will in part replace the ground-water supply.

If snow is present during the second phase, it will absorb part of the falling rain and through its storage effect delay the beginning of the next processes of the runoff cycle. If frost is present at a high moisture content it will reduce infiltration and increase surface runoff; if the ground is frozen at a low moisture content the general effect of the frost will be to increase the infiltration. The amount of water available for runoff will be augmented to the extent that thawing releases water stored in the snow, ice, and frost.

THIRD PHASE

The third phase of the runoff cycle is assumed to be associated with a continuation of rain at varying rates of intensity.

Figure XId-3 shows phenomena in the idealized cross section under varying rates of rainfall after an initial rain of uniform light intensity. As the rain (P) continues the capacity of the vegetation (V) to hold water is attained and the additional rain reaches the land surface and becomes a source of runoff. The capacity of the surface depressions (D) is reached, and additional inflow to the depressions is equaled by outflow—either as overland runoff (O) or by infiltration (I). Infiltration (I) continues in all areas of pervious soil.

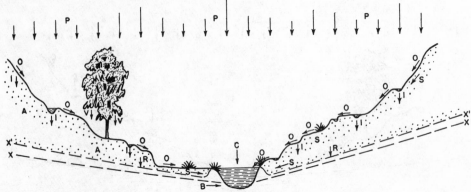

Fig. XId-3.—Third and fourth phases of the runoff cycle—continuation of rain.

When the net rate at which the water reaches the land surface exceeds the infiltration rate overland runoff (O) occurs. This runoff may or may not reach defined stream channels, depending on the absorptive or retentive capacity of the land surface over which it flows on its way toward the streams.

During the rainfall period there is a general increase of water in the upper part of the zone of aeration, especially in the root zone, which suffered greatest depletion and is nearest the new source of supply $(A$ to $A_1)$. When the deficiency of field moisture in the root zone has been satisfied water begins to move downward to the water table. If the rain continues the replenishment of the zone of saturation continues and the water table rises (from X to X_1 in Fig. XId-3). The rise in the stage of ground water from X to X_1 depends on the amount of water that reaches the water table and the effective porosity, or specific yield, of the rock material that becomes saturated.

During the rainfall period there may be subsurface storm flow (S) into the stream channels from water that has infiltrated to parts of the zone of aeration where layers of relatively low permeability intercept or retard downward movement to the water table.

If the stream channel was dry prior to the rainfall period, the rise of the water table may be sufficient to restore a normal slope in the water table toward the stream channel and thus to restore groundwater discharge into the stream. If the stream channel was not dry the net effect of the ground-water recharge during the rainfall period is to increase the hydraulic gradient or slope of the water table, and thus to increase the rate of discharge of ground water into the stream channel. However, if the stream rises rapidly its surface may temporarily be above the adjacent water table. The flow of ground water into the stream may then be stopped and water may seep from the stream into the adjacent formation, to be returned to the stream during its recession. This is sometimes called bank storage.

Evaporation and transpiration take place at a very low rate during a rainfall period, and the rain that falls on the stream surfaces is a direct increment to stream flow.

If snow is present during the third phase and its capacity to retain rain has been reached, the additional rain will become a source of runoff, augmented by the release of water resulting from a breakdown of the snow cover. To the extent that frost is present, the passage of water into the soil is retarded and runoff is increased. When frost leaves the soil there is generally a brief period of very rapid ground-water recharge, which at once diminishes the overland runoff and often also the subsurface storm flow but increases the flow of the streams in subsequent periods through ground-water discharge.

FOURTH PHASE

The fourth phase of the runoff cycle assumes a continuation of rainfall until the condition is approached when all available natural storage has become utilized.

As the rain continues unabated, with the storage capacity of the surface depressions, the interception capacity of vegetation, and the moisture capacity of the soil fully reached, infiltration probably takes place at a rate about equal to the rate of transmission of water through the zone of aeration either to the water table or into stream channels as subsurface storm flow.

Under some conditions the subsurface storm flow may reach the stream channels almost as promptly as the overland runoff, especially in areas where layers of relatively low permeability prevent or greatly retard downward percolation and divert infiltrated water back to the surface or into the stream channels.

As the rain continues the water table rises persistently until it may reach the land surface or the limiting levels so that ground-water outflow equals the maximum possible rate of recharge, and all further rain results in direct increment to runoff.   Such an extreme peak in the ground-water storage is probably never fully reached but it is approximately reached in flat swampy areas, such as those of the Southeast, after periods of very heavy and prolonged rainfall.

The effects of snow, ice, and frost during the fourth phase are similar to those described for the third phase.   If the snow melts faster than it falls, it may cause the rate of runoff to exceed the aggregate rate of precipitation as rain or snow.   On the other hand, if the weather turns cold and there is snowfall without melting, there is surface storage of snow, the stream flow diminishes, and there may also be depletion of ground water as a result of ground-water discharge without corresponding recharge.

FIFTH PHASE

The fifth phase of the runoff cycle occurs when the rain has ceased but sufficient time has not elapsed for the channel storage and surface retention to have become depleted to the stage that characterizes the first phase.

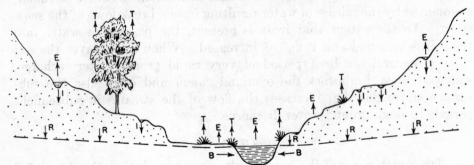

Fig. XId-4.—Fifth phase of the runoff cycle—following cessation of rain.

Figure XId-4 shows the hydrologic phenomena in the idealized section shortly after the rain has ceased.   Evaporation is then taking place at an active rate from all water held in surface depressions and retained on trees or other vegetation and from the soil moisture.   All the vegetation is transpiring water.   Evaporation and transpiration are shown by the symbols E and T in Figure XId-4.   Water held in surface depressions or on its way over the land surface to stream channels is infiltrating (I). Water in the zone of aeration is reaching the water table (R) or the stream channels (S).   Stream flow is being sustained by draining out of storage in stream channels, subsurface storm flow, and base flow or ground-water discharge.   The water table is rising or falling, depending on its peak stage and on the amount of water that is still draining out of the zone of aeration.

To the extent that temperatures are below freezing, the phenomena are not materially modified by the presence of snow and ice.   When the temperature is above freezing, the net effect of snow and ice is to prolong this phase by the time necessary for the depletion of the snow and ice storage.

MODIFICATIONS OF THE CYCLE

As Snyder [10] has pointed out, over a basin of considerable size with differing conditions as to slopes, vegetative cover, soil, and geology, the processes that have been described are not all synchronized, and each process differs in magnitude in different parts of the drainage basin. Also, as Hoyt [4] and Langbein [5] state, certain of the phenomena may be more outstanding in some drainage basins than in others, depending on the extent to which the physiographic and edaphic features of a drainage basin have been developed by the geologic and climatic history of the particular province in which it lies.

In this outline the processes relating to the groundwater have been greatly oversimplified. The movement and discharge of the ground water are complicated processes, determined by the complex geologic structure. Some of the ground water is not discharged under water-table conditions but under artesian conditions, which may cause perennial and relatively constant discharge that is not much affected by recurring periods of rainy and fair weather and therefore constitutes a base flow in the truest sense.

REFERENCES

1. Horner, W., and Flynt, F. L., Rainfall and runoff from urban areas: Am. Soc. Civil Eng. Trans., 1936, vol. 101, pp. 140–206.

2. Horton, R. E., The rôle of infiltration in the hydrologic cycle: Am. Geophys. Union Trans., 1931, pp. 189–202; Surface runoff phenomena, pt. 1—Analysis of the hydrograph: Horton Hydrol. Laboratory Pub. 101; Hydrologic interrelations of water and soils: Soil Science Soc. America Proc., vol. 1, pp. 401–429, 1937.

3. Houk, I. E., Rainfall and run-off in Miami Valley, Ohio: Miami Conservancy District Tech. Repts., pt. 8, 1921.

4. Hoyt, W. G., Rainfall and run-off in the United States: U. S. Geol. Survey Water-Supply Paper 772. See also Hoyt, W. G., and Langbein, W. B., Some general observations of physiographic and climatic influences on floods: Am. Geophys. Union Trans., 1939, pt. 2, pp. 166–174.

5. Langbein, W. B., Channel-storage and unit-hydrograph studies: Am. Geophys. Union Trans., 1938, pp. 435–447.

6. Lowdermilk, W. C., Land use and flood flows: Am. Geophys. Union Trans., 1938, pt. 1, pp. 508–516.

7. Meinzer, O. E., Outline of ground-water hydrology, with definitions: U. S. Geol. Survey Water-Supply Paper 494, 1923.

8. Meyer, Adolph, The elements of hydrology, John Wiley & Sons, 1917.

9. Musgrave, G. W., The infiltration capacity of soils in relation to the control of surface runoff and erosion: Am. Soc. Agronomy Jour., vol. 27, No. 5, 1935.

10. Snyder, F. F., A concept of run-off phenomena: Am. Geophys. Union Trans., 1938, pt. 4, pp. 725–738.

11. Thornthwaite, C. W., The hydrologic cycle reexamined: Soil Conservation, vol. 3, No. 4, 1937.

XIe. THE UNIT HYDROGRAPH METHOD

Leroy K. Sherman[1]

INTRODUCTION

The unit hydrograph method is a procedure to derive the hydrograph of runoff due to any amounts of effective or excess rainfall. The method was first presented by Sherman [11] in 1932 and since then has been improved and supplemented by the work of Bernard [1], Horner and Flynt [5], Hoyt [7], and others [3, 8].

The unit hydrograph is the hydrograph of surface runoff (not including ground-water runoff) on a given basin, due to an effective rain falling for a unit of time. The term "effective rain" means rain producing surface runoff. The unit of time may be one day or preferably a fraction of a day. It must be less than the time of concentration.

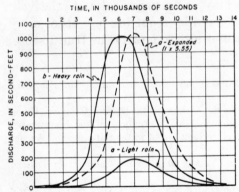

FIG. XIe-1.—Proportionality of unit hydrographs.

The unit hydrograph method takes cognizance of the facts

(a) That peak and other runoff rates are materially affected by variations of intensities of rainfall during a storm, that the single average rate of rainfall for the period of a storm (as commonly used) is not in accord with the varying rain pattern that takes place in nature.

(b) That, from a given basin, the observed hydrograph of runoff due to a given period of rainfall reflects all the combined physical characteristics of the drainage basin, including infiltration, surface detention and storage. It has further been found that, within close approximate limits,

(c) The ordinates of a unit hydrograph are proportional to the total volume of surface runoff from such unit time rains, irrespective of the amount or depth of such unit rainfalls [9, 13, and Fig. XIe-1].

(d) The base or time duration of the hydrograph of surface runoff, due to an effective rain in a unit of time, is practically a constant.

(e) The distribution of runoff, represented by the ratios of volume of runoff during a particular unit of time to the total runoff, is a constant for

[1] Consulting engineer, Chicago, Ill.

514

all unit hydrographs of runoff derived from the same basin. This holds true for all storms on the basin, without regard to their intensity. These percentages represent what is called the distribution graph [1].

(*f*) The complete hydrograph of runoff due to a storm is composed of the summation of a series of unit graphs, each representing the distributed runoff due to a rate of rainfall for a unit of time. The proportionality of ordinates (*c*) does not hold for the hydrograph composed of a series of unit graphs.

The unit hydrograph method does not apply to runoff originating from snow or ice.

The derivation of runoff from a given rainfall by this method for a particular drainage basin requires a hydrograph of runoff from the basin based on a stream flow record. It is desirable that this hydrograph be one that is due to a single unit-time period of rainfall, such as 24 hours or less. With such a record available, the method is quite simple. The procedure can best be presented by an example.

DISTRIBUTION GRAPH FOR 24-HOUR UNITS

The north Fabius River at Taylor, Mo., is a tributary of the upper Mississippi. The drainage area above Taylor is 930 square miles. The first step is to derive the typical graph of percentage distribution for this basin. We may use, on a basin as large as this, 24 hours as the unit of time. (Shorter units are preferable when hourly records of rain are available.)

An inspection of the United States Weather Bureau Monthly Climatological Data for Missouri in 1932 gives several 1-day segregated rainfalls. For the 24-hour rain of September 18, 1932, the corresponding record of stream flow is found in United States Geological Survey Water-Supply Paper 730, page 154.

TABLE 1.—*Derivation of distribution graph*

Date	Observed stream flow (c.f.s.)	Base flow (c.f.s.)	Surface runoff (c.f.s.)	Distribution graph (percent)
Sept. 16	40	40	0	
17	36	35	1	0.1
18	332	40	292	18.7
19	825	60	765	49.0
20	355	50	305	19.6
21	150	40	110	7.1
22	77	35	42	2.7
23	53	35	18	1.3
24	45	30	15	1.0
25	40	30	10	.5
			1,557	100.0

In table 1, the "base flow," after the day of rain was estimated as follows: On the 25th the observed stream flow was 40 c.f.s., and most of the surface runoff had passed. The base flow or ground-water outflow may be assumed as 30 c.f.s. By inspection of flow records at Taylor when there was evidently no surface runoff, it was found that the depletion curve ranged between about 60 and 30 c.f.s. in 7 days. This increase of ground water from observed 35 c.f.s. on the 17th to 60 c.f.s. on the 19th is a reasonable effect of infiltration from the rain. The column of base flow, though approximate, is within the necessary limits of accuracy for purposes of the distribution graph. The figures for this graph are those in the column "Surface runoff" converted to percentages of the total volume of runoff.

Comparison of this distribution graph with several similar 24-hour graphs showed that the peak of 49 percent was fair for storms centering near or below the middle of the basin, but it was too high for storms centering on the upper end of the Fabius Basin. The relative peak percentage reflects the position of the storm center in the basin.

In a similar manner, another distribution graph was derived from the runoff due to a rain on April 13, 1933, as follows:

April 1	1.7	April 6	7.6	April 11	2.7
2	4.6	7	5.3	12	2.5
3	17.2	8	4.2	13	2.2
4	34.8	9	3.5	14	1.8
5	8.8	10	2.9		100.0

The average of the two distribution graphs from the storms (centering in the lower and upper parts of the Fabius basin) with peaks of 49.0 and 34.8 percent, will give the distribution graph for a storm of uniform areal distribution or for storms centering at the middle of the basin. This average distribution graph is the one shown in column 5, tables 2 and 3.

In Weather Bureau records, rainfall readings at some stations are taken in the evening and at other stations the following morning. Inspection will frequently show that the separate records on the two days are both included in one 24-hour period. C. W. Sherman [10] gives 10 to 13 hours as the average duration of a 1-day storm.

APPLICATION OF THE DISTRIBUTION GRAPH TO DETERMINE RUNOFF FROM ANY RAINS ON THE GIVEN BASIN

During the period from July 30 to August 12, 1932, the Weather Bureau records for four stations in the North Fabius Basin above Taylor, Mo.—Downing, Labelle, Gorin and Memphis, Mo.—gave a weighted average of 3.32 inches of rain for the 24 hours ending on the morning of July 31. For August 7 the average was 1.18 inches. Table 2 shows the procedure recommended for tabulating and computing stream flow from these rainfall data.

Columns 1 and 2 give the weighted average rainfall on the basin. There was an antecedent rain of 1.11 inches on July 25, which affected the stream flow on July 31.   Column 4 is derived as explained hereinafter under the heading "Infiltration and losses."   Column 5 is the distribution graph derived as explained above.   Column 6 is the daily runoff due to rain on July 25 and 31 and August 7.   These figures are derived by multiplying the net runoff, 0.08 inch (in column 4) by each figure in the

TABLE 2.—*Computed runoff of North Fabius River at Taylor, Mo., July 25 to August 17, 1932*
[Drainage area 930 square miles]

1	2	3	4	5	6	6a	6b	7	7a	8	9
Date	Rain (inches)	Loss (inches)	Net rain (inches)	Distri-bution graph (percent)	Distributed runoff (inches) from			Total runoff		Base flow (c.f.s.)	Computed stream flow (c.f.s.)
					July 25	July 31	Aug. 7	Inches	c.f.s.		
1932											
July 25	1.11	1.03	.08	4	0.0032						
26	....	....	...	18	.0144						
27	....	....	...	43	.0394						
28	....	....	...	16	.0144						
29	.12	.12	0	7	.0056						
30	....	....	...	4	.0032	......	......	0.0032	80	20	100
31	3.32	2.71	.63	2.5	.0020	0.0252	......	.0272	680	20	700
Aug. 1	....	....	...	2.0	.0016	.1140	......	.1156	2,880	60	2,940
2	....	....	...	1.4	.0011	.2700	......	.2711	6,780	60	6,840
3	....	....	...	1.1	.0009	.1000	......	.1009	2,520	50	2,570
4	....	....	...	1.0	.0008	.0503	......	.0511	1,280	40	1,320
5	....	....	...	.....	......	.0252	......	.0252	630	30	660
6	....	....	...	.....	......	.0157	......	.0157	392	20	412
7	1.18	1.09	.10	.....	......	.0126	0.0040	.0166	415	20	435
8	....	....	...	.....	......	.0088	.0118	.0196	490	20	510
9	....	....	...	.....	......	.0069	.0430	.0499	1,245	20	1,265
10	....	....	...	.....	......	.0063	.0160	.0223	557	20	577
11	....	....	...	.....	......	......	.0070	.0070	175	20	195
12	....	....	...	.....	......	......	.0040	.0040	100	20	120
13	....	....	...	.....	......	......	.0025	.0025	60	20	80
14	....	....	...	.....	......	......	.0020	.0020			
15	....	....	...	.....	......	......	.0014	.0014			
16	....	....	...	.....	......	......	.0011	.0011			
17	....	....	...	.....	......	......	.0010	.0010			
			.81	100	.08	.63	.10	.7374			

distribution graph.   Columns 6a and 6b are derived in the same manner from the net runoff due to rain on July 31 and August 7.   The total of each of columns 6, 6a, and 6b, distributed runoff, in depth in inches equals the figures for net rain in column 4.   The figures in columns 6, 6a, and 6b begin opposite their corresponding day of rain.   Column 7 is the horizontal sum of columns 6, 6a, and 6b, expressed in inches, and column 7a is the same as column 7, expressed in c.f.s.   To column 7a is added the estimated base flow (column 8).   Base flow has been mentioned above and is further described by Hoyt and others [7].   Column 8 gives the computed stream flow for the North Fabius River at Taylor, Mo., for the period. It is in good agreement with the record contained in Water-Supply Paper 730.

FLOOD RUNOFF

On June 29, 1933, there was a weighted average rain of 5.84 inches on the Fabius River Basin. By means of the same distribution graph and procedure as given for table 2, the average 24-hour peak runoff on July 1, 1933, was computed as 25,800 c.f.s. The momentary peak, by graphic analysis, was estimated at 30,000 c.f.s. United States Geological Survey Water-Supply Paper 745 records the figures 26,400 and 30,300 c.f.s.

Table 3 illustrates the application of the unit hydrograph method in estimating the flood due to a storm with a frequency of once in 100 years.

TABLE 3.—*Computation of flood at Taylor, Mo., for 100-year 6-day storm*

1	2	2a	3	4	5	6	6a	6b	6c	7	7a
	Rain (inches)					Distribution of runoff					
Day	Center of storm	Average for basin (80 per-cent)	Loss (inches)	Net rain (inches)	Distribution graph (percent)	Third day	Fourth day	Fifth day	Sixth day	Total Inches	Total c.f.s.[a]
1	0.1	0.08	.08	0	4						
2	.1	.08	.08	0	18						
3	.6	.48	.35	.13	43	0.0052	......	......	......	0.0052	130
4	.9	.72	.43	.29	16	.0234	0.0116	......	......	.0350	875
5	1.3	1.04	.50	.54	7	.0560	.0522	0.0216	......	.1298	3,240
6	6.0	4.80	.98	3.82	4	.0208	.1220	.0972	0.1530	.3920	9,800
7	...	....	....	....	2.5	.0091	.0463	.2320	.6900	.9784	24,400
8	...	....	....	....	2.0	.0052	.0203	.0860	1.6100	1.7215	[b]43,300
9	...	....	....	....	1.4	.0032	.0116	.0378	.6110	.6636	16,550
10	...	....	....	....	1.1	.0026	.0073	.0216	.2670	.2985	7,460
11	...	....	....	....	1.0						
	9.0	7.20	2.42	4.78	100						

[a] c.f.s. per day = inches per day $\times$ 26.88 $\times$ drainage area in square miles.
[b] Peak = 50,000 c.f.s.

Column 2 shows the rain in the 6-day 100-year storm, given in the report on rainfall of the Miami Conservancy District, edition of 1936. It is applicable to the part of northeastern Missouri in which the Fabius Basin lies. The largest 1-day rains were used to make up the total of 9 inches of rain in 6 days. Slightly less runoff would have resulted with other grouping of daily rainfall, and the runoff would have been materially less on the assumption of a uniform daily rainfall.

Column 2a is 80 per cent of column 2. That is the distributed rain over the 930 square miles. It is taken as 80 per cent of the high-spot rain of 9 inches. The distribution graph, column 5, and all the rest of the procedure is the same as in table 2, except that some figures for falling stage are omitted. The flood due to a 100-year storm at Taylor, Mo., is 43,300 c.f.s. It is the average peak flow for a day. The instantaneous peak is 50,000 c.f.s.

INFILTRATION AND LOSSES

All formulas and methods for estimating runoff and rainfall require some expression of the relation between them. Surface runoff is the residual of rainfall minus losses. Infiltration and other losses vary according to season, temperature, and the infiltration capacity of the soil. The infiltration capacity is affected by antecedent precipitation. When rainfall data are based on self-recording gages, giving intensities and duration, the problem is capable of direct and definite solution. Such gage records are particularly essential for small drainage areas. Most of the available precipitation records of the United States Weather Bureau are given only for 24-hour periods. This 24-hour record can be used directly in the unit-hydrograph method only on areas greater than about 500 square miles because variation in rain intensity and duration is partly equalized by overland and channel flow and storage. If there is a recording rain gage on or near the basin, then the unit time can be taken as some fraction of a day, and the daily rain prorated. This method will give accurate results.

When only a daily record of precipitation is available, without hourly distribution, as illustrated in table 2, it does not show whether the rain fell in 24 hours, 3 hours, or whether it was continuous or intermittent. It is therefore impossible to apply hourly rates of infiltration to that record. The infiltration loss that may apply to any specific 1-day depth of rainfall is known to be greater in August than in April. The loss is known to be greater after a dry period than after a wet period. The loss for a particular 24-hour total rain record without a recorder cannot be precisely forecast, but the normal or average loss can be estimated. A method of evaluating net rainfall—that is, the portion of the rainfall that produces surface runoff—by the infiltration theory has been introduced recently by Sherman [14].

DIAGRAM OF RUNOFF

When the ratios of runoff to 24-hour rainfalls are platted in groups for a given month and given depth of rainfall, it will be found that the average figure for each group bears a consistent relation. This relation is better if cognizance is taken of antecedent rainfalls.

The author has platted such a diagram showing runoff-rainfall relation (Fig. XIᴇ-2). It is applicable particularly to certain streams in Indiana, Illinois, and eastern Iowa and Missouri. Results from its

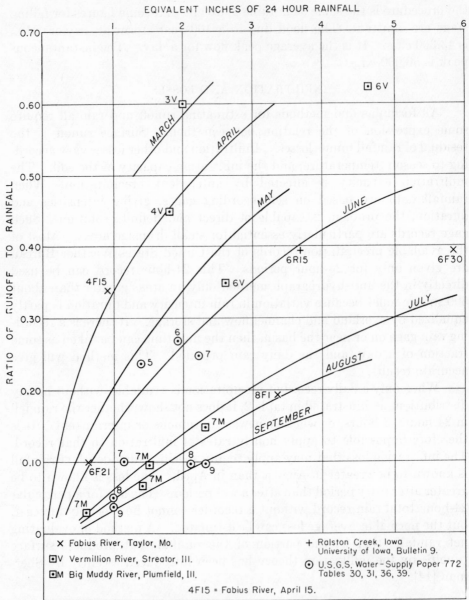

FIG. XIᴇ-2.—Relation of runoff to rainfall. For use in derivation of normal seasonal runoff when only 24-hour undistributed precipitation records are available. Data from records of certain streams in eastern Missouri and Iowa, Illinois, and western Ohio. To allow for the effect of antecedent rains add to the given rain the appropriate percentages of the antecedent rains shown below. This will give the equivalent inches of 24-hour rainfall for use in the diagram.

Intervening dry days	0	1	2	3	4	5	7	9
Percentage of antecedent rain	100	80	60	50	40	30	20	10

use will be good, fair, or poor, dependent on whether the particular problem for which it is used is one of average or abnormal infiltration. This diagram is similar in principle to the author's original diagram in the Engineering News-Record of April 7, 1932. The device is presented as a means for estimating the most probable amount of loss in infiltration when only 24-hour rainfall records are available.

In the example represented in table 2 figures in columns 3 and 4 were derived from the diagram as follows: The 24-hour distribution of rain on the Fabius Basin is unknown. Therefore it is necessary to use an estimated normal runoff with the aid of the diagram. The rain on July 31 was 3.32 inches. The infiltration capacity was affected by two antecedent rains. Using the empirical rule for effective antecedent rain, add to 3.32 inches, $0.12 \times 0.8 = 0.10$ inch for rain on July 29. Also add $1.11 \times 0.4 = 0.44$ for rain on July 25. This total is 3.86 inches. On the diagram for 3.86 inches rainfall and date as the later part of July, read "ratio runoff to rainfall" as 19 per cent. Then $3.32 \times 0.19 = 0.63$ inch as the total depth of net rainfall on July 31. Place 0.63 in column 4. All the other figures in column 4 were derived in the same manner. Although it is not essential in this particular problem, it is desirable to enter "losses" in column 3.

Whenever the distribution of 24-hour rain is known from a self-recording gage in the basin, then column 3 of losses is derived first. Under such conditions, this type of diagram will not be used, as a better method is available and will produce more accurate results and a shorter unit period can be applied. (See chapter VII, on infiltration.)

DERIVATION OF DISTRIBUTION GRAPHS
FROM COMPOUND HYDROGRAPHS

Some of the best distribution graphs are derived from hydrographs of large storms having durations of two, three, or several unit periods. Many ingenious procedures have been devised and used for obtaining unit hydrographs out of such composite storms. Examples of the procedure have been given by Collins [4], McCarthy [8] and Snyder [15]. The writer has used a procedure similar to the one described by McCarthy. Figure XIᴇ-3 shows, in heavy lines, the hydrograph of the Washita River at Durwood, Okla., for the storm of March 26–28, 1938. A chart is given showing the volume of rain excess in inch-miles for the five 12-hour periods of this storm. Period 3 had no excess precipitation. The observed hydrograph, therefore, is composed of four unit hydrographs. The relative volumes, or the relative peak ordinates or other ordinates, for each of these four unit hydrographs will be in proportion to the four given volumes of rain excess. The time from the peak, or a given point in the first unit hydrograph, to the time of the peak or similar given point in the fifth unit hydrograph is 48 hours. Draw any set of diagonal lines with the beginning in the morning, say, of March 30, and ending 48 hours later, on April 1, on the descending limb of the observed hydrograph. This is

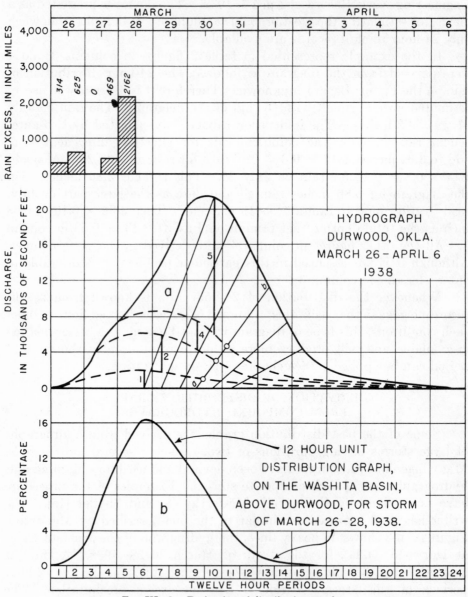

FIG. XIE-3.—Derivation of distribution graphs.

line ab. Measure ab with any scale. Prorate the distance ab into four parts, 1, 2, 4, and 5, each in proportion to the respective volumes of rain excess. Repeat this for lines similar to ab throughout the recession limb of the observed hydrograph. Now, starting at or near the diagonal corresponding to *ab* nearest the peak of the observed hydrograph, draw the vertical lines 1, 2, 4, and 5, each of these lines being in proportion to the given four volumes of inch-miles. On the rising side of the observed hydrographs, mark the beginning of the various 12-hour periods, as shown. The dotted lines of the superimposed unit graphs are continued by eye to

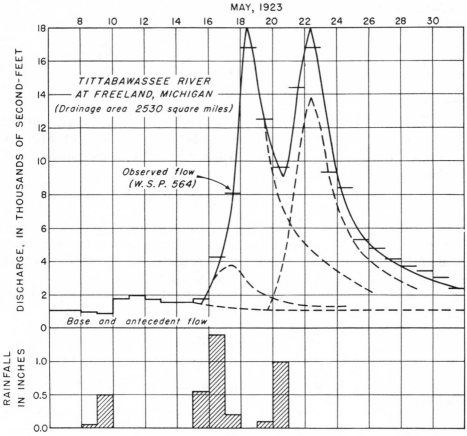

Fɪɢ. XIᴇ-4.—Segretation of unit hydrographs.

meet the lines heretofore platted by segregation along the descending limb of the hydrograph.

The ordinates of each of these four unit hydrographs will give the approximate form of the unit hydrographs, or the distribution graph when referred to a horizontal base line. Select the largest unit hydrograph, No. 5. Before adopting it, check the graphic derivation by applying the customary summation procedure to the given quantities for the five 12-hour periods of rain excess. Revise the preliminary distribution graph devised by the graphic process, so that the horizontal lines of summation are in reasonable accord with the figures for the observed hydrograph.

In this manner the 12-hour distribution graph for the Washita River above Durwood was derived as shown.

In the accompanying hydrograph for the Tittabawassee River at Freeland, Mich. (Fig. XIe-4), the two main overlapping hydrographs *A* and *B* can be segregated graphically as shown by the dotted line *A* and *B* prior to any tabulation work   The following distribution graph for the 15 days was derived from this figure:

1	3	5	12	9	3.5	13	1.7
2	9.7	6	8.5	10	2.9	14	1.4
3	25	7	6.5	11	2.5	15	1.0
4	16	8	4.5	12	2.1		100.0

This distribution graph, applied to the Miami Conservancy District 6-day 100-year storm, gives for the 24-hour peak runoff at Freeland (drainage area 2,530 square miles) 47,600 c.f.s.   The instantaneous peak is about 58,000 c.f.s.

TIME OF UNIT HYDROGRAPHS

Selection of a proper time period for unit hydrographs is important. For areas over 1,000 square miles use 12-hour units in preference to 24 hours.   For areas between 100 and 1,000 square miles use units of 6, 8, or 12 hours.   For areas of 20 square miles use 2 hours.   For smaller areas use a time unit of about one-third or one-fourth of the approximate concentration time of the basin.

REFERENCES

1. Bernard, Merrill, An approach to determinate stream flow: Am. Soc. Civil Eng. Trans., 1935, p. 347.

2. Boston Society of Civil Engineers, Report of committee on floods: Boston Soc. Civil Eng. Jour., September, 1930.

3. Brater, E. F., The unit-hydrograph principle applied to small watersheds: Am. Soc. Civil Eng. Proc., September, 1939, p. 1191; Discussion, reprint, January, 1940.

4. Collins, W. T., Runoff distribution graphs from precipitation occurring in more than one time unit: Civil Engineering, September, 1939, p. 559.

5. Horner, W. W., and Flynt, F. L., Runoff from small urban areas: Am. Soc. Civil Eng. Trans., 1936, p. 140.

6. Horton, R. E., Surface runoff phenomena, analysis of the hydrograph: Horton Hydrol. Lab., Voorheesville, N. Y., Pub. 101, 1935.

7. Hoyt, W. G., and others, Studies of relation of rainfall and runoff in the United States: U. S. Geol. Survey Water-Supply Paper 772, 1936.

8. McCarthy, G. T., The unit hydrograph and flood routing, U. S. Engineer Office, Providence, R. I., revised March 21, 1939.

8.1 Meyer, O. H., Analysis of runoff characteristics: Am. Soc. Civil Eng. Proc., vol. 64, No. 9, pp. 1769–1786, 1938.   Includes unit hydrographs and transposition.   Discussion. February, March, April, May, June, October, 1939.

9. Pettis, C. R., Appraisal of unit-hydrograph method of flood estimation: Civil Engineering, February, 1938, p. 114.

10. Sherman, C. W., Actual duration of "one-day" and "two-day" rainstorms: Civil Engineering, March, 1939, p. 179.

11. Sherman, L. K., Stream flow from rainfall by the unit-graph method. Eng. News-Record, April 7, 1932. Discussion, August 25 and September 1, 1932.

12. Sherman, L. K., Relation of hydrographs of runoff to size and character of drainage basins: Am. Geophys. Union Trans., 1932.

13. Sherman, L. K., The hydraulics of surface runoff: Civil Engineering, March, 1940, p. 165.

14. Sherman, L. K., The unit hydrograph and its applications: Associated State Eng. Soc. Bull., vol. 16, No. 2, 1941.

15. Snyder, F. F., Synthetic unit hydrographs: Am. Geophys. Union Trans., 1938, pt. I, pp. 447–454.

XIf. PREDICTION OF RUNOFF

Royal W. Davenport[1]

The constitution of the flow of rivers is complex and has responded slowly to efforts to discover any order or system. However, through critical scientific study of an increasing quantity of basic observations, considerable order and system have been disclosed in the relations between runoff and the meteorologic factors and physical characteristics peculiar to drainage basins. This knowledge is utilized in a variety of ways, notably in forecasts of stream flow. Such forecasts range from a few hours to a few days when rainfall is the source, up to a few weeks, in respect to total volume, when snow on the ground is the source. Considerable effort has been expended in attempting to define possible progressive cycles or systematic sequences of runoff that would furnish a basis for predicting the general conditions as to quantity of runoff weeks or even many months before the occurrence of the precipitation.

The prediction of stream flow by the definition of cycles is based upon an idea that the runoff records may display some conformity to cyclic occurrence and that the period and amplitude of such cycles can be determined with sufficient definiteness to permit their extension for some time in the future beyond the influence of known meteorologic and physical factors in order to show the stream flow to be expected. The situation is similar with respect to the application of evidence of systematic sequences.

Runoff has its source in precipitation, but viewed statistically it represents only what remains of precipitation after progress through the diverse processes of the hydrologic cycle and the subtractions by evaporation both directly and through the agency of vegetation [9, 12]. Both precipitation and evaporation are fundamental meteorologic phenomena, and the quantity of runoff is primarily the residual product of their interaction. It is common knowledge that periods of high or low runoff tend to conform respectively to periods of high or low precipitation. Moreover, under conditions of uniform precipitation periods of low runoff tend to be associated with periods of high evaporation, and conversely. It is not unreasonable to suppose, therefore, that if regularity of period and amplitude can be detected in the cycles of precipitation and other meteorologic data, a similar regularity might be reflected in cycles of runoff.

[1] Hydraulic engineer, Chief, Division of Water Utilization, Geological Survey, United States Department of the Interior, Washington, D. C.

Henry [6] discusses periodic fluctuations in climate and meteorologic effects of solar variability and briefly summarizes investigations in these fields. He concluded:

There seems not to be any definite evidence from the 100 years' instrumental observations available for examination that there are changes of a progressive or a cyclic character in the climate of any part of the earth.

Other results of investigations of periods and cycles in meteorologic data are briefly described by Weightman [11], who gives references to studies of cycles in droughts, temperature, precipitation, atmospheric pressure, and sunspots and makes the following statements concerning the results:

Investigators along these lines have produced some very interesting general relationships; but from the practical standpoint of predicting future occurrences in such a way as to be of commercial advantage, little has been accomplished and little has been claimed by conservative workers. From a consideration of the results obtained, investigations of cycles have not produced encouraging results.

On the basis of studies of the periodicities of solar variation Abbot [1] reports the discovery of corresponding periodicities in weather, integrally related to a 23-year cycle. He finds the effects of this cycle in the records of the levels of the Nile and of the Great Lakes.

Meteorologic literature shows that the search for periodicity and cycles is continuing, but apparently the results are not substantially more significant in a practical sense than those summarized by Weightman. The Monthly Weather Review, Supplement 39, "Reports of critical studies of methods of long-range weather forecasting," contains a group of papers by several authors, covering the work of investigators pertaining to various aspects of laws and principles underlying weather changes.

The Scripps Institution of Oceanography, La Jolla, Calif., has for several years, through Dr. George F. McEwen, professor of physical and dynamical oceanography, issued in mid-October indications of precipitation during the approaching rainfall season for a large part of the California coast and the probable temperature trend in southern California. The forecast is based upon a derived empirical relation between sea-surface temperatures during the summer and the precipitation of the following rainy season. McEwen also applies such deductions as can be made from discernible evidence of cycles in the data. Experience in the application of the method indicates that the forecast of precipitation will be accurate 75 to 80 percent of the time in respect to showing an excess or deficiency in relation to the average. The following is a quotation of McEwen's conclusion [8] with regard to the problems of weather forecasting:

In dealing with so complex a problem as long-range weather forecasting, the writer has proceeded along lines shown to be most promising by past experience, at the same time keeping an open mind for all possible methods of attack. It appears desirable to hold a forecasting system in a "fluid" state rather than in a rigid, unchangeable one. Here on the Pacific coast, where every clue as to the probable nature of the weather to be expected is so eagerly sought, it is imperative that careful unbiased consideration be given to the important question of evaluating the methods used. All interested hope that the combined efforts of those meteorologists who enter the field of long-range forecasting will meet with success commensurate with the increasing demands for such service. Finally, attempts to make long-range forecasts for one region continue to indicate that weather is not simply a local phenomenon having purely local causes. The value of indices relating to conditions far from the region for which forecasts are made is being demonstrated; thus long-range weather forecasting is necessarily a large-scale cooperative undertaking. Results commensurate with the increasing demand for such forecasts can evidently not come from only a few individuals giving part time to the problem.

Notable studies of cyclic variations or systematic sequences in annual stream flow have been made by Streiff [10], and the results are presented in a series of papers and discussions. In large hydroelectric projects, where through storage of the stream flow there is a high degree of utilization of the available water supply, there may be a strong commercial incentive to explore possibilities for forecasting the water supply as far in the future as possible. Successful prediction would afford a basis for planning the provision of adequate auxiliary or supplemental power by fuel plants or otherwise.

Streiff gives results to show that he has been able to predict runoff with significant reliability 2 years or more in advance. He states in respect to cyclic variations in annual stream flow:

> Systematic sequences are strongly evident on the great continental plains but are less regular in mountainous and coastal regions. But even in those areas nature, though infinitely complicated, will permit the separation of systematic sequences from the tangled mass of available data. In time it will be possible to predict the characteristic trends of stream flow with an accuracy not possible at present.

Other studies of the correlation among sun spots, rainfall, tree rings, and annual runoff have been made by Girand [4].

Several interesting studies of the relation between the growth of trees as shown by tree rings and precipitation or runoff have been made, of which those by Hardman [5] and by Davis and Sampson [3] are typical. These studies involve the complexity that exists because qualitative moisture values that are significant in producing tree growth may have little relation to quantitative moisture values expressed as annual precipitation or annual runoff.

The causes which conceivably may influence a cyclic type of occurrence in the meteorologic factors that are basic to the determination of quantities of river flow seemingly must have a comprehensive source, whether such source is terrestrial or extraterrestrial. The idea has been advanced by Teisserenc de Bort that certain well-defined centers of high and low pressure or "centers of action" may oscillate to and fro over considerable distances and in this way cause long period changes in weather [2].

The thought arises that if cycle- or sequence-producing causes operate in a comprehensive manner they may be associated with runoff results in such a way that the results at a given time, although varying widely on different rivers as to position in sequence, relative magnitude, and other aspects of cyclic occurrence, would nevertheless, when viewed together in a panoramic way, reflect an interrelation consistent with any associated basic cycle or sequence. Such relations might consist either of systematic repetitions of the same combination of conditions on different rivers or of a systematic march or oscillation across the earth's surface of a certain phase of a cycle (similar to the variation of the time of the maximum secular magnetic declination). If these relations exist, the prospect for the discovery and definition of the cycles will be more favorable the wider the areal representation of the river-flow records that are studied.

More than 40 years ago Horton [7] made the following general observation with regard to rainfall records:

> Many long records show no regularly recurring cycles, but in all cases which the writer has observed two or more successive dry or wet years occur with much greater frequency than would be the case if the sequence of wet or dry years were purely a matter of mathematical calculation. As a safe conclusion, it may be said that certain meteorological conditions underlying rainfall tend to recur in more or less obscure cycles. It seems not improbable that the causes of such cycles are general in their application and in their apparent effects in many instances are marked by local or secondary conditions.

This statement expresses reasonably well the consensus of present conservative opinion with respect to cyclic behavior of stream flow.

The attacks upon the problem of predicting river flow have produced very interesting results and have yielded methods of analysis which seem to those who have developed and used them to be valuable and helpful. Apparently one of the weaknesses of these methods has been their dependence on personal judgment as contrasted with rigorous mathematical procedures by which the same results would be obtained by any analyst. Moreover, the question seems to have arisen in the minds of some hydrologists whether the magnitude of the systematic cyclic element so far as it exists in runoff data may not be so small as to be obscured by other elements that behave in a fortuitous and unsystematic way. The present better-informed attitude appears to be to give full and sympathetic encouragement to investigators in this hopeful field of research.

REFERENCES

1. Abbot, C. G., Weather governed by changes in the sun's radiation: Smithsonian Inst. Ann. Rept., 1935, pp. 93–115.

2. Clayton, H. H., Centers of action and long-period weather changes: Am. Meteorol. Soc. Bull., vol. 19, pp. 27–29, 1938.

3. Davis, W. E., and Sampson, A. W., Experiment in correlation of tree-growth rings and precipitation cycles: Am. Geophys. Union Trans., 1936, pp. 493–496.

4. Girand, John, Weather records projected into the future: Civil Engineering, vol. 2, pp. 76–79, 1932.

5. Hardman, George, The relationship between tree growths and stream runoff in the Truckee River Basin, Calif.-Nev.: Am. Geophys. Union Trans., 1936, pp. 491–493.

6. Henry, A. J., Meteorological data and meteorological changes: Physics of the Earth, vol. 3, Meteorology, pp. 15–34, 1931.

7. Horton, R. E., report on the runoff and water power of Kalamazoo River, in Lane, A. C., Water resources of the Lower Peninsula of Michigan: U. S. Geol. Survey Water-Supply Paper 30, p. 29, 1899.

8. McEwen, G. F., Problems of long-range weather forecasting for the Pacific coast: Am. Geophys. Union Trans., 1936, pt. 2, p. 491.

9. Meyer, A. F., The elements of hydrology, 2d ed., pp. 298–315, John Wiley & Sons.

10. Streiff, A., Systematic sequences in annual stream flow: Civil Engineering, vol. 2, pp. 690–692, 1932.

11. Weightman, R. H., Physical basis of weather forecasting: Physics of the earth, vol. 3, Meteorology, pp. 234–279, 1931.

12. Williams, G. R., and others, Natural water loss in selected drainage basins: U. S. Geol. Survey Water-Supply Paper 846, 1940.

CLARENCE S. JARVIS[1]

A flood is a relatively high flow as measured by either gage height or discharge rate. Gage readings indicate levels of the water surface at measuring stations. Whenever the stream channel in an average section is overtaxed, causing overflow of adjacent land definitely outside the usual channel boundaries, the stream is said to have reached flood stage. Relative magnitudes of flood peaks may be expressed in various terms, including either height above low water, height above flood stage, or the corresponding rate of discharge.

Obviously the distinction between normal discharge and flood flow is determined by the usual discharge habits of the stream. A discharge constituting only a minor flood or even the average flow of such streams as the Delaware, Susquehanna, and Ohio Rivers or of a main tributary might be classed as a notable flood, far exceeding the maximum recorded on streams draining basins of equal size in semiarid or desert regions [63, app. I, pp. 393–426]. Thus 1.5 c.s.m. (cubic feet per second per square mile) may be equaled or exceeded by the average yield in rivers of the Appalachian region, whereas such a yield is seldom if ever attained at several stations on the lower Colorado River, Arizona, the lower Snake River, Idaho, or some of the larger streams of the Great Basin, such as the Sevier and Humboldt Rivers. Furthermore, any flow of sufficient volume or duration to impede traffic across an arroyo or other intermittent drainage channel may locally be called a flood, even though the yield per square mile of drainage area may be comparable to low or average flows in humid regions.

CAUSES OF FLOODS

Flood flows are normally the direct or indirect result of precipitation, even though the runoff may be delayed or modified by the processes of freezing and thawing, surface inequalities or indentations, interception on vegetal cover or through infiltration, underground flow, and temporary storage in or release from reservoirs through either natural or artificial means of detention and regulation.

Owing to differences in infiltration resulting from variations in initial soil moisture and the effects of land use, tillage, vegetal cover, and leaf

---

[1] Hydraulic engineer, Soil Conservation Service, United States Department of Agriculture, Washington, D. C.

mold or forest litter, and owing to differences in geologic structure, a given rainfall may produce only a moderate rise in the streams of one area and flood conditions in those of another area; and owing to the varying moisture content of the soil the same amount of rainfall on a given area may produce a greater rise in the stream at one time than at another. Moreover, a gentle rainfall extending over several hours or days may result in only slight increase of stream flow, whereas the same amount of precipitation in a few minutes or hours may produce high flood crests of brief duration. For example, during the disastrous flood on Monument Creek at Colorado Springs, Colo., in May 1935 the total volume discharged was only 10,000 acre-feet, but most of the water passed through the city in the course of 2 hours, in a channel that is normally dry most of the year and would have carried the entire volume in 20 hours with no appreciable damage. Obviously the torrential character of the runoff reflected both the steep slopes of the drainage system and the intensity of precipitation within most of the storm area, which ranged from 1 to 3 inches per hour throughout the 5-hour period of storm. Apparently the flood discharge at times was at least 1 inch per hour or nearly 1 cubic foot per second from each acre covered by the intense storm.

The runoff characteristics of a drainage basin—its extremes of discharge, the duration, volume, and frequency of floods of given types and magnitudes—may be largely determined through analysis of adequate records of stream flow within the basin, or within other basins of demonstrated similarity in principal factors influencing runoff behavior, with due regard to the interrelations of these factors. Thus it is known that the amount by which infiltration rate and surface detention are exceeded determines the rate and volume of surface runoff, which generally constitutes the greater part of flood runoff. In the final analysis, the composition, texture, and surface conditions of the soil, including the type and density of vegetal cover, antecedent moisture, and geologic structure, determine the rate of infiltration, the available storage capacity, and consequently the proportion of rainfall residue appearing as surface runoff.

Apart from direct relations with rainfall, the sudden release of water constitutes an immediate cause of floods. It may be due to rapid thawing of ice or snow on frozen ground, or to such thawing accompanied by rainfall, or to the release of stored water through failure of a reservoir dam or the breaking of log, ice, or debris dams. Occasionally damaging floods result merely from opening the outlet and flood gates of a storage reservoir to full capacity so suddenly as to produce well-defined transitory waves.

A study of the complicated network of drainage channels within a river system will often disclose substantial tributaries meeting the main channel almost in pairs, or in groups discharging within a short reach of the main stream.   Such conditions are favorable to occasional coincidence of flood crests, but close synchronization is generally broken by variation in storm patterns and in their direction as well as their velocity of motion, in distances traversed by the runoff, and in surface and channel gradients, cross section, and roughness, and therefore in channel velocities.

An analysis of flood phenomena pertaining to the principal river systems of the United States and other countries shows the important part played by alternation of flood peaks from different parts of the drainage basins, where synchronization would undoubtedly have produced record-breaking stages, with proportionately high property damage and probable loss of life.   At infrequent and thus far practically unpredictable intervals the timing of flood crests on the tributaries may be such as to produce in the trunk stream about the maximum peak commensurate with the rainfall volume and runoff rate—that is, proportional to the excess of rainfall over the infiltration and other detention factors.   It is against this rare occurrence that provisions are ordinarily planned in flood-protection programs, on the theory that proportional benefits will accrue during the recurrent stages of lesser magnitude.

Now that laboratory models have assumed prominence in the solution of many technical, research, and construction problems, it seems appropriate to deal with natural models and sample plots in the same manner. It is interesting to observe the distance traversed along a beaten path by a few gallons of water from an overturned pail and to compare the behavior of a like quantity applied to outcropping fractured or stratified rock, to a well-rooted grass plot, or to a soil surface covered with a mulch of leaf litter or other organic material.   Even when such a mulch is saturated it may be delivering a measurable flow by gravity, keeping pace with infiltration into the underlying soil and prolonging that process between showers to promote local utilization with proportionate decrease in surface runoff. Such elementary demonstrations show the differences in runoff characteristics, and therefore in flood potentialities, of different drainage basins and also of the same basin under different surface conditions.

RUNOFF AS INFLUENCED BY VEGETAL COVER

Figure XIG-1 summarizes the results of observations during a 4-year period of record in South Africa and portrays the fairly close coordination between overland or surface runoff and soil loss, the influence of natural veld sod, whether grazed, burned, or intact, and of other protective cover in stabilizing the soil and conserving the water.   Keeping in mind the fact that these graphs represent 4-year averages, we should expect a considerable range of values both above and below the eroded soil and runoff as plotted on the figure.   Furthermore, it seems advisable to consider that very steep, barren land, which would probably not be included in

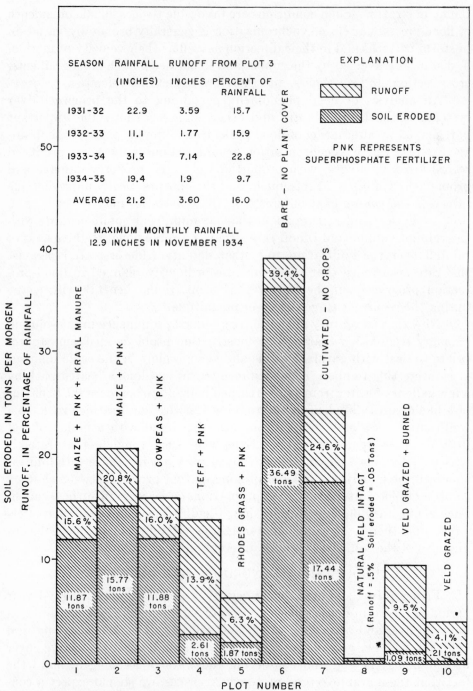

Fig. XIg-1.—Percentage of runoff and soil eroded, in tons per morgen (2.11 acres), as shown by experiments at the University of Pretoria, South Africa. (Average for the seasons 1931–32 to 1934–35.) (*After W. R. Thompson* [54].)

experimental plots, nevertheless constitutes an important element in both the genesis and assembly of flood volumes and in their attainment of peak flows.   The soil losses and runoff from such tracts or strips of deeply eroded, precipitous "badlands" should be considerably greater than the maximum shown for agricultural plots.   It is therefore conceivable that under extreme conditions favorable to high surface runoff the percentage might be more nearly double the maximum shown in Figure XIɢ-1 and thus approach equality with the rainfall causing it, or 100 percent yield, as a possible limit.   Between the 0.5 percent of rainfall appearing as surface runoff from the plot of "natural veld intact" (Fig. XIɢ-1) and the limiting value of nearly 100 percent, as above outlined, there is a range which suggests the use of a percentage scale in comparing maximum runoff yields from various river systems and their component tributaries— a device which has been approximated and submitted to practical tests under the title "Myers scale," as described below.   This was developed by modification and extension of the first known flood formula by an American author, Maj. E. D. T. Myers, chief engineer of a railway in Virginia, shortly after the Civil War [23, p. 994].

FLOOD FORMULAS

Perplexed and somewhat discouraged by divergent results from existing flood formulas, each seemingly designed for a restricted region, the writer undertook the assembly of the most authoritative, up-to-date, and representative flood data in this country, supplemented by samples from foreign records.   He then plotted this information on a single logarithmic chart, and superimposed thereon the most widely known and seemingly meritorious flood formulas, each one shown by its limiting curves, wherever a range of coefficients was provided.   Close study will demonstrate that the Myers formula as there modified is best suited for expansion and development to cover the entire field [23, Pl. IX, fig. 6].   The original formula was

$$a = C \sqrt{A}$$

in which a is the cross-sectional area of required waterway, in square feet, A is the area of the drainage basin, in acres, and C is a coefficient ranging from 1 to 4, which is indicative of the flood potentialities.   Or, transforming the area into square miles, M, and assuming that the average velocity of flow through the waterway is 10 feet per second, so that $10 \times a$ represents Q, the discharge in cubic feet per second (c.f.s.), we get

$$Q = 10a = 10C \times 25.3 \sqrt{\frac{A}{640}} = C \times 253 \sqrt{M}$$

Using 40 for C, and then neglecting the final digit of 253, we get

$$Q = 10,000 \sqrt{M}$$

for the upper range, representing 100 percent; or

$$Q = 100p \sqrt{M}$$

in which p is the numerical percentage rating on the Myers scale. Also, if q is the yield in cubic feet per second per square mile (c.s.m.),

$$Q = qM = 100p \sqrt{M}$$

therefore

$$q = 100p \frac{\sqrt{M}}{M} = \frac{100p}{\sqrt{M}}$$

and

$$p = \frac{q \sqrt{M}}{100}$$

or, with $\frac{Q}{M}$ substituted for q,

$$p = \frac{Q}{100 \sqrt{M}}$$

In spite of the simplicity of the modified Myers formula as above outlined and its adaptability for slide-rule calculations and for extension over the entire field of flood flows, even though the percentage ratings occasionally exceed 100, notably on certain turbulent streams of south-central Texas [63, app. 1], this formula needs further modification to be applicable to small drainage areas. For many areas below 9 square miles or for all areas below 4 square miles it is best to employ the first power of the drainage area, instead of the square root, as exemplified by what is often called the "rational formula,"

$$Q = CiA$$

in which Q = rate of discharge, in cubic feet per second.

C = a coefficient representing the percentage of the rainfall appearing directly as surface runoff.

i = average rainfall intensity, in inches per hour during the time of concentration—that is, during the period required for all parts of the drainage basin to contribute their quotas of stream flow.

A = drainage area in acres.

This formula is simplified by the coincidence that for a runoff depth of 1 inch per hour an acre will yield approximately 1 cubic foot per second, or nearly 2 acre-feet per day,[1] exclusive of ground-water contributions. A rainfall intensity of 2 inches per hour, with C equal to 0.50, might account for a discharge averaging 1 cubic foot per second per acre during a period equal to the time of concentration. If the existing conditions provide unusual facilities for detention and temporary storage, the period of runoff should be correspondingly prolonged, with a proportional decrease in the average rate of discharge.

Other flood formulas with considerable merit are presented and discussed in United States Geological Survey Water-Supply Paper 771 [28, pp. 32–67]. Even though some of them may serve certain regions exceptionally well, their results may all be expressed and compared to advantage by means of the Myers scale as above described and as illustrated in "Low Dams" [63, app. I]. Some of the approaches toward the evaluation of flood flows as there presented go far beyond the application of selected formulas; they amount to newly devised scientific procedures for analyzing the hydrometeorologic relations. The studies by the Miami Conservancy District relating the frequency, area, depth, intensity, duration, velocity, and direction of motion of storms to probable volume of runoff and peak discharge for each of the major storms of each region, opened new vistas for scientific research and analysis. Likewise, the unit hydrograph has done much to promote and to revolutionize the most advanced concepts in the hydrologic field. Finally, the use of records of rainfall intensity to derive the excess, hour by hour or for other time periods, beyond the reliable detention or other forms of depletion, including infiltration, affords an effective and unique approach with possibilities not yet fully realized or utilized.

ANALYSIS OF FLOOD DATA

Various methods of sampling flood data, together with either plotting or statistical procedure as steps in the analysis, have been employed to define and interpret trends, periodicities, and magnitude-frequency relations. Whether the basic data selected are annual, monthly, daily, or momentary flood peaks, the point toward which all graphs are directed, each in its distinctive way, is the maximum possible flow. Graphs representing various approaches to the analysis of flood records are discussed and illustrated in some detail elsewhere [28, pp. 58–60, 75].

After an array of flood data for a fairly long period has been arranged in either ascending or descending order, tabulated, and plotted, the addition of new data from time to time rarely disturbs the general-trend curve unless some marked change affecting infiltration, detention, and storage has occurred in the physical condition of the drainage basin. However, a short period of record may establish a curve considerably at

[1] 86,400 seconds in a day; 2 acre-feet = 87,120 cubic feet.

variance with that covering a long period. Thus, if a 60-year record is analyzed on the basis of short segments, such as 10, 15, or 20 years, the resulting curves may have only a general family resemblance to the graph covering the full period, and may serve as an effective warning against unqualified dependence on meager data, so well illustrated by the Tennessee River record at Chattanooga, Tenn. [28, p. 440].

The evaluation of flood potentialities on any area calls for the use of all relevant data on rainfall, runoff, and their interrelations as affected by the seasons, temperature, soil structure, land use, vegetal cover, storage and detention facilities (either natural or artificial), and opportunities for synchronization of maximum crests from the main stream with those from tributaries. Naturally, one of the first considerations is the relation of intensity and frequency of rainfall in the region, or for such portions of the drainage area as may be most productive of runoff, as this relation forms a dominant factor under general storm conditions. Thus, it is often a question whether the maximum flow will occur as the result of a local storm of high intensity or of a prolonged general storm, or of a succession of such occurrences.

For small drainage basins in humid regions the average rainfall intensity for the periods of concentration may occasionally amount to several inches per hour, and the maximum runoff rate may approach the same limit under extreme conditions favorable to high runoff coefficients. This initial peak may be either augmented or reduced by the algebraic sum of ground-water runoff and influent seepage or storage downstream.

RUNOFF FROM PLOTS, FIELDS, AND DRAINAGE BASINS

Table 1 contains runoff observations from plots, showing considerable ranges between runoff from sodded or wooded areas and runoff from row crop, fallow, or denuded ground. Naturally, among the numerous records of runoff from plots, fields, and small and large drainage basins, there are many percentage factors with narrow range and a few with wider range. For example, during several years rainfalls ranging from 1 inch to nearly 4 inches in depth per day were observed to cause frequent runoffs of 40 percent or more from corn or cotton with vetch cover at Tyler, Tex., even reaching 85 percent, whereas the surface runoff from nearby plots of well-established Bermuda grass did not exceed 1 or 2 percent of the rainfall, in spite of the 8.75 percent slope.

Such contrasts in surface runoff from small plots and experimental fields under a variety of cropping and land-use practices so far exceed the expectations of many practical-minded hydrologists as to invite a challenge. They assert that the problems of water conservation and flood control cannot be resolved so readily as such experimental data would imply. They emphasize the generally accepted fact that the

TABLE 1.—*Summary of runoff percentages from plots with various vegetal covers*

Experiment station	Plot No.	Cover	Length of record (years)	Average annual runoff Depth (inches)	Average annual runoff Percent	Plot area (acres)	Remarks
Blackland, Temple, Tex., Progress Report, 1931–36: Tables 16 and 17..........	3	Continuous corn	6	4.660	14.22	0.01	Slope 4.0 percent
	4	Rotation—corn, oats, cotton	6	2.469	7.54	0.01	
	6	Bermuda grass	6	.013	.039	0.01	
	12	Rotation—cane, grass, oats, etc.	5	.331	.95	.0463	Slope 3.5 percent
	13	Contour-row cotton	5	2.367	6.81	.0847	
	14	Rows down slope, cotton	5	5.435	15.63	.0309	Slope 3.5 percent
	18	Bermuda grass	4	.332	.95	.0286	Slope 4 to 6 percen
	24	Rows down slope, cotton	1	8.884	24.07	.1370	
Table 23..........	Lysimeter No. 1	Fallow	1	7.780	19.52	3 feet diam.	Level land
	Lysimeter No. 2	Bermuda grass	1	.171	.43	Do.	
	Lysimeter No. 8	Fallow	1	13.91	34.91	Do.	Slope 4 percent
Spur, Tex.:	Table 8	Cotton	14	3.09	15.4	....	Slope 2 percent
		Fallow	14	4.09	20.3	....	
Bulletin 587, July, 1940..........		Buffalo grass	14	1.04	5.2	....	About 0.34 inch in first year, from new grass.
	Table 9	Cotton	13	1.41	7.53	....	Rows on slope
		do	13	.88	4.70	....	Rows on contour
		do	13	0	0	....	Closed level terraces
Report covering 1934–36..........		Fallow	3	3.80	18.72		Slope 2 percent; years 1934–36
		Grass	3	7.73	38.10		
		Woods	6	1.52	7.50		Burned in March; slope 12.5 percent
		do	6	1.13	2.69		Virgin woods; slope 12.5 percent
Tyler, Tex.: Progress Report, 1931–36..........	1	Cotton	6	.227	.54	.01	Continuous; slope 8.75 percent
	2	do	6	7.48	18.32	.01	
	4	Clipped Bermuda grass	6	0.47	1.15	.01	
	8	Desurfaced cotton	6	10.75	26.33	.01	
Dec. 6, 1936[a]..........	8	Sod, dormant	..	.022	.70	.01	Slope 8.75 percent
	12	Cotton, dead	..	1.782	67	.01	
Nov. 15, 1937[a]..........	1	Cotton, 26 inches	..	1.016	63	.005	Do.
	8	Bermuda grass	..	.040	2	.01	
	9	Bare ground	..	1.112	69	.01	

[a] Runoff from individual storm.

multiplication of respective yields from small plots by thousands or millions will not necessarily indicate accurately either the total flood volumes or the corresponding peaks as affected by surface conditions. Even the most ardent advocate of careful land-use and conservation practices as features of the flood-control program must admit the validity of such comments and reservations. There is some intermediate ground, however, on which the divergent views might reasonably be reconciled. A significant contribution in this direction is to be found under the title "Giving areal significance to hydrologic research on small areas" in chapter III of the report of the Upstream Engineering Conference of 1936, which followed the World Power Conference [62]. In the preparation of that article Merrill Bernard undertook to incorporate the results of observations of runoff phenomena as influenced by land use and other factors within man's control made for several years at erosion experiment stations of the United States Department of Agriculture. The hydrographs shown in figure 21 of the report seem to demonstrate that the respective peak discharges from the 730-acre drainage area shown in figure 13 under conditions of 100 percent corn or 100 percent sod would be as 1,360 to 360 cubic feet per second; the corresponding runoff coefficients were 0.85 and 0.29, according to figure 23. Commenting on the data given in table 6 of the report, showing that 55 percent of the drainage area in sod would account for a 44 percent reduction in flood peak compared with the runoff behavior of the entire area in row crops, while 100 percent in sod would result in a 74 percent reduction, Bernard concluded that "on watersheds up to 730 acres, at least, the peak-reducing value of an effective cover varies almost directly as the degree to which the watershed is represented by such cover." According to figures 21 to 25 of the report, together with Bernard's analysis and further comments, it is evident that the runoff may be affected by vegetal cover in about the same manner as already observed for the peaks, with some range of variation either above or below. If the experimental plots are even approximately representative of the similarly treated tracts up to a square mile or more in area, then the main flaws in the index relations must develop with larger areas. This conclusion is amply confirmed by observation and practical experience, especially in connection with the routing and the evaluation of flood-flow phenomena.

Surely the flood waves assembled in the course of a few minutes from areas with dimensions of about a mile should reflect both the average rate, or excess rate, and the volume of rainfall, in suitable proportions; whereas areas so large as to require several hours or days for runoff assembly incline toward lower unit yields and peaks.

As explained above, flood discharge seems to be proportional to the drainage area up to a few square miles. For large areas the discharge peaks are more nearly proportional to the square root of the drainage area, or to some other fractional power under special conditions.   Naturally, such factors as shape of basin, slope and roughness of channels and of the land surface, amount and nature of vegetal cover, and soil characteristics vitally influence the runoff behavior and may partly mask the areal relations.

MAJOR FLOODS IN THE UNITED STATES

Major floods have been observed on many river systems of this country at average intervals of a few years, or occasionally at longer intervals such as two or three decades, and rarely they have been repeated during the same season or during consecutive years.   In this manner the average discharge for one year may become several times the mean for the period of record, and the associated peaks of discharge may likewise far exceed the average yearly peak, as shown by the data collected in "Low Dams" [63, app. I], sample items from which have been included in table 2, after being brought more nearly up to date.

Flood control or protection works designed on the basis of unusually severe runoff conditions may only rarely function to full capacity.   Thus, after the record-making floods of 1903 on the Delaware River, channel improvements were completed to accommodate like discharges without serious damage.   During the next 30 years the flood peaks at no time attained 60 percent of the peak of 1903; but the floods of 1936 and subsequent years in that region have fully justified the estimates of runoff potentialities both at Port Jervis and at Trenton, and presumably at intermediate and tributary stations as well.

The series of record-breaking flood stages and volumes during recent years, together with droughts of outstanding severity and extent, have raised questions concerning the stability of climatic conditions. Some find in these records a mounting severity of both floods and droughts, which can be ascribed in part to progressive denudation of land surfaces and consequent loss of soil structure and fertility, channel and storage capacity, surface mulch, twig and leaf litter, sod, top soil, and infiltration capacity.   This is based on the theory that with impaired surface detention the rainfalls capable of producing only moderate runoff under primitive conditions have given less than their normal quota to underground storage and correspondingly greater amounts to surface runoff, thereby aggravating the irregularities of stream flow through devastating floods and prolonged shortages of stream flow after the floods.   It is notable, however, that authentic records of floods on American streams are comparatively short.   It is natural that the longer such records become, the more excessive are the recorded floods likely to be.   Moreover, some entertain the possibility that periods that are wet or otherwise especially

TABLE 2.—Summary and comparison of discharge characteristics

[Items brought up to date from Low Dams, appendix I, National Resources Committee, 1938]

River and station	Drainage area (square miles)	Years of record — Average	Years of record — Maximum	Years of record — Final	Discharge, cubic feet per second — Average	Discharge, cubic feet per second — Maximum	Cubic feet per second per square mile — Average	Cubic feet per second per square mile — Maximum	Date of maximum	Myers rating (percent)
White, West Hartford, Vt.	690	23	23	1939	1,181	120,000	1.71	174	Nov. 4, 1927	45.7
Connecticut, Hartford, Conn.	(10,480)	11	301	1939	(20,000)	313,000	1.91	29.9	Mar. 20, 1936	30.6
Hudson, Mechanicsville, N.Y.	4,500	52	52	1939	7,435	120,000	1.65	26.7	March 1913	17.9
Delaware, Trenton, N.J.	6,796	26	26	1939	11,630	227,000	1.71	33.4	March 1936	27.6
West Branch of Susquehanna, Williamsport, Pa.	5,682	44	93	1939	8,830	264,000	1.56	46.5	March 1936	35.1
West Branch of Susquehanna, Harrisburg, Pa.	24,100	49	199	1939	34,570	740,000	1.43	30.7	March 1936	47.6
Rock Creek, Sherrill Drive, D.C.	62.2	10	46	1939	56	20,000	.89	322	June 1889	25.4
Potomac, Point of Rocks, Md.	9,651	43	51	1939	9,529	{480,000, 460,000}	.986	{49.7, 47.6}	Mar. 19, 1936; June 2, 1889	48.9; 46.8
James, Buchanan, Va.	2,084	40	44	1939	2,534	92,200	1.22	44.2	March 1913	20.2
James, Cartersville, Va.	6,242	39	40	1939	7,284	149,000	1.17	23.9	March 1936	18.9
Santee, Ferguson, S.C.	14,800	31	31	1939	18,930	368,000	1.28	24.8	July 22, 1916	30.3
Savannah, Augusta, Ga.	7,304	..	21	1939		350,000		47.9	Oct. 3, 1929	41.0
Suwanee, Ellaville, Fla.	6,580	12	12	1939	6,416	73,000	.98	11.1	Apr. 8, 1886	9.0
Alabama, Selma, Ala.	17,100	24	54	1939	26,730	221,000	1.56	12.9	Mar. 1, 1902	16.9
Tennessee, Knoxville, Tenn.	8,931	40	40	1939	13,280	195,000	1.49	21.8	Mar. 11, 1867	20.6
Tennessee, Chattanooga, Tenn.	21,390	65	65	1939	38,260	459,000	1.79	21.5	Mar. 24, 1897	31.4
Tennessee, Johnsonville, Tenn.	38,510	50	50	1939	63,650	460,000	1.65	11.9	Sept. 14, 1878	23.5
Kanawha, Kanawha Falls, W. Va.	8,367	62	62	1939	12,970	270,000	1.55	32.3	Mar. 18, 1936	29.5
Cheat, near Morgantown, W. Va.	1,380	14	54	1925	3,170	160,000	2.30	116	July 10, 1888	43.0
Kiskiminetas, Avonmore, Pa.	1,723	32	32	1939	3,007	200,000	1.74	116	Mar. 18, 1936	48.3
Ohio, Sewickley, Pa.	19,500	6	106	1939	30,470	574,000	1.56	29.4	Mar. 18, 1936	41.1
Miami, Hamilton, Ohio	3,639	20	20	1939	3,512	352,000	.965	96.8	Mar. 26, 1913	58.4
Wabash, Mount Carmel, Ill.	28,600	12	17	1939	26,710	428,000	.934	15.0	Mar. 30, 1913	25.4
Ohio, Metropolis, Ill.	203,000	6	57	1939	262,400	1,850,000	1.29	9.11	Feb. 1, 1937	41.1
Kansas, Topeka, Kans.	56,710	22	22	1939	3,791	{154,000, 250,000}	.067	{2.72, 4.41}	June 5, 1935; May 30, 1903	6.5; 10.5
Missouri, Fort Benton, Mont.	24,600	58	58	1939	8,344	140,000	.339	5.70	June 7, 1908	8.9
Missouri, Boonville, Mo.	505,700	14	14	1939	52,120	381,000	.103	.755	Apr. 23, 1927	5.4
Mississippi, St. Paul, Minn.	36,800	47	58	1939	8,866	107,000	.241	2.76	Apr. 29, 1881	5.4
Mississippi, LeClaire, Iowa	88,600	66	66	1939	47,780	250,000	.539	2.82	June 25, 1880	8.4
Mississippi, St. Louis, Mo.	701,000	20	69	1939	(149,700)	{649,000, 900,000}	.212	{.93, 1.28}	June 7, 1935; June 28, 1844	7.8; 10.7
Mississippi, Vicksburg, Miss.	1,144,500	12	69	1940	535,000	2,080,000	.467	1.82	Feb. 17, 1937	19.4
Mississippi, Natchez, Miss.	1,149,400	125	141	1940	(597,000)	(2,080,000)	.520	1.82	Feb. 17, 1937	19.4

Figures in parentheses are unofficial; derived or estimated.

TABLE 3.—*Maximum gage heights and discharges at Memphis, Tenn., and Vicksburg, Miss.*

Date	Gage readings (feet)		Discharge 1,000 cubic feet per second		Additional in floodway and valley storage (1,000 cubic feet per second)		Maximum river and floodway Discharge (1,000 cubic feet per second)	
	Memphis	Vicksburg	Memphis	Vicksburg	Memphis	Vicksburg	Memphis	Vicksburg
June 23, 1858	35.3	.....	(1,300)	....	(180)	.....	(1,480)	....
June 26, 1858	.....	46.98	....	....	.....	.....	....	(1,400)
Apr. 27, 1862	.....	51:10	....	....	.....	.....	....	(1,700)
Mar. 20–21, 1882	.....	48.75	....	....	.....	.....	....	(1,540)
Mar. 25, 1884	.....	49.00	....	....	.....	.....	....	(1,550)
Mar. 16–17, 1890	35.60	.....	1,400	....	170	.....	1,570	
Apr. 24–25, 1890	.....	49.05	....	....	.....	.....	....	(1,550)
Apr. 2–4, 1891	.....	48.1	....	....	.....	.....	....	(1,490)
May 10, 1892	.....	48.4	....	....	.....	.....	....	(1,500)
May 22–23, 1893	.....	48.3	....	....	.....	.....	....	(1,495)
Mar. 20–21, 1897	37.66	.....	....	....	.....	.....	(1,600)	
Apr. 16, 1897	.....	52.48	....	....	.....	.....	....	(1,800)
Apr. 10–11, 1898	37.22	.....	....	....	.....	.....	(1,600)	
Apr. 24–25, 1898	.....	49.4	....	....	.....	.....	....	(1,580)
Mar. 20, 1903	40.10	.....	....	....	.....	.....	(1,630)	
Mar. 28, 1903	.....	51.80	....	....	.....	.....	....	(1,800)
Apr. 11, 1904	39.20	.....	1,620	....	.....	.....	1,620	
Feb. 3, 1907	40.30	.....	....	....	.....	.....	(1,700)	
Feb. 12–13, 1907	.....	49.65	....	....	.....	.....	....	(1,700)
Mar. 22, 1909	38.60	.....	....	....	.....	.....	(1,600)	
Apr. 1–2, 1909	.....	48.00	....	....	.....	.....	....	(1,550)
Apr. 6, 1912	45.23	.....	(1,800)	....	240	.....	2,040	
Apr. 12, 1912	.....	51.65	....	(1,850)	.....	(300)	....	(2,150)
Apr. 9, 1913	46.55	.....	(2,030)	....	220	.....	2,250	
Apr. 27–28, 1913	.....	52.20	....	(1,900)	.....	(300)	....	(2,200)
Feb. 9, 1916	43.4	.....	(1,750)	....	.....	.....	1,750	
Feb. 15, 1916	.....	53.85	....	....	.....	.....	....	(1,700)
Apr. 23, 1917	.....	49.98	....	....	.....	.....	....	(1,730)
Apr. 27, 1920	.....	50.90	....	....	.....	.....	....	(1,825)
Apr. 1–2, 1922	42.5	.....	(1,560)	....	.....	.....	1,560	
Apr. 28, 1922	.....	54.85	....	....	.....	.....	....	1,826
Apr. 23–25, 1927	45.8	.....	(1,860)	....	500	.....	2,360	
May 4, 1927	.....	58.40	....	(2,145)	.....	(350)	....	2,495
July 12–16, 1928	.....	49.30	....	....	.....	.....	....	(1,670)
May 25, 1929	41.5	.....	(1,600)	....	.....	.....	1,600	
June 6–7, 1929	.....	55.2	....	1,741	.....	.....	....	1,741
Feb. 19, 1932	38.7	.....	1,308	....	.....	.....	1,308	
Feb. 28–29, 1932	.....	50.27	....	(1,410)	.....	.....	....	1,410
Apr. 9, 1933	40.1	.....	1,416					
June 10, 1933	.....	47.50	....	1,360			....	1,360
Mar. 19, 1934	30.0	.....	839					
Apr. 13–14, 1934	.....	34.58	....	877	.....	.....	....	877
Apr. 17, 1936	40.3	.....	1,360	....	.....	.....	1,360	
Apr. 30, 1936	.....	42.54	....	1,280	.....	.....	....	1,280
Feb. 7, 1937	50.4	.....	2,020	....	500	.....	2,520	
Feb. 17–22, 1937	.....	53.2	....	2,080	.....	.....	....	2,080

conducive climatically to the production of floods may occur in the manner of cycles and thereby tend to invalidate the evidence of apparent trends afforded by comparatively short records.   Some believe that because of these conditions evidence that floods are increasing or decreasing in severity is not satisfactorily convincing.

Table 3 shows in chronologic order the flood stages and peak discharges of the Mississippi River at Memphis, Tenn., and Vicksburg, Miss., from 1858 to the present time.   The increases in maximum recorded flood stages of 15.1 feet between 1858 and 1937 for Memphis and of 11.4 feet

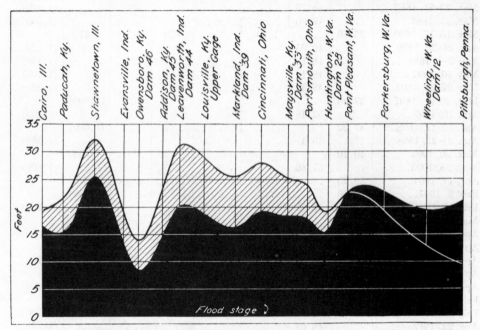

Fig. XIG-2.—Comparison of crest stages along the Ohio River in the flood of 1937 with the previous highest stages of record (black).   (*Data from U. S. Weather Bureau.*)

between 1858 and 1927 for Vicksburg (which may be influenced to some degree by the effects of levees or the regimen of the river), together with an increase of two-thirds in peak discharge for each of the stations, cannot be disregarded.

The recent developments in construction and operation of reservoirs to regulate stream flow in the interests of navigation, power, irrigation, municipal water supply, and flood control would make any upward trend of flood stages and peak discharges more significant.   Exclusion of high floods from reclaimed and protected areas formerly subject to overflow naturally provides some explanation of recent trends but does not fully account for the results.   Figures XIG-2 and XIG-3 show how new records were established by the flood of March 1937 on the Ohio and Mississippi Rivers.

Prior to the flood of June 1935 on the Republican River in Colorado, Nebraska, and Kansas, the highest rating on the Myers scale had been about 4 percent, but after that flood a rating of fully 25 percent, or six times as great, was found to be applicable to both the main stream and the average tributaries, both large and small, at rare intervals. Similarly the disastrous flood of June 1921 on the Arkansas River system at and near Pueblo, Colo., so far exceeded the flood crests observed through several decades of record (attaining about nine times the former maximum) as to challenge the use of all flood formulas based on experience in that locality. The percentage rating on the Myers scale attained by the Purgatoire River at Trinidad, in southeastern Colorado 75 miles south of Pueblo, in September 1904 was 17, and the ratings of the Arkansas River

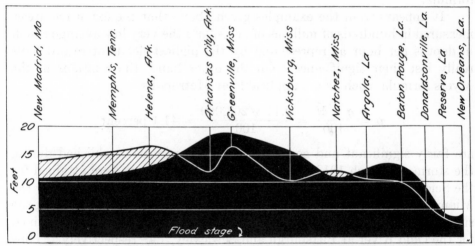

FIG. XIᴳ-3.—Comparison of crest stages along the lower Mississippi River in the flood of 1937 with the previous highest stages of record (black). (*Data from U. S. Weather Bureau.*)

at and below Pueblo in June 1921 were 15, 19, and 18. In view of the persistent similarity of topographic and other physical characteristics of this region along the eastern face of the Continental Divide, the conclusion is justified that an index of flood potentialities on the Arkansas River at Pueblo had been furnished at Trinidad nearly 17 years prior to the flood of 1921. However, this index had remained obscure and unrecognized, largely because of the difficulty in comparing flood crests and interpreting records from unequal drainage areas. This difficulty has been obviated, in part, by application of the Myers scale, described above, whereby the factor representing area seems to have been partly canceled out or made to vary proportionately to the probable flood build-up, so that ratings from either large or small tributaries tend to approach those for the main stream except as modified by other physical factors of the basins.

A COMMON DENOMINATOR FOR ALL FLOOD FORMULAS

The flood of January 1937 at the mouth of the Ohio River might be expressed in the form of the "rational formula" as

$$Q = CiA = 0.0142 \times 1.0 \times 640 \times 203,000 = 1,850,00$$

That is, runoff amounting to about one-seventieth of an inch per hour from the entire drainage basin, or 1 inch per hour from one-seventieth of the entire basin, was the maximum attained at Metropolis, Ill. Similarly, the maximum observed flood flows in the lower courses of the Columbia, Colorado, Missouri, and Mississippi Rivers would represent about 0.009, 0.002, 0.002, and 0.004 inch per hour, respectively, for use in the rational formula.

It appears from the examples given above that the extensive areas, measured in hundreds of millions of acres, and the very low average runoff in depths per hour as represented by the highest floods of record have really lost their significance. On the other hand, the relations of the Myers formula, such as are applicable at Metropolis—

$$p = \frac{q\sqrt{M}}{100} = \frac{9.11\sqrt{203,000}}{100} = 41.1 \text{ percent}$$

are fairly significant and consistent with the records established during the storm of March 1913, when ratings of 34.3 percent were attained for the Scioto River at Columbus, Ohio, and of 50.0 and 58.4 percent for the Miami River at Dayton and Hamilton, Ohio, respectively; and during the storm of March 1936, when ratings of 39.8 and 41.1 percent were attained for the Ohio River at Pittsburgh and Sewickley, Pa., respectively. Thus the flood peak of January 1937 at Metropolis, Ill., though exceeding the previous maximum record for that section of the river by about 52 percent, was also proving up on its inherent flood potentialities as indicated by the foregoing maxima on other parts of the drainage system. Furthermore, if steep topography and shallow or close-textured soils were prevalent in Indiana and Illinois instead of the relatively flat gradients and deep, permeable glacial soils, the floods on the lower Ohio River might reasonably be expected to approach a rating of 40 percent much more frequently.

Through similar use and interpretation of available data, including those from neighboring stations, the estimates tabulated under the column heading "Expected peaks" in table 2 of "Flood-flow characteristics" [23] forecast with fair accuracy the intensities to be expected during rare floods, closely approaching the probable limiting flood peaks at several stations. Thus, for item 919 in the table, Brazos River at Waco, Tex., the expected rare flood peak was recorded as 10 cubic feet per second per square mile, slightly more than double the maximum observed thereto-fore. Compared with the 9.0 cubic feet per second per square mile, actually measured by current meter during the notable flood of October 1936, the forecast of potentialities made 10 years earlier is a fair approximation. Likewise, a similarly determined forecast of 2.5 cubic feet per second per square mile for the Mississippi River at Helena, Ark., proved to be a satisfactory estimate of the flood peak of April 1927; to a lesser degree the same comment applies to the Colorado River at Austin, Tex., and to stations on the White River, Indiana, and on the Tennessee, Missouri, Susquehanna, and other rivers.

Figure XIG-4 shows maximum flood flows expressed as percentage ratings on the Myers scale plotted in geographic position, corresponding to the streams represented.

No matter what formula is chosen for estimating or evaluating flood flow, it has been found convenient to make comparisons by expressing results in terms of percentage rating on the Myers scale. If either of the variables is unknown, it may be readily determined from the other two, as outlined above under the heading "Flood formulas."

INTERPRETATION OF FLOOD HYDROGRAPHS BY VARIOUS STANDARDS

An outstanding example of recent progress in the analysis and adequate presentation of flood data is afforded by United States Geological Survey Water-Supply Paper 843 [38]. One of the many clear-cut illustrations that serve to strengthen the presentation is here reproduced as Figure XIG-5, showing graphs of mean daily discharge at several river-measurement stations. Careful selection of discharge scales resulted in an impressive array of daily peaks, mostly culminating on December 11, 1937. The time of maximum observed discharge extended from 1:00 a.m. December 11 to 10:00 p.m. December 12, a period of 45 hours. The variation of scales for the successive hydrographs is not suited to a ready comparison of discharges and might obscure other relations. For this reason, table 4 has been prepared, in order to provide additional comparisons of rainfall and flood discharge characteristics.

In view of the disparity in size of the drainage areas, which range from 6,600 to 268 square miles, or a maximum 24.6 times the minimum, it is not surprising that corresponding ratios of discharge for maximum calendar days and selected 24-hour periods (parts of two consecutive days) were 50.4 and 40.4 percent respectively; while such ratios for the peaks in cubic feet per second and cubic feet per second per square mile were 16.4 and 24.7 percent respectively; for the Myers ratings of the flood of December 1937 and other record-making floods, they were 14.7 and 10.6 percent respectively. For the December storm the maximum precipitation and runoff depths were respectively 2.6 and 24.0 times the minimum. Likewise, the runoff coefficients ranged from 48.4 to 5.2 percent, or a ratio of

9.3 to 1.   The final result of 24.5 for the ratio of maximum to minimum depths in inches per hour attained by the flood peaks at the eight stations

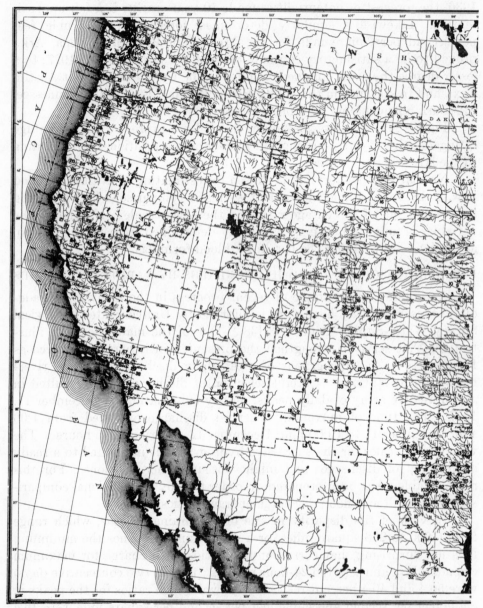

Fig. XIg-4.—(a) Map of the United States, western section, showing maximum flood flows based on stream gagings or estimates from observed physical data, expressed as percentage ratings on the Myers scale.

listed would have coincided with that given as 24.7 for the peak in cubic feet per square mile if the computations had been carried far enough into the decimals, but it provides a fair check as it stands.

Table 4 demonstrates that a station may record the maximum of one or more factors to be compared, and yet may fall far short of the maximum

Fig. XIg-4.—(b) Map of the United States, eastern section, showing maximum flood flows based on stream gagings or estimates from observed physical data, expressed as percentage ratings on the Myers scale.

in others. Thus the last four stations in the table provide most of the maximum values for comparison by various standards, and the first two, of widely different drainage areas and other physical features, provide

TABLE 4.—*Rainfall and discharge characteristics of flood of December 1937 in California*

Relating to hydrographs shown in fig. XIG-5 after U. S. Geol. Survey Water-supply Paper 843 [38, fig. 31, p. 83]

River and station	Drainage area		Maximum discharge (cubic feet per second)				Myers rating (percent)		Depth (inches)			Depth (inch per hour)		
	Square miles	Acres	Calendar day	24 hours	Peak	Peak (cubic feet per second per square mile)	December 1937	Other (maximum)	Precipitation	Runoff	Runoff ÷ precipitation (percent)	Maximum calendar day	Maximum 24 hours	Peak
Salinas near Spreckels	4,180	2,675,200	8,500	10,830	13,400	3.18	2.1	11.6	4.8	0.25	5.2	0.0063	0.0080	0.010
Tule near Porterville	268	171,520	2,880	3,876	11,300	41.9	6.9	7.6	9.4	1.1	11.7	.033	.045	.131
San Joaquin above Big Creek	1,042	666,880	31,700	32,480	52,500	50.0	16.1	5.6	8.8	2.05	23.3	.095	.097	.157
Merced at Pohono Bridge, near Yosemite	321	205,440	16,000	17,440	22,000	68.0	12.3	3.6	12.2	3.55	29.1	.155	.168	.212
American at Fair Oaks	1,921	1,229,440	81,100	83,400	114,000	58.9	26.0	32.0	9.0	3.5	38.9	.131	.135	.184
Yuba at Smartville	1,201	768,640	74,200	78,240	95,000	78.4	27.4	34.6	12.4	6.0	48.4	.191	.202	.245
Feather near Oroville	3,611	2,311,040	145,000	156,800	185,000	50.9	30.8	38.3	12.4	3.95	40.3	.124	.135	.159
Sacramento at Kennett	6,600	4,224,000	97,200	100,190	132,000	20.0	16.2	11.6	6.3	2.15	34.1	.046	.048	.062
Maximum	6,600		145,000	156,800	185,000	78.4	30.8	38.3	12.4	6.0	48.4	.191	.202	.245
Minimum	268		2,880	3,876	11,300	3.18	2.1	3.6	4.8	.25	5.2	.0063	.0080	.010
Ratio of maximum to minimum	24.6		50.4	40.4	16.4	24.7	14.7	10.6	2.6	24.0	9.3	30.4	25.2	24.5

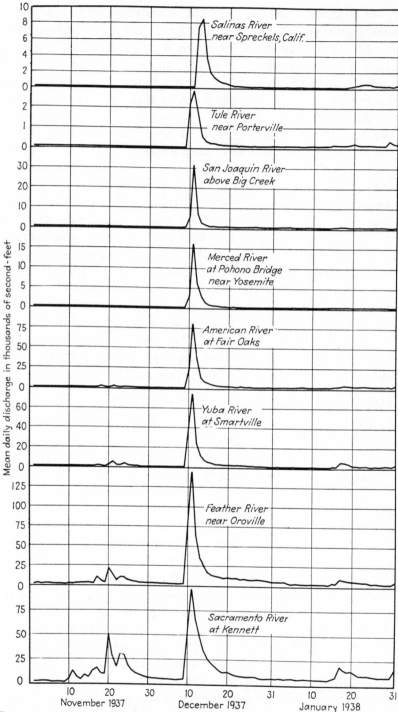

Fig. XIg-5.—Mean daily discharge at several river-measurement stations in northern California for the period November 1, 1937, to January 31, 1938.

most of the minimum values. Greater disparities in runoff and flood phenomena would probably have developed if the rainfall had encountered deep snow blankets in the high Sierra, or if any considerable part of the precipitation had been in the form of snow, or if there had been a succession of disturbances instead of the simple pattern of a single rainfall, developing both high intensities and great total depths over a considerable portion of the State.

Water-Supply Paper 843 [38, p. 1] states: "An interesting characteristic of the floods was the absence of high water along the lower reaches of the San Joaquin River, in contrast to the flooded areas along the lower Sacramento River. Large volumes of flood waters were withheld by the many storage reservoirs on tributaries of the San Joaquin River, whereas much smaller volumes were detained by the comparatively few storage reservoirs in the Sacramento River Basin. . . . A study of the conditions of antecedent precipitation and probable ground moisture associated with previous great floods supports the conclusion that the ground storage is generally a very critical factor in the development of floods in this region."

It would be difficult, if not impossible, to find a region where the comments above quoted would not apply in some degree, and in this conclusion authoritative opinion based on the behavior of large drainage basins coincides with experience on experimental plots, fields, and small drainage basins under varying conditions of soil, cover, culture, and land use.

FLOOD MAGNITUDES AS EXPRESSED IN VARIOUS UNITS

The diverse relations shown in table 4, depending on the respective features or units compared, suggest the need for a chart showing the relative magnitudes and conversion factors. Figure XIG-6, embodying the data of table 5, summarizes in graphic form the frequency-magnitude behavior of the Yuba River floods at Smartville, Calif., during the 32-year period 1903-34. The graph includes the peak of 120,000 cubic feet per second in March 1928 and would thus be subject to little change if the peak of 95,000 cubic feet per second in December 1937 were included.

The conversion factors or magnitude ratios between selected pairs of volumetric units, showing the value of the larger unit in terms of the smaller unit for each comparison, may be read from Figure XIG-6 with fair accuracy as follows: Begin where the curve lying in the lower part of the figure intersects the horizontal boundary of a decimal phase, such as 0.1, 1.0, 10, or 100, then move vertically from this point to the intersection with the upper curve to be compared, move horizontally to the left margin, and read the number directly, of course having regard to the decimals. Thus, for converting cubic meters per second to cubic feet per second, the factor is 35.3; or to million gallons per day (m.g.d.), 22.8; or to acre-feet per day, 70.0. This serves to illustrate the fact that 1 cubic foot per second will

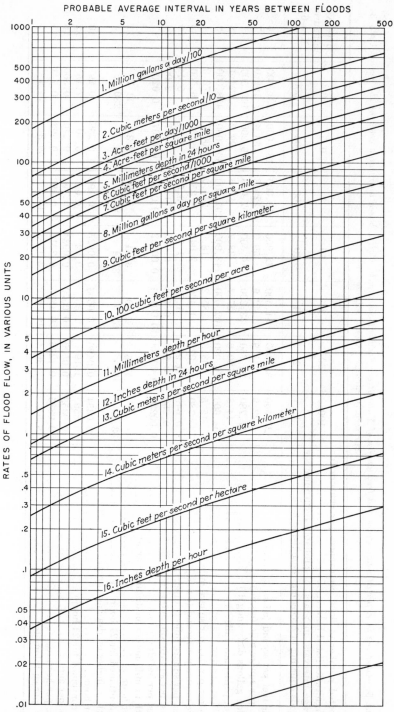

PROBABLE AVERAGE INTERVAL IN YEARS BETWEEN FLOODS

RATES OF FLOOD FLOW, IN VARIOUS UNITS

1. Million gallons a day/100
2. Cubic meters per second/10
3. Acre-feet per day/1000
4. Acre-feet per square mile
5. Millimeters depth in 24 hours
6. Cubic feet per second/1000
7. Cubic feet per second per square mile
8. Million gallons a day per square mile
9. Cubic feet per second per square kilometer
10. 100 cubic feet per second per acre
11. Millimeters depth per hour
12. Inches depth in 24 hours
13. Cubic meters per second per square mile
14. Cubic meters per second per square kilometer
15. Cubic feet per second per hectare
16. Inches depth per hour

FIG. XIG-6.—Expected magnitudes and frequencies of floods on the Yuba River at Smartville, Calif., in various units. Based on records for the period 1903–34.

TABLE 5.—*Observed or expected magnitudes and frequencies of Yuba River floods at Smartville, Calif., based on records covering the period 1903–34 expressed in various units of volume*

	Expected number of flood occurrences per century for magnitudes listed here							Curve No. in figure XIg-6
	100	50	25	10	1	0.5	0.2	
	Average intervals, in years, of probable recurrence for floods equaling or exceeding those listed here							
	1	2	4	10	100	200	500	
Cubic feet per second (c.f.s.)	27,500	38,300	51,500	72,000	150,000	184,000	231,000	6
C.f.s. per square mile (c.s.m.)	22.9	31.9	42.9	59.9	124.8	153.4	192.0	7
Million gallons daily (m.g.d.)	17,780	24,750	33,300	46,500	97,000	119,200	149,500	1
M.g.d. per square mile	14.8	20.6	27.7	38.7	80.6	99.2	124.1	8
Acre-feet per day	54,600	76,000	102,000	143,000	297,000	366,000	458,000	3
Acre-feet per day per square mile	45.5	63.3	85.2	118.9	244.0	300.0	376.0	4
Cubic meters per second (c.m.s.)	780	1,075	1,460	2,040	4,250	5,230	6,550	2
C.m.s. per square mile (c.m.m.)	0.649	0.904	1.21	1.69	3.53	4.34	5.44	13
C.m.s. per square kilometer (c.m.k.)	0.250	0.348	0.466	0.652	1.36	1.67	2.09	14
C.m.s. per hectare (c.m.h.)	0.00250	0.00348	0.00466	0.00652	0.0136	0.0167	0.0209	17
Depth in millimeters on drainage area:								
Per hour	1.40	1.95	2.60	3.64	7.60	9.35	11.7	11
If continued for 24 hours	33.5	46.9	62.5	87.4	182.0	224.0	280.0	5
Depth in inches on drainage-area:								
Per hour	0.0354	0.0496	0.0663	0.0925	0.193	0.238	0.298	10
If continued for 24 hours	0.850	1.19	1.59	2.22	4.64	5.70	7.15	12
C.f.s. per acre	0.0358	0.0500	0.0670	0.0934	0.195	0.240	0.300	16
C.f.s. per hectare	0.0885	0.1236	0.1655	0.231	0.482	0.593	0.741	15
C.f.s. per sq kilometer	8.85	12.36	16.55	23.1	48.2	59.3	74.1	9

deliver nearly 2 acre-feet per day, the deficiency being only 0.8 percent, as shown in foot-note 1, p. 537. Likewise, it is readily seen that in order to convert million gallons per day to cubic feet per second the proper factor for multiplication is 1.55. Similarly, the curves representing cubic meters per second per square mile and per square kilometer may serve for defining the areal relationship between square miles and square kilometers as 2.59. Furthermore, the relative lengths of miles and kilometers may be had by extracting the square root of the conversion factor of 2.59 for areas, the result being 1.61.

SLIDE-RULE SOLUTIONS FOR THE MYERS SCALE

A single setting of the ordinary slide rule will suffice for determining more than one factor. Thus, for the Ohio River flood of January 1937 at Metropolis, Ill., $M = 203,000$ square miles, and $Q = 1,850,000$ cubic feet per second; therefore, it is well to set 203 of scale B under the extreme right index of scale A, with the minimum displacement of the slide from its closed position. This insures the use of the right half of the scale B, to conform with the fact that an even number of digits expresses the area. For an odd number of digits the left half of the scale should be used for the setting under one of the end indexes, but never under the middle index of scale A if the best use of a single setting is desired.

Under 185 of the C scale, read 41.1, the percentage rating on the Myers scale. Then prove as follows: Without disturbing the setting, first read on A scale, above 185 of the B scale, the number 9.11, representing q, the average yield per square mile of drainage area for peak discharge. Now reset the slide, placing the right index of scale B under 203 of the right half of scale A. Then under 9.11 of scale C read 41.1 on scale D, furnishing the desired proof. It is evident that such manipulation of scales A and B either divides or multiplies by the square root of the drainage area expressed in square miles; and the readings on scales C and D supply the other needed factor and the desired result of the computation.

Even the most complicated formulas and technical procedures thus far introduced or likely to be devised require the determination of both the area of the drainage basin and the flood discharge, along with corresponding stage. As demonstrated above, it requires but a simple operation on the slide rule to determine the percentage rating on the Myers scale for purposes of comparison.

FLOOD RECORDS OF OUTSTANDING LENGTH

Incomplete records of several rivers in New England and along the Atlantic seaboard extend back well into the colonial period and thus partly cover two or three centuries, and the record for some stations on the Mississippi River and on some of its tributaries extends well beyond

100 years.   Concerning the Ohio River at Pittsburgh, Pa., for example, there was some relation between the welfare and security of the early colonists and their ability to keep their stores of powder dry at Fort Duquesne, precariously near the occasional flood marks of the 1760's. "It appears that the first two yearly maxima definitely recorded were 39.2 and 41.2 feet in January 1762 and March 1763, respectively, followed by 40.2 in November 1810, as compared with the 36.5 feet of February 1884, later superseded by the 38.7 feet of March 1907, the recognized 90-year maximum until the unprecedented flood of March 1936, when the gage reading attained 46.0 feet" [27, p. 163].

As would be expected, much longer records are available for some of the principal rivers of Europe, Asia, and Africa.   The records are usually intermittent, somewhat fragmentary, and more or less uncertain and are more qualitative than quantitative as derived from existing notes.   However, it is known that the floods of February 1658 and January 1910 on the Seine River at Paris were nearly equal in both stage and discharge, rating nearly 7 percent on the Myers scale.   Likewise, the floods of 1501 and 1899 on the Danube River were outstanding at 14 separate stations, the earlier one registering from 2.4 to 11.2 feet higher than the later one. According to the longest record with a claim to fair continuity, that of the Nile River at the Roda gage, Cairo, Egypt [25, fig. 19], the century maxima from the 7th century to the 20th seemed to rise about 9 feet, of which nearly 7 feet represents the normal rise from silting.

RECENT TRENDS IN FLOOD-CONTROL INVESTIGATIONS

The last two or three decades have witnessed a change in methods of approach and analytical treatment of basic data pertaining to flood assembly, routing, forecasting, damages, and warranted degrees of regulation, protection, and control.   The results achieved from the relatively meager and generalized data of 40 years ago, however, should stand as monuments to the engineering and other scientific professions responsible for those early investigations, designs, and construction projects on many river systems.

With the advent of greatly increased facilities for continuous automatic recording of rainfall, runoff, and associated physical phenomena, more rigorous scientific methods have been devised.   Groups recently organized to develop and carry on the newly defined relations of hydrology and meteorology have thus had the multiple advantages of more nearly adequate data and the step by step progress into what had been largely unexplored fields.

Some hydrologists are content to use daily records; others have required 12-hour, 6-hour, or even hourly rainfall and runoff data; and several others are inclined toward still further breakdown, using even

5-minute intervals. For application to specific drainage basins the resulting mass of detailed data and derivations may have to depend on rather broad assumptions, which may largely nullify the particularized information. However, out of the determined efforts of many groups have emerged some technical procedures and analyses that have much promise and have already been utilized to good effect in recent flood reports of the United States Geological Survey and of other Federal, State, and private or municipal agencies, some of which are listed under References.

HEADWATER STORAGE AND FLOOD CONTROL

Notable progress has been made both in this country and abroad toward storing or otherwise retaining rain water, either where it falls or as near thereto as practicable. Among the outstanding developments of this kind are the well-known terrace systems, which throughout many centuries, have retained valuable groves, vineyards, orchards, gardens, and tillage fields or plots, particularly in areas bordering the Mediterranean; the terrace systems of prehistoric times on the Andean slopes in Peru and Bolivia; and the Mangum broad-base and other earth terrace systems used in this country within the last few decades, to provide either storage or other detention capacity, both surface and underground, and at the same time to promote vegetative growth and attendant soil and water conservation. Small storage projects in headwater areas for domestic water supply, small power projects, recreation, stock watering, irrigation, fire protection, and general farm use have contributed toward the regulation and stabilization of adjacent ground-water levels and stream flow through holding back the crests and then augmenting the low flows.

If the objective in flood-control projects may be defined as reducing the peak discharge to one-half, one-third, or any other portion of the expected 100-year maximum and insuring the subsequent release of impounded water to augment low flows when most needed, then it appears practicable to make some progress toward this objective through proper use of the soil and its cover, as demonstrated strikingly by such data as those of figure XIg-1 and table 1. Although the more positive measures involving open storage in large reservoirs may be required for complete and satisfactory control of water resources in a designated region, a program of soil conservation is made more incumbent by reason of such major structures, in order to reduce sedimentation and thus prolong the useful life of the reservoir capacity.

REFERENCES

1. Bailey, Paul, The control of floods by reservoirs: California Dept. Public Works Bull. 14, 1928.

2. Bernard, Merrill, An approach to determinate stream flow: Am. Soc. Civil Eng. Trans., vol. 100, pp. 347–395 (including discussions), 1935.

3. Bernard, Merrill, Hydro-meteorological aspects of flood control and forecasting problems: Am. Meteorol. Soc. Bull., April 1939, p. 160.

4. Dickson, R. E., Langley, B. C., and Fisher, R. E., Water and soil conservation experiments at Spur, Tex.: Texas Agr. Exper. Sta. Bull. 587, July 1940.

5. Ellsworth, C. E., The floods in central Texas in September 1921: U. S. Geol. Survey Water-Supply Paper 488, 56 pp., 1923.

6. Follansbee, Robert, and Hodges, P. V., Some floods in the Rocky Mountain region: U. S. Geol. Survey Water-Supply Paper 520-G, pp. 105–129, 1925.

7. Follansbee, Robert, and Jones, E. E., The Arkansas River flood of June 3–5, 1921: U. S. Geol. Survey Water-Supply Paper 487, 44 pp., 1922.

8. Fuller, W. E., Flood flows: Am. Soc. Civil Eng. Trans., vol. 77, pp. 564–694, 1914.

9. Goodridge, R. S., A graphic method of routing floods through reservoirs: Am. Geophys. Union Trans., 1937, pp. 433–439.

10. Grover, N. C., The floods of March 1936, pt. 1, New England rivers: U. S. Geol. Survey Water-Supply Paper 798, 466 pp., 1937.

11. Grover, N. C., The floods of March 1936, pt. 2, Hudson River to Susquehanna River region: U. S. Geol. Survey Water-Supply Paper 799, 380 pp., 1937.

12. Grover, N. C., The floods of March 1936, pt. 3, Potomac, James, and upper Ohio Rivers: U. S. Geol. Survey Water-Supply Paper 800, 351 pp., 1938.

13. Grover, N. C., Floods of Ohio and Mississippi Rivers, January-February 1937: U. S. Geol. Survey Water-Supply Paper 838, 1938.

14. Hays, O. E., and Atkinson, H. B., Hydrologic studies—compilation of rainfall and runoff from the watersheds of the Upper Mississippi Valley Conservation Experiment Station, La Crosse, Wis.

15. Hazen, Allen, Flood flows; a study of frequencies and magnitudes, John Wiley & Sons, 1930.

16. Hill, R. A., Graphics of temporary flood storage: Eng. News-Record, vol. 100, No. 17, pp. 657–659, 1928.

17. Horton, A. H., and Jackson, H. J., The Ohio Valley flood of March-April 1913, including comparisons with some earlier floods: U. S. Geol. Survey Water-Supply Paper 334, 98 pp., 1913.

18. Horton, R. E., Flood frequency and flood control: Eng. Record, vol. 68, pp. 505–506, 1913.

19. Horton, R. E., Flood reduction by reservoirs: Inst. Civil Engineers Proc., 1924–25, pp. 1–2.

20. Horton, R. E., Discussion of the Report of the Committee on Floods, Boston Society of Civil Engineers: Boston Soc. Civil Eng. Jour., vol. 19, pp. 506–514, 1932.

21. Hoyt, W. G., and others, Studies of relations of rainfall and runoff in the United States: U. S. Geol. Survey Water-Supply Paper 772, 301 pp., 1936.

22. Jarvis, C. S., A general formula for waterways: Public Roads, vol. 6, pp. 253–259, 1926.

23. Jarvis, C. S., Flood-flow characteristics: Am. Soc. Civil Eng. Trans., vol. 89, pp. 985–1032, 1926.

24. Jarvis, C. S., Rainfall characteristics and their relation to soils and runoff: Am. Soc. Civil Eng. Trans., vol. 95, pp. 379–423, 1931.

25. Jarvis, C. S., Flood-stage records of the River Nile: Am. Soc. Civil Eng. Trans., vol. 101, pp. 1012–1071, 1936. (Records covering 1,300 years.)

26. Jarvis, C. S., Maximum stream flow with reference to flood formulas: Am. Geophys. Union Trans., 1937, pp. 409–419. Includes discussion by R. S. Goodridge.

27. Jarvis, C. S., Great floods in the United States: Am. Geophys. Union Trans., 1939, pp. 157–166.

28. Jarvis, C. S., and others, Floods in the United States, magnitude and frequency: U. S. Geol. Survey Water-Supply Paper 771, 497 pp., 1936.

29. Jarvis, C. S., and Murto, H. C., Graphic interpretation of hydrologic data as related to land use [in press as U. S. Dept. Agr. bulletin].

30. Kinnison, H. B., The New England flood of November 1927: U. S. Geol. Survey Water-Supply Paper 636-C, pp. 45–100, 1930.

31. Knoblauch, H. C., and Haynes, J. L., The effect of contour cultivation on runoff: Am. Geophys. Union Trans., 1940, pp. 499–504.

32. Krimgold, D. B., Runoff from small drainage basins: U. S. Dept. Agr., Soil Cons. Service, Tech. Pub. 17, June 1938.

33. LaRue, E. C., Water power and flood control of Colorado River below Green River, Utah: U. S. Geol. Survey Water-Supply Paper 556, 176 pp., 1925.

34. Lawson, L. M., and Keeler, Karl F., Special flood report, international portion of the Rio Grande, flood of September and October 1932, El Paso, Tex., Am. section, Internat. Boundary Comm., 1933.

35. Leach, H. R., Cook, H. L., and Horton, R. E., Storm-flow prediction: Am. Geophys. Union Trans., 1933, pp. 435–446.

36. Lynch, H. B., Transient flood peaks: Am. Soc. Civil Eng. Proc., November 1939, pp. 1605–1624.

37. McGlashan, H. D., and Ebert, F. C., Southern California floods of January 1916: U. S. Geol. Survey Water-Supply Paper 426, 81 pp., 1917.

38. McGlashan, H. D., and Briggs, R. C., The floods of December 1937 in northern California: U. S. Geol. Survey Water-Supply Paper 843, 1939.

39. Matthes, G. H., Floods and their economic importance: Am. Geophys. Union Trans., 1934, pp. 427–432.

40. Mead, D. W., Hydrology, New York, McGraw-Hill Book Co., 1919. Contains a chapter on floods and flood flows.

41. Meyer, A. F., Elements of hydrology, New York, John Wiley & Sons, 1917.

42. Meyer, O. H., Analysis of runoff characteristics: Am. Soc. Civil Eng. Trans., vol. 105, pp. 83–141 (including discussions), 1940.

43. Paulsen, C. G., and others, Hurricane floods of September 1938 (Long Island and New England): U. S. Geol. Survey Water-Supply Paper 867, 1940.

44. Pettis, C. R., Relation of rainfall to flood runoff: Military Engineer, vol. 28, pp. 94–98, 1936.

45. Posey, C. J., Functional design of flood-control reservoirs: Am. Soc. Civil Eng. Trans., vol. 105, pp. 1638–1674, 1940.

46. Ramser, C. E., Runoff from small agricultural areas: Jour. Agr. Research, vol. 34, pp. 797–823, May 1927.

47. Ramser, C. E., The rational method of estimating runoff from small agricultural areas: Engineering and Contracting, vol. 67, pp. 429–431, 1928.

48. Rutter, E. J., Graves, Q. B., and Snyder, F. F., Flood routing: Am. Soc. Civil Eng. Trans., vol. 104, pp. 275–313 (including discussions), 1939.

49. Ruff, C. F., Maximum probable floods on Pennsylvania streams: Am. Soc. Civil Eng. Proc., September 1940, pp. 1239–1276.

50. Sherman, L. K., Stream flow from rainfall by unit-graph method: Eng. News-Record, vol. 108, pp. 501–505, 1932. See also discussions in Eng. News-Record, vol. 109, pp. 223–226, 1932.

51. Sherman, L. K., The relation of hydrographs of runoff to size and character of drainage basins: Am. Geophys. Union Trans., 1932, pp. 332–339.

52. Thomas, H. A., Flood-retarding reservoir problem directly solved: Eng. News-Record, vol. 79, No. 5, p. 226, 1917.

53. Thomas, H. A., The hydraulics of flood movements in rivers: Carnegie Inst. Technology Bull., 1934; reprinted 1936.

54. Thompson, W. R., Rainfall, soil erosion, and runoff in South Africa, Univ. Pretoria, South Africa.

55. Report of the Flood Commission, Pittsburgh, Pa., 1911.

56. Hearings of the Committee on Flood Control, House of Representatives, 70th Congress, pts. 1–6, 1927–28.

57. Flood control, with special reference to the Mississippi River—a symposium: Am. Soc. Civil Eng. Trans., Paper 1709, vol. 93, pp. 655–969, 1929.

58. Report of the Committee on Floods, Boston Society of Civil Engineers, and discussion by others: Boston Soc. Civil Eng. Jour., vol. 19, pp. 492+, 1932.

59. Development of the rivers of the United States . . . to provide for the maximum amount of flood control, navigation, irrigation, and . . . hydroelectric power: 73d Cong. 2d sess., H. Doc. 395, 1934.

60. Storm rainfall of eastern United States: Miami Conservancy District Tech. Repts., pt. 5, revised 1936.

61. Engineering procedure as applied to flood control by reservoirs with reference to the Muskingum flood-control project, Ft. Belvoir, Va., Engineer School, 1936.

62. Headwaters control and use, papers presented at the Upstream Engineering Conference held in Washington, D. C., Sept. 22 and 23, 1936.

63. Low dams, a manual of design for small water-storage projects, Nat. Resources Comm., 1938.

64. Symposium on floods of the Section of Hydrology, American Geophysical Union: Am. Geophys. Union Trans., 1939, pt. 2.

65. Floods of August 1940 in Tennessee River Basin, Tennessee Valley Authority, 1940.

66. Engineering construction—flood control, Fort Belvoir, Va., Engineer School, 1940.

67. Report of cooperative hydrologic investigations, Pennsylvania Dept. Forests and Waters, U. S. Weather Bureau, and U. S. Geological Survey, 1940.

XIH. STORAGE IN RELATION TO FLOOD WAVES

Walter B. Langbein[1]

A rise in stream flow to a crest in response to runoff generated by precipitation and its subsequent recession after the cessation of precipitation constitute what is called a flood wave. A hydrograph of river flow is composed of a series of flood waves, varying in shape and size and occurring at irregular intervals. A flood wave may also be regarded as a temporary unbalance in river regimen resulting from the application of more water to the land in the form of precipitation or by the melting of snow than can be absorbed by the land itself. The rapid rise of the water in river channels produces unequal flow at different points, and the usual balance between frictional resistance and energy gradient that exists during steady flow is disturbed. The regimen during the resulting unsteady flow is determined in large part by complex local transfers of energy and of volume.

The general equations developed by Thomas [13] for unsteady flow in river channels are as follows:

Law of conservation of energy: Energy gradient equals slope of water
  surface plus instantaneous velocity gradient . . . . (1)
Law of conservation of matter: Total outflow between two sections during an interval of time equals total inflow plus or minus the change in storage during the same interval. Variously termed "equation of continuity" or "storage equation." . . . . (2)

Thomas emphasizes that the complexities of the general problem of unsteady flow in river channels, as well as the mathematical difficulties, are such as to require simplifying assumptions in order to obtain solutions under special conditions. Only particular solutions can be attained in engineering flood-routing investigations.

The process of determining progressively the timing and shape of a flood wave at successive points along a river is called flood routing. Some approximate methods for accomplishing this purpose are described below, but no attempt is made to appraise their accuracy in comparison with solution by exact formulas. In practice the approximate methods are

[1] Hydraulic engineer, Geological Survey, United States Department of the Interior, Washington, D. C.

checked by comparison with observed flood profiles and hydrographs, and adjustments are thereby made in the technique to improve the verification. However, such verification may be deficient to the extent that the data used in the derivation of the routing technique may have sampled only a small number of experiences. A later flood, representing an entirely different combination of events, may prove these empirical methods to be unreliable.

Seddon [10] is credited with having pointed out that the quotient between small changes in storage and the corresponding change in discharge (both sides of the ratio having the same sign) equals the time of travel of a uniformly progressive wave through the reach. This principle, however, can be expanded to cover other cases of flood-wave motion in river channels. Broadly there are two general classes of flood waves—namely, those in which momentum or accelerative forces predominate and those in which such forces have been largely counterbalanced by frictional resistance. Flood waves of the first class occur in power-regulated channels and in steep dry washes in the arid West as a result of cloud-burst rains. Most flood waves in natural river channels are of the second class, in which the time length of their base at any place greatly exceeds the time of travel from the headwater to the given place, and accelerative forces are therefore probably small.

The movement of such flood waves through natural river courses may be conceived to be subject to operations of two kinds—namely, uniformly progressive flow and reservoir (or pondage) action. The first process consists of downstream movement of a flood wave without change in shape, an occurrence that is approximated in those prismatic river channels in which stage and discharge are uniquely defined at all places and in which wave velocity remains constant throughout the range in stage experienced by the flood wave. Reservoir or pondage action refers to transformation of a flood wave that takes place as a result of reservoir action, with consequent attenuation of the maximum discharge and flattening of the wave. An ideal reservoir may be defined as a body of water whose depth is very great and in which the water velocity approaches zero. The surface of such a pool would be level, and the displacement produced by a mass of water placed in the pool (surge wave) would be transmitted to all parts of the pool almost instantly. Reservoirs as built in natural river courses for the storage, control, and regulation of river flow do not generally conform with these conditions; their pools are not level, and sharp distinctions cannot be made between the pool and the backwater reaches, which extend some distance upstream. Flood-wave movement in natural river courses is intermediate between the two limiting conditions cited whenever the ratio of the square of the water velocity to the product of gravitational acceleration and depth ranges between the limits of zero and unity.

Figures XIʜ-1 and XIʜ-2 show hydrographs of flood waves illustrative of the two processes mentioned. Figure XIʜ-1 shows movement of a flood wave in the North Platte River from Bridgeport to Lisco, Nebr., in June 1935, without appreciable change in shape; Figure XIʜ-2 shows the flow from an area of 502 square miles into the retarding basin on the Stillwater River at Englewood, Ohio, and the outflow from the basin during April 1938. The total drainage area above the Englewood station is 646 square miles; the flow from 144 square miles intervening was not

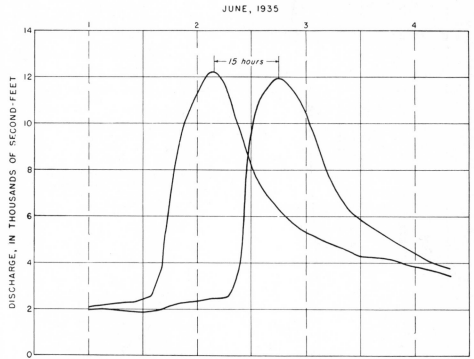

Fɪɢ. XIʜ-1.—Hydrographs of discharge of the North Platte River, June 1-4، 1935, at Bridgeport Neb. (first graph from the left), and Lisco, Neb. (second graph).

separately measured. The maximum rate of discharge into the retarding basin and adjoining channel reaches was probably about 16,000 second-feet. This was reduced to 8,800 second-feet by the storage in the reservoir.

The storage equation (2), supplemented by means for evaluating the volume of storage at appropriate intervals, is the basis of flood routing. Storage in a given basin or river reach intrinsically varies with stage, and in rivers unaffected by irregularly varying artificial regulation, storage may also be expressed in terms of discharge. River channels are rarely uniform canals; they usually consist of a succession of pools and rapids in which the height of the water surface and associated storage in reaches between rapids or other control features such as bends or constrictions are controlled or regulated to a variable extent by the stage-discharge relation of the control at the downstream end. The degree of control of a stable channel is complete when stage and discharge are uniquely related but is only partial when the stage-discharge relation is affected by rate of change

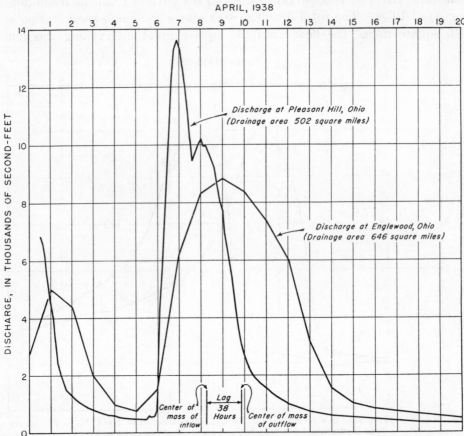

Fig. XIH-2.—Hydrographs of discharge of the Stillwater River at Pleasant Hill and Englewood, Ohio, April 1938.

of discharge, so that the discharge is greater for a given stage on the downstream part of a flood wave than on the upstream part of the wave [5].

The storage in a river reach depends primarily on the rates of discharge into and out of the reach, and on the shape and other hydraulic characteristics of the channel and its control features. The storage at a given time may accordingly be expressed as follows:

$$S_t = \frac{b}{a}\left[xI_t^{m/n} + (1 - x)D_t^{m/n} \right] \tag{3}$$

in which I_t is the inflow at time t, and D_t is the discharge or outflow from the reach, also at time t. The constants a and n express the stage-discharge characteristics of the control sections at the respective ends of the reach, and b and m evaluate the mean stage-volume characteristics of the reach in formulas of the type $Q = ah^n$ and $S = bh^m$, in which Q and S are discharge and volume respectively and h is the stage above the channel bed.

In uniform prismatic channels the exponent m/n generally ranges between 0.6 and 0.75, but in natural channels in which reaches with wide over-bank flood plains having little conveyance, indicative of large values of m, are subject to some degree of control by bends or narrows where the value of n would be low, the exponent m/n may be unity or even greater.

The factor x, which is dimensionless, defines the relative weights given to the rates of inflow and outflow in the determination of the storage volume within the reach. When the stages in a reach are determined by the control at its downstream end, as at the spillway of a reservoir, the storage is uniquely defined by the discharge at the downstream point alone and the value of x in equation 3 is zero. When, however, the discharge at upstream places also participates in the definition of the water profile, creating what McCarthy calls "wedge storage," the values of x increases, ultimately reaching 0.50 in uniform channels, where equal weight is given to inflow and outflow. The value of x for any given reach is determined by a trial and error process as explained below.

The relation expressed by equation 3 can be treated either graphically, as explained by Rutter, Graves, and Snyder [9], or analytically, as developed by McCarthy [7]. Each of these methods has its advantage, graphic treatment having greater flexibility, whereas the analytic method is adaptable to algebraic development.

In brief, in an analytic method that has found wide application it is assumed that the exponent m/n in equation 3 is unity through the entire range in flood discharge and that the volume of storage in a river reach or partial basin system at a given time may be evaluated in the following simplified form:

$$S = k[xI_t + (1 - x)D_t] \tag{4}$$

in which I_t and D_t have the same significance as before. The factor k, equal to b/a in equation 3, has the dimension of time and is the slope of the storage-discharge curve, which this method assumes to be linear within the range of flood discharges. This assumption may not always be correct, and its application to channels where the exponent m/n differs materially from unity may lead to greatly incorrect results. The factor x is dimensionless, as in equation 3, and defines the relative weights given to the rates of inflow and outflow in determining the volume of storage. These two factors have other physical significances, as explained below.

Discharge-storage relations can be computed on the basis of topo graphic surveys of the volume below defined river profiles throughout the range between low water and flood stage, supplemented by relations between discharge and stage and other factors such as slope at points of control in the river.　This method for routing floods through reaches affected by backwater from regulated navigation and power dams was used by Rutter, Graves, and Snyder [9].　But according to equation 3 discharge-storage relations for a specific river reach or a partial basin area unaffected by such artificial regulation may also be derived from records of stream flow during floods by the following method: Tabulations are

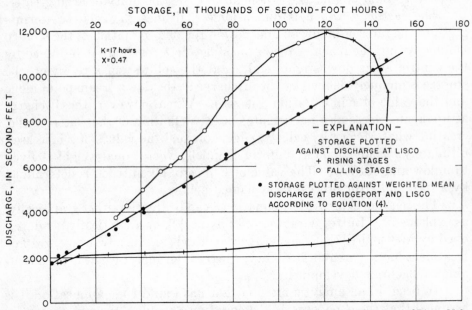

FIG. XIh-3.—Storage-discharge relation of the North Platte River between Bridgeport and Lisco, Neb.

prepared for the cumulative inflow at equal intervals from the beginning of the flood to the time the rivers have subsided to a stage nearly the same as that existing at the beginning.　The inflow into the reach is composed of measured inflow and of the inflow originating on areas not separately measured, estimated on the basis of that measured on nearby areas of comparable size, adjusted, if necessary, for differences in rainfall.　The total flood inflow so measured and estimated should equal the total measured outflow.　Wide discrepancy may be caused by errors in gaging or incorrect estimates of the unmeasured inflow.

The difference between the cumulative inflow and outflow at intervals during the flood are computed.　In accordance with the storage equation (2) the differences so computed are equal to the volume of water stored in the given reach from the beginning of the cumulation to the end of each selected interval. These volumes of storage are plotted against the weighted mean discharge through the reach at the end of each interval. The plotting procedure used is defined by equation 4. When the storage is plotted against outflow discharge ($x = 0$) the points define a loop, as shown in Figure XIH-3, with the rising branch plotting on the right. Accordingly successively larger values of x are selected, giving increasing influence to the inflow discharge, until the rising and falling branches approximately coincide. The slope of the graph is equal to k. A constant value of k (and consequently equation 4) will apply only over a range within which the curve approximates a straight line. This range may be fairly wide but does not by any means extend all the way from low-water flow to peak flood discharges.

Some rivers show an increase in k (lowered velocity) at higher stages, as in Figure XIH-4, and some show a decrease. In general, it does not add greatly to the work of solution to use the graph as plotted instead of a straight-line approximation.

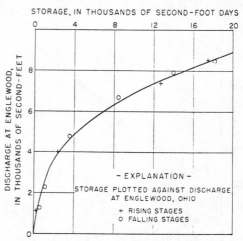

Fig. XIH-4.—Storage-discharge relation of the Stillwater River between Pleasant Hill and Englewood, Ohio, based on flood of April 1938.

Although serving to define the relative weights assigned to the inflow and outflow for evaluating the intervening storage, the factor x also defines the attenuation of the flood wave and therefore is known as the attenuation factor. Thus a condition of uniformly progressive flow or simple translation of the flood wave with no attenuation exists when $x = 0.50$, the maximum possible value, and k is a constant. In such a river course inflow and outflow are given equal weight in evaluating the storage. An example of uniformly progressive flow is shown in Figures XIH-1 and XIH-3. A value of $x = 0$, on the other hand, indicates that the storage is uniquely defined by the outflow alone. This is a condition that exists in reservoirs or ponded storage, of which an example is shown in Figures XIH-2 and XIH-4. The reduction in peak discharge effected by the reservoir storage above Englewood, Ohio, has already been noted. Figure XIH-4 shows that storage was defined by outflow discharge at Englewood on both rising and falling stages, without reference to rates of flow upstream at Pleasant Hill. The absence in Figure XIH-4 of the storage loop shown in Figure XIH-3 should be noted.

An expression for Seddon's wave velocity [10] may be generalized as illustrated in Figure XIH-5, where the weighted discharge in a river reach as defined by $[xI_t + (1 - x)D_t]$ of equation 4 is plotted against the cross-sectional area as defined by $\dfrac{\text{storage}}{\text{length}}$. The slope of a chord of the curve shown equals the wave velocity according to Seddon's principle. If point 1 represents initial or base conditions and point 2 represents a point on the flood wave, then $\dfrac{q_2 - q_1}{a_2 - a_1}$, in which q represents the weighted discharge and a represents the mean cross section of the reach, is equal to the mean wave velocity during the interval 1–2. The time required to traverse the reach is the lag and equals $\dfrac{S_2 - S_1}{q_2 - q_1}$, in which S is the storage in the reach. The lag between centers of mass of the entire wave equals the quotient of the sum of the lag for brief intervals during the wave multiplied by the volumes in the reach during these intervals, divided by the total volume. The result can be expressed as follows:

$$\text{lag} = \frac{\Sigma S}{\Sigma q} \tag{5}$$

in which ΣS is the sum of storage volumes in the reach at equal intervals during the passage of the wave in excess of the initial or base storage and Σq is the sum of the discharge (in excess of base flow) through the reach at corresponding intervals.

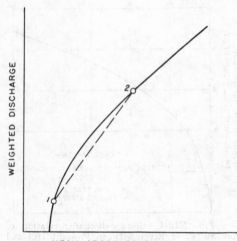

WEIGHTED DISCHARGE

MEAN CROSS-SECTIONAL AREA

FIG. XIH-5.—Graphic representation of velocity of a flood wave subject to friction control.

In many river reaches where the relation between weighted discharge and storage is linear within the range in flood discharges experienced, lag simply equals its slope, k, which can serve as a convenient measure of storage volumes and dependent characteristics.

The lag between the center of mass of effective rainfall and the center of mass of direct runoff at a gaging station is a concise measure of the hydraulic characteristics of the basin and in large part is definitive of the shape of the hydrographs of flood discharge from the basin. Thus it has been found that a general relation exists between the basin lag and its unit hydrograph [4, 12]. Figure XIH-6 shows a series of distribution hydrographs (unit hydrographs in which the ordinates are expressed in percentage of total runoff instead of second-feet per inch of runoff) for 6-hour storms classified in terms of the lag between centers of mass of inflow to the basin in the form of rainfall or snow melt and the outflow at a gaging station or other point.   The curves shown in Figure XIʜ-6 are based on an analysis of many unit hydrographs for basins ranging in area from 30 to 4,000 square miles.   The correlation shown in Figure XIʜ-6 assumes that the value of the attenuation factor, x in equation 4, is a constant for all basins and that k is constant through the range in flood discharge.

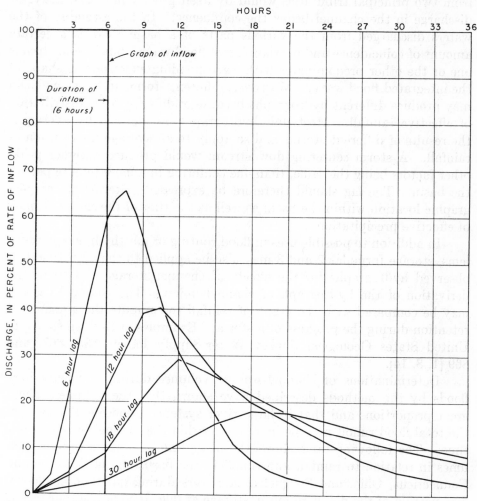

Fɪɢ. XIʜ-6.—Distribution hydrographs of direct runoff for six-hour periods of effective rainfall in terms of basin-lag intervals.

So far as the channel conditions in any particular basin may differ from the average, the curves shown in Figure XIʜ-6 may not fit.   For example, in two basins of equal lag the storage in one may be in simple channels with little overflow or pondage, whereas in the other there may be considerable pondage relative to its size.   In the first basin the attenuation would tend to be less than in the second.   As yet no guide can be given to the determination of the value of the attenuation factor for a particular basin in the absence of records of stream flow, although some investigations have been made of the relation between lag or shape of the unit hydrograph and topographic features [7, 12].   The position of the tributaries in the basin might have an appreciable influence.   The relative timing of floods from two principal tributaries would by itself greatly influence the crest discharge in the channel below the confluence.   In the assembly of the waters discharged from the various parts of a basin there is a certain amount of coincidence and overlapping of flood waves, but in some basins one or the other predominates with corresponding effect on the shape of the integrated flood wave.   Moreover, different storms in the same basin may produce different hydrographs because of differing areal distribution of effective rainfall.   Most unit hydrographs are derived by averaging the results of different storms and so apply to an average distribution of rainfall.   A storm centering downstream would produce a higher peak, other factors being the same, than one centering in a more remote part of the basin.   The lag should therefore be expressed in terms of the geographic location within the basin as well as the time of the center of mass of effective precipitation.

In addition to possible uses in flood routing or unit-hydrograph problems, storage formulas 2 and 3 may also be applied to the adjustment of observed hydrographs for the effects of channel storage and so to the derivation of the hydrograph of channel inflow.   The computed graph may be compared with the graph of rainfall to compute the amounts of retention during the progress of a storm.   Examples of this are shown in United States Geological Survey Water-Supply Papers 838, 867, and 869 [1, 8, 14].

Determinations of channel-storage volumes during unusually high floods by the methods described have shown that the volume reaches great proportions and that in large river systems a considerable part of the total flood runoff may be in storage within the channel system at one time.   The following table shows the magnitude of channel-storage volumes in relation to rainfall and runoff in the basins of the Muskingum, Connecticut, Ohio, and Susquehanna Rivers during outstanding floods. The portion of the direct runoff in storage at one time for the four basins ranged from 57 to 80 percent.   In terms of acre-feet of storage the range was from 720,000 acre-feet in the Muskingum River Basin during the flood of August 1935 to 56,000,000 acre-feet in the Ohio River Basin during the flood of January 1937.   It has been computed that in the latter flood the storage in the main channel and overflow areas of the Ohio River from Sewickley, Pa., to Metropolis, Ill., a channel distance of 932 miles, reached a maximum of 38,000,000 acre-feet, or about 1.4 times the capacity of Lake Mead, created by the Boulder Dam on the Colorado River, the largest artificial reservoir in the world. These enormous volumes suggest that any analysis of river-flood behavior must be based on thorough appreciation of the action of channel storage.

Volumes of channel storage in relation to rainfall and runoff during major floods

Basin	Date	Drainage area (square mile)	Mean areal precipitation (inches)	Direct runoff (inches)	Maximum volume of channel storage		Lag interval (days)
					Inches	Per-cent of direct runoff	
Muskingum River above McConnellsville, Ohio..	Aug. 8, 1935	7,411	4.15	2.3	1.83	80	3.5
Connecticut River above Hartford, Conn........	Sept. 22, 1938	10,480	7.55	4.05	2.90	72	3.4
Ohio River above Metropolis, Ill..............	Jan. 26, 1937	203,000	12.95[a]	8.9	5.1	57	15.
Susquehanna River above Marietta, Pa..........	Aug. 24, 1933	25,990	4.13	1.39	1.1	79	3.3

[a] Included 0.1 inch of snow-melt.

REFERENCES

1. Grover, N. C., Flood of Ohio and Mississippi Rivers, January-February 1937: U. S. Geol. Survey Water-Supply Paper 838, 746 pp., 1938.

2. Horton, R. E., Natural stream-channel storage: Am. Geophys. Union Trans., 1936, pp. 406–415.

3. Horton, R. E., Definitions and classification of flood waves: Permanent Internat. Assoc. Navigation Congresses, Brussels, Belgium, Bull. 25, 1938.

4. Hoyt, W. G., Studies of relations of rainfall and run-off in the United States: U. S. Geol. Water-Supply Paper 772, 301 pp., 1936.

5. Jones, B. E., A method of correcting river discharge for a changing stage: U. S. Geol. Survey Water-Supply Paper 375, pp. 117–130, 1916.

6. Langbein, W. B., Some channel-storage and unit-hydrograph studies: Am. Geophys. Union Trans., 1940, pp. 620–627.

7. McCarthy, G. T., The unit hydrograph and flood routing (unpublished manuscript presented at conference of North Atlantic Division, Corps of Engineers, U. S. Army, June 24, 1938).

8. Paulsen, C. G., and others, Hurricane floods of September 1938: U. S. Geol. Survey Water-Supply Paper 867, 562 pp., 1940.

9. Rutter, E. J., Graves, Q. B., and Snyder, F. F., Flood routing: Am. Soc. Civil Eng. Trans., vol. 104, pp. 275–313, 1939.

10. Seddon, J. A., River hydraulics: Am. Soc. Civil Eng. Trans., vol. 43, pp. 179–243, 1900.

11. Sherman, L. K., Stream flow from rainfall by the unit-graph method: Eng. News-Record, vol. 108, pp. 501–505, 1932.

12. Snyder, F. F., Synthetic unit-graphs: Am. Geophys. Union Trans., 1938, pp. 447–454.

13. Thomas, H. A., The hydraulics of flood movements in rivers: Carnegie Inst. Technology Eng. Bull., 70 pp., 1934.

14. Youngquist, C. V., and Langbein, W. B., Flood of August 1935 in the Muskingum River Basin, Ohio: U. S. Geol. Survey Water-Supply Paper 869, 116 pp., 1941.

XI₁. ARTIFICIAL STORAGE

WILLIAM G. HOYT[1]

Throughout the ages the degree to which people could either urbanize or carry on agricultural activities in arid or semiarid regions has depended largely upon the extent to which fluctuations in precipitation could be overcome through the storage and control of water. Storage was used in connection with municipal water supplies for irrigation and for flood control before the birth of Christ. Sextus Julius Frontinus, water commissioner of Rome, A.D. 97, in two reports on the water supply for the city of Rome, describes in detail a system of water collection, storage, transmission, and delivery, which, were the dates and quantities changed, would do credit to a modern metropolis.

The water supplies for Rome as well as other ancient cities were obtained partly from flowing streams but more generally from the earth's largest fresh-water storage reservoir—ground-water storage—and by diversion to points of use through canals and aqueducts. The remains of these early water systems still stand as evidence of a water-conscious people sufficiently versed in the knowledge of hydraulics and hydrology to comprehend that storage is essential in adapting most natural water supplies to man's use. As the writings of Frontinus indicate clearly, the Romans knew the significance of notable droughts, that contaminated and silty surface waters resulting from only moderate rainstorms should be used for irrigation rather than human consumption, that desilting reservoirs were desirable between points of diversion and conduit intakes, and that accurate measurements of storage and diversions were necessary to check unauthorized use and wastage of water.

After the fall of the Roman Empire little attempt seems to have been made to develop safe and reliable municipal water supplies. In fact, it is reported that during the eleventh century the per capita consumption of water in Paris, France, was as low as 1 quart a day. Storage for irrigation, however, persisted in all the countries bordering the Mediterranean and to the east in Mesopotamia, India, and China. In the United States irrigation was practiced in the Southwest before the advent of the Spanish explorers, and during the sixteenth century the Spanish missionaries constructed primitive irrigation works in what is now Arizona and New Mexico.

[1] Hydraulic engineer, Geological Survey, United States Department of the Interior, Washington, D. C.

572

Storage of water as a flood-control measure was practiced by the ancient Babylonians on the Euphrates River through the diversion of water into depressions in the Arabian deserts. Similar flood-control measures were used on the Nile. On the Nile, however, the diverted water was returned to the river after flood periods. Detention basins with a fixed opening were used on the River Loire for the protection of the city of Roanne, France, as early as 1711. In Germany, France, and Russia storage was developed in connection with river improvements as early as the fifteenth century. The number of reservoirs constructed was relatively small prior to about 1900.

Throughout the eastern part of the United States there is relatively an abundance of water, and storage was not essential for either early settlement or moderate utilization of surface-water supplies. With the economic development of the country there has been a remarkable growth in storage development until today there are in the United States few rivers whose flow is not regulated to some extent by storage. Although runoff conditions vary widely, and generalized statements do not clearly illustrate all conditions, it may be said that the possible use of water flowing in stream channels is extremely slight unless provision can be made to regulate the daily and seasonal flow to meet the demands.

In humid areas of the United States, where the annual rainfall exceeds 30 to 40 inches, between 50 and 70 percent of the total volume of stream flow occurs in the form of intermittent stream rises or flood waves, which result from the direct runoff from rains and melting snow. Except as such water may be used at the time of passing, it has little economic value unless it can be stored and released in conformity with more or less fixed requirements. In portions of the arid and semiarid regions of the United States, where stream flow is largely dependent on the runoff from melting snow, 75 percent or more of the total annual runoff flows out of each basin in the form of a huge wave, whose base may extend over several weeks but whose crest is in general considerably in advance of the peak of irrigation demands. Without artificial storage less than half of the runoff in humid areas can be depended upon for regular use, and in arid and semiarid areas only a relatively small part of the total can be used beneficially. By storing water of the peaks and flood rises, however, it is possible to synchronize stream flow more nearly with the demands for municipal water supply, irrigation, power, and navigation and to control flood runoff to some extent.

Beginning with early power development in New England, the regulation of the outflow from natural lakes by means of low dams and simple control structures afforded an inexpensive method of increasing the reliable power flow. As urban growth increased, natural low-water stream flow and ground-water supplies were often insufficient to meet the water requirements of municipalities, and the impounding of stream flow in reservoirs became a necessity. In arid States of the West, beginning about 1905, there was a spectacular development in storage for irrigation use, and the success thus attained has been reflected in a steady growth in

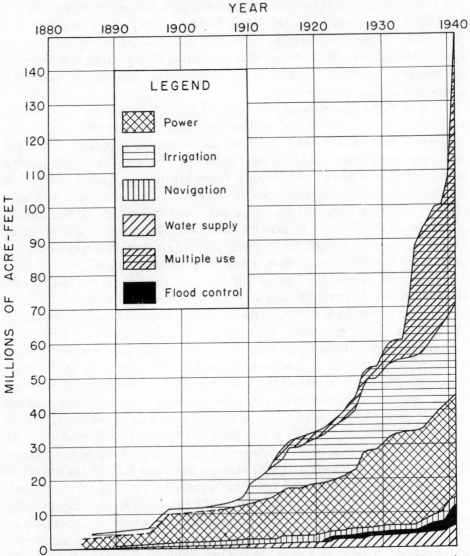

FIG. XII-1.—Growth of storage in the United States. (Developed reservoirs of 20,000 acre-feet capacity and over.)

storage development. The experience of the Miami River flood of March 1913 in Ohio led to the construction of reservoirs as detention basins solely for flood protection.

Prior to 1930 most storage reservoirs in the United States had been constructed for a single primary purpose, generally for municipal water supply, power, or irrigation. Beginning, however, with the construction on the Colorado River of Boulder Dam, creating Lake Mead, and later with funds made available through emergency relief appropriations, work was started on several reservoirs so large that the storage space can be dedicated to a multiplicity of uses without material conflict and with an adjustment of benefits not otherwise possible. The magnitude of these large reservoirs is emphasized by the fact that their capacity exceeds the combined capacity of all other reservoirs constructed in the United States to date.

The term "acre-feet," normally used only in connection with storage for irrigation, is here employed as a measure of capacity instead of "cubic feet" or "gallons," commonly used as a measure of the capacity of reservoirs whose primary purpose is municipal water supply and flood control, or "cubic yards," used as a measure of the capacity of reservoirs whose primary purpose is silt and debris control. The following factors may be useful in converting acre-feet into other units:

$$1 \text{ acre-foot} = 43,560 \text{ cubic feet.}$$
$$= 325,400 \text{ United States gallons.}$$
$$= 1,610 \text{ cubic yards.}$$
$$= 1.9835 \text{ second-feet flowing for 24 hours.}$$
$$= 0.01876 \text{ inch over 1 square mile.}$$
$$= 1,234 \text{ cubic meters.}$$

In general the capacity referred to herein represents the usable capacity above the outlet works and does not include so-called dead storage below the outlet works.

In January 1938 nearly 500 reservoirs having a capacity of 20,000 acre-feet (871,000,000 cubic feet, 6,500,000,000 gallons) or more had been constructed or were under construction in the United States. The classification of these reservoirs in relation to use is approximately as follows:

Use	Number	Capacity (acre-feet)	Percent of total
Multiple use	40	76,280,100	53.3
Irrigation	167	27,041,200	18.8
Power	164	27,001,100	18.8
Municipal water supply	65	5,791,400	4.0
Flood control	29	4,788,200	3.3
Navigation	14	2,636,000	1.8
	479	143,538,000	100

This table refers only to reservoirs of comparatively large size. There are innumerable reservoirs of less than 20,000 acre-feet, the combined capacity of which probably amounts to several million acre-feet. Most of the small reservoirs are located on small streams, and in general their operation has only a minor effect on the runoff from major basins.

The aggregate capacity of the large reservoirs is sufficient to hold a supply of 100 gallons a day for all the inhabitants of the United States during a period of 10 years. In terms of stream flow this capacity is equivalent to the aggregate runoff during a normal year of the Penobscot, Kennebec, Merrimack, Connecticut, Hudson, Delaware, Susquehanna, and Potomac Rivers and of the Ohio River at Pittsburgh, the Mississippi River at St. Paul, and the Missouri River at Kansas City. In terms of flowage it is equivalent to about 1 foot in depth over an area of 225,000 square miles, or enough water to flood all New England, New York,

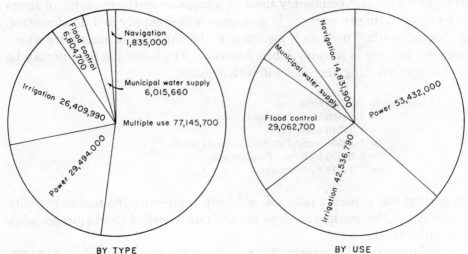

FIG. XI1-2.—Distribution of storage in the United States by type and by use.

Pennsylvania, Maryland, and Virginia to a depth of 1 foot; or to flood the entire surface of the United States to a depth of nearly an inch.

Figure XI1-1 shows the development of storage reservoirs of 20,000 acre-feet or more since 1885. An outstanding feature is the spectacular development in multiple-use reservoirs, beginning with the completion of Boulder Dam in 1935. Figure XI1-2 shows the distribution of the total developed storage by type and by use. Figure XI1-3 shows for major drainage basins of the United States the distribution of storage capacity, including that of multiple-use reservoirs, and the apportionment to the five primary uses—namely, municipal water supply, irrigation, power, flood control, and navigation. In making this classification, storage capacity dedicated to recreational centers, game refuges, and general uses such as water conservation has, in several instances, been included under "flood control." The line of demarcation is sometimes not distinct, and it is recognized that other investigators might make somewhat different

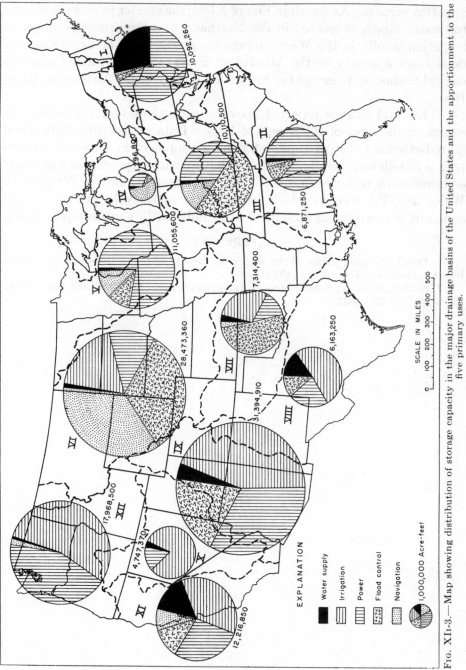

Fig. XII-3.— Map showing distribution of storage capacity in the major drainage basins of the United States and the apportionment to the five primary uses.

apportionments.   As shown in Figure XI1-3, the greater part of the storage for water supply is located in the Northeast and Southwest; storage for irrigation wholly in the West; storage for power in all areas; storage for flood control largely in the Mississippi River, Colorado, and California coastal basins; and storage for navigation largely in the Mississippi River Basin.

The total storage reported above is equivalent to 1.1 acre-feet per capita on the basis of the census of 1940.   Data reported by Sutherland [2] indicate that the per capita storage development in some other countries is as follows: Canada, a country that is sparsely populated but richly endowed with water resources, has 2.9 acre-feet per capita; New South Wales and Victoria, in which irrigation is extensively practiced, 0.70 acre-foot per capita; and South Africa, only 0.075 acre-foot per capita.

REFERENCES

1. Frontinus, Sextus Julius, Water supply for the city of Rome, translated by Clemens Herschel, Longmans, Green & Co., 1913.

2. Sutherland, R. A., Some aspects of water conservation: Am. Soc. Civil Eng. Trans., vol. 96, pp. 157–229, 1932.

CHAPTER XII

DROUGHTS

William G. Hoyt[1]

Considered as a natural phenomenon, drought "constitutes dryness, want of rain or water, especially such dryness of weather or climate as affects the earth and prevents the growth of plants" (Webster). Drought conditions, as ordinarily defined in humid areas, exist when there is insufficient moisture in the soil to maintain plant life [2]. Considered as an economic phenomenon, "Drought conditions may be said to prevail whenever precipitation is insufficient to meet the needs of established human activities" [6].

CAUSES

Nature supplies the earth with water largely in the form of rain and snow. Nature, however, has the first demands upon this precipitation, and there is left as stream flow or ground water only such water as escapes the demands of evaporation and transpiration. Any meteorologic condition that reduces the residual water available for man's use may be classified as drought-producing. The two principal meteorologic conditions that affect this residual adversely are absence of rainfall and high temperature, and the severity of a drought depends upon the degree in which these two major factors synchronize. The drought of 1936 in the Great Plains area is an excellent example of the synchronization of high temperature and deficient precipitation. Other drought-producing conditions include abnormal distribution of precipitation, not necessarily with deficiencies; high temperature, either with or without hot winds; and so far as droughts are related to stream flow and shallow ground-water supplies, long continued subfreezing periods.

Considered as an economic phenomenon, a droughty condition is created by man whenever he introduces and depends for his livelihood on a plant growth that requires an amount of moisture in excess of the demands of the native vegetation and neglects to supply by artificial means the additional water necessary for the growth and maturity of the crop or crops on which his livelihood depends. A droughty situation is also

[1] Hydraulic engineer, Geological Survey, United States Department of The Interior, Washington, D. C. In the preparation of this chapter the author has drawn heavily on Water-Supply Papers 680, and 820, by J. C. Hoyt [5, 6]. The reader is referred to those papers for a more exhaustive study of the subject.

created if, in the economic development of a region, man creates a demand for more water than is normally available. In connection with present-day activities of a highly organized civilization it is therefore increasingly difficult to define and delineate droughts on the basis of a study of meteorologic and hydrologic conditions alone.

DELINEATION OF DROUGHT AREAS

There is no simple way to delineate drought areas. Not only must the amount and distribution of the precipitation be taken into account, but other conditions that have a bearing on the quantity of the residual

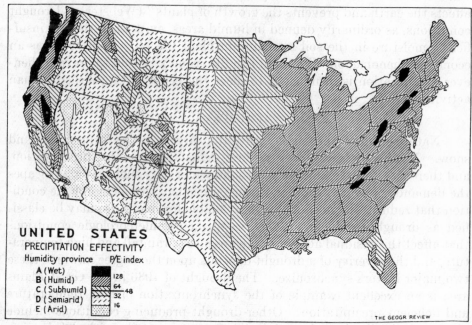

FIG. XII-1.—Map of the United States showing normal climatic regimen.

water available for man's use must be considered. Köppen [8], through an analysis of both precipitation and temperature, developed a classification of climates on a quantitative basis, which has been used by Russell [12] in delineating areas in the United States according to climate.

In 1931 Thornthwaite [13, 14], through a rigorous analysis of precipitation, temperature, and evaporation, made an advanced attempt to determine critical climatic limits by evaluating the effectiveness of precipitation in terms of the temperature at which it fell and gave numerical values to precipitation effectiveness and temperature efficiency. At low temperatures loss through evaporation is less than at high temperatures; thus the effectiveness of a given amount of rain would be greater in low-temperature areas. On the basis of temperature, precipitation, and evaporation data for monthly periods, Thornthwaite [13, 14] formulated the effectiveness of rain in terms of mean monthly temperature. As defined the effectiveness varies directly with precipitation and inversely with temperature. In figure XII-1 are shown the normal positions of the five major moisture provinces in the United States—(A) wet, (B) humid, (C) subhumid, (D) semiarid, and (E) arid—as delineated by Thornthwaite.

Climatic provinces as delineated by either Köppen [8] or Thornthwaite [13] are closely related to characteristic plant associations and soil distribution and as such are of value to ecologists, soil scientists, and agriculturists. They also have a direct bearing on hydrologic problems relating to droughts, as a primary function of the classification is the determination of the degree of aridity. It is axiomatic that these classifications are a measure of the drought-resistant qualities of an area with reference to agriculture in that all wet or humid areas are naturally drought-resistant and that all subhumid, semiarid, and arid regions are less resistant to drought. Provinces thus defined are also, to a great extent, based on their drought-resistant qualities as related to water supply.

Another definite index of the drought-resistant qualities of an area as related to water supply is the difference between precipitation on the one hand, and evaporation and transpiration on the other. The magnitude of this difference is a direct measure of all the water available for man's use, either in the form of stream flow or as an increment to ground water. The drought-resistant qualities of an area depend in part upon the stability and amount of its ground-water supplies. In general the larger and more stable the residual the greater is the margin available for resisting droughts. Figure XII-2 shows the normal amount of this residual in the United States and affords a basis for the study of the stability of the country's water supplies. The delineation of these provinces has been based on a study of precipitation, temperature, evaporation, and transpiration in the humid areas and of the runoff in the subhumid, semiarid, and arid areas. The drought-resistant provinces shown in this figure correspond closely with the five major divisions relating to humidity as delineated by Thornthwaite.

Extending north and south across the United States in close proximity to the 97th meridian is an area in which the evaporation and transpiration demands are about equal to the average annual precipitation. In this area there is very little residual water available to supply stream flow or to recharge ground water. Some water escapes the demands of evaporation, however, and there is recharge to ground water, especially during the winter, when losses are low, and there is some stream flow when rains of high intensity or melting snow exceed the infiltration capacity. In general, however, a line north and south through this area separates the eastern half of the United States, where the mean annual precipitation normally exceeds the evaporation and transpiration, from the western half, where, except in mountainous areas and along the coast, the mean annual precipitation is normally less than the demands of evaporation and transpiration.

Powell in 1878 recognized the significance of this line of demarcation. If his recommendations had been followed millions of dollars of drought relief would have been saved, and what is even more important, many

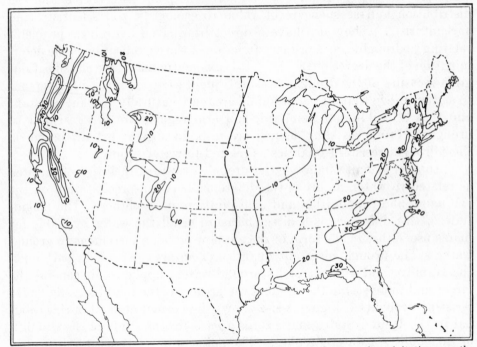

FIG. XII-2.—Map of the United States showing average annual excess of precipitation over the demands of evaporation and transpiration, in inches. (West of the zero line there is generally no annual excess except in mountain areas and in the Pacific Northwest.)

present-day problems of rehabilitation, resettlement, and soil conservation would be largely nonexistent, for Powell saw with exceptional foresight the necessity for the adaptation of man to soil and climate. In his report on the lands of the arid region of the United States [11] he says:

"The limit of [rainfall for] successful agriculture without irrigation has been set at 20 inches. . . . At 20 inches agriculture will not be uniformly successful from season to season. Many droughts will occur; many seasons in a long series will be fruitless; and it may be doubtful whether, on the whole, agriculture will prove remunerative. . . . Extending from the 100th meridian eastward to about the line of 28 inches, the district of the country thus embraced will be subject to more or less disastrous droughts. . . . In the western portion disastrous droughts will be frequent; in the eastern part, infrequent."

That his recommendations were not followed is shown as early as 1894, when Hay [4], in discussing the water resources of a portion of the Great Plains, stated:

"The almost boundless extent of tillable lands, the ease with which large areas can be cultivated, and the wonderful fertility of the soil have attracted settlement farther and farther from the Mississippi Valley out upon the Great Plains, and even into and across the regions which from the scantiness of rainfall are known to be subhumid or semiarid. The tide of settlement rolling westward has been thrown back again and again by the almost insurmountable barrier interposed by the meagerness of rainfall."

It seems futile to discuss droughts in an area where they are but a manifestation of normal climatic conditions, the frequency of occurrence of which has been predicted for over 50 years. Eastward from this area there is an increase in precipitation and a corresponding increase in the residual amount available for recharge to ground water and to maintain stream flow. In this area, however, where the average annual residual is 10 inches or more, as Powell pointed out, droughts of considerable severity are likely to occur. Even in the more humid area there are periods of drought, but they seldom attain great severity. The eastward limits of what might be called the subhumid area can be roughly defined as the area where differences between the average precipitation and the normal variations from the average exceed the normal demands of evaporation and transpiration. East of this area droughts of sufficient intensity to affect water supplies seriously are infrequent. In general this situation exists throughout the eastern third of the United States. West of the zero line, except in the higher mountainous areas and the Pacific coast region from San Francisco northward, where conditions are generally humid, precipitation is usually less than the demands of evaporation and transpiration, and there is little water available for recharge to ground water or stream flow. The degree of aridity increases rapidly with the decrease in precipitation from a subhumid or semiarid region to desert conditions.

DROUGHT FREQUENCY

As deficiencies in precipitation are considered the prime cause of droughts, most measures of drought frequency have been based on studies of such deficiencies, on either an annual, a seasonal, or a monthly basis. Deficiencies in precipitation, however, are not the sole cause of drought, and, moreover, it is difficult to set a limit for precipitation above which drought does not exist and below which a drought may be produced; consequently there is no definite statistical index that can be universally used. J. C. Hoyt [5, 6] in his drought studies concludes that in humid and semiarid States drought conditions exist when there is an annual deficiency in precipitation of 15 percent or more. C. G. Bates [10] in a study of climatic characteristics of the plains region in relation to the possibility of shelter-belt planting used two methods as a base—(1) full calendar years having less than 75 percent of the normal precipitation, and (2) 4-month droughts in which the precipitation during each month was less than 60 percent of the normal precipitation for that month. Russell [12] uses the Köppen classification of dry years and desert years

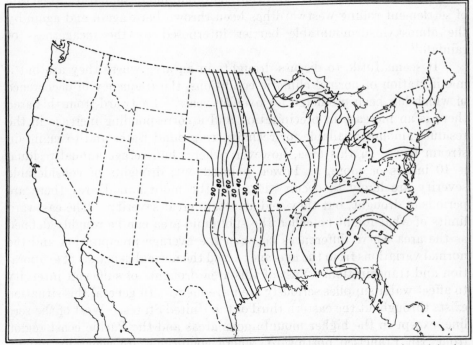

Fig. XII-3.—Map of the United States showing percentage of years that annual precipitation has been less than demands for evaporation and transpiration. (Throughout the West, except in mountain areas and the Pacific Northwest, annual demands of evaporation and transpiration, always or nearly always exceed annual precipitation.)

and shows frequency of such years for the period 1901 to 1920. Thornthwaite [10], using his index values for subhumid climates, shows frequency of occurrences of years having subhumid climate in the plains region for the period 1910–33. Naturally, frequencies based on statistical analyses using both precipitation and temperature, such as those devised by Köppen or Thornthwaite, define drought conditions more accurately than analyses based on precipitation alone. Figure XII-3 shows the results of a frequency study based on the number of years in which the precipitation was less than the demands of evaporation and transpiration as measured by the difference between precipitation and runoff. It was found that in humid and subhumid areas in the United States the normal annual consumption by evaporation and transpiration so computed ranged from about 18 inches at 39° F. to 33 inches at 64° F. The frequency of droughts sufficient to affect water supplies, shown in Figure XII-3, is directly related to the extent to which the area is drought-resistant, shown in Figure XII-2. The frequency increases as the residual available for man's use becomes less. The critical areas and the area of greatest variability lie between the lines representing 80 percent and 20 percent frequency and are generally coincident with the Great Plains. The area east of the 20 percent line is the area of least variability and in general has adequate precipitation for normal crops. East of the Mississippi River years of insufficient rainfall to meet the demands of transpiration and evaporation occur less than 5 percent of the time.

PRINCIPAL DROUGHTS IN THE UNITED STATES

During the period 1881 to 1936 five of the fifteen worst drought years occurred during the last 7 years. Studies by the writer [7] indicate that since 1930 there has been a general decline in precipitation and rise in temperature. These two meteorologic conditions have combined to produce aggravated conditions of drought. It is possible that since the settlement of the country there has not been in the humid or semihumid States another drought period of the extent or severity experienced between 1930 and 1936. The early history of lakes in sections of the West indicate that in the late 1840's their beds were dry and were crossed by emigrant trails [3]. Data from the records of early settlers as compiled by Lynch [9] indicate that in southern California about 1830 there was a period of deficient precipitation which has not been surpassed. Composite tree-ring studies in northern California indicate a 5-year period ending in 1850 when tree rings were prevailingly thin [1]. All these evidences seem to point to a severe drought of wide extent about the period 1830 to 1850. None of the students of climatic cycles and trends have definitely determined any trend that would indicate a change in climate or a definite cyclic recurrence of drought conditions. If it is true that our climate is not changing, then the present precipitation is best thought of as a low in an indeterminate and variable cycle.

DROUGHT MAGNITUDES

As droughts result from a combination of events there is no direct measure of their magnitude. Two measures most commonly used are deficiencies in precipitation and extent of area affected. Other partial measures of drought magnitude include crop yields, stream flow, groundwater levels, and (since 1930) work and direct-relief funds. Based on deficiencies in annual precipitation and area affected, the relative ranking

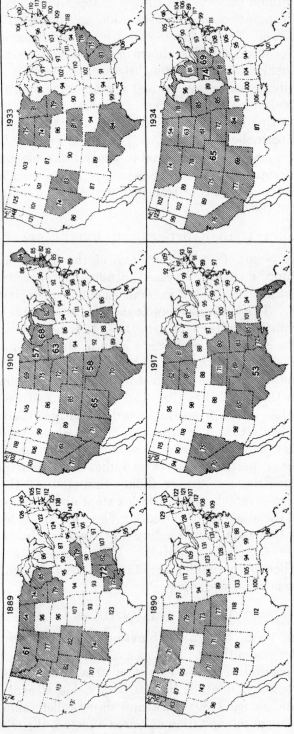

Fig. XII-4A.—Maps of the United States showing, by States, precipitation during eleven major drought years, in percentage of the mean.

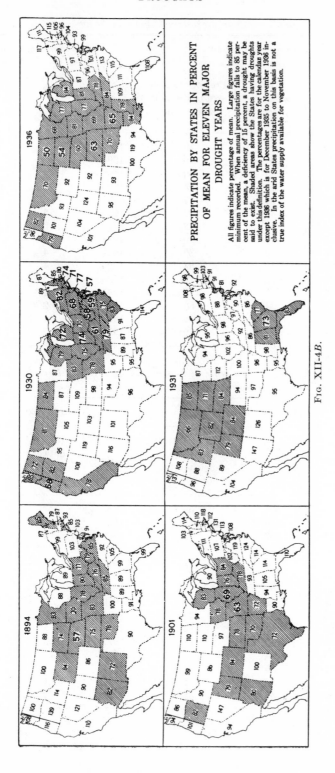

PRECIPITATION BY STATES IN PERCENT OF MEAN FOR ELEVEN MAJOR DROUGHT YEARS

All figures indicate percentage of mean. Large figures indicate minimum recorded. When annual precipitation falls to 85 percent of the mean, a deficiency of 15 percent, a drought may be said to exist. Shaded areas show the States having droughts under this definition. The percentages are for the calendar year except 1936 which is for December 1935 to November 1936 inclusive. In the arid States precipitation on this basis is not a true index of the water supply available for vegetation.

FIG. XII-4B.

TABLE 1.—*Fifteen worst drought years in the humid states*

No.	In order of extent			In chronologic order		
	Year	Area affected (percent)	Precipitation in area of drought (percent of mean)	Year	Interval between droughts (years)	Order of extent of area affected
1	1930	63	74	1889		5
2	1936	54	76	1894	5	3
3	1894	45	80	1895	1	12
4	1901	34	75	1896	1	14
5	1889	32	77	1901	5	4
6	1934	32	80	1904	3	11
7	1910	30	72	1910	6	7
8	1917	30	80	1917	7	8
9	1925	30	80	1921	4	10
10	1921	30	84	1925	4	9
11	1904	29	78	1930	5	1
12	1895	27	77	1931	1	15
13	1933	24	80	1933	2	13
14	1896	18	82	1934	1	6
15	1931	18	79	1936	2	2

TABLE 2.—*Fifteen worst drought years in the semiarid states (North Dakota, South Dakota, Nebraska, Kansas, and Oklahoma)*

No.	In order of extent			In chronologic order		
	Year	Area affected (percent)	Precipitation in area of deficiency (percent of mean)	Year	Interval between droughts (years)	Order of extent of area affected
1	1936	100	58	1887		15
2	1934	100	65	1888	1	10
3	1910	100	71	1890	2	6
4	1894	80	70	1893	3	9
5	1917	78	71	1894	1	4
6	1890	68	76	1895	1	11
7	1933	66	77	1901	6	13
8	1931	65	80	1910	9	3
9	1893	57	74	1913	3	12
10	1888	57	82	1914	1	14
11	1895	45	78	1917	3	5
12	1913	44	84	1931	14	8
13	1901	35	75	1933	2	7
14	1914	35	83	1934	1	2
15	1887	35	85	1936	2	1

for 15 drought periods in 1881 to 1936 is shown quantitatively in tables 1 and 2, and the areal extent of 11 major droughts is shown graphically in Figure XII-4. The No. 1 drought of 1936 in the humid States had only a temporary effect on stream flow and ground-water levels. Records of scattered wells showed that exceptionally low ground-water levels were reached during the summer of 1936. On the other hand, during the winter of 1936–37 there was sufficient recharge to restore the levels to their normal position, thus indicating the drought-resistant qualities of the humid States. In the subhumid States the continuity of droughts since 1930 has resulted in a lowered water table, which has been only partly restored.

EFFECT OF DROUGHTS ON GROUND WATER AND SURFACE WATER

The immediate effects of droughts are (1) cessation of all surface runoff, with a corresponding reduction in stream flow; (2) a depletion in soil moisture; and (3) a lowering of the ground-water table and decrease in ground-water runoff.

So far as stream flow is dependent on surface runoff from rains the drought effect is immediate and continuous throughout rainless periods or periods when precipitation is less than the rate of infiltration. As normally all surface runoff that may have accumulated in river channels flows out of the average-sized drainage basin in from 8 to 12 days after a rain, rainless periods exceeding 8 to 12 days constitute drought in respect to streams whose flows depend on surface runoff.

The effects of droughts on soil moisture are shown directly by the growth of plants whose roots penetrate the moisture zone. Shallow-rooted grasses may be able to draw moisture only from a soil zone containing 1 or 2 inches of water. Such supplies are quickly exhausted during the summer, and rainless periods of short duration result in a tendency for such grasses to wither. Deep-rooted vegetation draws from a large reserve and is therefore more drought-resistant.

In general, ground water is the last to reflect drought effects and also the last to reflect the cessation of a drought. Inasmuch as outflow from ground water furnishes most of the sustained part of stream flow and is the source of practically all rural and many urban water supplies, the effect of droughts on the stability of ground water is of vital importance. All observations of ground-water levels in areas where there is normally an excess of 10 to 20 inches of precipitation over the demands of evaporation and transpiration (see Fig. XII-2) indicate that whereas outstanding droughts, such as those of 1930 and 1936, cause rapid declines in ground-water levels, with resultant decrease in stream flow and drying up of springs and wells, the return of normal precipitation brings rapid recharge and return to normal conditions. There seems to be nothing in the ground-water records in humid areas to indicate that any droughts so far experienced in such areas have had anything more than a temporary effect upon ground-water levels.

In progressing from the humid to the subhumid and semiarid areas, however, the residual between precipitation and evaporation becomes less and less, and not only is the effect of droughts more immediately severe but the rate of recovery is correspondingly slow. There seems to be no reason to doubt that for the last 10 years or more in parts of the subhumid and semiarid areas precipitation has been less than the demands of evaporation and transpiration. In these areas progressive downward trends of ground-water levels have been noted. Even in these areas, however, it is encouraging to note that in years such as 1935, when precipitation was more nearly normal, there was a general tendency for recharge of ground water to take place. It is confidently expected that eventually ground-water levels in these areas will return to normal except in localities of heavy pumping from wells.

ALLEVIATION OF DROUGHT

Man can do little to modify the natural climatic phenomena that combine to cause droughts. He can, however, do much to lessen their impact on his activities through foresightedness in maintaining hold-over storage; in digging deeper wells or in lowering intakes to ground-water supplies; in adopting all practices known to conserve water; in limiting or adjusting economic development to assured sources of water supply; and in adopting a mode or scale of living in conformity with the dictates of nature.

In humid areas the normal excess of water is such that the maintenance of reliable water supplies is rarely a serious problem. From east to west, however, the residual between rainfall and runoff becomes less and less and the problem of its conservation becomes greater and greater. In much of the subhumid plains area water conservation revolves around the saving of as little as an inch or less of water. In such areas complete control of all surface runoff through strip cropping, terracing, and other measures of soil conservation, or storage in farm ponds, back of check dams, and in water holes will normally involve annually less than half an inch of water. The portion of this half inch that escapes evaporation forms an increment to soil moisture, and where the geologic conditions are favorable the small part that percolates through the zone of soil moisture aids in maintaining a ground-water table. In these plains areas the outflow from ground water that appears as stream flow may be considerably less than half an inch. This amount of water if stored in reservoirs would provide for municipal water supply or if diverted would provide for a moderate amount of irrigation. Complete conservation and storage measures in much of the Great Plains area would thus involve an amount of water sufficient in general to maintain domestic supplies but insignificant as a basis for crop production.

In the arid and semiarid regions droughts relate largely to shortages in water supply for irrigation. Through the development of excess storage sufficient to retain the runoff from occasional large floods, through snow surveys and studies by which spring runoff available for storage can be forecast, and through close coordination of land use to available water supply, losses and suffering can be kept at a minimum. The greatest danger in such areas, however, results from man-made droughts through overdevelopment based on inadequate information as to what constitutes a reliable water supply. If development is based on runoff during years in which the precipitation may be above normal and sufficient to provide water supply at a ratio of 2 acres for every 100 acres of contributing area, serious economic loss will result during subnormal years when the yield from 100 acres may be sufficient to irrigate only 1 acre.

REFERENCES

1. Bowman, Isaiah, Our expanding and contracting deserts: Geog. Rev., January, 1935, pp. 43–61.

2. Condra, G. E., Relation of drought to water use in Nebraska: Nebraska Univ., Dept. Conservation and Survey Div., Bull. 6, 1934.

3. Harding, S. T., Changes in lake levels in the Great Basin area: Civil Engineering, vol. 5, No. 2, pp. 87–92, 1935.

4. Hay, Robert, Water resources of a portion of the Great Plains: U. S. Geol. Survey 16th Ann. Rept., pt. 2, pp. 535–588, 1895.

5. Hoyt, J. C., Droughts of 1930–34: U. S. Geol. Survey Water-Supply Paper 680, 106 pp., 1936.

6. Hoyt, J. C., Drought of 1936, with discussion of the significance of drought in relation to climate: U. S. Geol. Survey Water-Supply Paper 820, 62 pp., 1938.

7. Hoyt, W. G., and others, Studies of relations between rainfall and run-off in the United States: U. S. Geol. Survey Water-Supply Paper 772, 301 pp., 1936.

8. Köppen, Wladimer, Versuch einer Klassification der Klimate: Geog. Zeitschr., Band 6, pp. 593–611, 657–679, 1900.

9. Lynch, N. B., Rainfall cycles historically deduced: Eng. News-Record, Sept. 17, 1931.

10. Possibilities of shelter-belt planting in the Plains region, 201 pp., U. S. Forest Service, 1935.

11. Powell, J. W., Lands of the arid region: 45th Cong., 2d sess., Ex. Doc. 73, p. 3, 1878.

12. Russell, R. J., Dry climates of the United States: California Univ., Pub. in Geography, vol. 5, No. 1, pp. 1–41, 1931; No. 5, pp. 245–274, 1932.

13. Thornthwaite, C. W., The climates of North America according to a new classification: Geog. Rev., vol. 21, pp. 633–655, 1931.

14. Thornthwaite, C. W., The climates of the earth: Geog. Rev., vol. 23, pp. 433–440, 1933.

15. Thornthwaite, C. W., The Great Plains, in migration and economic opportunity chapter 5, pp. 202–250, Pennsylvania Univ., 1936.

CHAPTER XIII

PHYSICAL CHANGES PRODUCED BY THE WATER OF THE EARTH

XIIIA. INTRODUCTION

WILLIAM H. TWENHOFEL[1]

GENERAL CONDITIONS

Water is one of the two most important of the media or agents of transportation of sediments, the atmosphere being the other. Water is considered to transport a greater quantity of sediments than the atmosphere. The work of water involves the acquirement, transportation and deposition of sediments. Acquirement and transportation are usually termed "erosion." Deposition is an essential process of sedimentation.

All free waters on the land and most of the free waters in the rocks are on their way to the sea or to some inland body of water. In passage the waters acquire burdens from the soils and rocks over and through which they flow, and they thus perform the work of erosion. These acquired burdens are deposited over stream channels and flood plains, over the bottoms of the bodies of standing or impounded water into which the streams ultimately empty, and to some extent within the rocks themselves. The burdens carried consist of materials in solution and suspension, of colloidal particles, and of material rolled or pushed on the bottoms of channels. The last is commonly designated the bed or tractional load, and the transportation is said to be effected by traction.

The dissolved load is largely acquired by solution of materials in the soils and rocks over and through which the waters flow. Some is acquired from the atmosphere. The colloidal load is acquired by contact of water with soil and rock containing colloidal materials or materials that may assume colloidal form on contact with water and contained substances. Suspended loads are acquired by abrasion, impact, grinding, or hydraulic action and transported because of turbulence in the water whereby upward-directed currents prevent settling. Transportation by rolling or sliding depends on the pushing and lifting effects of currents.

Ability to transport materials in solution depends on the solvent power of the water for each material, and this ability is absolutely independent of velocity, as is also the ability to transport colloidal materials. Transportation of materials in suspension depends upon the dimensions,

[1] Professor of Geology, University of Wisconsin, Madison, Wisc.

specific gravities, and shapes of the particles and upon the velocity and turbulence of the water, and turbulence is directly or indirectly due to velocity. Particles of spherical shape are more difficultly transported in suspension than particles of other shapes, owing to the greater ease with which spherical particles settle. Large particles or particles of high specific gravity require greater velocity and correspondingly higher turbulence for transportation in suspension than small particles or particles of low specific gravity.

According to Lane [4] an upward velocity of 1 centimeter per second is required to maintain in suspension a particle of quartz 0.1 millimeter in diameter, but only an upward velocity of 0.25 centimeter per second for particles 0.05 millimeter in diameter. Thus it is more difficult to transport large particles in suspension than small particles, and the degree of turbulence necessary for transportation of particles decreases very rapidly as the particles become smaller.

Transportation by traction is also dependent upon velocity but is greatly modified by the shapes of the particles. Spherical and ellipsoidal particles are more readily rolled than those of other shapes. Particles of two large and one small dimension—that is, disk-shaped—may roll on edge if they are very thin; otherwise they travel at times by leaping or saltation, or they roll over parallel to one of the longer axes and finally may be expected to come to rest with the inclination of one of the longer axes upcurrent.

Ability to transport in terms of the dimensions of the particles transported is termed "competency;" ability to transport in terms of the total weight of the particles is termed "capacity." Loads are quantities actually carried and are rarely equal to capacity. Both capacity and competency are affected by the density and viscosity of the water. Density and viscosity depend upon the temperature of the water and the quantity of materials in solution and colloidal form and also upon the quantity of materials in suspension. Transportation by traction bears little relation to density.

Any checking of velocity causes decrease of turbulence, settling of a part of the suspended load, and possibly transformation of that which settles to tractional load and cessation of movement of a part of the tractional load.

Colloidal particles carry electric charges, and this load may be deposited when the colloidal particles become aggregated or flocculated. This takes place on contact of the transporting waters with other waters carrying electrolytes in solution, or waters containing colloidal particles carrying electric charges of opposite sign. This contact may occur at or below the junction of two streams or where streams enter the sea. It may also occur where streams enter lakes, particularly salt lakes. The dissolved load may be deposited if chemical reactions take place to produce substances which for the existing conditions are relatively insoluble. The chief methods of deposition of dissolved materials, however, seem to be connected with organic processes.

PROCESSES OF ACQUIREMENT OF LOAD

Acquirement of load by flowing water is accomplished by both physical and chemical processes. Physical processes consist of wear or abrasion and impact, resulting from passage of water and its load over soils and rocks. The wear or abrasion produced by the direct action of pure water on rocks is not great unless velocities are high. Indirectly it may be great because of undermining. The wear on soils may be great, as particles may be detached from others by reason of expansion due to absorption of water and also by direct abrasion. The wear or abrasion may become great when caused by waters carrying such abrasive materials as silts, sands, and large particles, and is somewhat commensurate with the hardness of the abrasives carried and the softness of the rock or the soil acted upon. This is illustrated by the rapid cutting through of elbows in oil lines leading from wells that yield large quantities of quartz sand with their oils. As quartz is probably the most abundant abrasive material carried by water and is also one of the hardest of minerals, it follows that extensive cutting may be expected. Most of this is done on the surface, but a little may be done in caves. Impact on materials over which the water flows by particles carried in suspension or by traction also adds to load.

Chemical load is acquired by solution or by decomposition followed by solution. Such rocks as limestone, gypsum, anhydrite, and rock salt are readily removed in solution by surface and ground waters, and as a result soluble rocks may have mazes of underground passages, as illustrated by the caverns of Virginia, the Mammoth Cave of Kentucky, the Carlsbad Caverns of New Mexico, and others. In rocks composed of relatively insoluble materials, such as granites or gabbros, decomposition first leads to destruction of the silicates, releasing both soluble and colloidal materials, both of which may be removed.

FACTORS CONTROLLING RATES OF LOAD ACQUIREMENT

The rates at which soils and rocks yield loads to aqueous transportation depend upon so many variables that general statements are difficult. Important variables are the physical, chemical, and mineral character of the soils and rocks, the structure of the rocks, climate, plant growth, and slope or relief.

Character of rock and soils.—There are great differences in the character of rocks with respect to abrasion, impact, and grinding. Soft rocks yield more readily than hard, brittle rocks more readily than tough, porous rocks more readily than compact, soluble more readily than insoluble. Such soft rocks as clays, shales, and limestones are readily cut. The absorptive capacities of rocks are important for two reasons. If their textures permit large absorption, there is much less water to flow off over the surface, and correspondingly physical erosion is reduced, as the absorbed water moves too slowly to have much effect. Rocks of high absorption are extremely susceptible to destruction in regions where freezing takes place, as the freezing of the water in the pores leads to rupture of the rock.

The physical characters of the soils are large factors in the acquirement of load. Soils that have fine texture are composed largely of clay minerals in the dispersed condition. Not much absorption is possible, and water is thus forced to flow off over the surface and soil is removed to the extent permitted by other factors. If these same soils have the colloidal particles in a flocculated or granulated condition, their absorptive capacities are increased, runoff is decreased, and removal of materials through runoff is lessened. Soils that contain organic matter have higher absorptive capacities than otherwise similar soils in which organic matter is lacking, and thus they undergo physical erosion less readily.

The chemical and mineral characteristics of rocks and soils may exert a greater influence in the acquirement of load than the physical characteristics, particularly with respect to the loads carried in solution. This is especially true of such soluble rocks as limestone, gypsum, anhydrite, and rock salts. Rock salts are soluble in any water. Waters containing carbon dioxide and the various organic acids and other acids derived from the atmosphere and decomposition are strong solvents for limestones and many minerals. Even such resistant minerals as the feldspars undergo some solution in waters of this class, and most minerals that are not readily soluble undergo decompositional changes, with the production of substances that are more readily soluble. Thus feldspars change to carbonates, hydrous silicates, and silicon dioxide; and the ferromagnesian minerals result in ferric hydroxides, silicon dioxide, and carbonates. The carbonates are soluble and may be removed as they are formed. The hydroxides, hydrous silicates, and silicon dioxide are colloids when formed and may be removed at the same rate.

The chemical characters of soils are also important in determining the aqueous load. Soils that have been leached of soluble constituents are very likely to have the soil particles in a dispersed condition and thus poorly or nonabsorptive. This increases runoff and favors physical acquirement of load. Soils that contain soluble materials are likely to have the particles in a flocculated condition and thus have greater absorptive capacity and less runoff.

Rock structure.—Structural features of rocks that have influence on acquirement of load are the position of the stratification in sedimentary rocks and the extent of jointing and faulting in rocks of all kinds. Strata that are inclined permit the entrance of water more readily than strata in a horizontal position. Moreover, weak horizontal strata may be protected against aqueous attack by overlying resistant strata. Rocks broken by numerous joints and faults permit greater entrance and passage of water than those that are not so broken.

Climate.—Climate is extremely important in the acquirement of load by water. The most influential factor is precipitation, but the extent of acquirement of load is not a direct function of the quantity of precipitation. There is a direct effect resulting from precipitation and also an indirect effect because of the plant cover, which is controlled by precipitation as the most important factor. The total quantity of precipitation is less important than the rate at which it falls. A fall of 3 inches of rain spread over a week, with a small quantity falling over most of each day, may have little erosive effect, whereas, if the 3 inches should fall in less than an hour on one day, the soils and underlying rock would be unable to absorb the water, the runoff would be great, and there would be acquirement of load to some degree commensurate with the runoff. If the rapid fall of rain should be coincident with or immediately follow thawing of the soil materials, the acquirement of load would be greater than at other times. However, it should not be forgotten that a spread precipitation does not altogether prevent acquirement of load, as the water that is absorbed and thus enters the ground acquires some dissolved and colloidal matter.

Vegetable cover.—Some sort of vegetation develops on all lands that are not too cold and receive sufficient moisture to support plant life. The living plants break the blows of the falling water, and the water drops more or less gently from leaves and branches upon the dead litter that accumulates to a greater or less extent wherever plants grow. There the waters find lateral movement restrained or prevented. Passage over the surface is retarded, and time is provided for soaking into the substratum. The water is effectively filtered in its passage through the plant litter and thus enters the soil with little or nothing in suspension. Downward movement is aided by root passages and the numerous burrows made by the organisms that always dwell in greater or less abundance in all soils supporting plant growth. Runoff is greatly lessened and often prevented, and physical erosion of the surface ordinarily proceeds at a pace that is usually more than balanced by additions to the soil cover at its base through decomposition of underlying rocks. A soil cover thus protected tends to be thick. Data do not seem to be available with respect to the merits of forest, bush, or grass in retarding runoff and the limitations in acquirement of loads from these different growths. Studies [1] have been made of interception and holding of water by certain grasses and weeds, and it was found in a series of experiments that fully developed wheat held 50 to 80 percent of the water that fell, depending on the rate of application; an open growth of needle grass on upland prairie retained approximately 50 percent of rain applied at the rate of a quarter of an inch in 30 minutes; little bluestem 50 to 60 percent when applied at the rate of half an inch in 30 minutes; big bluestem and tall panic grass 47 percent when applied at a rate of 1 inch an hour and 87 percent when applied at a rate of an eighth of an inch in 30 minutes. Bind weed intercepted 17 percent when water was applied a the rate of half an inch in 30 minutes and 50 percent when an eighth of an inch was applied in the same interval. Buffalo grass retained 30 percent when half an inch was applied in 30 minutes and 74 percent when an eighth of an inch was applied in 30 minutes. Some of this water ultimately entered the ground, but most of it was probably evaporated from the plants.

However, erosion is not prevented even if all the water enters the ground. The water in its passage through the plant litter acquires solvents in the form of carbon dioxide and organic acids and is thus well equipped to dissolve, or decompose and dissolve, the soils and rocks with which it comes into contact. Thus when the water returns to the surface at some lower level it has acquired a load in the form of dissolved and colloidal materials.

Removal of a plant cover alters conditions. The soil loses its armor and has no protection against aqueous attack on its surface. When rain strikes the defenseless soil, the water immediately becomes turbid with suspended matter, is absorbed by the soil and filtered of its suspended materials. The openings in the soil quickly become clogged, so that additional falling water must flow away on the surface with consequent erosion of the soil. If a forest is cut away and the cutting is not followed by burning or cultivation, the defense may be little impaired, but if either of these follow deforestation, the soil becomes defenseless. The same is true of cultivation of a prairie. Unless the defenseless soils are given artificial protection, physical erosion on the surface is inevitable, and large loads are acquired. The first few years of cultivation may not cause very severe damage, as the soil materials contain much humus, so that their absorptive properties may be considerable, but more or less proportional with disappearance of the humus are an increase in runoff, a decrease in infiltration, a relative increase in suspended and tractional loads, and a relative decrease in the dissolved load. The increased runoff and decreased infiltration also result in fall of the water table, development of intermittency of brooks and creeks, and decline of springs and shallow wells.

Grazing may have a somewhat similar but perhaps lessened effect, depending upon its extent. If the grazing is moderate, little harm may be done, but if extensive, the results may not be greatly different from those of cultivation.

Slope or relief.—Movement of flowing water is a response to gravity, and thus the slope determines velocity of flow. A quadruple increase of slope causes a doubling of velocity. Abrasion, impact, and grinding are more or less direct geometrical functions of velocity and so likewise is ability to transport suspended and tractional loads. Suspended and tractional loads are much more readily acquired on steep than on gentle slopes, or, stated differently, the steeper the slopes, other factors being equal, the more readily is a surface eroded and a load acquired.

EROSION AND DEPOSITION IN STREAMS

Erosion in the streams is done on banks and beds. Pure waters do not have great effects, but waters provided with tools in the form of small to large particles have much erosive power. Most streams are crooked, and the currents alternately impinge on banks wherever the sides of channels are concave toward the streams. Crookedness favors turbulence, which in turn favors detachment of particles from banks and beds and also gives large increase in ability to transport the detached materials. Both banks and beds are eroded on the convex sides of currents (that is, along the concave banks of the bends), bottoms are deepened there to form the deeps, bends are extended into the flood plains, and thus the currents progressively become more convex. Turbulence is greatest in times of high water, and the deeps then attain greatest depths and the banks are also then most actively cut. At times of low water the currents may have little effect on either banks or beds, and deposition may take place where previously there had been erosion.

The flow of streams may be lamellar or turbulent. The lamellar flow exists commonly only at low velocities and hence may be disregarded here. The turbulence arises from friction to flow caused by irregularities of banks and bed and from differences in velocity in different parts of the stream. For simplicity of consideration a stream may be considered to have one single thread of maximum velocity of flow. On each side of this thread are areas of maximum turbulence, and on the outer sides of these in turn are areas of less rapid flow and little turbulence. Turbidity bears a direct ratio to turbulence. From the areas of maximum turbulence there are turbidity gradients into the thread of maximum velocity of flow and also into the areas of little turbulence. In the thread of maximum velocity the sediments moving from the areas of maximum turbulence are carried downstream and deposited elsewhere. The sediments carried into the marginal areas of little turbulence may be deposited there, with greatest deposition on the outer borders. In a straight stream with a channel of symmetrical profile the thread of maximum velocity may be expected to have a symmetrical position with respect to the marginal areas of maximum turbulence and the quiet marginal waters. On the convex side of the current in a crooked stream the area of maximum turbulence is narrow but very strong, and there is little or no area of quiet water, whereas on the other side the areas of maximum turbulence and of little turbulence may be expected to be wide. The turbidity gradient drops very steeply on the concave side of the current, but on the convex side turbulence may extend both to the edge of the current and downward to the bottom of the channel [5].

Turbulence lifts sediments from the bottom, and in straight streams with symmetrical profiles the bottoms are deepened and the materials of the sides are undermined and drop to the bottoms, whence they are removed. The channels thus deepen and widen. In crooked streams where the area of maximum turbulence is on the convex side of the channel, there is deepening and widening of the stream channel on that side and deposition on the other side. The widening on the convex side is done by undermining of the concave bank. The channel thus progressively becomes more crooked, and meander curves develop. The bottom of the stream progressively migrates over the area of travel. Bottoms change in depth owing to cutting in times of flood and filling in times of low water. Cutting prevails in degrading streams.

The bank eroded is termed "undercut" and the other bank the "slip-off slope." The bank of the slip-off slope is usually lower than that of the undercut slope, and the migration of a stream replaces the area eroded on one side by an approximately equal but somewhat lower area on the other side. Flood plains are thus lowered, and remnants of older flood plains may be left at asymmetrical levels on the valley sides.

If streams bring to valley bottoms more than they can carry away the processes are somewhat different. Filling takes place more or less generally over the bottoms of the channels. These may in time become filled to or even above the flood-plain surfaces, after which a new course is ultimately selected elsewhere. Cut and fill still take place, but the dominant process is fill. Under degrading conditions the dominant process is cut, the result being that the channels have a considerable degree of permanence, although there is much lateral migration. Under degrading conditions flood plains are covered to a greater or less extent during times of high water; under aggrading conditions they are certain to be extensively covered during times of high water. At times of flood the turbulence is very high in the channels and much less at the banks. Thus maximum deposition takes place on and near the banks, and natural levees are formed. Natural levees are also formed in aggrading streams, but deposition in the channels makes for instability of channel position and from time to time complete change of position. The results are that flood plains of aggrading streams are progressively buried beneath deposits of sediments.

The mineral matter carried in solution, in suspension, and by traction is abundant and bears a relation in both quantity and quality to the various factors considered. The streams of areas with dry climate carry greater loads of suspended and dissolved materials than those of areas with humid climate, and cultivated areas provide greater loads of suspended and dissolved materials than uncultivated areas. Streams of such uncultivated areas as most of Newfoundland, where the climate is humid, rarely carry muddy waters, whereas those of dry uncultivated areas like New Mexico and Arizona may carry very large loads at flood times. The streams of cultivated areas in some sections of the country at flood times carry loads comparable to those of arid and semiarid areas, particularly with respect to suspended matter.

METHODS OF RETARDING EROSION

Under natural conditions, runoff and physical erosion of the surface are retarded by a cover of dead and living vegetable matter and by root and animal passages in the soil. These conditions favor entrance of water into the ground. However, aqueous erosion cannot be prevented as long as water has access to rocks and soils. If all the water were compelled to enter the soil and rocks, there would be little or no physical erosion but increased chemical erosion. Cultivation and intense grazing destroy the protective plant covering and eliminate the various passages made by organisms. To retain the soil, runoff must be artificially controlled. This has been done in many regions through the construction of terraces by which the water is conducted from tops to bottoms of slopes by crooked channels, thus producing slow flow, little physical or surface erosion, and large infiltration. Dams have been constructed on many streams to prevent floods or to impound waters for irrigation or water supplies, for the maintenance of navigable waters or for the development of power. These dams have accomplished one or several of the desired objectives, have provided settling basins for sediments, and have prevented deposition on flood plains, but they have had little influence in preventing acquirement of load except that which might have been acquired from stream banks and beds if the waters had not been held back. The fundamental problem is prevention of erosion at the sources—that is, on the cultivated and pastured lands that are the places of stream beginnings. To retard such headwater erosion, vegetative covering of steep lands and removal of such lands from cultivation and close grazing are advocated.

WORK OF GROUND WATER

The work of the ground water consists of addition, subtraction (solution, leaching), and replacement. Abrasion, grinding, and impact are accomplished to a minor extent in caves, but each is small and may be disregarded.

Addition consists of the deposition of mineral matter from solution. This may be done in various kinds of small to large cavities in all places where these occur. Mineral matter may be deposited between grains of sand and particles of gravel, between and within shells, and in cracks and caves. Deposition between particles changes sand into sandstone and gravel into conglomerate. The cementing materials thus deposited may be any of those carried in solution, but the most common are calcite and quartz. The waters may be hot or cold; hot waters are not within the field of sedimentation. Most addition is probably effected below the water table, but there may be some above. For this reason the region beneath the water table has been termed the "zone of cementation," in contrast to the region above, which has been termed the "zone of weathering or subtraction."

Subtraction, or leaching, is effected through solution. Pure water does not have much solvent ability for most soil and rock materials, but water provided with carbon dioxide and organic, sulphuric, nitric, hydrochloric, hydrofluoric, and other acids has great solvent ability. These acids are acquired in the passage of rain through the air in falling, or from organic and soil materials through which the water filters after falling. Sulphuric acid is formed in the decomposition of sulphides, and some nitric acid may be formed in the decomposition of organic materials in the soils and from atmospheric discharge of electricity. Hydrochloric and hydrofluoric acids are discharged by volcanoes. Waters thus provided with solvents rather thoroughly leach the soils through which they percolate. Thus, in general, the easily soluble materials are removed, and only those soil materials remain which are insoluble under the prevailing conditions. If the soils and rocks contain decomposable materials, these may change to hydroxides, carbonates, and hydrous silicates, and, if any of these substances are soluble, they are removed. It thus results that soils of regions with vegetative cover are composed of some combinations of iron hydroxides, clay minerals, aluminum hydroxide, and quartz. Under some conditions the iron hydroxides are reduced to iron carbonate, which, being soluble in waters containing carbon dioxide, is removed. In certain regions the clay minerals may separate into aluminum hydroxide and quartz, and the quartz may be removed, leaving a soil composed of ferric and aluminum hydroxides. Sandstone and conglomerate have cements which may be removed by percolating waters to leave sand and gravel.

Some limestones are sufficiently porous and pervious to permit circulation of water, and crumbling may take place as a consequence.   In many rocks water is circulated along structural planes, and extensive solution takes place in such rocks as limestone, gypsum, anhydrite, and rock salt, so that these rocks become honeycombed by large and small passages.   Rock salt is so soluble that it does not appear on the surface except in very dry climates.

Replacement consists of the substitution of material in solution for something present in a rock, which in turn enters into solution.   The principle involved is that a mineral that is less soluble under the existing conditions takes the place of one that is more soluble, the more soluble mineral entering the solution.   Thus when water carrying silica flows over a carbonate the carbonate enters the solution and silica takes its place. The detailed structure of the replaced materials may be preserved.   Thus, wood replaced by silica may show the cell structure excellently, as in fossil cycad trunks in the Jurassic Sundance formation of the Black Hills region. Certain constituents dissolved in hot magmatic waters may replace other constituents in rocks such as limestone.

SEDIMENTATIONAL WORK IN IMPOUNDED WATERS

The sediments brought into the lakes and the sea are introduced in part by the streams—in solution, colloidal form, suspension, and by traction; in part they are derived by erosion from the shores and bottoms of these bodies of water through the work of the waves and currents in them; and in part they are dropped by the atmosphere.   The last are not here considered.

The sediments introduced by streams into impounded waters drop the tractional loads and the coarsest materials of the suspended loads as the current velocities decrease on meeting the resistance of the impounded waters.   In some places the currents and waves of the impounded waters aid stream currents, so that the sediments are not immediately dropped but are carried some distance from the shores.   Ordinarily the coarser parts of the loads are left adjacent to the mouths of streams to form what are known as the top-set, fore-set, and bottom-set deposits of deltas. Where the currents of bodies of impounded water aid the entering currents of streams the loads are carried beyond the mouths of the streams and are deposited to become a part of the offshore deposits.

The finer parts of the suspended loads and the materials in colloidal suspension float until flocculated into sufficiently large particles so as to sink under the influence of gravity.   Flocculation takes place on mingling of stream waters with other waters containing electrolytes in solution or colloids of electric charges opposite to those on the particles in suspension in the stream waters.   It is certain to take place in the sea, where fresh and salt waters mingle. Flocculation may be confined to a very small area if the waters are mingled rapidly. Under some conditions, however, the currents extend long distances into bodies of salt water, the fresh water because of less density flowing above the salt water, so that flocculation of the colloidal sediments takes place gradually and over an extensive area. Thus fine sediments may be carried tens and even hundreds of miles from the mouths of large streams. Flocculated particles contain large quantities of water and are hence of low density. Thus, they float readily in waters of little turbulence and may be transported long distances and may ultimately be deposited far from the places of entry; indeed, their deposition may be ocean-wide.

The colloidal loads of streams and their loads of fine materials in suspension consist of hydrous aluminum silicates, aluminum hydroxide, ferric hydroxides, manganese hydroxide, silicon dioxide, and rarer substances. Some of these have the capacity for base exchange and hence are changed in character when stream water mingles with salt water. If the settling takes place where the coarser parts of the suspended load and the tractional load are deposited, the colloids and fine suspended material are mingled with the other materials, but, if the colloids do not readily settle after flocculation or if flocculation is postponed until the other parts of the load are laid down, they may make a relatively pure deposit. It is also possible that under some conditions only colloidal and very fine materials are transported, and thus pure deposits are formed.

The dissolved loads are precipitated to some degree by chemical reactions and evaporation, but chiefly by organic processes. As transportation in solution is relatively easy, it follows that deposition is ocean-wide and there is little relation between the places of entry and the places of deposition.

The sediments derived from the shores and adjacent shallow bottoms are produced through the work of waves and currents in abrasion and impact, but there is some solution and also some decomposition of the materials. Impact and abrasion continue after dislodgement, there is grinding or crushing and materials ranging from colloidal particles to boulders are produced.

On most shores waves roll in with force related to the winds that cause most of them and to the size of the water body in which they are present. Large waves are rarely produced on small bodies of water. Waves strike shores at some angle that is seldom directly normal for any great distances. The energies of the waves are dissipated as they roll up the beaches or over shallow bottoms, and the water flows back under the influence of gravity. The velocity of the backward flow is ordinarily less than that of the onrush, hence the capacity and competency of the returning waters are less than those of the incoming waters. Incoming waters loaded to capacity and competency leave the coarsest materials on the beach, and even if they are not loaded to capacity they carry particles up to the extent of their competency and hence leave the coarsest parts of their loads on the beach. Only that which is within the range of competency of the returning waters is returned.

Waves and currents cut the bottoms to some level which is determined by the existing conditions. This is the baselevel of erosion for those conditions and is by some termed "wave base."

The backward-flowing waters form shore currents or undertow. The shore currents flow more or less parallel to the shores if the waves strike the shores obliquely. Thus they may carry sediments into the heads of bays to build bayhead beaches, or they may cross bays to build spits and bars.

Undertow, or movement of water outward, should take place on shores where the incoming waves are about normal to the shores, or in bays into which currents are moving on both shores. As the movement of waves is rarely normal to the shores, it should follow that undertow from such causes is rare. If currents move into a bay on both shores the water may be expected to return outward over the deeper parts of the bay. Such movement is known to be very strong at times and to have much competency and capacity. The currents coming into a bay may have less competency and capacity than the outgoing waters, and hence the bayhead shores may be eroded and coarse sediments may be carried outward to be deposited in the deeper parts of a bay and even beyond the threshold of a bay, whereas the shallower bottoms on the sides of the bay may contain finer sediments.

Water carried landward by waves is also returned seaward by rip currents which are seaward-moving bands of surface waters. These carry loads of suspended fine sediments outward from the shore (6).

If a sea bottom is up to the level at which waves and currents may erode it, the waves may break some distance from the shores, and ultimately there may be formed a barrier beach inland from the places of breaking. However, as the waters are deepened by erosion of the bottom outward from the barrier beach, the beach may ultimately be attacked and removed and its composing materials carried to deeper bottoms.

REFERENCES

No attempt has been made to give complete references here, but Nos. 2, 6, 7, and 8 give extensive bibliographies, to which the reader is referred.

1. Clarks, O. R., Interception of rainfall by herbaceous vegetation: Science, new ser., vol. 86, pp. 591–592, 1937.

2. Gilbert, G. K., The transportation of debris by running water: U. S. Geol. Survey Prof. Paper 86, 1914.

3. Hjulström, F., Studies of the morphological activity of rivers as illustrated by the River Fjris: Upsala Univ., Geol. Inst., Bull., vol. 25, pp. 221–527, 1935.

4. Lane, E. W., Notes on the formation of sand: Am. Geophys. Union Trans., 19th Ann. Meeting, pp. 505–508, 1938.

5. Leighly, J. B., Toward a theory of the morphological significance of turbulence in the flow of streams: California Univ. Pub. in Geology, vol. 6, No. 1, pp. 1–22; 1932; Turbulence and the transportation of rock debris by streams: Geog. Rev., vol. 24, pp. 453–464, 1934.

6. Shepard, F. P., Emery, K. O., and LaFond, E. C., Rip currents: a process of geological importance: Jour. Geology, vol. 49, pp. 337–369, 1941.

7. Trask, P. D., Modern marine sediments, Tulsa, Okla., Am. Assoc. Petroleum Geologists, 1939.

8. Twenhofel, W. H., and collaborators, Treatise on sedimentation, Baltimore, Md., Williams & Wilkins Co., 1932.

9. Twenhofel, W. H., Principles of sedimentation, New York, McGraw-Hill Co., 1939.

XIIIB. SOIL EROSION

HARRY R. LEACH[1]

In the geomorphic development of land forms and drainage channels, water is the chief agent of land sculpture. Coincident with or following geologic uplifts and movements, erosional processes become active in sculpturing mountain massifs, dissecting plateaus, carving canyons, and developing other land forms. From the initial disintegration of crystalline rock by exfoliation and hydrolysis to the ultimate assortment and consolidation of sediments in the sea, water plays a remarkable rôle. Rock surfaces are disintegrated by the action of water, frost, and ice as a preliminary step to soil formation. Decomposition of mineral crystals and granules begins with hydrolysis, which leads to solution and hydration and to the breakdown into finely divided material. The products of these processes are transported from their source to their final resting place mainly through the work of ice and water.

The development of the soil and its subsequent natural erosion is but part of the long cycle of geologic and geomorphic processes that slowly but continuously circulate the material forming the surface of the lithosphere. It is, however, that phase of the cycle which most intimately affects mankind and his welfare. The more majestic and spectacular erosional work of water shown in the sculpturing of high mountain peaks and deep canyons is of relatively little economic importance in comparison with the depletion of agricultural lands by accelerated erosional processes; and the preservation of irreplaceable productive soils is a matter of grave concern. The present discussion is therefore confined to erosional processes and their control on such lands.

As early as the middle of the eighteenth century a few of the more observing planters in the United States recognized the growing menace of uncontrolled erosion to their lands, but it is only within the last two decades that the general public has awakened to the irreparable consequences that follow the careless and unintelligent use of productive lands. In 1935 the Soil Conservation Service of the Department of Agriculture published a map and supporting tables showing the extent of erosion in the United States. These were based on a reconnaissance survey deline-

---

[1] Soil conservationist, Head, Section of Land-Use Studies, Hydrologic Division, Soil Conservation Service, United States Department of Agriculture, Washington, D. C. Died June 24, 1941.

ating areas affected by erosion. The approximate areas affected by different types and degrees of erosion are given in the following table.

Areas within which at least 25 percent of the land has been affected by erosion
[Reconnaissance erosion survey of the United States, 1935]

Type and degree of erosion	Million acres	Percent
Little or no erosion..................................	576	30.3
Moderate sheet and gully erosion......................	776	40.7
Severe sheet and gully erosion........................	193	10.2
Principally wind erosion..............................	213	11.2
Mountains, badlands, mesas, canyons...................	145	7.6
Total, excluding large cities and bodies of water........	1,903	100.0

In this table "moderate sheet erosion" designates a loss of 25 to 75 percent of the topsoil. "Severe sheet erosion" indicates a loss of 75 to 100 percent of the topsoil and in some areas part of the subsoil. Both processes affect areas having scattered gullies. "Severe gully erosion" indicates the formation of numerous gullies, generally deep, usually accompanied by more or less sheet or wind erosion, processes which in the more arid regions are generally active.

The widespread extent of erosion on agricultural lands has led the Federal Government to initiate investigations into the underlying causes of such erosion and the measures by which it can be stopped or controlled. It has been found that the normal geologic erosion has in most areas been greatly accelerated by the detrimental farming practices used on the land and that much of this damage can be corrected by moderate changes in the practices.

The character of the soil itself greatly affects its susceptibility to erosion. The soil is a product of the material from which it was derived and the environment under which it developed, and the environment is the more influential in determining its characteristics. The unceasing physical, chemical, and biologic processes that have gradually changed the parent material into the present-day soil have been profoundly affected by climatic and physiographic environment. The influence of climate has been exerted through numerous factors, including the extent and frequency of wetting and drying of the soil, the amount of precipitation that has infiltrated into and percolated through the soil body, the soil temperature and its stimulus on biotic activity, and the kind and density of the vegetation the soil has supported. Topography has affected the drainage of the soil and likewise its stability against creep and slippage. The vegetal cover has not only profoundly modified the composition and structure of the soil but has protected it from the erosive agencies of wind and water and given it increased stability. Both of these effects have fostered the uninterrupted continuance of soil-forming processes.

Throughout the greater part of the United States the soil is between 2 and 10 feet in depth. Areas where the soil is less than 2 feet or more than 10 feet deep are relatively small. The manner in which the soil has been formed has led to the development of a profile—the vertical section from the ground surface to the parent material—consisting of a series of successive layers that grade from the more or less thoroughly changed surface layers to the but slightly changed layers lying on the parent material.

It is in the uppermost layers, the topsoil, that the complex processes of soil development have been most active. This is the mellow, fertile, productive layer that furnishes the bulk of the plant food for crops. There is an almost abrupt change in fertility and productivity from the topsoil to the subsoil on which it rests, and the change is much more pronounced in cropped lands because of the limitation imposed by the depth of plowing on the stirring, mixing, and fertilizing of the soil. This underlying subsoil, however, performs an invaluable service in providing a reservoir for the storage of soil water from which the plants may draw needed moisture.

The topsoil generally averages about 7 or 8 inches in depth. The relative infertility of the subsoil makes the loss of the topsoil of major economic importance, because even with intensive effort the productivity of the subsoil can be made to approach that of the topsoil only after a long period of time. The loss of topsoil is the greatest factor in reducing valuable crop lands to the status of marginal or submarginal lands. Under such circumstances the agrarian population gradually migrates to virgin or fertile tracts, while the abandoned lands with their more sparse and inferior vegetal cover are left subject to the accelerated effects of erosion.

The principal types of water erosion are sheet erosion and gully erosion. Both may be operative within a single tract, but the dominant type is usually used as the basis of classification.

Sheet erosion is the process of slowly removing soil from all parts of the sloping surface of a field or tract, resulting in the gradual planation of the entire surface. It is naturally more active on the steeper and more exposed parts of the area, and in these parts the topsoil has suffered its greatest loss, not infrequently having been entirely removed, leaving the subsoil exposed. Erosion of this type frequently manifests itself in discolored, galled spots, areas of less vigorous crop growth, accumulations at the foot of slopes, and discernible soil and vegetal differences. Sheet erosion is caused by storm runoff that develops innumerable rills and streamlets, which score the surface with more or less minute channels. The scars and channels thus developed are subsequently eradicated before they can stabilize into permanent rills, gullies, and watercourses, either by tillage operations or through the resistance and choking by natural vegetation and soil wash. This recurring process causes the gradual planation of the land surface without definite change in configuration. Sheet erosion is much more widespread than is generally suspected, because the gradual loss is not easily observed from year to year except as the loss of fertility is reflected in poor crops. Sheet erosion is illustrated in Figure XIIIb-1.

Gully erosion consists of the development of relatively deep, steep-sided channels from small rills and watercourses that have not been eradicated by tillage and have become too deep to permit normal farming

Fig. XIIIb-1.—Sheet erosion following an intense rain on a field having a 2-inch stand of fall oats, McLennan County, Texas.

operations. They are caused by concentration of runoff waters on steep slopes and the high erosive power in the large volumes and rapid velocities of the concentrated flows. Two rather distinct processes are involved—the cutting back of the head of the gully by torrential runoff in intense storms, and the undercutting and caving of the sides by moderate but more protracted runoff. Conditions conducive to gully erosion are steep slopes, main watercourses materially lower than the surrounding terrane, and high rainfall intensities. Gullies are frequently cut back from the steep hillsides of a stream or flood plain into the relatively flat but higher-lying agricultural lands. They may also develop in cultivated fields from careless field operations that allow concentration of runoff or provide a channel more accessible for rapid runoff. They may develop in a rut caused by a wagon wheel driven up or down hill on soft ground. Gully erosion is illustrated in Figure XIIIb-2.

The process of erosion is directly dependent on three factors—the erodibility of the soil, the energy of the erosive agents, and the protective influence of the vegetal cover. In water erosion the erosive agents are precipitation and runoff.

Erodibility of the soil is its susceptibility to erosion. No satisfactory measure of erodibility has yet been found. It is known to depend on several more or less intimately related factors, the chief of which appear to be the structure of the soil, its stratification and depth, the permeability of the upper horizons, and the amount of instability created by the

Fig. XIIIв-2.—Beginning of gully encroachment on farming land, Houston County, Minn.

slope on which it lies. Up to a certain point soil moisture is an important factor. Owing to the fact that cohesion is reduced by lack of moisture, soils are more erodible when dry than when moist or damp. This condition is not unusual in subhumid and semiarid regions where dry periods are frequent. More obscure factors are the organic and colloidal content, the dispersability of its textural components, the presence of minerals promoting flocculation, and other factors whose importance is not yet fully known.

The erosive power of rainfall and runoff arises through the dissipation of the energy possessed by the falling raindrops and the water flowing over the soil surface. In rains of sufficient intensity to produce surficial runoff the energy expended by the rain falling on a slope of ordinary length may and usually does exceed the energy expended by the runoff. The erosive power of raindrops definitely increases with the size of the drop, but what little evidence there is indicates that in a given locality there is only a slight increase in drop size with increase in intensity. The increase in drop velocity, however, combined with the greater mass of rain, increases the erosive power of rainfall at a rate greater than the increase in intensity. Surface soil packing by the impact of rain and clogging of soil pores by sediment carried in the infiltrated water introduce secondary effects that modify the erosive action of rainfall.

The erosive power of runoff is derived from the turbulence possessed by the flowing water. Laminar or stream-line flow, having no turbulent motion, is not erosive, but it is improbable that any part of the surficial runoff during a storm is ever laminar. The impact of falling rain and the relative roughness of the surface over which it flows maintain a state of turbulence that precludes the presence of stream-line flow. Turbulent motion causes both the lossening and scouring of the surface soil and the transportation of the abraded material. The erosive power of runoff increases rapidly with increase of the volume and velocity of flow. On steep slopes erosion may be produced by direct impact of runoff, this effect ranging from undercutting of dense sod cover to scouring and under-mining at the heads of large gullies. The capacity to produce erosive action can be called potential erosivity. It is dependent on the combined energy of the rainfall and runoff but is not entirely independent of the character of the surface on which it acts, as surface roughness causes part of the turbulence that makes the runoff erosive.

The intimate relation between the intensity of rainfall and the rate of runoff it produces renders the isolation of single factors and their experimental probing difficult, even on bare soils. In general, high rates of erosion are promoted by loose, friable soils, steep slopes, high rainfall intensities, intricately dissected topography, and sparse cover, and the improvement or reduction of any of these factors results in more or less decrease in the erosion rate. The amount of erosion is dependent on the factors that affect the rate and on the duration and frequency of storms and the depth of the soil.

The protection against erosion given to a soil by its vegetative cover is effected through the binding force of the root system, the dissipation of rain impact by the aerial canopy, the retardation and detention of runoff by plant stems and root crowns, and the reduction of runoff through the increase in infiltration caused by the more open soil which a good cover promotes. The effectiveness of vegetal cover is dependent on the kinds of plants composing it and their density, condition, and stage of growth. It ranges from the complete protection found in mature forests with undisturbed litter and in dense grass sods to the negligible protection given by the sparse xerophytes of semiarid and arid regions. The seasonal changes that plants undergo during their normal growth introduce somewhat corresponding seasonal variations in their effectiveness, but these are more pronounced for agricultural crops than for natural vegetation.   Climatic cycles embracing series of consecutive wet or dry years introduce hazards that often adversely affect vegetal cover. This is particularly the case in subhumid and semiarid regions, where a series of drought years may so seriously dwarf or deplete the natural vegetation as to render it wholly ineffective as a protective cover.

Measures by which erosion on the agricultural lands utilized for cropping and grazing can be mitigated or eliminated involve not only the more effective handling of cropped lands but also a complete change in the use of tracts not suitable for intensive farming.   Due account must be taken of the fact that clean-tilled row crops, such as corn, cotton, and tobacco, although seriously conducive to erosion, are nevertheless essential to the national economy, and the acreage devoted to them is controlled mainly by economic considerations.   The initial step in introducing erosion-control measures is the development of a land use plan that takes into account, among other things, the agriculture of the region, the adaptability of the different land tracts to various types of farming, the use of appropriate control measures on cropped lands, and the withdrawal of lands unsuited for cultivation, because of their steep slope or other characteristics, from annual cropping and the substitution of protective perennial cover.

Erosion-control practices hinge on the establishment and maintenance of protective vegetal covers and the reduction of the volume and velocity of runoff.   On farm lands withdrawn from cultivation permanent cover is established by reforestation and the seeding of permanent meadows and pastures.   Crop rotation is used on cultivated lands to prevent the continuous planting of clean-tilled row crops on the same tracts and to improve the quality and condition of the soil.   On rolling lands terraces— low, broad-based dikes 18 to 30 inches high running nearly parallel to the land contour—are used to reduce the velocity of runoff and divert it to safe outlets.   On steeper lands bench terraces giving the hillside a steplike appearance are sometimes used.   Contour cultivation—furrows coinciding with the contours—increases infiltration and reduces runoff. Gully control is practiced by diverting runoff away from the head of the gully, stabilizing and protecting the sides with vegetation, and using small structures to prevent undercutting.   Numerous other practices are applied, but intensive measures are necessarily confined largely to the more productive lands.

The protection of the great tracts of unoccupied or sparsely populated forest, grazing, and idle lands presents a much more difficult problem, because on such tracts the widespread use of the intensive practices applied to farm lands is out of the question. Furthermore, the seeding and reforestation of any great proportion of these lands are not feasible. The only practical approach is prevention of the abuse and destruction of the natural cover. Fire protection and the control of cutting in timber and woodlands and the prevention of overgrazing on range lands all contribute to the preservation of the natural vegetation. On the range lands of the semiarid regions, however, climatic cycles bring serious hazards, and a series of dry or drought years can deplete almost to the extent of complete obliteration the short-grass vegetation of the region.

Aside from the protection of agricultural lands, erosion control may be considered in relation to other situations affecting a region. Surface erosion and soil wash account for much of the sediment carried in many streams and rivers during flood periods. Where the sediment carried is sufficient in amount to cause damaging deposits on fertile flood plains, material shortening of the useful life of storage reservoirs by sedimentation, or heavy sedimentation in the channel, which seriously affects the utility of the stream, erosion-control measures may be considered in relation to their ability to reduce the silt load. In such situations the improvement of the agricultural value of the lands on which the measures are used may in some localities be a minor consideration, although control measures that are effective in substantially reducing the silt content of the stream can hardly fail to effect a marked improvement on the lands.

REFERENCES

1. Comber, N. M., An introduction into a scientific study of the soil, London, Edw. Arnold, 1929.

2. Cook, H. L., The nature and controlling variables of the water erosion process: Soil Sci. Soc. America Proc., vol. 1, pp. 487–494, 1936.

3. Marbut, C. F., Soils of the United States: Atlas of American Agriculture, pt. 3, 1935.

4. Middleton, H. E., Properties of soils which influence soil erosion: U. S. Dept. Agr. Tech. Bull. 178, 15 pp., 1930.

5. Middleton, H. E., and Slater, C. S., Extent to which the erosibility of a soil can be anticipated by laboratory physical and chemical measurements: Amer. Soil Survey Assoc. Report, 15th Ann. Meeting, pp. 128–130, 1935.

6. Woolridge, S. W., and Morgan, R. S., Physical basis of geography, New York and London, Longmans, Green & Co., 1937.

7. National Resources Board, Soil erosion, supplementary report of Land Planning Committee, pt. 5, 1935.

XIIIc. MECHANICS OF RIVERS

Lorenz G. Straub[1]

PHYSICAL CHARACTERISTICS

Rivers differ greatly from one another in their physical characteristics and general behavior; hardly two can be found alike. The characterizing elements are so interwoven that it is extremely difficult if not impossible to describe them independently. The variation in mobility of the stream bed together with variation in discharge, both over wide ranges, results in exceedingly complex phenomena of a progressively changing nature. In their natural condition rivers seldom reach a state of equilibrium, even over short stretches. A state of change is the rule rather than the exception.

The nature of the source region of a river has a very significant relation to the behavior of its main stem, because the conduct of the river with reference to variation in the hydrologic cycle and sedimentary load is largely dependent thereon. Certain fundamental principles are evident as a result of long studies of river behavior under varying conditions of flow. These principles indicate definite relations between the fall, width, depth, and rate of discharge of a river.

In the source region the quantity of water is small, but it flows down very steep slopes. Here the detritus is of greatest diameter and is carried by small quantities of water in much greater masses than is possible farther downstream. On the other hand, the movement of heavy sedimentary load in the upper course is much more intermittent than in the lower course. In general the slopes of the source streams are steep and flatten progressively as the middle watercourse is approached, while the water discharge and sedimentary load normally increase. However, as the quantity of water increases in a much greater measure than the quantity of solid material, the relative proportion of detritus usually becomes smaller toward the river mouth. The width and depth of the watercourse also increase, while the gradient continually becomes flatter. These changes continue in the same manner as far downstream as the main stem of the lower course. The quantity of detritus does not necessarily increase as the lower stream is approached. Lakes that are present in the courses of some rivers act as clarification basins, such as Lake Pepin on the

[1] Professor of hydraulics, University of Minnesota, Minneapolis, Minn. Assistance in the preparation of this section was furnished by the personnel of Work Projects Administration official project No. 65-1-71-140, subproject No. 326.

Mississippi River, Lake Constance on the Rhine, and also artificial lakes such as Lake Mead on the Colorado River and the Fort Peck Reservoir on the upper Missouri. Such lakes may reduce the amount of both suspended and bed loads.

At the mouths of rivers discharging into the ocean, because of the influence of varying tides, the conditions may be entirely different from those prevailing elsewhere. Here the current is intermittently reversed in direction. As a general rule, however, in river stretches not influenced by the sea or intermediate lakes there is usually a gradual decrease in slope together with an increase in flow, width, and depth from the source to the mouth.

RIVER BEDS

Rivers are not always characterized by a uniformity of the stream bed. Branching commonly occurs, also vague loops and serpentines of the course. Bed forms and gradients that are suited to the nature of a river in some regions may be impeded in their formation where the river passes through terrane involving swamps or rock formations that lie between the stream source and the point of discharge. Gradual variations are characteristic, but individual stretches often deviate from the rule. Rivers, particularly those which undergo wide variations in discharge, are observed to change their regimen continuously. Space does not permit detailed discussion of these vagaries; suffice it to say that for each condition of flow there is a new regimen which the river approaches but never reaches, because the influence of time lag does not permit establishment of equilibrium before a new and changing condition of flow is encountered.

The reason for rivers "running wild" in their natural condition lies in their tendency to seek a state of equilibrium through the irregularities of gradient and terrane they traverse. Thus an obstacle found in a stream—a stranded tree, for example, or a gravel bar deposited by a rapidly subsiding high-water stage—forces the water of a straight stretch to the opposite shore. Here the water washes out a widening, thereby causing the start of a bend. The flow does not follow the old direction downstream after passing the newly formed bend but takes an oblique course. To attain equilibrium the stream must attack the shore on the other side below the obstruction, and here, if the shore material is erodible, it forms a new bend. If the shore material is hard, the bend continues to be one-sided; generally, however, the first bend develops a sinuous curve involving a succession of bends farther downstream. It seldom happens that a curve is followed by a straight stretch of any considerable length.

As the water tends to flow in a rectilinear course, it continually impinges on the concave shore, where a large depth is attained and scour occurs; at the convex side sedimentation takes place and sand banks are formed. (See Fig. XIIIc-1.) Thus under normal conditions the stream continually scours the concave side and deposits material on the convex side. River bends in this way continually move forward. The speed with which they move depends, of course, among other things, upon the erodibility of the stream banks and the nature of the hydrologic cycle.

In uncontrolled rivers fantastic nooses and loops often develop. These courses remain intact during long periods of low water; but in a period of high water, particularly when this is followed abruptly by another low-water period, the river often fails to return to the naturally created course. The high-water flow breaks through narrow necks of land between successive loops. In this way new river reaches are formed. The former loops become detached abruptly from the channel and then become filled progressively by sedimentation—at first rapidly, then more

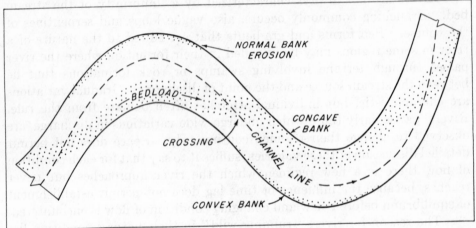

FIG. XIIIc-1.—Plan of serpentine stretch of river.

slowly, depending upon the frequency of overflow stages of the river. The Mississippi River and many of its tributaries show the remains of such action by the existence of crescent-shaped lakes which formerly were bends of the main channel of the river.

The route of strongest flow of a river is referred to as the channel line (Fig. XIIIc-1). It usually coincides or nearly coincides with the thalweg, which is the line joining the points of greatest depth. Both lines alternate from one bend to another, from one shore back to the other. Between bends, where the depth is relatively great, the river traverses "crossings" where the depth is relatively shallow. In the normal cycle of flow during high-water periods the bed within the bends is scoured deeper, while at the crossings or transitions between bends the level of the bed rises (fig. XIIIc-2). During the succeeding lower-water period the bends are subjected to sedimentation and a rise of the stream bed, while the crossings are scoured to lower levels.

The rise of a crossing becomes particularly troublesome on many navigable rivers. Upon the return of a low-water period following a long period of high water, it becomes necessary at many crossings on navigable rivers to dredge a channel through the crossing in order to provide sufficient draft for commercial shipping.

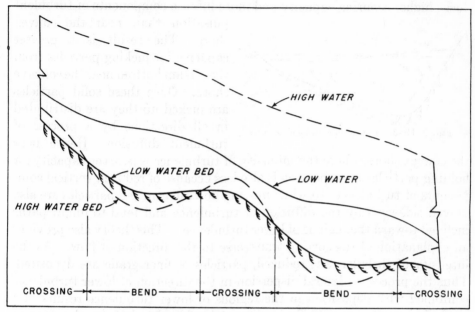

FIG. XIIIc-2.—Profile along channel line of river.

MODE OF MOVEMENT OF DETRITUS

The mode of detritus movement in natural watercourses is complex. In some rivers having relatively steep slopes for their size and fine-grained alluvial material forming the stream bed general transportation of the material takes place even at very low stages, but in most rivers uninterrupted movement of detritus usually occurs only at high water. The bed load for this situation follows the shortest path—that is, the particles move from one convex shore to another, the transition between two bends apparently being crossed diagonally (Fig. XIIIc-1). This situation was long attributed solely to the condition of helical flow, which is more or less pronounced at bends (Fig. XIIIc-3). In the region of higher velocity near the water's surface the flow is inclined toward the concave shore of the bend—that is, on the convex side of the stream—while in the lower portion of the stream near the bed the flow is inclined toward the convex shore. The length of the helix is ordinarily many times the breadth of the river. More recent studies seem to indicate that this is not the complete explanation of the phenomenon [16]. The particles of sediment seem to move at an inclination transverse to the channel at an angle greater than the resultant direction of water flow near the stream bottom [32]. A turbulence theory provides a more complete explanation of this phenomenon, particularly for rivers that are very broad and therefore relatively shallow. The velocity of the stream and also the intensity of turbulence are greatest near the concave shore of the bend. This produces higher scouring capacity and more intense components of turbulent pulsation than near the convex shore. The result is a greater capacity for picking particles from the stream bottom near the concave shore. Once these solid particles are picked up they are distributed in all directions by a process of turbulent diffusion. Hence near

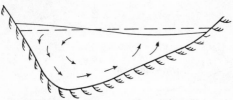

FIG. XIIIc-3.—Helical flow in bend of river.

the convex shore, where the intensity of turbulence is less, the capacity for holding particles in suspension is also less because of reduced vertical components of turbulence; so while moving downstream the particles are also moved sideways by the diffusion of turbulence and tend to follow paths inclined toward the regions of lower turbulence. This theory also provides an explanation of the sorting transverse to the direction of flow. As the intensity of turbulence is reduced, particles of finer grade are deposited. Thus the process of lateral dispersion in the direction of lower turbulence combined with deposition in the regions of lower turbulence results in a gradation from coarse to fine sediment in river bends from the deep of the pool to the edge of the convex shore.

A fairly complete explanation of the phenomenon of bed-load movement along the course of a serpentine river is probably provided by a combination of the helical-flow theory and the turbulence theory. In deep and relatively narrow channels the motion of the sedimentary load along the stream bottom is probably influenced

FIG. XIIIc-4.—Transverse flow in reaches and at crossings.

more particularly by helical flow, but in broad shallow channels the turbulence is probably the principal cause. In reaches and at crossings a double helical flow is observed (Fig. XIIIc-4), but the maximum turbulence is also found near the stream bed at the two low troughs on opposite sides of the channel [16].

RIVER GRADIENT

The gradient of a river—that is, its hydraulic slope—changes considerably with stage (Fig. XIIIc-2). Obviously the total drop in the gradient over a long stretch of river cannot change appreciably, regardless of the variation of discharge. Local changes, however, can be very pronounced. The gradient at pools (which develop at bends) and transitions is approximately uniform at high-water stages. With the return of a low-water stage the least resistance to flow is met in the deep sections of bends. Conversely, at high water the detritus is carried over the crossings from one concave shore to another. The bends are separated by crossings that are built up during high water. In effect these diagonal crossing bars act somewhat as low submerged dams, so that there is a steep gradient at the crossing. The high velocity so developed at the crossing results in scouring of the bar and deposition of particles in the pool beyond. Under some conditions a selective process develops, the result being that the finer particles are transported into the pool and the coarser materials are left at the crossing, so that the crossing becomes "armored" with a highly resistant layer of gravel [25]. In this way a state of equilibrium is produced during the low-water period, with virtually no further change in conformation of the stream bottom. The river becomes a succession of pools and shoals. In small rivers with gravel beds and serpentine courses the variation in gradient along the river channel is obvious during low-water periods, because the drops in elevation at the shoals are pronounced; in large rivers having fine-grained beds the situation is less evident to the naked eye but can be determined by hydrographic surveys.

Not always is the low-water temporal state of permanence entered into by a river immediately after the subsidence of high water. The nature of the river or the cycle of events preceding the return of low water may result in a complex readjustment before a reasonable state of equilibrium can be attained. Thus caving banks, redistribution of sedimentary deposits in the channel, and erosion of crossings are sometimes extensive on alluvial rivers during the early days of the low-water season.

The foregoing brief descriptive sketch of the behavior of rivers as related to their sedimentary load provides only a perspective. Some brief amplifications by theory and observation follow. A comparison of various rivers with one another indicates that although the hydraulic characteristics—namely, the slope, rate of discharge, variation in discharge, and the like—might be similar for two or more rivers, these rivers may differ greatly from one another in other respects. One river may have a gently serpentined course with a reasonably uniform bed; another may develop very pronounced shoals and deep pools, which offer great difficulty to engineers in their efforts to develop a navigable channel. The difference lies largely in the sedimentary characteristics of the river —the magnitude of the sedimentary load and the mechanical composition of the sediment. To be sure, the hydraulic and sedimentary characteristics are not independent; thus the hydraulic slope and the velocity of flow are influenced by the magnitude and nature of the sedimentary load as well as by the water discharge. The mechanics defining the interrelation of these quantities is of fundamental importance.

ORIGIN OF SEDIMENTARY LOAD OF RIVERS

Many factors are influential in producing erosion. Alternate freezing and thawing of saturated rock and soil, wind action, and the dynamic action of rain combine in varying degrees in the process of eroding the surface of the ground. Particles that have been loosened are transported by surface runoff. The greater the velocity of the water the greater will be its capacity to transport solid particles; moreover, the greater the intensity and duration of rainfall the higher will be the percentage of runoff. Loose, unvegetated soil composed of finely divided materials on steep slopes suffers serious erosion if subjected periodically to high rates of precipitation.

Several modes of erosion are more or less distinguishable from one another. In the source district the sedimentary load of the river consists largely of detritus formed by the weathering and wearing down of mountains. The river slopes are steep and, at least during high stages, the water flows at torrential velocities—that is, at velocities greater than those of waves in open channels ($V > \sqrt{gd}$, in which V = velocity of the water, in feet per second, g = acceleration due to gravity or 32.2 feet per second per second, and d = depth of water, in feet). During periods of extremely high rates of runoff (after cloudbursts) detritus avalanches take place; the stream then moves immense quantities of rock toward the sedimentary cone. Boulders are rolled long distances, with the finer gravel apparently forming a lubricating medium for them. The sedimentary particles progressively become rounded and smaller, owing to the abrasion incurred as they move along the river course. Simultaneously a process of sorting takes place, with the finer particles transported downstream more continuously than the coarser particles.

In contrast to the avalanches and detritus transportation of torrential rivers, the erosion in plain country, although often just as devastating, ordinarily takes place more gradually. Here the erosion is of two types—sheet erosion and gullying. These two processes normally take place simultaneously; the relative importance assumed by each is largely dependent upon the nature of the topography and the type of vegetation.

Although detailed observation of the erosion on areas throughout the United States has indicated very high rates of removal of the topsoil in certain localities, these rates do not afford a measure of the sedimentary load of the river to which the drainage area is tributary. This was especially evident in connection with an extensive investigation of the Missouri

River under the writer's supervision. Much of the material scoured from the highlands comes to rest in the lowlands without being carried into the rivers. A computation based upon the silt load of the Missouri, for example, would indicate an average annual erosion of 0.0031 inch from the drainage area tributary to the river above Kansas City for the 2-year period ending June 30, 1931. The amount of erosion is extremely variable from place to place; it varies with the nature of the soil, the slope, the vegetative cover, and the treatment of the land. Studies made on strips of land having slopes ranging from 0 to 3 percent and subject to an annual precipitation of 21 inches showed rates of erosion many times that indicated by the average silt load of the Missouri River distributed over the drainage basin.

The economic importance of soil erosion had until comparatively recently received far too little consideration. Costly reservoirs have become practically valueless within a period of a very few years in consequence of the unanticipated sedimentary load of the stream that supplied the water. Farm lands have become denuded of fertile topsoil because insufficient attention was given to the effect of the dynamic action of rain and surface runoff. Large areas of valuable grazing land have been virtually ruined by gullying, which might have been avoided if suitable precautions had been taken in the early stages of such development.

TRANSPORTATION OF SEDIMENTS

No simple all-inclusive rule can be set up regarding the general phenomenon of the transportation of sediments in its relation to the complex behavior of rivers. The movement of sediments along the beds and in suspension in natural watercourses, with the associated changes in conformation in the stream bed, has long been a most perplexing and yet most fascinating type of occurrence confronting the hydraulic engineer concerned with the regulation, improvement, and economic development of rivers. Probably in no other field of hydraulics have there been more confusing and opposing statements made in the last several decades. There are now, however, several focal points which lead to sound fundamental analysis based upon a careful study of fragmentary data derived from both field and laboratory observations.

Considerable progress was made by taking into account factors of bulk flow such as are presented with the Du Boys theory [5], which considers the computed traction along the stream bed. A reasonable result in idealized cases and the analysis in laboratory experiments have been obtained with this theory. Similar and possibly more empirical formulas have been proposed from time to time. The method is useful for idealized studies and serves to provide a tool for the hydraulic engineer.

More recently gratifying analytical approaches have been made to the phenomenon of fluid turbulence, particularly as regards flow through pipes made ideally rough by spherical grain projections of uniform size; however, even here there is still uncertainty over the detailed treatment in case of roughness different from the idealized. The turbulence theory in its fundamental form has been carried over to the mechanics of the flow of rivers and the transportation of sediments and seems to provide explanations for phenomena that previously have been obscure. The basic knowledge of the theory of turbulence as presented by Prandtl, Von Kármán, Taylor, and others and verified in part by experimental studies has been used as a framework and expanded to encompass the movement of sediments. A pioneer effort in this direction, in part verified by laboratory studies, was made by Shields [22] and presented in a discussion of the applications of the principles of the mechanics of turbulence research to bed-load movement.

Most analyses of sediment transportation by rivers have considered the bed load and suspended load independently. In some rivers the line of demarcation between these two loads is fairly distinct; in others the division is less apparent. Rivers like the Colorado, having relatively steep slopes for their size and fine-grained particles forming the stream bed, can hardly be analyzed satisfactorily in a rational procedure by independent consideration of suspended and bed loads. On the other hand, many rivers have beds composed of relatively coarse sand or gravel, while the suspended load is finely divided material consisting of silt and clay, which seldom comes to rest in the river channel once washed in from the tributary drainage area but rather is carried continuously to the river mouth. Here there is a logical and reasonable possibility of treating the two modes of transporting sediments independently.

SUSPENDED LOAD OF RIVERS

If the sedimentary load of rivers is considered in two classifications— that which is carried in suspension and that which is principally carried along the stream bed—a schematical separation for the purposes of description is obtained. The amount of material transported by suspension in a stream is largely dependent on the amount of finely divided material that finds its way to the stream. The quantity in suspension can be readily measured, and a mathematical analysis of the distribution of this material based upon the turbulence theory has been proposed [17] and its applicability reasonably well verified [4, 18]. The present status of the procedure, however, necessitates knowledge of the quantity and mechanical composition of the sediment at some point in the vertical profile of the stream, and also the distribution of velocity in the vertical and the resistance of the stream bottom to shear.

The turbulence theory of suspended-load transportation by rivers is based upon a knowledge of the internal mechanism of flow of water. At very low velocities, such as are seldom found in rivers, the flow is laminar— that is, the water particles in the stream follow substantially parallel paths, and no eddy motion occurs. At higher velocities turbulence develops— that is, superimposed upon the mean forward velocity, particles of water are continually moving in random directions very haphazardly with reference to time and at varying speeds. These variations are a result of eddies that have the power of diffusing entrained sediment particles.. The upward components of the velocity have the power of raising particles of silt to higher levels in the stream. Of course at any point the upward and the downward motion must counterbalance each other. However, with the concentration of the silt greater near the bottom of the stream than near the top, the downward components carry less material than the upward components. Thus, although there is continual action of gravity pulling downward on particles of sediment in suspension, material is maintained in suspension with the forward-moving stream by virtue of the continual process of diffusion, the upward components of turbulence continually lifting more sediment into the stream than is moved downward by the downward velocity components of turbulent motion. Of course the size of the largest particle that can be transported by suspension is dependent upon the maximum temporal vertical velocity of the turbulence. This vertical component must be greater than the settling velocity of the particle in still water. Formulas based upon a statistical theory of turbulence have been derived to express this relation.

It will be readily recognized that the turbulence theory also explains the lateral diffusion of suspended particles. Inasmuch as the larger particles have rates of sedimentation much greater than the smaller ones, in a pulsating lateral and vertical eddy motion the larger particles can be raised off the bottom only for short periods, because the intensity of the particular turbulent pulsation in which they become entrained will decrease before the particles reach a very high level and thus will permit them to fall again toward the stream bed. Thus both vertical and lateral diffusion take place simultaneously superimposed upon the main-stream current forward. The coarser sedimentary particles will drop out of the current when points of lesser turbulence are approached. Hence in the process of erosion particles move from points of high turbulence toward points of lower turbulence, where they eventually fall to the bottom of the stream. This phenomenon, in part at least, accounts for the rapid lateral shifting of channels in an alluvial stream having a bed of fine material. For example, in the Missouri River the writer has observed in the course of a day a lowering of the stream bed at a single cross section as much as 10 to 15 feet, with a corresponding rise at a point in the same cross section transverse to the direction of flow. Similar situations have been noted on other rivers, including the Platte River of Nebraska, the Niobrara, and the Colorado.

Conceivably it might be possible to predict the suspended load of a river by means of a statistical analysis of the fluctuations in velocity and a mechanical analysis of the sediments forming the stream bed. In this way it might be possible to get an index of the upward velocity components of turbulence and their duration at the stream bed, and by knowing the relative duration of the velocity components for the various grades of material that are lifted into the moving stream it might be possible to determine their percentages. Such a procedure has been suggested, and a mathematical analysis proposed [15]. It probably has its greatest possibility in channels that are in silty equilibrium, with no material entering from tributary drainage area. Possibly an additive factor could be worked out to account for suspended material that comes into the river from tributary area but never forms a part of the stream bed.

Ordinarily the percentage of solid matter contained in a silt-laden stream is small—usually no more than 20,000 parts per million by weight, or about 2 percent. The suspended load of the lower Mississippi, frequently considered a very muddy stream, seldom if ever exceeds 5,000 parts per million, and even that of the Missouri, known as the "Big Muddy," seldom reaches 20,000 parts [26]. Exceptions may be found among such streams as the Colorado and some of its tributaries during flood stages, a few tributaries of the Missouri when subjected to cloudbursts, and possibly also the Rio Grande and the Yellow River of China during high stages. On some streams this limit is greatly exceeded for very short periods, amounts up to 30 percent or more of solid material having been reported.

It is generally known that the law governing the rate of fall of solid particles through still water is different for very small particles from the rate for larger particles. For the small particles both the viscosity and the density of the fluid come into consideration, and the rate of fall is well defined by Stokes' law; here the resistance to fall is proportional to the first power of the velocity. For the larger particles Newton's law controls the relation between velocity and resistance to fall, the resistance being proportional to the square of the velocity. In water at a temperature of about 50° F. silt particles having a specific gravity of about 2.65 will follow Stokes' law up to diameters of about $\frac{1}{16}$ millimeters (0.0025 inch). For diameters greater than 1 millimeter Newton's relation is closely followed, the viscosity and therefore the temperature of the water being relatively unimportant. Between these two limits there is a transition region.

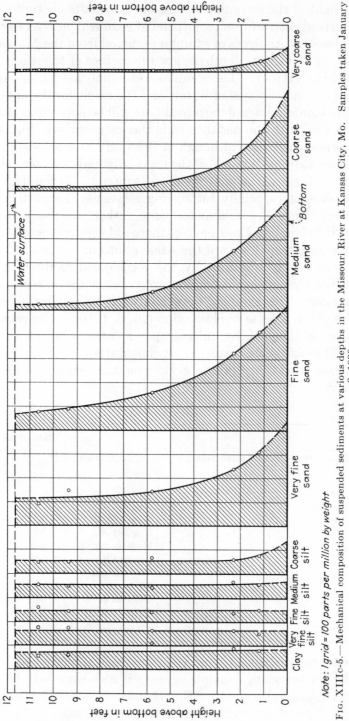

Note: 1 grid = 100 parts per million by weight

FIG. XIIIc-5.— Mechanical composition of suspended sediments at various depths in the Missouri River at Kansas City, Mo. Samples taken January 3, 1930.

In the light of the foregoing discussion the results of studies to determine the vertical distribution of suspended sediment in rivers are of considerable interest. Analyses of samples gathered from the Missouri River at Kansas City at various depths below the surface of the water are summarized in Fig. XIIIc-5. The samples were analyzed for amount of suspended load per unit volume of water, and the mechanical composition of the suspended material was determined. It will be noted that the concentration increased with the distance from the water surface (Fig. XIIIc-5). This is a normal condition, although in the study here presented the condition is rather extreme because of the especially high viscosity of the cold water. (The observations were made in winter.) Mechanical analyses of samples showed especially interesting relations: the particles having diameters less than $\frac{1}{16}$ millimeter were rather uniformly distributed throughout the river cross section, but those of larger diameters were very much more concentrated toward the stream bottom. The data indicated in Fig. XIIIc-5 were obtained by the mechanical analysis of samples taken from the river at five different depths below the water surface in a vertical section. The samples were analyzed by separation into constituent sizes by a process of elutriation [26, p. 1210]. The rates of sedimentation were checked by microscopic measurement of the size of particles. The following rates of sedimentation through still water at 22° C. were used; the specific gravity of the sediment was approximately 2.6.

Elutriation divisions

Diameter of particle (millimeter)	Classification	Rate of fall of particle (centimeter per second)
Less than $\frac{1}{256}$	Clay	
$\frac{1}{256}$–$\frac{1}{128}$	Very fine silt	0.0022–0.0091
$\frac{1}{128}$–$\frac{1}{64}$	Fine silt	.0091– .037
$\frac{1}{64}$–$\frac{1}{32}$	Medium silt	.037 – .124
$\frac{1}{32}$–$\frac{1}{16}$	Coarse silt	.124 – .38
$\frac{1}{16}$–$\frac{1}{8}$	Very fine sand	.38 –1.16
$\frac{1}{8}$–$\frac{1}{4}$	Fine sand	1.16 –2.60
$\frac{1}{4}$–$\frac{1}{2}$	Medium sand	2.60 –5.33
$\frac{1}{2}$–1	Coarse sand	5.33 –9.95
1–2	Very coarse sand	

The sediment-distribution curves in the vertical section of the river as indicated by the foregoing example agree well with what is to be expected from the turbulence theory [10, 17]. It must of course be kept in mind in the application of the turbulence theory as presented by the formulas thus far developed that no account is taken of the influence of time lag which necessarily exists in a natural watercourse because of the continued change in cross section from point to point along the stream.   It is largely the influence of time lag which causes the suspended load transverse to the river as well as in the direction of flow to be fairly well distributed, despite the fact that the relative turbulence as defined by shear resistance along the stream bed and velocity-distribution curves would indicate comparatively wide variations.

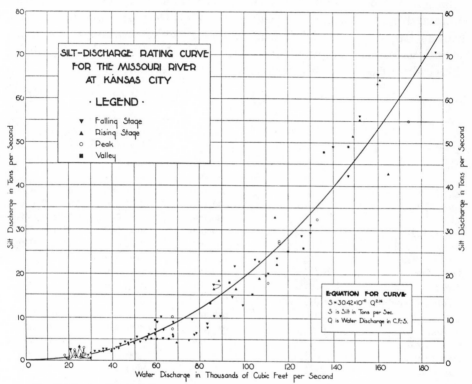

Fig. XIIIc-6.—Silt-discharge rating curve for the Missouri River at Kansas City, Mo.

Although a wide range of circumstances influence the amount of suspended material carried by a stream, observations indicate that over a long period, at least for many rivers, there is a reasonably well defined relation between the stream discharge and the amount of sediment transported in suspension.   In Figure XIIIc-6 are presented the writer's results of 2 years of daily measurements of the suspended load of the Missouri River at Kansas City.   Of course the amount of material found in suspension on any particular day may deviate greatly from the average for the existing stage, depending upon the condition of the surface of the drainage area at the time, the location of concentrated precipitation in the area, and many other factors.   This is well shown in the chart (Fig. XIIIc-6), in which the various plotted points give the values for individual measurements. The equation for the curve for average conditions at Kansas City is

$$S = 30.4 \times 10^{-11} Q^{2.16}$$

in which S is the suspended load in tons per second, and Q is the water discharge in cubic feet per second. For other rivers, and even for other localities on the Missouri, both the coefficient and the exponent in the equation will be different from those here given. A comparison of the computed and measured suspended load of the Missouri River past Kansas City is presented in the following table. Although the daily deviations of the computed and measured value were great, it will be observed that the monthly figures are in close agreement.

Comparison of measured and computed suspended load carried by the Missouri River past Kansas City

Period	Water discharge (acre-feet)	Suspended load (tons)	
		Measured	Computed
May 8–31, 1929	3,660,000	19,200,000	24,200,000
June 1929	10,600,000	153,000,000	151,000,000
July 1929	5,600,000	44,000,000	48,300,000
August 1929	2,180,000	6,660,000	6,190,000
September 1929	1,360,000	2,040,000	2,200,000
October 1929	1,730,000	3,900,000	3,410,000
November 1929	1,890,000	4,840,000	4,420,000
December 1929	916,000	1,050,000	878,000
Total, May 8 to December 31, 1929	27,936,000	234,690,000	240,598,000
January 1930	972,000	2,210,000	1,050,000
February 1930	2,040,000	8,740,000	6,890,000
March 1930	3,840,000	24,500,000	20,000,000
April 1930	3,460,000	18,500,000	15,900,000
May 1930	5,610,000	43,400,000	47,100,000
June 1930	4,370,000	31,400,000	27,600,000
Total, January 1 to June 30, 1930	20,292,000	128,750,000	118,540,000
Grand total, May 8, 1929 to June 30, 1930	48,228,000	363,440,000	359,138,000

Other investigators have since observed that relations similar to those set forth above exist on other rivers, including, for example, the Po River of northern Italy [11] and the Red River of the southwestern United States [1]. For the Red River an equation of the form

$$S = 95 \times 10^{-10} Q^{2.036}$$

was obtained. Usually the suspended load seems to vary approximately as the square of the water discharge, although this relation is entirely empirical.

Observations on many rivers indicate that for very high rates of flow the suspended load no longer increases at a rate as high as the square of the water discharge, on some rivers even decreasing when the duration of a high-flow rate is long. This situation is due, at least in part, to the reduced availability of material in the river channel susceptible to being held in the flowing stream by the mechanism of fluid turbulence.

Based upon a mathematical analysis involving the systematic integration of the product of suspended-load distribution curves and stream-velocity distribution curves in river verticals, a procedure was set up by the writer [26, p. 1189] to arrive at a systematic method of sampling rivers for determining the suspended load. The equation developed is of the form

$$S = (\tfrac{3}{8}s_{0.8d} + \tfrac{5}{8}s_{0.2d})q$$

in which S is the sediment discharge per unit width of stream; $s_{0.8d}$ and $s_{0.2d}$ are the sediment concentrations at 0.8 and 0.2 depth from the water surface respectively; and q is the water discharge of the river per unit width at the point of observation. This procedure provides a method of determining the suspended load of a river, somewhat analogous to the customary scheme of stream gaging for water discharge by measuring velocity at 0.2 depth and 0.8 depth. This relation has also been found suitable for determining the silt load of rivers by other investigators [3, 11].

RETENTION OF SEDIMENT IN SUSPENSION

Another question that frequently arises concerns the retention of sediment in suspension. A number of observations on rivers indicate that the material transported in suspension, particularly in heavily laden rivers, remains in suspension unless the flow is artificially retarded. A typical example of this is presented in Figure XIIIc-7. Observations on the discharge of suspended material were made for about a month at two stations on the Missouri River, at Kansas City and Waverly, about 80 miles apart. At these two stations the maximum and minimum suspended loads occur about 1 day apart almost invariably. With a mean velocity of about 3 miles an hour, this would be the time required for the silt-laden water to flow from Kansas City to Waverly. The duration curves of the two stations for the silt discharge are almost identical, as are also the duration curves for the water discharge. Furthermore, although there was considerable variation in the character of the material from day to day, the mechanical compositions of the finer grades of sediment gathered at the two stations on successive days were practically identical. These observations are in agreement with what might reasonably be expected, except for stretches where the river is in the process of changing its regimen.

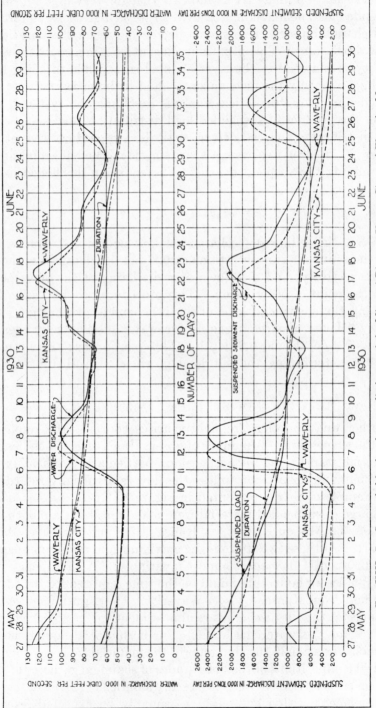

Fig. XIIIc-7.—Suspended-load and water discharge of the Missouri River at Kansas City and Waverly, Mo.

In some stretches of the Colorado River the process of transporation by suspension and along the stream bed is less well defined. Here the stream bed is composed of very fine material, and it seems likely that material is transported through some stretches along the stream bed, whereas in other stretches it goes into suspension, so that while the process of transporation might be continuous the mode of transportation may vary for a part of the sedimentary load. On the Missouri River the bed sediment is in general rather coarse as compared with the suspended material.

ANALYSIS OF RIVER-BED CHANGES AS RELATED TO TRANSPORTATION OF BED-SEDIMENT

The detailed mechanism of the transportation of sediment along stream beds is still vaguely known, although in recent years definite progress has been made in its analysis. In studying major changes in the conformation of streams with variation in flow the writer has found that considerable success can be obtained by consideration of major static and dynamic forces. Certain fundamental principles that relate primarily to factors of bulk flow and bed-load movement make it possible to estimate variations in the stream bed. A channel over a movable bed in contrast to one over a rigid bed tends toward a condition of equilibrium within itself, which is dependent upon bed load for different conditions of flow. In a stream with rigid bed, variations in cross section along the stream are reflected by variations in level of the water surface. In a stream with movable bed these changes are reflected in changes in shape of the stream bottom as well as in the water surface. Disregarding tributary inflow for the moment, we may say that the river channel for a given discharge approaches an equilibrium condition in which the flow past various sections and also the sedimentary load remain constant.

An approach to the analysis of such equilibrium conditions for a river requires the formulation of a law defining approximately the rate of movement for various cross sections. For straight stretches of river it is believed that some degree of success has been achieved in this regard, at least in determining the proper order of magnitude of the bed load or the relative quantity for the different types of sand ordinarily encountered. The procedure is based upon the general acceptance of the Du Boys relation, which can be derived [26, p. 1127] upon idealized assumptions regarding the method of bed-load movement, in the form

$$G = \psi \frac{\tau}{\gamma} \left(\frac{\tau}{\gamma} - \frac{\tau_0}{\gamma} \right)$$

in which G is the quantity of sediment transported along the stream bed per unit width of channel, ψ is the coefficient depending upon the mechanical properties of the sediment, τ is the shear force along the stream bed resulting from the flowing water, τ_o is the shear force at which sediment transportation begins, and γ is the unit weight of the water. Admittedly this leaves out of direct consideration the mechanism of turbulent flow. The Manning formula, which might be written in the form

$$V = CR^{\frac{2}{3}}S^{\frac{1}{2}}$$

is also accepted as applicable. Here V is the mean velocity of flow, R the hydraulic radius (or mean depth in the case of very wide channels), S the slope of the energy gradient, and C a coefficient depending upon the roughness of the channel. Experience has shown that a formula of this type gives satisfactory results over a wide range of flow conditions with and also without movement of bed load [29].

Various forms of the equation have been set up by the writer, accepting these two more or less empirical relations. Both of the relations have been verified over a fairly wide range of conditions and to this extent at least should be acceptable.

Several forms of the relation have proved useful in studying the effect of artificial structures upon the regimen of rivers and have been checked in different ways by comparison with river investigations and by laboratory experiments. Algebraic analysis is here dispensed with; suffice it to say that for the idealized case of a rectangular channel of large breadth, where the frictional resistance due to the sides is negligible, the relation takes the form

$$G = \psi[S^{1.4}/C^{1.2}]\, Q^{\frac{3}{5}}[Q^{\frac{3}{5}} - Q_0^{\frac{3}{5}}]$$

in which Q is the water discharge per unit width of channel, Q_o is the discharge per unit width of channel for slope S at which sediment transportation begins, and G, C, and ψ are as described in the preceding equations. C, ψ, and Q_0 must be experimentally determined. The values of ψ and Q_0 depend upon the mechanical composition (variation in size of grains as determined by sieve analysis or elutriation), specific gravity, and form of the stream particles; C depends upon the character of the sediment and also upon the rugosities of the channel itself, independent of the roughness due solely to the mechanical composition of the sediment. Thus C is influenced by the degree of turbulence.

A typical example of the comparison of the results by the above equation with experiments of Schaffernak [21] is indicated by Figure XIIIc-8. In this figure the dot-dash lines represent the theoretical bed load for the maximum and minimum sizes of sediments used in the experimental studies. In general they enclose the experimental results. Here for the coarser material $\psi = 28,000$, where G is measured in pounds per second per foot of breadth of channel; $\tau_0 = 0.115$ pound per square foot;

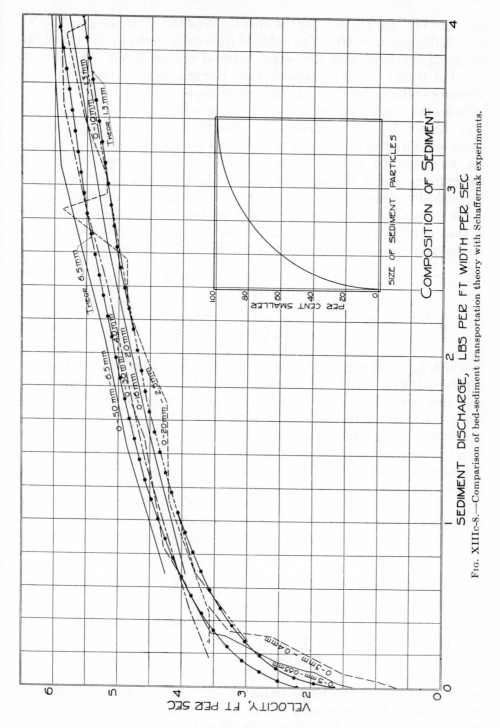

Fig. XIIIc-8.—Comparison of bed-sediment transportation theory with Schaffernak experiments.

and $C = 71$. In the curve for the finer material the values are $\psi = 92,000$, $\tau_0 = 0.275$, and $C = 90$. The value of Q_0 is determined by the use of the foregoing equations with the proper value of τ_0 substituted.

The theory has been expanded mathematically to explain the equilibrium conditions for channel-contraction works. The principle involved includes the conditions explained in the foregoing discussion and, in addition, the fact that the sediment transported through the contracted section of the stream as well as the water discharge must be the same as through the uncontracted section. Contracting the stream results in greater power for erosion in the beginning, but finally a state of equilibrium must be reached in which there is both a change in slope and a change in depth of the stream in consequence of the contraction. Algebraically the depth in the contracted section in terms of the flow conditions in the uncontracted section may be expressed as follows for a rectangular channel:

$$d_2 = \frac{\dfrac{d_1}{(1-\alpha)^{3/7}} \left\{ -\dfrac{\tau_0}{\gamma S_1} + \left[\left(\dfrac{\tau_0}{\gamma S_1}\right)^2 + \dfrac{4d_1\left(d_1 - \dfrac{\tau_0}{\gamma S_1}\right)}{(1-\alpha)} \right]^{1/2} \right\}^{3/7}}{\left[2\left(d_1 - \dfrac{\tau_0}{\gamma S_1}\right) \right]^{3/7}}$$

in which d_2 = the depth of water at the stretch of channel that has been contracted; d_1 = water depth before contraction (or the depth upstream and downstream of the contracted region); τ_o = the traction force (tangential force of the water against the stream bed per unit area of bed) at which transportation of sediment begins ($\tau_o = \gamma dS$, in which γ = unit weight of water, d = depth of stream at which bed sediment transportation begins with a slope S of the hydraulic gradient); S_1 = the natural slope of the hydraulic gradient of the stream in the uncontracted part; α = the amount of contraction—that is, $B_2 = (1 - \alpha) B_1$, B_2 and B_1 being the breadths of the channel at the contracted and normal sections respectively. The relation expressed by this formula agrees well with laboratory experiments and field observations [23].

MISCELLANEOUS CONSIDERATIONS IN RIVER BEHAVIOR

The foregoing description of the mechanics of river behavior presents only a perspective of a few of the major occurrences. Many phenomena of importance have scarcely been touched upon, if mentioned at all. Problems of practical significance are continually confronted and must be solved as well as possible with the present status of our knowledge. In many problems recourse has been had to river models, many with erodible beds [7, 33]. But even with practical efforts of this type there is still much that remains to be learned regarding the fundamental principles of similarity between the model and the prototype [19, 22] and regarding the limitations in the use of the different grades of sedimentary material in the performance of the experiments [2, 12].

The question of stable channels in erodible material has been much mooted, particularly in connection with navigation and irrigation projects, both in this country and abroad [14, 27]. The different types of bed movement referred to variously as sliding, rolling, and saltation [8] and their relation to suspended load [15] are of great importance. The formation of sand ripples on the stream bottom [31] and change with dynamic flow conditions and bed load [24], boundary layer and fluid turbulence [6, 22], and the progressive movement of sand bars downstream much as sand dunes [34] all come into consideration in analysis of river occurrences. The effects of transportation of sediment upon sorting and abrasion have practical significance [20]. The extensive work that is currently in progress and has been done during the last several years in Europe as well as in America is evident by bibliographic reviews of articles presented on this subject in various publications [28, 35, 36].

REFERENCES

1. Campbell, F. B., and Bauder, H. A., A rating-curve method for determining silt discharge of streams: Am. Geophys. Union Trans., 1940, pt. 2, pp. 603–607.

2. Casey, J., Über Geschiebebewegung: Preuss. Versuchsanstalt f. Wasserbau u. Schiffbau Mitt., No. 19, Berlin, 1935.

3. Chang, Y. L., Laboratory investigation of flume traction and transportation: Am. Soc. Civil Eng. Trans., vol. 104, pp. 1246–1284, 1939.

4. Christiansen, J. E., Distribution of silt in open channels: Am. Geophys. Union Trans., 1935, pt. 2, pp. 478–485.

5. Du Boys, P., Le Rhone et les rivières à lit affouillable: Annales des Ponts et Chaussées, 1879.

6. Exner, F. M., Über die Wechselwirkung zwischen Wasser und Geschiebe in Flüssen: Akad. Wiss., Math.-naturw. Klasse, Sitzungsber., Band 134, pt. 2, pp. 181–205, 1925.

7. Freeman, J. R. (editor), Hydraulic laboratory practice, 868 pp., Am. Soc. Mech. Eng., 1929.

8. Gilbert, G. K., The transportation of debris by running water: U. S. Geol. Survey Prof. Paper 86, 1914.

9. Griffith, W. M., A theory of silt transportation: Am. Soc. Civil Eng. Trans., vol. 104, pp. 1733–1748, 1939.

10. Hayami, Shôitirô, Hydrological studies on the Yangtze River, China, II, A theory of silt transportation by running water: Shanghai Sci. Inst. Jour., sec. 1, vol. 1, p. 196, 1938.

11. Indri, Egidio, Sulla determinazione della portata solida nei corsi d'acqua naturali: 8th Nat. Cong. Waters Proc., Padova, 1935; reprinted by Industrie grafiche italiane stucchi, 24 pp., Milan, 1936.

12. Kramer, Hans, Sand mixtures and sand movement in fluvial models: Am. Soc. Civil Eng. Trans., vol. 100, pp. 798–838, 1935.

13. Lacey, Gerald, Stable channels in alluvium: Engineering, vol. 129, pp. 179–180, 1930.

14. Lane, E. W., Stable channels in erodible material: Am. Soc. Civil Eng. Trans., vol. 102, pp. 121–142, 1937.

15. Lane, E. W., and Kalinske, A. A., The relation of suspended to bed material in rivers: Am. Geophys. Union Trans., 1939, pt. 4, pp. 637–641.

16. Leighly, J. B., Toward a theory of the morphologic significance of turbulence in the flow of water in streams: California Univ. Pub. in Geography, vol. 6, No. 1, pp. 1–22, 1932.

17. O'Brien, M. P., Review of the theory of turbulent flow and its relation to sediment-transportation: Am. Geophys. Union Trans., 1933, pp. 487–491.

18. Rouse, Hunter, Experiments on the mechanics of sediment suspension: 5th Internat. Cong. Applied Mechanics Proc., pp. 550–554, New York, John Wiley & Sons, Inc., 1939.

19. Rouse, Hunter, Criteria for similarity in the transportation of sediment: Iowa Univ. Studies in Engineering, Bull. 20, pp. 33–49, 1940.

20. Russel, R. D., Effects of transportation of sedimentary particles, in recent marine sediments, a symposium, edited by P. D. Trask, pp. 32–47, Am. Assoc. Petroleum Geologists, 1939.

21. Schaffernak, F., Neue Grundlagen für die Berechnung der Geschiebeführung im Fluss-läufen, 48 pp., Leipzig and Vienna, Franz Deuticke, 1922.

22. Shields, A., Anwendung der Aehnlichkeitsmechanik und der Turbulenzforschung auf die Geschiebebewegung: Preuss. Versuchsanstalt Wasserbau u. Schiffbau Mitt., Berlin, 1936.

23. Straub, L. G., Effect of channel-contraction works upon regimen of movable-bed streams: Am. Geophys. Union Trans., 1934, pp. 454–463.

24. Straub, L. G., Discussion of "Sand mixtures and sand movement in fluvial models," by Hans Kramer, Am. Soc. Civil Eng. Trans., vol. 100, pp. 867–873, 1935.

25. Straub, L. G., Some observations of sorting of river sediments: Am. Geophys. Union Trans., 16th Ann. Meeting, pp. 463–476, 1935.

26. Straub, L. G., Missouri River: 73d Cong., 2d sess., H. Doc. 238, app. 6, pp. 1032–1245, 1935.

27. Straub, L. G., A practical theory of detritus transportation and design of stable channels, Reports and Papers for the Postponed Meeting of the International Association for Hydraulic Structures Research, 1939. Liége (Published by Oskar Eklunds Boktrykri, Stockholm, pp. 37–69, 1940.)

28. Straub, L. G., Report of committee on dynamics of streams, 1934–35: Am. Geophys. Union Trans. 16th Ann. Meeting, pp. 443–451, 1935; idem, 1936–37; Trans. 18th Ann. Meeting, pp. 329–42, 1937; idem, 1938–39: Trans. 20th Ann. Meeting, pp. 555–579, 1939; idem, 1939–40: Trans. 21st Ann. Meeting, pp. 443–450, 1940.

29. Strickler, A., Beiträge zur Frage der Geschwindigkeitsformel und der Rauhigkeits zahlen für Ströme, Kanäle und geschlossene Leitungen: Amt f. Wasserwirtschaft Mitt., No. 16, Bern, Switzerland, 1923.

30. Trask, P. D., and co-authors, Recent marine sediments, a symposium: 736 pp., Am. Assoc. Petroleum Geologists, 1939.

31. Velikanov, M. A., Formation of sand ripples on the stream bottom (question 3, report 3, presented at Washington meeting of Commission of Potamology, Internat. Union of Geodesy and Geophysics), 17 pp., 1939, not yet published.

32. Vogel, H. D., and Thompson, P. W., Flow in river bends: Civil Engineering, vol. 3, pp. 266–268, 1933.

33. Vogel, H. D., Hydraulic-laboratory results and their verification in nature: Am. Soc. Civil Eng. Trans., vol. 101, pp. 597–629, 1936.

34. Wittman, Der Einfluss der Korrektion des Rheins zwischen Basel und Mannheim auf die Geschiebebewegung des Rheins: Deutsche Wasserwirtschaft, Nos. 10–12, 1927.

35. Williams, G. R., and others, Selected bibliography on erosion and silt movement: U. S. Geol. Survey Water-Supply Paper 797, 1937.

36. Bibliography on the subject of transportation of solids by flowing water in open channels, U. S. Bur. Reclamation, Denver, 1933.

XIIID. TRANSPORTATION OF MINERAL MATTER BY SURFACE WATER

CHARLES S. HOWARD[1]

The mineral matter carried in solution and suspension by streams is derived from the soils and rocks of the drainage basin. The rocks disintegrate through solution, oxidation, and hydration, and a part of the material is removed by solution and by the mechanical agency of running water. All the principal rock minerals are attacked by water and are soluble to some extent, but only a few of their constituents are present in appreciable quantities in natural waters.

Only small quantities of dissolved matter are brought to the earth in rain water [7], but atmospheric moisture is an influential agent in the disintegration of rocks [5]. The amount of material dissolved by rain water after it reaches the earth depends on the nature of the rocks with which the water comes into contact and the length of time that the water is in contact with the rock materials. The carbon dioxide in rain water and that added through organic processes after the rain reaches the earth assists in the solution of rock minerals, particularly in the formation of bicarbonates, which are abundant constituents of all natural waters.

In the disintegration and decomposition of rocks silica is set free, and it dissolves to some extent in the waters flowing over and percolating through the disintegrated material. The carbonates in natural waters come primarily from the decomposition products of feldspars and from the solution of limestones. Large quantities of sulphate are derived from beds of gypsum and in some areas from residual soluble salts on irrigated lands. Chlorides are present in small quantities in most surface waters but occur in high concentrations in waters that drain regions of sedimentary rocks containing marine deposits. Nitrates are usually present in small quantities in natural waters but may be present in considerable quantities in waters that drain certain soils. Calcium, magnesium, sodium, and potassium are common constituents of all surface waters. Calcium and magnesium usually predominate in waters draining areas of carbonate rocks, and sodium usually predominates in waters draining arid areas. Potassium is usually present in small quantities in natural waters.

The disintegration of igneous rocks is a slow process, and as a consequence streams that drain a region of igneous rocks usually carry

[1] Chemist, Geological Survey, United States Department of the Interior, Washington, D. C.

relatively small amounts of dissolved and suspended matter. The dis-integration of sedimentary rocks takes place extensively, and streams that drain regions of sedimentary rocks carry large quantities of suspended matter and often have high concentrations of dissolved matter. Streams separate the different sizes of particles, carrying the largest particles only short distances. The finer particles stay in suspension at very low velocities and are carried for long distances.

Solid material is carried in suspension in the main body of the stream, and some is rolled or dragged along the bed of the stream. The method of transportation depends on the type of material, the sizes of the par-ticles, and certain hydraulic characteristics of the stream. The methods of transportation have been studied and are discussed in chapter XIIIc. Streams rarely lose any appreciable quantities of their loads of dissolved material but are constantly changing their loads of suspended matter. Slight amounts of solid material go into solution during long contact with the water, but the greatest changes in the loads of solid material come through deposition and subsequent scouring as changing conditions affect the carrying capacity of the stream. Under certain conditions suspended fine material flows considerable distances beneath the clear water of reser-voirs [9, 10, 11].

DISSOLVED MATTER

Headwaters.—In the headwaters of a stream the water comes from springs, rainfall, and melting snow, and the quantities of dissolved mate-rial are usually low.

Main body of the stream.—Contributions to the flow of the stream come from ground water and from tributary streams. The quantities and nature of the dissolved material from these sources are variable, but as a rule the concentrations are greater during periods of low flow, when most of the water represents runoff from ground water. In arid regions the maximum concentrations often occur during periods of flash floods, when the run-off is caused chiefly by rainfall of high intensity in a desert country or in a country having little vegetation. To the natural flow of the stream there is often added an appreciable quantity containing sewage and other wastes, which add materially to the load of dissolved material carried in the stream. Brines from oil fields [31] and drainage from mines [19] are sources of stream pollution and may provide a part of the load of dissolved material carried in a few streams. In some irrigated regions streams carry high concentrations and greater loads of dissolved material below the irrigated district than was present in the stream above the district [23]. This increase is caused by the leaching of salts from the soil by the irrigation waters and the subsequent return of some of these waters to the stream. This is undoubtedly the cause of the increase in the concentration of Colorado River water between certain points.   Figure XIIID-1 gives the increase for one year between Cameo and Grand Junction, Colo.   Cameo is at the head of a large irrigated district about 20 miles above Grand Junction, and several drains between Cameo and Grand Junction carry water into the Colorado River.

A great many streams near the coast have high concentrations of dissolved material in their lower reaches because of tidal influences.   These high concentrations are of importance to those using the water, and large expenditures [3] have been planned to prevent extensive invasion of the salt waters, but the quantities of dissolved material in such streams are of no significance in the computation of the removal of mineral matter from the land.

Loads of dissolved material carried by streams.—The loads of dissolved material carried by streams can be computed only from the results obtained by analysis of an adequate number of samples over a period of several years.   For most streams it is necessary to have samples collected frequently at regular intervals in order to have all changes in concentration

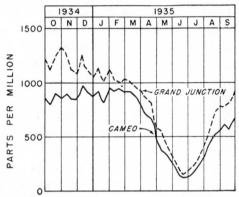

Fig. XIIID-1.—Dissolved solids in the Colorado River at Cameo and Grand Junction, Colo.

represented.   Usually one point can be selected in the section which will be representative of the quantity of dissolved material carried through the entire section.   The sampling station should be at or near a gaging station where the flow of the stream is measured.   Comprehensive analyses are usually made on composite samples, made from about 10 daily samples.   Additional information may be obtained concerning variations during the period represented by the composite by making determinations of some characteristic constituent on each of the individual daily samples.

The loads of dissolved material carried by some of the streams in the United States have been computed, but except for a few streams the records cover only single years.   The annual loads have been computed for the Colorado River and some of its tributaries [14].   The average for the Colorado River at the Grand Canyon during the 10 years ending September 30, 1935, was about 11,000,000 tons.   The load of dissolved material carried by the streams in the upper and lower basin areas of the southern coastal plain in California during the year ending September 30, 1932, was computed to be 139,000 tons [4].   The total quantities of dissolved material carried by the streams of the United States were computed by Dole and Stabler [8] on the basis of analyses of composite samples representing frequent sampling of a number of the larger streams of the country over periods of 1, 2, or 3 years. These authors estimated that the annual load of dissolved material carried by the streams of the United States was about 270,000,000 tons. Clarke [6], on the basis of the available data, estimated the annual load of dissolved material carried by all the streams of the world as about 3,000,000,000 tons.

SUSPENDED MATTER

Headwaters.—Most streams are clear at their sources, and many streams—for example, mountain streams and streams draining a country of igneous rocks—are clear for the greater part of their courses. Some mountain streams that have steep slopes move considerable quantities of sand, gravel, and sometimes boulders, but the total quantities moved are relatively small, and the material is not carried very far in any flood period. In certain areas where large snowbanks are formed, melting of the snow may produce large loads of suspended matter. Rockie [22] reports that large quantities of material are moved in this manner in the Palouse region, Washington. The intensity of a rainfall has a large influence on the quantity of material carried into the streams, particularly in regions that have scant vegetative cover.

Main body of the stream.—When the flow in the main stream is made up chiefly of ground water the stream is usually clear, and most of the solid material it carries has been scoured from the bottom or the banks of the stream and represents material that had been deposited at some previous stages. The material thus carried consists of relatively large particles, which settle rapidly and may be deposited at points farther downstream. When the flow in the main stream is primarily the result of rains or melting snow along the river or its tributaries, any increase in stream flow is usually accompanied by an increase in the quantity of suspended matter. During floods caused by rainfall of high intensity streams often show rapid fluctuations in their loads of suspended matter. At these times they generally carry the maximum loads, and during a few days they may carry a large proportion of the annual load. Love [20] shows that for almost every area of the 34 he studied "the greater part of the total load of suspended matter was removed from the drainage area in a very few days out of a total of about 450 days of record. In the area drained by Coon Creek at Coon Valley, Wis., 90 percent of the total load was carried in 10 days, and in the area drained by West Tarkio Creek near Westboro, Mo., 90 percent of the total load was carried in 12 days."

Different parts of the drainage area contribute varying proportions of the total load of suspended matter. Stabler [25] has shown that less than 50 percent of the drainage area of the Colorado River above the Grand Canyon furnishes 75 percent of the load of suspended matter carried by this stream past the Grand Canyon gaging station.

Sampling.—An accurate estimate of the quantities of suspended matter carried by a stream can be made only from the results obtained by an adequate sampling program and from an interpretation of the results based on a knowledge of conditions along the river in the vicinity of the sampling points.

The quantity of suspended matter is usually greater near the bottom of the stream than at the surface and varies throughout the cross section, so that samples must be taken at several points across the stream and must include water from different depths in order to determine the total load of suspended matter carried past the sampling station. The sampling station should be located at or near a gaging station where the flow of the stream is being measured.

Various types of samplers have been developed for the collection of representative samples. The simplest method of sampling is to obtain a bottleful of water at the desired point in the cross section. In deep water and in high velocities it is difficult to collect such samples without special apparatus. Different methods have been devised to open a bottle at a desired depth, and at an appreciable depth it is necessary to have some way to close the bottle in order to be certain that it contains water from that depth alone. Solid material will drop into an open bottle after it is full of water, and any full bottle may contain material that does not belong in the volume of the sample collected. For this reason it is desirable to close or remove the bottle before it is quite full. A great many investigators have apparently ignored the need of such apparatus for the collection of samples at a definite point. Straub [27] has described a sampler that closes automatically when the desired sample has been obtained. Cooperative studies of methods used in the measurement and analysis of sediment loads in streams were planned and conducted jointly by the Tennessee Valley Authority, Corps of Engineers, Department of Agriculture, Geological Survey, Bureau of Reclamation, Indian Service, and Iowa Institute of Hydraulic Research. Reports on these studies were prepared and released for the cooperating parties through the facilities of the Iowa Institute of Hydraulic Research. These reports [32, 33, 34, 35, and 36] describe the methods and equipment used for the collection of samples of suspended sediment and bed load, the analytical study of methods of sampling suspended sediment, methods of analyzing sediment samples, and laboratory investigations of suspended sediment samples.

Another method that has been used to some extent consists in collecting samples at given points in the cross section in such a manner that each sample contains water from all depths [15]. These "integrated" samples are obtained by having the bottle open at all depths. In shallow water a bottle with a small opening can be lowered to the bottom and raised to the surface at a uniform rate before it is completely filled. In deeper water it is necessary to have a device to open the bottle at the bottom and raise the bottle at a uniform rate so that it is nearly full when it comes to the surface of the stream.

There seems to be no definite relation between the flow of a stream and its load of suspended matter. In general the quantity of suspended matter increases with an increase in discharge, and with data from a large number of frequently collected samples it is possible to interpolate values for periods when no samples were taken. Love [20] has given the quantities of suspended matter carried by several streams during different periods of flood runoff and concludes that the only way to estimate or compute the suspended load is on the basis of careful and frequent sampling during floods. Faris [10] found for certain Texas streams that there was no direct relation between the suspended load and the velocity of the water.

The choice of satisfactory sampling points can best be made on the basis of the results obtained from a large number of samples in the cross section, and for a great many streams these observations must be made frequently. Faris [10] used as the mean percentage in the cross section the mean of the percentages in samples at 0.6 depth in verticals at one-sixth, one-half, and five-sixths of the entire width. Straub [27] shows mathematically that the "mean silt content" of the stream may be obtained by taking the sum of five-eighths of the average of the silt concentration at 0.2 depth across the stream for a particular measurement and three-eights of the average of the silt concentration in the samples at 0.8 depth.

Sizes of the particles.—The sizes of the particles in material carried in suspension and deposited along streams has been discussed by Fortier and Blaney [12], Straub [27], Faris [10], and others. In certain flood periods the load of suspended matter consists chiefly of the larger particles, and in other floods the smaller sizes predominate. Straub found that the material carried by the Missouri River during the winter was relatively coarse, but during the spring, when high rates of rainfall occur in the drainage basin, the suspended matter frequently consisted of finer particles. Similar results have been found for the Colorado River, in which during the spring floods most of the suspended material consists of particles whose diameters are greater than 50 microns, but in the summer floods the material often consists chiefly of particles whose diameters are less than 20 microns. The state of dispersion of the particles in suspension depends to some extent on the nature and quantity of the dissolved solids.

Breazeale [2] has discussed the results of laboratory experiments on the dispersion of Colorado River silt.

Bed load.—Estimates of the quantities of material carried as bed load have been made for some streams, but no satisfactory method has been found for determining this load.   Straub [27] gave figures for the Missouri River and some of its tributaries showing that the quantity of bed load ranged from one-eighth to one-one hundred eightieth of suspended load. Shulits [24] has discussed the Schoklitsch bed-load formula and suggested that studies should be made to determine its applicability.   The movement of material out of the bed of a stream has been discussed by many authors.   Wright [30] has given the results of laboratory experiments which show that clear water flowing out of a reservoir probably has a greater scouring power than turbid water under the same conditions. The changes that may occur in a stream bed below a reservoir have been discussed by Lane [18], Grover [13], Vetter [29], and others.

Loads of suspended matter in various streams.—The loads of suspended matter carried by individual streams can be computed only when adequate records of stream flow are available and when adequate samples have been obtained.   Each stream has certain characteristics affecting the load of suspended matter it may carry, and the results obtained for one stream are not representative of another stream.   The quantities of suspended matter carried by a few streams over short periods have been determined, but the data available are not sufficient to determine accurately the average load carried by any one stream, and the total load carried by all the streams of the United States cannot be closely estimated. Stevens [26] has listed the data available concerning the loads of suspended matter carried by the larger streams of the United States and by some of the streams of other countries.   The loads of suspended matter carried from small drainage areas have been determined in connection with the studies of soil erosion on cultivated plots in different agricultural regions [1].   The loads of suspended matter carried by streams draining small areas are given by Love [20] for 34 stations in different parts of the United States.   The maximum loads on these areas ranged from 154 to 127,000 tons a day.   The data from which these maximum loads were obtained show the total load for 1 year ranging from 200 tons to the square mile for a stream in Washington to nearly 8,000 tons to the square mile for a stream in Texas, and a large proportion of the total load may be carried in a few days.   An estimate of the loads of suspended matter carried by several streams over a period of years can be obtained from the results given by Eakin [9] in his report on the silting of reservoirs.

Nickle [21] in discussing Stevens' paper gave further data concerning the suspended matter carried by Texas streams.   Reports of the International Boundary Commission [17] give recent data for the Rio Grande.

Reports of the United States Waterways Experiment Station at Vicksburg, Miss., give the results of studies of the suspended matter carried and deposited by the Mississippi River [28]. The average annual load of suspended matter carried by the Colorado River past the Grand Canyon gaging station during the 10 years ending September 30, 1935, was 250,000,000 tons [16].

REFERENCES

1. Bennett, H. H., The quantitative study of erosion technique and some preliminary results: Geog. Rev., vol. 23, pp. 423–432, 1933.

2. Breazeale, J. F., A study of the Colorado River silt: Arizona Univ. Tech. Bull. 8, 1926.

3. Variation and control of salinity in Sacramento-San Joaquin delta and upper San Francisco Bay: California Dept. Public Works, Div. Water Resources, Bull. 27, 1931.

4 South Coastal Basin investigation, Quality of irrigation waters: California Dept. Public Works, Div. Water Resources, Bull. 40, p. 83, 1933.

5. Clarke, F. W., The data of geochemistry, 5th ed.: U. S. Geol. Survey Bull. 770, p. 479, 1924.

6. Clarke, F. W., A preliminary study of chemical denudation: Smithsonian Misc. Coll., vol. 56, No. 5, 1910.

7. Collins, W. D., and Williams, K. T., Chloride and sulfate in rain water: Ind. and Eng. Chemistry, vol. 25, p. 944, 1933.

8. Dole, R. B., and Stabler, Herman, Denudation: U. S. Geol. Survey Water-Supply Paper 234, pp. 78–93, 1909.

9. Eakin, H. M., Silting of reservoirs: U. S. Dept. Agr. Tech. Bull. 524, 1936.

10. Faris, O. A., The silt load of Texas streams: U. S. Dept. Agr. Tech. Bull. 382, 1933.

11. Fiock, L. R., Records of silt carried by the Rio Grande and its accumulation in Elephant Butte Reservoir: Am. Geophys. Union Trans., 1934, pt. 2, pp. 472–473.

12. Fortier, Samuel, and Blaney, H. F., Silt in Colorado River and its relation to irrigation: U. S. Dept. Agri. Tech. Bull. 67, 1928.

13. Grover, N. C., Discussion of Stevens, J. C., The silt problem: Am. Soc. Civil Eng. Trans., vol. 101, pp. 284–286, 1936.

14. Howard, C. S., Quality of water of the Colorado River, 1928–30: U. S. Geol. Survey Water-Supply Paper 638, pp. 145–158, 1932.

15. Howard, C. S., Suspended matter in the Colorado River in 1925–28: U. S. Geol. Survey Water-Supply Paper 636, pp. 15–44, 1929.

16. Howard, C. S., Suspended matter in the Colorado River, 1925–35: Am. Geophys. Union Trans., 1936, pt. 2, pp. 446–447.

17. Flow of the Rio Grande and tributary contributions, 1931. Internat. Boundary Comm., United States and Mexico, Water Bull. 1, 1932. Reports for years 1932, 1933, 1934, and 1935 published as Water Bulletins 2, 3, 4, and 5.

18. Lane, E. W., Retrogression of levels in river beds below dams: Eng. News-Record, vol. 112, pp. 836–838, 1934.

19. Leitch, R. D., The acidity of several Pennsylvania streams during low flow: U. S. Bur. Mines Rept. Inv. 3119, 1931.

20. Love, S. K., Suspended matter in several small streams: Am. Geophys. Union Trans., 1936, pt. 2, pp. 447–452.

21. Nickle, H. G., Discussion of Stevens, J. C., The silt problem: Am. Soc. Civil Eng. Trans., vol. 101, pp. 251–255, 1936.

22. Rockie, W. A., Snowdrifts and the Palouse topography: Geog. Rev., vol. 24, pp. 380–385, 1934.

23. Scofield, C. S., Stream pollution by irrigation residues: Ind. and Eng. Chemistry, vol. 24, pp. 1223–1224, 1932.

24. Shulits, Samuel, The Schoklitsch bed-load formula: Engineering, vol. 139, pp. 644–646, 687, 1935.

25. Stabler, Herman, Discussion of Stevens, J. C., The silt problem: Am. Soc. Civil Eng. Trans., vol. 101, pp. 277–284, 1936.

26. Stevens, J. C., The silt problem: Am. Soc. Civil Eng. Trans., vol. 101, pp. 207–250, 1936.

27. Straub, L. G., Missouri River: 73d Cong., 2d sess., H. Doc. 238, pp. 1032–1245, 1935.

28. Sediment investigations on the Mississippi River and its tributaries prior to 1930: U. S. Waterways Exper. Sta., Vicksburg, Miss., Paper H, 1930: idem, 1930–31: Paper U, 1931; Studies of river-bed materials and their movement, with special reference to the lower Mississippi River: Paper 17, 1935.

29. Vetter, C. P., Why desilting works for the All-American Canal?: Eng. News-Record, vol. 111, pp. 321–326, 1927.

30. Wright, C. A., Experimental study of the scour of a sandy river bed by clear and muddy water: Nat. Bur. Standards Jour. Research, vol. 17, pp. 193–206, 1936.

31. Wilhelm, C. J., Thorne, H. M., and Pryor, M. F., Disposal of oil-field brines in the Arkansas River drainage area in western Kansas: U. S. Bur. Mines Rept. Inv. 3318, 1936.

32. Iowa Institute of Hydraulic Research report on cooperative studies, Field practice and equipment used in sampling suspended sediment: Report No. 1, 1940.

33. Iowa Institute of Hydraulic Research report on cooperative studies, Equipment used for sampling bed-load and bed-material: Report No. 2, 1940.

34. Iowa Institute of Hydraulic Research report on cooperative studies, Analytical study of methods of sampling suspended sediment: Report No. 3, 1940.

35. Iowa Institute of Hydraulic Research report on cooperative studies, Methods of analyzing sediment samples: Report No. 4, 1941.

36. Iowa Institute of Hydraulic Research report on cooperative studies, Laboratory investigations of suspended sediment samplers: Report No. 5, 1941.

XIIIᴇ. CHEMISTRY OF GROUND WATER

Margaret D. Foster[1]

The water that falls upon the earth as rain or snow contains only small quantities of dissolved mineral matter [5]. As soon as it reaches the earth, however, it begins to react with the minerals of the soil and rocks with which it comes into contact. The amount and character of the mineral matter dissolved by meteoric waters depend upon the chemical composition and physical structure of the rocks with which they have been in contact, the temperature, the pressure, the duration of the contact, and the materials already in solution. The solvent action of the water is assisted by the presence in solution of carbon dioxide, derived from the atmosphere as the water fell as rain or from the soil through which it passes, where it is formed by organic processes.

WATER IN IGNEOUS ROCKS

The mean mineral composition of igneous rocks is estimated by Clarke and Washington [4] as follows:

	Per Cent
Quartz	12.0
Feldspars	59.5
Pyroxene and hornblende	16.8
Mica	3.8
Accessory minerals	7.9
	100.0

These minerals, though relatively insoluble, are not absoluteily so. The rate of solution is slow, and the amount in solution at any one time is small. Chemically these minerals, with the exception of quartz, are the alkali or alkaline earth salts of silicic, alumino-silicic, or ferro-silicic acids —salts of a strong base or bases combined with a weak acid. The action of meteoric waters on these minerals involves, first, solution of the mineral and then hydrolysis; reaction between the ions of the water and those of the dissolved mineral. The amount of dissociation of pure water into ions is small: at ordinary temperatures a liter of water contains only 10^{-7} grams of hydrogen in the ionic form. The hydrogen-ion concentration of meteoric waters is greater, however, because of the carbon dioxide universally present in them, and the action of the water on the minerals is accelerated, the amount of acceleration depending on the amount of

[1] Chemist, Quality of Water Division, Geological Survey, United States Department of the Interior, Washington, D. C.

carbon dioxide in solution. There is some divergence of opinion as to whether hydrolysis or the action of carbonic acid predominates. It is probable that near the surface, or as long as the percolating waters contain carbonic acid, the action of carbonic acid is the stronger, but as the carbonic acid is used up in the reaction the effects of hydrolysis becomes predominant. By that time, however, the water contains salts in solution, which also influence further action.

The action of water upon the silicate minerals takes place in definite steps and gives rise to definite compounds. Of the alteration products formed, the silica freed is soluble, and some of it is taken into solution by the water, although much remains behind in an intimate mixture with the clay minerals formed. These clay minerals (hydrous aluminosilicates) are relatively insoluble and tend to accumulate where they are formed. The potash developed, though soluble, is largely absorbed by the residual materials of the decaying rock. This is shown by the fact that natural waters contain much less potassium than sodium although the quantity of the two elements in the earth's crust is nearly the same. On the other hand, clays, shales, and soils contain more potassium than sodium.

If the mineral involved in the reaction is one that contains sodium, calcium, or magnesium instead of potassium, these elements are carried away in solution as the bicarbonates.

As a rule any iron-bearing mineral is apt to alter readily on attack by water, the iron uniting with oxygen to form iron oxide, which is very insoluble and remains in the soil.

The action of water on the different silicate minerals results in the formation of secondary minerals, but the general tendency is toward solution of the alkaline earths or of sodium, with some of the potassium, as the bicarbonates or hydroxides (generally the former, as carbon dioxide is so universally present in meteoric waters) and the production of simpler compounds from more complex. Compound silicates break up into simpler silicates, often hydrated, or to oxides, hydrates, or carbonates. As a rule, the chemical processes are incomplete; some of the minerals are not entirely altered, and the product exhibits many variations.

Even in the presence of carbonic acid, however, the silicate minerals that make up the igneous rocks are relatively resistant to attack. In experiments by Liegeois [8] to determine the action of carbonated water on rocks, quartzite and compact granite, syenite, and diabase showed no alteration on microscopic examination and comparison with fresh specimens after immersion in carbonated water for 6 months to a year, except one granite, in which the feldspar was attacked.

Water from silicate rocks is therefore usually low in dissolved mineral matter, containing only small quantities of calcium, magnesium, sodium, and potassium as bicarbonates, sulphates, and chlorides. The basic constituents are frequently present in nearly equivalent amounts. The percentage of silica in the dissolved mineral matter is usually high—as much as 50 percent or even more—although the actual amount is low.

WATER IN SEDIMENTARY ROCKS

Calcium bicarbonate waters.—In point of abundance in the earth's crust the sedimentary rocks are insignificant, constituting only about 5 percent [4]. They are, however, the most common rocks at the surface of the earth, covering approximately 75 percent of the land surface [1] and forming, at the top of the earth's crust, a layer that ranges in thickness from a little more than zero to 40,000 or 50,000 feet. With reference to ground water, therefore, they are much more important than the igneous rocks.

The three main types of sedimentary rocks, in the order of their estimated abundance, are shale, 82 percent of all sedimentary rocks; sandstone, 12 percent; and limestone (including chalk and dolomite), 6 percent [1]. Shale and sandstone are made up of the weathered residues of igneous and sedimentary rocks, to which more or less cementing material, usually calcium carbonate, silica, or iron oxide, has been added. They are estimated by Clarke [4] to have the following average mineral composition:

	Shale per cent	Sandstone per cent
Quartz	22.3	66.8
Feldspar	30.0	11.5
Clay	25.0	6.6
Limonite	5.6	1.8
Carbonates	5.7	11.1
Other minerals	11.4	2.2
	100.0	100.0

He estimates the average limestone to be 76 percent calcium carbonate.

The principal soluble material in the sedimentary rocks is carbonate, chiefly of calcium. The clastic constituents of the shales and sands, being the weathered residues of older rocks, have already been more or less altered by hydrolysis and leached of their soluble constituents. The solution of calcium carbonate, with some magnesium carbonate, is therefore the primary action when meteoric waters containing in solution carbon dioxide from the air and soil pass down through sedimentary deposits.

Calcium carbonate is relatively insoluble in pure water: 1 liter of distilled water dissolves only 0.014 gram of calcium carbonate at 25°C. [7]. Calcium bicarbonate, formed by the reaction between calcium carbonate and water containing carbonic acid, is, however, much more soluble. The amount that can be held in solution depends on the carbon dioxide content of the water. The net result of the action of meteoric waters on calcium carbonate, as on the silicate minerals, may represent the summation of three steps—solution of calcium carbonate, hydrolysis of calcium carbonate, and reaction between calcium ions and bicarbonate ions to form calcium bicarbonate.

Waters containing carbon dioxide attack calcium carbonate much more readily than they attack the silicate minerals. Waters from limestone or from sandstones or shales cemented with calcium carbonate may contain several hundred parts per million of dissolved mineral matter. The amount of calcium carbonate (or magnesium carbonate) taken into solution depends both on the carbon dioxide content of the percolating waters and on the calcium and magnesium carbonate content of the sedimentary beds.

The carbon dioxide content of meteoric waters is derived both from the atmosphere and from the oxidation of organic matter in the soil. It is probable that the greater part of the carbon dioxide content of meteoric waters is derived from the soils through which they pass. The proportion of carbon dioxide in the atmosphere is very nearly uniform and amounts, in round numbers, to 0.03 percent. The proportion of carbon dioxide in soil air is much larger [9]. Air in grassland soils, for example, may contain as much as 1.5 percent. The amount in the soil varies with the organic content of the soil and the energy of microbiologic decomposition.

In deposits that are relatively calcareous the capacity of the percolating waters to take calcium and magnesium carbonate into solution by virtue of their content of carbon dioxide is exhausted at shallow depths. In general, waters from such formations do not increase in mineral content with increasing depth in the formation. Wells 20 to 40 feet deep in these formations yield water containing as much dissolved mineral matter as those several hundred feet deep. In deposits that contain little calcareous material, however, the waters must travel farther to exhaust their capacity to take calcium carbonate into solution. Waters from shallow depths in such formations are usually low in dissolved mineral matter. As the waters percolate downward they continue to dissolve calcium and magnesium carbonate until their carbon dioxide content is exhausted. With greater depth the mineral content then tends to remain relatively constant. The water from the sandy phase of the Lissie formation in the vicinity of Houston, Tex., furnishes a good example of this phenomenon (Fig. XIIIᴇ-1, diagrams A–E). Some formations are apparently devoid of calcareous material, and even the deeper waters in them are very low in dissolved mineral matter. Some of these deeper waters carry considerable carbon dioxide in solution.

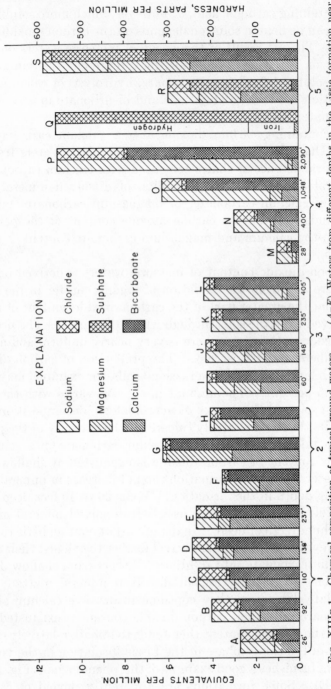

Fig. XIIIe-1.—Chemical composition of typical ground waters. 1. (A–E) Waters from different depths in the Lissie formation near Houston, Tex. 2. (F–H) Waters from dolomite. 3. (I–L) Waters from different depths in the Black Creek formation, South Carolina. 4. (M–P) Waters from different depths in the Willis (?) formation near Houston, Tex. 5. (Q–S) Acid, neutral, and alkaline sulphate waters.

This solvent action on the carbonate minerals of meteoric waters carrying carbon dioxide constitutes the primary action between the percolating meteoric waters and the rock minerals. As a result calcium bicarbonate is the predominant constituent of many waters from limestone and other sedimentary rocks cemented with calcium carbonate. As these rocks make up a large percentage of the surface of the earth, calcium bicarbonate waters are the most common type of natural ground waters. In some waters from such rocks calcium and bicarbonate make up 90 percent of the total dissolved mineral matter.

Dolomite yields water that contains practically equivalent amounts of calcium and magnesium. The double molecule of dolomite goes into solution as such and not according to the solubility of the separate carbonates. Calcium and magnesium are present in the water in the same proportion that they are in the rock (Fig. XIIIE-1, diagrams F–H). A magnesian limestone may yield a water resembling one from dolomite, but in this water the calcium and magnesium carbonates have gone into solution according to the solubility of the separate salts and are not present in the water in the same proportion that they are present in the rock.

Sodium bicarbonate waters.—Many waters from sedimentary deposits contain sodium and bicarbonate as the predominant basic and acidic constituents, and some contain approximately equal quantities of calcium and sodium. Many such waters are found in the Atlantic and Gulf Coastal Plain. The same formation may yield both calcium and sodium bicarbonate waters. In such a formation the calcium bicarbonate waters are usually the shallower waters, and the sodium bicarbonate waters are the deeper waters. The waters appear to undergo an alteration in character with increasing depth in the formation. The calcium and magnesium content decreases and the waters become softer; at the same time the sodium content increases but the bicarbonate and total mineral content often remain approximately the same. This phenomenon is illustrated in Figure XIIIE-1 by diagrams I–L, which represent analyses of waters from different depths in the Black Creek formation in South Carolina. These waters appear to be the result of a secondary action between the waters and the rock materials—exchange of calcium and magnesium in solution in the waters for the sodium of base-exchange minerals in the rock materials. The most important of these base-exchange minerals is glauconite, or greensand, a green granular silicate of potassium and iron that is formed near the mud line off continental shores and that is consequently often found in sedimentary deposits. Certain hydrous aluminosilicates that are derived from the weathering of crystalline rocks and that may make up part of the clastic material of the sedimentary deposits are also capable of base exchange

The depth at which softening begins depends upon the relative pro-portion of calcium and magnesium carbonates to base-exchange minerals in the beds through which the water passes. If the base-exchange miner-als are present in at least an equivalent amount to the carbonates, the two processes may be almost simultaneous, the calcium being exchanged almost as soon as it is taken into solution. For example, in the Willis (?) formation in the vicinity of Houston, Tex., the shallow waters are low in dissolved mineral matter and soft. With increasing depth in the forma-tion the waters continuously increase in total mineral content and in content of sodium bicarbonate, but the hardness and the content of the other constituents in these waters remain practically constant (Fig. XIIIᴇ-1, diagrams M–P). If the carbonates are present in the rock materials in amounts more than equivalent to the exchange minerals, or if the exchange capacity of the base-exchange minerals has been exhausted in the shallower materials, the ground waters must travel farther before being softened. In formations that contain little or no base-exchange materials, or in the limestone formations, the deep waters, as well as the shallow waters, are calcium bicarbonate waters.

Sulphate in ground water.—Sulphate is derived from various sources in the soil and rocks and from materials added by human agencies—from sulphates resulting from the oxidation and hydrolysis of metallic sul-phides, from gypsum, or from fertilizers containing sulphates. Iron sul-phide, by oxidation and hydrolysis, yields iron oxide (usually hydrated) and sulphuric acid:

$$2FeS_2 + 7H_2O + 15O = 2Fe(OH)_3 + 4H_2SO_4$$

Waters from shale characteristically carry sulphate, sometimes in consider-able amounts, derived, most probably, from the pyrite so often associated with shale. The sulphuric acid formed in the oxidation and hydrolysis of pyrite acts strongly on the other rock constituents and intensifies the action of the percolating water. Some waters, particularly in the vicinity of coal mines, where pyrite has been exposed to the action of air and water, are acid because of their content of sulphuric acid. When these acid waters move downward through lime-bearing rocks, the sulphuric acid acts on calcium carbonate and the waters become neutral and then more and more alkaline but still contain considerable sulphate and iron (Fig. XIIIᴇ-1, diagrams Q–S):

$$H_2SO_4 + CaCO_3 = H_2CO_3 + CaSO_4$$
$$H_2CO_3 + CaCO_3 = Ca(HCO_3)_2$$

Clarke [4] considers that the deposition of calcium sulphate from such waters is the most common primary cause of the formation of gypsum. In arid or semiarid regions calcium sulphate may be precipitated as a crust on the surface of the ground by the evaporation of sulphate-bearing waters, and, through re-solution by rain water, give rise to the alkali waters found in such regions.

Waters from gypsum characteristically contain calcium and sulphate as their most predominant mineral constituents. The action of meteoric waters on gypsum is one of solution only; the presence of dissolved carbon dioxide in the water has no effect on the solution of the gypsum, as calcium sulphate does not hydrolyze in water. Consequently, water continues to take calcium sulphate into solution as long as it is in contact with gypsum, until it is saturated.

In the waters in many sedimentary formations, however, notably in the Coastal Plain, the sulphate content is low and does not increase with increasing depth in the formation. This suggests that the sulphate may be present as an impurity in the calcium carbonate cementing materials, where it is accessible for solution only as the calcium carbonate is taken into solution; when solution of carbonate ceases, solution of sulphate ceases also. On contact with base-exchange minerals, the calcium of calcium sulphate in solution in ground waters may be exchanged for sodium in a manner analogous to the exchange of the calcium of calcium bicarbonate, giving rise to sodium sulphate waters.

Chloride in ground waters.—Chloride is dissolved in small quantities from many rock materials. Near the coast the ground waters may be contaminated by salt water from the sea. Along most coasts fresh water is usually obtainable at shallow depths, even very near the shore. The distance inland to which salt water may be found in deeper wells depends upon the relation between fresh water and salt water in the water-bearing formation, which in turn depends upon the rainfall, the seasonal fluctuations of the water table, the topography, and the permeability and structure of the rocks [2]. The chemical composition of many of the salty waters found along the coast shows them to be normal ground waters to which more or less sea water has been added. Some are sufficiently contaminated with sea water to contain sodium and chloride as the predominant mineral constituents. The problem of finding sufficient fresh water for a municipal supply is a serious one for many cities on the coast. The deep formations may all yield salty water, and the superficial deposits, while yielding fresh water, may not yield sufficient water for the use of a city. Waters high in sodium chloride may also be found in deep wells that penetrate to salt deposits or to connate waters entrapped in the older marine sediments or in wells contaminated by the salt water usually found associated with salt domes.

As sodium chloride is also a characteristic constituent of sewage, many shallow wells that are polluted by household or barnyard drainage yield waters containing more chloride than is normal for the formation and area. An abnormal chloride content in water due to pollution is usually accompanied by an abnormal nitrate content, as nitrate is a final oxidation product of nitrogeneous organic materials.

Nitrate in ground waters.—Many waters contain less than 1 part per million of nitrate, although waters containing more than 100 parts per million are sometimes found. Nitrate in shallow waters in excess of a few parts per million usually indicates present or past pollution. The interpretation of the presence of abnormal amounts of nitrate with reference to the sanitary condition of the water should be made, however, with extreme caution and only after careful consideration of the sanitary surroundings of the source of the water, the nature of the rock materials from which the water is derived, and the composition of other waters from the same formation. Abnormal nitrate due to pollution is usually found only in waters from shallow wells near the source of pollution, although waters from wells in cavernous limestone may contain abnormal nitrate derived from a source of pollution distant from the well.

Nitrate may also be leached from rocks, although few rocks contain appreciable amounts of nitrate except in regions where there are nitrate deposits. Waters high in nitrate are sometimes found in areas where caliche occurs, and it is probable that the nitrate in these waters is derived from this source. The caliche is not ordinarily related to any particular bed that may be regarded as a source of nitrate, although locally richer accumulations of nitrate may be associated with particular layers. In areas where nitrate fertilizer is used nitrate may be washed from the soil. Nitrate derived from such soil may appear in both shallow and deep waters in a considerable area.

As a rule nitrate is not a predominant constituent of natural waters. Only in waters otherwise low in mineral content that are badly polluted is nitrate likely to be the predominant acidic constituent.

The mineral matter dissolved in a water is not a collection of random quantities of the different constituents. The quantities of the basic constituents—calcium, magnesium, sodium, and potassium—dissolved in a water are together chemically equivalent to the sum of the acidic constituents—bicarbonate, sulphate, chloride and nitrate. In addition to these constituents that are in chemical equilibrium with each other, all waters contain iron, aluminum, and silica, which are generally supposed to be present in the colloidal state as oxides. If one basic and one acidic constituent make up the greater part of the mineral matter dissolved in a water it is customary to refer to the water as characterized by the name of the compound made up of these constituents. Thus if calcium and bicarbonate are the predominant basic and acidic constituents in a water, the water is referred to as a calcium bicarbonate water. If, however, the quantities of two or more of either the basic or acidic constituent are of about the same magnitude, it is unjustifiable and misleading to characterize the water by the name of a single compound.

The waters from some formations show a family likeness to one another; they are similar in mineral content and in chemical character. Waters from other formations differ greatly in mineral content and chemical composition. These differences are usually due to local variations in the mineral composition of the rock materials, except where the composition of the waters has been altered through contamination by salt water or pollution by domestic or commercial wastes. Some waters pass through several formations or are composites of waters from different sources and are not representative of any particular formation.

REFERENCES

1. Branson, E. B., and Tarr, W. A., Introduction to geology, p. 173, New York and London, McGraw-Hill Book Co., 1935.

2. Brown, J. S., A study of coastal ground water, with special reference to Connecticut: U. S. Geol. Survey Water-Supply Paper 537, 1925.

3. Byers, H. G., The constituents of the inorganic soil colloids [mimeographed], U. S. Dept. Agr., Bur. Chemistry and Soils.

4. Clarke, F. W., and Washington, H. S., The composition of the earth's crust: U. S. Geol. Survey Prof. Paper 127, p. 31, 1924.

5. Collins, W. D., and Williams, K. T., Chloride and sulphate in rain water: Ind. and Eng. Chemistry, 25, p. 944, 1933.

6. Getman, F. H., and Daniels, F., Outlines of theoretical chemistry, p. 401, New York, John Wiley & Sons, 1931.

7. Kendall, J., The solubility of calcium carbonate in water, Phil. Mag., 23, p. 958, 1912.

8. Liegeois, P. G., The action of carbonated waters on rocks: Soc. geol. Belgique Annales, tome 51, pp. 232–236, 1928.

9. Robinson, G. W., Soils, their organic constitution and classification, Murby, London, 1932.

CHAPTER XIV

HYDROLOGY OF LIMESTONE TERRANES

Allyn C. Swinnerton[1]

INTRODUCTION

Definition of limestone terrane.—Limestones constitute between 5 and 10 percent of the sedimentary rocks [4, pp. 32–34]; their outcrop areas measure several million square miles. Limestone terranes, however, are those natural regions or other well-defined areas which are underlain by dominantly calcareous rocks to the virtual exclusion of rocks of other kinds and whose surface and subsurface features are determined by the characteristic responses of soluble rocks to weathering and erosion. Such a region is commonly designated by the term "karst."

Rock solubility, with its corollary of progressive erosional change. is the paramount consideration in all elements of limestone hydrololgy Frequent repetition of emphasis on this factor in its varied relations wil, be found in this chapter.

Occurrence and distribution of limestone terranes.—Limestone terranes are found throughout the world, mainly on the continents. Some oceanic islands also have limestone terranes of small area. Space does not permit a review of the salient features of many such regions. In outlining the nature of a few areas the purpose is to indicate that such terranes occur on rocks of distinctly different ages, structure, and relief.

The plateau of the western Balkans is the classical area of limestone physiography. From it come the name "karst" and other terms that are slowly invading English and American geologic literature. The region is underlain by thick Triassic and Cretaceous limestones which were deformed by Tertiary folding and faulting [44, pp. 392–409]. The characteristic features of the Dalmatian karst include caves such as those at Adelsberg, interior drainage in large basins with only subsurface outlet, many varieties of sinkholes known as ponors, dolinas, uvalas, and polje, many "lost rivers" and large springs [6, 33]. All these characteristics have produced a reaction on human geography resulting in a concentration of population in the interior basins and along the resurgences of the "lost rivers" and an avoidance of the barren, waterless, thin-soiled uplands.

In the United States the distribution of thick Mississippian limestones from central Indiana southward through Kentucky to central Tennessee

[1] Professor of Geology, Antioch College, Yellow Springs, Ohio.

has created in some ways a more typical limestone terrane than the karst itself [23, pp. 285–286]. The rocks are well consolidated and have gentle dips, presenting relatively undisturbed masses to the effects of erosion. In this area are found many caves, of which Mammoth and Wyandotte are the best known, thousands of square miles of sinkholes, and number- less "lost rivers" and springs, while surface drainage is limited to a few major streams. The relief is least in the northern and southern portions of the belt; the caves are simple and the sink holes small but numerous. In the central area the relief reaches 400 feet, and complex, many-leveled caves and deep, nested sinkholes are found [8, 19, 22, 30, 41, 42].

The Appalachian Mountains, from New England to northern Ala- bama, contain many narrow, elongate limestone valleys. The Shenan- doah Valley of Virginia is the largest and best known of such valleys and should certainly be considered a limestone terrane. The rocks of the valley are of early Paleozoic age and include many thick limestone forma- tions, which are involved in complex folding and faulting. Several physiographic cycles are evident in the present relief, although the ground- water effects—caverns, sinkholes, and springs—appear to be related to the present stage [21, p. 13].

Many of the larger oceanic archipelagoes and islands such as the Bermudas, Bahamas, Cuba, and Puerto Rico, may be said to have lime- stone terranes. The larger islands have uplifted reef terraces; the Ber- mudas have a complicated recent history of changes of sea level that have resulted in a series of calcareous sand dunes, interbedded soils, and marine limestones—all in various stages of consolidation [34, pp. 381–468]. In the Bermudas the permeability is so well developed that no fresh water is available except that collected from rainfall.

The Floridian peninsula is a low-lying limestone terrane. Of par- ticular hydrologic interest are the artesian conditions set up in the Ocala (Eocene) limestone, which crops out in the northwest-central part of the peninsula and dips gently in all directions from its outcrop area. [36]. It carries water to considerable depth and is reached by drilling on both the east and the west coasts. A few offshore springs tap the aquifer. In the outcrop region there are both recharge and discharge areas. The large springs, Silver Springs, Rainbow (formerly Blue) Springs, and others, lie in the outflow district peripheral to the slightly higher intake area. Outside the outcrop area the Ocala is unconformably overlain by less permeable limestones and marls, which help to retain the artesian head. However, there is some very permeable limestone of more recent age near the surface in the southern part of the State.

"Fossil" limestone terranes are known. The structural character of the Boone formation in the Joplin district, Missouri, is attributed, at least in part, to the karst character of the pre-Pennsylvanian surface

[35, p. 32].   Nye [10, pp. 180–189] has pointed out compelling reasons for regarding the greater part of the present permeability of the aquifer in the Roswell artesian basin, New Mexico, as caused by karst action on a Permian land surface.   (See also Bretz [2].)

Composition of limestone.—Pure calcium carbonate contains 56.04 percent of CaO and 43.96 percent of CO_2.   Clarke [4, p. 564], giving a composite analysis of 345 specimens by Stokes, indicates that the average content of limestone is CaO 42.61 percent and CO_2, 41.58 percent.   Other analyses cited by Clarke show percentages as high as 47.5 CaO and 43.38 CO_2.   In limestones, as in other rocks, much variation is to be expected.   Dolomites are commonly grouped generically with limestones, and, to the extent that they show the physiographic effects of solution, their outcrop areas should be included as limestone terranes.

SOLUBILITY

Solubility of limestone in water is the factor which, more than any other, differentiates the hydrology of limestone terranes from that of terranes underlain by other rocks.   In most hydrologic studies the rocks serving as the reservoir can be regarded as static; in limestone areas the rock itself, because of its solubility, plays a dynamic part.   Hence infiltration and runoff ratios, permeability, ground-water motion, reservoir characteristics, quality of water, and its availability and permanence of supply—all these elementary hydrologic relations in limestone terranes must be studied with due consideration of the part played by the changing characteristics of the rock itself.

Figures indicating the solubility of calcite are not of great significance, for the reason that the observed concentrations of calcium and bicarbonate ions in ground water imply greater solution of calcium carbonate than data on solubility would indicate as possible.   Kendall [16, pp. 958–976], Wells [43, p. 617], and Johnston [13, pp. 2001–2020] show the ordinary solubility of $CaCO_3$ as ranging from 14.3 to 74 parts per million.   Analyses of ground water (see chapter XIIIᴇ) leave little doubt that the calcium carbonate, although $CaCO_3$ is not shown as such, commonly ranges from 100 to 200 parts per million and may reach well over 400 parts.

The study by Johnston and Williamson [14, pp. 975–983] of the complete solubility curve of calcium carbonate as the CaO-H_2O-CO_2 system, at 16° C., shows three stable solid phases—the hydroxide, the carbonate, and the bicarbonate—corresponding to three pressure ranges— up to 10^{-14} atmospheres, 10^{-14} to 15, and above 15.   In nature, at the earth's surface partial pressures exceed the first of these ranges and are normally less than the third.   Consequently, for this discussion, the effect of the partial pressure of CO_2 on the solubility of the solid $CaCO_3$ phase is the critical relation.

Under ordinary atmospheric conditions, when air exerts a pressure of 1 atmosphere, the partial pressure due to carbon dioxide is 0.0003 atmosphere. At this pressure, at 16^c C., about 63 parts per million of calcium carbonate can be dissolved. The partial pressure of CO_2 required to dissolve 400 parts per million is approximately 0.065 atmosphere. As the observed concentrations of $CaCO_3$ commonly fall between 100 to 400, it seems apparent that some enrichment of the environment in CO_2 is necessary.

Adams and Swinnerton [1, pp. 504–508] have discussed the possible causes of increased partial pressures of CO_2 leading to the high ground-water concentrations of calcium and bicarbonate ions and have pointed out that the soil is a potential source of enrichment of ground water in CO_2 content. The CO_2 present in the soil, from a variety of sources, will exert pressure on water passing through the soil several hundred times as great as the CO_2 in atmospheric air, and the solubility of $CaCO_3$ by ground water subjected to such conditions will be increased manyfold.

Carbon dioxide enrichment of the ground water through the medium of the soil may not be the complete answer, although under many conditions it is an adequate one, and some experimental work [28, pp. 1467–1475] and observations [40] tend to confirm its effectiveness.

The temperature factor is not highly significant in the ordinary ranges, but it is complicated. In general it may be said, after comparing Wells' and Kendall's figures [43, 16], that whereas the solubility of calcium carbonate in air free from carbon dioxide increases slightly with increase in temperature, the reverse is true in the presence of carbon dioxide.

Another problem concerns the differences of solubility of different limestones. It seems apparent that in addition to the varying capacities of solvents there is a real difference in the capacity of limestones to be dissolved. The solubility of certain limestones has been commonly attributed to their purity. On this contention, however, the partial analyses of the cavernous Virginia limestones shed interesting light, as shown by the following table:

Partial analyses of limestones from Virginia caves
[By J. H. Yoe, M. C. Goldberg, and Leopold Sender; adapted from McGill [21, p. 143]]

	1	2	3	4	5	6
Al_2O_3	0.42	2.12	3.48	0.46	2.44	1.14
Fe_2O_3						
$CaCO_3$	98.36	75.09	76.50	89.81	64.13	64.45
$MgCO_3$	.57	8.34	13.09	.53	1.84	30.10
Insoluble residue	.47	14.05	9.07	9.79	30.79	4.20
	99.82	99.60	102.14	100.59	99.20	99.89

1. Stones River limestone, Endless Caverns.
2. Stones River limestone, Massanutten Caverns.
3. Beekmantown limestone, Luray Caverns.
4. Conococheague limestone, Shenandoah Caverns.
5. Conococheague limestone, Grand Caverns.
6. Elbrook limestone, Dixie Caverns.

The range in insoluble residue from 0.47 to 30.79 percent, together with the range of $CaCO_3$ from 64.13 to 98.36 percent, clearly indicates that "purity"—that is, high $CaCO_3$ content—is not an essential factor in solubility. It is apparent that the physical characteristics of rocks may be significant in explaining variations in solubility. Texture, pore space, and the presence of colloidal matter or other impurities may eventually be found to be effective.

The time factor in solution cannot be ignored. The longer the period of contact of solvent with solute the greater the concentration of the solution so long as it remains below saturation. Volume of solvent, area of contact surface, and rate of flow are other factors of significance. For example, a large volume of solvent of low concentration flowing over a large area is probably more effective in producing solution than more stagnant solvents of lesser volume and contact. The common ion effect— for instance, that produced by the presence of calcium sulphate in solution with calcium bicarbonate in the presence of limestone—should, according to chemical dicta, depress the solubility of the $CaCO_3$. There is some geologic evidence that the reverse may be true for the example cited, but for the time being judgment must be suspended.

Enough has been written here to indicate that the phenomenon of solution is an extremely complex matter, depending on the interplay of a great many factors. It is on the particular combinations of these varied factors that many of the relations of the hydrology of limestone terranes need to be considered. Unfortunately it is still necessary to treat of solubilities in general terms.

PERMEABILITY

Permeability, meaning the capacity of rock to permit the passage of fluids, depends on the porosity, the size of the openings, and the fracture pattern. It is important to note that porosity does not always mean permeability.

The permeabilities of limestone are in general of two kinds—(1) that provided by primary porosity, in which permeability is attained by the presence of the initial, communicating pore space that remains in incompletely consolidated rocks, and (2) that achieved largely through the network of a joint-fracture pattern produced secondarily in the limestone by diastrophic forces. The first type of permeability may be designated as primary; the second as secondary. Both kinds of permeability may be present in the same rock. Studies by petroleum geologists have considered extensively the porosity and permeability of limestones in relation to rock fluids [12, p. 1155].

The solubility of the rocks permits a modification by circulating water of permeability of both kinds. Hence in a limestone region the permeability, undergoing progressive development, ordinarily increases.

Figures on the degree of permeability are not commonly available. Where permeability can be measured the data are sometimes amazing. Stringfield [37] reports:

Some of the most permeable limestone formations are in Florida and the Coastal Plain of Georgia. These include the Ocala limestone, of Eocene age, in Florida and Georgia, and limestone of Pleistocene and Pliocene age in Dade County, in southern Florida. The permeability in these formations appears to be chiefly secondary in origin. However, part of it may be primary. . . . These rocks contain both artesian and non-artesian water, and their capacity to yield water to wells is notably different from that of limestone formations, which yield water only from fractures or joints or a few solution channels. . . .

Few if any of the wells drilled into the Ocala are dry. It is not unusual for the larger wells to yield more than 1,000 gallons a minute, and a yield of 7,500 gallons a minute with a drawdown of only 9 feet has been recorded for one well. The Ocala is the principal source of ground water in the coastal area of Georgia, where it yields to wells in the six counties bordering the coast more than 80 million gallons a day. . . .

Observations indicate that the limestone will transmit at Savannah, Ga., about 250,000 gallons of water a day through each mile width of the formation for each foot per mile of hydraulic gradient. This means, of course, that with a hydraulic gradient of 10 feet per mile, which is comparable to some of the gradients in the Savannah area, each mile width of the formation will yield 2,500,000 gallons a day. Observations at Brunswick, Ga., . . . indicate that the rate at which the limestone will transmit water is several times that at Savannah. . . . The permeability [of the Ocala formation] in areas where the formation is at or near the surface, as in Marion County, Fla., is much larger than that where the formation is deeply buried, as in the southern part of Florida.

Although not as extensive as the Ocala formation, limestones of Pleistocene and Pliocene ages in Dade County, Fla., are notable for their permeability. Observations indicate that these formations will transmit at Miami about 3,000,000 gallons of water a day through each mile width of the formation with a hydraulic gradient of 1 foot per mile, or about 12 times the capacity of the Ocala under the same gradient at Savannah.

The effect of this marked permeability is strikingly indicated by the very shallow drawdown in one of the Miami well fields, as shown on the map (Fig. XIV-1) submitted by W. P. Cross, of the United States Geological Survey.

The following brief discussion is also furnished by Mr. Cross:

"The limestone in the Miami area is highly productive, and thousands of wells, from about 20 to 200 feet deep, are used for public, industrial, and domestic supplies. The surface is very flat, with altitudes from sea level to about 30 feet. The soil is sandy, is usually thin, and has a high infiltration capacity. There is no direct surface runoff, except in paved areas. The average rainfall is about 60 inches a year, and much of the rainfall reaches the water table.

"Conditions in the Miami well field, shown on the accompanying map (Fig. XIV-1), are typical. Fifteen municipal wells, with depths from 55 to 100 feet, supply Miami and nearby cities. Well logs indicate about 3 feet or less of sandy soil, underlain by about 20 feet or less of oolitic limestone (Miami oolite). The oolite in this area has many vertical solution channels, up to a foot or more in diameter and usually filled with permeable siliceous sand.

"The Miami oolite is variably underlain by about 45 feet of cavernous sandy limestone, including lenses and pockets of permeable siliceous sand. This stratum is extremely permeable, and most of the wells are seated in it. Below it is about 60 feet of a similar siliceous though less permeable limestone underlain by an impermeable glauconitic sandy and clayey marl.

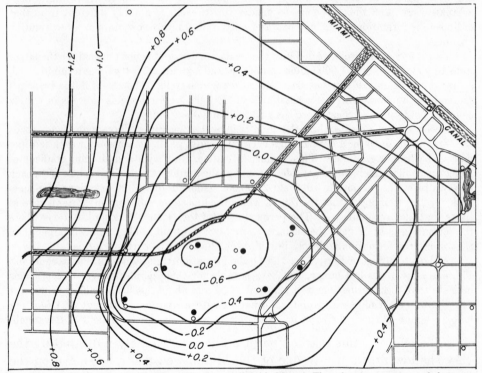

Fig. XIV-1.—Map of the Miami Springs well field, Miami, Fla., showing contours of the water table during heavy pumping. After W. P. Cross. Datum is mean sea level. Contour interval is 0.2 foot. Open circles, observation wells; solid circles, supply wells. Scale, one inch equals 2,000 feet.

"On February 12, 1940, the day for which the water-table map was drawn, approximately 20,000,000 gallons was pumped from the eight wells shown on the map. Based on the slope of the cone of depression, the coefficient of transmissibility was computed as 3,300,000."

The coefficient of permeability cannot be computed definitely until the thickness of the strata that are functional in supplying these wells has been more definitely determined. However, it appears to be well over 100,000, or higher than any coefficient of permeability previously determined by the United States Geological Survey.

The coefficients of transmissibility and permeability are defined in chapter XB.

It is clear from such data, not only that the permeability of limestone may be very great but also that such permeability may be of both primary and secondary nature and that it may be generally distributed in the formations as a rock characteristic. Such conditions may be contrasted with those prevailing in the older rocks of the Kentucky-Tennessee region, where the permeability is mainly secondary, and, although it may be very great because of large cavern channels, nevertheless the availability and permanence of supplies of water obtained by drilling are very uncertain. Elsewhere—for example, in the limestone areas of Iowa and Minnesota [11, 29], where the permeability, here also mainly secondary, is relatively low—the regional dip, carrying the beds underground and blocking circulation, causes the network of joints to be filled with water. Hence, even though the permeability is not great, water is relatively accessible.

Permeability and its development may, under certain specific circumstances, be independent of any particular physiographic stage; it may have been inherited from a previous cycle or it may depend upon an ancient karst underlying an unconformity. Under such conditions permeability may be superposed upon a terrane in somewhat the same manner as surface streams are said to be superposed. It is exceedingly difficult to prove conclusively that channels now functioning had their origin as part of a "fossil" karst, but for specific areas such an origin is strongly suspected [10, 2].

HYDROLOGIC CONDITIONS

RUNOFF, INFILTRATION AND DISCHARGE

In many parts of limestone terranes, because of their great permeability runoff is lacking, and springs and surface streams are few. The high infiltration in such areas leads to great ground-water recharge. Hence, in contrast to the dry surfaces there is commonly a counterpart area where the ground water is discharged in large springs, giving rise to streams that fluctuate with changes in the discharge of the springs. They are generally more constant in flow than streams in terranes of other rocks supplied by runoff.

The relations of runoff and infiltration in limestone terranes are changed progressively by the solutional modification of the rocks by ground water. In a region at the beginning of a physiographic cycle the ratios of runoff and infiltration will be similar to those in other terranes of the same relief and physical characteristics. However, in an area in which the erosional cycle has proceeded toward maturity the infiltration will be markedly increased, because the underground passageways are enlarged, and sinkholes are prominent surface features. Under these conditions the surface water promptly finds its way below the surface, and stream runoff, except for major drainage lines, is largely lacking or

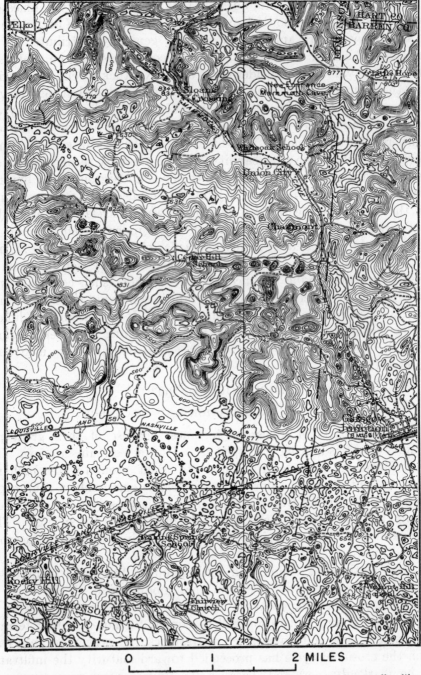

FIG. XIV-2.—Map of a part of the Mammoth Cave quadrangle, Ky., showing large valley-like sink-holes in the upper part and many small sinkholes and several lost rivers in the lower part.

only short-lived. (See Fig. XIV-2.) Ground-water flow and discharge from springs correspondingly will be very great.

Where the physiographic cycle has reached old age the effect of decreased topographic relief masks the effect of increased permeability. Runoff becomes greater again, because the capacity for infiltration is diminished by the reduction of flow induced by relief head.

GROUND-WATER CIRCULATION AND THE WATER TABLE

Theoretically ground water moves in arcuate paths following lines of flow that have their origin at the water table, curve downward below the water table for some distance, and then rise to the outlet. (See chapter XB.) Diagrammatically these flow lines can be represented by a family of curves, the spacing of which is closest near the area of outlet and becomes wider along the water table as the distance from the outlet increases. A similar family of curves can be drawn showing equipotential surfaces that represent the ratio between head and length of path. Such lines cross the flow lines at right angles. The volume of flow is equal between the lines representing flow.

In ordinary isotropic media where structural control does not intervene the arcuate pattern will probably be maintained with little modification. In limestones, on the assumption of a distribution of primary permeability or of joint spacing equivalent to an isotropic medium, the initial stages of ground-water circulation will undoubtedly have an arcuate pattern of motion. However, because of solution the lines of flow will be modified as soon as movement has begun. The concentration of flow lines at the outlet area, together with the greater velocities in this zone, will result in an enlargement of the outlet area and a consequent shallowing of the more remote arcuate paths. Hence the more direct paths will become larger than the less direct paths and will permit progressively larger flows at the expense of other passageways. This accelerating relation is certainly not a direct proportionality; too many variables enter as factors, but the general relation is clear.

In a practical sense the circulation of ground water in simple limestone terranes is separable into two elements—that which supplies water to the water table, largely vertical movement, and that which drains the water below the water table, largely horizontal movement. The depth and configuration of the water table at any time depend not only on the infiltration but also on the extent to which the enlargement of vertical passageways and of lateral drainage systems has progressed at the depth of the major surface valleys.

In some limestone terranes the water table conditions are so anomalous that many foreign investigators, notably Cramer [5, pp. 306–323] and Martel [25], disregard entirely the concept of the water table. However, the conclusion seems inescapable that a zone of water saturation exists below limestone areas, even those well advanced toward physiographic maturity.

Under relations of structure and stratigraphy that create artesian conditions in limestone terranes the behavior of ground water is very similar to that of water in other aquifers. The chief differences relate to the greater development of permeability and hence to a greater velocity of flow, greater reservoir capacity, and greater availability of water in limestones than in other rocks.

THE GROUND-WATER RESERVOIR

From the hydrologist's point of view the water that is in circulation between the sites of infiltration and discharge can be regarded as a ground-water reservoir. The character of the rock permeability and the extent of its development are significant factors in determining the features of the reservoir and the availability of its water. A second element is of equal significance: in some situations the structural relations of the limestone control the behavior of the ground-water circulation and, in consequence, affect the nature of the reservoir—for example, in areas where artesian conditions exist.

In a simple limestone terrane having predominantly primary permeability—that is, overlapping pore space—in a region where the topographic relief is moderate and structural control of flow is slight, infiltration will ordinarily exceed runoff, at least until the pore space of the limestone is filled to capacity. The gravity discharge of this mass of water by means of springs and seepages will permit slow circulation to the outlets and will result in the lowering of the water table until it is replenished and raised by further infiltration from precipitation. In this situation the availability of water will ordinarily be great: the water in wells will rise to the level of the water table and will fluctuate with the water table. The amount of fluctuation will depend upon the frequency of precipitation and upon the permeability. The greater the permeability the more rapid the flow through the reservoir to the discharge points, and in consequence the fluctuations of the water table will be great.

In a limestone terrane in which the permeability is mainly secondary—that is, by means of a network of joints—in a region where the topographic relief is moderate and structural control of flow insignificant, the infiltration will depend upon the physiographic development. In the early stages of the erosion cycle runoff will be relatively large and infiltration will be slight. After slow circulation along the joint network has enlarged the joint planes by solution, the infiltration will increase at the expense of the runoff. By the time maturity is reached the joint network may be so enlarged that these channels will be only partly filled. Those which have become greatly enlarged may rob the smaller openings of water except at times of copious infiltration. In such a region water supply from wells is very uncertain; some wells may reach the streams flowing through the large openings and so obtain plentiful supplies, others may cut relatively dry rock between the joints, and still others may tap the small fissures with intermittent supplies of water. Water will not rise in any of these wells, and fluctuations of level, even in those of abundant supply, may be very great.

In some limestone terranes a subterranean drainage system has developed that is somewhat comparable with the surface drainage system in a terrane of relatively impermeable rock, the part of the limestone above the subterranean stream channels being merely a sieve and the surface drainage system being almost completely abandoned. In such terranes there may be comparatively little water in storage, and the water table is not a prominent feature.

In regions where the limestone is involved in folded or tilted structure, so that artesian or pseudo-artesian conditions occur, the availability of water is dependent on the nature of the permeability. If the permeability is of the primary type, water will be generally available and will rise in wells to the level of the piezometric surface. In regions where the structural conditions are similar but where permeability is secondary, the availability of water to a well will depend upon the intersection of the well with joint openings. Ordinarily, as the openings are completely filled with water and under artesian pressure, the supply will be abundant. In such regions water will also rise in wells to the piezometric surface. The fluctuation of level of the piezometric surface is commonly not great except during long periods of drought or in regions where the supply of water has been overdeveloped by too much drilling.

Natural outlets occur in both the simple gravity type of circulation and the artesian type. In areas of the first type springs and seepages occur along the river valleys at approximately the level of the streams. In the artesian reservoirs natural outlets occur where faults or continuous joint zones cut through the aquifer and the overlying impermeable zones. Outlets may also occur peripheral to the artesian intake area just inside the line of outcrop of the overlying less permeable rocks. This situation occurs only where the recharge is abundant and the aquifer has little or no outlet down its dip. For example, in Florida the artesian conditions in the Ocala formation (see p. 657) are such that an area of surface discharge surrounds the intake area. It is well known that discharge from the aquifer also occurs from submarine springs off the Atlantic coast and that transverse as well as down-dip circulation takes place. However, in large parts of Florida recharge is so great that the piezometric level remains above the topographic surface outside of the intake area.

Complex limestone hydrology

The foregoing more or less theoretical discussion of hydrologic relations has been, of necessity, oversimplified. Likewise no integrated picture of the whole regimen of precipitation, runoff, infiltration, circulation, and discharge has been attempted. An example of actual conditions will serve to correct the preceding disproportionate emphasis.

In the vicinity of San Antonio, Tex., the hydrologic resources are largely determined by the character, distribution, and structure of the Edwards limestone. Two adjoining sets of conditions—one a simple gravity reservoir in the Edwards Plateau, the other down-dip and artesian

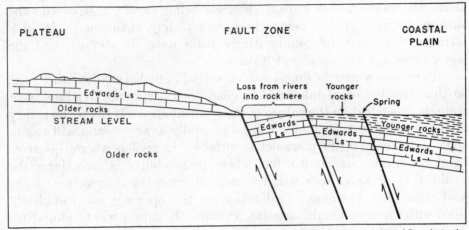

Fig. XIV-3.—Idealized diagram of structure controlling ground water in the vicinity of San Antonio, Texas. After Livingston, Sayre, and White.

circulation in the Balcones fault zone—combine to give a unique and instructive picture of ground-water behavior in limestones. Livingston, Sayre, and White [18] have reported the conditions vividly and in detail. (See Fig. XIV-3.) They say:

The Edwards limestone is more soluble than most other limestones [in the region] and has become honeycombed or cavernous by solution channeling over wide areas both on the Edwards Plateau and in the Balcones fault zone. . . . These openings are interconnected for long distances and form extensive underground reservoir systems, which, to a large extent, control the available supply of water in the region—both surface and underground. . . . [18, p. 72].

The plateau reservoir system [north and west of San Antonio] is located in areas in which the Edwards formation caps a large part of the interstream uplands and absorbs a high proportion of the rainfall. In these areas the water sinks through cracks and solution channels to the lower part of the formation, where it is prevented from going deeper by the relatively impermeable beds of the underlying formations. The water table in the body of ground water thus accumulated in many places is above the valleys of the larger streams, and the water moves laterally by gravity in the beds of the limestone, which are almost horizontal, and largely appears in the valleys as springs, usually along the base of the·Edwards limestone. . . . These contact springs are the source of the perennial rivers of the Edwards Plateau, which are famous for the clearness of their waters and the relative constancy of their flow. . . .

The lower or fault-zone reservoir occurs in the body of the formation that extends Gulfward from the Balcones escarpment [18, pp. 72–73].

In the outcrop area of the Edwards limestone along the Balcones escarpment the beds usually dip to the south or southeast at an angle materially greater than the slope of the surface. . . . The [structural] arrangement is ideal for the intake of water by the permeable beds of the limestone. The streams cross the outcrop area nearly at right angles to the strike, and most of them flow for miles on the Edwards limestone. In these stretches the water level in the Edwards reservoir is below the level of the streams, and the streams lose heavily into the reservoir. Ground-water recharge is also provided from rainfall on the outcrop by direct penetration and by seepage from innumerable small drainage channels that ordinarily carry water only during and for brief periods after exceptionally heavy rains [18, p. 75].

It appears probable that the combined annual losses into the Edwards from the Medina, Frio, Dry Frio, Nueces, and Sabinal Rivers and Hondo Creek may average as much as 150,000 acre-feet, the equivalent of a continuous flow of about 134,000,000 gallons a day [18, p. 77].

The principal natural outlets of the reservoir are springs that emerge along fault planes, among the largest of which are the Barton Springs, at Austin; the San Marcos Springs, at San Marcos; the Comal Springs, at New Braunfels; the San Antonio and San Pedro Springs, at San Antonio; the Las Moras Springs, at Brackettsville; and San Felipe Springs, at Del Rio. These springs are among the largest and best known in the southwestern part of the United States and are the sources of good-sized rivers and creeks [18, p. 74].

In 1934 the combined discharges of San Antonio and San Pedro Springs averaged nearly 12,000,000 gallons per day [18 p. 90].

The regimen of the streams of the Edwards Plateau has an important effect on the performance of the underground reservoir in the fault zone. The streams are fed in large part from the underground water systems of the plateau, and this ground-water inflow is nearly uniform for long periods. After heavy rains the ground-water discharge usually increases greatly and may be sustained at relatively high but slowly declining stages for a long time. In some dry years, such as 1925, the discharge of the streams of the plateau consists almost entirely of ground water. The rainfall in 1925 was exceedingly low, among the lowest on record at San Antonio and Uvalde. Nevertheless, the combined ground-water discharge of the Medina, Nueces, and Frio Rivers in that year amounted to about 70,000 acre-feet, most of which was derived from the Edwards reservoir of the plateau ᵃnd entered the lower part of the Edwards reservoir in the Balcones fault zone [18, p. 77].

PHYSIOGRAPHIC FORMS

Sinkholes.—Precipitation finds its way to the water table in limestone areas largely through the medium of depressions, or sinkholes, which lead the water generally downward through enlarged joint openings. In regions of well-developed subsurface drainage the land surface is pockmarked with sinkholes to the extent that such terms as "sinkhole plain" or "karst flat" may be used. In the Mitchell Plain, in southern Indiana, Malott [23, p. 289] counted over a thousand sinkholes in 1 square mile.

Commonly shaped like inverted cones, sinkholes show much variation in both shape and size. They range from small vertical openings to gigantic valley-shaped land forms. Some sinkholes contain water, either temporarily or permanently. (See Fig. XIV-2.)

The origin of some sinkholes and karst valleys may be attributed to such complex developments as the piracy of surface streams by subsurface drainage [24, p. 1984], or to the intersection of caves by surface tributaries. More commonly sinkholes are the result of the erosion by surface concentrations of infiltering ground water [32, pp. 120–122; 17] or represent the connection between surface and cave resulting from the collapse of the rock above the cave. In regions where a thin cover of insoluble rock overlies the limestone the collapse type is likely to predominate. The textural pattern in the distribution and dimensions of sinkholes may be determined, as Meyerhoff [27, pp. 279–295] has pointed out, by the relation to baselevel, or it may be controlled by the structure [39, pp. 218–219].

Subsurface forms.—The common subsurface erosional form is the tunnel-shaped cavern. It is usually nearly level, and generally linear in pattern or broadly curving. In places a two- or even three-dimensional network of tubes is present. Jointing is commonly the cause of the ground plan of a cave; jointing and structure, of its profiles and form. Locally some notable structural feature may determine the position of a cave. For example, the Timpanogos Cave, near Provo, Utah, has been excavated along a fault in thick limestones.

Vertical openings, other than fissure-form caves, are of two general types. Both are spectacular. Collapse of the ceiling may increase the height of a passageway, usually at the point of intersection of a cross passage. A second type of vertical opening is represented by the pit-and-dome shaft found in the cavern systems of the Mammoth Cave plateau. They are vertical tubes or prisms, of relatively small diameter but of considerable vertical extent.

The separation between chemical and corrasional work in the enlargement of the cave tubes themselves is especially difficult, because of the absence of distinguishing criteria. Mechanical erosion is undoubtedly effective, but its extent has not been adequately evaluated.

Stalactites, stalagmites, and columns formed by the intergrowth of the two, curtain deposits hanging from ceiling and wall, and travertine domes and half-domes are the ordinary deposits of calcium carbonate. Lobeck [19, pp. 377–387] and McGill [21, pp. 119–134] have described in detail the many depositional forms. In general cave deposits occur only in the upper levels of cavern systems, where infiltering ground water has access to the caves through many slightly enlarged joint openings.

In addition to the drip- and flow-stone deposits of calcium carbonate, most caves have slight and some caves abundant deposits of iron oxides, manganese oxides, and more rarely dolomite [20]. In a few caves gypsum crystals in prismatic curving forms are found on the ceilings; more rarely mats of acicular gypsum crystals are present. In a few places there are caves lined with calcite crystals, making immense geodelike openings.

Sand, silt, and clay deposits, washed in by cave streams or left as residual material, are found in practically all caves except those swept free by rapidly moving water [17, 31].

Several writers [7, 30, 38] have discussed the origin of caves. Briefly summarized, three hypotheses are differentiated on the basis of the relation of the cave to the water table at the time of formation. The vadose-water hypothesis places the site of formation above the level of the water table; the two-cycle hypothesis attributes the major solutional activity to slowly moving water far below the water table; and the hypothesis of lateral water-table flow ascribes the formation of caves to the sideward drainage of the fluctuating water zone immediately below the water table.

These views assume highly idealistic conditions, which are rarely found in specific cave areas. Whichever hypothesis may be accepted as the general principle governing cave development, the local application to any particular cave area must take into account the influence of the regional physiography, structure, stratigraphy, permeability, soil cover, the amount and frequency of the precipitation, and the theoretical sites of circulation. In Virginia the first three factors are important; in the Mammoth Cave district the regional dip, the permeability, and the differences in solubility are influential; in north-central Florida artesian conditions control. Malott [23, p. 314] who has studied the Indiana caves extensively, finds that a choice between the hypotheses of two cycles and lateral water-table flow is of little moment, provided that the importance of the sapping of the surface streams by ground-water underflow is recognized.

A discussion of the stages of the physiographic evolution of a limestone terrane is not appropriately included in an outline of hydrologic relations. Such material may be found in Lobeck's description of Mammoth Cave [19, pp. 351–370] and in Cvijić's work on the Dalmatian karst [6; 33, pp. 593–604]. In principle, the development of surface and sub-surface forms progresses simultaneously with the secular modifications of permeability and ground-water circulation, which have already been emphasized. In turn, permeability and circulation are modified to some extent by the changes in relief.

SPRINGS

Large springs are not uncommon in limestone terranes. Of the 199 springs listed by Meinzer [26, p. 4] as having a maximum discharge of at least 100 second-feet, 76 occur in limestone. Several kinds of limestone springs have been recognized—fluctuating springs in which the changes in discharge are closely related to precipitation, ebb-and-flow springs, springs of changing outlet, and springs of constant discharge.

It is typical of the first variety that careful records of discharge and of rainfall correspond sufficiently to demonstrate the immediate relation between the area of infiltration and the ground-water outflow. Slight discrepancies are attributable to a minor reservoir effect in the passageways between intake and outlet. One of the most completely studied springs of this type in the United States is at Huntsville, Ala. [41, p. 8, pl. 5; 14a, pp. 271–272]. The relation of precipitation to discharge is such that estimates of ground-water deficiency have been based on it. Other well-known springs of this class are the Meramec, Greer, and Bennett Springs, in Missouri [26, pp. 19–27, pls. 3–5, fig. 7]. The Fontaine de Vaucluse [15, pp. 284–291], the largest spring in France, belongs also in this group.

Fluctuating springs of quite a different character are the ebb-and-flow or periodic springs, which probably occur only in limestone terranes. Such springs have a relatively constant flow interrupted at more or less regular intervals by short periods during which there is no discharge or greatly decreased discharge. Springs of this type are briefly described by Meinzer in chapter XA.

Ebb-and-flow springs of another sort occur along coasts in the intertidal range. In the Bermuda Islands, at low tide, the shore line is marked in a few localities by seaward seepages from solution passageways. The flow of these seepages is undoubtedly reversed at high tide, as there is a tidal fluctuation in the caverns.

Springs with changing outlet represent another anomalous condition. Theis [41, p. 40] describes one in south-central Tennessee as follows:

This spring . . . furnishes water to several hydraulic rams to supply the needs of inhabitants in the community of Bigbyville. According to reports, after each of several heavy rains in a recent wet year the spring ceased flowing and another normally dry opening about 100 yards up the creek and at nearly the same altitude began to flow. This continued so long . . . that the rams were moved to the new spring. . . . Unfortunately, however, the new spring would soon cease to flow and Bigby Spring would begin again, necessitating the return of the rams. . . . Such behavior can be explained on the basis of a hydraulic system involving siphons whereby one channel is put in operation when the water table is high and the other when it is low.

Limestone springs of constant flow are those having extensive passageways, usually below the average water-table level, which serve as reservoirs and smooth out the irregularities of precipitation before the intake is discharged. Such springs are not constant in the sense that no variation of flow occurs, but rather in the sense that the changes are not sudden, and the slow rate of change is related to the secular adjustment of the water table over a large area. Meinzer [26, p. 12] gives the following data on Silver Springs in Florida:

The discharge of the basin [Silver Spring] . . . ranges from 342 to 822 second-feet [about 221 million to 531 million gallons a day]. . . . Comparison of the daily gage height from May 25, 1906, to December 31, 1907, with the daily precipitation at Ocala, 6 miles from Silver Spring, . . . shows some unexplained anomalies but otherwise seems to indicate that the discharge is not greatly affected by single rainstorms, even though the precipitation is heavy, but increases gradually in rainy seasons and decreases even more gradually in dry seasons.

Another type of spring with relatively constant flow is formed by the "rise" of lost rivers. In such localities excessive precipitation is cared for by surface flow in the area of the sinks. Springs of similar type are occasionally to be found on the downstream side of incised meanders, where subsurface piracy is occurring through the meander neck. Such springs are relatively constant in flow, because the ground-water channels are filled as long as there is water in the stream.

QUALITY OF WATER IN LIMESTONE TERRANES

The chemical characteristics of water obtained from limestone are described by Dr. Margaret Foster in chapter XIIIE. Other factors affecting the quality of water are turbidity and contamination.

The degree of turbidity and the amount of suspended matter may vary greatly from time to time in springs and wells in a limestone region. This is particularly true in those springs where rapid runoff into sinkholes and flow through enlarged cavern channels permit the maintenance of some turbulence during periods of great infiltration. Under these conditions heavy precipitation in the intake area is reflected in high turbidity, as well as in high volume, at the discharge points. On the other hand, extended ground-water circulation—for example, under artesian conditions—will enable the water to free itself of mechanically carried material. Where the increases in recharge are not immediately followed by increases in discharge—that is, where there is sufficient reservoir effect to mask the irregularities in precipitation—the discharge water is normally clear.

Bacterial contamination is commonly high in water in limestone areas, frequently so high as to render the water unfit for human consumption without treatment. The high infiltration means that bacteria from soil and from surface waste reach the water table quickly. Unless there is an established ground-water reservoir in which the water will sterilize itself or a natural filtering medium in which the organic sediment and suspended matter can be removed by adsorption, contamination will be high. In general, supplies from springs of constant flow and from artesian sources are more likely to be free from contamination than water from other sources, though their hardness may be greater.

ENGINEERING PROBLEMS OF LIMESTONE TERRANES

The marked permeability of some limestones, the general imperviousness of others except where the network of joints and bedding planes has been enlarged by solution, the relatively large fluctuations of the water table in short periods, and the invisible extent of the underground passageways and weakened zones create varied conditions affecting engineering works in limestone terranes. The types of projects seriously influenced by the presence of limestone include water supply, waste disposal, reservoirs, and canals, where permeability is the essential factor, and to a lesser extent foundation construction for dams, buildings, and other works, where the supporting strength of the rock is significant. The conditions are so varied that space does not permit a review of them [3, 9, 10, 30, 36, 41]. A few of the conventional techniques that are employed in typical situations are indicated below.

It is always desirable to determine the nature of the rock permeability, whether primary or secondary, and the capacity and distribution of the passageways or zones of permeability.

Where the permeability is primary, observations of water levels in wells will show whether the ground water is under artesian or gravity pressure. These data will also indicate whether the permeability is relatively constant over wide areas or varies locally. The amount of lowering of the water table and the shape of the area of drawdown surrounding a well from which excessive withdrawal is taking place and the recovery after pumping ceases will usually form the basis of estimates of permeability, rates of flow, and supply.

On the other hand, where the permeability is secondary some information about amount and direction of ground-water flow can be obtained from the observation of the alinement of sinkholes and of the relation of precipitation to the fluctuations of discharge of springs. Dye tests, using fluorescein or other chemicals, may be used to confirm these preliminary observations. However, it must be emphasized that no indirect method will determine the size of hidden cavern chambers. Even close exploratory drilling will sometimes miss large openings. When drilling is used to locate rock weakened by weathering, water levels in the holes should be measured and pressures applied to learn if the weak rock is actually permeable. If the water levels in wells are lower than the level of a stream that is to be dammed, heavy leakage out of the reservoir may occur after the dam is built.

In projects involving water supply it is essential to know where the water comes from, as well as the capacity; in waste disposal it is essential to know where the material goes. In dams the supporting strength of the rock and the tightness of the reservoir are paramount considerations. Leakage through enlargement of passages by solution is not so much to be feared, although this has been known to occur, as the washing out of clay and silt fillings of fissures that are assumed to be tight. In some reservoirs the capacity has been larger than was estimated because of the bank storage permitted by cavern systems.

REFERENCES

To give a comprehensive list of titles on limestone hydrology and physiography would require more than a thousand references. The publications cited below will serve as an introduction to the various aspects of limestone terranes; those of general interest have been briefly annotated.

1. Adams, C. S., and Swinnerton, A. C., Solubility of limestone: Am. Geophys. Union Trans., 1937, pt. 2, pp. 504–508.

2. Bretz, J H., Solution cavities in the Joliet Limestone of northeastern Illinois: Jour. Geology, vol. 48, pp. 337–384, 1940. The case against the interpretation of these cavities, filled with an overlying shale, as a fossil karst.

3. Bryan, Kirk, Geology of reservoir and dam sites: U. S. Geol. Survey Water-Supply Paper 597-A, pp. 1–38,.1929. Refers to problems to be anticipated in reservoir construction in rocks of all kinds, including limestones.

4. Clarke, F. W., The data of geochemistry, 5th ed.: U. S. Geol. Survey Bull. 770, pp. 32–34, 564, 1924.

5. Cramer, Helmuth, Höhlenbildung und Karsthydrographie: Zeitschr. Geomorphologie, vol. 8, pp. 306–323, 1935. A review of Davis' paper (see No. 7), comparing it with the views of several European cavern investigators.

6. Cvijić, Jovan, The evolution of Lapiés—a study in karst physiography: Geog. Rev., vol. 14, pp. 26–49, 1924. Many excellent photographs of land forms in the Dalmatian karst; for a more general statement of Cvijić's work see No. 33.

7. Davis, W. M., Origin of limestone caverns: Geol. Soc. America Bull., vol. 41, pp. 475–628, 1930. A comprehensive survey of cavern literature and the presentation of the hypothesis of the phreatic origin of caverns.

8. Dicken, S. N., and Brown, H. B., Jr., Soil erosion in the karst lands of Kentucky: U. S. Dept. Agr. Soil Conservation Service Circ. 490, 1938. The problem of soil conservation in limestone terranes is related directly to the hydrologic regimen.

9. Eckel, E. C., and others, Engineering geology of the Tennessee River system: Tennessee Valley Authority Tech. Mon. 47, 1940. Nearly half of the Tennessee Valley Authority region is underlain by limestone; hence much of the engineering geology of the region deals with limestone hydrology.

10. Fiedler, A. G., and Nye, S. S., Geology and ground-water resources of the Roswell artesian basin, N. Mex.: U. S. Geol. Survey Water-Supply Paper 639, 1933. Contains (pp. 180–189) excellent reasoning for regarding the limestone aquifer in the Roswell area as a fossil karst.

11. Hall, C. W., Meinzer, O. E., and Fuller, M. L., Geology and underground waters of southern Minnesota: U. S. Geol. Survey Water-Supply Paper 256, 1911.

12. Howard, W. V., A classification of limestone reservoirs: Am. Assoc. Petroleum Geologists Bull., vol. 12, p. 1155, 1928.

13. Johnston, J., The solubility-product constant of calcium and magnesium carbonates: Am. Chem. Soc. Jour., vol. 37, pp. 2001–2020, 1915.

14. Johnston, J., and Williamson, E. D., The complete solubility curve of calcium carbonate: Am. Chem. Soc. Jour., vol. 38, pp. 975–983, 1916.

14a. Johnston, W. D., Jr., Ground water in the Paleozoic rocks of northern Alabama: Alabama Geol. Survey Special Rept. 16, 414 pp., 1933.

15. Keilhack, K., Lehrbuch der Grundwasser- und Quellenkunde, pp. 284–291, Berlin, 1935. A standard German textbook of hydrology.

16. Kendall, J., The solubility of calcium carbonate in water: Philos. Mag., ser. 6, vol. 23, pp. 958–976, 1912.

17. Lee, W. T., Erosion by solution and fill: U. S. Geol. Survey Bull. 760, pp. 107–121, 1925. Preliminary account of Carlsbad Caverns.

18. Livingston, P., Sayre, A. N., and White, W. N., Water resources of the Edwards limestone in the San Antonio area, Texas: U. S. Geol. Survey Water-Supply Paper 773-B, pp. 72–90, 1936. Describes the ground-water regimen in a terrane of diverse elements in which limestone is abundant.

19. Lobeck, A. K., The geology and physiography of the Mammoth Cave National Park: Kentucky Geol. Survey, ser. 6, vol. 31, pp. 327–403, 1929. Excellent nontechnical description of the Mammoth Cave region; many block diagrams.

20. Lord, R. C., unpublished manuscript.

21. McGill, W. M., Caverns of Virginia: Virginia Geol. Survey Bull. 35, pp. 13, 119–134, 1933. Contains maps of the principal caves of Virginia and many fine photographs.

22. Malott, C. A., Handbook of Indiana geology, pp. 94–98, 187–210, 233–247, Indiana Div. Geology, 1922. Description of the karst areas, the Lost River, and the American Bottoms of Indiana.

23. Malott, C. A., Lost River at Wesley Chapel Gulf, Orange County, Ind.: Indiana Acad. Sci. Proc., vol. 41, pp. 285–286, 289, 314, 1931 [1932].

24. Malott, C. A., Karst valleys: Geol. Soc. America Bull., vol. 50, p. 1984, 1939.

25. Martel, E. A., Nouveau traité des eaux souterraines, 838 pp., Paris, 1921. Many plans, cross sections, and pictures of European caverns, and examples of tracing ground-water circulation.

26. Meinzer, O. E., Large springs in the United States: U. S. Geol. Survey Water-Supply Paper 557, pp. 4, 12, 19–27, pls. 3–5, 7, fig. 7, 1927. Describes many springs issuing from limestone, giving data of flow and geologic conditions.

27. Meyerhoff, H. A., The texture of karst topography in Cuba and Puerto Rico: Jour. Geomorphology, vol. 1, pp. 279–295, 1938. Discusses the Cuban and Puerto Rican karst features and relates their spatial distribution to the heights of erosion surfaces above baselevel.

28. Murray, A. N., and Love, W. W., Action of organic acids upon limestone: Am. Assoc. Petroleum Geologists Bull., vol. 13, pp. 1467–1475, 1929.

29. Norton, W. H., Hendrixson, W. S., Simpson, H. E., Meinzer, O. E., and others, Underground water resources of Iowa: U. S. Geol. Survey Water-Supply Paper 293, 1912.

30. Piper, A. M., Ground water in north-central Tennessee: U. S. Geol. Survey Water-Supply Paper 640, 1932. Excellent discussion of behavior of ground water in limestone, circulation, physiographic effects, and origin of caves.

31. Pohl, E. R., Geologic investigations at Mammoth Cave, Kentucky: Am. Geophys. Union Trans., 1936, pt. 2, pp. 332–334.

32. Purdue, A. H., On the origin of limestone sinkholes: Science, new ser., vol. 26, pp. 120–122, 1907.

33. Sanders, E. M., The cycle of erosion in a karst region (after Cvijić): Geog. Rev., vol. 11, pp. 593–604, 1921. A review in English of one phase of the work of a famous European physiographer.

34. Sayles, R. W., Bermuda during the Ice Age: Am. Acad. Arts Sci. Proc., vol. 66, pp. 381–468, 1931.

35. Siebenthal, C. E., Zinc and lead deposits of the Joplin region: U. S. Geol. Survey Bull. 606, p. 32, 1915.

36. Stringfield, V. T., Artesian water in the Florida Peninsula: U. S. Geol. Survey Water-Supply Paper 773-C, 1936. The fundamental geologic and hydrologic data on the artesian water of Florida.

37. Stringfield, V. T., personal communication.

38. Swinnerton, A. C., Origin of limestone caverns: Geol. Soc. America Bull., vol. 43, pp. 663–693, 1932. The theory of lateral subwater-table flow to account for the origin of caverns.

39. Swinnerton, A. C., Structural control of the form and distribution of sinkholes: Science, new ser., vol. 85, pp. 218–219, 1937.

40. Terzaghi, Karl von, Beitrag zur Hydrographie und Morphologie des Kroatischen Karstes: Ungar. geol. Reichs-Anstalt Mitt. Jahrb., Band 20, Heft 6, 1913.

41. Theis, C. V., Ground water in south-central Tennessee: U. S. Geol. Survey Water-Supply Paper 677, p. 8, pl. 5, p. 40, 1936. Excellent example of current hydrologic work in a limestone terrane.

42. Weller, J. M., The geology of Edmonson County: Kentucky Geol. Survey, ser. 6, vol. 28, 1927. The geology of the Mammoth Cave region, with much material on the caverns.

43. Wells, R. C., The solubility of calcite in water in contact with the atmosphere, and its variation with temperature: Washington Acad. Sci. Jour., vol. 5, p. 617–622, 1915.

44. Wray, S. A., The karstlands of western Yugoslavia: Geol. Mag., vol. 59, pp. 392–409, 1922. Brief account of the general geology; special descriptions of many karst features.

CHAPTER XV

HYDROLOGY OF VOLCANIC TERRANES

Harold T. Stearns[1]

INTRODUCTION

Volcanic terranes consist of extrusive rocks erupted from volcanoes and deposited on the earth's surface and intrusive rocks that congealed below the surface. They may be classified according to their composition as (1) basalt, a dark-colored rock, low in silica and high in ferromagnesian minerals; (2) rhyolite, a light-colored rock, high in silica and low in ferromagnesian minerals, and (3) a whole series of rocks having a composition intermediate between basalt and rhyolite, such as andesite, dacite, latite, and trachyte. The silica-rich rocks are commonly more viscous than basalt and are more often erupted in fragmental condition. For these reasons they tend to pile up close to their vents and build steep volcanoes such as Mount Lassen, California; Mount Hood, Oregon; and Mount St. Helens, Washington. The basalts, being more fluid, usually spread in wide sheets and form plains, such as the Modoc lava beds, in northern California; the Columbia River Plateau, in Oregon and Washington; and the Snake River Plain, in Idaho; or build shield-shaped domes, such as Kilauea and Mauna Loa volcanoes, in Hawaii.

Volcanic rocks are classified also according to their physical state when erupted. If poured out as molten lava they are flows, if blown out as fragments they are pyroclastic rocks, if solidified in cracks or other voids in the earth's crust they are intrusive rocks, and if they consist of fragments deposited in pipe-shaped vents they are throat breccias.

The flows with billowy and ropy surfaces distributed to the margin through tubes of their own making are called pahoehoe. With minor exceptions only basaltic or closely related rocks form lava of this type. The flows with clinkery or jumbled surfaces are called flow breccias. These are of two types—those of basaltic rocks, called aa, and those of silica-rich flows, called block lavas.

Dikes, sills, plugs, and bosses are the chief shallow intrusive bodies. All have low permeability, and most of them are practically impermeable. Where dikes form swarms cutting permeable rocks they commonly confine valuable water, as in the Hawaiian Islands. Sills interrupt the down-

[1] Geologist in charge of ground-water investigations in Hawaii, Geological Survey, United States Department of the Interior, Honolulu, Hawaii.

ward movement of water through permeable rocks and in such places cause perched water. Scattered dikes tend to retard the movement of ground water, and water moving downward along them causes serious drainage problems in some mines.

Figure XV-1 is a map of the western part of the United States showing areas in which Tertiary and Quaternary volcanic rocks are at or near

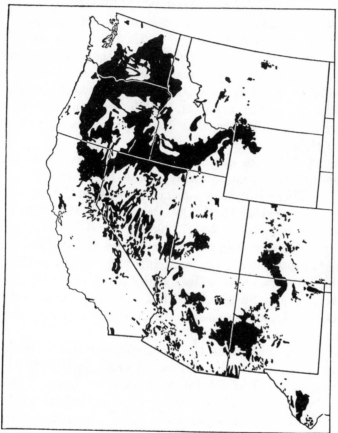

Fig. XV-1.—Map of the western part of the United States, showing areas in which Tertiary or Quaternary volcanic rocks are at or near the surface. After U. S. Geol. Survey Water-Supply Paper 489.

the surface. Most of these rocks are basalt. The most striking characteristic of basaltic lava, as related to its hydrologic properties, is its perviousness. This fact is commonly overlooked or even stated to the contrary.

A marked difference is shown in the amount of ground water available in islands that are emerged submarine volcanoes, such as are found in Micronesia, and those that are subaerial volcanoes, such as are found in Polynesia. Submarine volcanoes are chiefly explosive, and the pyroclastic rocks from them are poorly sorted and commonly laid down with ashy shales and other sediments of low permeability. Lava flows poured out beneath the sea are usually pillow lavas or breccias that would normally be highly permeable, but the great quantities of steam associated with such volcanoes impregnate these rocks and seal up most of the openings with secondary minerals.

PREVIOUS WORK AND LITERATURE

The geologic study of ground water in volcanic terranes was begun in 1900 in Idaho by Russell [15] and in Hawaii by Lindgren [6]. At an early date several engineers, well drillers, and others on the island of Oahu, Hawaii, were contributing to local journals facts and theories relating to the occurrence of water on that island [31]. However, it was not until O. E. Meinzer, W. O. Clark, and H. S. Palmer, of the United States Geological Survey, arrived in 1920 that systematic study of the occurrence of water in the Hawaiian Islands began.

A mass of literature has appeared regarding water in the rocks of Oahu. This has been annotated by Norah D. Stearns [31]. The chief publications dealing with the occurrence of water in the Hawaiian Islands are those by Meinzer [11], Clark [20], Palmer [14], McCombs [7], Vaksvik [23, 26], and Stearns [20, 23, 26, 27, 29, 30].

The outstanding treatise on the occurrence of water in volcanic rocks in the United States was written by Meinzer [9]. Other publications dealing with the subject are those by Landes [5], Calkins [1], Schwennesen [16], Meinzer [8], and Stearns [18, 21, 24, 25, 28]. One of these papers [25] describes in detail the occurrence of water in about 16,000 square miles of the Snake River basalt plain.

Much is now known about the occurrence of water in basalt, as shown by the detailed studies mentioned, but surprisingly little is known about the occurrence of water in volcanic rocks of other kinds. This is chiefly because basalt tends to build flat areas where agriculture can be pursued profitably and because it has proved to be so reliable and voluminous as a water bearer. Although nonbasaltic volcanic rocks cover large areas in the United States, they are found generally in more rugged country than basalt. Also, they have a much more variable and generally lower permeability than basaltic rocks, a fact which has tended to retard development of water in them.

EFFECT OF BASALT FLOWS ON DRAINAGE

Great changes are wrought in any drainage system inundated by lava flows. Most basalt flows are fluid when erupted, and in an eroded area they invariably follow stream channels. If enough lava is produced, all the valleys may be obliterated, and a gently sloping plain or dome may result. If a valley is not entirely filled with lava, the stream may return to the valley. At first it loses water rapidly in traversing the porous lava fill, but in time the stream, if a large one, generally silts up its channel sufficiently to find its way across the lava. Because of the hummocky

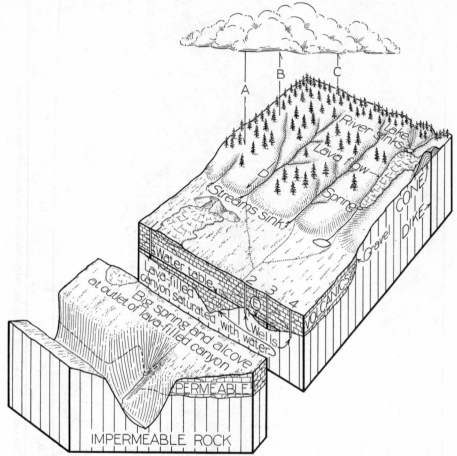

FIG. XV-2.—Diagram illustrating the source and disposal of rainfall and the hydrology of a basalt terrane. *A*, Rainfall; *B*, evaporation; *C*, transpiration from vegetation; *D*, runoff; *E*, infiltration and recharge to the zone of saturation. In the right upper corner a lava flow is shown filling a stretch of canyon, thereby making a lake on its upstream end, where the water sinks into the lava, and a spring at the downstream end where the water emerges. All streams sink in the permeable lavas where they reach the plain. The water moves chiefly along the ancestral prelava canyons which are indicated by dotted lines, and emerges where the main lava-filled canyon in the lower block is cut by a transverse valley. This valley was cut at the contact of the volcanics and impermeable rock. The alcove or amphitheater is typical of large springs in a lava terrane. Wells 1 and 3 penetrate saturated lavas and encounter water (solid black), but wells 2 and 4 are dry because they encounter only lavas above the water table and impermeable rock. The broken line in the lower block indicates the contact of the volcanics and underlying rock. Gravels lie in the ancient stream beds under the lava (indicated by small stippled area in the main lava-filled canyon) and as interfingering fans at the foot of the mountains.

surface of the lava the stream usually meanders from one side to the other, and later, when it cuts down to its former valley floor, benches of lava are left in the elbows of the meanders. If the valley was wide before the lava

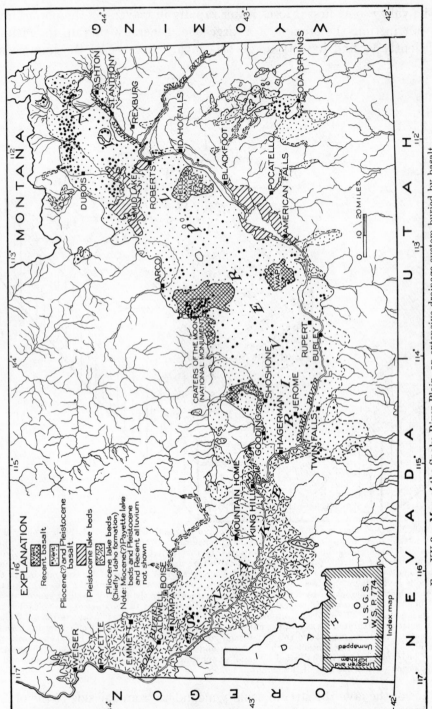

Fig. XV-3.—Map of the Snake River Plain, an extensive drainage system buried by basalt.

was poured out, and if it has several tributaries from each side, usually two streams are formed—one on each side of the lava fill. Lava flows partly filling valleys are known as intracanyon basalts. Their number is legion. They occur in practically every basaltic area. The great eruption in Iceland from the Skaptár Jökull fissure in 1783 [4] produced so much lava that it partly filled one valley for 50 miles and another for 40 miles, with lava in places 600 feet deep. A striking example in the United States is the copious flow that inundated the headwaters of the Deschutes and Crooked Rivers in Oregon. This lava flow filled or partly filled the Crooked River Canyon for about 30 miles and then continued for at least 8 miles down the Deschutes River. It was so voluminous that it flowed up the Deschutes River for more than 4.5 miles from the mouth of the Crooked River, where it is 900 feet thick [21, pp. 143–146]. This lava gives rise to numerous springs fed by water finding its way through the basalt along the buried drainage channels.

Smaller lava flows tumbling into river valleys commonly create lakes on their upstream sides and springs at their terminal margins, as in McKenzie Valley, Oreg. [18], or in the Lung Chiang Province, Manchuria [12]. This hydrologic condition is illustrated in Figure XV-2.

The Snake River Plain, Idaho, is an example of a vast drainage pattern obliterated by lava flows (Fig. XV-3). For 200 miles along the north side of this extensive lava plain all the rivers descending from the mountains sink into the porous lava. The volume of water is so great that the basalts are saturated for a considerable thickness above the impermeable basement rock, and the water table slopes gently southwestward. Near the west end of the plain, where the lava ends, great quantities of ground water discharge from the ancient lava-filled canyons of the Snake River [24]. This hydrologic condition is represented diagrammatically in Figure XV-2, in which wells are shown to illustrate why some obtain water and others do not.

The marked changes brought about by lava flooding an eroded surface sometimes have unforeseen economic effects. Thus, when the Blackfoot Reservoir, in southeastern Idaho was built, leakage from it ruined land 6 to 9 miles away in another drainage area and formed three lakes. This was due to the fact that the present divide between the two drainage basins is different from the underlying pre-lava divide. The upper end of the reservoir lay south of the pre-lava divide, and water leaking from it flowed south toward Soda Springs and underground, whereas leakage from the rest of the reservoir flowed north [32].

WATER-BEARING PROPERTIES OF BASALTIC ROCKS

Lava flows.—All basaltic flows except massive ones are very permeable (Figs. XV-4 and XV-5). The cavities and crevices within and between lava flows, named in the order of their potential yield of water, are interstitial spaces in clinker or flow breccia, cavities between beds, shrinkage cracks, gas vesicles, lava tubes, cracks produced by mechanical forces after the flows have come to rest, and vegetation-mold holes. This order varies slightly for different areas. Clinker is lacking in pahoehoe flows, but doughy slaggy material may be present (Fig. XV-4). The lava flows in the Triassic rocks of Connecticut are so massive that even the shrinkage cracks transmit very little water. A well at Hartford, Conn., obtained less than 4 gallons a minute after penetrating 169 feet of basalt [3]. These flows are so impermeable that they confine water under pressure [13]. Gas vesicles are rare in thick dense flows. In the Snake River lava plain

Fig. XV-4.—Highly permeable pahoehoe basalt containing many small tubes, shrinkage cracks, and thin layers of slaggy lava, near Olowalu, Maui, Hawaii.

aa lava flows are scarce but tubes in the pahoehoe are large and numerous. Open rifts and earthquake cracks are also present. Pahoehoe tubes are likewise great water carriers in the Pleistocene basalts of Oregon. The cracks produced by mechanical forces after the flows have come to rest are of the greatest importance where much faulting has occurred. In treeless areas covered by lava vegetation molds are too scarce or too small to be of value as carriers of water.

Numerous cities, villages, farms, and irrigated tracts in the northwestern part of the United States and the city of Honolulu and large sugar-cane plantations in the Hawaiian Islands obtain their water supplies from basalt. It was computed several years ago that the voluminous springs issuing from basalt in the Snake River Canyon near Twin Falls, Idaho, yielded enough water to supply all the cities in the United States of more than 100,000 inhabitants with 120 gallons a day for each inhabitant [10, p. 44].

Subaqueous basalt flows have water-bearing properties distinct from either aa or pahoehoe. Lava poured into bodies of water, or apparently even lava congealing in the presence of large quantities of steam, assumes physical properties that readily distinguish it from lava in ordinary subaerial flows. Pillow lava, or ball-like masses of basalt 1 foot or more in diameter, with glass rinds and internal radiating gas vesicles, lying in a matrix of comminuted glass, typifies such basalts. The interstices between the pillows may be only partly filled, and hence water may pass freely through them. Most of the great springs in the Snake River Canyon near Twin Falls, Idaho, issue from pillow lava [24, p. 433]. On the other hand, the pillow lavas in the lower 150-foot sheet of basalt in the Triassic of Connecticut and those in the island of Guam have relatively low permeability, because the interstices have been largely filled with secondary minerals.

Pyroclastic rocks.—The basaltic pyroclastic rocks are of two physical types if classified according to the process by which they are made— (1) the product of fire fountains, comprising fine glassy ash, pumice, spatter, and cinders; and (2) the

Fig. XV-5.—An aa basalt flow, showing pervious clinker beds and impervious dense layers, near Olowalu, Maui, Hawaii.

product of catastrophic explosions, comprising ash, lapilli ash, agglomerate, and vent breccia. Either of these types may be water-bearing and may later become non-water bearing through consolidation.

WATER-BEARING PROPERTIES OF HIGHLY SILICIC ROCKS

Lava flows.—Highly silicic flows in the United States of Tertiary or older age generally have low permeability, because they are massive and their brecciated parts are firmly compacted. Such water as moves through them usually follows narrow cracks produced or widened by later deformation or faulting, and wells drilled into them yield little or no water.

Some notable exceptions occur, chiefly in the glassy rocks. Big Springs, Idaho, discharges about 180 second-feet [10, pm. 53] fro spherulitic obsidian and rhyolite, and copious springs issue at Obsidian Cliff, in Yellowstone National Park.

Dams and reservoirs built in Tertiary silicic rocks are generally successful, but careful investigations should be made to determine whether permeable zones occur in them.

Thick, highly brecciated Quaternary silicic flows and their associated loose pumice deposits, such as those in the Medicine Lake and Mono Lake regions of California and on Newberry Volcano, Oregon, are extremely permeable, and rain and snow falling on their surfaces disappear without runoff.

Pyroclastic rocks.—Highly silicic consolidated pyroclastic deposits vary greatly in their permeability. Fractures in these rocks produced during consolidation or later flexing may be sufficiently numerous to yield water freely. However, some of the pyroclastic rocks are sufficiently compact and free from joints to serve as confining beds for artesian water where they are interstratified with permeable sedimentary rocks in synclines or homoclines. The unconsolidated pyroclastic deposits are very permeable.

WATER-BEARING PROPERTIES OF ROCKS OF INTERMEDIATE COMPOSITION

Lava flows.—The rocks of intermediate composition differ greatly in their influence on the movement of ground water. Their water-bearing properties depend on their physical form after they come to rest and the degree of subsequent compaction and alteration. Many are poured out as flows 300 to 600 feet thick, whereas others with low silica content approach basalts in form and water-bearing properties.

Clinker phases of massive trachyte flows transmit water freely in areas of heavy rainfall. Springs yielding as much as 500,000 gallons a day discharge from such rocks on the island of Maui, Hawaii. Dikes feeding these flows are commonly 15 feet or more wide and are very impermeable. They cut underlying permeable basalts and confine water in them more effectively than basaltic dikes. However, the rocks of the dike complex of Guam are so highly mineralized that they yield only about 600,000 gallons of spring water a day in dry weather to streams draining them. Under the same conditions of rainfall, but without mineralization, they would yield several millions of gallons a day.

A spring yielding 500 gallons a minute issues from a fault near the perifery of the trachytic plug forming Matafao Peak, Tutuila, Samoa. The spring is not thermal and fluctuates with the rainfall, indicating that it is supplied by percolation through the closely spaced joint system in the trachyte.

Pyroclastic rocks.—Lava rocks of intermediate composition make up the major part of the volcanoes in the regions bordering the Pacific Ocean. Most of these rocks in the islands bordering the Asiatic continent are pyroclastic and, if Tertiary or older, are generally compacted and deformed. Their water-bearing properties are little known, as hydrologists have made few studies of them.

Deformation may or may not increase the water-bearing properties of such pyroclastic rocks. Consolidated tuffs and agglomerates are generally brittle, and when deformed even slightly they develop numerous joint cracks. Thus, in the south end of the island of Guam the poorly sorted coarse agglomerates that normally would not be permeable carry water in the fissures produced by warping.

Tumalo Reservoir, Oregon [2], failed because of joint cracks in a pink tuff. The andesitic breccias and mud flows of northwestern Wyoming, however, are nearly free from joint cracks and yield water sparingly.

Folding and faulting may be so intense as to render tuffs and permeable pyroclastic rocks virtually impermeable by compressing the beds into tight folds or making them very discontinuous, as in central Guam.

The unconsolidated pyroclastic deposits of intermediate composition are very permeable. Some of the spring-fed rivers of Japan and Java rise in such deposits.

The whole subject of the occurrence of water in silicic and intermediate volcanic rocks awaits further study, but as a group they are far less permeable than basalt.

FORM OF THE WATER TABLE

The water table in lava plains is generally very flat, but its gradient is largely determined by the slope of the impermeable pre-lava terrane. The water-table gradient averages less than 4.5 feet to the mile in the 100-mile stretch of basalt between Idaho Falls and Minidoka, Idaho, but averages 25 feet to the mile in some other stretches. These variations are believed to result from different slopes in the underlying surface of the impermeable basement. A short distance downstream from Roberts, Idaho, the water table passes beneath the Snake River with a steep gradient and does not become tributary to the river again until the American Falls Reservoir is reached, 95 miles downstream.

The high porosity of basalt causes the water table to be close to the impermeable basement rock if the outlet of a lava-filled basin is low. Thus, if the lava is thick the depth to water will generally be great. The depth to the water table in the Snake River lava plain is generally more than 400 feet, except near tracts where the water table has been raised by irrigation.   It is also far below the surface in most of the basalt plateaus of California, Oregon, and Washington.

The water table under a basalt plain is generally almost flat.   Thus the depth to ground water may be predicted with considerable accuracy providing a few wells have been drilled and the altitude of the surface is known.   If, however, clay beds interfinger with the basalt, complicated forms of the water table result, as at Mud Lake, Idaho (Fig. XV-6).   Water is at or close to the surface in the basalt on the north shore of this lake, whereas 3 miles away, on the south shore, ground water is recovered in

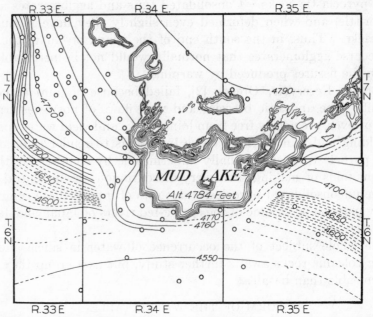

FIG. XV-6.—Water-table map of the Mud Lake Basin, Idaho, for 1929.   The lake is perched on clay beds and the land about it is flat.   The contours show that north of the lake there is only one water table, but that south of the lake there is a perched water table and below it the main water table with a ground-water cascade.

sandy clay by shallow dug wells, but the water in the basalt lies about 250 feet below the surface.   The gradient of the water table in this stretch is about 80 feet to the mile.   Similar ground-water cascades were found near Roberts, Rupert, Arco, and several other towns in southern Idaho.

The basement rock of a basaltic terrane is commonly rugged and impermeable.   Buried ridges of basement rock may project above the water table.   Thus, a well on one farm may be dry, whereas wells on adjacent farms may encounter water.   This condition, which exists near Twin Falls, Idaho, is illustrated by wells 2 and 3 in Figure XV-2.

The water table in basaltic islands is flat because of the high permeability of the rocks.   In general, it rises from sea level at the coast at the rate of 1 to 3 feet to the mile to a point below the wettest part, which may or may not be the highest point on the island. If no dikes or other intercepting structural features are present, the form of the water table will be essentially that of a flat dome near sea level. However, most basaltic islands are cut by a dike complex, so that the water table is not continuous across the island but lies at various levels between the dikes, as shown in Figure XV-7. All permeable rocks are saturated below the main water table.

WATER IN BASALTIC ISLANDS

Basal water.—The name "basal ground water" has been applied to all fresh water floating on salt water in permeable rocks below the water table in basaltic islands to distinguish it from perched bodies of ground water [11, p. 10]. Borings indicate that the rocks are saturated with fresh water for certain depths below the basal water table, and then salt water is encountered.

The Ghyben-Herzberg principle of the behavior of fresh water in contact with salt water in a pervious formation [23, p. 238] is applicable to the basal water in a basaltic island. Accordingly, the depth to salt water is a function of the specific gravity of the salt water and of the altitude of the water table above sea level. The depth to salt water is always less than the theoretical depth, because of chemical diffusion and mixing resulting from ground-water fluctuations. The zone of mixing for a given static head is usually thinner where large volumes of ground water are moving seaward than where the water is moving slowly in small quantities.

Perched ground water.—Features of six types are known to perch water or to hold it above the basal water table in a basaltic island. They are sills, ash or tuff beds, soil, alluvium, ice, and dense flow rock.

Sills that lie nearly horizontal intercept downward-percolating water and cause it to move along their upper surfaces if they are not so highly fissured as to allow the water to escape through them. Sills play an important part in regions where they are

FIG. XV-7.—Section of the island of Lanai, Hawaii, showing the lens of fresh water floating on salt water except in the dike complex, where the water table varies in height in the different dike compartments.. *A*, rainfall; *B*, evaporation and transpiration; *C*, runoff; *D*, recharge of zone of saturation.

numerous and extensive. Water is developed on sills by tunnels contouring their buried upper surface.

Ash or tuff beds interstratified with basalt intercept downward percolating water in much the same way as sills. They may perch exceedingly valuable water, as in the Kau District, Hawaii, where tunnels aggregating several miles in length have been driven to recover water on them, or they may be relatively unimportant, as on Oahu. If the ash is too coarse or not compact, all or most of the downward-moving water may percolate through it. Water is recovered from tuff beds by tunnels contouring their buried upper surface (Fig. XV-8).

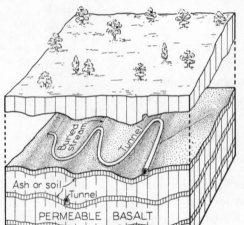

FIG. XV-8.—Diagram illustrating the position of a tunnel driven to recover water perched on an ash or soil bed between permeable lava flows. Three perching ash beds are shown one above the other each with its separate tunnel. The top part of the block is lifted to show the plan of the tunnel.

The effectiveness of soils interstratified with basalt for perching water depends partly upon their texture, continuity, and thickness. Soil 6 feet thick lying between the permeable Tantalus fire-fountain debris and the Koolau basalt gives rise to valuable springs in Honolulu. In the eastern part of Maui, Hawaii, tunnels aggregating several miles in length have been driven to develop small flows of water perched on thin soil beds lying between basalt flows. The yield from soil beds is usually small. The water is recovered by tunnels contouring their buried upper surfaces. Such a tunnel will be very crooked if the soil was formed on a rugged terrane prior to burial. (See Fig. XV-8.)

The alluvium in tropical islands usually contains much silt and is partly or completely weathered. This gives it a low permeability, and hence where it is overlain by basalt water sinking in the congealed lava will usually be perched by the alluvium. Numerous lava flows resting on alluvium in Oahu and Maui give rise to springs, some of which yield more than half a million gallons a day. Water is recovered by tunneling to the lowest part of the lava flow along its basal contact (Fig. XV-9).

Water is perched in basalt in regions of perennial ice, as on the tops of high mountains, such as Mauna Loa and Mauna Kea, Hawaii. The water cannot percolate downward, because the crevices are filled with ice. The quantity of such water is always small but may be valuable to hikers in out-of-the-way places. Such perched water was the only source of water supply in the Craters of the Moon National Monument, Idaho, for several years, and it affords the only perennial supply in the Modoc Lava Beds of California [17].

Small pools containing several gallons of water are found in a few places in rainy or foggy areas in shallow depressions on flat cakes of uncracked basalt. Such cakes are generally in pahoehoe flows and are simply natural rock tanks. In the Kona District, Hawaii, some lava

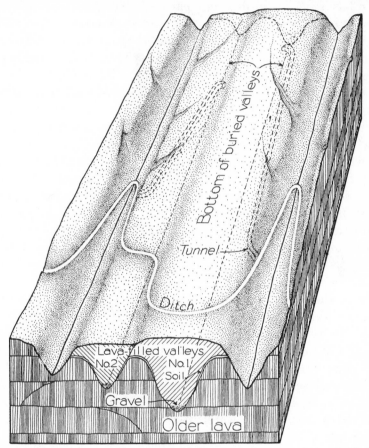

Fig. XV-9.—Diagram showing position of tunnels driven to recover perched water in lava-filled valleys.

tubes contain several hundred gallons of water. Apparently the cracks in the tube floor are silted sufficiently to perch water percolating through the roof of the tube and along the floor. The water collects in low places in the tube, generally at the mouth, where sufficient dirt has been washed in to seal the cracks in the floor. The water persists even during dry weather, because evaporation is slight. It is possible that heavy dew and fog condensing on the roof of the tube supply some of the water. Springs obviously supplied in part from dew occur near Ulupalakua, on the island of Maui, Hawaii. Some of these springs discharge from outcrops of permeable ash overlying impermeable lava that occurs in short flows about 1 foot thick on the sides of cinder cones.

Ground water confined in dike complexes.—Dike complexes underlie the rift zones of volcanoes. The dikes are progressively more numerous toward the heart of the complex and also at greater depths below the surface. Thus, the depth at which all extrusive basalt is replaced by intrusive basalt varies in different parts of the complex, but it is always least in the heart of the complex. In most complexes in Hawaii water is confined between nearly vertical dikes, and the rock is saturated to whatever depth the rocks are pervious below the water table. It is highly probable that the rocks are saturated with fresh water to the bottom of the pervious rock if the water table is 200 feet or more above sea level. If less than this height the fresh water may or may not be underlain by salt water, depending on whether permeable rocks extend to the depth required by the Ghyben-Herzberg principle.

A swarm of dikes cutting through permeable beds of basalt commonly confines ground water at high levels. This occurrence of water has world-wide significance, as most large basaltic volcanoes contain swarms of dikes. The dikes have low permeability and imprison the water in the intervening compartments of pervious lava beds. Such water is commonly very valuable, because it usually has a high head and uniform flow. The water is not perched in the usual sense, because the rock is saturated below the water table and is thus not a saturated body underlain by a zone of aeration. Individual dikes may be sufficiently impervious to resemble a sill in preventing the water from percolating to lower levels; such water is perched. However, in most dike swarms there are sufficient leaks through crevices in the dikes for the whole mass to be saturated below the water table, as shown in figure XV-7. Furthermore, the water table of any one of the dike-enclosed compartments may be at a different height from the one next to it, as shown in the same figure.

The dikes that confine water in a complex are in general sufficiently cracked to allow some water to move transversely through them. Even small cracks in dikes near sea level under a hydrostatic pressure of several hundred feet must allow considerable water to pass through them to join the adjacent basal zone of saturation. Tunnels driven into the dike complex develop water largely by reducing the pressure in the leaks from the compartments penetrated, and also by draining water through the dikes of adjacent compartments not penetrated, as a result of a hydraulic gradient being created toward the tunnel. It is chiefly for these reasons that the lower the altitude of a tunnel the wider will be its zone of influence and the greater its yield.

Many tunnels have been driven into the zones of water confined by dikes in the Hawaiian Islands. Such tunnels on Oahu alone yield about

12,250,000,000 gallons of water annually. Springs issue if the saturated part of a dike complex is cut by erosion or faulting. Such springs emerging from a dike complex on Oahu yield about 19,800,000,000 gallons annually.

When tunnels first cut the dike compartments they commonly drain large quantities of stored water. In the main Waiahole bore, Oahu, 16,348,000,000 gallons in excess of the normal daily ground-water yield of 8,600,000 gallons was drained from storage between the dikes in the period August 1913 to May 1916. It may take as long as 8 years for the stored water in a dike complex to drain out, as shown by the record of Waikane tunnel No. 1, Oahu.

It was recommended to the Oahu Sugar Co. in 1932 and to the United States Navy in 1934 that certain dikes in their tunnels be rebuilt by means of concrete plugs equipped with control gates, to store water in the ground during periods of rainy weather when the flow was not needed. These plugs were later installed and showed conclusively that many million gallons of water can thus be stored in the ground. The plug in Waikane tunnel No. 2 of the Oahu Sugar Co. stored more than 23,000,000 gallons in 22 days. Such utilization of underground reservoirs has great possibilities for the economic conservation of water.

ARTESIAN WATER

Artesian water may occur in basalt as follows: (1) In counterbalance with salt water in undisturbed lava beds with an upper confining bed of impermeable sedimentary rocks but without a lower restraining member; (2) confined within lava beds interstratified with impermeable sedimentary rocks and subsequently warped; (3) confined in unwarped lava beds laid down between impermeable sedimentary rocks that were deposited with a dip sufficient to cause artesian pressure.

The greatest known artesian basin in basalt is in Oahu, Hawaii. There relatively impervious sedimentary rocks and submerged soil blanket the basalt along the coast and confine the water under pressure. Such artesian conditions are very different, however, from those of ordinary artesian basins, because the lower restraining bed is lacking. The head is maintained by the counterpoise of the heavy sea water.

Several artesian areas with different static heads are found in some islands [14, p. 40]. They are caused by deeply submerged valleys and ridges, as shown in Figure XV-10. The difference in head between the areas is dependent upon the hydraulic gradient of the water table inland of them and upon loss in pressure caused by submarine leaks in the compartments.

Artesian water in basaltic islands is also found not in counterbalance with salt water but confined between impermeable beds. Two types of structure are known—(1) dike complexes in which the lower restraining member is intrusive basalt and the upper confining member is impermeable sedimentary rock [23, p. 268]; and (2) beds of permeable basalt

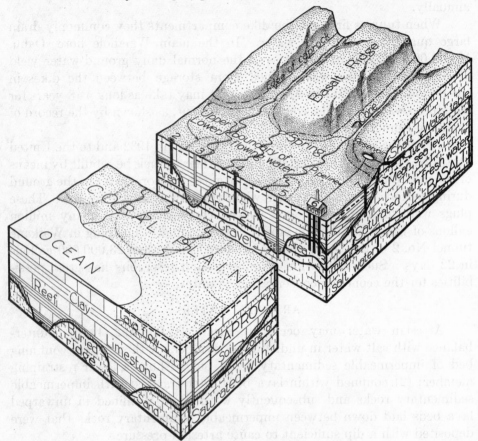

Fig. XV-10.—Diagram illustrating the hydrology of an artesian system in a partly submerged eroded volcanic island (based on conditions in Honolulu).

The fresh water occurs in basalt, floating on salt water, according to the Ghyben-Herzberg principle, and separated from it by a zone of mixture. The water is confined in the buried ridges under pressure by the sedimentary cap rock. The upper boundary of the area of artesian flow is determined by the height of the water table in the adjacent ridges, and the lower boundary by the seaward end of the fresh-water lens. A spring issues at the point where the cap rock is eroded below the upper boundary of the area of artesian flow. Drilled wells 1 and 5 (stippled) contain salt water, wells 2, 4, 6, and 7 (solid black) are flowing wells that yield fresh water, and well 3 (white) is dry because all ground water in the cap rock has been cased out and water-bearing basalt was not reached. The shaft will safely recover more water than drilled wells because it is far above the zone of mixture. Also, if the water is distributed from a reservoir as shown, less pipe line is necessary than if the water is pumped from wells on the plain. The partly buried cinder cone in one of the valleys was the source of the lava flow in the cap rock. Such lava yields water; if it is in contact with coral limestone or other pervious rocks the water in it will usually be brackish at or below sea level but fresh where the lava lies above sea level.

interstratified with (a) dense lava sheets in wet areas, or (b) impermeable sedimentary rocks in valleys or along the coast, generally resulting from secondary lava flows that have followed valleys seaward and become interstratified by subsequent deposition of the sediments in deltas or fans.

Basalt flows interstratified with fine-grained pyroclastic or impermeable sedimentary deposits having either an initial dip or a dip induced by subsequent earth movements yield artesian water to wells in a few localities in the United States. The water moves down the dip through the basalt and is confined above and below by the impermeable beds. Artesian water in large quantities is recovered at shallow depth by wells penetrating a basalt flow interstratified with unwarped clay beds at Hamer, Idaho [28, p. 43].

FLUCTUATIONS OF THE WATER TABLE

The water table in basaltic rocks, as well as in other permeable media, fluctuates in response to changes in the rate of recharge and discharge and to minor causes. In general these fluctuations are small compared to those in most other rocks, because the pore space is large.

The water table responds with a lag of a few days or a few months to changes in the rate of recharge, the time depending on the distance of the recharge area from the observation well. Records of water-table fluctuations at Blue Lakes Spring, Idaho [25, p. 61], indicates that the discharge of this spring increases $3\frac{1}{2}$ months after land is irrigated on the Hazelton tract, 15 miles to the east. Thus the average rate of movement of the water-table peak in this area is about 750 feet a day. If large quantities of irrigation water are suddenly applied the peak moves at the rate of about 850 feet a day.

The water table may rise progressively for long periods and may eventually give rise to drainage problems in regions where the natural ground-water outlet of the basalt is restricted, as in the South Side Twin Falls tract, Idaho. Irrigation water was first used in that tract in 1905, but the first well was not drilled until 1908. The water level rose 37 feet a year in this well during the first 5 years. In one part of the tract the average rise of the water table was 25 feet a year for the period 1909 to 1912. The rapid rise did not continue, however, as the measurements made in 1928 indicate an average rise of only 3.8 feet a year since 1913.

Directly across the Snake River Canyon from the South Side Twin Falls tract lies the North Side Twin Falls tract, in which more than 600,000 acre-feet annually (an average of about 535,000,000 gallons a day) is contributed to the underlying water table, yet no drainage problems exist. The water table rises and falls only about 5 feet a year and remains far below the surface, because the tract is underlain by several deep ancestral canyons of the Snake River filled with permeable basalt, which serve as natural drains.

Blowing and sucking wells are common in the lava regions of the United States. These are due to the pore space in the rock absorbing or emptying air according to changes in barometric pressure. At Jerome, Idaho, a home is cooled by means of the air from one of these wells.

The chief draft on the ground water may be transpiration from plants where the water table is close to the surface, as in the Mud Lake Basin, Idaho. In such places the water table declines rapidly during the growing season and recovers in the fall, when the plants cease growing.

In general the water tables in basaltic terranes in the continental United States have been rising or have remained practically stationary since measurements were first made. The rise has resulted from recharge from surface-water irrigation. Pumping has not yet begun on a sufficiently large scale to lower the water table except locally. The basaltic terranes contain very large quantities of water awaiting development.

In contrast to the mainland, pumpage from basalt has progressively increased in the Hawaiian Islands, especially on Oahu, where the average daily draft from wells entering basalt is 290,000,000 gallons. The average annual quantity of ground water visibly discharged from wells, springs, and tunnels on that island is 25.6 percent of the average annual rainfall as determined from existing records [23, p. 442]. The water table in Oahu has declined various amounts since artificial draft was begun. The greatest drop has been in artesian area 2 in Honolulu, where the static level fell 18.5 feet between 1881 and 1926. Since that time, owing to conservation, the sealing of leaky wells, and increased precipitation, the water level has risen about 10 feet.

The tide, the fluctuations in atmospheric pressure, and some earthquakes cause minor fluctuations of the water level in the artesian wells in Oahu. Between 1927 and 1940 the water levels of wells in Honolulu were affected by earthquakes in the United States, Turkey, China, Alaska, Japan, New Guinea, New Caledonia, Mexico, Peru, Fiji, Chile, the Philippine Islands, the Kurile Islands, the Aleutian Islands, New Zealand, Hawaii, the Carolina Islands, Burma, Nicaragua, the Solomon Islands, Bonin Island, and the Marianas Islands.

NATURAL AND ARTIFICIAL DISCHARGE OF GROUND WATER

The great natural reservoirs formed by basalt usually discharge through springs that may be spectacularly large. Of the 66 first-magnitude springs [10, p. 4; one spring in the Deschutes River Basin is added to Meinzer's list] in the United States, or those having an average discharge of 100 second-feet (about 65,000,000 gallons a day) or more, 36 issue from basalt (Fig. XV-11). Some individual vents discharge hundreds of second-feet of water. Most of these large springs issue from basalt occupying former valleys (Fig. XV-2), but some, such as those along the shore of Pearl Harbor, Oahu, discharge from flat-lying sheets of basalt at low points in the caprock of an artesian system (Fig. XV-10).

ARTIFICIAL RECHARGE OF THE ZONE OF SATURATION

Artificial recharge of ground-water reservoirs in basalt has been little tried, but as pumping is increased it will doubtless be more extensively practiced. The East Maui Irrigation Co. has for several years been running surplus irrigation water down gullies near its large wells to recharge the basal zone of saturation. Quantitative data are lacking to prove the efficacy of such recharge, but there can be little doubt that it is highly beneficial.

In general, reservoirs built in basalt terranes are so leaky that they afford good means for accomplishing artificial recharge where the surface water and reservoir sites are available and where careful study of the rock structure indicates that the water will percolate to the underground reservoir intended. Four reservoirs in the Nuuanu Valley, belonging to the City and County of Honolulu, leaked so badly after they were built that they were abandoned. It was erroneously thought that these reservoirs were not a total loss, because the seepage from them was supposed to reach the Honolulu artesian system and hence supplement the city wells. Geologic investigations, substantiated by drilling, showed that this water

Fig. XV-11.—Burney Falls, Calif., a basalt spring discharging about 150 second-feet of water (approximately 100,000,000 gallons a day).

found its way to the sea through lava flows perched on alluvium, and that the water was not recovered again by wells, nor did it enter the artesian system.

It is feasible on the island of Lanai to pump basal water from a well near the coast to a well shaft penetrating the zone of saturation in the dike complex, and there to store it in the rock from which natural stored water has been pumped. The Oahu Sugar Co. has for several years been running stream water into a shaft and infiltration gallery from which basal water is pumped, thereby decreasing the salt content and increasing the amount of fresh water stored in the rocks.

It is possible to recharge basalt by running water down drilled wells. Caution must be used to avoid pollution in artificially recharging a ground-water reservoir from which drinking water is taken.

SURFACE WATER

STREAMS

Permeability, topography, nearness of the water table to the surface, and intensity and quantity of rainfall are the chief factors governing the character of runoff from volcanic terranes. Hundreds of square miles of the lava plains of Idaho, Oregon, California, and New Mexico and of the recent basaltic cones on islands in the Pacific have no runoff. In some places runoff is lacking even though the rainfall may reach 200 inches annually or 24 inches during a single day. These areas are great sponges, and their capacity to absorb rainfall is phenomenal. Some of them are densely covered with jungle forests and some are bare, hence vegetation plays virtually no part. All are relatively flat terranes, underlain by relatively fresh basaltic lavas or pumice and by low water tables. Most of them do not even have drainage channels developed on them, even though they may be as old as Pleistocene. If, however, the terrane is steep, runoff may occur during heavy rains. Contiguous rock bodies of high permeability are found near Hilo, Hawaii, one steep enough to have runoff during storms and the other flat enough to absorb all the rainfall.

It is not unusual for the trunk stream crossing basaltic terranes to gain for long distances, then abruptly to start losing water and finally, after flowing many miles, to regain all the water previously lost. This action is due to hills and valleys in the impermeable basement rock. Where steep drops occur in the basement, the water cascades to a lower level through the very permeable lava. Usually nothing on the surface indicates the presence of this underground cascade, which changes the river from a gaining to a losing stream. The river may regain the lost water farther downstream if its valley intersects the same water-bearing lavas.

An area of about 10,000 square miles in southern Idaho underlain by basalts has no surface runoff, and most of the streams from the bordering mountains sink at the margin of the plain. The Snake River, with an annual flow of about 6,000,000 acre-feet where it reaches the plain, manages to reach the lower end of the lava fields without sinking by hugging their margin most of the way in a channel underlain by other rocks. In some stretches where the stream flows against basalt it loses heavily, but in other stretches, where it has cut a channel below the water table, it gains. Thus in the 60-mile stretch between Blue Lakes and King Hill its average gain is 6,180 second-feet [25, pp. 199–201].

The Deschutes River, Oregon, is typical of streams without flood flows draining large areas underlain by andesitic pumice and basalt. It heads in a group of spring-fed pools near Bend. As it flows northward to the Columbia River it picks up about 4,500 second-feet of spring water. It has a more uniform flow than any other river of its size in the United States [21, p. 162]. Most of the great rivers of the North Island of New Zealand have a similar regimen. They drain extensive areas of silicic pumice.

Streams on basaltic islands in the Tropics old enough to have developed soil and drainage channels are flashy and intermittent because of their steep gradients and the high porosity of the rocks. Floods of 6,260 second-feet per square mile of drainage basin have been recorded on Oahu, Hawaii [33]. Such streams deposit very little sand, the usual sediment being either mud or a bouldery alluvium resembling a mud flow. The small proportion of fine to coarse sediment results from the fact that low-stage velocities are very low and flood velocities extremely high. Some rivers, as for example the Rogue River, Oregon, disappear into lava tubes and reappear where the tubes again reach the surface. Some streams fail to reappear because the water finds its way through crevices to the water table or to a different stream.

Large perennial streams may erode channels across lava fields in spite of a water table far below the stream bed. They do so by slowly silting up the crevices in their channels. Disturbing the regimen of such a stream by diverting the water for part of the year may cause great losses as a result of the silt drying in the crevices and being eroded away when the stream returns to its channel. Losses in a 45-mile stretch of the Big Wood River, Idaho, have increased 145 second-feet since it was dammed in 1920 [25, p. 261].

Seepage losses are extremely variable because the stream beds may within short distances be on fresh or on deeply weathered lava or on relatively impermeable alluvium.

Structural features within permeable lavas may also greatly influence the regimen of a stream. Thus, the streams on the southwest side of the deeply eroded Koolau Volcano, on Oahu, are intermittent, and those on the northeast side are perennial. Such an anomalous condition is caused by the streams on the northeast side cutting into a swarm of impermeable dikes which cut across the permeable lava beds and give rise to an effluent water table.

Surface water dissolves very little mineral from lava terranes, hence the quality is generally excellent. The chloride content of the water of moderate floods on Pacific islands is usually greater than for low flows because during heavy rains the salt spray that had been carried inland during periods of dry weather is washed from the vegetation.

LAKES

Many lakes have been formed where lava flows have damned streams —for example, Davis Lake, Oregon. Such lakes generally have underground outlets, the water reappearing many miles downstream at the lower end of the lava flow. Some lakes have neither a surface inlet nor a surface outlet. They generally lie in the depression between two or more lava flows of different ages that have partly filled a stream valley.

Where streams carrying large quantities of silt sink at the margin of a lava plain they may develop intermittent lakes, which are filled only during times of heavy runoff. The water is dissipated from such lakes by evaporation and by percolation through the silt floor into the underlying lavas.

Small ponds are found in depressions in lava fields where animals have puddled the crevices with mud. Examples are the water holes north of St. Anthony, Idaho, puddled by the hoofs of the buffalo that formerly roamed this area in large numbers. Small ponds exist in cinder cones in regions of high rainfall where decaying swamp vegetation seals the floor.

Some lakes, such as those near Camperdown, Australia, occupy craters that indent the water table of a basaltic terrane. They have no surface inlet or outlet, and they rise and fall annually with the regional water table. The evaporation from these large groups of lakes is one of the chief elements of the discharge of this great underground reservoir [22]. Evaporation may equal the inflow, and a salt lake may result if the water can move freely into such a crater or other depression but has no way to escape through the walls, as in Salt Lake Crater, Oahu.

Many crater lakes are due to the impermeability of the rocks that form the walls. Such lakes dot the landscape of New Zealand, Java, Japan, and Alaska. These lavas are of the silicic type and are practically impermeable. Lakes occupying the craters of active volcanoes may cause great catastrophes if the water is suddenly blown out or cracking of the rim allows the water to escape quickly. The Dutch Government has driven a tunnel into the bottom of the crater lake in the summit of Keloed Volcano, Java. When the temperature of the lake rises high enough to indicate that an eruption is imminent the water is drained from the lake through the tunnel to prevent it being hurled over the countryside.

IRRIGATION SYSTEMS

Several irrigation projects have failed because such factors as the high permeability of volcanic terranes and the position of the water table were not recognized. Losses on the North Side Twin Falls tract, Idaho, bordering the Snake River, amount to 600,000 acre-feet annually. It is obvious that money would be saved if the water were used on lands not underlain by permeable basalt. Great quantities of water have been used to irrigate the South Side Twin Falls tract, Idaho, because of the extremely low water table and the high permeability of the volcanic terrane. It is estimated that 6,000,000 acre-feet of water went into permanent ground-water storage in this tract between 1906 and 1928 [25, p. 129]. Now certain areas must be drained. The projects succeeded largely because the unused flow of the Snake River was plentiful at that time.

The form of the water table along the Snake River is such that it is much more beneficial to irrigate land on the south and east sides of the river between Firth and Milner, Idaho, than land on the opposite side. The underground flow from such lands will return to the river above certain large reservoirs and diversions, but that used on the north side will return below these diversions, where it will have no value for re-use [25, p. 181].

Success and failure of reservoirs and dams in basalt

Basalt in any part of a reservoir site should be regarded with suspicion. Reservoirs in basalt generally fail because the water table is far below the floor of the reservoir, with only permeable rock intervening, or because there is nearby a canyon or coulee of an ancient stream course, now buried, into which the water may percolate through the permeable basalt.

Any conclusions regarding the success or failure of reservoirs in basalt are affected by economic considerations that should not be overlooked. A reservoir may leak large volumes of water and still be successful if a certain amount of water must be discharged past the dam to supply prior water rights downstream. An important difference exists between a reservoir built to detain water for a few weeks and one built to store water for the greater part of the year. Furthermore, the time and duration of runoff are influential factors. Thus, heavy leakage from an irrigation reservoir in one of the Pacific coast drainage basins, where most of the runoff occurs prior to the irrigation season, might mean failure, but equal leakage from a reservoir in one of the drainage basins in the high Rocky Mountains, where the high runoff occurs later and during part of the irrigation season, might not prevent success. A leaky reservoir built for both power and storage may be successful for irrigation and a failure for power if the seepage around the dam returns to the stream above the diversion point of the irrigation canal but so far below the dam as to make it worthless for power. A reservoir built for flood control, whether to regulate a stream for power or navigation or to prevent destruction of man's handi-work, will retard the water sufficiently to iron out the flood peaks, even if there is considerable leakage past the dam. Therefore reservoirs constructed for flood control in basaltic areas might be successful where hold-over irrigation reservoirs would be failures. Finally, in such reservoirs as the Blackfoot Reservoir, Idaho, the initial cost of storage has been so small that they have proved economically successful in spite of considerable leakage [19].

Reservoirs built where large springs issue close to the dam may fail because the pressure of the reservoir water on the springs may cause them to find new outlets downstream from the dam.

The greatest leakage occurs where reservoirs are built in basins high above the water table, with permeable basalt filling the space intervening between the reservoir and the water table. The lowest seepage losses occur where the adjacent water table is tributary to the reservoir basin with a slope steep enough to preclude a reversal of ground-water gradient at high stages, or where the basalt is underlain by or interstratified with impermeable rock.

REFERENCES

1. Calkins, F. C., Geology and water resources of a portion of east-central Washington: U. S. Geol. Survey Water-Supply Paper 118, 96 pp., 1905.

2. Dubuis, John, Report on Tumalo project (unpublished rept. to the Desert Land Board, State of Oregon, pp. 15–16, Dec. 28, 1916).

3. Gregory, H. E., and Ellis, A. J., Ground water in Hartford, Stanford, Salisbury, Willimantic, and Saybrook areas, Connecticut: U. S. Geol. Survey Water-Supply Paper 374, p. 24, 1916.

4. Henderson, E., Iceland, p. 229, 1819.

5. Landes, Henry, Preliminary report on the underground waters of Washington: U. S. Geol. Survey Water-Supply Paper 111, 85 pp., 1905.

6. Lindgren, Waldemar, The water resources of Molokai, Hawaiian Islands: U. S. Geol. Survey Water-Supply Paper 77, 62 pp., 1903.

7. McCombs, John, Methods of exploring and repairing leaky artesian wells on the island of Oahu, Hawaii: U. S. Geol. Survey Water-Supply Paper 596, pp. 1–33, 1927.

8. Meinzer, O. E., and Kelton, F. C., Geology and water resources of Sulphur Spring Valley, Ariz.: U. S. Geol. Survey Water-Supply Paper 320, pp. 68–70, 1913.

9. Meinzer, O. E., The occurrence of ground water in the United States: U. S. Geol. Survey Water-Supply Paper 489, 321 pp., 1923.

10. Meinzer, O. E., Large springs in the United States: U. S. Geol. Survey Water-Supply Paper 557, 94 pp., 1927.

11. Meinzer, O. E., Ground water in the Hawaiian Islands: U. S. Geol. Survey Water-Supply Paper 616, pp. 1–28, 1930.

12. Ogura, T., and others, Volcanoes of the Wu Ta Lien Chih District, Lung Chiang Province, Manchuria: Ryojun Coll. Engineering Survey Rept. 1, 96 pp., Ryojun, Manchuria, 1936.

13. Palmer, H. S., Ground water in the Southington-Granby area, Connecticut: U. S. Geol. Survey Water-Supply Paper 466, pp. 37–38, 1921.

14. Palmer, H. S., The geology of the Honolulu artesian system: Honolulu Sewer and Water Comm. Rept., Suppl., 68 pp., 1927.

15. Russell, I. C., Geology and water resources of Nez Perce County, Idaho, pt. 1: U. S. Geol. Survey Water-Supply Paper 53, 85 pp., 1901; Geology and water resources of the Snake River Plains of Idaho: U. S. Geol. Survey Bull. 199, 192 pp., 1902.

16. Schwennesen, A. T., and Meinzer, O. E., Ground water in Quincy Valley, Wash.: U. S. Geol. Survey Water-Supply Paper 425, pp. 147–150, 1919.

17. Stearns, H. T., Lava Beds National Monument, Calif.: Geol. Soc. Philadelphia Bull. 26, No. 4, pp. 239–253, 1928.

18. Stearns, H. T., Geology and water resources of the upper McKenzie Valley, Oreg.: U. S. Geol. Survey Water-Supply Paper 597, pp. 171–188, 1928.

19. Stearns, H. T., Success and failure of reservoirs in basalt [abstract]: Am. Inst. Min. Met. Eng. Trans., Tech. Pub. 215 (class 1, Mining geology, No. 26), pp. 111–112, 1929.

20. Stearns, H. T., and Clark, W. O., Geology and water resources of the Kau District, Hawaii: U. S. Geol. Survey Water-Supply Paper 616, 194 pp., 1930.

21. Stearns, H. T., Geology and water resources of the middle Deschutes River Basin, Oreg.: U. S. Geol. Survey Water-Supply Paper 637, pp. 125–212, 1931.

22. Stearns, H. T., Notes relating to ground water in New Zealand and Australia: U. S. Geol. Survey Water-Resources Bull., Dec. 11, 1933, pp. 40–42.

23. Stearns, H. T., and Vaksvik, K. N., Geology and ground-water resources of the island of Oahu, Hawaii: Hawaii Div. Hydrography Bull. 1, 479 pp., 1935.

24. Stearns, H. T., Origin of the large springs and their alcoves along the Snake River in southern Idaho: Jour. Geology, vol. 14, No. 4, pp. 429–450, 8 figs., 1936.

25. Stearns, H. T., Crandall, Lynn, and Steward, W. G., Geology and ground-water resources of the Snake River Plain in southeastern Idaho: U. S. Geol. Survey Water-Supply Paper 774, 268 pp., 1938.

26. Stearns, H. T., and Vaksvik, K. N., Records of the drilled wells on the island of Oahu, Hawaii: Hawaii Div. Hydrography Bull. 4, 213 pp., 1938.

27. Stearns, H. T., Geologic map and guide of the island of Oahu, Hawaii: Hawaii Div. Hydrography Bull. 2, 75 pp., 1939.

28. Stearns, H. T., Bryan, L. L., and Crandall, Lynn, Geology and water resources of the Mud Lake region, Idaho: U. S. Geol. Survey Water-Supply Paper 818, 125 pp., 1939.

29. Stearns, H. T., Supplement to Geology and ground-water resources of the island of Oahu, Hawaii: Hawaii Div. Hydrography Bull. 5, 164 pp., 1940.

30. Stearns, H. T., Geology and ground-water resources of the islands of Lanai and Kahoolawe, Hawaii: Hawaii Div. Hydrography Bull. 6, 177 pp., 1940.

31. Stearns, N. D., Annotated bibliography and index of geology and water supply of the island of Oahu, Hawaii: Hawaii Div. Hydrography Bull. 3, 74 pp., 1935.

32. Umpleby, J. B., The leakage near the head of the Blackfoot Reservoir, Idaho (unpublished report to the United States Indian Service, 1914; most of it is published in U. S. Geol. Survey Prof. Paper 152, pp. 325–328, 1927).

33. Surface water supply of Hawaii, July 1, 1936, to June 30, 1937: U. S. Geol. Survey Water-Supply Paper 835, p. 47, 1939.

INDEX

CATALOGUE OF DOVER BOOKS

ENGINEERING AND TECHNOLOGY

General and mathematical

ENGINEERING MATHEMATICS, Kenneth S. Miller. A text for graduate students of engineering to strengthen their mathematical background in differential equations, etc. Mathematical steps very explicitly indicated. Contents: Determinants and Matrices, Integrals, Linear Differential Equations, Fourier Series and Integrals, Laplace Transform, Network Theory, Random Function . . . all vital requisites for advanced modern engineering studies. Unabridged republication. Appendices: Borel Sets; Riemann-Stieltjes Integral; Fourier Series and Integrals. Index. References at Chapter Ends. xii + 417pp. 6 x 8½.   S1121 Paperbound **$2.00**

MATHEMATICAL ENGINEERING ANALYSIS, Rufus Oldenburger. A book designed to assist the research engineer and scientist in making the transition from physical engineering situations to the corresponding mathematics. Scores of common practical situations found in all major fields of physics are supplied with their correct mathematical formulations—applications to automobile springs and shock absorbers, clocks, throttle torque of diesel engines, resistance networks, capacitors, Fourier series and integrals, microphones, neon tubes, gasoline engines, refrigeration cycles, etc. Each section reviews basic principles of underlying various fields: mechanics of rigid bodies, electricity and magnetism, heat, elasticity, fluid mechanics, and aerodynamics. Comprehensive and eminently useful. Index. 169 problems, answers. 200 photos and diagrams. xiv + 426pp. 5⅜ x 8½.   S919 Paperbound **$2.50**

MATHEMATICS OF MODERN ENGINEERING, E. G. Keller and R. E. Doherty. Written for the Advanced Course in Engineering of the General Electric Corporation, deals with the engineering use of determinants, tensors, the Heaviside operational calculus, dyadics, the calculus of variations, etc. Presents underlying principles fully, but purpose is to teach engineers to deal with modern engineering problems, and emphasis is on the perennial engineering attack of set-up and solve. Indexes. Over 185 figures and tables. Hundreds of exercises, problems, and worked-out examples. References. Two volume set. Total of xxxiii + 623pp. 5⅜ x 8.
S734 Vol I Paperbound **$1.85**
S735 Vol II Paperbound **$1.85**
The set **$3.70**

MATHEMATICAL METHODS FOR SCIENTISTS AND ENGINEERS, L. P. Smith. For scientists and engineers, as well as advanced math students. Full investigation of methods and practical description of conditions under which each should be used. Elements of real functions, differential and integral calculus, space geometry, theory of residues, vector and tensor analysis, series of Bessel functions, etc. Each method illustrated by completely-worked-out examples, mostly from scientific literature. 368 graded unsolved problems. 100 diagrams. x + 453pp. 5⅝ x 8⅜.   S220 Paperbound **$2.00**

THEORY OF FUNCTIONS AS APPLIED TO ENGINEERING PROBLEMS, edited by R. Rothe, F. Ollendorff, and K. Pohlhausen. A series of lectures given at the Berlin Institute of Technology that shows the specific applications of function theory in electrical and allied fields of engineering. Six lectures provide the elements of function theory in a simple and practical form, covering complex quantities and variables, integration in the complex plane, residue theorems, etc. Then 5 lectures show the exact uses of this powerful mathematical tool, with full discussions of problem methods. Index. Bibliography. 108 figures. x + 189pp. 5⅜ x 8.
S733 Paperbound **$1.35**

Aerodynamics and hydrodynamics

AIRPLANE STRUCTURAL ANALYSIS AND DESIGN, E. E. Sechler and L. G. Dunn. Systematic authoritative book which summarizes a large amount of theoretical and experimental work on structural analysis and design. Strong on classical subsonic material still basic to much aeronautic design . . . remains a highly useful source of information. Covers such areas as layout of the airplane, applied and design loads, stress-strain relationships for stable structures, truss and frame analysis, the problem of instability, the ultimate strength of stiffened flat sheet, analysis of cylindrical structures, wings and control surfaces, fuselage analysis, engine mounts, landing gears, etc. Originally published as part of the CALCIT Aeronautical Series. 256 Illustrations. 47 study problems. Indexes. xi + 420pp. 5⅜ x 8½.
S1043 Paperbound **$2.25**

FUNDAMENTALS OF HYDRO- AND AEROMECHANICS, L. Prandtl and O. G. Tietjens. The well-known standard work based upon Prandtl's lectures at Goettingen. Wherever possible hydrodynamics theory is referred to practical considerations in hydraulics, with the view of unifying theory and experience. Presentation is extremely clear and though primarily physical, mathematical proofs are rigorous and use vector analysis to a considerable extent. An Enginering Society Monograph, 1934. 186 figures. Index. xvi + 270pp. 5⅜ x 8.
S374 Paperbound **$1.85**

Catalogue of Dover Books

FLUID MECHANICS THROUGH WORKED EXAMPLES, D. R. L. Smith and J. Houghton. Advanced text covering principles and applications to practical situations. Each chapter begins with concise summaries of fundamental ideas. 163 fully worked out examples applying principles outlined in the text. 275 other problems, with answers. Contents: The Pressure of Liquids on Surfaces; Floating Bodies; Flow Under Constant Head in Pipes; Circulation; Vorticity; The Potential Function; Laminar Flow and Lubrication; Impact of Jets; Hydraulic Turbines; Centrifugal and Reciprocating Pumps; Compressible Fluids; and many other items. Total of 438 examples. 250 line illustrations. 340pp. Index. 6 x 8⅞.   S981 Clothbound **$6.00**

THEORY OF SHIP MOTIONS, S. N. Blagoveshchensky. The only detailed text in English in a rapidly developing branch of engineering and physics, it is the work of one of the world's foremost authorities—Blagoveshchensky of Leningrad Shipbuilding Institute. A senior-level treatment written primarily for engineering students, but also of great importance to naval architects, designers, contractors, researchers in hydrodynamics, and other students. No mathematics beyond ordinary differential equations is required for understanding the text. Translated by T. & L. Strelkoff, under editorship of Louis Landweber, Iowa Institute of Hydraulic Research, under auspices of Office of Naval Research. Bibliography. Index. 231 diagrams and illustrations. Total of 649pp. 5⅜ x 8½.   Vol. I: S234 Paperbound **$2.00**
Vol. II: S235 Paperbound **$2.00**

THEORY OF FLIGHT, Richard von Mises. Remains almost unsurpassed as balanced, well-written account of fundamental fluid dynamics, and situations in which air compressibility effects are unimportant. Stressing equally theory and practice, avoiding formidable mathematical structure, it conveys a full understanding of physical phenomena and mathematical concepts. Contains perhaps the best introduction to general theory of stability. "Outstanding," Scientific, Medical, and Technical Books. New introduction by K. H. Hohenemser. Bibliographical, historical notes. Index. 408 illustrations. xvi + 620pp. 5⅜ x 8⅜.   S541 Paperbound **$3.50**

THEORY OF WING SECTIONS, I. H. Abbott, A. E. von Doenhoff. Concise compilation of subsonic aerodynamic characteristics of modern NASA wing sections, with description of their geometry, associated theory. Primarily reference work for engineers, students, it gives methods, data for using wing-section data to predict characteristics. Particularly valuable: chapters on thin wings, airfoils; complete summary of NACA's experimental observations, system of construction families of airfoils. 350pp. of tables on Basic Thickness Forms, Mean Lines, Airfoil Ordinates, Aerodynamic Characteristics of Wing Sections. Index. Bibliography. 191 illustrations. Appendix. 705pp. 5⅜ x 8.   S558 Paperbound **$3.25**

WEIGHT-STRENGTH ANALYSIS OF AIRCRAFT STRUCTURES, F. R. Shanley. Scientifically sound methods of analyzing and predicting the structural weight of aircraft and missiles. Deals directly with forces and the distances over which they must be transmitted, making it possible to develop methods by which the minimum structural weight can be determined for any material and conditions of loading. Weight equations for wing and fuselage structures. Includes author's original papers on inelastic buckling and creep buckling. "Particularly successful in presenting his analytical methods for investigating various optimum design principles," AERONAUTICAL ENGINEERING REVIEW. Enlarged bibliography. Index. 199 figures. xiv + 404pp. 5⅝ x 8⅜.   S660 Paperbound **$2.50**

Electricity

TWO-DIMENSIONAL FIELDS IN ELECTRICAL ENGINEERING, L. V. Bewley. A useful selection of typical engineering problems of interest to practicing electrical engineers. Introduces senior students to the methods and procedures of mathematical physics. Discusses theory of functions of a complex variable, two-dimensional fields of flow, general theorems of mathematical physics and their applications, conformal mapping or transformation, method of images, freehand flux plotting, etc. New preface by the author. Appendix by W. F. Kiltner. Index. Bibliography at chapter ends. xiv + 204pp. 5⅜ x 8½.   S1118 Paperbound **$1.50**

FLUX LINKAGES AND ELECTROMAGNETIC INDUCTION, L. V. Bewley. A brief, clear book which shows proper uses and corrects misconceptions of Faraday's law of electromagnetic induction in specific problems. Contents: Circuits, Turns, and Flux Linkages; Substitution of Circuits; Electromagnetic Induction; General Criteria for Electromagnetic Induction; Applications and Paradoxes; Theorem of Constant Flux Linkages. New Section: Rectangular Coil in a Varying Uniform Medium. Valuable supplement to class texts for engineering students. Corrected, enlarged edition. New preface. Bibliography in notes. 49 figures. xi + 106pp. 5⅜ x 8.   S1103 Paperbound **$1.25**

INDUCTANCE CALCULATIONS: WORKING FORMULAS AND TABLES, Frederick W. Grover. An invaluable book to everyone in electrical engineering. Provides simple single formulas to cover all the more important cases of inductance. The approach involves only those parameters that naturally enter into each situation, while extensive tables are given to permit easy interpolations. Will save the engineer and student countless hours and enable them to obtain accurate answers with minimal effort. Corrected republication of 1946 edition. 58 tables. 97 completely worked out examples. 66 figures. xiv + 286pp. 5⅜ x 8½.
S974 Paperbound **$1.85**

FLUID MECHANICS THROUGH WORKED EXAMPLES, D. R. L. Smith and J. Houghton. Advanced text covering principles and applications to practical situations. Each chapter begins with concise summaries of fundamental ideas. 163 fully worked out examples applying principles outlined in the text. 275 other problems, with answers. Contents: The Pressure of Liquids on Surfaces; Floating Bodies; Flow Under Constant Head in Pipes; Circulation; Vorticity; The Potential Function; Laminar Flow and Lubrication; Impact of Jets; Hydraulic Turbines; Centrifugal and Reciprocating Pumps; Compressible Fluids; and many other items. Total of 438 examples. 250 line illustrations. 340pp. Index. 6 x 8⅞. S981 Clothbound **$6.00**

THEORY OF SHIP MOTIONS, S. N. Blagoveshchensky. The only detailed text in English in a rapidly developing branch of engineering and physics, it is the work of one of the world's foremost authorities—Blagoveshchensky of Leningrad Shipbuilding Institute. A senior-level treatment written primarily for engineering students, but also of great importance to naval architects, designers, contractors, researchers in hydrodynamics, and other students. No mathematics beyond ordinary differential equations is required for understanding the text. Translated by T. & L. Strelkoff, under editorship of Louis Landweber, Iowa Institute of Hydraulic Research, under auspices of Office of Naval Research. Bibliography. Index. 231 diagrams and illustrations. Total of 649pp. 5⅜ x 8½. Vol. I: S234 Paperbound **$2.00**
Vol. II: S235 Paperbound **$2.00**

THEORY OF FLIGHT, Richard von Mises. Remains almost unsurpassed as balanced, well-written account of fundamental fluid dynamics, and situations in which air compressibility effects are unimportant. Stressing equally theory and practice, avoiding formidable mathematical structure, it conveys a full understanding of physical phenomena and mathematical concepts. Contains perhaps the best introduction to general theory of stability. "Outstanding," Scientific, Medical, and Technical Books. New introduction by K. H. Hohenemser. Bibliographical, historical notes. Index. 408 illustrations. xvi + 620pp. 5⅜ x 8⅜. S541 Paperbound **$3.50**

THEORY OF WING SECTIONS, I. H. Abbott, A. E. von Doenhoff. Concise compilation of subsonic aerodynamic characteristics of modern NASA wing sections, with description of their geometry, associated theory. Primarily reference work for engineers, students, it gives methods, data for using wing-section data to predict characteristics. Particularly valuable: chapters on thin wings, airfoils; complete summary of NACA's experimental observations, system of construction families of airfoils. 350pp. of tables on Basic Thickness Forms, Mean Lines, Airfoil Ordinates, Aerodynamic Characteristics of Wing Sections. Index. Bibliography. 191 illustrations. Appendix. 705pp. 5⅜ x 8. S558 Paperbound **$3.25**

WEIGHT-STRENGTH ANALYSIS OF AIRCRAFT STRUCTURES, F. R. Shanley. Scientifically sound methods of analyzing and predicting the structural weight of aircraft and missiles. Deals directly with forces and the distances over which they must be transmitted, making it possible to develop methods by which the minimum structural weight can be determined for any material and conditions of loading. Weight equations for wing and fuselage structures. Includes author's original papers on inelastic buckling and creep buckling. "Particularly successful in presenting his analytical methods for investigating various optimum design principles," AERONAUTICAL ENGINEERING REVIEW. Enlarged bibliography. Index. 199 figures. xiv + 404pp. 5⅝ x 8⅜. S660 Paperbound **$2.50**

Electricity

TWO-DIMENSIONAL FIELDS IN ELECTRICAL ENGINEERING, L. V. Bewley. A useful selection of typical engineering problems of interest to practicing electrical engineers. Introduces senior students to the methods and procedures of mathematical physics. Discusses theory of functions of a complex variable, two-dimensional fields of flow, general theorems of mathematical physics and their applications, conformal mapping or transformation, method of images, freehand flux plotting, etc. New preface by the author. Appendix by W. F. Kiltner. Index. Bibliography at chapter ends. xiv + 204pp. 5⅜ x 8½. S1118 Paperbound **$1.50**

FLUX LINKAGES AND ELECTROMAGNETIC INDUCTION, L. V. Bewley. A brief, clear book which shows proper uses and corrects misconceptions of Faraday's law of electromagnetic induction in specific problems. Contents: Circuits, Turns, and Flux Linkages; Substitution of Circuits; Electromagnetic Induction; General Criteria for Electromagnetic Induction; Applications and Paradoxes; Theorem of Constant Flux Linkages. New Section: Rectangular Coil in a Varying Uniform Medium. Valuable supplement to class texts for engineering students. Corrected, enlarged edition. New preface. Bibliography in notes. 49 figures. xi + 106pp. 5⅜ x 8. S1103 Paperbound **$1.25**

INDUCTANCE CALCULATIONS: WORKING FORMULAS AND TABLES, Frederick W. Grover. An invaluable book to everyone in electrical engineering. Provides simple single formulas to cover all the more important cases of inductance. The approach involves only those parameters that naturally enter into each situation, while extensive tables are given to permit easy interpolations. Will save the engineer and student countless hours and enable them to obtain accurate answers with minimal effort. Corrected republication of 1946 edition. 58 tables. 97 completely worked out examples. 66 figures. xiv + 286pp. 5⅜ x 8½. S974 Paperbound **$1.85**

Catalogue of Dover Books

GASEOUS CONDUCTORS: THEORY AND ENGINEERING APPLICATIONS, J. D. Cobine. An indispensable text and reference to gaseous conduction phenomena, with the engineering viewpoint prevailing throughout. Studies the kinetic theory of gases, ionization, emission phenomena; gas breakdown, spark characteristics, glow, and discharges; engineering applications in circuit interrupters, rectifiers, light sources, etc. Separate detailed treatment of high pressure arcs (Suits); low pressure arcs (Langmuir and Tonks). Much more. "Well organized, clear, straightforward," Tonks, Review of Scientific Instruments. Index. Bibliography. 83 practice problems. 7 appendices. Over 600 figures. 58 tables. xx + 606pp. 5⅜ x 8. S442 Paperbound **$3.25**

INTRODUCTION TO THE STATISTICAL DYNAMICS OF AUTOMATIC CONTROL SYSTEMS, V. V. Solodovnikov. First English publication of text-reference covering important branch of automatic control systems—random signals; in its original edition, this was the first comprehensive treatment. Examines frequency characteristics, transfer functions, stationary random processes, determination of minimum mean-squared error, of transfer function for a finite period of observation, much more. Translation edited by J. B. Thomas, L. A. Zadeh. Index. Bibliography. Appendix. xxii + 308pp. 5⅜ x 8. S420 Paperbound **$2.25**

TENSORS FOR CIRCUITS, Gabriel Kron. A boldly original method of analyzing engineering problems, at center of sharp discussion since first introduced, now definitely proved useful in such areas as electrical and structural networks on automatic computers. Encompasses a great variety of specific problems by means of a relatively few symbolic equations. "Power and flexibility . . . becoming more widely recognized," Nature. Formerly "A Short Course in Tensor Analysis." New introduction by B. Hoffmann. Index. Over 800 diagrams. xix + 250pp. 5⅜ x 8. S534 Paperbound **$2.00**

SELECTED PAPERS ON SEMICONDUCTOR MICROWAVE ELECTRONICS, edited by Sumner N. Levine and Richard R. Kurzrok. An invaluable collection of important papers dealing with one of the most remarkable developments in solid-state electronics—the use of the p-n junction to achieve amplification and frequency conversion of microwave frequencies. Contents: General Survey (3 introductory papers by W. E. Danielson, R. N. Hall, and M. Tenzer); General Theory of Nonlinear Elements (3 articles by A. van der Ziel, H. E. Rowe, and Manley and Rowe); Device Fabrication and Characterization (3 pieces by Bakanowski, Cranna, and Uhlir, by McCotter, Walker and Fortini, and by S. T. Eng); Parametric Amplifiers and Frequency Multipliers (13 articles by Uhlir, Heffner and Wade, Matthaei, P. K. Tien, van der Ziel, Engelbrecht, Currie and Gould, Uenohara, Leeson and Weinreb, and others); and Tunnel Diodes (4 papers by L. Esaki, H. S. Sommers, Jr., M. E. Hines, and Yariv and Cook). Introduction. 295 Figures. xiii + 286pp. 6½ x 9¼. S1126 Paperbound **$2.25**

THE PRINCIPLES OF ELECTROMAGNETISM APPLIED TO ELECTRICAL MACHINES, B. Hague. A concise, but complete, summary of the basic principles of the magnetic field and its applications, with particular reference to the kind of phenomena which occur in electrical machines. Part I: General Theory—magnetic field of a current, electromagnetic field passing from air to iron, mechanical forces on linear conductors, etc. Part II: Application of theory to the solution of electromechanical problems—the magnetic field and mechanical forces in non-salient pole machinery, the field within slots and between salient poles, and the work of Rogowski, Roth, and Strutt. Formerly titled "Electromagnetic Problems in Electrical Engineering." 2 appendices. Index. Bibliography in notes. 115 figures. xiv + 359pp. 5⅜ x 8½. S246 Paperbound **$2.25**

Mechanical engineering

DESIGN AND USE OF INSTRUMENTS AND ACCURATE MECHANISM, T. N. Whitehead. For the instrument designer, engineer; how to combine necessary mathematical abstractions with independent observation of actual facts. Partial contents: instruments & their parts, theory of errors, systematic errors, probability, short period errors, erratic errors, design precision, kinematic, semikinematic design, stiffness, planning of an instrument, human factor, etc. Index. 85 photos, diagrams. xii + 288pp. 5⅜ x 8. S270 Paperbound **$2.00**

A TREATISE ON GYROSTATICS AND ROTATIONAL MOTION: THEORY AND APPLICATIONS, Andrew Gray. Most detailed, thorough book in English, generally considered definitive study. Many problems of all sorts in full detail, or step-by-step summary. Classical problems of Bour, Lottner, etc.; later ones of great physical interest. Vibrating systems of gyrostats, earth as a top, calculation of path of axis of a top by elliptic integrals, motion of unsymmetrical top, much more. Index. 160 illus. 550pp. 5⅜ x 8. S589 Paperbound **$2.75**

MECHANICS OF THE GYROSCOPE, THE DYNAMICS OF ROTATION, R. F. Deimel, Professor of Mechanical Engineering at Stevens Institute of Technology. Elementary general treatment of dynamics of rotation, with special application of gyroscopic phenomena. No knowledge of vectors needed. Velocity of a moving curve, acceleration to a point, general equations of motion, gyroscopic horizon, free gyro, motion of discs, the damped gyro, 103 similar topics. Exercises. 75 figures. 208pp. 5⅜ x 8. S66 Paperbound **$1.75**

STRENGTH OF MATERIALS, J. P. Den Hartog. Distinguished text prepared for M.I.T. course, ideal as introduction, refresher, reference, or self-study text. Full clear treatment of elementary material (tension, torsion, bending, compound stresses, deflection of beams, etc.), plus much advanced material on engineering methods of great practical value: full treatment of the Mohr circle, lucid elementary discussions of the theory of the center of shear and the "Myosotis" method of calculating beam deflections, reinforced concrete, plastic deformations, photoelasticity, etc. In all sections, both general principles and concrete applications are given. Index. 186 figures (160 others in problem section). 350 problems, all with answers. List of formulas. viii + 323pp. 5⅜ x 8. S755 Paperbound **$2.00**

PHOTOELASTICITY: PRINCIPLES AND METHODS, H. T. Jessop, F. C. Harris. For the engineer, for specific problems of stress analysis. Latest time-saving methods of checking calculations in 2-dimensional design problems, new techniques for stresses in 3 dimensions, and lucid description of optical systems used in practical photoelasticity. Useful suggestions and hints based on on-the-job experience included. Partial contents: strained and stress-strain relations, circular disc under thrust along diameter, rectangular block with square hole under vertical thrust, simply supported rectangular beam under central concentrated load, etc. Theory held to minimum, no advanced mathematical training needed. Index. 164 illustrations. viii + 184pp. 6⅛ x 9¼. S720 Paperbound **$2.00**

APPLIED ELASTICITY, J. Prescott. Provides the engineer with the theory of elasticity usually lacking in books on strength of materials, yet concentrates on those portions useful for immediate application. Develops every important type of elasticity problem from theoretical principles. Covers analysis of stress, relations between stress and strain, the empirical basis of elasticity, thin rods under tension or thrust, Saint Venant's theory, transverse oscillations of thin rods, stability of thin plates, cylinders with thin walls, vibrations of rotating disks, elastic bodies in contact, etc. "Excellent and important contribution to the subject, not merely in the old matter which he has presented in new and refreshing form, but also in the many original investigations here published for the first time," NATURE. Index. 3 Appendixes. vi + 672pp. 5⅜ x 8. S726 Paperbound **$3.25**

APPLIED MECHANICS FOR ENGINEERS, Sir Charles Inglis, F.R.S. A representative survey of the many and varied engineering questions which can be answered by statics and dynamics. The author, one of first and foremost adherents of "structural dynamics," presents distinctive illustrative examples and clear, concise statement of principles—directing the discussion at methodology and specific problems. Covers fundamental principles of rigid-body statics, graphic solutions of static problems, theory of taut wires, stresses in frameworks, particle dynamics, kinematics, simple harmonic motion and harmonic analysis, two-dimensional rigid dynamics, etc. 437 illustrations. xii + 404pp. 5⅜ x 8½. S1119 Paperbound **$2.00**

THEORY OF MACHINES THROUGH WORKED EXAMPLES, G. H. Ryder. Practical mechanical engineering textbook for graduates and advanced undergraduates, as well as a good reference work for practicing engineers. Partial contents: Mechanisms, Velocity and Acceleration (including discussion of Klein's Construction for Piston Acceleration), Cams, Geometry of Gears, Clutches and Bearings, Belt and Rope Drives, Brakes, Inertia Forces and Couples, General Dynamical Problems, Gyroscopes, Linear and Angular Vibrations, Torsional Vibrations, Transverse Vibrations and Whirling Speeds (Chapters on vibrations considerably enlarged from previous editions). Over 300 problems, many fully worked out. Index. 195 line illustrations. Revised and enlarged edition. viii + 280pp. 5⅝ x 8¾. S980 Clothbound **$5.00**

THE KINEMATICS OF MACHINERY: OUTLINES OF A THEORY OF MACHINES, Franz Reuleaux. The classic work in the kinematics of machinery. The present thinking about the subject has all been shaped in great measure by the fundamental principles stated here by Reuleaux almost 90 years ago. While some details have naturally been superseded, his basic viewpoint has endured; hence, the book is still an excellent text for basic courses in kinematics and a standard reference work for active workers in the field. Covers such topics as: the nature of the machine problem, phoronomic propositions, pairs of elements, incomplete kinematic chains, kinematic notation and analysis, analyses of chamber-crank trains, chamber-wheel trains, constructive elements of machinery, complete machines, etc., with main focus on controlled movement in mechanisms. Unabridged republication of original edition, translated by Alexander B. Kennedy. New introduction for this edition by E. S. Ferguson. Index. 451 illustrations. xxiv + 622pp. 5⅜ x 8½. S1124 Paperbound **$3.00**

ANALYTICAL MECHANICS OF GEARS, Earle Buckingham. Provides a solid foundation upon which logical design practices and design data can be constructed. Originally arising out of investigations of the ASME Special Research Committee on Worm Gears and the Strength of Gears, the book covers conjugate gear-tooth action, the nature of the contact, and resulting gear-tooth profiles of: spur, internal, helical, spiral, worm, bevel, and hypoid or skew bevel gears. Also: frictional heat of operation and its dissipation, friction losses, etc., dynamic loads in operation, and related matters. Familiarity with this book is still regarded as a necessary prerequisite to work in modern gear manufacturing. 263 figures. 103 tables. Index. x + 546pp. 5⅜ x 8½. S1073 Paperbound **$2.75**

Optical design, lighting

THE SCIENTIFIC BASIS OF ILLUMINATING ENGINEERING, Parry Moon, Professor of Electrical Engineering, M.I.T. Basic, comprehensive study. Complete coverage of the fundamental theoretical principles together with the elements of design, vision, and color with which the lighting engineer must be familiar. Valuable as a text as well as a reference source to the practicing engineer. Partial contents: Spectroradiometric Curve, Luminous Flux, Radiation from Gaseous-Conduction Sources, Radiation from Incandescent Sources, Incandescent Lamps, Measurement of Light, Illumination from Point Sources and Surface Sources, Elements of Lighting Design. 7 Appendices. Unabridged and corrected republication, with additions. New preface containing conversion tables of radiometric and photometric concepts. Index. 707-item bibliography. 92-item bibliography of author's articles. 183 problems. xxiii + 608pp. 5⅜ x 8½. S242 Paperbound **$2.85**

OPTICS AND OPTICAL INSTRUMENTS: AN INTRODUCTION WITH SPECIAL REFERENCE TO PRACTICAL APPLICATIONS, B. K. Johnson. An invaluable guide to basic practical applications of optical principles, which shows how to set up inexpensive working models of each of the four main types of optical instruments—telescopes, microscopes, photographic lenses, optical projecting systems. Explains in detail the most important experiments for determining their accuracy, resolving power, angular field of view, amounts of aberration, all other necessary facts about the instruments. Formerly "Practical Optics." Index. 234 diagrams. Appendix. 224pp. 5⅜ x 8. S642 Paperbound **$1.75**

APPLIED OPTICS AND OPTICAL DESIGN, A. E. Conrady. With publication of vol. 2, standard work for designers in optics is now complete for first time. Only work of its kind in English; only detailed work for practical designer and self-taught. Requires, for bulk of work, no math above trig. Step-by-step exposition, from fundamental concepts of geometrical, physical optics, to systematic study, design, of almost all types of optical systems. Vol. 1: all ordinary ray-tracing methods; primary aberrations; necessary higher aberration for design of telescopes, low-power microscopes, photographic equipment. Vol. 2: (Completed from author's notes by R. Kingslake, Dir. Optical Design, Eastman Kodak.) Special attention to high-power microscope, anastigmatic photographic objectives. "An indispensable work," J., Optical Soc. of Amer. "As a practical guide this book has no rival," Transactions, Optical Soc. Index. Bibliography. 193 diagrams. 852pp. 6⅛ x 9¼. Vol. 1 S366 Paperbound **$3.50**
Vol. 2 S612 Paperbound **$2.95**

Miscellaneous

THE MEASUREMENT OF POWER SPECTRA FROM THE POINT OF VIEW OF COMMUNICATIONS ENGINEERING, R. B. Blackman, J. W. Tukey. This pathfinding work, reprinted from the "Bell System Technical Journal," explains various ways of getting practically useful answers in the measurement of power spectra, using results from both transmission theory and the theory of statistical estimation. Treats: Autocovariance Functions and Power Spectra; Direct Analog Computation; Distortion, Noise, Heterodyne Filtering and Pre-whitening; Aliasing; Rejection Filtering and Separation; Smoothing and Decimation Procedures; Very Low Frequencies; Transversal Filtering; much more. An appendix reviews fundamental Fourier techniques. Index of notation. Glossary of terms. 24 figures. XII tables. Bibliography. General index. 192pp. 5⅜ x 8. S507 Paperbound **$1.85**

CALCULUS REFRESHER FOR TECHNICAL MEN, A. Albert Klaf. This book is unique in English as a refresher for engineers, technicians, students who either wish to brush up their calculus or to clear up uncertainties. It is not an ordinary text, but an examination of most important aspects of integral and differential calculus in terms of the 756 questions most likely to occur to the technical reader. The first part of this book covers simple differential calculus, with constants, variables, functions, increments, derivatives, differentiation, logarithms, curvature of curves, and similar topics. The second part covers fundamental ideas of integration, inspection, substitution, transformation, reduction, areas and volumes, mean value, successive and partial integration, double and triple integration. Practical aspects are stressed rather than theoretical. A 50-page section illustrates the application of calculus to specific problems of civil and nautical engineering, electricity, stress and strain, elasticity, industrial engineering, and similar fields.—756 questions answered. 566 problems, mostly answered. 36 pages of useful constants, formulae for ready reference. Index. v + 431pp. 5⅜ x 8. T370 Paperbound **$2.00**

METHODS IN EXTERIOR BALLISTICS, Forest Ray Moulton. Probably the best introduction to the mathematics of projectile motion. The ballistics theories propounded were coordinated with extensive proving ground and wind tunnel experiments conducted by the author and others for the U.S. Army. Broad in scope and clear in exposition, it gives the beginnings of the theory used for modern-day projectile, long-range missile, and satellite motion. Six main divisions: Differential Equations of Translatory Motion of a projectile; Gravity and the Resistance Function; Numerical Solution of Differential Equations; Theory of Differential Variations; Validity of Method of Numerical Integration; and Motion of a Rotating Projectile. Formerly titled: "New Methods in Exterior Ballistics." Index. 38 diagrams. viii + 259pp. 5⅜ x 8½. S232 Paperbound **$1.75**

GEOLOGY, GEOGRAPHY, METEOROLOGY

PRINCIPLES OF STRATIGRAPHY, A. W. Grabau. Classic of 20th century geology, unmatched in scope and comprehensiveness. Nearly 600 pages cover the structure and origins of every kind of sedimentary, hydrogenic, oceanic, pyroclastic, atmoclastic, hydroclastic, marine hydroclastic, and bioclastic rock; metamorphism; erosion; etc. Includes also the constitution of the atmosphere; morphology of oceans, rivers, glaciers; volcanic activities; faults and earthquakes; and fundamental principles of paleontology (nearly 200 pages). New introduction by Prof. M. Kay, Columbia U. 1277 bibliographical entries. 264 diagrams. Tables, maps, etc. Two volume set. Total of xxxii + 1185pp. 5⅜ x 8. S686 Vol I Paperbound **$2.50**
S687 Vol II Paperbound **$2.50**
The set **$5.00**

TREATISE ON SEDIMENTATION, William H. Twenhofel. A milestone in the history of geology, this two-volume work, prepared under the auspices of the United States Research Council, contains practically everything known about sedimentation up to 1932. Brings together all the findings of leading American and foreign geologists and geographers and has never been surpassed for completeness, thoroughness of description, or accuracy of detail. Vol. 1 discusses the sources and production of sediments, their transportation, deposition, diagenesis, and lithification. Also modification of sediments by organisms and topographical, climatic, etc. conditions which contribute to the alteration of sedimentary processes. 220 pages deal with products of sedimentation: minerals, limestones, dolomites, coals, etc. Vol. 2 continues the examination of products such as gypsum and saline residues, silica, strontium, manganese, etc. An extensive exposition of structures, textures and colors of sediments: stratification, cross-lamination, ripple mark, oolitic and pisolitic textures, etc. Chapters on environments or realms of sedimentation and field and laboratory techniques are also included. Indispensable to modern-day geologists and students. Index. List of authors cited. 1733-item bibliography. 121 diagrams. Total of xxxiii + 926pp. 5⅜ x 8½. Vol. I: S950 Paperbound **$2.50**
Vol. II: S951 Paperbound **$2.50**
Two volume set Paperbound **$5.00**

THE EVOLUTION OF THE IGNEOUS ROCKS, N. L. Bowen. Invaluable serious introduction applies techniques of physics and chemistry to explain igneous rock diversity in terms of chemical composition and fractional crystallization. Discusses liquid immiscibility in silicate magmas, crystal sorting, liquid lines of descent, fractional resorption of complex minerals, petrogenesis, etc. Of prime importance to geologists & mining engineers, also to physicists, chemists working with high temperatures and pressures. "Most important," TIMES, London. 3 indexes. 263 bibliographic notes. 82 figures. xviii + 334pp. 5⅜ x 8. S311 Paperbound **$2.25**

INTERNAL CONSTITUTION OF THE EARTH, edited by Beno Gutenberg. Completely revised. Brought up-to-date, reset. Prepared for the National Research Council this is a complete & thorough coverage of such topics as earth origins, continent formation, nature & behavior of the earth's core, petrology of the crust, cooling forces in the core, seismic & earthquake material, gravity, elastic constants, strain characteristics and similar topics. "One is filled with admiration . . . a high standard . . . there is no reader who will not learn something from this book," London, Edinburgh, Dublin, Philosophic Magazine. Largest bibliography in print: 1127 classified items. Indexes. Tables of constants. 43 diagrams. 439pp. 6⅛ x 9¼. S414 Paperbound **$3.00**

HYDROLOGY, edited by Oscar E. Meinzer. Prepared for the National Research Council. Detailed complete reference library on precipitation, evaporation, snow, snow surveying, glaciers, lakes, infiltration, soil moisture, ground water, runoff, drought, physical changes produced by water, hydrology of limestone terranes, etc. Practical in application, especially valuable for engineers. 24 experts have created "the most up-to-date, most complete treatment of the subject," AM. ASSOC. of PETROLEUM GEOLOGISTS. Bibliography. Index. 165 illustrations. xi + 712pp. 6⅛ x 9¼. S191 Paperbound **$3.50**

SNOW CRYSTALS, W. A. Bentley and W. J. Humphreys. Over 200 pages of Bentley's famous microphotographs of snow flakes—the product of painstaking, methodical work at his Jericho, Vermont studio. The pictures, which also include plates of frost, glaze and dew on vegetation, spider webs, windowpanes; sleet; graupel or soft hail, were chosen both for their scientific interest and their aesthetic qualities. The wonder of nature's diversity is exhibited in the intricate, beautiful patterns of the snow flakes. Introductory text by W. J. Humphreys. Selected bibliography. 2,453 illustrations. 224pp. 8 x 10¼. T287 Paperbound **$2.95**

PHYSICS OF THE AIR, W. J. Humphreys. A very thorough coverage of classical materials and theories in meteorology . . . written by one of this century's most highly respected physical meteorologists. Contains the standard account in English of atmospheric optics. 5 main sections: Mechanics and Thermodynamics of the Atmosphere, Atmospheric Electricity and Auroras, Meteorological Acoustics, Atmospheric Optics, and Factors of Climatic Control. Under these headings, topics covered are: theoretical relations between temperature, pressure, and volume in the atmosphere; composition, pressure, and density; circulation; evaporation and condensation; fog, clouds, thunderstorms, lightning; aurora polaris; principal ice-age theories; etc. New preface by Prof. Julius London. 226 illustrations. Index. xviii + 676pp. 5⅜ x 8½. S1044 Paperbound **$3.00**

URANIUM PROSPECTING, H. L. Barnes. For immediate practical use, professional geologist considers uranium ores, geological occurrences, field conditions, all aspects of highly profitable occupation. Index. Bibliography. x + 117pp. 5⅜ x 8. T309 Paperbound **$1.00**

SELECTED PAPERS IN THE THEORY OF THERMAL CONVECTION: WITH SPECIAL APPLICATION TO THE EARTH'S PLANETARY ATMOSPHERE, Edited by Barry Saltzman. An indispensable volume for anyone interested in the motions of the earth's atmosphere. 25 basic theoretical papers on thermal convection by major scientists, past and present: Helmholtz, Overbeck, Jeffreys, Rayleigh, G. I. Taylor, Chandrasekhar, A. R. Low, Rossby, Davies, Charney, Eady, Phillips, Pellew and Southwell, Elbert, Fjortoft, and H.-L. Kuo. Bibliography. x + 461pp. 6⅛ x 9¼. S171 Paperbound **$3.00**

THE FOUNDERS OF GEOLOGY, Sir Archibald Geikie. Survey of the high moments and the work of the major figures of the period in which the main foundations of modern geology were laid—the latter half of the 18th century to the first half of the 19th. The developments in the science during this era centering around the lives and accomplishments of the great contributors: Palissy, Guettard, Demarest, Pallas, Lehmann, Füchsel, Werner, Hutton, Playfair, Sir James Hall, Cuvier, Lyell, Logan, Darwin, Agassiz, Nicol, and others. Comprehensive and readable. Index. xi + 486pp. 5⅜ x 8½. T352 Paperbound **$2.25**

THE BIRTH AND DEVELOPMENT OF THE GEOLOGICAL SCIENCES, F. D. Adams. Most thorough history of the earth sciences ever written. Geological thought from earliest times to the end of the 19th century, covering over 300 early thinkers & systems: fossils & their explanation, vulcanists vs. neptunists, figured stones & paleontology, generation of stones, dozens of similar topics. 91 illustrations, including medieval, renaissance woodcuts, etc. Index. 632 footnotes, mostly bibliographical. 511pp. 5⅜ x 8. T5 Paperbound **$2.25**

A HISTORY OF ANCIENT GEOGRAPHY, E. H. Bunbury. Standard study, in English, of ancient geography; never equalled for scope, detail. First full account of history of geography from Greeks' first world picture based on mariners, through Ptolemy. Discusses every important map, discovery, figure, travel, expedition, war, conjecture, narrative, bearing on subject. Chapters on Homeric geography, Herodotus, Alexander expedition, Strabo, Pliny, Ptolemy, would stand alone as exhaustive monographs. Includes minor geographers, men not usually regarded in this context: Hecataeus, Pythea, Hipparchus, Artemidorus, Marinus of Tyre, etc. Uses information gleaned from military campaigns such as Punic wars, Hannibal's passage of Alps, campaigns of Lucullus, Pompey, Caesar's wars, the Trojan war. New introduction by W. H. Stahl, Brooklyn College. Bibliography. Index. 20 maps. 1426pp. 5⅜ x 8. T570-1, clothbound, 2 volume set **$12.50**

DE RE METALLICA, Georgius Agricola. 400-year old classic translated, annotated by former President Herbert Hoover. The first scientific study of mineralogy and mining, for over 200 years after its appearance in 1556, it was the standard treatise. 12 books, exhaustively annotated, discuss the history of mining, selection of sites, types of deposits, making pits, shafts, ventilating, pumps, crushing machinery; assaying, smelting, refining metals; also salt, alum, nitre, glass making. Definitive edition, with all 289 16th century woodcuts of the original. Biographical, historical introductions, bibliography, survey of ancient authors. Indexes. A fascinating book for anyone interested in art, history of science, geology, etc. Deluxe edition. 289 illustrations. 672pp. 6¾ x 10¾. Library cloth. S6 Clothbound **$10.00**

GEOGRAPHICAL ESSAYS, William Morris Davis. Modern geography & geomorphology rest on the fundamental work of this scientist. 26 famous essays presenting most important theories, field researches. Partial contents: Geographical Cycle, Plains of Marine and Subaerial Denudation, The Peneplain, Rivers and Valleys of Pennsylvania, Outline of Cape Cod, Sculpture of Mountains by Glaciers, etc. "Long the leader & guide," ECONOMIC GEOGRAPHY. "Part of the very texture of geography . . . models of clear thought," GEOGRAPHIC REVIEW. Index. 130 figures. vi + 777pp. 5⅜ x 8. S383 Paperbound **$2.95**

Prices subject to change without notice.

Dover publishes books on art, music, philosophy, literature, languages, history, social sciences, psychology, handcrafts, orientalia, puzzles and entertainments, chess, pets and gardens, books explaining science, intermediate and higher mathematics, mathematical physics, engineering, biological sciences, earth sciences, classics of science, etc. Write to:

Dept. catrr.
Dover Publications, Inc.
180 Varick Street, N.Y. 14, N.Y.